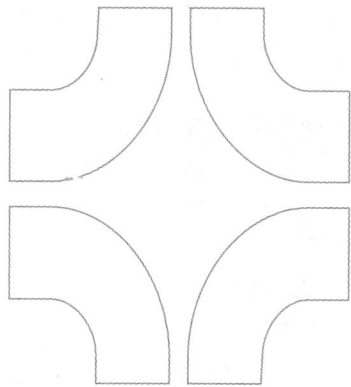

# Programming WITH MICROSOFT VISUAL BASIC 2005:

## An Object-Oriented Approach

### Second Edition

Michael Ekedahl
University of Nevada, Reno

THOMSON
COURSE TECHNOLOGY

**THOMSON**

**COURSE TECHNOLOGY**

**Programming with Microsoft Visual Basic 2005: An Object-Oriented Approach, Second Edition**

by Michael Ekedahl

**Publisher:**
Bob Woodbury

**Managing Editor:**
Tricia Coia

**Developmental Editor:**
Jill Batistick

**Production Editor:**
Jill Klaffky

**QA Manuscript Reviewers:**
Chris Scriver, Teresa Storch,
Serge Palladino

**Marketing Coordinator:**
Suelaine Frongello

**Interior Designer:**
David Vogin
314 Design

**Cover Designer:**
Steve Deschene

**Compositor:**
Integra

**Senior Manufacturing
Coordinator:**
Justin Palmeiro

**Copy Editor:**
Karen Annett

**Proofreader:**
Wendy Benedetto

**Indexer:**
Liz Cunningham

# TABLE OF CONTENTS

# TABLE OF CONTENTS

# CHAPTER 4
## INTRODUCTION TO NUMERIC DATA TYPES AND VARIABLES

# CHAPTER 5

# TABLE OF CONTENTS

# CHAPTER 6
## UNDERSTANDING THE STRUCTURE OF AN APPLICATION: PROCEDURES, MODULES, AND CLASSES

# CHAPTER 7
## DECISION MAKING

# TABLE OF CONTENTS

# CHAPTER 9

# CHAPTER 10
## SEQUENTIAL FILES AND STRUCTURES

# PREFACE

*Programming with Microsoft Visual Basic 2005: An Object-Oriented Approach, Second Edition* is designed to provide the beginning Visual Basic programmer with the tools to create Visual Basic applications that conform to well-adopted Windows standards. This textbook assumes that students have little or no programming experience. It assumes familiarity with basic Windows 98, Windows 2000, or Windows XP concepts.

## ORGANIZATION AND COVERAGE

*Programming with Microsoft Visual Basic 2005: An Object-Oriented Approach, Second Edition* begins by discussing how to get started using Visual Studio .NET and Visual Basic .NET. No previous experience with Visual Basic is required, although any experience with Basic or general programming concepts will be helpful.

After the reader understands how to maneuver in Visual Basic .NET, the book presents the following:

- » An introduction to programming and the Visual Basic programming language
- » Use of the Visual Studio developer interface to create a first program
- » Creating Windows forms applications and the essentials of event-driven applications
- » Numeric data types and variables, including examples related to creating expressions and data type conversion
- » Use of the String and DateTime data types
- » The structure of a Visual Basic application, including classes, modules, and procedures
- » Decision-making and the use of controls related to decision-making
- » Looping and the different types of looping statements
- » Using looping statements with lists
- » Processing data with arrays
- » Reading and writing sequential files
- » Processing database data with ADO.NET
- » Drawing graphical objects on a form
- » Creating a user interface with the MenuStrip, StatusStrip, and ToolStrip controls
- » Tools to help debug applications
- » Introduction to printing
- » The deployment of an application

New to this edition, each chapter is divided into two lessons. The first lesson is a concept lesson designed to teach core programming concepts. Each concept lesson has a corresponding Visual Studio application with which you can further explore core concepts discussed in the text. The second lesson is an application lesson. In each application lesson, you will implement a real-world business application utilizing the concepts presented in the current chapter and in previous chapters.

## FEATURES

*Programming with Microsoft Visual Basic 2005: An Object-Oriented Approach, Second Edition* is a superior textbook because it also includes the following features:

» **Read This Before You Begin Page.** This page is consistent with Thomson Course Technology's unequaled commitment to helping instructors introduce technology into the classroom. Technical considerations and assumptions about hardware, software, and default settings are listed in one place to help instructors save time.

» **Step-by-Step Methodology.** This unique Thomson Course Technology methodology keeps readers on track. They write program code always within the context of solving the problems posed in the chapter's application lesson. The text constantly guides users and lets them know where they are in the process of solving the problem. The numerous illustrations guide readers in creating useful, working programs.

» **Tips.** These notes provide additional information on Graphical User Interface (GUI) design, programming, and computer performance. For example, they might identify an alternative method of performing a procedure, some background information on a technique, or a commonly-made error to watch out for.

» **Mini-Quizzes.** In each concept lesson, there are three to five new mini-quizzes to review key concepts. Answers to the mini-quizzes appear after the chapter summary.

» **Summaries.** Following each chapter is a summary that recaps the programming concepts and commands covered in each section.

» **Key Terms.** Following the chapter summary is a list of the key terms introduced in the chapter.

» **Review Questions and Programming Questions.** Each chapter concludes with meaningful, conceptual review questions that test readers' understanding of what they learned in the chapter. These questions are divided into two types: multiple choice questions and programming questions that require the reader to write small code segments.

» **Hands-On Projects.** Each chapter concludes with hands-on projects that give readers additional practice with the skills and concepts they learned in the chapter. These exercises increase in difficulty and are designed to allow the student to explore the language and programming environment independently.

» **Additional Online Content.** New online appendices have been created to discuss new Visual Studio 2005 printing capabilities and deployment features.

» **Interior Design.** The interior of the book has been redesigned, presenting a cleaner, more streamlined look and feel, which allows for ease of reading and freedom to concentrate on the topics.

## THE VISUAL BASIC ENVIRONMENT

This book was written using Microsoft Visual Studio 2005 – Professional Edition installed on a Windows XP personal computer. The Express Edition of Visual Basic 2005 will produce the same results. Screen shots were captured using Windows XP. Specific instructions for installing Visual Studio 2005 are provided in the Instructor's Manual.

This book can be purchased with Microsoft Visual Basic 2005 Express Edition or Microsoft Visual Basic 2005 Professional Edition (180-day version). All the material in the text will work with either version. Please contact your sales representative for more information about ordering the book with this software.

## TEACHING TOOLS

All the teaching tools for this text are found on the Instructor's Resource CD-ROM, or at *www.course.com*. Additional teaching tools, including standard naming conventions, can also be found on this site.

You should be familiar with the following:

» **Instructor's Manual.** The Instructor's Manual was written by the author of the text and all solutions were thoroughly quality-assurance tested. It is available on the Instructor's Resource CD-ROM or at *www.course.com* (instructor material is password protected). The Instructor's Manual contains the following items:

– Answers to all the Review Questions and solutions to all the Hands-On Projects in the book. The files contain instructor's notes about each solution and its expected difficulty level.

– Teaching notes to help introduce and clarify the material presented in the chapters. As Visual Studio 2005 differs from previous versions of Visual Studio, the author has made significant efforts to include transition material in the teaching notes.

– Technical notes that include troubleshooting tips.

» **ExamView.** This textbook is accompanied by ExamView, a powerful testing software package that allows instructors to create and administer printed, LAN-based, and Internet exams. ExamView includes hundreds of questions that correspond to the topics covered in this text, enabling students to generate detailed study guides that include page references for further review. The computer-based and Internet testing components allow students to take exams at their computers and also save the instructor time by grading each exam automatically.

» **Solution Files.** Solution Files contain a possible solution to every program readers are asked to create or modify in the chapters and projects. Each solution contains numerous comments to help explain the code found in the solution file. (Due to the nature of programming, readers' solutions will likely differ from these solutions and still be correct.)

» **Data Files.** Data Files containing all the data that students will use for the chapters and exercises in this textbook are provided through *www.course.com* and on the Instructor's Resource CD-ROM. A Help file includes technical tips for lab management. See the "Read This Before You Begin" page before Chapter 1 for more information on the data files and their organization.

» **Distance Learning.** Thomson Course Technology is proud to present online test banks in WebCT and Blackboard to provide the most complete and dynamic learning experience possible. Instructors are encouraged to make the most of the course, both online and offline. For more information on how to access the online test bank, contact your local Thomson Course Technology sales representative.

## ACKNOWLEDGEMENTS

Our appreciation goes to each of the reviewers whose efforts helped to improve the organization and content of this book, including Frank Friedman, Temple University; Larry Langellier, Moraine Valley Community College; Ann Rovetto, Horry-Georgetown Technical College; Neal Stenlund, Northern Virginia Community College; and Melinda White, Seminole Community College. Thanks also to the editorial and production staff at Thomson Course Technology for making this book possible, including Tricia Coia, Managing Editor; Jill Klaffky, Production Editor; as well as Teresa Storch, Serge Palladino, and Chris Scriver, Quality Assurance Testers.

Special thanks to Jill Batistick, our developmental editor. Her tireless efforts, attention to detail, and positive spirit made creating this book a more rewarding experience than I thought possible.

I would also like to thank Christina Robinson who helped in the development and testing of the exercises and test bank. Christina is a Graduate Student at the University of Nevada, Reno.

Michael V. Ekedahl would like to dedicate this book to his dog Rio for his companionship and his wife Sharon for her understanding and patience while completing this text.

# READ THIS BEFORE YOU BEGIN

The following information will help you as you prepare to use this textbook.

## TO THE USER OF THE DATA FILES

To complete the steps and projects in this book, you will need data files that have been created specifically for this book. Your instructor will provide the data files to you. You also can obtain the files electronically from the Thomson Course Technology Web site by connecting to *www.course.com* and then searching for this book title. Note that you can use a computer in your school lab or your own computer to complete the Hands-On Projects in this book.

The data files for this book are organized such that the examples and exercises are divided into folders named Chapter.*xx*, where *xx* is the chapter number. The completed program for the concept lesson appears in the folder Chapter*xx*ConceptLesson. A preview of the completed application lesson appears in the folder Chapter*xx*ApplicationPreview and the startup program appears in the folder Chapter*xx*ApplicationStartup within the Chapter.*xx* folder. Compiled solutions to selected Hands-On Projects appear in the Chapter.*xx*\HandsOnProjects folder. Use these precompiled solutions to help you visualize the end result of the steps. You can save the student files anywhere on your system unless specifically indicated otherwise in the chapter. Data files appear in a folder named Data beneath the Chapter.*xx* folder.

## USING YOUR OWN COMPUTER

To use your own computer to complete the steps and Hands-On Projects, you will need the following:

» **Software.** Microsoft Visual Studio 2005 Professional Edition or Microsoft Visual Basic 2005 Express Edition including the Microsoft .NET Framework version 2.0.

» **Hardware.** A Pentium II-class processor, 450 MHz or higher, personal computer, Windows 2000, or Windows XP.

» **Data Files.** You will not be able to complete the chapters and projects in this book using your own computer unless you have the data files. You can get the data files from your instructor, or you can obtain the data files electronically from the Thomson Course Technology Web site by connecting to *www.course.com* and then searching for this book title.

## VISIT OUR WORLD WIDE WEB SITE

Additional materials designed especially for this book might be available for your course. Periodically search *www.course.com* for more details.

# 1

# AN INTRODUCTION TO PROGRAMMING AND THE .NET FRAMEWORK

**After completing this chapter, you will be able to:**

Explain the software development life cycle

Describe selected tools used to help design software systems

Understand the control structures used in programming

Describe the evolution of programming languages

Understand the characteristics of object-oriented programming languages

Understand the syntax of programming languages

Understand the structure of a Visual Basic application

Write executable statements

Use the Command Prompt window to compile and execute
a Visual Basic application

# CONCEPT LESSON

## INTRODUCTION TO SOFTWARE DEVELOPMENT

Organizations must develop complex software systems in a timely manner that correctly solves a business problem. These software systems often consist of several computer programs that work together to form an effective system. Effective and efficient software systems can improve the overall efficiency of an organization. Ineffective and inefficient software systems can cost an organization millions of dollars or even cause an organization to fail. Thus, developing a software system made up of one or more computer programs involves much more than just sitting down at a computer, typing in a program, and then deploying that program to its end users.

The development of a software system involves performing a well-defined sequence of steps. Collectively, these steps are referred to as the **software development life cycle**. The steps involved in the software development life cycle are typically not performed by a single person. Rather, a software development team consists of end users, systems analysts, and programmers who work together to perform the following steps that make up the software development life cycle.

» *Problem identification*: In this first step, the business problem to be solved must be clearly defined. A problem might exist with an existing software system that needs to be rectified, or the problem might require automating a manual system. It is also quite common that a software system needs to be upgraded to provide new capabilities or to deal with changes in a business process.

» *System design*: In this step, the software development team clearly defines how the proposed system will solve the business problem or automate a business process. In essence, the development team builds the plans for the software system that will be later implemented. Several tools and techniques exist to help developers design software systems. Some of these tools are discussed in the next section of this chapter.

» *System implementation*: After the system design phase is complete, the software system can be implemented in this step using the chosen development environment and programming language. In practice, the development team must make conscious choices about which software development tool and programming language to use. Often, several programming languages may be used in the development of a complex software system. In this book, Visual Studio is used as the development environment and Visual Basic is used as the programming language.

» *System documentation*: Every good system has documentation. Some of the documentation in this step is designed for use by the software developers who will ultimately maintain the software system. Other documentation is intended for the end users who will be using the software system.

» *System testing*: Testing is an important part of the software development process. During this step, all of the features of the software system should be exhaustively tested to ensure that no errors exist and that the software system correctly solves the business problem that was identified in the problem identification phase. The testing should also ensure that the system implementation matches the original systems design. In addition, system testing involves the use of realistic test data. That is, if a system is designed to support 100,000 customers, it should be tested using 100,000 customers.

» *System deployment*: After a software system has been designed, implemented, and tested, it must be deployed in this step to the end users who will use the system. A software system is often deployed via removable media such as a CD-ROM or DVD, or deployed to the Internet or company intranet where it can be easily downloaded. The Visual Studio tools used to deploy applications are discussed in Appendix D.

» *Postimplementation audit*: After all the preceding steps have been performed, a postimplementation audit is performed to determine whether the system has fully met its objectives and if further development needs to be undertaken.

The software development life cycle is iterative. That is, after the postimplementation audit has been performed, errors might be detected that were not found during the design, implementation, or other phases. In such a case, the process begins again. In addition, the needs of businesses are dynamic. Thus, software systems are constantly undergoing modification to account for changes in business requirements and changes in business processes.

In this book, you will learn how to write Visual Basic applications, so much of this book is devoted to implementing systems rather than designing them. Where appropriate, flowcharts, pseudocode, and other diagrams will appear to help you visualize how an application or a particular part of an application works.

# SOFTWARE DESIGN METHODOLOGIES AND TOOLS

The simplest of computer applications can be created without much consideration to their design. For example, an application to tally a list of numbers or an application to determine whether a number is a prime number is simple enough that a single developer could implement it without spending much, if any, time designing the best solution to the problem. However, few applications are so simple.

To illustrate the importance of application design, think of a carpenter. If a skilled carpenter were to build a shed, that carpenter could likely do so without a set of plans, or at most, a very simple set of plans. However, when building a house, the problem becomes more complex and a set of plans becomes essential. As the house becomes larger and more intricate, those plans become even more important and detailed. Now expand the problem and think about building a skyscraper. Complex interacting systems, including power, heating and cooling, and water and sewage, must work together for the building to be useful to its occupants. Without detailed plans describing each system and how these systems interact with each other, building the skyscraper would be near impossible. In summary, the complexity of plans and models are a function of a system's complexity.

As software systems become more complex, the design and planning of those software systems becomes increasingly important. Just as a carpenter would not begin building a house without a set of plans, a software development team should not begin creating an application without first understanding the problem and designing the best solution to that problem. After the design is complete, developers can go to work implementing that design, testing the implementation, and finally deploying the application to the end users.

Several methodologies exist to help software developers design software systems that work correctly and that accurately solve a business problem or set of business problems. These tools all apply some type of model to help developers fully understand and describe the software system being developed. Simply put, a **model** is a simplified, and often visual, representation of reality. Just as architects often create elaborate physical models of buildings before they are actually built, good software systems are designed and modeled. The following list summarizes selected system analysis methodologies, tools, and models discussed in this chapter:

» *Pseudocode*: Pseudocode uses English-like statements to depict the actions performed by an application, and the order in which those actions are performed.

» *Top-down design*: Using the top-down design process, general tasks are broken down or subdivided into more specific tasks, which are then broken down into even more specific tasks. After the general tasks have been decomposed into small tasks, they can be solved more easily. This design approach is often called the divide-and-conquer approach.

» *Flowcharting*: Using flowcharting, standardized graphical symbols are used to depict the actions performed by an application, and the order in which those actions are performed.

**»** *The Unified Modeling Language*: One of the predominant software design tools in use today is the Unified Modeling Language (UML). The UML supplies numerous graphical templates to specify how various end users will interact with the system. Other graphical templates are used to define how the system itself is organized and the actions performed by each component that makes up the system.

In the following sections, each of these tools is described along with how they might be used to design or model a common business process: an ATM withdrawal transaction.

## PSEUDOCODE

Pseudocode lies somewhere between English and the programming statements that are written to solve the business problem at hand. Using **pseudocode**, English-like statements are used to describe the specific steps that must be performed to complete a given task. The following pseudocode describes the steps necessary to perform an ATM withdrawal:

```
Start
Get the PIN number.
Validate the PIN number.
If the PIN number is valid, then perform the following steps:
    Get the desired withdrawal amount from the customer.
    Validate that the account contains sufficient funds.
    If the account contains sufficient funds, then perform the
    following steps:
        Dispense the cash.
        Deduct the amount withdrawn from the available balance.
    Otherwise
        Reject the transaction.
    End of decision
Otherwise
    Reject the transaction.
End of decision
Stop
```

As you can see, pseudocode describes the activities that an application or part of an application needs to perform. Of course, the preceding example is simplified. It does not account for other types of transactions, such as deposits, credit lines, or balance inquiries.

Pseudocode is not an exact science. That is, just as different authors use different words and sentences to express a thought, different developers might write pseudocode differently, but most pseudocode shares the following characteristics:

**»** The words "start" and "stop" are typically used to denote the beginning and end of a process.

» The word "if" is used to indicate a decision. The actions taken as a result of the decision are indented for readability.

» Decisions can be nested. That is, one decision can appear inside of another decision. Nested decisions are also indented.

## TOP-DOWN DESIGN

Top-down design is another approach to the design process. Using **top-down design**, the general tasks to be accomplished are first defined. Those general tasks are then decomposed into more specific tasks, which can then be further decomposed into more specific tasks. The goal of top-down design is to divide a complex problem into its individual component parts. One of the visual tools used to represent the top-down design approach is the **Hierarchical Input Process Output (HIPO)** chart. Figure 1-1 illustrates the HIPO chart for an ATM withdrawal.

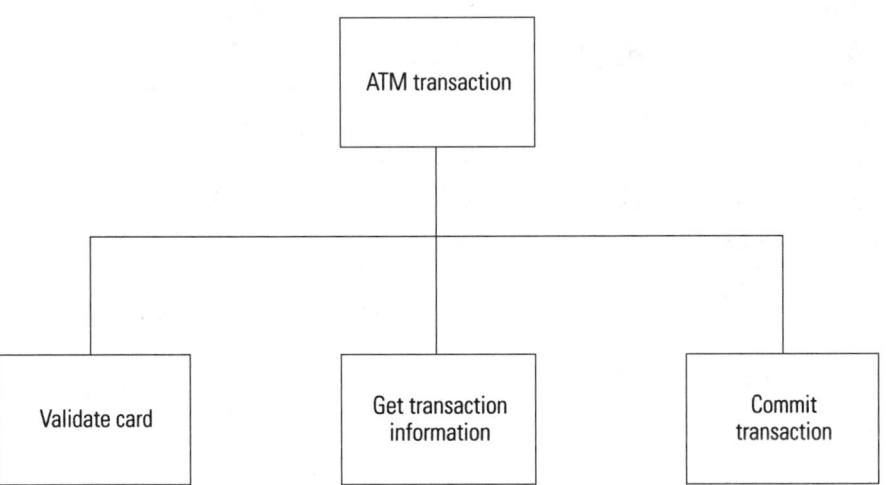

Figure 1-1: HIPO chart for an ATM withdrawal

As shown in Figure 1-1, the general task is the ATM transaction. That general task is subdivided into validating the card, getting the transaction information from the customer, and finally committing the transaction.

In the ATM example shown in Figure 1-1, only one level of subtasks exists. However, more complex problems might require several levels of subtasks. To illustrate, the HIPO chart shown in Figure 1-1 could be further decomposed into more specific steps, as shown in Figure 1-2.

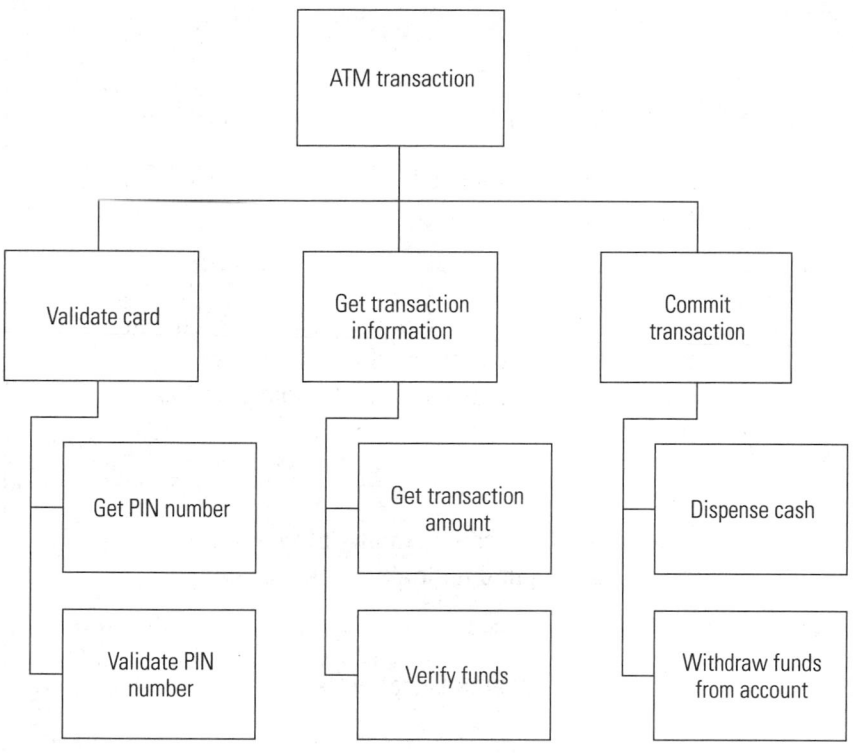

Figure 1-2: Expanded HIPO chart

As shown in Figure 1-2, the step of validating the card is further decomposed into getting the PIN number and validating the PIN number. The task to get the transaction information and committing the transaction are also divided into two steps. The steps to get the transaction information are decomposed into getting the transaction amount and verifying that the account has sufficient funds. The steps to commit the transaction are also divided into dispensing the cash and withdrawing the funds from the customer's account.

## FLOWCHARTING

Flowcharting is another graphical technique used to diagram the activities performed by an application. A **flowchart** consists of standard graphical symbols connected together to depict the processing that occurs in an application or in part of an application. Each graphical symbol denotes a specific type of operation, as shown in Table 1-1.

> **»»NOTE**
> Top-down design is also known as hierarchical application design or design-by-explosion.

| Symbol | Purpose |
|---|---|
| | A box represents a single step or multiple steps in a process. |
| | A diamond is used to mark a decision or branching point. Lines representing different decision outcomes emerge from different points on the diamond. |
| | The polygon represents input data entering the system or output data leaving the system. |
| | This icon represents stored data. |
| | This icon represents manual keyboard input. |
| | This icon represents a database file. |
| | This icon denotes displaying data to the screen or other soft copy device. |
| | This icon represents some terminal activity such as the start of a process or the end of a process. |
| | This icon marks a subroutine or a sequence of actions embedded in a larger process. |

Table 1-1: Flowchart symbols *(Continued)*  ▶

| | |
|---|---|
| ○ | A connector is used to connect two execution paths. The two execution paths are typically formed as a result of a decision. |
| ⬠ | This icon marks an off-page reference. That is, it is used to denote a flowchart or part of a flowchart that appears elsewhere. |
| → | The flow lines connect the preceding elements in this table to illustrate the flow of information in a process. |

Table 1-1: Flowchart symbols

Figure 1-3 shows various flowchart elements and how they can be used to create a generic flowchart.

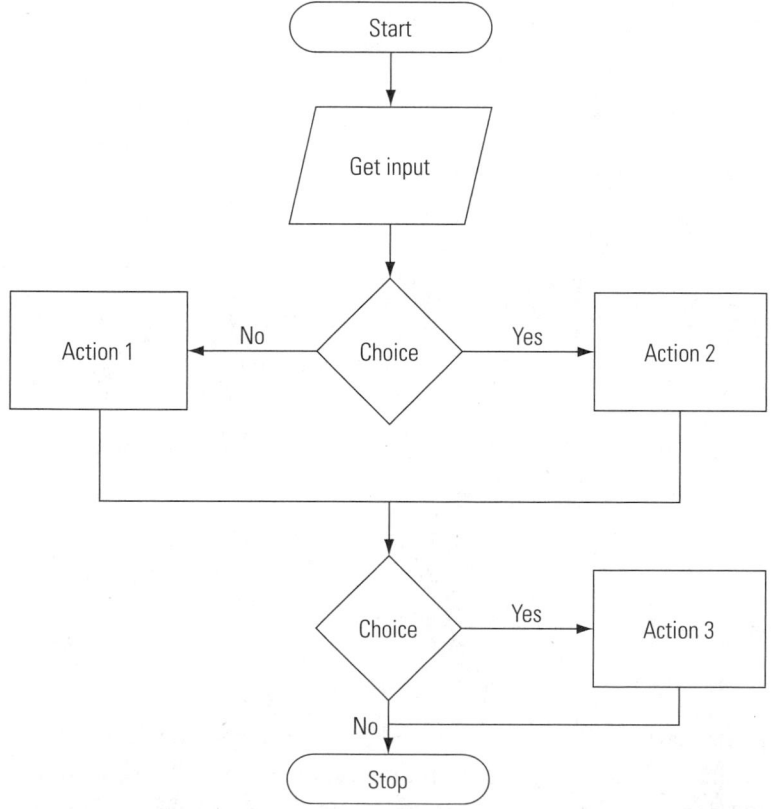

Figure 1-3: Generic flowchart

As shown in Figure 1-3, the Start element indicates the entry point for the task. The end user then enters an input value. A choice is then made. If the end user enters "No," "Action 1" is performed. If the end user enters "Yes," "Action 2" is performed. A second choice is then made. If "Yes" is chosen, "Action 3" is performed and the activity exits. If "No" is chosen, no more actions are performed and the activity exits.

Figure 1-4 illustrates the flowchart to perform the same ATM withdrawal transaction discussed in the previous section of the chapter.

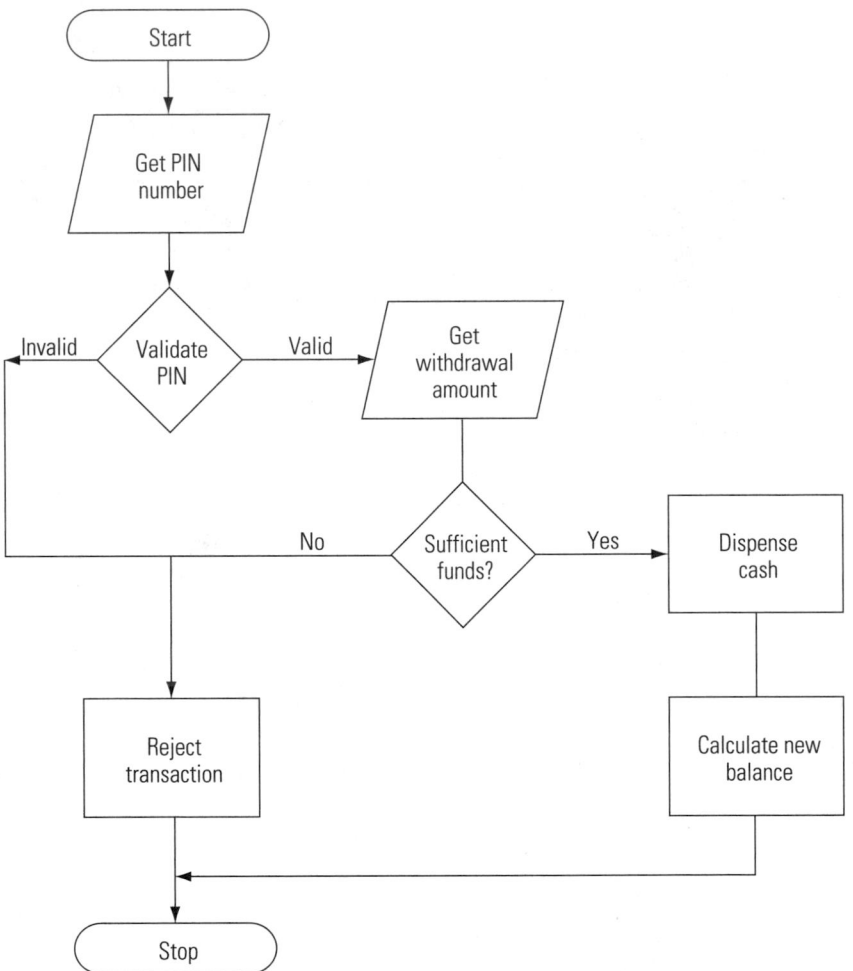

Figure 1-4: ATM withdrawal flowchart

The start and stop symbols mark the beginning and end of the process. The first input to the process is the PIN number entered by the customer. As mentioned in Table 1-1, the diamond-shaped symbol denotes a decision. That is, the PIN number is checked to see whether it is valid. If the PIN number is not valid, the transaction is rejected and the process ends. If the PIN number is valid, the requested withdrawal amount is obtained from the customer. Then, a second decision is made based on whether the customer has sufficient funds in his account. This second decision has two possible outcomes. If there are sufficient funds, the cash is dispensed, the new balance is calculated, and the process ends. If there are insufficient funds, the transaction is rejected and the process ends.

Unlike a HIPO chart, a flowchart diagrams the activities that occur in a business process and the order in which those activities occur. Note that the two diagrams have similarities though. Both list the activities being performed.

## THE UNIFIED MODELING LANGUAGE

The **Unified Modeling Language (UML)** is a standard language used to model complex software systems in a visual way. The UML consists of several diagrams, each of which models a specific aspect of the system. Some of these UML diagrams can be used in place of the other diagrams discussed in the preceding section. For example, the UML activity diagram can be used in place of a flowchart.

The following list describes three of the common UML diagrams and their purpose:

> » A *class diagram* models the conceptual and physical aspects of a system. In other words, it models the data maintained by the system and the possible actions that can be performed on that data. Going back to the ATM transaction, a customer's balance and PIN number are both data items. Making a withdrawal is considered an action. Performing the action causes a change in the data. That is, the customer's balance is reduced by the amount of the withdrawal.

> » *Use case* diagrams model the actors (users) of the system and the interaction between those actors with the system itself. In the ATM transaction example, the customer is the actor.

> » *Activity diagrams* show the actions performed by the system and the order in which those actions are performed. Conceptually, activity diagrams are similar to flowcharts.

Figure 1-5 shows the UML class diagram for the ATM transaction.

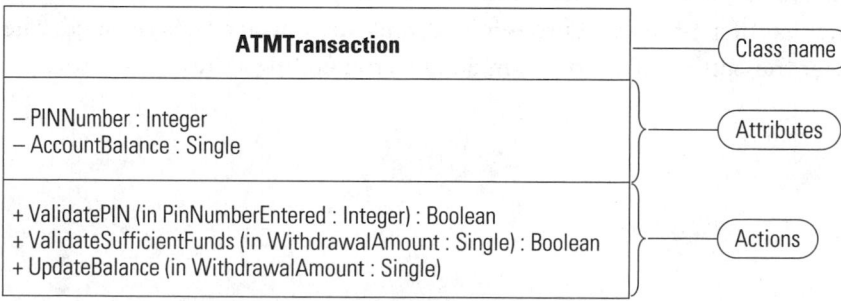

Figure 1-5: UML class diagram

As shown in Figure 1-5, a UML class diagram is made up of three sections. The top section contains the name of the class. The middle section contains the attributes (data) of the class. The attributes shown in Figure 1-5 are the PIN number and the account balance. The operations make up the bottom section. The data passed to the operation appear in parentheses. The three operations involved in the ATM transaction are validating the PIN number, dispensing the cash, and updating the account balance.

Figure 1-6 shows the UML use case diagram for the ATM transaction.

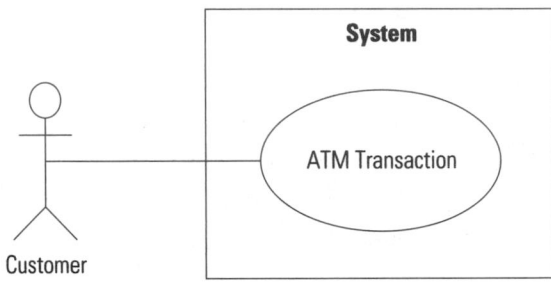

Figure 1-6: UML use case diagram

As shown in Figure 1-6, a rectangular box defines the boundaries of the system. The ATM transaction itself is considered the use case and the customer is the only actor.

Figure 1-7 illustrates the UML activity diagram for an ATM transaction. Note that the UML activity diagram resembles a flowchart. The solid black circle at the top of the diagram represents the activity's initial state. The next state is called an "activity state." The activity is to get the PIN number from the customer. The next state denotes that the PIN number has been entered. The top horizontal black bar represents a decision. In UML terms, this is called a "fork transition." If the PIN number is valid, the withdrawal amount is obtained from the customer and the funds are verified. Again, these are both activity states. A final fork transition is made depending on whether there are sufficient funds. If the customer's account has sufficient funds, the cash is dispensed, and the withdrawal amount is deducted from the customer's balance. The final element in the diagram is the "join transition." Here, the outcome of the invalid PIN number and insufficient funds states is joined, and the transaction is rejected. The bordered circle at the bottom of the diagram denotes the ending state.

**»NOTE**

Applications like Visio support visual diagrams that describe the structure of a software system or specific tasks performed by a software system. These diagrams include flowcharts and UML diagrams to name a few.

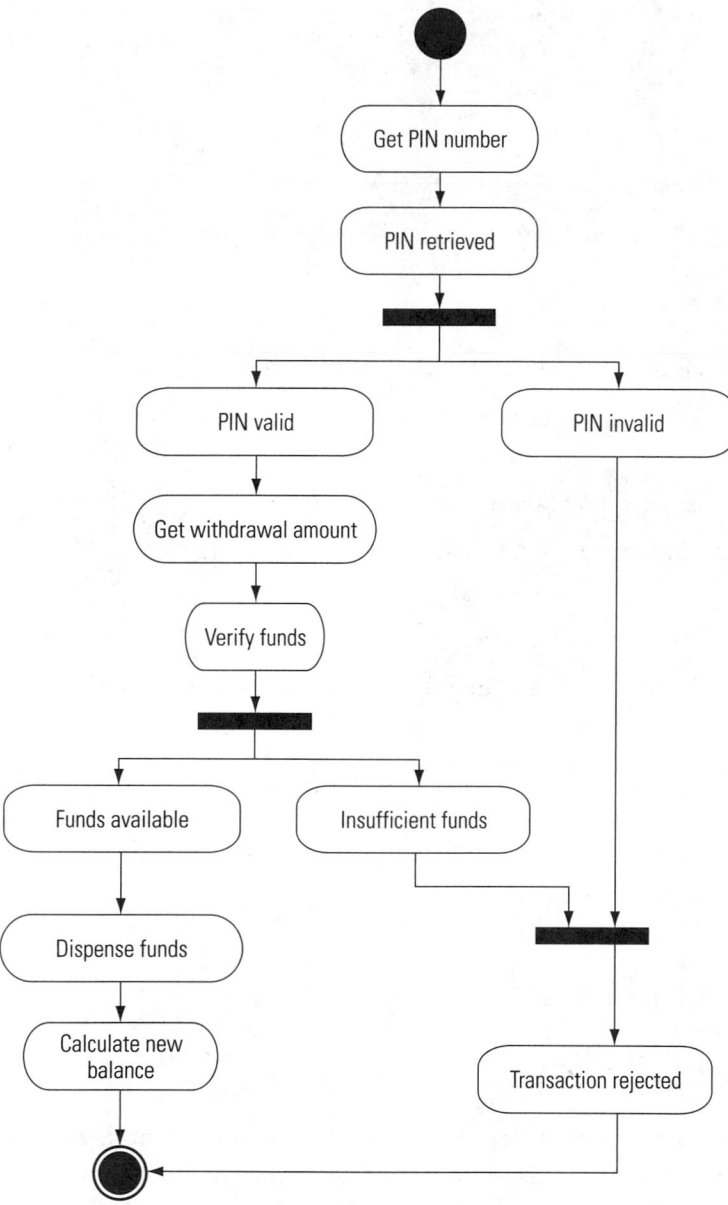

Figure 1-7: UML activity diagram

The diagrams appearing in Figures 1-1 through 1-7 model an extremely simple task. However, most applications are much more complex, making the models more useful for explaining complex sets of tasks and the relationships between those tasks. As you progress through this book, UML diagrams, flowcharts, and other diagrams will be used to describe various programming concepts.

## MINI-QUIZ 1

1. List the steps in the software development life cycle.

2. If you were using the top-down design model, which would be the most appropriate chart to use?

   a. flowchart

   b. UML use case diagram

   c. HIPO chart

   d. UML activity diagram

3. What is the name of the UML diagram that has characteristics similar to a Flowchart?

4. What does a UML class diagram attempt to model?

   a. the activities performed by the system and the order in which those activities are performed

   b. how the users interact with the system

   c. the data maintained by the system and the possible actions performed on that data

   d. none of the above

# INTRODUCTION TO PROGRAMMING CONTROL STRUCTURES

All computer applications are written using three control structures. These **control structures** define the order in which tasks are performed, whether a certain set of tasks is performed, and how many times a task is performed. These three control structures are the sequence, selection, and repetition structures. Each is discussed in turn in the following sections of the chapter, along with how control structures are used together.

## THE SEQUENCE STRUCTURE

As the name implies, the **sequence structure** defines the order or sequence in which a task is performed. For example, when you follow a recipe, you perform a well-defined sequence of steps. These steps are followed in the order in which they appear in the recipe. Figure 1-8 shows the generic flowchart for a sequence structure.

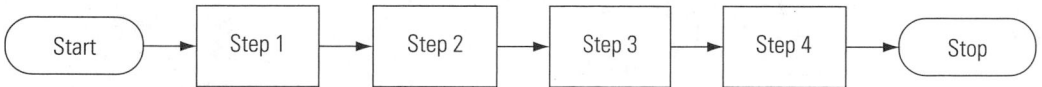

Figure 1-8: Sequence structure

Figure 1-8 depicts the sequence structure using a flowchart. As shown in Figure 1-8, the sequence structure has a starting and ending state. After the starting state, a series of steps is performed one after another in a sequence. After the steps have been performed, the sequence ends, and the ending state is reached.

## THE SELECTION STRUCTURE

The **selection structure** is used to make decisions. In the preceding section about modeling, the selection structure was used to make a decision about whether a PIN number was valid and whether a customer had sufficient funds in their account. The selection structure is used in conjunction with the sequence structure. That is, based on a particular decision, sequential steps are performed or other decisions are made. To illustrate, some recipes vary based on the altitude. A decision is made to follow one sequence of steps for high-altitude baking and another sequence of steps for low-altitude baking.

The selection structure takes three forms; the single-alternative decision structure, the dual-alternative decision structure, and the multiple-alternative decision structure. Each form of decision structure is discussed next.

### THE SINGLE-ALTERNATIVE DECISION STRUCTURE

The single-alternative decision structure causes specific tasks to be performed only if the decision outcome is true. If the decision outcome is false, those tasks are not performed and sequential statement execution continues. This type of decision structure is commonly called a one-way decision structure or a unary decision structure. Figure 1-9 shows a generic flowchart for a one-way decision structure.

### THE DUAL-ALTERNATIVE DECISION STRUCTURE

The dual-alternative decision structure causes one group of tasks to be performed if a decision's outcome is true, and another group of tasks to be performed if the outcome of the decision is false. Then, sequential execution continues at the statements following the dual-alternative decision statement. This form of selection structure is also called a two-way decision structure or a binary decision structure. Figure 1-10 shows the flowchart for a two-way decision structure.

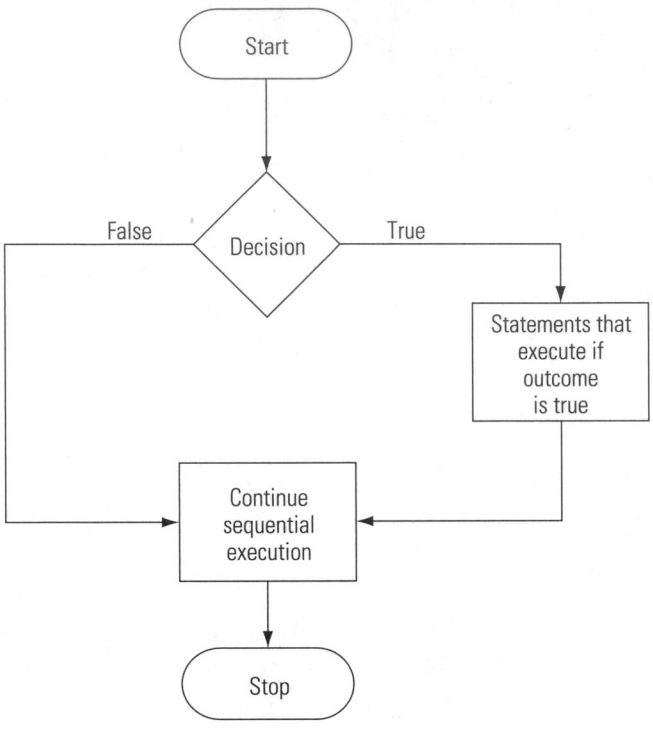

Figure 1-9: One-way decision structure flowchart

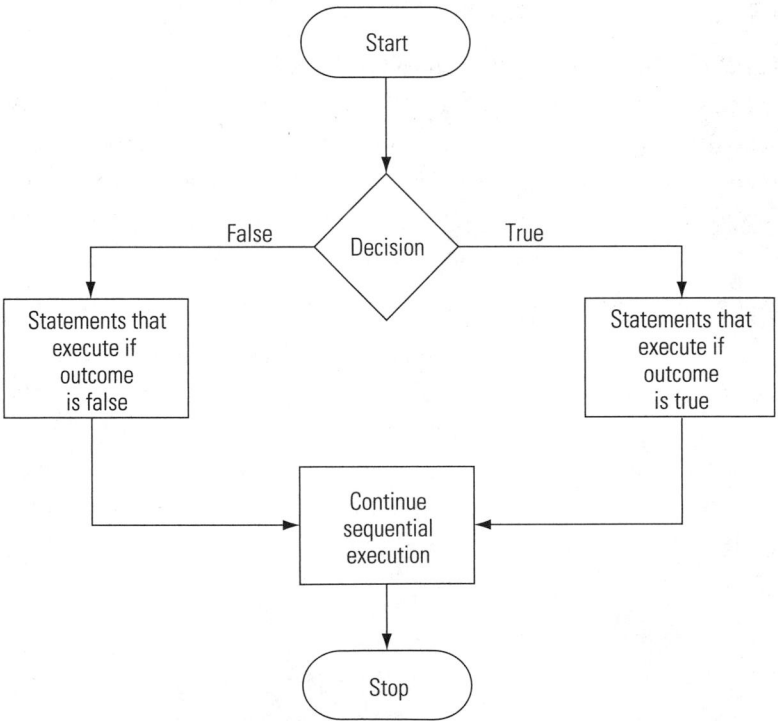

Figure 1-10: Two-way decision structure flowchart

## THE MULTIPLE-ALTERNATIVE DECISION STRUCTURE

The multiple-alternative decision structure has three or more possible outcomes. This decision structure is also called a multiway decision structure. Figure 1-11 shows the flowchart for a multiway decision structure.

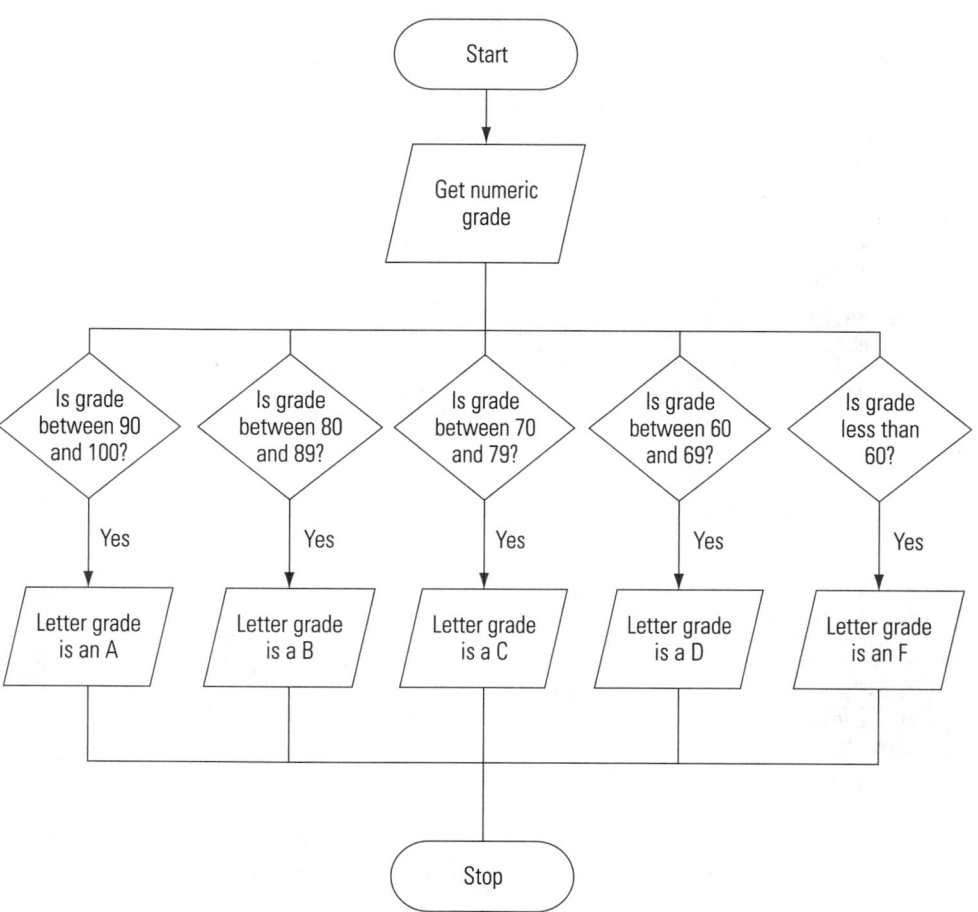

Figure 1-11: Multiway decision structure flowchart

Figure 1-11 uses the example of converting a numeric grade into a letter grade. Because letter grades are typically A, B, C, D, and F, there are five possible outcomes to the decision based on the numeric grade.

## THE REPETITION STRUCTURE

The **repetition structure** is used to perform a given task repeatedly, hence the name. Repetition structures are often called loops. Going back to the ATM transaction example, most ATM machines allow the customer to try three times to enter a valid PIN number. After three failed attempts, the ATM machine keeps the card. The repetition structure also involves making a decision about whether a particular set of steps need to be repeated. Figure 1-12 shows the flowchart for a repetition structure again using the same ATM example.

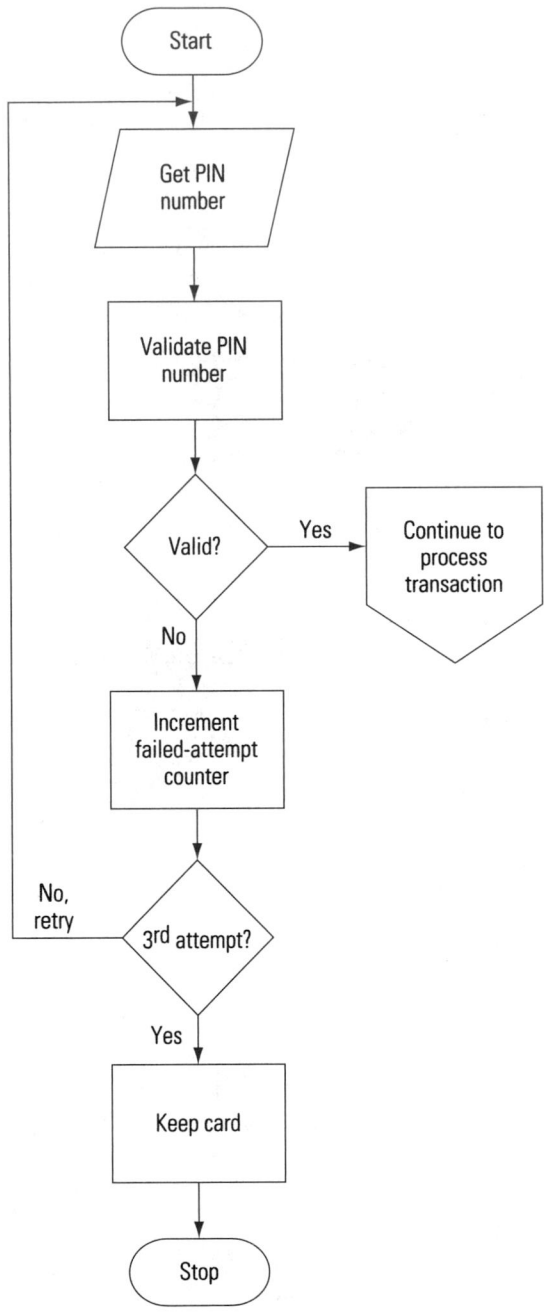

Figure 1-12: Repetition structure flowchart

As shown in Figure 1-12, the repetition structure works in conjunction with the selection structure, as the selection structure is used to determine whether to repeat the sequence. If the customer enters an invalid PIN number, a counter is incremented to keep track of the number of failed attempts. A decision is then made to continue based on the value of the counter. If there have been three failed attempts, the ATM machine is instructed to keep the card. Otherwise, the customer can try again to enter a valid PIN number.

## COMBINING CONTROL STRUCTURES

Most applications use the preceding three control structures together to get input from the end user, process that input, and produce the required output. In other words, a decision structure will likely contain statements having a sequence structure. Or a repetition structure might contain decision-making statements. Furthermore, decision-making structures might contain other (nested) decision-making structures, and loops might contain other (nested) loops. Figure 1-13 shows how the preceding three control structures can be combined.

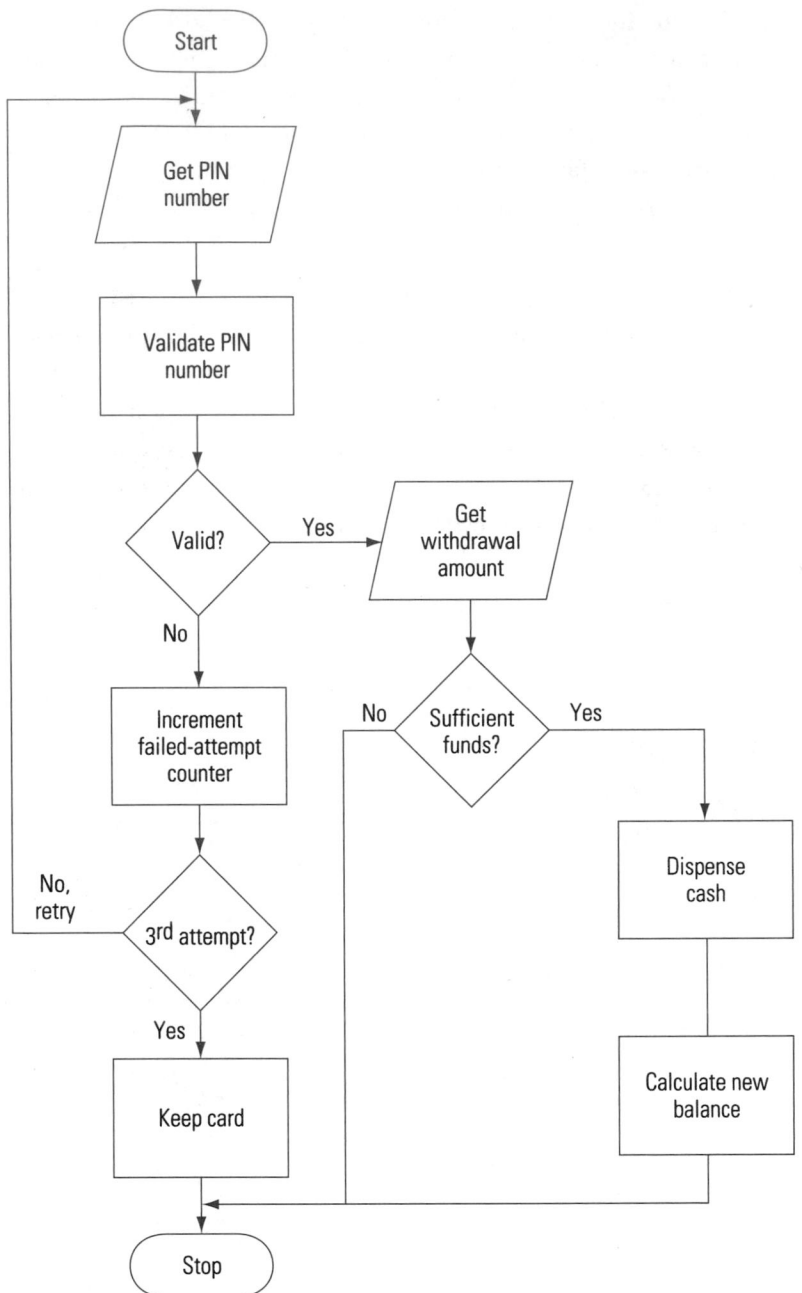

Figure 1-13: Combining control structures

Having introduced some of the modeling techniques used to design software systems and the control structures used to implement those systems, you will now learn about the characteristics of programming languages and how they are used to implement software systems.

# THE EVOLUTION OF COMPUTER PROGRAMMING LANGUAGES

After a software system has been designed, it must be implemented so as to create a computer application that can be run by the end user. Of course, in this book, all the applications you create will be implemented using Visual Basic. However, other programming languages such as C#, Java, or C++ could be used too. All of these programming languages share similar characteristics and features. For example, each of the preceding programming languages supports the sequence, selection, and repetition structures. In addition, each of the preceding languages is an object-oriented language.

Just as all technologies mature, so too has the technology surrounding computer programming and computer programming languages. Computer programming languages are often categorized into first-, second-, third-, and fourth-generation languages. The generations of programming languages and their characteristics are discussed next.

## FIRST-GENERATION MACHINE LANGUAGES

**Machine languages** were the first generation of programming languages. Using a machine language, a computer program was written in the binary 1s and 0s that would then execute on the corresponding computer hardware. Each type of computer had its own unique machine language because the hardware differed from one computer type to the next. To illustrate, the following hexadecimal values represent the machine language instructions required to add the numbers 2 and 5 together on a MOS 6502 processor, which was used in the original Apple II computer:

```
1000   A9   02   69   05   8D   A0   0F   60
```

A machine language consists of operation codes that correspond to the operations supported by the underlying computer hardware. In the preceding machine language program, A9 is the operation code to load a register called the accumulator with the value 2. A register is a storage location within a CPU. 69 is the operation code to add two values. The value 5 is added to the value stored in the accumulator. In addition to operation codes, machine language uses operands. Operands are data, such as the numbers 2 and 5 used in the preceding example.

The following code segment illustrates these same machine instructions expressed in binary:

```
1000   10101001   00000010   01101001   00000101   10001101   10100000
00001111   01100000
```

As you can see, machine languages are extremely cryptic. The cryptic nature of machine languages made programming them slow, tedious, and error prone. Thus, machine language developers were not very efficient.

## SECOND-GENERATION ASSEMBLY LANGUAGES

Assembly languages were the second generation of programming languages. An **assembly language** is made up of mnemonic operation codes (opcodes) that correspond to the binary machine language instructions understood by the underlying computer hardware. For example, the assembly language instruction LDA (load accumulator) corresponds to the machine language instruction A9 on a MOS 6502 processor. The assembly language instruction ADC (add with carry) performs the addition and corresponds to the machine language instruction 69.

Just as each type of CPU has its own unique machine language, each type of CPU has its own assembly language. A program called an **assembler** translates the assembly language instructions into the machine language instructions understood by the underlying CPU. Figure 1-14 illustrates the relationship between assembly language statements, an assembler, and machine language statements.

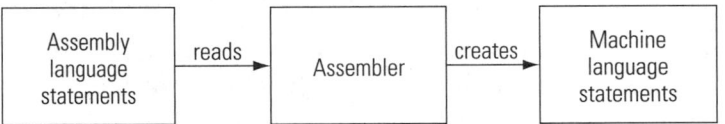

Figure 1-14: Relationship between assembly language and machine language

The following code segment illustrates the assembly language program to add the numbers 2 and 5 together on a MOS 6502 processor. The second column group contains the actual machine language code expressed as hexadecimal values, and the rightmost column group contains the assembly language statements.

```
1000      A9 02        LDA  #$02
1002      69 05        ADC  #$05
1004      8D A0 0F     STA  $0FA0
1007      60           RTS
```

Examining the preceding code segment, the first column lists a pseudo memory address. The second column group contains the machine language operation codes and operands. These are the same machine language operation codes and operands (expressed in hexadecimal) shown in the preceding machine language example. The third column group contains the assembly language instructions and the operands for those instructions.

The first of the preceding statements (load accumulator) loads the value 2 into the accumulator, which is a CPU register. The second statement (add with carry) performs the addition, thereby adding 5 to the value stored in the accumulator. As a result of the addition, the value 7 is stored in the accumulator. The third statement (store accumulator) stores the value of the accumulator into memory, and the final statement (return from subroutine) returns from the subroutine.

Assembly language was a big improvement over machine language. However, developers were still forced to understand and work with the underlying computer hardware. Thus, assembly languages were very primitive compared to the more English-like statements provided by the third- and fourth-generation programming languages used today.

## THIRD-GENERATION PROGRAMMING LANGUAGES

Third-generation programming languages represented a significant improvement over second-generation languages. Third-generation programming languages are characterized by more human-readable statements that do not rely on the underlying computer hardware. The FORTRAN programming language, short for FORmula TRANslation, was introduced in 1957 and was the first third-generation programming language. Using FORTRAN, a developer could write more English-like statements to perform a given task, as shown in the following statements:

```
Total = 2 + 5
Write(6, 100) Total
```

The first of the preceding statements adds the values 2 and 5 together and stores the result in the variable named Total. The second statement displays the result of the arithmetic operation. Even without understanding the FORTRAN programming language, you could guess that two values are being added together to calculate a result.

To execute a computer program written in a third-generation language, source statements, written in a language such as FORTRAN, are translated into assembly language by another program called a **compiler**. Those assembly language statements are then translated into machine language statements by an assembler. This is the same assembler discussed in the previous section about second-generation programming languages. Figure 1-15 illustrates the relationships between a third-generation language program, a compiler, the assembly language statements produced by the compiler, the assembler, and the machine language that is produced.

One significant benefit of third-generation programming languages was **machine independence**. A machine-independent program could be written once and compiled by different compilers to execute on different CPUs. That is, a single FORTRAN program could be passed through different compilers producing different assembly and machine language for the target computer. Clearly, this capability increased the efficiency of developers and made a program available to the broadest number of end users. Figure 1-16 illustrates the compilation of a machine-independent program.

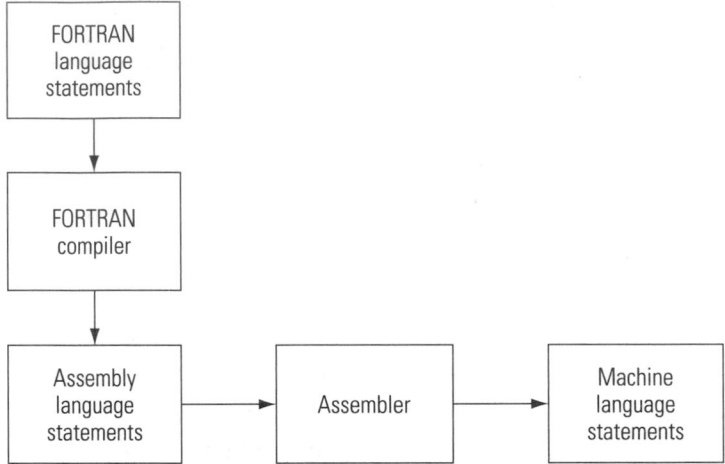

Figure 1-15: Compiling third-generation programs

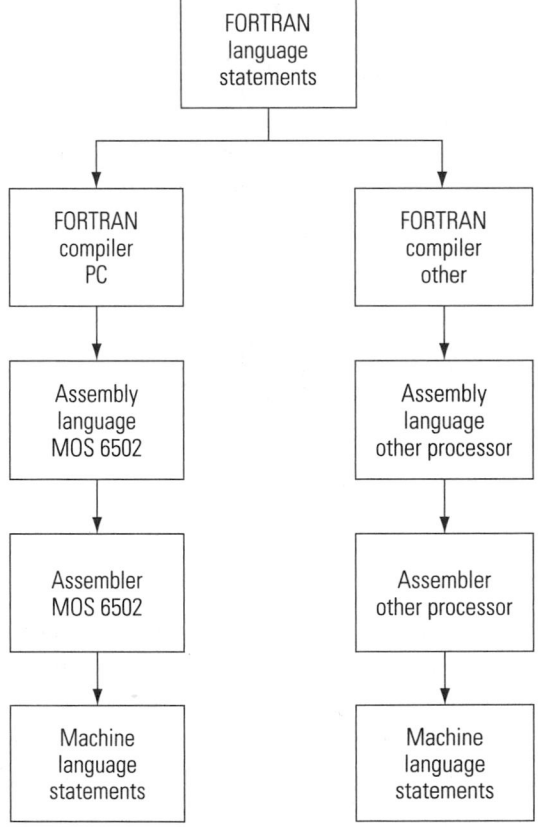

Figure 1-16: Compiling a machine-independent program

Following FORTRAN, numerous other third-generation programming languages were developed, including the Common Business Oriented Language (COBOL), which is used to solve business problems. BASIC, Pascal, and C are also third-generation programming languages. Each of these languages uses a compiler to translate source statements into assembly language statements, which are then translated into an executable application.

Visual Studio compiles a program's source statements into a machine-independent form of assembly language called intermediate language (IL). The following Visual Basic statements:

```
Dim Total As Integer
Total = 2 + 5
Console.WriteLine(Total)
```

are translated into the following IL:

```
IL_0000:        nop
IL_0001:        call    string
[mscorlib/*23000001*/]System.Console/*01000002*/::ReadLine()/*
0A000001 */
IL_0006:        stloc.0
IL_0007:        ldloc.0
IL_0008:        call    void
[mscorlib/*23000001*/]System.Console/*01000002*/::WriteLine
(string) /*  0A000002 */
IL_000d:        nop
IL_000e:        nop
IL_000f:        ret
```

As you can see, IL bears a striking resemblance to assembly language. However, there is one big difference between IL and assembly language. IL is the same no matter the underlying CPU. When a computer program written in any .NET programming language is compiled, the same IL is produced. When a .NET program is executed, the IL is translated into an executable form that is understood by the target CPU architecture using another utility program called the just-in-time compiler (JIT).

## FOURTH-GENERATION PROGRAMMING LANGUAGES

Fourth-generation languages are characterized as nonprocedural software tools that enable end users to create applications with little or no technical assistance. Fourth-generation languages are often called **natural languages**. The Microsoft Access Report Writer and

Microsoft Access Query-by-Example utility are good examples of fourth-generation languages. Using these tools, end users can create reports and queries without any knowledge of computer programming. Fourth-generation languages continue to evolve but their capabilities remain limited. As yet, they have not replaced third-generation programming languages nor are they likely to do so in the near future.

# INTRODUCTION TO OBJECT-ORIENTED PROGRAMMING LANGUAGES

Although the cost of computer hardware is falling, the cost to develop and maintain computer software is not. The software industry faces the challenges of developing increasingly complex software systems that are easy to maintain, modify, enhance, and reuse. To face these challenges, the software industry is turning more and more to object-oriented programming languages, which are languages that attempt to combine together data, and the processes acting on that data, so as to mimic a business process.

Visual Basic, along with the other Visual Studio programming languages, are considered **object-oriented programming languages**. In such a programming language, objects are created from classes. A **class** is a template or blueprint for an object that describes the data stored in the class and the actions that can be performed on that data. To illustrate the relationship between a class and an object, think back to the idea of building a house. The blueprints for a house are considered the template or class. Suppose that several houses are being built from the same set of blueprints. Each house (object) is created from its blueprint (class). Each house has the same characteristics (has the same number of rooms, for example). However, each object created from the class has its own data. That is, each house has a color but each house has its own color.

In Visual Basic, the buttons and boxes you create on a form are created from classes too. Button objects appearing on a form are created from the `Button` class, and boxes appearing on a form are created from the `TextBox` class. These are but two of the thousands of classes supported by Visual Studio.

Figure 1-17 illustrates how multiple objects are created from the same class.

**»NOTE**

In object-oriented programming, an object can be thought of as a black box. It is not necessary to understand how the black box works to use it. To illustrate, think of a DVD player as a black box. You press a button to play a DVD and it begins to play. However, it is not necessary for you to understand how the DVD player works to use it.

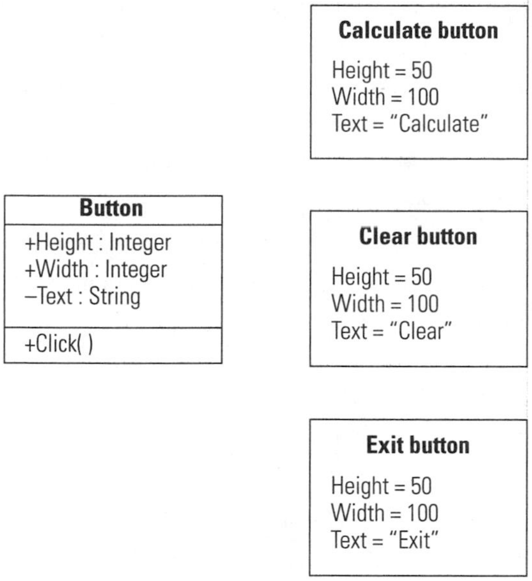

**Calculate button**

Height = 50
Width = 100
Text = "Calculate"

**Button**

+Height : Integer
+Width : Integer
−Text : String

+Click( )

**Clear button**

Height = 50
Width = 100
Text = "Clear"

**Exit button**

Height = 50
Width = 100
Text = "Exit"

Figure 1-17: Relationship between a class and objects created from the class

Figure 1-17 shows a partial UML class diagram for the Button class. The diagram shows three attributes named Height, Width, and Text. The figure also shows an event named Click. Assuming that a form has three buttons, there would be three instances of the Button control on the form, each storing their own data and performing a unique action when clicked.

## CHARACTERISTICS OF OBJECT-ORIENTED PROGRAMMING LANGUAGES

All object-oriented programming languages, including Visual Basic, C#, C++, and Java, use classes to mimic the behavior of real-world objects. That is, the Button class mimics a clickable button and the TextBox class is made up of a box in which the end user can enter text and text can be displayed.

All object-oriented programming languages share common characteristics, as mentioned in the following list:

» *Encapsulation*: In an object-oriented programming language, data and the processes that act on that data are coupled together. Encapsulation is a way of packaging data and processes such that the inner workings of the class are hidden from the developer using the class. Adhering to the rules of encapsulation requires that the data in a class can only be modified by a process of the class.

» *Inheritance*: Inheritance, simply put, allows a new class to be created from an existing class such that the new class inherits the data and processes from the existing class.

The concept of inheritance can be introduced via a metaphor. Recall the taxonomy of species from biology. It includes the following taxonomic categories: kingdom, phylum, class, order, family, genus, and species. There are two kingdoms: plant and animal. All plants have, or inherit, the general characteristics from the plant kingdom. All animals inherit the general characteristics from the animal kingdom. At each level in the taxonomy, new characteristics are added.

» *Information hiding*: Some information is hidden inside of a class. All computer programs perform operations on data. A customer name, an account balance, and a credit limit all represent data. Although a bank teller can look up a credit limit, the information about how the credit limit was calculated might be hidden from the teller. The principle of information hiding says that only the essential characteristics of information are exposed, and the internal details of how that information is determined are hidden.

» *Polymorphism*: In Greek, polymorphism means "having multiple forms." Applied to programming, suppose three classes named TextEmail, SoundEmail, and PictureEmail are inherited from a class named Email. Using polymorphism, executing a function from the Email class would cause the correct function to be called in the proper TextEmail, SoundEmail, or PictureEmail classes.

The preceding list described characteristics shared by all object-oriented programming languages. As you progress through this book, you will learn how to create your own classes and apply these object-oriented concepts. Having introduced general object-oriented concepts, you will now learn how Visual Studio implements those object-oriented programming concepts.

## THE VISUAL STUDIO IMPLEMENTATION OF OBJECT-ORIENTED PROGRAMMING

Let's look at classes and object-oriented programming from a more technical perspective. The only way for a developer to interact with a class is through its interface. In this context, the term interface does not mean user interface. The term **interface** refers to the formal specifications by which the developer writes statements to read and write data stored in a class, and perform the actions supported by the class.

The interface for all Visual Basic classes consists of the following elements:

» Objects are created from their underlying class. That is, Button objects are created from the Button class. To create an object from its underlying class, Visual Studio uses a **constructor**. A constructor is a procedure that is called to create an instance of a class.

» The data items defined by a class are called **properties**. For example, every button supports properties that define its size and position on the form, and the caption of the button. Building on the house example, the House class may define a Color property. Each class instance (object) has its own data copy. Thus, the house has a property named `Color`. However, each class instance (House object) can have a unique color because each class instance has its own data copy.

» In addition to storing data, classes can perform actions that might or might not modify the data (properties) stored in a class instance. For example, there are .NET classes that perform generic tasks such as opening, reading, and writing files. Using object-oriented terminology, these tasks or actions are called **methods**.

» A class can also handle events. The Windows operating system generates an **event** as a result of some end user activity such as clicking a button or moving the mouse. This action is referred to as *firing an event*. Windows can also fire events itself without any end user activity. For example, the `Timer` class generates an event at regular intervals, much like an alarm clock going off every 10 minutes or at some other constant interval. As a developer, you create statements in an **event handler** that execute in response to Windows firing a particular event. Event handlers are also known as *event procedures*. Procedures are discussed later in the chapter. The statements appearing inside an event handler execute when a specific event fires. For example, assume that a form has a button intended to exit the application when clicked by the end user. You, as the developer, create a `Click` event handler that will execute to call the `Close` method of the form. The statements in the event handler automatically run when the end user clicks the button.

In a typical event-driven application, the application sits idle waiting for an event to fire. When Windows fires an event, the application performs some action in response to the event. After the desired action is complete, the application sits idle again waiting for the next event to fire. Collectively, the preceding steps are known as the event processing loop. Figure 1-18 shows a flowchart for the event processing loop.

As shown in Figure 1-18, the application starts, and then waits for an event to fire. Based on end user interaction, Windows fires one of three events. When an event fires because the end user clicked a button, Windows executes the corresponding event handler (procedure). When execution of the event handler is complete, the application again enters the waiting state until Windows fires another event. In Figure 1-18, execution of the event handler for the Exit button causes the application to end.

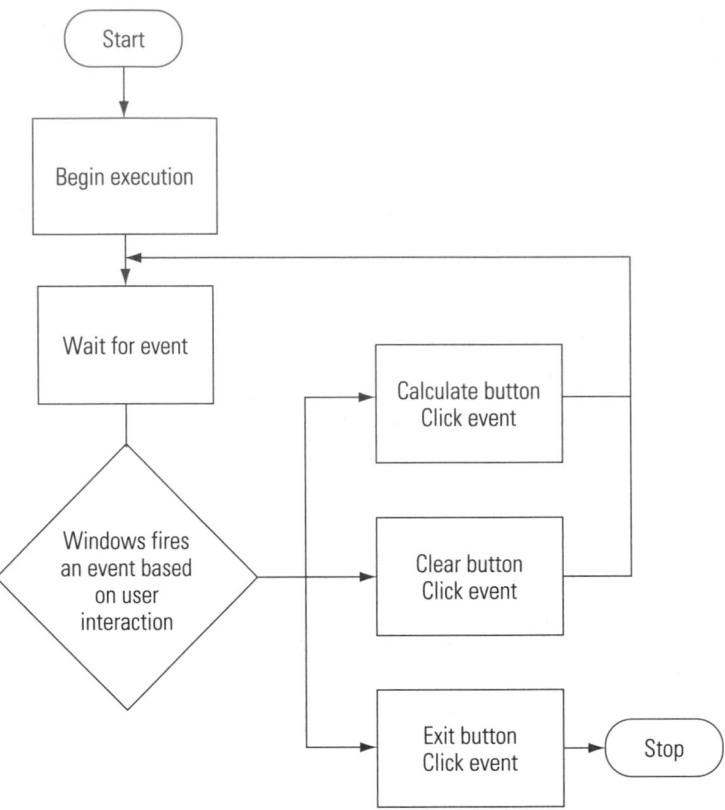

Figure 1-18: Event processing loop

# PROCEDURAL AND EVENT-DRIVEN LANGUAGES

A programming language, regardless of whether it is an object-oriented language, can also be categorized as either a procedural language or an event-driven language. Visual Basic can be used both as a procedural language or an event-driven language. In a **procedural language**, the sequence of actions can be predicted by the application. A procedural application has a known beginning, and the order that actions are performed is controlled by the application rather than events external to the application. That is, the execution path of an application can be determined in a procedural application. Figure 1-19 shows the operation of a procedural application.

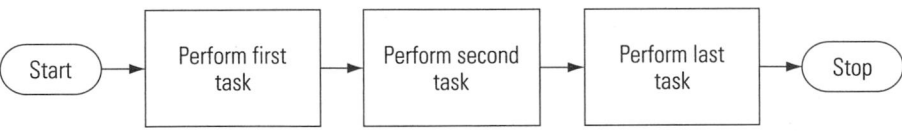

Figure 1-19: Operation of a procedural application

As shown in Figure 1-19, the application begins executing, the statements execute, and then the application ends. Figure 1-19 illustrates a very simple application containing only the sequence structure. However, it could also contain decision-making and repetition statements.

As mentioned, in an **event-driven language**, the application performs actions based on various events that Windows fires as the end user interacts with the application. Thus, using an event-driven language, the execution path of an application is controlled by events fired by Windows. The application cannot predict when the end user will perform a particular action, thereby causing Windows to fire the corresponding event.

Using Visual Basic, it is possible to create both procedural and event-driven applications. This chapter discusses how to create a procedural application. Chapter 3 introduces how to create a first event-driven application.

# MINI-QUIZ 2

1. Which of the following are control structures?

   a. the sequence structure      c. the repetition structure

   b. the decision-making structure      d. all of the above

2. What is the name of the program that translates third-generation programming statements into assembly language?

3. Which of the following is considered a third-generation programming language?

   a. COBOL      d. the Microsoft Access Report Writer

   b. machine language      e. none of the above

   c. assembly language

4. Which of the following statements is correct regarding first-, second-, and third-generation programming languages?

   a. Assembly language is considered a second-generation programming language.

   b. Third-generation programming languages are no longer used and have almost been completely replaced by fourth-generation programming languages.

   c. FORTRAN is considered a fourth-generation programming language.

   d. Assemblers translate applications written in a third-generation programming language into assembly language.

   e. none of the above

*(Continued)*      ▶

5. Which of the following statements is correct regarding programming languages?

a. All object-oriented languages must be procedural languages.

b. Object-oriented languages are considered second-generation programming languages.

c. A programming language can be a procedural language or an event-driven language, but not both.

d. Procedural and event-driven languages might or might not be object-oriented programming languages.

e. none of the above

# THE SYNTAX OF PROGRAMMING LANGUAGES

Just as an English sentence must conform to certain rules, all programming languages, including Visual Basic, have specific rules known as **syntax**. Each programming language has its own syntax meaning that the language rules vary from one language to another. Although the rules for an English sentence are somewhat flexible, the rules for the Visual Basic language or any other programming language are absolute. This section discusses syntax elements common to nearly all programming languages.

To illustrate, examine the following Visual Basic application, which prints the string "Hello World."

```
Module Hello
    Sub Main()
        System.Console.WriteLine("Hello World")
    End Sub
End Module
```

The preceding Visual Basic application prints the string "Hello World" to the Command Prompt window.

The C# language has a different syntax than Visual Basic but can be used to accomplish the same tasks. The following code segment illustrates the same classic "Hello World" program written in C#:

```
class Hello
{
[STAThread]
    static void Main(string[] args)
    {
        System.Console.WriteLine("Hello World");
    }
}
```

The syntax of the C# language differs from the syntax of Visual Basic. Opening and closing braces surround blocks. That is, braces surround the Main( ) procedure and the class named Hello. C# is case sensitive but Visual Basic is not. In C#, statements end with a semicolon. In Visual Basic, they do not. The point to be made is that both languages have syntax rules, but the syntax differs between the two languages.

Although an English sentence might be grammatically incorrect, the reader of that sentence will likely be able to understand its meaning. However, if you write a Visual Basic statement that is incorrect, the compiler will be unable to translate that statement into intermediate language and the statement is said to contain a **syntax error**. The following lines contain two syntax errors:

```
System.Console.WriteLine(Hello World)
System.Console.WritLine("Hello World")
```

In the first line, the double quotation marks surrounding the literal string "Hello World" are missing. In the second line, the call to the WriteLine() method is spelled incorrectly. Instead of WriteLine(), the method name is spelled WritLine(). Note that it is possible for a line to contain multiple syntax errors.

## TYPES OF PROGRAMMING STATEMENTS

A programming language, whether it is procedural or event-driven, whether it is an object-oriented programming language or not, uses words with a specific meaning, connected together in a specific order, to form a statement. A **statement** expresses a complete thought or action and is similar to a sentence in English. That is, both a programming statement and an English-language sentence must adhere to certain rules for them to be correct. Statements can be categorized into two types:

» *Declaration statements* are used to create variables and other elements used to define the structure of the application.

» *Executable statements* perform some action while the application is running.

To illustrate the difference between declaration and executable statements, again consider the "Hello World" application just discussed.

```
Module Hello
    Sub Main()
        System.Console.WriteLine("Hello World")
    End Sub
End Module
```

The statement `System.Console.WriteLine("Hello World")` is considered an executable statement. When the application is run, the statement will execute and the string "Hello World" is displayed in the Command Prompt window. All of the other statements are declaration statements. These declaration statements define the structure of the application.

## RESERVED WORDS AND OPERATORS

Language keywords, also known as **reserved words**, are part of every programming language, and every programming language has its own set of reserved words. That is, the reserved words of one language differs from the reserved words of another language. A reserved word is simply a word that has special meaning to a particular programming language. For example, `Module` and `Sub` are both reserved words in Visual Basic. Operators, as their name implies, perform an operation or task while an application runs. For example, + is the Visual Basic operator used to perform addition. Table 1-2 lists the Visual Basic reserved words and operators.

| | | | |
|---|---|---|---|
| AddHandler | AddressOf | Alias | And |
| AndAlso | Ansi | As | Assembly |
| Auto | Boolean | ByRef | Byte |
| ByVal | Call | Case | Catch |
| CBool | CByte | CChar | CDate |
| CDec | CDbl | Char | CInt |

Table 1-2: Visual Basic reserved words and operators *(Continued)*  ▶

| Class | CLng | CObj | Const |
|-------|------|------|-------|
| CShort | CSng | CStr | CType |
| Date | Decimal | Declare | Default |
| Delegate | Dim | DirectCast | Do |
| Double | Each | Else | ElseIf |
| End | EndIf | Enum | Erase |
| Error | Event | Exit | False |
| Finally | For | Friend | Function |
| Get | GetType | Global | GoSub |
| GoTo | Handles | If | Implements |
| Imports | In | Inherits | Integer |
| Interface | Is | Let | Lib |
| Like | Long | Loop | Me |

Table 1-2: Visual Basic reserved words and operators *(Continued)* ▶

| | | | |
|---|---|---|---|
| Mod | Module | MustInherit | MustOverride |
| MyBase | MyClass | Namespace | New |
| Next | Not | Nothing | NotInheritable |
| NotOverridable | Object | On | Option |
| Optional | Or | OrElse | Overloads |
| Overridable | Overrides | ParamArray | Preserve |
| Private | Property | Protected | Public |
| RaiseEvent | ReadOnly | ReDim | REM |
| RemoveHandler | Resume | Return | Select |
| Set | Shadows | Shared | Short |
| Single | Static | Step | Stop |
| String | Structure | Sub | SyncLock |
| Then | Throw | To | True |

Table 1-2: Visual Basic reserved words and operators *(Continued)*

| Until | Variant | Wend | When |
|---|---|---|---|
| Xor | #Const | #ExternalSource | #If...Then...#Else |
| #Region | - | & | &= |
| * | *= | / | /= |
| \ | \= | ^ | ^= |
| + | += | = | -= |

Table 1-2: Visual Basic reserved words and operators

In any programming language, reserved words and operators use named elements called identifiers.

## IDENTIFIERS AND THEIR NAMES

Just as a person has a name, so too do the elements of an application. In any programming language, the term **identifier** is used to describe the name of a particular programming element. The following code segment illustrates the use of identifiers:

```
Module Hello
    Sub Main()
    End Sub
End Module
```

In the preceding code segment, the module has a name of Hello, and the procedure has a name of Main. Thus, the identifiers are named Hello and Main. There are syntax rules that apply to the naming of identifiers as described in the following list:

» Identifier names must begin with a letter.

» Identifier names can only contain alphabetic characters, digits, or the underscore character.

> **»NOTE**
>
> In Visual Basic, identifier names are not case sensitive. That is, the names "Hello," "hello," and "HELLO" are all equivalent. In addition, it is possible for an identifier name to begin with the underscore (_) character. However, there are special rules that apply when an identifier name begins with an underscore. This chapter does not discuss or use identifier names that begin with an underscore character.

This section described the syntax of a programming language and the kinds of elements that make up all programming languages. The following section describes how those elements are used as building blocks to create a Visual Basic application.

# CREATING THE STRUCTURE OF A VISUAL BASIC APPLICATION

Every Visual Basic application has a similar structure. Just as a book is organized into chapters containing paragraphs, which, in turn, contain sentences, a Visual Basic application has a hierarchical structure too.

Visual Basic is a *block structured language*, meaning that many language elements consist of statements that mark the beginning and end of a block. The outermost block in any Visual Basic application is the `Namespace` block. `Namespace` blocks, in turn, contain other blocks such as `Module` blocks, which, in turn, contain `Sub` procedure blocks. Each of these types of blocks is discussed, in turn.

## NAMESPACE BLOCKS

**Namespaces** can be thought of as the file folders that store a hierarchy of classes, modules, and other types. An application can contain a single namespace or multiple namespaces. The `Namespace` keyword marks the beginning of a namespace block. Every namespace has a name (identifier). Following the `Namespace` keyword appears the name of the namespace. The `End Namespace` keywords mark the end of a namespace. The following code segment shows the declaration statements for a namespace named Chapter01:

```
Namespace Chapter01
End Namespace
```

As shown in the preceding code segment, the namespace named Chapter01 is enclosed in a `Namespace`, `End Namespace` block. Namespaces, in turn, can contain four different elements, each of which forms a block:

» A `Class` block is used to create a class, which, in turn, can contain properties and methods.

» A `Structure` block is similar to a `Class` block in that it can contain properties and methods.

» A `Module` block is also similar to a `Class` block but has unique characteristics too. For example, modules do not support inheritance in the same way that classes do.

» Interfaces are used in conjunction with classes and structures to create more complex object-oriented applications.

The following sections discuss `Module` blocks and how to use them.

## INTRODUCTION TO MODULE BLOCKS

A Namespace block can contain one or more Module blocks. The syntax of a Module block is similar to the syntax of a Namespace block. For example, both a Namespace and Module block have a name (identifier). The following code segment illustrates a module named Hello in the namespace named Chapter01:

```
Namespace Chapter01
    Module Hello
    End Module
End Namespace
```

The preceding code segment shows one Namespace block named Chapter01 containing one Module block named Hello. Note that the statements for the Module block are indented. Indenting statements is done solely to improve readability. Indenting is not required for the statements to be syntactically correct.

Module blocks cannot be nested. That is, one Module block cannot appear inside of another Module block. Thus, the following statements cause a syntax error:

```
Namespace Chapter01
    Module Hello
        Module Goodbye
        End Module
    End Module
End Namespace
```

Module blocks can appear inside of a Namespace block but the reverse is not true. That is, putting a Namespace block inside of a Module block causes a syntax error. The following statements generate a syntax error:

```
Module Hello
    Namespace Chapter01
    End Namespace
End Module
```

Module blocks, in turn, contain other blocks. One type of block appearing in a Module block is a procedure.

## INTRODUCTION TO PROCEDURE BLOCKS

A Module block can contain one procedure or it can contain many procedures. Collectively, the statements in a procedure are similar to an English paragraph. A Module block can contain many procedures just as a document can contain many paragraphs. A procedure, in turn, can contain additional declaration statements or executable statements. Procedures in a Module block can appear in any order but ordering procedures alphabetically makes them easier to locate. The following code segment illustrates a namespace containing one module containing one procedure:

```
Namespace Chapter01
    Module Hello
        Sub Main()
        End Sub
    End Module
End Namespace
```

The preceding code segment shows the namespace named Chapter01 with a single module named Hello. The module, in turn, contains one procedure. A procedure begins with the keyword Sub and ends with the End Sub keywords marking the beginning and end of the procedure, respectively. Just as a namespace and module have a name, so too does a procedure. The procedure name follows the Sub keyword. In the preceding example, the procedure is named Main. Following the name, parentheses appear to denote the argument list. In this case, the argument list is empty because the procedure does not accept any arguments.

Just as Module blocks cannot be nested, procedure blocks cannot be nested. That is, one procedure cannot appear inside of another procedure. Thus, the following statements cause a syntax error:

```
Namespace Chapter01
    Module Hello
        Sub Main()
            Sub NestedProcedure()
            End Sub
        End Sub
    End Module
End Namespace
```

Procedures can appear at the module-level (inside of a Module block), but not at the namespace-level. Thus, the following statements also generate a syntax error:

```
Namespace Chapter01
    Sub NestedProcedure()
    End Sub
    Module Hello
        Sub Main()
        End Sub
    End Module
End Namespace
```

The preceding statements also generate a syntax error because the procedure named NestedProcedure appears at the namespace-level instead of the module-level.

Figure 1-20 shows the relationships between a namespace, a module, and a procedure block.

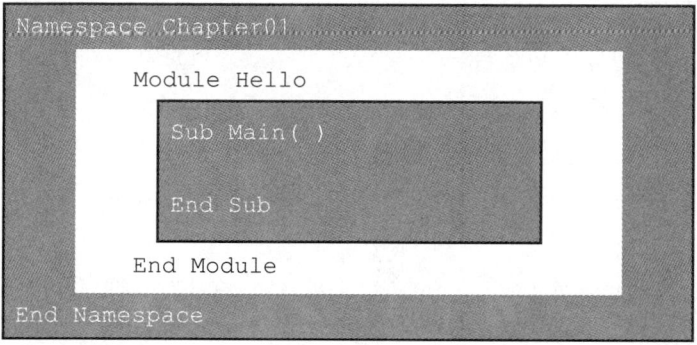

```
Namespace Chapter01
    Module Hello
        Sub Main( )

        End Sub
    End Module
End Namespace
```

Figure 1-20: Organization of a namespace, a module, and a procedure

Every Visual Basic application has what is called an entry point. An application's **entry point** marks where execution begins. In the case of the preceding code example, the application's entry point is the procedure named Main(). The procedure name Main() is significant. Although it is not a reserved word, the .NET Framework looks for the Main() procedure as an application's entry point.

# MINI-QUIZ 3

1. Which of the following statements is correct regarding programming language syntax?

   a. All programming languages have exactly the same syntax.

   b. All languages have syntax, but the syntax can vary from one programming language to the next.

   c. Compilers can correct most syntax errors.

   d. A statement can have one syntax error at most.

*(Continued)* ▶

2. List the two categories of programming statements.

3. Which of the following statements correctly describes the structure of a Visual Basic application?

    a. Modules can be nested. That is, one module can appear inside of another module.

    b. Procedures can be nested. That is, one procedure can appear inside of another procedure.

    c. A namespace can have one module or many modules. Each module can have one procedure or many procedures.

    d. Namespaces, modules, and procedures can have names (identifiers) but are not required to.

    e. A namespace declaration must appear inside of a module declaration, which must appear inside of a procedure declaration.

4. Describe the syntax error(s) in the following statement block:

```
Namespace
    Sub Main()
    End Sub
    Module Welcome
    End Module
End Namespace
```

# WRITING EXECUTABLE STATEMENTS

So far, the statements that have been presented have all been declaration statements. In this section, you will learn about executable statements, which perform some action as an application runs. Executable statements can be used for various purposes, as described in the following list:

» Executable statements can be used to call (execute) a procedure.

» Recall that decision-making and repetition statements are control structures. Executable statements can be used to make decisions and execute loops.

» One form of an executable statement is an assignment statement. Assignment statements are made up of a left side and a right side separated by an equal sign. The action on the right side is carried out and the result is stored on the left side.

In this section, you will learn how to write executable statements to call procedures belonging to the .NET Framework class library.

## CALLING A .NET FRAMEWORK CLASS LIBRARY METHOD

Recall that a class is a template or blueprint from which objects are created. When programming in Visual Basic or any other Visual Studio language, you work with thousands of predefined classes that were created by the developers of Visual Studio. Collectively, these classes are referred to as the **.NET Framework class library**. The .NET Framework class library supplies a general set of services used by nearly all Visual Studio applications. There are services to do just about anything, including communicating with the operating system, creating forms, reading and writing files, and so on.

This chapter introduces the following classes:

» The `Console` class contains methods used to read input from and write output to a Command Prompt window.

» The `SystemInformation` class, as the name implies, is used to get configuration information about the local computer.

The .NET Framework class library is made up of several physical disk files containing predefined classes stored in libraries. A **library** is a physical disk file containing one or more precompiled classes that can be used by all of the applications you create. Using the terminology of the .NET Framework, physical library files are called **assemblies**. Physical assemblies contain one or more logical namespaces. Namespaces organize classes and other types in a hierarchical way. The following list describes five of the most common logical namespaces. In all, the .NET Framework class library is made up of over 100 namespaces.

» The `System` namespace defines the primary data types provided by the .NET Framework class library. Its classes are used by nearly all .NET applications. For example, the `Console` class belongs to the `System` namespace.

» The `System.Data` namespace contains the classes that make up ADO.NET. ADO.NET supplies the means for Visual Studio applications to work with databases, including Microsoft Access, Microsoft SQL Server, and Oracle.

» The `System.Drawing` namespace supplies graphics functionality. That is, its classes are used to draw and fill graphical shapes such as lines, rectangles, and polygons, to name a few.

» The `System.Windows.Forms` namespace contains the classes used to create desktop Windows applications made up of visual forms.

» The `System.XML` namespace provides support for processing the Extensible Markup Language (XML). XML is used throughout the .NET Framework class library to manage data.

Namespaces are organized hierarchically. A period (.) separates each namespace name. As you can see from the preceding list, the namespace `System` is the primary or root namespace. The `System` namespace contains additional namespaces named `Data` and `Drawing`. As mentioned, a period separates each namespace name, as in `System.Data` and `System.Drawing`.

Namespaces, in turn, contain types. Using the terminology of the .NET Framework, the word *type* has a very specific meaning. All types supported by the .NET Framework can be categorized as value types or reference types. The primary difference between a value type and reference type is how the data is stored in memory. Value types can be categorized into built-in data types, which are used to store numbers, and enumerations, which are used to store a finite list of values. Reference types can be roughly categorized into classes and arrays. The concept of a class has already been discussed. Arrays are used to store lists of data. Figure 1-21 shows the relationship between selected types that make up the .NET Framework class library.

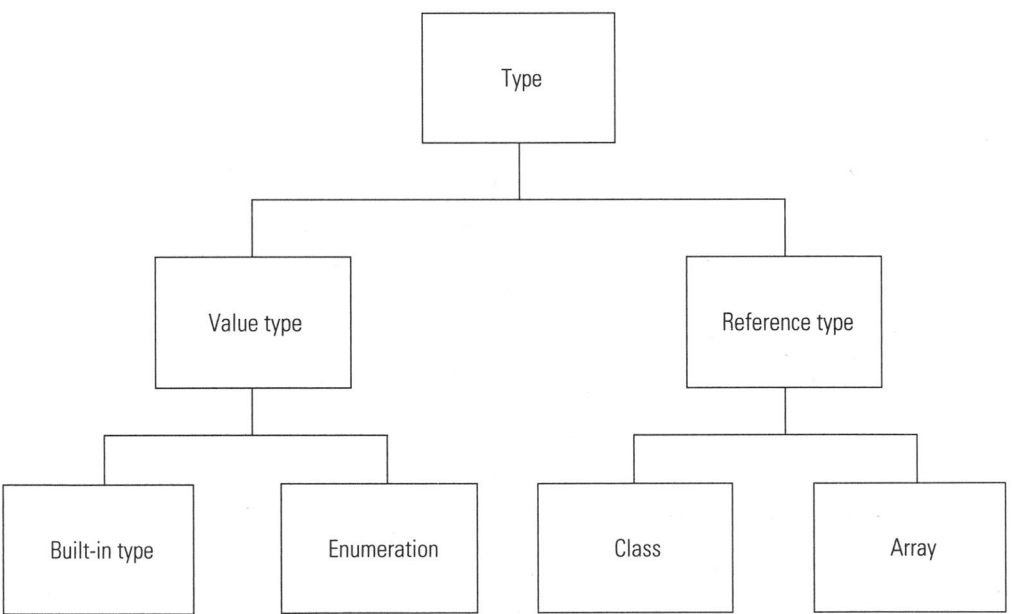

Figure 1-21: Categorization of types that make up the .NET Framework class library

As shown in Figure 1-21, all types are classified as either value types or reference types. Enumerations and built-in types are both value types. Classes and arrays are both reference types.

Remember that namespaces contain classes and modules, which, in turn, contain procedures. The .NET Framework class library is organized in the same way. That is, namespaces contain classes and other types, which, in turn, contain procedures called methods.

The syntax (language rules) to reference namespaces and the classes contained in those namespaces is simple. A period separates the namespace name and the class name. Thus, the following statement fragment references the `Console` class of the `System` namespace:

```
System.Console
```

The syntax to call a method (procedure) also involves separating the method name and the class name with a period, as the following executable statement shows:

```
System.Console.WriteLine()
```

The preceding statement calls the `WriteLine` method of the `Console` class of the `System` namespace.

Many methods accept one or more arguments. Method **arguments** provide the means to send, or pass, data to a method. Parentheses surround method arguments. If a method accepts multiple arguments, a comma separates each argument in the list. If a method accepts no arguments, no characters appear between the opening and closing parentheses. The `WriteLine` method can be called with one argument. That argument contains the data to be printed to the Command Prompt window. In the following code segment, the literal string value "Hello World" is passed as an argument to the `WriteLine` method. Thus, the string "Hello World" will be printed to the Command Prompt window. Note that double quotation marks surround literal string values.

```
System.Console.WriteLine("Hello World")
```

The `WriteLine` method can also be called without arguments to write a blank line to the Command Prompt window. As shown in the following statement, the argument list is empty:

```
System.Console.WriteLine()
```

The parentheses are optional if the argument list is empty. Thus, the following statement is equivalent to the preceding statement:

```
System.Console.WriteLine
```

All executable statements must appear in a procedure. The following procedure named Main( ) contains one executable statement to print the text "Hello World" to the Command Prompt window:

```
Module Hello
    Sub Main()
        System.Console.WriteLine("Hello World")
    End Sub
End Module
```

If an executable statement appears outside of a procedure block, a syntax error is generated. Thus, the following code segment causes a syntax error because the call to the WriteLine method appears outside of the procedure:

```
Module Hello
    System.Console.WriteLine("Hello World")
    Sub Main()
    End Sub
End Module
```

## CONTINUATION LINES

When writing a complicated statement, the statement might not fit on a single line. One statement can be divided into multiple lines by using the underscore character (_) at the end of a line to tell the Visual Basic compiler that the next line continues the statement on the current line. This second line is referred to as a **continuation line**. When used in this way, the underscore character is called a continuation character.

Several rules apply to the use of the continuation character, as described in the following list:

>> The continuation character must be the last character on a line.

>> A space must always precede the continuation character.

>> A continuation character can only appear between words. For example, a procedure name (identifier) cannot appear on multiple lines using a continuation character.

>> A comment cannot follow the continuation character. Comments are used to provide documentation for an application.

The continuation character appears at the end of a continuation line. In addition, continuation lines, which are the lines that follow the continuation character in a statement, are typically indented. The following statement illustrates the use of a continuation line:

```
System.Console.WriteLine( _
    "Hello World")
```

The preceding statement appears on two lines. On the first line, the continuation character appears to separate the lines. In addition, a statement can have multiple continuation lines as the following code segment shows:

```
System.Console. _
    WriteLine( _
    "Hello World")
```

The preceding statement is divided into three lines.

The following code segment illustrates illegal use of the continuation character:

```
System.Console._
    Write _
    Line( _
    "Hello World")
```

The preceding statement is illegal because a space does not precede the continuation character in the first line. In addition, the method `WriteLine`, like any method, cannot be divided across continuation lines.

## THE METHODS OF THE SYSTEM.CONSOLE CLASS

The `Console` class of the `System` namespace has methods to get input from the end user and to display output to the end user. The following list summarizes these methods:

» The `Read` method reads one character from the input stream. The Command Prompt window can be used as an input stream in which the end user enters characters.

» The `ReadLine` method reads a line from the input stream. A line is a sequence of characters terminated by a carriage return (the Enter key). While the `ReadLine` method reads the terminating carriage return character, the character is discarded. The `ReadLine` method only uses the carriage return character to determine the end of a line.

» The `Write` method writes a single character or string to the output stream. For example, characters can be written to the Command Prompt window.

» The `WriteLine` method writes a single character or string to the output stream, and then follows that character or string with a carriage return character.

## CALLING THE MEMBERS OF THE SYSTEMINFORMATION CLASS

The `System.Windows.Forms.SystemInformation` class is used to obtain information from the Windows operating system about the configuration of the current computer. The `System.Windows.Forms` namespace contains a class named `SystemInformation`, which supports the following properties to get configuration information about the local computer:

» The `ComputerName` property returns the name of the computer on which the application is running.

» The `MouseButtons` property returns the number of mouse buttons on the mouse. Most PC mice have two buttons but three-button mice are supported.

» The `MouseWheelPresent` property indicates whether the mouse has a mouse wheel.

» The `Network` property indicates whether the computer is attached to a network.

» The `PrimaryMonitorSize` property returns the size, in pixels, of the primary monitor attached to the computer. Note that many computers today have multiple monitors attached to them.

» The `UserName` property returns the name of the user currently logged on to the computer.

The following code segment illustrates an application that prints system information to the Command Prompt window:

```
Module SystemInformation
    Sub Main()
        System.Console.WriteLine( _
            System.Windows.Forms. _
            SystemInformation.ComputerName)
        System.Console.WriteLine( _
            System.Windows.Forms. _
            SystemInformation.MouseButtons)
        System.Console.WriteLine( _
            System.Windows.Forms. _
            SystemInformation.MouseWheelPresent)
        System.Console.WriteLine( _
            System.Windows.Forms. _
            SystemInformation.Network)
        System.Console.WriteLine( _
            System.Windows.Forms. _
            SystemInformation.UserName)
    End Sub
End Module
```

The structure of the preceding application looks just like the structure of the other applications presented in this chapter. That is, the application contains one module having a name of `SystemInformation` and a procedure named Main( ). The statements in the application write configuration information to a Command Prompt window. Note that continuation lines appear in many of the executable statements.

## MINI-QUIZ 4

1. Which of the following statements is correct of the .NET Framework class library?

   a. The root namespace is always the namespace named root.

   b. Syntactically, hierarchical namespaces are connected together using an exclamation point.

   c. It contains namespaces stored in physical assemblies.

   d. none of the above

2. Which of the following statements is correct about continuation lines?

   a. One statement can be separated to appear on two lines, but a statement cannot be separated into three lines.

   b. The exclamation point character is considered the continuation character.

   c. The continuation character must be the last character on a continuation line.

   d. A continuation character can appear anywhere in a statement.

3. Describe the error(s) in the following statement:

```
System.Console._
    WriteLine _ (
    "Hello World")
```

4. What is the name of the method that you would call to read a line from an input stream?

# USING A COMMAND PROMPT WINDOW

In Chapter 2, you will use the Visual Studio integrated development environment (IDE) to create an application. However, in this chapter, to illustrate the purpose of the compiler, you will see how to create and compile an application by hand using Notepad and a Command Prompt window. The Command Prompt window is briefly discussed in this section in case you are not familiar with its use.

There is a special Command Prompt window designed specifically for use with Visual Studio applications. The window is automatically configured so that it is possible to call the Visual Basic compiler and the compilers for other Visual Studio languages. To start the Visual Studio Command Prompt window, click Start, All Programs, Microsoft .NET Framework SDK v2.0, SDK Command Prompt.

The Command Prompt window has a command-line interface. That is, you type a command, press Enter, and Windows executes the command. After the command has executed, a prompt is displayed indicating that the Command Prompt window is ready for the next command. Figure 1-22 shows the Command Prompt window.

Figure 1-22: Command Prompt window

The Command Prompt window allows you to navigate through the Windows file system. This is the same file system navigated by Windows Explorer. In addition, as its name implies, the Command Prompt window allows you to execute commands.

The Windows file system is organized into hierarchical directories (folders) containing additional directories called subdirectories, along with zero or more individual files. Using the Command Prompt window to navigate between directories involves specifying a path. A **path** defines the hierarchical location of a directory or file within the Windows file system. Path references are of two types: absolute and relative.

## ABSOLUTE PATHS

To specify an absolute path, each directory in the hierarchy is separated by a path separator character, which is a backslash (\). A disk drive designator precedes the pathname. The following statements illustrate absolute path references:

```
C:\CourseTechnology\Chapter01
D:\Temp
```

The first of the preceding statements references the Chapter01 subdirectory of the CourseTechnology directory on the C:\ drive. The second statement references a directory named Temp on the D:\ drive.

## RELATIVE PATHS

In addition to absolute directory references, it is possible to create relative directory (path) references. Instead of referencing a file or directory with the full pathname including the disk drive designator, a relative directory reference references a directory or file based on the current working directory. The following statements illustrate relative directory references:

```
..\Data\Chapter.01
.\Chapter.01
```

When creating relative directory references, the character "." and the characters ".." have special meaning. The period means the current directory and the two consecutive periods denote the parent directory of the current directory. Thus, if the current directory were C:\System, the first of the preceding statements would reference the directory C:\Data\Chapter.01. The second statement would reference the directory named C:\System\Chapter.01.

## USING ABSOLUTE AND RELATIVE DIRECTORIES

Absolute and relative directories are used in various commands to change the directory considered the current working directory. The following list describes selected commands used to navigate and manipulate the file system:

» Without arguments, the DIR command lists the files and directories in the current directory. An optional *directoryname* argument lists the directories and files in the specified directory.

» The CD command changes the current working directory. It typically accepts one argument, a *directoryname*. Without an argument, the CD command prints the current working directory.

» The RENAME command is used to change the name of a file or directory. It accepts two arguments: the *oldfilename* followed by the *newfilename*. Note that the *newfilename* must not already exist.

» The DEL command accepts one argument: the *filename* to delete.

The following code segment illustrates the use of the preceding commands:

```
DIR
CD \
RENAME FileOld FileNew
DEL FileNew
```

The first of the preceding statements prints the contents of the current directory. The second statement changes the current working directory to the root directory on the current drive. The third statement renames the file named FileOld to FileNew, and the final statement removes the file named FileNew.

One way to compile a Visual Basic application is to call the compiler directly using the Command Prompt window. This topic is discussed next.

# COMPILING AND EXECUTING A VISUAL BASIC APPLICATION

The statements written in most programming languages are translated by a compiler into an executable form that is understood by the underlying computer hardware. In Visual Studio, the process is a bit more complex. As mentioned, the Visual Basic compiler translates the source Visual Basic statements into what .NET refers to as **intermediate language (IL)**. As mentioned, intermediate language is conceptually similar to a machine-independent assembly language. That intermediate language is the same no matter the type of computer (CPU) on which the application is running.

When a program containing IL statements executes, another .NET Framework utility called the just-in-time (JIT) compiler translates the IL statements into the machine language understood by the underlying computer hardware. Figure 1-23 illustrates how source code is translated into IL, which is then translated into machine language.

The JIT compiler is called automatically when a .NET application is run, so the process is transparent to both the end user and the developer.

The Visual Basic compiler is named vbc.exe (Visual Basic Compiler), and by default is stored in the folder named C:\Windows\Microsoft.NET\Framework\v2.0.50727. Note that the final directory named v2.0.50727 represents the version and build number of the .NET Framework.

**»» NOTE**
This version and build number will vary based on the version of the .NET Framework that you are running.

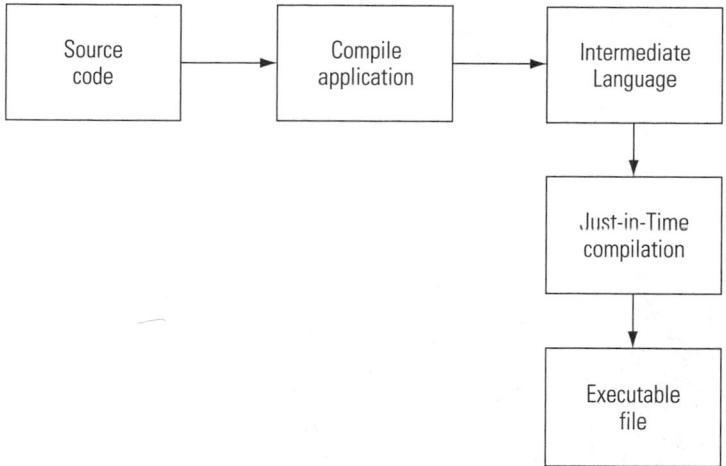

Figure 1-23: Translation of .NET source code to executable code

To compile a Visual Basic application from a Command Prompt window, you call the Visual Basic compiler directly, with the source filename as an argument. In the following example, the source file is named `Hello.vb`. In addition to supplying the filename to compile, you supply the command-line directives that describe how the application should be compiled, any external references that are necessary to compile the application, and the name of the output (executable) file that will be produced.

The syntax to call the Visual Basic compiler is simple. Each compiler directive (option) is preceded by the forward slash character (/). The following optional argument is separated from the compiler directive by a full colon. Either a space or a comma separates each compiler directive and argument pair. The following list describes the compiler directives used in this chapter:

» The `/main` directive specifies the class or module that contains the Main() procedure. The `/main` directive can also specify the name of the form designated as the start-up form. Remember that the Main() procedure is the entry point for an application.

» The `/out` directive defines the filename of the executable file produced. If omitted, the output file has the same name as the module name containing the Main() procedure.

» The `/verbose` directive causes the compiler to display additional descriptive information about the compilation.

The following statement illustrates how to call the compiler to produce an executable file:

```
vbc /main:Chapter01.Hello /out:Hello.exe Hello.vb
```

The preceding statement shows that the Visual Basic compiler is named `vbc.exe`. The file named `Hello.vb` will be compiled. The `/main` directive is used to specify the namespace and module name containing the Main( ) procedure used as the application's entry point. The optional /out directive specifies that the executable file will be stored in the file named Hello.exe.

Figure 1-24 shows the Command Prompt window with the statements to call the compiler and the output from the compiler.

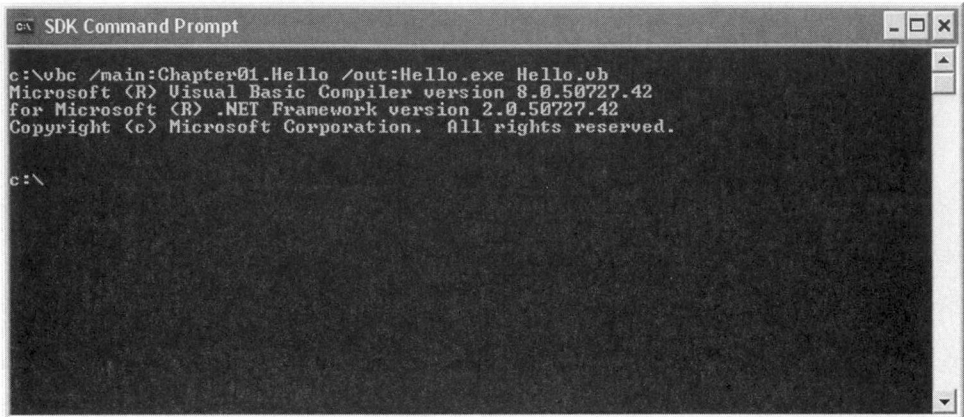

Figure 1-24: Using the Command Prompt window to compile a Visual Basic application

If an application contains syntax errors, the Visual Basic compiler will not be able to compile it and will report any errors that it finds, as shown in Figure 1-25.

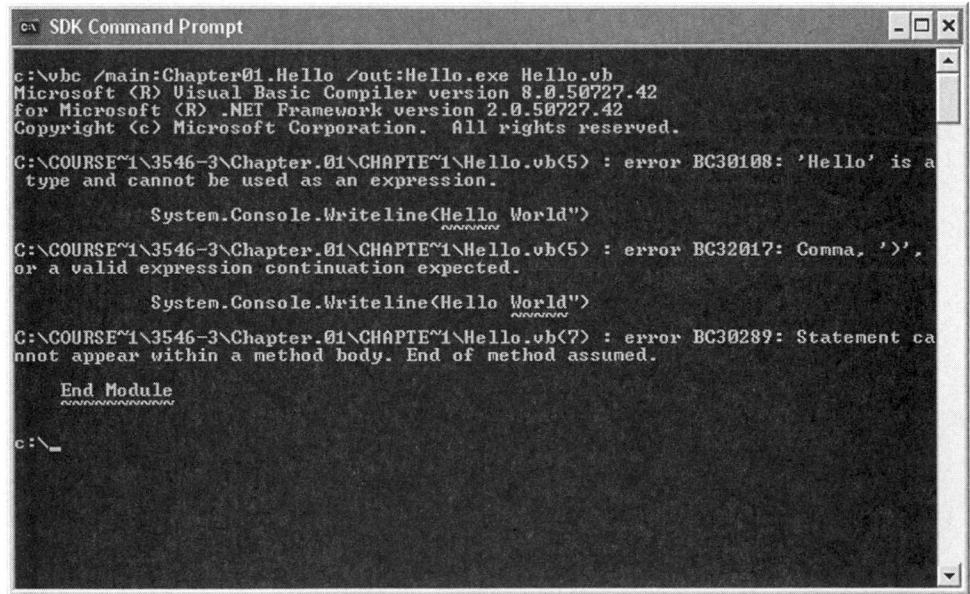

Figure 1-25: Syntax errors

In Figure 1-25, the following statement produced a syntax error because the first double quotation mark is missing in the argument to the `WriteLine` method:

```
System.Console.WriteLine(Hello World")
```

The Visual Basic compiler reports the error as occurring on line 5, and underlines the offending statement.

## MINI-QUIZ 5

1. Which of the following is a correct relative pathname?

   a. `C:\..\CourseTechnology`

   b. `..\CourseTechnology`

   c. `\Parent\CourseTechnology`

   d. None of the above are relative pathnames.

2. Write the statement to change the current working directory to C:\CourseTechnology\3546-3\Temp. Use an absolute directory reference.

3. What is the name of the utility program that translates IL into executable code?

4. Write the statement to compile the Visual Basic application stored in the file named Quiz.vb. Assume that the Main( ) procedure is in the module named Quiz in the namespace named CourseTechnology.

# APPLICATION LESSON

## CREATING A CONSOLE APPLICATION

Each chapter in this book is made up of two lessons. The concept lesson appears first and describes key concepts. The application lesson appears second. In the application lesson, you will apply those key concepts to create a new working application or to finish a partially completed one.

In this application lesson you will create a Console application that will print information about the current computer system to a Command Prompt window. The application will be created in Notepad, although you could use any other text editor. After you have created the application, you will call the Visual Basic compiler as discussed in this chapter.

## APPLICATION LESSON—DESIGN

The design of this application is very simple. It uses the sequence structure to print the following system information to a Command Prompt window:

» The computer name

» The number of mouse buttons on the mouse, and whether there is a mouse wheel present

» Whether the computer is connected to the network

» The name of the user currently logged on to the computer

For each of the preceding display items, a descriptive prompt is also printed. After all the output has been written, a prompt is displayed asking the end user to press a key to exit the application. Figure 1-26 shows a flowchart for the application.

The flowchart shown in Figure 1-26 has a starting point and an ending point. After execution begins, the application prints the computer name, and the remaining information in order. Then, a message is displayed asking the end user to press a key to exit the application. When the character is read, the application ends.

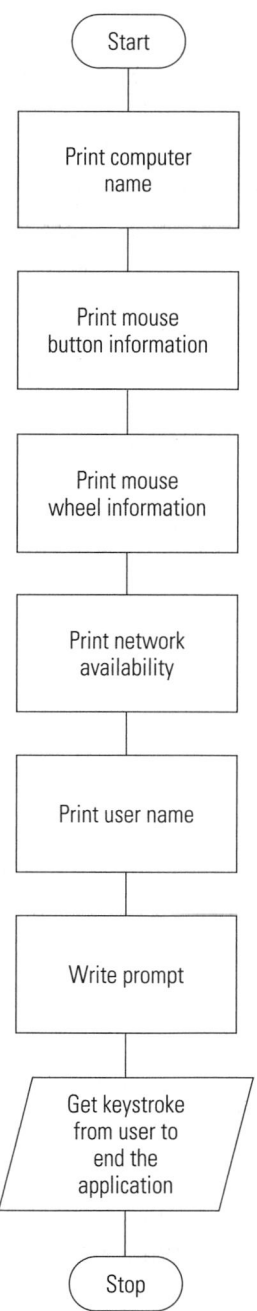

Figure 1-26: Application flowchart

## APPLICATION LESSON—IMPLEMENTATION

To implement this application, you will perform three distinct steps. First, you will create the application using a text editor. Second, you will compile the application using a Command Prompt window. Finally, you will run the application to test it.

The implementation of this application lesson is similar to the "Hello World" application shown throughout the chapter. The application has a single procedure named Main( ) in a module named SystemInformation, in a namespace named CourseTechnology, as shown in the following code segment:

```
Namespace CourseTechnology
    Module SystemInformation
        Sub Main()
        End Sub
    End Module
End Namespace
```

Five groups of code print a message, and then the value of a specific property from the System.Windows.Forms.SystemInformation class. They all resemble the following statements:

```
System.Console.Write("ComputerName=")
System.Console.WriteLine( _
    System.Windows.Forms. _
    SystemInformation.ComputerName)
```

Finally, the following statements execute to print a message to the end user and wait until the end user presses the Enter key.

```
System.Console.Write("Press [Enter] to quit")
System.Console.Read()
```

To create a console application:

1. Start Notepad or other text editor of your choice. If you use another text editor, be sure to save the file as a text file rather than as another file type. If the file is not in text format, the Visual Studio compiler will not be able to compile the file.

2. Enter the following statements to create the namespace, module, Main( ) procedure and the statements to print the system information to the Command Prompt window:

```
Namespace CourseTechnology
    Module SystemInformation
        Sub Main()
            System.Console.Write("ComputerName=")
            System.Console.WriteLine( _
                System.Windows.Forms. _
                SystemInformation.ComputerName)
```

```
        System.Console.Write("MouseButtons=")
        System.Console.WriteLine( _
            System.Windows.Forms. _
            SystemInformation.MouseButtons)

        System.Console.Write("MouseWheelPresent=")
        System.Console.WriteLine( _
            System.Windows.Forms. _
            SystemInformation.MouseWheelPresent)

        System.Console.Write("Network=")
        System.Console.WriteLine( _
            System.Windows.Forms. _
            SystemInformation.Network)

        System.Console.Write("UserName=")
        System.Console.WriteLine( _
            System.Windows.Forms. _
            SystemInformation.UserName)

        System.Console.Write("Press [Enter] to quit")
        System.Console.Read()
      End Sub
    End Module
  End Namespace
```

3. Using Notepad, click **File**, **Save** and navigate to a folder of your choosing. Name the file **SystemInformation.vb**. Make sure that **All Files** is selected in the Save as type list box. If this option is not selected, Notepad will change the file extension to ".txt". Click **Save**.

4. Exit Notepad.

Next, the application must be compiled. To do this, the Command Prompt window must be able to locate the Visual Basic compiler named "vbc.exe."

1. Your first step is to open an instance of the Command Prompt window. To do so, click **Start**, **All Programs**, **Microsoft .NET Framework SDK v2.0**, **SDK Command Prompt**, if you are running the Professional edition of Visual Studio.

> **》》NOTE** If you are running the Visual Basic Express edition, you must run a batch file that accompanies this book so that the vbc.exe compiler can be found. To do so, you need to open the Command Prompt window and then run the batch file by typing **vsvars2005.bat** and pressing **Enter**. (This file can be found in the Chapter.01 folder in the data files accompanying this book.)

2. Change the current directory to the one where you saved the file named SystemInformation.vb.

3. Enter the following statement to compile the application. Even though the following command appears on two lines, enter it as a single command (note that there is a space before both forward slashes), and then press **Enter**.

```
vbc /main:CourseTechnology.SystemInformation
/out:SystemInformation.exe SystemInformation.vb
```

4. Test the application by typing **SystemInformation.exe**, and pressing **Enter**. The application runs and the output is produced, as shown in Figure 1-27.

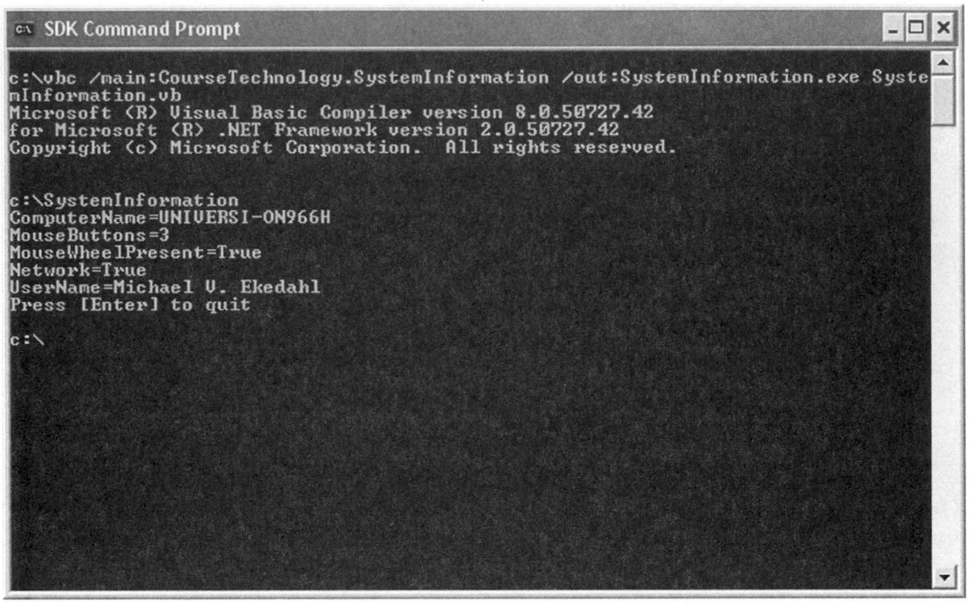

Figure 1-27: Application output

# CHAPTER SUMMARY

» The development of a software system involves performing a well-defined series of steps collectively called the software development life cycle. These steps include problem identification, systems analysis, system implementation, system documentation, system testing, and a postimplementation audit. This software development process is iterative.

» Complex software systems must be designed before they are implemented. Various models and methodologies are used to design software systems. These models and methodologies include pseudocode, top-down design, flowcharting, and the Unified Modeling Language (UML).

» All applications are written using one or more control structures. The sequence structure is used to execute statements in the order that they appear in a procedure. The selection structure is used to make a decision (selection). The repetition structure or loop is used to perform a task over and over again. These control structures are often combined together.

» After a software system has been designed, it must be implemented. A choice must be made as to which programming language should be used to implement an application. Available languages include C#, Java, Visual Basic, and C++ among others.

» Programming languages are often categorized into first-, second-, third-, and fourth-generation programming languages. First-generation languages are machine languages. Assembly languages represent second-generation languages. Third-generation languages include FORTRAN, COBOL, Pascal, and C. Fourth-generation languages are characterized as natural languages.

» One category of programming language is an object-oriented programming language. Object-oriented programming languages attempt to reduce software costs by creating code that is reusable. Object-oriented programming languages use classes that are templates for objects. Classes have properties that store data and methods that act on that data. All object-oriented programming languages share common characteristics, such as encapsulation, inheritance, information hiding, and polymorphism. The only way for a developer to interact with a class is through its interface. An interface consists of the properties, methods, and events supported by a class.

» The .NET Framework class library contains the classes that are part of Visual Studio. These classes are stored in physical library files. These physical library files are called assemblies. Physical assemblies are organized into logical namespaces in a hierarchical way. These namespaces, in turn, contain classes and other types.

» All programming languages have a set of rules called syntax. The syntax of a language varies from one language to another. The syntax rules of a programming language are absolute. That is, an application with syntax errors cannot be compiled.

» Statements express a complete thought or action and are enclosed in a procedure. Statements can be categorized as declaration statements and executable statements. One type of executable statement is an assignment statement. Assignment statements have a right side and a left side. The expression on the right side is evaluated and the result stored in a variable on the left side. In an assignment statement, an equal sign separates the left side from the right side.

» A procedure is conceptually similar to an English paragraph. Procedures are contained in a `Class` or `Module` block, which, in turn, is contained in a `Namespace` block.

» This chapter discussed two classes. The `System.Console` class is used to read and write information to the Command Prompt window. The members of the `System.Windows.Forms.SystemInformation` class get information about the local computer.

» Statements written in a source language, such as Visual Basic, are translated by a compiler into intermediate language, and then into machine language.

» The Visual Basic compiler can be called from a Command Prompt window. The name of the Visual Basic compiler is "vbc.exe."

# KEY TERMS

**.NET Framework class library**—The classes and other types that are part of Visual Studio .NET.

**argument**—Method arguments provide the means to send or pass data to a method.

**assembler**—A program that translates assembly language into machine language.

**assembly**—An assembly is a physical library file containing one or more namespaces.

**assembly language**—The second-generation programming languages characterized by mnemonic names replacing binary machine instructions.

**class**—A template or blueprint for an object.

**code**—A general term used to refer to the statements, procedures, and other elements that make up an application.

**compiler**—A program that translates statements written in a machine-independent, third-generation programming language into assembly language.

**continuation line**—A continuation line is used to create a statement that appears on multiple lines. The underscore character is the continuation character used to create a continuation line.

**constructor**—A procedure called by Windows to create an instance of a class is called the constructor.

**control structure**—The definition of the order in which program statements execute. The sequence, selection, and repetition structures are the three programming control structures.

**entry point**—When an application starts running, a specific procedure executes. That procedure is called the application's entry point.

**event**—Windows fires events as a result of some end user activity such as clicking a button or moving the mouse. Statements in event handlers are created that execute in response to the event.

**event-driven language**—A programming language that performs actions based on events that fire. The execution path of the application is controlled by the events fired by Windows.

**event handler**—An event handler is a procedure that executes when an event fires. An event typically fires as a result of some end user interaction.

**flowchart**—A pictorial representation using standardized graphical symbols that are used to depict the actions performed by an application, and the order in which those actions are performed.

**HIPO chart**—A visual tool used to represent the top-down design approach to software modeling.

**identifier**—The name of a particular programming element is called an identifier.

**intermediate language**—A machine-independent assembly language. All applications created with Visual Studio are compiled to intermediate language.

**interface**—The formal specifications of a class. The properties and methods of a class make up the interface.

**library**—A physical file containing one or more precompiled classes.

**machine independence**—Third-generation programming languages allowed a program to be compiled for different CPUs.

**machine language**—The first-generation programming languages. Programs written in machine language are written in binary 1s and 0s.

**methods**—The actions a class can perform.

**model**—A simplified and often visual representation of reality used to describe a software system or other system.

**namespace**—The hierarchical organization of .NET classes and other types.

**natural languages**—The nonprocedural software tools are called fourth-generation or natural languages.

**object-oriented programming languages**—The languages in which objects are created from classes, which are templates or blueprints for objects.

**path**—A path defines the hierarchical location of a directory or file within the Windows file system.

**pseudocode**—The English-like statements used to define specific steps necessary to perform a particular task.

**procedural language**—A type of language in which the sequence of actions can be predicted by the application.

**properties**—The data items defined by a class are called properties.

**repetition structure**—One of the three programming structures used to execute statements over and over again until some condition occurs causing the repetition process to end.

**reserved words**—The keywords that are part of a programming language. Reserved words vary from one language to the next.

**selection structure**—One of the three programming structures used to make decisions.

**sequence structure**—One of the three programming structures used to execute a series of sequential steps.

**software development life cycle**—A well-defined series of steps used to develop complex software systems.

**statement**—A program statement expresses a complete thought or action. There are two types of statements, declaration statements and executable statements.

**syntax**—Programming languages have specific rules known as syntax.

**syntax error**—A condition that occurs when a statement violates one or more rules defined by a programming language. An application with a syntax error cannot be compiled.

**top-down design**—A modeling technique where general tasks are defined, and then decomposed into more specific tasks so as to divide a problem into simple component parts.

**UML**—The Unified Modeling Language contains various diagrams used to model complex software systems.

# ANSWERS TO MINI-QUIZZES

### MINI-QUIZ 1
1. Problem identification, systems design, system implementation, system documentation, system testing, deployment, and postimplementation audit.

2. c. HIPO chart

3. A UML activity diagram

4. c. the data maintained by the system and the possible actions performed on that data

### MINI-QUIZ 2
1. d. all of the above

2. A compiler

3. a. COBOL

4. a. Assembly language is considered a second-generation programming language.

5. d. Procedural and event-driven languages might or might not be object-oriented programming languages.

### MINI-QUIZ 3

1. b. All languages have syntax, but the syntax can vary from one programming language to the next.

2. Declaration statements and executable statements

3. c. A namespace can have one module or many modules. Each module can have one procedure or many procedures.

4. First, the namespace has no identifier. Second, the procedure must appear inside of the module block.

### MINI-QUIZ 4

1. c. It contains namespaces stored in physical assemblies.

2. c. The continuation character must be the last character on a continuation line.

3. In the first line, a space must be inserted before the continuation character. In the second line, the continuation character must be moved so that it appears as the last character on the line.

4. `ReadLine`

### MINI-QUIZ 5

1. b. `..\CourseTechnology`

2. `CD C:\CourseTechnology\3546-3\Temp`

3. The just-in-time compiler

4. `vbc /main:CourseTechnology.Quiz /out:Quiz.exe Quiz.vb`

# REVIEW QUESTIONS

1. Which of the following statements is correct of the Unified Modeling Language?

   a. A flowchart and HIPO chart are both UML diagrams.

   b. UML programs are written in Visual Basic.

   c. The UML can be used to model and document complex software systems.

   d. Visual Studio provides the means to edit UML documents.

   e. none of the above

2. Which of the following statements is correct related to pseudocode?

   a. Pseudocode is exact. In other words, there exists only one way to express a particular task using pseudocode.

   b. UML models and pseudocode models are synonymous.

   c. The Visual Basic compiler translates source statements into pseudocode statements when an application is compiled.

   d. Pseudocode uses English-like statements to depict the actions performed by a software system.

   e. none of the above

3. What is the name of the program that translates source statements written in a programming language into an executable program?

   a. language translator          b. execution generator

   c. compiler                     d. the UML

   e. none of the above

4. Which of the following comprise the interface for a class?

   a. attributes and actions        b. namespaces and modules

   c. properties, methods, and events   d. data items and action items

   e. none of the above

5. Which of the following statements about object-oriented programming is correct?

   a. All object-oriented programming languages support encapsulation, which is the packaging together of data and the processes that act on that data.

   b. All objects are created from a template called a root.

   c. Although not a requirement, some object-oriented programming languages support inheritance.

   d. All object-oriented programming languages store classes in folders called templates.

   e. none of the above

6. Which of the following statements about the Visual Basic programming language is correct?

   a. An application contains namespaces having modules with one or more procedures. Procedures, in turn, can contain declaration and executable statements.

   b. An application contains one or more executable statements. Executable statements appear inside of a namespace but outside of a module.

c. Procedures can be nested. That is, one procedure block can appear inside of another procedure block.

d. A module must contain exactly one procedure.

e. The rules of a programming language are called semantics.

7. Which of the following statements is correct regarding `Module` blocks?

   a. `Module` blocks can be nested. That is, one `Module` block can appear inside of another `Module` block.

   b. A `Module` block cannot appear inside of a `Namespace` block.

   c. A `Namespace` block can contain multiple `Module` blocks.

   d. A `Module` block cannot contain a procedure named Main.

   e. none of the above

8. Which of the following statements is correct regarding procedures?

   a. A procedure cannot appear inside of a `Module` block.

   b. A procedure can appear inside of a `Namespace` block, but cannot appear inside of a `Module` block.

   c. All procedures must be named Main.

   d. Procedures can have zero, one, or many arguments.

   e. none of the above

9. Which of the following statements correctly writes a blank line to the Console window?

   a. `System.Console.WriteBlank()`

   b. `System.BlankLine()`

   c. `System.Console.WriteLine()`

   d. `System.Console.WriteLine(Blank)`

   e. none of the above

10. What is meant by the term entry point?

    a. The entry point refers to the point in a procedure at which execution of the procedure begins.

    b. An application has one entry point. This can be the procedure named Main() where execution begins when the application runs.

    c. An application's entry point refers to the main namespace where execution begins.

d. An entry point marks the event procedure where execution of the application begins. Thus, the terms entry point and event procedure are synonymous.

e. none of the above

11. Which of the following statements related to the continuation character is correct?

a. In Visual Basic, the continuation character is the ampersand "&" character.

b. The continuation character allows a Visual Basic statement to appear on multiple lines instead of just a single line.

c. The continuation character appears at the beginning of the continuation line.

d. The continuation character can be used to connect the statements in one procedure to the statements in another procedure.

e. all of the above

12. What is the purpose of the `System.Windows.Forms.SystemInformation` class?

a. Its methods are used to get information about the open windows on the desktop.

b. Its methods are used to get information about the current form.

c. Its methods are used to get information about the assemblies currently residing in the global assembly cache.

d. Its methods are used to get configuration information about the local computer.

e. none of the above

13. Which of the following statements correctly calls the Visual Basic compiler to compile an application named Questions.vb? Assume that the namespace is named CourseTechnology, and the module containing the Main procedure is named Questions.

```
a. vbc /root:CourseTechnology.Questions Questions.exe
   Questions.vb
```

```
b. vbc /main:CourseTechnology.Questions
   /execute:Questions.exe Questions.vb
```

```
c. vbc /CourseTechnology.Questions /out:Questions.exe
   /input:Questions.vb
```

```
d. vbc main:CourseTechnology.Questions
   out:Questions.exe Questions.vb
```

```
e. vbc /main:CourseTechnology.Questions
   /out:Questions.exe Questions.vb
```

14. List and describe the steps involved in the software development life cycle.

15. List and describe characteristics of first-, second-, and third-generation programming languages.

16. What is meant by the term interface? List the members of a class's interface.

17. Describe the organization and contents of the .NET Framework class library.

18. Describe how a Visual Basic program is translated from source code into an executable file. In your answer, be sure to discuss the role of intermediate language and the role of the just-in-time compiler.

19. List and describe the syntax errors in the following namespace and module declaration:

```
Namespace
    Module
    End Module
End Namespace
```

20. List and describe the syntax errors in the following statements:

```
Sub Main()
    Sub Demo()
        System.Console.WritLine("Question)
    End Sub()
End Sub
```

# PROGRAMMING QUESTIONS

1. Write the statements to print your name to the Command Prompt window. Print a blank line before and after your name. Create the statements in a procedure named Main.

2. Write the statements to write a blank line, and the text "Chapter 1," followed by another blank line to the Command Prompt window. Create the statements in a procedure named Main. The procedure should appear in a module named Question.

3. Create a procedure named Main with the statements to write the string "Visual Basic" to the Command Prompt window. Create the procedure in a module named Question in a namespace named Chapter01. Do not write a carriage return at the end of the line.

4. Write the statement to compile the program source file named Test.vb to produce an executable file named Test.exe. Use the default values for the application's entry point.

5. Write the statement to compile the program source file named `Question.vb` to produce an executable file named `Question.exe`. Use the default values for the application's entry point. Assume that the namespace named QuestionList has a module named Question containing the application's entry point.

6. Write the statements to create a namespace named Question having a module named ModuleTest with a procedure named Test. The code in the procedure should display the text "Enter a line:".

7. Write the statements to create a namespace named CourseTechnology having a module named ComputerInformation. The `System.Windows.Forms.SystemInformation` class contains methods named `ComputerName`, `KeyboardDelay`, and `KeyboardSpeed`. Create a Main procedure to display descriptive prompts along with the values of these properties.

8. The `System.IO.File.Copy` method is used to copy files. The method accepts two arguments. The first argument is a string containing the source file, and the second argument is a string containing the destination file. Write the statement to copy the file named `Demo.txt` to the file named `Demo.bak`. The statement should appear in a module named CopyFile in a namespace named FileOperations.

9. Create a procedure named Main in a module named Question to produce the following output:

```
Visual Basic
Course Technology
```

10. Write statements that would be used in the Command Prompt window to change the current directory to the directory named C:\Chapter.01\Questions. Delete the file named Junk.txt in that directory.

# HANDS-ON PROJECTS

1. In this project, you will create a flowchart to model the processes involved in transferring funds from a checking account to make a credit card payment. Using the flowchart discussed in the chapter related to an ATM withdrawal, create a flowchart to make a credit card payment using funds from a checking account. Your flowchart will need to do the following:

   » Get the amount of the payment.

   » Verify that there are sufficient funds in the checking account to make the payment.

» If there are sufficient funds, deduct the payment amount from the checking account. Deduct the payment amount from the credit card balance due.

2. In this project, you will create an application that will write output to the Command Prompt window.

 a. Using Notepad or another text editor, create a module file named **Ch01HandsOnProject2.vb**.

 b. The namespace for the application should be CourseTechnology. The module should be named Address.

 c. Create a Main procedure to act as the application's entry point. Write the necessary statements to display the following output:

```
**********

Course Technology
25 Thomson Place
Boston MA
**********
```

 d. After displaying the preceding output, display a prompt to the end user to press Enter to quit the application.

 e. Write the statement that will wait until the end user presses the Enter key. When the end user presses the Enter key, the application should exit.

 f. Compile the application such that the output file is named **Ch01HandsOnProject2.exe**.

3. In this project, you will create an application that will read input from a Command Prompt window, and write output to a Command Prompt window.

 a. Using Notepad or another text editor, create a file named **Ch01HandsOnProject3.vb**.

 b. In the file, create a module named Information in a namespace named Course Technology.

 c. Create a Main procedure to act as the application's entry point.

 d. Write the statements to display the following message replacing *computername* with the actual name of your computer and *n* with the number of mouse buttons attached to the computer.

```
My computer is named computername.
It has n mouse buttons.
```

 e. After displaying the preceding data, display a message with the caption "Press any key to exit . . ." and read a character from the keyboard.

 f. Compile the program such that the output file is named **Ch01HandsOnProject3.exe**.

4. In this project, you will create an application that prints additional properties of the `System.Windows.Forms.SystemInformation` class beyond those discussed in the chapter.

a. Using Notepad or another text editor, create a module file named **Ch01HandsOnProject4.vb**.

b. The namespace should be named CourseTechnology and the module should be named Information.

c. Create a Main procedure to act as the application's entry point.

d. Display the contents of the following informational properties. All of these properties apply to the `System.Windows.Forms.SystemInformation` class. Display the data such that each property appears on a single line and a descriptive prompt appears to the left of each property.

» The `ScreenOrientation` property describes the orientation of the monitor. Monitors can be rotated 0, 90, 180, or 270 degrees. Display the monitor orientation to the Command Prompt window.

» Display the value of the `MonitorCount` property, which indicates the number of monitors installed on the system.

» Referring to double-clicking the mouse, the `DoubleClickSize` and `DoubleClickTime` properties describe the size of the rectangle in which the mouse must be double-clicked, and the maximum amount of time that can pass between two mouse clicks.

» Referring to the keyboard, the `KeyboardDelay` and `KeyboardSpeed` properties indicate the amount of time that must pass before the repeating characters will be entered and the rate at which repeating keystrokes appear.

e. After displaying the various informational system data, display a message with the caption "Press any key to exit . . ." and read a character from the keyboard. When the character is read, write the message "Program ended" to the Command Prompt window, to indicate to the end user that the program has ended.

f. Compile the program such that the output file is named **Ch01HandsOnProject4.exe**.

# 2

# CREATING A CONSOLE APPLICATION WITH VISUAL STUDIO

**After completing this chapter, you will be able to:**

Describe the Visual Studio IDE and Configure Visual Studio for use with Visual Basic

Describe the organization of the Visual Studio Help system

Navigate the Visual Studio Help system

Use the Visual Studio Object Browser

Explore the different types of Visual Studio applications

Work with Visual Studio solutions and projects

Explore the Visual Studio IDE and its windows

Use Visual Studio to create and compile a Visual Basic project

Create application comments and work with the My object

# CONCEPT LESSON

# INTRODUCTION TO VISUAL STUDIO

Chapter 1 discussed how to create a Console Application without Visual Studio to demonstrate the role of the Visual Basic compiler and how to use it. Although this technique might be adequate for very simple applications, more complex applications are not developed in this way. More commonly, the Visual Studio integrated development environment (IDE) is used to simplify the process of creating, compiling, and testing applications.

Visual Studio can be used to create applications written with programming languages such as Visual Basic, Visual C++, C# (pronounced C Sharp), or J# (pronounced J Sharp). No matter which Visual Studio programming language you choose, the tools used to develop Visual Studio applications are the same.

The Visual Studio developer interface is called an integrated development environment (IDE), which you, as the developer, use to create applications for end users or to create programming tools intended for use by other developers. The **Visual Studio IDE** includes all of the tools necessary to create and test applications.

Visual Studio can be started from the Start menu or via a desktop icon if one exists. Figure 2-1 shows the Visual Studio IDE with selected windows and development tools that are discussed in this chapter.

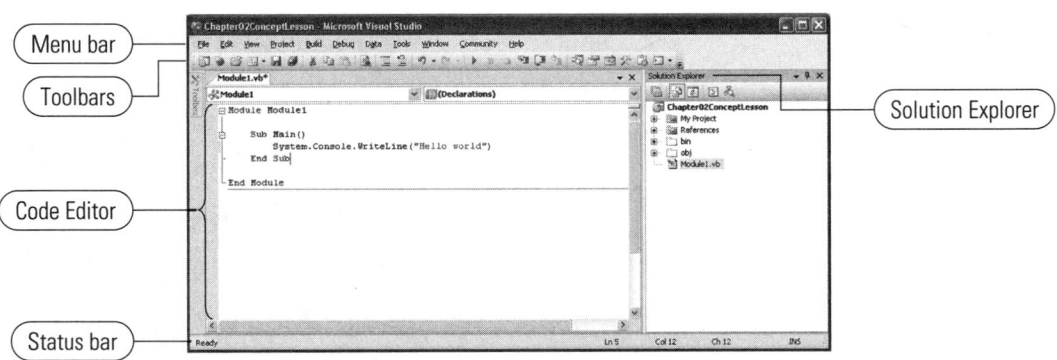

Figure 2-1: The Visual Studio IDE

As shown in Figure 2-1, the Visual Studio IDE interface is similar to that of other applications. The interface is made up of menus, toolbars containing toolbar buttons, a status bar, and many windows that are specific to Visual Studio. The windows that make up the IDE each have a particular purpose. For example, Figure 2-1 shows the Solution Explorer, which is used to manage the parts of an application. There are many different types of applications that can be built using the Visual Studio IDE. This chapter describes how to create Console Application projects.

In Chapter 1, you developed a Console Application using a text editor and called the compiler directly instead of using the Visual Studio IDE. In this chapter, you will see how the Visual Studio IDE can be used to create, compile, and execute applications. The information maintained by Visual Studio and the Solution Explorer allows Visual Studio to compile and test an application automatically with the click of a button.

The Code Editor, also shown in Figure 2-1, is used to create the Visual Basic statements that will execute when the end user runs the application. The Code Editor is used to create the same Visual Basic statements as those discussed in Chapter 1. However, the Code Editor, as you will see later in the chapter, does more for you as a software developer: It detects syntax errors, formats the code you write, and performs other tasks to simplify the development process and make it less error-prone.

In addition to the Solution Explorer and Code Editor, several other windows exist for testing and debugging applications. These windows are discussed in this chapter and in Chapter 3 as they are used for the first time.

# CONFIGURING VISUAL STUDIO FOR USE WITH VISUAL BASIC

Visual Studio can be configured based on the preferences of an individual developer using the Options dialog box. In total, there are hundreds of configurable settings. In this section, only those settings relevant to this and subsequent chapters are discussed.

The Options dialog box has a drill-down interface made up of two panes. A **drill-down interface** is one in which you navigate from the most general information to the most specific information. Folders appear in the left pane. These folders can be expanded to display more specific configuration categories. Some subfolders, in turn, contain additional subfolders. The list of configurable items varies based on the installed Visual Studio edition and whether the Show all settings check box is checked. If this check box

**»»NOTE**

The figures in this chapter assume that the Visual Basic Professional edition is being used. Other Visual Studio editions have different configuration options. Note that the configuration options discussed in this chapter are supported by the Visual Basic Express edition too.

is not checked, only the most common configuration options appear. If it is checked, it is possible to configure all of the possible settings applicable to the installed Visual Studio or Visual Basic edition. This section assumes that the Show all settings check box is checked and the Visual Studio Professional edition is installed. Like most Microsoft applications, clicking Tools, Options will activate the Options dialog box.

Figure 2-2 shows the Options dialog box with the Environment folder expanded and the General subfolder selected.

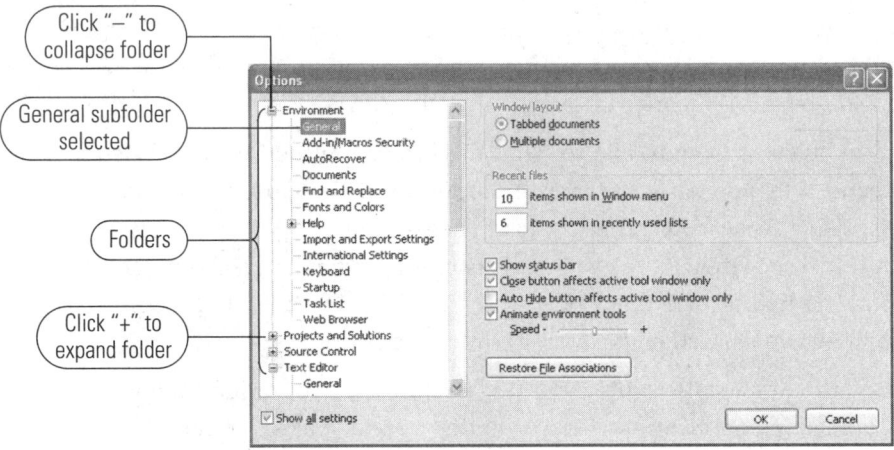

Figure 2-2: Options dialog box—General subfolder

The Environment folder's General subfolder contains settings to define how the IDE windows appear to the developer. The IDE can be configured to operate in two modes based on the Window layout setting.

» In Tabbed documents mode, windows appear on one or more tabs, are docked along an edge of the IDE, or appear as floating windows. Floating windows can appear anywhere on the desktop. This book uses Tabbed documents mode because it is the newer developer interface mode.

» In Multiple Document Interface (MDI) mode, the region of each window appears inside another window called an MDI parent window. MDI mode operates similarly to Microsoft Excel. That is, in Excel, each workbook appears inside the region of an MDI parent window. Multiple Document Interface mode was used by versions of Visual Basic prior to the introduction of Visual Studio .NET.

The Environment folder has a Help subfolder that controls how the Help system is displayed to the developer. Figure 2-3 shows the Options dialog box displaying the Help settings.

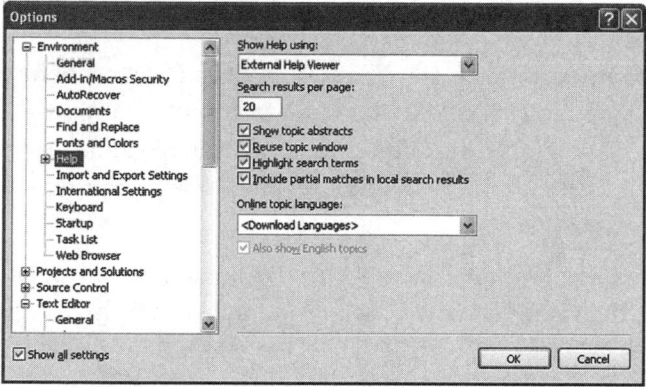

Figure 2-3: Options dialog box—Help subfolder

The Show Help using combo box controls whether the Help system is displayed inside of the Visual Studio IDE or in a separate browser window. This chapter assumes that the Help system is displayed in a separate browser window, which is the default. The check boxes control how topic windows appear when they are displayed. By default, all of these options are enabled.

The Projects and Solutions folder contains options used to configure the actions taken when a project is compiled and options specific to Visual Basic. Figure 2-4 shows the Options dialog box with the Build and Run subfolder selected.

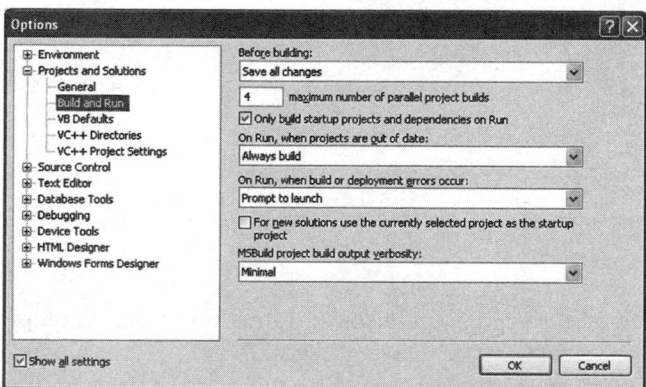

Figure 2-4: Options dialog box—Build and Run subfolder

Proper configuration of two of the settings can help avoid some common problems. Remember from Chapter 1 that you created an application using a text editor, saved it, and called the Visual Basic compiler to generate an executable application. Finally, you ran the application. The options on the Build and Run subfolder control how the Visual Studio IDE automatically saves files and compiles an application.

The Before building combo box is set to "Save all changes" by default. Thus, before attempting to compile an application, any unsaved changes are automatically saved. This setting prevents the possibility of compiling and running an outdated application version during the debugging and testing process thinking that you are running the current version.

The second combo box titled "On Run, when projects are out of date" defines what happens when you run an application from the Visual Studio IDE, when one or more files have been modified since the executable application was created. The default setting "Always build" causes the Visual Studio IDE to rebuild the application before running it. This setting also prevents Visual Studio from running an outdated version of an application.

The Text Editor folder contains the settings applicable to the editing environment. The editing environment can be customized for particular programming languages or particular file types. Figure 2-5 shows the Options dialog box with the Basic, General subfolder selected.

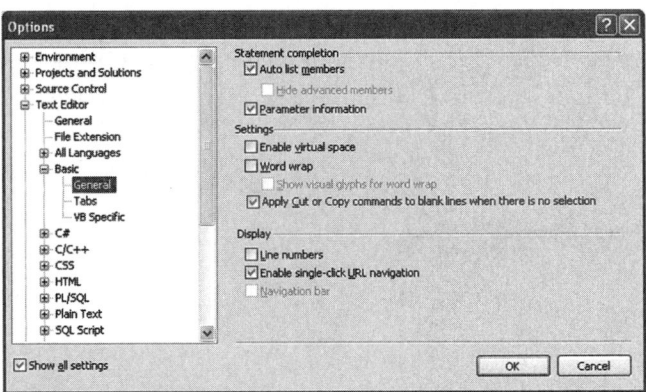

Figure 2-5: Options dialog box—Basic, General subfolder

The Basic, General subfolder contains options relevant to Intellisense technology. **Intellisense** technology helps you to write Visual Basic statements by displaying the properties, methods, and events applicable to an object, the arguments to a method call, and other helpful tips. Intellisense technology is discussed in detail later in this chapter. The following settings are significant:

» Checking the Auto list members check box causes Visual Studio to display a pop-up list box identifying the properties, methods, and other members applicable to a class or other type. The list box appears as statements are entered into the Code Editor.

» Checking the Parameter information check box causes Visual Studio to display a ToolTip listing the arguments and data types for a particular method call. Again, the ToolTips appear as a method call is entered into the Code Editor.

» Checking the Enable virtual space check box is useful for aligning comments. It's possible to click at a specific column position and enter a comment.

» Checking the Word wrap check box causes long lines to appear on multiple lines in the Code Editor. However, to the compiler, the statement exists on a single line. That is, if the code were to be viewed in another editor such as Notepad, the statement would appear on one line. This book does not use word wrap. Rather, long lines are broken up manually using continuation characters. Chapter 1 discussed continuation characters.

» When using the Visual Studio IDE with a printed copy of a module, you might want to check the Line numbers check box. Line numbers are a useful way to locate segments of code.

The Basic, Tabs subfolder controls how Visual Studio automatically performs indenting of blocks, decision-making statements, and continuation lines. Figure 2-6 shows the Basic, Tabs subfolder.

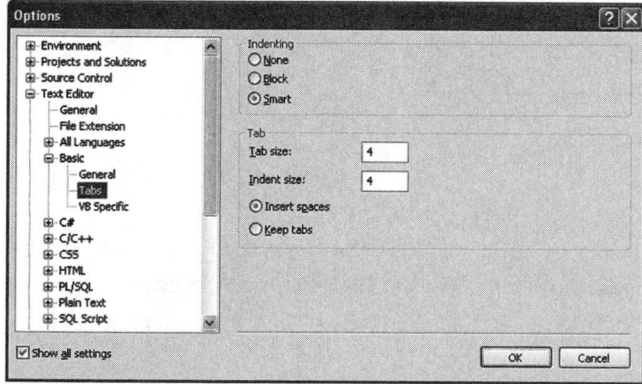

Figure 2-6: Options dialog box—Basic, Tabs subfolder

In the Indenting group, if you click the Smart radio button, Visual Studio automatically indents the statement blocks you write as follows:

» `Module` blocks and `Class` blocks are indented when they appear inside of a `Namespace` block.

» Procedure blocks appearing inside of a `Module` or `Class` block are indented.

» The statements appearing inside of a procedure block are indented.

» The statements appearing in a decision-making or repetition block are indented.

» Continuation lines are indented.

The number of spaces used to indent a block appears in the Tab group. The Insert spaces and Keep tabs radio buttons determine whether space characters are converted to tab characters or vice versa.

The final option folder discussed in this chapter, VB Specific, contains those editing options applicable to the Visual Basic language. Figure 2-7 shows the VB Specific sub-folder.

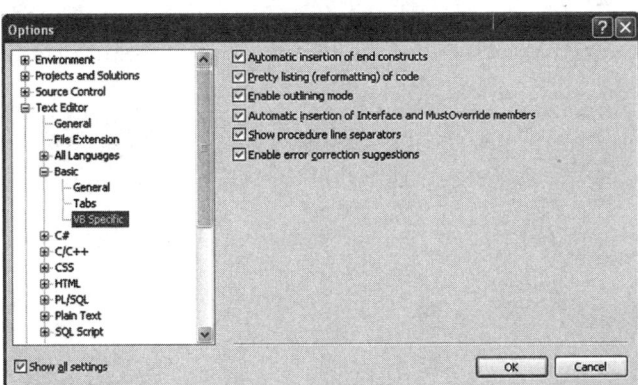

Figure 2-7: Options dialog box—VB Specific subfolder

The VB Specific subfolder contains check boxes used to enable or disable specific options applicable only to Visual Basic. By default, all of the check boxes are checked indicating that the options are enabled. The following list describes the purpose of selected options:

» Checking the Automatic insertion of end constructs check box causes the Visual Studio IDE to automatically create a closing block after an opening block is typed and the Enter key pressed. For example, had you created the Main( ) procedure that you created in Chapter 1, Visual Studio would have automatically generated the corresponding End Sub statement. Visual Studio also adds end constructs for decision-making and repetition statements.

» Checking the Pretty listing (reformatting) of code check box causes Visual Studio to recase keywords and variable names to make them consistent, and to align code based on well-accepted standards of indenting modules and procedures. In addition, Visual Studio attempts to add missing quotation marks to strings.

» The Enable outlining mode check box causes the Visual Studio Code Editor to display code using a drill-down interface. Procedures in a module can be expanded or collapsed. Enabling this feature makes it easier to locate those procedures under development and to hide those that are working properly. Entire Module and Class blocks can also be expanded or collapsed.

» The Automatic insertion of Interface and MustOverride members check box is used when creating classes that inherit from other classes. Enabling this option causes Visual Studio to create inherited procedures automatically.

» The Show procedure line separators check box causes Visual Studio to draw a horizontal line between the procedures appearing in the Code Editor.

» The Enable error correction suggestions check box causes Visual Studio to make suggestions to help fix syntax errors.

Having discussed how to configure the Visual Studio IDE for use with Visual Basic, you will now learn how to use the Visual Studio Help system.

> **»NOTE**
> The remaining text editor options apply to programming in other languages or working with documents other than Visual Basic code files and are not discussed in this chapter.

# INTRODUCTION TO THE VISUAL STUDIO HELP SYSTEM

Visual Studio supports an extensive Help system that provides information about the Visual Basic language, the statements that make up the Visual Basic language, along with those of the other Visual Studio languages. The Help system also contains documentation for the members of the .NET Framework class library. In addition, numerous technical articles, tutorials, and more are available.

> **»NOTE**
> The Help system and the topics in it are constantly being updated. Thus, various links to the content for a particular Help topic might change slightly.

> **»NOTE** The Visual Basic Express edition has a streamlined Help system that contains topics relevant only to Visual Basic. Other Visual Studio editions, such as the Professional edition, contain the full Microsoft Developer Network (MSDN) library. The figures in this chapter correspond to the Visual Studio Professional edition.

# UNDERSTANDING THE ORGANIZATION OF THE HELP SYSTEM

The Help pages for Visual Studio, the Visual Basic programming language, and the .NET Framework class library are organized similarly and can be categorized roughly into three types:

» A Language Help page relates to the statements that make up the Visual Basic language itself. These Help pages list the syntax for a particular statement and how to use the statement.

» A Class Help page describes the general purpose of the class or other type, and contains links to various examples that have been created.

» A Members Help page lists all of a type's members organized hierarchically. Members Help pages usually have sections for the supported properties, methods, and events.

Each Help page category is made up of sections having common names. For example, each category of a Help page has a See Also section containing links to related topics. Individual a Help page sections can be expanded or collapsed. These three categories of Help pages and the sections they contain are discussed next.

Note that the first time the Help system is started, the dialog box appearing in Figure 2-8 will be displayed.

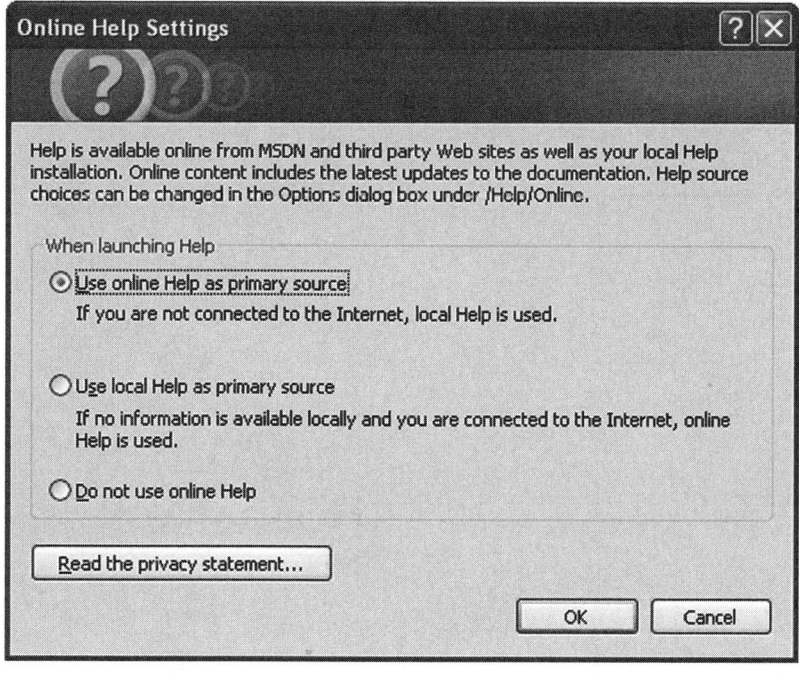

Figure 2-8: Online Help Settings dialog box

The settings in Figure 2-8 allow you to configure how local Help files will be integrated with online Help files.

» The setting Use online Help as primary source causes Visual Studio to use the online MDSN library as the primary source for Help files. If your computer is connected to the Internet, selecting this option provides you with the most up-to-date Help files. Because of the volume of information communicated over the network, you will experience delays with a dial-up modem connection.

» The setting Use local Help as primary source causes Visual Studio to first use local Help files, and then to look for Help files on the Internet.

» The setting Do not use online Help causes the online Help files to be ignored.

## LANGUAGE HELP PAGES

The purpose of a Language Help page is to describe how to use a particular Visual Basic statement or other Visual Basic language element. Figure 2-9 shows the Language Help page for the `Module` statement. This is the same `Module` statement discussed in Chapter 1.

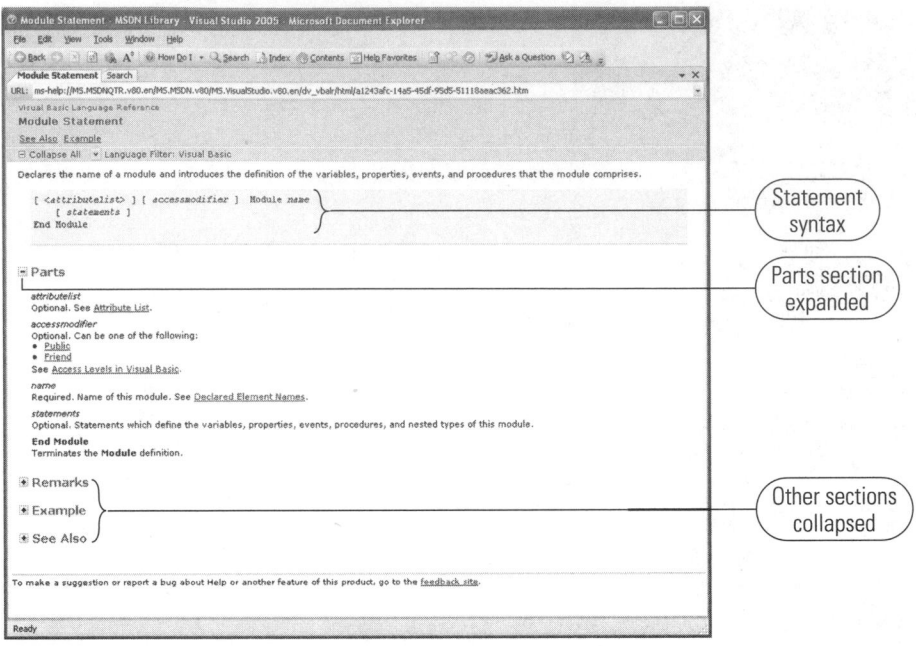

Figure 2-9: Language Help page

As shown in Figure 2-9, the Language Help page is divided into sections. Each section can be expanded or collapsed by clicking the plus and minus signs, respectively. Figure 2-9 shows the Parts section expanded and the other sections collapsed.

At the top of a Language Help page appears the syntax of the language statement or keyword along with a brief description of the statement or keyword. The syntax for all statements and keywords appears the same way.

» Reserved words appear in a monospace courier font.

» Square brackets [ ] surround optional data or arguments.

» Placeholder data appears in italics.

Additional sections appear following the syntax. The content of each of the sections is discussed next.

## THE PARTS SECTION

The Parts section describes the elements appearing in the Syntax section at the top of the Help page. As shown in Figure 2-9, the Parts section describes the purpose and require-ments for each placeholder.

» The *attributelist* argument contains any attributes defined for the `Module` block. The concept of an attribute is discussed later in the chapter.

» The *accessmodifier* defines the visibility of the `Module` block.

» As you know, each `Module` block must have a name (identifier). The *name* place-holder contains the name of the `Module` block.

» As you know, a `Module` block can contain declaration and executable statements. The placement of these statements is indicated by the *statements* placeholder. Because the *statements* block is optional, it is possible, although not useful, to create a module without any statements.

In addition to fully describing the syntax of a particular statement, the Parts section also contains links to related topics. These links vary from Help page to Help page.

## THE REMARKS SECTION

The Remarks section applies to nearly every category of Help page. For a Language Help page, it contains additional information about how to use the statement, and the rules for the statement's use. For Class Help pages, the section contains information necessary to use the class and its members. Most remarks provide a brief tutorial about how to use the statement, class, or other type. Most keywords appearing in the Remarks section are links to other Help pages making cross-referencing related topics easy.

The Remarks section can contain additional subsections. For example, the Help page for the `Module` statement contains subsections titled Classes and Modules, Rules, and Behavior. The subsections of the Remarks section vary from one Help page to the next.

## THE EXAMPLE SECTION

The Example section contains one or more sample applications or application fragments to demonstrate the use of a particular statement, class, or other type. In most cases, examples are supplied for all of the Visual Studio languages. Code examples can be easily copied from the Help system into a Visual Basic application by clicking Copy Code at the top of the example. The code is then copied to the Windows Clipboard. To paste the code example into a Visual Basic application, activate the Code Editor, and paste the code example from the Clipboard. In most applications, including Visual Studio, you can paste data from the Clipboard by clicking Edit, Paste on the menu bar, or by clicking the Paste button on a toolbar. Copying code examples assists you in exploring how to use a particular statement, class, or method because you can quickly run operational examples to see how they work. The following code segment shows a code example taken from the `Module` statement. Note that a continuation line has been inserted in the example for formatting reasons.

```
Public Module thisModule
    Sub Main()
        Dim userName As String = _
            InputBox("What is your name?")
        MsgBox("User name is" & userName)
    End Sub
    ' Insert variable, property, procedure, and event
    ' declarations.
End Module
```

This code should look extremely familiar. The `Module` is named "thisModule." It contains a procedure named Main. The statements in the procedure display two dialog boxes: an input box and a message box.

### THE SEE ALSO SECTION

The See Also section contains links to related topics. For the `Module` statement, the See Also section contains links to other related Visual Basic statements. The See Also section is also divided into subsections based on the Help topic. Note that almost all Help pages contain a See Also section.

## MEMBERS HELP PAGES

Most classes have a Members Help page that lists the members of the class, or other type, hierarchically organized by property, method, and event. Figure 2-10 shows the Members page for the `Console` class of the `System` namespace.

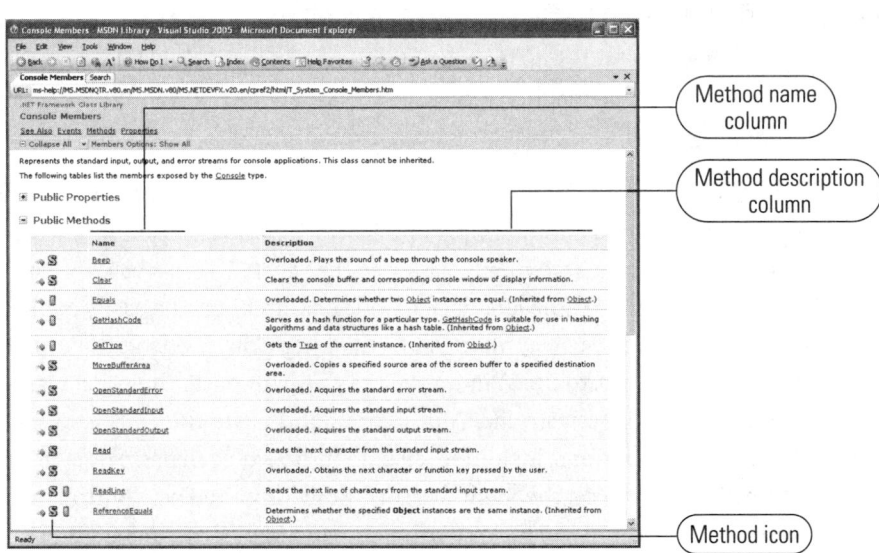

**▶▶ NOTE**

The Public Properties category (shown in Figure 2-10) and the Public Methods category (which is visible in Figure 2-10 if you scroll down) work similarly to the Public Methods category.

Figure 2-10: Console Members Help page

Like other Help pages, the Members Help page has a drill-down interface that displays an overview of the properties, methods, events, and other members of the type. As shown in Figure 2-10, the Public Properties category appears collapsed and the Public Methods category is expanded and lists the methods in alphabetical order. For each method, an icon indicating the method's type appears in the first column. The method name appears in the second column, and a brief description appears in the third column. Clicking on a method name, such as Beep, causes a detailed Help page to appear describing the method. If the method is overloaded, an intermediate Help page appears requesting you to select the desired version of the overloaded method.

## CLASS HELP PAGES

The purpose of a Class Help page is to describe a particular class, and give general information related to how to use the class. Figure 2-11 shows the Class Help page for the System.Console class.

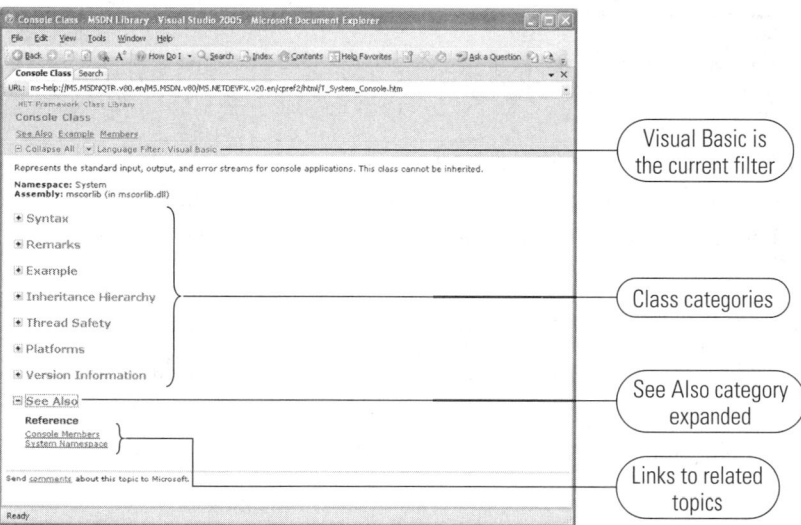

Figure 2-11: Class Help page for the System.Console class

Figure 2-11 shows all of the categories collapsed with the exception of the See Also category. Note that Class Help pages have similar sections as Language Help pages. That is, both types of Help pages have Remarks, Example, and See Also sections. The purpose of these sections is the same for both types of Help pages. Next, the various sections common to most Class Help pages are discussed.

## THE SYNTAX SECTION

The Syntax section shows the syntax declaration for the class or class member. Figure 2-12 shows the Syntax section expanded for the Console class of the System namespace.

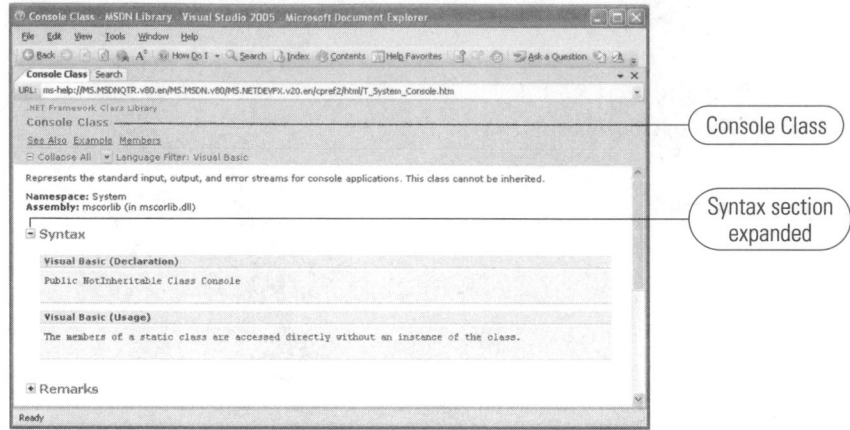

Figure 2-12: Console Class Help page—Syntax section

As shown in Figure 2-12, the Syntax section shows the declaration for the `Console` class of the `System` namespace. Examining the Visual Basic statement, the full declaration of the class is shown. The following list introduces the meaning of each term shown in the declaration in Figure 2-12.

» The reserved word `Public` means that the class can be used by any other class.

» The `NotInheritable` keyword indicates that the `Console` class cannot be inherited by another class.

» The `Class` keyword denotes that the `Console` type is a class.

» The final word `Console` defines the name (identifier) of the class.

As you progress through this book, you will better understand the purpose of each of these keywords. For now, just realize that the Syntax section, as the name implies, lists the syntax of a particular member.

## THE INHERITANCE HIERARCHY SECTION

Remember that all object-oriented programming languages support inheritance and Visual Basic is no exception. In Visual Basic, all types inherit from the `System.Object` superclass. The Inheritance Hierarchy category shows the types from which the current class inherits. For example, the `System.Console` class inherits directly from the `System.Object` class, as shown in Figure 2-13.

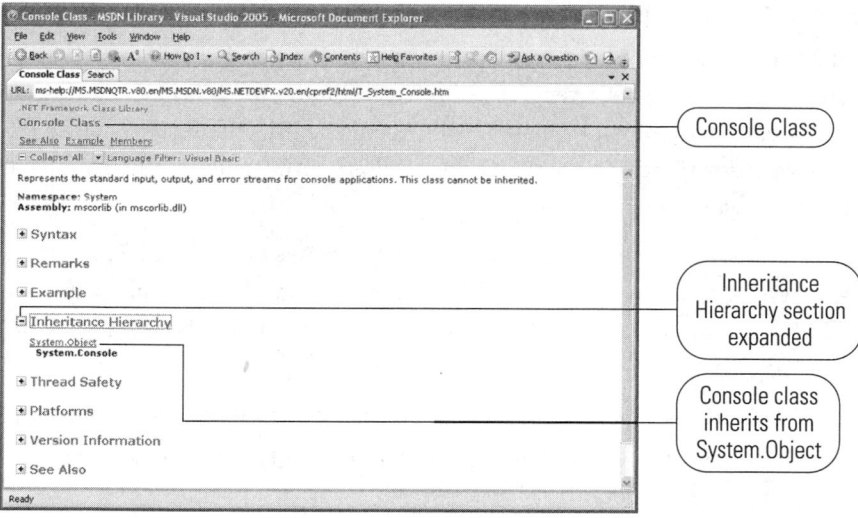

Figure 2-13: Console Class Help page—Inheritance section

The inheritance hierarchy for some classes is not so simple. To illustrate, the following code segment shows the inheritance hierarchy for the `System.Windows.Forms.Form` class:

```
System.Object
    System.MarshalByRefObject
        System.ComponentModel.Component
            System.Windows.Forms.Control
                System.Windows.Forms.ScrollableControl
                    System.Windows.Forms.ContainerControl
                        System.Windows.Forms.Form
                            Derived Classes
```

At this point, explaining the purpose of each of the previous classes is beyond the scope of this chapter. However, as the Help page shows, the `System.Windows.Forms.Form` class inherits from a complex hierarchy of classes, but just as with all Visual Studio classes, the superclass is `System.Object`.

## THE THREAD SAFETY, PLATFORMS, AND VERSION INFORMATION SECTIONS

The final three common Help page sections require little explanation, beyond the following facts:

» The Thread Safety section describes how a particular class is shared among multiple processes. Multiple processes and thread safety is not discussed further in this book.

» The Platforms section describes whether the class or method is supported by a particular version of Windows and lists any usage differences between versions of Windows. Platforms are categorized into development platforms and target platforms. Creating applications using Visual Studio requires a development platform. Target platforms can run applications created with Visual Studio so long as the .NET Framework is installed.

» The Version Information section describes which versions of the .NET Framework class library support the class or method. The version of the .NET Framework class library for Visual Studio 2005 is 2.0. Previous versions of the .NET Framework class library are 1.0 and 1.1.

Having described the various types of Help pages and the sections that make up those Help pages, you will now learn the different ways to search for specific Help pages within the Help system.

# NAVIGATING THROUGH THE HELP SYSTEM

Just as searching for a particular topic on the Internet can be difficult because of the volume of both relevant and irrelevant pages, navigating through the Visual Studio Help system poses a set of challenges. Unlike the Web, however, the Visual Studio Help system is well organized and managed. It also gives the developer a variety of ways to search for information.

The following list describes different ways to navigate through the Help system to find a particular topic:

» The Contents tab displays Help topics hierarchically, as you would typically see the table of contents appearing in a book. Content topics are expanded and collapsed using a drill-down interface. To activate the Contents tab, click Help, and then click Contents.

» The Index tab displays an alphabetical list of Help topics. It works the same way as a book index. To activate the Index tab, click Help, and then click Index.

» In the Search tab, Help topics are located by keyword. Those topics matching the specified search parameters appear in another window called the Search Results window. To activate the Search tab, click Help, and then click Search.

» Most of the Help system is feature-based. That is, the Help topics describe a particular Visual Studio, Visual Basic, or .NET Framework feature. The How Do I tab provides task-based help instead of feature-based help.

» Help Favorites can be used to store a list of frequently used Help topics. Help Favorites work the same way as Favorites created in Microsoft Internet Explorer.

» The Dynamic Help option causes a tool window called the Dynamic Help window to appear inside of the Visual Studio IDE. As you write statements or perform other tasks, the Dynamic Help window is automatically updated to show relevant topics.

## INTRODUCTION TO HELP FILTERS

The topics appearing in a table of contents, index, or search can be restricted to those for a particular language by applying a **help filter**. In addition to filtering topics by language, topics can be filtered according to other categories such as those types belonging to the .NET Framework class library.

The following list describes common Help filters applicable to the Visual Studio Professional edition and the full MSDN library:

» The .NET Framework filter displays a broad set of topics applicable to the .NET Framework class library. When searching the Help system for .NET Framework classes and their methods, apply this Help filter. Note that applying this filter excludes those topics applicable only to the Visual Basic language.

» The Visual Basic filter restricts Help topics to those pertaining to the .NET Framework, Visual Basic programming language, Windows forms, and Web development. When developing desktop Visual Basic applications, choose this filter.

» Filters named Visual C#, Visual C++, and Visual J# exist for each respective programming language.

» The Web Development (.NET) development filter includes documentation relevant to developing applications for use on the Internet or intranet. Do not use this filter when developing desktop applications.

» The Windows Forms development filter contains the documentation for forms-based (desktop) applications. Topics included in this filter are also included in the Visual Basic filter.

## USING THE TABLE OF CONTENTS

The table of contents can be an invaluable tool to locate information within the Help system. The table of contents is also a useful tool to help you learn about Visual Studio and Visual Basic because the topics are organized along functional boundaries and related tasks. To use the table of contents, you navigate through a drill-down interface moving from the most general topics to the most specific topics. The Development Tools and Languages folder and the .NET Development folder contain the information most applicable to the Visual Basic programmer. Figure 2-14 shows the Contents window with these two folders expanded.

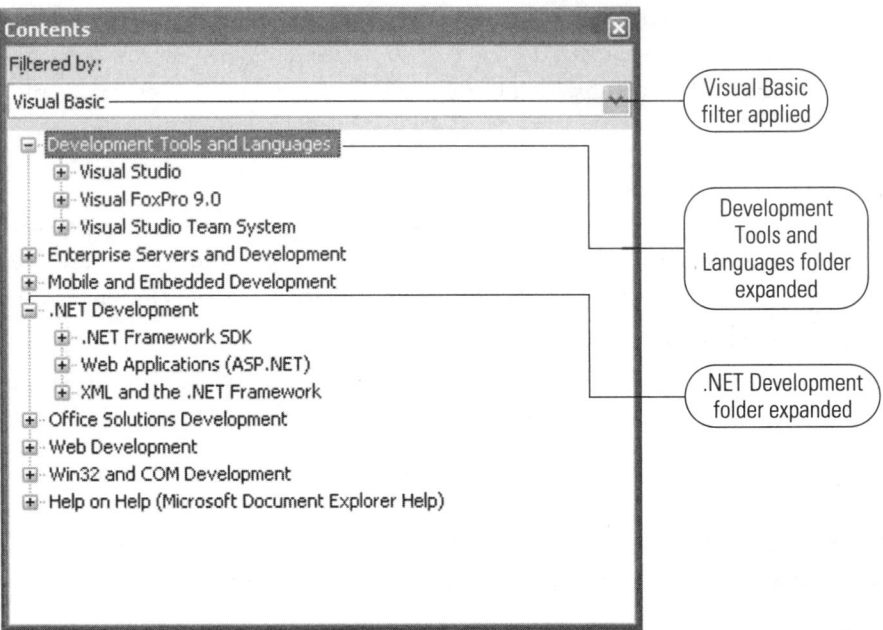

Figure 2-14: Contents window

First, note that the Visual Basic filter is selected. The Development Tools and Languages folder lists three products: Visual Studio, Visual FoxPro 9.0, and the Visual Studio Team System. Only the Visual Studio product applies to programming with Visual Studio 2005. The Visual Studio folder contains Help topics for the Visual Studio IDE along with help for each programming language including Visual Basic. This chapter does not discuss the other development tools or languages. The .NET Development folder contains Help topics relevant to the .NET Framework class library itself.

## HELP CONTENTS—DEVELOPMENT TOOLS AND LANGUAGES

Nearly all of the general topics applicable to Visual Studio and Visual Basic, appear in the Visual Studio subfolder of the Development Tools and Languages folder, as shown in Figure 2-15.

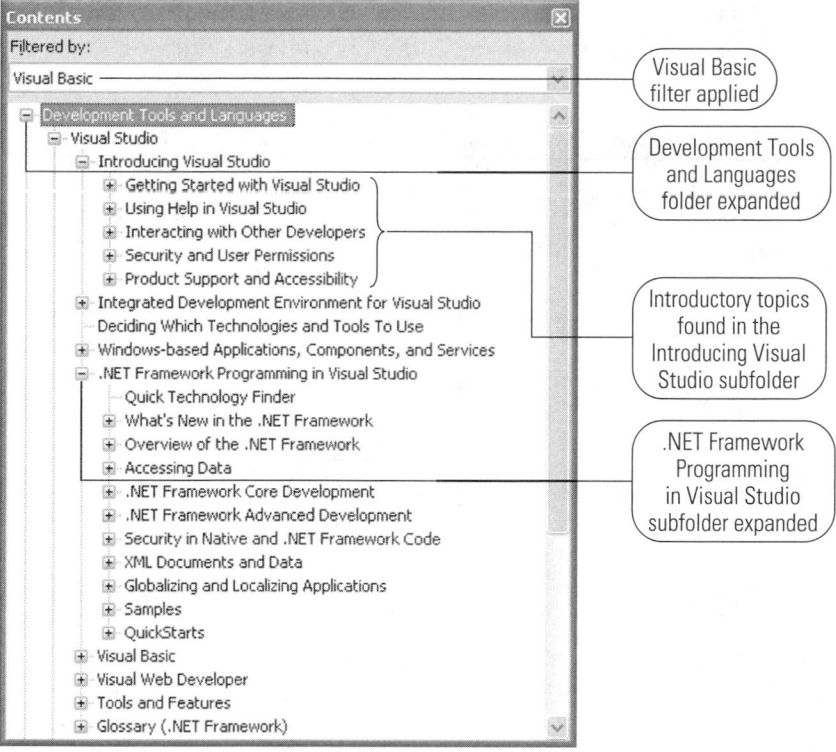

Figure 2-15: Contents window—Visual Studio subfolder

The following list describes selected subfolders of the Visual Studio subfolder:

» The subfolder titled Introducing Visual Studio contains additional subfolders titled Getting Started with Visual Studio and Using Help in Visual Studio. The Getting Started with Visual Studio subfolder contains introductory material describing how to install Visual Studio, how to use the Visual Studio IDE, and new features found in Visual Studio 2005. The Using Help in Visual Studio folder, as its name implies, shows you how to use the Help system.

» The subfolder titled .NET Framework Programming in Visual Studio contains topics related to using Visual Studio with the .NET Framework class library. The subfolder titled Overview of the .NET Framework describes the design philosophy behind the .NET Framework and its operation. The folder titled Accessing Data contains additional subfolders describing how to use the Visual Database Tools and ADO.NET. Chapters 11 and 12 discuss these topics.

» The folder titled Visual Basic contains help related to the Visual Basic language itself.

Topics related to the Visual Basic language itself appear in the Visual Basic subfolder. Figure 2-16 shows selected subfolders appearing in the Visual Basic folder.

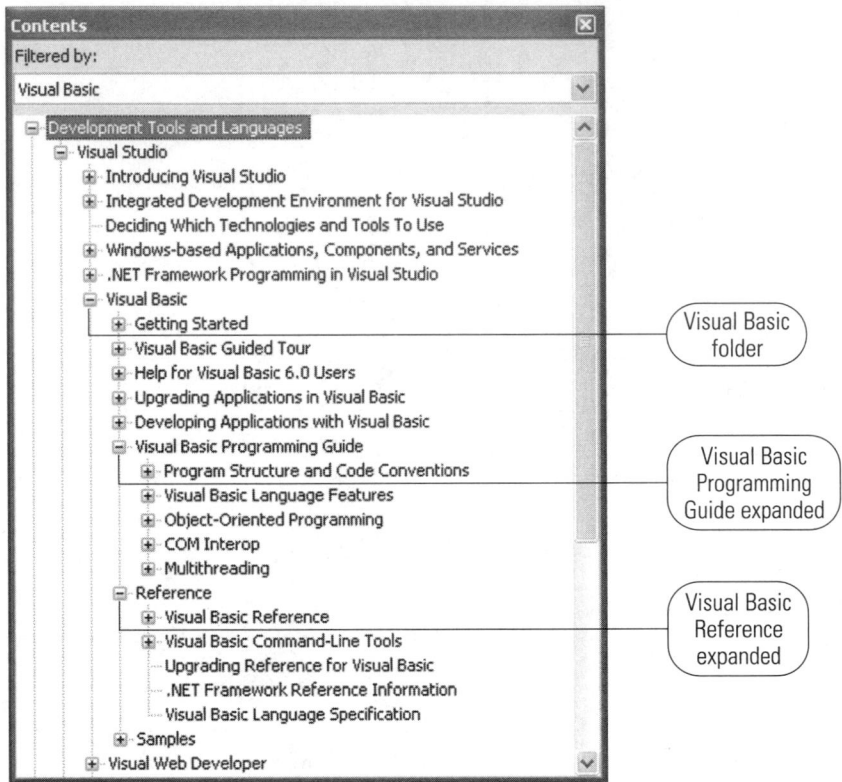

Figure 2-16: Contents window—Visual Basic subfolder

Programmers new to Visual Basic will find the tutorials in the Getting Started subfolder and the Visual Basic Guided Tour subfolder useful. For example, the Visual Basic Guided Tour subfolder contains tutorials to create a first application, and to explore the elements of the Visual Basic language.

The Visual Basic Programming Guide contains five subfolders:

» The Program Structure and Code Conventions subfolder describes the structure of a Visual Basic application and the naming requirements for identifiers. This material is similar to the syntax material discussed in Chapter 1.

» The Visual Basic Language Features subfolder has additional subfolders that describe the elements of the Visual Basic language.

» The Object-Oriented Programming subfolder contains topics related to how classes, inheritance, and other objects work in Visual Basic.

» The final two subfolders named COM Interop and Multithreading contain more advanced topics and are beyond the scope of this chapter.

The Visual Basic subfolder also contains a subfolder named Reference. The Visual Basic Reference subfolder, as its name implies, contains a complete reference of the Visual Basic language. A reference to all of the Visual Basic reserved words and operators can be found in this section.

## HELP CONTENTS—.NET DEVELOPMENT

The .NET Development subfolder contains Help topics related to the .NET Framework itself. Its folders are shown in Figure 2-17.

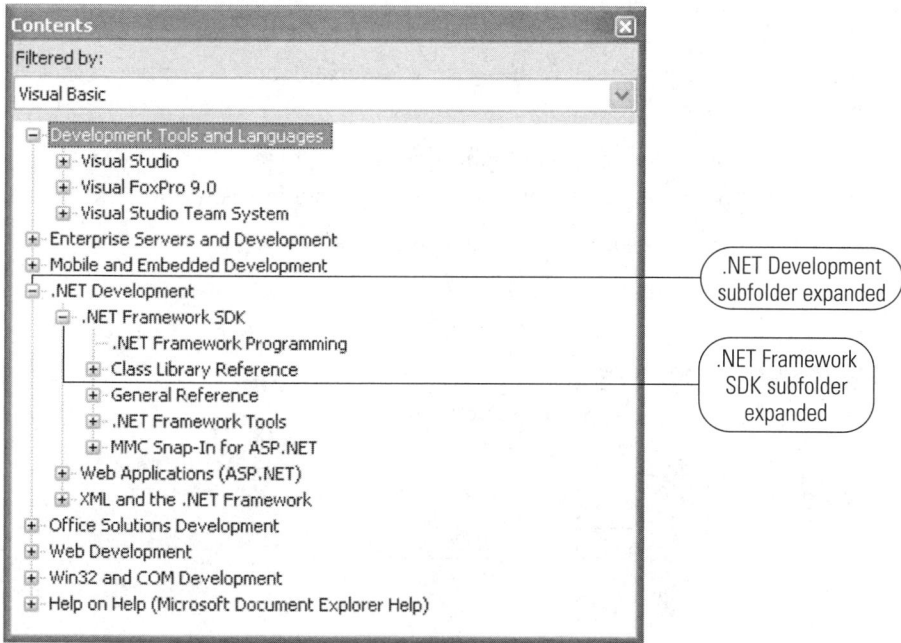

Figure 2-17: Contents window—.NET Development subfolder

Two subfolders in the .NET Development folders might be useful. The .NET Framework Programming subfolder contains a discussion of the .NET Framework itself. The second folder titled Class Library Reference contains an alphabetical list of all the types that make up the .NET Framework class library. This list can be useful if you know the class or other type for which you are seeking help. However, this list will not assist you to determine which class to use to perform a particular task.

## USING THE INDEX WINDOW

Whereas the Contents window displays information from the Help system hierarchically, the Index window contains Help topics in the form of an alphabetized list. Thus, if you are searching for Help on a term or a keyword, the Index window can be very useful. Note that the Index window ultimately displays the same Help pages as the Contents window. The following general points can be made about the Index window:

» Just as a filter can be applied to the topics in the Contents window, a filter can be applied to the Index window.

» Index entries appear sorted alphabetically.

» Many index entries appear organized by namespace and class name. A period separates the namespace and class names just as a period separates these elements when writing code.

» If you know the name of a particular namespace, class, method, or other type, the Help Index window is the easiest way to locate a particular Help topic.

» The search for Help topics is made in a case-insensitive way.

Figure 2-18 shows the Help Index window.

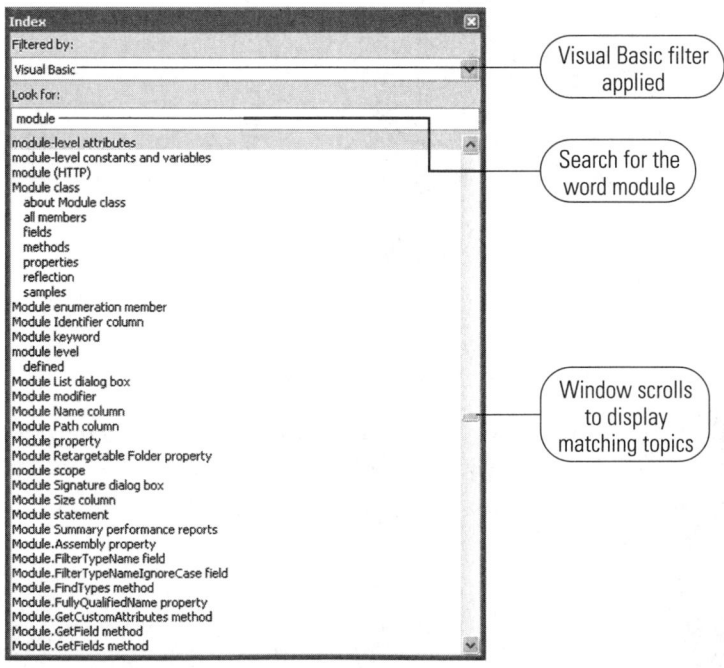

Figure 2-18: Help Index window

As shown in Figure 2-18, the Help Index window contains a combo box with which to apply a filter. In the Look for combo box, you enter the search text. As you do, the section containing the topics found is updated accordingly. As many Help pages have keywords matching a particular topic, there can be many matching entries. Click any matching entry to display the corresponding Help topic.

## USING THE SEARCH WINDOW

Selected words in the Help pages are marked as keywords. Using these keywords, it is possible to search for a particular Help topic using the Help Search window shown in Figure 2-19.

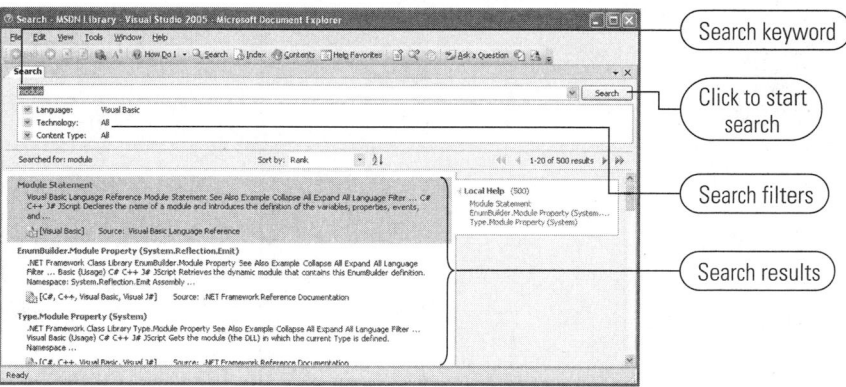

Figure 2-19: Help Search window

As shown in Figure 2-19, the Help Search window is made up of two sections. In the top section, you define the search parameters. In the bottom section, the Help topics that most closely match those parameters appear. The following list describes how to specify the search parameters in the top section:

» In the top combo box, you enter the search topic. In Figure 2-19, the search topic is "module."

» In the following combo boxes, you apply search filters. It is possible to restrict the search to a particular Visual Studio language. By selecting an item from the Technology combo box, it's possible to restrict the search to a particular Microsoft product. Microsoft divides content into various types. For example, there are technical articles, knowledge base articles, and others.

After the Search button is clicked, the matching Help topics appear in the lower window. When using the search feature, use the most specific keywords possible to restrict the search to the fewest possible items.

**»NOTE**

How Do I Help is new to
Visual Studio 2005.

## USING HOW DO I HELP

While most of the Help system is feature-based, How Do I Help is task-based. There exists How Do I Help for general Visual Studio features along with How Do I Help for Visual Basic.

Figure 2-20 shows the main How Do I Help window.

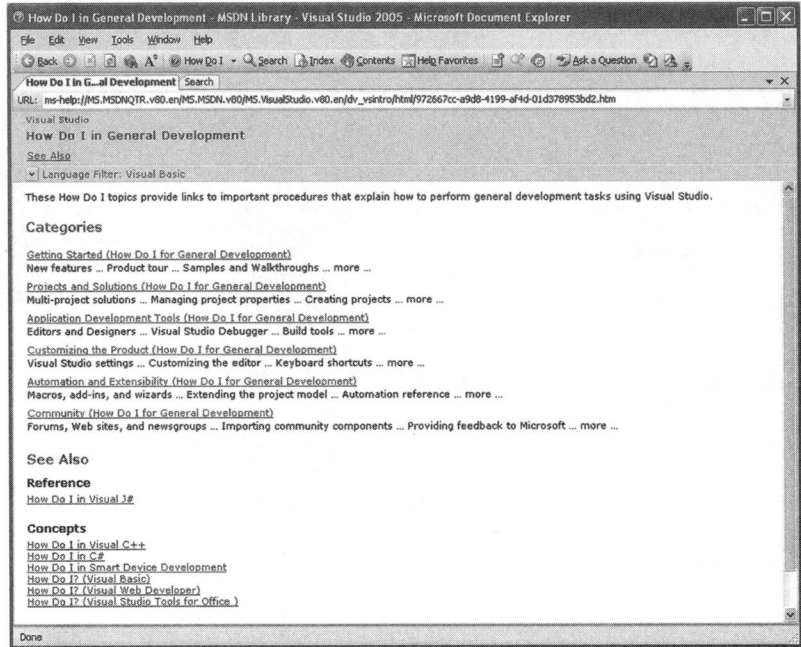

Figure 2-20: How Do I Help window

The following general points can be made about How Do I Help:

» Help filters can be applied to How Do I Help, just as Help filters are applied to the Help Contents and Help Index windows.

» How Do I Help topics are organized hierarchically. Thus, you drill-down through various Help pages to locate a particular How Do I Help topic.

» Each How Do I Help topic contains a hands-on tutorial describing how to complete a particular task.

» Most How Do I Help topics are introductory but there are a few advanced examples.

In addition to the Help system, another Visual Studio tool called the Object Browser will help you to learn about the hundreds of classes supported by the .NET Framework class library. That tool is discussed next.

# INTRODUCTION TO THE VISUAL STUDIO OBJECT BROWSER

In addition to the Help system, Visual Studio supports a tool used to explore the namespaces, classes, and all of the other types that make up the .NET Framework class library. In addition, it can be used to examine the types in the applications that you create. This tool, called the **Object Browser**, appears in Figure 2-21.

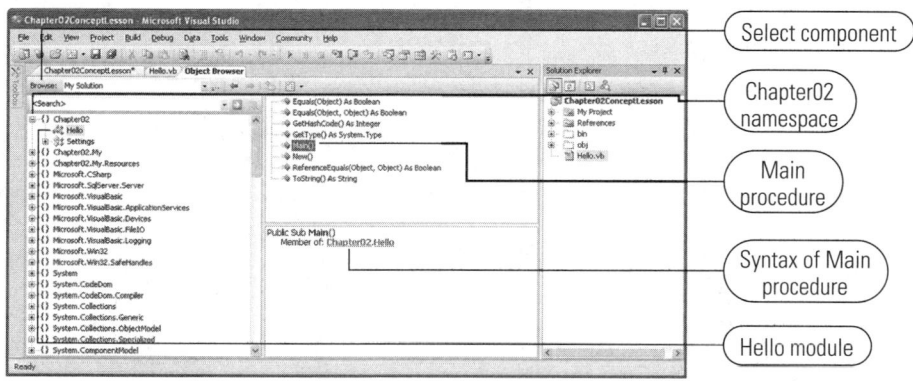

Figure 2-21: Object Browser—My Solution component selected

At the top of the Object Browser appears a combo box from which components are selected. Figure 2-21 shows the My Solution component selected. This setting causes the components from the current application, along with those belonging to the .NET Framework class library to appear in the Object Browser. The setting .NET Framework class library causes only those components belonging to the .NET Framework class library to appear.

The user interface for the Object Browser is made up of three panes. The left pane has a drill-down interface with which to select the namespaces and types that compose the .NET Framework class library or the current application. Remember that assemblies are physical files containing logical namespaces, which are organized hierarchically.

The concept lesson for this chapter uses the same "Hello World" application discussed in Chapter 1. Figure 2-21 shows the namespace for the concept lesson expanded. This namespace is named Chapter02. That namespace, in turn, contains one `Module` block named Hello.

Members of a class or other type appear in the upper-right pane. In Figure 2-21, the methods of the module named Hello appear. If a namespace is selected in the left pane, the upper-right pane is blank. In the lower-right pane, detailed information about the selected namespace, class, or class member appears. In Figure 2-21, the syntax of the procedure named Main appears. Again, this is the same Main procedure discussed in Chapter 1.

In addition to using the Object Browser to display the members of the current application, the Object Browser can be used to display the members of the .NET Framework class library itself, as shown in Figure 2-22.

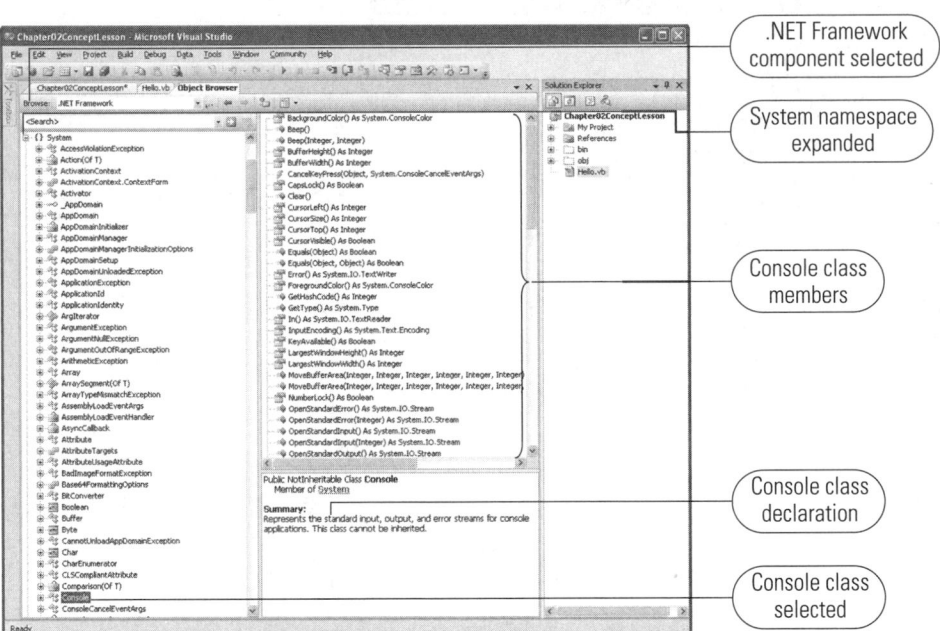

Figure 2-22: Object Browser—.NET Framework component selected

**» NOTE**

Each element appearing in the Object Browser has an icon that corresponds to the type. That is, there are different icons for namespaces, classes, properties, methods, and so on. These are the same icons that appear in the Help pages and in Intellisense pop-ups.

Figure 2-22 shows the `System` namespace expanded with the `System.Console` class selected. Recall that classes have properties and methods. Figure 2-22 shows the properties and methods of the `System.Console` class appearing in the upper-right pane of the Object Browser. Because the `Console` class is selected, its declaration appears in the lower-right pane.

In this exploration exercise, you will start Visual Studio and explore the Help system along with the Object Browser.

1. Using the Start menu or desktop icon, start Visual Studio.

2. On the Visual Studio menu bar, click **Help**, **Index** to activate the Help system. The Help system should appear in a separate browser window.

3. Select **Visual Basic** in the Filtered by list box.

4. In the Look for text box, type **My.Application**. Note that you will use this object in the application lesson.

5. In the list area, click **My.Application object**. The Help page appears, as shown in Figure 2-23.

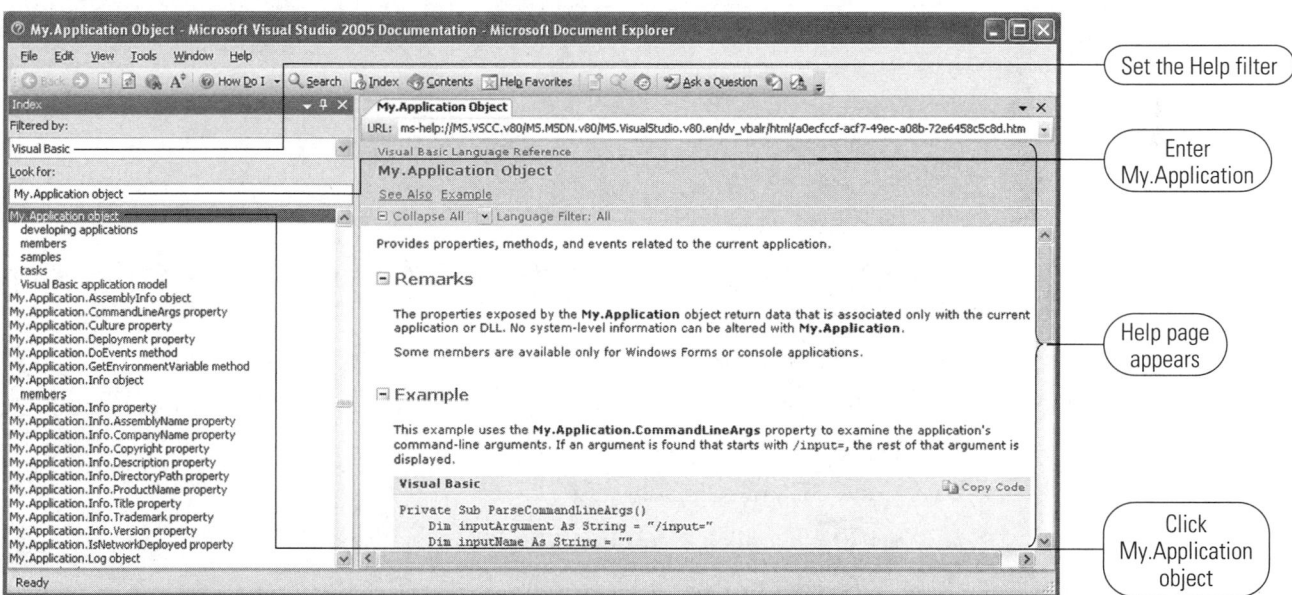

Figure 2-23: My.Application object Help page

6. Note that the Help page is divided into categories. Click the **See Also** category to see the change on the screen.

7. Close the Index window and the Help page.

8. In the main Help window, click the **Search** tab. Set the filters as shown in Figure 2-24. Type the text **My.Application**, and click the **Search** button. (Click the **Use local Help as primary source** radio button if prompted, and then click **OK**.) The topics found appear as shown in Figure 2-24.

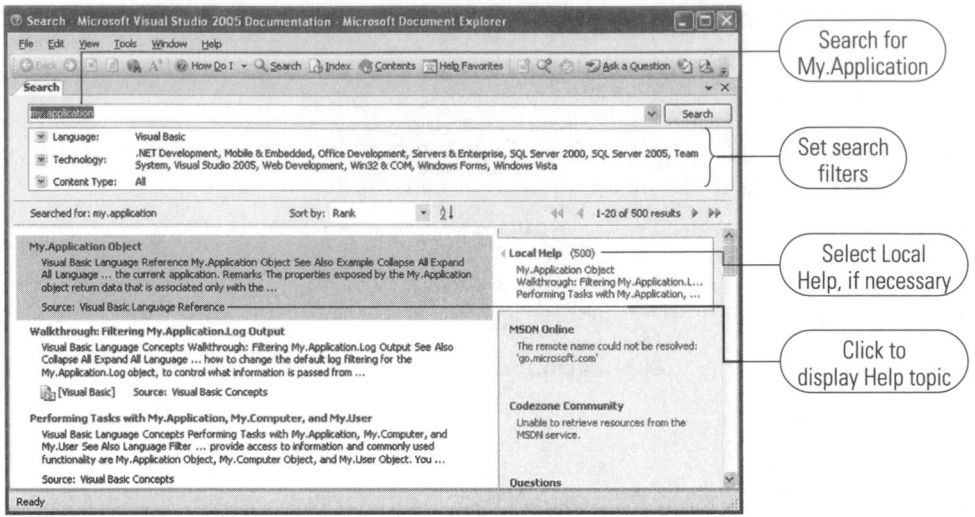

Figure 2-24: Searching for the My.Application topic

9. Double-click the first topic. The same Help page appears as the one shown in Figure 2-23.

10. Close the Help window.

11. Next, you will explore the Object Browser. In the Visual Studio IDE, click **View**, **Object Browser**.

12. In the Browse list box, select **.NET Framework**, if necessary.

13. In the left pane of the Object Browser, locate and expand the **System** namespace. The types in the System namespace appear.

14. Locate and click the **Console** class.

15. In the right pane, click **ReadLine( ) As String** to display its syntax.

16. Close the Object Browser.

## MINI-QUIZ 1

1. What is Intellisense technology?

   a. Intellisense technology is used by Visual Studio to compile Visual Basic projects.

   b. Intellisense technology displays object members as statements are entered in the Code Editor.

*(Continued)* ▶

c. Intellisense provides the means to display Help topics.

d. Intellisense is used in all of these situations.

2. Which of the following statements is correct regarding the Visual Studio Help system?

a. Help pages for the .NET Framework class library can be roughly categorized as Class Help pages, Members Help pages, or Language Help pages.

b. The Help pages for most .NET Framework class library objects display data hierarchically.

c. Sample code can be copied into an application from a Help page.

d. all of the above

3. What is the name of the Visual Studio utility used to look at the namespaces, classes, and other types that make up the .NET Framework class library?

# TYPES OF VISUAL STUDIO APPLICATIONS

The Visual Studio IDE supports templates, which are used to create different types of applications designed for use on the Windows desktop or on the Web. Each type of Visual Studio application can be created with the Visual Studio IDE using its corresponding template. Creating applications from Visual Studio templates is not a requirement, however. These same applications could just as well be created by hand using any text editor, such as Notepad, and calling the Visual Basic compiler directly. However, creating applications by hand is considerably more work, and, in most cases, is neither practical nor desirable. The following list of Visual Studio application templates will vary based on the Visual Studio edition installed on your computer:

» The Console Application template is used to create an application that operates from a Command Prompt window, such as the one shown in Chapter 1. In this chapter, you will see how to create a Console Application project using Visual Studio, rather than creating one by hand.

» The Windows Application template is used to create visual applications designed to run on a computer that might or might not be connected to a network. A Windows Application consists of one or more rectangular forms that appear on the desktop. A form contains boxes in which the user enters text, buttons that the user clicks, and other visual elements, such as scroll bars and radio buttons. Chapter 3 introduces how to create a Windows Application project.

**»NOTE**

Visual Studio also allows you to create several other types of application templates in addition to those appearing in this list. Additional download-able templates are also available from Microsoft. If you are using the Visual Basic Express edition, only selected templates are available.

» The Class Library template is used to create a component designed for use by another application and developer. Class libraries are not intended to be used by end users. Rather, class libraries are used by developers in the same way that you use the classes that make up the .NET Framework class library.

» ASP.NET Web Applications and Web Service Applications are templates designed for use on the Web. Another set of templates exists to create applications designed for mobile devices such as Pocket PCs, smart phones, and Windows CE. These templates are not discussed in this chapter nor this book. These templates are not available with the Visual Basic Express edition.

# INTRODUCTION TO VISUAL STUDIO SOLUTIONS AND PROJECTS

A developer interface is an extremely valuable software tool that can be used to simplify the development, testing, and debugging process. Here is where the Visual Studio IDE enters the picture. The Visual Studio IDE is made up of numerous visual tools used to create Console Applications and Windows Applications. The Visual Studio IDE supplies additional tools to compile and execute those applications, along with even more tools to debug applications as errors are detected.

Chapter 1 described how to create a simple application with a single `Module` block and a single procedure. However, most applications are more complex, containing many modules each having several procedures. Visual Studio organizes each application that you create into a solution. A Visual Studio **solution** is made up of multiple folders (directories) containing files and additional folders. Visual Studio manages all of the folders and files that make up a solution.

Every application that you create using Visual Studio has a well-defined structure and the **solution** file is the heart of an application's structure. A solution file gets created when you create an application based upon one of the templates discussed in the preceding section. Solution files have a suffix of .sln, which should never be changed. The solution file controls how the projects in a solution will be translated into one or more executable files. Thus, when a Console or Windows Application project is created, Visual

Studio creates a solution file and a directory for that solution. The following list describes some of the ways that Visual Studio uses the solution file:

» Visual Studio uses the solution file to keep track of one or more projects. Each project in a solution has a specific purpose and is created from a project template. For example, one type of project is a Console Application project. In this chapter, you will see how to create a solution with a single Console Application project.

» The solution file controls how the projects in a solution will be compiled into executable files. Visual Studio also uses the solution file to call the Visual Basic compiler with the correct command-line arguments. This is the same Visual Basic compiler used in Chapter 1. In fact, when a solution gets compiled, the Visual Studio Output window shows the call to the compiler and the results of the compilation.

A solution file contains references to one or more **project** files. Each project file is compiled to an assembly. That is, Visual Studio uses a project file to create an executable file. Chapter 1 showed how to compile an application using a command-line interface. A project is analogous to the application discussed in Chapter 1. To understand the purpose of a project, examine Figure 2-25, which shows the Project property page for a project.

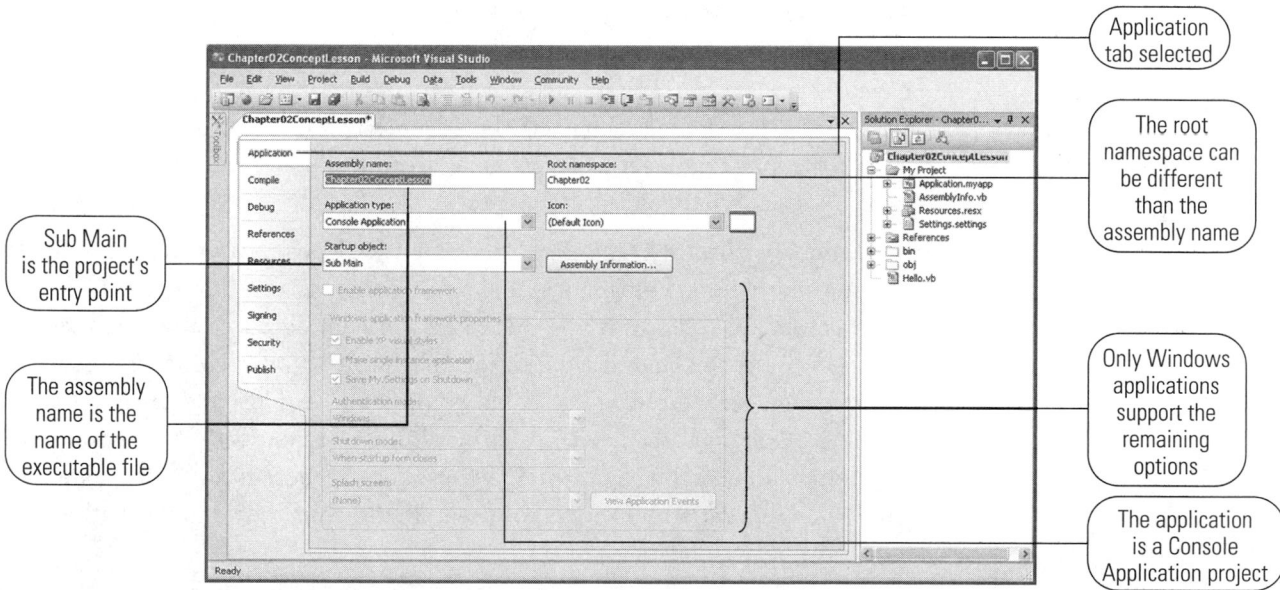

Figure 2-25: Project property page—Application tab

**» NOTE**

Figure 2-25 shows several shaded options related to Windows application framework properties. These options are shaded because they are only applicable to Windows Application projects. These options are discussed in Chapter 3 when you create your first Windows Application project.

The Project property page uses a drill-down interface. Figure 2-25 shows the Application tab selected. To activate the Project property page, right-click the project name in the Solution Explorer, and then click Properties from the context menu. The following application properties define how the application (project) is compiled into an executable file and the name of the assembly produced:

» The Assembly name text box contains the name of the executable file produced when Visual Studio compiles the project. By default, the assembly name is the same as the project name. The names might differ, however, if the developer chooses to change them.

» Remember from Chapter 1 that Visual Studio assemblies contain one or more namespaces. The projects you create are no exception. Every project has a root namespace. Technically, this namespace is no different than the namespaces defined by the .NET Framework class library or the root namespace you created for the application in Chapter 1. By default, the name of the root namespace is the same as the name of the project. Again, the names might differ if the developer chooses to change them.

» In addition to belonging to one or more namespaces, every project has a type. The project type is set when a project gets created from a template. However, it is possible to change a project's type after it has been created.

» Remember from Chapter 1 that an application (project) has an entry point. The startup object contains the procedure or module name that will execute when the executable file is run. For example, the entry point for the application discussed in Chapter 1 was a procedure named Main appearing in a `Module` block. Figure 2-25 shows the startup object as `Sub Main`, denoting that the Main procedure in a `Module` block will be the startup object.

When you compiled the applications in Chapter 1, it was necessary to add arguments to the command line when calling the Visual Basic compiler to reference various .NET Framework assemblies. This was not much of a problem because only two assemblies were used. However, imagine an application that used 10 or 20 different assemblies. Clearly, calling the compiler directly would be difficult, tedious, and error-prone. The Visual Studio IDE obviates the need for this by adding common assembly references to a project by default, and supplying a visual way to add references to additional assemblies. Based on this configuration information, Visual Studio calls the compiler with the correct command-line arguments.

A Visual Studio project also contains assembly references. The References tab on the Project property page lists the assemblies used by the project and appears in Figure 2-26.

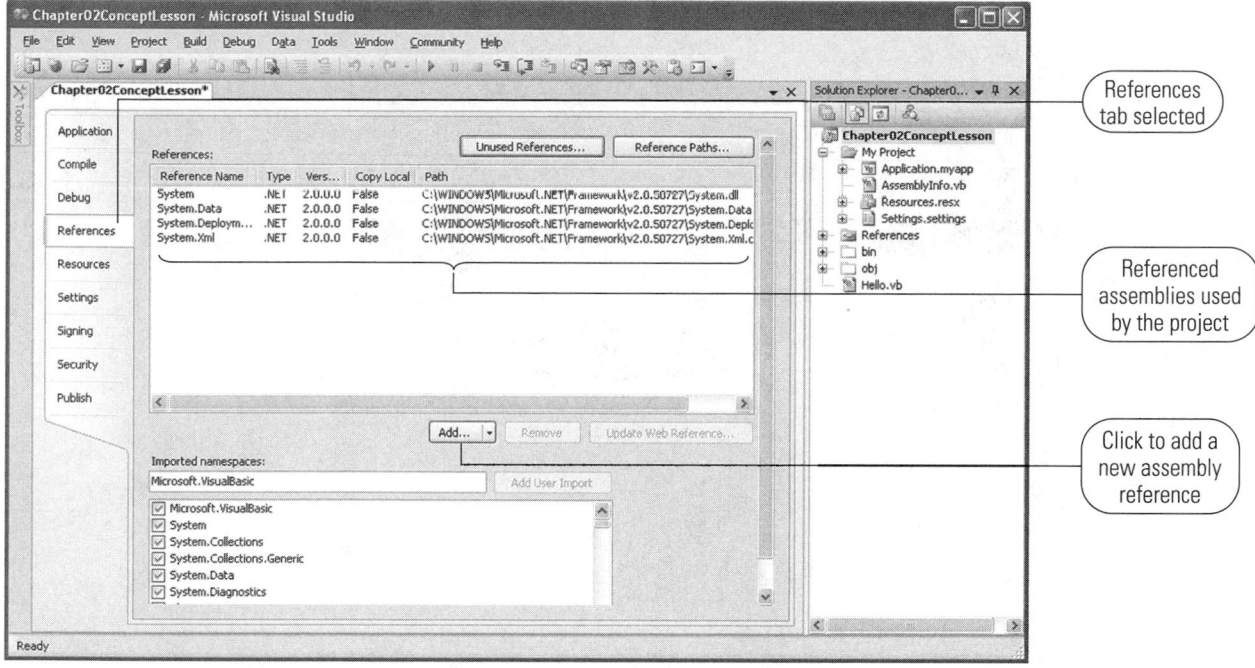

Figure 2-26: Project property page—References tab

Remember that a project references one or more assemblies and those assemblies contain one or more namespaces. When a project gets created from a template, Visual Studio adds references to commonly used assemblies automatically. Figure 2-26 shows that references have been added to four assemblies. As its name implies, the Add button is used to add references to additional assemblies.

In addition to listing the referenced assemblies, the References tab contains a section titled Imported namespaces. The concept of importing namespaces is discussed in Chapter 4.

In addition to application settings and namespace references, projects also have the following elements:

>> A project and its corresponding assembly contain data global to the project, including the textual description, version information, and copyright information. Global project data is discussed in more detail later in the chapter.

>> A project contains references to the files (modules) that make up the project. These files include forms, HTML documents, modules, and other file types. For example, the projects discussed in this chapter contain references to the module file containing the application's code.

Having discussed the purpose of a Visual Studio solution and project, you will now learn how to create a new Visual Basic solution, save that solution to the disk, and understand the organization of a Visual Basic solution.

## CREATING A VISUAL STUDIO SOLUTION

To create a new solution with Visual Studio, you begin by creating a new solution file with one project. That project is typically created from a template. Figure 2-27 shows the New Project dialog box displaying the currently installed Visual Basic templates. Again, the templates appearing in Figure 2-27 are found in the Visual Studio Professional edition.

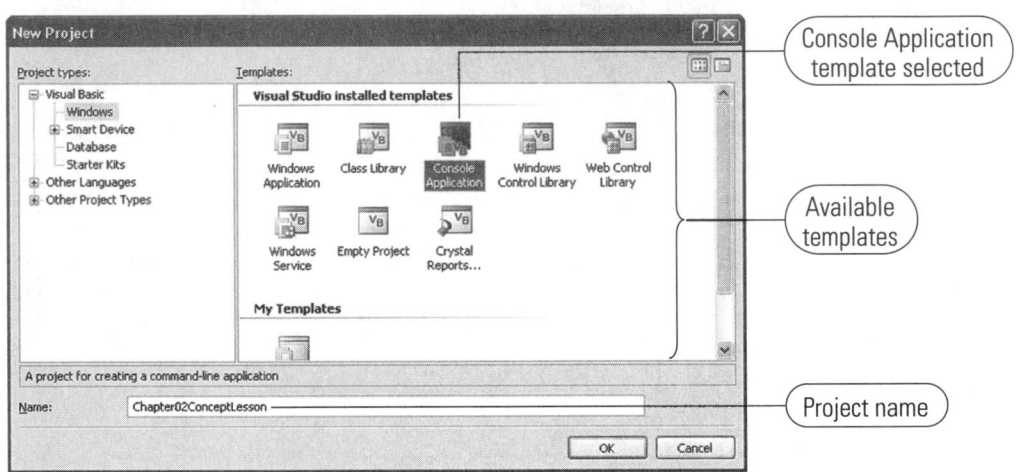

Figure 2-27: New Project dialog box

As shown in Figure 2-27, the New Project dialog box lists the currently installed Visual Studio templates. The My Templates section contains any custom templates you have created, along with those that have been downloaded from the Web. The Name text box contains the name of the solution and project. Visual Studio uses this name to set the default assembly name and the name of the root namespace.

## SAVING A VISUAL STUDIO SOLUTION

After a solution has been created, it must be saved to a folder (directory) on the disk. When a solution is saved for the first time, Visual Studio creates the directory structure for the solution and project. To save a solution, you click File, Save All on the Visual Studio menu bar. Visual Studio then displays the Save Project dialog box shown in Figure 2-28.

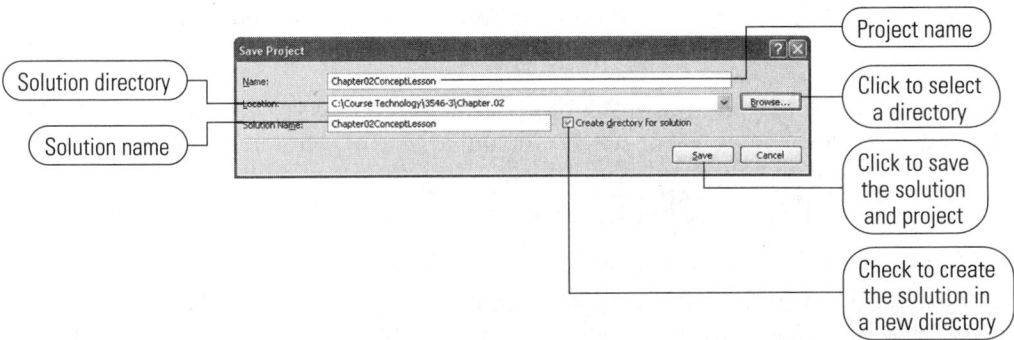

Figure 2-28: Save Project dialog box

As shown in Figure 2-28, the Save Project dialog box allows you to specify the following items related to saving the solution:

» In the Name text box, you specify the name of the project. By default, the project and solution have the same name.

» In the Location combo box, you specify the directory (folder) where the solution directory will be created.

» The Solution Name text box contains the name of the solution and solution directory.

» If the Create directory for solution check box is checked, Visual Studio creates the solution file in a new directory having the same name as the solution. This book follows the convention of creating a solution in a new solution directory.

The Save Project dialog box only appears the first time the solution is saved. After that, the solution and its files are automatically saved to the same directory, when File, Save All is clicked.

## ORGANIZATION OF A VISUAL STUDIO SOLUTION

Having seen how to start Visual Studio, and how to create and save a solution, you will now explore the elements of a solution and its projects in more detail. A Visual Studio window called the Solution Explorer is used to manage the files and other resources required by the solution and its projects.

Figure 2-29 shows the Solution Explorer for a Console Application project. The Solution Explorer displays information hierarchically similar to the way that Windows Explorer displays folders and files hierarchically. In Figure 2-29, all of the folders have been expanded so that you can see the files that make up the solution and their organization. In addition, note that all the solution files appear because the Show All Files button is selected.

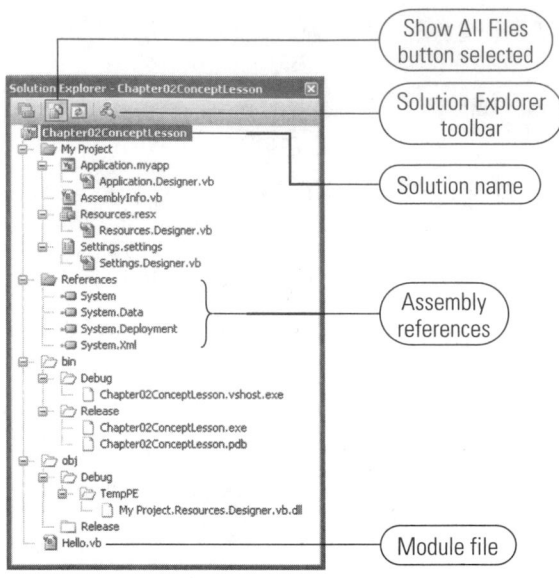

Figure 2-29: The Solution Explorer with all folders expanded

As shown in Figure 2-29, a solution is much more complex than just a single Visual Basic module file. The topic of using the Solution Explorer is discussed in a moment, but for now, focus on the different parts of a solution, which appear in the following list:

» The solution file is named Chapter02ConceptLesson. The solution file is stored in a directory having the same name as the solution. The solution directory contains one project directory, which, in turn, contains the project file and other files related to the project. Even though the two files have the same name, they have different file extensions and are stored as separate physical files on the disk. The solution file has a suffix of .sln, whereas the project file has a suffix of .vbproj. The Solution Explorer does not display the file extensions for solution files or project files.

» The My Project folder contains configuration files common to all projects. The file named Application.myapp is an XML document. The Application.myapp file defines such things as the type of application and whether the application is a single instance application. This file is automatically generated by Visual Studio and is not discussed further in this chapter.

» Remember from Chapter 1 that when you compile an application, the Visual Basic compiler produces an executable file called an assembly. The file named AssemblyInfo.vb contains descriptive information that is compiled into the assembly, such as copyright, trademark, and other product information. This file is generated automatically when a project is created from a template. The contents of the AssemblyInfo.vb file are discussed further later in the chapter.

» Visual Studio makes it easy to create applications that work with multiple languages. Resource files are used to create multilingual (internationalized) applications. The file named Resources.resx is a resource file. Resource files are XML documents. The file Resources.Designer.vb contains the executable code corresponding to the resource file. Resource files are not discussed further in this chapter.

» An application might have additional settings containing data used to configure the application. The files Settings.settings and Settings.Designer.vb contain these application defined settings.

» Remember from Chapter 1 that an application uses assemblies and namespaces from the .NET Framework class library. The References folder lists those assemblies that are used by the project. Assembly references added through the Project's property pages appear in this list.

» The bin\Debug folder contains the executable file named Chapter02 ConceptLesson.exe. This is the executable file that will ultimately be run by the end user. By default, the executable file has the same name as the assembly.

» The obj folder contains additional folders that Visual Studio uses to compile and debug the project. These files are discussed in more detail in subsequent chapters.

» The file named Hello.vb contains the Visual Basic module. This file contains a `Module` block similar to the one you created in Chapter 1.

The files managed by a solution are stored in a tree of folders (directories). Figure 2-30 shows Windows Explorer displaying selected directories for the solution displayed in Figure 2-29.

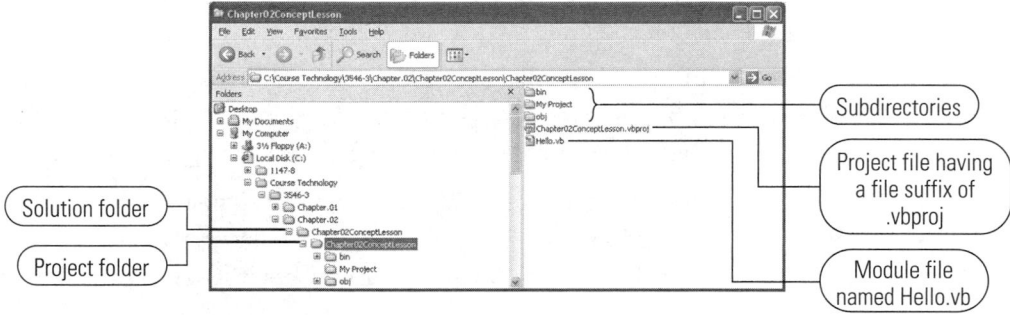

Figure 2-30: Solution files appearing in Windows Explorer

As shown in Figure 2-30, the solution folder and project folder have the same name as the solution itself. Remember that a solution could have multiple projects. In such a case, the solution folder would contain multiple project folders. The project folder contains the following:

» The file named Chapter02ConceptLesson.vbproj is also an XML document. Its members describe how to compile the project, the namespace references, and the modules that make up the project.

» The file named Hello.vb corresponds to the module file containing the application's code.

» The folder named My Project contains files shared by the entire project. These are the same files that appear in the My Project folder in the Solution Explorer.

» The folders named bin and obj contain the compiled application files.

Having learned about the files managed by the Solution Explorer, you will now learn how to use it.

## USING THE SOLUTION EXPLORER

The Solution Explorer is a tool window with a drill-down interface. Each line in the Solution Explorer includes the following items:

» For folders containing additional files or references, a box containing a plus or a minus sign. Clicking the plus sign opens a folder and displays its contents. Clicking the minus sign closes the folder so that its contents are hidden.

» An icon identifying the type of module (file). Use care not to change file suffixes. Visual Studio uses a file's suffix to identify the type of the file. In most cases, Visual Studio displays a warning message if you attempt to change a file suffix.

» The filename of the module saved on the disk, or the name of a namespace reference.

The Solution Explorer also has a toolbar displaying one or more of the following buttons. The buttons that appear vary depending on the type of module selected. These buttons appear just below the window's title bar.

» The Properties button is used to display a window used to edit the properties of the currently selected object.

» The View Code button appears only for certain types of files. These are typically module files having a file suffix of .vb and contain Visual Basic code. For example, a module file named Hello.vb contains code and can be edited using the Code Editor.

» The View Designer button opens the Windows Forms Designer for the module. Note that other types of modules have custom designers but these other designers are not discussed in this chapter. Chapter 3 discusses the Windows Forms Designer in detail.

» The Refresh button allows multiple developers to synchronize files.

» The Show All Files button causes the Solution Explorer to display all the folders and files that make up a solution. If this button is not clicked, most of the files automatically generated and managed by Visual Studio are hidden.

» The View in Diagram button displays a form or other class in a hierarchical view.

This completes the discussion of a Visual Studio solution and project. You will now learn how to use the Visual Studio IDE to create solutions and projects, set their properties, and create the code that executes as the end user runs an application.

**»» NOTE**

When renaming files, use the Solution Explorer instead of Windows Explorer. Otherwise, the Solution Explorer will not be able to locate the files that constitute the solution.

# WINDOWS OF THE VISUAL STUDIO IDE

How and where a Visual Studio window appears depends on the window's type. The Visual Studio IDE windows are categorized into two types: tool windows and document windows. These two window types are discussed in turn.

## TOOL WINDOWS

Tool windows do as their name implies: They provide common tools used in the creation of all applications developed with the Visual Studio IDE. The same tool windows are used no matter which Visual Studio programming language is being used or the type of application that is being created. The following list describes common tool windows:

» The Solution Explorer groups all of the elements needed to compile and test an application.

» The Properties window is used to set selected solution and object properties. It is most often used to view and set object properties. Properties and the Properties window are discussed in detail in Chapter 3.

» The Toolbox contains the controls that are created on a form. Forms, controls, and the Toolbox are discussed in Chapter 3 when Windows Application projects are introduced.

» There are several tool windows used to debug applications. These windows include the Command and Watch windows to name a few. Appendix A discusses the various debugging windows and how to use them. Note that the Visual Basic Express edition supports only some of the debugging windows available in the Professional edition.

» The Error List window displays any errors detected when the project is compiled. The Error List window is discussed later in the chapter when the topic of compiling a project is discussed.

» The Output window displays information as a project is compiled. This is the same compiler output produced when calling the Visual Basic compiler directly.

The items on the View menu are used to make tool windows visible. The most common windows appear directly on the View menu. The Other Windows submenu on the View menu is used to view lesser-used windows. In addition, the Windows submenu on the Debug menu is used to display the windows related to debugging.

As stated, the same tool windows are used in the creation of all Visual Studio applications. That is, you use tool windows to manage the contents of the document windows. The following list describes the four ways that the Visual Studio IDE displays tool windows:

» A tool window can be docked. A docked tool window is anchored along an edge of the Visual Studio IDE. Although the Properties window and the Solution Explorer are commonly docked along the right edge of the Visual Studio IDE, they can be docked along any other edge. Debugging and output windows are typically docked along the bottom edge of the IDE.

» Tool windows can appear as floating windows. A floating window is not anchored (docked) to another window, and can appear anywhere on the Windows desktop.

» Docked windows appearing along an edge of the Visual Studio IDE window can be Auto Hidden. When Auto Hide is enabled, the window name appears on a tab along the edge of the IDE window where the tool window is docked. Moving the mouse over the tab causes the window to be displayed. Moving the mouse off of the Auto Hidden window causes the window to disappear. The Auto Hide feature is useful as it allows more room to view document windows.

» Tool windows, such as the Solution Explorer and the Properties window, can also be configured to appear as document windows by dragging the window to a tab group. Again, when and how windows are displayed is a matter of personal preference.

Figure 2-31 shows how tool windows can be configured to appear differently inside of the Visual Studio IDE.

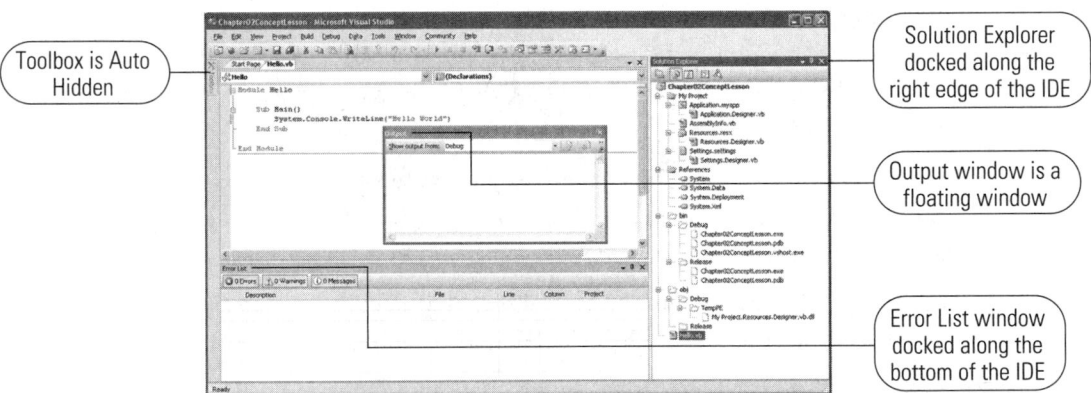

Figure 2-31: The appearance of tool windows in the Visual Studio IDE

The Toolbox is Auto Hidden along the left edge of the IDE. The Error List and the Solution Explorer are docked. The Output window is configured to appear as a floating window.

Visual Studio makes docking windows easy. To dock a window, begin to drag the Window's title bar. As the window is dragged over a drop button, the new position of the docked window appears shaded, as shown in Figure 2-32.

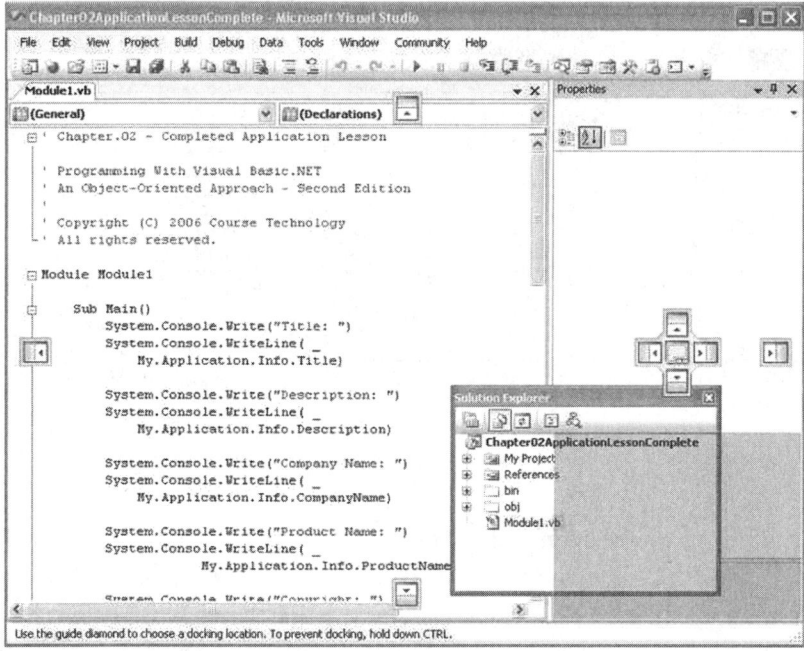

Figure 2-32: Docking tool windows

Figure 2-32 shows the Solution Explorer in the process of being docked to the Properties window. The shaded area shows where the docked window (the Solution Explorer) will appear.

To Auto Hide a window, first dock the window along an edge of the Visual Studio IDE. Then, right-click the title bar of the tool window to be docked. Finally, click Auto Hide from the context menu.

## DOCUMENT WINDOWS

**Document windows** correspond to the individual files (modules) that make up a project. The Windows Forms Designer and Code Editor are the primary document windows used to create Windows Application projects. The Windows Forms Designer is used to create a form's visual interface and is discussed in Chapter 3 when Windows Application projects are discussed.

Chapter 1 showed how to use Notepad to create the code for the most simple of Visual Basic applications. In practice, the Visual Studio IDE and the Code Editor are used to write an application's code. The **Code Editor** is an intelligent text editor specifically designed to edit Visual Basic code and Visual Studio code written in other .NET languages. It can also be used to edit text files, HTML files, and other file types. Figure 2-33 shows the Code Editor.

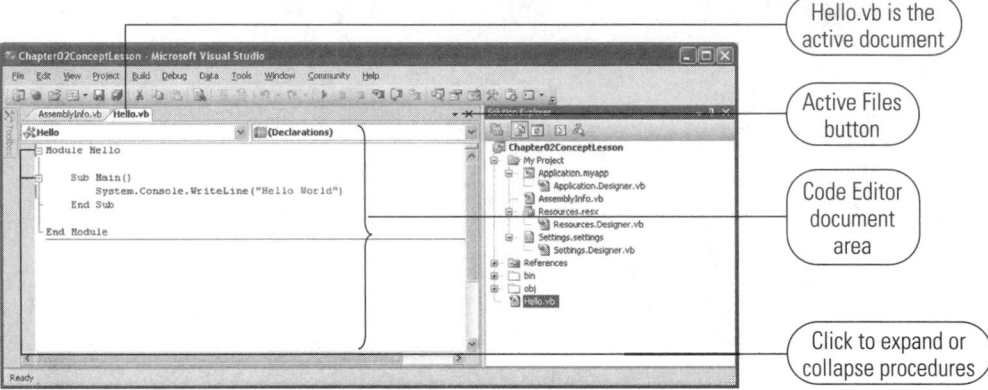

Figure 2-33: The Code Editor

Multiple document windows can be open at the same time. Figure 2-33 shows the Visual Studio IDE with two open document windows. The Open document windows appear on a tab group. Clicking on a tab in a tab group activates the document window for the selected document. The module named Hello.vb is the active document window and appears in the Code Editor. The file named AssemblyInfo.vb is inactive. The Solution Explorer is docked along the right edge of the Visual Studio IDE.

## USING THE CODE EDITOR

As shown in Figure 2-33, one tab group appears containing two document windows. To switch between open document windows, click the tab for the desired document. In addition, the Active Files button displays a list of the open files. Selecting a file from the list causes the selected file to be displayed.

As shown in Figure 2-33, the main region of the Code Editor is a document window containing Visual Basic statements. In Figure 2-33, the Code Editor shows a `Module` block with statements similar to those you created in Chapter 1. When viewed in color, you will see that the Code Editor displays Visual Basic reserved words in blue, string literal values in maroon, and everything else in black. A horizontal line separates one procedure from another.

Two combo boxes appear across the top of the Code Editor. These combo boxes are called the Class Name and Method Name combo boxes, respectively, and are used to select procedures. Along the left side of the Code Editor appear plus (+) and minus (-) signs. These buttons are used to expand or collapse procedures and other code segments. In Chapter 3, you will create an application with multiple procedures so using the Class Name and Method Name combo boxes is discussed there.

**▶▶NOTE**

Although not discussed in this chapter, it is possible to open multiple tab groups.

## USING INTELLISENSE WITH THE CODE EDITOR

The Code Editor uses Intellisense technology to display various types of pop-up menus and ToolTips while you write a statement. Roughly speaking, Intellisense technology displays the following two types of ToolTips:

» As you type the name of a namespace, Intellisense displays the members of that namespace. As you continue to enter a class name or the name of another type, Intellisense also displays the members of that type. These tips appear in list boxes.

» After you type a method name and enter the opening parenthesis, Intellisense displays the possible arguments to the method.

Figure 2-34 shows an Intellisense pop-up menu appearing while a statement is being entered in the Code Editor.

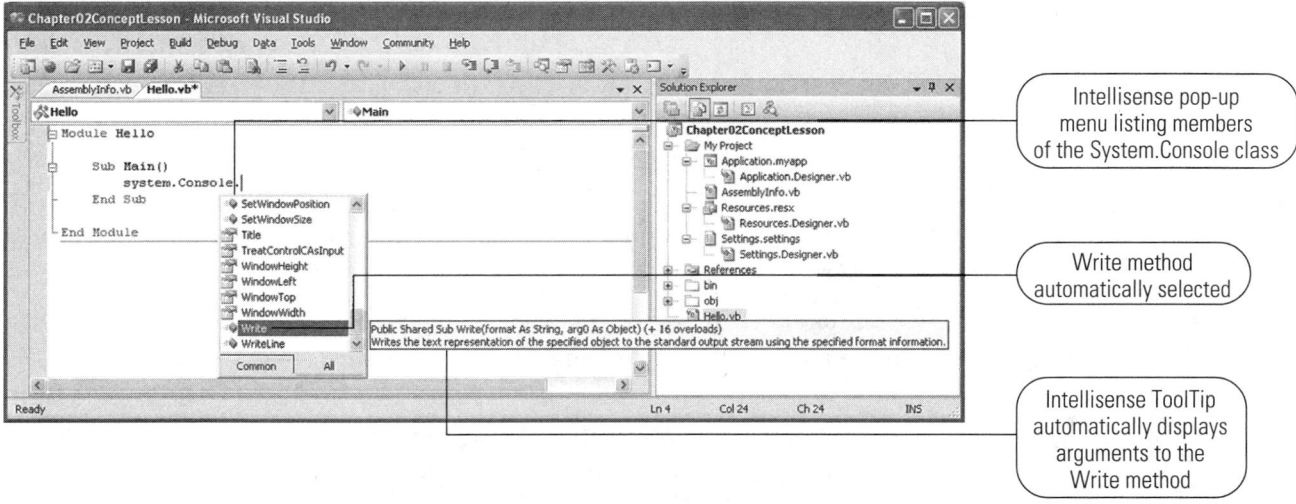

Figure 2-34: Intellisense pop-up menu

As you enter class names and method names in the Code Editor, Intellisense technology displays the members supported by that class or displays a method's arguments. Figure 2-34 shows Intellisense displaying the members of the System.Console class. Note that the pop-up has two tabs named Common and All. As their names imply, the Common tab displays only the more frequently used members, whereas the All tab displays all members. Intellisense technology automatically selects the most common member name from a list. For example, the Write method is automatically selected. The ToolTip listing the function arguments is also displayed automatically.

In addition to the Intellisense pop-up menus, Intellisense technology also displays ToolTips displaying a method's arguments. Again, after Visual Studio has detected that a method is being called, the ToolTip appears listing the method arguments. Figure 2-35 shows Intellisense displaying method arguments for the `System.Console.Write()` method.

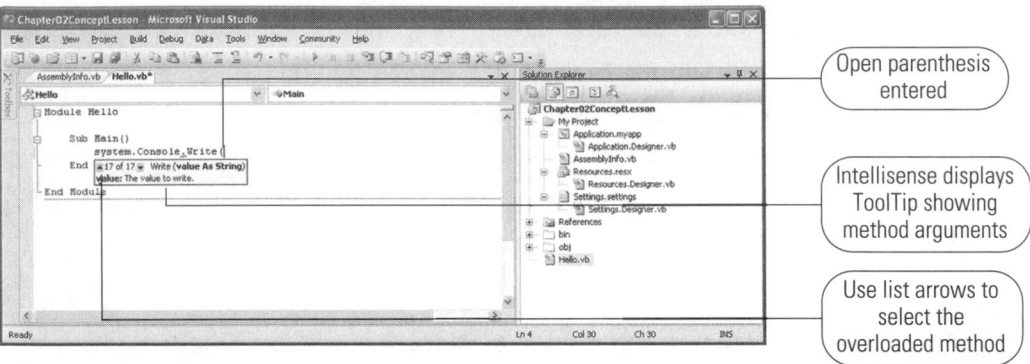

Figure 2-35: Intellisense ToolTip

Remember that the `Write()` method applies to the `System.Console` class. When the open parenthesis is typed, Visual Studio displays the method arguments in an Intellisense ToolTip. If the method is overloaded, arrows appear allowing you to select the desired overloaded method from a numbered list.

The Code Editor also checks the syntax of the statements that you write. After a statement is entered and the insertion point is moved to another line, Visual Studio checks the syntax of the statement just entered. If a statement contains a syntax error, the syntax error appears underlined, and a description of the error appears in another window called the Error List window. It is possible that one line (statement) contains multiple syntax errors. Figure 2-36 shows a statement with one syntax error and another statement with two syntax errors. The error descriptions appear in the Error List window.

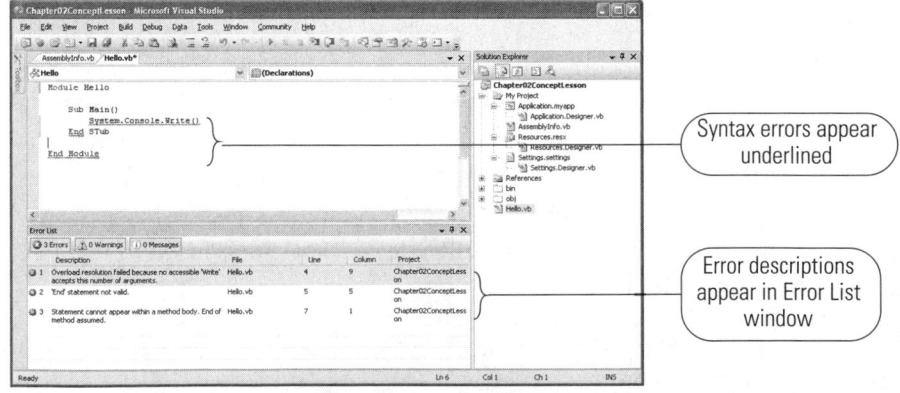

Figure 2-36: Code Editor and Error List window displaying syntax errors

As shown in Figure 2-36, the Error List window contains three tabs. The Error tab lists syntax errors that will prevent the project from being compiled. The Warnings tab lists errors that should be corrected but will not prevent a project from compiling. The Messages tab displays any informational messages.

Three syntax errors appear in Figure 2-36. The first syntax error arises because the argument to the `Write` method is missing. The second and third syntax errors are caused by the same error. Note that the `End Sub` statement is spelled incorrectly. Because the end of the procedure cannot be located, a third syntax error appears indicating that the `End Module` statement is incorrect.

> **»TIP** In the Error List window, double-click a line containing a syntax error. The insertion point position is updated in the Code Editor to the line and character position where the error was discovered. Note also that one error can cause the compiler to detect multiple syntax errors in the statements that follow the syntax error. Thus, when multiple syntax errors appear, check the first one carefully and correct it to make sure that it is not the cause of other errors.

# MINI-QUIZ 2

1. Visual Studio creates a solution from templates installed locally or templates obtained from the Web.

   a. True

   b. False

2. Which of the following statements correctly describes the relationship between a solution and its projects?

   a. A solution has one or more projects.

   b. A project has one or more solutions.

   c. For every solution file, there exists exactly one project file.

   d. The name of a solution and its projects must be the same.

   e. Information about a solution and its projects are stored in a file called a master file.

*(Continued)* ▶

3. Which of the following are characteristics of a project?

   a. A project file contains exactly one module file, which in turn contains all of the Visual Basic statements for the project.

   b. When a project gets compiled, an assembly is produced.

   c. Some projects have a root namespace, whereas others do not.

   d. none of the above

4. What is the name of the document window used to edit Visual Basic code?

# COMPILING AND EXECUTING A VISUAL BASIC PROJECT WITH VISUAL STUDIO

After an application has been created, the source code must be compiled to produce an executable file. Instead of calling the Visual Basic compiler directly as you did in Chapter 1, Visual Studio calls the compiler based on the various solution and project settings.

## COMPILING A VISUAL BASIC PROJECT

Clicking Build *projectname* causes Visual Studio to compile or recompile the selected project. *Projectname* is a placeholder for the actual name of the project.

When a project is compiled, Visual Studio calls the Visual Basic compiler with the proper options to specify the referenced namespaces and create the executable file.

While a project is being compiled, Visual Studio displays the actions taken in the Output window, as shown in Figure 2-37.

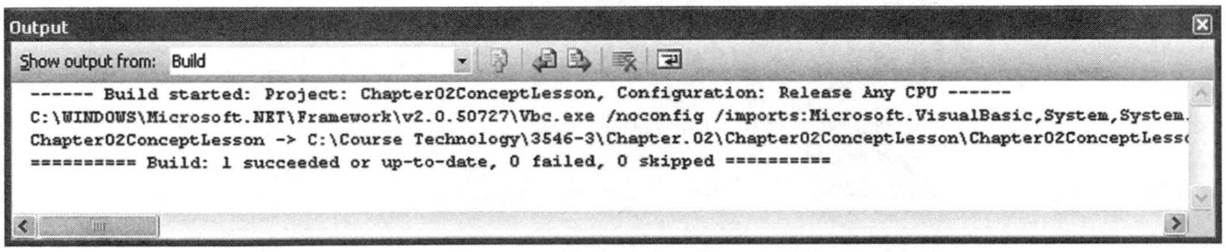

> **▶▶ NOTE**
>
> In this context, the terms "build" and "compile" are synonymous. That is, the terms building a project and compiling a project mean the same thing.

```
Output                                                                                    ☒
Show output from:  Build              ▾  | 🗗 | 🗗 🗗 | 🗐 🗐

------ Build started: Project: Chapter02ConceptLesson, Configuration: Release Any CPU ------
C:\WINDOWS\Microsoft.NET\Framework\v2.0.50727\Vbc.exe /noconfig /imports:Microsoft.VisualBasic,System,System.
Chapter02ConceptLesson -> C:\Course Technology\3546-3\Chapter.02\Chapter02ConceptLesson\Chapter02ConceptLesso
========== Build: 1 succeeded or up-to-date, 0 failed, 0 skipped ==========
```

Figure 2-37: The Output window

The Output window shown in Figure 2-37 shows that the Visual Basic compiler named Vbc.exe was called. It also shows the options passed to the compiler along with the module file to compile. Again, this is the same Visual Basic compiler that you called directly in Chapter 1.

## EXECUTING A VISUAL BASIC PROJECT

After a project has been compiled and the executable file created, the executable application can be run directly from Visual Studio. Of course, it could just as well be run from a Command Prompt window as you did in Chapter 1. Either of the following steps can be used to execute a compiled project from the Visual Studio IDE:

» Press F5. Visual Studio compiles (builds) the project if necessary, and then runs it.

» Click Debug, Start Debugging on the menu bar to run the project. Again, the project will be recompiled if necessary.

When a Console Application project is run from inside of the Visual Studio IDE, the console output is sent to a Command Prompt window that appears only while the application is running. If run from a Command Prompt window, the output appears in the same Command Prompt window from which the application was run.

In this exploration exercise, you will open an existing Visual Studio project and run it to see how to navigate the windows of the Visual Studio IDE, and how to compile and execute a project. In addition, you will explore how Intellisense technology can help write code.

1. Start Visual Studio, and open the solution file named **Chapter.02\Chapter02 ConceptLesson\Chapter02ConceptLesson.sln**.

2. Open the Solution Explorer, if necessary, by clicking **View**, **Solution Explorer**.

3. In the Solution Explorer, double-click the file named **Hello.vb**. The Visual Basic code appearing in the file appears in the Code Editor.

4. Click **View**, **Error List** to display the Error List window.

5. Modify the statement that reads `System.Console.Writeline("Hello World")` so that it reads `System.Console.Writeline("Hello World)`. That is, remove the second quotation mark. Move the insertion point to the next line. Visual Studio checks the syntax of the statement you just edited. Because the statement contains a syntax error, it appears underlined in the Code Editor, and the error description appears in the Error List window.

6. Correct the error.

7. To see the effect of Intellisense technology, enter the following statement after the line that you just modified and fixed. As you do, pay attention to the pop-ups that appear, and the method prototype:

```
System.Console.WriteLine("Message")
```

8. Compile the application by clicking **Build** and then clicking **Build Chapter02ConceptLesson**.

9. Display the Output window by clicking **View**, **Other Windows**, **Output**. The output from the Visual Basic compiler appears in the Output window. If there are syntax errors in the module, the compiler messages indicate that the project could not be compiled.

# CREATING APPLICATION COMMENTS

Although some code might be self-explanatory, other code is not. Comments are used to document an application's code for you and other developers. A comment is a full or partial line of text that is ignored by Visual Studio. A comment block is simply one or more comment lines grouped together. Comments are for the benefit of developers rather than end users. In other words, comments describe to a developer how particular code works. Comments are not used to describe to an end user how to use the application.

Comprehensive and standardized comments will help you and other developers understand what an application is doing and how. Although there are no strict rules governing the use of comments, the following guidelines generally apply:

» Comments should be created as an application is developed. As an application is modified, relevant comments should be changed or expanded to reflect any new behavior.

» A comment block should generally appear at the beginning of a `Class` or `Module` block to describe the purpose of that block, the developer who created it, and a history of revisions.

» Each procedure often has a comment block to describe the purpose of the procedure.

» Comments can be used to describe specific statements whose purpose might be unclear to other developers.

» Don't overuse comments. For example, don't add comments to describe a statement whose purpose and meaning is clear to almost any developer.

Like other elements in an application, syntax rules apply to comments too. First, any line beginning with an apostrophe (`'`) is considered a comment line and is ignored by the Visual Basic compiler. If a Visual Basic statement is followed by an apostrophe and additional text all on the same line, Visual Studio ignores the text following the apostrophe considering that text a comment. A space must appear after the end of the statement and before the apostrophe that marks the beginning of the comment.

> **»TIP**
>
> Comments often account for 50% or more of the lines in an application. Increasing the number of comments does not affect an application's execution speed because the comments are removed when Visual Studio compiles a project into an executable file.

The following code segment illustrates two different comments:

```
' This line is a comment.
System.Console.WriteLine("Hello") ' Write a string.
```

The first of the preceding lines contains only a comment. The second line contains a statement followed by a comment. Note that in the second statement, a space separates the method call and the apostrophe that begins the comment. A space must separate the end of the statement and the beginning of the comment. Thus, the following comment causes a syntax error:

```
System.Console.WriteLine("Hello")' Write a string.
```

Blank lines can also be included between comments or statements. Blank lines are referred to as white space and are ignored by Visual Studio. Inserting white space between declarations of groups of related variables or between other statements can improve code readability. Too much white space, or the inconsistent use of white space can decrease code readability, however. Including the comment character on a blank line is optional.

The sample data files accompanying this book use comments to provide additional information about the application or particular code segments as a means to further explain a particular concept.

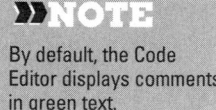

**»NOTE**

By default, the Code Editor displays comments in green text.

# INTRODUCTION TO THE MY OBJECT

Visual Studio supports an object named My. The My object simplifies programming by encapsulating commonly used classes into a single class. The following list describes selected objects of the My object:

» The My.Application object has properties that get information about the current application.

» The My.Computer object gets configuration information for the computer on which the application is running.

» The My.Computer.Network object allows you to work with the network. For example, it is possible to ping other hosts and copy files using the FTP protocol.

» The My.User object gets information about the user currently logged on to the computer.

Each of these objects is discussed in the following sections.

## THE MY.APPLICATION OBJECT

Remember that a project contains a file named AssemblyInfo.vb, and that this file contains descriptive information about an assembly. The AssemblyInfo.vb file contains what are called attributes. One purpose of **attributes** is to store descriptive information about an assembly. Remember when Visual Studio compiles a project, an assembly is created. That assembly can contain descriptive information through the use of attributes. The following code segment shows how to declare an attribute named AssemblyTitle. This attribute appears in the AssemblyInfo.vb file for a project.

```
<Assembly: AssemblyTitle("Chapter 2 - Concept Lesson")>
```

As shown in the preceding code segment, an attribute declaration is enclosed in less-than and greater-than signs. The keyword `Assembly:` indicates that the attribute applies to the entire assembly. The remainder of the attribute declaration looks like a method call. `AssemblyTitle` is the name of the attribute. The string "Chapter 2—Concept Lesson" is passed as the argument to the attribute.

The following statements show how to set other attributes that describe an assembly:

```
<Assembly: AssemblyDescription("")>
<Assembly: AssemblyCompany("Course Technology")>
<Assembly: AssemblyProduct( _
    "Visual Basic .NET - An Object-Oriented Approach")>
<Assembly: AssemblyCopyright( _
    "Copyright @ Course Technology 2006")>
<Assembly: AssemblyTrademark("")>
```

The preceding statements set the `AssemblyDescription`, `AssemblyCompany`, `AssemblyProduct`, `AssemblyCopyright`, and `AssemblyTrademark` attributes.

In addition to the preceding attributes, an assembly also contains version information. The following code segment shows the attributes to store the assembly version information:

```
<Assembly: AssemblyVersion("1.0.0.0")>
<Assembly: AssemblyFileVersion("1.0.0.0")>
```

After assembly attributes have been declared, they can be used by reading the properties of the `My.Application.Info` class. These properties have the same or similar name as their corresponding attribute. The following code segment shows how to print these attributes to the Command Prompt window:

```
System.Console.WriteLine(My.Application.Info.Title)
System.Console.WriteLine(My.Application.Info.Description)
System.Console.WriteLine(My.Application.Info.CompanyName)
System.Console.WriteLine(My.Application.Info.ProductName)
System.Console.WriteLine(My.Application.Info.Copyright)
System.Console.WriteLine(My.Application.Info.Trademark)
System.Console.WriteLine(My.Application.Info.Version)
```

**>> NOTE**

The property names of the Info class are similar but not exactly the same as the corresponding attribute names.

The preceding statements resemble those that you wrote in the first chapter to print system information. However, instead of using the `SystemInformation` class, these statements use the `My.Application.Info` class.

## THE MY.COMPUTER OBJECT

The `My.Computer` object supports a class named `FileSystem`. The methods of the `FileSystem` class can be used to create and copy files and directories. Its methods can also be used to determine information about a file.

One property of the `My.Computer.FileSystem` class is the `CurrentDirectory` property. As an application executes, one directory (folder) is considered the current working directory. The following statement prints the current working directory to the Command Prompt window:

```
System.Console.Writeline( _
    My.Computer.FileSystem.CurrentDirectory)
```

The `My.Computer` object supports another class named `Info`, whose members are used to get configuration information about the local computer system. The following list describes these members:

» The `AvailablePhysicalMemory` property returns the physical memory currently not in use. The unit of measure is bytes.

» The `AvailableVirtualMemory` property returns the total available virtual memory not in use. Again, the value is expressed in bytes.

» The `TotalPhysicalMemory` property returns the physical memory installed in the computer. The unit of measure is bytes.

» The `TotalVirtualMemory` property returns the total virtual memory on the system. Again, the unit of measure is bytes.

» The `OSFullName` property stores the name of the operating system.

» The `OSPlatform` property returns the current family of the operating system. Operating system platforms such as Windows 2000 and Windows XP have a value of Win32NT. Windows 95 and Windows 98 have values of Win32Windows. The value for the Windows CE operating system platform is WinCE.

» The `OSVersion` property returns the version of the operating system installed.

## THE MY.COMPUTER.NETWORK OBJECT

Ping is a commonly used program to determine whether an Internet host is alive. The `My.Computer.Network.Ping` method supplies an implementation of the Ping program. The following code segment illustrates how to ping a host on the Internet:

```
My.Computer.Network.Ping(131.216.39.3)
```

The `Ping` method accepts one argument, the Internet address or host name to ping. The method returns `True` if the host is alive and `False` otherwise.

In addition to the `Ping` method, the `My.Computer.Network` object supplies numerous other methods to copy files using the FTP protocol, and to perform other tasks.

# MINI-QUIZ 3

1. What is the name of the Visual Studio window that shows the call to the Visual Basic compiler and the results of that compile?

2. What is the name of the class that has properties corresponding to the general assembly attributes?

   a. `My.Assembly`

   b. `My.Attributes`

   c. `My.Application.Attributes`

   d. `My.Application.Info`

   e. `System.Attributes`

3. What information can be obtained from the `My.Computer.Info` class?

   a. the name of the user logged on to the computer

   b. the amount of logical and physical memory installed on the computer

   c. the number of disk drives installed on the computer

   d. assembly information

   e. all of the above

# APPLICATION LESSON

## CREATING A CONSOLE APPLICATION WITH VISUAL STUDIO

In this application lesson, you will create a Console Application project using the Visual Studio IDE. The code in this project will display general information about an assembly, the computer, and miscellaneous information. In addition, you will create comments for the application. The purpose of this application lesson is twofold. First, it allows you to further explore the Visual Studio IDE. Second, it allows you to work with the members of the My object.

### APPLICATION LESSON—DESIGN

This application is not that much different than the Console Application project discussed in Chapter 1. Like all Console Applications, it has a Module block containing a Main procedure that marks the application's entry point. Executable statements appear in the Main procedure to display three categories of information. Figure 2-38 shows the flowchart for this application.

As shown in Figure 2-38, four sequences are performed. The first sequence displays information about the current assembly, the second sequence displays information about the current computer, and the next sequence displays other miscellaneous information including the current working directory. Finally, the end user is prompted to exit the application.

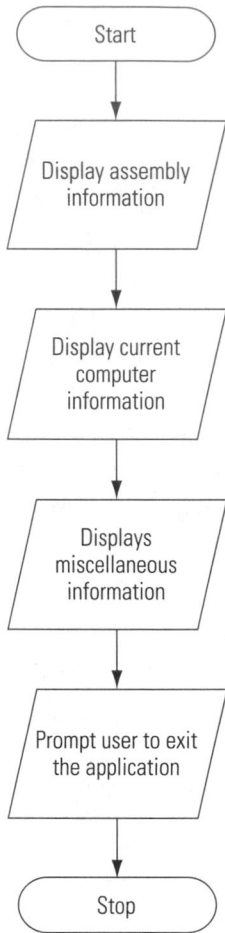

Figure 2-38: Application lesson flowchart

## APPLICATION LESSON—IMPLEMENTATION

From this chapter forward, the beginning of each application lesson will contain a series of hands-on steps designed so that you can preview the completed application. The purpose of exploring the completed application is to provide a road map of the application's operation.

After you preview the completed application, you will create a new project or open a partially completed one, and then complete another series of hands-on steps. After completing these hands-on steps, you will end up with the completed application discussed in the preceding section. Note also that the code for the completed application might have additional comments beyond those that you are asked to enter when completing the application lesson yourself. These extra comments serve to further document the program you are creating in the application lesson.

To preview the completed application project:

1. Start Visual Studio, if necessary.

2. On the Visual Studio menu bar, click **File**, and then click **Open Project**.

3. In the Open Project dialog box, select the solution file named **Chapter.02\
Chapter02ApplicationLessonPreview\Chapter02ApplicationLessonPreview.sln**.

4. Run the solution by pressing **F5**. When the solution is run, the output shown in Figure 2-39 appears in the Console window.

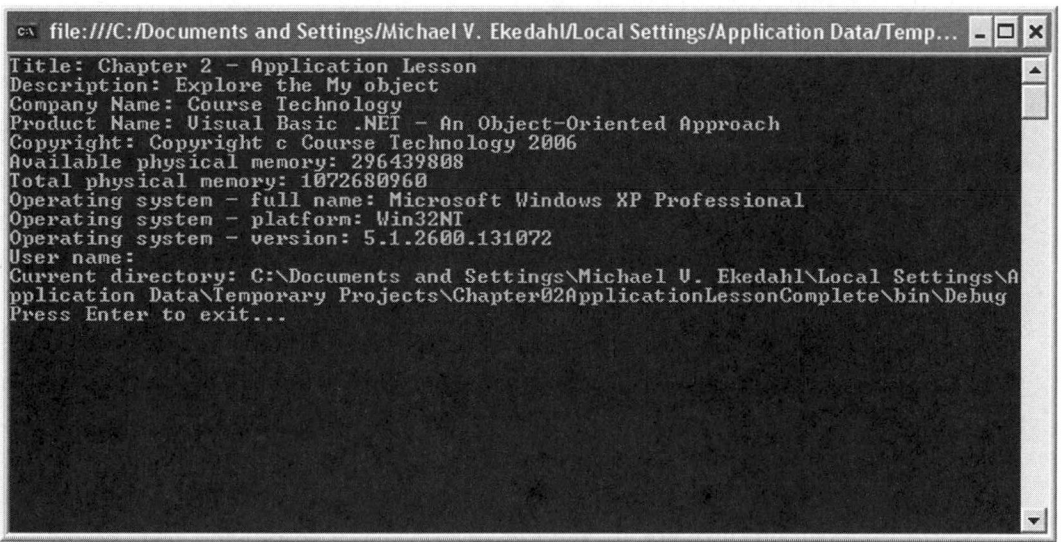

Figure 2-39: Console window displaying application output

5. In the Console window, press **Enter** to end the application.

6. Exit Visual Studio .NET.

The application in this lesson prints status information to a Console window along with descriptive prompts. Next, you will create the application you just previewed using the Visual Studio IDE.

To start Visual Studio and create a new Console Application project:

1. Start Visual Studio, if necessary.

2. Using the menu bar, click **File**, **New Project** to display the New Project dialog box.

3. In the New Project dialog box, click **Console Application** to select the application template.

4. In the New Project dialog box, set the Name to **Chapter02ApplicationLessonStartup**.

5. Click **OK** to close the New Project dialog box and create the project.

Next, the new solution and project must be saved the first time using the Save Project dialog box.

To save a Visual Studio solution and project:

1. On the Visual Studio menu bar, click **File**, **Save All** to display the Save Project dialog box.

2. The project name and new solution name should already be set to Chapter02ApplicationLessonStartup. Set the location as necessary to the folder where Visual Studio will create the new solution and solution directory.

3. Click **Save** to save the solution and close the dialog box.

The Solution Explorer displays the modules that make up the application and is usually docked along the right edge of the Visual Studio IDE.

Remember that the file named AssemblyInfo.vb declares attributes that describe the application (assembly). Next, you will use the Code Editor to configure those attributes from their default values.

To configure assembly attributes:

1. Activate the Solution Explorer, if necessary, by clicking **View**, **Solution Explorer**.

2. In the Solution Explorer, click the **Show All Files** button.

3. Expand the **My Project** folder.

4. Click the **AssemblyInfo.vb** file, and then click the **View Code** button. The module should appear in the Code Editor.

5. Modify the following statements by adding the code shown in bold. Insert the continuation lines, as necessary. Replace the default values as necessary:

```
<Assembly: AssemblyTitle("Chapter 2 - Application Lesson")>
<Assembly: AssemblyDescription("Explore the My object")>
<Assembly: AssemblyCompany("Course Technology")>
<Assembly: AssemblyProduct( _
    "Visual Basic .NET - An Object-Oriented Approach")>
<Assembly: AssemblyCopyright( _
    "Copyright @ Course Technology 2006")>
```

Having configured the AssemblyInfo.vb file, the code needs to be written to get the assembly information and display it to the end user when the application is run.

1. Activate the Code Editor, if necessary, by selecting the module named **Module1.vb** in the Solution Explorer, and then clicking **View**, **Code**.

2. Click **View**, **Error List** to activate the Error List window. This window displays any syntax errors as you enter statements in the Code Editor.

3. Enter the following statements (shown in bold) into the Code Editor. While entering the statements, pay particular attention to the Intellisense technology features discussed in the chapter. Also, make sure that the statements have no syntax errors. Visual Studio underlines syntax errors in the Code Editor as they are discovered along with displaying them in the Error List window. Note that the Main procedure has already been created in the module because the project was created from a template.

```
Sub Main()
    System.Console.Write("Title: ")
    System.Console.WriteLine(My.Application.Info.Title)
    System.Console.Write("Description: ")
    System.Console.WriteLine(My.Application.Info.Description)
    System.Console.Write("Company Name: ")
    System.Console.WriteLine(My.Application.Info.CompanyName)
    System.Console.Write("Product Name: ")
    System.Console.WriteLine(My.Application.Info.ProductName)
    System.Console.Write("Copyright: ")
    System.Console.WriteLine(My.Application.Info.Copyright)
End Sub
```

4. The `My.Computer.Info` class has properties to get the computer's configuration information. Enter the following statements (shown in bold) at the end of the Main procedure to get the current computer's configuration information:

```
    System.Console.WriteLine(My.Application.Info.Copyright)
    System.Console.Write("Available physical memory: ")
    System.Console.WriteLine( _
        My.Computer.Info.AvailablePhysicalMemory.ToString)

    System.Console.Write("Total physical memory: ")
    System.Console.WriteLine( _
        My.Computer.Info.TotalPhysicalMemory.ToString)

    System.Console.Write("Operating system - full name: ")
    System.Console.WriteLine(My.Computer.Info.OSFullName)

    System.Console.Write("Operating system - platform: ")
    System.Console.WriteLine(My.Computer.Info.OSPlatform)

    System.Console.Write("Operating system - version: ")
    System.Console.WriteLine(My.Computer.Info.OSVersion)
End Sub
```

5. Enter the following statements (shown in bold) at the end of the Main procedure to get the username and current directory, and to display a prompt before exiting the application:

```
System.Console.WriteLine(My.Computer.Info.OSVersion)
System.Console.Write("User name: ")
System.Console.WriteLine(My.User.Name)
System.Console.Write("Current directory: ")
System.Console.WriteLine( _
    My.Computer.FileSystem.CurrentDirectory)
System.Console.Write("Press Enter to exit . . .")
System.Console.Read()
End Sub
```

Finally, you will create a comment block at the beginning of the module to describe the application.

To create a comment block:

1. Activate the Code Editor, if necessary, for the module named Module1.vb. Enter the following statements, shown in bold, at the beginning of the module:

```
' Chapter.02 - Application Lesson
' Programming With Visual Basic.NET
' An Object-Oriented Approach Second Edition
Module Module1
```

Having created the statements for the application, it can now be compiled and tested.

To compile a Visual Studio project:

1. Press **F5** to compile the project and run it. As the project gets compiled, diagnostic messages appear in the Command Prompt window. If a syntax error was made while entering the statements, those errors appear in the Error List window.

2. When the application is run, the output is displayed, as shown in Figure 2-39.

# CHAPTER SUMMARY

» The Visual Studio IDE is the primary tool used to work with Visual Basic applications, and applications created in other Visual Studio languages. It contains a robust set of tools to create, test, and debug the applications you create. The appearance of Visual Studio can be customized using the Options dialog box.

» Visual Studio supplies a Help system that describes how to use Visual Studio itself, and how to use the members of the .NET Framework class library. The Help system for the Visual Basic Express edition is streamlined. Other Visual Studio editions include the full

Microsoft Developer Network (MSDN) library. It is possible to search for Help topics, locate a Help topic through an index, or via a table of contents. Help topics can be restricted through a filter. Help topics pertaining to members of the .NET Framework class library have three types of summary pages. Class Help pages describe the general purpose of a class, and the Members Help pages lists the members of a particular class. Language Help pages apply to a particular Visual Studio language.

» The Object Browser is another tool used to explore the members of the .NET Framework class library. The Object Browser uses a drill-down interface to view the assemblies, namespaces, and types that constitute the .NET Framework class library, along with other assemblies.

» Visual Studio supports different types of applications based on templates. Two common templates are Console Application projects and Windows Application projects. The available templates will vary based on the installed Visual Studio edition.

» Visual Studio organizes an application into a solution containing one or more projects. Each project in a solution is compiled into an executable file (assembly). A project has properties that define the name of the assembly, the name of the root namespace, how the project is compiled, and the assembly's entry point. These options are configured using the Project property pages.

» The New Project dialog box is used to create a new Visual Basic solution based on one of the installed templates. After a solution has been created, it must be saved for the first time. When a solution is saved the first time, the solution folder, solution name, and project name are specified. When the solution is saved the first time, Visual Studio creates the structure of the solution and its projects.

» The solution and its files are managed using a window called the Solution Explorer. The Solution Explorer has a drill-down interface listing the modules that constitute the application. Plus and minus signs are used to expand or collapse folders. Icons appear next to files to describe the file's type. Buttons appear across the top of the Solution Explorer to open the Code Editor or Windows Forms Designer. The Show All Files button controls whether the files automatically managed by Visual Studio appear in the Solution Explorer.

» Visual Studio categorizes windows into two types: document windows and tool windows. Document windows include the Windows Forms Designer and the Code Editor. Tool windows provide common tools used in the creation of all applications. The Solution Explorer, Properties window, Toolbox, Command, Watch, Error List, and Output windows are all tool windows. Tool windows can appear in different ways. A tool window can be configured to float on the desktop or docked along an edge of the Visual Studio IDE. A tool window can also be Auto Hidden. An Auto Hidden tool window appears as an icon along an edge of the Visual Studio IDE. The Auto Hidden tool window is made visible when the mouse is passed over the icon.

» The Code Editor is the primary window used to create and edit the code for an application. It is an intelligent text editor designed specifically to edit Visual Basic applications and applications created in other Visual Studio languages. Two combo boxes appear across the top of the Code Editor with which you select modules and procedures. Intellisense technology displays pop-ups helping you to complete statements as you write them.

» Visual Studio uses the solution and project to compile an application. That is, Visual Studio calls the Visual Basic compiler for you automatically.

» The My object simplifies programming by encapsulating commonly used classes into a single object. Using the My object, it is possible to read the values of assembly attributes, get information about the current computer's configuration, get information about the user logged on to the computer, and other information.

# KEY TERMS

**attributes**—Descriptive information about a class are stored in what are called attributes. Assembly attributes are stored in the file named AssemblyInfo.vb.

**Code Editor**—A document window specially designed to edit Visual Basic code and code developed in other Visual Studio .NET languages.

**document window**—A window that provides the means to create an application's code (the Code Editor) and the visual interface for an application (the Windows Forms Designer).

**drill-down interface**—A hierarchical interface in which you navigate from general information to specific information.

**help filter**—A filter that restricts the Help topics being displayed to those of a particular language or the .NET Framework class library.

**Intellisense**—The technology that helps you to write Visual Basic statements by completing or suggesting class members and method arguments.

**Object Browser**—A Visual Studio tool that allows you to look at the members of the .NET Framework class library or the members of the applications that you create.

**project**—A file that contains the necessary information to compile an application into an assembly (executable file).

**solution**—A solution is the building block for all Visual Basic applications and is made up of one or more projects. Each project is compiled to its own assembly. Solutions are managed using the Solution Explorer.

**tool windows**—The windows, such as the Solution Explorer and Properties window, used to create all applications. They operate the same way no matter the Visual Studio language being used or the type of project being created.

**Visual Studio IDE**—The integrated development environment used to create, compile, and test applications.

# ANSWERS TO MINI-QUIZZES

### MINI-QUIZ 1

1. b. Intellisense technology displays object members as statements are entered in the Code Editor.

2. a. Help pages for the .NET Framework class library can be roughly categorized as Class Help pages, Members Help pages, or Language Help pages.

3. the Object Browser

### MINI-QUIZ 2

1. a. True

2. a. A solution has one or more projects.

3. b. When a project gets compiled, an assembly is produced.

4. the Code Editor

### MINI-QUIZ 3

1. the Output window

2. d. `My.Appliction.Info`

3. b. The amount of logical and physical memory installed on the computer.

# REVIEW QUESTIONS

1. Which of the following statements is true regarding the Visual Studio IDE?

   a. All windows have a fixed position within the Visual Studio IDE and cannot be moved.

   b. Tools windows can be docked, be Auto Hidden, or be configured to float on the desktop.

c. Both document windows and tool windows can be Auto Hidden.

d. The Visual Studio IDE works very differently based on the Visual Studio programming language being used. That is, different tool windows are used to edit Visual Basic programs than C# programs.

e. To configure the Visual Studio IDE, you edit an XML document.

2. Which of the following statements is correct regarding the Visual Studio Help system?

a. The same Help contents are available for all Visual Studio editions.

b. A Help filter can be applied to restrict the topics displayed to those related to a particular Visual Studio language or Visual Studio product.

c. Visual Basic Help is read from local Help files. Help files cannot be downloaded from the Internet.

d. all of the above

3. Which of the following statements is true regarding a solution and the files that make up a solution?

a. A solution contains one or more projects.

b. A solution always contains exactly one project.

c. A code file contains the statements that execute when a solution is run. The code file is stored on the disk with a file suffix of .cod. All Visual Studio code in a solution appears in this code file.

d. Visual Studio stores a solution file, and all of the data necessary to compile a solution in a single file having a suffix of .sol. Conceptually, this file works similarly to a Microsoft Access .mdb file.

e. none of the above

4. Which of the following statements is true regarding Visual Studio projects?

a. A project file is compiled into a solution.

b. A project file is compiled into an assembly.

c. Every project has a root namespace of `System.Project`.

d. A project has multiple types. That is, a single project could contain both a Windows Application and a Console Application.

e. none of the above

5. Which of the following statements is true of the Solution Explorer?

    a. It displays references to the .NET assemblies used by a project.

    b. It is used to set the properties of both the solution and the projects contained by the solution.

    c. The Solution Explorer is considered a document window.

    d. all of the above

    e. none of the above

6. Which of the following statements is correct regarding the Code Editor?

    a. Files edited with the Code Editor must have a file extension of .cod.

    b. The Code Editor is an intelligent text editor specifically designed to edit Visual Basic applications and applications written in other Visual Studio languages.

    c. The Code Editor is used only by Visual Basic. Other languages, such as C#, use other specialized editors.

    d. The files edited using the Code Editor have a special format. Thus, files created with the Code Editor cannot be created or edited with any other text editor.

    e. none of the above

7. Which of the following are categories of Visual Studio windows?

    a. code windows and editing windows

    b. editing windows and properties windows

    c. tabbed windows and floating windows

    d. document windows and tool windows

    e. none of the above

8. What type of window is the Solution Explorer?

    a. document window

    b. management window

    c. primary window

    d. tool window

    e. none of the above

9. What is the name of the Visual Studio window that displays syntax errors?

    a. document window

    b. Error List window

    c. Syntax window

    d. Compile window

    e. none of the above

10. Which of the following would be displayed in the Output window?

    a. data produced by calling the `WriteLine()` method of the `Console` class

    b. information resulting from compiling a project

    c. assembly information

    d. all of the above

    e. none of the above

11. What is the term for the technology used to display members of a particular object or list the arguments to a member?

    a. Code Wizard

    b. command completion

    c. Intellisense

    d. rapid application development

    e. program helper

12. Which of the following statements correctly describe an attribute?

    a. An attribute is the same as an executable statement.

    b. Attributes can be used to store descriptive information about a class.

    c. Attributes are used to describe the purpose of a procedure.

    d. Every project contains exactly one attribute file having a file suffix of .attrib.

    e. none of the above

13. What is the name of the file that stores assembly-related attributes?

    a. Attributes.vb

    b. AssemblyAttributes.vb

    c. AssemblyInfo.vb

d. Project.vb

e. none of the above

14. Which of the following statements is correct regarding the My object?

    a. The My object is used to call procedures in a module.

    b. The My.Computer.Information object is used to get the configuration of the current computer.

    c. The My.Current.Application object is used to get information about the running application.

    d. The My object is primarily used to debug applications having syntax errors.

    e. The My object supports classes to get information about the current application, computer, and user.

15. Describe the relationship between a project file and a solution file.

16. List and describe the purpose of the four application templates supported by Visual Studio and discussed in this chapter.

17. List and describe the different ways to navigate the Help system.

18. Describe the differences between tool windows and document windows.

19. Describe the different ways a tool window can be displayed inside of the Visual Studio IDE. List and describe the three ways tool windows can appear on the desktop or inside the main window of the Visual Studio IDE.

20. Describe how to create application comments and the purpose of comments.

# PROGRAMMING QUESTIONS

1. Write the statement to declare an attribute that will set an assembly's description to "Object-oriented program".

2. Write the statements to declare two attributes that will set the assembly product to "Course Technology", and the copyright to "Copyright Course Technology".

3. Write the statement that will declare the necessary attribute so that the assembly version will be 1.2.2.2.

4. Using the `My` object, write the statement to print the assembly description to the Console window.

5. Using the `My` object, write the statements to print the assembly company name and assembly product name to the Console window.

6. Using the `My` object, write the statement to print the current working directory to the Console window.

7. Using the `My` object, write the statement to print the assembly version to the Console window.

8. Create a `Sub` procedure named Main( ) in a `Module` block named Question that will print the total available physical and logical memory to the Console window. Display a prompt to the left of each item.

9. Use the Help system to get information about the `My.User` class. Using that information, display the name of the current user and whether the user is authenticated.

10. Using the Help system to get information about the `My.Computer.Audio` class, write the statement to create a Console Application that will play the audio file named "Demo.wav."

11. Using Visual Studio, create a blank Console Application project. Using the Help system, locate the Language Help page for the `Module` statement. Paste the code example into the application you created and test it.

12. Using the Help system, look up the Members Help page for the `My.Computer.Keyboard` object. Using the information you found, write the statements to determine the status of the Alt, Caps Lock and Control keys.

13. Using the Help system, write a paragraph describing the purpose of the `My.Resources` object.

14. Using the Help system, determine the inheritance hierarchy for the `System.IO.File` class.

15. Using the Help system, determine whether the `My` object is supported by versions 1.0 or 2.0 of the .NET Framework class library.

# HANDS-ON PROJECTS

1. In this hands-on project, you will create a Console Application that will configure assembly information and display that assembly information to the Console window.

   a. Start Visual Studio and create a new Console Application project named **Ch02HandsOnProject1**. Save the solution and project, as necessary.

   b. Configure the AssemblyInfo.vb file so that the title of the assembly is "Chapter 2— Hands-on Project 1." Set the project assembly description to "Display assembly information." Set the Copyright to "Copyright Course Technology."

   c. Set the necessary attribute to set the assembly version to 1.0.0.1.

   d. Create the code for the module that will print the preceding assembly information to the Console window. For each item printed, display a descriptive prompt.

   e. Prompt the user before exiting the application.

   f. Using the Project property pages, set the root namespace to Chapter2Project1.

   g. Create comments that describe the purpose of the statements you write.

2. In this project, you will create a Console Application that will use the `My` object to get information about the keyboard and mouse.

   a. Start Visual Studio and create a new Console Application project named **Ch02HandsOnProject2**. Save the solution and project, as necessary.

   b. Set the project properties so that the executable file will be named KeyboardStatus.

   c. Set the root namespace to Chapter2Project2.

   d. Use the Help system to determine the members of the `My.Computer.Keyboard` class. This class contains shared properties that contain the state of various keyboard keys.

   e. In the module for the Console Application, write the statements to display the status of the Alt, Caps Lock, Control, Num Lock, Scroll Lock, and Shift keys. Display the data such that each line displays a prompt and the status of a particular keyboard key. Create comments that describe the purpose of the statements that you write.

f. Use the Help system to determine the members of the `My.Computer.Mouse` class. This class contains shared properties to get information about the mouse.

g. In the module for the Console Application, write the statements to display whether the mouse has a mouse wheel, and the information about the wheel scroll lines. In addition, there is a property that displays whether the mouse buttons have been swapped. Mouse buttons are sometimes swapped for left-handed mouse users. Again, display the data with a descriptive prompt followed by the data item.

h. After displaying the information, write the statement to display a prompt and to read a line. When the line is read, exit the application.

3. In this project, you will create a Console Application that will get information about the system clock.

a. Start Visual Studio and create a new Console Application project named **Ch02HandsOnProject3**. Save the solution and project, as necessary.

b. Set the project properties so that the executable file will be named ClockInformation.

c. Use the Help system to investigate the members of the `My.Computer.Clock` class.

d. In the module for the Console Application, write the statements to display the Greenwich mean time, the local time, and the number of elapsed ticks.

e. Again, display a prompt to indicate the content of each property. Display each property value on a single line.

f. Display a message to indicate whether the computer is connected to a network.

g. After displaying the information, write the statement to display a prompt and to read a line. When the line is read, exit the application.

# 3

# INTRODUCTION TO EVENT HANDLERS AND WINDOWS FORMS APPLICATIONS

**After completing this chapter, you will be able to:**

Compare command-line interfaces and forms-based interfaces

Design the user interface for a Windows application

Create a Windows Application project using the Visual Studio IDE

Use the Visual Studio IDE to create and configure control instances

Use controls to create the user interface for a Windows Application project

Create code for a Windows Application project

# CONCEPT LESSON

## COMPARING COMMAND-LINE AND FORM-BASED INTERFACES

Chapter 2 discussed how to create a Console Application project that ran inside of a Command Prompt window. The application's user interface consisted of textual prompts and output data that was displayed one line at a time. This type of user interface is often called a **command-line interface**. However, the user interface for most Windows applications is a **form-based visual interface**. That is, the end user interacts with an application via a visual form containing buttons, text boxes, check boxes, scroll bars, and other visual elements. Figure 3-1 compares a command-line and form-based user interface for the Hello World application from Chapters 1 and 2.

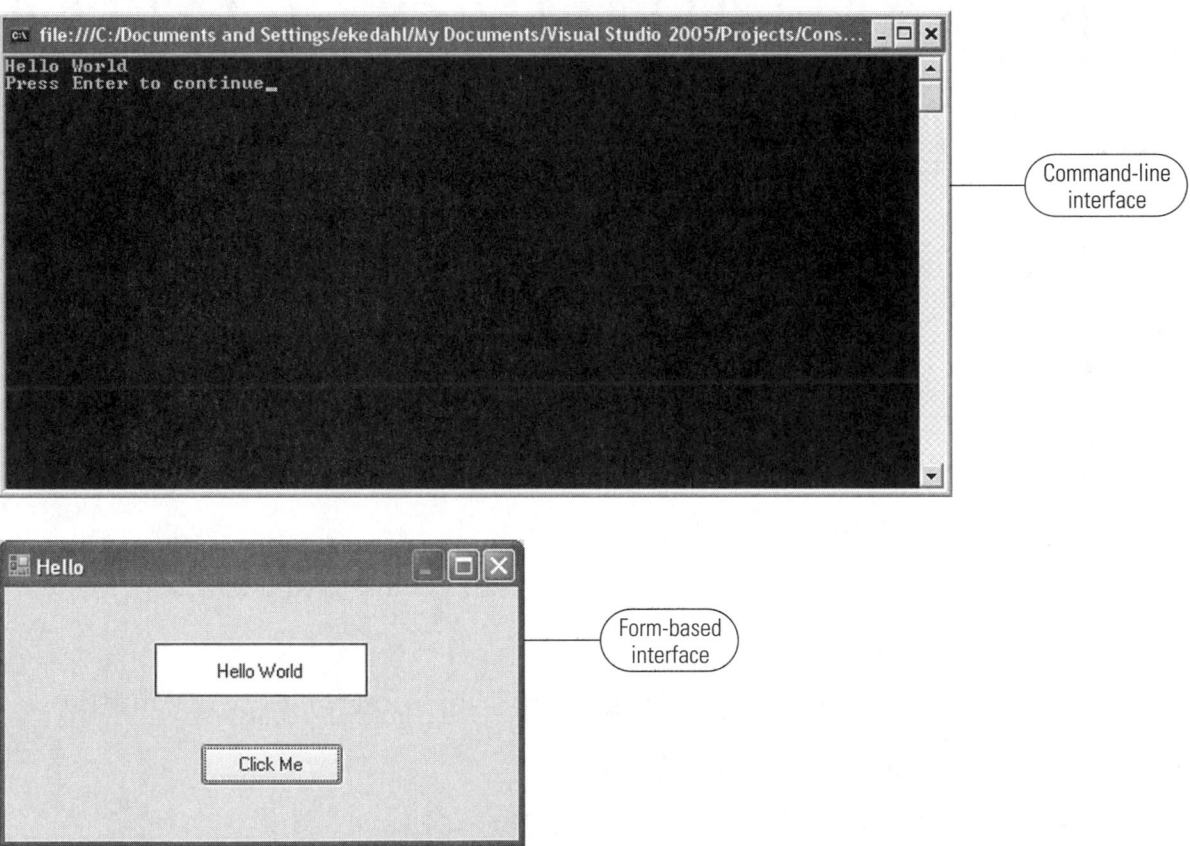

Figure 3-1: Comparing a command-line interface and a form-based interface

As shown in Figure 3-1, a command-line interface displays text in a Command Prompt window. The form-based interface consists of a visual form. When the form's button is clicked, the output text (Hello World) appears on the form.

This concept lesson is composed of three parts. The design elements common to all Windows applications are discussed in the first part of the chapter. The second part of the concept lesson describes how to use the Visual Studio IDE and the Windows Forms Designer to create the visual elements that make up a Windows Application project. The third and final part of the concept lesson describes how to use the Code Editor to create the event handlers and the statements that execute as the end user interacts with the application's visual elements. This is the same Code Editor discussed in Chapter 2.

# DESIGNING A USER INTERFACE—PART 1

The user interface is an important part of any application. A well-designed and intuitive user interface makes an application easy to use. A poorly designed user interface has the opposite effect, making an application seem cumbersome and difficult to use. Designing a user interface requires an artistic eye and adherence to several principles described in Table 3-1.

| Principle | Description |
|---|---|
| Control | The end user should always control the application, rather than the other way around. |
| User-friendliness | The interface should help the end user accomplish tasks and not call attention to itself. Too many different fonts or images tend to distract the end user from the task at hand. |
| Intuitiveness | The interface should follow a direct style that proceeds logically. For example, if an end user needs to complete consecutive steps to accomplish an activity, the steps should be grouped together and proceed one after another. |

Table 3-1: Principles of a good user interface *(Continued)*  ▶

| Principle | Description |
|---|---|
| Consistency | The interface should be conceptually, linguistically, visually, and functionally consistent. For example, the font style used should be consistent throughout the interface. Avoid using more than one or two different fonts on a form. Too many fonts can cause the interface to appear cluttered and unbalanced. If there are several buttons on a form, those buttons should all have the same shape and size. |
| Feedback | The interface should provide immediate and clear feedback to the end user. For example, if the end user adds a record to a file, the interface should inform the end user that the record was added. Likewise, if an end user makes an error when entering data, the interface should communicate the cause of the error and describe possible solutions to the problem. |
| Graphics | The interface should not be cluttered with graphics that serve no useful purpose. Graphics can cause an application to run more slowly, and can detract from the form objects that are necessary to complete a particular task. Logos, icons, and pictures can be used to guide the end user. For example, an icon of a stop sign or exit sign is an intuitive metaphor to use as a button to end the application. Play, rewind, and fast forward icons commonly found on a DVD player are common metaphors to locate the next, previous, and last record in a list. |

Table 3-1: Principles of a good user interface *(Continued)*  ▶

| Principle | Description |
|---|---|
| Input | The interface should minimize situations in which the end user needs to switch input modes from the mouse to the keyboard and back again. This strategy allows tasks to be completed more quickly and efficiently. In addition, the interface should allow the end user to execute commands using the mouse or keyboard so as to provide the end user with maximum flexibility. |
| Screen resolution | Different computers operate at different screen resolutions. Thus, be careful that a form will fit on the end user's screen. Also, some screens, such as those on laptops, are small. This problem is even worse when working with mobile devices such as PDAs and cellular telephones because their displays are so small. There are two solutions to the screen resolution problem. The simplest solution is to create applications for the computer having the lowest screen resolution. A better but more complex solution is to determine the screen resolution of the computer running the application. Then, resize and reposition the visual elements based on the current screen size. |

Table 3-1: Principles of a good user interface

Using the principles described in Table 3-1, a sketch of the user interface is often prepared before creating it on the computer. Microsoft Visio supports tools to sketch a user interface or a simple pencil-and-paper sketch will suffice. Figure 3-2 shows the user interface design for the form that will be used in this chapter's application lesson. This user interface was created in Microsoft Visio.

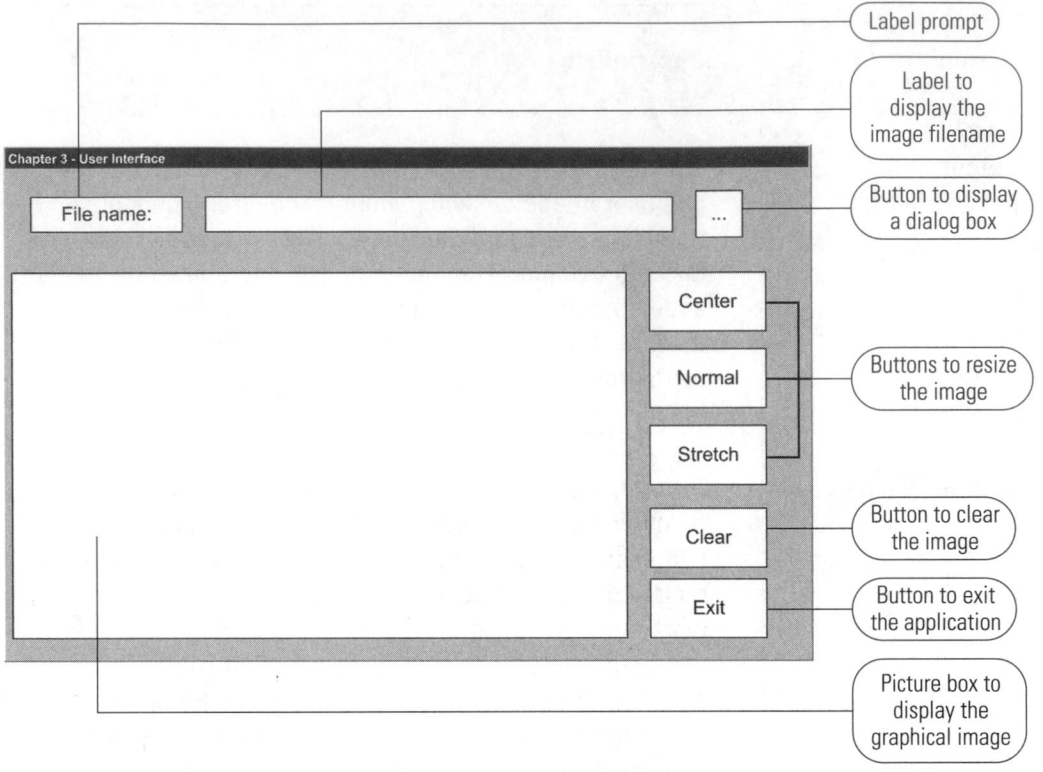

Figure 3-2: Designing a user interface

The user interface shown in Figure 3-2 contains three types of visual elements.

» There are six clickable buttons. The topmost button contains an ellipsis. Clicking the topmost button causes a dialog box to open in which the end user selects a file-name. The second, third, and fourth buttons resize the image. The fifth button clears the image, and the final button exits the application.

» Two labels are used to display a descriptive prompt and the filename of the image displayed. Informational labels, called **prompts**, are commonly used to describe the purpose of another visual element, such as a text box in which the end user enters text, or the purpose of another label.

» The final visual element is the picture box in which a graphical image is displayed.

In addition to the general guidelines described in Table 3-1, the visual elements that you create on a form should adhere to the following principles appearing in Table 3-2. As you will learn later in the chapter, the visual elements created on a form are called controls.

| Principle | Description |
| --- | --- |
| Alignment | Control instances appearing in a column should be aligned vertically. Control instances appearing in a row should be aligned horizontally. |
| Balance | Control instances should be distributed evenly about the form. That is, they should not all appear on the left side or the right side of the form. |
| Appropriate color | Although color can improve a user interface, it can also be abused. Use soft colors such as blue, green, or gray for most forms. Use bright colors, such as red, only for emphasis. Make sure that the foreground and background colors have adequate contrast. That is, make sure that any text and the background appearing behind the text has adequate contrast so as to improve readability. Also, remember that users might be color-blind. Similar visual elements should have similar colors. That is, all labels on a form used as prompts should have the same color text and the same background color behind the text. |
| Function grouping | Control instances that have a similar purpose should be grouped together. |
| Consistent sizing | Control instances should be consistent in size. For example, when a form has multiple buttons, they should all be the same size. |

Table 3-2: Principles of control design

Figure 3-3 illustrates a poor user interface, and Figure 3-4 illustrates a redesigned version of that same user interface.

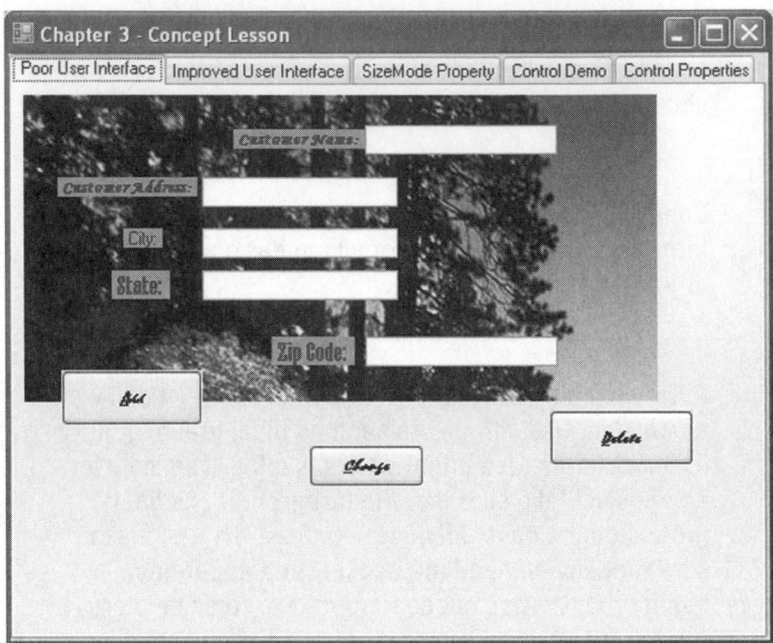

Figure 3-3: A poor user interface

As shown in Figure 3-3, the control instances are not balanced on the form nor are they visually aligned. In addition, the numerous hard-to-read fonts add unnecessary complexity to the form. Finally, the image used as the background is distracting and serves no useful purpose. Figure 3-4 corrects the problems of the poorly designed user interface by aligning the control instances, eliminating the background picture, and simplifying the fonts and colors.

In this exploration exercise, you will examine the poor and improved user interfaces shown in Figures 3-3 and 3-4.

1. Start Visual Studio and open the solution named **Chapter.03\Chapter03 ConceptLesson\Chapter03ConceptLesson.sln**.

2. Press **F5** to run the application.

3. Examine the poor user interface. Click the **Improved User Interface** tab. Although the two user interfaces have exactly the same content, note how the improved user interface adheres to the general design principles and the control design principles described in Tables 3-1 and 3-2.

4. End the application.

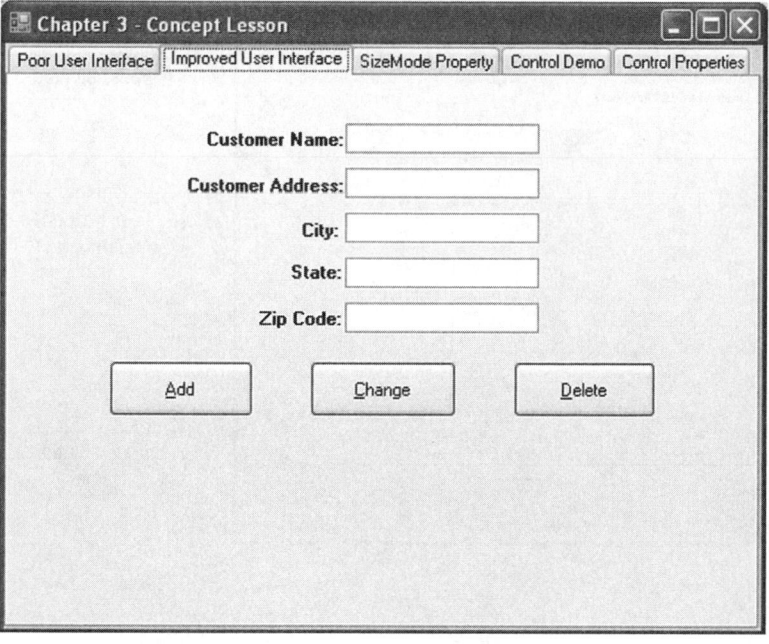

Figure 3-4: An improved user interface

# USING THE VISUAL STUDIO IDE TO CREATE WINDOWS APPLICATION PROJECTS—PART 2

Chapters 1 and 2 described how to create Console Application projects with a single module having a single procedure. In the second part of this concept lesson, you will learn how to create a Windows Application project made up of one form.

The steps to create a new Windows Application project are almost the same as the steps to create a Console Application project. That is, you use the New Project dialog box to create a solution from one of the installed templates. Instead of using the Console Application template, however, the Windows Application template is used. Figure 3-5 shows the New Project dialog box with the Windows Application template selected.

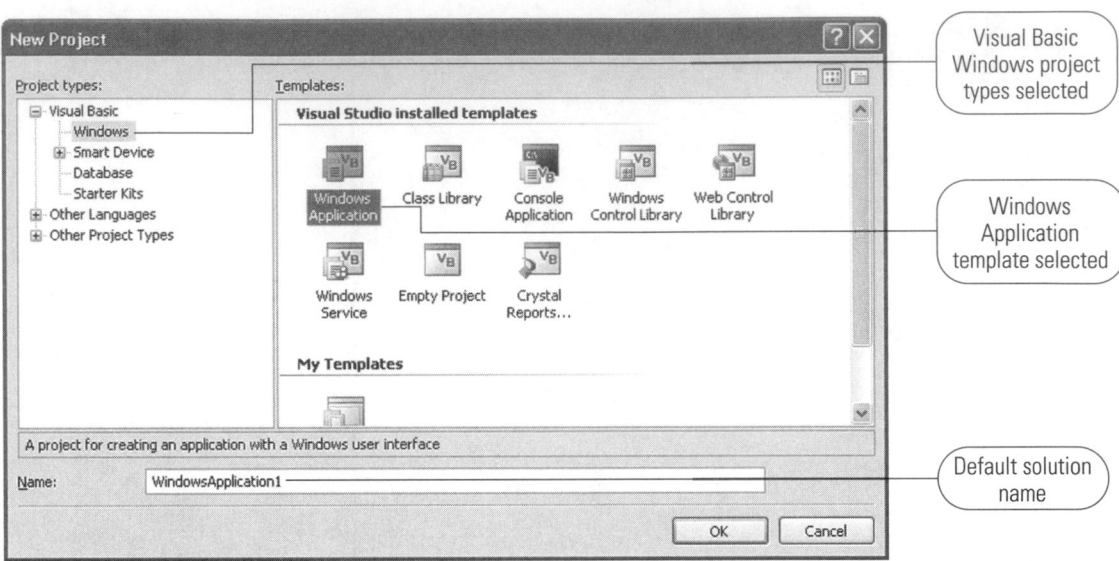

Figure 3-5: New Project dialog box

**»»NOTE** The New Project dialog box shown in Figure 3-5 will differ based on the Visual Studio edition running on your computer. Figure 3-5 shows the New Project dialog box for the Professional edition. In addition, when Visual Studio is run for the first time, you are asked to choose a default editing environment. The New Project dialog box will also appear differently if the default editing environment is not Visual Basic. Specifically, the available templates will vary based on the Visual Studio edition installed. Also, the solution and solution location might not appear depending on your configuration.

Upon creating a Windows Application project from its template, Visual Studio creates the solution and displays the files that make up the solution in the Solution Explorer. When the solution is saved for the first time, the Save Project dialog box might open, allowing you to give both the project and solution a name and set the folder (directory) where the solution will be created.

Although Windows Application projects and Console Application projects are created from a template, these two types of projects have significant differences, some of which are described in the following list:

» The only visual parts of a Console Application project are the textual messages that are displayed in a Command Prompt window. Windows Application projects are graphical applications having one or more windows with which the end user interacts.

» Console Application projects are procedural. As discussed in Chapter 1, a procedural application has a known beginning, and the order in which the actions are performed is controlled by the application itself.

» Windows Application projects, on the other hand, are event driven. That is, in an event-driven application, the application starts running, and then waits for Windows to fire events as the end user interacts with the control instances created on the form.

Before describing how to create the visual interface for a Windows Application project, the structure of a Windows Application project is discussed.

## THE ANATOMY OF A WINDOWS APPLICATION PROJECT

There are similarities and differences between Console Application projects and Windows Application projects. To illustrate the similarities and differences between the files that constitute the two project types, examine the Visual Studio IDE for the Windows Application project shown in Figure 3-6. Figure 3-6 shows the Visual Studio IDE displaying the windows commonly used to create the user interface for a Windows Application project.

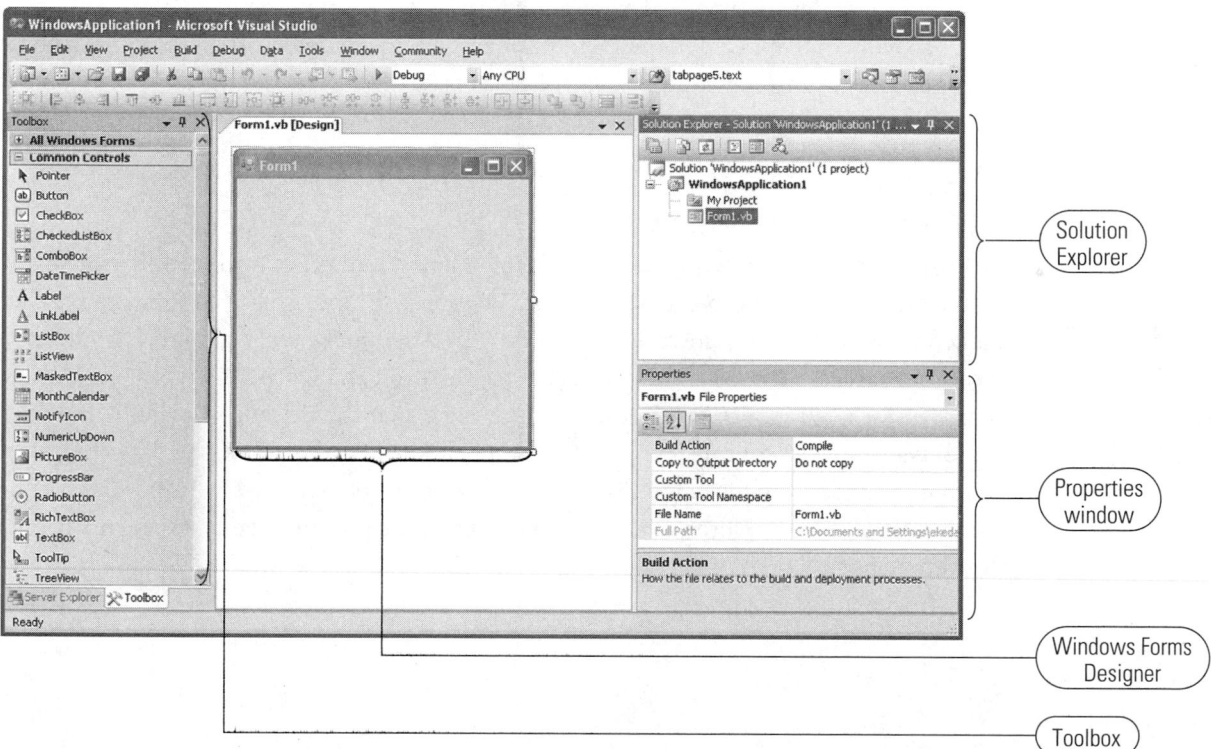

Figure 3-6: Selected windows of the Visual Studio IDE

The following list describes the purpose of the windows appearing in Figure 3-6:

» The Solution Explorer, which was discussed in Chapter 2, is used to manage the files that make up the solution and project(s). Unlike the solution created in Chapter 2, this solution contains different files because it is based on a Windows Application template rather than a Console Application template. That is, the form file replaces the module file. Note that a Windows Application project can have module files too.

» A form's visual interface gets created in a window called the **Windows Forms Designer**. The Windows Forms Designer displays the visual elements, called controls, appearing on the form, and their relative position on the form.

» The visual interface is created by dragging controls appearing in the **Toolbox** to the form's visual surface (Windows Forms Designer). By default, the Toolbox appears along the left margin of the Visual Studio IDE with Auto Hide enabled.

» The final window is the Properties window. Remember that classes support properties. The Properties window provides a visual way to set the properties for an object at design time. For example, a form has a property named `Text` containing a string that appears in the form's title bar. In this chapter, the Properties window is used extensively to set the various properties of a form and the control instances created on the form.

The purpose and use of each of these windows is discussed in the following sections.

## THE SOLUTION EXPLORER

The role of the Solution Explorer is the same for both a Windows Application project and a Console Application project. That is, the Solution Explorer is used to manage the files that compose a solution. However, some of the files that make up a Windows Application project differ from those for a Console Application project. Figure 3-7 shows the Solution Explorer for a Windows Application project. Note that the default solution name for a Windows Application project is WindowsApplication1. Furthermore, the default project contains a single form file named Form1.vb. This file can be renamed by right-clicking the file in the Solution Explorer, clicking Rename from the pop-up menu, and then entering the new name.

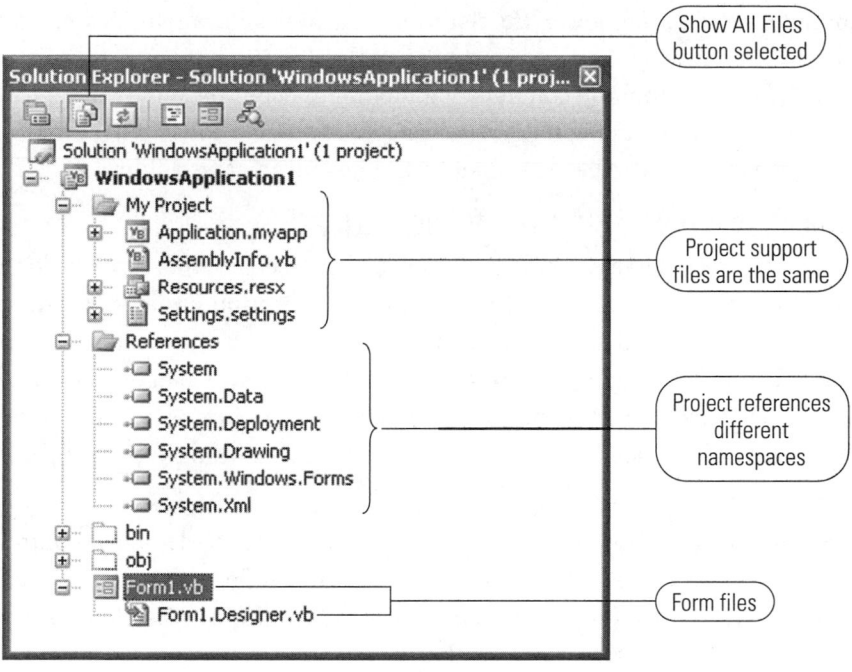

Figure 3-7: Solution Explorer for a Windows Application project

A Windows Application project has the same support files as a Console Application project. That is, both project types have a My Project folder containing an AssemblyInfo.vb file, which describes the assembly. In addition, the My Project folder contains the other support files. Both types of projects have folders named bin and obj. These two folders store the compiled application. Both project types also have namespace references. However, the two types of projects reference different namespaces because they use different .NET Framework assemblies. Specifically, a Windows Application project contains references to the following namespaces:

» All projects, no matter their type, contain a reference to the System namespace.

» The System.Data namespace contains classes used to work with databases.

» The System.Deployment namespace contains classes used to distribute an application to other computers.

» The System.Drawing namespace is used by Windows Application projects to render (draw) the form and the objects appearing on the form.

» The System.Windows.Forms namespace contains those classes that make up the visual forms and the objects created on those forms.

» The System.XML namespace contains classes used to work with XML documents.

Instead of a module named Module1.vb, the Solution Explorer shows two files named Form1.vb and Form1.Designer.vb. As you will see in the third section of the chapter, the contents of these files differ from the contents of a module file, but for now, just realize that together, these two files contain all the Visual Basic code for a form. Furthermore, these files are text files so they can be viewed and edited using any text editor.

## THE TOOLBOX AND WINDOWS FORMS DESIGNER

The Windows Forms Designer and the Toolbox are discussed in the same section because they are almost always used together. Windows Application projects are made up of one or more windows called *forms*. A form has two parts: the user interface (form) and the code behind the form. The user interface is made up of a rectangular window containing visual components such as buttons and boxes. The buttons and boxes on a form are called **control instances**. Control instances are created from controls appearing in the Toolbox.

The Windows Forms Designer is used to create a form and the visual elements (control instances) that appear on the form. A form's visual elements include buttons, text boxes, and other control instances. A more general term for the Windows Forms Designer is **visual designer**. This name stems from the fact that a form's user interface is created in a visual way by clicking and drawing directly on the form. Note that Visual Studio supports additional visual designers in addition to the Windows Forms Designer. The Windows Forms Designer, like the Code Editor, always appears as a document window on a tab group and cannot be docked like a tool window. The Windows Forms Designer can be activated in the following ways:

» Selecting the form name in the Solution Explorer and then clicking the View Designer button in the Solution Explorer's toolbar displays the Windows Forms Designer for the selected form.

» Selecting the form in the Solution Explorer and then clicking View, Designer on the menu bar also activates the Windows Forms Designer.

A form consists of a rectangular region having an optional border and title bar, and a region containing control instances. The .NET Framework class named `System.Windows.Forms.Form` represents the visual form appearing on the desktop and has the following general characteristics:

» At the top of the form appears a *title bar* having an optional caption. The caption can contain spaces and other special characters. However, the caption should fit on the visible title bar.

» The optional *control box* appears along the right edge of the title bar. The control box has buttons to minimize, maximize, and restore a maximized form to its original size. The leftmost *Minimize* button is used to hide the form causing it to

**» NOTE**

All classes are made up of properties, methods, and events. The syntax of a class is presented in a manner consistent with the class interface and the Visual Studio Help system. That is, the various members appear as bulleted lists of properties, methods, and events.

appear as a button on the taskbar. Clicking the button on the Windows taskbar restores the form. The *Restore* button appears as the center button in the control box and operates as a toggle switch. The *Maximize* button causes the form to maximize, thus filling the desktop. The *Restore* button restores the form to its size before the form was maximized. The *Close* button closes the form or application. The control box buttons can be made visible or hidden.

» Below the form's title bar appears an optional *menu*.

» The region inside a form's border, excluding the title bar, is called the form's *client area*. It is here that the form's control instances appear.

As you know, classes support properties, methods, and events, and the `System.Windows.Forms.Form` class is no exception.

## Syntax

`System.Windows.Forms.Form class`

## Public Properties

» The `AcceptButton` property contains the name of a `Button` control instance designated as the Accept button. There can be only one Accept button per form. Pressing the Enter key causes the `Click` event to fire for the button designated as the Accept button.

» The `BackColor` property specifies the background color of the form.

» If the `ControlBox` property is set to `True`, the control box appears on the form's title bar. If set to `False`, the control box does not appear. Note that the Close button always appears and is enabled when the control box is visible.

» The `MaximizeBox` property, if set to `True`, causes the Restore/Maximize buttons to be enabled. If set to `False`, the buttons are disabled.

» The `MinimizeBox` property defines whether the Minimize button is enabled or disabled. Note that if both the `MaximizeBox` and `MinimizeBox` properties are set to `False`, neither button is visible.

» The `FormBorderStyle` property is used to specify the appearance of the border surrounding a form, and whether the form is resizable. It can be set to a fixed set of values. If set to `None`, no border surrounds the form. The settings `FixedSingle` and `Fixed3D` cause the form to appear with a flat and three-dimensional border, respectively. The end user cannot resize the form when either of these settings is used. The setting `FixedDialog` appears the same to the end user as the `FixedSingle` setting. That is, the end user cannot resize the form. Dialog boxes are used to display forms that must be closed before the end user can interact with the other forms in the application. The setting `Sizable` configures the form so that it can be resized by dragging the form's border. The settings `FixedToolWindow` and `SizableToolWindow` cause the form to appear with a shorter title bar. These types of windows are called tool windows. The appearance of

*(Continued)* ▶

tool windows is similar to the appearance of Visual Studio tool windows. If the `BorderStyle` property is set to `FixedToolWindow`, the end user cannot resize the form. If set to `SizableToolWindow`, the end user can resize the form.

» The `CancelButton` property contains the name of a `Button` control instance designated as the Cancel button. Pressing the Escape key causes the `Click` event to fire for the associated button. This property works in tandem with the `AcceptButton` property. Only one button on a form can be designated as the Cancel button.

» The `Icon` property contains the image appearing in the upper-left corner of the form's title bar. The form's icon also appears on the taskbar when the form is minimized.

» The `Text` property contains the text that appears in the form's title bar. The text in the title bar can include spaces and punctuation characters. Although it can contain any number of characters, the text should fit in the form's title bar.

» The `Width` and `Height` properties define the size of the form. By default, Visual Studio uses pixels as the unit of measure.

» The `StartPosition` property is used to specify where on the desktop the form will appear when it is displayed. If set to `CenterScreen`, the form is displayed in the center of the desktop. If set to `Manual`, the position of the form is defined by the `X` and `Y` properties.

» The `X` and `Y` properties define the position of the form relative to the desktop. These properties are only used when the `StartPosition` property is set to `Manual`. If both of these properties are set to zero (0), the form appears in the upper-left corner of the desktop.

## Public Methods

» The `Close` method closes the form, thereby unloading it from memory.

» The `Hide` method makes a form invisible but the form is not unloaded from memory.

## Public Events

» The `Load` event fires when a form is loaded into memory each time the application is run.

When working with a form, it is necessary to reference the current instance of that form. For example, to exit an application, the `Close` method must be called on the current form instance. To reference the current instance of a class (form), you use the `Me` keyword. To illustrate, the following statement shows how to close the current form instance, thereby ending the application:

```
Me.Close()
```

The Toolbox contains all of the visual tools (controls) necessary to create a form's user interface. You use the controls on the Toolbox to create control instances on the Windows Forms Designer. By default, the Toolbox appears along the left edge of the IDE with Auto Hide enabled. Like many other windows, the Toolbox has a drill-down interface. Each tab can be expanded or collapsed by clicking the plus or minus signs, respectively. Figure 3-8 shows the Toolbox with the Common Controls tab expanded and the other tabs collapsed.

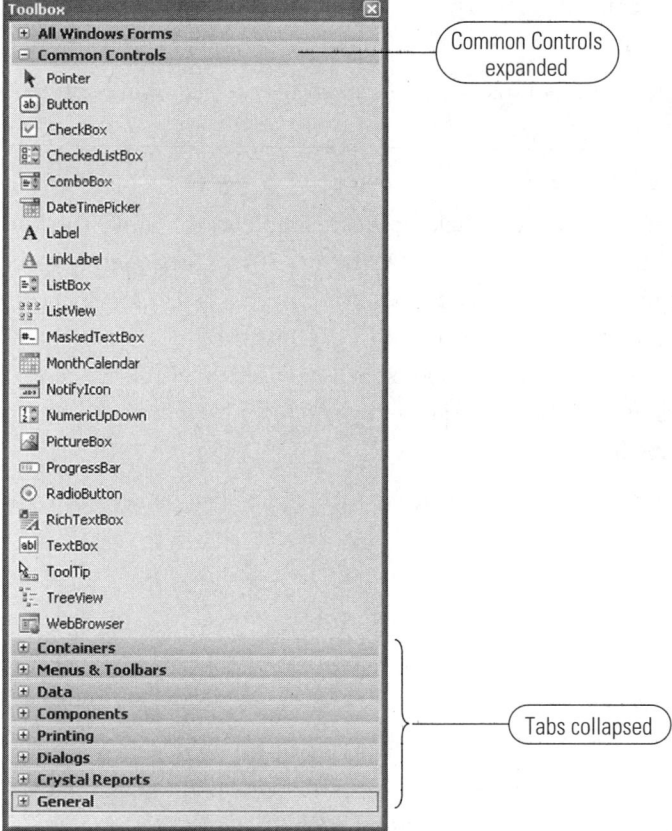

Figure 3-8: The organization of controls in the Toolbox

All controls appearing in the Toolbox are organized into tabs based on their purpose, as described in the following list:

» The All Windows Forms tab lists all of the controls applicable to Windows Application projects.

» The Common Controls tab lists those controls used most frequently.

» The Containers tab lists those controls that contain or group other control instances.

» As the name implies, the Menus & Toolbars tab contains those controls used to create the menu system for a form and to create toolbars on a form.

» The Data tab contains controls used to establish a database connection, to retrieve database data, and to make changes to that data.

» The Components tab contains controls that work with various Windows services, such as global event logs and messaging.

» The Printing tab contains those controls used to send output to a printer.

» The Dialogs tab contains controls that display standard dialog boxes used to open and save files, print files, and so on.

» The Crystal Reports tab contains those controls used by the reporting software package known as Crystal Reports.

» By default, the General tab is empty.

Creating a control instance on a form involves clicking the desired control in the Toolbox. The selected control appears highlighted. Then, in the Windows Forms Designer, drag the outline of the control instance to define its visible region. It's also possible to create a control instance by double-clicking the control in the Toolbox. All control instances are created in this manner. If the control instance is being created from an invisible control, the control instance automatically appears in the resizable tray below the form no matter where the control instance is created on the form.

After a control instance has been created on a form, its properties can be set using the Properties window.

## INTRODUCTION TO THE PROPERTIES WINDOW

As you know, a property is class data, such as a button's caption, screen location, or size. The properties of an object, such as a form, or the control instances created on a form are set using the Properties window. Figure 3-9 shows the Properties window.

The Properties window is a tool window. Thus, docking can be enabled or disabled and the window can be Auto Hidden. The Properties window is divided into four sections, as described in the following list:

» The Object combo box is used to select an object such as a form or control instance created on the form. The combo box displays the currently selected object. The list arrow to the right of the combo box is used to select the form or control instance created on a form.

» The toolbar area contains buttons used to change the order in which the properties appear in the Properties window and the information to view. The toolbar area also contains two buttons used to display either the properties of the currently selected object or the events applicable to the currently selected object.

» The list section is made up of two columns. The Name column lists the name of each property. The Value column lists the current value assigned to a property. Scroll bars appear automatically when all of the properties do not fit in the list section of the Properties window. The Name and Value columns can be resized by dragging the vertical line separating the two columns. Some properties are hierarchical. The plus and minus indicators appearing in the left margin expand or collapse the hierarchy, respectively.

» The Description section appearing at the bottom of the window contains a brief description of the selected property. Right-clicking on the Description section, and then clicking Description from the pop-up menu hides this section.

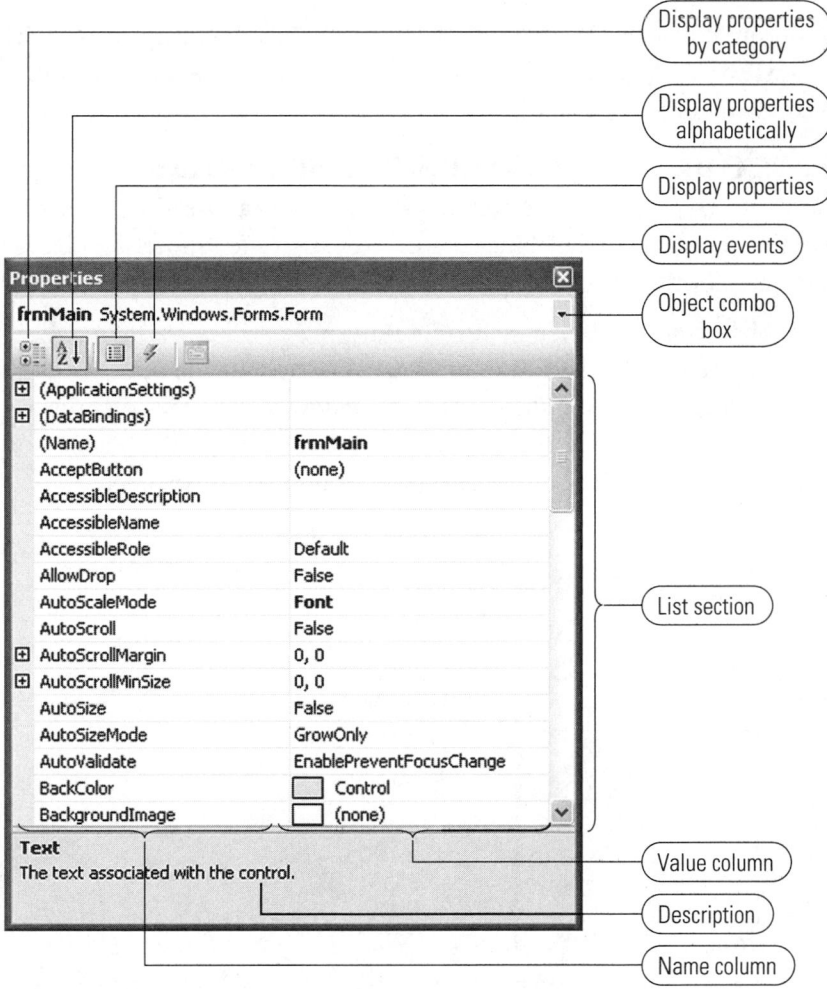

Figure 3-9: The Properties window

The leftmost two buttons in the Properties window control the order in which properties are displayed in the list section. When the Categorized button is active, the properties are organized based on the purpose of the property. Individual property categories can be expanded or collapsed. When the Alphabetic button is active, the properties appear sorted in alphabetic order. Last, if the Properties button is selected, the properties pertaining to the selected object appear, and if the Events button is active, the events pertaining to the selected object appear.

To change the current value of a property, you edit the contents of the Value column. The Value column operates differently depending on the contents of the property. To set the properties for a form, click the form in the Windows Forms Designer. Sizing handles surround the form. The form name appears in the Object combo box at the top of the Properties window. The Properties window is updated to display the properties for the form.

Note that different properties store different types of data. For example, some properties store textual values whereas others store numeric values. The steps to set a property vary based on the type of data stored in the property.

## CONFIGURING TEXTUAL AND HIERARCHICAL PROPERTIES

Properties such as the Name property store textual values. In such a case, the property is edited by typing in the new value in the Value column. Note that the Properties window displays the text (Name) for the Name property.

Some properties are hierarchical and their values are set using a drill-down interface. To illustrate, consider the size and position of a control instance on a form. The Location and Size properties appear hierarchically in the Properties window. The Location property has X and Y properties. The Size property has Width and Height properties. Figure 3-10 shows the Properties window with the Location and Size properties expanded.

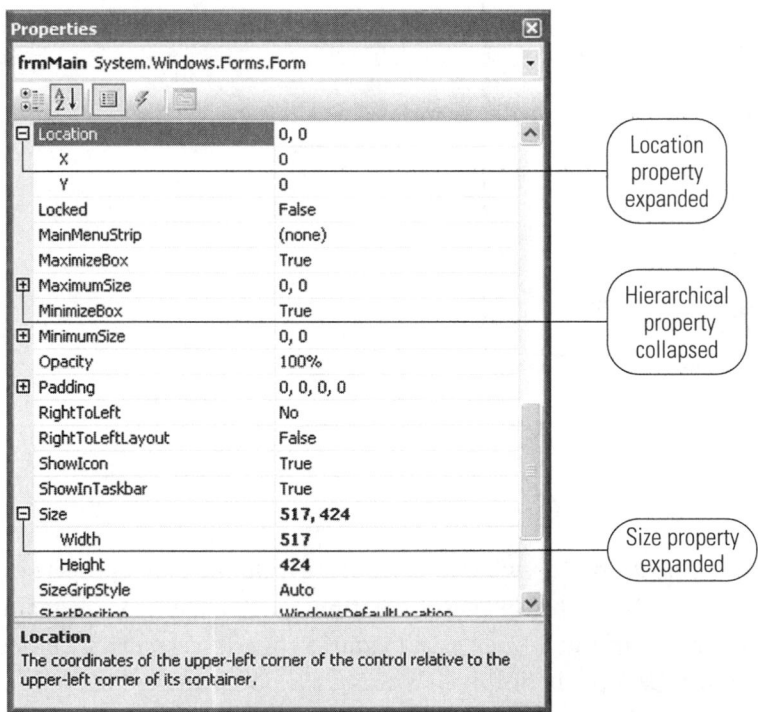

Figure 3-10: Hierarchical properties in the Properties window

Properties involving color, such as the `BackColor` and `ForeColor` properties, are set using a color palette. The same color palette is used to set both of these properties and any other property involving color. Figure 3-11 shows the Properties window with a color palette displayed.

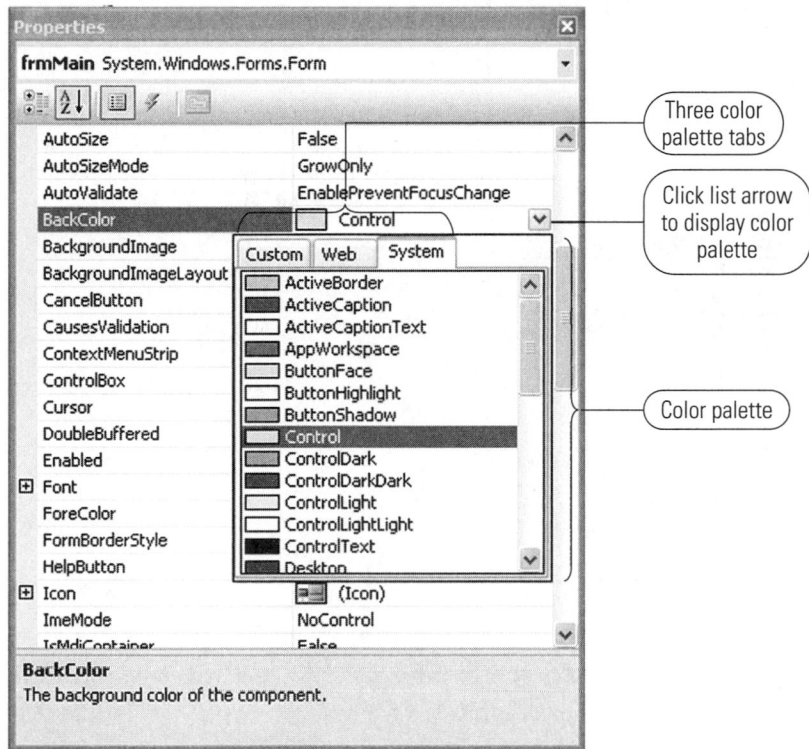

Figure 3-11: Properties window displaying a color palette

As shown in Figure 3-11, the color palette has three tabs. The Custom tab is used to create custom colors. The Web tab lists those colors supported by the Web. The final tab, System, causes the color of a control instance to be the same as the color defined by a common Windows system property. The system colors can be set using the Display properties dialog box in the Control Panel.

Some properties, such as the `SizeMode` property of the `PictureBox` control, have a fixed set of valid values from which a value can be selected. The desired value is selected from a drop-down list, as shown in Figure 3-12.

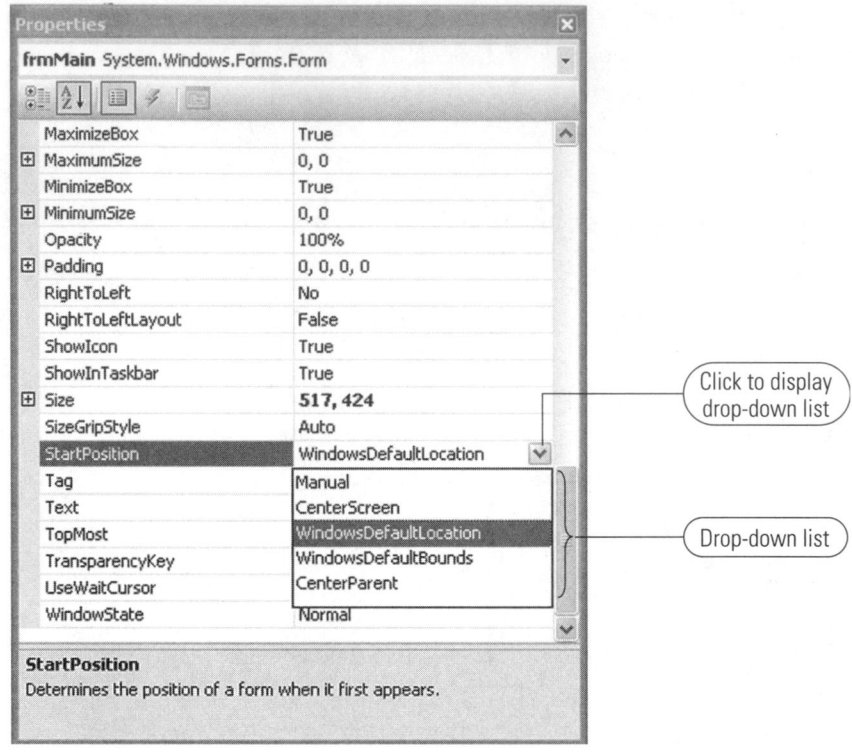

Figure 3-12: Properties window displaying a drop-down list

**NOTE**

When a property is set using a dialog box, ellipses appear in the Properties window instead of a list arrow.

When setting properties of this type, a property value must be selected from the drop-down list. Any other property value is prohibited.

Some properties, such as the Font property, display a dialog box, allowing you to select the typeface, size, and formatting attributes. Figure 3-13 shows the Font dialog box.

Setting the desired property value is as simple as selecting the desired items in the dialog box, and then clicking the OK button.

Other properties, such as the TextAlign property, have a visual editor allowing you to set the property. Figure 3-14 shows the visual editor for the Label control's TextAlign property.

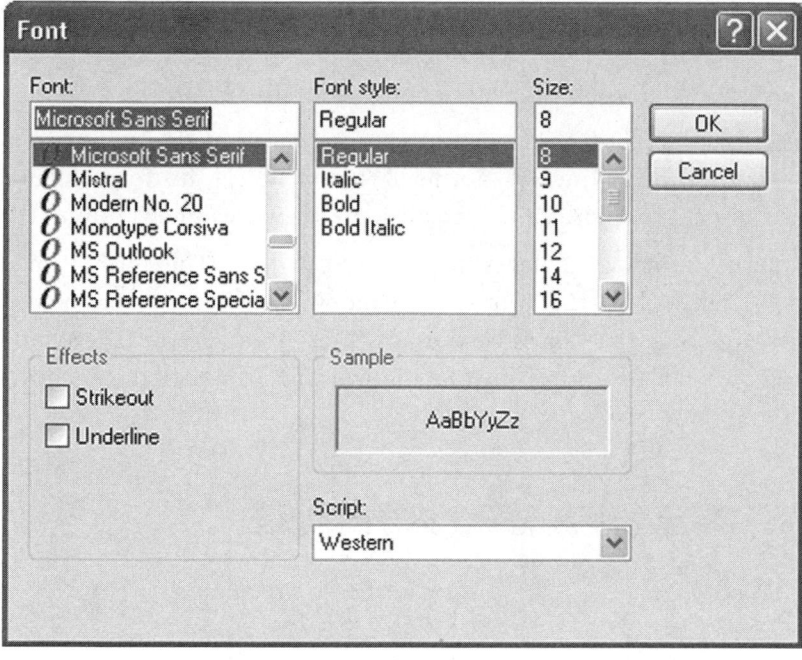

Figure 3-13: Font dialog box

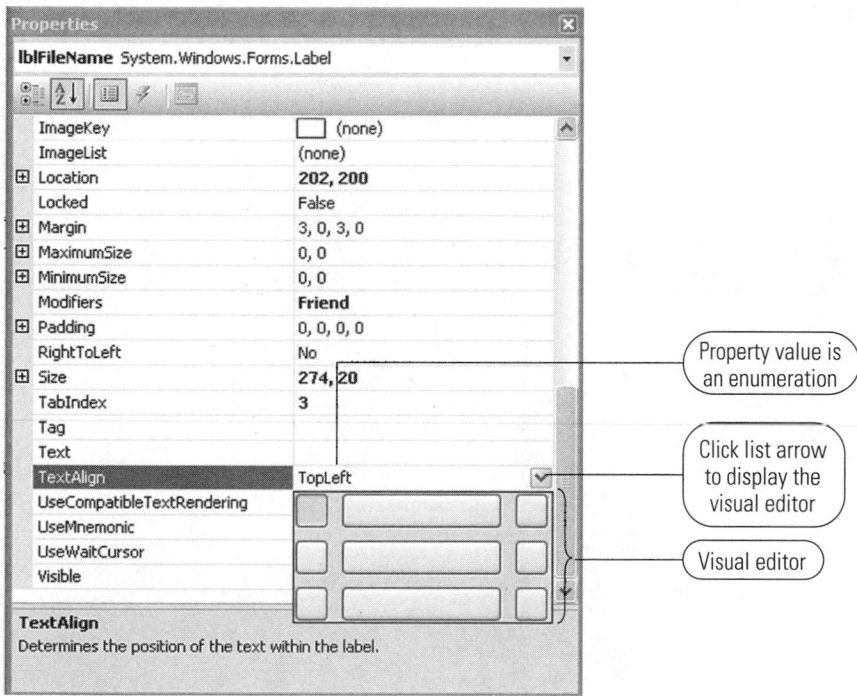

Figure 3-14: Visual editor for the TextAlign property

As shown in Figure 3-14, the visual editor for the `TextAlign` property makes it easy to set the property's value.

In this exploration exercise, you will see how to set properties for a form.

1. Your first step is to make sure that the Windows Forms Designer is active in the Visual Studio IDE. To activate the Windows Forms Designer, click the form named **frmMain.vb** in the Solution Explorer, and then click the **View Designer** button.

2. Activate the Properties window, if necessary, by pressing **F4**. The form named frmMain should be selected in the Properties window. Select the form named **frmMain**, if necessary, using the Object combo box. The Visual Studio IDE should resemble the one shown in Figure 3-15. Note that the size and position of the windows might vary from those shown in Figure 3-15.

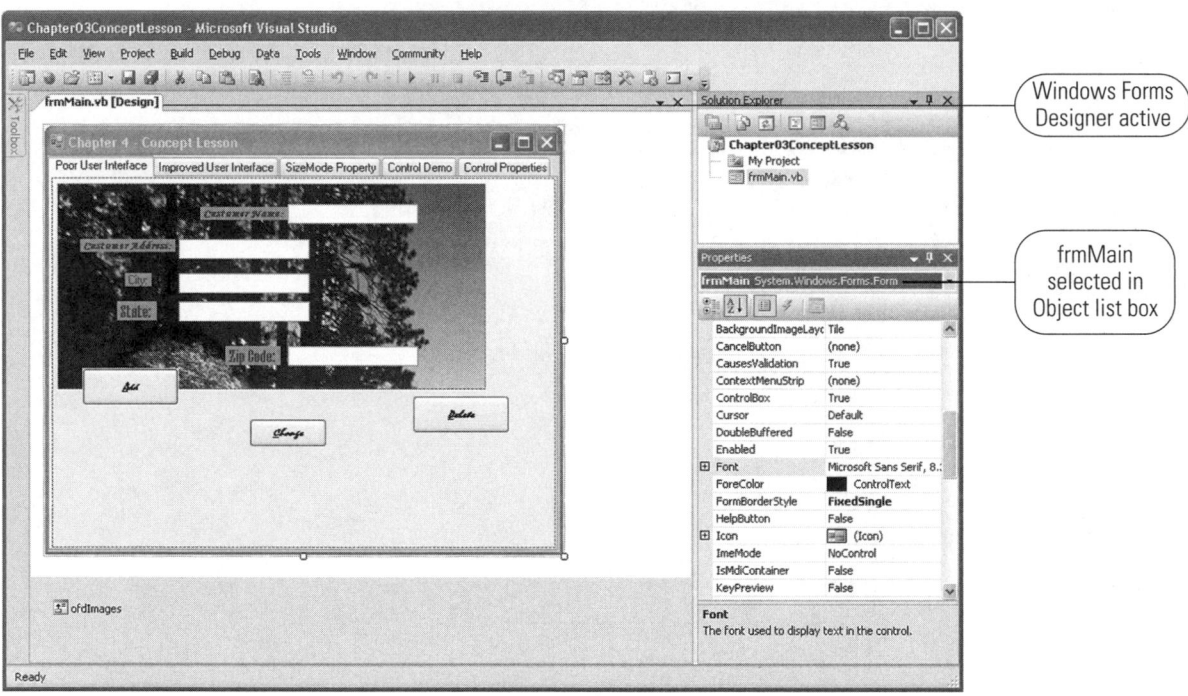

Figure 3-15: Setting properties for a form

3. Using the Properties window, set the `ControlBox` property to `False` by clicking the **Value** column and selecting **False**. Note that you might need to use the scroll bars to locate the property. The control box disappears from the Windows Forms Designer. Set the property back to **True**. As you can see, as you set individual property values, the Windows Forms Designer updates the form as necessary.

4. Set the `FormBorderStyle` property to **FixedToolWindow**. The height of the title bar is updated in the Windows Forms Designer. Set the `FormBorderStyle` property back to **FixedSingle**.

5. Set the `StartPosition` property to **CenterScreen**. When the application is run, the window appears in the center of the desktop.

# MINI-QUIZ 1

1. Windows Application projects are made up of one or more forms that make up the application's user interface.

   a. True                             b. False

2. Which of the following are characteristics of Windows forms?

   a. A form has a title bar and an optional control box.

   b. The region inside a form's border is called the client area.

   c. The default name for the first form in a Windows Application project is Form1.

   d. A form derives from the `System.Windows.Forms.Form` class.

   e. all of the above

3. What two properties would you use to make the form resizable, and appear in the center of the desktop when the application is run?

4. The Properties window is made up of two columns. List the names of the two columns and describe their purpose.

# USING THE VISUAL STUDIO IDE TO CREATE AND CONFIGURE CONTROL INSTANCES

As mentioned, to create control instances on a form, the Toolbox and Windows Forms Designer are used together. Visual Studio makes it surprisingly easy to create and modify an application's user interface. In the following section, you will see how to create and delete control instances on a form, and how to reposition and resize those control instances.

## CREATING CONTROL AND DELETING CONTROL INSTANCES

To create control instances on a form, both the Windows Forms Designer and Toolbox should be active. You can create a control instance on the form in two ways.

» In the Toolbox, double-click the desired control. The control instance is created on the form using a default size.

» In the Toolbox, click the desired control. Move the mouse pointer to the form. The mouse pointer changes to a crosshair along with an icon of the control. Click and drag the mouse to define the initial size and position of the control instance.

All control instances are created in this way. Of course, it's possible to create multiple instances of the same control.

Occasionally, a control instance needs to be deleted because it is no longer needed or because it was created by mistake. Again, Visual Studio supplies different ways to delete a control instance.

» In the Windows Forms Designer, click the control instance to select it. Then, press the Delete key.

» Right-click the control instance to select it. Click Delete from the context menu that appears.

## MOVING AND RESIZING CONTROL INSTANCES

After a control instance has been created on a form, its position might need to be changed because a design specification has changed or because the control instances are not visually aligned. Any control instance on a form can be moved (repositioned) by clicking the control instance to select it, and then using the mouse to drag the control instance to its new position. The same task can also be performed by setting the X and Y properties in the Properties window.

A control instance can be resized by clicking the control instance in the Windows Forms Designer to select it, and then doing one of the following:

» Pressing the arrow keys moves the selected control instance in the direction of the arrow.

» Holding down the Control key while pressing the arrow keys moves the control instance in the direction of the arrow using snap lines to align the control instance with other control instances appearing on the form.

» Holding down the Shift key while pressing the arrow keys resizes the control instance. Pressing the down and up arrows increases and decreases the height of the control instance, respectively. The left and right arrows decrease and increase the width, respectively.

» The mouse can be used to drag the sizing handles, which are the small boxes that appear around any selected control instance. The corner sizing handles are used to resize the control instances both vertically and horizontally. Note that sizing handles do not appear if the AutoSize property is set to True.

» The Properties window can also be used to resize control instances by setting the Height and Width properties.

In addition to sizing and positioning a single control instance, it is also possible to set the size and position of several control instances at the same time.

## WORKING WITH MULTIPLE CONTROL INSTANCES

It is possible to work with multiple control instances at the same time so as to align them with each other or adjust their spacing relative to each other or relative to the form. It is also possible to set properties for multiple control instances at the same time using the Properties window. Note that only those properties common to all the selected control instances can be set in this way.

The following list describes the two ways to select multiple control instances:

» Using the Pointer tool in the Toolbox, drag a rectangular region marking the control instances to be selected. If the selected region surrounds only part of a control instance, the control instance is selected.

» While holding down the Shift key, click each control instance to select it. Sizing handles surround the selected control instances. Clicking a selected control instance causes that control instance to be deselected.

After multiple control instances have been selected, various operations can be performed on them.

## ALIGNING MULTIPLE CONTROL INSTANCES

The Format menu, which appears only while the Windows Forms Designer is active, has menu items used to align the selected control instances. Of the selected control instances, one control instance is considered the active control instance. The other control instances are aligned or resized based on which selected control instance is the active control instance. The active control instance appears with white sizing handles. The remaining selected control instances appear with black sizing handles.

The following list summarizes the different alignment commands appearing on the Format menu:

» The Align command aligns the left, right, top, or bottom margins of the selected control instances based on the position of the active control instance.

» The Make Same Size command, as its name implies, resizes the selected control instances to match the size of the active control instance. The width, height, or both dimensions can be resized.

» The Horizontal Spacing and Vertical Spacing commands align the control instances with the form horizontally or vertically. There are options to make the spacing the same or to increase or decrease the spacing.

» The Center in Form command centers the selected control instances between either the top and bottom margins of the form or the left and right margins.

Each of these commands works the same way, and each uses the active selected control instance to determine the size and/or alignment of the other control instances. The Windows Forms Designer also supplies a visual way to align control instances. By clicking a control instance to select it, and dragging that control instance, lines called snap lines appear temporarily, as shown in Figure 3-16.

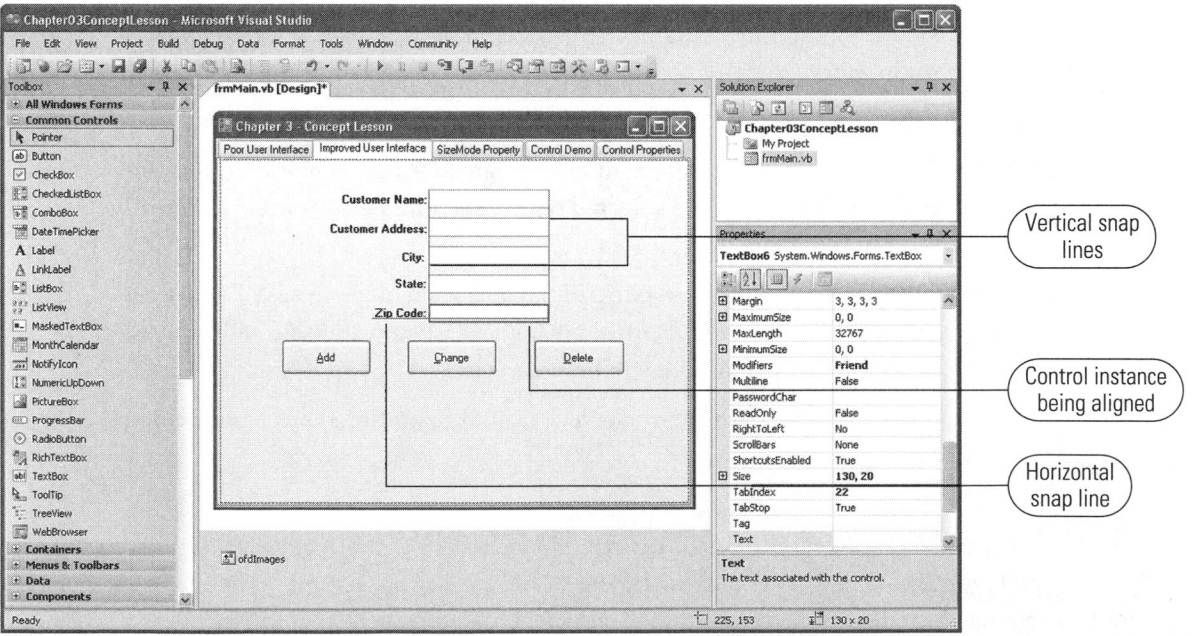

Figure 3-16: Snap lines in the Windows Forms Designer

As shown in Figure 3-16, as a control instance is dragged across the form, snap lines appear allowing one control instance to be aligned with another.

No matter the type of visual control you create, they are created in the same way. That is, you create control instances by drawing them on the form. After being created, control instances can be resized and repositioned.

# INTRODUCTION TO VISUAL STUDIO CONTROLS

Having learned how to create control instances, you will now learn how to use selected controls supplied by Visual Studio. The following list describes the controls discussed in this chapter and their purpose:

>> The `PictureBox` control is used to display graphical images.

>> The `Label` control displays text. Other than displaying text, the end user has no interaction with `Label` control instances.

>> The `Button` control performs a specific task when clicked by the end user.

>> The `OpenFileDialog` control displays a dialog box allowing the end user to select a file to open.

>> The `ToolTip` control displays an informational pop-up message when the mouse hovers over another control instance for a few seconds.

**>>NOTE**

In this chapter, only five controls are discussed. In total, Visual Studio supports nearly 100 different controls. As you progress through this book, additional controls are presented as they are used.

## THE SYSTEM.WINDOWS.FORMS.CONTROL CLASS

As you have learned, a form is a class having properties, methods, and events. Visual Basic controls are also classes that are part of the .NET Framework class library. Each control created on a form is called a control instance. In other words, a control instance (object) is created from its underlying control (class). All control instances created from the same class share the same properties. For example, all of the buttons on a form have a position on the form, a size, and a caption. All controls share another common characteristic—they each have a visual representation on the form. The `System.Windows.Forms.Control` class is the base class from which all visible controls are derived. The `Control` class supplies the basic functionality to get input from the keyboard and mouse, and to display output. Figure 3-17 shows the organization of the control classes discussed in this chapter.

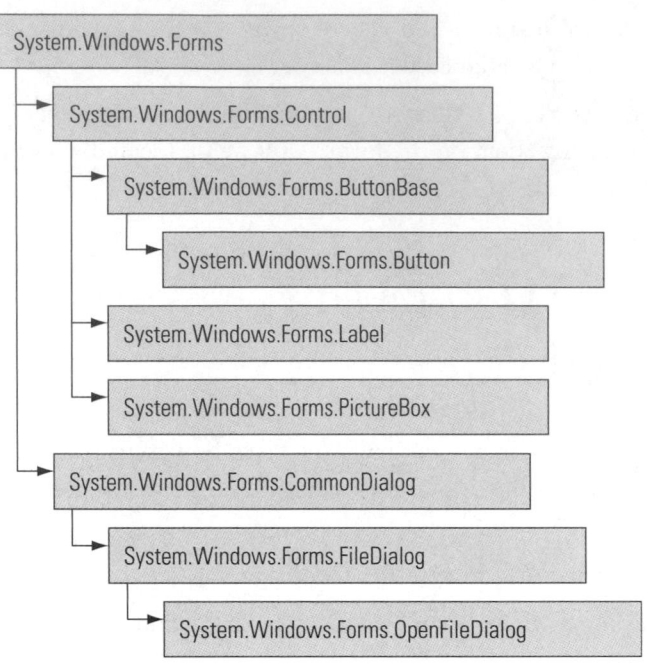

Figure 3-17: Hierarchical organization of control classes

As shown in Figure 3-17, the System.Windows.Forms.Control class is the base class for all visual controls. The Label and PictureBox controls derive directly from the Control class. All clickable buttons, including the Button control, derive from the ButtonBase class.

There are a group of controls that appear as dialog boxes. These controls all derive from the CommonDialog class.

## UNDERSTANDING THE NAME PROPERTY

When you create a form or control instance on a form, Visual Studio assigns a default name to that form or control instance. The default name of the first form created in a project is Form1. The default name for the second form would be Form2 and so on. Control instances, such as a Button, are similarly named Button1, Button2, Button3, and so on. As you will see later in the chapter, you use the name of a form or control instance when writing code.

In this book, meaningful and consistent names are used for forms and the control instances created on a form. Form names are created beginning with the prefix "frm" to denote a form. A descriptive name follows the prefix. For example, an application's main form is named "frmMain". Control instances are similarly named with a descriptive prefix.

**»NOTE**

The naming convention of using a prefix followed by a descriptive name is called *Hungarian notation* and was pioneered by a Microsoft developer named Charles Simonyi.

The Name property of a form or control instance must adhere to the following rules:

» The first character of the name must be a letter.

» The subsequent characters of the name can be letters, numbers, or the underscore character.

» The name must be fewer than 255 characters in length.

» Names cannot contain spaces.

» A name cannot include any special characters other than the underscore character.

» The name of each form and the control instances created on the form must be unique. Control instances created on different forms can have the same value for the Name property, however.

The following list contains the prefixes for the control types discussed in the chapter:

» The Button control has a prefix of "btn".

» The Label control has a prefix of "lbl".

» The prefix for the OpenFileDialog control is "ofd".

» The PictureBox control has a prefix of "pic".

» The ToolTip control has a prefix of "tip".

As other controls are introduced, the standard naming prefix for a particular control type is noted.

In addition to the prefix denoting the type of control, control instance names are chosen to describe the purpose of the control instance. For example, a Label control instance displaying a filename might have a name of lblFileName. A Button control instance used to exit the application might have a name of btnExit.

One common error made when setting properties is trying to set the Name property of two forms or two control instances on a form to the same value. In such a case, the dialog box in Figure 3-18 appears indicating the error.

Figure 3-18 shows the message that appears when an attempt is made to set the Name property for two forms or control instances to the same value. Another common error made is trying to use the Properties window to set properties while the Visual Studio IDE is running the application. The Properties window can only be used to edit properties while Visual Studio is in design mode.

» NOTE

The naming of a form and the control instances appearing on a form can be a subjective decision. In general, choose meaningful names and be consistent. Use whole words and avoid obscure abbreviations.

Figure 3-18: Properties Window error dialog box

## MEMBERS OF THE CONTROL CLASS

Because all visible controls are derived from the `Control` class, they all share similar members (properties and methods). The following members are defined by the `Control` class:

### Syntax

`System.Windows.Forms.Control`

### Public Properties

» The `ForeColor` and `BackColor` properties define the text color and color appearing behind the text, respectively.

» The `Enabled` property stores values of `True` or `False` indicating whether the control instance will respond to user interaction.

» All visible controls have a size. The `Height` and `Width` properties store the size of the control instance. Valid values are positive whole numbers.

» Control instances can be configured so that they will resize based on their contents. If the `AutoSize` property is set to `True`, the control instance is resized based on its contents. The `MinimumSize` property defines the minimum size of the control instance, and the maximum size is defined by the `MaximumSize` property.

» All visible control instances have a position on the form. The position of a control instance is relative to the upper-left corner of the form's client area. The `Location` property is used to set the position of the control instance on the form.

*(Continued)* ▶

» The Name property of the Control class has the same meaning as the Name property of the Form class. It is used to uniquely identify the control instance. Two control instances on the same form cannot have the same value for the Name property.

» The Text property contains the text that appears in the control instance.

» The Visible property stores the values True or False and indicates whether the control instance is visible or hidden from the end user.

## Public Methods

» The Hide method makes the control instance invisible. Thus, the Visible property is set to False when the Hide method is called.

» The Show method makes the control instance visible. Thus, the Visible property is set to True when the Show method is called.

## Public Events

» Some events fire as a result of the user clicking and moving the mouse. The Click event fires when the user clicks in a control instance.

The preceding properties all apply to the Control class. Thus, all controls derived from the Control class support these properties. The following sections describe selected controls derived from the Control class. These classes are, of course, also part of the .NET Framework class library.

### THE LABEL CONTROL

The Label control displays text and is derived directly from the System.Windows.Forms.Control class. It is typically used as a prompt to identify the purpose of other control instances appearing on the form, or to display data. Labels are used for display (output) purposes only; the end user cannot input text into a label. The following members apply to the Label control:

**»NOTE**

The Label control does support methods and events. However, they are not discussed in this chapter because they are rarely used. The reason is simple. The Label control is used solely to display text. The end user typically has no other interaction with a label.

## Syntax
```
System.Windows.Forms.Label class
```

## Public Properties

» The BorderStyle property can be set to one of three constant values. If set to None, no border surrounds the label. If set to FixedSingle, a flat border surrounds the label. If set to Fixed3D, the Label control instance appears recessed.

» The Font property defines the typeface and the size of the text appearing in the label. Like the Size and Position properties, the Font property is hierarchical. Fonts support the Name and Size attributes to describe the typeface, and the size of the font, which is measured in points. The Font property also supports attributes, including Bold, Italic, Strikeout,

*(Continued)* ▶

and `Underline`. These attributes are enabled and disabled by setting the respective property to `True` or `False`.

» The `TextAlign` property determines how the textual characters are aligned inside the region of the label. Text can be left-, right-, or center-aligned. Text can also be aligned along the top or bottom of the control instance. Again, the Properties window has a visual editor with which you set the `TextAlign` property.

## THE BUTTON CONTROL

The .NET Framework supports a group of controls that derive from the `System.Windows.Forms.ButtonBase` class, which provides a foundation for a clickable button. The following three controls are derived from the `ButtonBase` class:

» The `Button` control supplies a clickable button.

» The `CheckBox` control is a two-state control with a visible check box. The box becomes checked or unchecked when the box is clicked.

» Multiple instances of the `RadioButton` control are typically used to create a mutually exclusive list. That is, only one `RadioButton` control instance can be selected from a list of radio buttons.

In this chapter, the `Button` control is discussed. The `CheckBox` and `RadioButton` controls are discussed in subsequent chapters.

Like all visible controls, the `Button` control supports the `X`, `Y`, `Height`, and `Width` properties to define its position and size on the form, respectively. A button typically has a descriptive prompt that appears inside the button's visible region to identify the button's purpose. The `Button` control can also display graphical images.

When clicked, Windows raises the `Click` event, and executes the corresponding `Click` event handler. Events and event handlers are discussed in part three of this concept lesson. In addition to the properties shared by the `Label` control, the `Button` control supports the following members:

## Syntax
`System.Windows.Forms.Button class`

## Public Properties
» The `Enabled` property can be either `True` or `False`. If `True`, Windows fires a `Click` event when the end user clicks the button. If `False`, the button text appears shaded and `Click` events are not fired.

» The `FlatStyle` property can be set to one of four values. If set to `Flat`, the button appears flat on the form. If set to `Popup`, the button appears raised when the mouse pointer is placed over the button at run time. If set to `Standard`, the default, the button appears raised off of

*(Continued)*                                                                                    ▶

the form's surface. If set to `System`, the appearance of the control instance is the same as the one used by the operating system and defined by the Control Panel.

» The `Image` property contains a picture that appears in the button along with the button text.

» The `ImageAlign` property is used to indicate where the image will appear within the button's visible region. The `Image` and `ImageAlign` properties work in tandem.

» The `Text` property contains the text that appears in the button's visible region. You can also create a **hot key** for a button by inserting an ampersand character (&) in the `Text` property just before the character that should act as the hot key. A hot key is a set of keystrokes, such as Alt+C, that, when typed by the end user, produces the same result as clicking the button. Each hot key on a form should be unique.

## Public Events

» The `Click` event is derived from the `Control` class. Windows fires the `Click` event when the end user clicks the button.

## THE PICTUREBOX CONTROL

The `PictureBox` control displays a graphical image inside the visible region of the control instance and is derived directly from the `System.Windows.Forms.Control` class. Based on the setting of the `SizeMode` property, the image is resized based on the size of the visible control instance. The `PictureBox` control can display JPEG, bitmap, and other image formats and has the following members:

## Syntax

```
System.Windows.Forms.PictureBox class
```

## Public Properties

» The `BorderStyle` property defines the appearance of the border surrounding the control instance. The control instance can appear with a flat border, a three-dimensional border, or no border at all.

» The `Image` property contains the image displayed in the control instance.

» The `ImageLocation` property contains the name of the disk file where the image is stored.

» The `SizeMode` property defines how the image appears inside the region of the control instance. The various settings for the `SizeMode` property are discussed in the next section.

## Public Events

» By handling the `Click` event, a `PictureBox` control instance can be made to work as if it were a `Button` control instance.

Images have a fixed size, which might differ from the size of the `PictureBox` control instance displaying the image. The `SizeMode` property controls how the image appears inside the region of the `PictureBox` control.

Figure 3-19 illustrates the effect of scaling an image with the `SizeMode` property.

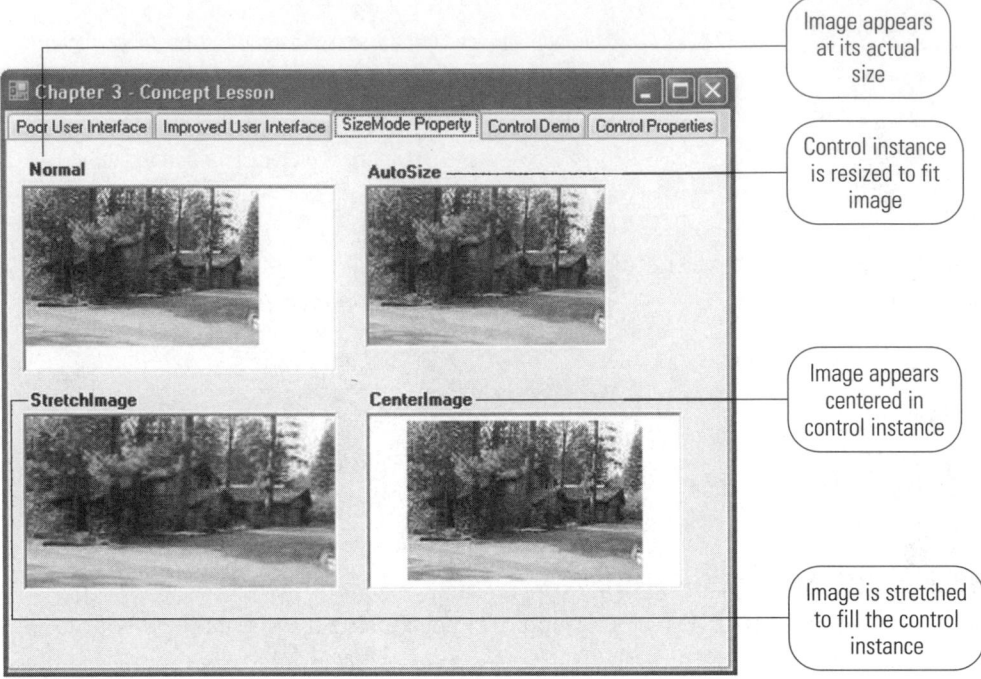

Figure 3-19: Using the SizeMode property to scale images

If the SizeMode property is set to Normal, the image appears at the upper-left corner of the control instance. The image is not resized. The setting StretchImage causes the image to be resized such that it fills the region of the control instance. If the property is set to AutoSize, the control instance resizes to fit the image. The setting CenterImage causes the image to be centered in the control instance.

## THE OPENFILEDIALOG CONTROL

Visual Studio supplies a group of controls allowing the end user to select files to open and save, to print documents, and to select colors and fonts. These standard dialog boxes are derived from the CommonDialog class instead of the Control class. In this chapter, the OpenFileDialog control is introduced.

Unlike the other controls discussed so far in this chapter, the OpenFileDialog control does not appear within the visible region of the form. Rather, the control instance appears in its own dialog box when the ShowDialog method is called. Figure 3-20 shows the dialog box displayed as a result of calling the ShowDialog method.

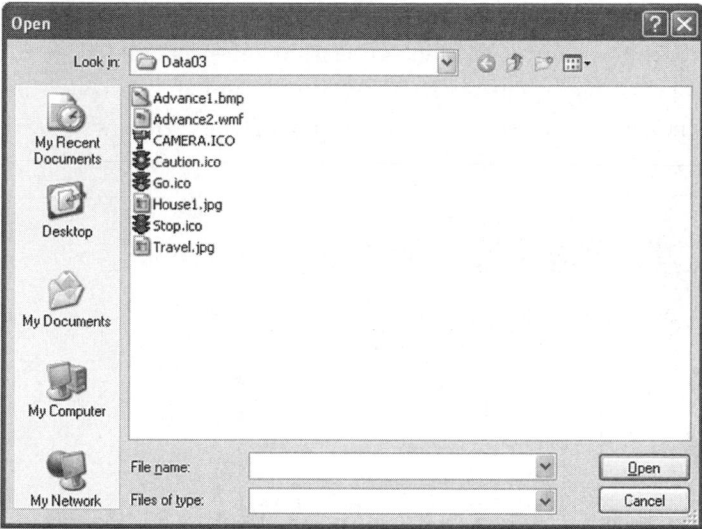

Figure 3-20: Open dialog box

As shown in Figure 3-20, the OpenFileDialog control displays a dialog box allowing the end user to select a file to open. This dialog box allows the end user to navigate through folders to locate a particular file. Contrary to its name, the OpenFileDialog control does not actually open a file. Rather, when the end user selects a file to open, the name of the selected file is stored in the FileName property. It is up to you, the developer, to actually open the file or to process it in some way.

One method and one property are all that is needed to use the OpenFileDialog control, as follows:

» Calling the ShowDialog method displays the dialog box to the end user. The method accepts no arguments.

» The filename selected by the end user is stored in the FileName property.

The following code segment shows how to display the OpenFileDialog control instance named ofdImages, and write the filename to the Console window.

```
ofdImages.ShowDialog()
System.Console.WriteLine(ofdImages.FileName)
```

The first of the preceding statements displays the OpenFileDialog control instance. The filename specified by the end user is stored in the FileName property. Thus, the final statement writes the filename selected by the end user to the Console window or Output window.

Another difference between the `OpenFileDialog` control and the other controls presented in this chapter is where the control instance appears when it is created on the form's visual surface. Instances of the `OpenFileDialog` control and all other invisible control instances appear in a resizable tray at the bottom of the Windows Forms Designer, as shown in Figure 3-21.

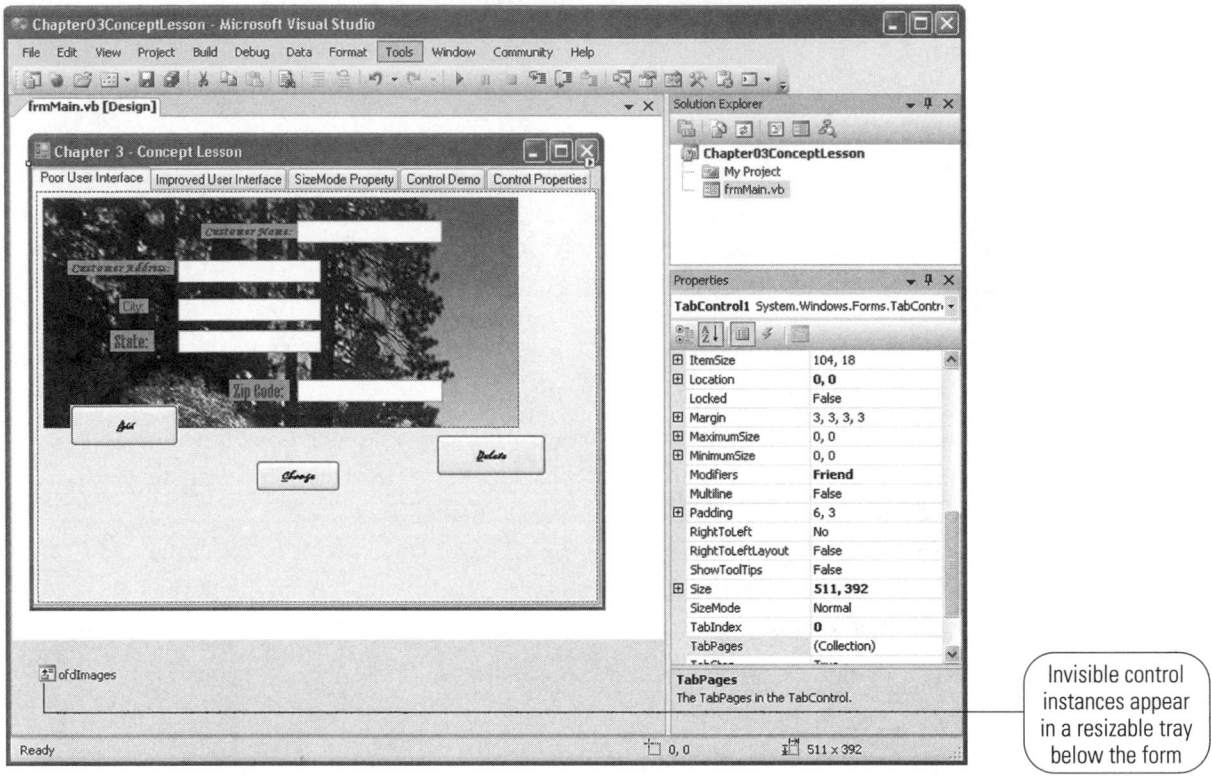

Figure 3-21: Invisible control instance

The final control discussed in this chapter is the ToolTip control.

## CREATING TOOLTIPS

ToolTips appear when the mouse hovers over a control instance at run time. ToolTips further improve the user interface by providing a visual clue as to the purpose of a control instance. To create ToolTips, you create an instance of the `ToolTip` control on a form, and then associate other control instances with that `ToolTip` control instance. The `ToolTip` control belongs to a category of controls called provider controls. A provider control does not do its work alone. Rather, a **provider control** works in conjunction with other control instances. That is, one `ToolTip` control instance can provide ToolTips for all of the other control instances appearing on a form. In addition, the `ToolTip` control is an invisible control so it appears in the resizable tray below the Windows Forms Designer.

The `ToolTip` control supports the following properties:

### Syntax
`System.Windows.Forms.ToolTip control`

### Definition
The `ToolTip` control displays a pop-up ToolTip when the mouse hovers over a control instance for a few seconds.

### Public Properties
» The `InitialDelay` property defines the amount of time the mouse must hover over a control instance before the ToolTip appears. The time is measured in milliseconds. 1000 milliseconds is equivalent to 1 second.

» The `AutomaticDelay` property defines the amount of time that the ToolTip appears after the `InitialDelay` interval has elapsed.

As mentioned, the `ToolTip` control is a provider control that works in conjunction with a form or another control instance. After an instance of the `ToolTip` control has been created on a form, the Properties window displays another property named ToolTipOn*ControlInstanceName*, where *ControlInstanceName* is the name of the `ToolTip` control instance created on the form. The value of this property is the text string that appears in the ToolTip at run time.

In this exploration exercise, you will see the effect of various property settings and their effect on the visual appearance of selected controls.

1.  Click the **Control Demo** tab in Chapter03ConceptLesson.sln. This tab contains several control instances that have different sizes and are poorly aligned, as shown in Figure 3-22. In the following steps, you will use the Visual Studio IDE to align these control instances.

2.  As shown in Figure 3-22, there are four `Label` control instances appearing along the left side of the form. Click the top **Label** control instance to select it. White sizing handles appear indicating that this is the active control instance. Hold down the Shift key and click the remaining **Label** control instances to select them.

3.  On the menu bar, click **Format**, point to **Make Same Size**, and then click **Both** to make the selected control instances the same size. Click **Format**, point to **Align**, and then click **Lefts** to left-align the selected `Label` control instances.

4.  Using the Pointer tool, select all of the four buttons. Click **Format**, point to **Align**, and then click **Rights** to right-align the `Button` control instances. When complete, the form should resemble Figure 3-23.

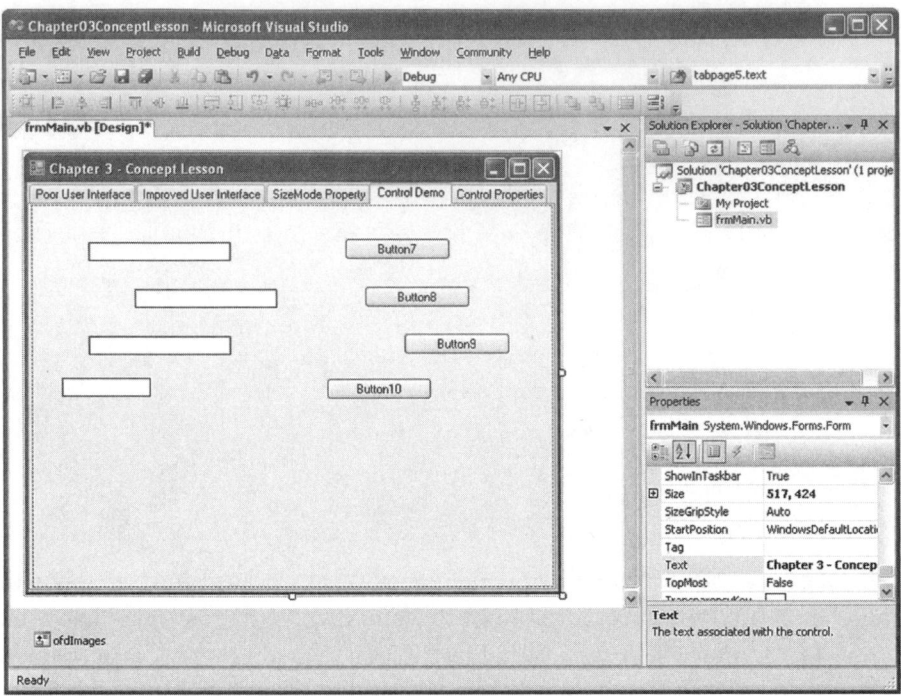

Figure 3-22: Chapter 3 Concept Lesson—Control Demo tab

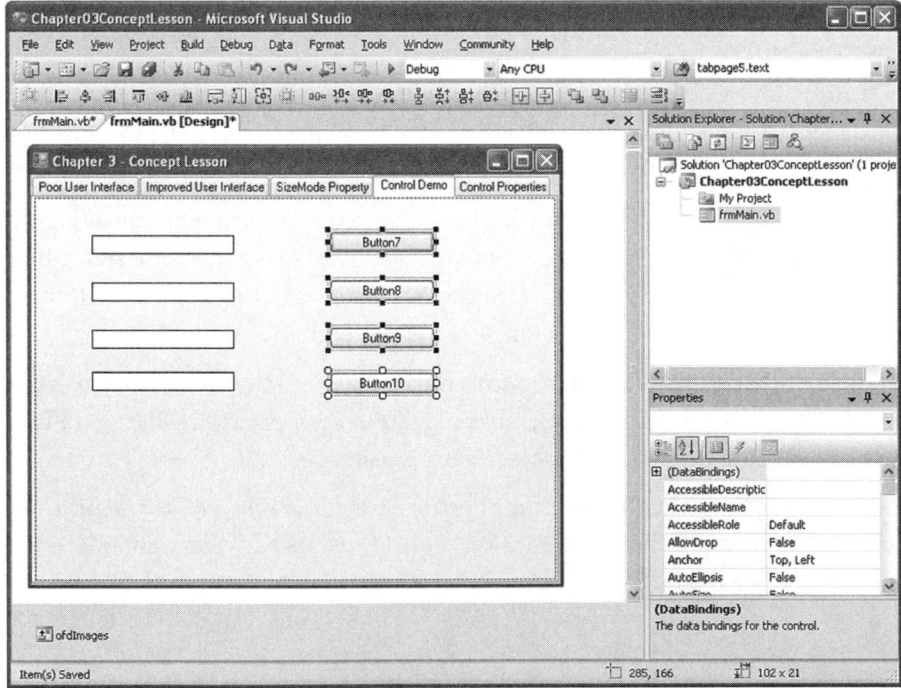

Figure 3-23: Chapter 3 Concept Lesson—Control Demo tab with control instances aligned

5. Run the application. Click the **Control Properties** tab. Figure 3-24 shows the Control Properties tab with various options selected.

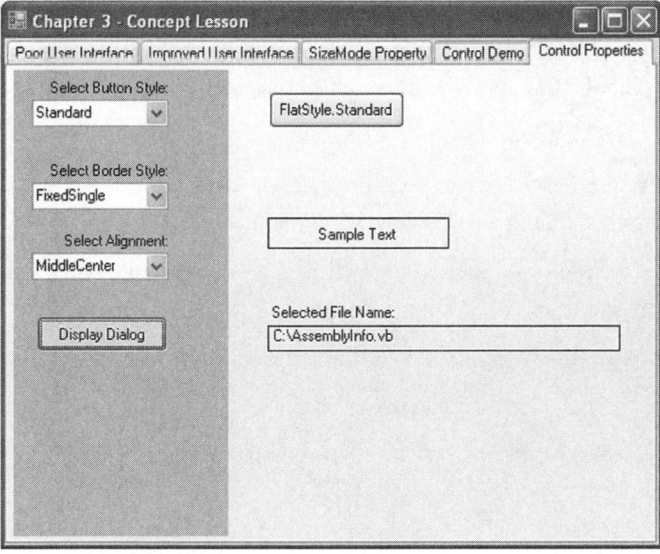

Figure 3-24: Chapter 3 Concept Lesson—Control Properties tab

6. In the combo box titled Select Button Style, select different style elements. The appearance of the Button control instance appearing to the right of the combo box changes.

7. In the combo box titled Select Border Style, select different border styles. The appearance of the Label control instance to the right of the combo box changes.

8. In the combo box titled Select Alignment, select different text alignments. The appearance of the Label control instance to the right of the combo box changes.

9. Click the **Display Dialog** button. In the Open dialog box that appears, select a file of your choosing, and then click **Open**. The file appears to the right of the button in the Label control instance.

10. End the application to return to Design mode. Click the **Control Demo** tab. Explore setting various properties by selecting a control instance of your choosing, and then setting properties using the Properties window.

## MINI-QUIZ 2

1. What two windows do you use to create control instances on a form?

2. What is the term used for labels that describe another visual element on a form?

3. What is meant by the term *Hungarian notation*?

4. Describe what would happen if you tried to set the Name property to the same value for two control instances using the Properties window.

5. Which of the following statements is correct regarding the Name property for a form and the control instances created on a form?

   a. Multiple control instances on a form can have the same name.

   b. Names can contain spaces but other special characters are prohibited.

   c. Names must contain letters, numbers, or the underscore character. Other characters are prohibited.

   d. A form and a control instance on that form can have the same value for the Name property.

   e. none of the above

# CREATING CODE FOR A WINDOWS APPLICATION PROJECT

Just as a Console Application project has code that executes when the application is run, Windows Application projects also contain code that executes when the application runs. This code is often referred to as the *code behind the form*.

The code behind the form is made up of two parts. One part is the code automatically generated by Visual Studio and the Windows Forms Designer, which is used to create the control instances on the form when the application runs. The second part consists of the statements that execute as the end user interacts with the form's control instances. This code is created by you, the developer.

## INTRODUCTION TO CLASS BLOCKS AND PARTIAL CLASSES

When a form is created, and as control instances are created on a form, Visual Studio and the Windows Forms Designer generate and edit the code in the *frmName*.Designer.vb file. Developer-created code appears in the *frmName*.vb file. Note that the italicized text *frmName* is a placeholder for the actual form name. Remember that the default filename for the first form in a Windows Application project is Form1.vb. The form filename for this concept lesson has been changed to frmMain.vb to denote the main form. The following code segment shows the structure of a form named frmMain with a filename of frmMain.vb.

```
Public Class frmMain
    ' statements
End Class
```

The syntax of the preceding `Class` block looks much like a `Module` block. Looking at the syntax, the `Class` keyword replaces the `Module` keyword.

Although `Class` and `Module` blocks have the same structure, they work somewhat differently. The following list describes selected differences between classes and modules:

» A `Module` block can have a procedure named Main marking the application's entry point. Although a `Class` block can have a procedure named Main, it is not the application's entry point.

» As you know, objects are created from templates called classes, and that multiple objects (class instances) can be created from the same class. Because the form named frmMain is a class, multiple forms (objects) can be created from the same class. Modules work differently. As an application runs, there is exactly one instance of a module.

» When a class instance gets created, a `Sub` procedure named New is automatically executed. This procedure, when appearing in a class, is called a constructor. Modules do not have constructors. Think of a constructor as the entry point for a form or other class instance.

Having introduced the structure of the frmMain.vb file, the contents of the frmMain.Designer.vb file are discussed. Visual Studio and Visual Basic support what are called partial classes. A **partial class** is a class whose code appears in more than one physical file.

Partial classes are useful for two reasons:

» Suppose that a complex class was being created by several developers. Using partial classes, each developer could work with a separate physical file, allowing other developers to work on other parts of the class contained in other files. When development is complete, all of the files that compose the class can be compiled together.

» Visual Studio and the Windows Forms Designer use partial classes. As mentioned, Visual Studio splits the class for a form into two files. One file is managed entirely by the Windows Forms Designer. Developer-created code is created in the other file. This division of code prevents accidental modification or corruption of code generated by the Windows Forms Designer.

> **» NOTE**
>
> Partial classes are new to Visual Studio 2005. Prior to Visual Studio 2005, a form class appeared in a single file.

The following code segment shows the structure of the frmMain.Designer.vb file.

```
Partial Public Class frmMain
    Inherits System.Windows.Forms.Form
    ' Windows Forms Designer generated code.
End Class
```

The preceding `Class` block introduces a new keyword: `Partial`. The `Partial` keyword denotes that the class is a "partial" class. A partial class is just a class that is split across multiple physical files.

The preceding class declaration also contains the following `Inherits` statement:

```
Inherits System.Windows.Forms.Form
```

The .NET Framework supports inheritance, so one class can inherit the members of a base class. The preceding statement indicates that the class named frmMain inherits from the base `System.Windows.Forms.Form` class. Thus, the new frmMain class supports all of the properties and methods and other types of the base `System.Windows.Forms.Form` class.

When a Windows Application project is created from a template, Visual Studio creates code automatically in the frmMain.Designer.vb file. In addition, code is automatically generated in this file when you create control instances on a form. Figure 3-25 shows some of the automatically generated code for the form named frmMain. This code appears in the file named frmMain.Designer.vb.

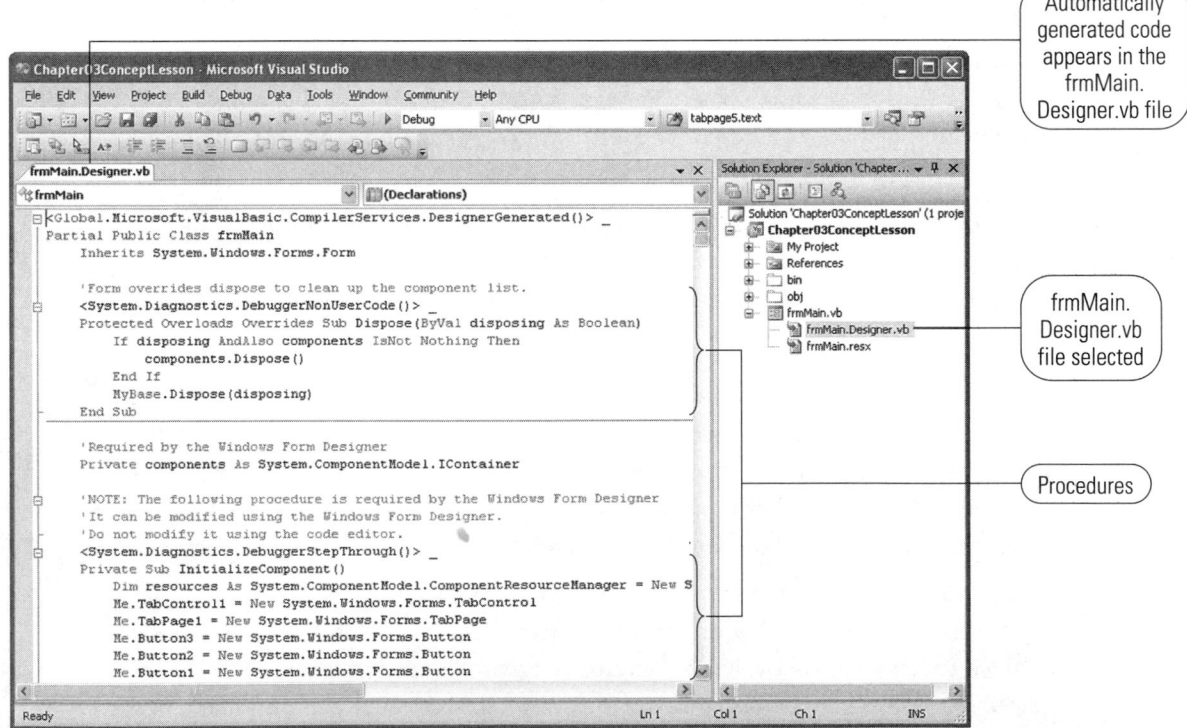

Figure 3-25: Windows Forms Designer generated code

Compare the following statement with the attributes discussed in Chapter 2, as the following statement declares an attribute:

```
<Global.Microsoft.VisualBasic.CompilerServices. _
    DesignerGenerated()>
```

The attribute declaration appears between less-than and greater-than signs as do all attributes. The `DesignerGenerated()` attribute tells Visual Studio or any other application, that this class was generated by the Windows Forms Designer.

The goal of this section is not to explain all of the code generated by the Windows Forms Designer. In fact, you never need to edit this code directly. The purpose of this section is to explain how a form works and the relationship between the two files that constitute a form.

## INTRODUCTION TO EVENT HANDLERS

In Chapters 1 and 2, you created a Console Application project with a `Sub` procedure named Main( ) that executed when the application started. After the statements in the Main( ) procedure executed, the application ended. Unlike Console Application projects, Windows Application projects are event-driven applications. An event-driven application works differently than a procedural application. In an event-driven application, the application starts running, and then waits for Windows to fire events as the end user interacts with the control instances created on the form.

An **event handler** is a procedure containing one or more Visual Basic statements that Windows executes when the end user performs an action, such as clicking a button on a control instance. Windows executes different event handlers as different events fire. For example, a `Click` event fires for a button when the end user clicks the button.

Other events are applicable to other controls such as a `TextBox` control. For example, each time that the end user enters a character into a `TextBox` control instance, a `TextChanged` event fires. In this event handler, you can write code to detect the character pressed by the end user and perform some conditional processing. This chapter introduces event handling using a button's `Click` event. In subsequent chapters, different events and the concept of event handling is discussed in more detail. Figure 3-26 shows the process of executing an event handler.

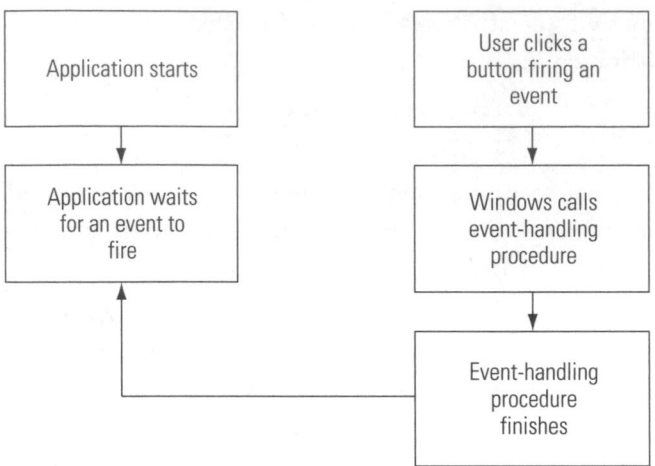

Figure 3-26: Executing an event handler

As shown in Figure 3-26, the application initializes, and then waits for an event to fire. When the end user clicks a button, thereby causing Windows to fire a Click event, the corresponding event handler and its statements execute until the procedure completes, and then the application begins waiting again for another event to fire. This process continues until the application ends.

An event handler is nothing more than a Sub procedure with a couple of unique characteristics. To illustrate, the following statements make up a Click event handler for a Button control instance named btnDemo:

```
Private Sub btnDemo_Click(ByVal sender As System.Object, _
    ByVal e As System.EventArgs) Handles btnDemo.Click
End Sub
```

The meaning of the Sub and End Sub keywords is the same as their meaning used to declare the Main( ) procedure shown in Chapters 1 and 2. That is, these keywords declare the beginning and end of the procedure block. Instead of the procedure being named Main( ), the procedure is named btnDemo_Click. Remember that procedure names can contain the underscore character.

Unlike the Main( ) procedure shown in Chapters 1 and 2, this procedure has two arguments. These arguments are used to send information about the event to the event handler. The purpose of these arguments is discussed in subsequent chapters. For now, just do not modify the arguments to an event handler or Visual Basic will mark the statement as containing a syntax error. Following the event arguments appears the Handles clause. It is the Handles clause that marks a procedure as an event handler. Note that the name of the procedure is not significant. Following the Handles clause appears the control instance name and the event name separated by a period. Thus, the statement fragment Handles btnDemo.Click indicates that the procedure handles the Click event for the Button control instance named btnDemo.

Fortunately, you do not have to enter all of the statements to create an event handler (procedure) as Visual Studio gives you two ways to create event handlers automatically:

» Double-clicking a control instance in the Windows Forms Designer activates the Code Editor and creates the event handler for the control instance's most commonly used event. For example, double-clicking a button in the Windows Forms Designer causes the Visual Studio to create the Click event handler for that button.

» The second technique for automatically creating an event handler is to use the Code Editor along with the Class Name and Method Name combo boxes.

The Class Name combo box displays a drop-down combo box listing the form, along with the control instances created on the form, as shown in Figure 3-27.

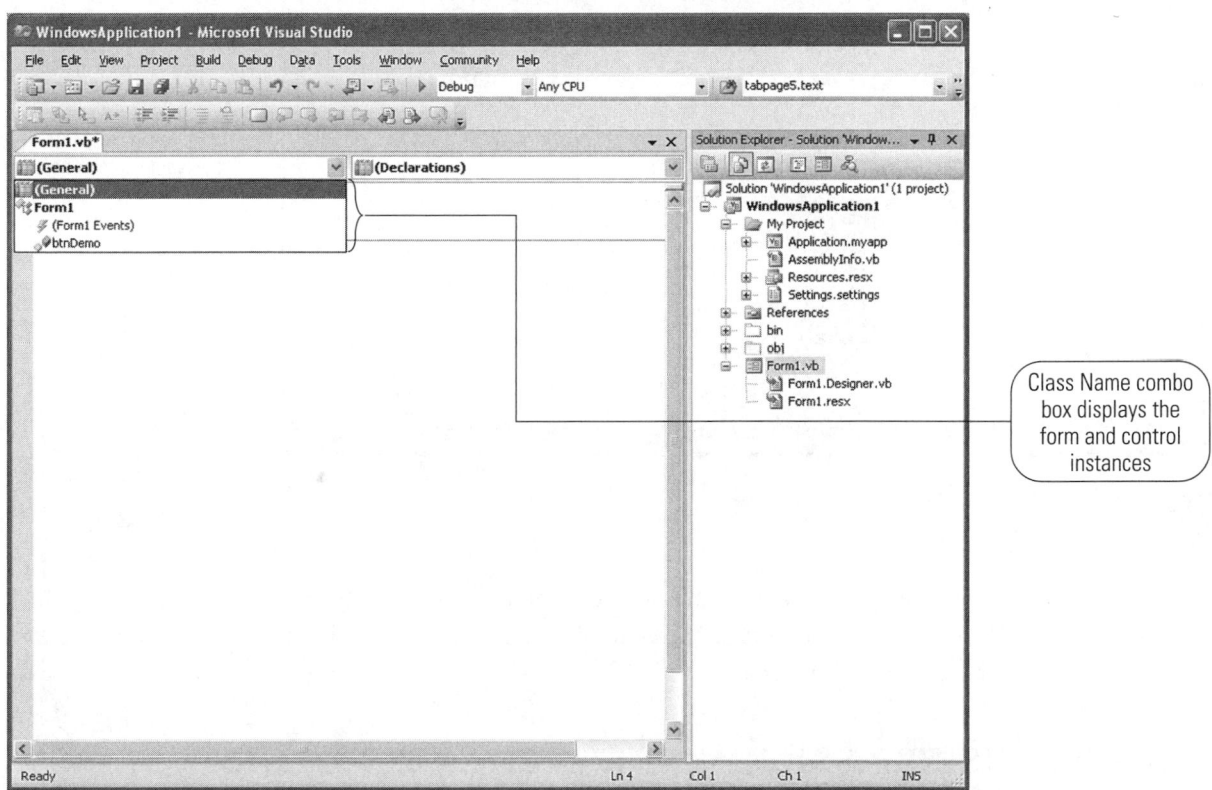

Figure 3-27: Class Name combo box

Figure 3-27 shows a default Windows Application project with a single Button control instance named btnDemo. As additional control instances are created on the form, they will appear in the Class Name combo box too.

After the form or a control instance is selected, the Method Name combo box is updated listing the events applicable to the selected form or control instance. To create or select the desired event handler, click the event name from the list. Visual Studio will either create the event handler or select the event handler if it has already been created. Figure 3-28 shows the Method Name combo box.

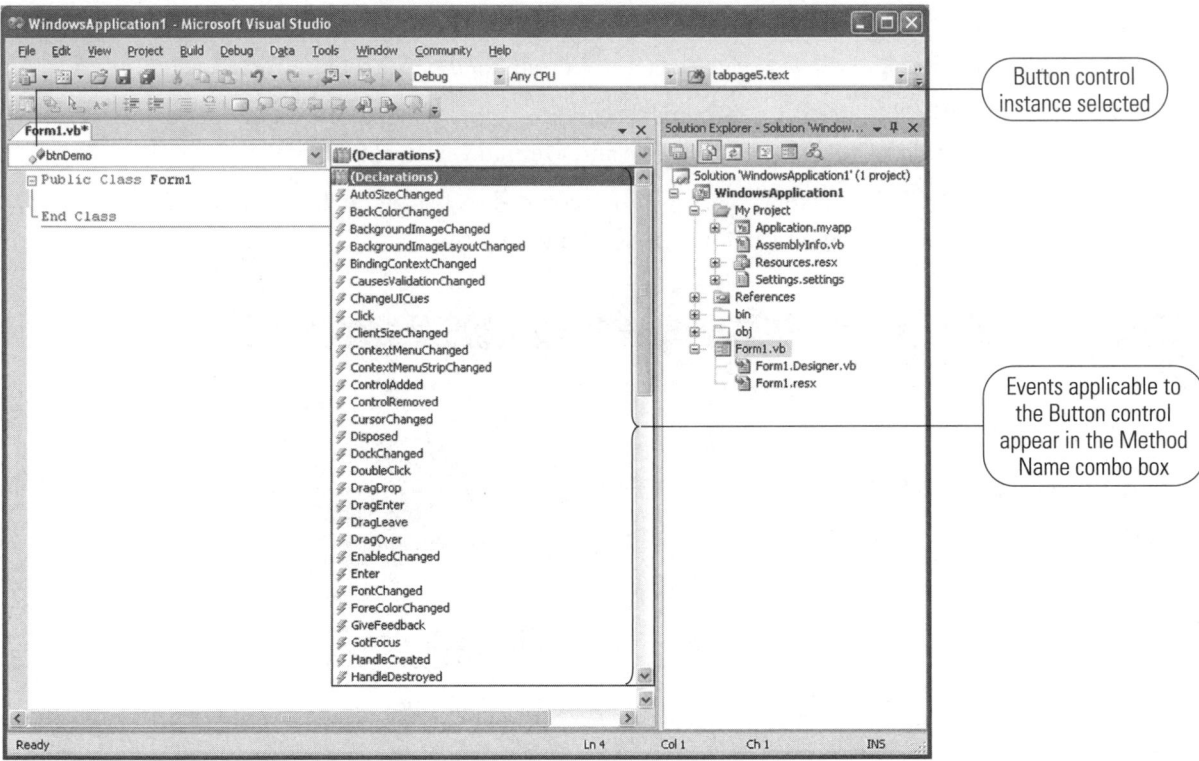

Figure 3-28: Method Name combo box

After the event handler has been created, code can be created in the procedure. Declaration statements and executable statements appear in event handlers just as they do in other procedures.

## USING ASSIGNMENT STATEMENTS TO READ AND WRITE PROPERTIES

Chapters 1 and 2 described how to call methods and read property values using executable statements. There exists another category of statement called an assignment statement. Similar to an algebraic statement, an **assignment statement** is made up of a left side and a right side separated by an equal sign (=). When an assignment statement executes, the expression on the right side is evaluated and the result is stored in the expression appearing on the left side of the assignment statement. The following code segment illustrates a simple assignment statement using a literal string value:

```
Me.Text = "Chapter 3 - Concept Lesson"
```

As shown in the preceding statement, an equal sign separates the left and right sides of the assignment statement. The right side of the assignment statement contains a literal string value. As always, literal string values must be enclosed in quotation marks. Remember that the Me keyword is used to reference the current form instance. Thus, the statement Me.Text is used to reference the Text property of the form. The value of the form's Text property appears in the form's title bar. Thus, when the statement executes, the literal string value appears in the form's title bar.

Some properties, such as the positional properties of a form or control instance, store numeric values instead of string values. When used in assignment or other statements, quotation marks do not surround numeric values. The following code segment stores values in the Top and Left properties of the PictureBox control instance named picCurrent:

```
picCurrent.Top = 0
picCurrent.Left = 0
```

The preceding statements set the Top and Left properties to 0, thereby causing the upper-left corner of the picture box to appear in the upper-left corner of the form itself.

In addition to using literal values on the right side of an assignment statement, it's possible for properties to appear on the right side of an assignment statement as the following statements show:

```
picCurrent.Width = Me.Width
picCurrent.Height = Me.Height
```

The preceding statements reset the Width and Height properties of the picture box named picCurrent. The height and width of the picture box is set to the height and width of the form. Remember that the Me keyword references the current form instance.

Some properties store what are called Boolean values. That is, they store the values True or False. To illustrate, examine the following statements:

```
btnDemo.Visible = False
picCurrent.Enabled = True
```

The preceding statements assume that btnDemo and picCurrent are control instances. The first statement sets the Visible property to False, thereby making the control instance invisible. The second statement sets the Enabled property to True, thereby causing the control instance to respond to events.

In addition to textual and numeric values, you saw that some properties, such as the SizeMode property of a PictureBox, can be set to a value chosen from a list of values. This type of property is called an enumeration. An enumeration is nothing more than a descriptive name used in place of a numeric value.

The SizeMode property can be set using the Properties window or programmatically. The following statements illustrate how to set the SizeMode property of the picture box named picDemo:

```
picDemo.SizeMode = PictureBoxSizeMode.AutoSize
picDemo.SizeMode = PictureBoxSizeMode.CenterImage
picDemo.SizeMode = PictureBoxSizeMode.Normal
picDemo.SizeMode = PictureBoxSizeMode.StretchImage
```

As shown on the left side of the preceding assignment statements, the SizeMode property of the PictureBox control instance named picDemo is being set. The right side of the assignment statement specifies the value to be assigned. For the SizeMode property of the PictureBox control, the possible legal values that can be assigned are predefined as part of an enumeration. Enumerations are discussed more fully in subsequent chapters. For now, you need to know that an enumeration gives meaningful names to a fixed set of values. The possible enumeration values are AutoSize, CenterImage, Normal, and StretchImage. These are the only possible values for the SizeMode property of a PictureBox control.

In addition to properties storing textual values, numeric values, or enumerations, some properties themselves store objects. The primary purpose of the PictureBox control is to display an image, and the image displayed is stored in the Image property. Unlike some properties that store numbers and strings, the Image property references another object having a data type of System.Drawing.Image. This class, in turn, supports a method named FromFile that reads an image from a disk file, and stores it as an Image object.

The following code segment illustrates how to read an image by calling the FromFile method and storing that image in a PictureBox control instance named picDemo:

```
picDemo.Image = _
    System.Drawing.Image.FromFile("C:\House1.jpg")
```

The preceding statement calls the FromFile method of the System.Drawing.Image class. The method accepts one argument: the filename to read. Calling the FromFile method returns an Image object, which is stored in the Image property of the PictureBox control instance.

The syntax to call a method of a control instance is no different than the syntax to call methods of any other class. Suppose that a Label control instance existed and that it is named lblDemo, as shown in the following code:

```
lblDemo.Show()
lblDemo.Hide()
```

The first of the preceding statements displays the control instance and the second statement makes the control instance invisible. Both of the preceding methods accept no arguments.

## MINI-QUIZ 3

1. What is the term used to describe a procedure whose code executes in response to an event?

2. Event procedures are always Sub procedures having two arguments.

   a. True

   b. False

3. What is the keyword that marks a procedure as an event procedure?

4. Describe the syntax error in the following statement:

   ```
   Me.Text = Chapter 3
   ```

# APPLICATION LESSON

# CREATING A WINDOWS APPLICATION PROJECT WITH VISUAL STUDIO

This application lesson contains instructions for using the Visual Studio IDE to create an application's visual interface and the code behind that interface. The application you will develop allows the end user to display graphical images and to stretch and resize them. The Visual Basic PictureBox control makes creating this application surprisingly easy.

## APPLICATION LESSON—USER INTERFACE

The application to display images is an event-driven application made up of the following control instances:

» An instance of the `Label` control displays the filename of the currently displayed image. A second instance of the `Label` control displays a descriptive prompt.

» An instance of the `PictureBox` control displays graphical images.

» A button containing an ellipsis, when clicked, displays an instance of the `OpenFileDialog` control to get the filename from the end user, to load the image file into memory, and, finally, to display the image.

» Three buttons having captions of Center, Normal, and Stretch resize the image appearing in the `PictureBox` control instance.

» The button named Clear removes the displayed image from memory and deletes the text in the `Label` control instance used to display the filename.

» The button named Exit, as the name implies, exits the application.

## APPLICATION LESSON—DESIGN

As mentioned, this application is an event-driven one. In this application lesson, you will create six `Click` event handlers for the `Button` control instances as described in the following list:

» The first displays an `OpenFileDialog` to the end user. The application code then loads the image into the `PictureBox` control instance.

» The next three buttons are used to change how the image in the `PictureBox` control instance are displayed.

» The Clear button's `Click` event handler clears the image from the `PictureBox` control instance.

» The final button's `Click` event handler exits the application.

Figure 3-29 shows the completed flowchart depicting the actions of the form's buttons.

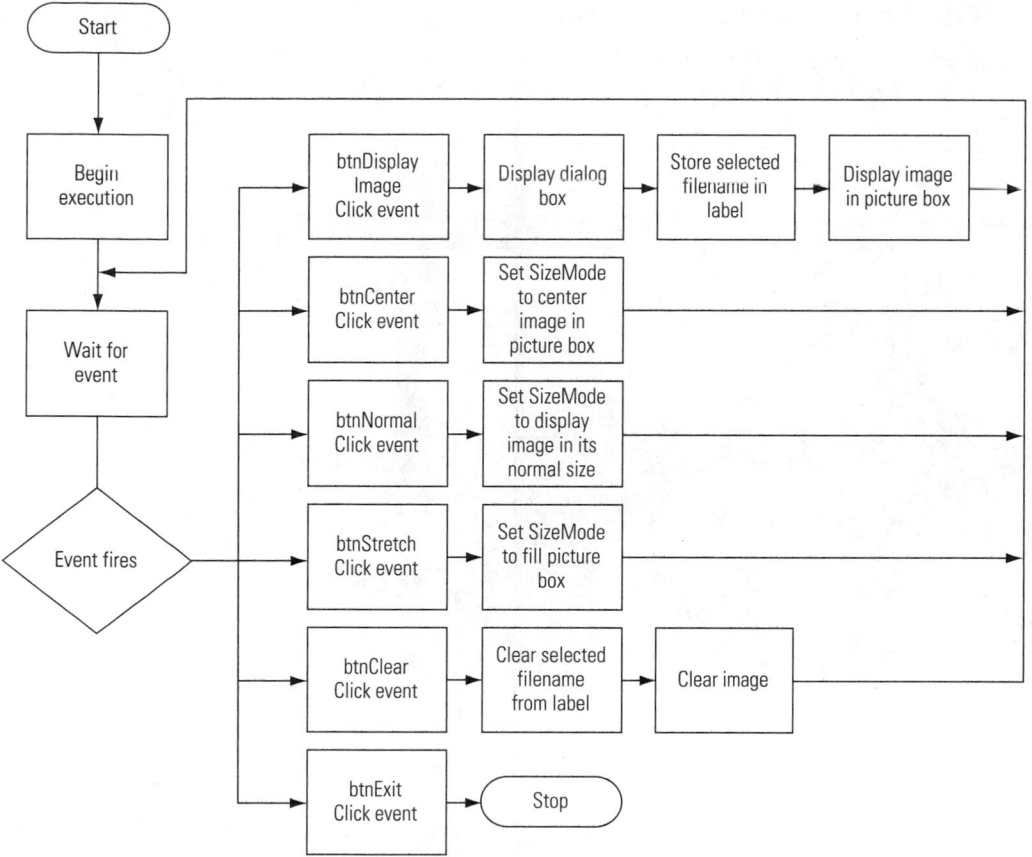

Figure 3-29: Application lesson flowchart

## PREVIEWING THE APPLICATION

At the beginning of each application lesson, you will preview the application that you will create in the hands-on steps. Previewing the application will help you visualize the goals for each application lesson.

To preview the completed application:

1. Start Visual Studio, if necessary, and open the solution file named **Chapter.03\Chapter03ApplicationLessonPreview\Chapter03ApplicationLessonPreview.sln**.

2. Press **F5** to run the solution.

3. Click the **Display Image** button. (This is the button at the upper-right corner of the window with three dots.)

4. In the Open dialog box, navigate to the **Chapter.03\Data03** folder, and then select the file named **Travel.jpg**.

5. Click **Open** to open the file and display the image on the form. The image appears, as shown in Figure 3-30. The name of the file appears in the label at the top of the form. Figure 3-30 shows the visual interface for the completed form while the application is running.

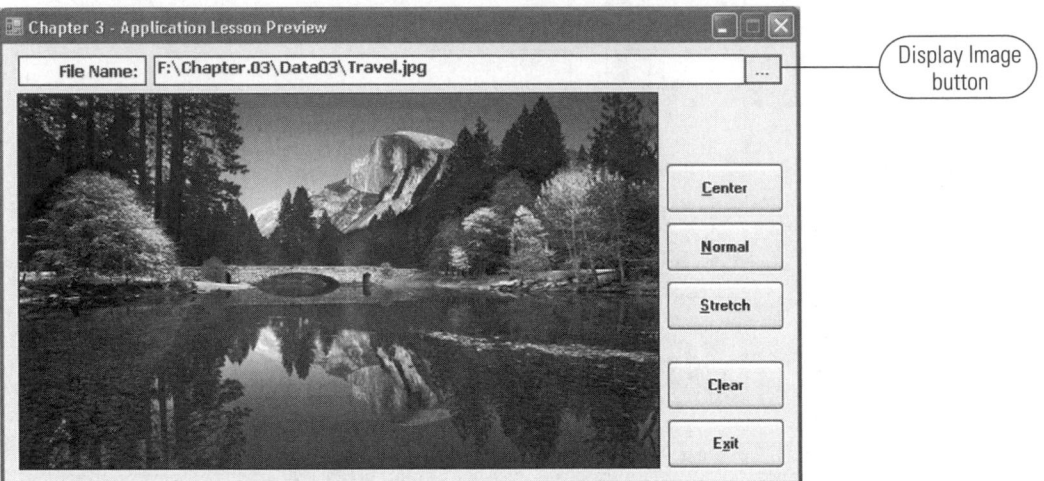

Figure 3-30: Completed form with image displayed

6. Click the **Center**, **Normal**, and **Stretch** buttons to see the effect of the image in the control instance.

7. Click the **Clear** button to clear the image and the filename.

8. Click the **Exit** button to exit the application.

Now that you have explored both the design and implementation of a Windows Application project, you can carry out the steps to create a Windows Application project, create the form and its control instances, and then create the code behind the form.

To create a Windows Application solution:

1. Visual Studio should have already been started. On the menu bar, click **File**, and then click **New Project**. (Note that these steps vary if you are not using the Visual Basic Professional edition.)

2. In the Templates pane, click **Windows Application**, if necessary.

3. Set the project name to **Chapter03ApplicationLesson.sln**, and then click **OK**.

4. Click **File**, **Save All** to display the Save Project dialog box. Save the project in the folder of your choosing.

Properties applicable to the form were discussed previously in the chapter. In this case, the form will be configured so that it is not resizable. From a design perspective, this is reasonable because the control instances have not been configured to be resized if the form were resized. In addition, the form's caption and control box will be configured. The form's caption will be set so as to describe the form's purpose. The Maximize button will be disabled because the control instances will not resize if the form were resized.

To set properties for a form:

1. In the Solution Explorer, right-click the form named **Form1.vb**, and then click **Rename** from the context menu. Type **frmMain.vb**, and then press **Enter**.

2. Activate the Windows Forms Designer, if necessary, by selecting the **frmMain.vb** form in the Solution Explorer, and clicking the **View Designer** button. The form's border appears highlighted and sizing handles appear in the lower-right corner of it.

3. Press **F4**, if necessary, to display the Properties window.

4. Locate and expand the **Size** property. Set the value of the Width property to **652**, and press **Enter**. Set the value of the Height property to **387**, and then press **Enter**. Note that selecting a different property will also change the value of the first property.

5. In the Properties window, expand the **Location** property. Set both the X and Y properties to **72**.

6. Locate the Text property. In the Value column, change the text "Form1" to **Chapter 3 – Application Lesson**, and then press **Enter**. The form's title bar is updated with the new value in the Windows Forms Designer.

7. Locate the FormBorderStyle property in the Properties window. Click the **Value** column to display the list arrow. Click the list arrow to display the list of possible values. Select **FixedSingle**. This setting prohibits the end user from resizing the form at run time.

8. Set the MaximizeBox property to **False** to disable the Maximize button on the form's control box. Note that the Maximize button appears disabled in the Windows Forms Designer.

9. Set the StartPosition property to **Manual** so that the X and Y properties will be used to position the form on the desktop when the application is run.

10. Using the Properties window and the color palette (via the Web tab), set the BackColor property to **WhiteSmoke**.

The next step in the development of the application's user interface is to create the control instances on the form and configure them. As you create the user interface, refer to Figure 3-31, which shows the completed user interface along with the name of each control instance.

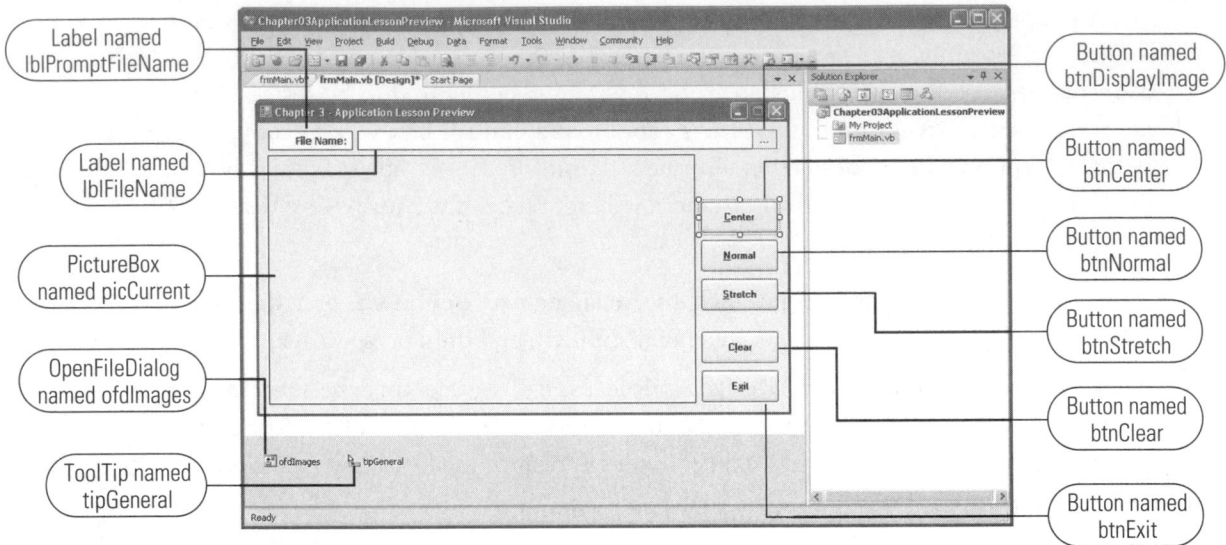

Label named lblPromptFileName

Label named lblFileName

PictureBox named picCurrent

OpenFileDialog named ofdImages

ToolTip named tipGeneral

Button named btnDisplayImage

Button named btnCenter

Button named btnNormal

Button named btnStretch

Button named btnClear

Button named btnExit

Figure 3-31: Completed user interface

To create a form's user interface:

1. Create the first instance of the Label control by first clicking the **Label** control in the Toolbox on the Common Controls tab. Click **View**, **Toolbox**, if necessary to make the Toolbox visible. In the Windows Forms Designer, click and hold down the left mouse button to draw the control instance on the form.

2. Create a second **Label** control instance to the right of the control instance that you just created.

3. Create an instance of the **PictureBox** control, as shown in Figure 3-31.

4. Create six instances of the **Button** control, as shown in Figure 3-31.

5. Create an instance of the **OpenFileDialog** control on the form. Because the control is not visible at run time, the control instance appears in the resizable tray below the form.

6. Using the alignment tools discussed in the concept lesson, align and size the control instances to match Figure 3-31.

Having created the form's control instances, you can now set the properties of those control instances.

To configure the form's control instances:

1. In the Windows Forms Designer, click the **Label1** control instance.

2. Activate the Properties window for the control instance, if necessary, by pressing **F4**.

>> TIP

You could have just as well created each control instance, and then set the properties for each control instance as it was created.

3.  In the Properties window, set the AutoSize property to **False**. Sizing handles surround the selected control instance.

4.  Set the Name property to **lblPromptFileName**. Set the Text property to **File Name:**. Set the BorderStyle property to **FixedSingle**.

5.  To change the font appearing in the label, you need to set the Font property. Locate the Font property in the Properties window. Click the **Value** column. Click the **Build** button (the button with the ellipses) to display the Font dialog box. Set the font style to **Bold**, and then click **OK**.

6.  Locate the BackColor property in the Properties window. Click the **Value** column. Click the **List arrow**, click the **Custom** tab, and then select the first row, first box. When you click the color, it is applied as the background color behind the label text.

7.  Locate the TextAlign property in the Properties window, and then click the **Value** column. Using the visual editor, select **MiddleRight**.

8.  In the Windows Forms Designer, click the **Label2** control instance. Set the Name property to **lblFileName**. Remove the text from the Text property. Set the remaining properties to the same values you used for the control instance named lblPromptFileName.

9.  Activate the Properties window for the PictureBox control instance. Rename the PictureBox control instance so that it is named **picCurrent**. Set the BorderStyle property to **FixedSingle**.

10. Rename the OpenFileDialog control instance so that it is named **ofdImages**.

11. Set the properties for the remaining control instances, as shown in Table 3-3. Use the Object combo box in the Properties window to select the control instances. Use Figure 3-31 to guide you in identifying the correct control instances. Note that the ampersand character marks the button's hot key.

| Name property | Property and values |
|---|---|
| btnDisplayImage | Text: . . . |
| btnCenter | Text: &Center |
| btnNormal | Text: &Normal |
| btnStretch | Text: &Stretch |
| btnClear | Text: C&lear |
| btnExit | Text: E&xit |

Table 3-3: Button control instance settings

Next, you will create ToolTips for the form's Button control instances.

To create ToolTips:

1. Using the ToolTip control in the Toolbox, create an instance of it on the form. Because the ToolTip control is invisible to the end user when the application runs, it appears in the resizable tray below the form. It does not matter where you position the control instance. Using the Properties window, set the Name property to **tipGeneral**.

2. In the Properties window, select the control instance named **btnDisplayImage**. Set the ToolTip on the tipGeneral property to **Click to display an image**.

At this point, you have completed the form's visual interface. Next, you will create the Click event handlers for the various buttons. There are two ways to easily create the Click event handlers for a Button control instance. Double-clicking on a Button control instance in the Windows Forms Designer causes the event handler to be created and the Code Editor to be activated so that it displays the event handler.

The second way to create an event handler is to activate the Code Editor for the form, select the control instance in the Class Name combo box, and then select the event name in the Method Name combo box. In the following steps, you will create the Click event handler for the button named btnDisplayImage.

To create an event handler by double-clicking a button:

1. In the Windows Forms Designer, double-click the **Display Image** button (the one with the ellipsis). Visual Studio creates the Click event handler for the button and activates the Code Editor.

2. Enter the following statements (shown in bold) in the event handler:

```
ofdImages.ShowDialog()
lblFileName.Text = ofdImages.FileName
picCurrent.Image = _
        System.Drawing.Image.FromFile(ofdImages.FileName)
```

The first of the preceding statements displays the OpenFileDialog. The second statement displays the filename selected by the end user in the Label control instance named lblFileName. The final statement displays the image in the PictureBox control instance. Note that a continuation line is used in the statement.

Next, you will create the Click event handler for the Clear button. The code in this event handler will remove the image currently displayed in the control instance by setting the Image property to Nothing.

To clear the image from the picture box:

1. Create the **Click** event handler for the **Clear** button, and then enter the following statements:

```
lblFileName.Text = ""
picCurrent.Image = Nothing
```

Next, the event handler for the Exit button needs to be created. The code in this event handler will exit the application:

To exit the application:

1. Create the **Click** event handler for the **Exit** button, and then enter the following statement:

```
Me.Close()
```

The next group of statements that need to be written control how the image will appear in the PictureBox control instance. Each of these statements will set the SizeMode property to a different enumeration value.

To create event handlers to resize the image:

1. Create the **Click** event handler for the button named **btnCenter**, and then enter the following statement:

```
picCurrent.SizeMode = PictureBoxSizeMode.CenterImage
```

2. Create the **Click** event handler for the button named **btnNormal**, and then enter the following statement:

```
picCurrent.SizeMode = PictureBoxSizeMode.Normal
```

3. Create the **Click** event handler for the button named **btnStretch**, and then enter the following statement:

```
picCurrent.SizeMode = PictureBoxSizeMode.StretchImage
```

At this point in the solution's development, you have created all of the code for the application. Next, you need to test that the code you wrote works correctly.

To test the application:

1. Click the **Start Debugging** button on the Debug toolbar or press **F5**. Visual Studio runs the solution and displays the form. The Visual Studio title bar displays status information, including the text "(Running)" to indicate that the application is running. The application is now waiting for an event to fire.

2. Click the **Display Image** button. The Click event fires for the button. In the dialog box that opens, navigate to the folder named **Chapter.03\Data03**, and then select the file named **Travel.jpg**.

3. In the dialog box, click **Open** to open the file and display the image on the form.

When you stop a solution from running, you change the operating mode from run mode to design mode. As you develop and test solutions, you will frequently run and end an application as you make changes to it.

4. Click the **Exit** button. Visual Studio stops running the application and returns to design mode.

# CHAPTER SUMMARY

» The user interface is an important part of any application. Good design principles include control, user-friendliness, intuitiveness, consistency, feedback, and appropriate use of graphics. Control instances should be vertically or horizontally aligned about the form, and be evenly distributed about the form. In addition, color should be used appropriately.

» This chapter introduced Windows Application projects. Although structurally similar to Console Application projects, Windows Application projects are made up of forms instead of modules. Both types of projects are created using the New Project dialog box. Windows Application projects also reference different namespaces.

» A Windows application project is made up of a form and the code behind the form. The code behind the form is divided into two parts. The first part contains the code automatically generated by the Windows Forms Designer. The second part is made up of the developer-created event handlers. Note that the code automatically generated by the Windows Forms Designer should never be modified directly. Visual Studio implements forms and partial classes. The code automatically generated by the Windows Forms Designer appears in a partial class.

» All Windows forms share certain characteristics. A title bar appears across the top of the form. The title bar has a control box that displays buttons to maximize, minimize, restore, or close the form. Below the title bar appears an optional menu. The region inside the form's border is called the client area.

» Visual control instances appearing on a form are derived from the `System.Windows.Forms.Control` class. Controls created on a form are referred to as control instances. Controls support properties and methods and can be configured to handle events.

» The `Label` control is used to display prompts and application output. Other than that, the end user typically has no interaction with the `Label` control.

» Clickable buttons are derived from the `System.Windows.Forms.ButtonBase` class. These include the `Button`, `CheckBox`, and `RadioButton` controls. This chapter discussed the `Button` control. The `Button` control fires a `Click` event when the end user clicks the button. A button can be configured to display text, an image, or both.

» The `PictureBox` control displays an image based on the setting of the `Image` property. An image is loaded by calling the `System.Drawing.Image.FromFile` method. The size of the image appearing in the control instance can be configured by setting the `SizeMode` property.

» The `OpenFileDialog` control is part of a group of controls collectively referred to as `CommonDialog` controls. The `OpenFileDialog` control supports the `ShowDialog` method to display the dialog box to the end user. The filename selected by the end user is stored in the `FileName` property. As the control instance is not visible to the end user at run time, it appears in the resizable tray below the form.

» The `ToolTip` control is used to create a ToolTip, which is a message that appears when the mouse hovers over a control instance for a few seconds. The `ToolTip` control is called a provider control because it works in conjunction with other control instances.

» Control instances are created on a form by clicking a control in the Toolbox, and then drawing the visible region of the control instance in the Windows Forms Designer.

Sizing handles can be used to resize control instances. Selecting a control instance and dragging it to a new position on the form moves the control instance. The Format menu contains other menus used to align control instances or make the spacing between control instances the same.

» The Properties window supplies the primary means to set properties for control instances. The selected control instance appears in the Object combo box in the Properties window. If multiple control instances are selected, the Object combo box is empty. Properties having different data types support various visual editors used to simplify the process of setting a property's value. Properties are edited using the Value column in the Properties window.

» The code for Windows Application projects appears in event handlers. An event handler is just a form of a Sub procedure. The Handles clause marks a procedure as an event handler. Following the Handles clause appears the control instance name followed by the event name. Event handlers can be created easily using the Code Editor's Class Name and Method Name combo boxes. All event handlers accept two arguments that should not be changed.

# KEY TERMS

**assignment statement**—An assignment statement is made up of a left side and a right side, which are separated by an equal sign. The expression on the left side is evaluated and stored in the expression on the right side.

**command-line interface**—An interface in a Console Application project that displays textual prompts one line at a time.

**control instance**—The buttons and boxes and other visual elements that appear on a form. Control instances are created from controls appearing in the Toolbox.

**event handlers**—The procedures that are automatically executed by Windows as the end user interacts with a form and the control instances created on a form.

**form-based visual interface**—A visual interface that is made up of visual buttons containing control instances.

**hot key**—A set of keystrokes that will produce the same result as clicking a button.

**partial class**—A class whose code appears in two or more physical files. Visual Studio and the Windows Forms Designer implement forms using partial classes.

**prompt**—A message that is commonly used to describe the purpose of another visual element, such as a text box or other control instance.

**provider control**—A type of control that works in conjunction with other control instances. The `ToolTip` control is an example of a provider control.

**Toolbox**—A set of tools containing the visual tools, called controls, which are used to create a form's user interface.

**visual designer**—A general term used to describe an interface or other application element that is created in a visual way. The Windows Forms Designer is a visual designer.

**Windows Forms Designer**—The visual tool used to create a form and the visual elements (control instances) appearing on that form. A more general term for the Windows Forms Designer is a visual designer.

# ANSWERS TO MINI-QUIZZES

## MINI-QUIZ 1

1. a. True

2. e. all of the above

3. `FormBorderStyle` and `StartPosition`

4. The Name column contains an alphabetized or categorized list of property names. The Value column contains the current value of the property. The Value column is used to set the value of properties at design time.

## MINI-QUIZ 2

1. The Toolbox and Windows Forms Designer

2. Prompt

3. The naming convention of using a prefix followed by a descriptive name is called Hungarian notation. For example, the three-character prefix for a button is "btn".

4. The Properties window would display a dialog box indicating that the proposed property value is not valid.

5. c. Names must contain letters, numbers, or the underscore character. Other characters are prohibited.

**MINI-QUIZ 3**

1. event handler

2. a. True

3. `Handles`

4. The literal string on the right side of the assignment statement must be enclosed in quotation marks.

# REVIEW QUESTIONS

1. Which of the following describe guidelines of a good user interface?

   a. Avoid displaying data in rows and columns.

   b. Bright colors should be used wherever possible to create an enticing application.

   c. On any form, use several different fonts to set apart various functional elements.

   d. User interface elements, such as the `Button` control instances on a form, should have the same size and be aligned vertically or horizontally.

   e. all of the above

2. Which of the following is a characteristic of a Windows Application project?

   a. It contains exactly the same physical files as a Console Application project.

   b. Unlike a Console Application project, Windows Application projects do not contain namespace references.

   c. The code for each form in a Windows Application project is stored in two physical files.

   d. Whereas a Console Application project can contain a module, a Windows Application project cannot.

   e. none of the above

3. Which of the following lists of properties defines the size and position of a form or control instance?

   a. `X, Y, Z, Height, Width`

   b. `Top, Left, Height, Width`

   c. `Top, Left, Length, Width`

   d. `X, Y, Height, Width`

   e. none of the above

4. Which of the following statements is correct regarding selecting multiple control instances on a form?

   a. The Shift key and left mouse button can be used to select multiple control instances.

   b. The Pointer tool can be used to select multiple control instances.

   c. Any number of control instances can be selected.

   d. When multiple control instances are selected, only one control instance can be the active selected control instance.

   e. all of the above

5. The Name property of a control instance must _____.

   a. have a letter as its first character, contain less than 255 characters, and contain no spaces

   b. have a letter as its first character, be between 8 and 40 characters in length, and contain only letters of the alphabet (A-Z)

   c. not contain the underscore character or any special character

   d. not contain numbers

   e. all of the above

6. What is the name of the method to unload a form?

   a. Quit

   b. Close

   c. Exit

   d. Remove

   e. none of the above

7. Which of the following statements is correct regarding inheritance related to controls?

   a. The OpenFileDialog control inherits from the Control class.

   b. All clickable buttons inherit from the ButtonBase class, which inherits from the Control class.

   c. All visible controls inherit from the System.Windows.Forms.Form class.

   d. All controls ultimately inherit from the VisibleControl class.

   e. none of the above

8. Which of the following statements is true about controls?

   a. The `Name` property contains the name used to reference the control instance using code.

   b. You use the Toolbox to create control instances on a form.

   c. Multiple instances of the same control can be created on a form.

   d. The Properties window is used to set control instance properties at design time.

   e. all of the above

9. Which of the following statements is true regarding the `Button` control?

   a. It can display text, an image, or both.

   b. Multiple buttons can be created on a form.

   c. It responds to (handles) the `ButtonClick` event.

   d. The `Button` control derives from the `AbstractButton` class.

   e. both a and b

10. Which of the following statements is true regarding the `Label` control?

   a. It is visible to the user at run time.

   b. The `ForeColor` and `BackColor` properties define the color of the text and background, respectively.

   c. The `TextAlign` property determines the alignment of the text within the label.

   d. The `Text` property identifies the text appearing in the label.

   e. all of the above

11. Which of the following statements is correct regarding the `PictureBox` control?

   a. The `PictureBox` control is derived from the `PictureBoxBase` class.

   b. The `Resize` property defines how the image will be resized to fit inside the visible region of the control instance.

   c. The `PictureBox` control can only be used to display bitmap images. Other image formats are not supported.

   d. Like a `Button` control, the `PictureBox` control can handle a `Click` event.

   e. none of the above

12. What is the name of the method supplied by the System.Drawing class used to read an image into an instance of the PictureBox control?

    a. ImageFromFile

    b. ReadFile

    c. ReadImage

    d. Read

    e. FromFile

13. Which of the following statements is correct regarding the OpenFileDialog control?

    a. The OpenFileDialog opens a file. The filename to be opened is passed as an argument to the OpenFile method.

    b. When the end user selects a file in the OpenFileDialog control, the selected file is stored in the FileName property.

    c. To display the dialog box, call the Show method of the underlying System.Windows.Forms.Form class.

    d. Like all visible controls, the OpenFileDialog control derives from the System.Windows.Forms.Controls class.

14. Which of the following statements is correct regarding event handlers?

    a. All event handlers have two arguments that must not be modified.

    b. All event handlers are Sub procedures.

    c. The Code Editor can be used to locate and create event handlers.

    d. Double-clicking a control instance in the Windows Forms Designer creates the most commonly used event handler for the selected control instance.

    e. all of the above

15. What is the name of the keyword used to mark a procedure as an event handler?

    a. EventHandler

    b. Handles

    c. Click

    d. Handler

    e. none of the above

16. List and describe elements of a good user interface. Describe the effect of control positioning and color on the user interface.

17. What is a partial class? Discuss how the Windows Forms Designer uses partial classes to implement forms.

18. List and describe the valid settings for a form's border. In your answer, discuss how these settings affect the end user's ability to resize the form.

19. What is the purpose of the control box? Describe the buttons on the control box, and the properties used to configure those buttons.

20. What is an event handler? In your answer, describe the purpose of the `Handles` clause and the purpose of the `Sub` keyword.

# PROGRAMMING QUESTIONS

1. Write a statement to store the string "Enter a value" into the text of the label named lblQuestion.

2. Write a statement to store the string "Exit" into the caption of the button named btnQuestion.

3. Write a statement to store the caption of the label named lblQuestion into the caption of the button named btnQuestion.

4. Write the statement to make the `Button` control instance named btnDemo invisible.

5. Write the statement to disable the `Button` control instance named btnDemo.

6. Write the statement to exit the application.

7. Write a statement to display the `OpenFileDialog` control instance named ofdQuestion. Display the filename entered by the user in the `Label` control instance named lblQuestion.

8. Write a statement to load the picture named "A:\Pic1.bmp" into the `PictureBox` named picOne.

9. Write a statement to load a picture into the `PictureBox` named picOne, assuming that the filename is stored in the label named lblOne.

10. Write the `Click` event handler for the button named btnOK. The statements in the event handler should store your name, address, city, state, and zip code into each of the following labels: lblName, lblAddress, lblCity, lblState, lblZipCode.

11. Write the `Click` event handler for the button named btnClear. The statements in the event handler should clear the text from the `Label` control instances named lblName, lblAddress, lblCity, lblState, lblZipCode.

12. Write the statement to configure the `PictureBox` control instance named picDemo so that the image will be resized to match the size of the control instance.

13. Write the statements to configure the `PictureBox` control instance named picDemo so that its position is the upper-left corner of the form. Make the size of the control instance the same size as the form.

14. Assume that a form contains a `Label` control instance named lblDemo and a `Button` control instance named btnDemo. Write the statements to make the button visible and the label invisible. Set the size and position of the button so that they are the same as the size and position of the label.

15. Write the statements to remove the image from the `PictureBox` control instance named picDemo. In addition, make the control instance invisible.

# HANDS-ON PROJECTS

1. In this hands-on project, you will create a solution that simulates the effect of a stoplight. A stoplight can be green, yellow, or red. To accomplish this task, you will need to create an instance of the `PictureBox` control and call the `FromFile` method of the `Image` class to display three similar pictures. Each picture shares a common characteristic—they all resemble a stoplight. Each picture, however, has a slightly different appearance. That is, each displays the same stoplight but illuminates a different light. To demonstrate the effect of the stoplight, you will create three buttons (Stop, Caution, and Go) that display the correct image when clicked. Each control instance should have an appropriate name and caption. When a particular button is clicked, the image corresponding to that button should appear in the `PictureBox` control instance.

a. For selected exercises in this book, an executable version of the solution is provided so that you can visualize the completed solution. To run these executable files, double-click the file from Windows Explorer. Run the executable file named **Chapter.03\HandsOnProjects\Ch03HandsOnProject1.exe**. Set the drive designator as necessary. Click each button, noting how the icon changes as each button is clicked. (For the solution to work properly, the icon files must reside in the same folder as the executable application.)

b. Create a new solution file named **Ch03HandsOnProject1**.

c. Rename the form and set the filename of the form to **frmMain** and **frmMain.vb**, respectively.

d. Set the appropriate property so that the title bar of the form contains the text **Chapter 3 – Hands-on Project 1**. Also, set the necessary property so that the form appears in the center of the desktop when the solution runs. Set the necessary properties so that the end user cannot resize, maximize, or minimize the form.

e. Resize the form.

f. Create an instance of the `PictureBox` control on the form. Refer to the completed executable version for an example.

g. Set the name of the control instance to **picStopLight**.

h. Set the necessary property so that the picture will fill in the region of the `PictureBox` control instance. Set the necessary property so that a single line border surrounds the picture box.

i. Create three buttons on the form. Set the `Text` properties of the buttons to **Go**, **Caution**, and **Stop**, respectively. Create a fourth button and set its `Text` property to **Exit**. Create hot keys for the `Button` control instances.

j. Set the `Name` property for each button using the correct prefix. Make sure the name conveys the purpose of each control instance.

k. Using the formatting tools described in the chapter, align the buttons and make them the same size. Also, selecting all of the buttons at once, make the font bold.

l. Write the necessary statement to exit the solution when the end user clicks the Exit button.

m. Display the image named **Chapter.03\Data03\Stop.ico** in the object named **picStopLight**, using the following statement. This statement should appear in the `Click` event handler for the Stop button. Change the drive designator and pathname, depending on the location of the student files on your computer.

```
picStopLight.Image = System.Drawing.Image.FromFile( _
    "A:\Chapter.03\Data03\Stop.ico")
```

n. Write the necessary statements in the `Click` event handler for the Caution and Go buttons to display the corresponding bitmap file in the `PictureBox` control instance. The relevant images are stored in the files **Chapter.03\Data03\Caution.ico** and **Chapter.03\Data03\Go.ico**.

o. Create a `ToolTip` control instance on the form and name it **tipGeneral**.

p. In the `PictureBox` control instance, display the text "Image appears here" in the ToolTip.

q. Test the solution. Click each button to make sure a sign appears with the green, yellow, and red light visible.

2. In this hands-on project, you will create an image viewer. This image viewer will demonstrate the effect of each setting pertaining to the `SizeMode` property of the `PictureBox` control.

a. Run the executable file named **Chapter.03\HandsOnProjects\Ch03HandsOn Project2.exe**. Click the **Display** button to display the Open dialog box. Load the image named **Chapter.03\Data03\Advance1.bmp**. Note that the image appears in three `PictureBox` control instances. Exit the solution by clicking the **Exit** button.

b. Create a new solution file named **Ch03HandsOnProject2**.

c. Change the form size and caption. Refer to the completed executable version for an example. Rename the form to **frmMain.vb**, and set the start-up object as necessary.

d. Configure the form so that it cannot be resized or maximized. It should be possible to minimize the form, however.

e. Create the buttons, labels, and picture boxes. Set the captions and button names as appropriate. Use the Arial font and a bold typeface for all text, and use a single line border to surround all control instances. Center the text in the descriptive labels above the picture boxes.

f. Configure the first picture box to display the image using its original size. The second picture box should display the image stretched. The final picture box should center the image in the control instance.

g. Create hot keys for the buttons.

h. Create an instance of the `OpenFileDialog` control, and set its `Name` property as appropriate.

i. Create the code for the **Display** button to display an `OpenFileDialog`, allowing the end user to select a filename. The code should display the image selected by the end user in the three `PictureBox` control instances. Also, display the filename in the descriptive `Label` control instance.

j. Create the code for the **Clear** button to remove the text from the descriptive label, and remove the image from the three picture boxes.

k. Create the code for the **Exit** button to end the solution.

l. Save and test the solution.

3. In this hands-on project, you will create an application that will resize the contents of a `PictureBox` control instance while the application runs.

a. Run the executable file named **Chapter.03\HandsOnProjects\Ch03HandsOn Project3.exe**. A form appears with a `PictureBox` control instance and `Label` control instances used as prompts and several buttons. Click the **Open File** button. In the dialog box that opens, select the image file named **House1.jpg**. Click the buttons titled **Normal Image**, **Center Image**, and **Stretch Image**. Note the image is updated in the picture box. A label appearing above the picture box is also updated to reflect the status of the picture box. Click the **Exit** button to end the application.

b. Create a new solution file named **Ch03HandsOnProject3**.

c. Configure the form's border style so that the form cannot be resized and the control box does not appear.

d. The background color of the form should be silver.

e. Create the control instances on the form using the completed project as an example.

f. Create the code for the Open File button. The code for the button's `Click` event handler should display an instance of the `OpenFileDialog` control. Using the filename selected by the end user, display the corresponding image in the `PictureBox` control instance. Display the filename in the corresponding `Label` control instance.

g. Create the code for the Normal Image, Center Image, and Stretch Image buttons. The code for each button should cause the `PictureBox` control to display the image normally, centered in the control instance, and stretched to fit inside the region of the control instance, respectively. In addition, display the current status of the picture box in the label appearing just above the picture box.

h. Write the necessary statement in the `Click` event handler to exit the application.

4. In this hands-on project, you will work with the `My.Computer` object discussed in Chapter 2. The first button in the completed form displays information about the mouse, the second button displays information about the computer hardware and the operating system version, the third button displays information about the network, and the final button exits the application.

a. Run the executable file named **Chapter.03\HandsOnProjects\Ch03Hands OnProject4.exe**. Click each of the different buttons. As you click each button, note that a label below the button becomes visible indicating which information is being displayed. In addition, the labels displaying the output also become visible and invisible based on the number of rows of information displayed. That is, if one row of information is being displayed, only one row of output labels is visible. Each output row is made up of a descriptive prompt and an output data item.

b. Create a new solution file named **Ch03HandsOnProject4**.

c. Change the form size and caption using the completed executable version as an example. Make sure the end user cannot resize the form, and that the form appears in the center of the desktop when run.

d. Create 10 instances of the Label control to display the output data. The left column will display a descriptive prompt and the right column will display the value of a property of the My object. Create four buttons along the bottom of the form. Set their names and captions as appropriate. Create meaningful names for these control instances.

e. Create three more Label control instances below the buttons that will display the data. These buttons will just display a background color to indicate the data that is currently being displayed.

f. Next, you need to create the code for the buttons. For the first button, use the My object to determine whether a mouse wheel is present and whether the mouse buttons are swapped. For this button, update the descriptive prompt and data for the first and second output rows. Make the control instances in the remaining three rows invisible.

g. For the second button, display information about the current computer, including the available physical memory, the available virtual memory, the full name of the operating system, the platform, and the version of the operating system. As there are five data items, make all five output rows visible, and update the prompts and data contents as necessary.

h. For the final button, display whether the network is available. For this button, there is only one data item. Thus, only the first output row should be visible, and the remaining output rows should be invisible.

i. As each of the preceding buttons is clicked, update the label below the button to make it visible, and make the other labels invisible.

j. When the application is first started, only the buttons should be visible. Configure the control instances accordingly.

k. Finally, create the code for the button to exit the application.

# 4

# INTRODUCTION TO NUMERIC DATA TYPES AND VARIABLES

**After completing this chapter, you will be able to:**

Process numeric data

Describe different data types and reference types

Declare and use variables

Create user-defined constants and use expressions

Work with numeric data types and convert data between
numeric and string data types

Work with intrinsic functions and methods

Learn how to use the `TextBox` control

Define the order in which control instances get input focus

# CONCEPT LESSON

The first three chapters of this book described the structure of a Console Application project and a Windows Application project and how to use selected predefined .NET Framework classes, along with their properties and methods, to perform tasks such as displaying system information and loading images. However, most applications must get input data from the end user, store that input, perform calculations on that input, and display the results of those calculations.

This chapter describes how to create control instances on a form in which the end user enters text. This text must then be converted into a numeric form and arithmetic and financial calculations must be performed on that numeric data. The results (outputs) of those calculations must be displayed back to the end user as textual data.

## INTRODUCTION TO DATA TYPES AND DATA TYPE STORAGE

In Chapters 1 through 3, you stored data in the properties of objects such as the `Text` property of a `Label` control instance, or the `Image` property of a `PictureBox` control instance. However, the topic of how that data is stored in memory or how data is converted from one data type to another was not discussed. In this section of the chapter, you will learn how different types of data are stored in memory.

The reason to study this topic might not be obvious because Visual Studio takes care of storing data in memory automatically. However, understanding how data is stored in memory will help to explain why data must be converted from one data type to another and the problems that arise when type conversion between data types is performed.

In Chapters 2 and 3, you learned that objects have properties that store data. Every property has a **data type** that determines the kind of data the property can store. Some data types store numbers and are referred to as numeric data types. Numeric data types can be subdivided into two categories:

>> Numeric data types can store floating-point numbers (numbers with a decimal point).

>> Numeric data types can also store integral values. An integral data type can store a positive or negative number and the value 0. Integral numbers have no fractional value and, thus, have no decimal point.

Other data types store strings of characters or dates. Finally, other data types store object references.

## INTEGRAL DATA TYPES

Visual Studio supports different data types to store integral values. The differences between these data types are the amount of memory allocated to store the data, and whether the stored value can be negative. Table 4–1 lists the Visual Basic integral data types and the possible ranges of values for these types.

| Data type | Storage size | Possible values |
|-----------|--------------|-----------------|
| Byte | 1 byte | Numbers between 0 and 255 |
| SByte | 1 byte | Positive and negative numbers between −128 and +127, and the value 0 |
| UShort | 2 bytes | Numbers between 0 and 65,535 |
| Short | 2 bytes | Positive and negative numbers between −32,768 and 32,767, and the value 0 |
| UInteger | 4 bytes | Numbers between 0 and 4,294,967,295 |

Table 4-1: Integral data types *(Continued)*   ▶

| Data type | Storage size | Possible values |
|-----------|--------------|-----------------|
| Integer | 4 bytes | Positive and negative numbers between −2,147,483,648 and 2,147,483,647, and 0 |
| ULong | 8 bytes | Numbers between 0 and 18,446,744,073,709,551,615 |
| Long | 8 bytes | Positive and negative numbers between −9,223,372,036,854,775,808 and 9,223,372,036,854,775,807, and 0 |

Table 4-1: Integral data types

**»NOTE**

Unsigned data types are new to Visual Basic 2005.

All integral values are stored as binary numbers. Table 4–2 illustrates how the counting numbers from 0 to 15 are stored in binary using the SByte data type. The Decimal column shows the counting number. The Binary column shows the number expressed in binary.

To understand why the range of an SByte is a value between −128 and +127 and an Integer value is between −2,147,483,648 and 2,147,483,647, recall that an SByte can be positive or negative or 0. That is, an SByte value is *signed*. One bit in the SByte value is called the **sign bit**, and it is used to denote whether the value is positive or negative. Thus, of the 8 bits used to store the SByte, 7 bits store the value itself and one bit denotes the value's sign. Most computer languages, and Visual Basic is no exception, use the leftmost or high-order bit as a number's sign bit. If the SByte value is positive or zero, the sign bit is 0. If the value is negative, the sign bit is 1.

| Decimal | Binary | Decimal | Binary |
|---------|--------|---------|--------|
| 0 | 00000000 | 8 | 00001000 |
| 1 | 00000001 | 9 | 00001001 |
| 2 | 00000010 | 10 | 00001010 |
| 3 | 00000011 | 11 | 00001011 |
| 4 | 00000100 | 12 | 00001100 |
| 5 | 00000101 | 13 | 00001101 |
| 6 | 00000110 | 14 | 00001110 |
| 7 | 00000111 | 15 | 00001111 |

Table 4-2: Decimal and binary values

Because each bit can store two possible values, 0 or 1, and there are 7 bits available to store the actual value, the largest possible positive value for the SByte data type is $2^7 - 1$ or 127. This number has the following binary pattern:

```
01111111
```

It is possible to compute the value of this representation in much the same way the base ten representation of a number is computed. Thus, the preceding sequence of 1s represents the value (reading left to right) as follows:

```
= 2^6 + 2^5 + 2^4 + 2^3 + 2^2 + 2^1 + 2^0
=  64 +  32 +  16 +   8 +   4 +   2 +   1
= 127
```

Expressed in binary, the arithmetic appears as follows:

```
00000001 (2^0)
00000010 (2^1)
00000100 (2^2)
00001000 (2^3)
00010000 (2^4)
00100000 (2^5)
01000000 (2^6)
01111111 (2^6 + 2^5 + 2^4 + 2^3 + 2^2 + 2^1 + 2^0)
```

The `Integer` data type works similarly. The `Integer` data type is stored in 32 bits, so the largest value is $2^{31} - 1$ or 2,147,483,647. This number has the following binary pattern:

```
0111 1111 1111 1111 1111 1111 1111 1111
```

In the preceding code segment, all of the value bits are turned on. The sign bit is turned off indicating that the number is positive. Spaces were inserted every four bits to improve readability.

The largest negative value that can be stored in an `SByte` is $2^7$ or –128, and the largest negative value that can be stored in an `Integer` is $2^{31}$ or –2,147,483,648. How Visual Basic, and most computer languages for that matter, store negative integral values requires a bit of explanation. Given what has been said so far, the high-order bit in an `SByte` or `Integer` represents a value's sign. Because negative numbers have a sign bit value of 1, you might think that the value (–1) would be stored as follows:

```
1000 0001 (SByte)
1000 0000 0000 0000 0000 0000 0000 0001 (Integer)
```

This is not the case, however. Negative integral values are represented in a form called **two's complement**. Computers represent negative integral values in this way for two reasons. First, using two's complement, there is only one representation of the value 0. Without two's complement, the following binary patterns would represent positive 0 and negative 0:

```
0000 0000
1000 0000
```

Second, it is very efficient for the computer hardware to perform addition and subtraction of integral values using two's complement arithmetic.

The rules to represent a negative integral value using two's complement consist of the following three steps:

1. Start with the binary representation of a positive number.

2. Flip the value of each bit. That is, if the value is 0, it becomes 1, and if the value is 1, it becomes 0. This step forces the sign bit to have a value of 1 because the sign bit of all positive integral numbers is 0.

3. Finally, add one to the number created in Step 2.

The following example shows how to calculate the binary two's complement value of the number –42.

First, start with the positive representation of the number:

```
0010 1010
```

Second, flip each bit as follows:

```
1101 0101
```

Finally, add one to the value so that the result becomes:

```
1101 0110
```

Visual Studio supports an unsigned `Byte` data type, an unsigned short data type (`UShort`), and an unsigned integer (`UInteger`) data type among others. For these data types, all 8, 16, or 32 bits are used to store the value because there is no need for the sign bit. Thus, the largest possible value for an unsigned `Integer` is $2^{\wedge}32 - 1$ or 4,294,967,295.

In this exploration exercise, you will see how signed and unsigned integral types are stored in memory.

1. Start Visual Studio, if necessary, and open the solution file appearing in the folder named **Chapter.04\Chapter04ConceptLesson**.

2. Run the application. The Binary Format tab should be active.

3. Click the **Maximum Value (Integer)** and **Minimum Value (Integer)** buttons. The maximum and minimum values for the `Integer` data type appear in the form's control instances, and the binary representation of the value appears, as shown in Figure 4–1.

4. Click the **Maximum Value (UInteger)** and **Minimum Value (UInteger)** buttons. The maximum and minimum values for the `UInteger` data type appear in the form's control instances and the binary representation of the value appears.

5. Enter a value of your choosing in the Value text box. Click the **Show Format (Integer)** button. The number is converted to its binary representation and displayed in the form's labels.

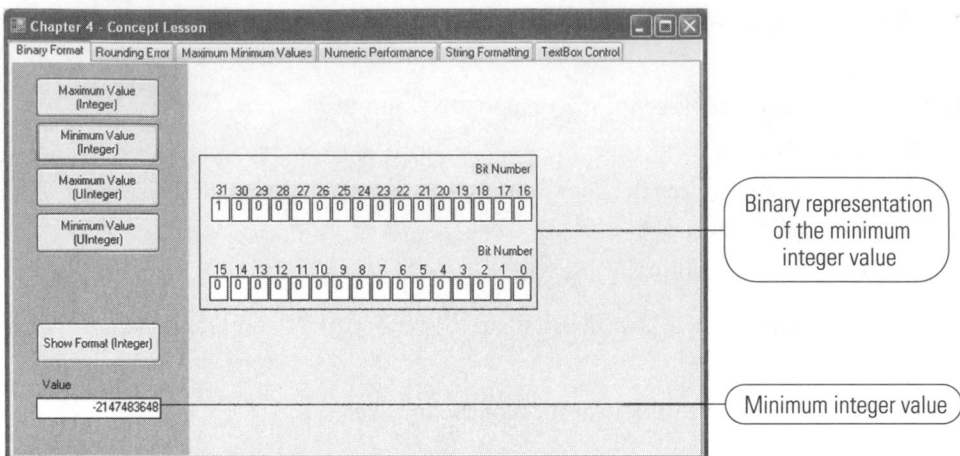

Figure 4-1: Concept lesson—Binary Format tab

## FLOATING-POINT DATA TYPES

In addition to integral data types, Visual Basic has data types to store numbers containing a decimal point. These numbers are called **floating-point numbers**. Table 4–3 lists the Visual Basic floating-point data types.

| Data type | Storage size | Possible values |
| --- | --- | --- |
| Single | 4 bytes | A positive or negative floating-point number having at most seven digits of precision (digits to the right of the decimal point). |
| Double | 8 bytes | A positive or negative floating-point number having at most 15 digits of precision (digits to the right of the decimal point). |
| Decimal | 16 bytes | The Decimal data type has the greatest precision of all numeric types and is commonly used in financial calculations to avoid loss of precision. |

Table 4-3: Floating-point data types

A floating-point number is stored much differently than an integral number. The Visual Basic `Single` data type stores a floating-point number as a 32-bit value according to a standard defined by the Institute of Electronics and Electrical Engineers (IEEE). This 32-bit value is expressed in a form of scientific notation and is divided into the following parts:

» One bit is designated as the sign bit.

» A 23-bit mantissa is used to represent a number greater than or equal to 1.0 and less than 2.0. The mantissa describes the fractional part of the number. The high-order bit is always 1, so it is not stored in the mantissa's value. Thus, the mantissa is actually a 24-bit value.

» The exponent is stored in the remaining 8 bits.

Figure 4–2 illustrates the format of the `Single` data type and the representation of the value –0.25.

Decimal value is –0.25

| Bit 31 | Bits 30–23 | Bits 22–0 |
|---|---|---|
| Sign bit | Exponent | Mantissa |
| 1 | 01111101 | 00000000000000000000001 |

Figure 4-2: Representation of a 32-bit single precision value

The problem with storing a floating-point number as a fixed-size binary value is that a floating-point number is an approximation of an actual value. Because only 23 bits are allocated to store the decimal part of the number, a fraction such as 2/3 repeats indefinitely. Because such a value must be stored in 32 bits, it must be rounded in some way. That is, the decimal equivalent of 2/3 is 0.6666666666, which repeats indefinitely. Thus, the number must be rounded to be stored as a binary value in 32 bits. The value 2/3 stored as a `Single` data type is represented as 0.6666667. This required rounding introduces a small amount of error in the representation of a real number using the floating-point model. Unless many computations are performed on the floating-point values, the error might not be noticed.

When arithmetic operations are performed on floating-point values, an error is introduced. This error is called a **rounding error**. To illustrate, suppose an average is being calculated on a list of numbers. If the list contains 10 numbers each having a value of 0.6666667, the average value would obviously be 0.6666667. However, because of rounding errors, the average values can become inaccurate. Table 4–4 shows the total and average values for lists having 10, 20, and 30 items, each having a value of 0.6666667. As you can see, at 10 and 30 iterations, the value is incorrect due to a rounding error.

| Number of items with the value of 0.6666667 | Total | Average |
|---|---|---|
| 10 | 6.66666600000 | 0.6666666 |
| 20 | 13.33333000000 | 0.6666667 |
| 30 | 20.00000000000 | 0.6666666 |

Table 4-4: Rounding errors

When working with currency values, rounding errors can become problematic. To address this problem, Visual Basic supports the Decimal data type. Like the other primary data types, the Decimal data type is a value type. The MinValue and MaxValue fields define the minimum and maximum values. The Decimal data type stores data as a 128-bit signed number. 96 bytes store an integral value. The remaining 32 bits store the scaling factor, which represents the number of digits to the right of the decimal point.

When programming, it is up to the developer to choose the data type that provides the most accurate representation of actual data being stored. Thus, choosing the correct data type is critical.

## PROPERTIES OF NUMERIC DATA TYPES

Each of the numeric data types has two constant fields that identify the minimum and maximum values for the specified data type. These fields are named MinValue and MaxValue, respectively. The following statements print the minimum and maximum values for the Int16 (Short) and Single data types:

```
System.Console.WriteLine(System.Int16.MinValue)
System.Console.WriteLine(System.Int16.MaxValue)
System.Console.WriteLine(System.Single.MinValue)
System.Console.WriteLine(System.Single.MaxValue)
```

The preceding statements print the minimum and maximum values for the two data types to the Console window.

In this exploration exercise, you will see how rounding errors can affect floating-point operations, and you will see the minimum and maximum values that can be stored in numeric data types.

1. Run the concept lesson's application named **Chapter04ConceptLesson**.

2. Click the **Rounding Error** tab.

3. The value 1,000,000 (minus the commas) is automatically selected in the combo box. This value contains the number of iterations that will be performed.

4. Click the **Show Rounding Error (Single)** button. The fractional value 2/3 (0.6666667) is being accumulated and the average value is calculated using the `Single` data type. The form's text box displays the iteration count, the total value, and the average value in the list every 100,000 iterations, as shown in Figure 4–3.

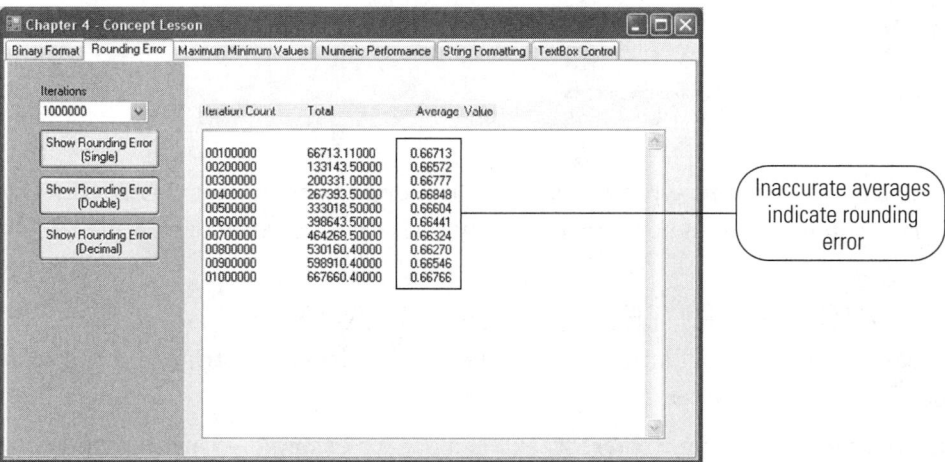

Figure 4-3: Concept lesson—Rounding Error tab

As you can see, the larger the number of iterations, the greater the rounding error.

5. Click the **Show Rounding Error (Double)** button and the **Show Rounding Error (Decimal)** button. The same arithmetic operations are performed using the `Double` and `Decimal` data types. Note that the rounding error is less for the `Double` data type, and even less for the `Decimal` data type.

6. Click the **Maximum Minimum Values** tab.

7. Click the **Show Minimum Maximum Values** button. The minimum and maximum values for the respective data types appear, as shown in Figure 4–4.

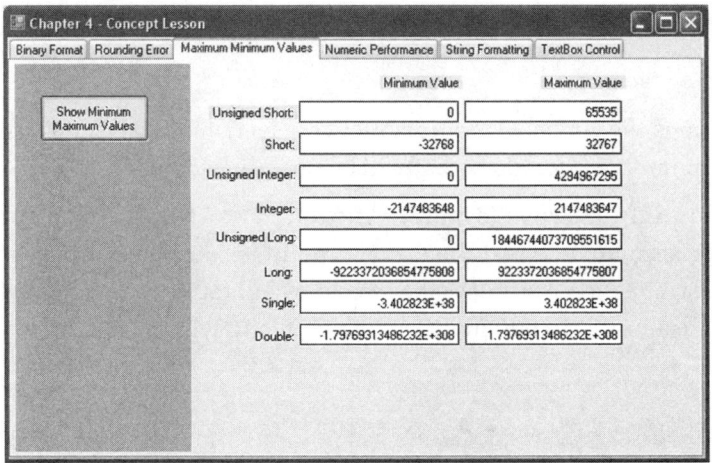

Figure 4-4: Concept lesson—Maximum Minimum Values tab

In addition to numeric data types, Visual Basic also supports nonnumeric data types. One of the most commonly used nonnumeric data types is the `String` data type.

## INTRODUCTION TO THE STRING DATA TYPE

This section contains a brief introduction to the `String` data type. Strings are important in programming for three reasons.

» First, they are used to represent textual data. For example, strings are important for representing and manipulating names and addresses.

» When the end user enters data, that data is represented as a string of characters. That data must be converted to numeric data before arithmetic operations can be performed on the data.

» Strings are also used to display output of numeric and other data types. Later in this chapter, you will see how to convert numeric data types to and from strings.

Unlike the numeric data types, each character making up a string of characters is stored as an individual character rather than as a binary number. Internally, Visual Basic stores strings as Unicode characters. Using the Unicode character set, each character is stored as a 2-byte (16-bit) coded value. In this way, 65,535 unsigned values can be stored in 16 bits. This is the same number of values that can be stored in an unsigned `Short` (`UShort`). Unicode characters are represented as follows:

**»NOTE**

Additional string-processing techniques and string applications are discussed in more detail in Chapter 5.

» The first 127 values store the letters, numbers, and symbols appearing on U.S. computer keyboards. For example, the code for the lowercase letter "a" is 97, and the code for the digit "1" is 49.

» The values 128 to 255 are for special characters such as the keyboard arrows and function keys.

» The values 256 to 65,535 are used to store most of the common international characters and diacritical marks. For example, French uses a grave accent and German uses an umlaut.

Suppose that the end user entered the value 15. When the end user enters a value at the keyboard, that value is stored as a string rather than as a number. To illustrate how the same value can be stored differently, the value 15 expressed using the `Short` data type would be represented in binary as:

**»NOTE**

Refer to Appendix B for a list of textual characters.

```
0000 0000 0000 1111
```

However, stored as two Unicode characters, the value would be expressed much differently, as shown in Figure 4–5.

Digit "1"
```
0000 0000 0011 0001
```

Digit "5"
```
0000 0000 0011 0101
```

2 bytes per character (16 bits)

2 bytes per character (16 bits)

2 characters stored in 32 bits

Figure 4-5: Representation of a Unicode string

As shown in Figure 4–5, each Unicode character is stored in two bytes. The character "1" is stored in the first two bytes, and the character "5" is stored in the third and fourth bytes. The important point to be made is that these are two entirely different representations of the value 15.

The purpose of this section is not to describe every topic related to the storage and use of Unicode characters. Rather, the purpose is to show how character strings are stored differently than integral or floating-point numbers. Because integral numbers, floating-point numbers, and strings are represented in memory differently, it becomes clear that data must be converted from one data type to another as operations are performed on that data. Such conversion is important to ensure that the results obtained when manipulating these data types are correct.

## SUMMARY OF DATA TYPE STORAGE

As you will see while working through this chapter, choosing the correct data type for a variable is important. For example, if a variable will contain only integral data, the SByte, Short, Integer, or Long data types should be used. You should use the Single or Double data types for floating-point values, and you should use the Decimal data type when numbers represent currency values.

## PERFORMANCE OF NUMERIC DATA TYPES

The preceding sections discussed the amount of memory consumed by the various numeric data types and how data is stored in memory. There are performance implications for the various numeric data types too. Performance is a key characteristic of any application. That is, the application must be responsive to the end user. In most simple applications, performance is not a problem. However, when creating mathematical applications that perform calculations millions of times, or business applications that process data files containing millions of records, overall application performance and response time must be considered.

Each numeric data type has performance characteristics. Arithmetic operations using the Long data type perform more slowly than arithmetic operations using the Integer or Short data types. Arithmetic performed using the Double and Single data types is faster than arithmetic performed using the Decimal data type.

In this exploration exercise, you will examine the performance of arithmetic operations using different numeric data types. Although a full explanation of the code for this exercise is beyond the scope of the chapter, you will see arithmetic operations performed many times for each of the various data types.

1. Run the concept lesson's application named **Chapter04ConceptLesson**.

2. Click the **Numeric Performance** tab.

3. In the Number of Iterations combo box, select the number of times the arithmetic operations should be performed. Click the **Start Tests** button. As each test starts and ends, messages are displayed in the text box. Checking and unchecking the form's check boxes enables and disables a particular test. The elapsed time to perform the arithmetic operations appear in the form's output labels, as shown in Figure 4–6.

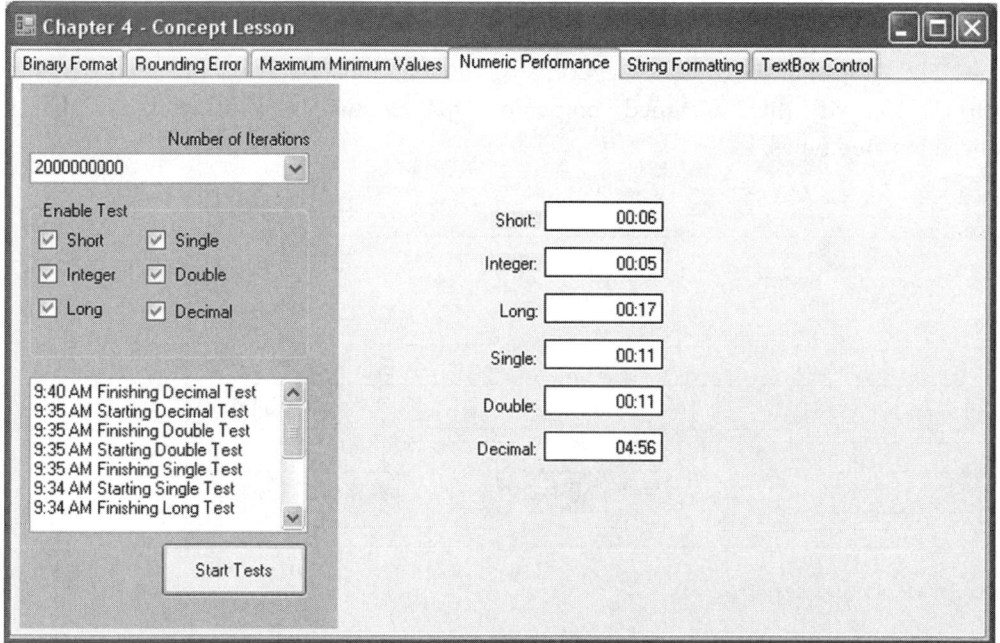

Figure 4-6: Concept lesson—Numeric Performance tab

As you can see from Figure 4–6, the performance of the Short and Integer data types is the fastest. The performance of the Single and Double data types are comparable. The performance of the Decimal data type is comparably quite slow. Because of other operations that Windows may be performing, it is possible that your results may vary from those shown in Figure 4–6.

4. End the application.

# VALUE TYPES AND REFERENCE TYPES

The preceding section discussed how a value is stored in memory based on its data type. In this section, you will learn where data is stored in memory. As described in Chapter 1, all Visual Studio data types can be categorized into either value types or reference types.

## VALUE TYPES

For **value types**, Visual Studio stores the data value in the memory allocated to the variable. The SByte, Short, Integer, Long, Single, and Double data types are all value types, along with their unsigned companion types. Figure 4–7 illustrates how data is stored in value types.

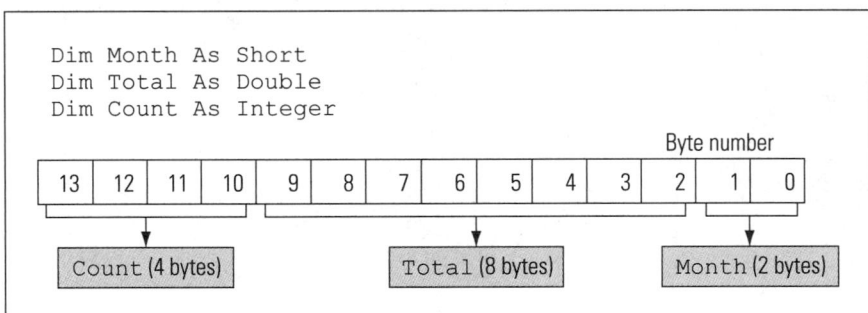

Figure 4-7: Storage of value types

As shown in Figure 4–7, value type variables are stored in consecutive memory addresses. The data for the value type is stored directly in the memory allocated to the variable. In Figure 4–7, a total of 14 bytes is used to store the three variables.

Examining the .NET Framework object hierarchy, you will notice that all value types are derived from the System.ValueType class. Figure 4–8 shows selected value types and their location within the .NET Framework object hierarchy.

As shown in Figure 4–8, the System.ValueType class derives from the System.Object class. All value types derive from the System.ValueType class.

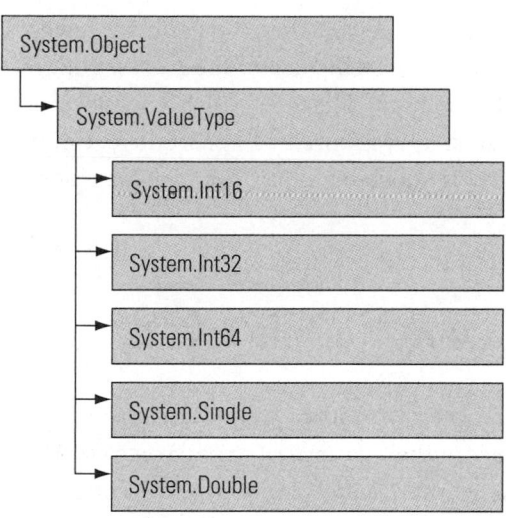

Figure 4-8: Organization of value types

## REFERENCE TYPES

Reference types work quite differently than value types. All reference type variables are 32 bits in size and store an integral value. Instead of storing data however, **reference type** variables store a memory address. The data stored in this memory address, in turn, points to (references) the actual data or object. The term pointer or pointer variable is often used to describe a reference type. Figure 4–9 illustrates how data is stored using reference types.

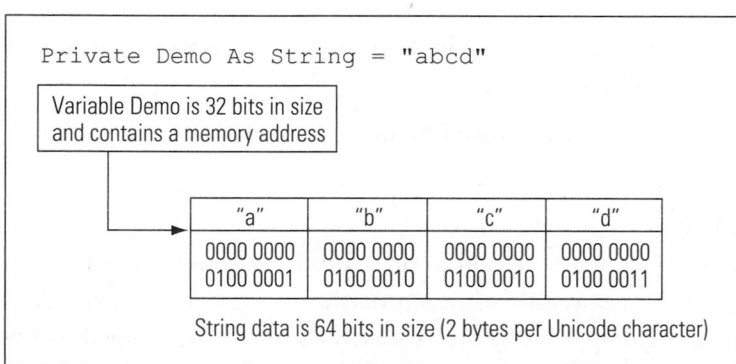

Figure 4-9: Storage of reference types

The `String` data type is a reference type rather than a value type, so variables having a type of `String` store a memory address instead of the string itself. The memory address stored in the `String` variable points to the memory allocated to the actual string. Remember from the previous section that strings are stored as consecutive Unicode characters. Figure 4–9 illustrates how memory is allocated to a string variable made up of four characters.

# INTRODUCTION TO VARIABLES

Until now, any data stored in an application has been stored in the property of an object. For example, you have read data from the properties of the `SystemInformation` class. Using an assignment statement, you stored a value in the `Image` property of a `PictureBox` object. In addition to storing data in an object's properties, data can be stored in variables.

A **variable** stores data for an application in memory while the application runs. Just as a property has a data type, so too does a variable. The process of creating a variable is known as declaring a variable. When a variable is declared, that variable is assigned a data type and a name (identifier). The rules for naming variables are the same as the naming rules for all identifiers.

All variables have three characteristics, as described in the following list:

» A variable has a *lifetime*, which is the period of time that a variable exists, and memory is allocated to store the variable.

» A variable has a *scope*. The scope of a variable refers to which statements can use (reference) the variable.

» *Accessibility* controls how a variable can be used by other classes and modules. Scope and accessibility are closely related.

Each of these variable characteristics is discussed in turn.

## VARIABLE LIFETIME

The term **variable lifetime** refers to the period of time during program execution that the variable exists. Some variables exist only while a procedure executes. Other variables exist whenever a form instance or module exists. A variable's lifetime is defined by the keyword used to declare the variable along with where in a `Module` or `Class` block a variable is declared.

A variable can have roughly two lifetimes, as follows:

» A variable can exist while a procedure executes. When execution of the procedure begins, the variable is created and memory is allocated to store the variable's data. When execution of the procedure is complete, the variable is destroyed and the memory allocated to the variable is released back to the system. If the procedure executes again, the variable is re-created and new memory is allocated to store the variable.

» A variable can exist while the `Module` or `Class` block containing the declaration exists.

Variables can be declared inside of a procedure block (between the `Sub` and `End Sub` statements) or outside of a procedure block. Variables declared inside a procedure have a **local lifetime** because they exist only while the procedure executes. The memory for a local variable is allocated when the procedure starts executing and released back to the system when the procedure ends. Thus, the value of a local variable and the local variable itself are destroyed when the statements in a procedure have executed.

Another category of variable lifetime is module-level lifetime. A variable with a **module-level lifetime** exists while a class instance, such as a form instance, or a module, exists. Module-level variables can be declared inside of a `Class` or `Module` block. If declared in a `Class` block, the module-level variable exists while the class instance exists. If declared in a `Module` block, the variable exists for the entire time that the application is executing.

## VARIABLE SCOPE AND ACCESSIBILITY

In addition to a variable's lifetime, a variable has a scope. The term **variable scope** refers to the statements that can use a variable. Variables declared inside of a procedure have local scope. That is, only the statements appearing in a procedure can reference a variable having local scope. Variables having local scope are referred to as *local variables*. Local variables are declared inside a procedure block with the `Dim` keyword, as shown in the following code segment:

```
Sub Main()
    Dim Counter As Integer
End Sub
```

The preceding statement in the Main procedure declares a local variable named Counter.

**Variable accessibility** defines how a variable can be used by other classes and modules. A variable's accessibility is defined by the keyword used to declare a variable. In Visual Basic, the keywords `Public`, `Protected`, `Friend`, `Protected Friend`, and `Private` are used to define a variable's accessibility. The term **access modifier** is often used to describe these keywords as they are used to control a variable's accessibility.

In this chapter, the `Dim` keyword is used to declare local variables. The access modifiers described previously are discussed in detail when applications containing multiple forms and modules are discussed.

# THE SYNTAX TO DECLARE VARIABLES

Having introduced the lifetime, scope, and accessibility of a variable, you will now learn the Visual Basic syntax to declare local variables. Variables are declared using a declaration statement, which has the following general syntax:

## Syntax

```
[Dim | Static] varName As type [= initexpr]
```

## Dissection

» The `Dim` keyword is used to declare a local variable. That is, it declares a variable accessible only to the procedure containing the declaration. Local variable declarations appear inside of a procedure block.

» The `Static` keyword is also used to declare variables having local scope. That is, variables declared with the `Static` keyword can be referenced only from the procedure containing the declaration. However, the lifetime of a static variable is the same as the lifetime of a module-level variable. That is, unlike a local variable declared with the `Dim` keyword, the value of a static variable persists from one procedure invocation to the next. Thus, the lifetime of a `Static` variable is the same as a variable declared with the `Private` keyword. Static variable declarations must appear inside of a procedure block.

» *varName* is the name (identifier) by which the variable is referenced in an executable statement.

» The `As` *type* clause defines the data type of the variable. Data types are discussed throughout this chapter and in Chapter 5.

» The optional *initexpr* assigns an initial value to the variable.

To illustrate how to declare variables, and the effect of a variable's scope, examine the following event procedure for the button named btnDemo:

```
Public Class frmMain
    Private Sub btnDemo_Click( _
        ByVal sender As System.Object, _
        ByVal e As System.EventArgs) Handles btnDemo.Click
        Static CallCounter1 As Integer
        Dim LocalCounter1 As Integer
        CallCounter1 = CallCounter1 + 1
        LocalCounter1 = LocalCounter1 + 1
    End Sub
End Class
```

The variable named CallCounter1 is declared with the Static keyword. The lifetime of the variable is the same as the lifetime of the form instance (frmMain). The scope of the variable is the procedure containing the variable declaration (btnDemo_Click).

The variable named LocalCounter1 is declared as a local variable with the Dim keyword. The memory for the variable is allocated when the procedure starts executing, and released back to the system when the procedure ends. Thus, the value of the variable LocalCounter1 does not persist from one procedure call to the next.

## INITIALIZING VARIABLES

In the statements in the preceding section, the variable's value was not initialized in the code. By default, variables having numeric data types, such as an Integer, are automatically initialized to zero (0) when the variable is declared. String data types are initialized to an empty string. Note, however, that an initial value can be assigned to a variable when it is declared, as shown in the following statements:

```
Dim CurrentYear As Integer = 2006
Dim CurrentBalance As Double = 100000.52
```

The first of the preceding statements declares a variable named CurrentYear having a data type of Integer and initializes its value to 2006. The second statement declares the variable CurrentBalance having a data type of Double and assigns the floating-point value 100000.52 to the variable.

Numeric initialization values cannot contain commas or other formatting characters. For example, the following statements are not valid because the value on the right side of the first assignment statement contains a comma and the value on the right side of the second assignment statement contains both a comma and a dollar sign:

```
Dim InitialValue As Double = 100,000.52
Dim InitialValue As Double = $100,000.52
```

Remember that variables having a numeric data type also have a valid range of values. For example, the range of the Short data type is –32,768 to +32,767. Thus, the following statements cause syntax errors because the initialization values are outside the valid range of values:

```
Dim Value1 As Short = -55555
Dim Value2 As Short = 55555
```

In the preceding statements, each variable was declared on a single line. Visual Basic also allows multiple variables to be declared on the same line (in the same statement). A comma, as shown in the following statements, separates each variable name and data type:

```
Dim IntegerValue As Integer, DoubleValue As Double
```

The preceding statement declares two variables named IntegerValue and DoubleValue. The first has a data type of Integer, and the second has a data type of Double.

If two or more variables are to have the same data type, the following shorthand declaration syntax can be used:

```
Dim IntegerValue1, IntegerValue2 As Integer
```

The preceding statements declare two variables named IntegerValue1 and IntegerValue2. Both variables have a data type of Integer. Using the same syntax, it is also possible to declare three or more variables in the same statement.

## VARIABLE NAMING CONVENTIONS

Just as every control instance has a name (the value of the Name property), every variable has a name. A scheme of naming variables is called a **naming convention**. A naming convention is nothing more than a consistent way of naming variables, control instances, or other objects. These naming conventions are for the benefit of you, the developer. So long as a variable name adheres to the naming requirements for an identifier, statements to declare and use the variable are legal. That is, the following variable declarations are legal although they give no indication to the variable's purpose:

```
Dim a1, b2, c2, d3 As Integer
```

Thus, most applications use one or more of the three variable naming conventions described in the following list:

» **Hungarian notation** was pioneered by Microsoft. It utilizes a standard prefix to denote a variable's data type. Microsoft has recently abandoned declaring variables using Hungarian notation in favor of Pascal case and Camel case. However, Hungarian notation is still commonly used for naming control instances. For example, a `TextBox` control instance to store a person's name might be named txtName. The prefix for a text box is "txt". This book uses Hungarian notation for control instances in the same way that Hungarian notation was used in Chapter 3 to name control instances.

» **Pascal case** uses whole words to name variables. When a variable name contains multiple words, the first character of each word is capitalized. Using Pascal case, whole words should be used in favor of obscure abbreviations. For example, a variable to store the gain on an investment might be named GainOnInvestment. However, GOI is clearly an obscure abbreviation. This book uses Pascal case for most variable names.

» **Camel case** is similar to Pascal case. However, the first word in the variable name appears as all lowercase characters. The first character of subsequent words is capitalized. Camel case is commonly used with the Java programming language. Using Camel case, the variable name to store the investment gain would be gainOnInvestment. In this book, Camel case is used for procedure arguments as Microsoft tends to use Camel case for procedure arguments for members of the .NET Framework class library.

# INTRODUCTION TO USER-DEFINED CONSTANTS

When a variable is declared, Visual Studio allocates memory to store the variable's data and assigns a name (identifier) to that memory address. An application can also store values in memory that remain constant while the application runs.

A **user-defined constant** is one that a developer declares to allocate memory and to assign a name (identifier) to that memory similar to the way that memory is allocated for a variable. Like a literal value, the value of a user-defined constant (hereafter, the term "constant" is used for brevity) cannot change while an application runs. Trying to assign a value to a constant causes Visual Studio to display the following syntax error: "Constant cannot be the target of an assignment," which indicates that it is illegal to assign a value

**» NOTE**

One common naming convention for constants is to declare them with all uppercase characters. Constants are named this way in this book. The underscore (_) character is used to separate words in a constant name.

to a constant. Like a variable, a constant has a name. The rules for naming constants are the same as the rules for naming variables and other identifiers.

To illustrate the benefit of using constants instead of literal values, suppose that an application computes sales tax at a rate of 7% and that several different statements use that sales tax rate. If several statements used the same literal value 0.07 (which is 7% written in decimal format) and the sales tax rate increased, the literal values would need to be changed each time they appeared. By defining a constant and using that constant throughout an application's code, however, the value assigned to the constant would need to be changed only once. Furthermore, suppose that the value 0.07 was used elsewhere in the application but had a different meaning. In such a case, performing a global search-and-replace operation would cause one or more literal values to be changed incorrectly.

A constant is declared with the Const statement, which has the following syntax:

### Syntax

```
Private Const constantName [As type] = initexpr
```

### Definition

The Const statement declares a user-defined constant.

### Dissection

» The Private keyword has the same meaning as it does when declaring variables. It declares a module-level constant. It is legal but uncommon to declare local constants inside of a procedure block with the Dim statement.

» The constantName assigned to a constant defines the name of the constant. Constant names follow the same rules as those for all other identifiers.

» Constants can be declared having any of the Visual Basic primary data types using the As type clause.

» The initexpr contains a Visual Basic expression that becomes the value of the constant. An expression appears on the right side of an assignment statement. The initexpr can be a literal value, such as a price, or it can contain other constants and arithmetic operators (such as +, −, *, and /). The value of the constant must be assigned when the constant is declared. It cannot be assigned using a run-time assignment statement. The operands in such a statement must be literal values or other constants.

### Code Example

```
Private Const PI_VALUE As Single = 3.14159
Private Const TWO_PI_VALUE As Single = PI_VALUE * 2
```

### Code Dissection

The first statement declares a Private constant named PI_VALUE (the value of PI). The second statement declares and initializes a constant named TWO_PI_VALUE. Its initialized value is PI_VALUE * 2. Note that the constant TWO_PI_VALUE is declared using another constant value in an arithmetic operation.

It is not possible to assign values to a constant using an executable statement. That is, the following assignment statement in the Main procedure is illegal:

```
Private Const TWO_PI_VALUE As Single = PI_VALUE * 2
Sub Main()
    TWO_PI_VALUE = 3.14159 * 2
End Sub
```

**»NOTE**

Instead of declaring a constant to store the value of Pi, the `System.Math.PI` constant stores the value of Pi.

Variables cannot be used when initializing a constant's value because constant values are evaluated when the application is compiled, rather than when the application is run. Because the application is not running, values have not yet been assigned to the application's variables.

The following constant declaration is invalid because PIValue is a variable rather than a constant:

```
Private PIValue As Single = 3.14159
Private Const TWO_PI_VALUE As Single = PIValue * 2
```

# MINI-QUIZ 1

1. Which of the following statements is correct regarding numeric data types?

   a. They are reference types.

   b. They are value types.

   c. All numeric data types are 32 bits in size.

   d. Numeric data types are made up of one or more Unicode characters. Each digit is stored as a Unicode character.

   e. none of the above

2. Which of the following statements is correct regarding the String data type?

   a. Strings are value types.

   b. The memory allocated to store a string variable varies based on the length of the string.

   c. String variables are always 32 bits in size because they are reference types. The variable contains a pointer to the memory allocated to store the actual string.

   d. none of the above

*(Continued)*  ▶

3. Which of the following statements is correct regarding variable scope?

   a. Scope refers to the period of time that a variable exists.

   b. Scope refers to the statements and procedures that can use a variable.

   c. Variables declared inside a procedure with the `Dim` keyword have module-level scope.

   d. Variables declared with the `Private` keyword have local scope.

   e. none of the above

4. If a variable was named "TotalValue," which naming convention is being used?

   a. Pascal case

   b. Camel case

   c. Whole word case

   d. Hungarian notation

5. Describe the error(s) in the following declarations:

   ```
   Dim SomeVariable As Double = 1,234.45
   Dim LittleVariable As Byte = 9000
   ```

After variables have been declared, they are commonly used in assignment statements and in arithmetic expressions, which are discussed next.

# INTRODUCTION TO EXPRESSIONS

In Chapter 3, you wrote assignment statements having a left side and a right side. However, these assignment statements were very simple. That is, on the right side of the assignment statement, a property reference or method call appeared. The result was stored in a property appearing on the left side of the assignment statement. In this section, assignment statements are discussed in more detail, along with how to create assignment statements using more complex expressions.

Any application generally needs to read some input from the end user, perform calculations on that input, and display the results (outputs) of those calculations. After a variable has been declared, data can be stored in the variable. Of course, by initializing a variable when it is declared, data can also be stored in a variable. Literal values can be stored in a variable, along with object properties, or the value of other variables. The following statements show how to assign values to variables having a data type of `Integer`:

```
Dim Result As Integer
Dim Example As Integer = 4
Result = 3                    ' Literal value
Result = txtExample.Height    ' Property
Result = Example              ' Another variable
```

The first two statements declare the variables used in this example. The first assignment statement stores the literal value 3 in the `Integer` variable named Result. A **literal value**, also known as a constant value, is a value that does not change while an application runs. The literal value is an `Integer`. The second assignment statement stores the current value of the `Height` property of the `TextBox` control instance named txtExample into the variable named Result. Note that both the `Height` property and variable have a data type of `Integer`. The final assignment statement contains a variable on the right side of the assignment statement. This assignment statement stores the contents of the variable named Example into the variable named Result. Again, both variables have the same data type.

Assignment statements involving incompatible types cause the Visual Basic compiler to generate syntax errors. To illustrate, the following assignment statement is illegal:

```
Dim SomeInteger As Integer
SomeInteger = txtExample.Font
```

Assuming that txtExample is a `TextBox` control instance, the second of the preceding statements will produce a syntax error with the description "Value of type 'System.Drawing.Font' cannot be converted to 'Integer'." In other words, a data type of `Font` cannot be converted to a data type of `Integer`. This point involving type conversion is significant and is discussed in more detail in the next section of this chapter.

Assignment statements can also contain literal floating-point values and literal text strings, as the following statements show:

```
Dim SingleValue As Single
SingleValue = 1234.56
txtDemo.Text = "Hello"
```

The second of the preceding statements stores a literal value in the variable SingleValue having a data type of `Single`. Assuming that txtDemo is an instance of the `TextBox` control, the final statement stores the literal string "Hello" in the `Text` property of the control instance. The data type of the `Text` property is `String`. As you have seen, double quotation marks always surround literal string values.

To complete the discussion, examine the following illegal assignment statements involving literal values:

```
Dim Count As Integer = 1.23
Dim Total As Double = "12.34"
```

The first of the preceding statements is illegal because the value 1.23 is a floating-point value, which cannot be converted to an `Integer`. Remember that double quotation marks surround literal string values. Thus, in the second of the preceding statements, the value 12.34 is treated as a `String` data type because double quotation marks surround the literal value. Again, the assignment statement is illegal because the `String` data type cannot be implicitly converted to the `Double` data type.

When an assignment statement performs a calculation, the right side of the assignment statement contains an expression. A Visual Basic expression, like an algebraic expression, is made up of operators and operands.

» The **operators** in an expression consist of arithmetic operators (+, −, *, /, ^, \), comparison operators, and logical operators. Arithmetic operators are discussed in this chapter.

» The **operands** in an expression are made up of literal values, constants, variables, object properties, and the results of method calls.

The following statements illustrate a simple expression having two literal values appearing as operands, and one arithmetic operator (*), which is the multiplication operator:

```
Dim Result As Integer
Result = 3 * 2
```

The preceding assignment statement multiplies the literal values 3 and 2 using the multiplication operator and stores the result (6) in the variable Result.

Table 4–5 lists selected arithmetic operators that work with numeric data, describes them, and provides examples of their use.

| Operators in order of precedence | Description | Example |
|---|---|---|
| ^ | Raises a number to the power of an exponent | 2 ^ 3 is equal to 8 |
| *, / | Multiplication and division | 2 * 3 is equal to 6<br>8 / 4 is equal to 2 |
| \ | Integer division | 10 \ 3 is equal to 3<br>5 \ 2 is equal to 2 |
| Mod | Modulus arithmetic; returns the integer remainder of a division operation | 10 Mod 3 is equal to 1 |
| +, – | Addition and subtraction | 2 + 3 is equal to 5<br>2 – 3 is equal to –1 |

Table 4-5: Operators and precedence

The following statements illustrate the use of variables, literal values, and arithmetic operators:

```
Dim Numerator As Double = 10
Dim Denominator As Double = 5
Dim Result As Double
Result = Numerator / Denominator * 100
```

The preceding statements declare and initialize two variables named Numerator and Denominator each having a data type of Double. The third statement declares a variable named Result to store the result of the assignment statement. The assignment statement performs a division operation using the two variables, multiplies the intermediate result (2) by the literal value 100, and stores the result in the variable Result. Thus, the value 200 is stored in the variable Result.

Use of the multiplication, division, addition, and subtraction operators is straightforward, as the following statements illustrate. The following statements show the order in which an arithmetic expression is evaluated:

```
Dim Result As Integer
Result = 4 / 2 + 4 / 4 - 1 * 3
Result = 2 + 1 - 3
Result = 0
```

In the preceding code segment, the division and multiplication are performed first from left to right. Then, the addition and subtraction operations are performed from left to right in the order they appear.

Use of `Integer` division and the `Mod` operator requires a bit more explanation. Using `Integer` division, the result of the arithmetic operation is always converted to an integral value such that the value is truncated rather than rounded. The following statements show the results of various `Integer` division operations:

```
Result = 4 \ 3   ' The result is 1.
Result = 5 \ 2   ' The result is 2.
Result = 10 \ 6  ' The result is 1.
```

The `Mod` operator calculates the `Integer` remainder of a division operation. This calculation is the same as the one used when performing long division by hand, which can produce a remainder. The following statements illustrate the use of the `Mod` operator:

```
Result = 5 Mod 2 ' The remainder is 1.
Result = 4 Mod 2 ' The remainder is 0.
```

In the preceding statements, 5 Mod 2 evaluates to 1 because the result of 5/2 is 2 with a remainder of 1. 4 Mod 2 evaluates to 0 because the result of 4/2 is 2 with no remainder. In both assignment statements, the expression is evaluated and stored in the variable named Result.

## PRECEDENCE IN EXPRESSIONS

All programming languages, including Visual Basic, evaluate arithmetic expressions containing operators and operands from left to right in a predefined order known as **precedence**. Expressions in Visual Basic apply the rules of precedence in the same way as algebraic expressions.

Thus, when an arithmetic expression is evaluated, the expression is scanned from left to right looking for the operator with the highest-level precedence, which is exponentiation. If no operators are found at that level, the expression is scanned again and the next-level operations (multiplication and division) are evaluated from left to right. After performing the multiplication and division, integer division is performed. After any integer division is performed, the `Mod` operator is applied. Finally, addition and subtraction are performed. This pattern of "search and execute" continues until all of the arithmetic operations have been completed. If more than one operator in an expression has the same level of precedence, each operator is applied from left to right as it appears.

## CHANGING THE DEFAULT PRECEDENCE

In many cases, it is necessary to alter the standard evaluation order of arithmetic operators. The standard evaluation order is altered by applying parentheses to an expression just as parentheses are applied to algebraic expressions. Expressions appearing in parentheses are evaluated starting with those appearing in the innermost parenthesis working toward the outermost parenthesis. For example, in the formula $(Var1 + Var2)^{Var3}$, the addition would take place before the exponentiation because the addition operator and its operands are enclosed in parentheses. Without the parentheses, the exponentiation would be performed first. That is, Var2 would be raised to the power of Var3, and then the intermediate result would be added to Var1.

As a further discussion of precedence, consider that in the formula $((Var1 + Var2) - (Var3 + Var4))^{Var5}$ the parentheses are nested, which means that the innermost and left operations (Var1 + Var2) would be evaluated first, (Var3 + Var4) would be evaluated second, and the result of each addition would be subtracted next ((Var1 + Var2) - (Var3 + Var4)). Finally, the result would be raised to the power $^{Var5}$. Figure 4–10 shows another algebraic formula using the standard order of evaluation.

$$\left( \frac{Var1 + Var2}{Var3 - Var4} \right) Var5^{Var6}$$

Figure 4-10: Algebraic expression

The order of operations shown in Figure 4–10 can be easily determined through the way the formula is written. If you transformed this formula directly into a Visual Basic expression, it would resemble the following statement fragment:

```
Dim Result As Integer
Result = ((Var1 + Var2) / (Var3 - Var4)) * (Var5 ^ Var6)
```

Without parentheses, the order of execution of the operators would follow the standard order of precedence. The parentheses change the standard evaluation order, as shown in Figure 4–11.

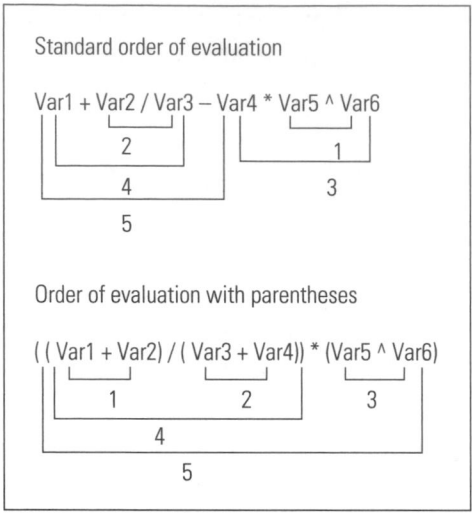

Figure 4-11: Evaluation order with and without parentheses

Additional parentheses can improve the readability of a statement, so they should be used whenever there is a question about the readability or clarity of an expression. For example, including parentheses around the subexpression (Var5$^{Var6}$) in Figure 4–10 does not change the order of evaluation but can improve readability.

# MINI-QUIZ 2

1. Every property or variable has a data type.

   a. True

   b. False

2. What value is stored in the variable named Result after the following assignment statement has executed?

```
Dim Result As Integer
Result = 14 \ 5
```

   a. 3

   b. 2

   c. 2.7

   d. 2.8

   e. none of the above

*(Continued)* ▶

3. Write the statement to declare a constant named TAX_RATE having a data type of `Double`. Initialize the constant's value to 20.1.

4. Assuming that lblDemo is an instance of the `Label` control, describe the error(s) in the following statements.

```
Dim Result As Integer
Result = lblDemo.Font
Result = "123"
```

# NUMERIC DATA TYPES AND TYPE CONVERSION

As discussed previously in this chapter, every declared variable has a data type, and the data type of a variable indicates the kind of data a variable can store and how that data is represented in memory. In this section, numeric data types or those data types that store integral and floating-point numbers are discussed in detail. In addition, the errors caused by arithmetic operations are discussed, along with the topic of type conversion. Finally, the topics of strict type checking, explicit variable declaration, explicit type conversion, and the formatting of strings are discussed.

## INTEGRAL DATA TYPES

As you have seen, the `Byte`, `Short`, `Integer`, and `Long` data types all store integral data. All of these integral data types are also signed types meaning that the value can be either positive or negative. The choice of which integral data type to use depends on the range of possible values that will be stored in a variable. For example, if a variable were to store a number representing the months of the year, the range of possible values would be from 1 to 12, so the `Byte` data type would be the most suitable choice. The other integral data types would work correctly but would waste memory.

## FLOATING-POINT DATA TYPES

Visual Basic supports two signed floating-point data types. The `Single` and `Double` data types can store values that have a fractional part. The difference between the two data types lies in the magnitude of the value and the number of digits of precision. The number of digits to the left of the decimal point is referred to as the magnitude. The number of digits to the right of the decimal point is referred to as the precision. The `Single` data type can store values with seven significant digits of precision, whereas the Double data type can store values with 15 significant digits of precision. In other words, the Single data type can have up to seven digits to the right of the decimal point, whereas the Double data type can have up to 15 digits to the right of the decimal point.

## COMMON ARITHMETIC ERRORS

Exceptions (run-time errors) can arise when performing arithmetic operations on numeric data. One of the most common arithmetic errors is arithmetic overflow. Arithmetic overflow occurs when a statement attempts to store a value in a variable that is outside the possible bounds of that variable's data type. For example, the Short data type can store values between –32,768 and +32,767. If a statement tries to store a value outside of this range in a Short variable, an arithmetic overflow exception is thrown.

Some arithmetic overflow exceptions can be detected at compile time, whereas others cannot be detected until run time. Examine the following statement in which an arithmetic overflow error will be detected at compile time:

```
Dim SmallValue As Short = 50000
```

The preceding statement declares and initializes a variable having a data type of Short. The statement is marked as a syntax error because the largest possible value that can be stored in the Short data type is 32,767. The compiler can detect this error because the literal value (50,000) is known when the application is compiled. However, consider the following example in which the compiler cannot detect the arithmetic overflow error:

```
Dim SmallValue As Short
Dim Operand As Short = 2500
SmallValue = Operand * Operand
```

The assignment statement is not evaluated until run time, so the value of the variable SmallValue is not known until the assignment statement executes. Because the results of the multiplication operation are greater than 32,767, an arithmetic overflow exception is thrown. To fix the arithmetic overflow problem, you might think that declaring the result variable (SmallValue) with an Integer data type would solve the problem, as shown in the following statements:

```
Dim IntegerValue As Integer
Dim Operand As Short = 2500
IntegerValue = Operand * Operand
```

On the surface, the preceding statements would appear to solve the arithmetic overflow problem because the result value has a data type of Integer. However, because all of the values on the right side of the expression have a data type of Short, the expression is evaluated as a Short, even though the result is stored in an Integer. It is in these situations that understanding how Visual Studio performs type conversion is necessary.

## UNDERSTANDING TYPE CONVERSION

An operation called **type conversion** must often be performed to convert a value from one data type to another. For example, an Integer might need to be converted to a Single when used in an assignment statement. Visual Studio performs type conversion in two ways:

» *Implicit type conversion* is automatically performed as expressions are evaluated.

» Using *explicit type conversion*, a value is explicitly converted from one data type to another by calling a method of the System.Convert class.

How type conversion is performed depends on whether **strict type checking** is disabled or enabled. When strict type checking is disabled, the .NET Framework attempts to perform type conversion as necessary (implicitly), as shown in the following statements:

```
Dim Result As Integer
Result = 5 / 2      ' The result is 2.5 which is rounded to 2.
Result = 7 / 2      ' The result is 3.5 which is rounded to 4.
```

The arithmetic operation 5/2 produces a floating-point value as its result. However, the assignment statement attempts to store that floating-point value in a variable having a data type of Integer. Applying the implicit type conversion rules, the value 2.5 is rounded to 2. The arithmetic expression 7/2 also produces a floating-point value. In this case, the value is rounded to 4. The Visual Basic rounding rules work such that if the fractional value is exactly 1/2, then the value is rounded up if the integral part of the number is odd, and rounded down if the integral part of the number is even.

When strict type checking is disabled, the .NET Framework attempts to perform implicit type conversion where possible. However, rounding errors and truncation errors are possible if the underlying values are not compatible. In addition, arithmetic overflow errors are possible. Thus, implicit type conversion can cause errors that are difficult to find and diagnose. This book enables strict type checking for all applications.

## INTRODUCTION TO STRICT TYPE CHECKING

If strict type checking is enabled, the rules surrounding implicit type conversion are much different, as described in the following list:

» Strings are not implicitly converted to numeric data types.

» Numeric data types are implicitly converted from more restrictive types to less restrictive types through a process called *widening type coercion*. For example, a Short is implicitly converted to an Integer or Long, and a Single is implicitly converted to a Double. Integral data types, such as a Short or Integer, are implicitly converted to floating-point data types, such as a Single or a Double.

These implicit type conversion rules are logical as it is not possible for any data to be lost or for an arithmetic overflow error to occur.

» Attempts to force implicit type conversion from less restrictive types to more restrictive types cause syntax errors. For example, a `Double` is not implicitly converted to a `Single`. Furthermore, a `Long` is not implicitly converted to an `Integer` or a `Short`. Floating-point types are not converted to integral types. Implicit type conversion is prohibited because loss of data or loss of precision is possible. The following syntax error is generated in these cases: "Option Strict On disallows implicit conversions from '*type*' to '*type*'", where *type* is the data type of the operands in the expression.

The `Option Strict` statement enables or disables strict type checking, as shown in the following statements:

```
Option Strict On
Option Strict Off
```

The first of the preceding statements enables strict type checking and the second of the preceding statements disables strict type checking. The `Option Strict` statement must appear at the beginning of a module file, although white space or a comment can precede the `Option Strict` statement. The following code segment shows the placement of the `Option Strict` statement in a `Class` block for the form named frmMain:

```
Option Strict On
Public Class frmMain
    ' statements
End Class
```

To understand the implications of strict type checking, examine the following statement to declare and initialize an `Integer` variable:

```
Dim Size As Integer = 1.822
```

The preceding statement declares an `Integer` variable but tries to initialize that variable to a floating-point value. If strict type checking is enabled, the Visual Basic compiler marks the statement as containing a syntax error. If strict type checking is disabled, the Visual Basic compiler performs the assignment, rounds the value, and stores the number 2 in the variable named Size. Obviously, any statement that uses this variable is using the wrong value for Size.

## ENFORCING EXPLICIT VARIABLE DECLARATION

In addition to enabling strict type checking with the `Option Strict` statement, it's possible to require explicit **variable declaration** with the `Option Explicit` statement.

> **»»NOTE**
>
> When enabled, strict type checking is performed for the module file containing the `Option Strict` statement. Thus, each module file in an application should enable strict type checking by including the `Option Strict On` statement at the beginning of the module.

Suppose that you tried to use a variable in a statement without declaring it first. If explicit variable declaration is enabled, the Visual Basic compiler considers any statements that use the undeclared variable as having the following syntax error: "Name '*varname*' is not declared.", where *varname* contains the name of the undeclared variable. If explicit variable declaration is disabled, the Visual Basic compiler automatically (implicitly) declares a variable when it is used for the first time.

To illustrate the benefit of explicit variable declaration, suppose that you misspell a variable name in an assignment statement. If explicit variable declaration is enabled, the Visual Basic compiler checks that the variable is declared. Because of the typographical error, the variable is not declared and the statement is marked as containing a syntax error.

```
Dim Total As Double = 13.33
Dim CurrentValue As Double = 4.28
Total = Totol + CurrentValue
```

In the third of the preceding statements, the variable Total is misspelled. If explicit variable declaration is enabled, the statement is marked as a syntax error.

The `Option Strict` and `Option Explicit` statements have the same syntax as the following statements show:

```
Option Explicit On
Option Strict On
Public Class frmMain
    ' statements
End Class
```

Both the `Option Strict` and `Option Explicit` statements must appear at the beginning of a module. The `On` and `Off` keywords enable and disable explicit variable declaration, respectively. The order of the `Option Explicit` and `Option Strict` statements does not matter.

## PERFORMING EXPLICIT TYPE CONVERSION

The .NET Framework supports a class named `System.Convert` containing methods used to perform explicit type conversion. These methods are commonly used when strict type checking is enabled. The syntax to call the methods of the `System.Convert` class is the same as the syntax to call any other method.

## Syntax

```
result = System.Convert.ToInt16(value)

result = System.Convert.ToInt32(value)

result = System.Convert.ToInt64(value)

result = System.Convert.ToDecimal(value)

result = System.Convert.ToDouble(value)

result = System.Convert.ToSingle(value)

result = System.Convert.ToString(value)
```

## Definition

The preceding methods convert the *value*, supplied as an argument, from one data type to another. If the value cannot be converted to the destination type, an exception is thrown. If the value can be converted, it is stored in *result*.

## Dissection

» The `ToInt16` method converts the argument to a short integer (`Short`) data type.

» The `ToInt32` method converts the argument to the `Integer` data type.

» The `ToInt64` method converts the argument to a long integer (`Long`) data type.

» The `ToDecimal` method converts the argument to the `Decimal` data type.

» The `ToDouble` method converts the argument to a double precision number (`Double`) data type.

» The `ToSingle` method converts the argument to a single precision number (`Single`) data type.

» The `ToString` method converts the argument to the `String` data type.

## Code Example

```
Dim DoubleValue1 As Double = 123.44

Dim DoubleValue2 As Double = 123.59

Dim IntegerResult1 As Integer

Dim IntegerResult2 As Integer

Dim StringResult As String

IntegerResult1 = System.Convert.ToInt32(DoubleValue1)

IntegerResult2 = System.Convert.ToInt32(DoubleValue2)

StringResult = System.Convert.ToString(DoubleValue1)
```

## Code Dissection

The first two assignment statements convert a `Double` to an `Integer`. The `ToInt32` method rounds floating-point numbers so IntegerResult1 stores the value 123 and the variable IntegerResult2 stores the value 124. The converted string value is "123.44."

The following code segment solves the type conversion problem caused by short arithmetic being used instead of integer arithmetic discussed previously in the chapter:

```
Dim IntegerValue As Integer
Dim Operand As Short = 2500
IntegerValue = System.Convert.ToInt32(Operand) *
    System.Convert.ToInt32(Operand)
```

The preceding assignment statement does not cause an arithmetic overflow error because the operands are explicitly converted to the Integer data type before the arithmetic operation is performed. Thus, the arithmetic is performed using the Integer data type instead of the Short data type, and the result also has a data type of Integer.

In addition to converting textual (string) data to numeric data, numeric data must often be converted to a string. For example, a numeric value must be converted to a string when it is displayed and formatted in a control instance such as a Label. If strict type checking is enabled, a numeric value is not implicitly converted to a string. If strict type checking is disabled, the .NET Framework attempts to convert the value to a string and throws an exception if the value cannot be converted.

```
Dim Count As Integer = 3
txtResult.Text = Count ' Error when Option Strict On
txtResult.Text = System.Convert.ToString(Count)
```

The second of the preceding statements causes a syntax error because the Text property of a text box has a data type of String, while the variable Count is an Integer. To correct the type conversion error, the final statement calls the ToString method of the System.Convert class to explicitly convert the Integer to a String.

In addition to calling the methods supported by the System.Convert class to convert a numeric value to a string, all data types also support the ToString method. Thus, the following equivalent statements convert the variable Count to the String data type and store the result in the text box named txtResult:

```
txtResult.Text = Count.ToString()
txtResult.Text = System.Convert.ToString(Count)
```

## FORMATTING OUTPUT STRINGS

The ToString method can also be used to format a numeric value when converting that value to a string. To do so, an argument, called a **format specifier**, is passed to the ToString method. Format specifiers are not case sensitive. A format specifier consists of a single alphabetic character followed by an optional numeric precision specifier. Table 4–6 lists the supported format specifiers.

| Specifier | Name | Description |
|---|---|---|
| C | Currency | The number is formatted as a currency value, and a leading currency symbol appears. The number is formatted with a thousands and decimal separator. |
| D | Decimal | The Decimal specifier is used with integral types. The precision specifier defines the minimum number of digits in the formatted string. Values are padded with zeros, as necessary. |
| F | Fixed | The Fixed specifier displays at least one digit to the left of the decimal specifier and two digits to the right of the decimal specifier. |
| P | Percent | The number is expressed as a percentage. |

Table 4-6: Format specifiers

The following code segment illustrates how to use various format specifiers:

```
Dim DoubleValue1 As Double = 12345678.12345678
Dim IntegerValue1 As Integer = 1234
System.Console.WriteLine(DoubleValue1.ToString("C"))
System.Console.WriteLine(DoubleValue1.ToString("F"))
System.Console.WriteLine(DoubleValue1.ToString("F4"))
System.Console.WriteLine(IntegerValue1.ToString("D"))
System.Console.WriteLine(IntegerValue1.ToString("D6"))
```

The preceding statements produce the following formatted values:

```
$12,345,678.12
12345678.12
12345678.1235
1234
001234
```

In addition to using the predefined format specifiers, it is also possible to create custom format specifiers. In this case, the argument to the `ToString` method contains special characters called placeholder characters. Table 4–7 describes selected placeholder characters.

| Placeholder character | Description |
|---|---|
| 0 | The (0) is a digit placeholder. If the number corresponding to this position does not contain a value, the value 0 appears. |
| # | The (#) is a digit placeholder. If the number corresponding to this position does not contain a value, nothing appears in the character position. |
| . | The (.) is a decimal placeholder. The period (.) defines the character position of the decimal point. |
| ' | The (,) is the thousands separator. |
| % | The (%) sign is the percentage placeholder. The expression is multiplied by 100, and the (%) character is inserted where it appears in the format string. |
| − + $ ( ) | These are literal characters embedded into the format string. |

Table 4-7: Placeholder characters

The placeholder characters shown in Table 4–7 are used to build the format argument. Table 4–8 shows how different values will be formatted using the respective format strings.

| Value | Format string (mask) | Formatted value |
|---|---|---|
| 123.45 | 000000.000 | 000123.450 |
| 1234.4 | ###,###.00 | 1,234.40 |
| 1234.4 | $###,###.00 | $1,234.40 |
| 0.08 | ###% | 8% |
| 0.08 | ##.00% | 8.00% |
| 1234.4 | C | $1234.40 |
| 1234.4 | F | 1234.40 |

Table 4-8: Format strings

The following statements show how to use a custom format string:

```
Dim FormatValue As Single = 123.45
txtFormattedValue.Text = _
    FormatValue.ToString("$###,###.00")
```

In this exploration exercise, you will see how named format specifiers and custom format strings can be used to format numeric values.

1. Run the concept lesson program named **Chapter04ConceptLesson**.

2. Click the **String Formatting** tab. In the Value to Format text box, enter the number shown in Figure 4–12, and then click the **Format** button. The results are formatted and displayed, as shown in Figure 4–12.

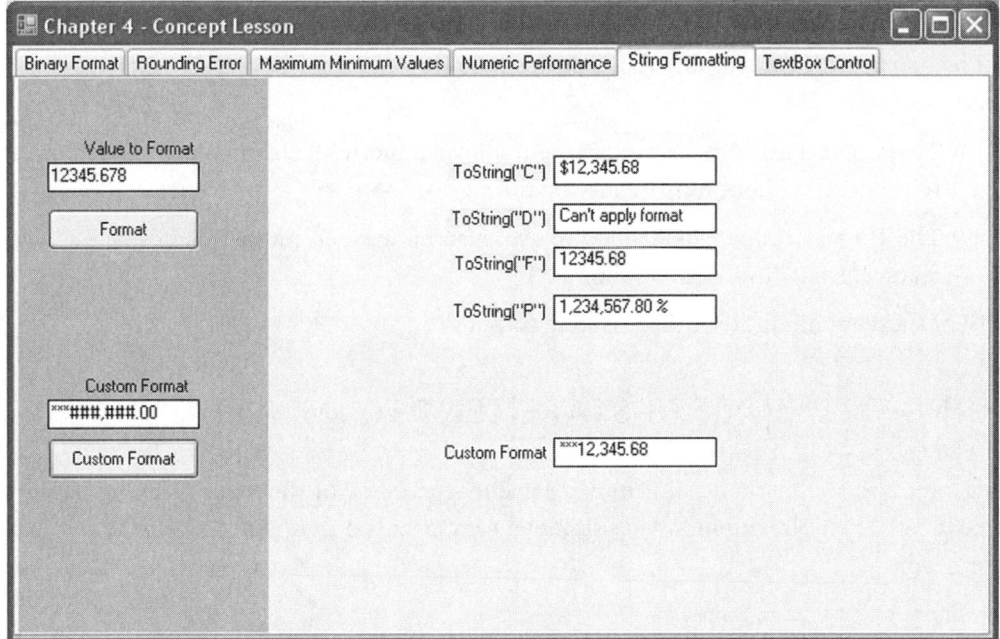

Figure 4-12: Concept lesson—String Formatting tab

3. In the Custom Format text box, enter the format shown in Figure 4–12, and then click the **Custom Format** button. The value is formatted and displayed in the output label as a check amount might be displayed.

4. Continue to experiment with other custom formats.

Strings can also be converted to numeric values. For example, you might need to convert the text stored in the `Text` property of a text box to a number, and store the result in a numeric variable, as shown in the following statements:

```
Dim Count As Integer
Count = System.Convert.ToInt32(txtInput.Text)
```

The preceding assignment statement converts the value stored in the text box named txtInput into an `Integer` and stores the value in the variable Count. If the `Text` property of the text box named txtInput contains a noninteger value such as 123.45, or "12A," an exception is thrown. Otherwise, the value is converted to the `Integer` data type and stored in the variable Count.

# THE IMPORTS STATEMENT

One of the difficulties in referencing the classes of various namespaces is that statements can become quite long, and typing them repeatedly becomes tedious. For example, typing `System.Convert` every time a method of the `System.Convert` class needs to be called causes much unnecessary typing.

There are two ways to simplify the code used to reference a particular namespace, class, or other type:

» The Visual Basic `Imports` statement allows a method, class, or namespace to be referenced without fully qualifying the class or namespace reference.

» The Project Properties dialog box can also be used to import namespaces. This feature is new to Visual Studio 2005.

Both of these techniques are discussed in turn.

## USING THE IMPORTS STATEMENT TO IMPORT NAMESPACES AND CLASSES

The `Imports` statement accepts one argument—the name of the namespace or class to import. For example, the following statement imports the `System.Convert` class just discussed:

```
Imports System.Convert
```

By importing the `System.Convert` class, it is possible to call its methods without fully specifying the `System` namespace or `Convert` class. Thus, the following two assignment statements are equivalent:

```
Dim Result As Integer
Result = System.Convert.ToInt32("42")
Result = ToInt32("42")
```

Both of the preceding statements call the `ToInt32` method of the `System.Convert` class. The first of the statements uses the fully qualified class name. The second statement assumes that the `System.Convert` class has been imported using the `Imports` statement.

The `Imports` statement appears in a code file after the `Option Strict` and `Option Explicit` statements, and before the declaration of the `Class` or `Module` block, as the following code segment shows:

```
Option Explicit On
Option Strict On
Imports System.Convert
Public Class frmMain
    ' statements
End Class
```

In the preceding statements, the `System.Convert` class is being imported. However, a code file can contain multiple `Imports` statements, as shown in the following code segment:

```
Imports System.Convert
Imports System.Windows.Forms.SystemInformation
```

The preceding statements import two classes instead of one. It's possible to import any number of namespaces or classes. In addition, the order in which namespaces and classes are imported does not matter.

## IMPORTING NAMESPACES USING THE PROJECT PROPERTIES DIALOG BOX

In addition to using the `Imports` statement, it is also possible to import namespaces using the Project Properties dialog box, as shown in Figure 4–13.

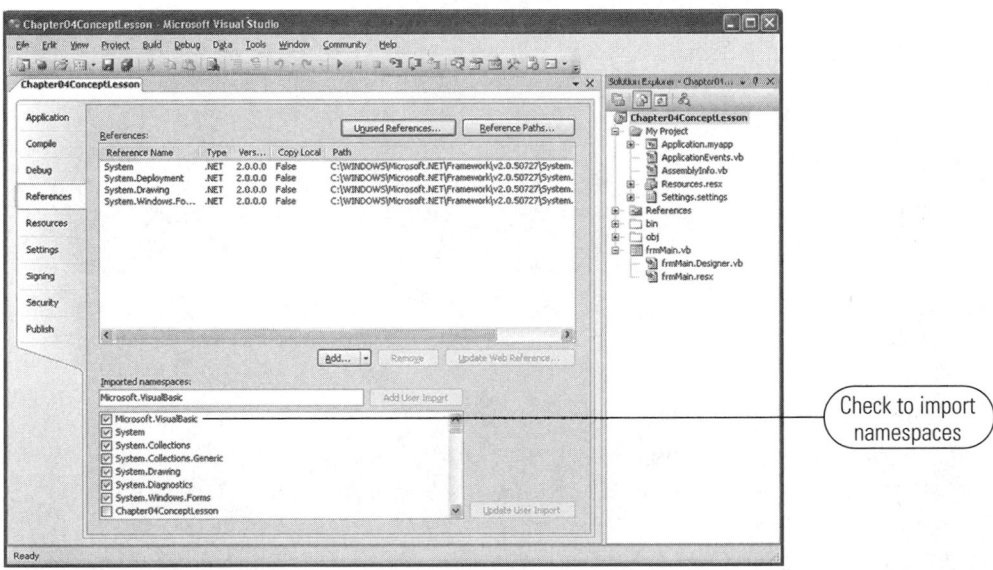

Figure 4-13: Project Properties dialog box

As shown in Figure 4–13, the lower portion of the Project Properties dialog box contains a section titled Imported namespaces. Checking the check boxes causes Visual Studio to import the selected namespace(s) into the project. The imported namespaces appear in the corresponding project file. Using this technique, it is not necessary to import the namespace or class using the `Imports` statement.

# INTRINSIC FUNCTIONS COMPARED TO METHODS

**Intrinsic functions** are functions that are built in to a programming language. As an example, think of the square root button on a calculator as an intrinsic function. You press the square root button and the calculator computes the square root of a number. To send information to an intrinsic function, you supply arguments just as you supply arguments to methods. After an intrinsic function executes, it returns a value, such as the square root of a number, or an object such as a graphical image. Again, in this way, intrinsic functions work the same way as methods.

The subtle difference between intrinsic functions and methods is that intrinsic functions need not be qualified using a namespace and class reference. Thus, an intrinsic function is called using only its name, rather than having to specify a particular namespace and class. The intrinsic `FV` function has the following syntax:

## Syntax
```
result = FV(rate, periods, payment [, presentValue ][, type ])
```

## Definition
The intrinsic `FV` function computes the future value of an annuity (investment). The data type of the resulting value is `Double`.

## Dissection
» The *rate* argument represents the interest rate per period. The value should be expressed as a decimal. That is, a 7% interest rate is represented at 0.07.

» The *periods* argument stores the number of time periods the investment is held.

» If regular payments are made, they are identified by *payment*. To compute the future value of a fixed amount, which does not involve regular payments, the value of *payment* would be 0. A regular payment is equivalent to making a deposit into an investment account for each period.

» The next two arguments are optional and, therefore, are enclosed in brackets. This book uses the convention of showing optional arguments in square brackets. The *presentValue* contains the initial amount (or current value). If the initial value is 0, the argument can be omitted.

*(Continued)* ▶

» The optional *type* argument describes when payments are made. If they take place at the end of the period, *type* is given a value of 0. If they are made at the beginning of a period, *type* is given a value of 1. The default value is 0.

» The FV function returns the future value of an investment and stores the value in *result*.

## Code Example

```
Dim MonthRate As Integer = 0.01
Dim MonthTerm As Integer = 12
Dim InitialValue As Single = 1000.00
Dim FutureValue As Double
FutureValue = FV(0.01, 12, 0, 1000)
FutureValue = FV (MonthRate, MonthTerm, 0, _
    InitialValue)
```

## Code Dissection

The first call to the Future Value (FV) function computes the future value of $1000.00 for 12 periods at an interest rate of 1 percent per period. The regular payment amount is 0. The second call to the FV function uses variables to compute the same result.

The FV function, by default, returns a negative number. To convert this number to a positive number, you could multiply the result by –1, or call the Abs (absolute value) method of the System.Math class, as the following statements show:

```
FutureValue = FV(0.01, 12, 0, 1000)
FutureValue = System.Math.Abs(FutureValue)
```

In this chapter's application lesson, the end user needs to enter textual input values into control instances on the form. These input values are used to calculate the future value of an investment. Visual Basic supports a control suited for editing text: the TextBox control.

>> **NOTE**

With the release of Visual Studio 2005, many intrinsic functions have equivalent class methods. For example, the Microsoft.Visual-Basic.Financial class contains an FV method that is equivalent to the intrinsic FV function.

# THE TEXTBOX CONTROL

Visual Studio supports three controls that allow the user to edit text: the TextBox, MaskedTextBox, and RichTextBox controls. Each of these controls derives from the TextBoxBase class, which derives from the System.Windows.Forms.Control class. In this chapter, the TextBox control is discussed.

## Syntax

```
System.Windows.Forms.TextBox class
```

## Definition

The TextBox control gets textual input from the end user and displays output to the end user.

## Public Properties

» The BorderStyle property defines the type of border surrounding the control instance. If set to None, no border appears. If set to FixedSingle, a flat border appears, and if set to Fixed3D, a three-dimensional border surrounds the text box.

» The ForeColor and BackColor properties define the color of the text and background color appearing behind the text, respectively.

» The Enabled property can be set to True or False. If set to True, the text box can get input focus and responds to events. If set to False, the text box is disabled, cannot get input focus, and does not respond to events. The topic of input focus is discussed in detail in the next section of this chapter.

» The ReadOnly property can be set to True or False. If True, the end user can select text and copy it to the Windows Clipboard. However, the end user cannot change the text. If set to False, the end user can modify the text appearing in the control instance.

» The MultiLine property can be set to True or False. If True, the text box displays text on multiple lines. The MultiLine property works in tandem with the ScrollBars and WordWrap properties.

» The MaxLength property defines the maximum number of characters that the end user can enter into the text box.

» The purpose of the Name property is the same as with other controls. The Name property uniquely identifies a control instance and is used to reference the control instance when writing code.

» The ScrollBars property defines whether scroll bars appear in a multiline text box. If set to None, scroll bars do not appear. If set to Horizontal, a horizontal scroll bar appears across the bottom of the text box, if necessary. If set to Vertical, a vertical scroll bar appears down the right side of the text box when the text will not fit in the visible region. If set to Both, both vertical and horizontal scroll bars appear, as necessary.

» The Text property contains the text string appearing in the control instance.

» The TextAlign property defines whether the text appearing in the control instance appears left-justified, right-justified, or centered within the region of the control instance.

» The X, Y, Height, and Width properties define the position and size of the control instance.

## Public Methods

» The Focus method sets the input focus to the specified text box.

## Events

» The Enter event fires when the control instance gets input focus.

» The Leave event fires when the control instance loses input focus.

One of the most common operations performed with the TextBox control is to store text into the text box or to copy text from the text box into a variable. The following code segment illustrates these operations, assuming that the TextBox control instances are named txtInput and txtMessage:

```
Dim Amount As Single
Amount = System.Convert.ToSingle(txtInput.Text)
txtInput.Text = ""
txtMessage.Text = "This is a string"
```

The first of the preceding statements declares a variable to store the contents of the text box after they have been converted to a numeric value. The second statement converts the contents of the text box to a Single data type and stores the result in the variable named Amount. Note that if the value cannot be converted, an exception is thrown. The next statement stores an empty string in the text box named txtInput. The final statement stores the textual message "This is a string" in the TextBox control instance named txtMessage.

When working with a Windows Application project and a form, the order in which control instances get focus is important as it can improve an application's user interface.

# INTRODUCTION TO TAB ORDER

Every form has exactly one active control instance at run time. When the end user types text in a text box, that text box is, by definition, the **active control instance** and has input focus. When running the application, the end user can change the input focus between one control instance and another by pressing the Tab key or by clicking the mouse in the desired control instance. The order in which control instances get input focus as the end user presses the Tab key is referred to as the **tab order**.

**» TIP**

Defining an appropriate tab order is not an exercise in randomness. The tab order should be arranged so that as the end user presses the Tab key, the control instances get focus in a vertical or horizontal order.

If a control instance can get input focus, the control instance supports the TabIndex property. The TabIndex property determines the order in which control instances get focus as the end user presses the Tab key. A form's tab order is determined initially by the order in which the control instances were created on the form.

Assume that a form has three control instances and that each control instance supports the TabIndex property. Each control instance has a value in the TabIndex property to indicate the order in which it gets focus. The control instance that gets focus first has a TabIndex property value of 0, the second has a TabIndex value of 1, and so on.

>>**TIP**  Although you do not have to set the tab order for labels, which never get focus, labels do play a role in the tab order. You can define a hot key for a label by embedding an ampersand (&) character in the label's Text property. When the end user activates the hot key for the label, the next control instance in the tab order will get focus. If the next control instance is a text box, that text box will get focus. This technique allows the user to select a text box using a hot key.

Visual Studio supports two ways to set the tab order for a form's control instances. First, the tab order can be set using the TabIndex property in the Properties window. The second technique allows you to set the tab order by clicking View, Tab Order on the menu bar, and then clicking the control instances in the Windows Forms Designer in the order that they should get input focus. The Windows Forms Designer must be active for this menu item to appear. Figure 4–14 shows the Windows Forms Designer while setting the tab order.

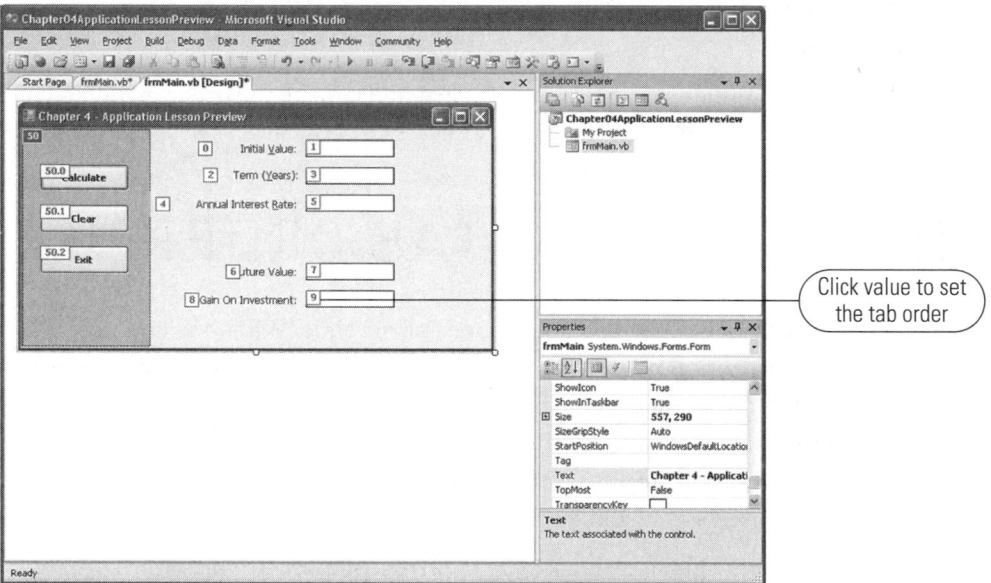

Figure 4-14: Setting the tab order

As shown in Figure 4–14, the tab order value appears in a box at the upper-left corner of each control instance. To set the tab order, click each control instance in the order that it should receive input focus. As you click each control instance, the numeric values are updated indicating the tab order. After having set the tab order for the form's control instances, click View, Tab Order again to record the changes.

In this exploration exercise, you will see how the various properties of the `TextBox` control change the behavior and appearance of the control instance:

1. Run the concept lesson program named **Chapter04ConceptLesson**.

2. Click the **TextBox Control** tab.

3. Click the various check boxes to set the various Boolean properties.

4. Select different scroll bar configurations. The horizontal scroll bar appears if only word wrap is turned off. Figure 4–15 shows the TextBox Control tab.

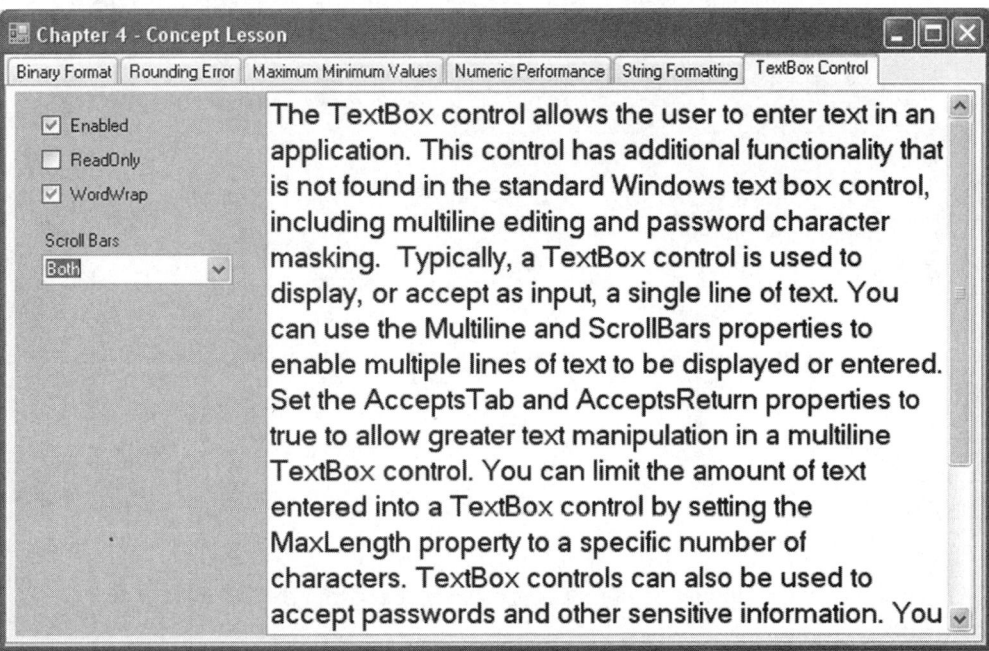

Figure 4-15: Using the TextBox control

# MINI-QUIZ 3

1. Which of the following statements is correct regarding numeric data types?

   a. The `Integer` data type can store values with a decimal point.

   b. A signed whole number data type can store a larger positive value than an unsigned whole number data type.

   c. The `Double` data type can store a value with greater precision than the `Single` data type.

   d. The `Long` data type requires 32 bits of memory.

   e. none of the above

2. Given the following declarations:

   ```
   Dim Var1 As Integer
   Dim Var2 As Single
   Dim Var3 As Double
   ```

   which statement is illegal assuming that strict type checking is enabled?

   a. `Var2 = Var3 * 2`

   b. `Var3 = Var1 * Var2`

   c. `Var2 = Var1 * 2`

   d. `Var3 = Var1 + Var2 + Var3`

3. Which of the following statements is correct regarding the `TextBox` class?

   a. If text appears on multiple lines, that text is stored in the `MultiLine` property.

   b. The control can be configured to display horizontal or vertical scroll bars but not both.

   c. It can accept textual input and display textual output.

   d. Text appearing in the control instance is always left-justified.

   e. none of the above

# APPLICATION LESSON

## CREATING A FUTURE VALUE CALCULATOR

In this application lesson, you will develop an investment calculator. The application's user interface is made up of text boxes in which the end user enters the input values, labels to describe the input fields and to display the output, and, finally, buttons the end user clicks to perform the following tasks:

» Reset the calculator.

» Calculate the future value of an investment.

» Exit the application.

### APPLICATION LESSON—USER INTERFACE

The application's user interface is made up of three text boxes in which the end user enters the following input values:

» The initial value of an investment

» The investment's term, expressed in years

» The annual interest rate

The three buttons are used to calculate the investment's future value, clear the calculator, and exit the application, respectively. Labels are used to display the output values. The output values are formatted as necessary. Figure 4–16 shows the completed user interface for the application.

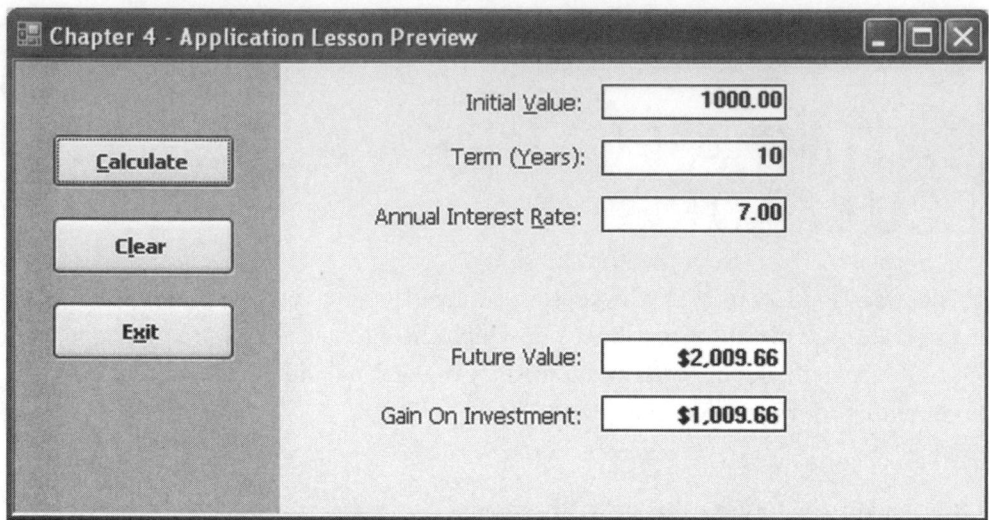

Figure 4-16: Application lesson—user interface

The user interface adheres to the guidelines discussed in Chapter 3. The control instances are balanced and are of the same size. Prompts describe each of the input fields and the output is appropriately formatted. Hot keys have been defined for the buttons. The Calculate button is designated as the form's Accept button, and the Exit button is designated as the Cancel button.

## APPLICATION LESSON—DESIGN

Similar to the application lesson from Chapter 3, this application lesson is an event-driven one. Buttons are used to fire `Click` events, as discussed in Chapter 3. Figure 4–17 shows a flowchart for the application.

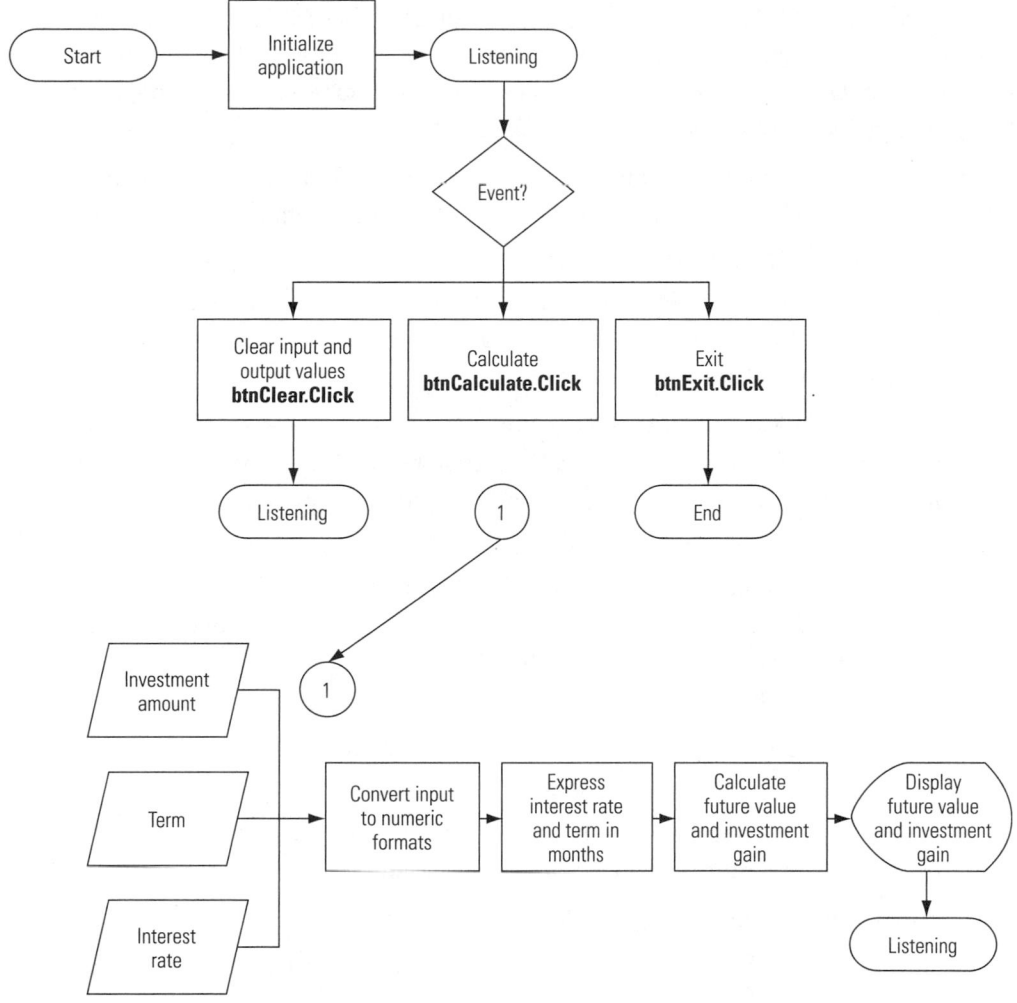

Figure 4-17: Application flowchart

As shown in Figure 4–17, the application is first initialized and general control properties are set. The application then begins to listen for events. In this application, the `Click` event is handled for each button. When the Clear button is clicked, the text appearing in the input and output labels is cleared. When the Exit button is clicked, the form is closed and the application ends.

When the Calculate button is clicked, the three input values are converted to numeric values and stored in variables. Conversions are made to the input values, which are expressed in years, to express those values in months. This is because the interest is calculated monthly, rather than annually. Next, the calculations are performed and the output is displayed. Then, the application waits for the next event to fire.

## APPLICATION LESSON—IMPLEMENTATION

The input data, stored in text boxes, must be converted to numeric data types and stored in local variables. The following list describes the input data used in this application, and the local variable names used to store that data:

» The TextBox named txtInitialValue stores the initial investment amount entered by the end user. The value is converted to a Double data type and stored in the variable named InitialValue.

» The TextBox control instance named txtAnnualInterestRate stores the interest rate entered by the end user. This value is converted to a Double and stored in the variable named AnnualInterestRate.

» The variable MonthlyInterestRate stores the annual interest rate expressed as a monthly interest rate. The AnnualInterestRate is divided by 12 to calculate the MonthlyInterestRate. The TextBox control instance named txtAnnualInterestRate stores the annual interest rate.

» The TextBox control instance named txtYearlyTerm stores the investment term entered by the end user. The investment term, expressed in years, is converted to an Integer and stored in the variable YearlyTerm.

» The variable MonthlyTerm contains the investment term expressed in months. The variable YearlyTerm is multiplied by 12 to calculate this value.

» The constant named MONTHS_PER_YEAR stores number of months in a year (12). This constant is used in the arithmetic expressions to convert values, expressed in months, to values expressed in years.

The following two calculations are performed on the input data:

» The future value of the investment is calculated and stored in the variable FutureValue.

» The variable Gain stores the gain on the investment. The investment gain is calculated by subtracting the initial value of the investment from the future value.

Finally, the output values are formatted and displayed in the output labels.

To preview the completed application:

1. In Visual Studio, open the solution file appearing in the folder named **Chapter.04\Chapter04ApplicationLessonPreview**.

2. Run the solution. Enter the input values shown in Figure 4–16, or input values of your choosing, and then click the **Calculate** button. Figure 4–16 shows the application's input and output.

3. Click the **Clear** button to clear the input and output values.

4. Click the **Exit** button to return to design time.

Instead of creating this application from scratch, the data files accompanying this book contain a partially completed application that you will complete in the hands-on steps in this application lesson. All of the control instances have already been created for the partially completed application. However, none of the code has been written for these control instances.

To open the partially completed solution file:

1. In Visual Studio, open the solution file appearing in the folder **Chapter.04\Chapter04ApplicationLessonStartup**.

2. Activate the Windows Forms Designer. Note that all of the control instances have already been created on the form. In addition, those control instances have been configured and formatted.

First, you will declare the constant and variables to store the application's input and output. These variables only need to be used by the `Click` event handler for the Calculate button. Thus, they should be declared as local variables inside of that event handler.

To declare a constant and local variables:

1. Click **frmMain.vb** in the Solution Explorer, if necessary. Click **View**, and then click **Code** to open the Code Editor for the form named **frmMain**.

2. Enter the following statement (shown in bold) at the module level to declare the constant that stores the number of months per year:

```
Public Class frmMain
    Private Const MONTHS_PER_YEAR As Integer = 12
```

3. Enter the following variable declarations, shown in bold, into the **Click** event handler for the button named **btnCalculate**. (Create the `Click` event handler, as necessary.)

```
Private Sub btnCalculate_Click( _
    ByVal sender As System.Object, _
    ByVal e As System.EventArgs) Handles btnCalculate.Click
    Dim AnnualInterestRate As Double
    Dim MonthlyInterestRate As Double
    Dim InitialValue As Double
    Dim YearlyTerm As Integer
    Dim MonthlyTerm As Integer
    Dim FutureValue As Double
    Dim Gain As Double
End Sub
```

These local variables store the input and calculated values. As each variable stores and generates fractional values, the `Double` data type is used. Both the FV intrinsic function and method expect arguments having a data type of `Double` and return a `Double`.

Next, you will write the statements to clear the input and output values, and exit the application, respectively.

1. Create the **Click** event handler for the **Button** control instance named **btnClear**. Enter the following statements in the event handler to clear the text boxes and to explicitly set focus to the TextBox control instance named **txtInitialValue**:

```
txtInitialValue.Text = ""
txtYearlyTerm.Text = ""
txtAnnualInterestRate.Text = ""
lblFutureValue.Text = ""
lblGain.Text = ""
txtInitialValue.Focus()
```

2. Create the **Click** event handler for the **Button** control instance named **btnExit**, and then enter the following statement to unload the form, thereby exiting the application:

```
Me.Close()
```

Finally, the statements to calculate the future value of an investment must be written using the input values supplied by the end user. The first statements get the input values and convert those values to the appropriate data type as follows:

```
InitialValue = _
    System.Convert.ToDouble(txtInitialValue.Text)
AnnualInterestRate = _
    System.Convert.ToDouble(txtAnnualInterestRate.Text) _
    / 100
YearlyTerm = System.Convert.ToInt32(txtYearlyTerm.Text)
```

Next, the following statements convert the input values, expressed in years, so that they are expressed in months. This step is necessary because interest is calculated monthly rather than annually.

```
MonthlyInterestRate = AnnualInterestRate / MONTHS_PER_YEAR
MonthlyTerm = YearlyTerm * MONTHS_PER_YEAR
```

Finally, the future value and investment gain are calculated and the results are displayed using the following statements:

```
FutureValue = FV(MonthlyInterestRate, MonthlyTerm, 0, _
    InitialValue)
FutureValue = System.Math.Abs(FutureValue)
Gain = FutureValue – InitialValue
lblFutureValue.Text = FutureValue.ToString("C")
lblGain.Text = Gain.ToString("C")
```

The FV function calculates the future value of the investment. Calling the Abs method of the System.Math class converts the result to a positive number. The investment gain is calculated by subtracting the initial investment value from the future value. The output is then formatted and displayed in the form's labels.

To calculate the future value of an investment:

1. Select the **Click** event handler for the **Button** control instance named **btnCalculate**, and then enter the following statements to calculate the future value of the investment:

```
Dim Gain as Double
InitialValue = _
    System.Convert.ToDouble(txtInitialValue.Text)
AnnualInterestRate = _
    System.Convert.ToDouble( _
    txtAnnualInterestRate.Text) / 100
YearlyTerm = System.Convert.ToInt32(txtYearlyTerm.Text)
MonthlyInterestRate = AnnualInterestRate / MONTHS_PER_YEAR
MonthlyTerm = YearlyTerm * MONTHS_PER_YEAR
FutureValue = FV(MonthlyInterestRate, MonthlyTerm, 0, _
    InitialValue)
FutureValue = System.Math.Abs(FutureValue)
Gain = FutureValue - InitialValue
lblFutureValue.Text = FutureValue.ToString("C")
lblGain.Text = Gain.ToString("C")
```

2. Test the application using input values of your choosing or use those appearing in Figure 4–16.

# CHAPTER SUMMARY

» All properties and variables have a data type. Integral data types store numeric values without a decimal point. Integral data types are stored using two's complement arithmetic. Floating-point values have a decimal point. The String data type stores its values as a list of consecutive Unicode characters. Other properties and variables have data types that are themselves objects.

» All data types can be categorized as either value types or reference types. Value types store their data directly in the memory allocated to the variable. All reference type variables are 32 bits in size. The variable stores the memory address of the actual data or object.

» Variables store data while an application runs. The process of creating a variable is known as declaring a variable. Variables have three characteristics: lifetime, scope, and accessibility. Variables can have a module-level lifetime or a local lifetime. Scope and accessibility refer to the procedures and other modules that can use a variable. The Private, Dim, and Static keywords are used to declare variables.

» Variable names should follow a naming convention. Hungarian notation was pioneered by Microsoft and utilizes a prefix denoting a data type followed by a descriptive name. Pascal case and Camel case use whole words to name variables. Pascal case uses uppercase characters for the first letter of each word. Camel case uses a lowercase character for the first letter of the first word and uppercase characters as the first letter of the subsequent words.

» Constants can be declared instead of using a literal value to improve code readability. Constants are declared using the `Const` statement. The value of a constant cannot be changed while an application runs.

» Assignment statements are made up of a left side and a right side. The right side of an assignment statement contains an expression that is evaluated. Arithmetic expressions are made up of operators and operands. Operators are applied in a specific order known as precedence. Operands are made up of literal values, constants, variables, and object properties. Type conversion is performed on operands either implicitly or explicitly. Explicit type conversion is performed by calling the members of the `System.Convert` class.

» How type conversion is performed is based on whether strict type checking is enabled or disabled. When disabled, the .NET Framework attempts to implicitly convert data between data types. When strict type checking is enabled, data is only implicitly converted from more restrictive types to less restrictive types. Explicit type conversion can be performed by calling the members of the `System.Convert` class.

» The `Option Explicit` statement is used to force variables to be declared before they can be used in an executable statement. Enabling explicit variable declaration prevents hard-to-find bugs resulting from typographical errors.

» For most numeric data types, the `ToString` method can be called to format the numeric value as it is being converted to a string. By passing a named format specifier or a custom format specifier made up of placeholder characters to the `ToString` method, the string value can be formatted as a currency value, a whole number, or a custom format.

» To reduce typing and simplify code, the `Imports` statement can be used to import a particular namespace or class. By importing a namespace or class, it is not necessary to fully qualify the namespace or class name to call a method or reference a property. Namespaces can also be imported using the Project Properties dialog box.

» Both the `TextBox` control and the `Label` control display text. The `TextBox` control allows the end user to enter text. The text entered by the end user is stored in the `Text` property.

# KEY TERMS

**access modifier**—A keyword used to specify a variable's accessibility.

**active control instance**—The control instance on a form having input focus.

**Camel case**—A naming convention similar to Pascal case. The first word appears in all lowercase characters and the first character of subsequent words appear as uppercase characters.

**data type**—The kind of information the property or variable can store is determined by the data type of a property or variable. Every property or variable has a data type.

**floating-point number**—A numeric value having a decimal point and a fractional part.

**format specifier**—A special character or string of characters passed to the `ToString` method that is used to format a numeric value.

**Hungarian notation**—A naming convention that uses a prefix to denote the variable's data type, followed by a descriptive name. The Hungarian naming convention was pioneered by Microsoft.

**intrinsic functions**—Intrinsic functions work like methods but do not belong to a class or namespace. Most intrinsic functions are supported only for backward compatibility with previous versions of Visual Basic and Visual Studio .NET.

**literal value**—Also known as a constant value, a value that does not change while an application runs.

**local lifetime**—Variables that exist only while a procedure executes and are declared with the `Dim` statement inside of a procedure block. Variables declared in a procedure have local lifetime.

**module-level lifetime**—Variables that exist while the class instance exists or the module is loaded. Module-level variables are declared with the `Private` keyword. Module-level variables are declared inside of a `Class` or `Module` block but outside of a procedure.

**naming convention**—A consistent way of naming variables, control instances, or other objects. Pascal case, Camel case, and Hungarian notation are three common naming conventions.

**operands**—Literal values, constants, and object properties used in arithmetic expressions are called operands.

**operators**—Arithmetic, comparison, or logical operations are performed using operators.

**Pascal case**—A naming convention that uses whole words for variable names. The first character of each word is capitalized.

**precedence**—The rules for evaluating arithmetic and other types of expressions.

**reference type**—Variables that store a memory address instead of data are called reference type variables. The memory address, in turn, points to the actual data.

**rounding error**—Arithmetic operations performed on binary floating-point values introduce error because of how the values are rounded. This error is called rounding error.

**sign bit**—A bit designated in a numeric data type to determine whether the number is positive or negative.

**strict type checking**—A form of type checking that prohibits implicit type conversion from less restrictive types to more restrictive types. Strict type checking is enabled and disabled using the `Option Strict` statement.

**tab order**—The order in which control instances get input focus.

**two's complement**—Negative integral values are expressed as two's complement values. The sign bit has a value of 1. The value of all other bits is flipped. Finally, 1 is added to the number.

**type conversion**—The process of converting one data type to another so that an expression can be evaluated. Type conversion can be performed implicitly or explicitly.

**user-defined constant**—A user-defined constant is similar to an initialized variable whose value cannot be changed. User-defined constants are declared with the `Const` statement.

**value type**—A type of property or variable where data is stored directly in the memory allocated to the variable or property. For example, the data for a 32-bit `Integer` variable is stored directly in the 32 bits allocated to the variable.

**variable**—While the application runs, data is stored in memory using what is called a variable.

**variable accessibility**—How a variable can be used by other classes and modules is defined by a variable's accessibility.

**variable declaration**—The process of creating a variable.

**variable lifetime**—The period of time that a variable exists.

**variable scope**—The executable statements and procedures that can use a variable.

# ANSWERS TO MINI-QUIZZES

### MINI-QUIZ 1

1. b. They are value types.

2. c. String variables are always 32 bits in size because they are reference types. The variable contains a pointer to the memory allocated to store the actual string.

3. b. Scope refers to the statements and procedures that can use a variable.

4. a. Pascal case

5. The initialization value in the first declaration statement contains a comma. In the second statement, the value 9000 is too large to be stored in the `Byte` data type.

### MINI-QUIZ 2

1. a. True

2. b. 2

3. `Private Const TAX_RATE As Double = 20.1`

4. In the second statement, the data type `Font` cannot be converted to the data type `Integer`. In the second statement, the double quotation marks should be removed from the literal value 123.

### MINI-QUIZ 3

1. c. The `Double` data type can store a value with greater precision than the `Single` data type.

2. a. `Var2 = Var3 * 2`

3. c. It can accept textual input and display textual output.

# REVIEW QUESTIONS

1. Which of the following are valid Visual Basic data types?

    a. `Number`, `Float`, and `String`

    b. `Numeric` and `Character`

    c. `Short`, `Integer`, `Long`, `Single`, and `Double`

    d. `Integer16`, `Integer32`, `Integer64`, `Float32`, and `Float64`

    e. none of the above

2. Which of the following statements correctly describes the difference between value types and reference types?

a. A reference type stores data directly in the memory allocated to the variable, whereas a value type stores a memory address, which, in turn, points to the memory allocated to the variable.

b. A value type stores data directly in the memory allocated to the variable, whereas a reference type stores a memory address, which, in turn, points to the memory allocated to the variable.

c. The amount of memory needed to store a value type or a reference type is always 32 bits.

d. The `Integer`, `Single`, and `Double` data types are all reference types.

e. none of the above

3. Which of the following are characteristics of a variable?

a. persistence and inheritance

b. lifetime, scope, and accessibility

c. physical storage and virtual storage

d. availability and exposure

e. none of the above

4. Which of the following is the keyword to declare a local variable?

a. `Declare`

b. `Dim`

c. `Create`

d. `New`

e. `Private`

5. Which of the following statements is true regarding variable declaration?

a. Module-level variables can be used by all of the event handlers in a module and are declared with the `Private` statement.

b. Local variables can be used by all of the event handlers in a module and are declared with the `Local` statement.

c. Variable names (identifiers) can contain spaces.

d. When strict type checking is enabled, variables can have a data type but a data type is not required.

e. none of the above

6. Which of the following keywords is used to declare a local variable whose value will persist from one procedure invocation to the next?

   a. `Exposed`

   b. `Persistent`

   c. `Private`

   d. `Static`

   e. `Friend`

7. Which of the following statements is correct regarding the placement of a variable declaration?

   a. Local variables cannot be declared inside of a procedure block (between the `Sub` and `End Sub` statements).

   b. Local variables can be declared inside of a procedure block with the `Private` access modifier but module-level variables cannot.

   c. Module-level variables can be declared inside of a procedure block but local variables cannot.

   d. Module-level variables must be declared inside of a `Declaration` and an `End Declaration` block.

   e. none of the above

8. Which of the following lists arithmetic operators in their correct precedence order?

   a. $+-, */, \wedge$

   b. $\wedge, +-, *, /$

   c. $\wedge, */, +-$

   d. $*+, /-, \wedge$

   e. none of the above

9. Which of the following are valid type conversion methods?

   a. `ToShort, ToInteger, ToLong, ToSingle, ToDouble`

   b. `ToInt16, ToInt32, ToInt64, ToSingle, ToDouble`

   c. `ConvertToNumeric, ConvertToString`

   d. `ToTypeInt, ToTypeLong, ToTypeSingle, ToTypeDouble`

   e. none of the above

10. What is the most restrictive data type that can store the value 4023?

    a. Short

    b. Integer

    c. Long

    d. Single

    e. Double

11. What is the most restrictive data type that can store the value 1234.55553333432?

    a. Short

    b. Integer

    c. Long

    d. Single

    e. Double

12. Which arithmetic operator should be used to calculate the integer remainder of an integer division operation? _____

13. What value is stored in the variable VarResult after the following statements have executed: _____

    ```
    Dim VarCount As Integer = 3
    Dim VarResult As Double
    VarResult = (VarCount - 1) * (VarCount + 1) ^ 2
    ```

14. Which of the following statements correctly describes the error in the following code segment:

    ```
    Dim FICARate As Double = 7.5
    Private Const TAX_RATE As Double = 20.1
    Private Const TOTAL_RATE = FICARate + TAX_RATE
    ```

    a. The statement declaring the constant TOTAL_RATE is not legal because the initialization value contains a variable.

    b. The statement declaring the constant TOTAL_RATE contains a type conversion error.

    c. The variable FICARate cannot be initialized in the declaration statement.

    d. A constant cannot be declared with the Private keyword.

    e. There is no error in the preceding statements.

15. What is the difference between a constant and a literal value?

16. What is the primary difference between a text box and a label?

17. Describe the type conversion rules pertaining to Visual Basic assuming that strict type checking (Option Strict) is enabled.

18. What is the purpose of the Option Explicit statement?

19. Describe the difference between a signed data type and an unsigned data type.

20. What is the difference between an intrinsic function and a method?

# PROGRAMMING QUESTIONS

1. Write the statements to declare two local variables named Counter and Total. The first should store an integer and the second a single precision number. Declare two more local variables named Count1 and Count2 having a data type of Integer such that both variable declarations appear on the same line.

2. Write the assignment statement(s) to add the literal values 1, 2, and 3 together, multiply the intermediate result by 4, and then raise that intermediate result to the power of 2 (squared). Store the result in a variable named Result.

3. Write the statement to declare a module-level constant named TAX_RATE having a data type of Double. Initialize the value to 0.20.

4. Write the statement to convert the Text property of the TextBox control instance named txtCurrent to a double precision number. Store the result in the variable Current.

5. Assume that the variables named Var1 and Var2 have a data type of Integer and that the variable Result has a data type of Long. Write the statement to add the variables Var1 and Var2 together and store the result in the variable Result. Perform the necessary type conversion so that long arithmetic is used to evaluate the right side of the expression instead of integer arithmetic.

6. Write the statement(s) to format the single precision value stored in the variable OutputValue with two decimal places and a leading dollar sign. Two zeros should appear to the left of the decimal point if there is no value for the character position. Include a thousands separator. Store the formatted result in a variable named FormattedOutput having a data type of `String`.

7. Write the statement(s) to format the double precision value stored in the variable OutputValue with four decimal places. Store the formatted result in the variable named FormattedOutput having a data type of `String`.

8. Write the statement to format the numeric value stored in the variable Percent as a percentage. Assume that Percent is declared as a `Single` data type. Format the variable as a percentage with three decimal places. The percent symbol should appear at the end of the formatted string. Store the result in the variable FormattedOutput.

9. Write the statement(s) to compute the future value of an investment having an initial value of $2500.00 and an interest rate of 10 percent per year for 30 years. Store the result in a variable named FutureValue. Make sure to compound the interest monthly rather than annually. Declare additional variables, as necessary.

10. Assume that the variables Var1, Var2, Var3, and Var4 are declared each having a data type of `Double`. Write the statement to compute the average of the list of numbers and store the result in the variable named Result also having a data type of `Double`.

11. Assume that two `TextBox` control instances exist named txtNumber and txtPower. Write the statements to raise the value stored in txtNumber to the exponent stored in txtPower. Convert the input to the `Double` data type before performing the calculations. Store the result in the text box named txtResult converting the output to a data type of `String`. Declare any intermediate values, as necessary.

12. Create the `Click` event handler for the button named btnAverage. The code in the event handler should calculate the average of the variables named Value1, Value2, Value3, and Value4. Store the result in the variable Average. Assume that all variables have a data type of `Double`. In another statement, convert the variable Average to a string and format it with two decimal places. Store the formatted result in the label named lblAverage.

13. The area of a circle is calculated with the formula $\pi * R^2$, where $R$ is the radius of a circle. Assume that a `TextBox` control instance exists named txtRadius, which stores the radius of a circle. Write the statements to convert this input value and store it in a variable having a data type of `Double` named Radius. Declare a constant to store the value of $\pi$. Calculate the area of the circle storing the result in a variable having a data type of `Double`. Declare the variable. Finally, convert the output to a string and display the result in a `Label` control instance named lblCircleArea.

14. One of the earliest mathematical theorems known to ancient civilizations was the Pythagorean theorem, which can be used to calculate a side of a right triangle when the length of the other two sides is known. The formula for the Pythagorean theorem is $a^2 + b^2 = c^2$. Assume that two `TextBox` control instances named txtSideA and txtSideB store input values containing two sides of the right triangle. Write the statements to declare variables named SideA and SideB to store the input values. Use a data type of `Double`. Write the statements to perform the necessary type conversion on the input values. Write the assignment statements to calculate the length of the triangle's hypotenuse. Convert the result to a data type of `String` and store the result in the output text box named txtHypotenuse. *Hint*: Use the `Sqrt` method.

15. Write the statements to declare variables named HoursWorked, HourlyRate, GrossPay, and NetPay having a data type of `Double`. Write the statements to multiply the hours worked by the hourly rate to calculate the gross pay. Calculate the net pay by multiplying the gross pay by 0.80. Finally, convert the net pay to a string and store the result in the label named lblOutput.

# HANDS-ON PROJECTS

1. In this hands-on project, you will create an application that computes the straight-line depreciation of an asset for a period. The application should provide an interface through which the end user inputs the initial cost of an asset, the value of the asset at the end of its useful life (its salvage value), and the life of the asset. To create the application, you will use the intrinsic `SLN` function.

a. Run the executable file named **Chapter.04\HandsOnProjects\Ch04HandsOn Project1.exe**. Enter input values, and then click the **Calculate** button. Note the blue color scheme of the form. You will re-create this interface in the hands-on project. Exit the solution.

b. Create a new solution named **Ch04HandsOnProject1**.

c. Write the statements to enable strict type checking and explicit variable declaration.

d. Set the form's caption. Also create the descriptive labels along the left side of the form. Use a bold typeface and right-justify the label control instances. Set the text color to Navy.

e. Create three `TextBox` control instances to the right of the labels. Change the `Name` properties of the text boxes to **txtCost**, **txtSalvageValue**, and **txtLife**, starting from the top text box. Remove the text from each of the text boxes.

f. Format the text boxes to use a bold font and right-justify the text.

g. Create a label to store the output. Set its `Name` property to **lblDepreciation**. Set the properties so that the appearance is similar to the text boxes.

h. Create three buttons to the right of the text boxes. Use a standard style for all of the buttons applying a similar design.

i. Set the `Name` property of the top button to **btnCalculate** and change its caption. Define it as the Accept button and use the character **C** as the hot key.

j. Set the `Name` property of the center button to **btnClear**; set the caption and hot key.

k. Set the `Name` property of the bottom button to **btnExit**. Designate this button as the Cancel button.

l. Write the code for the **Exit** button to end the solution.

m. Write the statement to import the `System.Convert` class.

n. Create the code for the **Calculate** button to compute the straight-line depreciation for an asset and store the result in the output label named **lblDepreciation**. Store the value of the text boxes in local variables that you declare. Use the `SLN` intrinsic function to calculate the depreciation. As the arguments to the function, use the local variables you declared in the previous steps. Format the output as a currency value. The `SLN` function has the following syntax:

```
SLN(cost, salvage, life)
```

The *cost* argument contains the initial cost of the asset. The *salvage* argument contains the value of the asset (salvage value) at the end of its useful life. The *life* argument contains the number of periods in the asset's life. For further information, refer to the `SLN` Help topic.

o. Create the code for the **Clear** button to clear the text from the three text boxes and the output label. Each object should display a blank (empty) string. Set the focus to the text box named **txtCost**.

p. Set the tab order so that the input focus moves from the top text box to the bottom text box.

q. Create an instance of the `ToolTip` control. Associate the `ToolTip` control instance with the three buttons. For the Calculate button, display the text "Calculate the straight-line depreciation of an asset." For the Clear button, display the text "Clear the input and output values." For the Exit button, display the text "Exit the application."

r. Run and test the application as necessary.

2. In this hands-on project, you will create an application that determines the cost of a printing order. The cost of the order is based on the paper size and the number of pages printed.

Note that part of the project is to align the numerous control instances and create a visually appealing user interface. A color theme was chosen in the sample solution for this project. You will use your artistic eye to develop a different color scheme by applying the user interface principles discussed in Chapter 3 so as to present a pleasing user interface.

a. Run the executable file named **Chapter.04\HandsOnProjects\Ch04HandsOn Project2.exe** to view the user interface. Enter values in each of the quantity text boxes, and then click the **Calculate** button to calculate the extended prices and order total. Click the **Clear** button to clear the user interface. Exit the solution.

b. Create a new solution named **Ch4HandsOnProject2**.

c. Change the title bar of the form.

d. Create the descriptive labels. These labels all have similar formatting characteristics, so you can set the color and border for all of them simultaneously. Use boldface text and center-align the text.

e. Create three text boxes to store a quantity-ordered value for each of the different paper sizes, and set the visual properties. Remove the initial text for each of the text boxes.

f. Create three `Label` control instances to the right of the text boxes you created in the previous step to store the extended price for each item. Also, create another `Label` control instance to store the order total. Right-justify the contents of these labels.

g. Create three buttons on the form to calculate the extended prices and order total, clear the input and output fields, and exit the solution.

h. Set the Name property of all the control instances using the appropriate Hungarian prefix.

i. Write the statements to enable strict type checking and explicit variable declaration. Also, write the statement to import the System.Convert class.

j. Declare three constants to store the price per page for each of the three different products.

k. Declare the necessary local variables to store the quantity ordered and extended price for each of the three items. Also, declare a local variable to store the total quantity ordered of all products along with the order total. Again, choose appropriate variable names and use Pascal case.

l. In the Click event handler for the Calculate button, write the necessary statements to store the contents of the three text boxes in the local variables performing type conversion, as necessary. In the same event handler, write the statements to calculate the extended price for each paper size. Compute the extended price by multiplying the quantity by the price per page. Use the constants you declared to store the price per page. The output displayed in the extended price labels should be formatted with a leading dollar sign and two decimal places.

m. In the same event handler, write statements to add the extended prices of the individual items together, format the result, and display it in the total label. Total and display the total quantity ordered appropriately.

n. In the Click event handler for the Clear button, write statements to remove the contents from the input and output control instances. Store the value 0 in the text boxes and an empty string in the labels.

o. Set the tab order as appropriate. Define the **Calculate** button as the Accept button, and the **Exit** button as the Cancel button. Create ToolTips for the buttons as appropriate.

p. In the event handler for the **Exit** button, write the statements to exit the application.

3. In this hands-on project, you will create an application that will estimate a buyer's closing costs and payment amount for the purchase of a home.

a. Run the executable file named **Chapter.04\HandsOnProjects\Ch04HandsOn Project3.exe**.

b. Enter a purchase price of 100000 and an interest rate of 0.07, and then click the **Calculate** button. The output values are computed based upon standard formulas used by the loan company. Exit the application.

c. The end user input consists of the home purchase price and the annual interest rate expressed as floating-point values. That is, a value of 0.07 represents a 7% interest rate. The following list describes the computations your code must perform to calculate the output values:

» The down payment is 20% of the purchase price.

» The closing costs are 2.5% of the purchase price.

» Cash required to close the loan is equal to the down payment plus the closing costs.

» Principal and interest can be computed by calling the PMT function. Assume that the term of the loan is 30 years or 360 months.

» Property taxes are 2.5% of purchase price per year. The value displayed on the form should be expressed in months, however.

» Homeowner's insurance is 0.8% of the purchase price per year. This value should also be expressed in months.

» The monthly payment is equal to the sum of the principal and interest, property taxes, and homeowner's insurance.

d. Create a new solution named **Ch04HandsOnProject3**.

e. Change the form title.

f. Create the user interface for the solution. Use the completed example as a model. Make sure that you select appropriate names for each of the control instances and align them.

g. Configure the form so that it is not resizable and so that the Maximize button on the control box is disabled.

h. Write the statements to enable strict type checking and explicit variable declaration.

i. Declare the necessary local variables to store the input and any intermediate values.

j. Declare constants to store the percentages for the down payment, closing costs, property taxes, and homeowner's insurance. Declare other constants, as necessary.

k. Create the **Calculate** button and the code to calculate all of the output values using the rules defined in the preceding list. Display the output formatted as currency with two decimal places. To calculate the payment (principal and interest), use the PMT function, which has the following syntax:

```
PMT(rate, nper, pv [, fv [, type ]])
```

The *rate* argument contains the interest rate of a loan. The *nper* argument contains the number of periods of the loan. The *pv* and *fv* arguments contain the starting and ending value of a loan. A loan that is paid off has an ending value of zero. The *type* argument indicates whether payments are made at the start or end of the period. For further information, refer to the PMT function Help topic. As shown in the chapter, convert the necessary values so that they are expressed in months before calculating the payment.

l. Write the code for the **Clear** button to clear the contents of the input text boxes and output labels. Set the contents for all of the values to an empty string.

m. Create ToolTips for each of the buttons, and define the **Calculate** button as the Accept button, and the **Exit** button as the Cancel button.

n. Create the code to exit the solution when the **Exit** button is clicked.

4. In this hands-on project, you will create an application that will convert measurements between U.S. and metric values. In other words, the application needs to perform tasks such as converting feet to meters. To perform these conversions, you need to know that there are 2.54 centimeters per inch and 100 centimeters per meter. From this knowledge, you can calculate that there are 0.394 inches per centimeter.

a. Run the executable file named **Chapter.04\HandsOnProjects\Ch04HandsOn Project4.exe**. Type in a value in the **Input Measurement** text box, and then click the buttons on the form to display the result of each conversion.

b. Create a new solution named **Ch04HandsOnProject4**.

c. Write the statements to enable strict type checking and explicit variable declaration.

d. Declare constants to store the conversion values.

e. Change the form title to a meaningful name.

f. Create the user interface, using a color scheme of your choice and the appropriate control instances.

g. In the `Click` event handler for the four conversion buttons, write the necessary statements to convert the input unit of measure to the output unit of measure. That is, write the code to convert feet to meters, meters to feet, and so on. Remember that there are 2.54 centimeters per inch and 100 centimeters per meter. Display the result in the output label.

h. Test the solution. To validate the computations, approximate that there are roughly 3 feet per meter. From this information, you will be able to derive the number of units per inch.

# 5

# THE STRING AND DATETIME DATA TYPES

**After completing this chapter, you will be able to:**

Understand the use of characters and strings

Use the `Char` data type and understand character encoding systems

Use the `String` data type

Call members of the `String` class to manipulate string data

Understand the basics of using dates

Work with the `System.DateTime` data type

Perform arithmetic operations on dates

Use the `DateTimePicker` control as a means for the end user to select dates from a calendar

Use the `Timer` control to generate events at regular intervals

Use strings and dates to create a form letter

# CONCEPT LESSON

## INTRODUCTION TO CHARACTERS AND STRINGS

Chapter 4 introduced the `String` data type solely to show how data is converted from a numeric data type to a string and back. This chapter discusses, in more detail, characters and strings and the operations that can be performed on them. In addition, the `DateTime` data type is introduced as a means to store date and time data. The arithmetic operations that can be performed on dates are also discussed.

The controls presented in the preceding chapters all fired events as a result of end-user interaction, such as clicking a button. In this chapter, you will work with the `Timer` control. Windows fires events for the `Timer` control at regular intervals, rather than as a result of end user interaction with the control instance. This chapter also explains how to work with a control that allows the end user to select dates and times called the `DateTimePicker` control.

## INTRODUCTION TO THE CHAR DATA TYPE AND CHARACTER ENCODINGS

The process of representing a single character seems simple. For example, in the English character set, there exists a small set of characters (the uppercase and lowercase letters A–Z and a–z), digits (0–9) and a few special characters such as !, @, #, $, %, ˆ, &, *, ( , ), . . . . Representing them should be as easy as storing a coded binary value in a single byte. However, some international character sets are much more complex consisting of many more characters. For example, the German language has umlauts and the French language has grave accents, just to name a few of the special international characters. The umlaut is the diacritical symbol used in the German language over vowels to indicate a sound change or change in inflection. The following characters show umlauts:

    Ä ë ï ö ü ÿ

Furthermore, some languages have entirely different character sets than the English character set. This section introduces some history of character sets and the different ways to represent the characters in those character sets as binary data.

## THE ASCII CHARACTER SET

There was a time when different computer manufacturers used different character sets. For example, IBM mainframe computers used (and some still do use) a character set called the Extended Binary Coded Decimal Interchange Code (EBCDIC). Other computer manufacturers had their own unique character sets too. These character sets, or the way in which characters were represented in memory, were not standardized from one computer manufacturer to the next. That is, different computer manufacturers used different binary values to represent each character. Furthermore, the number of bits used to store a character varied from one computer manufacturer to the next. Thus, communicating information from one computer to another was difficult if not impossible. To solve this problem, the ASCII character set was created in 1961 by Bob Bemer of IBM. This character set allowed different computers to share data because every character was coded using the same standard binary value and was stored in the same number of bits.

ASCII was, and still is, a very popular character encoding scheme. An **encoding scheme** is a way of representing each character in a language with a unique binary value. The ASCII encoding scheme represents each character in one unsigned 8-bit byte. Thus, there are 256 possible character codes. Remember that a byte can store 256 possible values. The first 128 character codes (0 to 127) define those of the English character set. For example, the capital "A" is represented by the decimal value 65, and a lowercase "a" is represented by the decimal value 97. The second 128 character codes (128 to 255) are used for special keyboard keys such as the arrow keys and function keys. Characters that are not represented in the basic 256 codes are made up of an Escape character (typically a backslash), followed by an extended character code. Extended character codes are not discussed in this chapter.

While ASCII works well for the English character set, it was not adequate to represent script-based character sets or international character sets that have diacritical marks. In other words, some languages have more than 256 characters in their character set. As a result, the Unicode character set was introduced, which is discussed next.

**»NOTE**
The 256 codes that make up the ASCII character set appear in Appendix B.

## INTRODUCTION TO UNICODE

In the 1980s, computer manufacturers realized the need to represent all characters in all languages and to define a standard for multilingual character-encoding systems. It was hoped that this standard would be adopted by all computer systems worldwide. From this work, the "Unification code" was born, which is now known as **Unicode**.

Instead of representing each character in a 1-byte value, Unicode stores a character in an unsigned 2-byte value. Thus, up to 65,536 unique characters can be represented with the Unicode character encoding scheme. Each unique binary pattern representing a character is called a **code point**. Like the ASCII character set, the first 128 code points correspond

**»NOTE**

Although not mentioned in this book, there are actually multiple Unicode character encoding schemes. For complete information about Unicode encoding and the Unicode standard, refer to *www.unicode.org*.

to the letters and symbols appearing on a U.S. keyboard. The second 128 code points represent special characters. The remaining code points from 256 to 65,535 store a wide variety of symbols and diacritical marks commonly used by other languages.

## INTRODUCTION TO THE CHAR DATA TYPE

The Char data type stores a Unicode character in one 16-bit (2-byte) value. The steps to declare variables having a data type of Char are identical to the steps to declare a variable having any other data type, as the following statement shows:

```
Dim LetterA, Result As Char
```

As shown in the preceding declaration statement, variables having a data type of Char are declared in the same way that any other variable is declared.

Storing data in a variable having a data type of Char requires that explicit type conversion be performed as the following statements show:

```
LetterA = System.Convert.ToChar(65)
LetterA = System.Convert.ToChar("A")
```

The System.Convert class supports a method named ToChar, which converts its argument to the Char data type. In the first statement, a code point (65) is converted to a Char. As mentioned, the code point for a capital "A" is 65, so that character is stored in the variable LetterA. The second statement initializes the variable using the ToChar method of the System.Convert class. Thus, a capital "A" is stored in the variable LetterA. The two preceding statements produce the same result.

Because a letter is just a single character, you might think that the following assignment statement will work to assign a literal value to a variable having a data type of Char:

```
Dim LetterA As Char
LetterA = "A"
```

However, if strict type checking is enabled, the preceding assignment statement causes a syntax error to be generated because the value on the right side of the assignment statement is a String rather than a Char. The Char data type is a more restrictive type than the String data type so the value is not implicitly converted. The reverse is not true, however. The Char data type is always implicitly converted to a String data type. Of course, the string is one character in length.

Assignment statements are also possible using the Char data type as the following statement shows:

```
Result = LetterA
```

The preceding statement assumes that both variables have a data type of Char. The value in the variable LetterA is stored in the variable Result.

## REPRESENTING UNICODE STRINGS

As mentioned, a string is made up of a sequence of characters. Each character in a string has a data type of Char and stores one Unicode character (code point). For example, the Unicode code point for the space character is 32. Both printable and nonprintable characters have an associated Unicode code point.

The Microsoft.VisualBasic.Strings class contains two methods that work with Unicode characters. They are the Asc method and the Chr method.

The Asc method has the following syntax:

### Syntax

```
Public Shared Function Asc(ByVal string As Char) As Integer
Public Shared Function Asc(ByVal string As String) As Integer
```

### Definition

The Asc method accepts either a character or string argument and returns the Unicode code point corresponding to the character, or first character in the string, respectively.

### Dissection

» In the first method, *string* contains a single character having a data type of Char. Note that the name of the argument is a bit of a misnomer because the data type of the argument is not String.

» In the second method, *string* contains multiple characters. The Asc method returns the character code (code point) of the first character in the string. The remaining characters are ignored.

### Code Example

```
Dim Result As Integer

Result = Asc("A")

Result = Asc("This is a string")
```

### Code Dissection

In the first assignment statement, the character "A" (a string having a length of 1) is converted to its numeric code point and the value is stored in the variable Result. The code point for the letter "A" is 65, so the value 65 is stored in the variable Result. In the second assignment statement, the first character in the string "T" is converted to its numeric code point. The code point for the letter "T" is 84, so the value 84 is stored in the variable Result. The remaining characters in the string are ignored.

In addition to converting a character or string to its corresponding code point, a code point can be converted to its corresponding Unicode character by calling the `Chr` method, which has the following syntax:

### Syntax

```
Public Shared Function Chr(ByVal charCode As Integer) As Char
```

### Definition

The `Chr` method accepts one argument, an `Integer` character code (code point), and returns the Unicode equivalent of that character.

### Dissection

» The *charCode* argument contains the code point to convert to a Unicode character. An exception is thrown if the character code cannot be converted to a Unicode character.

### Code Example

```
Dim CurrentChar As Char = Chr(32)
```

### Code Dissection

The preceding statement converts the code point 32 into a `Char` data type. The character code 32 represents a space so a space is stored in the variable CurrentChar.

This exploration exercise shows how to convert characters to their Unicode code points and how to convert code points back to their equivalent character values.

1. Start Visual Studio, if necessary, and open the solution file in the folder named **Chapter.05\Chapter05ConceptLesson**.

2. Run the application.

3. Click the **Character Conversion** tab, if necessary. Type **a** in the form's text box next to the prompt titled "Enter a Character", and click the **Asc** button. The code point for the character entered appears in the output label. The code in the event handler calls the `Asc` method on the contents of the text box, as shown in the following code segment:

   ```
   lblCodePoint.Text = Asc(txtCharacter.Text).ToString
   ```

4. Type **97** in the "Enter a Unicode Code Point" text box. Click the **Chr** button. The code in the event handler calls the `Chr` method on the code point stored in the text box, as shown in the following code segment:

   ```
   lblCharacter.Text = Chr(ToInt32(txtCodePoint.Text))
   ```

The corresponding Unicode code point appears as shown in Figure 5-1.

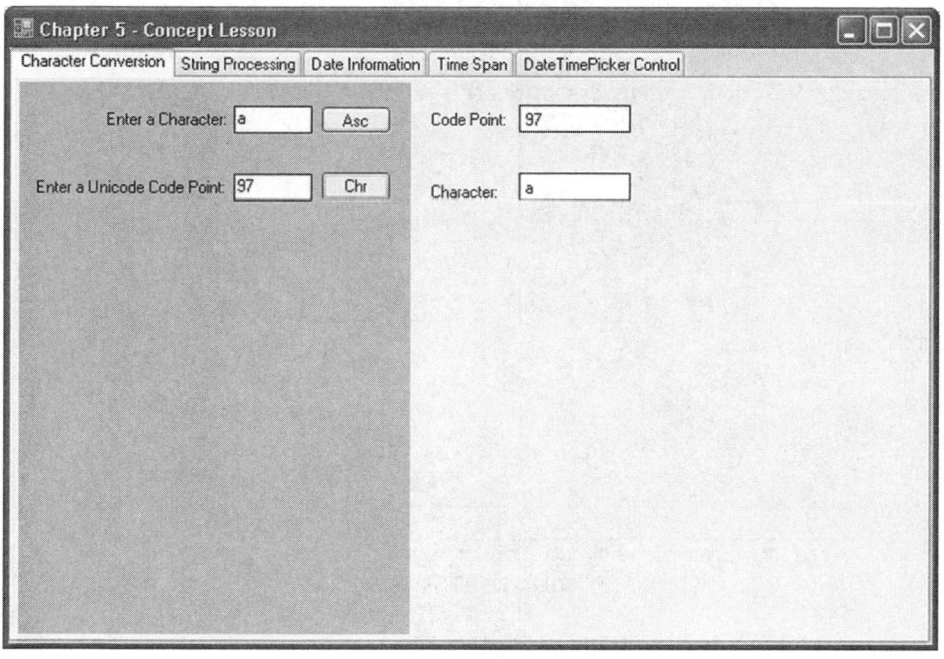

Figure 5-1: Concept lesson—Character Conversion tab

Having discussed the `Char` data type, the `String` data type will now be discussed in detail. Strings are nothing more than a collection of characters. In other words, a string is a collection of `Char` data types.

# INTRODUCTION TO THE STRING DATA TYPE

Many properties, such as the `Text` property of a text box, store data as consecutive characters called a **string**. A string is nothing more than a collection of characters having a data type of `Char`.

The `String` data type, which is a class, was introduced in Chapter 4, as you converted strings to numeric data types so as to perform arithmetic operations on the converted numeric data. Classes are reference types, so when declaring a variable having a data type of `String`, the memory allocated to the string variable contains another memory address. This second memory address stores the actual string of characters. Figure 5-2 illustrates how a `String` is stored in memory.

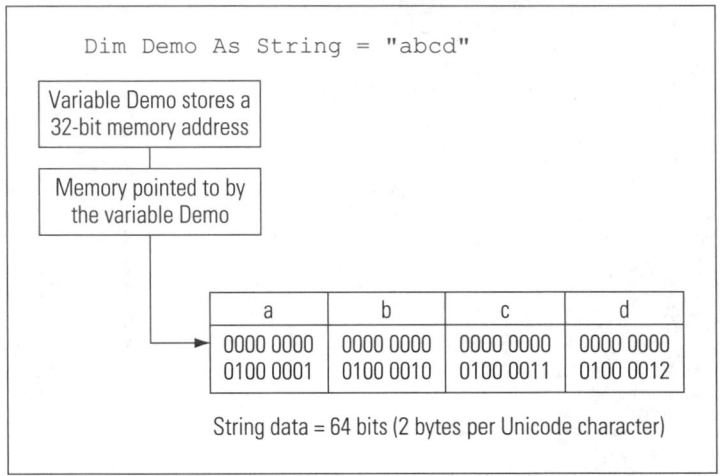

Figure 5-2: Storing data in a string

## STATEMENTS TO DECLARE A STRING

The statements to declare a string are no different than the statements to declare a variable of any other data type. The `Private` keyword is used to declare module-level `String` variables. The `Dim` keyword is used to declare local `String` variables. The following statements illustrate how to declare module-level variables having a data type of `String`:

```
Private Class frmMain
    Private Prefix As String
    Private FirstName, LastName As String
    Private CurrentName As String = "Joe Smith"
    ' procedures
End Class
```

The first of the preceding statements declares a module-level `String` variable named Prefix. The second statement shows that multiple `String` variables can be declared in the same statement, just as multiple numeric variables can be declared in the same statement. The variables FirstName and LastName both have a data type of `String`. The final statement declares and initializes a `String`. Double quotation marks always surround literal `String` values such as "Joe Smith."

Local `String` variables are declared in the same way as any other local variable. The variable is declared with the `Dim` keyword inside of a procedure, as shown in the following statements:

```
Sub Main()
    Dim CompanyName As String = "Course Technology"
    System.Console.WriteLine(CompanyName)
End Sub
```

The preceding statements declare a local `String` variable and write the contents of that variable to the Console window.

Variables having a data type of `String` can be used in assignment statements just as numeric variables can be used in assignment statements, as the following statements show:

```
Dim PersonName As String
Dim CurrentName As String = "Joe Smith"
PersonName = CurrentName
PersonName = txtName.Text
```

The first and second of the preceding statements declare variables named PersonName and CurrentName, respectively, each having a data type of `String`. The second statement initializes the string with a literal value of "Joe Smith." In the third statement, the contents of the variable CurrentName are stored in the variable PersonName. Thus, both variables store the same value. The final statement assumes that txtName is an instance of the `TextBox` control and stores the contents of the `Text` property into the variable named PersonName. The preceding assignment statements are valid because the data on the left and right side of the assignment statements have the same data type, which is `String`.

## TYPE CONVERSION

Type conversion must be performed when working with strings just as type conversion must be performed when working with numeric variables. So long as two variables or properties have the `String` data type, assignment statements are possible without performing explicit type conversion. If strict type checking is enabled with `Option Strict On`, then strings must be explicitly converted to numeric data types, and numeric data types must be explicitly converted to the `String` data type, as shown in the following statements:

```
Dim DataValue As Double = 1234.56
Dim FormattedOutputValue As String
FormattedOutputValue = DataValue.ToString("C")
```

The first two of the three preceding statements declare variables having the `Double` and `String` data types, respectively. The third statement explicitly converts the `Double`

value stored in the variable DataValue to a `String`, and formats that value as currency using the "C" format specifier. Thus, the variable FormattedOutputValue would contain the following string:

```
$1,234.56
```

Other numeric data types are converted in a similar manner by calling the `ToString` method of the underlying numeric data type.

As mentioned in Chapter 4, a variable having a data type of `String` must be explicitly converted to a numeric data type when strict type checking is enabled using a member of the `System.Convert` class, as the following statements illustrate:

```
Dim IntegerDataValue As Integer
Dim SingleDataValue As Single
IntegerDataValue = System.Convert.ToInt32(txtInput.Text)
SingleDataValue = System.Convert.ToSingle(txtInput.Text)
```

The first and second of the preceding statements declare `Integer` and `Single` variables to store the converted textual data. The final two statements assume that txtInput is an instance of the `TextBox` control. The first of the assignment statements converts the contents of the `Text` property, which is stored as a `String`, to an `Integer` data type and stores the value in the variable IntegerDataValue. The final statement converts the text to a `Single` data type and stores the result in the variable SingleDataValue. Note that an exception is thrown if the value cannot be converted to its respective data type.

## STRING OPERATIONS

Just as numeric variables can be used in expressions, so too can strings. One common string operation is concatenation. Strings are **concatenated**, or appended together, using the `&` operator, as shown in the following statements:

```
Dim FirstName As String = "John"
Dim LastName As String = "Brown"
Dim FullName As String
FullName = FirstName & " " & LastName
```

The preceding statements concatenate three strings. The first two statements declare variables and initialize them to the literal values "John" and "Brown", respectively. The final statement concatenates the two string variables and a literal value, which, in this case, is a space. Remember that a literal value is a value that does not change. When working with strings, a space is considered a character just as the letter "a" is considered a character. The space character is a literal value so it is surrounded by double quotation marks just as double quotation marks surround all literal string values.

Constants also can have a `String` data type, as shown in the following statements:

```
Dim Const COMMA As String = ","
Dim FirstName As String = "John"
Dim LastName As String = "Brown"
Dim FullName As String
FullName = LastName & COMMA & " " & FirstName
```

The preceding code segment stores the string "Brown, John" in the variable FullName. The constant COMMA stores a comma as its constant value, and is used in the assignment statement. Figure 5-3 illustrates how the preceding string concatenation operation works.

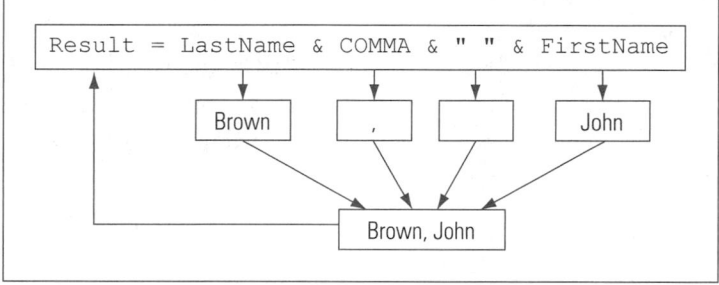

Figure 5-3: String concatenation

## CONTROL CHARACTERS AND SPECIAL CHARACTERS

In addition to containing visible characters, strings can also contain embedded characters called control characters. **Control characters** include such characters as the Tab character and the carriage return character. The Tab character is used to move text over on a line by a fixed number of spaces, and the carriage return is used to cause the subsequent text to appear on the next line.

The `Microsoft.VisualBasic.ControlChars` class contains fields that correspond to special (control) characters. The following list summarizes selected constants corresponding to commonly used control characters:

» The `Back` constant embeds a backspace character into a string.

» The `CrLf` constant embeds a carriage return, line feed sequence in a string, causing the cursor to advance to the first character of the next line.

» The `NewLine` constant embeds the same character sequence as the `CrLf` constant.

» The `NullChar` constant embeds a binary zero in a string. Assigning `NullChar` to a string variable creates an empty string.

» The `Quote` constant embeds a double quotation mark in a string.

» The `Tab` constant embeds a Tab character in a string.

Suppose that you want a string to appear on multiple lines in a text box named txtOutput. A control character can be embedded in the string, as shown in the following statement:

```
Imports Microsoft.VisualBasic
 . . .
txtOutput.Text = "John" & ControlChars.CrLf & "Brown"
```

The preceding statement creates a string that will appear on two lines. The string "John" will appear on the first line and the string "Brown" will appear on the second line. The CrLf property of the ControlChars class embeds a carriage return, line feed between the two strings. In the preceding code segment, the Microsoft.VisualBasic namespace was imported to reduce typing.

Control characters have unique Unicode code points just as printable characters have unique Unicode code points. For example, the decimal value (code point) 9 is the Unicode code point for the Tab key, and the decimal value 0 is the Unicode code point for the null character. Recall that the Chr method converts a Unicode code point to its equivalent character. As such, the following statements show two equivalent ways to accomplish the same task of concatenating a Tab character into a string:

```
Dim StringCurrent As String
StringCurrent = "Joe" & ControlChars.Tab & "Smith"
StringCurrent = "Joe" & Chr(9) & "Smith"
```

Both of the preceding statements store a string containing the name "Joe Smith" with the Tab character embedded between the first name and the last name. The first uses the Tab property of the Microsoft.VisualBasic.ControlChars class. That same Tab character is produced by calling the Chr(9) method.

## EMBEDDING QUOTATION MARKS IN STRINGS

Given that double quotation marks are used to enclose literal string values, you might wonder how to embed double quotation marks in a string. The following statements illustrate how to accomplish this task using the Quote field of the Microsoft.VisualBasic.ControlChars class:

```
Dim QuotedString As String = "The " & _
    ControlChars.Quote & "Fox" & ControlChars.Quote & _
    " Ran Fast."
```

Embedding a double quotation mark in a string is no different than embedding any other special character into a string. The preceding statement produces the following string value:

```
The "Fox" Ran Fast.
```

To delete the contents of a string, it is possible to assign either an empty string or the NullChar constant, as shown in the following statements:

```
Imports Microsoft.VisualBasic
. . .
Dim EmptyString As String
EmptyString = ""
EmptyString = ControlChars.NullChar
```

Both of the preceding assignment statements remove the text from the variable named EmptyString.

## WORKING WITH MULTILINE TEXT BOXES

As you know, the Text property of a text box stores data having a data type of String. In addition to displaying a string on a single line, a TextBox control instance can be configured to display a string on multiple lines. A multiline text box is one that is capable of displaying, but that is not required to display, text on more than one line. To create a multiline text box, set the MultiLine property to True for the TextBox control instance.

The ScrollBars property works in conjunction with the MultiLine property and defines whether horizontal or vertical scroll bars appear along the right side or bottom of the control instance. The following settings control the appearance of the scroll bars:

» If the ScrollBars property is set to None, scroll bars do not appear.

» If the ScrollBars property is set to Horizontal, a horizontal scroll bar appears along the bottom of the control instance.

» If the ScrollBars property is set to Vertical, a vertical scroll bar appears along the right side of the control instance.

» Finally, if the ScrollBars property is set to Both, both horizontal and vertical scroll bars appear, as necessary.

The WordWrap property works in conjunction with the MultiLine property. If set to True, lines wrap on word boundaries. Figure 5-4 shows two TextBox control instances containing identical text. In the upper text box, the WordWrap property is set to False. In the lower text box, the WordWrap property is set to True.

When the WordWrap property is set to False, the text does not wrap around lines. Rather, horizontal scroll bars appear if the ScrollBars property is set to Horizontal. Scroll bars also appear if the ScrollBars property is set to Both.

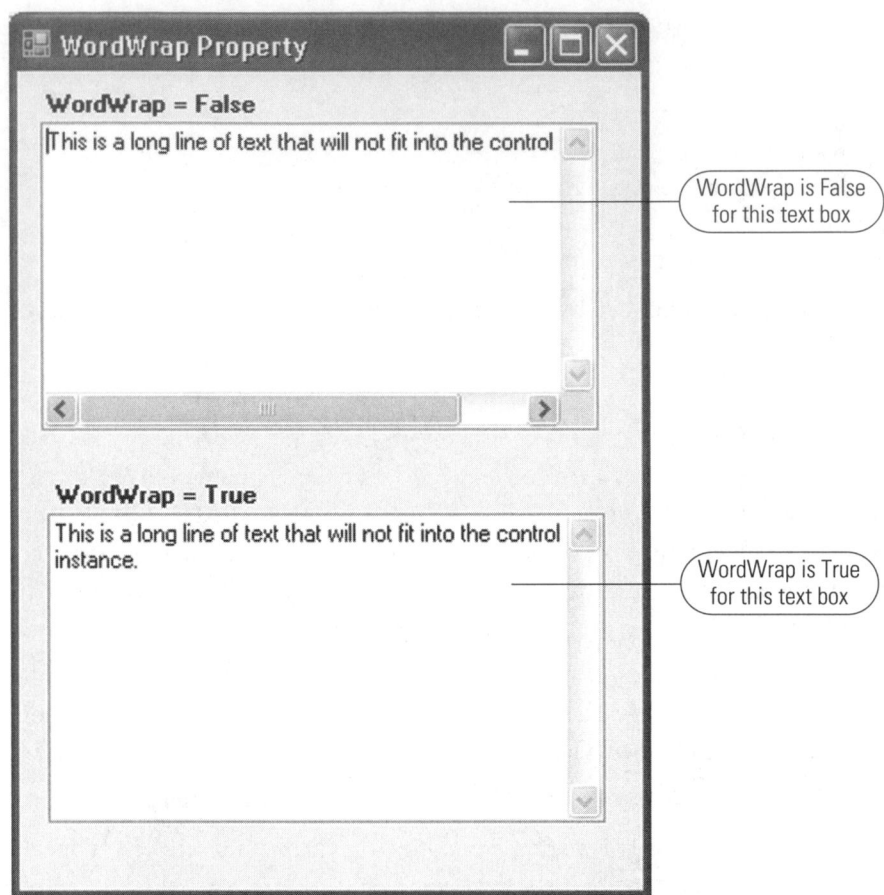

Figure 5-4: The effect of the WordWrap property

# STRING MANIPULATION METHODS

**>>NOTE**

Several intrinsic functions exist that operate on strings. These intrinsic functions are supplied for backward compatibility with older versions of Visual Basic. This chapter does not discuss these older intrinsic functions.

The String class supports properties and methods, just as other classes support properties and methods. These methods can be used to determine the length of a string and to convert a string to a particular form, such as all uppercase or all lowercase characters. Methods are also available to determine whether a string contains a particular pattern, and to extract a substring from an existing string.

This section discusses most of the available String operations and the methods used to perform string operations.

## DETERMINING THE LENGTH OF A STRING

Operations are performed on strings by calling the methods and referencing the properties of the `String` class. To begin, the `Length` property of the `String` class returns an `Integer` containing the number of characters in a string. If the string is empty, the `Length` property returns 0. This property is useful for validating the maximum size of a string or validating that a string is not empty. The following statements illustrate how to determine the length of a string:

```
Dim FullName As String = "Mr. Ed Jones"
Dim LengthOfString As Integer
LengthOfString = FullName.Length()
```

The first statement declares and initializes a `String` variable, and the second statement declares an `Integer` variable to store the length of the string. The final statement reads the value of the `Length` property to determine the length of the string. The string contains 12 characters, so the value 12 is stored in the variable named LengthOfString.

Just as it is possible to determine the length of a string stored in a variable, it is also possible to determine the length of a string stored in a text box, or the length of a literal string value, as shown in the following statements:

```
Dim LengthOfString As Integer
LengthOfString = txtName.Text.Length()
LengthOfString = ("Mr. Ed Jones").Length()
```

The second of the preceding statements determines the number of characters in the `Text` property of the text box named txtName. The final statement determines the length of a literal string. Note that the parentheses were added to the final statement to improve readability.

**»NOTE**

The `Length` property counts all the characters in the string, including spaces and nonprinting characters.

## CONVERTING THE CASE OF A STRING

The `ToUpper` and `ToLower` methods of the `String` class convert all of the characters in a string to uppercase and lowercase characters, respectively, as the following statements show:

```
Dim CurrentString As String = "John Brown"
Dim UpperString, LowerString As String
UpperString = CurrentString.ToUpper()
LowerString = CurrentString.ToLower()
```

In the third and fourth of the preceding statements, the string is converted to all uppercase characters and all lowercase characters, respectively. If you ran the code in the preceding example, the result of the conversion would be as follows:

```
JOHN BROWN
john brown
```

## WORKING WITH PARTS OF A STRING

The IndexOf method of the String class determines whether a string contains a specific substring and has the following syntax:

### Syntax

```
Public Function IndexOf(ByVal value As String) As Integer

Public Function IndexOf(ByVal value As String, ByVal
startIndex As Integer) As Integer

Public Function IndexOf(ByVal value As String, ByVal
startIndex As Integer, count As Integer) As Integer
```

### Definition

» The IndexOf method searches the value argument to determine whether the string contains a particular substring. If the IndexOf method finds the substring, it returns the character position (leading character) within the string where the substring first appears. The IndexOf method is 0-based. Thus, the first character in a string has a value of 0. If the substring is not found, the IndexOf method returns negative 1 (–1). If the string is empty, an exception is thrown. If the substring appears more than once in the string, the character position of the first occurrence is returned.

» In the second method, IndexOf accepts a second argument indicating the character position where the search will begin. Again, the character position is 0-based.

» In the final method, IndexOf accepts a third argument indicating the number of characters to search along with the character position of where the search will begin.

### Code Example

```
Dim Position As Integer
Dim States As String = "Arizona California Nevada"
Position = States.IndexOf("California")        ' 8
Position = States.IndexOf("California", 10)    ' -1
Position = States.IndexOf("Arizona",0 , 5)     ' -1
```

### Code Dissection

The first call to the IndexOf method searches the string "Arizona California Nevada" for the substring "California." The search begins at the first character in the string. The pattern is found at position 8 (the ninth character). In the second statement, the second argument marks the character position where the search will begin. Because the search begins at character position 10, the search string "California" is not found. Thus, the method call returns –1. In the final statement, the search begins at character position 0, but only five characters are searched so the method again returns –1 because the substring is not found.

The `Substring` method returns a selected number of characters from a string and has the following syntax:

## Syntax

```
Public Function Substring(ByVal startIndex As Integer) As
String

Public Function Substring(ByVal startIndex As Integer, ByVal
length As Integer) As String
```

## Definition

» The `Substring` method returns a selected number of characters from a string. For example, it allows a specific word or phrase from a string or any other consecutive sequence of characters to be extracted from a string.

## Dissection

» In both methods, the `Substring` method returns a string starting at *startIndex*. *startIndex* is 0-based so the first character in a string has a *startIndex* value of 0.

» The *length* argument appearing in the second method is used to specify the number of characters to return. The `Substring` method throws an exception if *startIndex* is less than zero; calling the second method throws an exception if *length* is greater than the length of the string.

## Code Example

```
Dim SSN As String = "555-12-3456"
Dim Part1, Part2, Part3 As String
Part1 = SSN.Substring(0, 3)
Part2 = SSN.Substring(4, 2)
Part3 = SSN.Substring(7, 4)
```

## Code Dissection

The preceding statements declare string variables to store the Social Security number and the parts of the Social Security number. The last three statements extract substrings from the string named SSN. The first three characters are extracted and stored in the variable named Part1. The fifth and sixth characters are extracted and stored in the variable named Part2. The last four characters are stored in the variable named Part3.

Figure 5-5 illustrates the operation of the `Substring` method to extract the first three characters from a Social Security number. The first part of the Social Security number is stored in a `String` variable named Part1.

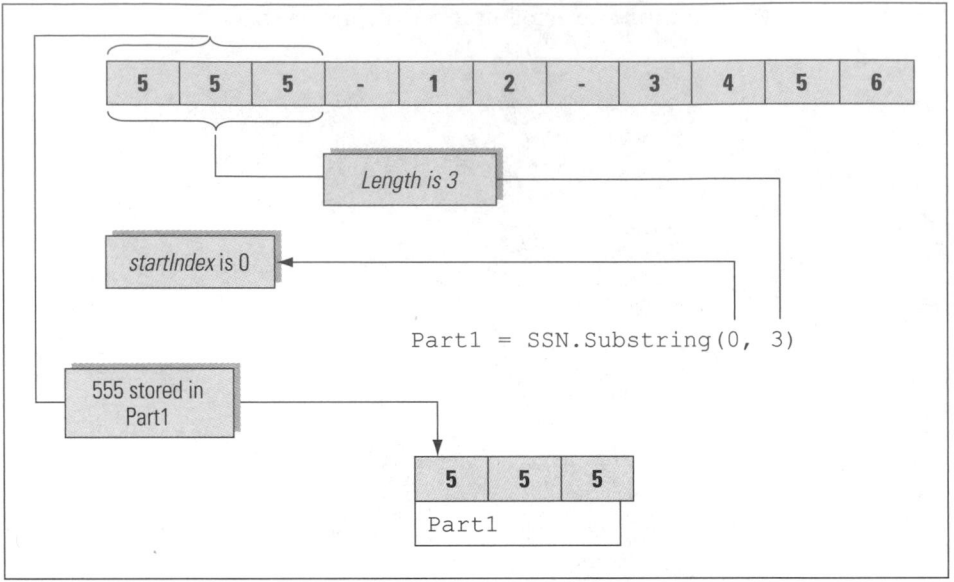

Figure 5-5: Operation of the Substring method

As shown in Figure 5-5, the `Substring` method is called to extract the first three characters from the Social Security number.

## INSERTING AND REMOVING CHARACTERS FROM A STRING

The `Insert` method inserts a string into an existing string and has the following syntax:

### Syntax
```
Public Function Insert(ByVal startIndex As Integer, ByVal
value As String) As String
```

### Definition
The `Insert` method of the `String` class inserts a string of characters into an existing string at some defined position. The character previously existing in that defined position, and those to the right of that character position are shifted to the right, as necessary.

### Dissection
» *startIndex* contains the character position of the existing string where the new string will be inserted. This property is 0-based. An exception is thrown if *startIndex* is less than 0 or greater than the string's length.

» *value* contains the string that will be inserted.

*(Continued)*  ▶

## Code Example

```
Dim SSN As String = "590123456"

SSN = SSN.Insert(5, "-")

SSN = SSN.Insert(3, "-")
```

## Code Dissection

The first of the preceding statements declares a string and initializes the variable's value to a Social Security number with the dashes removed. The second and third statements insert the string "-" at the character positions five and three. Thus, after the statements have executed, the value of the variable SSN is "590-12-3456".

The Insert method inserts a string before the character position rather than after the character position. Thus, if characters were being inserted at character position 0, the inserted characters would appear at the beginning of the string. Characters to the right of the inserted position are moved to the right, as necessary. If you were to insert a string at character position 0, it would be easier to just use the string concatenation operator.

Figure 5-6 illustrates the operation of the Insert method.

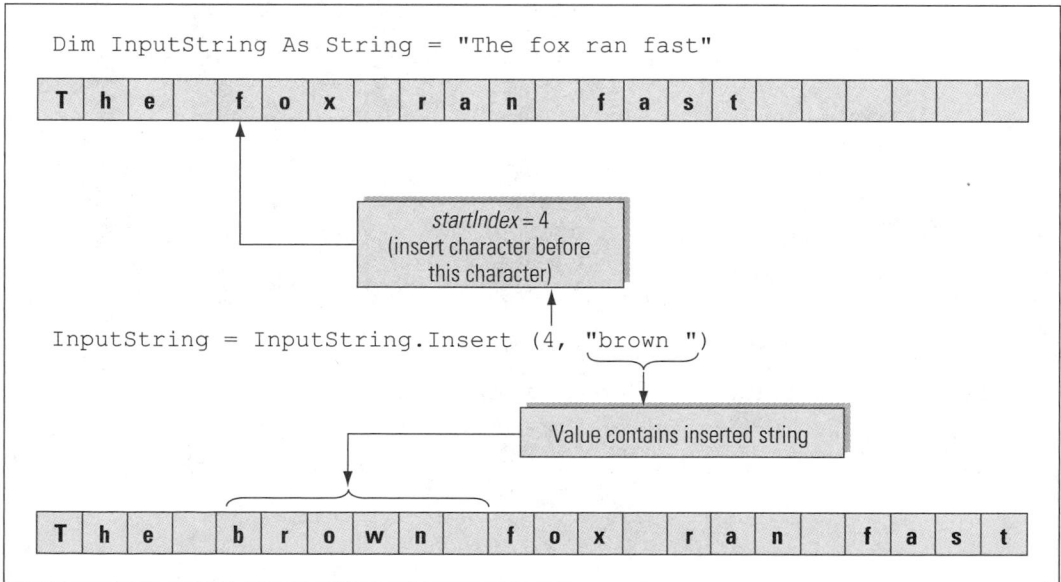

Figure 5-6: Operation of the Insert method

Characters can be removed from a string by calling the Remove method of the String class, which has the following syntax:

## Syntax

```
Public Function Remove(ByVal startIndex As Integer) As String

Public Function Remove(ByVal startIndex As Integer, count
As Integer) As String
```

## Definition

The Remove method removes one or more characters from a string.

## Dissection

» The first method removes all the characters from the string starting at the character position specified by the *startIndex* argument, through the end of the string. Again, *startIndex* is 0-based. An exception is thrown if *startIndex* is less than zero or greater than the length of the string.

» The second method removes *count* characters from the string starting at the character position specified by the *startIndex* argument. An exception is thrown if *startIndex* plus *count* is greater than the length of the string.

## Code Example

```
Dim Telephone As String = "702-555-1212"

Dim TelephoneNoAreaCode As String

TelephoneNoAreaCode = Telephone.Remove(0, 4)
```

## Code Dissection

The preceding statements remove the area code from a telephone number by calling the Remove method of the String class. The first four characters are removed from the string so the resulting value stored in the variable TelephoneNoAreaCode is "555-1212".

Figure 5-7 shows the operation of the Remove method.

Visual Studio makes the task of string replacement easy. The Replace method of the String class is used to replace one character with another or one string with another depending on which method is called. The Replace method has the following syntax:

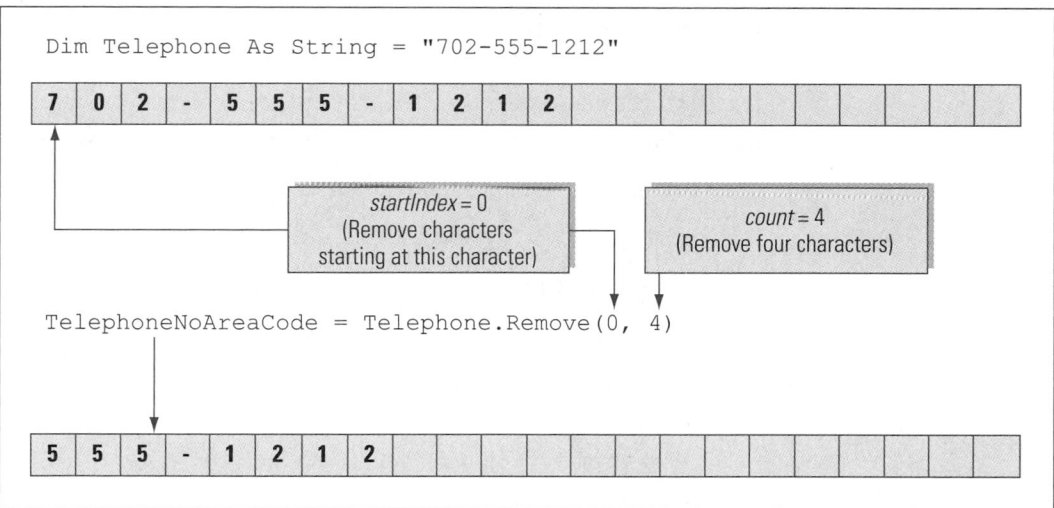

```
Dim Telephone As String = "702-555-1212"
```

| 7 | 0 | 2 | - | 5 | 5 | 5 | - | 1 | 2 | 1 | 2 |  |  |  |  |  |  |  |  |  |  |  |  |

*startIndex* = 0
(Remove characters
starting at this character)

*count* = 4
(Remove four characters)

```
TelephoneNoAreaCode = Telephone.Remove(0, 4)
```

| 5 | 5 | 5 | - | 1 | 2 | 1 | 2 |  |  |  |  |  |  |  |  |  |  |  |  |  |  |  |  |

Figure 5-7: Operation of the Remove method

## Syntax

```
Public Function Replace(ByVal oldChar As Char, ByVal
newChar As Char) As String

Public Function Replace(ByVal oldValue As String, ByVal
newValue As String) As String
```

## Definition

The `Replace` method replaces characters within a string or substrings within a string. All instances of the character or substring are replaced, rather than just a single instance.

## Dissection

» The first method replaces one character with another character in a string. *oldChar* is replaced by *newChar*.

» The second method replaces one substring with another substring in a string. *oldValue* is replaced by *newValue*.

## Code Example

```
Dim InputString As String = "A B C D E"

InputString = InputString.Replace(" ", "")
```

## Code Dissection

The first of the preceding statements declares and initializes a `String` variable. The second statement calls the `Replace` method replacing a space with a null character, thereby removing all of the spaces from the string. Thus, the resulting string contains the value "ABCDE".

## DELETING LEADING OR TRAILING SPACES

At times, a string appears with leading or trailing spaces. These leading or trailing spaces must often be removed before the string data can be processed. Three methods of the `String` class are used to remove leading and trailing spaces from a string, as described in the following list:

» The `Trim` method removes both leading and trailing spaces from a string.

» The `TrimEnd` method removes trailing spaces from a string.

» The `TrimStart` method removes leading spaces from a string.

The following code segment illustrates the use of the various `Trim` methods:

```
Dim InputString As String = " Joe Smith "
Dim ResultString As String
ResultString = InputString.TrimStart    ' "Joe Smith "
ResultString = InputString.TrimEnd      ' " Joe Smith"
ResultString = InputString.Trim         ' "Joe Smith"
```

In the third of the preceding statements, the leading spaces are removed. In the fourth statement, the trailing spaces are removed. In the final statement, both the leading and trailing spaces are removed.

In this exploration exercise, you will see how to perform various operations on strings.

1.  Run the solution named **Chapter05ConceptLesson**, and click the **String Processing** tab. Figure 5-8 shows the String Processing tab.

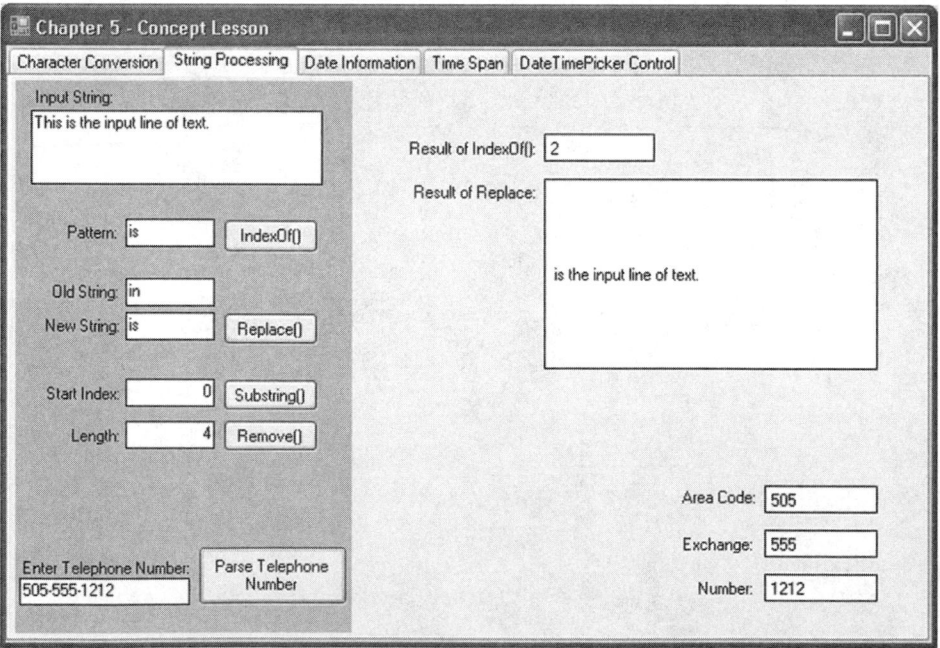

Figure 5-8: Concept lesson—String Processing tab

2. The Input String text box contains a predefined input string. Default input values have also been supplied for the other input fields. Click the **IndexOf( )**, **Replace( )**, **Substring( )**, and **Remove( )** buttons to call the methods of the same name pertaining to the `String` class and display the output values. Examine the `Click` event handlers for these buttons to see the syntax to call the respective methods.

3. Click the **Parse Telephone Number** button. The telephone number is broken down into its component parts and displayed in the output labels. The `Click` event handler for this button contains statements similar to those shown previously in the chapter to parse a Social Security number.

# MINI-QUIZ 1

1. Which of the following statements is correct regarding the `String` data type?

   a. The `String` data type is a reference type.

   b. The `String` class supports methods to manipulate strings.

   c. Strings are made up of one or more Unicode characters.

   d. all of the above

   e. none of the above

2. What is the name of the method to determine the character position of a substring within a string?

   a. `Pos`

   b. `Index`

   c. `IndexOf`

   d. `InString`

   e. none of the above

3. What value is stored in the variable named StringValue1 after the following statements have executed?

   ```
   Dim StringValue1 As String = "James Smith"
   StringValue1 = StringValue1.Replace("James", "Jim")
   StringValue1 = StringValue1.Insert(4, "R. ")
   ```

4. Describe the error in the following set of statements:

   ```
   Dim StringValue1 As String = "James Smith"
   StringValue1 = StringValue1.Remove(-1, 1)
   ```

# INTRODUCTION TO DATES

The next data type discussed in this chapter is the `System.DateTime` data type, which is used to store dates and perform operations on dates.

You have two problems to address when working with dates. First, it is necessary to uniquely represent a point in time in a binary form. Second, it is necessary to display that point in time in a way that is meaningful, using a well-known calendar.

Every calendar defines, somehow, the beginning of time. For example, the Gregorian calendar in use today defines the beginning of time as the year 1 B.C., which has a value of 0. The term used to define a calendar's beginning of time is called the **epoch**. Different calendars have different epochs.

As you likely know, the Gregorian calendar measures time as elapsed years, months, and days, since the epoch. Computer systems represent dates and times much differently and use a different epoch. For example, the UNIX operating system stores a date as the number of elapsed milliseconds since January 1, 1970, which happens to be the date that UNIX was originally released. That is, UNIX stores the date January 1, 1970, as the value 0 and increments that value by one for every millisecond that elapses from that date. Dates prior to January 1, 1970, are represented as negative numbers. Thus, using the UNIX timekeeping system, the epoch is January 1, 1970.

Windows uses a very different representation to store date values as described in the following list:

» The earliest date in the past that can be stored in the `DateTime` data type is January 01, 0001.

» The farthest date in the future that can be stored in the `DateTime` data type is December 31, 9999. Thus, there will be a year 10,000 problem.

» The date January 01, 0001, is the epoch.

Understanding that different calendars and computers represent a point in time differently, it follows that different calendars and computers increment that point in time differently. The Gregorian calendar, UNIX, and Windows have a different way of counting points in time, as described in the following list:

» Using the Gregorian calendar, time is incremented daily. That is, the time interval is one day. More granular time increments are referred to as timekeeping.

» The UNIX operating system increments time in milliseconds. Thus, the UNIX measurement of time is the number of elapsed milliseconds since January 1, 1970.

» Windows increments time in 100 nanosecond units, called *ticks*, from January 01, 0001.

# THE SYSTEM.DATETIME DATA TYPE

To store dates and perform operations on dates, Visual Basic uses the `System.DateTime` data type. A variable having the `System.DateTime` data type is 64 bits in length. Two of the bits represent the time zone where the date was created. The remaining bits store an unsigned `Integer` counting the number of ticks since January 1, 0001.

The `System.DateTime` data type is represented as a structure and is, thus, a value type. Remember that the memory allocated to a value type stores the actual data. The `System.DateTime` data type supports properties and methods designed specifically to perform operations on dates and to display dates using different formats.

The syntax to declare a variable having the `DateTime` data type is the same as the syntax to declare any other variable. The following statements illustrate how to declare and initialize `DateTime` variables:

```
Dim CurrentDate As DateTime
Dim PastDate, FutureDate As DateTime
Dim InitializedDate As DateTime = #3/22/2006#
```

The first of the preceding statements declares a variable of type `DateTime`. The second statement declares two variables having a data type of `DateTime`. Again, multiple variables can be declared in the same statement. The final statement declares a `DateTime` variable and initializes its value to 3/22/2006. When a literal value is used to initialize a variable having the `DateTime` data type, pound signs (#) surround the literal value. To illustrate a common error made when initializing a date, suppose that you wrote the following statement to declare and initialize a date:

```
Dim InitializedDate As DateTime = 3/22/2006
```

The preceding statement causes a syntax error because 3/22/2006 is interpreted as 3 divided by 22 divided by 2006, and the result of such a division operation has a data type of `Double`. The `Double` data type cannot be implicitly converted to a `DateTime` data type.

If strict type checking is enabled, the following statement would also produce a syntax error:

```
Dim CurrentDate As DateTime = "3/22/2006"
```

The preceding statement causes a syntax error because the value "3/22/2006" is considered a literal `String` data type, which cannot be implicitly converted to a date.

## MEMBERS OF THE SYSTEM.DATETIME STRUCTURE

Just as other structures support properties and methods, so too does the `System.DateTime` structure. There are two fields named `MaxValue` and `MinValue`, which store the largest possible date (12/31/9999 11:59:59 PM), and the smallest possible date (01/01/0001 12:00:00 AM), respectively. The following code segment shows how to read the values from these properties:

```
Dim MaximumDate As DateTime = System.DateTime.MaxValue
Dim MinimumDate As DateTime = System.DateTime.MinValue
```

The `System.DateTime` structure supports two properties that get the current date and time and the current date.

» The `Now` property returns the current local date and time as a `DateTime` structure. The resolution (granularity) of the time value is roughly 10 milliseconds.

» The `Today` property returns the current date as a `DateTime` structure. The time is set to 00:00:00.

The following statements show how to get the current date and time from the system and the current date from the system:

```
Dim CurrentDateAndTime As DateTime = System.DateTime.Now
Dim CurrentDate As DateTime = System.DateTime.Today
```

The `DateTime` data type supports several properties to get the various parts of a date or time as described in the following list:

» The `Day`, `Month`, and `Year` properties return the day of the month, month of the year, and year, respectively as `Integer` values. Valid day values are between 1 and 31. Valid month values are between 1 and 12. Years are stored as four-digit values. That is, the year 2006 is represented as 2006 rather than 06.

» The `Hour`, `Minute`, and `Second` properties return the time elements having the same name. Each of these properties stores an `Integer`. Valid hour values range from 0 to 23. Valid minute values range from 0 to 59, and valid second values range from 0 to 59.

» The `Millisecond` property gets the milliseconds part of the date.

» The `DayOfWeek` and `DayOfYear` properties return an `Integer` containing the day of the week and the day of the year, respectively. Sunday is considered the first day of the week and has a value of 0. Saturday is considered the last day of the week and has a value of 6. The first day of the year is 1.

To illustrate the use of the preceding properties, the following statements store the current date in a variable, and then read the values of the various properties.

```
Dim CurrentDay, CurrentMonth, CurrentYear As Integer
Dim CurrentHour, CurrentMinute, CurrentSecond As Integer

Dim CurrentDateAndTime As DateTime = System.DateTime.Now
CurrentYear = CurrentDateAndTime.Year
CurrentMonth = CurrentDateAndTime.Month
CurrentDay = CurrentDateAndTime.Day
CurrentHour = CurrentDateAndTime.Hour
CurrentMinute = CurrentDateAndTime.Minute
CurrentSecond = CurrentDateAndTime.Second
```

## METHODS THAT WORK WITH DATES

Two classification methods work with dates as summarized in the following list:

» The `IsDaylightSavingTime` method returns a `Boolean` value indicating whether daylight savings time is in effect for the date.

» The `IsLeapYear` method accepts one argument—an integer containing the year. The method returns a `Boolean` value indicating whether the year is a leap year.

The following code segment illustrates how to use these methods:

```
Dim DaylightTime, LeapYear As Boolean
Dim CurrentDateAndTime As DateTime = System.DateTime.Now
DaylightTime = CurrentDateAndTime.IsDaylightSavingTime()
LeapYear = _
    System.DateTime.IsLeapYear(CurrentDateAndTime.Year)
```

The first of the preceding statements declare `Boolean` variables to store the results from the classification methods. The second statement stores the current date and time in a variable named CurrentDateAndTime. The third statement calls the `IsDaylightSavingTime` method on the current date. The `IsLeapYear` method accepts one argument, an `Integer` containing a year. The final statement calls the `IsLeapYear` method using the current year as the argument.

Just as all other objects support a method named `ToString` so too does the `DateTime` data type. In fact, the `DateTime` data type supports variations of the `ToString` method to format dates and times in different ways as mentioned in the following list:

» The `ToString` method converts a `DateTime` structure to a string. The `ToString` method of the `System.Convert` class can also be used.

» The `ToLongDateString` and `ToShortDateString` methods convert a `DateTime` structure to a string using the computer's long date format and short date format, respectively. Assuming the date is 8/27/2006, the default long date string would be "Sunday, August 27, 2006," and the default short date string would be "8/27/2006." The Control Panel is used to set the short date format and the long date format.

» The `ToLongTimeString` and `ToShortTimeString` methods convert a `DateTime` structure to a string using the computer's long and short time formats, respectively. A long time string would appear as 10:49:48 AM while a short time string would appear as 10:49 AM. Again, the Control Panel is used to set the short and long time formats.

The following statements get the current date and time from the system and format the output:

```
Dim CurrentDate, CurrentDateAndTime As DateTime
CurrentDate = System.DateTime.Today
CurrentDateAndTime = System.DateTime.Now
System.Console.WriteLine(CurrentDate.ToString)
System.Console.WriteLine(CurrentDateAndTime.ToString)
```

The first statement declares two variables having the `DateTime` data type. The next two statements store the current date and current date and time in the two variables. Calling the `ToString` method on a date causes Visual Basic to convert the date to a string containing both the date part and the time part. The following code segment shows how the two dates are formatted using the `ToString` method:

```
7/29/2006 12:00:00 AM
7/29/2006 12:17:54 PM
```

The `ToShortDateString` and `ToLongDateString` methods display only the date part of a `DateTime` variable and exclude the time part.

The following statements get the current date and format it by calling the `ToLongDateString` and `ToShortDateString` methods, respectively:

```
System.Console.WriteLine( _
    System.DateTime.Today.ToLongDateString)
System.Console.Writeline( _
    System.DateTime.Today.ToShortDateString)
```

The first statement converts the current date to a string using the long date format and the second statement converts the current date to a string using the short date format. The results are printed to the Console window. The following strings show a date formatted as both a long date string and a short date string. Note that these formats might vary based on the date format settings on your computer.

```
Saturday, July 29, 2006
7/29/2006
```

In this exploration exercise, you will see how various properties are used to get information about a date.

1. Run the solution named **Chapter05ConceptLesson**, and click the **Date Information** tab. Figure 5-9 shows the Date Information tab.

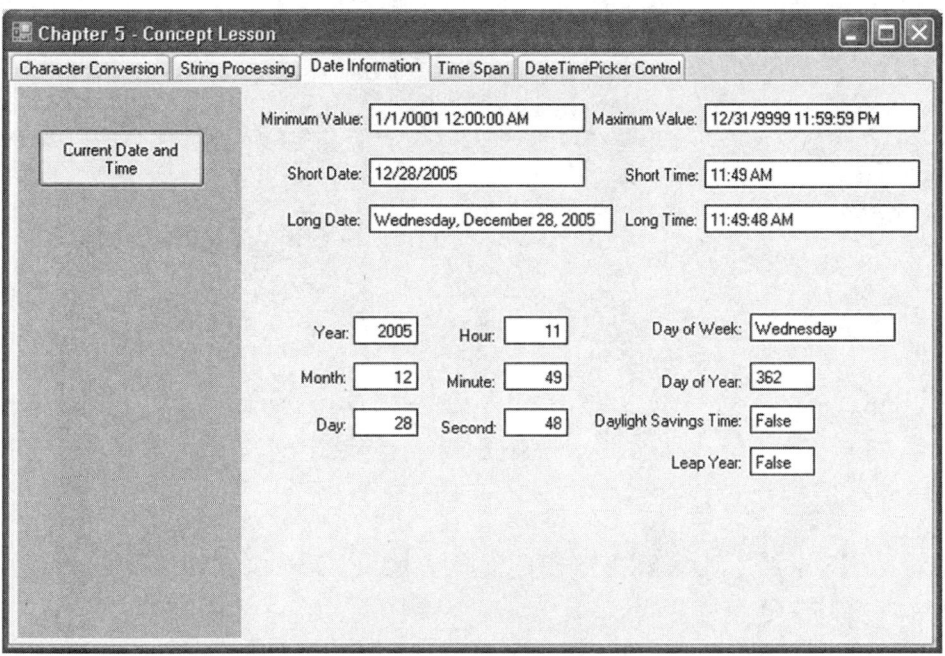

Figure 5-9: Concept lesson—Date Information tab

2. Click the **Current Date and Time** button. The current date appears in the form's controls instances. Examine the Click event handler for the Button control instance. The code in the event handler gets the current date and prints the respective informational values to the output labels appearing on the form.

## MINI-QUIZ 2

1. What is the term used to describe a calendar's beginning of time?

2. Which of the following statements is correct regarding the System.DateTime data type?

    a. It is a reference type.

    b. It is a value type 64 bits in length.

    c. To get the current date and time, you would call the DateTime method.

    d. The GetYear, GetMonth, and GetDay methods get the current year, month, and day from the current date.

    e. none of the above

3. Describe the error in the following statements:

```
Dim CurrentDateAndTime As DateTime = _
    System.DateTime.Now
Dim LeapYear As Boolean
LeapYear = _
    System.DateTime.IsLeapYear(CurrentDateAndTime)
```

# PERFORMING CALCULATIONS ON DATES

It is possible to perform arithmetic operations on variables having a data type of DateTime using the methods appearing in the following list:

» The AddHours, AddMinutes, and AddSeconds methods add a fixed number of intervals (hours, minutes, or seconds) to an existing DateTime structure and return a DateTime structure. If negative numbers are added to a time, the value is subtracted from the time.

» The AddYears, AddMonths, and AddDays methods add years, months, and days to a date, respectively, and return a DateTime structure. Again, negative values cause the value to be subtracted from the date.

» The `DaysInMonth` method returns the number of days in a particular month. The method does account for leap year.

» The `Subtract` method subtracts a date from another date and returns a `DateTime` structure containing the time difference.

Each of the preceding methods accepts one argument having a data type of `Double`, and each returns a `DateTime` structure. If the argument's value is positive, a fractional number of years, months, or days is added to the date. If the value is negative, a fractional number of years, months, or days is subtracted from the date. That is, if the `AddYears` method were called with an argument value of 1.5, then 1.5 years would be added to the date. The following statements illustrate the date arithmetic methods:

```
Dim NextDay As DateTime = Today.AddDays(1)
Dim NextMonth As DateTime = Today.AddMonths(1)
Dim NextYear As DateTime = Today.AddYears(1)
Dim LastDay As DateTime = Today.AddDays(-1)
Dim LastMonth As DateTime = Today.AddMonths(-1)
Dim LastYear As DateTime = Today.AddYears(-1)
```

The first three of the preceding statements add one day, one month, and one year to the current date, respectively, and store the result in the corresponding variable. The last three statements subtract one day, one month, and one year from the current date, respectively.

In addition to adding a fixed number of days, months, or other units to a date, it is possible to add a specific time interval to a date.

## INTRODUCTION TO THE TIMESPAN STRUCTURE

The `TimeSpan` structure is a data type that represents a time interval. In this way, the `TimeSpan` structure stores elapsed time much like a stopwatch. The `TimeSpan` structure has the following members:

### Syntax
`System.TimeSpan structure`

### Public Properties
» The `Milliseconds` property stores the number of whole milliseconds in the interval. The `Days`, `Minutes`, and `Seconds` properties store the number of whole days, minutes, and seconds in the interval. Suppose that 121 seconds had elapsed. In such a case, the `Minutes` property would have a value of 2 and the `Seconds` property would have a value of 1, because 2 minutes and 1 second had elapsed. Each of these properties has a data type of `Integer`.

*(Continued)*

The `TimeSpan` constructor accepts three arguments: the number of elapsed hours, minutes, and seconds. The following code segment shows the use of the `TimeSpan` structure:

```
Dim Span1 As New TimeSpan(1, 1, 1)
Dim Span2 As New TimeSpan(2, 2, 2)
Dim Span3 As TimeSpan = Span2 + Span1
Console.WriteLine(Span3.Hours.ToString)         ' 3
Console.WriteLine(Span3.Minutes.ToString)       ' 3
Console.WriteLine(Span3.Seconds.ToString)       ' 3
Console.WriteLine(Span3.TotalHours.ToString)    ' 3.0508333
Console.WriteLine(Span3.TotalMinutes.ToString)  ' 183.05
Console.WriteLine(Span3.TotalSeconds.ToString)  ' 10983
```

The first two statements create instances of the `TimeSpan` structure. The variable Span1 is set to 1 elapsed hour, minute, and second. The variable Span2 is set to 2 elapsed hours, minutes, and seconds. The third statement adds the two `TimeSpans` together. The total elapsed time is 3 hours, 3 minutes, and 3 seconds. The final statements display the total number of elapsed hours, minutes, and seconds. That is, three hours, three minutes, and three seconds is equal to 10983 seconds.

## INTRODUCTION TO THE DATEDIFF METHOD

In addition to using the `TimeSpan` structure to perform arithmetic on dates, the `DateDiff` method of the `Microsoft.VisualBasic.DateAndTime` class computes the elapsed time between two date values. The `DateDiff` method returns a `Long` containing the number of elapsed date or time units. It is possible to specify different time units. That is, the `DateDiff` method will return such date and time units as years, months, days, hours, minutes, and seconds. The `DateDiff` method has the following syntax:

## Syntax

```
result = DateDiff(interval, date1, date2 [, firstDayOfWeek
[, firstWeekOfYear]])
```

## Definition

The `DateDiff` method calculates the number of intervals between two dates and returns a long integer (`Long`). For example, the `DateDiff` method returns the number of elapsed years, months, or days between two dates. The `DateDiff` method truncates, rather than rounds, the elapsed intervals. For example, the number of elapsed months between 3/5/2007 and 4/30/2007 is one month because only one full month has elapsed.

## Dissection

» The `Microsoft.VisualBasic` namespace contains an enumeration named `DateInterval`, which is used with the `DateDiff` method. Valid intervals are `Day`, `DayOfYear`, `Hour`, `Minute`, `Month`, `Quarter`, `Second`, `Weekday`, `WeekOfYear`, and `Year`. The required *interval* argument must contain one of these enumerations.

» The required *date1* and *date2* arguments define the two dates used in the calculation. If *date1* is more recent than *date2*, the result is negative. Otherwise, the result is positive. Both *date1* and *date2* have a data type of `DateTime`.

» The optional *firstDayOfWeek* argument specifies which day is considered the first day of the week. The `Microsoft.VisualBasic` namespace has an enumeration named `FirstDayOfWeek`. Valid enumeration values are `Sunday`, `Monday`, `Tuesday`, `Wednesday`, `Thursday`, `Friday`, and `Saturday`.

» The optional *firstWeekOfYear* argument allows you to change how Visual Studio determines the first week of the year. By default, the first week of the year is the week containing January 1. Again, the `Microsoft.VisualBasic` namespace supplies the `FirstWeekOfYear` enumeration having the following values: The value `Jan1` causes the week containing January 1 to be considered the first week of the year. The enumeration `FirstFourDays` causes the week containing four full days to be considered the first week of the year. The enumeration `FirstFullWeek` causes the first full week of the year to be considered the first week.

## Code Example

```
Dim StartDate, EndDate As DateTime
Dim Elapsed As Long
StartDate = System.DateTime.Today
EndDate = System.DateTime.Today.AddMonths(22)
Elapsed = DateDiff(DateInterval.Month, StartDate, _
    EndDate, FirstDayOfWeek.Monday, FirstWeekOfYear.Jan1)
Elapsed = DateDiff(DateInterval.Year, StartDate, _
    EndDate, FirstDayOfWeek.Monday, FirstWeekOfYear.Jan1)
```

*(Continued)* ▶

## Code Dissection

These statements declare two `DateTime` variables named StartDate and EndDate, and then store the current date and a date 22 months in the future in those variables. The variable Elapsed stores the elapsed intervals. The `DateDiff` method computes the number of elapsed months and years between the two dates. In the first statement, the number of elapsed months is 22. In the second statement, the number of elapsed years is 1. In both statements, the first day of the week is Monday, and the first week of the year is the week containing January 1.

In this exploration exercise, you will see how the `TimeSpan` structure is used to determine a time interval and compare the `TimeSpan` structure with the `DateDiff` method.

1. Run the solution named **Chapter05ConceptLesson**, and click the **Time Span** tab. Figure 5-10 shows the Time Span tab.

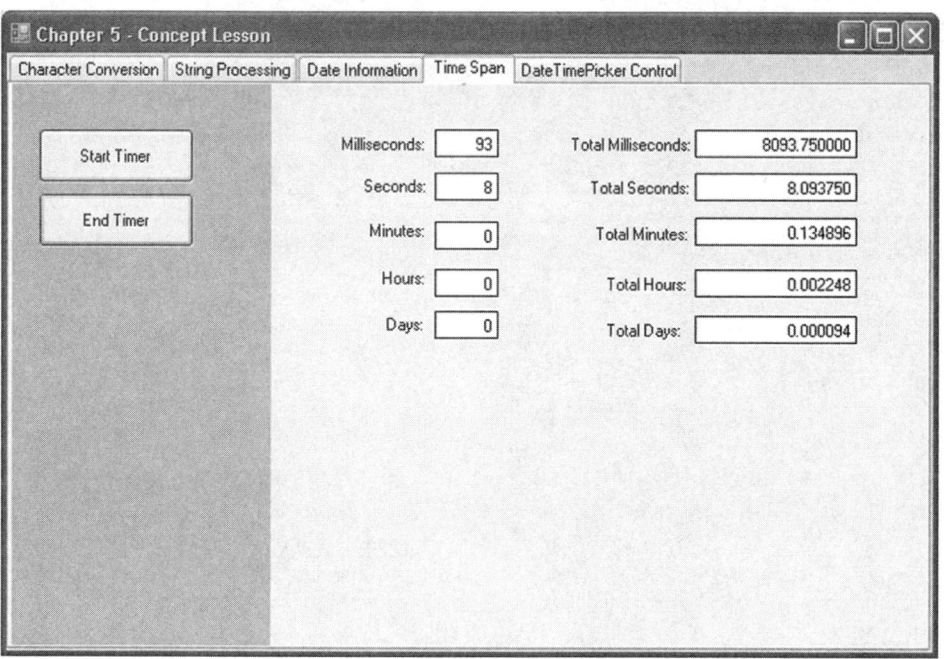

Figure 5-10: Concept lesson—Time Span tab

2. Click the **Start Timer** button. The current time is marked. Every 100 milliseconds, the control instances on the form are updated to display the elapsed time by displaying the properties of a `TimeSpan` structure. Note that an instance of the `Timer` control is used to calculate the elapsed time and is discussed later in the chapter.

3. Click the **End Timer** button. The control instances are no longer updated.

## MINI-QUIZ 3

1. Which of the following statements is correct regarding operations on dates?

   a. Methods such as AddDays or AddMonths return an Integer.

   b. To subtract one day from a date, you call the SubtractDays method.

   c. Methods such as AddDays return a TimeSpan structure.

   d. none of the above

2. What is the output produced by executing the following statements?

   ```
   Dim Date1 As DateTime = #3/24/2006#
   Dim Date2 As DateTime = #4/27/2007#
   Dim Span As TimeSpan = Date2 - Date1
   System.Console.WriteLine(Span.Hours.ToString)
   System.Console.WriteLine(Span.Days.ToString)
   ```

3. What is wrong with the following statements?

   ```
   Dim Result As Integer
   Dim Span1, Span2 As TimeSpan
   Result = DateDiff(DateInterval.Day, Span1, Span2)
   ```

In addition to the DateTime structure, Visual Basic supports a control specifically designed to work with dates called the DateTimePicker control, which is discussed next.

# THE DATETIMEPICKER CONTROL

The DateTimePicker control gives the end user an easy way to select a date using a visual calendar. Visually, the control instance consists of two parts: a list box to display and edit dates and a drop-down calendar to select dates. Figure 5-11 shows a DateTimePicker control instance at run time with the drop-down calendar exposed.

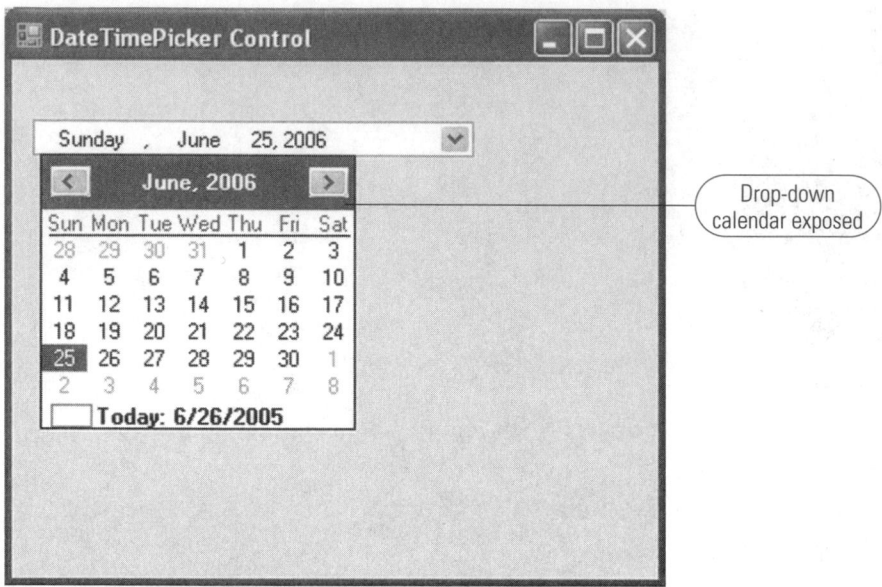

Figure 5-11: DateTimePicker control instance with calendar exposed

## SELECTING A DATE USING THE DATETIMEPICKER CONTROL

The DateTimePicker control supports several ways for the end user to select a date.

» To select a month, click the forward and back arrows appearing on the month calendar.

» Clicking the month name displays a pop-up menu containing a list of months.

» Clicking the year activates an up-down control from which the end user can increment or decrement the year.

» Selecting a date from the calendar causes the drop-down calendar to close, thereby setting the current date.

The DateTimePicker control supports the following members:

### Syntax

System.Windows.Forms.DateTimePicker class

### Definition

The DateTimePicker control allows the end user to select dates and times from a drop-down calendar, or from an up-down (spin) button.

*(Continued)*                                                                                              ▶

## Public Properties

» The Font property defines the font appearing in the list portion of the control.

» The CalendarFont property defines the font appearing in the drop-down calendar.

» The CalendarForeColor property defines the foreground color of the drop-down calendar.

» The CalendarMonthBackgroundColor property defines the background color of the drop-down calendar.

» The CalendarTitleBackColor and CalendarTitleForeColor properties define the background and foreground color of the title bar appearing at the top of the drop-down calendar.

» The Format property contains one of four enumeration values. If set to Long, the date appears using the system's long date format. If set to Short, the date appears using the system's short date format. The enumeration Time displays the time. The final enumeration Custom allows custom date formats to be defined. When set to Custom, this property works in tandem with the CustomFormat property. Custom date formats are not discussed in this chapter.

» The MaxDate and MinDate properties define the maximum and minimum dates that the end user can select from the calendar.

» The ShowUpDown property, if set to False, causes a drop-down combo box to appear. Clicking the combo box displays a month calendar. If set to True, spin-buttons appear. Clicking the spin-buttons increments or decrements the date or time.

» The Value property contains the currently selected date. The property has a data type of DateTime.

## Events

» The CloseUp event fires when the end user closes the drop-down calendar.

» The ValueChanged event fires when the Value property changes. The event fires when the end user selects a different date.

In this exploration exercise, you will see how arithmetic operations can be performed on dates using the DateDiff method and how to use the DateTimePicker control.

1. Run the solution named **Chapter05ConceptLesson**, and click the **DateTimePicker Control** tab. Figure 5-12 shows the DateTimePicker Control tab.

2. Using the instances of the DateTimePicker control appearing on the form, select different dates. The code for this application handles the ValueChanged event. The DateDiff method is called on the two date values and the results displayed in the form's labels whenever the ValueChanged event fires.

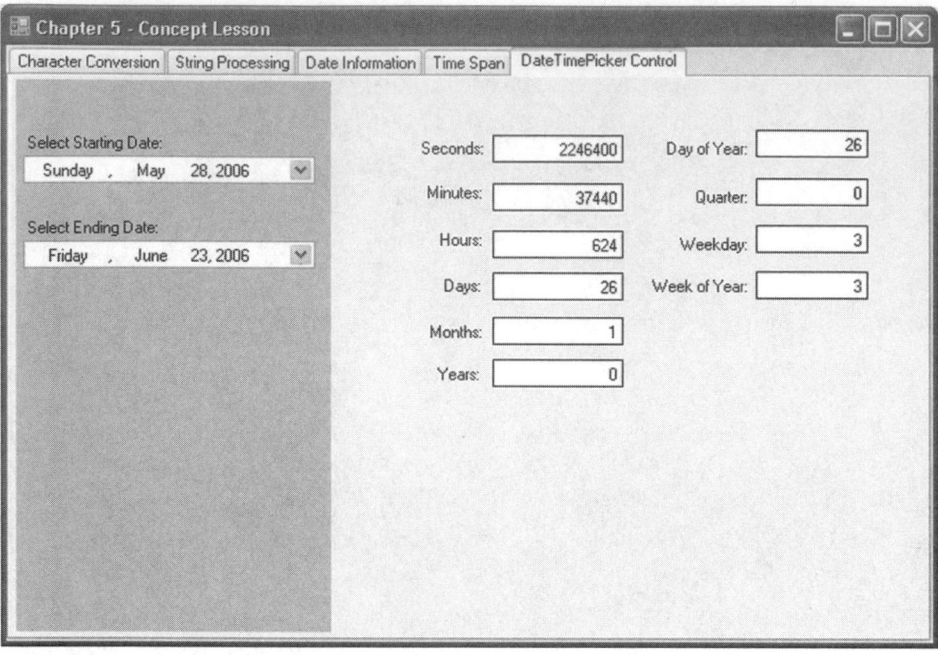

Figure 5-12: Concept lesson—DateTimePicker Control tab

The final control presented in this chapter is the `Timer` control. The only purpose of the `Timer` control is to fire events at regular intervals.

# THE TIMER CONTROL

With the controls you have used thus far in this book, Windows has fired an event as a result of some end-user activity, such as clicking a button or pressing the Tab key, which changes input focus from one control instance to another. The `Timer` control, however, works a bit differently. Instead of an end-user action causing an event to fire, Windows fires a `Tick` event at regular intervals. The benefit of this is that you can force an action to occur without end-user intervention. For example, if you had an application that worked with data files, a `Timer` could be used to save files at regular intervals.

The `Timer` control is not visible to the end user so, like the `OpenFileDialog` control, it appears in the resizable tray below the form in the Windows Forms Designer, as shown in Figure 5-13.

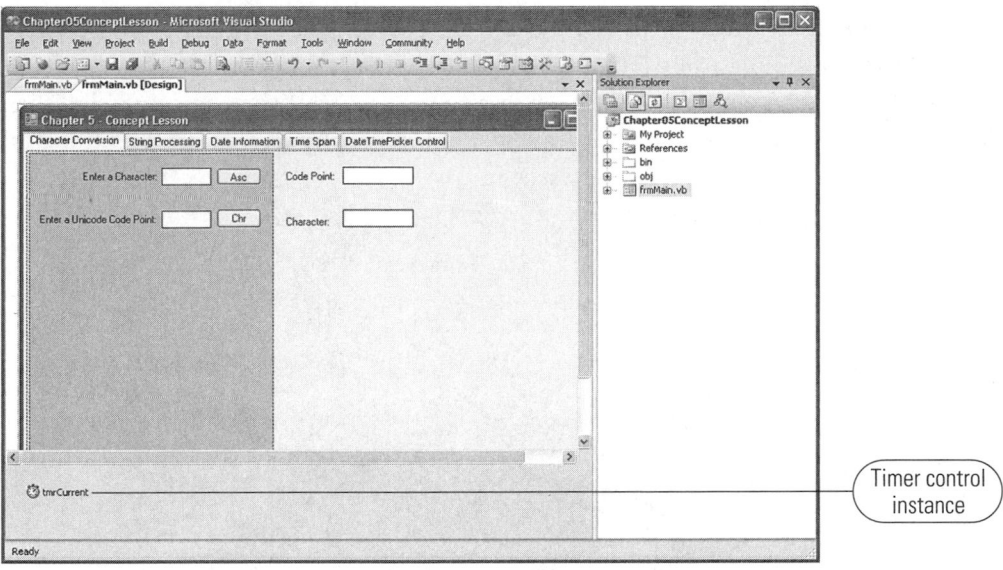

Figure 5-13: Timer control

## THE SYNTAX OF THE TIMER CONTROL

The Timer control has the following members:

### Syntax

`System.Windows.Forms.Timer class`

### Definition

The Timer control fires a Tick event at regular intervals while the control instance is enabled.

### Public Properties

» The Enabled property has values of True or False. If True, the Tick event fires at regular intervals based on the value of the Interval property. If set to False, the control instance is disabled and Tick events do not fire. By default, a Timer control instance is disabled when it is first created on the form.

» The Interval property stores an Integer. The value contains the number of milliseconds that elapse between Tick events. 1000 milliseconds is equivalent to 1 second.

### Events

» The Tick event fires at regular time intervals based on the setting of the Interval property when the Enabled property is set to True. Again, if the Enabled property is set to False, Tick events do not fire.

## USING THE TIMER CONTROL

> NOTE

Note that the firing of the Tick event is not exact. That is, if the Interval property is set to 1000 (1 second), Tick events fire roughly every second, but the duration might be slightly longer.

To illustrate the simplest possible use of the Timer control, the following Tick event handler displays the current time of day in a Label control instance named lblClock, thereby implementing a simple clock. If the Interval property were set to 1000, the clock would be updated roughly every second.

```
Private Sub tmrClock_Tick(ByVal sender As System.Object, _
    ByVal e As System.EventArgs) Handles tmrClock.Tick
        lblClock.Text = System.DateTime.Now.ToLongTimeString
End Sub
```

## MINI-QUIZ 4

1. In regard to the DateTimePicker control, which of the following properties define the range of allowable date values?

    a. MaxDate, MinDate

    b. Minimum, Maximum

    c. MinimumDate, MaximumDate

    d. StartDate, EndDate

    e. none of the above

2. Which of the following statements is correct regarding the Timer control?

    a. The Tick always fires once per second.

    b. For the Tick event to fire, the Enabled property must be set to True.

    c. The Timer control fires a Click event at regular intervals.

    d. none of the above

3. What is the name of the Timer property that defines the frequency at which Tick events fire?

# APPLICATION LESSON

## USING STRINGS AND DATES TO CREATE A FORM LETTER

In this application lesson, you will create a program that processes strings and dates to fill in the variable elements in a form letter, much in the same way that Microsoft Word uses templates. That is, special patterns will be embedded into an existing letter. Based on end user input, the actual data will replace these special patterns. In this application lesson, all these patterns appear in square brackets.

The following list describes the patterns (codes) that are substituted in the letter:

» The embedded code [FULLNAME] contains the full name of the letter recipient.

» The embedded code [FIRSTNAME] contains the first name of the letter recipient.

» The embedded code [LASTNAME] contains the last name of the letter recipient.

» The embedded code [ADDRESS] contains the recipient's address.

» The embedded code [CITYSTATEZIP] contains the recipient's city, state, and zip code.

» The embedded code [CURRENTDATE] is replaced by the current date or a date selected by the end user in a `DateTimePicker` control instance.

» The embedded code [SAVINGS] contains the payment savings.

» The embedded code [NEWPAYMENT] contains the amount of the new payment.

» The embedded code [OLDPAYMENT] contains the amount of the old payment.

The completed application contains an input region and an output region. The buttons in the input region are used to view either the template or the form letter that is generated as output. The input values are used in string replacement operations to generate the form letter from the template (this form letter is the output). In addition to the input values, the current date is also used in the replacement operations.

## APPLICATION LESSON—USER INTERFACE

The application's user interface is made up of text boxes and a `DataGridView` control instance in which the end user enters the following input values:

» The name, address, city, state, and zip code of the recipient

» The current payment and remaining number of payments on an existing loan

» A new loan amount

» The date of the letter

Two buttons appear across the top of the form. These buttons are used to view two different text boxes. One text box displays the template letter. The other text box displays the form letter after the recipient's information has been substituted in the template letter. The form's remaining buttons generate the form letter, clear the output, and exit the application. Figure 5-14 shows the user interface for the application lesson at design time.

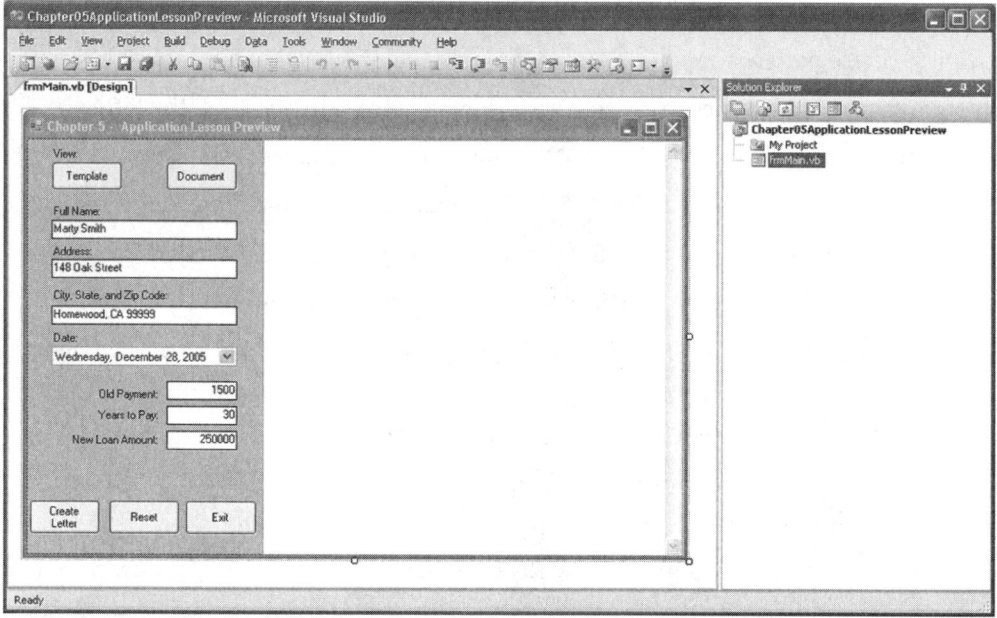

Figure 5-14: Application lesson user interface

## APPLICATION LESSON—DESIGN

Similar to the application lesson from Chapters 3 and 4, this application lesson is an event-driven one. Buttons are used to fire `Click` events as discussed in Chapter 3. Figure 5-15 shows a flowchart for the application.

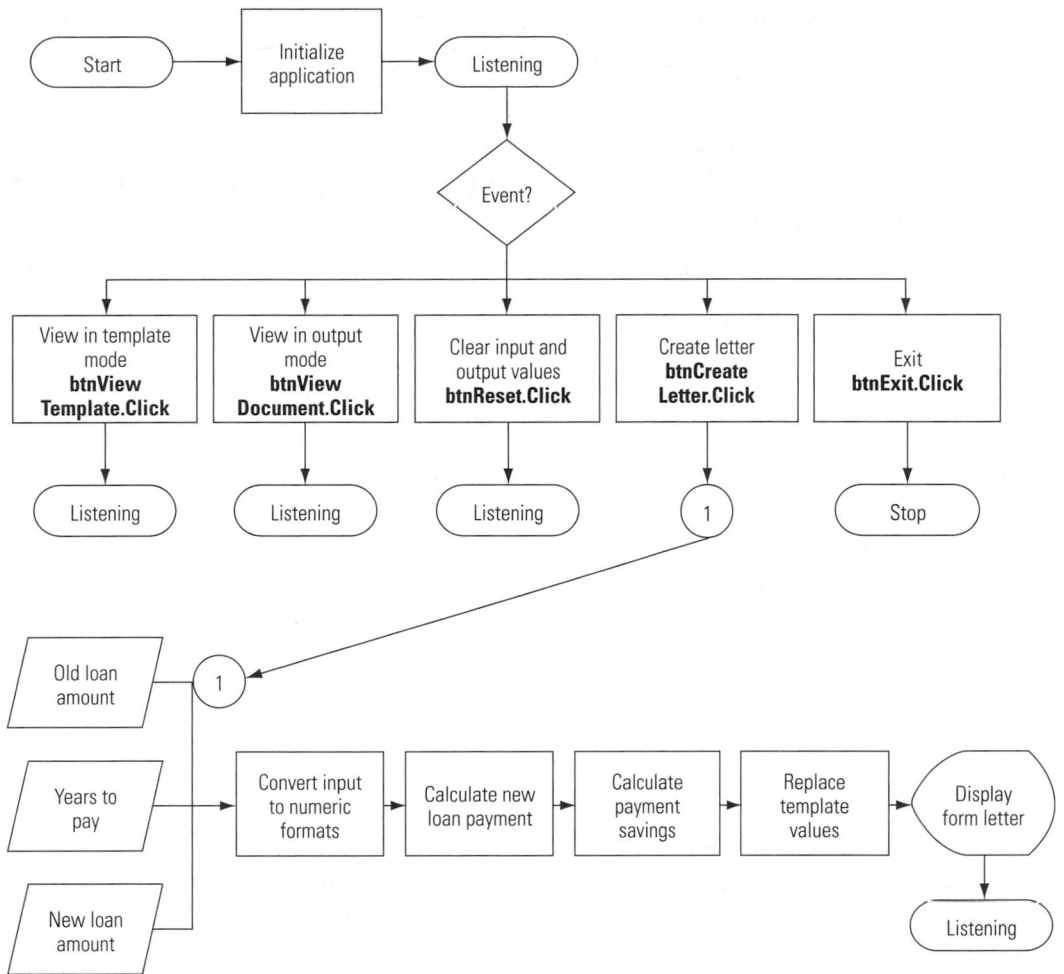

Figure 5-15: Application flowchart

As shown in Figure 5-15, the application's processing is performed by five `Click` event handlers, each fired by one of the five `Button` control instances on the form.

## APPLICATION LESSON—IMPLEMENTATION

Most of the input data is entered by the end user as strings. Some of this data is textual and some must be converted to numeric data and stored in variables. The textual data is stored in `TextBox` control instances having the following names:

» The text box named txtFullName stores the full name of the recipient. The full name is assumed to consist of a first name and a last name separated by a space.

» The address of the recipient is stored in the text box named txtAddress.

» The city, state, and zip code of the recipient are stored in the text box named txtCityStateZipCode.

The contents of the following text boxes must be converted to numeric data before the input can be processed. The following text boxes and numeric variables are used to store the input data and converted input data:

» The text box named txtOldPayment stores the payment on the original loan. This input is converted to a numeric value and stored in the variable named OldLoanPayment.

» The text box named txtYearsToPay stores the number of periods (months) remaining on the existing loan. The input is converted to the Double data type and stored in the variable named YearsToPay.

» The text box named txtNewLoanAmount contains the amount of the new loan. The input is stored in the variable NewLoanAmount.

The application operates in two modes: input mode and output mode. In input mode, the text box containing the template appears. In output mode, the text box containing the form letter appears. The Click event handlers for the buttons named btnViewTemplate and btnViewDocument make the respective text boxes visible and invisible, as shown in the following code segment:

```
txtTemplate.Visible = True
txtOutput.Visible = False

txtTemplate.Visible = False
txtOutput.Visible = True
```

Although it would have been possible to edit the Text property of the text box containing the template, this application reads the text from a text file using the following statements (these statements already exist in the start-up application):

```
Dim ofdMain As New OpenFileDialog
ofdMain.ShowDialog()
Dim CurrentReader As New _
    System.IO.StreamReader(ofdMain.FileName)
txtTemplate.Text = CurrentReader.ReadToEnd()
CurrentReader.Close()
```

Although a full discussion of these statements is beyond the scope of this chapter, the OpenFileDialog control instance is used to get a filename from the end user. Creating an instance of the StreamReader class opens the file. Calling the ReadToEnd method reads the file and stores the text in the text box named txtTemplate. Finally, the file is closed.

Most of the processing takes place in the `Click` event handler for the Create Letter button. The first name and last name are extracted from the full name entered by the end user, as shown in the following statements:

```
FirstName = txtFullName.Text.Substring(0, _
    txtFullName.Text.IndexOf(" "))
LastName = txtFullName.Text.Substring( _
    txtFullName.Text.IndexOf(" ") + 1)
```

The first statement calls the `Substring` method to extract characters starting with the first character up to the first space character detected. The second statement extracts characters starting with the first character after the space to the end of the string. Incorrect results are produced if the input string does not have the correct format.

The following statements calculate the new loan payment and the payment savings:

```
NewLoanPayment = Pmt( _
    0.05 / 12, YearsToPay * 12, NewLoanAmount, 0)
NewLoanPayment = System.Math.Abs(NewLoanPayment)
PaymentSavings = OldLoanPayment - NewLoanPayment
```

The first of the preceding statements calculates the new loan payment by calling the `Pmt` method. For brevity, the annual interest rate is assumed to be 5%. However, the application could be modified to get this value from the end user. The second statement converts the payment to a positive value, and the final statement calculates the payment savings by subtracting the new loan payment from the old loan payment.

Next, the fields are substituted by calling the `Replace` method of the `String` class:

```
CurrentString = txtTemplate.Text
CurrentString = CurrentString.Replace( _
    "[FULLNAME]", txtFullName.Text)
    ' Statements to replace other fields.
txtOutput.Text = CurrentString
```

The preceding statements store the contents of the template in the variable CurrentString. The `Replace` method is called to replace the "[FULLNAME]" field with the actual value. Other fields are replaced using similar statements. Finally, the contents of the variable CurrentString are stored in the output text box.

Dates are also substituted into the form letter. The following statement substitutes the date from the `DateTimePicker` control instance:

```
CurrentString = CurrentString.Replace("[CURRENTDATE]", _
    dtpDate.Value.ToLongDateString)
```

Finally, the `Insert` method of the `String` class is called to insert a disclaimer at the end of the letter, as the following statements show:

```
CurrentString = CurrentString.Insert( _
    CurrentString.Length, ControlChars.CrLf & _
    ControlChars.CrLf & _
    "This offer expires in 30 days on " & _
    Today.AddDays(30).ToLongDateString & ".")
```

The preceding statement inserts a string at the end of the temporary string variable named CurrentString.

As in the preceding chapters, a completed version of the application lesson appears with the data files accompanying this book.

To preview the completed application:

1. In Visual Studio, open the solution appearing in the folder **Chapter.05\Chapter05 ApplicationLessonPreview**.

2. Run the solution. The Open dialog box appears. Select the **Chapter.05\Data\ Template.txt** file. Click the **Template** button, if necessary. The completed solution in input mode appears, as shown in Figure 5-16. Note that default input values appear in the form's text boxes.

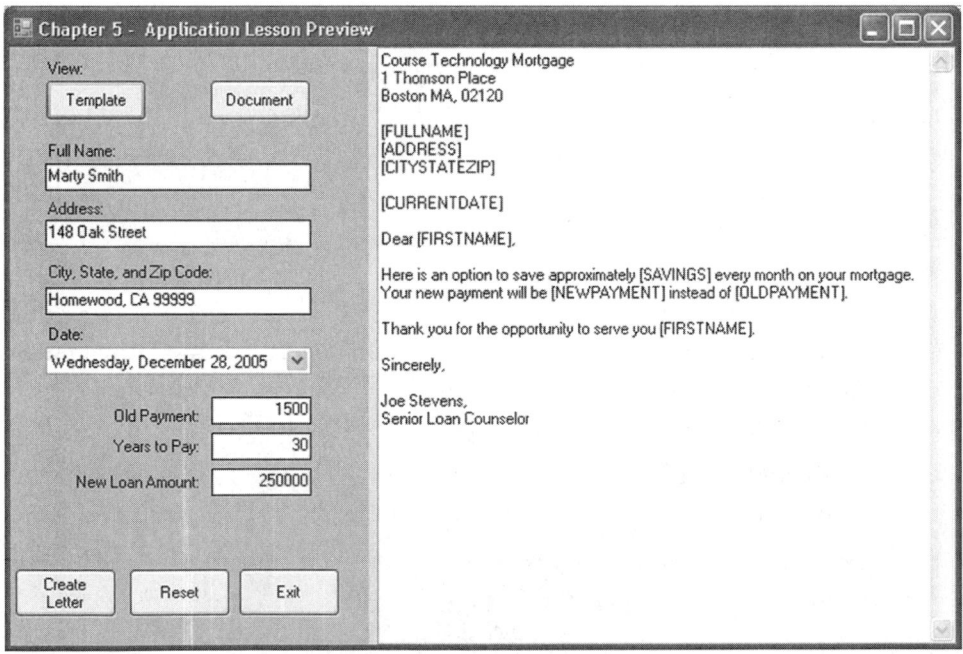

Figure 5-16: Completed form—input mode

3. Click the **Create Letter** button. Click the **Document** button, if necessary. The form letter appears, as shown in Figure 5-17.

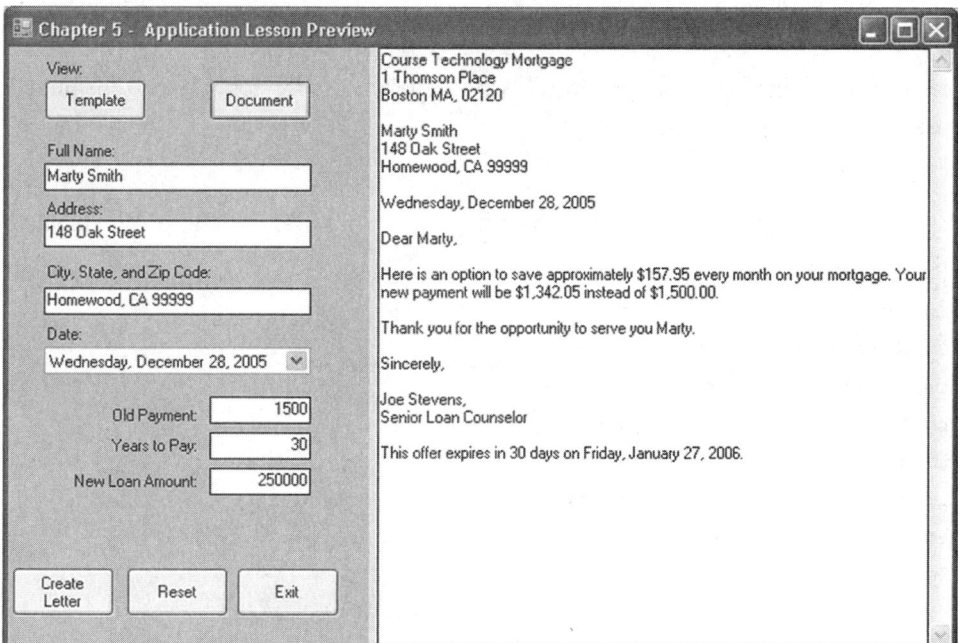

Figure 5-17: Completed form—output mode

As shown in Figure 5-17, the template replacements have been made. In addition, a final line was added to the letter to show the expiration date of the offer.

Having seen the implementation of the application lesson, you will now write the code to complete that implementation.

1. In Visual Studio, open the solution appearing in the folder **Chapter.05\Chapter05 ApplicationLessonStartup**.

2. Enter the following statements into the **Click** event handler for the button named **btnViewTemplate**:

```
txtTemplate.Visible = True
txtOutput.Visible = False
```

3. Enter the following statements into the **Click** event handler for the button named **btnViewDocument**:

```
txtTemplate.Visible = False
txtOutput.Visible = True
```

4. Enter the following statements in the **Click** event handler for the button named **btnReset**:

```
txtOutput.Clear()
txtTemplate.Visible = True
txtOutput.Visible = False
```

5. Enter the following statements into the **Click** event handler for the button named **btnExit**:

```
Me.Close()
```

6. Enter the following statements into the **Click** event handler for the button named **btnCreateLetter**:

```
Dim CurrentString As String
Dim FirstName As String
Dim LastName As String
Dim OldLoanPayment As Double
Dim YearsToPay As Integer
Dim NewLoanAmount As Double
Dim NewLoanPayment As Double
Dim PaymentSavings As Double
OldLoanPayment = ToDouble(txtOldPayment.Text)
YearsToPay = ToInt32(txtYearsToPay.Text)
NewLoanAmount = ToDouble(txtNewLoanAmount.Text)
FirstName = txtFullName.Text.Substring(0, _
    txtFullName.Text.IndexOf(" "))
LastName = txtFullName.Text.Substring( _
    txtFullName.Text.IndexOf(" ") + 1)
NewLoanPayment = Pmt(0.05 / 12, YearsToPay * 12, _
    NewLoanAmount, 0)
NewLoanPayment = System.Math.Abs(NewLoanPayment)
PaymentSavings = OldLoanPayment - NewLoanPayment
CurrentString = txtTemplate.Text
CurrentString = CurrentString.Replace("[FULLNAME]", _
    txtFullName.Text)
CurrentString = CurrentString.Replace("[ADDRESS]", _
    txtAddress.Text)
CurrentString = CurrentString.Replace("[CITYSTATEZIP]", _
    txtCityStateZipCode.Text)
CurrentString = CurrentString.Replace("[FIRSTNAME]", _
    FirstName)
```

```
CurrentString = CurrentString.Replace("[LASTNAME]", _
    LastName)
CurrentString = CurrentString.Replace("[SAVINGS]", _
    PaymentSavings.ToString("c"))
CurrentString = CurrentString.Replace("[NEWPAYMENT]", _
    NewLoanPayment.ToString("c"))
CurrentString = CurrentString.Replace("[OLDPAYMENT]", _
    OldLoanPayment.ToString("c"))
CurrentString = CurrentString.Replace("[CURRENTDATE]", _
    dtpDate.Value.ToLongDateString)
CurrentString = CurrentString.Insert( _
    CurrentString.Length, _
    ControlChars.CrLf & ControlChars.CrLf & _
    "This offer expires in 30 days on " & _
    Today.AddDays(30).ToLongDateString & ".")
txtOutput.Text = CurrentString
```

7. Test the completed solution.

# CHAPTER SUMMARY

» An encoding scheme is a way of uniquely representing every character in a language with a binary number. There was a time when different computer manufacturers used different character-encoding schemes, which made it difficult, if not impossible, to communicate information between computers. Today, character-encoding schemes have become standardized. Two common character encoding schemes include ASCII and Unicode. The binary representation of a Unicode character is called a code point. Each code point is stored in 2 bytes.

» Visual Studio supplies the Char data type to store a single Unicode character. The Asc method accepts a character or string argument and returns the corresponding code point for the character. The Chr method works in reverse. It returns the character corresponding to a given code point.

» The String data type is used to represent a collection of characters. Strings are concatenated together using the & operator. Special characters, called control characters, are embedded into a string using the members of the Microsoft.VisualBasic.ControlChars class.

» Multiline text boxes work with strings. By setting the MultiLine property to True, text appears on multiple lines. The WordWrap property controls how the text wraps from one line to another in a multiline text box. The ScrollBars property is used to determine whether scroll bars appear.

» The String class supports numerous methods to manipulate strings. The Length property gets the length of a string. The ToUpper and ToLower methods convert a string to all uppercase or lowercase characters, respectively. The IndexOf method is used to determine whether a string contains a particular substring. The Substring method returns selected characters from an existing string. The Insert method inserts a string into another string at a specific character position. The Remove method removes one or more characters from a string. The Replace method replaces one character in a string with another character. The Trim, TrimStart, and TrimEnd methods remove leading and trailing white space from a string.

» The System.DateTime data type is a structure used to store dates. Arithmetic operations can also be performed on dates. Numerous properties are used to get information about a date such as the day of the week, year, month, or day, or various time values.

» The System.TimeSpan data type is a structure used to represent a time interval. The properties of the TimeSpan structure are used to determine the parts of the time interval, such as the number of elapsed days, hours, minutes, or seconds.

» The DateDiff method calculates the number of intervals between two dates. The method truncates, rather than rounds, date intervals.

» The DateTimePicker control is used to work with dates. The end user can select a date from a month calendar. The control supports extensive formatting capabilities. The selected date is stored in the Value property.

» The Timer control is an invisible control. If enabled, a Tick event is fired at regular intervals. The Interval property defines the time interval over which the event is fired.

# KEY TERMS

**code point**—The unique binary pattern used to represent each Unicode character. Code points are 2 bytes (16 bits) in size.

**concatenation**—The operation to append strings together.

**control characters**—The special characters such as the Tab and carriage return character. The Microsoft.VisualBasic.ControlChars class contains fields that correspond to common control characters.

**encoding scheme**—A way of uniquely representing a character in a language with a binary number.

epoch—The term used to define a calendar's beginning of time.

string—A collection of characters (the Char data type). All strings are represented by the String class.

Unicode—A character-encoding scheme in which each character is stored as a 2-byte value. Unicode was designed to be able to represent English as well as international character sets.

# ANSWERS TO MINI-QUIZZES

### MINI-QUIZ 1

1. d. all of the above

2. c. IndexOf

3. Jim R. Smith

4. The first argument to the Remove method, which defines the starting character position, cannot be negative.

### MINI-QUIZ 2

1. the epoch

2. b. It is a value type 64 bits in length.

3. The argument to the IsLeapYear method should be an Integer containing the year rather than a DateTime data type.

### MINI-QUIZ 3

1. d. none of the above

2. 0

   399

3. The DateDiff method requires the second and third arguments have a data type of DateTime rather than a data type of TimeSpan.

### MINI-QUIZ 4

1. a. MaxDate, MinDate

2. b. For the Tick event to fire, the Enabled property must be set to True

3. Interval

# REVIEW QUESTIONS

1. Which of the following statements is true pertaining to strings?

   a. The `String` data type supports methods to convert strings to numeric and date data types.

   b. Strings are concatenated using the ampersand (&) operator.

   c. The `Size` property returns the number of characters in a string.

   d. The `RemoveChars` method removes selected characters from a string.

   e. none of the above

2. Assuming that the variable named Result is declared as a `String` data type, which of the following statements is valid to concatenate strings?

   a. `Result = "Joe" and "Brown"`

   b. `Result = "Joe" & "Brown"`

   c. `Result = "Joe" "&" Space "&" "Brown"`

   d. `Result = "Joe" Concat "Brown"`

   e. All the above are valid.

3. What is the purpose of the `Asc` and `Chr` methods?

   a. The `Ascii` method converts an ASCII character into its corresponding character code. The `Char` method converts a character code into its equivalent Unicode character.

   b. The `Asc` method converts a character into its `Integer` character code. The `Chr` method converts an `Integer` character code into its equivalent Unicode character.

   c. The two methods are equivalent. They are supported for backward compatibility with older versions of Visual Basic.

   d. The methods are used to convert strings from Unicode format to ASCII format.

   e. none of the above

4. Which of the following are properties of the `Microsoft.VisualBasic.ControlChars` class?

   a. `SingleQuote`

   b. `DoubleQuote`

   c. `Space`

d. Tab

e. none of the above

5. What is the name of the method that will determine the character position of a character or substring within a string?

   a. Position()

   b. Index()

   c. CharPos()

   d. IndexOf()

   e. Location()

6. After the following statements have executed, what value is stored in the variable ResultString?

```
Dim InputString As String = "Smith, Joe"
Dim ResultString As String
ResultString = InputString.Substring(1, 3)
```

   a. Smi

   b. mit

   c. Smit

   d. Joe

   e. none of the above

7. What can be said of the following statements assuming that the variable StringCurrent has been initialized and has a data type of String?

```
StringCurrent = StringCurrent.TrimStart
StringCurrent = StringCurrent.TrimEnd
```

   a. All spaces will be removed from the string.

   b. The statements are not legal because both the TrimStart and TrimEnd methods cannot be called on the same string.

   c. Leading and trailing spaces will be removed from the string but any intervening spaces will remain.

   d. The preceding statements are not legal because TrimStart and TrimEnd are not methods of the String class.

   e. none of the above

8. Assuming that the variable StringCurrent has a data type of `String`, what can be said of the following statement?

   `StringCurrent = StringCurrent.Replace("Mrs.", "Ms.")`

   a. The first time the string "Mrs." is found, it will be replaced by the string "Ms."

   b. All occurrences of the string "Mrs." will be replaced by the string "Ms."

   c. All occurrences of the string "Ms." will be replaced by the string "Mrs."

   d. The statement will throw an exception if the variable StringCurrent does not contain the string "Mrs."

   e. none of the above

9. Which of the following statements is true pertaining to dates?

   a. Dates are declared using the `DateTime` data type.

   b. When storing literal values in a `DateTime` variable, pound signs surround the literal value as in #04/22/2007#.

   c. The `ToDateTime` method converts a string to a `DateTime` structure.

   d. The `DateTime` structure is a value type.

   e. all of the above.

10. Which of the following properties are supported by the `DateTime` structure?

    a. `Hours, Minutes, Seconds`

    b. `Weeks, Days, Months, Years`

    c. `Hour, Minute, Second`

    d. `HourOfDay, MinuteOfDay, SecondOfDay`

    e. none of the above

11. What is the purpose of the `TimeSpan` structure?

    a. It is used to represent a point in time.

    b. It is used to represent an elapsed time interval.

    c. The `TimeSpan` and `DateTime` structures are the same. The `TimeSpan` structure is supported only for backward compatibility with older versions of Visual Basic.

    d. The `GetTimeSpan` method is used to get the timespan representing the difference between two dates.

    e. none of the above

12. Which of the following are properties of the `TimeSpan` structure?

    a. `DaySpan, HourSpan, MinuteSpan, SecondSpan`

    b. `SpanInterval, SpanRange`

    c. `ElapsedDays, ElapsedHours, ElapsedMinutes, ElapsedSeconds`

    d. `TotalDays, TotalHours, TotalMinutes, TotalSeconds`

    e. none of the above

13. Which of the following statements is correct regarding the `DateDiff` method?

    a. The `DateDiff` method is a member of the `System.DateTime` structure.

    b. The method returns a value having a data type of `TimeSpan`.

    c. Based on the setting of the interval argument passed to the method, it returns the number of elapsed hours, minutes, seconds, or other time period.

    d. The return data type of the method is `DateTime`.

    e. none of the above

14. Which of the following statements is true about the `DateTimePicker` control?

    a. The current date is stored in the `Text` property.

    b. When the end user selects a new date in the control instance, the `Change` event fires.

    c. The `MinDate` and `MaxDate` properties define the minimum and maximum allowable date values.

    d. all of the above

    e. none of the above

15. Which of the following statements is correct of the `Timer` control?

    a. The `Timer` control is granular to one second.

    b. The `Timer` control automatically fires a `Click` event every second.

    c. The `Timer` control fires a `Tick` event at regular intervals based on the setting of the `Interval` property.

    d. Only one instance of the `Timer` control can be created on a form.

    e. none of the above

16. After the following statements have executed, what value is stored in the variable ResultString? _____

```
Dim InputString As String = "James Brown"
Dim SpaceIndex As Integer = InputString.IndexOf(" ")
Dim ResultString As String
ResultString = InputString.Substring(SpaceIndex + 1) _
    & ", " & InputString.Substring(0, SpaceIndex)
```

17. What value is stored in the variable ResultDays after the following statements have executed? _____

```
Dim ResultDays As Long
ResultDays = DateDiff(DateInterval.Day, _
    #4/22/2006#, #5/2/2006#)
```

18. List and describe the methods used to convert date and time values to strings. In your answer, describe the differences of each resulting method call.

19. Referring to the DateTime structure, what is the purpose of the Today and Now properties? What is the data type returned by these properties?

20. Discuss the purpose of the Timer control. In your answer, discuss how and when events are raised for an instance of the Timer control.

# PROGRAMMING QUESTIONS

1. Write a statement to concatenate the String variables named FirstName, MiddleInitial, and LastName and store the result in the variable named FullName. Embed a space between the first name, middle initial, and last name.

2. Assume that the variable named SearchString contains a string. Write the statement to extract the first 10 characters from the string and store the result in the variable named Result.

3. Many types of credit cards have the same format. This format is *XXXX-XXXX-XXXX-XXXX* where *X* is a digit. The dashes are embedded into the string containing the card number. Write the statements to extract each four-digit segment into String variables

named Part1, Part2, Part3, and Part4, respectively. Assume that the credit card number is stored in the variable InputString.

4. Assume that a variable named InputString exists and is initialized to the literal string value "Peter Paul Mary." Write the statement to extract the substring "Mary" from the input string. Store the result in the variable named ResultString.

5. Write the statement to determine whether the string variable named InputString contains the substring "Paul." Store the result in the `Integer` variable CharacterIndex.

6. Write the statement to remove any leading and trailing white space from the string variable named InputString. Store the result in the variable named OutputString.

7. Assume that a string exists named LogMessageInput. Write the statements to remove all white space from the string. Remove all Tab characters from the string too. Finally, replace all periods (.) with commas (,). Store the resulting string in the variable LogMessageOutput.

8. Assume that an input string variable named InputString has the format *firstname middleinitial lastname*. Write the statements to remove the middle initial from the input string. Assume that the middle initial does not have a period following the middle initial. Store the result in the variable OutputString. Declare any local variables, as necessary.

9. Write the statement to get the current date from the system and store the result in the variable CurrentDate. Write a second statement to get the current time from the system and store the result in the variable CurrentTime. Assuming that two `String` variables exist named CurrentDateFormatted and CurrentTimeFormatted, convert the current date and time to a string using the system's long date and time format respectively.

10. Assume that a variable named SomeDate has been declared having a `DateTime` data type. Write the statements to get the current year, month, day, hour, minute, and second from the variable. Display the results to the Console window.

11. Assume that a variable named FutureDate has a data type of `DateTime`. Write the statements to add one month, one day, and one hour, to the variable.

12. Assume that an instance of the `DateTimePicker` control exists named dtpDemo. Write the statements to set the minimum allowable date to 1/1/2006 and the maximum allowable date to 12/31/2006. Finally, write the statement to set the current date to 6/1/2006. Use literal values in the assignment statements.

13. Assume that an instance of the `DateTimePicker` control exists named dtpDemo. Write the statements to set the minimum allowable date to one year prior to the current date and the maximum allowable date to one year past the current date. Finally, store the current date as the value of the control instance.

14. Assume that two date values exist and are stored in the variables named StartingDate and EndingDate. Write the statements that will display, to the Console window, the number of elapsed days, hours, minutes, and seconds between the two dates. Use the `TimeSpan` structure to store the interval.

15. Assume that an instance of the `Timer` control exists named tmrCurrent. Create the necessary `Tick` event handler to display the current time of day in the `Label` control instance named lblTime. Format the time as a long time string.

# HANDS-ON PROJECTS

1. In this hands-on project, you will implement a stopwatch that displays the elapsed number of milliseconds, seconds, minutes, and hours between two time values. The end user should be able to perform the following tasks:

» The stopwatch can be reset, thereby setting all of the elapsed time counters to zero. When the stopwatch is reset, the elapsed and active time should begin incrementing. That is, the stopwatch should be started automatically when reset.

» The stopwatch can be paused. When paused, the elapsed time and paused time are incremented but the active time is not. Note that the elapsed time values are not refreshed until the stopwatch begins running again.

» When started and running, the elapsed and active time are incremented but the paused time is not.

The critical code for the application is the code for the `Timer` control's `Tick` event handler.

a. Run the executable file named **Chapter.05\HandsOnProjects\Ch05HandsOn Project1.exe**. Click the **Start** button to activate the stopwatch. Pause and reset the stopwatch. As you click the buttons, note that the elapsed time intervals are updated. In addition, the application displays the total time the application has been running along with the current time of day.

b. Create a new solution file named **Ch05HandsOnProject1.sln**.

c. Rename the form to **frmMain**. Configure the form so that it is not resizable. Hide the control box.

d. Create the control instances on the form, using the sample application as a template. Designate the Exit button as the Cancel button.

e. Create a `Timer` control instance to display a clock along the bottom of the form. The clock should be updated once every second. In addition, display the total elapsed time that the application has been running in a second `Label` control instance.

f. Create a second instance of the `Timer` control to implement the stopwatch. Configure the control instance so that the `Tick` event fires every millisecond.

g. The stopwatch should be implemented such that clicking the Reset button resets the stopwatch. That is, the starting time for the stopwatch is set to the current time. Write the statements to clear all of the accumulated time values when the stopwatch is reset.

h. Clicking the Start and Pause buttons should start and pause the stopwatch, respectively. That is, the active time will not continue to tick but the total elapsed time will continue to tick while the stopwatch is paused. *Hint*: Use module-level variables to keep track of the starting time and the total elapsed paused time.

i. Create the code for the Exit button to exit the application.

2. In this hands-on project, you will create a word-jumbling game. The end user will enter a word into a text box. The characters in the word will then be jumbled based on character positions selected by the end user. In addition, it is possible to use an autojumble feature that will jumble random characters automatically. So that the end user can visualize how the process of switching characters works, informational messages will be displayed as the characters are switched.

a. Run the executable file named **Chapter.05\HandsOnProjects\Ch05HandsOn Project2.exe**. A default word has been supplied to jumble. In the form's text boxes, enter the position of the characters to jumble or use the default values, and then click the **Jumble** button. Informational messages appear as the characters are exchanged.

b. Click the **Start Auto Jumble** button. Random characters are jumbled roughly every 2 seconds.

c. Click the **Stop Auto Jumble** button. Automatic character jumbling is suspended.

d. Click the **Reset** and **Exit** buttons to reset the application and exit the application, respectively. Note that clicking the Reset button resets the control instances to their initial values.

e. Create a new solution file named **Ch05HandsOnProject2**.

    f.  Rename the form to **frmMain**.

    g.  Create the control instances on the form, using the sample application as a template.

    h.  The `Click` event handler for the Jumble button performs most of the application's processing switching the two characters selected by the end user. Use the `Insert` and `Remove` methods of the `String` class to switch the characters. *Hint*: Declare a local variable to temporarily store the character that is being switched.

    i.  Using a module-level variable, keep track of the number of switches performed on the current string.

    j.  Create the code for the Start Auto Jumble and Stop Auto Jumble buttons. This code should enable and disable a `Timer` control instance.

    k.  Create a `Timer` control instance on the form. In the `Tick` event, write the code to jumble random characters. *Hint*: Use the milliseconds or ticks part of the time of day to get a random value and use the `Mod` function to get random chararacter positions.

    l.  Create the code for the **Reset** button. The statements in this event handler should clear the text from the input and output text boxes and labels, and reset the first and second character position to 1 and 2, respectively.

    m.  Create the code for the **Exit** button to exit the application.

3.  In this hands-on project, you will create an application that will calculate the cost of a car rental based on the number of days that the car is rented. The cost of the car rental includes the cost of the car itself, the cost of insurance, and the cost of fuel.

    a.  Run the executable file named **Chapter.05\HandsOnProjects\Ch05HandsOn Project3.exe**. Select dates for the date rented and date returned. Enter a floating-point value for the gallons of fuel necessary to fill the car. Click the **Calculate** button to calculate the cost of a car rental.

    b.  Create a new solution file named **Ch05HandsOnProject3**.

    c.  Rename the form to **frmMain**.

    d.  Create the control instances on the form, using the sample application as a template. The input control instances consist of the date the car was rented and the date the car was returned. In addition, the number of gallons of fuel is entered as a floating-point value.

    e.  Declare constants to store the following values:

       »  The cost of fuel is $2.65 per gallon.

       »  The cost of the car is $49.99 per day.

       »  The cost of insurance is $14.99 per day.

   f. In the `Click` event handler for the Calculate button, write the statements to read the input data and store that data in variables of the appropriate data types. Perform the following calculations on the input data:

     » Convert the input data to the appropriate data types as necessary.

     » Determine the number of days that the car was rented.

     » Calculate the cost of the car based on the daily rate and display the output.

     » Calculate the cost of the insurance based on the daily rate and display the output.

     » Calculate the cost of the fuel by multiplying the number of gallons used by the fuel cost per gallon.

     » Calculate the grand total of the car rental using these intermediate values.

   g. Display the output values and format those values as currency.

   h. Create a `Timer` control instance to display a clock along the bottom of the form. The clock should be updated every second.

   i. Create the code for the Reset button to reset the control instances to their default values.

   j. Create the code for the Exit button.

   k. Test your application using input values of your choosing.

4. In this hands-on project, you will create an application that builds an activity log of television viewing habits.

   a. Create a new solution file named **Ch05HandsOnProject4**.

   b. Rename the form to **frmMain**.

   c. Create four instances of the `DateTimePicker` control on the form to display the starting and ending date and time of the program watched.

   d. Create a text box so that the end user can enter the name of the televison show watched.

   e. Create a multiline text box to display a log of the television shows watched.

   f. Create a Record button on the form. Each time the end user clicks the Record button, the application should get the starting and ending date and time from the `DateTimePicker` control instances appearing on the form. Using the starting and ending dates and times, along with the television show appearing in the text box, calculate the elapsed time watched. Concatenate a message in the `TextBox` control instance containing the elapsed time and the name of the television show.

   g. Maintain a total of the number of hours, minutes, and seconds that the television was watched.

h. Create the code for the Reset button that will reset the starting and ending dates and times to the current date and time, and clear the output from the form's text boxes.

i. Create the code to exit the application.

j. Create a `Timer` control instance to display a clock along the bottom of the form. The clock should be updated every second.

# 6

# UNDERSTANDING THE STRUCTURE OF AN APPLICATION: PROCEDURES, MODULES, AND CLASSES

**After completing this chapter, you will be able to:**

Use multiple forms and classes to build an application

Describe the purpose of procedures

Understand applications with multiple modules

Communicate data between forms

Create and use Property procedures

# CONCEPT LESSON

# USING MULTIPLE FORMS AND CLASSES TO BUILD AN APPLICATION

Until this chapter, all of the applications discussed in this book were made up of a single form containing event handlers, or a Console Application with a single procedure named Main. However, most applications are not so simple and contain additional elements, as discussed in the following list:

» *Procedures*: In addition to event handlers, most applications contain other procedures. These procedures can be reused throughout an application, thereby reducing the amount of code that must be written. Procedures can also be grouped into classes, which can be used throughout an application or used by multiple applications.

» *Splash screens*: Most applications are made up of multiple forms instead of just a single form. For example, applications such as Microsoft Word or Microsoft Excel have a start-up form called a **splash screen** that appears while the application is loaded into memory. In addition to the splash screen and main form, an endless array of dialog boxes is used to configure the software itself and to perform various other tasks.

» *User-defined classes*: You have used members of the .NET Framework class library to perform mathematical operations and get information about an assembly. It is also possible to create your own *user-defined classes* in addition to those supplied by the .NET Framework class library.

» *Scope and visibility*: The concepts of scope and visibility become important in applications with multiple forms and multiple modules. That is, data and procedures can be configured such that they are accessible only to the current form or module, accessible to other forms and modules, or accessible to other assemblies.

This chapter explains how to create different types of procedures, how to create applications with multiple modules and forms, and how to communicate data between those modules and forms. In addition, you will learn how to create classes that work the same way as those supplied by the .NET Framework class library itself, so as to create components that can be reused by multiple applications.

The topics appearing in the preceding list are interrelated. That is, procedures can appear in `Class` and `Module` blocks. Access modifiers, such as `Public`, `Friend`, and `Private`, define whether a variable or procedure can be referenced from other forms, classes, or assemblies.

# THE PURPOSE OF PROCEDURES

**Procedures** facilitate code reuse because they can be called by multiple event handlers and by other procedures. After a procedure has been developed and tested, it can be used repeatedly by the other procedures in an application or by other applications.

To illustrate the significance of procedures, think of the classes supplied by the .NET Framework class library and the methods supported by those classes. These methods are nothing more than procedures appearing inside of a `Class` or `Module` block. Methods are exposed to other classes and are considered part of the class interface rather than part of the implementation. These classes can be used by any application, thereby simplifying the development process. That is, by using the classes of the .NET Framework class library, you need not write the same code over and over again. For example, you can call the `System.Console.WriteLine()` method from any application.

Procedures are usually grouped together in classes to further facilitate code reuse. For example, the `System.Math` class of the .NET Framework class library contains methods, which are nothing more than procedures. In general, the `System.Math` class contains methods to perform mathematical tasks and each method performs a specific mathematical task. The following code segment illustrates how the `Abs` method of the `System.Math` class might be implemented:

```
Public Class Math
    Public Shared Function Abs(ByVal arg As Double) As Double
        If arg < 0 Then
            Return arg * -1
        Else
            Return arg
    End Function
End Class
```

**»NOTE**

One strategy for writing successful applications is to divide repetitive tasks into procedures, which can be reused within the same application or in different applications.

The Class keyword along with the Public access modifier denotes that the Math class is globally accessible. Thus, any application can use the Math class. The preceding sample class contains one method named Abs. (The syntax of the Function procedure is discussed in detail in the next section.)

# INTRODUCTION TO FUNCTION PROCEDURES

All procedures accept arguments, which are used as input to the procedure. The code in the **Function procedure** performs its processing using these arguments and returns a value. The value returned by a Function procedure has a data type that is typically assigned to a variable or property. Thus, Function procedures work just like methods that return a value. To illustrate, examine the following call to the Abs method of the System.Math class:

```
Dim Result As Double
Result = System.Math.Abs(-123.456)
```

The following points can be made about the preceding statements:

» The Abs method accepts one argument, which is used as input to the method. In this case, the argument is a literal value but it could be a variable, object property, or constant.

» The Abs method calculates the absolute value of a number passed as an argument, and returns a value having the same data type as the argument. In the preceding code segment, the returned value is stored in the variable Result.

Function procedures have the following syntax:

## Syntax
```
[ Public | Friend | Private] Function name [ (argumentList)]
[ As type]

    [ statements]

    [ Exit Function]

    [ Return expression]

End Function
```

## Definition
The Function keyword declares a Function procedure.

*(Continued)*                                                                          ▶

## Dissection

» The optional `Public`, `Friend`, and `Private` keywords denote the procedure's accessibility. The `Public` keyword indicates that all of the modules or classes in a project can use the procedure. Other projects (assemblies) can also use procedures declared with the `Public` keyword. The `Friend` keyword indicates that the modules in the current project (assembly) can use the procedure but other assemblies cannot. The `Private` keyword indicates that the procedure is accessible only to the procedures in the module or class in which the procedure is declared. The meaning of the `Public`, `Friend`, and `Private` keywords is the same when declaring procedures as their meaning when declaring variables. Visual Basic supports other access modifiers but they are not discussed in this chapter.

» The required *name* argument contains the `Function` procedure name and must be unique within a `Class` or `Module` block. The naming rules for procedures are the same as the naming rules for variables or other identifiers.

» The optional *argumentList* contains the argument names and the data types passed to the `Function` procedure. Literal values, constants, variables, and object properties can be passed as procedure arguments. Declaring the *argumentList* is discussed in detail in the next section of the chapter.

» A `Function` procedure returns exactly one value. The optional `As` *type* clause defines the data type of the value returned by the `Function` procedure. The `As` *type* clause is required when strict type checking is enabled (`Option Strict On`). `Function` procedures always return one value having a data type, such as an `Integer`. `Function` procedures can also return object data types. That is, a `Function` procedure could return an object, such as an instance of the `TextBox` class.

» The required `Return` statement causes the `Function` procedure to return a result. The `Return` statement takes one argument—the value to return. The value must have the same data type as the return data type specified in the procedure's `As` *type* clause. When the `Return` statement executes, the `Function` procedure exits and the value is returned to the calling procedure. Execution continues at the statement following the statement that called the `Function` procedure. A `Function` procedure can have multiple `Return` statements. When the `Return` statement is encountered, the `Function` procedure ends and the value is returned, regardless of whether more statements in the procedure remain to be executed.

» The optional `Exit Function` statement causes the `Function` procedure to exit immediately. Execution continues at the statement following the statement that called the `Function` procedure. A `Function` procedure can contain zero or more `Exit Function` statements. The `Exit Function` statement is most often used for error conditions.

» The required `End Function` statement defines the end of the `Function` procedure. After this statement is reached, execution continues at the statement following the statement that called the `Function` procedure.

## UNDERSTANDING PROCEDURE ARGUMENTS

An important part of using procedures is understanding the purpose of arguments and how arguments are passed to procedures. As mentioned, an argument is the mechanism by which data is communicated to any procedure. You have used arguments to supply values to methods such as the FV method, which calculates the future value of an investment. No matter the type of procedure, the syntax and meaning of an argument are the same.

### Syntax

```
[ ByRef | ByVal] argName [ ( )] [As argType]
```

### Definition

Each argument in the argument list defines how the argument is passed to the procedure, the argument name, and its data type.

### Dissection

» The optional `ByRef` keyword indicates that the argument is passed by reference. Passing arguments by reference is not discussed in this chapter.

» The optional `ByVal` keyword (the default) indicates that the argument is passed by value.

» The required *argName* contains the name (identifier) of the argument. The naming rules for arguments are the same as the naming rules for all identifiers. The *argName* can be used in a procedure as if it were a local variable. In this text, Camel case is used to name arguments to remain consistent with the Visual Studio Help system. The Camel case naming convention specifies that the first word appears in all lowercase characters. The first character of subsequent words appears in uppercase characters.

» The `As` *argType* clause defines the data type of the argument passed to the procedure. Because this book assumes that `Option Strict` is enabled, a data type must be defined for all procedure arguments.

» A comma separates each argument in the argument list and a procedure can accept any number of arguments. It is also possible that a procedure accepts no arguments.

### Code Example

```
Public Function Square(arg As Double) As Double
    Dim LocalResult As Double
    LocalResult = arg * arg
    Return LocalResult
End Function
```

*(Continued)* ▶

**Code Dissection**

The preceding code segment declares a Function procedure named Square that multiplies a number by itself, thereby squaring the value passed as an argument. Following the name of the Function procedure (Square), the argument named arg appears having a data type of Double. Thus, the variable arg can be used as a local variable in the Function procedure. Following the argument list, the return data type of the procedure appears. The As Double keywords in the Function declaration indicate that the procedure will return a double precision number. The code in the Function procedure multiplies the value of the argument by itself and the result is then stored in the local variable LocalResult. Because the variable is only used by this Function procedure, a local variable is appropriate. Finally, the Return statement causes the Function procedure to end and return the value stored in the variable LocalResult to the calling procedure.

The preceding Function procedure can be written a bit differently so as to eliminate the local variable, as shown in the following code segment:

```
Public Function Square(arg As Double) As Double
    Return arg * arg
End Function
```

As shown in the preceding code segment, the local variable has been omitted. The variable arg is multiplied by itself and the result of the expression is returned to the calling procedure.

## EXECUTING A PROCEDURE

Now that you have seen how to declare and create a Function procedure, it can be called (executed), as shown in the following event handler:

```
Private Sub btnDemo_Click(. . .) Handles btnDemo.Click
    Dim Result As Double
    Result = Square(34.55)
End Sub
```

The syntax to call a Function procedure that you create is identical to the syntax used to call a method such as FV. In the preceding example, the literal value 34.55 is passed to the Function procedure as the argument, although the argument could be a variable or object property. The Function procedure then executes, and the returned value is stored in the variable named Result.

Figure 6-1 illustrates how an argument is passed to a Function procedure, and how a value is returned from a Function procedure.

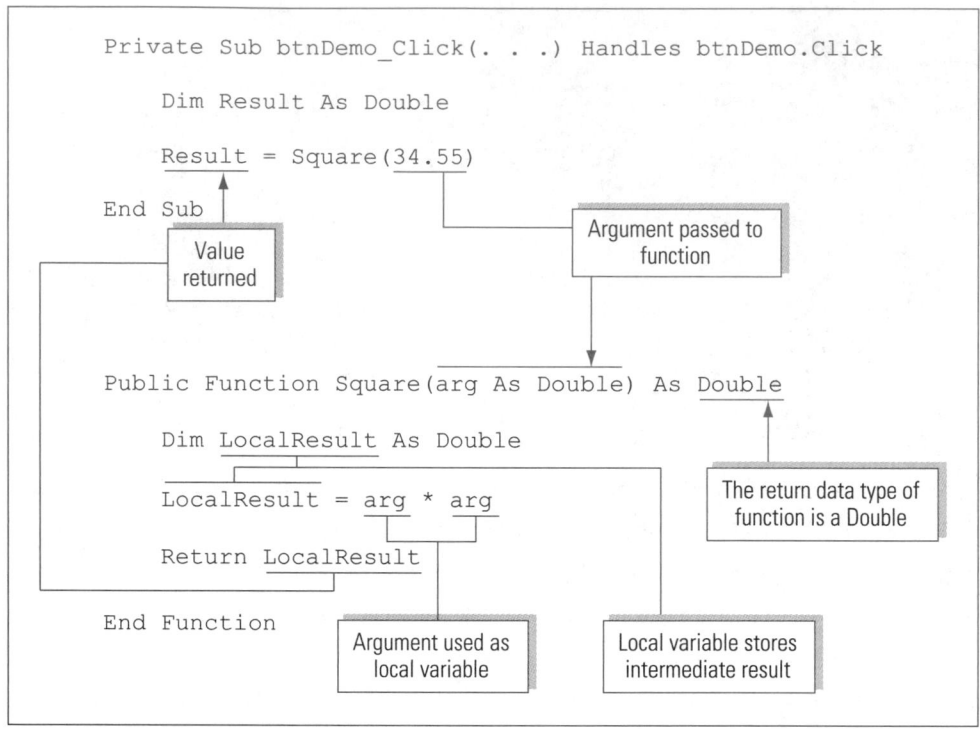

Figure 6-1: Execution flow of a Function procedure call

## COMMON PROCEDURE ERRORS

Chapters 4 and 5 discussed the importance of data types and type conversion between data types. Data types also play a role in the creation and use of procedures. To illustrate, examine the following erroneous version of the Square procedure discussed in the preceding section:

```
Public Function Square(arg As Double) As Integer
    Return arg * arg
End Function
```

If strict type checking is enabled, Visual Studio produces the following syntax error: "Option Strict On disallows implicit conversions from 'Double' to 'Integer'." The reason for this error is that the result of the expression `arg * arg` is a `Double`, but the procedure is declared to return a data type of `Integer`. The syntax error occurs because Visual Basic does not implicitly convert less restrictive types to more restrictive types.

Another error that can arise is calling a procedure with arguments having an incorrect data type or calling a procedure with the wrong number of arguments. To illustrate, examine the following version of the Square procedure, which accepts an argument having a data type of Single, and returns a value having a data type of Single:

```
Public Function Square(arg As Single) As Single
    Return arg * arg
End Function
```

The preceding Square procedure is the same as the one previously discussed. However, the procedure returns a Single instead of a Double data type. A common problem is calling a procedure with arguments having incorrect data types or the wrong number of arguments, as shown in the following statements:

```
Dim DoubleVariable As Double = 3.2444432355
Dim Result As Double
Result = Square(DoubleVariable)
Result = Square(DoubleVariable, DoubleVariable)
```

Two points can be made about calling the preceding Square procedure. The first call to the Square procedure causes the following syntax error: "Option Strict On disallows implicit conversions from 'Double' to 'Single'." The reason for this error is that the Function procedure expects an argument having a data type of Single, but the data type of the argument passed to the procedure has a data type of Double. Again, Visual Studio does not implicitly convert less restrictive types to more restrictive types. The final call to the Square procedure also causes a syntax error because two arguments are passed to the procedure but the procedure expects only one argument.

The second point to be made is related to the return data type of the Function procedure. The Function procedure returns a data type of Single, but the variable Result has a data type of Double. Because the .NET Framework implicitly converts more restrictive types to less restrictive types, this condition is not an error because the Single data type can be implicitly converted to the Double data type.

## CREATING PROCEDURES IN MODULES

As you know, all procedures must appear inside of a Class or Module block. In addition, procedures cannot be nested. That is, one procedure block cannot appear inside of another procedure block. The following code segment illustrates how a Function procedure would appear inside of a Module block named MathDemo:

```
Public Module MathDemo
    Public Function Square(ByVal arg As Double) As Double
        Return arg * arg
    End Function
End Module
```

The preceding code segment illustrates a `Module` block named MathDemo containing a single `Function` procedure named Square. Although this `Module` block contains a single `Function` procedure, it could, and likely would, contain several procedures. Procedures can appear in any order inside of a `Class` or `Module` block. The `Function` procedure is declared with the `Public` access modifier, so it can be called by any statement in the current project (assembly) or from other assemblies.

To call a `Function` procedure appearing in a `Module` block, the module name appears followed by a period, and then the procedure name, as the following statements show:

```
Dim Result As Double
Result = MathDemo.Square(34.55)
```

To illustrate the role of an access modifier, assume that the Square procedure is declared with the `Private` access modifier instead of the `Public` access modifier, as shown in the following code segment:

```
Public Module MathDemo
    Private Function Square(ByVal arg As Double) As Double
        Return arg * arg
    End Function
End Module
```

If this procedure is declared with the `Private` access modifier, the `Function` procedure can only be called from statements appearing inside of the MathDemo module.

# INTRODUCTION TO SUB PROCEDURES

Other than not returning a value, the syntax of a `Sub` procedure is identical to the syntax of a `Function` procedure. Like a `Function` procedure, a `Sub` procedure can be declared with the `Public`, `Friend`, or `Private` access modifiers, and can accept zero or more arguments. A `Sub` procedure, however, cannot appear on the right side of an assignment statement because it does not return a value. Also, a `Sub` procedure has no `As` *type* clause because it does not return a value. Finally, the `End Sub` keywords replace the `End Function` keywords.

## CREATING SUB PROCEDURES

Because Sub procedures do not return a value, they are most commonly used to perform a generic task that does not produce a result. The following list contains examples in which Sub procedures might be useful:

» Suppose that a form exists, in which the contents of several input text boxes needs to be cleared. A Sub procedure could be created to perform this task. The Sub procedure would likely be created to accept no arguments.

» Suppose that a form has various control instances that require similar formatting. For example, it might be necessary to apply the same foreground and background colors to several control instances. A Sub procedure would again be useful in this case. The control instance to be formatted would be passed as an argument to the procedure.

The following code segment shows a Sub procedure to remove the text from multiple text boxes:

```
Private Sub ClearTextBoxes()
    txtPrefix.Text = NullChar
    txtFirstName.Text = NullChar
    txtLastName.Text = NullChar
End Sub
```

The Sub procedure appearing in the preceding example is named ClearTextBoxes and accepts no arguments. The code in the Sub procedure clears the text from three different text boxes by setting the Text property to a null character. This Sub procedure can only be called from a procedure in the class where ClearTextBoxes is declared because the procedure is declared with the Private access modifier. Thus, this procedure would appear in the Class block (form) containing the declaration for the referenced TextBox control instances.

Consider a second example in which a Sub procedure accepts an argument, as shown in the following code segment:

```
Private Sub FormatTextBox(ByVal txtArg As TextBox)
    txtArg.ForeColor = Color.LightBlue
    txtArg.BackColor = Color.DarkBlue
End Sub
```

The preceding Sub procedure accepts one argument having a data type of TextBox. The contents of the TextBox control instance passed as an argument are formatted. Thus, arguments of any data type can be passed to procedures.

Having seen how to create a Sub procedure, it is also necessary to know how to call one.

## CALLING SUB PROCEDURES

The syntax to call a Sub procedure differs slightly from the syntax to call a Function procedure. To call a Sub procedure, the Call statement is used, which has the following syntax:

### Syntax

```
[ Call] procedureName(argumentList)
```

### Definition

The Call statement executes a Sub procedure. The Sub procedure executes, and then execution continues at the statement following the Call statement.

### Dissection

» The required *procedureName* indicates which Sub procedure is being called. That is, *procedureName* contains the name of the Sub procedure being called.

» The optional *argumentList* contains the arguments that are communicated to the Sub procedure. Again, a Sub procedure can accept zero or more arguments.

### Code Example

```
Call ClearTextBoxes()

Call FormatTextBox(txtDemo)
```

### Code Dissection

The first of the preceding statements calls the ClearTextBoxes Sub procedure. The Sub procedure is called with zero arguments. The second of the preceding statements calls a Sub procedure named FormatTextBox. One argument is passed to the procedure—an instance of the TextBox control named txtDemo.

The Call keyword is optional when calling a Sub procedure. However, the examples in this book include the Call keyword for clarity. Thus, the following two statements are equivalent:

```
Call ClearTextBoxes()
ClearTextBoxes()
```

Figure 6-2 illustrates the call to the ClearTextBoxes Sub procedure.

As shown in Figure 6-2, the Call statement executes a Sub procedure. When execution of the Sub procedure is complete (that is, when the End Sub statement is reached), the Sub procedure returns, and then execution continues at the statement following the statement that called the Sub procedure.

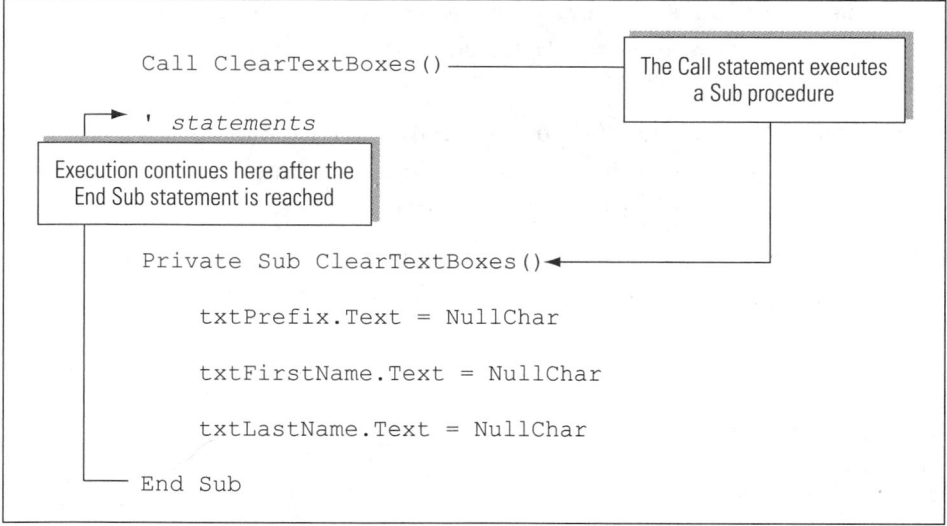

```
        Call ClearTextBoxes()                    The Call statement executes
                                                  a Sub procedure

          ' statements

    Execution continues here after the
    End Sub statement is reached

        Private Sub ClearTextBoxes()

            txtPrefix.Text = NullChar

            txtFirstName.Text = NullChar

            txtLastName.Text = NullChar

        End Sub
```

Figure 6-2: Calling a Sub procedure

In this exploration exercise, you will see how to call `Function` and `Sub` procedures and how to pass arguments to those procedures.

1. Start Visual Studio, if necessary, and open the solution file in the folder named **Chapter.06\Chapter06ConceptLesson**. Run the solution, and click the **Calling Procedures** tab, if necessary. Note that an introductory screen called a splash screen appears when the application is first started. The splash screen is discussed later in this chapter. Figure 6-3 shows the Calling Procedures tab.

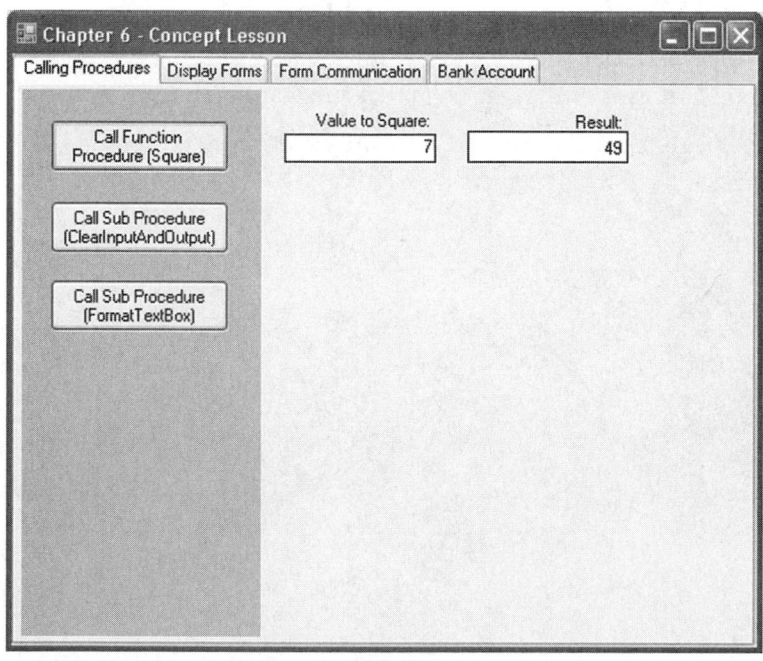

Figure 6-3: Concept lesson—Calling Procedures tab

2. Click the **Call Function Procedure (Square)** button. The Square procedure discussed previously appearing in the MathDemo module is called and the result is displayed in the output label.

3. Click the **Call Sub Procedure (ClearInputAndOutput)** button. The code in the event handler calls a Sub procedure named ClearInputAndOutput to remove the text from the input and output control instances.

4. Click the **Call Sub Procedure (FormatTextBox)** button. The code in the event handler calls the Sub procedure named FormatTextBox with one argument: the name of the text box to format.

# MINI-QUIZ 1

1. Describe the primary difference between a Function procedure and a Sub procedure.

2. What is the name of the keyword used to return a value from a Function procedure?

3. Which of the following statements is correct regarding a Function procedure?

   a. A procedure must have at least one argument to be syntactically correct.

   b. A Function procedure can accept zero or more arguments.

   c. An object reference, such as a reference to a TextBox control instance, cannot be used as an argument to a Function procedure.

   d. If multiple arguments are passed to a Function procedure, those arguments must all have the same data type.

   e. none of the above

4. Describe the error(s) in the following code segment:

```
Public Function Cube(ByVal arg As Double) As Integer
    Dim Result As Double
    Result = arg ^ 3
    Return arg
End Function
```

# INTRODUCTION TO APPLICATIONS WITH MULTIPLE MODULES

The first part of this concept lesson described how to create procedures, pass arguments to them, and call procedures. This section discusses how to organize those procedures across different `Module` and `Class` blocks and how to communicate information between modules and forms.

Most applications require multiple forms such as an introductory form called a splash screen, a login form, a main form, about dialog boxes, and other forms each having a particular purpose. In addition to multiple forms, an application can have additional `Class` and `Module` blocks. These additional `Class` and `Module` blocks contain procedures that can be used by other parts of the application or by multiple applications.

This section discusses how to work with multiple forms, add forms to an application, and designate a particular form as the start-up form.

## ORGANIZATION OF AN APPLICATION WITH MULTIPLE MODULES

All of an application's forms, classes, and modules appear in the Solution Explorer, and each form, class, and module is saved as a separate physical disk file. Figure 6-4 shows the Solution Explorer displaying the classes and modules appearing in this concept lesson.

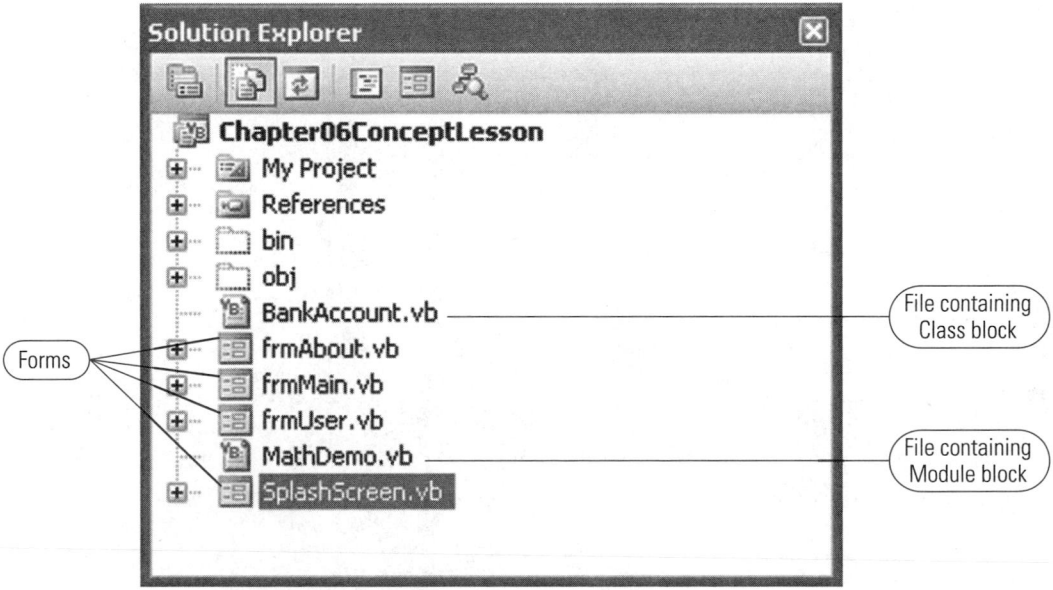

Figure 6-4: The Solution Explorer containing multiple modules

As shown in Figure 6-4, the Solution Explorer displays the files that make up the solution. Instead of just a single module or form file, the Solution Explorer displays several different files, as described in the following list:

» The module named BankAccount.vb contains a `Class` block. The class contains methods to implement a bank account.

» The form named frmAbout.vb describes the application using information obtained from the assembly itself.

» The form named frmMain.vb is the application's main form.

» The form named frmUser.vb contains text boxes allowing the end user to enter a name and an ID number. The purpose of this form is to show how to communicate data between forms.

» The module named MathDemo.vb contains a `Module` block with `Function` procedures used to perform mathematical operations.

» The form named SplashScreen.vb contains an introductory splash screen.

» The other files appearing in the Solution Explorer are the same project files discussed in Chapters 2 and 3.

## ADDING A FORM MODULE TO AN APPLICATION

The Add New Item dialog box is used to add a new form, module, or class to a project. Clicking Project, Add New Item activates the Add New Item dialog box shown in Figure 6-5.

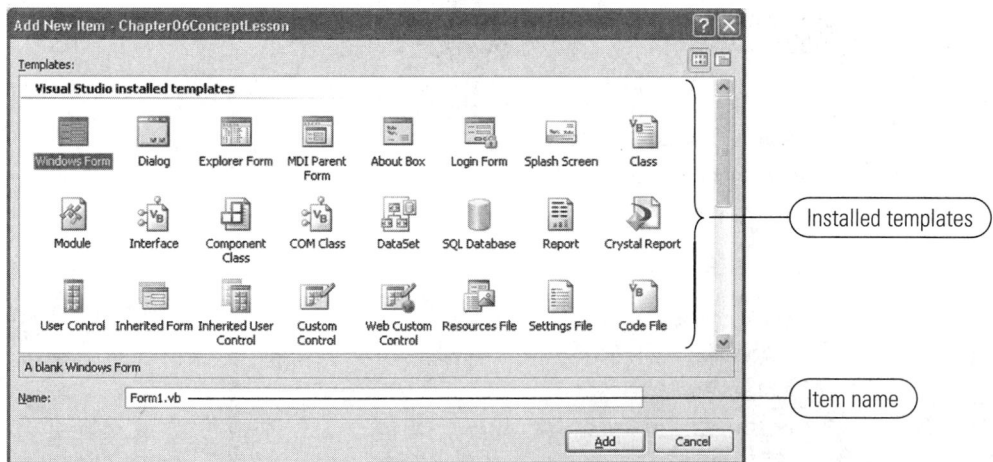

Figure 6-5: Add New Item dialog box

As shown in Figure 6-5, the Add New Item dialog box lists the installed templates for different types of modules. There is nothing special about these templates. That is, templates are nothing more than forms or other file types, with common configuration information already completed.

The following list describes the purpose of a few of the Visual Studio templates:

» The About Box template contains control instances and the necessary code to display information about the assembly. This is the same assembly information discussed in Chapter 2.

» The Class template creates an empty class (a `Class`, `End Class` block).

» The Module template creates an empty `Module`, `End Module` block.

» The Login Form template creates a form with login and password control instances. The template does not contain any code to process this information in any way.

» The Windows Form template contains a blank form. Use this template to add additional custom forms to a project.

In addition to creating a new module, class, or other item from a template, it is also possible to add an existing module or class file to a project. To do this, copy the disk file containing the class or module to the desired project directory. Then, in Visual Studio, click Project, Add Existing Item. In the dialog box that opens, select the file to be added to the project.

## SETTING THE START-UP OBJECT FOR A MULTIFORM APPLICATION

In any application containing multiple forms or modules, it is necessary to designate the application's entry point. In other words, it is necessary to define where execution of the application should begin. The entry point for the Console Application projects created in the first two chapters of this book was the procedure named Main.

In a Windows Application project, there are two possible entry points:

» A procedure named Main in a `Module` block can be designated as an application's entry point.

» Any form in the project can also be designated as an application's entry point. In this case, when the application is run, an instance of the form is created, and that form instance is displayed to the end user on the desktop.

An application's entry point is specified using the Project's property pages. These are the same property pages discussed in Chapter 2. As mentioned before, the Application tab contains options to define the namespace, assembly name, and other application-specific information. It also contains the options to define the project's start-up object, as shown in Figure 6-6.

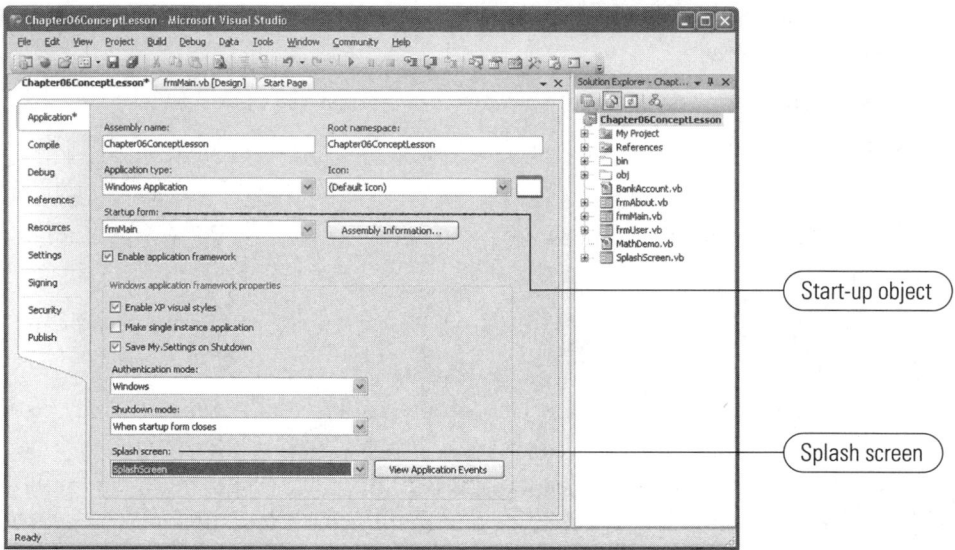

Figure 6-6: Project property pages

The Startup form drop-down list displays the forms in the project that can be designated as the start-up object. In Figure 6-6, the form named frmMain is designated as the start-up form. Checking the Enable application framework check box causes those options applicable only to Windows Application projects to be enabled. The following list describes these options:

» The Enable XP visual styles check box causes buttons to appear using the new rounded XP visual style standard.

» The Make single instance application check box causes the system to prohibit more than one copy of the application from running.

» The Save My.Settings on Shutdown check box causes the application's current settings to be saved so that they persist from one application invocation to the next. The topic of persisting application settings is not discussed in this chapter.

» The Authentication mode drop-down list controls how users will authenticate themselves to the system. Security and authentication are not discussed in this chapter.

» The Shutdown mode drop-down list has two settings. The When startup form closes setting causes the application to close when the start-up form is closed. The When last form closes setting causes the application to close when the last remaining form instance is closed.

» The final drop-down list, titled Splash screen, defines the application's initial form or splash screen. The form designated as the splash screen appears while the start-up object loads.

The Project's property pages also contain an Assembly Information button. This button allows you to configure descriptive information about the assembly. This is the same information appearing in the AssemblyInfo.vb file discussed in Chapter 2. Figure 6-7 shows the Assembly Information dialog box.

Figure 6-7: Assembly Information dialog box

The following code segment shows the settings for the corresponding attributes:

```
<Assembly: AssemblyTitle("Chapter06ConceptLesson")>
<Assembly: AssemblyDescription("")>
<Assembly: AssemblyCompany("University of Nevada, Reno")>
<Assembly: AssemblyProduct("Chapter06ConceptLesson")>
<Assembly: AssemblyCopyright("Copyright © University of
Nevada, Reno 2005")>
<Assembly: AssemblyTrademark("")>
```

As shown in the preceding statements and discussed in Chapter 2, the preceding statements set global assembly attributes, which can be read by the application at run time. These statements are automatically created when an About form is created from a template.

# CREATING AND DISPLAYING MULTIPLE FORM INSTANCES

In any application having multiple forms, operations need to be performed on those forms:

» Just as it is necessary to create instances of controls and other classes, it is necessary to create instances of a form.

» After a form instance has been created, it can be displayed.

» Visible forms must be hidden or closed.

» Windows fires events as the end user interacts with a form instance. Like any other event, form-related events can be handled.

## CREATING A FORM INSTANCE

As you know, when a control instance gets created on a form, the Windows Forms Designer writes the statements in the form's partial class to create that control instance at run time. Conceptually, creating an instance of a form is no different than creating an instance of a control such as a Label, Button, or TextBox.

To illustrate a form class and how to create an instance of that class, suppose that a form (class) named frmAbout existed in the current project. The following code segment shows the sample declaration for the class:

```
Public Class frmAbout
    Inherits System.Windows.Forms.Form
    ' statements
End Class
```

Like any class, an instance of the form class must be created before it can be used. You can create an instance of a form and display it in three ways:

» Explicitly create an instance of the form class by calling the form's constructor, and call the Show method to display the form.

» The My.Forms object provides a default form instance for every form in the project. Call the Show method using the default instance of the form class supplied by My.Forms.

» A default form instance is also supplied through an automatically generated property having the same name as the form class.

Each of these techniques to create and display a form instance is discussed in the following sections.

## CREATING A FORM INSTANCE EXPLICITLY

The first way to create and display a form involves creating an instance of the underlying form class and storing a reference to that form instance in a variable. After the form instance has been created, its properties can be used as with any other object.

```
Dim frmNewInstance As New frmAbout
frmNewInstance.Text = "About Form"
```

The first of the preceding statements creates an instance of the form class named frmAbout and stores a reference to that form instance in the variable named frmNewInstance. The New keyword is used to create an instance of a class by calling the form's constructor. The New keyword and constructors are discussed in more detail later in the chapter. The second statement sets the Text property of the form, thereby resetting the form's caption.

To illustrate a common error when creating and displaying a form, examine the following statements:

```
Dim frmNewInstance As frmAbout
frmNewInstance.Text = "About Form"
```

Note that the New keyword does not appear in the preceding declaration, so an instance of the form class is not created. Thus, the second statement causes a NullReferenceException because the object does not exist.

## DISPLAYING A FORM USING THE MY.FORMS COLLECTION

Remember that the My object is used to reference other commonly used objects. The My.Forms collection has a property used to reference each form in an assembly. The name of the property is always the same as the name of the form. Thus, as different projects have different form names, the My.Forms collection contains different property names. The following statement illustrates the second way to set the `Text` property for an instance of the form named frmAbout using the `My.Forms` collection:

```
My.Forms.frmAbout.Text = "About Form"
```

Assuming that the project contains a form named frmAbout, the preceding statement stores a string in the form's caption. Note that the `Text` property is set without creating an instance of the form. On the surface, it might seem that a `NullReferenceException` would occur but it does not. One of the features of the `My.Forms` object is that it creates a default form instance automatically.

> **»NOTE** Visual Basic 6.0 supported a similar default form instance. However, in Visual Studio 2002 and 2003, the only way to work with a second form was to explicitly create a form instance as discussed in the preceding section. By implicitly creating a default instance of each form, it is much easier to navigate between forms and communicate data between forms.

## DISPLAYING A FORM USING THE MY OBJECT'S DEFAULT PROPERTY

In addition to referencing the default form instance through the `My.Forms` object, it is possible to reference the same form using its name as the following statement shows:

```
frmAbout.Text = "About Form"
```

On the surface, the following statement makes it appear that the form's class name is being used to set the `Text` property. If that were true, the statement would cause an error. However, Visual Studio 2005 automatically supplies a default form instance having the same name as the form class, and supplied through the `My.Forms` object. That is, it is not necessary to explicitly create a form instance before displaying it or calling its methods.

To summarize, each of the preceding statements to set a form's `Text` property is equivalent:

```
Dim frmNewInstance As New frmAbout
frmNewInstance.Text = "About Form"
My.Forms.frmAbout.Text = "About Form"
frmAbout.Text = "About Form"
```

## DISPLAYING FORMS

After a form instance exists, it can be explicitly displayed. Only the start-up form and optional splash screen are displayed implicitly when an application starts. How the end user navigates from one form to another works differently based on how the form is displayed. This concept of form interaction is called **modality**.

» A form can be displayed as a *modal form*. When a modal form is visible, the form that displayed the modal form cannot get input focus. Focus returns to the form that displayed the modal form after the modal form is hidden or closed. The `ShowDialog` method is used to display a form as a modal form.

» When a form is displayed as a *modeless form*, the end user can change input focus between the other open forms in the application. The `Show` method is used to display a form as a modeless form.

The following statements illustrate how to display a form as a modeless form and as a modal dialog box. The following statements assume that the identifier named frmAbout is the default form instance supplied through the `My.Forms` object:

```
frmAbout.ShowDialog()
frmAbout.Show()
```

The first of the preceding statements displays the form named frmAbout as a modal form and the second statement displays the same form as a modeless form.

Another important point needs to be made related to displaying a form as a modal form, as shown in the following statements:

```
frmAbout.ShowDialog()
' statements
```

When the `ShowDialog` method is called, execution of the current procedure is suspended until the modal form is either closed or hidden. Thus, *statements* following the call to the `ShowDialog` method call do not execute until the form named frmAbout is closed or hidden.

## HIDING AND CLOSING A FORM

Just as a form can be displayed, it can also be closed or made invisible, as follows:

» When a form is made invisible, its objects still exist. That is, even though a form is invisible to the end user, the other forms in an application can reference the form's data (properties) and call the form's methods.

» When a form is closed, the form's data is destroyed and the memory is released back to the operating system. In other words, all of the form's control instances and variables are destroyed. Thus, after a form is closed, a new instance of the form must be re-created before its properties can be used or the form can be displayed.

The `Hide` method of the `Form` class makes a form invisible. In addition, setting the `Visible` property of a form to `False` also makes a form invisible. The following statements show two ways to hide the form named frmAbout using the same default form instance discussed previously:

```
frmAbout.Hide()
frmAbout.Visible = False
```

Calling the `Close` method of a form unloads the form from memory. The following statement unloads the form named frmAbout, thereby destroying the form and its control instances. The memory for the form and its objects is released back to the operating system with the following statement:

```
frmAbout.Close()
```

As forms are loaded, displayed, hidden, and unloaded, Windows fires various events applicable to the form. These events are discussed next.

## INTRODUCTION TO FORM EVENTS

Chapter 3 introduced selected events that fire as a form is loaded and as a form gets and loses input focus. However, these events were not discussed in detail because the application contained only a single form. When an application contains multiple forms, handling these events becomes useful.

Remember that one control instance on a form has input focus at a time. Thus, it follows that only one form among an application's visible forms can have input focus. Several events are related to a form's focus, as described in the following list:

» The `Activated` event fires each time a form gets input focus.

» The `Deactivate` event fires each time a form loses input focus. Thus, if the end user changed input focus from the form named frm1 to the form named frm2, the `Deactivate` event would fire for the form named frm1, and then the `Activated` event would fire for the form named frm2.

» The `Load` event fires when a form is loaded into memory for the first time. However, this event does not fire as a form gets focus again. Only the `Activated` event fires in this case. Initialization processing is typically performed in the form's `Load` event. Initialization can also be performed in the form's constructor. If a form was closed and the memory allocated to the form released, the form would be re-created and the `Load` event would fire.

» A `FormClosing` event fires just before a form is unloaded. Final housekeeping chores are typically performed in this event handler.

» After a form has closed, the `FormClosed` event fires.

Figure 6-8 illustrates the order in which form events fire as a main form loads and as focus switches from one form to another.

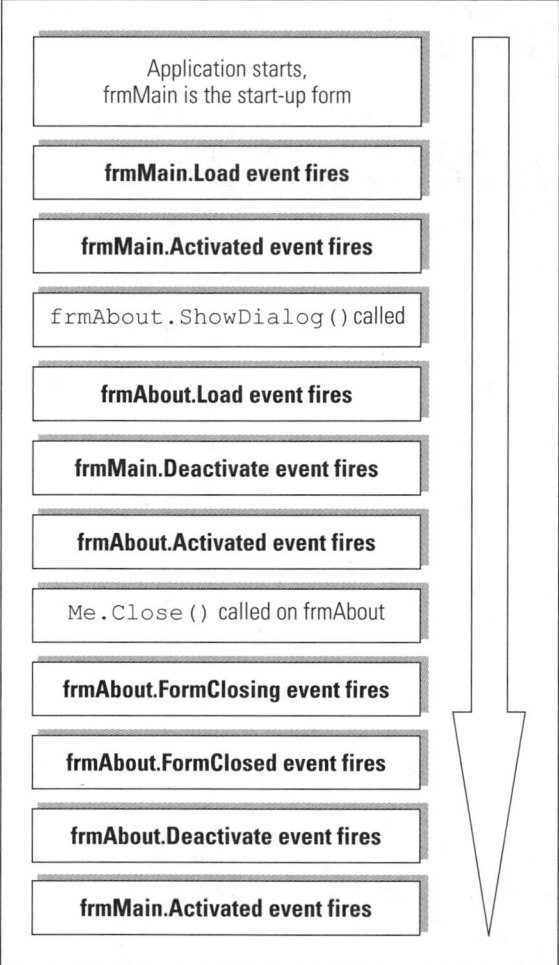

Figure 6-8: Order of form events

In this exploration exercise, you will see how to display and hide modal and modeless forms in an application and examine the events that fire as input focus changes from one form to another.

1. Run the solution named **Chapter06ConceptLesson**.

2. Click the **Display Forms** tab. Figure 6-9 shows the Display Forms tab. As you display and change input focus from form to form, a text box on the main form is updated displaying the focus events as they fire. A message appears in the multiline text box each

time a `Load`, `Activated`, `Deactivate`, `FormClosing`, or `FormClosed` event fires for forms named frmMain, frmAbout, and frmUser.

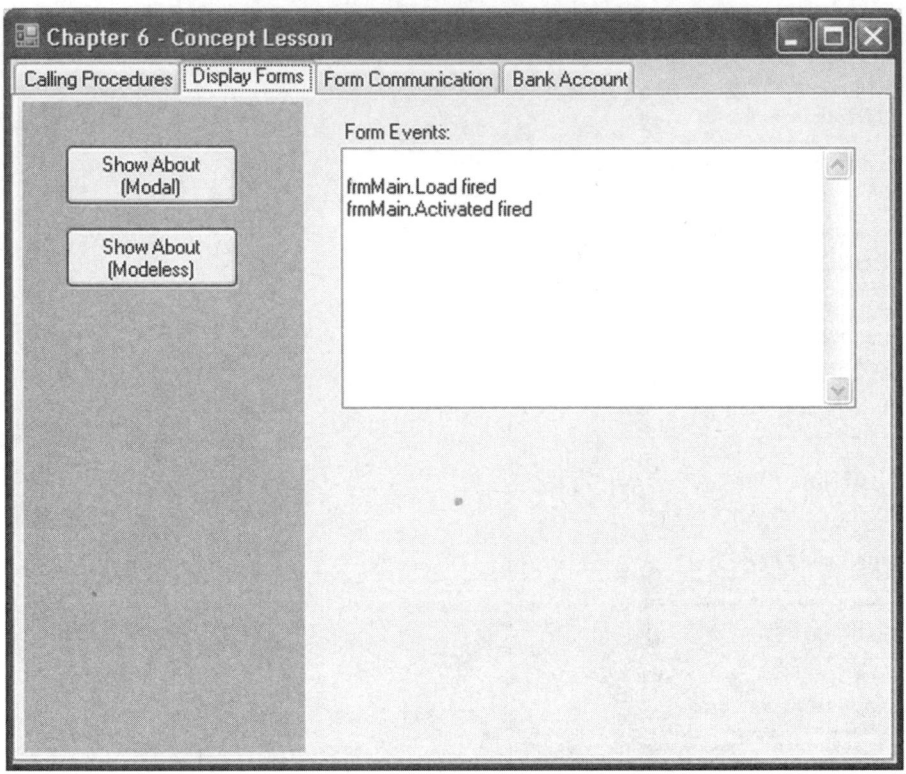

Figure 6-9: Concept lesson–Display Forms tab

3. Click the **Show About (Modal)** button. The form named frmAbout appears as a modal dialog box. Click the main form. Note that it cannot get focus because the modal dialog box is still open. Close the modal dialog box.

4. Click the **Show About (Modeless)** button. The form named frmAbout appears as a modeless dialog box. Note that it is possible to toggle focus back and forth between the two forms. Close the dialog box by clicking the OK button.

# MINI-QUIZ 2

1. What are the possible options for an application's start-up object?

2. Which of the following statements will correctly display the form named frmDemo as a modeless form?

   a. `frmDemo.Show()`

   b. `My.Forms.frmDemo.Show()`

   c. `Dim f As New frmDemo()`

   `f.Show()`

   d. all of the above

   e. none of the above

3. Write the statements to display the form named frmDemo as a modal and modeless form, respectively. Use the `My.Forms` object to display the form.

4. Assuming the frmDemo is a form class, describe the error in the following statements:

```
Dim frmNewDemo As frmDemo
frmNewDemo.Text = "Mini Quiz"
```

In addition to displaying and hiding multiple forms, it is also necessary to communicate data between forms. This topic is discussed next:

# COMMUNICATING DATA BETWEEN FORMS

To understand how to communicate data between forms, the concepts of scope and visibility become important. The `Public`, `Friend`, and `Private` access modifiers have been mentioned throughout this book. However, fully understanding their purpose was difficult because the applications were made up of a single class (form). In this section, you will learn how to communicate data between forms.

## REVIEWING THE ACCESSIBILITY OF PRIVATE DATA

Remember that the accessibility of a `Private` module-level variable is the `Class` or `Module` block containing the declaration. That is, only the `Class` or `Module` block containing the declaration can reference a variable or procedure declared with the `Private` access modifier. Thus, the following variable named HiddenVariable can only be referenced from the class named frmMain, which contains the declaration:

```
Public Class frmMain
    Private HiddenVariable As Integer
End Class
```

Thus, to communicate data between forms or other modules, another access modifier must be used.

## THE ACCESSIBILITY OF FRIEND DATA

To illustrate how data can be communicated between forms, suppose that an application has two forms named frmMain and frmUser and that the form named frmUser has two text boxes named txtUserName and txtUserID. In addition to referencing the control instances on the current form, it is also possible to reference those control instances appearing in the other forms of an application because the Windows Forms Designer creates control instances with the `Friend` access modifier by default.

As you know, when the Windows Forms Designer creates control instances on a form, statements are automatically generated to create those control instances in the corresponding partial class, as shown in the following code segment:

```
Friend WithEvents txtUserName As System.Windows.Forms.TextBox
Friend WithEvents txtUserID As System.Windows.Forms.TextBox
```

The preceding declaration statements look similar to other declaration statements that you have written with two exceptions: the `Friend` access modifier replaces the `Private` access modifier, and the `WithEvents` keyword appears to indicate that the control instance will handle events. When a variable or procedure (identifier) is declared with the `Friend` access modifier, that identifier is visible to all of the modules in an assembly, rather than just the `Class` or `Module` block containing the declaration. Thus, `Friend` identifiers can be shared across the entire assembly. Figure 6-10 compares the accessibility of the `Private` and `Friend` access modifiers.

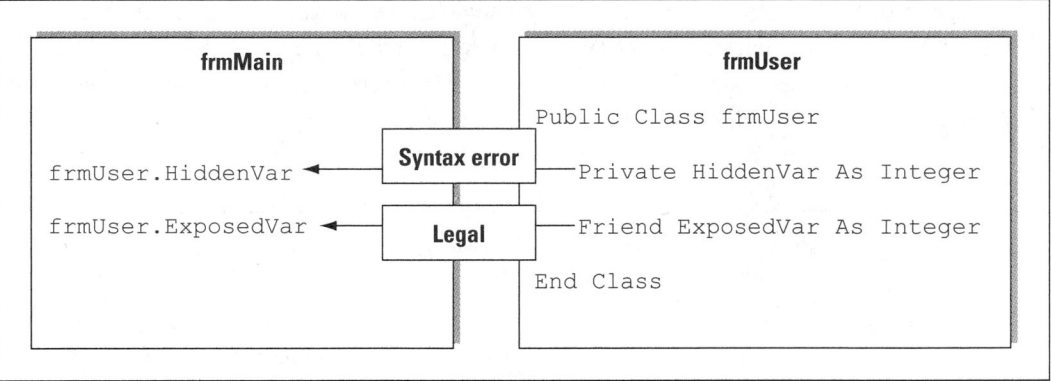

Figure 6-10: Controlling accessibility with the Friend and Private access modifiers

Because the variable named HiddenVar is declared with the `Private` access modifier, it can only be referenced from the frmUser class. Thus, the statement in frmMain that tries to reference the variable will cause a syntax error. Because the variable named ExposedVar is declared with the `Friend` access modifier, that variable can be referenced by the other modules in the application.

When referencing a control instance or variable appearing on the current form, that control instance or variable is referenced using the control instance name or the variable name. However, when referencing a control instance or variable on another form, the form name must also be specified. The following statements illustrate this:

```
ExposedVar = 1
frmUser.ExposedVar = 1
```

The first of the preceding statements tries to reference the variable named ExposedVar declared in the form (class) named frmUser. However, the statement does not work because the variable is not declared in the current form. Visual Studio, therefore, generates the following syntax error: "Name 'ExposedVar' is not declared". The reason for this error is simple: Without qualifying the form name, the compiler cannot locate the variable appearing in a different form (class). Thus, the second statement corrects the error by specifying the default form instance named frmUser.

## THE ACCESSIBILITY OF PUBLIC DATA

If a variable or procedure is declared with the `Public` access modifier, that variable or procedure can be used throughout the current assembly as well as by other assemblies. To illustrate, examine the following sample variable declarations appearing in a form named frmUser:

```
Public Class frmUser
    Private HiddenVariable As Integer
    Friend FriendVariable As Integer
    Public ExposedVariable As Integer
End Class
```

The preceding statements declare variables having `Private`, `Friend`, and `Public` visibility. The variable named ExposedVariable is visible to the current assembly but is also visible to other assemblies because it is declared with the `Public` access modifier. Figure 6-11 illustrates the accessibility of these variables.

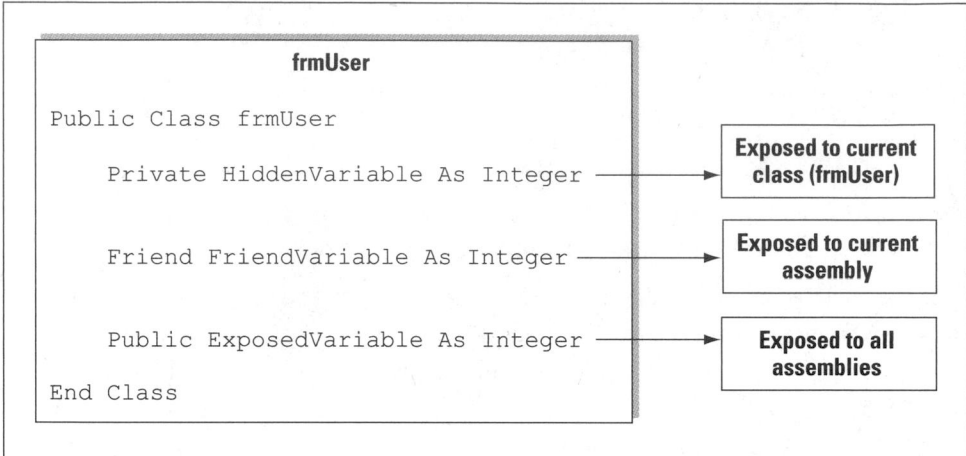

Figure 6-11: Variable accessibility

# INTRODUCTION TO PROPERTY PROCEDURES

Remember that encapsulation rules dictate that the data in a class should only be modified by a process of the class. However, as shown in the preceding section, declaring a `Friend` or `Public` variable in a class violates the encapsulation rules because data can be modified directly using an assignment statement. `Property` procedures solve this problem.

Syntactically, **Property procedures** are similar to `Function` and `Sub` procedures. That is, code executes when the procedure is called. However, the purpose of `Property` procedures differs slightly from the purpose of `Function` and `Sub` procedures, as described in the following list:

» As you know, classes of the .NET Framework support properties and methods. `Function` and `Sub` procedures are used to implement methods. `Property` procedures, as their name implies, are used to implement properties.

» The syntax to execute the code in a `Property` procedure differs slightly from the code to execute a `Function` or `Sub` procedure.

`Property` procedures are discussed in this section because they are used to store exposed data without violating the rules of encapsulation, and can be used to share data between the forms in an application. `Property` procedures have the following syntax:

## Syntax

```
[ ReadOnly | WriteOnly | Property]  varName ([ parameterList
]) [ As type]
    [ Get
         [ statements]
    End Get]
    [ Set(ByVal value As type)
        [ statements]
    End Set]
End Property
```

## Definition

The `Property` statement declares a `Property` procedure. `Property` procedures, like other procedures, cannot be nested and must appear inside of a `Class` or `Module` block.

## Dissection

» Read-only properties are declared with the `ReadOnly` keyword.

» Write-only properties are declared with the `WriteOnly` keyword.

» The required *varName* argument defines the name (identifier) of the property. Use the Pascal case naming conventions for properties and methods. That is, use whole words and nouns, and capitalize the first letter of each word.

» The *parameterList* contains the list of arguments passed to the `Property` procedure. The syntax of the *parameterList* is the same as the syntax of a procedure's argument list. Properties can accept zero or more arguments.

» The `As` *type* clause contains the data type of the property. Just like `Function` procedures, `Property` procedures have a data type. If strict type checking is enabled, the `As` *type* clause is required.

» The statements in the `Get` block execute when the property's value is read.

» The statements in the `Set` block execute when the property's value is written. The `Set` block contains an *argumentList* that specifies the variable and data type passed as an argument when the property's value is set.

*(Continued)* ▶

## Code Example

```
Private HiddenName As String
Public Property EmployeeName() As String
    Get
        Return HiddenName
    End Get
    Set(ByVal value As String)
        HiddenName = value
    End Set
End Property
```

## Code Dissection

The preceding code segment is used to implement a property named EmployeeName having a data type of `String`. The property is a read-write property so both the `Get` and `Set` blocks appear. The code in the `Set` block executes when a value is stored in the property. The statement stores the value, passed as an argument, in the module-level variable named HiddenName. The code in the `Get` block executes when the property is read. The statement in the `Get` block returns the value stored in the module-level variable named HiddenName. `Property` procedures almost always store their data to a hidden variable and retrieve data from that hidden variable.

**»TIP**

When creating a Property procedure, the Code Editor and Intellisense technology create the procedure template after you enter the property declaration.

`Property` procedures are called with the same *object.property* syntax used to reference any other property or variable. Assuming that the preceding EmployeeName property was declared in the current form, the following statements write and read the property's value, respectively. Remember that the Me keyword is used to reference the current form or other class instance.

```
Me.EmployeeName = txtEmployeeName.Text
txtEmployeeName.Text = Me.EmployeeName
```

When the first of the preceding statements executes, the code in the `Property` procedure's `Set` block executes, thereby storing a value in the hidden variable named HiddenName. When the second statement executes, the code in the `Property` procedure's `Get` block executes, thereby reading the value from this hidden variable. Figure 6-12 illustrates how `Property` procedures execute.

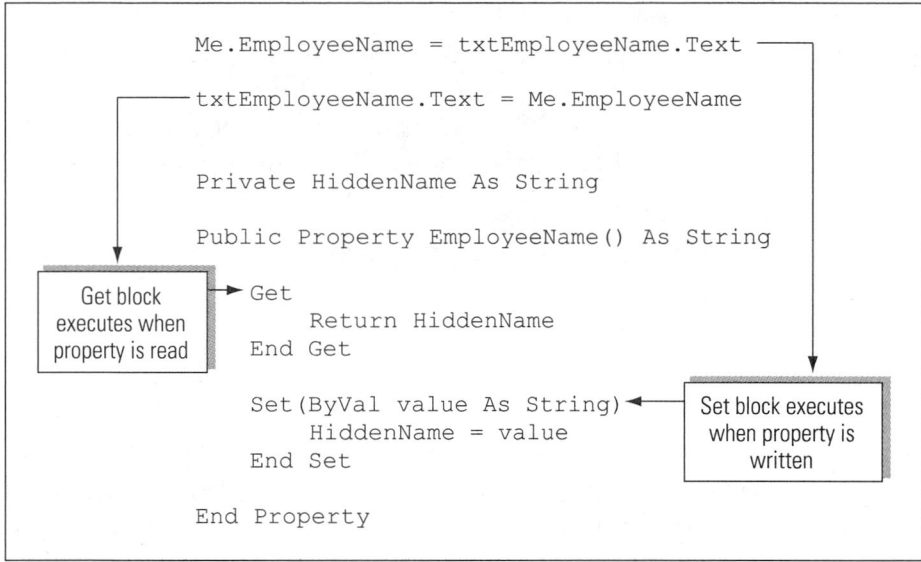

```
              Me.EmployeeName = txtEmployeeName.Text

              txtEmployeeName.Text = Me.EmployeeName


              Private HiddenName As String

              Public Property EmployeeName() As String

    Get block      Get
 executes when          Return HiddenName
property is read    End Get

                   Set(ByVal value As String)      Set block executes
                       HiddenName = value           when property is
                   End Set                              written

              End Property
```

Figure 6-12: Executing Property procedures

In addition to read-write properties, it is also possible to create read-only properties and write-only properties, which are discussed next.

## CREATING READ-ONLY PROPERTIES

A read-only property is created by adding the ReadOnly keyword to the Property procedure's declaration. The Set block cannot appear in a read-only Property procedure because the property's value cannot be written. Trying to include a Set block in a read-only property causes the following syntax error to be generated: "Properties declared 'ReadOnly' cannot have a 'Set'." The following code segment illustrates how to declare a read-only property named ReferenceCounter:

```
Private ReferenceCounterHidden As Integer
Public ReadOnly Property ReferenceCounter() As Integer
    Get
        Return ReferenceCounterHidden
    End Get
End Property
```

Because the ReferenceCounter property is read-only, the Set block does not appear. The statement in the Get block returns the value of the module-level variable named ReferenceCounterHidden. Of course, some other statement in the class must update the value of this variable.

Here, a read-only property enforces encapsulation rules. That is, the data stored in the variable ReferenceCounterHidden cannot be modified outside of the class containing the declaration. It can only be accessed through the Public Property procedure.

## CREATING WRITE-ONLY PROPERTIES

Although not frequently used, it is possible to create write-only properties. When creating a write-only property, the `WriteOnly` keyword appears in the property declaration. In addition, the property cannot have a `Get` block as the property cannot be read. The following statements illustrate a write-only `Property` procedure named SecureUser:

```
Private SecureUserHidden As String
Public WriteOnly Property SecureUser() As String
    Set(ByVal value As String)
        SecureUserHidden = value
    End Set
End Property
```

As shown in the preceding code segment, the write-only property named SecureUser contains a `Set` block, but the `Get` block is omitted. The `WriteOnly` keyword appears in the property declaration. Again, it is assumed that some other statements in the class read the variable named SecureUserHidden.

In this exploration exercise, you will see how to communicate information between the forms in an application and how `Property` procedures operate.

1. Run the solution named **Chapter06ConceptLesson**. Click the **Form Communication** tab. Figure 6-13 shows the Form Communication tab.

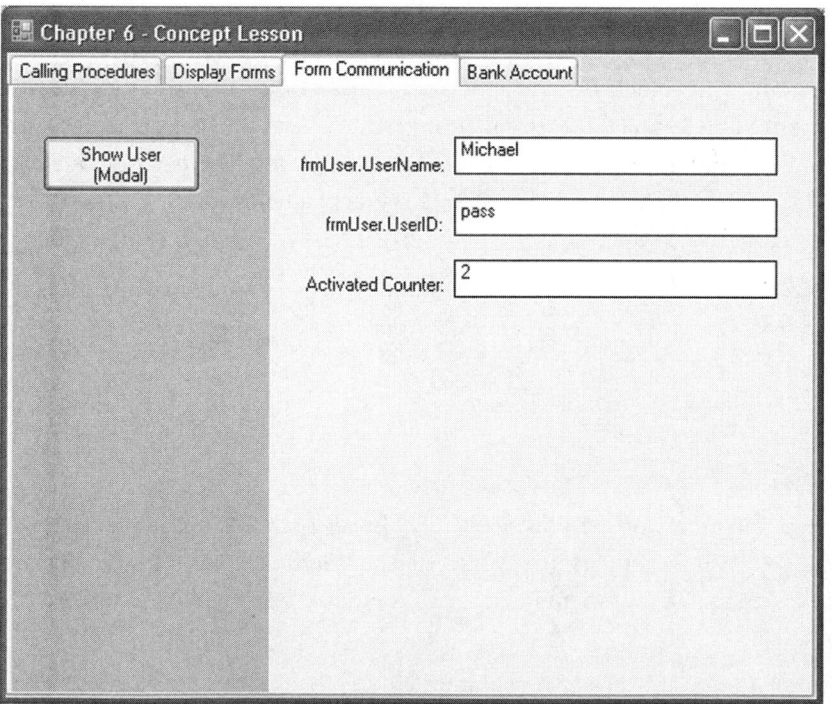

Figure 6-13: Concept lesson—Form Communication tab

2. Click the **Show User (Modal)** button to display the User form, as shown in Figure 6-14. Enter sample values for a username and user ID.

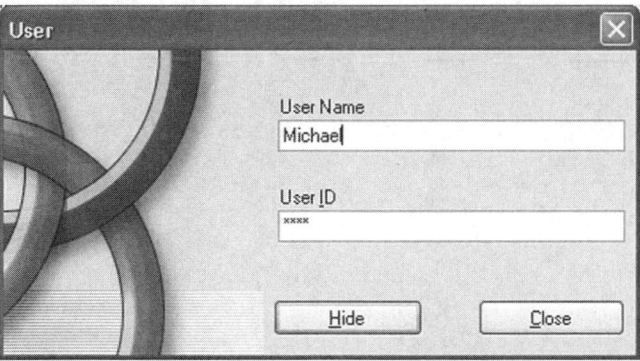

Figure 6-14: Concept lesson—User form

3. Click the **Hide** button to make the form invisible. The code for the button's `Click` event handler calls the `Hide` method to make the form invisible but preserve its objects. The following statements on the form named frmMain execute to get the contents of the text boxes from the User form. The final statement reads a counter indicating the number of times the form has been activated since it was loaded. This counter is implemented using a `Property` procedure.

```
lblUserName.Text = frmUser.txtUserName.Text
lblUserID.Text = frmUser.txtUserID.Text
lblReferenceCounter.Text = frmUser.ReferenceCounter.ToString
```

4. Click the **Show User (Modal)** button to display the User form. This time, enter the same information, if necessary, but click the **Close** button. Instead of being hidden, the form is closed by calling the `Close` method, so the form's objects are destroyed. Thus, when the preceding statements execute, a new form instance is implicitly created and the text boxes are blank. The reference counter is also reset.

## MINI-QUIZ 3

1. Describe the accessibility of procedures and variables declared with the `Friend` access modifier.

2. Which of the following variables is accessible only to the class containing the declaration?

   a. `Private Data As Integer`

   b. `Friend Data As Integer`

   c. `Public Data As Integer`

   d. `Global Data As Integer`

   e. none of the above

3. Describe the error in the following `Property` procedure:

```
Public Property Demo() As String
    Get
        Return Now.ToString
    End Get
End Property
```

# CREATING REUSABLE APPLICATIONS WITH CUSTOM CLASSES

In addition to the classes that make up the .NET Framework class library, you can create custom classes. These custom classes can then be reused by other applications. In fact, when you create a form, that form is nothing more than a class that extends the `System.Windows.Forms.Form` class of the .NET Framework class library. The following list describes elements common to most custom classes:

» A class has a constructor, which executes when a developer creates an instance of the class. A class instance is created with the `New` keyword.

» Classes typically have methods, which are procedures declared with the `Public` access modifier.

» Classes typically have properties. Properties can be implemented as fields by declaring a variable with the `Public` access modifier. Properties can also be implemented using `Property` procedures.

» Classes can support events. Class events are not discussed in this chapter.

The following sections introduce how to design classes, and the elements of classes, including constructors, shared and instance data, and methods.

## INTRODUCTION TO CLASS DESIGN

Chapter 1 introduced several key concepts related to object-oriented programming. The following list contains a review of these concepts:

» Encapsulation refers to the coupling of data and the methods that act upon that data. By calling a method (process), the value of one or more properties (data) is often changed. Again, it should not be possible to modify data directly so exposed variables should be avoided.

» Classes have both an interface and an implementation. The interface consists of the properties, methods, and events by which a developer interacts with the class. The implementation of a class forms the hidden part of the class. The hidden part of the class is only accessible from within the class itself.

» A primary goal of object-oriented programming is to create classes that can be reused by an application or by many applications. Each class should be designed to mimic a process or related group of processes.

Chapter 1 briefly introduced the concept of a model, which is an abstract description of a system. This abstract description is often expressed using a modeling language or as a series of diagrams. The preceding chapters used flowcharts to model the processing that took place in an event handler. In this chapter, you will use the Unified Modeling Language (UML) and class diagrams to model the methods and properties of a class. After modeling a simple class, you will see how to implement that class.

### MODELING A BANK ACCOUNT

To begin, consider a person's bank account as a class used to implement a business process. Such a class would likely perform the following actions:

» Create a new bank account.

» Allow withdrawals to be made from a bank account, thereby decreasing the account balance.

» Allow deposits to be made into a bank account, thereby increasing the account balance.

» Obtain the current account balance. However, the only possible way to update the account balance is to make a deposit or a withdrawal.

» Maintain a log of the transactions as transactions are made (deposits and withdrawals), so as to create an audit trail of transactions.

A bank account has attributes (properties) to store data related to the account as described in the following list:

» The account number

» The account balance

» The date the account was created

» A log of account transactions

## INTRODUCTION TO UML CLASS DIAGRAMS

In UML, a class is modeled using a class diagram. Each class in a **UML class diagram** is drawn as a rectangle divided into three compartments with horizontal lines. The top compartment contains the name of the class. The middle compartment contains the class attributes (properties), and the lower compartment contains the class operations (methods). Figure 6-15 shows a sample UML class diagram for the BankAccount class.

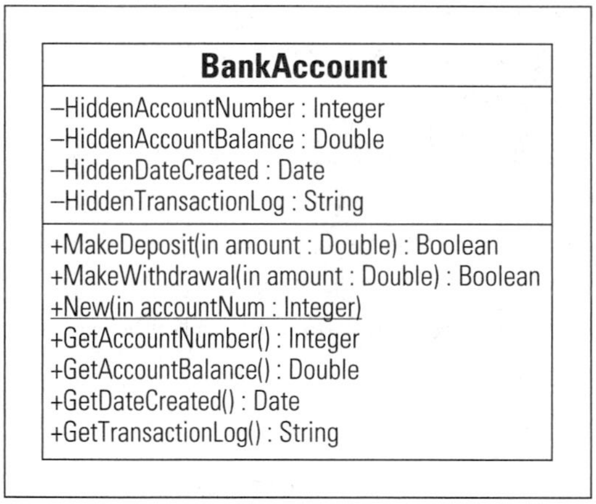

```
┌─────────────────────────────────────────────┐
│                BankAccount                   │
├─────────────────────────────────────────────┤
│ −HiddenAccountNumber : Integer               │
│ −HiddenAccountBalance : Double               │
│ −HiddenDateCreated : Date                    │
│ −HiddenTransactionLog : String               │
├─────────────────────────────────────────────┤
│ +MakeDeposit(in amount : Double) : Boolean   │
│ +MakeWithdrawal(in amount : Double) : Boolean│
│ +New(in accountNum : Integer)                │
│ +GetAccountNumber() : Integer                │
│ +GetAccountBalance() : Double                │
│ +GetDateCreated() : Date                     │
│ +GetTransactionLog() : String                │
└─────────────────────────────────────────────┘
```

Figure 6-15: UML class diagram

As shown in Figure 6-15, the class name (BankAccount) appears in the top compartment. The data (attributes) appears in the middle compartment along with the data type. Attributes also have visibility. Attributes marked with a plus sign (+) are public, meaning that they are exposed to other classes. Attributes marked with a minus sign (–) are private. In Figure 6-15, the attributes are hidden. This hidden data is made visible through `Property` procedures so that encapsulation rules are not violated. In other words, the data is not directly accessible to other classes.

The operations (methods) appear in the lower compartment. Like attributes, operations have a name. Operations also have visibility. Again, a plus sign (+) denotes that the operation is public, and a minus sign (–) denotes that the operation is private. Operations also accept zero or more arguments and have an optional data type. Referring back to the BankAccount class shown in Figure 6-15, the operations (methods) named MakeDeposit and MakeWithdrawal accept one argument named amount having a data type of `Double`. The "in" keyword denotes that the parameters are input parameters. Both of the operations (methods) return a value having a data type of `Boolean` to indicate whether the operation was successful.

Another operation shown in Figure 6-15 is a procedure named New. The procedure named New accepts one argument: the bank account number. In Visual Basic, the New procedure is called a constructor, which is discussed next. The final four public methods are used to retrieve the values of the corresponding hidden data items. These methods will be implemented as `Property` procedures.

## ASSOCIATIONS

The class diagram appearing in Figure 6-15 is very simple. In most cases, multiple related classes are required to solve a business problem or describe a business process. In such a case, these classes are said to have associations. For example, a person might have multiple bank accounts. Figure 6-16 illustrates a simplified UML class diagram containing an association.

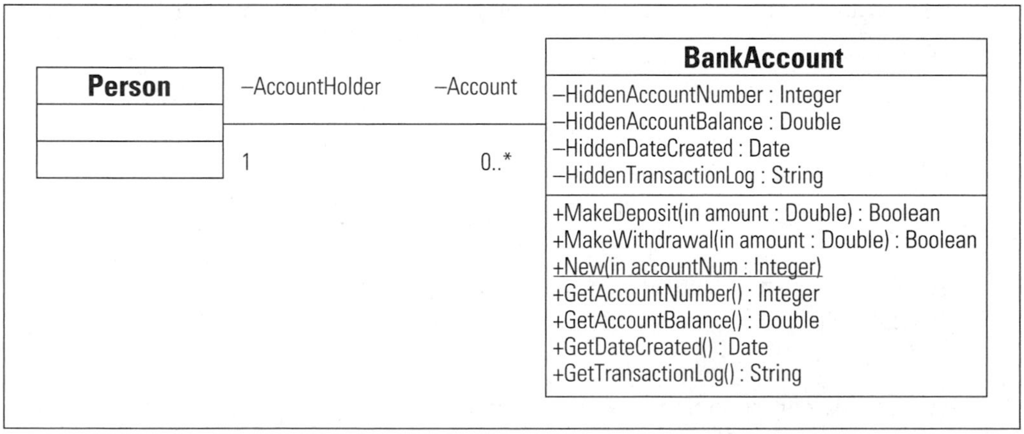

Figure 6-16: UML class diagram with an association

After modeling a class with the UML, that class must be implemented by translating the class diagram into Visual Basic code. The remaining sections of this chapter show how to translate the UML diagram appearing in Figure 6-15 into a working Visual Basic class.

> **»NOTE** UML class diagrams do not replace flowcharts or UML activity diagrams. Each diagram performs a different task and models a different part of a system. For example, you might create a flowchart or UML activity diagram for each operation (method) supported by the class.

## INTRODUCTION TO CONSTRUCTORS

In Visual Basic, all classes can have a special procedure called a constructor. A **constructor** is a procedure that gets called automatically when an instance of a class gets created. In Visual Basic, a constructor is always a Sub procedure named New appearing in a Class block.

The following statements show a sample constructor for the BankAccount class:

```
Public Class BankAccount
    Private HiddenDateCreated As Date
    Public Sub New()
        HiddenDateCreated = Now
    End Sub
End Class
```

The preceding class named BankAccount contains a single Sub procedure named New, which is the constructor. In the preceding statement, the Sub procedure (constructor) accepts no arguments. The statement in the constructor sets the value of a hidden variable named HiddenDateCreated to store the date and time that the class instance was created.

Constructors can also accept arguments just as all procedures can accept arguments. The following code segment shows a constructor that accepts one argument named accountNum:

```
Public Class BankAccount
    Private HiddenDateCreated As Date
    Private HiddenAccountNumber As Integer
    Public Sub New(accountNum As Integer)
        HiddenDateCreated = Now
        HiddenAccountNumber = accountNum
    End Sub
End Class
```

In the preceding constructor, an account number is passed as an argument to the procedure (constructor), which is then stored in a hidden variable. As you will see in a moment, read-only Property procedures will be created to read the HiddenDateCreated and the

HiddenAccountNumber variables from the class instance, thereby adhering to the encapsulation rules.

Unlike ordinary `Sub` procedures, a constructor is not called with the `Call` statement. Instead, the constructor is called automatically when the class instance is created. The following statements show how to create instances of the preceding BankAccount class, thereby calling the two different constructors:

```
Dim DemoInstance1 As New BankAccount()
Dim DemoInstance2 As New BankAccount(12345)
```

The first of the preceding statements calls the constructor that accepts no arguments, and the second statement calls the constructor that accepts one argument. Just as the `New` keyword is used to create an instance of a .NET Framework class such as a `TextBox` or a form, it is also used to create an instance of a developer-defined class. Thus, the preceding statement creates an instance of the BankAccount class, thereby calling the constructor. Figure 6-17 illustrates the process of calling a constructor.

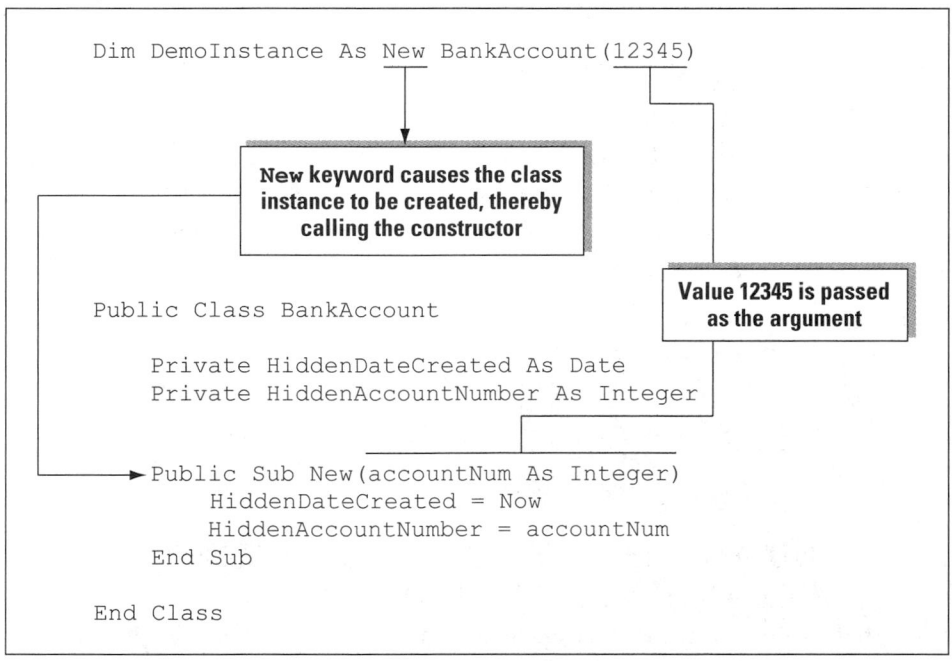

Figure 6-17: Calling a constructor

Compare the preceding statement with the following two statements:

```
Dim DemoInstance As BankAccount
DemoInstance = New BankAccount(12345)
```

The first of the preceding statements declares a variable named DemoInstance having a data type of BankAccount. However, an instance of the class is not created. In the second statement, an instance of the class is created because the New keyword appears in the assignment statement. After the second statement has executed, the variable DemoInstance references an instance of the BankAccount class. Thus, it is possible to create a class instance with the New keyword when declaring a variable or by using an assignment statement. As with any class, it is essential to create a class instance before referencing the members of a class. For example, the following statements cause a NullReferenceException because an instance of the BankAccount class does not exist.

```
Dim DemoInstance As BankAccount
DemoInstance.GetAccountBalance()
```

Constructors are not called directly. Thus, the syntax error "Constructor call is valid only as the first statement in an instance constructor" would be generated by Visual Studio in the second of the following statements:

```
Dim DemoInstance As Demo
DemoInstance.New()
```

## THE DIFFERENCE BETWEEN CLASS AND MODULE BLOCKS

Although Class and Module blocks have a similar structure, they work much differently. Most notably, it is not possible to create an instance of a module. Thus, modules do not have constructors. To illustrate, the following New procedure appearing inside of a Module block is not legal and causes a syntax error:

```
Public Module Module1
    Public Sub New()
        ' Statements
    End Sub
End Module
```

## UNDERSTANDING THE DIFFERENCE BETWEEN SHARED DATA AND INSTANCE DATA

Remember that each class instance has its own data copy. For example, two instances of a TextBox control can have different values for the Text property because each class instance has a separate copy of the data (properties). Modules work differently. That is, exactly one copy of the data stored in a module exists. Data can be categorized as shared data or instance data. To understand the difference between the two, examine the following declarations:

```
Public Module DemoModule
    Public Counter As Integer
End Module

Public Class DemoClass
    Public Counter As Integer
End Class
```

The preceding `Class` block is almost identical to the `Module` block. Both contain a declaration for a variable named Counter. Although the two variable declarations look identical, they work much differently. To understand the difference, look at how data is stored in the variable. The following statement stores a value in the variable named Counter in the module:

```
DemoModule.Counter = 1
```

First, notice that you do not create an instance of the module to store data in its variables. In fact, it is not legal to create an instance of a module. Exactly one copy of the variable exists. This variable is referred to as a **shared variable** or shared data because it is shared by the entire application (assembly).

Data stored in a class works differently than data stored in a module. First, given the class named DemoClass shown in the preceding code segment, you must first create an instance of the class before referencing the variable named Counter. To illustrate, the following statements cause a `NullReferenceException`:

```
Dim DemoVar As DemoClass
DemoVar.Counter = 1
```

The reason for the exception is simple. The variable DemoVar is considered an **instance variable** or instance data meaning that there is one instance of the variable's data for each class instance. Because the class instance does not exist, the variable does not exist. To illustrate how an instance variable works, examine the following statements:

```
Dim DemoInstance1 As New DemoClass()
Dim DemoInstance2 As New DemoClass()
DemoInstance1.Counter = 1
DemoInstance2.Counter = 2
```

The preceding code segment declares two variables named DemoInstance1 and DemoInstance2, and then stores a different value in the Counter property of the two class instances. Because each class instance has its own data, DemoInstance1.Counter has a value of 1 and DemoInstance2.Counter has a value of 2.

It is possible to create a shared variable in a class by including the Shared keyword in a variable declaration. Including the Shared keyword causes the variable to work in the same way as a variable declared in a Module block. To illustrate, examine the following declaration:

```
Public Class DemoClass
    Public Shared SharedCounter As Integer
End Class
```

A variable declared in a class with the Shared keyword is shared across all class instances. In fact, the data for a shared variable exists even if a class instance has not been created. Compare the preceding statements with the following statements:

```
Dim DemoInstance1 As New DemoClass()
Dim DemoInstance2 As New DemoClass()
Dim NoInstance As DemoClass
DemoInstance1.SharedCounter = 1
Debug.WriteLine(DemoInstance1.SharedCounter)    ' 1
Debug.WriteLine(DemoInstance2.SharedCounter)    ' 1
Debug.WriteLine(NoInstance.SharedCounter)       ' 1
```

Even though two instances of the class named DemoClass have been created, there exists only one copy of the variable named SharedCounter. Thus, assigning a value to the variable in one class instance affects the other class instances because there exists only one copy of the variable. The variable can also be referenced even when no class instance exists, as shown in the final statement.

## CREATING METHODS

Using UML terminology, classes have a name, attributes, and operations. Using Visual Studio terminology, classes also have a name, but attributes are called properties and operations are called methods. Class methods are implemented using procedures appearing in a Class block. Exposed methods and properties are created using the Public access modifier. Class properties are implemented using public variables or public Property procedures. Again, public variables should be avoided as they violate encapsulation rules.

The UML class diagram shown in Figure 6-15 showed methods named MakeDeposit and MakeWithdrawal. Implementing these methods is as simple as creating two Function procedures declared with the Public access modifier, as the following code segment shows:

```
Public Class BankAccount
    Private HiddenAccountBalance As Double

    Public Function MakeWithdrawal( _
        ByVal amount As Double) As Double
        HiddenAccountBalance -= amount
    End Function
```

```
    Public Function MakeDeposit( _
        ByVal amount As Double) As Double
        HiddenAccountBalance += amount
    End Function
End Class
```

As mentioned previously in this chapter, `Public` procedures are exposed to other assemblies and, therefore, are part of a class's interface. Thus, the `Function` procedures named MakeWithdrawal and MakeDeposit form part of the interface, rather than being part of the implementation. The MakeWithdrawal method will deduct the amount from the account balance. The MakeDeposit method will add the amount to the account balance. The variable HiddenAccountBalance is part of the class's implementation rather than part of the interface. Thus, it is not possible for another class to reference the variable. This is logical because if the variable HiddenAccountBalance were declared as a `Public` variable, it would be possible to update the account balance directly without making a deposit or making a withdrawal. This situation would violate the business rule specified in the class design along with violating general encapsulation rules.

The following statements show how to create an instance of the BankAccount class, make a deposit, and make a withdrawal by calling the MakeDeposit and MakeWithdrawal methods:

```
Private CurrentAccount As BankAccount

CurrentAccount = New _
    BankAccount(ToInt32(txtAccountNumber.Text))
CurrentAccount.MakeDeposit(ToDouble(txtAmount.Text))
CurrentAccount.MakeWithdrawal(ToDouble(txtAmount.Text))
```

As shown in the preceding code segment, the first statement declares a module-level variable named CurrentAccount to store an instance of the BankAccount class. The second statement creates the class instance passing the account number to the constructor. The final two statements call the MakeDeposit and MakeWithdrawal methods. The preceding statements assume that the input data is stored in `TextBox` control instances. The data is explicitly converted to the correct data type by calling the methods of the `System.Convert` class.

Remember that the variable HiddenAccountBalance was declared with the `Private` access modifier so the data is part of the implementation rather than part of the interface. Thus, the following statement is not legal:

```
System.Console.WriteLine(CurrentAccount.HiddenAccountBalance)
```

Trying to execute the preceding statement causes the following syntax error: "Chapter06ConceptLesson.BankAccount.HiddenAccountBalance is not accessible in this context because it is 'Private'." because variables declared with the `Private` access modifier are not visible outside the `Class` or `Module` block containing the declaration.

## CREATING FIELDS AND PROPERTIES

Data can be stored inside of a class instance or a module block in two ways.

» First, variables can be declared with the `Public` access modifier.

» `Property` procedures can be used in conjunction with hidden variables.

These two ways of storing data in a class instance are discussed in the following sections.

### CREATING FIELDS

To make data accessible to other classes, variables can be declared with the `Public` access modifier, as the following statements show:

```
Public Class BankAccount
    Public Name As String
End Class
```

By declaring a variable with the `Public` access modifier, there are no restrictions on the other classes and modules that can reference the variable so the variable becomes part of the class interface. When a variable is declared with the `Public` keyword, that variable is considered a field of the class. Thus, in the preceding code segment, Name is a public field of the class named BankAccount. The same *object.property* syntax is used to reference these fields as the syntax to reference a .NET Framework class library field, as the following statements show:

```
Dim LocalString As String = "Joe Smith"
Dim CurrentAccount As New BankAccount(12345)
CurrentAccount.Name = LocalString
LocalString = CurrentAccount.Name
```

The assignment statements read and write the Name field from an instance of the BankAccount class, respectively. In many cases, implementing properties as fields violates a particular business rule. Furthermore, declaring properties in this way violates the rule of encapsulation. For example, in the BankAccount class, implementing the account balance as a field would allow any other class to directly modify the account balance, which violates the business process of maintaining an account. To solve this problem and properly implement a business rule, hidden data is used in conjunction with `Property` procedures.

### ENFORCING ENCAPSULATION WITH PROPERTY PROCEDURES

The BankAccount class, as it has been implemented so far, supports methods to make a withdrawal or make a deposit. However, there exists no way to get the current balance or the other hidden data (the account number and date created). By implementing read-only properties to get the current balance, account number, date created, and transaction log, it's possible to read the data but the data cannot be modified, thereby causing the business rule to be enforced correctly. The following code segment illustrates the implementation of the `Property` procedures in the BankAccount class:

```
Public Class BankAccount

    Private HiddenDateCreated As Date
    Private HiddenAccountNumber As Integer
    Private HiddenAccountBalance As Double
    Private HiddenTransactionLog As String

    Public ReadOnly Property GetAccountBalance() As Double
        Get
            Return HiddenAccountBalance
        End Get
    End Property
    Public ReadOnly Property GetAccountNumber() As Integer
        Get
            Return HiddenAccountNumber
        End Get
    End Property
    Public ReadOnly Property GetDateCreated() As Date
        Get
            Return HiddenDateCreated
        End Get
    End Property
    Public ReadOnly Property GetTransactionLog() As String
        Get
            Return HiddenTransactionLog
        End Get
    End Property
End Class
```

The preceding read-only `Property` procedures are quite simple. They merely return the value of the hidden variables named HiddenAccountBalance, HiddenAccountNumber, HiddenDateCreated, and HiddenTransactionLog. Thus, the actual data cannot be modified directly. The following statement shows how to use the GetDateCreated `Property` procedure assuming that CurrentAccount is an instance of the BankAccount class:

```
lblDateCreated.Text = CurrentAccount.GetDateCreated.ToString
```

Trying to assign a value to a read-only property is illegal. Thus, the following statement causes a syntax error to be generated:

```
CurrentAccount.GetDateCreated = Now
```

Because the GetDateCreated property is declared as a read-only property, the preceding statement generates the following syntax error:

```
"Property 'GetDateCreated' is 'ReadOnly'."
```

In this exploration exercise, you will see how to use the BankAccount class discussed in this section.

1. Run the solution file in the folder **Chapter06\Chapter06ConceptLesson**.

2. Click the **Bank Account** tab. Default input values appear for all of the input control instances.

3. Click the **Create Account** button. The account gets created (an instance of the BankAccount class is created) and a log record is generated as the following statements execute:

```
CurrentAccount = New _
    BankAccount(ToInt32(txtAccountNumber.Text))
lblCurrentBalance.Text = _
    CurrentAccount.GetAccountBalance.ToString
lblDateCreated.Text = _
    CurrentAccount.GetDateCreated.ToString
txtTransactionLog.Text = _
    CurrentAccount.GetTransactionLog
```

4. Click the **Make Deposit** and **Make Withdrawal** buttons. A deposit and withdrawal are made to the account and the transaction log is updated. Figure 6-18 shows the Bank Account tab.

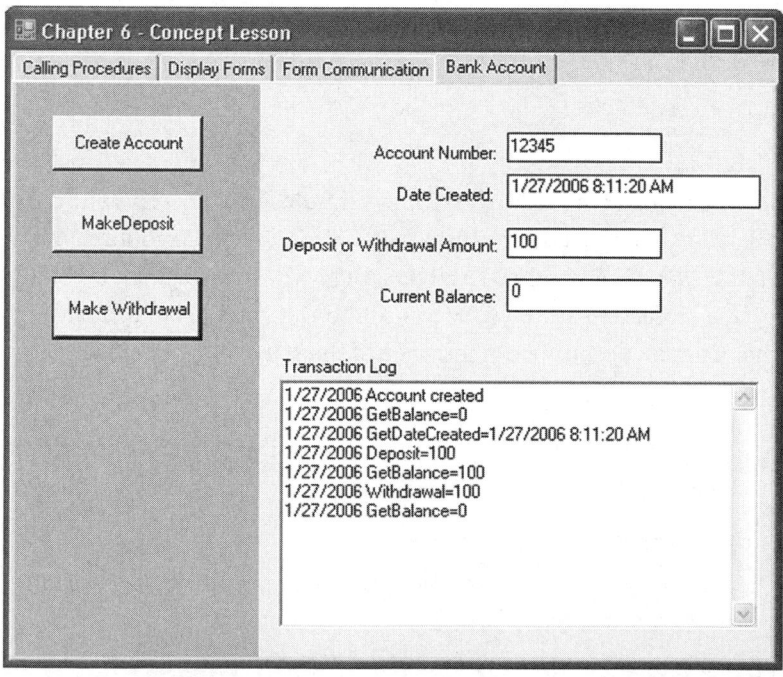

Figure 6-18: Concept lesson—Bank Account tab

# MINI-QUIZ 4

1. Which of the following statements correctly describes the sections in a UML class diagram?

   a. A UML class diagram contains three sections for the `Function` procedures, `Sub` procedures, and `Property` procedures.

   b. A UML class diagram contains three sections that describe the class name, class attributes, and class operations.

   c. A UML class diagram contains two sections describing attributes and operations that are part of the interface and attributes and operations that are part of the implementation.

   d. none of the above

2. When does a constructor execute?

3. A procedure declared with the `Public` access modifier is considered part of the class interface.

   a. True

   b. False

4. Given the following class declaration:

```
Public Class Quiz
    Public Shared Counter As Integer
End Class
```

   and the following statements:

```
Dim Quiz1 As New Quiz()
Dim Quiz2 As New Quiz()
```

   how many copies of the variable Counter exist?

# APPLICATION LESSON

## CREATING AN APPLICATION TO SUPPORT BUSINESS PROCESSES

Suppose that a gasoline storage company had a site with storage tanks of varying sizes. The size of a tank is determined by the radius of the tank and its height. Assume that the gasoline company needs to keep track of the product volume stored in each tank and that there are four tanks in the storage facility. As product is purchased and sold, product is added or removed from a particular tank. Given this scenario, the processing could be broken down into the following three functional areas:

» Mathematical functions are required to calculate the volume of a tank based on its height and radius. Other mathematical functions are needed to convert units of measure. For example, this application needs to convert cubic feet to gallons.

» The business rules require an instance of the Tank class be created to represent each fuel tank. Methods to add and remove product are required along with properties to determine the number of gallons of product in the tank, and the amount of product in a tank expressed as a percentage. Transaction logs are also produced on a tank-by-tank basis.

» A user interface is required so that the end user can add and remove fuel from a particular tank.

### APPLICATION LESSON—USER INTERFACE

The application's user interface has control instances divided into four groups. Each control instance group is used to add and remove product to and from a particular tank. Each time product is added or removed from the tank, the various output labels are updated. A log is kept of each transaction. A text box is used to add or remove product from a tank. Finally, there are buttons to display an About form and to exit the application. Figure 6-19 shows the user interface for the application's main form.

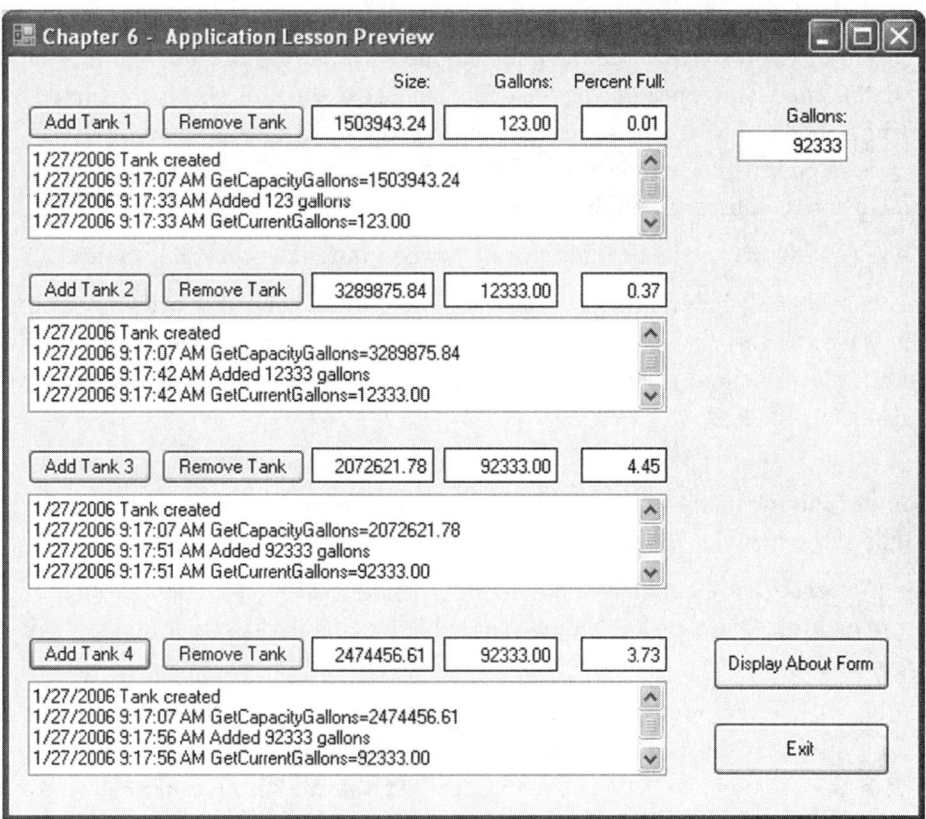

Figure 6-19: Application lesson—completed form

## APPLICATION LESSON—DESIGN

Unlike the applications you created in the preceding chapters in which all the application's code was grouped into the event handlers in one form module, the functionality of this application is divided into different classes based on the functional tasks described in the case introduction.

Mathematical procedures appear in a module named MathUtility. This module could be expanded and used by other applications. Figure 6-20 shows the class diagram for the module named MathUtility.

| **MathUtility** |
| --- |
| +GallonsPerCubicFoot : Double = 7.48 |
| +CylinderFace(in radius : Double) : Double<br>+CylinderVolume(in radius : Double, in height : Double) : Double<br>+CubicFeetToGallons(in cubicFeet : Double) : Double |

Figure 6-20: MathUtility class diagram

The MathUtility module contains two geometric methods named CylinderVolume and CylinderFace that calculate the volume of a cylinder and the face of a cylinder, respectively. A final method converts cubic feet to gallons because the tank size is calculated in cubic feet but needs to be expressed in gallons. All of these methods are public and, therefore, are exposed to other classes and assemblies. Because the code appears in a `Module`, all of the members are implicitly shared.

The following list describes the formulas needed to compute the preceding values:

» The face of a cylinder is expressed with the formula $A = \pi r^2$ where $A$ is the area (face) of the circle, $\pi$ is the value of PI, and $r$ is the circle's radius. The CylinderFace method accepts one argument, the radius of a circle, and returns the area.

» The volume of a cylinder is expressed with the formula $V = A * height$. The CylinderVolume method accepts two arguments: the area of the cylinder and the height of the cylinder. The method returns the volume of the cylinder.

» The CubicFeetToGallons method converts the value of its argument from cubic feet to gallons. There are 7.48 gallons per cubic foot. This value is stored as a public constant.

A second class is used to model a storage tank. Two arguments to the constructor are used to specify the tank's radius and height. Other methods are used to add and remove product from the tank and to get the current product volume in the tank. Figure 6-21 shows the UML diagram for the Tank class.

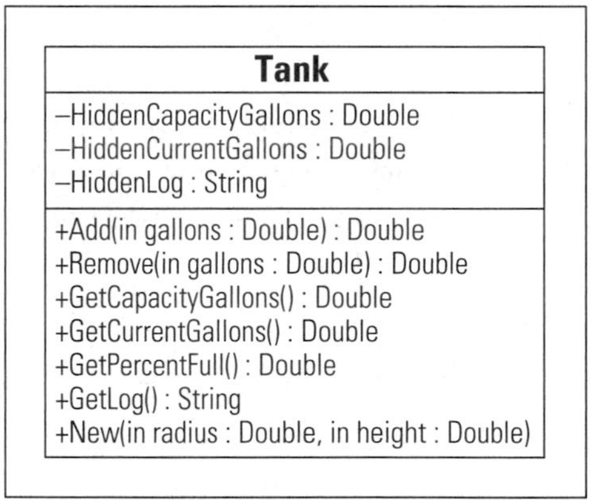

| **Tank** |
|---|
| −HiddenCapacityGallons : Double |
| −HiddenCurrentGallons : Double |
| −HiddenLog : String |
| +Add(in gallons : Double) : Double |
| +Remove(in gallons : Double) : Double |
| +GetCapacityGallons() : Double |
| +GetCurrentGallons() : Double |
| +GetPercentFull() : Double |
| +GetLog() : String |
| +New(in radius : Double, in height : Double) |

Figure 6-21: Tank class diagram

The following list describes the members of the Tank class:

» The radius and height of the tank are supplied as arguments to the constructor and are used to calculate the tank's size.

» The tank size is stored as hidden data in the variable HiddenCapacityGallons.

» A hidden variable named HiddenCurrentGallons stores the current product volume in the tank.

» A hidden variable named HiddenLog stores a transaction log.

» Methods named Add and Remove each accept one argument, the number of product gallons to add or remove from the tank.

» Read-only `Property` procedures named GetCapacityGallons and GetCurrentGallons return the tank capacity and the number of product gallons currently in the tank, respectively. Both of these properties rely on hidden data values.

» Another `Property` procedure named GetPercentFull returns the current amount of product as a percentage of the tank's capacity.

» A method named GetLog returns the transaction log.

## APPLICATION LESSON—IMPLEMENTATION

The application contains two forms. The form named frmMain is the application's main form. The form named frmAbout displays an about dialog box similar to the one presented in the chapter. These forms have already been created. As with all of the application lessons in this book, a finished version of the application has been provided so that you can preview the end result of the lesson's hands-on steps.

To preview the completed application:

1. Start Visual Studio if necessary and open the solution file in **Chapter.06\ Chapter06ApplicationLessonPreview**. Run the application.

2. In the Gallons text box, enter a new numeric value. Click the buttons to add and remove product from each of the four tanks. As you do, the output values are updated accordingly. In addition, the logs are updated accordingly.

3. Display the About dialog box by clicking the **Display About Form** button. Click **OK** to close the dialog box.

4. Exit the application.

In the following steps, you will implement the MathUtility and Tank classes just discussed. As you proceed with the implementation, you will create the MathUtility module first, as the Tank class will depend on the MathUtility class. Then, you will create the Tank class and, finally, the user interface.

To create and implement the MathUtility module:

1. Start Visual Studio, if necessary, and open the file named **Chapter.06\Chapter06ApplicationLessonStartup.sln**. Click **Project**, **Add Module** to display the Add New Item dialog box. Set the name of the module to **MathUtility**. Click **Add** to close the dialog box and add the module to the application.

2. Open the Code Editor for the **MathUtility** module, if necessary, and then enter the following methods (shown in bold):

```
Public Module MathUtility
        Public Const GallonsPerCubicFoot As Single = 7.48
        Public Function CylinderFace( _
            ByVal radius As Double) As Double
            Return radius ^ 2 * System.Math.PI
        End Function
        Public Function CylinderVolume(ByVal radius As Double, _
            ByVal height As Double) As Double
            Return CylinderFace(radius) * height
        End Function

        Public Function CubicFeetToGallons( _
            ByVal cubicFeet As Double) As Double
            Return cubicFeet * GallonsPerCubicFoot
        End Function

    End Module
```

Next, the Tank class can be created.

To create and implement the Tank class:

1. Click **Project**, **Add Class** to display the Add New Item dialog box. Set the name of the class to **Tank**. Click **Add** to add the class and close the dialog box.

2. Open the Code Editor for the Tank class, if necessary, and then enter the following methods and properties (shown in bold):

```
    Option Explicit On
    Option Strict On
    Imports Microsoft.VisualBasic.ControlChars
Public Class Tank
        Private HiddenCapacityGallons As Double
        Private HiddenCurrentGallons As Double
        Private HiddenLog As String

        Public Sub New(ByVal radius As Double, _
            ByVal height As Double)
            Dim CubicFeet As Double
            CubicFeet = MathUtility.CylinderVolume( _
                radius, height)
            HiddenCapacityGallons = _
                MathUtility.CubicFeetToGallons(CubicFeet)
            HiddenLog = Now & " Tank created"
        End Sub
```

```
    Public Function Add(ByVal gallons As Double) As Double
        HiddenCurrentGallons += gallons
        HiddenLog &= CrLf & Now & " Added " _
            & gallons.ToString & " gallons"
    End Function

    Public Function Remove(ByVal gallons As Double) As Double
        HiddenCurrentGallons -= gallons
        HiddenLog &= CrLf & Now & " Removed " _
        & gallons.ToString & " gallons"
    End Function

    Public ReadOnly Property GetCapacityGallons() As Double
        Get
            HiddenLog &= CrLf & Now & _
                " GetCapacityGallons=" & _
                HiddenCapacityGallons.ToString("f2")
            Return HiddenCapacityGallons
        End Get
    End Property

    Public ReadOnly Property GetCurrentGallons() As Double
        Get
            HiddenLog &= CrLf & Now & _
                " GetCurrentGallons=" & _
                HiddenCurrentGallons.ToString("f2")
            Return HiddenCurrentGallons
        End Get
    End Property

    Public ReadOnly Property GetPercentFull() As Double
        Get
            HiddenLog &= CrLf & Now & " GetPercentFull" _
                & HiddenCurrentGallons _
                / HiddenCapacityGallons * 100).ToString("f2")
            Return HiddenCurrentGallons / HiddenCapacityGallons * 100
        End Get
    End Property

    Public ReadOnly Property GetLog() As String
        Get
            Return HiddenLog
        End Get
    End Property
End Class
```

Finally, the code behind the application's user interface needs to be completed. The user interface will call upon the methods of the **Tank** class to manage the tank.

1. Activate the Code Editor for the form named **frmMain**, and enter the following statements (shown in bold) in the **Class** block. These statements create four instances of the Tank class specifying the radius and height of the tank to the constructor.

```
Public Class frmMain
    Private Tank1 As New Tank(80, 10)
    Private Tank2 As New Tank(100, 14)
    Private Tank3 As New Tank(70, 18)
    Private Tank4 As New Tank(90, 13)
```

2. Create the form's constructor to initialize the labels displaying the tank size by entering the following statements:

```
Public Sub New()
    InitializeComponent()
    lblSizeTank1.Text = Tank1.GetCapacityGallons.ToString("f2")
    lblSizeTank2.Text = Tank2.GetCapacityGallons.ToString("f2")
    lblSizeTank3.Text = Tank3.GetCapacityGallons.ToString("f2")
    lblSizeTank4.Text = Tank4.GetCapacityGallons.ToString("f2")
End Sub
```

3. Create the **Click** event handler for the **Button** control instance named **btnAddTank1** and enter the following statements:

```
Tank1.Add(ToDouble(txtGallons.Text))
lblGallonsTank1.Text = Tank1.GetCurrentGallons.ToString
lblPercentFullTank1.Text = Tank1.GetPercentFull.ToString
```

4. Create the **Click** event handler for the **Button** control instance named btnRemoveTank1 and enter the following statements:

```
Tank1.Remove(ToDouble(txtGallons.Text))
lblGallonsTank1.Text = Tank1.GetCurrentGallons.ToString
lblPercentFullTank1.Text = Tank1.GetPercentFull.ToString
```

5. Repeat Steps 3 and 4 for the remaining **Button** control instances. Be sure to replace the tank number to reflect the correct tank.

6. Test the application to validate that your application produces the same results as the one you previewed.

In this chapter, you have learned the basics of interform communication and how to design and implement a simple class. As you will see as you progress through this book, much more complex classes can be created to reflect much more complex business processes.

# CHAPTER SUMMARY

» Procedures are categorized as Function and Sub procedures and are created to perform repetitive tasks. Procedures are called by event handlers and other procedures. Both Function and Sub procedures accept zero or more arguments, which supply the means to send information to a procedure. Procedures can appear in a Class or Module block and cannot be nested. That is, one procedure block cannot appear inside of another procedure block.

» Most applications are more complex than just a single form, and consist of several classes, forms, and modules. The Add New Item dialog box is used to add new modules to an application. The templates that appear in this dialog box vary based on the edition of Visual Basic that is installed. It is also possible to add existing items to a project.

» When an application consists of multiple forms, the start-up object must be defined. The start-up object can be any form in an application or a Sub procedure named Main appearing in a Module block.

» Forms can be displayed as modal forms by calling the ShowDialog method, or as modeless forms by calling the Show method. When a form is displayed as a modal form, the form must be closed before the other forms in the application can get input focus. A form is made invisible by calling the Hide method or closed by calling the Close method. Calling the Hide method makes a form invisible, whereas calling the Close method removes the form and its objects from memory.

» Just as most objects support events, so too do forms. The Load event fires as a form is loaded. The Activated and Deactivate events fire as a form gets focus and loses focus, respectively. The FormClosing and FormClosed events fire as a form is closing and after the form has closed, respectively.

» Information must often be communicated between forms. Visual Basic supports two ways to communicate information between forms. A variable declared with the Public access modifier is considered a field and is accessible to all of the forms in the application as well as other assemblies. In addition, it is possible to create Property procedures. Property procedures can be created as read-write, read-only, or write-only procedures.

» The classes defined by the .NET Framework class library support methods and the classes that you create are no exception. Creating Function or Sub procedures in a class with the Public access modifier creates a class method.

» Classes can be modeled using UML class diagrams. UML class diagrams appear in three sections. The first section contains the name of the class. The second section contains the properties (attributes), and the third section contains the methods (operations).

» A constructor is a special procedure named New that is called when creating a class instance. It is not possible to call a constructor directly. It is always called automatically by Visual Studio. Constructors can accept arguments.

» Class data can be instance data or shared data. One copy of instance data exists for each class instance. One copy of shared data exists for all class instances.

# KEY TERMS

**constructor**—A procedure named New that executes when a class instance is created.

**Function procedure**—A form of general procedure. Function procedures accept zero or more arguments and return a value having a data type.

**instance variable**—A category of variable in which one copy of the data exists for each class instance.

**modality**—A form can be displayed as a modal form or as a modeless form. When displayed as a modal form, other forms in an application cannot get focus until the modal form is hidden or closed. When displayed as a modeless form, the user can change input focus from form to form.

**procedures**—A block of statements that facilitate code reuse is considered a procedure. Procedures are categorized as Function or Sub procedures. Function procedures return a value, whereas Sub procedures do not.

**Property procedure**—A type of procedure that is used to implement properties. Property procedures consist of Get and Set blocks, which contain the code that executes when a property's value is read or written, respectively.

**shared variable**—A variable for which one data copy exists and is shared by the entire application. Variables declared in a Module block are always shared. To declare a shared variable in a Class block, include the Shared keyword in the variable declaration.

**splash screen**—A form that appears while the remainder of an application loads.

**UML class diagram**—A diagram that models the attributes (properties) and operations (methods) supported by a class.

# ANSWERS TO MINI-QUIZZES

### MINI-QUIZ 1

1. `Function` procedures return a value. `Sub` procedures do not return a value.

2. `Return`

3. b. A `Function` procedure can accept zero or more arguments.

4. The variable returned from the procedure should be Result, rather than the argument named arg. In addition, the data type of the procedure's return value should be `Double`.

### MINI-QUIZ 2

1. Any form in an application can be configured as the start-up object. Also, a `Sub` procedure named Main in a `Module` block can be designated as the start-up object.

2. d. all of the above

3. `My.Forms.frmDemo.ShowDialog()`

   `My.Forms.frmDemo.Show()`

4. The first statement does not create an instance of the class, so the second statement causes a NullReferenceException.

### MINI-QUIZ 3

1. Variables and procedures declared with the `Friend` access modifier are visible to all of the modules in the current assembly but are not visible to other assemblies.

2. a. `Private Data As Integer`

3. The property is declared as a read-write property but the `Set` block does not appear. Either the property should be declared with the `ReadOnly` keyword or the `Set` block should be included.

### MINI-QUIZ 4

1. b. A UML class diagram contains three sections that describe the class name, class attributes, and class operations.

2. A constructor executes when a class instance is created. Class instances are created with the `New` keyword.

3. True

4. 1

# REVIEW QUESTIONS

1. Which of the following statements is true regarding variable lifetime and scope?

    a. Local variables exist whenever an application runs.

    b. Module-level variables are declared using the `Public` keyword.

    c. A class can contain module-level variables or local variables but not both.

    d. The lifetime of a variable declared with the `Static` keyword is while a class or module block exists.

    e. none of the above

2. Which of the following statements is true about procedures?

    a. A procedure cannot be called explicitly.

    b. Procedures can be categorized as `Function` procedures and `Sub` procedures.

    c. A procedure and an event handler are identical in that Windows calls them in response to some event.

    d. Procedures can be nested. That is, one procedure can appear inside of another procedure.

    e. none of the above

3. Which of the following statements is true regarding `Function` procedures?

    a. They have a name.

    b. They return a value.

    c. They can accept zero or more arguments.

    d. They can appear on the right side of an assignment statement.

    e. all of the above

4. Which of the following statements correctly returns the value of the variable Total from a `Function` procedure?

    a. `Return Total`

    b. `Function = Total`

    c. `As Total`

    d. `Exit Total`

    e. none of the above

5. Which of the following statements is true regarding Sub procedures?

   a. They have a name.

   b. They return a value.

   c. They can accept zero or more arguments.

   d. both a and c

   e. both b and c

6. Which of the following statements correctly calls the procedure named Format having one argument named txtDemo with a data type of TextBox?

   a. `Call Format(txtDemo)`

   b. `Call Format txtDemo`

   c. `Format txtDemo`

   d. `Call Format[ txtDemo]`

   e. none of the above

7. The _____ method will display a form, and the _____ method will make a form invisible while keeping it in memory.

   a. `Display, Invisible`

   b. `ShowForm, Close`

   c. `Visible, Invisible`

   d. `Display, Close`

   e. `ShowDialog, Hide`

8. Which of the following are valid entry points for a Windows application with multiple forms?

   a. An application's main form must have a procedure named Main, which is always designated as the start-up object or entry point.

   b. Multiple forms can be designated as start-up forms. In such a case, a form is displayed in the order it was selected.

   c. Any form in the project can be designated as the start-up object, but only one form can be designated as a start-up object.

   d. A splash screen must be designated as the start-up object.

   e. none of the above

9. Which of the following statements correctly displays the form named frmDemo as a modal dialog box?

    a. `Form.frmDemo.ShowDialog()`

    b. `Me.ShowDialog()`

    c. `frmDemo.ShowDialog()`

    d. `My.Form.frmDemo.Show(Type.Dialog)`

    e. all of the above

10. Which of the following statements is correct regarding the `Public` access modifier?

    a. The `Public` and `Private` access modifiers have exactly the same meaning.

    b. Variables declared with the `Public` and `Private` keywords have a different lifetime.

    c. Variables declared with the `Public` access modifier can be shared between forms.

    d. none of the above

11. Which events fire when a form gets and loses input focus?

    a. `Enter, Leave`

    b. `Load, Unload`

    c. `Activated, Deactivate`

    d. `InFocus, OutFocus`

    e. none of the above

12. Which of the following statements is correct regarding encapsulation rules?

    a. Public variables should be used in favor of `Property` procedures.

    b. `Property` procedures should be used in favor of public procedures.

    c. The purpose of `Sub` procedures is to encapsulate data.

    d. none of the above

13. List and describe the similarities and differences between `Function` procedures and `Sub` procedures.

14. What is the purpose of the `Call` statement?

15. Compare and contrast the `Public` and `Private` access modifiers.

16. What is the difference between a form displayed as a modal form and a form displayed as a modeless form?

17. List and describe three ways to create or use an instance of a form.

18. Describe how to communicate information between forms.

19. List and describe the three parts of a UML class diagram.

20. Describe the error(s) in the following statements assuming that frmMain is the name of a form class:

    ```
    Dim frmNew As frmMain()
    frmMain.ShowDialog()
    ```

# PROGRAMMING QUESTIONS

1. Write the statements to create a `Function` procedure named Area that determines the area of a rectangle (length * width), and then returns this value. The procedure should accept two arguments having a data type of `Double` and return a `Double`. The `Function` procedure should appear in a `Module` block named Geometry. Both the `Module` block and the procedure should be available to other assemblies.

2. Write the statements to create a `Sub` procedure named Active that accepts one argument, a reference to a `TextBox` control instance. The code in the `Sub` procedure should set the `Visible` and `Enabled` property of the text box to `True`.

3. Write the statements to create a `Sub` procedure named ClearAll. The procedure should accept no arguments. The statements in the procedure should remove the text from the following text boxes: txtName, txtAddress, txtCity, and txtState. The procedure should only be visible to the form containing the declaration.

4. Write the statements to create a `Function` procedure named Cat, with four string arguments. The `Function` procedure should concatenate the four arguments and return the result.

5. Write the statements to create a read-write `Property` procedure named ItemDescription. When the property is read or written, get or store the property value using the hidden variable named HiddenItemDescription. The property should have a data type of `String`.

6. Write the statements to create a read-only `Property` procedure named GetBalanceOwed having a data type of `Double`. The `Property` procedure should return the value of the hidden variable named HiddenBalance.

7. Write the statements to display the form named frmDemo as a modeless dialog box and as a modal dialog box. Use the `My.Forms` object.

8. Write the statements to display the form named frmDemo as a modeless dialog box and as a modal dialog box. Create an instance of the form by hand.

9. Write the statements to create a module named PlaneGeometry. Create two methods in the module. The first method should calculate one angle of a triangle given the other two angles. The sum of all angles in a triangle is 180 degrees. Name the first method CalculateTriangleAngle. The method should accept two arguments and return the third angle. The second method should calculate an angle in a quadrilateral. The sum of all angles in a quadrilateral is 360 degrees. The method named CalculateQuadrilateralAngle should accept three angles as arguments and return the fourth angle. For both methods, the data type of the arguments and the return value should have a data type of `Double`.

10. Write the statements to create a class named Person. Create a constructor for the class such that it accepts two arguments—a person's first name and a person's last name. Declare hidden variables named HiddenFirstName and HiddenLastName to store the values passed to the constructor.

11. Write the statements to create a class named Employee. Create a `Public` field named EmployeeName having a data type of `String`. Create a method named CalculatePayroll that accepts two arguments—the hours worked and the hourly wage. The method should multiply the two values to calculate and return the calculated payroll. Both the arguments and the return value of the method should have a data type of `Double`.

12. Write the statements to create a class named TimeStamp. Create a constructor that will store the current time in a hidden variable named HiddenTimeCreated. Create a read-only property named GetTimeCreated to return this hidden value. Create a method named GetElapsedTime. This method should return the `TimeSpan` between the current time and the time created.

13. Create a class named TelephoneNumber. The constructor should accept one argument—a string containing the telephone number with a format of *xxx-xxx-xxxx*, where *x* is a digit. Create three read-only properties named AreaCode, ExchangeCode, and Number. Each property should return the corresponding part of the telephone number. The constructor argument and each property should have a data type of `String`.

14. Write the statements to create a class named ZipManager. Create a constructor that accepts one argument, a zip code having the format *xxxxx–xxxx* where *x* is a digit. Store the zip code in a hidden variable. Create two read-only properties named GetZip and GetPlusFour to get the two parts of the zip code.

15. Write the statements to create a class named Person with two `String` fields named FirstName and LastName.

# HANDS-ON PROJECTS

1. In this hands-on project, you will expand on the application lesson by adding additional methods to the MathUtility class and support an additional business process.

   a. A preview of the completed hands-on project appears in the file **Chapter.06\HandsOnProjects\Ch06HandsOnProject1.exe**.

   b. Create a new solution file named **Ch06HandsOnProject1.sln**.

   c. Using the MathUtility module described in this chapter's application lesson, modify the class diagram to add two methods named GetHypotenuse and GetSide. These methods will use the Pythagorean theorem to determine the length of a right triangle's hypotenuse or side based on the length of the other two sides or side and hypotenuse. The following formula shows the Pythagorean theorem: $C^2 = A^2 + B^2$. The GetHypotenuse method should accept two arguments, the length of the two sides, and return the length of the hypotenuse. The GetSide method should also accept two arguments: the length of the hypotenuse and the length of a side. The method should return the length of the other side.

   d. Modify the UML class diagram for the Tank class by creating two more methods that will work similarly to the GetCurrentGallons and GetPercentFull methods named GetCurrentGallonsEmpty and GetPercentEmpty.

e. Using the first class diagram that you just created, modify the MathUtility module to implement the two methods. *Hint*: To determine the square root of a value, use the `System.Math.Sqrt` method.

f. Using the second class diagram that you created, modify the Tank class to implement the additional two methods. Make sure that you write the statements to update the transaction log, as necessary.

g. Modify the user interface using the sample application as a template, and test the methods created in the previous step.

h. Make sure that the application has an about box.

i. Add a splash screen to the application.

2. In this hands-on project, you will create a class to manage a credit card, along with a user interface to test that class. This class should mimic the activities that you would perform on a credit card, such as making charges and payments, updating the credit limit, and recording periodic interest. The CreditCard class should have the following characteristics:

» The credit card number should be passed as an argument to the constructor and stored in a hidden variable having a data type of `String`. The credit card number should be made available to other classes through a read-only property. In addition, the initial credit limit should be passed as the second argument to the constructor. The credit limit should also be made available to other classes by way of a read-only property.

» It should be possible to make payments on the credit card account along with making charges. Making payments and charges should decrease and increase the credit card balance, respectively. The credit card balance should be stored in a hidden variable and made available to other classes via a read-only property.

» It should be possible to increase or decrease the credit limit.

» A read-only property should be created to get the available credit. The available credit can be determined by subtracting the current balance from the credit limit. Another read-only property needs to be created to get the available balance.

» Create a method to charge interest on the account for the month. Pass the monthly interest rate as an argument to the method. The method should return the interest changes.

» For every transaction, a message should be written to a hidden transaction log.

a. Open the completed application named **Chapter.06\HandsOnProjects\ Ch06HandsOnProject2.exe**. Create a new account, and then perform various transactions on the account. Display the transaction log form and the other forms in the application.

b. Create a new solution file named **Ch06HandsOnProject2.sln**.

c. Create a UML class diagram to model the CreditCard class described in the preceding list.

d. Add a new class named CreditCard to the solution.

e. Implement the CreditCard class using the UML class diagram that you created. Again, hidden variables should store the card number, the card balance, and the credit limit. A final hidden variable should store the transaction log.

f. Create the user interface to test the class that you created in the previous step. The user interface should supply the means to create an instance of the CreditCard class, by specifying the account number and the initial credit limit. After the credit card has been created, the text boxes and the button to create an account number should be disabled.

g. Create buttons and the necessary code to record charges and payments, and get the available balance. In addition, it should be possible to increase or decrease the credit limit, obtain the balance due, and obtain the available credit. Again, call the members of the CreditCard class to determine these values.

h. Configure buttons for the credit card such that the button to create an account is enabled when the form loads and the other buttons are disabled. When the end user creates an account, the button to create a new account should be disabled and the other buttons should be enabled. Create procedures to enable and disable the buttons.

i. Create an About form to display assembly information similar to the one presented in the chapter. Create a button on the main form to display the About form as a modal dialog box.

j. Create another form to display the transaction logs for the account. *Hint*: Pass a reference to the current account class instance to the form's constructor.

k. Finally, create and configure a splash screen for the solution.

3. In this hands-on project, you will create multiple utility classes to perform common operations. The first utility class will work with a person's first name, last name, and full name. The second class will work with dates.

a. Create a new solution file named **Ch06HandsOnProject3.sln**.

b. Create a new class named NameManager. Create three `Property` procedures named FirstName, LastName, and FullNameFirstLast. When the FirstName property is set, the full name should be updated. When the LastName property is set, the full name should be updated. A space should separate the first name and the last name. When the FullNameFirstLast property is set, both the first name and last name should be updated.

c. Create a second class named DateManager. The constructor for the class should accept two arguments having a data type of `DateTime`. In this class, create read-only properties to get the number of elapsed days, hours, minutes, and seconds between the two dates. Each of these properties should have a data type of `Integer`.

d. Next, you will create a user interface that will work with these two classes. The application and its user interface will implement a simple timekeeping system.

e. Create a splash screen for the application.

f. Create a login form in which the end user enters their first name and last name into the system.

g. When the login form is closed, display the main form. The main form should display the user's full name in the form's title bar. Use the NameManager class to do this.

h. The timekeeping system on the main form should be designed such that there are two buttons. The first should denote the starting time when work begins on a project, and the second button should mark the time when work ends on a project. The user should enter a project name in a text box. Create the user interface using a design of your choosing.

i. Use the DateManager class to keep track of the number of minutes worked. On the main form, display a log of work activities and the number of minutes applicable to each work activity.

j. Create an About form. In the About form, display a message in a multiline text box describing how to use the system. Create a button on the main form to display the About form.

k. Create a button to exit the application.

4. In this hands-on project, you will design and implement a television remote control. The design will include a RemoteControl class. The implementation will include a `Class` block that implements the RemoteControl class and a corresponding user interface that uses the RemoteControl class. The RemoteControl class should have the following members:

   » A read-only property named CurrentChannel should retrieve the current channel from a hidden member.

   » A read-only property named CurrentVolume should retrieve the current volume from a hidden member.

   » Two methods named ChannelUp and ChannelDown should change the channel increasing or decreasing the channel's value by 1. The current channel should be stored in the hidden member described in the first bullet.

» Another method named SetChannel should accept one argument, an integer containing the channel. When the channel is set, be certain to set the value of the corresponding hidden variable.

» Two methods named VolumeUp and VolumeDown should change the volume increasing or decreasing the volume's value by 1. The current volume should be stored in the hidden member.

» Another method named SetVolume should accept one argument, an integer containing the volume. When the volume is set, be certain to set the value of the corresponding hidden variable.

a. Create a new solution file named **Ch06HandsOnProject4.sln**.

b. Create a UML class diagram to model the RemoteControl class described in the preceding list.

c. Add a new class named RemoteControl to the solution.

d. Create the members for the RemoteControl class as described in the preceding list. Make sure that the interface and implementation of the class corresponds to the UML class diagram that you created.

e. On the main form, create the user interface for the RemoteControl class. Create buttons to increase or decrease the channel value by 1. Create a button to explicitly change the channel. Create similar buttons to adjust the volume. Try to create the user interface to mimic that of a typical remote control.

f. Create an About form to display assembly information similar to the one presented in the chapter.

# 7

# DECISION MAKING

**After completing this chapter, you will be able to:**

- Use the `Boolean` data type in decision-making statements
- Use `If` statements and `Select Case` statements to make decisions
- Use logical operators to create complex conditions
- Create message boxes and input boxes
- Use decision-making statements to perform input validation
- Create structured exception handlers so that run-time errors will not cause an application to terminate
- Create instances of check boxes, scroll bars, group boxes, and radio buttons
- Group control instances

# CONCEPT LESSON

## INTRODUCTION TO DECISION-MAKING

Chapter 1 introduced the three control structures common to all applications: the sequence structure, the decision structure, and the repetition structure. In the previous chapters, the sequence structure was used, as all the statements executed sequentially one after another in the same order that they appeared in a procedure. In this chapter, you will write statements that make decisions and conditionally execute statements based on the outcome of that decision. In addition, selected Visual Basic controls that rely on decision-making are introduced in this chapter.

## INTRODUCTION TO BOOLEAN DATA

`Boolean` data operates similarly to an on/off switch. The keyword `True` signifies on, and the keyword `False` signifies off. Properties such as the `Visible` and `Enabled` properties store `Boolean` values. For example, the following assignment statements make the `Label` control instance named lblPrompt visible and invisible, respectively:

```
lblPrompt.Visible = True
lblPrompt.Visible = False
```

The syntax to declare a variable having the `Boolean` data type is the same as the syntax to declare any other variable, as shown in the following statements:

```
Dim Valid As Boolean
Dim BrowseMode As Boolean = True
Dim Test1, Test2 As Boolean
```

The first statement declares a local `Boolean` variable named Valid. By default, a `Boolean` variable is initialized to `False`. The second statement declares and initializes a `Boolean` variable, and the final statement declares two `Boolean` variables in the same statement.

The reserved words `True` and `False` can be assigned to `Boolean` variables, as shown in the following statements:

```
Valid = True
Valid = False
```

The preceding assignment statements store the values `True` and `False` in the `Boolean` variable named Valid.

In Visual Basic, `Boolean` values are not stored as numbers, and conversion of numeric data types should be avoided. When converting a numeric data type to a `Boolean` value, 0 is converted to `False` and all other values are converted to `True`. Conversion of a `Boolean` value to a numeric data type illustrates the conversion problem, as the following statements show:

```
System.Convert.ToInt32(True)    ' 1
CInt(True)                      ' -1
```

The preceding statements show that the `ToInt32` method converts `True` to positive 1, whereas the intrinsic `CInt` function converts `True` to negative 1 (–1).

# INTRODUCTION TO DECISION-MAKING

The statements you have written thus far in this book have executed sequentially in the same order that they appeared in a procedure. Most applications need the capability to execute one group of statements in certain circumstances and another group of statements in different circumstances. Collectively, these types of statements are referred to as **decision-making statements** or conditional statements.

To introduce the concept of decision-making, consider the following English sentence: "If the user inputs a date in the future, then alert the user that the input is invalid. Otherwise continue." A general form of this statement can be expressed with the following pseudocode:

```
If the input date is greater than the current date then
    Display a message box indicating the input is invalid.
End of If statement
```

Flowcharts can be used to model the decision-making process shown in the pseudocode, as shown in Figure 7-1.

Figure 7-1 depicts the logic of the pseudocode with a flowchart. A one-way decision is made based on the value of two dates. If the input date is after the current date, the conditional task of displaying a message box is performed, and execution ends. Otherwise, if the condition is false, the message box is not displayed and execution ends.

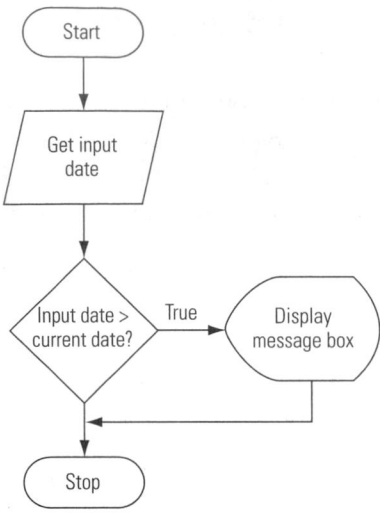

Figure 7-1: Flowchart of a decision-making statement

## USING IF STATEMENTS AND COMPARISON OPERATORS

When you understand that the English word "if" represents a decision, the transition to decision-making statements is easy. Conditional statements are used to determine which group of statements to execute and when. A conditional statement executes one group of statements when the condition is `True`, and, optionally, another group of statements when the condition is `False`.

When writing a conditional statement, **comparison operators** are used on two or more values or expressions. Visual Basic supports the following comparison operators: equal to (=), not equal to (<>), less than (<), greater than (>), less than or equal to (<=), and greater than or equal to (>=). These are all binary operators so two operands surround the comparison operator.

A conditional operation always produces a `Boolean` value as its result. Comparison operators all have the same precedence and are evaluated from left to right. When comparison operators are used in conjunction with arithmetic operators, the arithmetic operations are performed before the comparison operations. The following statements illustrate the use of comparison operators and arithmetic operators:

```
Dim Result As Boolean
Dim Value1 As Integer = 3, Value2 As Integer = 5
Result = Value1 < Value2                ' True
Result = Value1 + 2 < Value2 – 1        ' False
```

In the first of the preceding assignment statements, Value1 (3) is less than Value2 (5), so the result is `True`. In the second statement, the arithmetic operations are performed first. The value 5 (3 + 2) is not less than 4 (5 – 1), so the result is `False`.

The following statements illustrate the evaluation order of the same expressions with and without parentheses:

```
Result = Value1 + 2 < Value2 - 1
Result = (Value1 + 2) < (Value2 - 1)
```

The preceding two statements are equivalent. The arithmetic operations are performed first, and then the comparison operator is applied to the intermediate result. Thus, 2 is added to Value1, and 1 is subtracted from Value2. The two arithmetic values are then compared. The value 5 is not less than 4, so the result is `False`. Optional parentheses clarify the order of evaluation, as shown in the second statement. Figure 7-2 illustrates the order of evaluation used in the preceding statements.

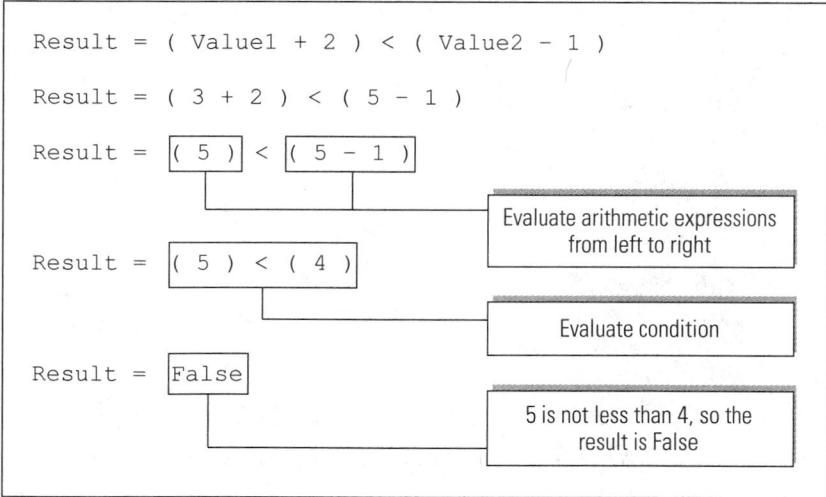

Figure 7-2: Evaluating a condition

Comparison operators are seldom used alone. Rather, they are used to build the condition in a decision-making statement. The simplest form of a decision-making statement executes a group of statements only if the condition is `True`. If the condition is `False`, the group of statements do not execute and execution continues at the statement following the decision-making statement. This form of an `If` statement is known as a **one-way If statement**. The group of statements that execute as a result of a conditional operation is called a *statement block*. A one-way `If` statement has the following syntax:

## Syntax

```
If condition Then

    statements

End If

statement
```

## Dissection

» The If statement tests the value of a *condition*, which must evaluate to a Boolean value. If the condition is True, the *statements* between the If and End If statements execute, and then execution continues at the *statement* following the End If statement. If the condition is False, these statements do not execute, and execution continues at the *statement* following the End If statement.

» *statements* include zero or more statements that execute when the condition is True and form a statement block.

## Code Example

```
Dim CurrentValue As Boolean = True

If CurrentValue = True Then

    ' Statements that execute when CurrentValue is True

End If

' statements
```

## Code Dissection

The variable CurrentValue is declared and assigned a value of True. When the If statement executes, the value of the variable is compared with the constant value True using the equal to (=) operator. The values are equal (True = True), so the statement block between the If and End If statements executes.

Figure 7-3 uses a flowchart to depict the execution flow of a one-way If statement.

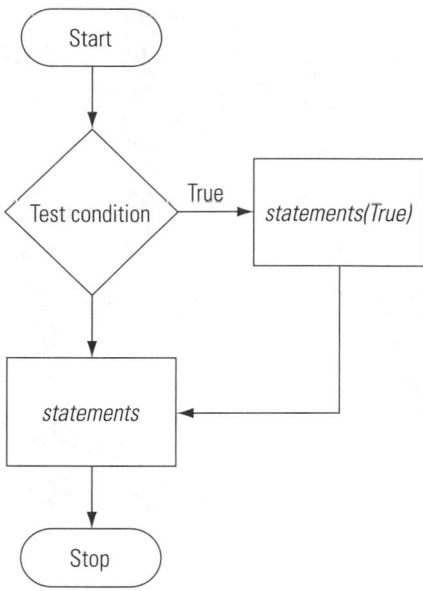

Figure 7-3: One-way If statement

As shown in Figure 7-3, a condition is tested. If the result of the condition is True, the statement block executes. Otherwise, those statements do not execute, and execution continues at the statement following the If statement.

The If statement in the preceding syntax diagram can be abbreviated as the following statements show (note that the (= True) clause is omitted because it is implied):

```
If CurrentValue Then
    ' Statements that execute when CurrentValue is True
End If
```

Most If statements contain more complex conditions. If statements can be made up of conditions that compare dates, numeric values, or strings. Conditions using each of these data types are discussed in the following sections.

## COMPARISON OPERATIONS INVOLVING DATES
Comparison operations can be performed on dates, as the following statements show:

```
Dim StartDate As DateTime = #3/22/2007#
Dim EndDate As DateTime = #3/24/2007#
If StartDate < EndDate = True Then
    EndDate = System.DateTime.Today
End If
' statements
```

If the start date is prior to (less than) the end date, the condition is `True` and the current date is stored in the variable EndDate. Again, the keyword `True` can be omitted, as shown in the following code segment:

```
If StartDate < EndDate Then
    EndDate = System.DateTime.Today
End If
```

## COMPARISON OPERATIONS ON NUMERIC DATA TYPES

In addition to conditions that compare values having data types of `DateTime`, conditions can be built using numeric data types, as shown in the following statements:

```
Dim Value1 As Integer = 90
If Value1 < 100 Then
    ' Statements execute when Value1 is less than 100
End If
' statements
```

The preceding statements use a numeric variable and literal value in a condition. Value1 is an `Integer` containing the value 90. 90 is less than 100, so the condition is `True` and the statement block between the `If` and `End If` statements executes.

## COMPARISON OPERATIONS ON STRINGS

In addition to performing comparison operations on dates and numeric data types, comparison operations can be performed on strings. Strings are compared character-by-character from left to right. Determining whether one character is less than or greater than another character depends on the **sort order**. Characters are compared using one of two sort orders. Using a *binary comparison*, characters are compared in a case-sensitive way based on a character's Unicode code point. The following code fragment shows the sort order of a binary comparison:

```
A < B < E < Z < a < b < e < z
```

As shown in the preceding code fragment, "A" is less than "Z," which are less than "a" to "z." The second type of comparison is a text comparison. Using a *text comparison*, characters are compared in a case-insensitive way as follows:

```
(A=a) < (B=b) < (E=e) < (Z=z)
```

Table 7-1 shows the equality of various strings using a text and binary comparison.

| String 1 | String 2 | Binary comparison | Text comparison |
|----------|----------|-------------------|-----------------|
| A | a | Less than | Equal to |
| Apple | APPLE | Greater than | Equal to |
| James | Jim | Less than | Less than |

Table 7-1: String equality using text and binary comparison

The `Option Compare` statement is used to determine whether string comparisons are made in a text or binary way, and has the following syntax:

```
Option Compare Text
Option Compare Binary
```

The `Option Compare` statement must appear at the beginning of a module. The `Option Compare` statement appears in the same section as the `Option Strict` and `Option Explicit` statements, as the following statements show:

```
Option Compare Text
Option Explicit On
Option Strict On
```

If the `Option Compare` statement is omitted, a binary comparison is used.

## TWO-WAY IF STATEMENTS

A one-way `If` statement can be expanded to execute specific statements when the condition is `True` and other statements when the condition is `False`. This type of `If` statement is referred to as an `If . . . Then . . . Else` statement, or a **two-way If statement**, and has the following syntax:

## Syntax

```
If condition Then
    statements(True)
Else
    statements(False)
End If
statements
```

## Dissection

» The two-way If statement differs from a one-way If statement in that it executes one statement block when the condition is True and another statement block when the condition is False. Then, the statements following the End If statement execute.

» If the *condition* is True, the *statements*(*True*) appearing between the If and Else statements execute, and then execution continues at the statement following the End If statement.

» If the *condition* is False, the *statements*(*False*) appearing between the Else and End If statements execute, and then execution continues at the statement following the End If statement.

## Code Example

```
Dim Pass As Boolean
Dim Grade As Integer = 80
If Grade > 75 Then
    Pass = True
Else
    Pass = False
End If
' statements
```

## Code Dissection

If the value of Grade is greater than 75, Pass is set to True. Otherwise, Pass is set to False, and then execution continues.

Figure 7-4 illustrates the execution flow of a two-way If statement.

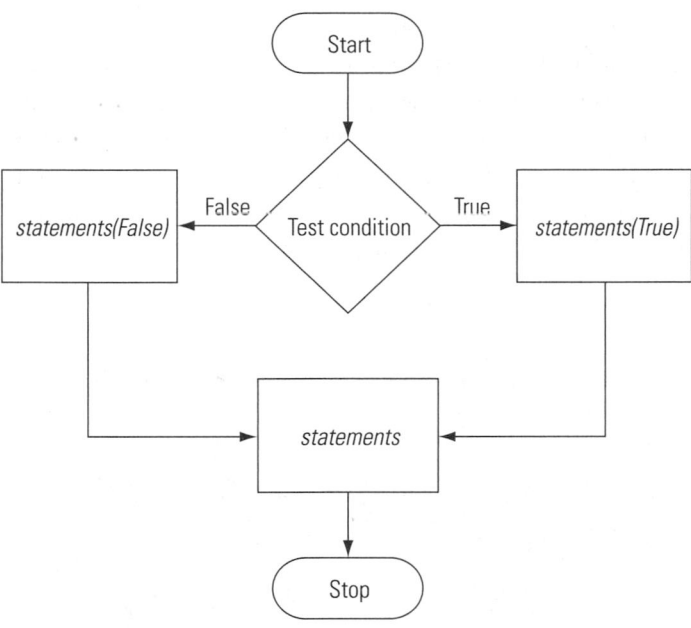

Figure 7-4: Two-way If statement

**>> TIP** When writing two-way If statements, the keyword Then always appears at the end of the line containing the If. The Else keyword appears on a line by itself. Finally, the End If keywords appear on their own line and mark the end of the If statement.

An If . . . Then . . . Else statement can be written in different ways. The following two-way If statement produces the same result as the two-way If statement shown in the previous syntax dissection:

```
If Grade <= 75 Then
    Pass = False
Else
    Pass = True
End If
```

The preceding If statement produces equivalent results to the one shown in the syntax dissection. However, the condition in the If statement is reversed. The condition in the first If statement checks whether the variable Grade is greater than 75, and the other checks whether the variable Grade is less than or equal to 75. Because the conditions are reversed, the statement blocks are reversed.

**» TIP**

When an If statement can be written in several ways to produce the same result, choose the most readable and intuitive statement. This decision is often subjective.

The statements between the If and Else statements appear indented, and the statements between the Else and End If statements appear indented. This convention makes the code more readable because it is visually apparent which statements execute when the condition is True and which statements execute when the condition is False. Furthermore, the words If, Else, and End If are aligned vertically in the same column, which helps to identify the beginning and end of the If statement. The Visual Studio Code Editor performs this indentation and alignment automatically.

## MULTIWAY IF STATEMENTS

The final variation of the If statement is the **multiway If statement**, which has three or more possible outcomes and has the following syntax:

### Syntax

```
If condition1 Then

    [ statements]

[ ElseIf condition2 Then

    [ elseifStatements]]

[ Else

    [ elseStatements]]

End If

statements
```

### Dissection

» The multiway If statement is used to make decisions having three or more possible outcomes.

» If condition1 is True, the statements between the If and the first ElseIf execute, and then execution continues at the statement following the End If statement. No further conditions are tested. If condition1 is False, condition2 is tested. If condition2 is True, the statements following the ElseIf execute, the multiway If statement exits, and execution continues at the statement following the End If statement. It is possible to create as many conditions as necessary. If condition2 is False, the next condition is tested, and so on.

» If no condition is True, the statements between the optional Else and End If statements execute, and execution continues following the End If statement. If the optional Else statement is omitted, execution continues at the statement following the End If statement.

*(Continued)* ▶

## Code Example

```
Dim NumericGrade As Integer = 84

Dim LetterGrade As String

If NumericGrade >= 90 Then

    LetterGrade = "A"

ElseIf NumericGrade >= 80 Then

    LetterGrade = "B"

ElseIf NumericGrade >= 70 Then

    LetterGrade = "C"

ElseIf NumericGrade >= 60 Then

    LetterGrade = "D"

Else

    LetterGrade = "F"

End If

' statements
```

## Code Dissection

The preceding If statement calculates a letter grade based on a numeric grade. The If statement first tests whether the numeric grade is greater than or equal to 90. If it is, the letter grade "A" is assigned to the variable LetterGrade. After a condition is found to be True, the If statement exits, and the statement following the End If statement executes. If the numeric grade is not greater than 90, the first ElseIf condition is tested to determine whether the numeric grade is greater than or equal to 80. If it is, the letter grade is a "B." The process continues examining the numeric grade to determine whether it is greater than 70 or greater than 60. If none of the ElseIf conditions are True, the Else clause executes, and the letter grade assigned is an "F." Thus, because the numeric grade is 84, the second condition is True, the letter grade "B" is assigned to the variable, and the If statement exits.

Figure 7-5 illustrates the execution flow of the preceding multiway If statement.

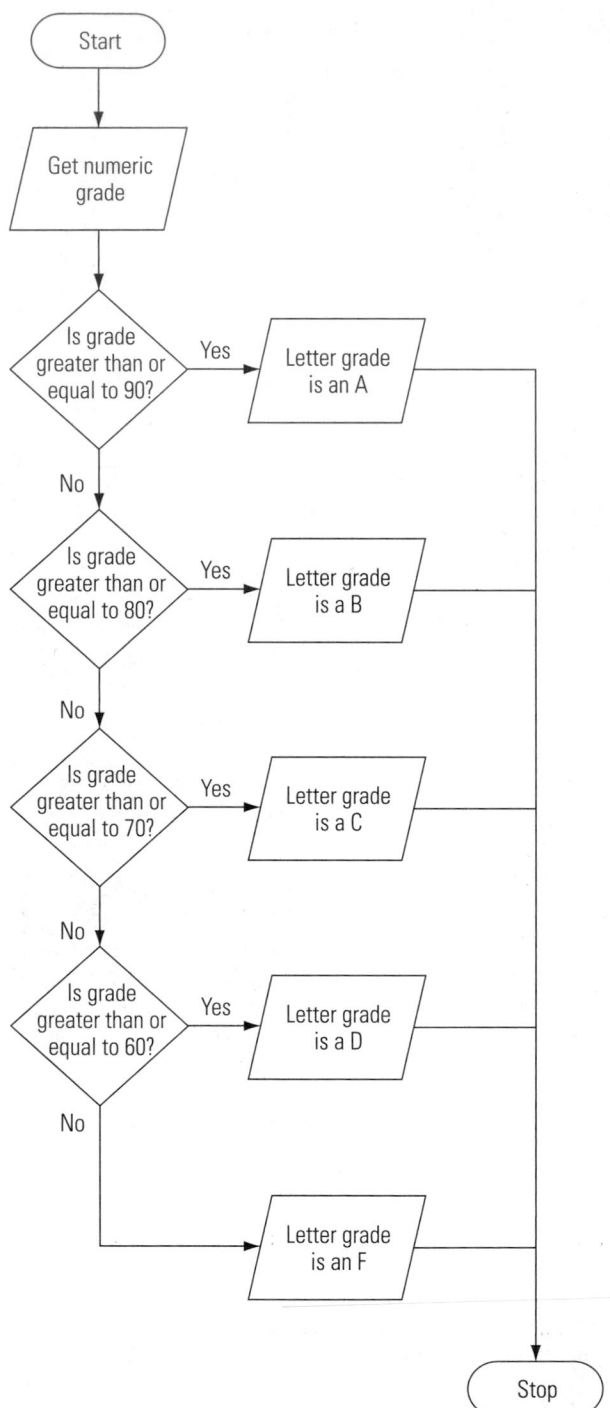

Figure 7-5: Multiway If statement

Carefully consider the order in which the conditions appear in the multiway If statement appearing in the syntax diagram. These conditions can be rewritten as follows and still produce the correct result:

```
If NumericGrade < 60 Then
    LetterGrade = "F"
ElseIf NumericGrade < 70 Then
    LetterGrade = "D"
ElseIf NumericGrade < 80 Then
    LetterGrade = "C"
ElseIf NumericGrade < 90 Then
    LetterGrade = "B"
Else
    LetterGrade = "A"
End If
```

Again, the preceding If statement shows how the conditions can be reversed and still produce the same result.

Next, examine a variation of the preceding If statement that will not work correctly:

```
If NumericGrade <= 90 Then
    LetterGrade = "B"
ElseIf NumericGrade <= 80 Then
    LetterGrade = "C"
ElseIf NumericGrade <= 70 Then
    LetterGrade = "D"
ElseIf NumericGrade <= 60 Then
    LetterGrade = "F"
Else
    LetterGrade = "A"
End If
' statements
```

The preceding If statement will not work correctly unless the numeric grade is greater than or equal to 90 or between 80 and 89. If the numeric grade is less than 90, the letter grade "B" is assigned and the If statement exits. The letter grades "C," "D," and "F" will never be assigned because those conditions are never tested. Thus, grades less than 79 are assigned a letter grade of "B," which is not correct.

## NESTED IF STATEMENTS

The statements between the `If` and `Else` keywords can include another `If` statement. That is, `If` statements can be nested, as shown in the following code segment:

```
If NumericGrade >= 90 Then
    LetterGrade = "A"
    If NumericGrade > 95 Then
        Note = "Deans List"
    End If
ElseIf NumericGrade >= 80 Then
    LetterGrade = "B"
ElseIf NumericGrade >= 70 Then
    LetterGrade = "C"
ElseIf NumericGrade >= 60 Then
    LetterGrade = "D"
Else
    LetterGrade = "F"
End If
```

The preceding statements illustrate the use of a nested `If` statement. If the grade is an A, the inner `If` statement executes to determine whether the grade is greater than 95. If so, the literal text "Deans List" is stored in the variable Note.

In this exploration exercise, you will see the operation of various forms of decision-making statements using different data types.

1. Start Visual Studio, if necessary, and then open the solution file in the folder named **Chapter.07\Chapter07ConceptLesson**. Run the solution, and click the **Numeric Comparison** button on the Decision Making 1 tab. Figure 7-6 shows the Decision Making 1 tab.

2. Use the default values provided or enter numeric, date, and string values in the respective text boxes and click the **Date Comparison** and **String Comparison** buttons. A message is displayed in the output label to indicate whether the two values are equal to, less than, or greater than one another based on the outcome of various `If` statements. Each of these `If` statements are multiway `If` statements. Exceptions are thrown if the data types are incorrect. Handling these exceptions is discussed later in the chapter.

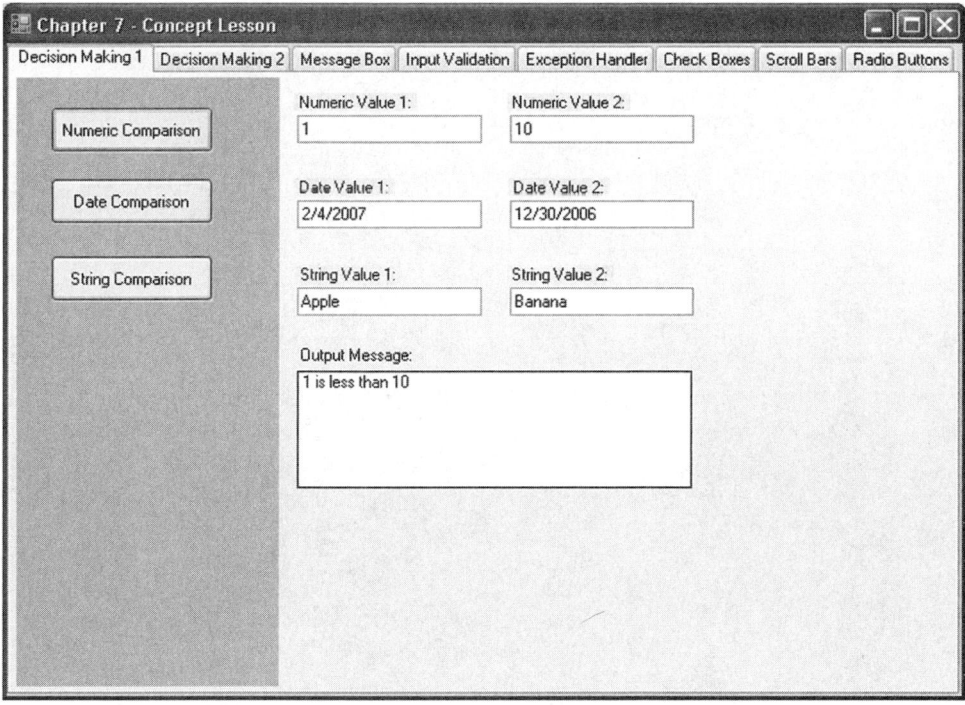

Figure 7-6: Concept lesson—Decision Making 1 tab

# MINI-QUIZ 1

1. What value is stored in the variable Result after the following statements have executed? Assume that the variable Result has a data type of `Boolean`.

   `Result = 3 + 2 >= 2 - 1`

2. Indicate whether the strings in the following table are less than, equal to, or greater than each other using both binary and text comparisons.

*(Continued)* ▶

| String1 | String2 | Binary | Text |
|---------|---------|--------|------|
| Jolt | JOLT | | |
| 099 | 100 | | |
| 99 | 100 | | |

3. What value is stored in the variable Valid after the following statements have executed?

```
Dim Q1 As Integer = 25
Dim Q2 As Integer = 26
Dim Q3 As Integer = 30
Dim Q4 As Integer = 24
Dim Total As Integer = 100
Dim Valid As Boolean
If Q1 + Q2 + Q3 + Q4 = Total Then
    Valid = True
Else
    Valid = False
End If
```

## THE SELECT CASE STATEMENT

You have seen how an `If` statement tests conditions and executes different statements based on those conditions. In circumstances in which all `ElseIf` conditions in an `If` statement use the same expression in each condition and compare it with a different value, the `Select Case` decision structure makes the code more readable. **Select Case statements** resemble `If` statements, but instead of evaluating multiple expressions, they evaluate only one expression, and execute different statements based on the result of that expression. The `Select Case` statement has the following syntax:

## Syntax

```
Select Case testExpression

    Case expressionList-1

        statement-block1

    [Case expressionList-2

        statement-block2]

    [Case expressionList-n

        statement-blockn]

    [Case Else

        statements]

End Select

' statements
```

## Dissection

» The Select Case statement evaluates the *testExpression* once when the Select Case statement first starts. It then compares *expressionList-1* with *testExpression*. If the condition is True, the statements in *statement-block1* execute, and then the Select Case statement exits. After a condition is found to be True, no further Case blocks are tested. If the first condition is False, *expressionList-2* is compared with *testExpression*. This process continues until no more expressions remain to be tested. Execution then continues with the statement following the End Select statement.

» If no *expressionList* matches *testExpression*, the statements in the optional Case Else block execute. If no *expressionList* matches *testExpression* and the Select Case statement does not include a Case Else clause, no statement block executes, and execution continues with the statement following the End Select statement. A Case Else clause is roughly equivalent to the Else in a multiway If statement.

» If more than one *expressionList* matches *testExpression*, only the statements in the first matching Case statement execute. Execution then continues with the statement following the End Select statement.

## Code Example

```
Dim Quarter As Integer = 1

Dim QuarterString As String

Select Case Quarter

    Case 1

        QuarterString = "First"

    Case 2

        QuarterString = "Second"

    Case 3

        QuarterString = "Third"
```

*(Continued)*

```
    Case 4
        QuarterString = "Fourth"
    Case Else
        QuarterString = "Error"
End Select
' statements
```

## Code Dissection

In the preceding `Select Case` statement, the *testExpression* stores an `Integer` value. Each `Case` block tests whether *testExpression* is 1, 2, 3, or 4, and assigns a string to the variable named QuarterString.

Figure 7-7 shows the execution flow of a `Select Case` statement.

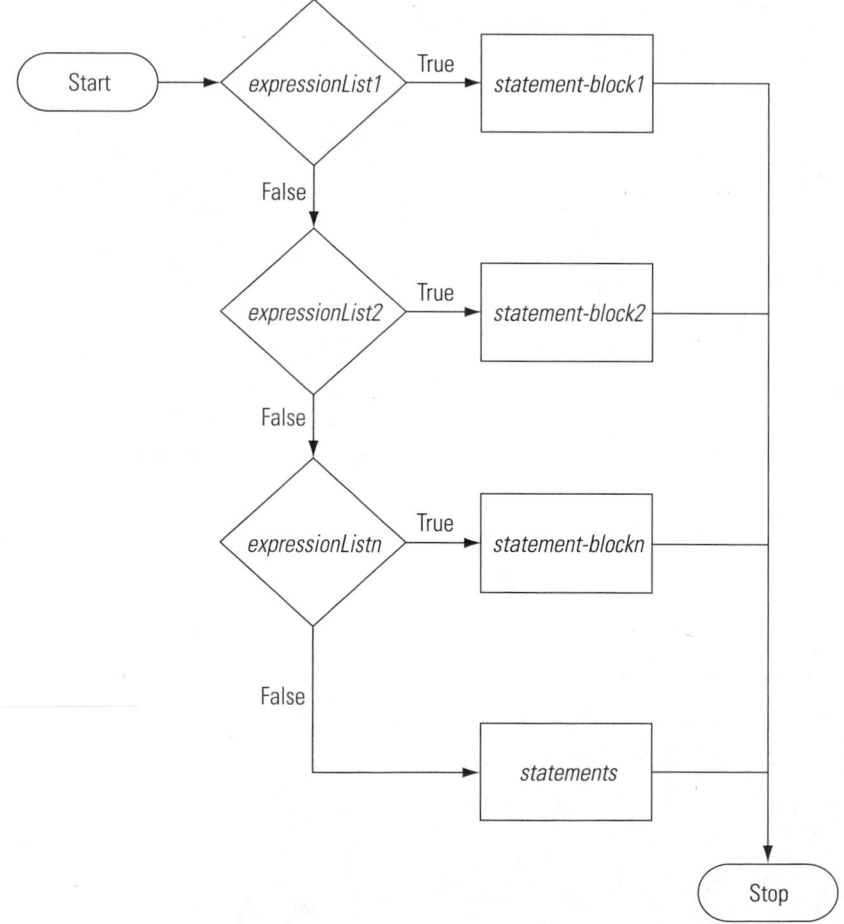

Figure 7-7: Select Case statement

A `Select Case` statement can be created with the `To` clause so as to test a range of values, as the following statements show:

```
Dim NumericGrade As Integer = 84
Dim LetterGrade As String
Select Case NumericGrade
    Case 90 To 100
        LetterGrade = "A"
    Case 80 To 89
        LetterGrade = "B"
    Case 70 To 79
        LetterGrade = "C"
    Case 60 To 69
        LetterGrade = "D"
    Case Else
        LetterGrade = "F"
End Select
```

**» TIP**

A `Select Case` statement always executes more quickly than a comparable `If` statement because the condition is only checked once, rather than many times in each `If` and `ElseIf` statement.

The preceding `Select Case` statement produces the same result as the multiway `If` statements discussed previously.

The `Select Case` statement in the preceding code example works properly if the grade is an `Integer`. However, what if the grade contained a fractional value such as 89.5? Given the preceding `Select Case` statement, none of the conditions would be `True`, so the `Case Else` statement would execute, which is not the correct outcome. To solve this problem, the `Select Case` statement can be written another way using comparison operators and the `Is` keyword, as shown in the following code segment:

```
Dim NumericGrade As Double = 89.5
Select Case NumericGrade
    Case Is >= 90.0
        LetterGrade = "A"
    Case Is >= 80.0
        LetterGrade = "B"
    Case Is >= 70.0
        LetterGrade = "C"
    Case Is >= 60.0
        LetterGrade = "D"
    Case Else
        LetterGrade = "F"
End Select
```

The following variation of the Select Case statement utilizes a list of values. To specify a list of values in a case, separate the list items with commas, as the following statements show:

```
Dim TestValue As Integer
Select Case TestValue
    Case 1, 3, 5, 7, 9
        ' The value is odd.
    Case 2, 4, 6, 8
        ' The value is even.
End Select
```

The preceding Select Case statement has two Case blocks. If the variable TestValue has a value of 1, 3, 5, 7, or 9, the statements in the first Case block execute. If the value is 2, 4, 6, or 8, the statements in the second Case block execute.

# LOGICAL OPERATORS

>> NOTE

Complex Select Case statements can be created by combining cases with comma-separated lists and the To and Is operators.

Logical operators are used with comparison and arithmetic operators to create the condition in a decision-making statement. Logical operators consist of words such as And and Or.

A **logical operator** performs the same task as a conjunction (and) or a disjunction (or) in English. In the sentence "If the value is a valid date and the value is greater than the current date, then the date is valid," the word *and* is used as a conjunction. If the phrases to the left and right of the conjunction are both True, the sentence is True. Table 7-2 lists the Visual Basic logical operators.

| Logical operator | Example | Result |
|---|---|---|
| And | `If 2 > 1 And 3 > 1 Then`<br>`    ' statements`<br>`End If` | True |
|  | `If 1 > 2 And 3 > 1 Then`<br>`    ' statements`<br>`End If` | False |

Table 7-2: Logical operators *(Continued)* ▶

| Logical operator | Example | Result |
|---|---|---|
| Or | ```
If 2 > 1 Or 3 > 1 Then
    ' statements
End If
``` | True |
| | ```
If 1 > 2 Or 3 > 1 Then
    ' statements
End If
``` | True |
| | ```
If 1 > 2 Or 1 > 3 Then
    ' statements
End If
``` | False |
| Xor | ```
If 2 > 1 Xor 3 > 1 Then
    ' statements
End If
``` | False |
| | ```
If 1 > 2 Xor 3 > 1 Then
    ' statements
End If
``` | True |
| | ```
If 1 > 2 Xor 1 > 3 Then
    ' statements
End If
``` | False |
| Not | ```
If Not 1 > 2 Then
    ' statements
End If
``` | True |
| | ```
If Not 2 > 1 Then
    ' statements
End If
``` | False |

Table 7-2: Logical operators

Logical, comparison, and arithmetic operators have an order of precedence. In any expression, all arithmetic operations are performed first. Second, the comparison operators are evaluated from left to right in the order they appear because comparison operators all have the same precedence. The logical operations are performed last in the following order: Not, And, Or, Xor from left to right.

To illustrate the use and precedence of arithmetic, comparison, and logical operators, examine the following statement. The arithmetic operations are performed first, the comparison operators are then applied, and, finally, the logical operation is evaluated.

```
Dim Result As Boolean
Result = (3 + 4) > 6 And (4 + 1) < 6
```

The operators appearing in the preceding assignment statement are evaluated in the following order:

```
Result = 7 > 6 And 5 < 6
Result = True And True
Result = True
```

The following example shows how multiple logical operators can be used in the same expression and the order in which the expression is evaluated:

```
Result = (7 > 9) Or (5 > 3) And (3 > 2)
Result = False Or True And True
Result = False Or True
Result = True
```

In the preceding statement, the comparison operations are performed first. That is, (7 > 9) is False, (5 > 3) is True, and (3 > 2) is True. Next, the And operator is applied. Last, the Or operator is applied.

The Xor operator is called an *exclusive or* and works similarly to the Or operator. However, when applying the Xor operator, only one expression can be True for the result to be True. If both expressions are True, the Xor operator returns False. If both expressions are False, the Xor operator returns False. The following code segment shows an expression using the Xor operator:

```
Dim Result As Boolean
Result = (7 > 6) And (5 > 3) Xor (3 > 2)
Result = True And True Xor True
Result = True Xor True
Result = False
```

In the preceding statement, the comparison operations are performed first. Second, the And operator is applied. Finally, True is compared with True using the Xor operator. Because both values are True, Xor returns False.

The logical Not operator performs negation. Unlike the other logical operators, the Not operator has one operand instead of two. Thus, the Not operator is considered a **unary operator** instead of a binary operator. The following statements illustrate the use of the Not operator:

```
Result = Not (True)     ' False
Result = Not (False)    ' True
Result = Not (4 > 3)    ' False
```

The result of the first two statements should be intuitive. That is, `Not (True)` is `False` and `Not (False)` is `True`. In the third statement, the expression (4 > 3) is `True`. `Not True` is `False`, so the result is `False`.

`Boolean` expressions containing comparison and logical operators are commonly used in decision-making statements. Assuming that the variables CurrentMin and CurrentMax have a data type of `Integer`, and Input is an `Integer`, the following statements test whether Input is between CurrentMin and CurrentMax:

```
If Input >= CurrentMin And Input <= CurrentMax Then
    Valid = True
Else
    Valid = False
End If
' statements
```

Assuming that the variable Input contained the value 150, CurrentMin contained the value 1, and CurrentMax contained the value 1000, the `If` statement would be evaluated as follows:

```
If 150 >= 1 And 150 <= 1000 Then
If True And True Then
If True Then
```

First, the comparison operations are evaluated from left to right. Then, the `And` operator is applied. Thus, the result of the `If` statement is `True`.

There are a few common mistakes made when writing a complex condition in a decision-making statement. To illustrate, examine the following statement, which incorrectly tests whether the variable TestValue is greater than or equal to 1 and less than or equal to 1000:

```
If TestValue >= 1 And <= 1000 Then
    ' statements
End If
```

On the surface, the preceding `If` statement might appear to work. However, it does not and the following syntax error is generated: "Expression expected." In English, the statement "If 150 is greater than or equal to 1 and less than or equal to 1000" makes sense. However, Visual Basic comparison operators require two operands, so the preceding conditional expression must be written as follows:

```
If TestValue >= 1 And TestValue <= 1000 Then
```

In this exploration exercise, you will examine variations of the Select Case statement and how to use logical operators in decision-making statements:

1. Run the solution named **Chapter07ConceptLesson**. Click the **Decision Making 2** tab. Click the various buttons to execute the different forms of Select Case statements. Figure 7-8 shows the Decision Making 2 tab after clicking the various buttons.

2. End the solution, and then examine the Click event handlers to see the various forms of Select Case statements.

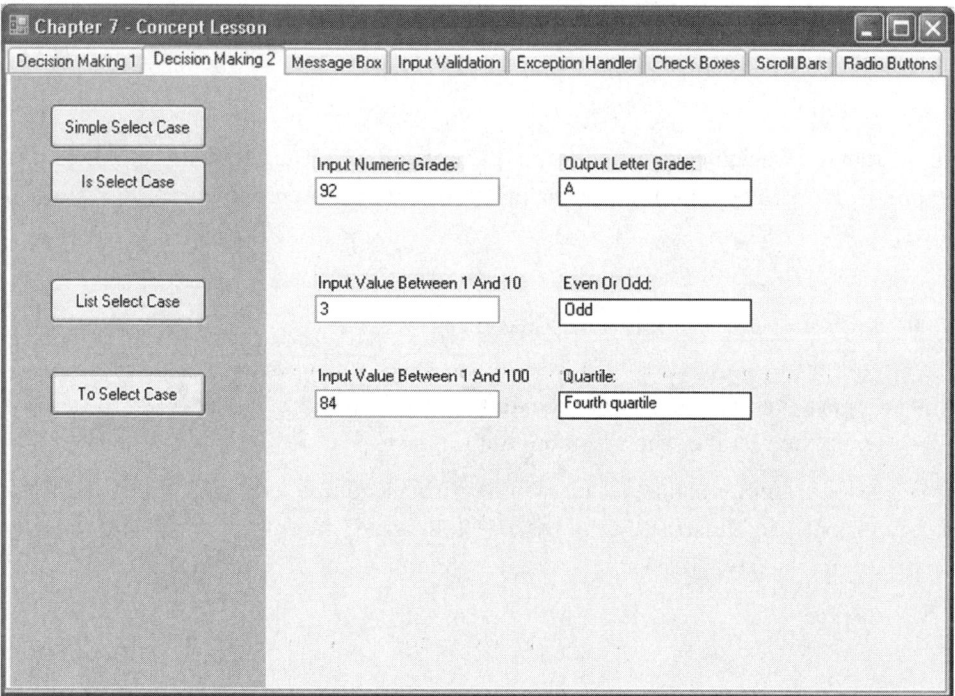

Figure 7-8: Concept lesson—Decision Making 2 tab

# MINI-QUIZ 2

1. Describe the error in the following `Select Case` statement. Assume that strict type checking is enabled.

```
Dim TestValue As Integer = 3
Select Case TestValue > 3
    Case 1
        ' statements
    Case 2
        ' statements
    Case 3
        ' statements
End Select
```

2. Which of the following lists the order in which operators are evaluated?

   a. Logical operators, comparison operators, arithmetic operators

   b. Comparison operators, arithmetic operators, logical operators

   c. Arithmetic operators, comparison operators, logical operators

   d. Comparison operators, logical operators, arithmetic operators

3. What value is stored in the variable Result after the following statements have executed?

```
Dim Result As Double
Dim Gender As String = "Female"
Dim Age As Integer = 19
If Gender = "Male" Then
    Select Case Age
        Case 16 To 25
            Result = 123.44
        Case 26 To 59
            Result = 99.48
        Case Else
            Result = 88.2
    End Select
```

(Continued) ▶

```
      ElseIf Gender = "Female" Then
          Select Case Age
              Case 16 To 25
                  Result = 115.2
              Case 26 To 59
                  Result = 94.23
              Case Else
                  Result = 84.22
          End Select
      End If
```

# THE MESSAGEBOX CLASS

Visual Basic supports a standard dialog box called a **message box** that displays a message, an icon to identify the importance or purpose of the message, and a set of buttons containing captions such as Yes, No, or OK. The MessageBox class is discussed in this chapter because decision-making statements are commonly used to determine which button from a list of buttons was clicked by the end user, and then conditionally perform some action. A message box is a standardized form that appears when the Show method of the MessageBox class is called. The Show method has the following syntax:

### Syntax

```
Public Shared Function Show(ByVal text As String, ByVal
caption As String, ByVal buttons As MessageBoxButtons,
ByVal icon As MessageBoxIcon) As DialogResult
```

### Definition

The Show method of the MessageBox class displays a dialog box with a caption, message, icon, and one or more predefined buttons. The Show method is a shared method so it is not necessary to create an instance of the MessageBox class before calling the method. Message boxes are always displayed as modal dialog boxes.

### Dissection

» The *text* argument contains the textual message that appears in the message box.

» The *caption* argument contains the text that appears in the title bar of the message box.

*(Continued)* ▶

» The *buttons* argument defines the number and caption of the buttons that appear in the message box. Valid buttons are defined by the `MessageBoxButtons` enumeration of the `System.Windows.Forms` namespace.

» The *icon* argument defines which icon appears in the message box. Valid icons are defined by the `MessageBoxIcon` enumeration of the `System.Windows.Forms` namespace.

» The `Show` method returns a value having a data type of `DialogResult`. This enumeration is also defined by the `System.Windows.Forms` namespace.

## Code Example

```
Dim Result As DialogResult
Result = MessageBox.Show("Do you want to quit?", "Exit", _
    MessageBoxButtons.YesNo, MessageBoxIcon.Question)
If Result = DialogResult.Yes Then
    Me.Close()
End If
```

## Code Dissection

These statements call the `Show` method of the `MessageBox` class with the necessary arguments to display the prompt "Do you want to quit?", two buttons with the captions "Yes" and "No", and a question mark icon. The button clicked by the end user is returned in the variable Result.

Figure 7-9 shows a sample message box.

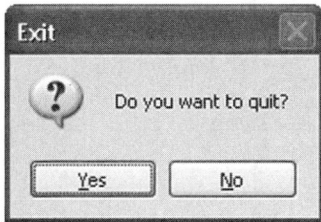

Figure 7-9: Message box

Table 7-3 illustrates the various enumerations related to the message box.

| MessageBoxButtons | MessageBoxIcon | DialogResult | MessageBox DefaultButton |
| --- | --- | --- | --- |
| AbortRetryIgnore | Asterisk | Abort | Button1 |
| OK | Error | Cancel | Button2 |
| OKCancel | Exclamation | Ignore | Button3 |
| RetryCancel | Hand | None | |
| YesNo | Information | OK | |
| YesNoCancel | None | Retry | |
| | Question | Yes | |
| | Stop | | |
| | Warning | | |

Table 7-3: Message box enumerations

The first column in Table 7-3 lists the valid enumerations for the buttons that will appear in the message box. The second column lists the valid enumerations for the icons. The third column lists the valid enumerations for the return value. This is the value returned by the `Show` method. The default button works like the Accept button on a form. When the end user presses Enter, the message box closes and the button designated as the default button is returned in the `DialogResult`.

> **»»TIP** Carefully consider which icon to display in a message box. If you are asking a question, display a question mark using the Question enumeration. Reserve the Error icon to indicate only very serious problems or consequences. Use the Warning icon for less critical problems. The Information icon is a good choice when you are explaining something.

# THE INPUTBOX CLASS

The `Microsoft.VisualBasic` class contains a method named `InputBox`, which is used to get an input string from the end user using a standardized dialog box. The `InputBox` method has the following syntax:

## Syntax

```
Shared Function InputBox(ByVal prompt As String, Optional
ByVal title As String, Optional ByVal defaultResponse As
String, Optional ByVal xPos As Integer, Optional ByVal yPos
As Integer) As String
```

## Definition

The `InputBox` method displays a modal dialog box to the end user, which is used to get an input string.

## Parameters

»  The *prompt* argument contains a textual prompt that appears inside the visible region of the input box.

»  The *title* argument contains a textual prompt that appears in the title bar of the input box.

»  The *defaultResponse* argument contains a string that will be the default response used if the end user does not enter a response.

»  The *xPos* argument contains the *x* position of the dialog box on the desktop.

»  The *yPos* argument contains the *y* position of the dialog box on the desktop.

*(Continued)* ▶

## Code Example

The following code segment displays an input box in the upper-left corner of the desktop:

```
Dim ResultString As String
ResultString = Microsoft.VisualBasic.InputBox( _
    "Enter a value", "Title", "Default Value", 0, 0)
```

## Code Dissection

The preceding code segment declares a string variable to store the string returned by calling the `InputBox` method. The second statement calls the `InputBox` method. The string entered by the end user is stored in the variable ResultString.

Figure 7-10 shows a sample input box.

Figure 7-10: Input box

In this exploration exercise, you will explore the possible buttons and icons supported by the `MessageBox` class along with examining an input box.

1. Run the solution named **Chapter07ConceptLesson**. Click the **Message Box** tab.

2. Click the various radio buttons to configure the message box, and then click the **Show Message Box** button. Note that the message box is displayed as a modal dialog box. Close the message box by clicking one of the message box buttons. The label on the form is updated to show which button was clicked.

3. Click the **Show Input Box** button to display a sample input box. Close the input box. A label on the form is updated to show the text returned by the call to the `InputBox` method. Figure 7-11 shows the Message Box tab.

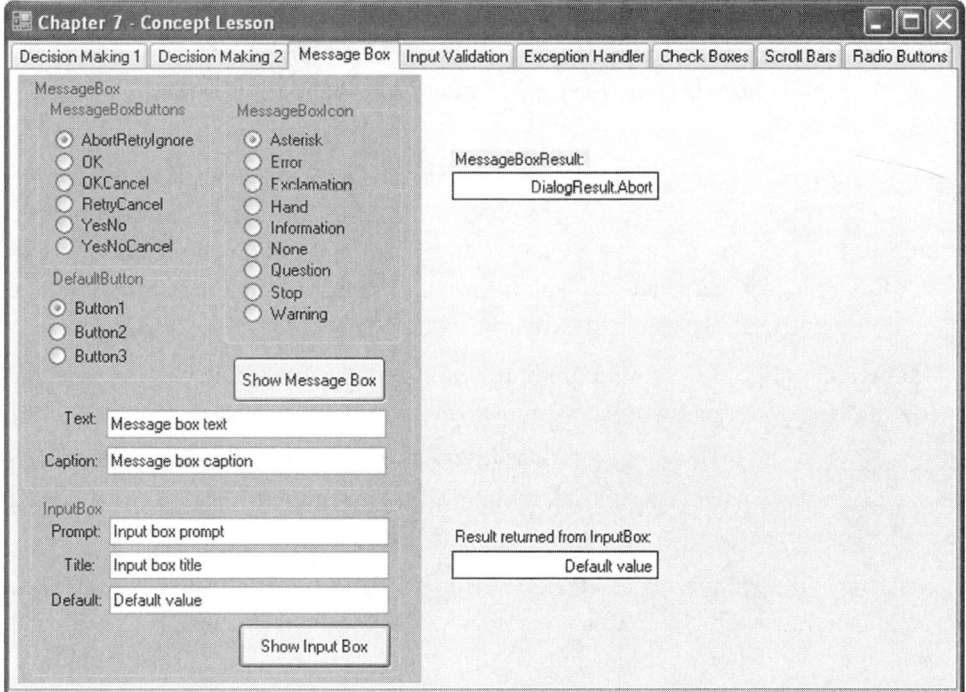

Figure 7-11: Concept lesson—Message Box tab

# DECISION-MAKING AND INPUT VALIDATION

You have written several applications in which the end user enters text in an instance of the TextBox control. Some of that input needed to be converted to numeric and date data types. If the end user were to enter invalid data into these text boxes, exceptions (run-time errors) would be thrown. Decision-making statements can be used to check the validity of input data. If the data is invalid, the end user can be advised of the error, and possibly how to correct it instead of exceptions being thrown. This concept is called **input validation**. The following list describes selected categories of input that can be validated:

» Some data must be represented as a date. The IsDate method determines whether a value can be converted to a date (the DateTime data type). Validating user-supplied date strings before trying to convert them prevents exceptions from being thrown.

» Some data must be numeric. For example, an employee's salary must contain a floating-point number and a person's age must be a positive number. The IsNumeric method determines whether a string can be converted to a number.

» Data must often fall within some range. For example, a valid date of birth cannot be a future date. A well-designed application should warn the end user when the input entered exceeds some reasonable value. This validation technique is called **range checking**.

» Sometimes data must have a particular format. For example, Social Security numbers contain a three-character region code, a dash, two digits, another dash, followed by four more digits. Thus, the format of a Social Security number can be validated. Postal zip codes, telephone numbers, and credit card numbers can be validated in the same way to make sure that they have the correct input format.

» Character strings often have a minimum or maximum length. For example, some computers restrict passwords to a minimum length of six characters.

Deciding when to validate input is an important topic. All input can be validated at once just before performing calculations on that input. Other common times to validate input are just before a particular control instance loses input focus.

Most controls support an event designed specifically for input validation. The `Validating` event fires just before a control instance loses focus. Thus, if an end user were navigating from control instance to control instance using the Tab key, Windows would fire the `Validating` event after the end user pressed the Tab key but before the next control instance gets focus. The `Enter` event fires when the text box first gets input focus. When the end user presses the Tab key or selects another control instance, thereby causing the `TextBox` to begin losing input focus, the `Validating` event fires. If the `Validating` event is not canceled, the `Validated` event fires, and the `Enter` event fires for the next control instance. If the event is canceled, the `Enter` event fires for the same text box again. Figure 7-12 shows the relevant order of events as focus moves from one text box to another.

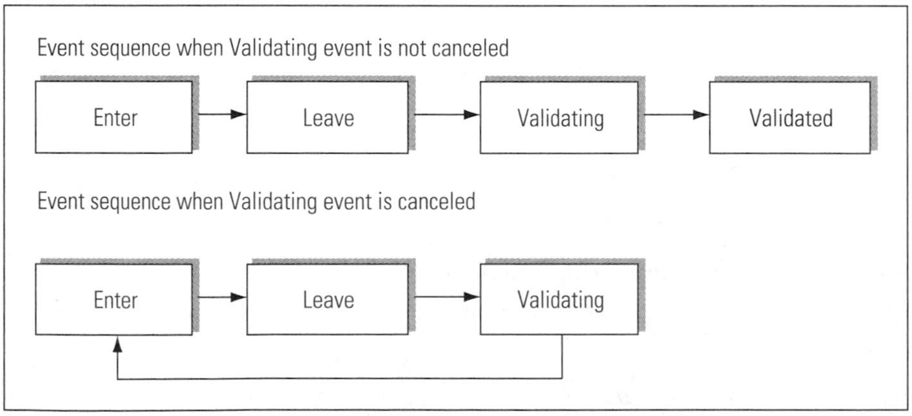

**»»NOTE**

Not all input can be validated. For example, a person's name might be spelled incorrectly, but the incorrect spelling cannot be detected. Furthermore, a Social Security number or credit card number might have the correct format, but still contain invalid digits.

Figure 7-12: Focus and Validating event sequence

The following procedure illustrates the `Validating` event handler for a `TextBox` control instance named txtDOB:

```
Private Sub txtDOB_Validating(ByVal sender As Object, _
    ByVal e As System.ComponentModel.CancelEventArgs) _
    Handles txtDOB.Validating
    If Not (IsDate(txtDOB.Text)) Then
        e.Cancel = True
    End If
End Sub
```

Note that the second argument of the event handler has a data type of `System.ComponentModel.CancelEventArgs`. This class has a property named `Cancel`, which when set to `True`, causes the event to be canceled. That is, the subsequent events do not fire and the control instance does not lose focus. If the `Cancel` property is not set to `True`, the event sequence fires normally and the next control instance gets focus.

The preceding event handler validates that the `TextBox` control instance contains a valid date. If it does not, the `Validating` event is canceled.

## APPLYING INPUT VALIDATION CONCEPTS

Chapter 6 discussed how to create reusable components that could be shared by the modules in an assembly or by multiple assemblies. Input validation is a case in which a class could be created and shared by multiple applications. This class could extend the `IsNumeric` and `IsDate` methods. The UML class diagram shown in Figure 7-13 lists some possible input validation methods.

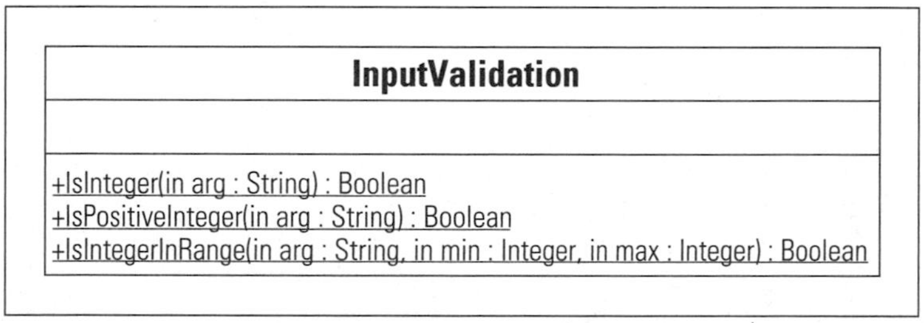

| **InputValidation** |
| --- |
| |
| +IsInteger(in arg : String) : Boolean<br>+IsPositiveInteger(in arg : String) : Boolean<br>+IsIntegerInRange(in arg : String, in min : Integer, in max : Integer) : Boolean |

Figure 7-13: InputValidation class diagram

Note that the behavior section at the top of the class diagram is blank because the class supports no properties. The following list describes the shared methods shown in Figure 7-13:

» The IsInteger method tests a string argument to determine whether it can be converted to the Integer data type.

» The IsPositiveInteger method tests a string argument to determine whether the value can be converted to the Integer data type, and whether the value is positive.

» The IsIntegerInRange method tests a string argument to determine whether the value is an integer that falls within a range of values.

The following code segment shows the implementation of this class:

```
Public Class InputValidation
    Public Shared Function IsInteger(ByVal arg As String) _
        As Boolean
        If IsNumeric(arg) Then
            If arg.IndexOf(".") < 0 Then
                Return True
            End If
        End If
        Return False
    End Function

    Public Shared Function IsPositiveInteger( _
        ByVal arg As String) As Boolean
        Dim IntegerValue As Integer
        If IsInteger(arg) Then
            IntegerValue = ToInt32(arg)
            If IntegerValue > 0 Then
                Return True
            End If
        End If
        Return False
    End Function

    Public Shared Function IsIntegerInRange(
        ByVal arg As String, _
        ByVal min As Integer, ByVal max As Integer) As Boolean
        Dim IntegerValue As Integer
        If IsInteger(arg) Then
            IntegerValue = ToInt32(arg)
```

```
            If IntegerValue >= min And IntegerValue <= max Then
                Return True
            End If
        End If
        Return False
    End Function
End Class
```

The IsInteger method first tests whether the argument contains a numeric value. If it does, the nested `If` statement tests whether the value is an `Integer` by checking the argument to determine whether it contains a decimal point.

The IsPositiveInteger method calls the IsInteger method. If the argument can be converted to an `Integer` data type, a second test is made to determine whether the value is greater than zero.

The IsIntegerInRange method determines whether the argument can be converted to an `Integer` data type and whether the value falls between a range of values. The minimum and maximum values are passed as arguments.

In this exploration exercise, you will see how input can be validated and events canceled, as necessary, when that input is not valid.

1. Run the solution named **Chapter07ConceptLesson**. Click the **Input Validation** tab. Figure 7-14 shows the Input Validation tab.

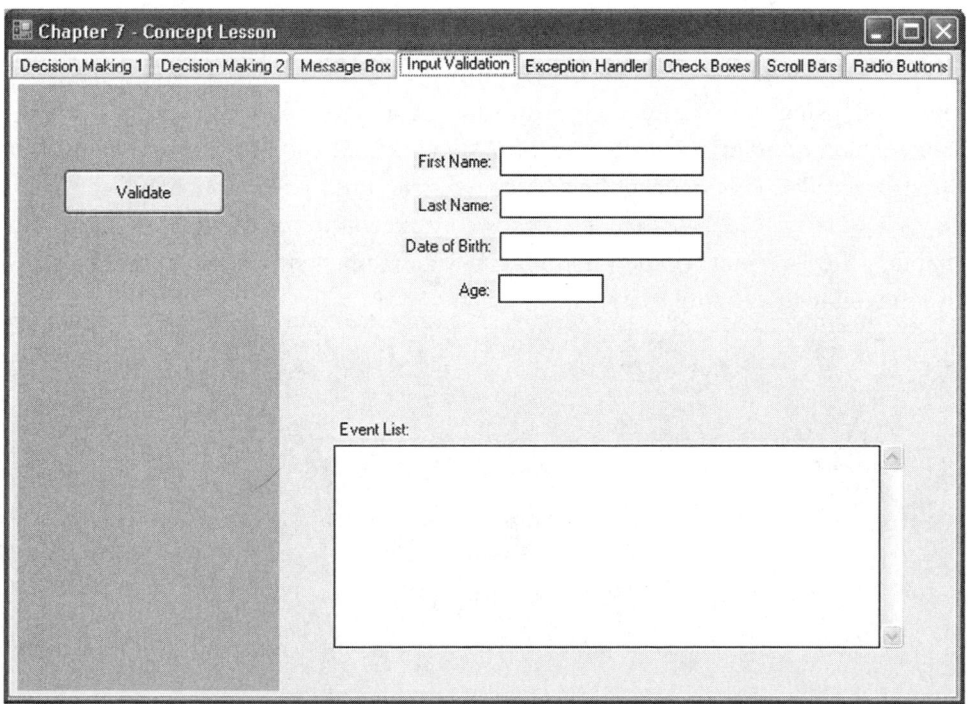

Figure 7-14: Concept lesson—Input Validation tab

2. The `Click` event handler for the Validate button contains code to check that the first and last names exist, that the date of birth is a valid date in the past, and that the age is between 18 and 100. If any of these fields are not valid, a message box appears listing the invalid fields. Enter invalid data in these fields and click the **Validate** button to see the message box. Note that as input focus moves from text box to text box, a log is updated indicating the events as they fire.

Some errors (exceptions) can be prevented by validating input. However, there are times when errors (exceptions) cannot be prevented. To deal with these types of errors, structured exception handling is used.

# INTRODUCTION TO STRUCTURED EXCEPTION HANDLING

The applications that you have created so far in this book would terminate whenever a run-time error (exception) was thrown. Exceptions can be thrown for several reasons. As you have seen, dividing a number by zero causes an exception to be thrown. Numeric overflow is another common cause of exceptions. Exceptions are also thrown when a file cannot be found.

In this section, you will learn how to write code that executes when an exception is thrown. This code will determine the cause of the exception and provide the end user with suggestions as to how to correct the error.

## THE SYNTAX OF A STRUCTURED EXCEPTION HANDLER

As mentioned, using .NET terminology, run-time errors are called exceptions. A **structured exception handler** processes exceptions and is made up of four statements that form a structured exception handling block. A structured exception handling block resembles a `Select Case` statement. That's why exception handlers are discussed in this chapter—they are a form of decision-making statement. A structured exception handler has the following general syntax:

**Syntax**
```
Try
    ' Place executable statements that might throw
    ' an exception in this block.
Catch
    ' This code runs if the statements in the Try block
    ' throw an exception.
```

*(Continued)* ▶

```
Finally
    ' This code always runs immediately before
    ' the Try block or Catch block exits.
End Try
```

## Definition
The Try, Catch, and Finally blocks make up a structured exception handler.

## Parameters
» The Try statement marks the beginning of a structured exception handler. Between the Try statement and the first Catch statement, the statements that might cause an exception to occur appear.

» The Catch statement marks the code that executes if an exception is thrown. A structured exception handler can have multiple Catch blocks. Multiple Catch blocks and different types of exceptions are discussed in a moment.

» The optional Finally statement marks a block of code that always executes, regardless of whether an exception occurred.

» The End Try statement marks the end of the exception handler.

## Code Example
```
Dim Value1 As Short = 100
Dim Value2 As Short = 0
Dim Result As Short
Try
    Result = Value1 / Value2
Catch ex As System.Exception
    MessageBox.Show(ex.Message, "Error")
End Try
```

## Code Dissection
The preceding statements illustrate an exception handler. The statement in the Try block attempts to divide a Short value by zero causing an exception to be thrown. Thus, the code in the Catch block executes. The Catch statement declares a variable named ex that has a data type of System.Exception. The System.Exception type supports a property named Message that contains a description of the error. The statement in the Catch block displays the error message in a message box and the application continues to execute.

Figure 7-15 illustrates the execution flow of a structured exception handler. The statements between the `Try` statement and the first `Catch` statement always execute. If an exception is thrown, the statements(s) in the `Catch` block execute. Regardless of whether an exception is thrown, the statements in the optional `Finally` block execute.

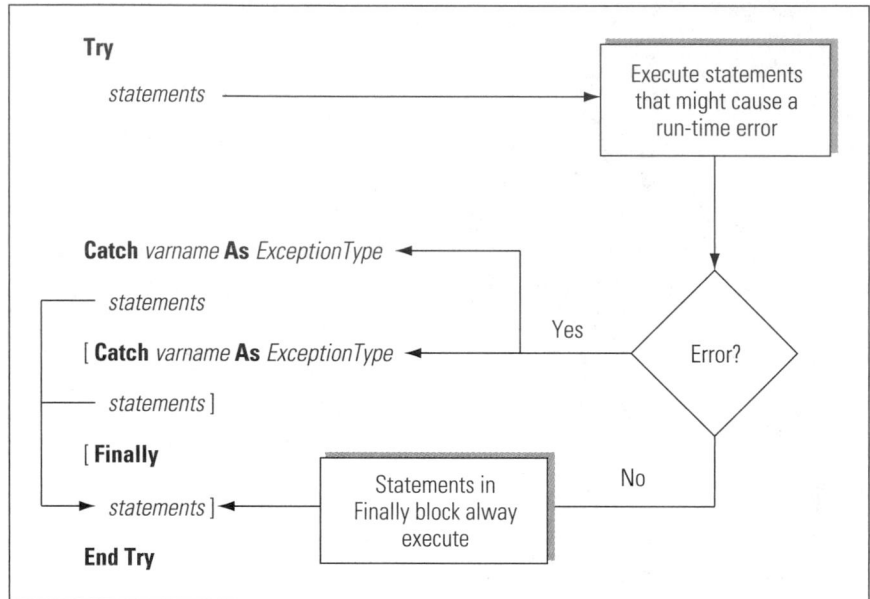

Figure 7-15: Execution flow of a structured exception handler

In .NET, all exceptions are derived from the `System.Exception` class. In addition to the `System.Exception` class, the .NET Framework class library supports additional classes to handle specific types of exceptions. For example, a division by zero operation causes a `DivideByZero` exception to be thrown. The `Exception` class and all exceptions derived from the `Exception` class have the following properties:

» The `Message` property gets the text message associated with the exception.

» The `Source` property gets a string containing the application name or object that caused the exception to be thrown.

» The `StackTrace` property returns a string defining where in the application the exception occurred.

## UNDERSTANDING DIFFERENT TYPES OF EXCEPTIONS

As mentioned, the .NET Framework class library supports several different exceptions. These different exceptions can be used in multiple `Catch` blocks to perform conditional processing based on the type of exception that was thrown. The following list describes selected predefined .NET Framework class library exceptions:

» Attempting to perform an invalid type conversion operation typically causes an `ArithmeticException` to be thrown.

» A `DivideByZeroException` is thrown if an arithmetic operation attempts to divide a number by zero.

» An `OverflowException` is thrown if an arithmetic expression causes numeric overflow or numeric underflow to occur.

» ADO.NET components cause a `DataException` to be thrown.

» Trying to reference an object that does not exist causes a `NullReferenceException` to be thrown.

Exceptions operate in a hierarchical manner and all exceptions are ultimately derived from the `System.Exception` class. Thus, if a `Catch` block is created to catch `System.Exception`, the `Catch` block executes no matter which type of exception is thrown.

The `System.ArithmeticException` class can be thought of as a more specific category of exception than `System.Exception`. A `Catch` block that catches errors of type `System.ArithmeticException` handles arithmetic exceptions, but does not handle other kinds of exceptions, such as exceptions that are thrown as a result of a failed file-handling operation.

Additional exception classes are derived from the `System.ArithmeticException` class. A `System.OverflowException` is thrown in cases of numeric overflow. A `System.DivideByZeroException` is thrown if a statement tries to divide a number by zero. Figure 7-16 illustrates part of the .NET Framework exception hierarchy.

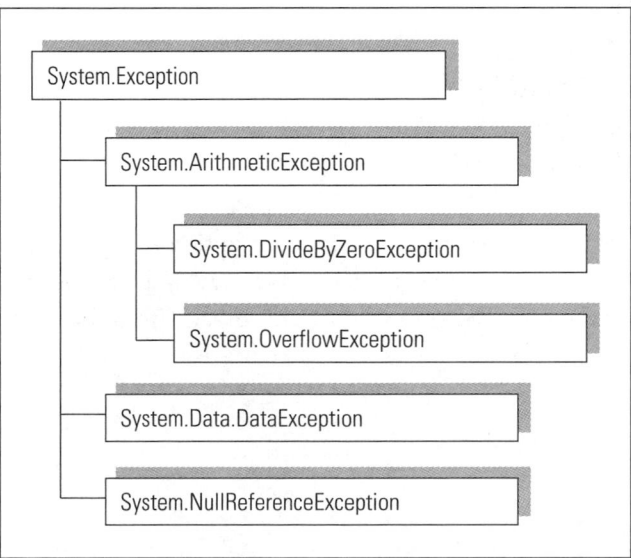

Figure 7-16: Exception hierarchy

As shown in Figure 7-16, `System.Exception` is the base class for all exceptions. `System.ArithmeticException` and `System.NullReferenceException` are derived from `System.Exception`. Additional exceptions derive from `System.ArithmeticException`.

The following structured exception handler contains two `Catch` blocks. Different `Catch` blocks execute based on the exception that was thrown.

```
Dim Value1 As Short = 10000
Dim Value2 As Short = 1000
Dim Result As Short
Try
    Result = Value1 * Value2
Catch exOverflow As System.OverflowException
    MessageBox.Show(exOverflow.Message, "Error")
Catch ex As System.Exception
    MessageBox.Show("Other Error", "Error")
End Try
```

The preceding exception handler catches all exceptions. The first `Catch` block handles only the numeric overflow exception. Note that the arguments to the `MessageBox.Show` method use the `Message` property of the `System.OverflowException` class instance named exOverflow. If the exception thrown is something other than numeric overflow, the second `Catch` block executes. Because this `Catch` block catches all exceptions, the code displays a message box for all errors other than numeric overflow errors.

The following exception handler is incorrect:

```
Try
    Result = Value1 * Value2
Catch ex As System.Exception
    MessageBox.Show(ex.Message, "Error")
Catch exOverflow As System.OverflowException
    MessageBox.Show(exOverflow.Message, "Error")
End Try
```

The preceding exception handler does not work correctly. If an exception is thrown, the first `Catch` block executes regardless of the exception that is thrown. Thus, the second `Catch` block never executes. The rule is, always organize `Catch` blocks from the most specific exception to the most general exception.

## THROWING AN EXCEPTION

In addition to handling an exception with a structured exception handler, it is also possible to create one. The term *throwing an exception* is used to describe the process of generating an exception. The Throw keyword is used to throw an exception, as shown in the following statement:

```
Throw New System.ArgumentException
```

The preceding statement throws a System.ArgumentException. When throwing an exception, it is necessary to create an instance of the desired exception class. Thus, the New keyword appears.

In this exploration exercise, you will see how various exceptions can be handled so that execution of an application can continue.

1. Run the solution named **Chapter07ConceptLesson**. Click the **Exception Handler** tab. Figure 7-17 shows the Exception Handler tab with the various boxes populated.

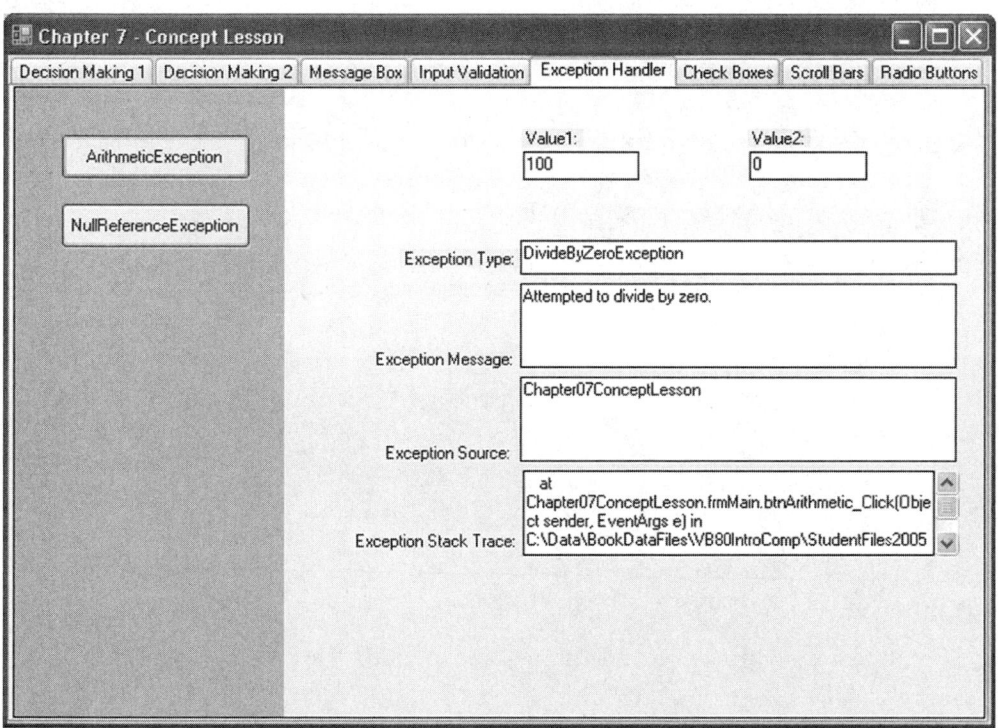

Figure 7-17: Concept lesson—Exception Handler tab

2. In the text box titled Value1, enter a number. In the text box titled Value2, enter the number **0**. Click the **ArithmeticException** button. The following statement throws a `DivideByZeroException`:

```
Result = Value1 \ Value2
```

3. In the text box titled Value1, enter the number **1000**. Enter the same value in the text box titled Value2. Click the **ArithmeticException** button. The following statement throws an `OverflowException`:

```
Result = ToInt32(Value1 ^ Value2)
```

4. Click the button titled **NullReferenceException**. The following statement throws a `NullReferenceException` because the `TextBox` control instance does not exist.

```
Dim txtTemp As TextBox
txtTemp.Text = "Some string"
```

# MINI-QUIZ 3

1. Write the statement to display a message box with the text "Continue?" in the title bar, and the message "Do you want to continue?" in the dialog box. Display the dialog box with Yes and No buttons and a question mark icon.

2. If a structured exception handler handled three separate exceptions, there would be three _____.

   a. `Catch` blocks          c. exceptions

   b. `Try` blocks            d. none of the above

3. Write the exception handler so that the following statements will be enclosed in a structured exception handler. Handle the `ArithmeticException`. If an exception is thrown, display a message box.

   ```
   Dim i, j, k As Integer
   k = i \ j
   ```

4. Will the following statements throw an exception? If so, what exception will be thrown?

   ```
   Dim Temp As TextBox
   Temp.Text = "Hello"
   ```

# CONTROLS THAT RELY ON DECISION-MAKING

This section discusses the Visual Studio controls that are commonly used with decision-making statements. The following list describes the controls discussed in this section:

» The CheckBox control is a two-state control, which allows the end user to select one of two possible values. Decision-making statements are typically used to determine whether the check box is checked or unchecked.

» The scroll bar controls allow the end user to select an integral value from a range of values. Visual Studio supports two scroll bar controls. The VScrollBar appears vertically on the form, and the HScrollBar control appears horizontally on the form.

These controls are discussed in the following sections.

## THE CHECKBOX CONTROL

The CheckBox control allows the end user to choose between two possible values and is useful in situations in which yes and no are the only choices. The CheckBox control can also be configured such that a third choice is possible. This third choice is typically used to indicate that the end user has not yet checked or unchecked the box. The CheckBox control supports the following members:

### Syntax
System.Windows.Forms.CheckBox control

### Definition
The CheckBox control creates a box that can be checked or unchecked. It contains three visible regions: a box that indicates whether the box is checked, a descriptive prompt, and an optional icon. The Hungarian prefix for a check box is "chk".

### Public Properties
» The CheckAlign property defines where the box appears within the visible region of the control instance.

» The Checked property stores the values True or False to indicate whether the check box is checked.

» The value of the Text property appears in the visible region of the control instance to describe its purpose.

» The TextAlign property indicates how the text is aligned within the region of the control instance (right, left, or center).

### Events
» The CheckedChanged event fires whenever the value of the Checked property changes.

The following statements illustrate how to set the Checked property for a check box named chkDemo:

```
chkDemo.Checked = True
chkDemo.Checked = False
```

As mentioned, the CheckBox control is commonly used with decision-making statements. To illustrate, the following code segment uses an If statement to test the value of the CheckBox control while configured as a two-state control:

```
If chkDemo.Checked = True Then
    txtState.Text = "Checked"
Else
    txtState.Text = "Not checked"
End If
```

In this exploration exercise, you will examine the events related to check boxes.

1. Run the concept lesson for the chapter and click the **Check Boxes** tab.

2. Click the check box, as shown in Figure 7-18. The check box is configured to operate as a two-state check box. An event handler for the CheckBox control instance displays the status in the corresponding Label control instance.

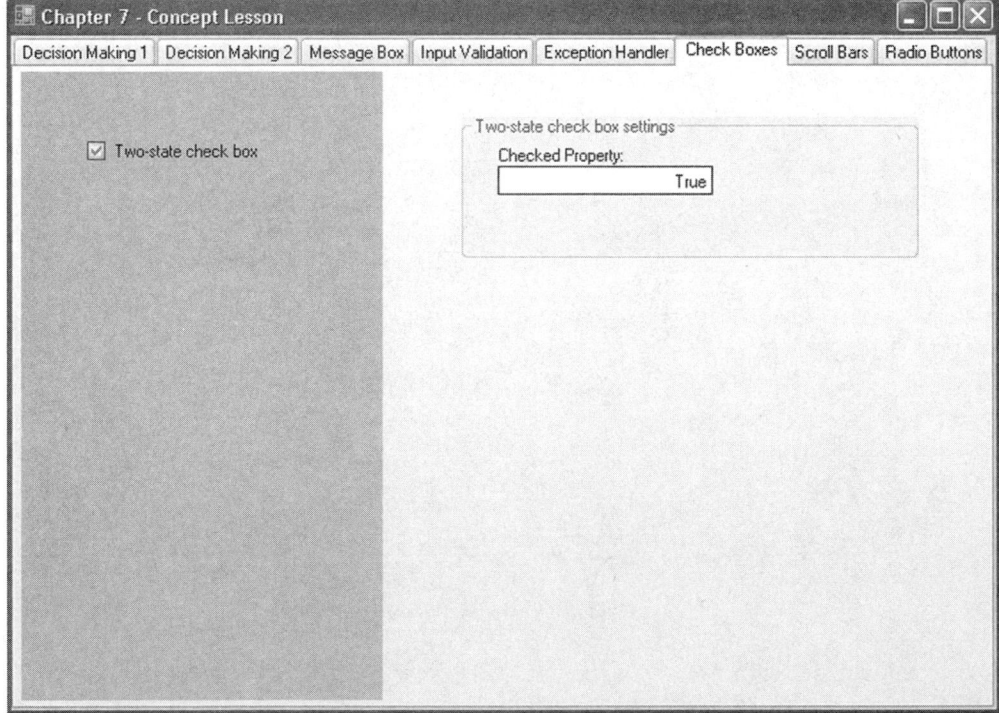

Figure 7-18: Concept lesson—Check Boxes tab

In addition to the CheckBox control, Visual Basic supports other controls designed for a particular purpose. The scroll bar controls store an integral value between a range of values.

## THE HSCROLLBAR AND VSCROLLBAR CONTROLS

Frequently, an end user needs to select a value from a range of values. For example, the end user might need to specify a percentage between 1 and 100, or scroll to a particular position in a document. Visual Studio supports two scroll bar controls with which the end user can increment and decrement an integral value. Scroll bars work the same way as scroll bars in most Windows applications. The two controls share the same properties, so the choice of which one to use depends on the user interface requirements.

### Syntax

```
System.Windows.Forms.HScrollBar control

System.Windows.Forms.VScrollBar control
```

### Definition

The HScrollBar control and the VScrollBar control store an Integer that represents a value within a specified range of values. The Hungarian prefix for a vertical scroll bar (VScrollBar) control is "vsb", and the prefix for a horizontal scroll bar (HScrollBar) control is "hsb".

### Public Properties

» The valid range of values are defined by the Maximum and Minimum properties. By default, the value for the Maximum property is 100 and the value for the Minimum property is 0. The value of the Maximum property cannot be less than the value of the Minimum property.

» The Value property has a data type of Integer and contains the current value of the scroll bar. The Value property must be between the values of the Minimum and Maximum properties.

» When the end user clicks the arrows at either end of the scroll bar, the Value property increases or decreases by the value stored in the SmallChange property. The default value of the SmallChange property is 1.

» When the end user clicks the region between the arrows (the scroll area), the Value property changes by the value of the LargeChange property. The default value of the LargeChange property is 10. The value of both the LargeChange and SmallChange properties must be greater than zero.

### Events

» The Scroll event fires as the end user scrolls the value by clicking in the scroll area or scroll arrows, or by dragging the scroll indicator. When this event fires, the Value property has not yet been changed.

» The ValueChanged event fires whenever the value of the scroll bar changes. The ValueChanged event fires after the Scroll event.

A scroll bar is divided into two regions, as shown in Figure 7-19.

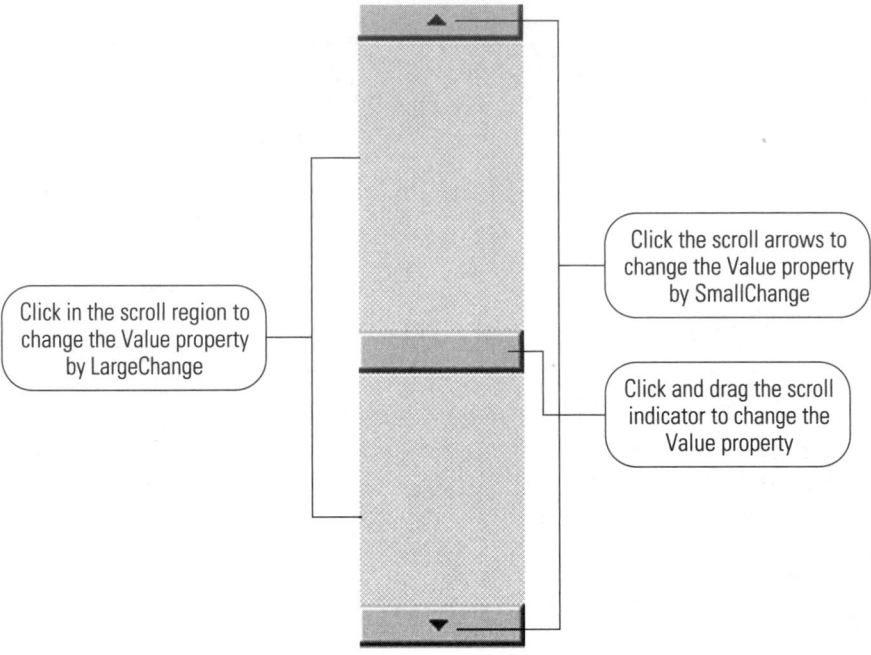

Click in the scroll region to change the Value property by LargeChange

Click the scroll arrows to change the Value property by SmallChange

Click and drag the scroll indicator to change the Value property

Figure 7-19: Changing the Value property of a vertical scroll bar

The end user can change the Value property in one of three ways: by clicking the arrows at the ends of the scroll bar, by dragging the scroll indicator, or by clicking the region between the scroll indicator and the scroll arrows. The Value property of a vertical scroll bar increases as the bar moves downward. Think of a vertical scroll bar as scrolling down through a page in a document; the down arrow repositions the document from line 1 of the page to the next line. The line number continues to increase as the position of the scroll bar is moved farther down the page, as illustrated in Figure 7-20.

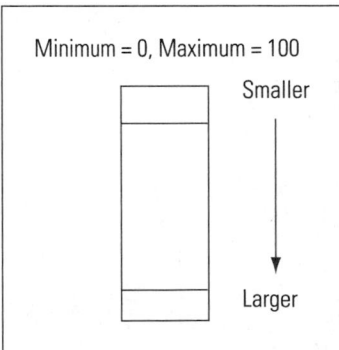

Minimum = 0, Maximum = 100

Smaller

Larger

Figure 7-20: The Maximum and Minimum properties of a vertical scroll bar

Usually, some action needs to be taken when the value of a scroll bar changes. Whenever the value of a scroll bar changes, the Scroll event fires. The following statements illustrate a Scroll event handler for a scroll bar named vsbDemo.

```
Private Sub vsbDemo_Scroll(ByVal sender As System.Object, _
    ByVal e As System.Windows.Forms.ScrollEventArgs) _
    Handles vsbDemo.Scroll
    txtValue.Text = vsbDemo.Value.ToString
    txtOldValue.Text = e.OldValue.ToString
    txtNewValue.Text = e.NewValue.ToString
End Sub
```

The data type of the second event argument is ScrollEventArgs. This class supports the following properties used to determine information about the scroll bar's position and the reason for the event:

» The NewValue property contains the new or proposed value of the scroll bar.

» The OldValue property contains the value of the scroll bar before it was changed.

» The Type property describes what caused the Scroll event to fire and has a data type of ScrollEventType.

**»TIP**

Horizontal scroll bars are well suited for measures of distance, such as inches, because the metaphor of a ruler on a map tends to be a left-to-right sliding scale. In circumstances in which the type of scroll bar is irrelevant, consider using the one that will best balance the layout of the form.

In this exploration exercise, you will see the events that fire as the end user interacts with the scroll bar.

1. Run the concept lesson for the chapter and click the **Scroll Bars** tab. Figure 7-21 shows the various boxes already populated on the Scroll Bars tab.

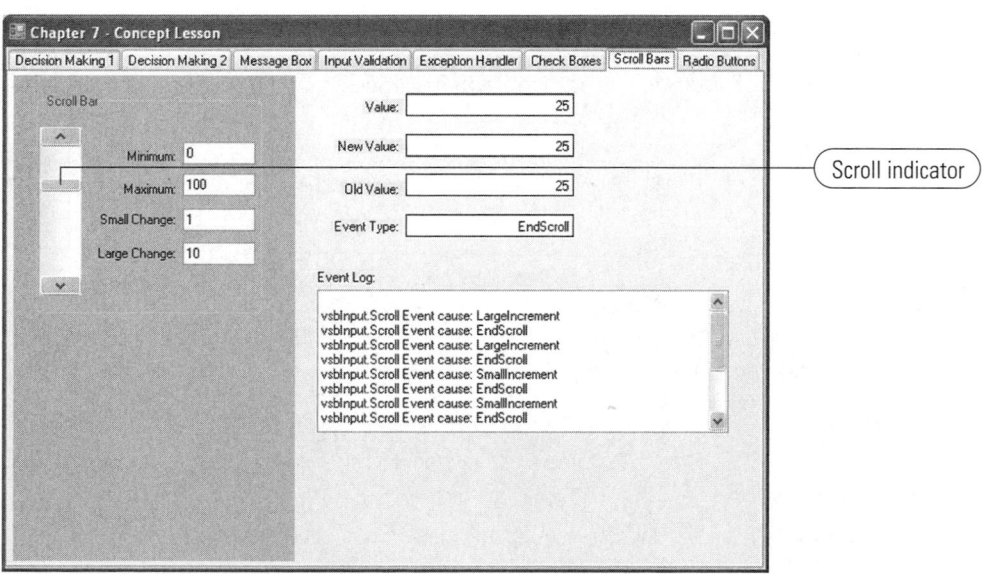

Figure 7-21: Concept lesson—Scroll Bars tab

When the form loads, the initial value of the scroll bar's `Maximum`, `Minimum`, `LargeChange`, and `SmallChange` properties are displayed in the appropriate text boxes. Each of these text boxes has a `Validating` event handler. If the input is correct, the corresponding scroll bar property is updated. The IsInteger method discussed previously validates that the value can be converted to an `Integer` data type. If the input is valid, the `Minimum` property of the `VScrollBar` is updated.

2. In the vertical scroll bar, drag the scroll box to change the value. As you do, statements in the `Scroll` event handler execute to display the current scroll bar values on the right side of the form. As you move the scroll box, pay particular attention to how the new and old values are updated.

3. Using the first two text boxes on the left side of the form, update the values of the scroll bar properties. As you do, the corresponding values are reflected in the scroll bar.

# CONTROL GROUPS

It is possible to group control instances together inside of another control instance generally referred to as a **container control**. A container control gets its name from the fact that the control instance contains other control instances. One such container is the `GroupBox` control. When you create a `GroupBox` to group control instances, such as radio buttons (which are discussed in detail in the next section), you must create an instance of the `GroupBox` control (container) first, and then create the other control instances inside the `GroupBox` control instance.

## THE GROUPBOX CONTROL

The `GroupBox` control contains other control instances and supports the following members:

**Syntax**

`System.Windows.Forms.GroupBox control`

**Definition**

The `GroupBox` control visually identifies sections on the form or groups other control instances together. The Hungarian prefix for a `GroupBox` control is "grp".

**Public Properties**

» The `BackColor` and `ForeColor` properties define the background and foreground colors of the `GroupBox`, respectively.

» The `Text` property contains the caption that appears along the top of the `GroupBox`.

RadioButton control instances are grouped together in an instance of the GroupBox control to form a **button group**.

## THE RADIOBUTTON CONTROL

The RadioButton control allows you to create a group of buttons from which the end user can select only one button at a time from the group of buttons. Radio buttons are usually positioned and operated on as a group from inside a group box. When you create a group box and place radio buttons inside it, the radio buttons form a button group. Only one radio button in a button group can be selected at a time. The RadioButton control has the following members:

### Syntax

System.Windows.Forms.RadioButton control

### Definition

The RadioButton control instances are generally used as a group. Within a group of radio buttons, only one radio button can be selected at a time. The RadioButton control has a Hungarian prefix of "rad".

### Public Properties

» The Text property contains the text that appears in the radio button.

» The Checked property can be either True or False. When True, the radio button is selected. When False, the radio button is deselected. When a radio button that is part of a button group is selected, the Checked property for the other radio buttons in that button group are automatically set to False.

### Events

» The CheckedChanged event fires when the end user clicks a radio button.

Before discussing event handling for a group of RadioButton control instances, it is necessary to introduce a new concept related to event handlers. For the control instances you have worked with so far, there has been a one-to-one correspondence between a control instance and a particular event handler. For example, there existed one Click event handler for a particular Button control instance. When working with radio buttons in a button group, it is often desirable to have one event handler handle the CheckedChanged event for all of the RadioButton control instances in a button group.

To do this, you create what is called a **multicast event handler**. The following code segment illustrates a multicast event handler:

```
Private Sub radChoices_CheckedChanged( _
    ByVal sender As System.Object, ByVal e As System.EventArgs) _
    Handles radFirstChoice.CheckedChanged, _
    radSecondChoice.CheckedChanged, radThirdChoice.CheckedChanged
    Dim CurrentRadioButton As RadioButton
    CurrentRadioButton = CType(sender, RadioButton)
    Select Case CurrentRadioButton.Name
        Case "radFirstChoice"
        Case "radSecondChoice"
        Case "radThirdChoice"
    End Select
End Sub
```

As shown in the preceding statements, a multicast event handler resembles any other event handler. That is, the event handler accepts two arguments. The first argument, as always, has a data type of System.Object and the second argument has a data type of System.EventArgs or a class that derives from System.EventArgs. The only difference between this event handler and others is the Handles clause. In the case of a multicast event handler, the Handles clause contains a comma-separated list of the control instances and events to be handled. That is, the CheckedChanged event is being handled for the RadioButton control instances named radFirstChoice, radSecondChoice, and radThirdChoice.

Examine the following statement appearing in the event handler:

```
CurrentRadioButton = CType(sender, RadioButton)
```

The CType function converts one type to another. The first argument contains the object to be converted. The second argument contains the data type. In the preceding statement, the object "sender" is being converted to the RadioButton data type.

In this exploration exercise, you will see how to work with group boxes and radio buttons.

1. Run the application corresponding to this chapter's concept lesson. Click the **Radio Buttons** tab. The Radio Buttons tab appears in Figure 7-22 with the various boxes already populated.

Note that the radio buttons are divided into two control groups contained by GroupBox control instances.

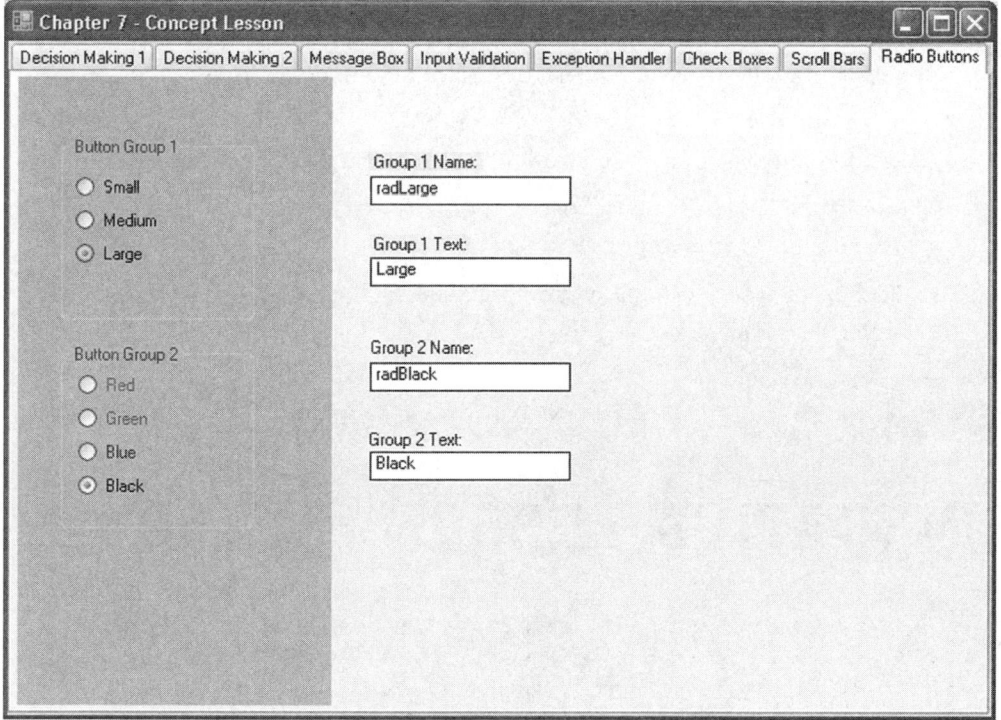

Figure 7-22: Concept lesson—Radio Buttons tab

2. Click the radio buttons appearing on the form. As you do, multicast event handlers execute, thereby updating output labels to indicate which radio button is selected.

# MINI-QUIZ 4

1. Write the statements to determine whether the check box named chkCurrent is checked or not checked. If it is checked, display a message box with the text "The check box is checked."

2. Assuming that strict type checking is enabled, what is wrong with the following statement? Assume that hsbQuiz is an instance of the HScrollBar control.

```
hsbQuiz.Value = 3.5
```

*(Continued)*     ▶

3. Which of the following statements describes how to create a multicast event handler?

   a. Include the `Multicast` keyword in the event handler declaration.

   b. Modify the `Handles` clause so that each control instance and event appears in a comma-separated list.

   c. Declare an event as a multicast event by setting the `Multicast` property of each control instance using the Properties window.

   d. none of the above

# APPLICATION LESSON

# CREATING A DECISION-MAKING APPLICATION TO CALCULATE THE COST OF A CAR RENTAL

In this application lesson, you will create an application that will calculate the cost of a car rental. The cost of the car rental is dependent on several factors:

» The number of weeks and days that the car was rented are part of the cost.

» The cost varies based on the category of car rented. There are four car categories.

» The customer can optionally accept or decline insurance. Insurance is charged at a fixed rate per day.

» The customer must pay for the fuel used.

» The business rules require that the customer be 25 years of age or older.

## APPLICATION LESSON—USER INTERFACE

The user interface for the application consists of the various controls discussed in the chapter. The end user selects the car category using radio buttons. A check box allows the end user to accept or decline insurance. A scroll bar allows the end user to select the gallons of fuel. `DateTimePicker` control instances provide the means for the end user to select the date that the car was rented and returned. Finally, the end user enters the customer's age in a `TextBox` control instance. Figure 7-23 shows the user interface for the completed application lesson.

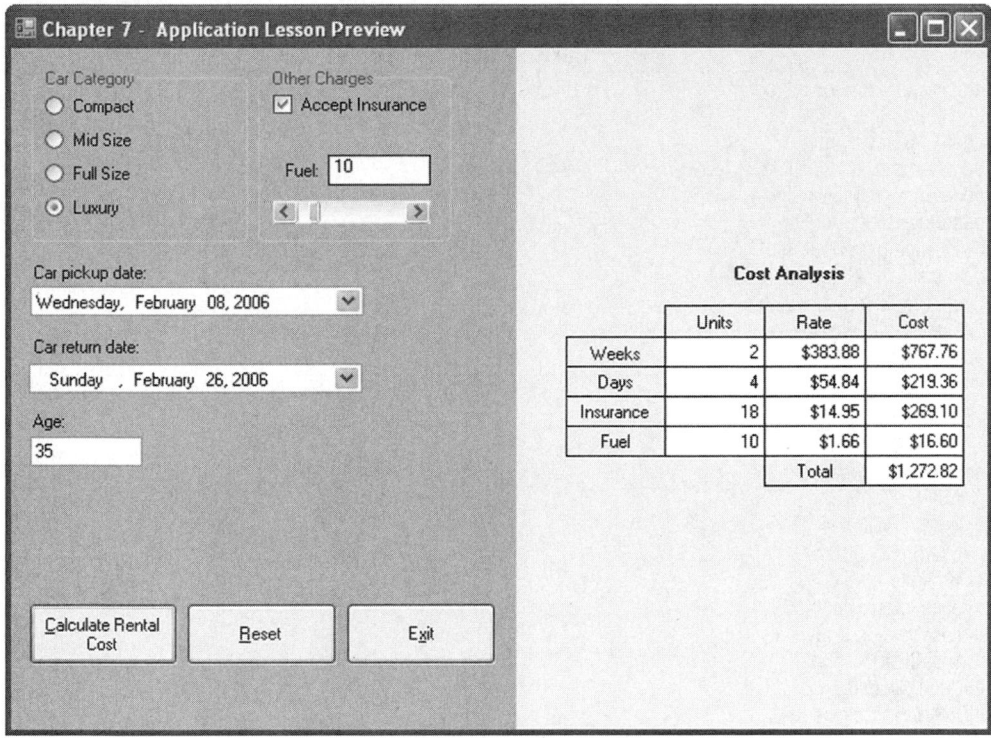

Figure 7-23: Application lesson—completed form

## APPLICATION LESSON—DESIGN

The design of this application is similar to the application lesson discussed in Chapter 6. The application has been divided into three separate classes each performing a similar task. The following list describes the classes that make up this application:

» The class named InputValidation is the same as the one presented in the chapter.

» The class named CarRental contains the business logic to calculate the cost of a car rental based on the supplied input values. The constructor for the class accepts the input values as arguments. All of the calculations are then performed in the constructor. All of the data is made available through read-only properties.

» The form named frmMain contains the user interface for the application. It calls upon the services provided by the InputValidation and CarRental class.

Figure 7-24 shows the UML class diagram for the CarRental class.

| CarRental |
|---|
| −HiddenWeeks : Integer |
| −HiddenDays : Integer |
| −HiddenTotalDays : Integer |
| −HiddenCurrentRate : Double |
| −HiddenWeeksRate : Double |
| −HiddenDaysRate : Double |
| −HiddenTotalCost : Double |
| −HiddenInsuranceSelected : Boolean |
| −HiddenInsuranceCost : Double |
| −HiddenFuelGallons : Double |
| −HiddenFuelCost : Double |
| +New(in carClass : Single, in startDate : Date, in endDate : Date, in insurance : Boolean, in fuelGallons : Integer) |
| +WeeksRented() : Integer |
| +DaysRented() : Integer |
| +WeeklyRate() : Double |
| +DailyRate() : Double |
| +WeeksCost() : Double |
| +DaysCost() : Double |
| +HoursCost() : Double |
| +InsuranceRate() : Double |
| +InsuranceUnits() : Double |
| +InsuranceCost() : Double |
| +FuelRate() : Double |
| +FuelUnits() : Double |
| +FuelCost() : Double |
| +TotalCost() : Double |

Figure 7-24: CarRental class diagram

## APPLICATION LESSON—IMPLEMENTATION

Nearly all of the processing for this application lesson takes place in the constructor for the CarRental class. The following significant points can be made about the code:

» Hidden constants store the rate of each car class, the fuel rate, and the insurance rate.

» Based on the starting and ending date, the number of weeks and days that the car was rented are calculated.

» The weekly and daily cost are calculated.

» The cost of insurance and fuel are calculated, if applicable.

» Finally, the total cost is calculated.

Because most of the work takes place in the InputValidation and CarRental class, the form's code is quite simple. The button to calculate the cost of the car rental calls the constructor for the CarRental class. Then the read-only properties are read to get the output values. A second button resets the input fields and clears the output fields. A final button exits the application after displaying a confirmation message.

To preview the completed application lesson:

1. Start Visual Studio, if necessary, and open the solution file appearing in the folder **Chapter.07\Chapter07ApplicationLessonPreview**. Run the solution.

2. The Accept Insurance check box appears checked. When the box is checked, the cost of insurance is added to the cost of the car.

3. Click each radio button. Only one radio button from the group of buttons can be selected at a time. As you click each radio button, the previously selected radio button is deselected. The radio buttons define the selected car category.

4. The scroll bar indicates the amount of fuel used. The renter pays to fill the tank. Use the scroll bar to select a different value.

5. Dates are selected using the `DateTimePicker` control instances. Using the list arrow, select a date in the calendar. The car pick-up date must be prior to the return date.

6. Click the **Calculate Rental Cost** button to calculate the cost of the rental car. The application calculates the number of weeks and days that the car was rented along with the extended cost, the cost of insurance, and the cost of fuel. The Reset and Exit buttons do as their names imply. They clear the input and output values, and exit the application, respectively.

Much of the application that you will create has already been finished. For example, the InputValidation class is complete because it is the same class as the one presented in the chapter. In addition, the form's control instances have been created. The CarRental class has been created but its code is only partially complete.

To finish the implementatioin of the CarRental class:

1. Open the solution file appearing in the folder named **Chapter.07\ Chapter07ApplicationLessonStartup**.

2. Enter the following statements (shown in bold) in the constructor for the `Class` block named CarRental. Refer to the comments appearing in the completed application lesson for a detailed description of the calculations. Note that the constants, hidden variables, and read-only `Property` procedures have already been declared.

```
Public Class CarRental
. . .
Private HiddenFuelCost As Double

 Public Sub New(ByVal carClass As String, _
      ByVal startDate As Date, ByVal endDate As Date, _
      ByVal insurance As Boolean, ByVal fuelGallons As Integer)

      HiddenInsuranceSelected = insurance
      HiddenFuelGallons = fuelGallons

      Select Case carClass
          Case "Luxury"
              HiddenCurrentRate = LUXURY_RATE
          Case "Full Size"
              HiddenCurrentRate = FULLSIZE_RATE
          Case "Mid Size"
              HiddenCurrentRate = MIDSIZE_RATE
          Case "Compact"
              HiddenCurrentRate = COMPACT_RATE
      End Select

      HiddenWeeks = ToInt32(DateDiff(DateInterval.Day, _
          startDate, endDate))
      HiddenWeeks = HiddenWeeks \ 7
      HiddenTotalDays = ToInt32(DateDiff(DateInterval.Day, _
          startDate, endDate))
      HiddenDays = HiddenTotalDays - (HiddenWeeks * 7)

      If HiddenDays < 0 Then
          HiddenDays = 7 + HiddenDays
          HiddenWeeks = HiddenWeeks - 1
      End If

      HiddenWeeksRate = HiddenCurrentRate * 7
      HiddenDaysRate = HiddenCurrentRate

      HiddenWeeksCost = HiddenWeeksRate * HiddenWeeks
      HiddenDaysCost = HiddenDaysRate * HiddenDays

      If HiddenInsuranceSelected Then
          HiddenInsuranceCost = HiddenTotalDays * _
              INSURANCE_RATE
      Else
          HiddenInsuranceCost = 0
      End If
```

```
      HiddenFuelCost = HiddenFuelGallons * FUEL_RATE
      HiddenTotalCost = HiddenWeeksCost + HiddenDaysCost + _
          HiddenInsuranceCost + HiddenFuelCost
    End Sub
End Class
```

Having created the CarRental class, you will now create the code behind the user interface that will use the CarRental class to calculate the cost of a car rental based on the end user input.

To implement the code behind the user interface:

1. Activate the Code Editor for the form named **frmMain**.

2. Create the following statements in the **Click** event handler for the button named **btnCalculate**:

```
If dtpStartDate.Value >= dtpEndDate.Value Then
    Exit Sub
End If
StartDate = dtpStartDate.Value
EndDate = dtpEndDate.Value
Dim CarCurrent As New CarRental(CurrentCarClass, _
    StartDate, EndDate, chkInsurance.Checked, hsbFuel.Value)
lblUnitsWeeks.Text = CarCurrent.WeeksRented.ToString
lblUnitsDays.Text = CarCurrent.DaysRented.ToString
lblRateWeeks.Text = CarCurrent.WeeklyRate.ToString("c")
lblRateDays.Text = CarCurrent.DailyRate.ToString("c")
lblCostWeeks.Text = CarCurrent.WeeksCost.ToString("c")
lblCostDays.Text = CarCurrent.DaysCost.ToString("c")
lblUnitsInsurance.Text = CarCurrent.InsuranceUnits.ToString
lblRateInsurance.Text = CarCurrent.InsuranceRate.ToString("c")
lblCostInsurance.Text = CarCurrent.InsuranceCost.ToString("c")

lblUnitsFuel.Text = CarCurrent.FuelUnits.ToString
lblRateFuel.Text = CarCurrent.FuelRate.ToString("c")
lblCostFuel.Text = CarCurrent.FuelCost.ToString("c")

lblCostTotal.Text = CarCurrent.TotalCost.ToString("c")
```

3. Create the following statements in the **Click** event handler for the button named **btnExit**:

```
Dim Result As DialogResult
Result = MessageBox.Show("Do you want to Exit?", "Confirm", _
    MessageBoxButtons.YesNo, MessageBoxIcon.Question)
If Result = Windows.Forms.DialogResult.Yes Then
    Me.Close()
End If
```

4. Create the following multicast event handler for the radio button group:

```
Private Sub radCarClass_CheckedChanged( _
    ByVal sender As System.Object, _
    ByVal e As System.EventArgs) _
    Handles radCompact.CheckedChanged, _
    radMidSize.CheckedChanged, radFullSize.CheckedChanged, _
    radLuxury.CheckedChanged
    Dim radCurrent As RadioButton
    radCurrent = CType(sender, RadioButton)
    CurrentCarClass = radCurrent.Text
End Sub
End Class
```

5. Create the following **Validating** event handler for the text box named **txtAge**:

```
If Not InputValidation.IsIntegerInRange( _
    txtAge.Text, 25, 100) Then
    MessageBox.Show( _
        "Customer must be at least 25 to rent a car", _
        "Error", MessageBoxButtons.OK, MessageBoxIcon.Warning)
End If
```

6. Run the application to test it.

# CHAPTER SUMMARY

» The `Boolean` data type operates similarly to an on/off switch. The keyword `True` signifies on, and the keyword `False` signifies off.

» Decision-making statements are used to execute different statement blocks based on the outcome of a conditional operation. `If` statements appear in three forms: one-way `If` statements, two-way `If` statements, and multiway `If` statements.

» Conditional statements are made up of arithmetic operators, comparison operators, and logical operators and must produce a `Boolean` result. In a conditional expression, the arithmetic operators are evaluated first. Then the comparison operators are applied, and, finally, the logical operators are applied in the following order: `Not`, `And`, `Or`, `Xor` from left to right.

» In cases in which the same expression is compared with a different value, a `Select Case` statement can be used in place of a multiway `If` statement.

» The `MessageBox` class along with the `Show` method are used to display a standardized modal dialog box with a message, icon, and fixed set of buttons. The `InputBox` method is used to get a text string from the end user using a standard modal dialog box.

» In some cases, run-time errors (exceptions) cannot be prevented. In these cases, a structured exception handler is useful. A structured exception handler is made up of a `Try` block containing the code that might cause an exception to be thrown. One or more `Catch` blocks can be created to handle various exceptions. An optional `Finally` block can be included, which contains code that executes regardless of whether an exception was thrown.

» The `CheckBox` control can be configured to operate as a two-state or a three-state control. When operating as a two-state control, the `Checked` property is used to determine whether the box is checked.

» Visual Basic supports two scroll bar controls: the `HScrollBar` and `VScrollBar`. The end user can select an integral value, thereby setting the `Value` property.

» A container control, such as the `GroupBox` control, is used to group other controls such as radio buttons. Multiple radio buttons contained in a `GroupBox` control instance are called a button group.

» A multicast event handler is often used with radio buttons. In this case, one event handler serves multiple control instances.

# KEY TERMS

**button group**—A group of `RadioButton` control instances appearing inside of the same container control, such as a `GroupBox` control.

**comparison operators**—The operators used to compare the values of two arithmetic expressions. Visual Basic supports the following comparison operators: equal to (=), not equal to (<>), less than (<), greater than (>), less than or equal to (<=), and greater than or equal to (>=).

**container control**—A control instance in which multiple control instances can be grouped or contained. The `GroupBox` control is a container control.

**decision-making statement**—The statements Visual Basic uses to make decisions having two or more outcomes, such as the `If` and `Select Case` statements. Decision-making statements are also called conditional statements.

**input validation**—The concept of validating input to make sure that it is correct or at least plausible.

**logical operator**—An operator that performs the same task as a conjunction (and) or a disjunction (or) in English.

**message box**—A standardized dialog box displaying a message and various categories of buttons. The message box is implemented with the `MessageBox` class and the `Show` method.

**multicast event handler**—An event handler that handles events for multiple control instances. The `Handles` clause contains a comma-separated list of control instances and events.

**multiway If statement**—A form of an `If` statement in which there are three or more possible outcomes.

**one-way If statement**—A form of an `If` statement in which a statement block executes when a condition is `True`.

**range checking**—An input validation technique in which the range of a value is tested to make sure that the value is at least plausible.

**Select Case statements**—A statement that resembles an `If` statement but evaluates a single expression instead of several expressions.

**sort order**—The means by which characters in a string are compared. Using a binary comparison, characters are compared in a case-sensitive way based on a character's Unicode code point. Using a text comparison, characters are compared in a case-insensitive way.

**structured exception handler**—A form of decision-making statement used to catch exceptions that are thrown so that an application can continue to run.

**two-way If statement**—A form of `If` statement that executes one statement block if a condition is `True` and another statement block if that same condition is `False`.

**unary operator**—An operator that has only one operand instead of two.

# ANSWERS TO MINI-QUIZZES

## MINI-QUIZ 1

1. True

2.

| String1 | String2 | Binary | Text |
|---------|---------|--------|------|
| Jolt | JOLT | Greater than | Equal to |
| 099 | 100 | Less than | Less than |
| 99 | 100 | Greater than | Greater than |

3. False

## MINI-QUIZ 2

1. The test expression returns a data type of `Boolean`. Thus, the valid case values are `True` and `False`, rather than `Integer` values.

2. c. Arithmetic operators, comparison operators, logical operators

3. 115.2

## MINI-QUIZ 3

1. 
```
MessageBox.Show("Do you want to continue?", _
    "Continue?", MessageBoxButtons.YesNo, _
    MessageBoxIcon.Question)
```

2. a. Catch blocks

3. 
```
Dim i, j, k As Integer
Try
    k = i \ j
Catch ex As ArithmeticException
    MessageBox.Show(ex.Message, "Error")
End Try
```

4. A NullReferenceException will be thrown.

## MINI-QUIZ 4

1. 
```
If chkCurrent.Checked Then
    MessageBox.Show("The check box is checked.")
End If
```

2. The `Value` property of a scroll bar must be an integral value.

3. b. Modify the `Handles` clause so that each control instance and event appears in a comma-separated list.

# REVIEW QUESTIONS

1. Which of the following statements is true regarding `Boolean` data?

   a. The valid values are `True` and `False`.

   b. `Boolean` data is often used in an `If` statement's condition.

   c. Many properties, such as the `Visible` property of a `TextBox` or `Label` control, store their data as a `Boolean` value.

   d. A `CheckBox` control, when configured as a two-state control, typically works with `Boolean` data.

   e. all of the above

2. Which of the following groups of Visual Basic comparison operators is valid?

    a.  >, <, =, !>, <=, <=

    b.  >, <, =, <>, >=, <=

    c.  >, <, = <>, =>, =<

    d.  +, –, =, <>, <=, >=

    e.  +, –, =, <>, =>, =<

3. Which of the following are logical operators?

    a. `And, Or, Xor, Not`

    b. >, <, =, <>, >=, <=

    c. `True, False`

    d. all of the above

    e. none of the above

4. Which of the following statements is correct regarding the evaluation order of expressions?

    a. Logical operators are evaluated before arithmethic operators.

    b. Arithmetic operators are evaluated before logical operators.

    c. Logical operators are evaluated before comparison operators. Comparison operators are evaluated before arithmetic operators.

    d. Comparison operators each have different precedence.

    e. Logical operators all have the same precedence.

5. Which of the following is true regarding `If` statements?

    a. The condition must evaluate to a `Boolean` data type.

    b. There can only be one comparison operation in an `If` statement.

    c. The `Exit If` statement marks the end of the `If` statement.

    d. `If` statements cannot be nested. That is, one `If` statement cannot appear inside of another `If` statement.

    e. none of the above

6. Which of the following `Case` blocks is invalid?

    a. `Case Is > 1 And < 2`

    b. `Case 1 To 5`

c. `Case 1 To 5, 10`

d. `Case Is < 3`

e. all of the above are valid

7. Which of the following statements make up a structured exception handler?

a. `Error, HoldError, ResumeError`

b. `BreakError, RepairError`

c. `Try, Catch, Finally`

d. `Exception, HandleException`

e. none of the above

8. Which of the following statements is correct regarding structured exception handlers?

a. A structured exception handler must have exactly one `Catch` block.

b. A structured exception handler can have multiple `Finally` blocks.

c. The statements in a `Finally` block execute regardless of whether an exception is thrown.

d. all of the above

e. none of the above

9. Which of the following statements is true regarding the `CheckBox` control?

a. The `CheckBox` control can display text, graphics, or both.

b. The `CheckStatus` property defines the possible values for the check box.

c. The `CheckBox` control responds to a `CheckedChanged` event when the value of the check box changes.

d. The `CheckBox` control can be configured as a three-state or a four-state control.

e. all of the above

10. Assuming that a scroll bar control named hsbDemo exists, what is wrong with the following statements?

```
hsbDemo.Minimum = -100
hsbDemo.Maximum = 200
hsbDemo.Value = 300
```

a. The value of the `Minimum` property cannot be negative.

b. The value of both the `Minimum` and `Maximum` properties must be between 0 and 100.

c. The value must be between the value of the `Minimum` and `Maximum` properties.

d. All of the above are errors.

e. There is no error. The preceding statements are legal.

11. What is a multicast event handler?

a. A multicast event handler is a special event handler typically used with scroll bars.

b. A multicast event handler handles an event for multiple control instances.

c. A multicast event handler is typically used to handle different events for the same control instance.

d. A multicast event handler is used to handle events when an application contains multiple forms.

e. none of the above

12. Which of the following statements is true about scroll bars?

a. The `Orientation` property is used to define whether a scroll bar appears vertically or horizontally.

b. The `Max` and `Min` properties define the range of the scroll bar.

c. The `ValueChanged` event fires when the value of the scroll bar changes.

d. The current value of the scroll bar is stored in the `Text` property.

e. none of the above

13. Which of the following statements correctly describes how to create a multicast event handler?

a. In the procedure designated as the multicast event handler, include the `Multicast` keyword.

b. In the `Handles` clause for the event handler, include the control instance name and the event name as a comma-separated list.

c. Instead of creating a `Sub` procedure, create a `Multicast` procedure.

d. Create multiple event handlers such that the `Multicast` keyword appears in each event handler

e. none of the above

14. What is the result of the following expression?

```
Result = Not((3 + 4) > (2 - 1) And (4 > 2) Xor (2 < 3))
```

15. What is the relationship between arithmetic, logical, and comparison operators in the condition of an `If` statement? Describe the order of evaluation (precedence) of each operator type.

16. Describe the relationship between a multiway `If` statement and a `Select Case` statement. Describe when a `Select Case` statement can be used in place of a multiway `If` statement and when a `Select Case` statement cannot be used.

17. Describe the various forms of the `Case` blocks in a `Select Case` statement.

18. Discuss how exceptions work. In your answer, discuss how exceptions are derived from the `System.Exception` class.

19. Describe the operation of a `CheckBox` control when it is configured to operate as a two-state control.

20. What is a button group? Describe how to create a button group and the purpose of a `GroupBox` control in creating a button group.

# PROGRAMMING QUESTIONS

1. Write the statement to set the current value of a scroll bar named hsbPercent to 60. Set the minimum and maximum values to 10 and 90, respectively.

2. Write a statement to check the check box named chkAccept.

3. Write an `If` statement to determine if the radio button named radCurrent is selected. If it is, set the value of the `Boolean` variable StatusOK to `True`. Otherwise, set the variable's value to `False`.

4. Write an `If` statement that determines whether the variable CurrentBalance is greater than 1000.01. If it is, multiply the variable CurrentBalance by 1.005. Otherwise, multiply CurrentBalance by 1.007.

5. Write an `If` statement to determine whether the check box named chkDeduction is checked. If it is, make the text box named txtDeductionAmount visible. Otherwise, make the same text box invisible.

6. Write an `If` statement to evaluate the following condition. Assume that a person's age is stored in the `Integer` variable named Age. Set the value of the `Boolean` variable LowRisk to `True`, if the person's age is greater than 25 and less than 35. Otherwise, set the value of the `Boolean` variable to `False`.

7. Write the statements to get the current date and time and store the value in the variable CurrentDate. If the time is after 3:00 p.m. and before 6:00 p.m., set the value of the variable PeakMultiplier to 1.5. If the value is between 6:00 p.m. and 11:00 p.m., set the variable PeakMultiplier to 0.9. Otherwise, set the value of the variable PeakMultiplier to 1.0.

8. Write the statement that will obtain the current day of the year and store it in the `Integer` variable named CurrentDayOfYear. Write a multiway `If` statement that will set the value of the string variable named CurrentPeriod to "First," "Second," or "Third" depending on whether the value of the variable CurrentDayOfYear is between 1 and 122, 123 and 244, and 245 to 366, respectively.

9. Write an `If` statement to determine whether a string named Data contains one of the following values: "NV", "CA", or "AZ". If the string does contain one of the preceding values, set the variable named Valid to `True`. Otherwise, set the variable's value to `False`.

10. Write a `Select Case` statement that tests the value of the `Integer` variable named Category. If the Category is 100, set the `String` variable named Description to "Asset". Set the `String` variable as follows for the other categories: 200 = "Liability", 300 = "Capital", 600 = "Income", 700 = "Expense". If an invalid category is found, set the value of the `String` variable to "Error".

11. Write a `Select Case` statement to determine the magnitude of the Long Integer value CurrentValue. If the value is between 10 and 99, store the value "Tens" in the `String` variable named Magnitude. If the value is between 100 and 999, store the value "Hundreds" in the variable. If the value is between 1000 and 9999, store the value "Thousands" in the variable. If the number is larger than 9999, store the value "Too large" in the variable.

12. Write the statements to display a message box having a caption of "Do you want to continue?" Display the text "Continue" in the title bar. Use a question mark icon and Yes/No buttons. Write an `If` statement such that if the end user clicks Yes, a statement sets the value of the variable ContinueProcessing to `True`. Otherwise, set the value of the variable to `False`. Store the result of the message box in the variable Result.

13. Create a `Function` procedure named IsValidZipCode. The procedure should accept one argument, a string to validate, and return a `Boolean` value. A valid zip code contains either five characters or 10 characters. The 10-character Zip + four codes have the format *xxxxx–xxxx*, where *x* is a digit.

14. Create a `Function` procedure named IsValidTelephone. The procedure should accept one argument, a string to validate, and return a `Boolean` value. The format for a valid telephone number is *(xxx) xxx–xxxx*, where *x* is a digit. The function should return `True` if the argument is valid and `False` otherwise.

15. Create a `Function` procedure named IsValidBirthDate. The procedure should accept one argument, a string to validate, and return a `Boolean` value. To be valid, the argument must be a valid date in the past.

# HANDS-ON PROJECTS

1. In this hands-on project you will create an application that validates the input fields representing sales taken over the telephone. The input fields include two types of credit cards having different formats, a telephone number, the length of a person's first and last name, and a sales amount.

   a. A completed version of the solution appears in the file **Chapter.07\ HandsOnProjects\Ch07HandsOnProject1.exe**.

   b. Create a new solution named **Ch07HandsOnProject1.sln**.

   c. Create the control instances on the form, using the sample application as a template.

d. Create the necessary event handler and code so that when the form loads, it will display the current date in an instance of the Label control.

e. Create a class named InputValidation with shared members named, IsValidVCard, IsValidAXCard, and IsValidTelephone number. The AX card type has the format *xxxx–xxxxxx–xxxxx*. The V card type has the format *xxxx-xxxx-xxxx-xxxx*. A telephone number has the format *xxx-xxx-xxxx*. Create methods that accept an argument containing the data to validate and return a Boolean data type to indicate whether the data is valid. Create other validation procedures, as necessary.

f. All input should be validated in a Validating event handler and again when the end user clicks the Validate button. If an input field is not valid, the foreground color of the text should be changed to red. Otherwise, the foreground color of the text should be black.

g. Validate that the first and last name fields are between 1 and 20 and 1 and 25 characters in length, respectively.

h. Sales can be either Cash or Credit. Write the code to make the Credit Card Type group box visible only if the sales type is Credit.

i. If the sales type is Credit, the credit card must be validated. Call the appropriate method in the class that you created in the preceding steps to validate the credit card based on the credit card type.

j. Validate the telephone number using the IsValidTelephoneNumber method you created.

k. When the text box containing the first or last name loses focus, convert the text to proper case.

l. The sales amount must be a number greater than zero (0). Verify that the content of the field is valid.

m. Create a procedure named ResetValues. The procedure should clear the contents from the text boxes, select the Cash radio button, and make the Credit Card Type group box invisible. Reset the input focus to the First Name text box.

n. Create the code for the Reset button to call the procedure that you just created.

o. Create an Exit button that, when clicked, will display a message box to obtain confirmation from the end user. Designate the Exit button as the Cancel button.

2. In this hands-on project, you will calculate the property taxes for a home. The property taxes are based on the square footage of the home, the square footage of the land, and the age of the home.

a. A completed version of the solution appears in the file **Chapter.07\ HandsOnProjects\Ch07HandsOnProject2.exe**.

b. Create a new solution named **Ch07HandsOnProject2.sln**.

c. Validate the input according to the following rules:

» The owner name must not be blank and must be 30 characters or less in length.

» The owner address must not be blank and must be 40 characters or less in length.

» The home square footage, land square footage, and year built must be positive integral values. The land square footage must be greater than the home square footage. To be valid, the year built must be equal to or prior to the current year.

d. Part of the property tax is based on the square footage of the home. The tax is a graduated tax. That is, the rate for a larger home is greater than the rate for a smaller home. The following rates apply to home square footage:

» 0–1000 square feet is $0.10/square foot.

» 1001–2000 square feet is $100.00 plus $0.11/square foot greater than 1000.

» 2001–3000 square feet is $210.00 plus $0.12/squre foot greater than 2000.

» 3001–4000 square feet is $330.00 plus $0.13/square foot greater than 3000.

» 4000 or greater square feet is $460.00 plus $0.14/square foot greater than 4000.

e. Part of the property tax is based on the square footage of the land. Again, the tax is graduated. The following rates apply to the land square footage:

» 0–10000 square feet is $0.02/square foot.

» 10001–20000 square feet is $200.00 plus $0.03/square foot greater than 10000.

» 20001–30000 square feet is $500.00 plus $0.04/square foot greater than 20000.

» 30001–40000 square feet is $900.00 plus $0.05/square foot greater than 30000.

» 40000 or greater square feet is $1400.00 plus $0.06/square foot greater than 40000.

f. A deduction is given for the age of the home. If the home is more than five years old, the following deduction schedule applies:

» $\frac{1}{2}$ of 1 percent of the tax amount applies to the home for each year of the home's age. Thus, the discount is $\frac{1}{2}$ of 1 percent for the total tax applied to the home.

» 1 percent of the tax applies to the land for each year of the home's age. Thus, a one percent discount applies to the total land tax.

g. Convert the contents of the owner name and property address fields to proper case when the corresponding control instances are validated.

h. Write the code to validate the input.

i. Write the code to calculate the property tax using the rules described previously.

j. Write the code for the Clear button to clear the input and output values.

k. Write the code for the Exit button to exit the application after getting confirmation from the user.

3. In this hands-on project, you will create a calculator that will determine the present value of an investment, future value of an investment, payment, or interest rate, based on a radio button selection. When a radio button is selected, enable or disable the various text boxes, as necessary, so the current output value is disabled. Also, set the foreground color of the corresponding label prompts to indicate which text boxes are currently being used for input and which text boxes are being used for output.

a. A completed version of the solution appears in the file **Chapter.07\ HandsOnProjects\Ch07HandsOnProject3.exe**.

b. Create a new solution named **Ch07HandsOnProject3.sln**.

c. Create the control instances using the sample application as a template. Configure the form so that it appears on the center of the desktop when the application is run.

d. To communicate to the end user which values are for input and which values are for output, set the foreground color of the label prompt for the input values to blue and set it to gray for the output value, depending on which radio button is clicked. Also, disable the text box that will display the output value.

e. Write the code to calculate the output values, after validating the input. Use the FV method to calculate the future value, the PV method to calculate the present value, the PMT method to calculate the payment, and the Rate method to calculate the interest rate. Use the Help system to assist you with the syntax of these methods. Format the output values as appropriate.

f. Create the code for the Reset button to clear the input and output values. Also, reset the solution so that the Present Value radio button is selected. Configure the label prompts and text boxes as appropriate.

g. Create the code for the Exit button to exit the solution. Display a message box to get user confirmation.

4. In this hands-on project, you will create an application to write a check. The application should have two forms. In the first form, the end user will enter the input. The second form should display the check. The check should display the following items:

» The check date, which should be the current date.

» The payee.

» The check amount formatted numerically.

» The check amount spelled out. For example, One Hundred Ninety Five Dollars and 93/100 is (195.93).

a. Create a new solution named **Ch07HandsOnProject4.sln**.

b. Create the application's main form. The main form should contain control instances for the payee, the amount, and the check number.

c. Create the code for the constructor that will convert the dollar amount to a string. The string should contain the written amount of the check. This task will require various decision-making statements. The code you write should be able to convert dollar amounts up to $9,999.99. The minimum check amount is $1.00.

d. Create a second form representing the check. Use your imagination to create the check itself. The check should display the payee, the amount, and the amount spelled out. Spelling out the check amount is the difficult part of this hands-on project. You will need to write numerous decision-making statements to write out the check based on the numeric amount.

# USING REPETITION WITH LOOPS AND LISTS

**After completing this chapter, you will be able to:**

Write `Do` loops to execute statements repeatedly

Write `For` loops to execute statements repeatedly

Use generic collections of objects to locate items in a list and to add, change, and delete list items

Use controls that operate on lists, including the `ListBox` and `ComboBox` controls

Use the `DataGridView` control to work with tabular data

# CONCEPT LESSON

## INTRODUCTION TO LOOPS

Chapter 7 discussed how to use decision-making statements as a means to control the execution flow of an application's statements. In this chapter, you will use another category of statements called repetition statements. **Repetition statements** cause one or more statement blocks to be executed over and over again. Thus, after completing this chapter, you will have learned about the three primary programming control structures:

» The sequence structure

» The decision-making structure

» The repetition structure

These three programming structures are used in nearly every application you write.

## EXECUTING STATEMENTS REPEATEDLY

Loops alter the sequential execution of statements by executing the same statement block over and over again. Just as repetition statements are used to solve specific types of problems, so too are loops. The following list describes common situations in which loops are used in programming:

» Suppose payroll was being calculated for 10 employees. The same calculations would be used for all 10 employees. Thus, a loop would execute 10 times, calculating the payroll for one employee each time through the loop. If the number of employees changed, the loop would execute additional times but the application itself would not need to be modified.

» Reading files often requires loops. For example, many data files contain multiple lines called records. A loop is commonly used to read and process each line (record) until the end of the file has been reached. Loops are also used when writing files, with one record being written each time through the loop. For example, payroll data might be read or written in the form of records.

» Graphics or shapes can be moved across the screen, thereby creating an animation. Loops are commonly used to perform animations. Each time the statement block in the loop executes, the position of the graphic or shape is updated.

» Loops are also used in many accounting problems such as calculating the depreciation on an asset. Depreciation is calculated for each period. Loops are also used to calculate the amortization schedule for a loan.

Loops are categorized as pre-test loops or post-test loops. Using a **pre-test loop**, a condition is tested first, and then the statements in the loop execute based on the outcome of the condition. Thus, the statements in a pre-test loop might not execute at all, depending on the outcome of the condition. Using a **post-test loop**, the statement block in the loop executes first, and then the condition is tested. Thus, the statements in a post-test loop will always execute at least once. Visual Basic supports two types of loops: Do loops and For loops. Do loops can be created as either pre-test or post-test loops. For loops are always pre-test loops.

## DO WHILE AND DO UNTIL LOOPS

A Do loop executes statements repeatedly while some condition is True or until a condition becomes True, and has the following syntax:

### Syntax

```
Do [While | Until] condition

    [statements]

    [Exit Do]

    [statements]

Loop

statements
```

### Definition

The Do While and Do Until loops repeatedly execute a statement block while a condition remains True or until a condition becomes True, respectively.

### Dissection

» The Do While and Do Until loops evaluate the *condition* before executing the statement block appearing inside the loop. Thus, they are pre-test loops. The condition in a Do loop has the same syntax as the condition in an If statement. That is, the condition can contain arithmetic, relational, and logical operators. Like an If statement, the condition must evaluate to a Boolean value.

» Using the While keyword, the statements in the loop execute while the condition remains True. Just before executing the statements in the loop, the condition is tested, and if it is True, the statements in the loop execute. When the condition becomes False, the loop exits, and the statement after the Loop statement executes.

*(Continued)*  ▶

» If the `Until` keyword is used, the statements in the loop execute until the condition becomes `True`. Then the loop exits, and the statement after the `Loop` statement executes. In a `Do` loop, either the `While` or `Until` keywords are used but not both.

» The `Exit Do` statement causes the `Do` loop to exit immediately. Execution continues at the statement following the `Loop` statement. The `Exit Do` statement typically appears in a decision-making statement and is used to exit a loop as a result of some abnormal condition or error.

## Code Example

```
Dim Counter As Integer = 1
Do Until Counter > 10
    Debug.WriteLine(Counter)
    Counter += 1
Loop
' statements
```

## Code Dissection

The statements in the preceding `Do Until` loop execute 10 times. The first time the `Do Until` statement executes, the variable Counter has a value of 1. Because 1 is not greater than 10, the two statements inside the loop execute. The statements inside the loop print the value of the variable Counter to the Immediate window, and then add 1 to the value of the variable. The next time through the loop, the value of Counter is 2, and then 3, and so on, until the variable Counter has a value greater than 10. When this condition becomes `True`, execution of the statements in the loop ends, and the statement following the `Loop` statement executes.

Figure 8-1 illustrates the logic flow of the preceding `Do Until` loop.

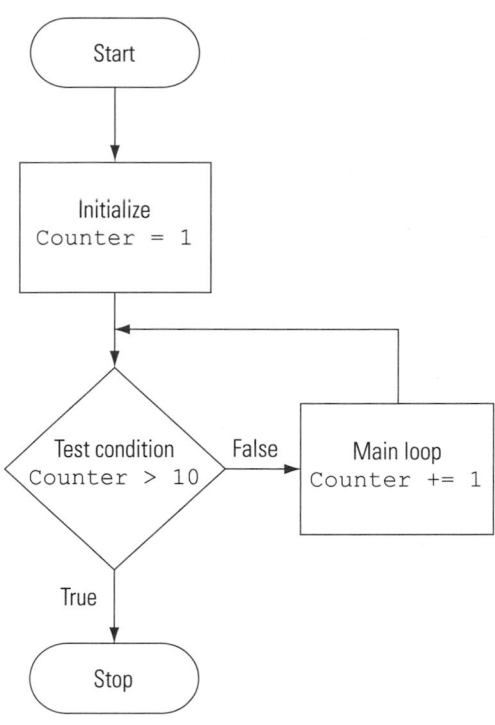

Figure 8-1: Execution flow of a Do Until loop

In Figure 8-1, the variable Counter is incremented by 1 each time the statements in the loop execute. This variable is known as a counter. A **counter's** value increases by a constant value (usually one) each time some activity occurs. A counter takes the following general form:

```
Counter = Counter + 1
Counter += 1
```

Any Do Until loop can be written as a Do While loop as the following code segment shows:

```
Dim Counter As Integer = 1
Do While Counter <= 10
    Debug.WriteLine(Counter)
    Counter += 1
Loop
```

The preceding Do While loop produces exactly the same output as the previous loop written with the Do Until statement. The condition has been reversed, however, so the loop executes while Counter is less than or equal to 10.

**»TIP**

Which variation of the Do loop to use is a matter of personal preference. You should write looping statements in the form that appears most intuitive and readable.

Figure 8-2 illustrates the execution flow of the preceding Do While loop.

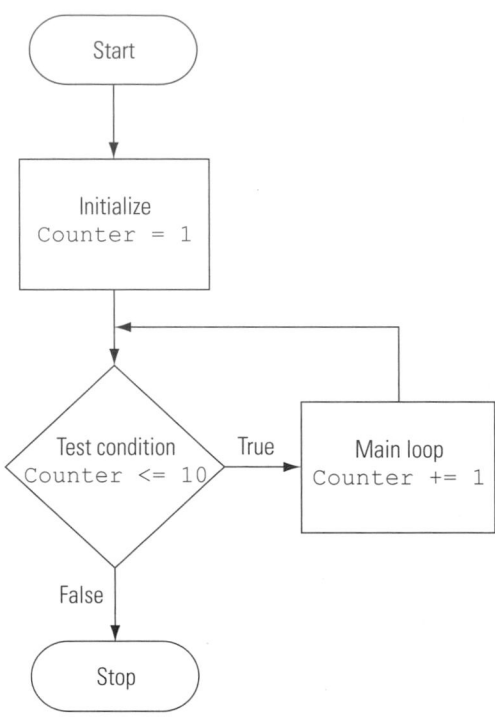

Figure 8-2: Execution flow of a Do While loop

**»TIP**

When you use the Code Editor to create any form of a Do loop, Visual Studio automatically adds the Loop keyword for you as you write the loop. In addition, the statement block appearing inside of the loop is automatically indented.

The preceding Do Until and Do While loops are both pre-test loops because both loops test the condition before executing the statements in the loop. Thus, depending on the value of the condition, the statements inside the loop might never execute.

## POST-TEST DO LOOPS

Visual Basic supports another variation of a Do loop that first executes the statements in the loop, and then tests the value of the condition. Thus, the statements in the loop always execute at least once. This type of loop is called a post-test loop and has the following syntax:

## Syntax

```
Do

    [statements]

    [Exit Do]

    [statements]

Loop [While | Until] condition

statements
```

## Definition

The `Do Loop While` and `Do Loop Until` statements repeatedly execute a block of statements while a condition remains `True` or until a condition becomes `True`, respectively. The condition is tested for the first time after the statements in the loop have executed. Thus, this form of a `Do` loop is considered a post-test loop.

## Dissection

The preceding `Do` loop is similar to the first version. The only difference is that the condition appears at the end of the loop instead of at the beginning of the loop.

## Code Example

```
Dim Counter As Integer = 1

Do

    Debug.WriteLine(Counter)

    Counter += 1

Loop While Counter < 10

' statements
```

## Code Dissection

The statements inside the preceding `Do` loop always execute at least once because the condition is not tested until the statements in the loop have executed. The first time through the loop, Counter has a value of 1, so the value 1 is written to the Immediate window. When the variable named Counter has a value greater than or equal to 10, the loop exits, and the statement following the `Loop While` statement executes. Thus, the preceding statements print the counting numbers 1 through 10 to the Immediate window.

Figure 8-3 illustrates the execution flow of the preceding `Do` loop.

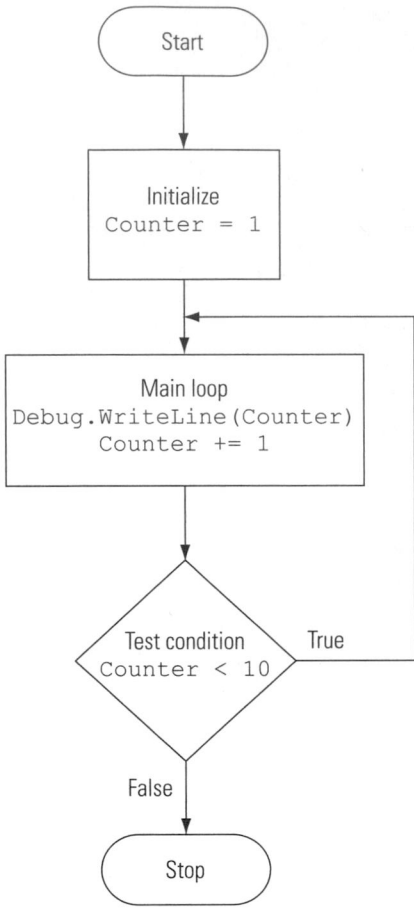

Figure 8-3: Execution flow of a post-test Do loop

## THE ROLE OF AN ACCUMULATOR

Closely related to a counter is the concept of an **accumulator**. Just like the value of a counter, the value of an accumulator is updated each time the statements in a loop execute. The statements in a loop increment the value of an accumulator typically to calculate a total. An accumulator takes the following general form:

```
Accumulator = Accumulator + value
Accumulator += value
```

The following code segment illustrates the use of an accumulator:

```
Dim Counter As Integer = 1
Dim Accumulator As Integer = 0
Do While Counter <= 10
    Debug.WriteLine(Counter)
    Accumulator += Counter
    Counter += 1
Loop
```

In the preceding statements, the variable named Accumulator stores the sum of the counting numbers 1 through 10.

## THE PERILS OF INFINITE LOOPS

When writing a loop, some condition must ultimately occur that causes the loop to exit. Otherwise, the loop continues to execute forever. Consider what would happen if you wrote the following Do While loop:

```
Dim Counter As Integer = 1
Do While Counter < 10
    Debug.WriteLine(Counter)
Loop
```

This loop will execute forever because no statement in the loop changes the value of the variable Counter. As a result, the loop executes indefinitely, printing the value 1 to the Immediate window. An **infinite loop** is one of the most common errors in programming loops.

>> **TIP** If you create an infinite loop, Visual Studio appears to be locked in run mode. The buttons on the form do not respond to events because the statements in the loop are executing indefinitely. Clicking the Break button on the Debug toolbar suspends execution. Visual Studio enters break mode and highlights the statement currently executing (typically a statement inside of the Do loop or the Do statement itself) in the Code Editor.

## NESTED DO LOOPS

Just as decision-making statements can be nested, so too can Do loops. To illustrate, the following code segment shows how to create a multiplication table for the counting numbers from 1 to 10:

```
Dim Factor1, Factor2, Result As Integer
Factor1 = 1
Do While Factor1 <= 10
    Factor2 = 1
    Do While Factor2 <= 10
        Result = Factor1 * Factor2
        Debug.Write(Result.ToString() & " ")
        Factor2 += 1
    Loop
    Debug.WriteLine("")
    Factor1 += 1
Loop
```

The preceding nested Do loops print a multiplication table. The outer Do loop iterates 10 times. Each time through the outer loop, the variable Factor1 is incremented by 1. The inner Do loop iterates 10 times for each factor. The statements in the inner Do loop multiply the two factors together and print the result. Thus, the preceding statements generate the following output:

```
1  2  3  4  5  6  7  8  9  10
2  4  6  8  10  12  14  16  18  20
3  6  9  12  15  18  21  24  27  30
4  8  12  16  20  24  28  32  36  40
5  10  15  20  25  30  35  40  45  50
6  12  18  24  30  36  42  48  54  60
7  14  21  28  35  42  49  56  63  70
8  16  24  32  40  48  56  64  72  80
9  18  27  36  45  54  63  72  81  90
10  20  30  40  50  60  70  80  90  100
```

## COMBINING LOOPING AND DECISION-MAKING STATEMENTS

As mentioned, the three primary programming control structures are the sequence structure, the decision-making structure, and the repetition structure. In most programming applications, these control structures are used together to create an application that solves a particular problem. To illustrate, examine the following Function procedure that determines whether a number is a prime number (a prime number is a number that is only divisible by 1 and itself):

```
Private Shared Function IsPrime(ByVal arg As Integer) As Boolean
    Dim Count As Integer = 2
    Do While Count < arg
        If (arg Mod Count) = 0 Then
            Return False
        End If
        Count += 1
    Loop
    Return True
End Function
```

The IsPrime Function procedure accepts one argument, an Integer containing the value to test. The Do loop iterates from 2 to the argument's value minus 1. The loop begins iterating at 2 because a prime number is always divisible by 1. The loop iterates to the argument's value minus 1 because a prime number is always divisible by itself. If the argument is evenly divisible by a value, the number is not prime and the Function procedure returns False. If the argument is not divisible by any number, the argument is prime and the Function procedure returns True.

In this exploration exercise, you will examine the execution of various forms of Do loops:

1. Run the concept lesson for the chapter and click the **Do Loops** tab, as shown in Figure 8-4.

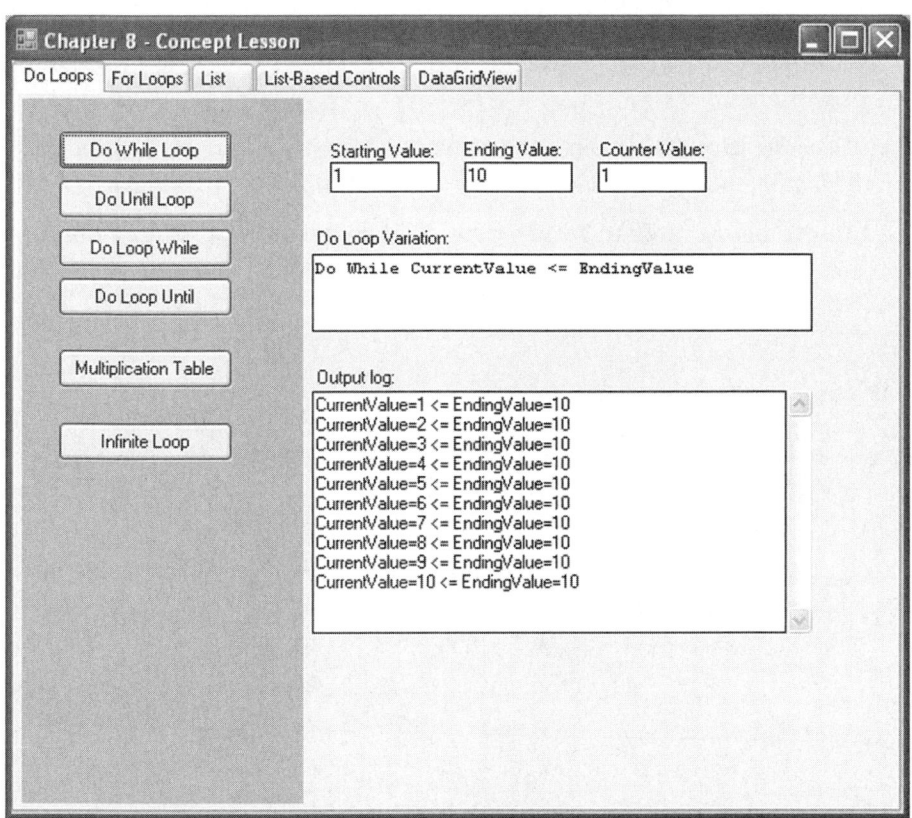

Figure 8-4: Concept lesson—Do Loops tab

The Click event handlers for the first four buttons contain code to demonstrate the use of the four variations of pre-test and post-test Do loops. For each of the four buttons, a procedure is called to store the contents of the text boxes into numeric loop variables. The following code segment shows the Click event handler for the Do While Loop button:

```
txtDoLog.Clear()
Call InitializeDoLoopVariables()
txtDoStatement.Text = "Do While CurrentValue <= EndingValue"
CurrentValue = StartingValue
Do While CurrentValue <= EndingValue
    Call AppendDoLoopLogMessage(" <=")
    CurrentValue += Increment
Loop
```

The first group of statements clears the text box containing the output log, initializes the loop variables, and displays the variation of the Do loop that is being executed. The remaining statements contain the loop itself. Each time the loop executes, a message is appended to a text box showing the current value of the condition.

2. Click each of the **Do Loop** buttons to see the execution path of the corresponding loop. Explore different starting, ending, and incremental values to see how they affect the loop's execution.

3. Click the **Multiplication Table** button. The multiplication table is created and displayed in the log text box using code similar to the code discussed previously.

4. Click the **Infinite Loop** button to begin execution of an infinite loop. Click **Debug** on the menu bar, and then click **Break All**. Execution is suspended, and the statement currently executing appears in the Code Editor.

## MINI-QUIZ 1

1. Which of the following statements is correct regarding the condition in a Do loop?

   a. All loops are pre-test loops. That is, the condition in all Do loops is tested before the statement block in the loop executes the first time.

   b. To execute the statements in a loop while a condition is True, the Do Until version of the loop should be used.

   c. The condition in a Do loop has the same format as the condition in an If statement.

   d. The condition in a Do loop must evaluate to a positive integer value.

   e. none of the above

2. A(n) _____ loop error occurs when there is no condition causing the loop to terminate.

   a. nonterminating          b. infinite

   c. perpetual               d. syntax

   e. none of the above

3. Describe the difference between a counter and an accumulator.

*(Continued)* ▶

4. What value is stored in the variable Result after the following statements have executed?

```
Dim Counter As Integer = 0
Dim Result As Integer = 0
Do While Counter <= 5
    Counter += 1
    Result += Counter
Loop
```

# FOR LOOPS

Just like the variations of the Do loop, the For loop executes statements repeatedly. However, a For loop can only be used when the number of iterations (times the loop will execute) is known in advance. A For loop works like a Do loop that uses a counter. Each time the statements in the loop execute, the counter's value is automatically incremented until the counter reaches some value causing the loop to exit. The For loop has the following syntax:

## Syntax

```
For counter = start To end [ Step increment]
    [statements]
    [Exit For]
    [statements]
Next [counter]
statements
```

## Definition

The For loop executes the statement block appearing between the For and Next keywords a fixed number of times.

## Dissection

» When the loop is initialized, *counter* is set to *start*. The statements in the loop execute until the value of *counter* is greater than *end*. Note that Visual Studio automatically updates the value of *counter*. Do not write statements inside of the loop that modify the value of *counter*. If you do, the loop will not iterate the correct number of times.

» By default, *counter* is incremented by 1 each time through the For loop. This value can be changed by including the Step *increment* clause. The *increment* typically contains an integral

*(Continued)*   ▶

value. If the value is positive, the value of *counter* is increased by *increment*. If the value is negative, the value of *counter* is decremented by the value of *increment*.

» The `For` loop can be terminated prematurely using the optional `Exit For` statement. The `Exit For` statement typically appears inside of a decision-making statement and executes in response to some abnormal condition.

## Code Example

```
Dim Counter As Integer
For Counter = 1 To 10
    Debug.WriteLine(Counter)
Next Counter
```

## Code Dissection

The preceding `For` statement uses the variable named Counter as the loop's counter. The statements in the loop execute 10 times. Each time the statements in the loop execute, the value of the variable Counter is incremented by 1, the default, and printed to the Immediate window.

## EXECUTION OF A FOR LOOP

A `For` loop is a repetition structure that works with a counter, as illustrated in Figure 8-5.

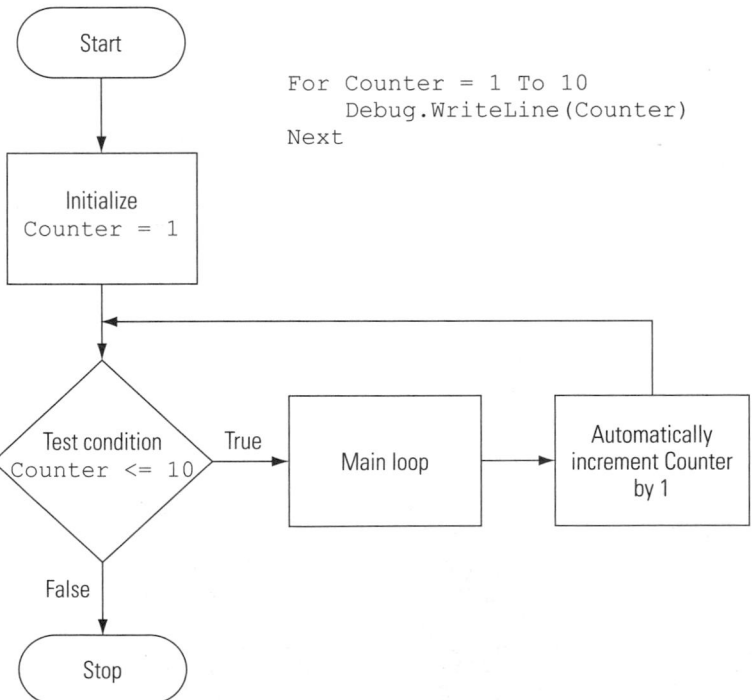

```
For Counter = 1 To 10
    Debug.WriteLine(Counter)
Next
```

Figure 8-5: Execution of a For loop

The `For` loop shown in Figure 8-5 increments a counter by 1 from 1 to 10. When the value of Counter is greater than 10, the `For` loop exits.

Just as `Do` loops can be nested, so too can `For` loops. The following code segment shows the same multiplication table discussed previously. This time, however, the loop is implemented using a nested `For` loop instead of a nested `Do` loop.

```
Dim Factor1, Factor2, Result As Integer
For Factor1 = 1 To 10
    For Factor2 = 1 To 10
        Result = Factor1 * Factor2
        Debug.Write(Result.ToString() & " ")
    Next
    Debug.WriteLine("")
Next
```

It is also possible to write `For` loops that decrement a counter, or modify the counter by a value other than 1, as shown in the following `For` loop:

```
Dim CurrentYear As Integer
For CurrentYear = 2000 To 1900 Step -5
    Debug.WriteLine(CurrentYear.ToString)
Next CurrentYear
```

The preceding `For` loop begins at 2000. Each time through the loop, CurrentYear is decremented by 5 until the variable CurrentYear is less than 1900. At that point, the loop exits.

## THE IMPLICATIONS OF LONG-RUNNING LOOPS

In the preceding code segments, the demonstration loops executed just a few times. However, many applications have loops that iterate thousands or millions of times. In these situations, two points must be considered:

» Some loops can run for minutes or hours as they perform their processing. In such a case, it is important to advise the end user that a process is working and operating normally. Otherwise, the end user might think that the application is locked or has crashed.

» Performance of long-running loops must be considered. To improve performance, minimize those statements appearing inside of the loop whenever possible.

To solve the first problem, displaying progress messages periodically in a long-running loop informs the end user that the loop is operating correctly. To illustrate, examine the following For loop:

```
Dim Counter As Integer
For Counter = 1 To Integer.MaxValue - 1
    If (Counter Mod 10000000) = 0 Then
        Debug.WriteLine("Iteration " & Counter.ToString)
    End If
Next
```

In the preceding code segment, a message is displayed to the end user every 10,000,000 iterations so that the operation's progress is monitored. Of course, the purpose of the preceding loop is to show relative progress. The loop itself does not accomplish any particular task.

The solution to the second problem should be fairly obvious. To illustrate this common problem, examine the following loop:

```
For Counter = 1 To 1000000
    ' statements
    Temp = 0
Next
```

The statement in the preceding loop initializes a variable named Temp to 0. However, the variable is initialized to the same value one million times, which is not necessary. To improve performance, this statement should be moved outside of the loop, as the following code segment shows:

```
Temp = 0
For Counter = 1 To 1000000
    ' statements
Next
```

In this exploration exercise, you will examine the operation of various For loops.

1. Run the concept lesson for the chapter and click the **For Loops** tab. Figure 8-6 shows the For Loops tab.

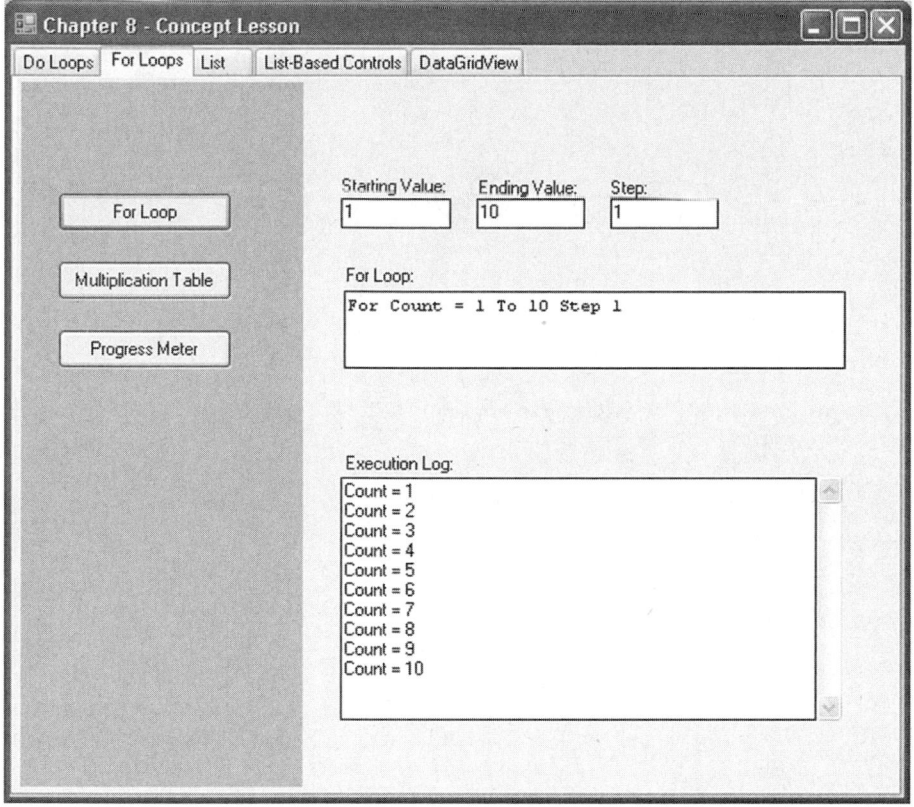

Figure 8-6: Concept lesson—For Loops tab

2. The form's text boxes are used to store the starting value, ending value, and incremental value for a For loop. Default values appear in these text boxes. Click the **For Loop** button. The following For loop executes to print the value of the counter to the output text box:

```
For Count = StartingValue To EndingValue Step Increment
    txtForLog.Text &= "Count = " & Count.ToString & CrLf
Next
```

3. Modify the default values appearing in the Starting Value, Ending Value, and Step text boxes, and click the **For Loop** button again to see how the For loop is evaluated.

4. Click the **Multiplication Table** button. A nested For loop prints the multiplication table discussed previously.

5. Click the **Progress Meter** button. A For loop executes from 1 to Integer.MaxValue – 1. A message appears in the output text box every 10 million iterations.

# MINI-QUIZ 2

1. Which of the following statements is true regarding For loops?

   a. The counter in a For loop is always incremented by 1.

   b. The counter in a For loop cannot be decremented. It can only be incremented.

   c. The starting and ending loop values must be positive integer values.

   d. Decision-making statements cannot appear in the statement block enclosed by a For loop.

   e. none of the above

2. Given the following statements, what value is stored in the variable Iterations after the For loop has executed?

```
Dim Counter, Iterations As Integer
For Counter = 1 To 5 Step 2
    Iterations += 1
Next
```

3. Given the following For loop, which of the statements can be moved outside of the loop without the result of the value of the variables changing?

```
Dim Counter, Total, Index, Temp As Integer
For Counter = 1 To 1000
    Total += 1
    Index = 0
    Temp = 0
Next
```

# USING COLLECTIONS TO STORE REPEATING DATA ITEMS

The first part of this chapter discussed the use of loops to process numeric data repeatedly. However, the first section of this chapter did not illustrate how to store repeating data items, such as multiple payroll records. Furthermore, Chapters 6 and 7 discussed how a class instance stores data and how to create the processes that act on that data. However, storing and managing multiple class instances was not discussed. In this part of the chapter, you will learn how to store and manage repeating data items as a list, which Visual Basic refers to as a collection.

## GENERAL CHARACTERISTICS OF LISTS

Sometimes, multiple class instances must be stored together as a list. For example, instead of working with a single employee, customer, or supplier, you have to work with a list of employees, customers, or suppliers. In such a situation, each employee, customer, or supplier is a class instance. Multiple class instances can be stored and managed as a list. Visual Studio implements lists as collections. A **collection** contains references to one or more objects having the same data type or varying data types.

Some collections store references to objects having different data types. For example, the predefined `Controls` collection stores a reference to each of the control instances created on a form. However, the data types of those control instances will likely vary.

Other collections require that each class instance referenced by the collection have the same data type. For example, a collection could store a list of Employee class instances but no other data type would be allowed.

**»NOTE**

In this section, the terms list and collection are used frequently. When referring to storing class instances, the general term "list" is used. When referring to a specific type of list supported by the .NET Framework class library, the term "collection" is used.

## METHODS AND PROPERTIES OF COLLECTIONS

All collections (lists) have similar methods, such as adding an item (class instance) to the collection, changing the contents of a collection item, and removing an item from the collection. Thus, all collections support the following members:

» The `Add` method adds a new item to the end of a collection.

» The read-only `Count` property returns the number of items in a collection. The `Count` property is 1-based.

» The `Item` method references an item (class instance) in the collection. Thus, the `Item` method is used to both read an item from a collection or to replace a collection item. The `Item` method accepts an integer argument containing the index of an item stored in the collection. The `Item` method is 0-based, so the first item in a collection has an index value of 0.

» Calling the `RemoveAt` method removes an item from a collection. The `RemoveAt` method accepts one argument: the numeric index of the item to be removed from the collection. Using the `RemoveAt` method, the item to be removed is specified using a 0-based index value.

## CREATING A LIST

Visual Studio collections (lists) can be roughly categorized into three types:

» One category of collection can store items having different data types.

» A second category of collection requires that each item has the same data type. However, the collection can store items having any data type. This type of list is called a **generic list**.

» A third category of collection requires that each item has the same data type, which is always the same.

This part of the chapter discusses the generic List class. The generic List class stores references to objects having the same data type. However, each instance of the List class can store references to objects having a different data type. In this section, you will see how to manage a list of employees.

The examples in the following section store repeating instances of the Employee class in an instance of the List class:

```
Public Class Employee
    Public EmployeeID As Integer
    Public EmployeeName As String
End Class
```

The preceding class has two public fields named EmployeeID and EmployeeName. To create a list that can store references to other class instances (in this example, Employee), you create an instance of the generic List class as follows:

```
Private EmployeeList As New List(Of Employee)
```

The argument to the List constructor specifies the data type of the items that can be stored in the collection. In the preceding example, the data type of each collection item is Employee. The Of keyword is required, followed by the class name, which in the preceding statement is Employee. A syntax error occurs if an attempt is made to add items to the preceding List class instance having a data type other than Employee.

## ADDING ITEMS TO A COLLECTION

When an instance of the List class is first created, it is empty. That is, the collection contains no references to other objects. An object reference is added to an instance of the List class by calling the Add method. The Add method of the generic List class accepts one argument: the object to be added. The item (object) is added to the end of the collection.

The following code segment shows how to add two instances of the Employee class to an instance of the `List` class named EmployeeList:

```
Dim EmpCurrent As New Employee
EmpCurrent.EmployeeID = 18223
EmpCurrent.EmployeeName = "Joe Smith"
EmployeeList.Add(EmpCurrent)
EmpCurrent = New Employee
EmpCurrent.EmployeeID = 24428
EmpCurrent.EmployeeName = "Mary Deems"
EmployeeList.Add(EmpCurrent)
```

The first of the preceding statements creates an instance of the Employee class. The second and third statements store values in the two properties. The next statement adds the employee to the collection named EmployeeList. The final four statements create a second instance of the Employee class, set its properties, and add the newly created employee object to the collection.

Just as all classes are reference types (reference types store the memory address of another object), so too are the `List` and Employee classes. Figure 8-7 shows how the `List` class instance named EmployeeList stores references to separate instances of the Employee class.

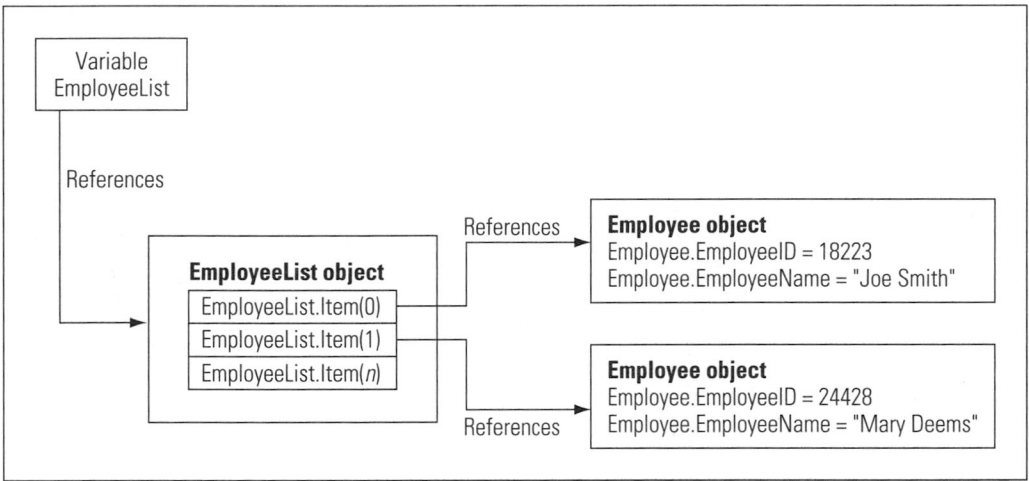

Figure 8-7: Memory allocation using the List class

The variable EmployeeList stores the 32-bit memory address of the `List` class instance, which, in turn, stores a reference to Employee class instances through the `Item` property.

An error is often made when working with collections. Most likely, each item in the collection should reference a different class instance. However, it's possible to erroneously create two list items that reference the same class instance, as the following statements show:

```
Dim EmpCurrent As New Employee
EmpCurrent.EmployeeID = 18223
EmpCurrent.EmployeeName = "Joe Smith"
EmployeeList.Add(EmpCurrent)
' EmpCurrent = New Employee
EmpCurrent.EmployeeID = 24428
EmpCurrent.EmployeeName = "Mary Deems"
EmployeeList.Add(EmpCurrent)
```

The statement to create the second instance of the Employee class has been commented, so only one instance of the Employee class exists. Thus, the four statements that set the object's properties are referencing the same Employee class instance through the variable named EmpCurrent. Furthermore, a reference to the same Employee class instance is added to the collection. Figure 8-8 illustrates this problem.

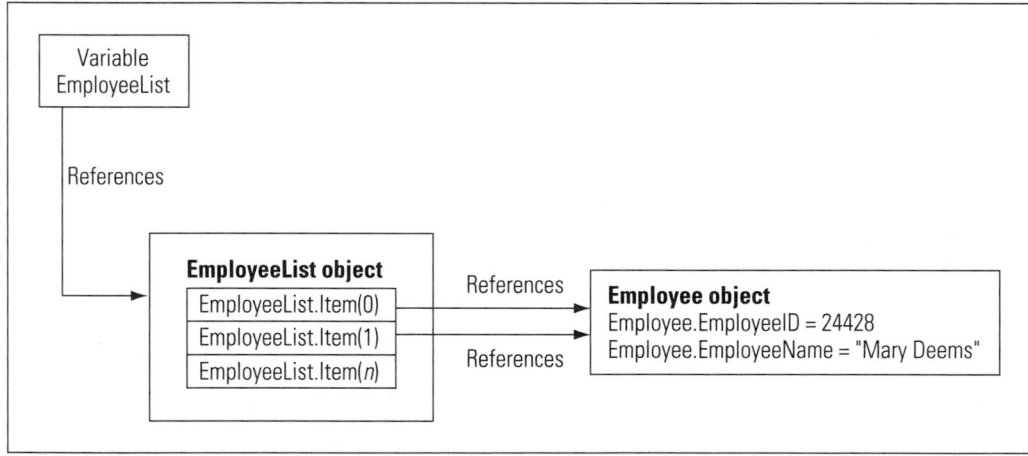

Figure 8-8: Incorrect list references

As shown in Figure 8-8, both collection elements reference the same instance of the Employee class.

Items stored in an instance of the List class must have the same data type. Again, the sample data type used in this example is the Employee class. Trying to store a reference to a data type other than an instance of the Employee class would cause a syntax error, as the following statements show:

```
Dim EmployeeList As New List(Of Employee)
Dim CustomerCurrent As New Customer
EmployeeList.Add(CustomerCurrent)
```

Assuming that EmployeeList is declared as a List of Employee, the third of the preceding statements has a syntax error because only items having a data type of Employee can be added to the List class instance.

## REFERENCING A LIST ITEM

The items in a collection can be read (referenced) after they have been added. To do so, the Item property is used. The Item property accepts one argument, the 0-based index value of the item to read, as shown in the following statements:

```
Dim EmpCurrent As Employee
EmpCurrent = EmployeeList.Item(0)
Debug.WriteLine(EmpCurrent.EmployeeID.ToString)     ' 18223
Debug.WriteLine(EmpCurrent.EmployeeName)            ' "Joe Smith"
EmpCurrent = EmployeeList.Item(1)
Debug.WriteLine(EmpCurrent.EmployeeID.ToString)     ' 24428
Debug.WriteLine(EmpCurrent.EmployeeName)            ' "Mary Deems"
```

The first of the preceding statements declares a variable named EmpCurrent, which is used to reference the employee retrieved from the list. The second statement references the first item in the list named EmployeeList and stores that reference in the variable named EmpCurrent. The property values are then printed to the Immediate window. The final three statements reference the second list item (employee) and print its property's values to the Immediate window.

The following statement attempts to reference the third item in a two-item list named EmployeeList:

```
EmpCurrent = EmployeeList.Item(2)
```

The preceding statement throws an `ArgumentOutOfRangeException` because the element having an index value of 2 does not exist. In cases in which this type of exception might be thrown, the statements that might cause the exception should be enclosed in an appropriate exception handler, as the following code segment shows:

```
Dim EmpCurrent As Employee
Try
    EmpCurrent = EmployeeList.Item(2)
Catch ex As System.ArgumentOutOfRangeException
    MessageBox.Show("Employee not found.")
End Try
```

The `Item` property is the default property of the `List` class, so explicitly specifying the property name is optional. Thus, the following two assignment statements are equivalent:

```
Dim EmpCurrent As Employee
EmpCurrent = EmployeeList.Item(0)
EmpCurrent = EmployeeList(0)
```

## UPDATING A COLLECTION ITEM

Conceptually, you can update an item in a collection in two ways. First, it is possible to replace the data stored in an existing item (class instance). Second, it is possible to replace the item entirely, thereby replacing one class instance with another. The following statements store new data for the first employee item (class instance) in the list named EmployeeList:

```
Dim EmpCurrent As Employee
EmpCurrent = EmployeeList.Item(0)
EmpCurrent.EmployeeID = 99999
EmpCurrent.EmployeeName = "Amy Stein"
```

In the preceding statements, the first assignment statement causes the variable named EmpCurrent to reference the first employee in the list. The third and fourth statements store values in the EmployeeID and EmployeeName properties, respectively, in the same instance of the Employee class. Figure 8-9 shows the operation of these statements.

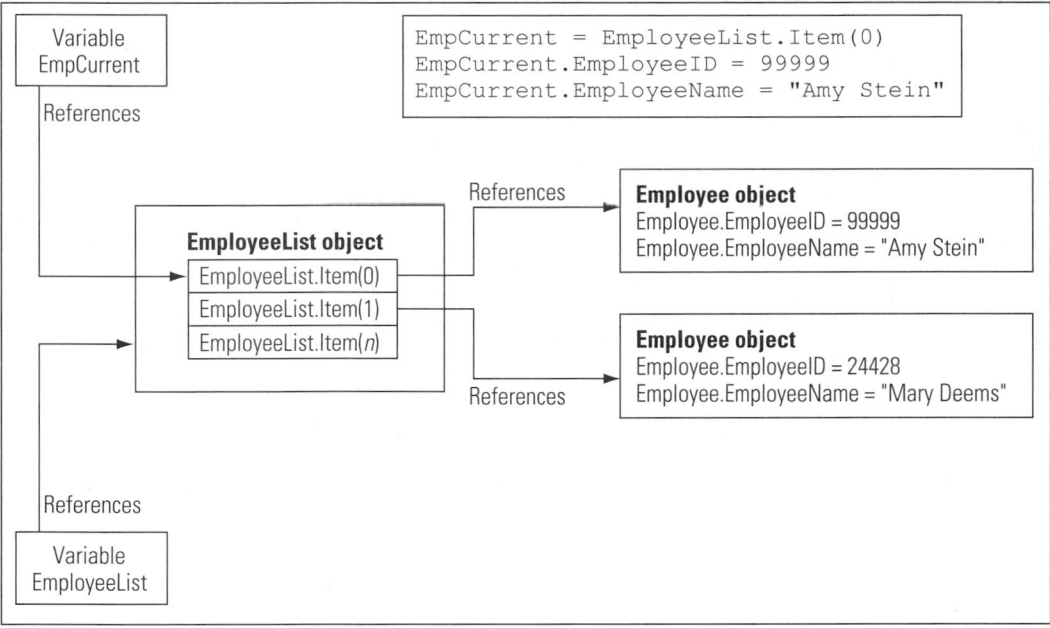

Figure 8-9: Updating list items

Instead of changing the data in an existing list item (class instance), it is also possible to update the `Item` property so that it references a different object, thereby deleting the reference to the original object and replacing it with a reference to another object, as the following statements show:

```
Dim EmpCurrent As New Employee
EmpCurrent.EmployeeID = 99999
EmpCurrent.EmployeeName = "Amy Stein"
EmployeeList.Item(0) = EmpCurrent
```

In the preceding statements, a new instance of the Employee class is created and its properties set. The final statement causes the first list item to reference the new instance of the Employee class. The reference to the old class instance is destroyed, thereby returning the object's memory back to the system. Figure 8-10 shows the process of replacing list items.

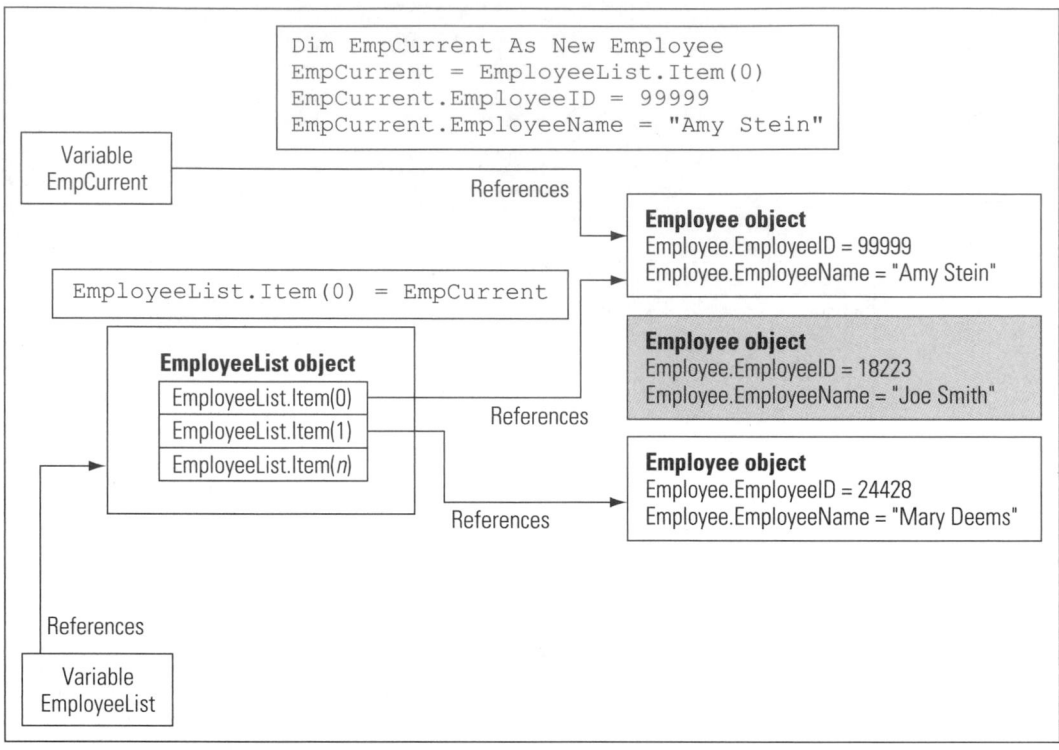

Figure 8-10: Replacing list items

## DELETING A COLLECTION ITEM

The RemoveAt method removes an item from a collection by referencing that item's index value. Thus, the RemoveAt method works similarly to referencing an item using the Item property. The RemoveAt method accepts one argument, the index of the item to remove from the collection. If no item in the collection having the specified index value exists, an ArgumentOutOfRangeException is thrown. The following code segment shows how to call the RemoveAt method:

```
Try
    EmployeeList.RemoveAt(0)
Catch ex As ArgumentOutOfRangeException
    MessageBox.Show("Employee not found.")
End Try
```

The preceding statements attempt to remove the first item from the list named EmployeeList. If no employee having that index value exists, an exception is thrown and handled. That is, an exception is thrown if the list is empty.

## DETERMINING THE SIZE AND CAPACITY OF A COLLECTION

As items are added to and removed from a collection, the Count and Capacity properties are updated.

The Count property returns the number of items contained in the collection. The Count property is incremented and decremented when the Add and RemoveAt methods are called. The property is 1-based, so an empty list has a Count of 0. The Count property is useful to examine the items in a collection with a For loop.

The Capacity property returns the number of items that the collection can contain. The value of the Capacity property is always greater than or equal to the value of the Count property. To improve the performance of the List class, items are not created one at a time. Rather, when an instance of the List class is created, the Capacity property is initially set to 4. That is, memory is allocated to store four collection items even though those items have not been added yet. When the fourth item is added to the collection, the Capacity property and the Count property will have the same value (4). When the fifth item is added to the collection, the Capacity doubles so the value of the Capacity property will be 8. When the ninth element is added, the value of the Capacity property doubles again to 16. Thus, when adding items to a collection, the Capacity always doubles when the value of the Count property would exceed the value of the Capacity property.

## ENUMERATING A COLLECTION WITH A FOR LOOP

The first section of this chapter showed how to use loops to process data repeatedly. Loops are also used to examine each item in a collection. For example, a loop might be used to examine each item in the preceding collection of employees so as to print an employee roster. Because the size of a collection is known in advance, a For loop can be used instead of a Do loop. The following code segment shows how to iterate through all of the items in a collection named EmployeeList using a For loop:

```
Dim Index As Integer
Dim EmpCurrent As Employee
For Index = 0 To EmployeeList.Count - 1
    EmpCurrent = EmployeeList(Index)
    Debug.WriteLine(EmpCurrent.EmployeeID.ToString)
    Debug.WriteLine(EmpCurrent.EmployeeName)
Next
```

The preceding For loop examines all of the items in the generic list named EmployeeList. The index value is initialized to 0 and the For loop iterates to the ending value of `EmployeeList.Count - 1`. The statement in the loop returns a reference to the current employee, and prints the value of the EmployeeID and EmployeeName properties to the Immediate window.

Suppose that the following `For` loop were written to examine the collection of employees:

```
Dim Index As Integer
Dim EmpCurrent As Employee
For Index = 0 To EmployeeList.Count
    EmpCurrent = EmployeeList(Index)
    ' Statements to reference the current employee.
Next
```

The preceding loop would throw an `ArgumentOutOfRangeException`. Because the `Count` property is 1-based, the loop tries to examine an item that is one item beyond the end of the collection.

## ENUMERATING A COLLECTION WITH A FOR EACH LOOP

All collections share a common characteristic—they can be enumerated using a form of a `For` loop called a `For Each` loop, which has the following syntax:

### Syntax

```
For Each object In group
    [statements]
    [Exit For]
    [statements]
Next
statements
```

### Definition

The `For Each` loop executes the statements appearing between the `For Each` and `Next` keywords, returning an *object* from the *group* each time the loop is evaluated.

### Dissection

» *object* contains a variable (object reference). Each time through the loop, *object* contains an item from the collection (*group*).

» *group* contains the collection to be enumerated.

» The meanings of the `Exit For` and `Next` keywords are the same for both `For` loops and `For Each` loops.

*(Continued)* ▶

**Code Example**
```
Dim EmpCurrent As Employee
For Each EmpCurrent In EmployeeList
    Debug.WriteLine(EmpCurrent.EmployeeID.ToString)
    Debug.WriteLine(EmpCurrent.EmployeeName)
Next
```

**Code Dissection**

Instead of using a numeric index value to examine each item in a collection, the `For Each` loop returns an object from the collection each time through the loop. Each time through the loop, an object from the generic `List` named EmployeeList is stored in the variable named EmpCurrent. The statements inside of the loop print the value of the EmployeeID and EmployeeName properties.

## INTRODUCTION TO PREDEFINED COLLECTIONS

Visual Studio supports predefined collections in addition to those collections that you create. One such collection is the `Controls` collection. Since the first chapters of this book, you have created control instances on a form and referenced those control instances via their `Name` property. However, there might be circumstances when it is necessary to reference all of the control instances on a form or only those control instances having a particular data type. For these situations, the `Controls` collection is useful.

The following code segment shows how to enumerate, or examine, the `Controls` collection of the `Form` class:

```
Dim CurrentControl As Control
For Each CurrentControl In Me.Controls
    ' Statements to reference the current control.
Next
```

The preceding code segment declares a variable of type `Control`, which is used to reference each control instance in the `Controls` collection. Remember that the `Me` keyword references the current instance of a class, which in this case is a form. Thus, `Me.Controls` references the current instance of the underlying `Form` class. Each time through the loop, the variable CurrentControl references the current control instance.

Suppose that you wanted to write a loop that would perform an action on all of the `TextBox` control instances created on a form. The previous code segment would reference all of the control instances created on the form including the text boxes, but there still needs to be a way to identify which of those control instances has a data type of

TextBox. To determine the underlying data type of an object, Visual Basic supports the TypeOf operator, which has the following syntax:

## Syntax

```
result = TypeOf objectExpression Is typeName
```

## Definition

The TypeOf operator compares a reference type variable with a data type to determine if their data types are the same. If the *objectExpression* has the same data type as the *typeName*, the TypeOf operator returns True. If the data types differ, the TypeOf operator returns False.

## Dissection

» *result* contains the Boolean result of comparing an object's type with a particular data type.

» *objectExpression* contains an instance of a reference type.

» *typeName* contains a data type.

## Code Example

```
Dim CurrentControl As Control
For Each CurrentControl In Me.Controls
    If TypeOf CurrentControl Is TextBox Then
        ' Statements to work with the current TextBox
        ' control instance.
    End If
Next
```

## Code Dissection

The preceding statements enumerate the Controls collection of the current form. An If statement is used with the TypeOf operator to determine whether the control instance has a data type of TextBox. If it does, the condition in the If statement returns True. Otherwise, the condition is False.

In this exploration exercise, you will see how to add, change, and delete items from a list and how to enumerate the items in a list with a For loop and a For Each loop.

1. Run the concept lesson for the chapter and click the **List** tab. Figure 8-11 shows the List tab. The List tab contains buttons to add, change, and delete list items, along with buttons to enumerate the list items. Refer to the commented code for additional information.

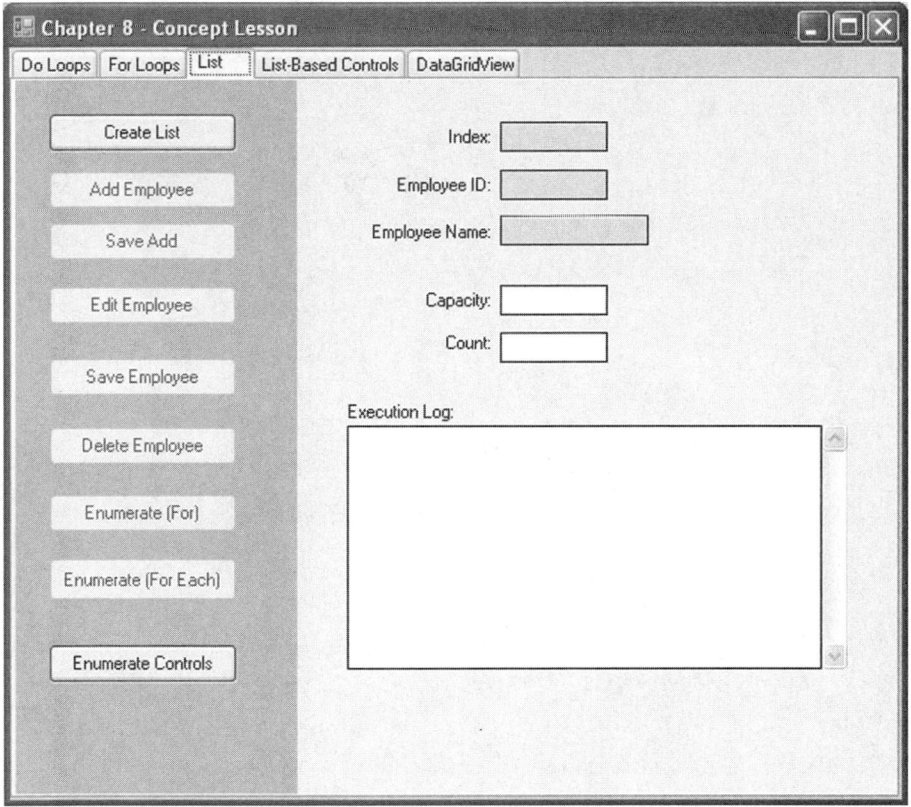

Figure 8-11: Concept lesson—List tab

2. Click the **Create List** button. The applicable buttons on the form are enabled.

3. Click the **Add Employee** button. The text boxes are enabled. Enter an Employee ID of **12345** and an Employee Name of **Joe Smith**. Click the **Save Add** button. The employee is added to the list and the Capacity and Count fields are updated.

4. Add a second employee having an Employee ID number of **23456** and an Employee Name of **Mary Deems**. Click the **Save Add** button again.

5. Click the **Edit Employee** button. Enter a value of **0** in the Respond dialog box to select the first employee from the list, and then click **OK**. Change the employee's name to **Marty Smith** and click the **Save Employee** button.

6. Click the **Delete Employee** button. Enter the value **0** in the input box to delete the first employee from the list, and then click **OK**.

7. Click the **Enumerate (For)** and **Enumerate (For Each)** buttons to enumerate the list and display the list items in the multiline text box.

8. Click the **Enumerate Controls** button. The control instances appearing on the current tab page are enumerated.

# MINI-QUIZ 3

1. Which of the following statements correctly creates an instance of the `List` class such that each element in the list will have a data type of Client?

   a. `Dim ClientList As New List Of Client`

   b. `Dim ClientList As New Client List`

   c. `Dim ClientList As New List(Of Client)`

   d. `Dim ClientList As New List()`

   e. none of the above

2. Assuming that PersonList is a list of Person, and that the Person class has a Name property, describe the error in the following statements:

   ```
   For Current = 1 To PersonList.Count - 1
       Debug.WriteLine(PersonList(Current).Name)
   Next
   ```

   a. The statement in the loop will cause a syntax error because the `Item` property is not specified.

   b. The collection is 0-based so the `For` loop should start at zero instead of one. The statements as currently written will not enumerate the first Person in the list.

   c. `For Each` loops must be used to enumerate a collection. `For` loops cannot be used to enumerate a collection.

   d. The preceding loop will operate correctly enumerating all elements in the list.

3. Write the statement(s) to remove the last item from the collection named Customers.

# INTRODUCTION TO CONTROLS INVOLVING LOOPS

The `ComboBox` and `ListBox` controls display lists of data. The `ComboBox` control displays a drop-down list when the end user clicks the list arrow so the visible region expands to display the drop-down list. The `ListBox` control does not display a drop-down list so the visible region has a fixed size. These two controls work similarly because they are both derived from the `System.Windows.Forms.ListControl` class.

Figure 8-12 shows the placement of the ComboBox and ListBox controls within the
.NET Framework inheritance hierarchy.

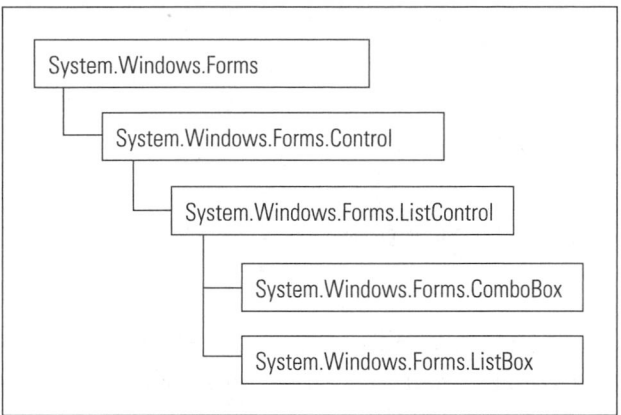

Figure 8-12: Hierarchical organization of the ListBox and ComboBox controls

The ListControl class supports the following members:

## Syntax
```
System.Windows.Forms.ListControl class
```

## Definition
» The ListControl class is the base class from which the ListBox and ComboBox controls derive.

## Public Properties
» The Items property is a collection containing a reference to the items stored in the control instance. The Items property can be set at design time using the Properties window, or at run time with code. Like all collections, the Items property supports methods to add and remove list items.

» Every list item referenced by an instance of the ListControl class has an associated 0-based index value stored in the SelectedIndex property and is used to identify the index of the currently selected item. Thus, if the end user selects the first item in the control instance, the SelectedIndex property has a value of 0. If no item is selected, the SelectedIndex property has a value of -1. Setting the value of this property programmatically also selects an

*(Continued)* ▶

item. Attempting to set the `SelectedIndex` property to an index value that does not exist causes an exception to be thrown.

» The `SelectedItem` property works in conjunction with the `SelectedIndex` property. Instead of returning the 0-based index of the item, the property returns a reference to the selected item itself. Each item in the collection has a data type of `System.Object`.

## Public Methods

» The `ClearSelection` method deselects all selected items.

## Public Events

» Windows fires the `SelectedIndexChanged` event when the end user selects an item from the list.

Having discussed the general members applicable to the `ListControl` class, you will examine the specific members of the `ComboBox` and `ListBox` controls in the following sections.

## INTRODUCTION TO THE COMBOBOX CONTROL

The `ComboBox` control displays a list of items when the list button is clicked. The `ComboBox` control supports the following members:

## Syntax

`System.Windows.Forms.ComboBox class`

## Definition

» A `ComboBox` control displays a list of items from which the end user selects one item. The `ComboBox` control typically displays a drop-down list of items when clicked.

## Public Properties

» Combo boxes appear in one of three styles defined by the `DropDownStyle` property.

» Setting the `DropDownStyle` property to `DropDown` allows the end user to select an item from a drop-down list of suggested items or to type in a new item. No items appear until the end user clicks the list arrow at the right of the combo box.

» Setting the `DropDownStyle` property to `Simple` displays a text box and a list that does not drop down. Instead, the list shows all choices at all times, causing the `ComboBox` to resemble a `ListBox`. If the list items will not fit inside the visible region of the combo box, a vertical scroll bar appears. The end user can also type in a new value not appearing in the list of suggested choices.

» Setting the `DropDownStyle` property to `DropDownList` allows a user only to select an item from a preset drop-down list of choices. As with the drop-down combo box, this list does not appear until the end user clicks the list arrow at the right of the combo box.

## INTRODUCTION TO THE LISTBOX CONTROL

The ListBox control is nearly identical to the ComboBox control. However, unlike the ComboBox control, the ListBox control does not drop-down, and the end user cannot type a value into the ListBox. The ListBox control has the following members:

### Syntax
System.Windows.Forms.ListBox class

### Definition
» A ListBox control displays items in the same way as the ComboBox control. However, the visible region of the ListBox control is fixed and does not drop down.

### Public Properties
» The SelectedItems property returns a collection of the items currently selected in the control instance.

» The SelectionMode property defines how the end user selects one or more items from an instance of the ListBox control.

### Public Methods
» The ClearSelected method clears all of the selected items.

» The GetSelected method accepts one argument, the integer index of a list box item. The method returns True if the item is selected and False otherwise.

» The SetSelected method accepts two arguments: The first argument contains the integer index of a list box item, and the second argument contains a Boolean value denoting whether the item should be selected.

## WORKING WITH A COMBOBOX OR LISTBOX

When working with the ListBox and ComboBox controls, a few operations are commonly performed, as described in the following list:

> » Items must be added to the list either at design time or at run time.

> » When the end user selects an item from the control instance, some conditional action must be performed based on the item selected.

> » At times, an item must be selected programmatically.

Each of the preceding tasks are discussed in the following sections.

### ADDING ITEMS TO A COMBOBOX OR LISTBOX

Items can be added to an instance of the ListBox or ComboBox control at design time using the Properties window, or programmatically at run time. To add items at design time, select the Items property in the Properties window, and then click the Build button to activate the String Collection Editor, as shown in Figure 8-13.

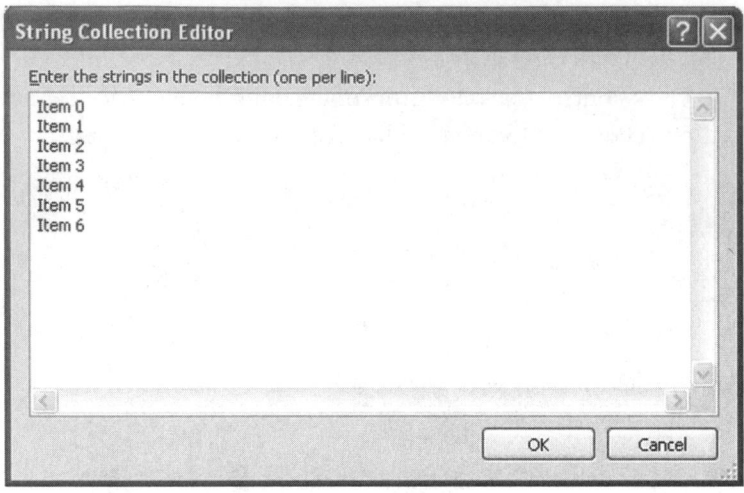

Figure 8-13: String Collection Editor dialog box

In the String Collection Editor, you enter each list item on one line, and then click the OK button to record any changes.

The process to add items programmatically at run time is the same as the process to add items to any collection. That is, the Add method is called as the following code segment shows:

```
For Count = 1 To 20
    lstDemo.Items.Add("Item " & Count.ToString)
Next
```

The preceding statements use a For loop to add 20 items to the list box named lstDemo having the values "Item 1", "Item 2", "Item 3", and so on.

## WORKING WITH THE SELECTED ITEM

When the end user selects an item in a ListBox or ComboBox control instance, the SelectedIndexChanged event fires. When this event fires, there are two properties of interest:

» The SelectedItem property, which references the object or other data referenced by the current item

» The SelectedIndex property, which returns the 0-based index of the currently selected item

The following code segment shows a sample `SelectedIndexChanged` event handler for a `ComboBox` control instance named cboSingleSelect:

```
Private Sub cboSingleSelect_SelectedIndexChanged( _
    ByVal sender As System.Object, _
    ByVal e As System.EventArgs) _
    Handles cboSingleSelect.SelectedIndexChanged

    lblSelectedComboBoxItem.Text = _
        cboSingleSelect.SelectedItem.ToString
    lblSelectedComboBoxIndex.Text = _
        cboSingleSelect.SelectedIndex.ToString
End Sub
```

The preceding event handler fires whenever the end user selects an item from the combo box. The statements in the event handler store the `SelectedItem` and `SelectedIndex` properties in corresponding `Label` control instances. Both values are converted to a string.

## SELECTING AN ITEM PROGRAMMATICALLY

By default, when an application runs and a form initializes, `ComboBox` and `ListBox` control instances have no selected item. It's possible to select an item by setting the `SelectedIndex` property to the index value of the item to select.

The following code segment shows how to select the first item in the `ComboBox` control instance named cboSingleSelect:

```
cboSingleSelect.SelectedIndex = 0
```

When an item is not selected from the list, the `SelectedIndex` property has a value of –1. The following statement shows how to deselect the current item:

```
cboSingleSelect.SelectedIndex = -1
```

In this exploration exercise, you will see how to work with the `ListBox` and `ComboBox` controls.

1. Run the concept lesson for the chapter and click the **List-Based Controls** tab. Figure 8-14 shows the List-Based Controls tab with some fields already populated.

**» TIP**

In cases where a particular list item is selected most frequently, set the value of the `SelectedIndex` property programmatically when the form loads or otherwise, as necessary.

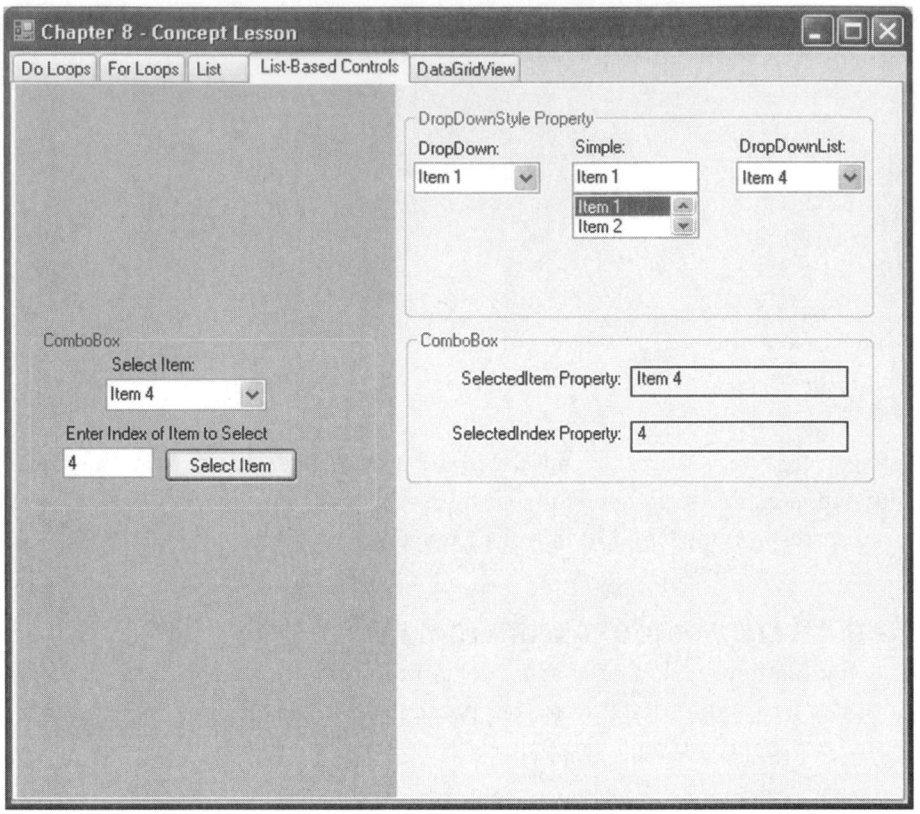

Figure 8-14: Concept lesson—List-Based Controls tab

2. In the DropDownStyle Property section, click the three combo boxes to see how each one works and how each one is affected by the `DropDownStyle` property.

3. In the ComboBox section on the left side of the form, select an item from the `ComboBox` control instance. The code in the `SelectedIndexChanged` event handler fires and updates the contents of the corresponding output labels on the right side of the form.

4. In the text box in the blue section of the form, enter an integer value and click the **Select Item** button. The button's `Click` event handler fires and sets the `SelectedIndex` property based on the text box input. This action causes the `SelectedIndexChanged` event for the combo box to fire causing the output labels to be updated. An exception is thrown if an item does not exist having the corresponding index value.

## MINI-QUIZ 4

1. Which of the following statements is correct regarding list boxes and combo boxes?

   a. The end user can enter text into the ListBox control at run time so as to create a new item.

   b. It is possible to select multiple items using a ComboBox control. It is not possible to select multiple items using a ListBox control.

   c. The items in a ListBox or ComboBox control instance can be enumerated with either a For loop or a For Each loop.

   d. The two controls derive from the List class.

   e. none of the above

2. Referring to a ComboBox or ListBox control, what is the value of the SelectedIndex property when a list item is not selected?

3. Write the statements to add the letters "A" through "Z" to the list box named lstQuiz. *Hint*: Use the Chr method and a For loop.

# INTRODUCTION TO THE DATAGRIDVIEW CONTROL

In the preceding section, loops were used to process the lists contained in instances of the ComboBox and ListBox controls. Loops can also be used to process tabular data stored in an instance of the DataGridView control. Figure 8-15 shows a sample DataGridView control instance displaying the multiplication table discussed in the section titled "Nested Do Loops."

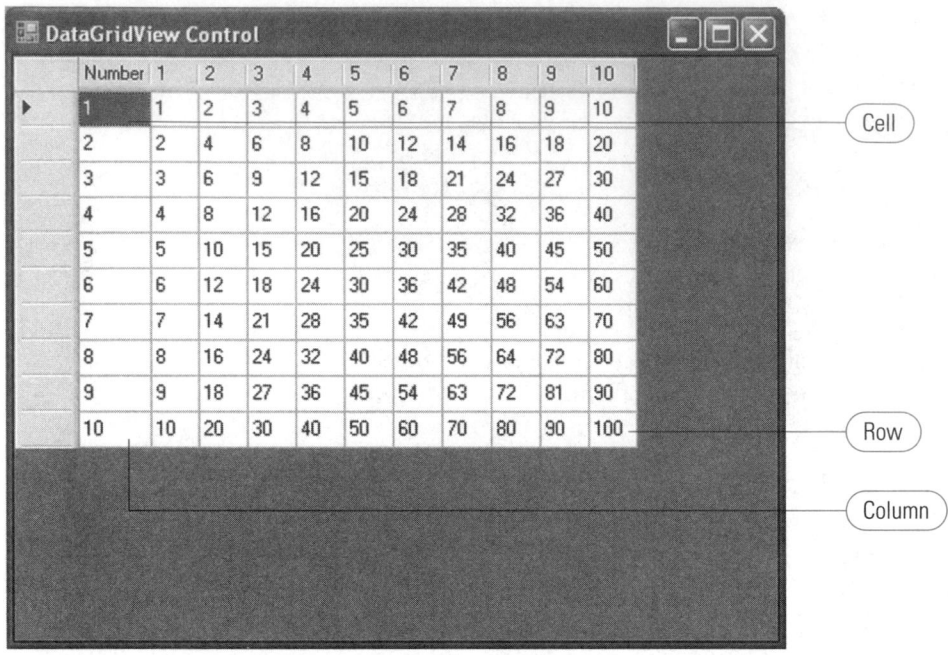

Figure 8-15: DataGridView control instance displaying a multiplication table

The `DataGridView` control displays data as a two-dimensional grid containing rows and columns, as shown in Figure 8-15. The intersection of a row and column is called a *cell*.

The `DataGridView` control operates in one of two modes, as described in the following list:

» The control instance can get its data from an underlying data source, such as a database. In this case, the control is said to be *bound* to a data source.

» It is also possible to programmatically add rows and columns to the grid, and to store and retrieve data from the individual cells. In this case, the `DataGridView` control is said to operate in an *unbound mode*. Use of the `DataGridView` in unbound mode is discussed in this chapter.

## WORKING WITH A DATAGRIDVIEW CONTROL

By default, the grid in a `DataGridView` control instance is empty when it is first created. That is, the control instance contains zero rows and zero columns. There are four steps to populating and removing items from the grid, as described in the following list:

» First, the columns are added to the grid.

» Second, the rows are added to the grid. In unbound mode, the columns must be added to the grid before the rows are added or an exception is thrown.

» Third, the cells need to be referenced and populated. Cells can be populated for each row as it is added or all of the cells can be populated at once after all the rows have been added.

» Finally, it's also possible to delete existing rows from the grid.

Each of these steps are discussed in the following sections.

## ADDING COLUMNS TO THE DATAGRIDVIEW

The `DataGridView` control supports a property named `Columns`, which is a collection. Each object in the collection represents one column in the grid. Thus, the `Columns` collection stores repeating data items.

To add columns to the `DataGridView` control, the `Add` method of the `Columns` collection is called. The `Add` method accepts two arguments. The first argument contains a string used to reference a particular column. The topic of referencing rows and columns is discussed in a moment. The second argument contains the text that will appear in the column header.

To illustrate how to add a column to the `DataGridView` control instance named dgvDemo, examine the following code segment:

```
dgvDemo.Columns.Add("Column1", "Visible Text")
```

The preceding statement adds a column to the `DataGridView` control instance named dgvDemo. The first argument to the `Add` method contains the string used to later reference the column. The second argument, "Visible Text", contains the text string that will appear in the column header. Columns are added sequentially. That is, each column that is added appears as the last column.

Examine the following statements, which call the `Add` method to add three columns:

```
dgvDemo.Columns.Add("Column1", "Header 1")
dgvDemo.Columns.Add("Column2", "Header 2")
dgvDemo.Columns.Add("Column3", "Header 3")
```

After columns have been added to the `DataGridView` control, the rows can be added.

## ADDING ROWS TO THE DATAGRIDVIEW

Adding rows to a `DataGridView` control instance is not that much different than adding columns. Just as the `DataGridView` control has a `Columns` collection, it has a `Rows` collection. Calling the `Add` method of the `Rows` collection creates a new row and adds it as the last row of the control instance. Without arguments, the `Add` method adds a single row, as shown in the following statement:

```
dgvDemo.Rows.Add()
```

To add multiple rows to the DataGridView, the Add method is called with an Integer argument containing the number of rows to add. Thus, the following statement adds 20 rows to the control instance at the end of the list.

```
dgvDemo.Rows.Add(20)
```

## REFERENCING AND POPULATING INDIVIDUAL GRID CELLS

When working with the DataGridView control, individual cells must be referenced so as to store data in a cell or to read data from a cell. Remember that a cell is the intersection of a row and column. To reference a cell, the Rows and Cells collections are used together, as the following statements show:

```
Dim CurrentCell As DataGridViewCell
CurrentCell = dgvDemo.Rows(0).Cells(0)
```

The preceding statements require some careful analysis. First, every row and column are referenced by a 0-based numeric index. Thus, the statement fragment dgvDemo.Rows(0) references the first row in the control instance. The second part of the statement Cells(0) references the first column (cell) in the row. Thus, the statement dgvDemo.Rows(0).Cells(0) references the cell corresponding to the first row and the first column.

Each cell in the DataGridView has a data type of DataGridViewCell. Thus, the preceding statements reference the first cell in the first row and return a reference to that cell. Having a reference to a particular cell, it is easy to store a value in the cell or to retrieve a value, as the following statements show:

```
CurrentCell.Value = 42
txtDemo.Text = CurrentCell.Value.ToString
```

The Value property of the DataGridViewCell class stores the value of the cell. The first of the preceding statements stores the value 42 in the current cell. The second statement reads the value from the current cell and stores that value in the text box named txtDemo.

**»NOTE**

In the statement to the right there exists a hierarchical relationship between the two collections. That is, a row in the Rows collection references another collection named Cells.

## DELETING ROWS FROM THE DATAGRIDVIEW

Deleting a row from the `DataGridView` is simple. Remember that the `RemoveAt` method removes an item from a collection. Because the `Rows` property is a collection, the following statement removes the first row from the `DataGridView` control instance named dgvDemo:

```
dgvDemo.Rows.RemoveAt(0)
```

## USING LOOPS TO EXAMINE THE CELLS IN A DATAGRIDVIEW CONTROL INSTANCE

Loops are commonly used to examine the rows in a particular column, or to examine all of the cells in the grid. The following code segment shows how to use an accumulator to tally the values of the first column for all of the rows appearing in the `DataGridView` control instance named dgvDemo:

```
Dim Total As Double = 0
Dim CurrentRow As Integer
For CurrentRow = 0 To dgvDemo.Rows.Count - 1
    Total += dgvDemo.Rows(CurrentRow).Cells(0).Value
Next
```

The preceding code segment looks similar to other loops that examine the items in a collection. The `For` loop examines each row in the collection. The statement in the loop references the first cell in the current row. The value of that cell is added to the accumulator variable named Total.

In this exploration exercise, you will examine how to add and remove rows from a `DataGridView` control and see how to use loops with the `DataGridView`.

1. Run the concept lesson for the chapter and click the **DataGridView** tab.

2. Click the **Add Columns** button. Three columns are added to the control instance.

3. Click the **Add Rows** button. The default value of 5 is read from the corresponding text box and five additional rows are added to the control instance.

4. Click the **Delete Row** button. Again, the default value 0 is read from the corresponding text box and the first row is removed from the control instance.

5. Click the **Multiplication Table** button. A nested For loop executes to create the multiplication table discussed previously in the chapter. Your screen should resemble Figure 8-16. Refer to the commented procedure for a detailed discussion of the code.

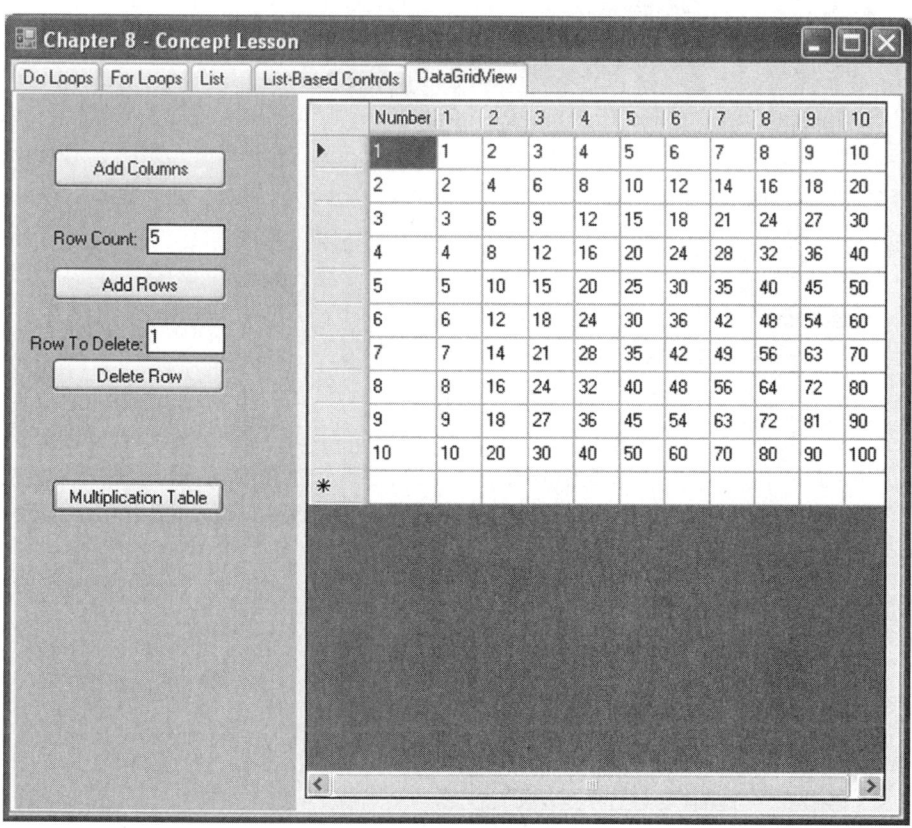

Figure 8-16: Concept lesson—DataGridView tab

## MINI-QUIZ 5

1. Describe the error that will occur when the following statements execute to add rows and columns to an instance of the DataGridView control.

```
dgvQuiz.Rows.Add(10)
dgvQuiz.Columns.Add("Name", "Title")
```

2. Which of the following statements references the cell occupying the second row and second column in the DataGridView control instance named dgvQuiz?

   a. CurrentCell = dgvQuiz.Rows(2).Cells(2)
   b. CurrentCell = dgvQuiz.Rows(1).Cells(1)
   c. CurrentCell = dgvQuiz.Cells(1, 1)
   d. CurrentCell = dgvQuiz.Cells(2, 2)
   e. CurrentCell = dgvQuiz.Columns(1).Rows(1)

3. Write a nested For loop to examine all of the cells in the DataGridView control instance named dgvQuiz. Using an accumulator named Total, tally the values of all the cells.

# APPLICATION LESSON

This application lesson contains instructions to display the future value of an investment in a DataGridView control instance, based on varying interest rates and varying recurring deposit amounts. Loops are used to change the interest rate and deposit amounts and to calculate the output for different scenarios.

## APPLICATION LESSON—USER INTERFACE

The application's user interface is made up of text boxes and combo boxes in which the end user enters the following input values:

» The end user specifies the minimum and maximum interest rates. A what-if analysis will be performed varying the interest rate between these two values. The end user will also specify the incremental interest rate.

» The monthly recurring investment amounts will work the same way. The end user will specify the minimum and maximum monthly investment amount. The end user will also specify the incremental investment amount.

» The initial investment amount is an input value.

» The investment term is an input value.

The combo boxes supply an alternative means for the end user to specify selected input values. When the end user selects an item in one of the combo boxes, the corresponding text box is updated.

The application's processing is all performed with four buttons.

» The Clear button clears the input and output values.

» The Calculate button performs the what-if analysis, thereby populating the DataGridView control instance.

» The Reset button resets the input values to their default values and clears the DataGridView control instance.

» The Exit button exits the application.

All of the output appears in an instance of the DataGridView control. Each cell contains the future value of the investment based on the interest rate and deposit amount. Figure 8-17 shows the completed user interface for the application.

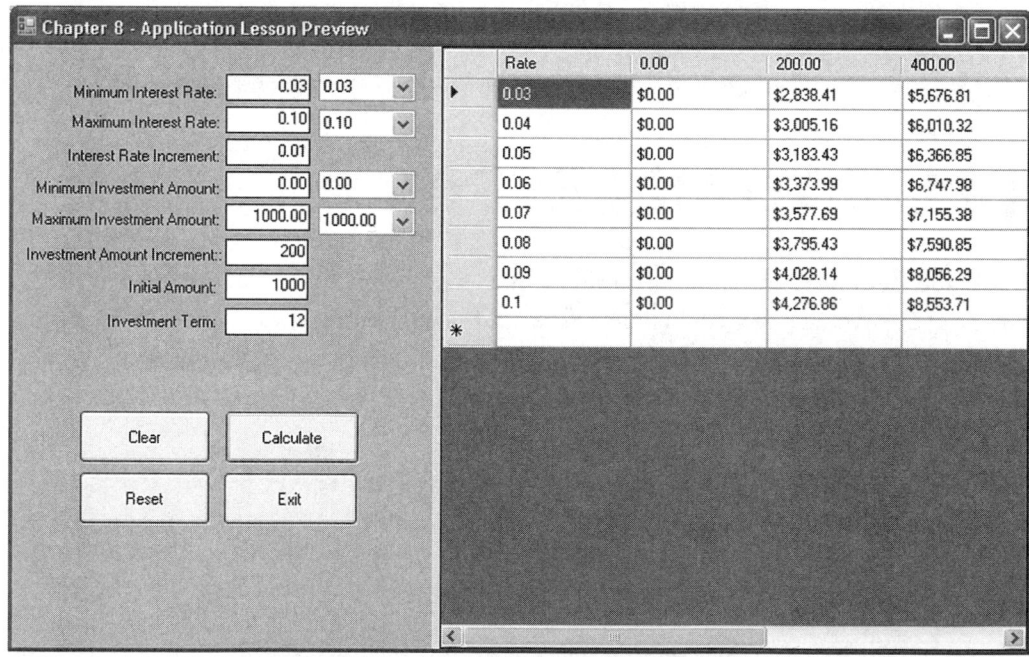

Figure 8-17: Application lesson—user interface

## APPLICATION LESSON—DESIGN

Initialization tasks are performed in the form's Load event handler. Here, the combo boxes are initialized based on hidden data stored in constants. The combo boxes are initialized such that the list contains items ranging from the minimum interest rate to the maximum interest rate varied by the incremental interest rate. The combo boxes displaying the investment amounts work the same way. A default item is selected for each combo box.

A SelectedIndexChanged event handler exists for each of the combo boxes. Each event handler works the same way. The event handler updates the contents of the corresponding text box so that the value is the same as the currently selected combo box text.

Nearly all of the processing takes place when the Calculate button is clicked. First, the input is validated by calling a Function procedure named ValidateInput. The procedure verifies that each text box contains a positive integer value. If the input is valid, the what-if analysis is performed. The following list summarizes the steps used to perform the what-if analysis that ultimately populates the DataGridView control instance:

- » First, the control instance is cleared.

- » Second, the input values are converted to numeric values.

- » Third, a loop is used to add the columns. The column headers contain the incremental investment amounts.

- » Finally, a second loop is used to add the rows. The first row contains the interest rate applicable to the row. The following rows contain the future value of the investment based on the current interest rate and the amount of the recurring deposit.

Figure 8-18 shows the flowchart for the actions performed by the Calculate button.

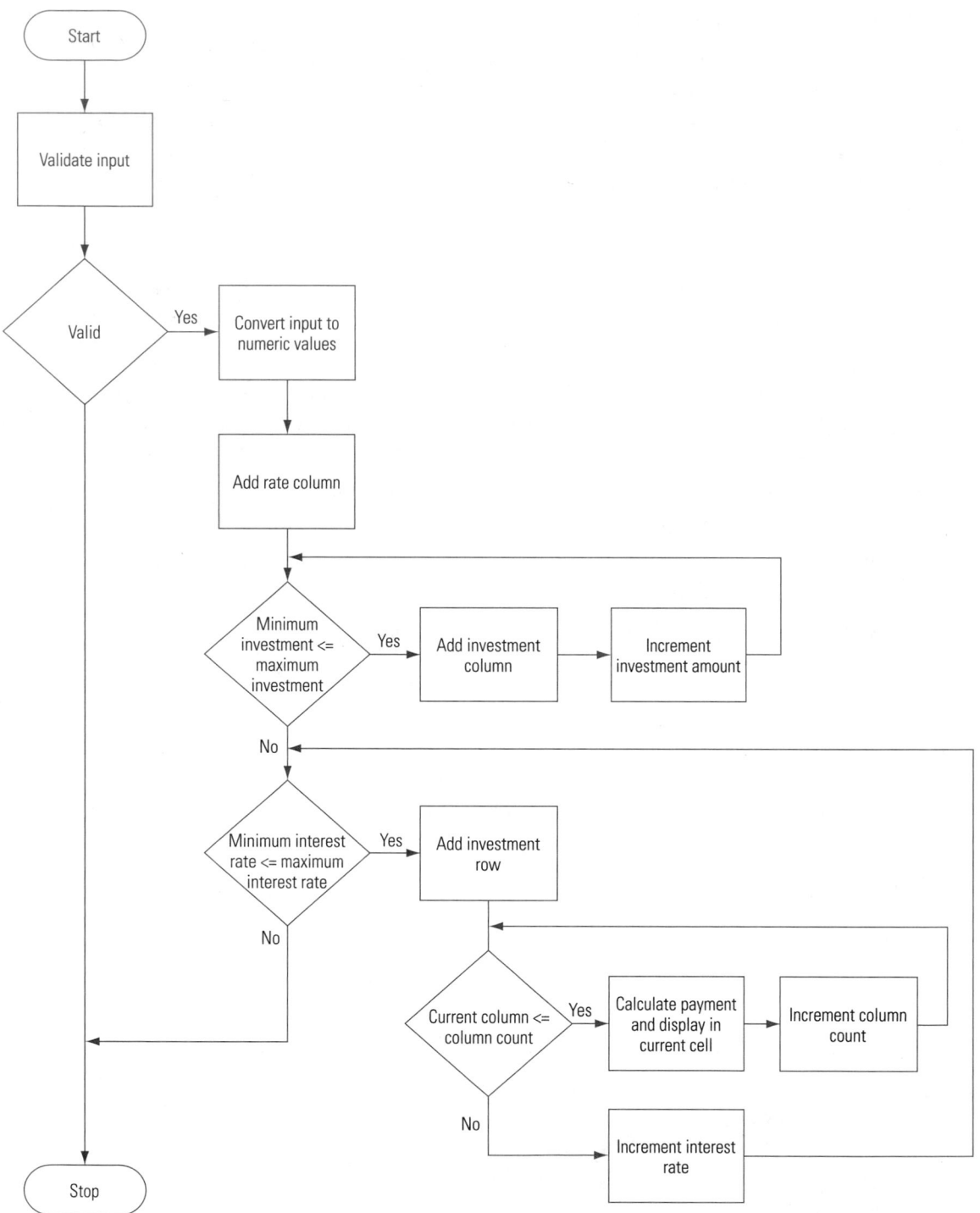

Figure 8-18: Calculate button flowchart

The code for the Reset and Clear buttons is fairly simple. The `Click` event handler for the Reset button resets the text boxes and combo boxes to their default values. Again, the default values are stored in constants. The Clear button clears the contents of the text boxes and deselects items in each of the combo box control instances.

## APPLICATION LESSON—IMPLEMENTATION

User input is supplied through the text boxes and combo boxes appearing on the form. The following points can be made of the application's code:

» Constants are used to store default values into these control instances.

» In the form's `Load` event handler, the combo boxes are initialized.

» A `SelectionChanged` event handler exists for each combo box. The code in these event handlers updates a corresponding text box.

» `Click` event handlers exist for each of the form's buttons.

As usual, a completed version of the application lesson appears in the data files accompanying this book, which you can preview next.

To preview the completed application lesson:

1. Start Visual Studio, if necessary, and open and run the solution file in the folder named **Chapter.08\Chapter08ApplicationLessonPreview**.

2. Click the **Calculate** button to use the default values and populate the grid with the investment results.

3. Click the **Clear** button. The input values are cleared and the data is removed from the grid.

4. Click the **Reset** button. The default values are reset in the text boxes and combo boxes.

5. Exit the solution.

As usual, the control instances have been created on the form for you in the start-up application. The first step in the process is to declare constants to store the default input values.

To create the application's constant data:

1. Start Visual Studio, if necessary, and open the solution file in the folder named **Chapter.08\Chapter08ApplicationLessonStartup**.

2. Enter the following statements in the `Class` block for the form named **frmMain**:

```
Private Const MinInvestmentDefault As Double = 0.0
Private Const MaxInvestmentDefault As Double = 1000.0
Private Const InvestmentIncrementDefault As Double = 200.0
Private Const MinInterestRateDefault As Double = 0.03
Private Const MaxInterestRateDefault As Double = 0.1
Private Const InterestRateIncrementDefault As Double = 0.01
Private Const InitialAmountDefault As Double = 1000.0
Private Const TermDefault As Double = 12
```

When the form loads, the combo boxes are initialized. Two combo boxes list the range of interest rates and two other combo boxes list the range of varying investment amounts. Each combo box is initialized using a similar `Do` loop. The following list describes the implementation:

» The current interest rate (list item) is initialized to the minimum interest rate.

» The loop consists of a single `Boolean` value, which is always `True`.

» The current interest rate is added to the two combo boxes.

» The current interest rate is incremented by the default interest rate increment.

» If the current interest rate is greater than the maximum interest rate, the loop exits using an `Exit Do` statement.

The loop to initialize the investment amounts works the same way.

To create the form's `Load` event handler to initialize the application:

1. Create the form's **Load** event handler, if necessary, and then enter the following statements:

```
Dim Initialized As Boolean
Dim CurrentRate As Double = MinInterestRateDefault
Do Until Initialized
    cboMaxInterestRate.Items.Add(CurrentRate.ToString("f2"))
    cboMinInterestRate.Items.Add(CurrentRate.ToString("f2"))
    CurrentRate += InterestRateIncrementDefault
    If CurrentRate > MaxInterestRateDefault Then
        Exit Do
    End If
Loop
```

```
cboMinInterestRate.SelectedIndex = 0
cboMaxInterestRate.SelectedIndex = _
    cboMaxInterestRate.Items.Count - 1
CurrentRate = MinInvestmentDefault
Do Until Initialized
    cboMinInvestment.Items.Add(CurrentRate.ToString("f2"))
    cboMaxInvestment.Items.Add(CurrentRate.ToString("f2"))
    CurrentRate += InvestmentIncrementDefault
    If CurrentRate > MaxInvestmentDefault Then
        Exit Do
    End If
Loop
cboMinInvestment.SelectedIndex = 0
cboMaxInvestment.SelectedIndex = _
    cboMaxInvestment.Items.Count - 1
```

The code for the Clear button clears all of the input text boxes, deselects the combo box items, and clears the contents of the output grid. The code for the Reset button also resets the input values to default values using the constants declared in the previous set of steps, and clears the output grid.

To create the event handlers for the Clear and Reset buttons:

1. Enter the following statements in the **Click** event handler for the **Clear** button:

```
Dim CurrentControl As Control
Dim CurrentTextBox As TextBox
For Each CurrentControl In Controls
    If TypeOf CurrentControl Is TextBox Then
        CurrentTextBox = CType(CurrentControl, TextBox)
        CurrentTextBox.Clear()
        CurrentTextBox.ForeColor = Color.Black
    End If
Next
dgOutput.Columns.Clear()
```

2. Enter the following statements in the **Click** event handler for the **Reset** button:

```
cboMinInterestRate.SelectedIndex = 0
cboMaxInterestRate.SelectedIndex = _
    cboMaxInterestRate.Items.Count - 1
cboMinInvestment.SelectedIndex = 0
cboMaxInvestment.SelectedIndex = _
    cboMaxInvestment.Items.Count - 1
```

```
txtMinInvestment.Text = MinInvestmentDefault.ToString
txtMaxInvestment.Text = MaxInvestmentDefault.ToString
txtInvestmentIncrement.Text = _
    InvestmentIncrementDefault.ToString
txtMinInterestRate.Text = MinInterestRateDefault.ToString
txtMaxInterestRate.Text = MaxInterestRateDefault.ToString
txtInterestRateIncrement.Text = _
    InterestRateIncrementDefault.ToString
txtInitialAmount.Text = InitialAmountDefault.ToString
txtTerm.Text = TermDefault.ToString
```

Most of the processing takes place in the Click event handler for the Calculate button. This code can be broken down into the following general tasks:

» Clear the output grid.

» Convert the input values stored in the text boxes to numeric values.

» Add the first column to the grid.

» Using a loop, add the remaining columns to the grid varying the investment amount from the minimum investment amount to the maximum investment amount.

» Using a second loop, add rows varying the interest rate from the minimum selected value to the maximum selected value. For each row added, populate the columns in the current row using another loop. This nested loop multiplies the investment's future value for each cell in the row.

To create the Click event handler for the Calculate button:

1. Enter the following statements in the **Click** event handler for the button named **btnCalculate**:

```
Dim MinInvestment, MaxInvestment, MinInterestRate, _
    MaxInterestRate As Double
Dim InvestmentIncrement, InterestRateIncrement As Double
If ValidateInput() = False Then
    Exit Sub
End If
dgOutput.Columns.Clear()

MinInvestment = ToDouble(txtMinInvestment.Text)
MaxInvestment = ToDouble(txtMaxInvestment.Text)
InvestmentIncrement = ToDouble(txtInvestmentIncrement.Text)

MinInterestRate = ToDouble(txtMinInterestRate.Text)
MaxInterestRate = ToDouble(txtMaxInterestRate.Text)
```

```
InterestRateIncrement = _
    ToDouble(txtInterestRateIncrement.Text)

Dim CurrentColumn, CurrentRow As Double
Dim ColumnCount As Integer

dgOutput.Columns.Add("Rate", "Rate")
ColumnCount += 1

For CurrentColumn = MinInvestment To MaxInvestment Step _
    InvestmentIncrement
    dgOutput.Columns.Add("Column" & CurrentColumn.ToString, _
        CurrentColumn.ToString("f"))
    ColumnCount += 1
Next

For CurrentRow = MinInterestRate To MaxInterestRate _
    Step InterestRateIncrement
    Dim Row As Integer
    Dim Col As Integer
    row = dgOutput.Rows.Add()

    Dim d As DataGridViewCell
    d = dgOutput.Rows(row).Cells(0)
    d.Value = CurrentRow.ToString
    For Col = 1 To ColumnCount - 1

        Dim CurrentRate As Double
        Dim CurrentPayment As Double
        Dim CurrentResult As Double
        d = dgOutput.Rows(row).Cells(0)
        CurrentRate = ToDouble(d.Value)

        CurrentPayment = _
            ToDouble(dgOutput.Columns(Col).HeaderText())
        CurrentResult = Abs(FV(CurrentRate, _
            ToDouble(txtTerm.Text), CurrentPayment, 0))

        d = dgOutput.Rows(row).Cells(col)
        d.Value = CurrentResult.ToString("c")

    Next
Next
```

2. Test the application to verify that it produces the same output as the completed application.

# CHAPTER SUMMARY

» Loops are used to execute statements repeatedly while a condition is true or until a condition becomes true. The syntax of a loop condition is the same as the syntax of the condition in an `If` statement. That is, both conditions must evaluate to a `Boolean` value. Loops can be categorized into two types. Using a pre-test loop, the condition is tested before the statement block inside the loop executes. Using a post-test loop, the statement block inside the loop executes, and then the condition is tested. Loops can be nested and can contain decision-making statements.

» A `For` loop is a form of a loop that can be used when the loop's iteration count is known in advance. Any `For` loop can be written as a `Do` loop, but not all `Do` loops can be written as `For` loops.

» Loops are often used to process lists. Lists store repeating data items or class instances. These lists are called collections. All collections have methods to add, change, and delete items appearing in the collection. One collection is the `List` class. The `List` class stores items having the same data type. The `Add` method is used to add an item to a collection. Individual items are referenced through the `Item` property. The `Item` property is the default property and need not be explicitly specified. The `RemoveAt` method is used to remove an item from a list. The index of the item is specified as an argument.

» Collections can be enumerated using a form of a `For` loop called a `For Each` loop. Each time the `For Each` loop iterates, an object is returned from the collection.

» Visual Basic supports predefined collections such as the `Controls` collection of the `Form` class. The `Controls` collection contains a reference to the control instances appearing on the form. The `TypeOf` operator is commonly used when enumerating a collection so as to determine the data type of a particular object.

» Visual Basic supports two list-based controls: the `ListBox` and `ComboBox` controls. Both controls work similarly. However, the end user can select multiple items from a `ListBox` control.

» The `DataGridView` control stores tabular data consisting of rows and columns. The intersection of a row and column is called a cell. In unbound mode, the columns must be added before the rows are added.

# KEY TERMS

**accumulator**—A variable used in a loop so as to calculate a total.

**collection**—A group of objects having the same data type or different data types. Collections have methods to add, update, and remove items. Loops are used to enumerate the items in a collection.

**counter**—A variable whose value is incremented or decremented by a constant value each time through a loop. Most often, a counter's value is incremented by 1.

**generic list**—A type of list that can store items having any data type but whose data type must be the same for all elements.

**infinite loop**—A loop error that causes a loop to execute forever because no condition exists that causes the loop to exit.

**post-test loop**—A form of loop, in which the statement block in the loop executes first, and then the condition is tested.

**pre-test loop**—A form of loop, in which the condition is tested first, and then the statements in the loop execute based on the outcome of the condition.

**repetition statements**—Statements that are executed over and over again.

# ANSWERS TO MINI-QUIZZES

### MINI-QUIZ 1

1. c. The condition in a Do loop has the same format as the condition in an If statement.

2. b. infinite

3. A counter is used to increment the value of a variable by a constant value. That constant value is typically 1. An accumulator is used in a loop to calculate a total.

4. 21

### MINI-QUIZ 2

1. e. none of the above

2. 3

3. Index = 0

   Temp = 0

### MINI-QUIZ 3

1. c. `Dim ClientList As New List(Of Client)`

2. b. The collection is 0-based so the `For` loop should start at zero instead of at one. The statements as currently written will not enumerate the first Person in the list.

3. `Customers.RemoveAt(Customers.Count - 1)`

### MINI-QUIZ 4

1. c. The items in a `ListBox` or `ComboBox` control instance can be enumerated with either a `For` loop or a `For Each` loop.

2. –1

3.
```
Dim Count As Integer
For Count = 65 To 90
      lstQuiz.Items.Add(Chr(Count))
Next
End Sub
```

### MINI-QUIZ 5

1. Columns must be added before the rows are added.

2. b. `CurrentCell = dgvQuiz.Rows(1).Cells(1)`

3.
```
Dim CurrentRow As Integer
Dim CurrentColumn As Integer
Dim Total As Integer
For CurrentRow = 0 To dgvQuiz.Rows.Count - 1
    For CurrentColumn = 0 To dgvQuiz.Columns.Count - 1
        Total += _
            ToInt32(dgvQuiz.Rows(CurrentRow). _
            Cells(CurrentColumn).Value)
    Next
Next
```

# REVIEW QUESTIONS

1. _____ statements are used to execute the same code repeatedly.

   a. Logical
   
   b. Decision-making

   c. Boolean
   
   d. Repetition

   e. none of the above

2. Which of the following statements is true regarding Do loops and For loops?

   a. Any For loop can be written as a Do loop.

   b. Any Do loop can be written as a For loop.

   c. A Do loop can only be written in one possible way.

   d. A For loop can be created as a pre-test loop or a post-test loop.

   e. none of the above

3. What is an accumulator?

   a. An accumulator is a Visual Basic data type specifically designed to calculate totals.

   b. An accumulator is a variable typically used to calculate a total. Accumulators are commonly used in loops.

   c. The terms accumulator and counter are synonymous.

   d. An accumulator must have a data type of Double.

   e. none of the above

4. Which of the following statements is correct regarding a collection?

   a. After a collection has been created, it is generally not possible to add items to that collection.

   b. A collection is a group or list of like objects.

   c. After an item has been added to a collection, it cannot be removed.

   d. Collections have a fixed size that is specified when the collection is created.

   e. none of the above

5. Assuming that PersonList is an instance of the `List` class storing elements having a data type of Person, what can be said regarding the following two statements?

```
CurrentPerson = PersonList.Item(3)
CurrentPerson = PersonList(3)
```

   a. The two statements are equivalent and return the fourth item from the list.

   b. The two statements are equivalent and return the third item from the list.

   c. The second statement causes a syntax error because no property or method name is explicitly specified.

   d. The preceding statements cause a syntax error only if strict type checking is enabled.

   e. none of the above

6. Referring to the `List` class, which of the following statements is correct regarding the `Count` and `Capacity` properties?

   a. The value of the `Count` and `Capacity` properties can never be equal.

   b. The value of the `Count` property is always less than or equal to the value of the `Capacity` property.

   c. The value of the `Capacity` property increases by a factor of 10. Thus, the value of the `Capacity` property is 10, 100, 1000, and so on.

   d. The value of the `Capacity` property is set when the list instance is created and cannot be changed.

   e. none of the above

7. What is the name of the method to add an item to a collection?

   a. `Create`

   b. `Add`

   c. `New`

   d. `AddItem`

   e. none of the above

8. Which of the following statements correctly removes the first item from the list named EmployeeList?

   a. `EmployeeList.RemoveAt(0)`

   b. `EmployeeList.Remove(0)`

   c. `EmployeeList.Remove(1)`

   d. `EmployeeList.Items(0).Remove`

   e. none of the above

9. Which of the following statements is correct regarding the `ListBox` control?

   a. The `ListBox` control can be configured such that the list items are always visible or such that the items are only visible when the drop-down list arrow is clicked.

   b. Only one item in a `ListBox` can be selected at a time.

   c. Depending on how the `ListBox` control is configured, it is possible to select a single item or to select multiple items.

   d. Items can be added programmatically at run time, but cannot be added at design time.

   e. none of the above

10. Assuming that lstQuestion is an instance of the `ListBox` control that has three items, which of the following statements causes an exception to be thrown?

    a. `lstQuestion.SelectedIndex = 2`

    b. `lstQuestion.SelectedIndex = -1`

    c. `lstQuestion.SelectedIndex = lstQuestion.Items`

    d. `lstQuestion.Items.Add("Demo")`

    e. none of the above

11. What is the term used to describe the intersection of a row and column in the `DataGridView` control?

    a. item                  b. grid

    c. element         d. cell

    e. none of the above

12. Which of the following statements is correct regarding the `DataGridView` control?

    a. Rows must be added to the control instance before the columns are added or a run-time error will occur.

    b. To reference a cell in the `DataGridView`, you use the `Cells` collection with the index of the row and column as arguments.

    c. The `Rows` and `Columns` collections are 0-based.

    d. Rows must be added one row at a time.

    e. none of the above

13. Which of the following statements correctly references the first row of the third column in the `DataGridView` control instance named dgvDemo?

    a. `dgvDemo.Rows(1).Cells(3)`  b. `dgvDemo.Rows(0).Cells(2)`

    c. `dgvDemo.Row(0).Columns(2)`  d. `dgvDemo.Row(1).Column(3)`

    e. none of the above

14. Assuming that the `DataGridView` control instance named dgvDemo exists, which of the following statements correctly adds a new row to the end of the control instance?

    a. `dgvDemo.Rows.Add()`  b. `dgvDemo.Add.Row()`

    c. `dgvDemo.Items.Add(1)`  d. `dgvDemo.Add.Rows(1)`

    e. none of the above

15. Describe the difference between a pre-test loop and a post-test loop. In your answer, describe the Visual Basic statements used to create pre-test and post-test loops.

16. What is the difference between a counter and an accumulator?

17. What is meant by the term "infinite loop"?

18. What value is stored in the variable Total after the following loop has exited?

```
For Counter = 1 to 5 Step 2
    Total = Total + 1
Next
```

19. How many times will the following loop execute?

```
Dim Count As Integer = 1
Do While Count > 10
    Count += 1
Loop
```

20. Describe the error in the following nested loop.

```
Dim Result As Integer
Dim X, Y As Integer
Do While X < 5
    Do While Y < 2
        Result = Result + 1
        X -= 1
        Y += 1
    Loop
Loop
```

# PROGRAMMING QUESTIONS

1. Write the statements that will increment the variable Count from 1 to 100 by 1 and add the current value of the counter to the variable named Total. Thus, the variable Total will be considered an accumulator. Use a pre-test Do loop to accomplish this task.

2. Write the preceding Do loop as a For loop.

3. Create a For loop that will enumerate 100,000 times (from 1 to 100,000), using a counter variable named Counter. Each time through the loop, print the value of the counter to the Immediate window using the Debug.WriteLine method only if the counter is divisible by 1000.

4. Create a For loop that will enumerate 100 times from 100 to 1. If the counter is divisible by 5, print the value of the counter to the Immediate window using the Debug.WriteLine method. Declare a counter as necessary.

5. Write the statement to create an instance of the List class named EmployeeList. The data type of the items in the list should be Employee. Next, write the statement to add an instance of the Employee class to the list. Create the instance of the Employee class and name it CurrentEmployee. Write the statements to determine the capacity of the list and the number of items stored in the list. Display the result to the Immediate window. Finally, write the statement to remove the first item from the list.

6. Assume that an instance of the List class named EmployeeList exists having items of type Employee. Write the statements to enumerate the list using a For Each loop. Assume that the Employee class has an EmployeeID property. Write the statements to print the EmployeeID property to the Immediate window. Declare local variables as necessary.

7. Write the statement to remove all of the items from the ComboBox control instance named cboCurrent. Then write the statements to add the letters "A" through "Z" to the control instance. Declare any local variables as necessary.

8. Assume that two list boxes exist named lstInput and lstOutput. Write the statements to first clear the list box named lstOutput. Then create a loop to copy all of the items from the list box named lstInput to the list box named lstOutput.

9. Assume that an instance of the DataGridView control named dgvDemo exists. Write the statements to store the value 100 in the first row and second column.

10. Write the statements to create three columns in the DataGridView control instance named dgvDemo. The columns should have captions of Column 1, Column 2, and Column 3, respectively.

11. Write the statements to create a single column in the DataGridView control instance dgvDemo having a caption of Count. Then add 100 rows to the grid having values from 1 to 100 storing these values in the column that you created.

12. Assume that a DataGridView control instance exists named dgvDemo. Write the statements to add five columns having captions of Name, Address, City, State, and Zip Code. Create the columns such that the name used to reference the column is colName, colAddress, colCity, colState, and colZipCode. Next create one new row and add your name, address, city, state, and zip code to that row.

13. Write the statement(s) to remove all of the rows from the `DataGridView` control instance named dgvQuestion.

14. Assume that a `DataGridView` control instance exists named dgvDemo. Write the statements to total the values in the first column for all of the rows.

15. Create two nested `For` loops to print multiplication tables and add the tables to an instance of the `DataGridView` control named dgvCurrent. Declare any local variables as necessary. Print the multiplication table for the numbers 1 through 12.

# HANDS-ON PROJECTS

1. In this hands-on project, you will create an application that works with lists. The application you create will allow the end user to add, change, and delete list items as well as locate items in the list. The list will be implemented as a collection.

   a. A preview of the completed hands-on project can be found in the file **Chapter.08\HandsOnProjects\Ch08HandsOnProject1.exe**.

   b. Start Visual Studio, if necessary, and create a new solution named **Ch08HandsOnProject1.sln**.

   c. Create a class named Employee having properties named EmployeeID, EmployeeType, EmployeeName, EmployeeAddress, and EmployeeSSN. Choose appropriate data types for each property. Use hidden variables and Property procedures to implement each property.

   d. Create the control instances on the form, as shown in the preview solution.

   e. Create an instance of the `List` class to store instances of the Employee class.

   f. Create a button and the necessary code that will allow the user to add an employee to the list. When the end user clicks the Add button, a new instance of the Employee class should be created. The ID number of the employee should correspond to the index of the item as it will appear in the corresponding list. Update the contents of the text box to display the current Employee ID number. The end user should not be able to modify the Employee ID number.

   g. Create a button that will allow the end user to save the changes to the current item in the list. The program should operate such that the current item in the list always appears in the form's text boxes. Validate that the format of the Social Security number is correct. The valid values for the employee type should be "Manager" and "Staff." The end user must not be able to change the value of the Employee ID number after it has been assigned. Create an InputValidation class similar to the one presented in Chapter 7 to do this.

h. Allow the end user to remove an item from the list. The item removed should always be the current item.

i. Create the control instances and event handlers to display the current number of employees in the list.

j. Create control instances that will allow the user to navigate to the next and previous record in the list. *Hint*: Declare a variable to keep track of the current list item. When the end user navigates to a different record, update the text boxes to display that record, as necessary. Consider creating a procedure to update the current record display. Write the necessary decision-making statement to prevent the end user from selecting the previous record when the first record is the current record, and the next record when the last record is the current record.

2. In this hands-on project, you will create an application that will display the depreciation schedule for an asset using the straight-line depreciation method. Using the straight-line depreciation method, the salvage value for an asset is subtracted from its original value to calculate the total depreciation. Then, the total depreciation is divided by the asset's life to calculate the annual depreciation amount. The depreciation schedule contains one row for each period that the asset is being depreciated. The input values required to compute the depreciation include the original cost of the asset, the life of the asset, and the value of the asset at the end of its useful life (known as the salvage value). Refer to the Help page for the SLN function if necessary.

a. A preview of the completed hands-on project can be found in the file **Chapter.08\HandsOnProjects\Ch08HandsOnProject2.exe**.

b. Create a new solution named **Ch08HandsOnProject2.sln**.

c. Create the input objects on the main form, as shown in the preview solution, along with the `DataGridView` control instance used to display the output.

d. Create a combo box control that will list the life span of common assets. These life spans should be 3, 5, 10, and 26 years. Update the corresponding text box when the end user selects an item in the combo box.

e. Validate that the input fields contain numeric data. In addition, validate that the salvage value is less than the initial value of the asset. All input values must be positive integral values. Indicate invalid input to the end user. Implement an InputValidation class to perform the input validation.

f. Write the necessary statements to calculate the depreciation for the asset. Display the columns in the grid.

g. Create the code for the Clear button to clear the rows from the `DataGridView`.

h. Create the code for the Exit button.

i. Display the current time of day on the main form and update the value each second.

3. In this hands-on project, you will develop a program that creates a simple tax table displayed in multiple columns. The input fields for the tax table include the minimum value, the maximum value, and the incremental value. These values should be used in a `For` loop that prints the tax amount starting with the minimum value, to the ending value, incrementing the tax amount by a constant value. For each value, multiply the amount by the effective tax rate. The information should be displayed in a `DataGridView` control instance. The first column should contain a value, and the second column should contain the tax for that value. The third and fourth columns should contain the same information. Create the tax table such that the data in the rows is evenly balanced.

   a. A preview of the completed hands-on project can be found in the file **Chapter.08\HandsOnProjects\Ch08HandsOnProject3.exe**.

   b. Create a new solution named **Ch08HandsOnProject3.sln**.

   c. Create the input objects on the main form, as shown in the preview solution, along with the `DataGridView` control instance used to display the output.

   d. Validate that the input fields contain numeric data. In addition, validate that the minimum tax rate is less than the maximum tax rate. Again, create an InputValidation class to do this.

   e. Create the code to generate the tax table based on the input values. Create column and row headers as appropriate. Make sure that the rows are balanced. That is, the first two columns should contain the same number of data items as the third and fourth columns.

   f. Create a button and the necessary code to clear the output values from the `DataGridView` control instance.

   g. Create a button to exit the application.

4. In this hands-on project, you will create a loan amortization schedule. That is, you will create a two-dimensional `DataGridView` displaying the principal and interest applied to a loan for each payment period along with the loan balance. The following list describes the application's input values:

   » The initial amount of the loan

   » The loan's interest rate expressed as an annual interest rate

   » The loan's term expressed in years

The processing for the application involves calculating the loan's payment. Use the Help system to discover the syntax of the Pmt method. The loan payment only needs to be calculated once as the payment will remain constant over the life of the loan. Convert the input values, which are expressed in years so that they are expressed in months. That is, a 30-year loan would have 360 payments and a 12% annual interest rate is equivalent to a 1% monthly interest rate.

Each payment period, the following processing must be performed:

» The amount of the payment applicable to interest must be calculated. Multiply the current loan balance by the effective monthly interest rate to determine the interest amount.

» The amount of the payment applicable to principal must be calculated. Subtract the interest amount from the payment amount to determine the amount of the payment applicable to the principal.

» Subtract the principal amount from the loan balance to get the new loan balance.

» Each of these calculations must be performed in a loop. The number of loop iterations is equivalent to the number of payments.

   a. Create a new solution named **Ch08HandsOnProject4.sln**.

   b. Create the control instances as you see fit.

   c. Configure the `DataGridView` control instance to display the column headers as necessary based on the information supplied in the preceding list. The column headers should be created when the form is loaded.

   d. Validate the input to make sure that it contains valid numeric data before trying to process that data. All of the numeric input must contain positive values.

   e. Write the necessary code to create the amortization schedule using the preceding description on how to perform the processing. Format the output values as appropriate.

   f. Calculate and display the total interest paid on the loan.

   g. Create the code for the Clear button to clear the input and output values.

   h. Create an Exit button and its necessary code.

# PROCESSING LISTS WITH ARRAYS

**After completing this chapter, you will be able to:**

Understand the concept of random numbers and how to generate random numbers

Describe the similarities and differences between arrays and collections

Understand and work with arrays, and use `Do` loops and `For` loops to examine array elements

Sort, reverse, and search for elements in an array

Find and diagnose common array errors

Work with multidimensional arrays and arrays of objects

# CONCEPT LESSON

In the first section of this chapter, you will learn about the characteristics of random numbers and how to generate them. Random numbers have uses in gaming and simulation applications, and are also useful to generate test data for an application.

Chapter 8 introduced the concept of a collection and how the List class can store references to multiple objects having the same data type. In this chapter, you will work with arrays, which operate similarly to collections. That is, both arrays and some collections store references to multiple objects having the same data type.

# INTRODUCTION TO RANDOM NUMBERS

Many applications require random numbers to perform their processing. Random numbers are numeric values that are generated by methods of the System.Random class. The following list describes several uses for random numbers:

» Gaming and casino gaming applications require random numbers to be selected each time a game is played. Random numbers can be used to shuffle a deck of cards or to pick a specific number. For example, the game of Keno uses 80 numbers having values between 1 and 80. The player usually selects between 1 and 10 numbers. Note that there are variations on the game of Keno. The casino then selects 20 random numbers from the 80 possible numbers. The amount won is based on how many numbers selected by the player were hit (selected by the casino).

» Computer simulations often require the use of random numbers. For example, a simulation might be created to determine the number of tellers required to service the customers entering a bank. In such a scenario, customers enter the bank at random intervals. The amount of time it takes for a teller to serve a customer is also a random value. The results of such a simulation are used to determine the optimal staffing level for the bank.

» Random values are also useful when generating test data. In any system, it is necessary to develop test data that models the data the system will ultimately process. For example, it is possible to generate random numbers to simulate telephone numbers or Social Security numbers.

## RANDOM NUMBER GENERATION

The process of creating a sequence of random numbers is called **random number generation**. A random number generator is initialized based on a numeric value called the **seed value**. Given the same seed value, the same sequence of random numbers is always generated. Conversely, different seed values cause different random number sequences to be generated. After a random number generator has been initialized, methods are called to get the next random number in the sequence.

The .NET Framework class library supports the System.Random class to initialize a random number generator and to generate random numbers. The System.Random class has the following members:

### Syntax
```
System.Random class
```

### Public Methods
» The overloaded Next method returns a random number having a data type of Integer.

» The NextDouble method returns a random number having a data type of Double. The value of the random number is always a fractional value between 0.0 and 1.0.

The overloaded constructor, which is shown in the code segment after the next paragraph, initializes an instance of the Random class. Without arguments, the class instance is initialized using a seed value based on the time of day. Thus, each time the constructor is called, the time of day varies so a different seed value is used. Using different seed values, different random number sequences are generated when subsequent calls to the Next or NextDouble methods are made. The second version of the overloaded constructor accepts one argument having a data type of Integer containing the seed value. If the specified seed value is negative, the absolute value of that number is used. Given a particular seed value, the same sequence of random numbers is always generated.

The following code segment illustrates how to create instances of the Random class using a seed value based on the time of day and fixed seed value, respectively:

```
Dim RandomSeed As New Random()
Dim FixedSeed As New Random(10)
```

The first of the preceding statements creates an instance of the Random class using a seed value based on the time of day. Thus, the sequence of random numbers generated by calls to the Next method varies for each class instance created. The second statement uses a constant seed value of 10. All class instances created with this seed value always produce the same sequence of random numbers.

## THE NEXT METHOD
After creating an instance of the Random class, the sequence of random numbers can be generated. The methods of the Random class can be used to generate Integer random

numbers or random numbers having a data type of Double. To generate an Integer random number sequence, the overloaded Next method is called, as the following statements show:

```
Dim RandomValue As Integer
RandomValue = RandomSeed.Next()
RandomValue = RandomSeed.Next(1, 10)
```

Each time the Next method is called, the next random number in the sequence is returned. Without arguments, the Next method generates a random Integer value greater than zero. With arguments, the Next method generates a random Integer value within a range. The two arguments define the range of possible values. Thus, the third of the preceding statements generates a random number between 1 and 10. When generating random numbers in a range, two numbers can repeat before all of the numbers in the range have been generated.

## THE NEXTDOUBLE METHOD

In addition to generating a sequence of random Integer values, the Random class supports the NextDouble method, which returns a fractional value between 0.0 and 1.0 having a data type of Double. The following statements show how to call the NextDouble method:

```
Dim RandomDouble As Double
RandomDouble = RandomSeed.NextDouble()
```

Assuming that the variable RandomSeed is an instance of the System.Random class, the second of the preceding statements generates a double precision random number between 0.0 and 1.0.

Most commonly, a random number generator is used to generate a sequence of random numbers rather than just a single random number. The following code segment shows how to generate a sequence of 100 random numbers and add them to an instance of the ListBox control named lstRandomList:

```
Dim CurrentRandom As New System.Random()
Dim CurrentIndex As Integer
Dim CurrentRandomValue As Double
For CurrentIndex = 1 To 100
    CurrentRandomValue = CurrentRandom.NextDouble()
    lstRandomList.Items.Add(CurrentRandomValue.ToString)
Next
```

The preceding code segment first creates an instance of the Random class using the time of day as the seed value. The For loop iterates 100 times. Each time the loop executes, the next value in the sequence is generated by calling the `NextDouble` method. That value is then added to the list box.

In this exploration exercise, you will see how to generate random integer and double precision numbers using random seed values and fixed seed values.

1. Start Visual Studio and open the solution file in the folder **Chapter.09\ Chapter09ConceptLesson**. Run the solution. Click the **Random Numbers** tab, if necessary. Figure 9-1 shows the Random Numbers tab.

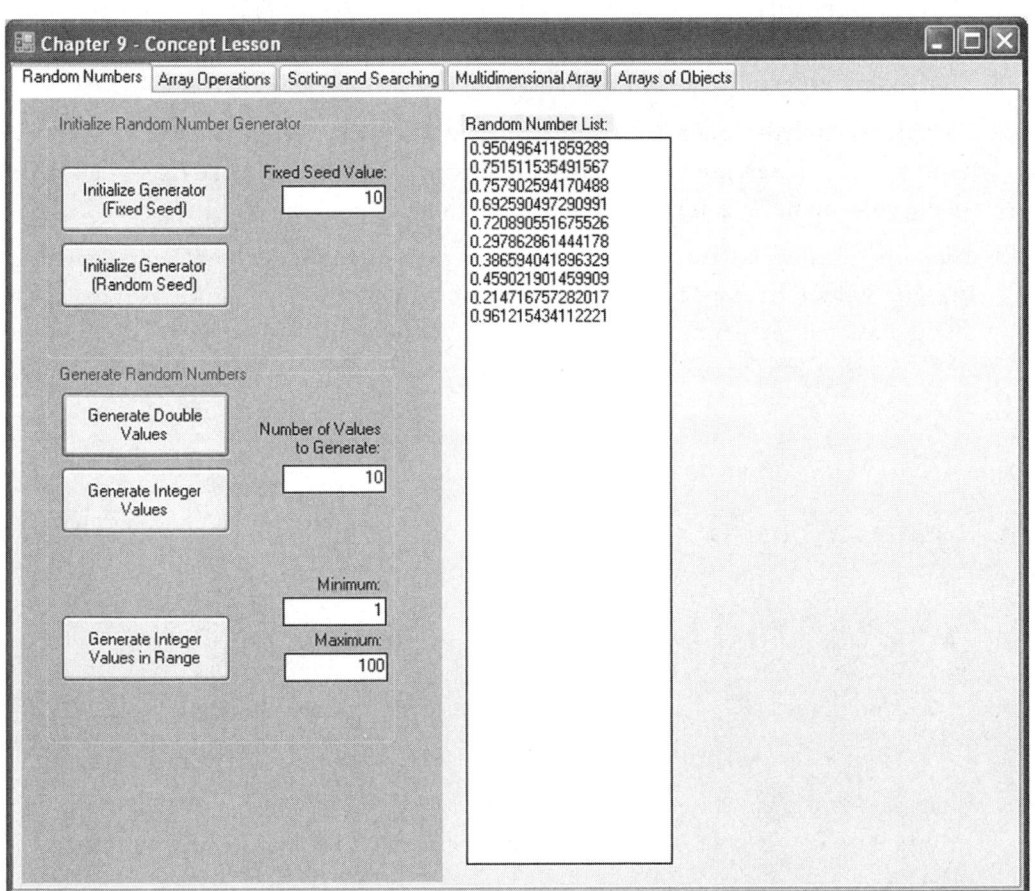

Figure 9-1: Concept lesson—Random Numbers tab

2. An input text box stores a fixed seed value. This value is used to initialize the random number generator. Click the **Initialize Generator (Fixed Seed)** button. The default value (10) stored in the text box is used as the seed value for the random number generator. You will not see any visual changes on the form.

3. Click the **Generate Double Values** button. A sequence of 10 double precision numbers is generated. The text box contains the number of random values to generate. The random values appear in the form's list box.

4. Examine the random number sequence that was generated. Click the **Initialize Generator (Fixed Seed)** and **Generate Double Values** buttons again. Note that the same random number sequence is generated because the seed value (10) is the same.

5. Click the **Generate Integer Values** button. A sequence of 10 random integers is generated.

6. Click the **Generate Integer Values In Range** button. A sequence of 10 random integers is generated having values between 1 and 100. The range of values appears in the corresponding text boxes.

7. Click the **Initialize Generator (Random Seed)** button to create a new instance of the Random class using a seed value based on the time of day instead of a fixed seed value. Again, you will not see any visual changes to the form.

8. Click the **Generate Double Values**, **Generate Integer Values**, and **Generate Integer Values In Range** buttons. The random values appear in the list box. If the random number generator is reinitialized, a new random number sequence is generated because a random seed value is used.

# MINI-QUIZ 1

1. Which of the following statements is correct regarding random number generation?

   a. Random numbers are always double precision values between 0.0 and 1.0.

   b. Random numbers are always integer values between 1 and 1,000,000.

   c. The methods of the System.Random class are static. That is, it is not necessary to first create an instance of the Random class before calling its methods.

   d. To create a random number sequence with the same seed value, call the constructor without arguments.

   e. none of the above

*(Continued)*  ▶

2. Which of the following statements creates an instance of the `System.Random` class such that the same sequence of random numbers will be generated?

   a. `Dim RndCurrent As New Random(Sequence.Repeat)`

   b. `Dim RndCurrent As New Random(15)`

   c. `Dim RndCurrent As New RandomSequence()`

   d. `Dim RndCurrent As New Random()`

   e. none of the above

3. Assume that RndCurrent is an instance of the `System.Random` class. Write the statements to generate 10,000 random numbers having values between 10,000 and 100,000. The random numbers generated should have a data type of `Integer`. Add the random numbers generated to a list box named lstQuiz.

# INTRODUCTION TO ARRAYS

Chapter 8 introduced the concept of a collection. Remember that the `List` class is a collection, which can store multiple data items having the same data type. In addition to collections, Visual Basic supports another data type called an array, which also stores one or more data items having the same data type. The following list describes similarities and differences between the `List` class and arrays:

» Both arrays and the `List` class store multiple items having the same data type.

» The size of both lists and arrays can be changed while an application executes. As discussed in Chapter 8, items are added to and removed from the `List` class by calling the `Add` and `RemoveAt` methods, respectively. However, the size of an array is changed through a process known as redimensioning.

» Arrays can have multiple dimensions. That is, arrays can be created as a list (one dimension), as a table containing rows and columns (two dimensions), or with three or more dimensions. The `List` class is linear, so it is similar to a one-dimensional array in this regard.

## CHARACTERISTICS OF ARRAYS

A variable that stores a single item of information, such as an interest rate or the term of a loan, is called a **scalar variable**. In addition to collections, arrays can be used to store several data items (scalar variables) each having the same data type. For example, suppose that it is necessary to store monthly sales totals for each month of the year. Although 12 variables could be declared such that one number is stored in each variable representing sales totals for the months January through December, this is not the easiest or most efficient solution to the problem. A better solution is to declare one variable to store all of the sales totals for the 12 months of the year. Sales totals for each month of the year could be stored as an array of double precision values.

Developers typically use the following terms when describing arrays:

» An **array** is a variable that stores multiple data items, each having the same data type. For example, an array can store a list of integers, a list of single precision numbers, or a list of strings. Arrays can also store lists of objects (reference types). For example, it's possible to create an array to store references to instances of `TextBox` controls or any other class.

» An array has one or more **dimensions**. The meaning of the word dimension is similar to its meaning in English. Think of a one-dimensional array as a columnar list of values. Two-dimensional arrays are made up of rows and columns. Think of a two-dimensional array as a grid or table. A Visual Basic array has between one and 60 dimensions, but arrays containing more than three dimensions are rarely used in business applications. This chapter discusses how to create one, two, and three-dimensional arrays.

» The number of dimensions in an array is called the **rank**. Thus, a one-dimensional array has a rank of 1, a two-dimensional array has a rank of 2, and so on.

» Each data item stored in an array is called an **element**.

» An array element is referenced by a unique index number known as a **subscript**. One subscript is used to reference the elements in a one-dimensional array. Two subscripts are used to reference the elements in a two-dimensional array. With a three-dimensional array, three subscripts are used. In Visual Studio, all arrays are 0-based. In other words, the value of the first subscript for each dimension is 0.

## THE ARRAY CLASS

In Visual Studio, arrays are classes; thus, they are reference types. Arrays have properties and methods, just as any class has properties and methods. The `Array` class supports the following members:

# COMMON ARRAY TASKS

Just as common tasks are performed with lists, similar tasks are commonly performed on arrays. The following list describes common array tasks:

» An array must be declared before it can be used. Arrays are declared in the same way scalar variables are declared, using the `Public`, `Friend`, `Private`, and `Dim` access modifiers. All elements in an array have the same data type.

» It's possible to declare and initialize an array in the same statement.

» It's possible to determine the bounds of an array.

» The number of elements in an array can be changed while an application runs. That is, an array can grow or shrink at run time.

» Data is retrieved from individual array elements and stored into those same array elements.

These common array tasks are discussed in the following sections.

## DECLARING ARRAYS

When an array is declared, Visual Basic allocates memory (RAM) to store the array's data in the same way that memory is allocated to store the data for a scalar variable. Arrays are classes so they are reference types, meaning that the memory allocated to the array variable stores a reference (memory address) to the actual array data.

To declare an array, the Public, Friend, Private, or Dim access modifiers are used, just as they are used to declare a scalar variable.

All Visual Basic arrays are dynamic. That is, their size can be changed at run time. An array can be given an initial size when it is declared or its initial size can be undefined. Arrays are declared using the following syntax:

### Syntax

```
[Public | Friend | Private | Dim] arrayName ([size]) As
dataType = initExpr
```

### Dissection

» The Public access modifier declares a global array available to all of the modules in a project and to other assemblies. The Friend access modifier declares an array that is accessible to the current project but is hidden from other assemblies. The Private access modifier declares a module-level array. The Dim keyword appears within a procedure to declare an array that is local to the procedure. The meaning of these access modifiers is the same as their meaning when declaring scalar variables or procedures.

» The arrayName contains the name of the variable used to reference the array. The naming rules for arrays are the same as the naming rules for any other variable.

» The optional size argument defines the initial value of the largest subscript. If omitted, the array has no initial size. An array without an initial size must be redimensioned before it is used. Otherwise, a System.NullReferenceException is thrown.

» The As dataType clause defines the data type of each array element. Each element in an array has the same data type and arrays can be declared having any data type.

» initExpr allows initial values to be assigned to the array's elements. Conceptually, the process is the same as initializing scalar variables.

*(Continued)* ▶

## Code Example

```
Dim EmptyArray() As Integer
Dim OneElementArray(0) As Integer
Dim IntegerArray(3) As Integer
Dim SingleArray(4) As Single
```

## Code Dissection

The first of the preceding statements declares an array with no initial size. The second statement declares a one-dimensional array. The array has one element having a subscript of 0. The third statement declares a one-dimensional array with four elements having subscripts ranging from 0 to 3. In the final statement, the one-dimensional array has five elements with subscripts ranging from 0 to 4. The first, second, and third statements declare an array with elements having a data type of `Integer`, and the final statement declares an array with elements having a data type of `Single`. Each of the preceding arrays has one dimension (a rank of 1).

Figure 9-2 shows how memory is allocated to an array when it is declared. The first array contains one element, and the second array contains four elements.

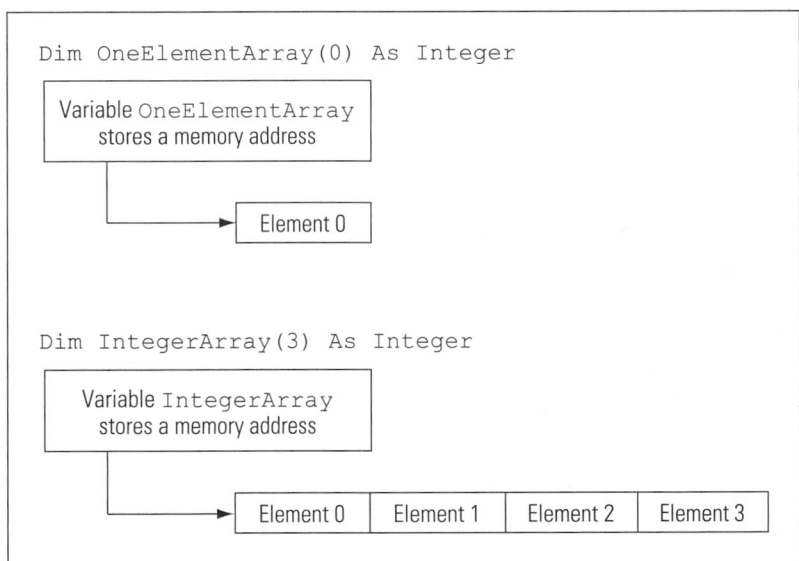

Figure 9-2: How memory is allocated to an array

In addition to arrays having a data type of `Integer`, arrays can have other data types such as `Boolean`, as the following statement shows:

```
Dim WeekDayArray() As Boolean
```

The preceding statement declares a dynamic array named WeekDayArray having a data type of `Boolean`.

## INITIALIZING AN ARRAY

An array can be declared and initialized in the same statement similar to the way a scalar variable can be declared and initialized in the same statement. The syntax to initialize an array differs from the syntax to initialize a scalar variable because a list of values is being initialized, rather than a single value. When initializing a one-dimensional array, the list of values appears in braces {}, and a comma separates each value in the list.

The following statement declares and initializes a dynamic, one-dimensional array having a data type of `Integer`:

```
Dim IntegerList() As Integer = {24, 12, 34, 42}
```

The preceding statement declares an array without an initial size, and then initializes the array. The array contains four `Integer` elements having values of 24, 12, 34, and 42. Remember that arrays are 0-based. Thus, element 0 has a value of 24, element 1 has a value of 12, and so on. The largest subscript value for the array is 3. Figure 9-3 shows the process of declaring and initializing an array.

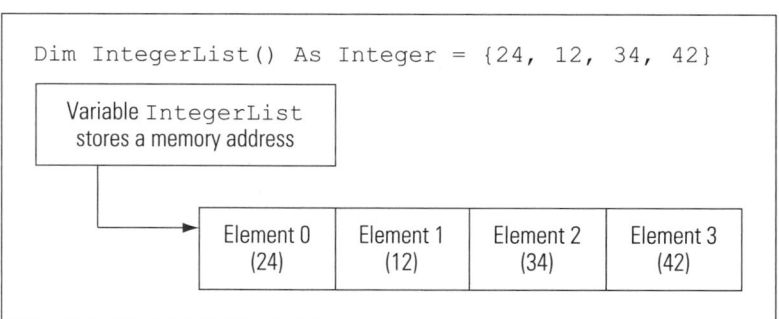

Figure 9-3: Declaring and initializing an array

When declaring and initializing an array, the array's size must not be specified in the declaration statement. Thus, the following statement causes the syntax error "Explicit initialization is not permitted for arrays declared with explicit bounds."

```
Dim IntegerList(3) As Integer = {24, 12, 34, 42}
```

In addition to initializing arrays having a data type of Integer, arrays having other data types such as Boolean can also be initialized, as the following statements show:

```
Dim WeekDayArray() As Boolean = _
    {False, False, True, True, True, True, True}
```

The preceding statement declares an array named WeekDayArray, and initializes its seven elements to Boolean values.

Arrays having the String data type can be declared and initialized too. For example, an array can be declared to store the month names January through December, as shown in the following code segment:

```
Dim MonthNames() As String = _
    {"January", "February", "March", "April", "May", _
     "June", "July", "August", "September", "October", _
     "November", "December"}
```

The preceding statement declares and initializes a dynamic array having a data type of String. Each array element contains a month name, and the array has a total of 12 elements. The elements in the list appear in braces and a comma separates each element as before. As always, double quotation marks surround literal string values.

The preceding array of month names works correctly. However, the subscript values for the month names are not intuitive. That is, most people associate the numeric value 1 with January. However, the subscript for January is 0 because it is the first array element. To improve readability in such a case, it's possible to leave the first subscript (array element) unused, as the following code segment shows:

```
Dim MonthNames() As String = _
    { "", "January", "February", "March", "April", "May", _
      "June", "July", "August", "September", "October", _
      "November", "December"}
```

In the preceding declaration, the first array element contains an empty string, and the second array element, having a subscript of 1, contains the string January.

## DETERMINING AN ARRAY'S BOUNDS

Arrays support methods to determine the smallest and largest subscript for a particular dimension. The `GetLowerBound` method gets the smallest subscript value for an array dimension, whereas the `GetUpperBound` method gets the largest subscript value for an array dimension. The methods require one argument: the dimension to examine. The argument is 0-based. That is, to examine the first dimension, the argument's value is 0, 1 for the second dimension, and so on.

```
Dim SmallestSubscript, LargestSubscript As Integer
SmallestSubscript = MonthNames.GetLowerBound(0)        ' 0
LargestSubscript = MonthNames.GetUpperBound(0)         ' 12
```

The preceding statements get the lower and upper bound of the first dimension of the array named MonthNames. The lower bound is 0 and the upper bound is 12. Thus, the array has 13 elements. Again, given the preceding example, the first element having a subscript of 0 is not used. Remember that arrays are 0-based, so the following statement throws a `System.IndexOutOfRangeException` for a one-dimensional array because `MonthNames.GetUpperBound(1)` references the second array dimension, which does not exist.

```
Dim LargestSubscript As Integer
LargestSubscript = MonthNames.GetUpperBound(1)
```

## REDIMENSIONING AN ARRAY

An array's size is determined by the number of dimensions in the array and the number of elements in each array dimension. Any array can be redimensioned at run time using the `ReDim` statement. Arrays must frequently be redimensioned when the number of array elements is not known in advance. Conceptually, redimensioning an array is similar to adding an item to a collection. For example, suppose a sequential file is being read into an array. If the number of records in the file is not known, it is not possible to determine the number of array elements needed. Two possible solutions are available for this problem:

» One possible solution is to declare an array with an arbitrarily large number of elements. In such a case, unused array elements cause memory to be wasted. Given this solution, it's also possible that the array will be too small at some point.

» The second solution is to dynamically change an array's size by **redimensioning** it.

An array is redimensioned with the ReDim statement, which has the following syntax:

## Syntax

```
ReDim [Preserve] varname(size)
```

## Dissection

» The ReDim statement redimensions an existing array. The ReDim statement cannot be used to change an array's data type. It is also not possible to use the ReDim statement to initialize an array's values. An array can only be initialized when it is declared. Furthermore, the ReDim statement must appear inside of a procedure because it is an executable statement rather than a declaration statement. There are also restrictions when using the ReDim statement to redimension arrays with two or more dimensions. Those restrictions are discussed later in the chapter when multidimensional arrays are discussed.

» If the optional Preserve keyword is used, and the array's size is increased, any data stored in the array is saved when the array is redimensioned. If the size of an array is increased, the new elements are initialized to zero for numeric arrays, and to an empty string for arrays having a data type of String. If the size of the array is decreased, the data stored in the deleted array elements is destroyed. If the Preserve keyword is not used, all of the values stored in the array elements are reinitialized when the array is resized. Visual Basic does not allow the number of array dimensions to be changed when using the Preserve keyword, in addition to other restrictions.

» The required *varname* argument contains the name of the array that was previously declared.

» The required *size* argument contains the new array dimensions and has the same syntax with which you are already familiar.

## Code Example

```
Dim IntegerList() As Integer = {24, 12, 34, 42}
ReDim IntegerList(4)
ReDim Preserve IntegerList(4)
```

## Code Dissection

The first statement declares and initializes an array named IntegerList. The second statement changes the size of the array named IntegerList so that it contains five elements and destroys the existing contents. The final statement resizes the same array but preserves the existing contents.

Figure 9-4 shows the process of redimensioning an array.

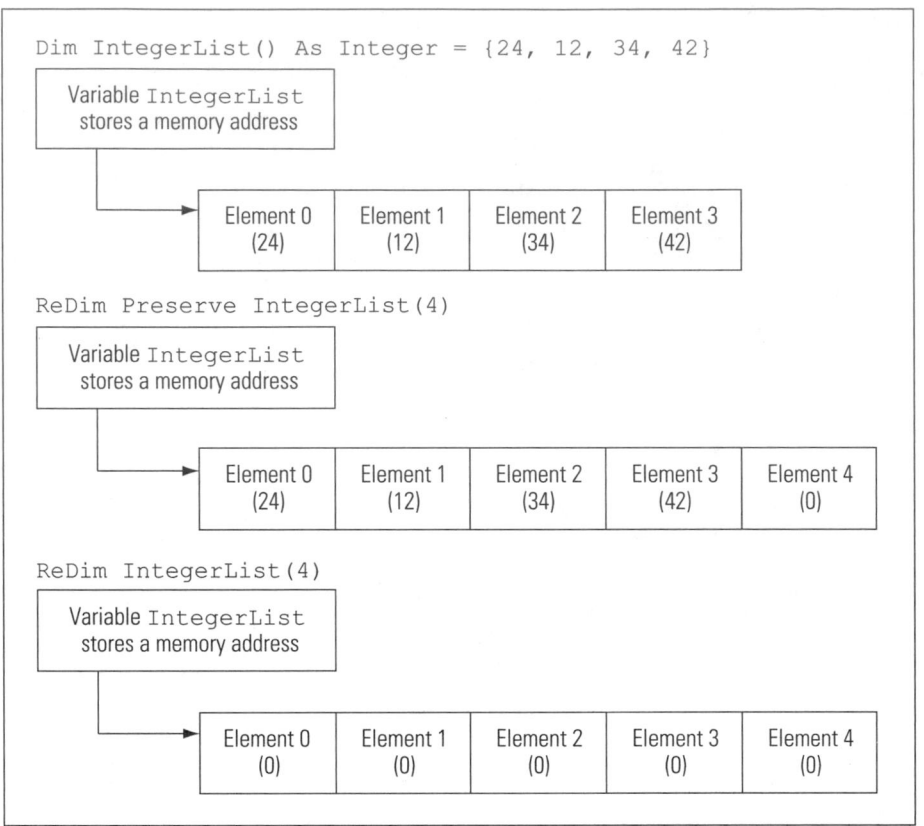

Figure 9-4: Redimensioning an array

> **»TIP** Use care when redimensioning arrays. When arrays are redimensioned, especially large arrays, a new array is actually created and the old array is destroyed. If the `Preserve` keyword is used, the data must be copied from the old array to the new array. This action can have a severe impact on performance.

## PERFORMING ASSIGNMENT STATEMENTS WITH ARRAYS

The process of storing and retrieving information from an array is similar to the process of storing and retrieving information using scalar variables. Storing data to and retrieving data from an array requires the use of a subscript to reference a specific array element, however.

To see how to store and retrieve array data, this example uses an array with 13 elements representing the months of the year. The statements in this section show how to store and retrieve data to and from those elements.

The following statement declares a 13-element array to store monthly sales data for each month of the year. Again, the first element of the array is not used in this example so that element 1 is associated with the first month of the year instead of element 0.

```
Dim SalesList(12) As Double
```

The array is named SalesList. The text within the parentheses defines the upper bound of the array, which is 12. Because the lower bound of all Visual Basic arrays is 0, the preceding statement declares a 13-element array rather than a 12-element array. Furthermore, each element in the array has a data type of Double.

After an array has been declared, data can be stored to and retrieved from the individual array elements. To reference a specific array element, a subscript is used. The subscript is an Integer value that appears in parentheses.

The following statements store and retrieve a value to and from the second array element, respectively. The second array element stores data for January and is identified by the subscript 1. Again, subscript 0 is unused.

```
Dim SalesListItem As Double
SalesList(1) = 84616.12
SalesListItem = SalesList(1)
```

The first assignment statement stores the literal value 84616.12 in the second array element, which has a subscript of 1. The second statement reads the value from the same array element and stores it in the scalar variable named SalesListItem.

Figure 9-5 illustrates how data is stored to and retrieved from an array element.

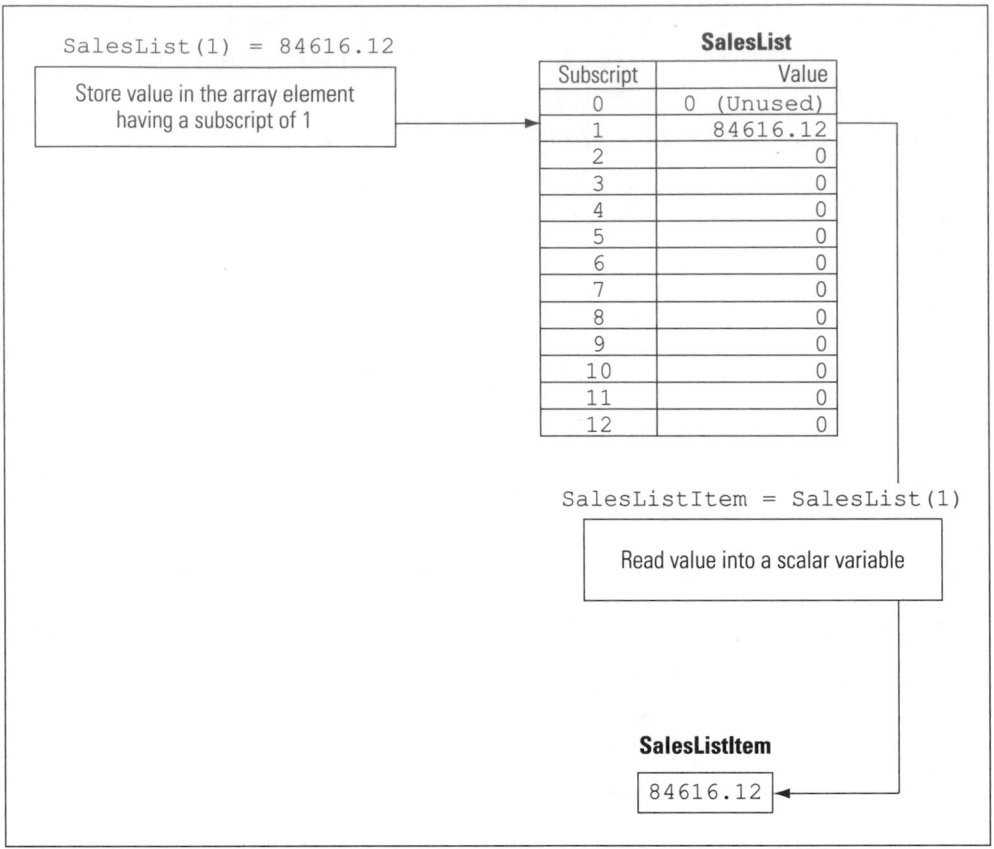

Figure 9-5: Storing and retrieving array values

Explicit type conversion of array elements is also possible just as explicit type conversion is possible with scalar data types. The elements in the array named SalesList have a data type of `Double`. The `ToString` method can be used to convert an array element to a data type of `String`, as the following statements show:

```
Dim OutputString As String
OutputString = SalesList(1).ToString
```

The preceding statement calls the `ToString` method on the second array element (having a subscript of 1), storing the result in the variable OutputString.

Compare the preceding call to the `ToString` method with the following statement:

```
OutputString = SalesList.ToString
```

In the preceding statement, the `ToString` method is called but the array subscript is omitted. Although the statement is legal, it does not return all of the elements converted to a `String` data type. Rather, the statement returns the following string:

```
System.Double[]
```

Calling the `ToString` method on an array returns the data type of the array elements, rather than the data contained in a particular element.

Explicit type conversion can also be performed when storing a value in an array element. The following statement assumes that txtSalesAmount is an instance of the `TextBox` control:

```
SalesList(1) = ToDouble(txtSalesAmount.Text)
```

The elements in the array named SalesList have a data type of `Double`. Thus, the string stored in the text box must be converted to the `Double` data type before being stored in an array element. An exception is thrown if the data cannot be converted to the appropriate type in the same way that exceptions are thrown with scalar variables.

In addition to literal values, variables can be used as array subscripts. The following statements retrieve the second element from the array named SalesList:

```
Dim SubscriptValue As Integer = 1
Dim SalesListItem As Double
SalesListItem = SalesList(SubscriptValue)
```

Instead of using a literal value for the array subscript, the preceding statements use the variable named SubscriptValue.

Subscripts cannot have a floating-point data type. Thus, the following statements cause a syntax error if strict type checking is enabled. If strict type checking is disabled, the value is converted to an `Integer` data type.

```
Dim DoubleValue As Double = 1.2
SalesList(DoubleValue) = 3
```

# USING LOOPS TO EXAMINE ARRAY ELEMENTS

Loops are commonly used to examine the elements in an array or to assign values to array elements sequentially. The following common array tasks require the use of loops:

» Calculating the total value of all array elements using an accumulator

» Calculating the minimum value stored in an array

» Calculating the maximum value stored in an array

» Calculating the average of an array's values

The following sections discuss each topic in turn. Then, one additional section discusses how to use arrays as function arguments.

## CALCULATING THE TOTAL VALUE OF AN ARRAY'S ELEMENTS

Calculating the total value of an array's elements involves writing a Do or For loop. Each time through the loop, an accumulator is used to store the total. The flowchart shown in Figure 9-6 shows the steps to examine each element in an array and calculate a total.

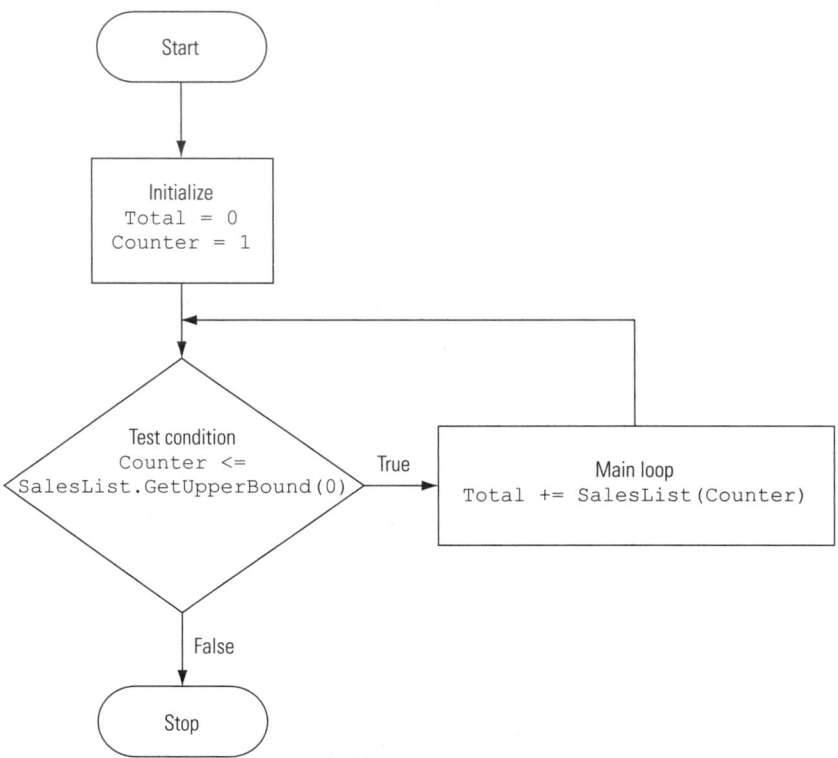

Figure 9-6: Using a loop to examine array elements

The following Do loop examines all the elements in the array named SalesList except for the first element, and calculates a total for those elements using the logic from the flowchart shown in Figure 9-6. In this case, the first element is ignored because data for the months January through December is stored in elements 1 through 12.

```
Dim Total As Double = 0.0
Dim Counter As Integer = 1
Do While Counter <= SalesList.GetUpperBound(0)
    Total += SalesList(Counter)
Loop
```

The preceding Do loop examines the array elements using the variable named Counter as a counter. The first time through the loop, Counter has a value of 1. Again, even though the first array element has a subscript value of 0, the value 1 is used to initialize the counter because the first array element is not used in this example. The statement in the loop executes for each array element. The variable Total is an accumulator and tallies the value for all of the used array elements.

Because the size of an array is known when writing a loop, a For loop can be used instead of a Do loop, as the following statements show:

```
Dim Total As Double = 0.0
Dim Counter As Integer
For Counter = 1 To SalesList.GetUpperBound(0)
    Total += SalesList(Counter)
Next
```

The preceding For loop examines the elements in the array named SalesList, just as the previous Do loop did. The loop iterates from 1 to the array's upper bound. Each time through the loop, the accumulator named Total is updated.

## DETERMINING THE MINIMUM VALUE OF AN ARRAY ELEMENT

Searching an array's elements to determine the value of the minimum array element value is a common operation. For example, you might want to determine the minimum sales amount from a list of sales amounts. As with most array operations, a For loop can be used to examine each array element. Each time through the loop, the value of the current array element is compared with the current minimum value. If the value of the current array element is less than the current minimum value, the current minimum value is replaced.

A key to solving the problem is initializing the current minimum value. There are two solutions to the problem. The first is to set the current minimum value to the maximum value for the corresponding data type, as the following statement shows:

```
Dim CurrentMinimum As Double = System.Double.MaxValue
```

By setting the current minimum value to the largest possible value for the Double data type, it is not possible for an array element to have a larger value. A second common solution is to set the current minimum value to the value stored in the first array element that is used, as the following statement shows:

```
Dim Counter As Integer = 1
Dim CurrentMinimum As Double = SalesList(Counter)
```

The following code segment determines the minimum value stored in the array named SalesList. Again, the first array element is not used in this example so Counter is initialized to 1 instead of to 0.

```
Dim Counter As Integer = 1
Dim CurrentMinimum As Double = SalesList(Counter)
For Counter = 1 To SalesList.GetUpperBound(0)
    If CurrentMinimum > SalesList(Counter) Then
        CurrentMinimum = SalesList(Counter)
    End If
Next
```

The preceding statements examine each element in the array named SalesList with the exception of the first element, which is unused. The current minimum value is compared with the value of the current array element. The first time through the loop, the current minimum value is always equal to the current value. After all of the array elements have been examined, the variable CurrentMinimum contains the minimum array value.

## DETERMINING THE MAXIMUM VALUE OF AN ARRAY ELEMENT

The steps to determine the maximum value stored in an array's elements are not that much different than the steps to determine the minimum value. Essentially, the process is reversed, as the following statements show:

```
Dim Counter As Integer = 1
Dim CurrentMaximum As Double = SalesList(Counter)
For Counter = 1 To SalesList.GetUpperBound(0)
    If CurrentMaximum < SalesList(Counter) Then
        CurrentMaximum = SalesList(Counter)
    End If
Next
```

The preceding statements initialize the variable named CurrentMaximum to the value of the second array element because the first array element is not used. The For loop again examines all of the array elements with the exception of the first unused element. If the current maximum value is less than the value of the current array element, the maximum value is reset. Thus, when the For loop has executed, the variable CurrentMaximum contains the maximum array element value.

## DETERMINING THE AVERAGE VALUE OF AN ARRAY'S ELEMENTS

To calculate the average value of an array's elements, an accumulator is used to tally all of the values. The average is then calculated by dividing the total by the number of array elements. The following code segment calculates the average value of the array named SalesList. Again, the example assumes that the first array element is unused.

```
Dim Counter As Integer = 1
Dim Total, Average As Double
For Counter = 1 To SalesList.GetUpperBound(0)
    Total += SalesList(Counter)
Next
Average = Total / SalesList.GetUpperBound(0)
```

The For loop examines all of the elements with the exception of the first element. The statement in the loop updates the accumulator named Total to tally the values. Finally, the total is divided by the array's upper bound, which is 12—the number of used array elements.

## ARRAYS AS FUNCTION ARGUMENTS

The code segments thus far have calculated the minimum, maximum, and average value of an array's elements. In addition, they all shared one common characteristic: They each operated on an array having a data type of Double. Furthermore, each code segment was designed to work with any one-dimensional array, regardless of the number of elements in the array. Thus, it's possible to create a class with Function procedures to calculate the minimum, maximum, and average values for any array by passing the array as an argument to the Function procedure.

Just as scalar variables can be passed as arguments to Function and Sub procedures, so too can arrays. To illustrate, suppose that you want to calculate the total value of all elements in an array such as the following array named SampleArray:

```
Private SampleArray() As Double = {6.11, 4.12, 5.88, 6.44}
```

To begin, examine the following Function procedure, which accepts a one-dimensional array as its argument. This Function procedure calculates the total of all array elements. Note that in the following generic example, the first array element is used:

```
Public Class ArrayStats
    Public Shared Function Total( _
        ByVal argList() As Double) As Double
        Dim Counter As Integer = 0
        Dim TotalValue As Double
        For Counter = 0 To argList.GetUpperBound(0)
            TotalValue += argList(Counter)
        Next
        Return TotalValue
    End Function
End Class
```

When passing an array as a procedure argument, the syntax of the argument is the same as the syntax to pass a scalar variable with one exception: The array being passed as an argument is declared with an empty argument list. That is, the syntax is the same as the syntax used to declare a dynamic array. Thus, in the preceding Function procedure, the argument named argList is a one-dimensional array.

The following code segment shows how to call the preceding Function procedure:

```
Dim Total As Double
Total = ArrayStats.Total(SampleArray)
```

# SORTING AND REVERSING ARRAY ELEMENTS

As mentioned, the System.Array class supports methods to sort an array's elements and to reverse an array's elements. These methods perform all of the work to sort the array, or reverse the array elements. As the developer, you need not worry about the sort or element exchanges that are performed.

## SORTING ELEMENTS

To sort all of the elements in a one-dimensional array in ascending order, the following call to the Sort method is used:

```
Private SampleArray() As Double = {6.11, 4.12, 5.88, 6.44}
System.Array.Sort(SampleArray)
```

The second of the preceding statements sorts all of the elements in the one-dimensional array named SampleArray.

In addition to sorting all of the elements in an array, it is possible to sort only a part of the array. To sort only part of an array, the Sort method is called with two additional arguments. The second argument contains the starting subscript of the element to be sorted. The third argument contains the number of elements to sort. Thus, the following statements sort the array named SampleArray but exclude the first element:

```
Private SampleArray() As Double = {0, 6.11, 4.12, 5.88, 6.44}
System.Array.Sort(SampleArray, 1, SampleArray.GetUpperBound(0))
```

In the preceding statement, the first element of the array is excluded from the sort. Thus, only elements 1 through 4 are sorted.

## REVERSING ELEMENTS

In addition to sorting an array, it's possible to reverse the order of the array elements by calling the Reverse method of the Array class. Again, it is possible to reverse all of the array elements or only a subset of the array elements. The following statements show how to reverse the order of the elements in the array named SampleArray:

```
Private SampleArray() As Double = {6.11, 4.12, 5.88, 6.44}
System.Array.Reverse(SampleArray)
```

The Reverse method can be called with the same arguments as the call to the preceding Sort method, so as to exclude the first element, as the following statements show:

```
Private SampleArray() As Double = {0, 6.11, 4.12, 5.88, 6.44}
System.Array.Reverse(SampleArray, 1, _
    SampleArray.GetUpperBound(0))
```

The preceding statement reverses the elements in the array named SampleArray. Only the order of elements 1 through 4 is reversed.

## USING SORTING AND REVERSING TOGETHER

Suppose that an array should be sorted in descending order instead of ascending order. To do this, call the Sort method, and then call the Reverse method, as follows:

```
System.Array.Sort(SampleArray)
System.Array.Reverse(SampleArray)
```

In this exploration exercise, you will examine and run an application to store and retrieve values from a one-dimensional array. The application will also calculate the minimum, maximum, and average values stored in an array. The code has been developed with a class named ArrayStats having shared methods to calculate the minimum, maximum, and average value. For each method, the array is passed as the first argument to the method. The second argument contains a Boolean value to indicate whether the first array element should be examined. Each method returns the result. You will also see how to sort an array and reverse the order of an array's elements. Finally, you will see the performance effect of redimensioning large arrays.

1. Run the solution for the concept lesson. Click the **Array Operations** tab. Figure 9-7 shows the Array Operations tab.

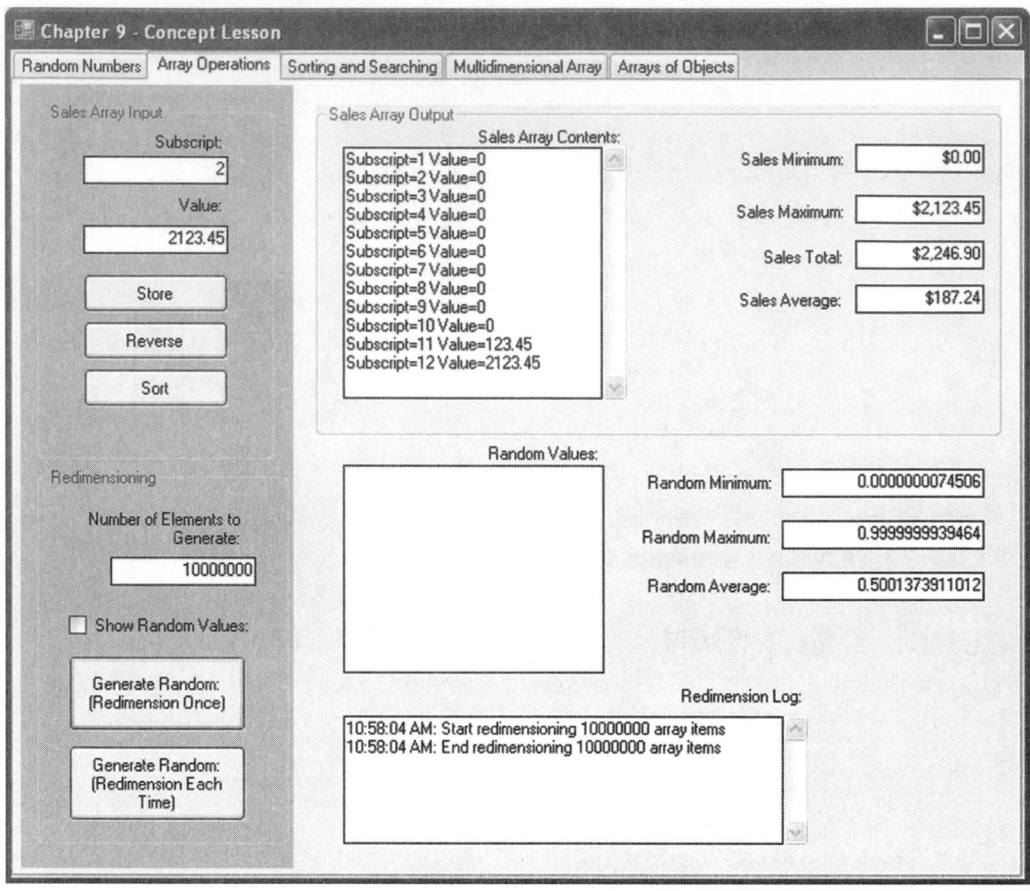

Figure 9-7: Concept lesson—Array Operations tab

2. The section titled Sales Array Input contains two text boxes titled Subscript and Value. When the Store button is clicked, the value is stored in the array element having the specified subscript. In addition, the array elements are enumerated and the current subscripts and values are displayed. Finally, the minimum, maximum, and average values of the array are calculated and displayed using the functions discussed previously in the chapter. Click the **Store** button; the value 123.45 is stored in the element having a subscript of 1. The array is enumerated, and the minimum, maximum, and average values are calculated. Explore the process by storing different values in other array elements.

3. Click the **Reverse** and **Sort** buttons to reverse the array elements and to sort them. Note that the first element is excluded from the sort.

The purpose of the Redimensioning section is to show the performance impact of redimensioning large arrays. Random numeric values are stored in an array. The text box appearing in the section contains the final size of the array. Checking the check box causes the array elements to be added to a `ListBox` control instance. Generating over 1000 elements will take quite a while if this check box is checked, because updating the visible contents of a list box is a time consuming operation.

4. Click the **Generate Random: (Redimension Once)** button. The array is redimensioned and the random values are generated. The starting and ending times are logged to the text box at thc bottom of the form.

5. Click the **Generate Random: (Redimension Each Time)** button. The array is redimensioned each time a random value is generated. Thus, the array's size is increased by one each time through a loop. A message appears every 10,000 iterations. Note that as the array becomes larger, the time to redimension the array increases significantly.

## MINI-QUIZ 2

1. Which of the following general statements is correct regarding arrays?

    a. An array with one dimension has a rank of 0.

    b. Individual array elements are referenced by a unique index value known as a subscript.

    c. In Visual Basic, arrays are value types.

    d. After being declared, the size of an array cannot be changed.

    e. All arrays must be declared having numeric data types, such as `Integer` or `Double`.

2. Which of the following statements is correct regarding the following array declaration?

    ```
    Dim CurrentList() As Integer = {1, 2, 3, 4, 5}
    ```

    a. The largest subscript for the array is 4.

    b. The largest subscript for the array is 5.

    c. If the `GetUpperBound` method were called on the array, the value 5 would be returned.

    d. The array has a rank of 5.

    e. none of the above

*(Continued)* ▶

3. Which of the following statements correctly declares an array with 10 elements having a data type of Integer?

a. `Dim Quiz() As Integer`

b. `Dim Quiz(10) As Integer`

c. `Dim Quiz(1 To 10) As Integer`

d. `Dim Quiz(9) As Integer`

e. `Dim Quiz(9) As Array(Of Integer)`

4. Write the statements to declare an array with 100 elements named Quiz. Each element should have a data type of Integer. Then, write the statements to store random integer values having values between 1 and 10 in the array.

# INTRODUCTION TO SEARCHING

In addition to using loops to perform operations on all of the elements in an array to calculate totals and averages, it is often necessary to locate a particular item in an array. In this section, you will learn how to develop algorithms for the following array tasks:

» Searching for an item in an unordered (unsorted) array using a sequential search

» Searching for an element in a sorted array using a type of search called a binary search

## SEARCHING FOR AN ARRAY ITEM IN AN UNORDERED ARRAY WITH A SEQUENTIAL SEARCH

One common task when working with arrays is to search for a particular array item. Suppose that an array contained an unordered (unsorted) list of values, and it was necessary to determine whether a particular value existed. To determine whether a particular value exists in an array, the array can be searched sequentially using a loop. If the current array element is equal to the search value, the list item is found and the loop exits. If all of the array elements have been examined and the element is not found, the element does not appear in the array. Figure 9-8 shows the flowchart to search for an element in an unordered array.

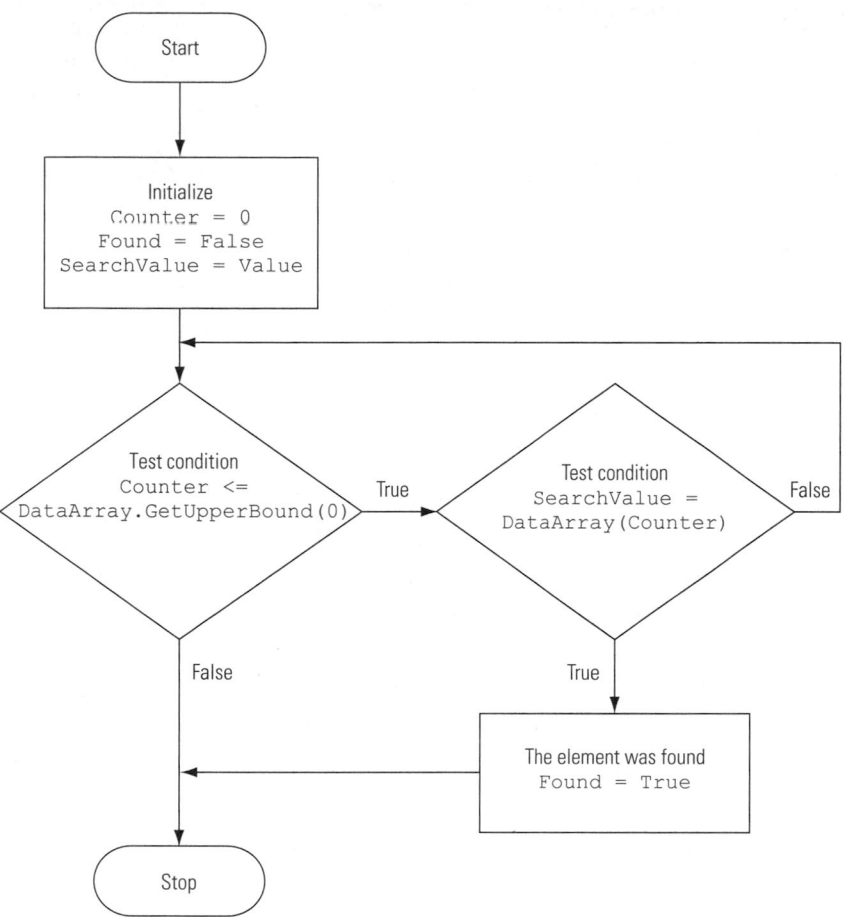

Figure 9-8: Searching for an element in an unordered array

The following code segment shows the code to search for an item in an unsorted array. The following code segment assumes that all elements in the array are used:

```
Dim Counter As Integer
Dim SearchValue As Integer
Dim Found As Boolean = False
SearchValue = ToInt32(txtSearch.Text)
For Counter = 0 To DataArray.GetUpperBound(0)
    If SearchValue = DataArray(Counter) Then
        Found = True
        Exit For
    End If
Next
```

As shown in the preceding code segment, a `For` loop is used to examine each array element. The current array element is compared with the search value. If the two values are the same, the element was found and the variable Found is set to `True`. The `For` loop then exits and no further array elements are examined. If all of the elements have been searched, the variable Found remains `False`, indicating that the search value was not found in the array.

## SEARCHING FOR AN ARRAY ITEM IN A SORTED ARRAY USING A BINARY SEARCH

If an array is sorted, there is a way to search for a particular element (the key) using a search called a **binary search**. In the worst case of the sequential search, every element of the array would have to be checked to see if it matched the key.

The performance of a binary search is much better than a sequential (linear) search because it is not necessary to check each array element. The binary search works by comparing the search value with the element at the middle position of the array. If the search value is less than the value of the middle element, the element must be in the first half of the array. If the search value is greater than the value of the middle element, the element must be in the second half of the array. For each iteration the process is repeated, so for each iteration, the part of the table searched is cut by one-half. The process continues until the element is found or not found. Figure 9-9 shows the operation of a binary search.

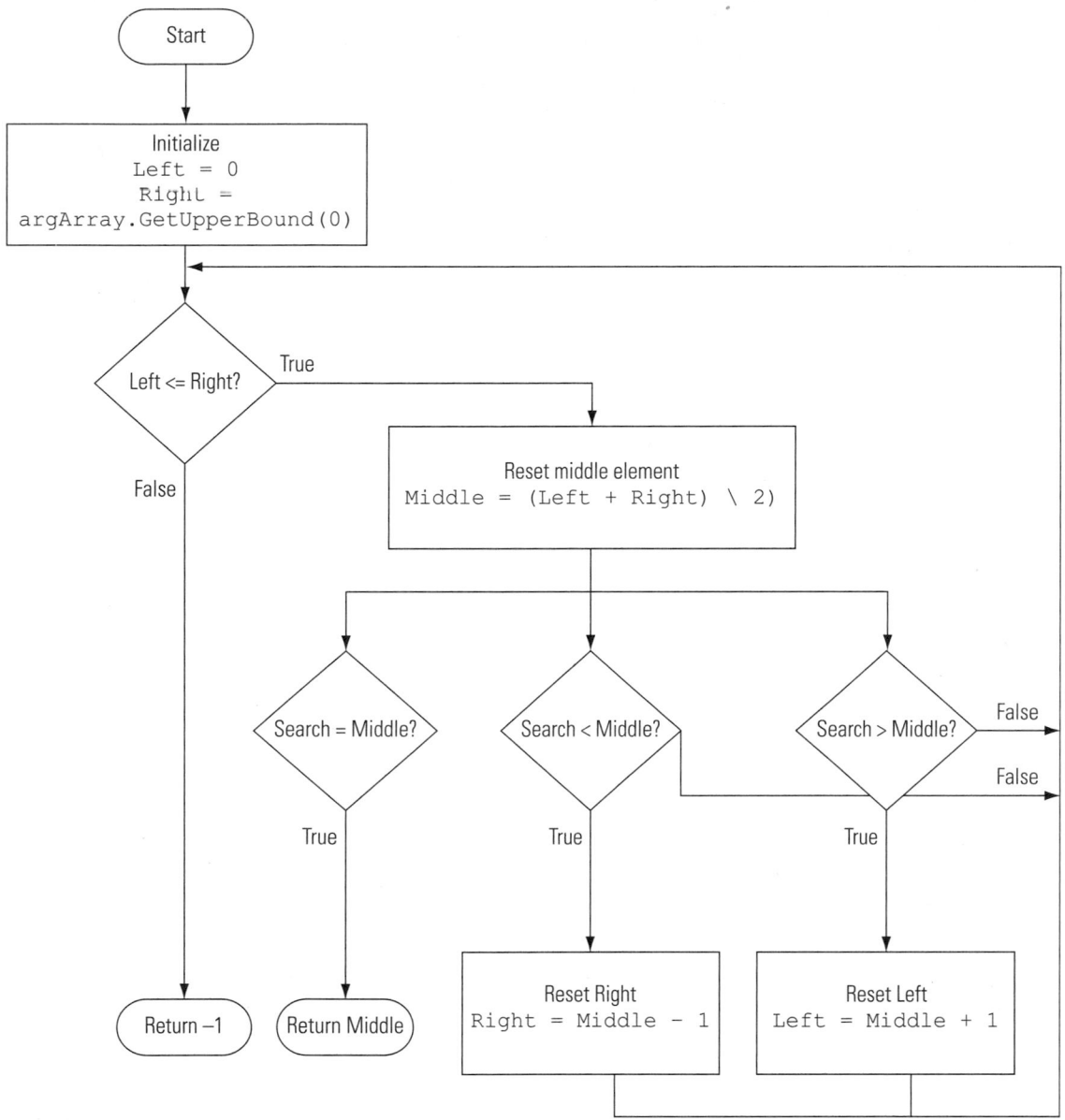

Figure 9-9: Binary search flowchart

As shown in Figure 9-9, the far-right element is initialized to the largest array subscript. A first test is made to determine whether the index of the left element is less than or equal to the far-right element. If it is, the index of the middle element is reset. If not, the element is not found and the procedure returns the value –1 indicating that the search element did not exist. If the search value and middle element are equal, the value is found, and the index of the elment is returned. Otherwise, the index of the middle element is reset, thereby cutting the part of the array being searched by one-half.

Figure 9-10 shows how an integer array containing a list of values is searched.

| Index | 0 | 1 | 2 | 3 | 4 | 5 | 6 | 7 | 8 | 9 | 10 |
|---|---|---|---|---|---|---|---|---|---|---|---|
| Iteration 1 | 0 | 2 | 4 | 6 | 8 | **10** | 12 | 14 | 16 | 18 | 10 |
| Iteration 2 | 0 | 2 | **4** | 6 | 8 | | | | | | |
| Iteration 3 | **0** | 2 | | | | | | | | | |
| Iteration 4 | 0 | **2** | | | | | | | | | |

Figure 9-10: Comparisons using the binary search

Figure 9-10 shows the binary search operating on 11 values. The figure assumes that the search is for the value 2. On the first pass, the element having a subscript of 5 is the middle element. On the second pass, the subscript having a value of 2 is the middle element. On the third pass, the first element is the middle element. On the final pass, the element having a subscript value of 1 is the middle element. This subscript value is returned.

The following code segment shows the implementation of the binary search:

```
Public Shared Function BinarySearch( _
    ByRef argArray() As Integer, ByVal value As Integer) _
    As Integer
    Dim Left As Integer = 0
    Dim Right As Integer = argArray.GetUpperBound(0)
    Dim Middle As Integer
    Dim Search As Integer
    Search = value
    Do While (Left <= Right)
        Middle = (Left + Right) \ 2
        If Search = argArray(Middle) Then
            Return Middle
        ElseIf Search < argArray(Middle) Then
            Right = Middle - 1
        Else
            Left = Middle + 1
        End If
    Loop
    Return -1
End Function
```

In the preceding `Function` procedure, the array to be searched is passed as an argument along with the value to find. The procedure returns an `Integer`. If the search value is found, the value returned is the subscript corresponding to the found element. If the value is not found, the value –1 is returned from the procedure.

The variables Left and Right contain the subscripts of the far-left and far-right array element. The variable Middle contains the subscript of the element halfway between the Left and Right elements. Each time through the `While` loop, the variable Middle is recalculated, thereby cutting the size of the part of the table to search by one-half. The value of the search element is compared with the middle element and the right and left boundaries are updated accordingly. If the two values are equal, the element is found, and the index of the element is returned to the calling procedure.

In this exploration exercise, you will see how to perform a linear search and a binary search of an array.

1. Run the concept lesson for the chapter and click the **Sorting and Searching** tab. Figure 9-11 shows the Sorting and Searching tab.

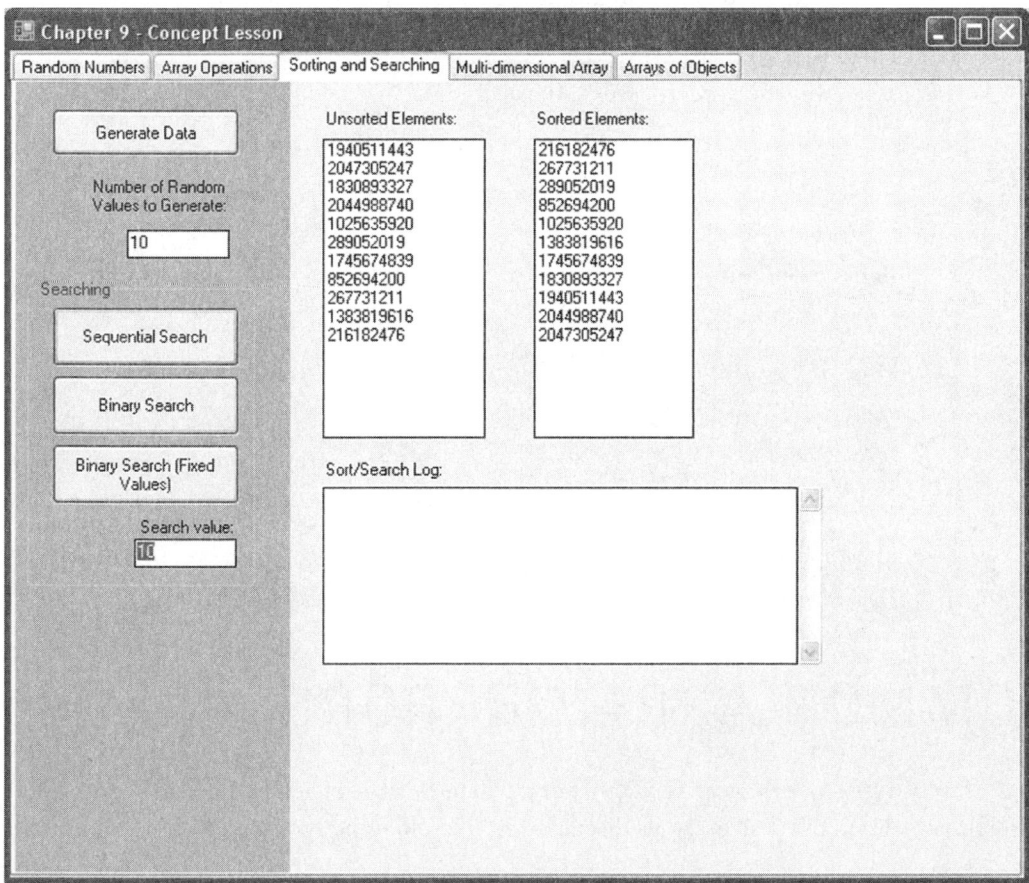

Figure 9-11: Concept lesson—Sorting and Searching tab

2. Click the **Generate Data** button. An array is initialized with random values. The text box contains the number of elements to generate. In addition, the unsorted and sorted elements appear in the list boxes.

3. Click the **Sequential Search** and **Binary Search** buttons. The sorted array is searched using a sequential search and a binary search, respectively. Change the Search value in the text box as necessary. A message box appears indicating whether the item was found in the array.

4. Click the **Binary Search (Fixed Values)** button. A binary search is performed on an arbitrary fixed array of values. A message box appears indicating whether the item was found in the array.

## MINI-QUIZ 3

1. Which of the following statements is correct regarding the binary search?

   a. It can be used to search for items in a sorted array or in an unsorted array.

   b. It can only be used on a sorted array.

   c. The performance of a binary search is always worse than the performance of a sequential search.

   d. none of the above

2. Which of the following statements is correct regarding a sequential search?

   a. For a sequential search to be used, the items in an array must be sorted.

   b. A sequential search can be used on an unsorted array.

   c. Using a sequential search, all of the array items must be examined in the worst possible case.

   d. both a and c

   e. both b and c

# COMMON ARRAY ERRORS

Different types of errors arise when storing data to and retrieving data from an array's elements. Each of these errors is discussed in the following sections.

## ERRORS ARISING FROM OMITTING AN ARRAY SUBSCRIPT

The first type of error occurs when an array reference does not contain a subscript, as shown in the following statement. When you do not include a subscript, you are, in effect, attempting to assign a value to an entire array, which is not legal.

```
Dim DemoArray(12) As Integer
DemoArray = 100
```

The preceding statement causes the following syntax error: "Value of type 'Integer' cannot be converted to '1-dimensional array of Integer'." The error arises because the value on the right side of the expression is an `Integer`, but the value on the left side of the expression is an array of type `Integer`.

## SUBSCRIPT OUT OF RANGE ERRORS

A second type of error occurs if a subscript is used that is beyond the array bounds. For example, the following statements cause a `System.IndexOutOfRangeException` to be thrown because the subscript value is greater than the upper and lower bound of the array, respectively:

```
Dim DemoArray(10) As Integer
DemoArray(20) = 100
DemoArray(-1) = 100
```

## LOGIC ERRORS THAT ARISE WHEN EXAMINING ARRAY ELEMENTS

Another common mistake made when examining all of the elements in the array is missing the first array element, as shown in the following code segment:

```
Dim DemoArray(12) As Double
Dim Total As Double
For Counter = 1 to DemoArray.GetUpperBound(0)
    Total += DemoArray(Counter)
Next
```

The preceding code segment runs correctly, but the value of the variable Total is incorrect because the array element having a subscript value of 0 is not included in the accumulator's value. Of course, the preceding loop is correct if the first array element is not used, as shown in several of the preceding examples. Thus, use care to include or exclude the first array element based on how the array is being used.

Conversely, another error occurs when a loop tries to access an element beyond the bounds of the array, as the following statements show:

```
Dim DemoArray(12) As Double
Dim Counter As Integer
Dim Total As Double
For Counter = 0 To 24
    Total += DemoArray(Counter)
Next
```

When the preceding loop executes, a `System.IndexOutOfRangeException` is thrown because the loop attempts to reference an array element that does not exist. Specifically, the statement in the loop tries to reference an array element with a subscript greater than 12.

# INTRODUCTION TO MULTIDIMENSIONAL ARRAYS

So far in this chapter, you have worked with arrays having a single dimension (a rank of 1). However, arrays can also have multiple dimensions. This part of the chapter introduces two- and three-dimensional arrays.

## INTRODUCTION TO TWO-DIMENSIONAL ARRAYS

A two-dimensional array has rows and columns. Thus, a two-dimensional array is similar to a table or grid. The syntax to declare a two-dimensional array is a bit different than the syntax to declare a one-dimensional array, as the following statements show:

```
Dim Table(,) As Integer
Dim Table(9, 9) As Integer
```

The preceding statements declare two-dimensional arrays. The first statement declares a two-dimensional array having no initial size. Note that a comma appears in the declaration to indicate that there are two dimensions. The second statement also declares a two-dimensional array. The array has 10 rows and 10 columns. Thus, the array has a total of 100 elements. The data type of the elements in both arrays is `Integer`.

## INITIALIZING TWO-DIMENSIONAL ARRAYS

Just as one-dimensional arrays can be initialized when they are declared, so too can two-dimensional arrays. To illustrate how to initialize a two-dimensional array, Table 9-1 shows sample quarterly sales data for four different sales regions.

| | North | South | East | West |
|---|---|---|---|---|
| Quarter 1 | 150 | 140 | 170 | 178 |
| Quarter 2 | 155 | 148 | 182 | 190 |
| Quarter 3 | 162 | 153 | 191 | 184 |
| Quarter 4 | 181 | 176 | 201 | 203 |

Table 9-1: Sample sales data

The following statement illustrates how to declare and initialize a two-dimensional array to store the sales data appearing in Table 9-1:

```
Private SalesArray(,) As Integer = { _
    {150, 140, 170, 178}, _
    {155, 148, 182, 190}, _
    {162, 153, 191, 184}, _
    {181, 176, 201, 203} _
    }
```

Again, for the array to be initialized, it must be declared with no initial size. Initializing a two-dimensional array involves using a nested initialization list. The inner list represents the rows. The outer list represents the columns. Braces separate the inner and outer lists.

## REFERENCING ELEMENTS IN A TWO-DIMENSIONAL ARRAY

Referencing the elements in a two-dimensional array requires that two subscripts be used instead of a single subscript. Thus, the following statements reference the first row of the first column of the array named SalesArray and store the value in the variable named Cell:

```
Dim Cell As Integer
Cell = SalesArray(0, 0)
```

Recall the multiplication table discussed in Chapter 8; that same multiplication table could be implemented as a two-dimensional array using the following code segment:

```
Private MultiplicationTable(9, 9) As Integer
Dim Row, Column As Integer
For Row = 0 To 9
    For Column = 0 To 9
        MultiplicationTable(Row, Column) = Row * Column
    Next
Next
```

The preceding code segment uses nested `For` loops to initialize the two-dimensional array. The outer loop is used to initialize the rows and the inner loop is used to initialize the columns. Each cell stores a value for the multiplication table.

## REDIMENSIONING TWO-DIMENSIONAL ARRAYS

It is possible to redimension two-dimensional arrays with the `ReDim` statement. However, there are restrictions, as described in the following list:

» It is illegal to change the number of array dimensions with the `ReDim` statement. For example, the `ReDim` statement cannot be used to change a two-dimensional array to a three-dimensional array.

» When using the `Preserve` keyword, only the size of the last dimension can be changed. The size of the other dimensions cannot be changed or a `System.ArrayTypeMismatchException` is thrown.

## INTRODUCTION TO THREE-DIMENSIONAL ARRAYS

In addition to arrays having one or two dimensions, it is also possible to create three-dimensional arrays. The syntax to declare a three-dimensional array is consistent with the syntax to declare a two-dimensional array. That is, a three-dimensional array has three subscripts instead of two. The following statements declare three-dimensional arrays:

```
Dim Cube(,,)
Dim Cube(9, 9, 9)
```

The first of the preceding statements declares a three-dimensional array with no initial size. The second statement declares a 10 by 10 by 10 three-dimensional array. Thus, the array will have 1000 elements.

## REFERENCING THE ELEMENTS IN A THREE-DIMENSIONAL ARRAY

To reference the elements in a three-dimensional array, three subscripts are used, as the following statements show:

```
Dim Cell As Integer
Cell = Cube(1, 1, 1)
```

In this exploration exercise, you will see how to initialize a two-dimensional array and how to store and retrieve values from a two-dimensional array.

1. Run the concept lesson for the chapter and click the **Multidimensional Array** tab.

2. Click the **Multiplication Table** button. The multiplication table discussed in this section is initialized and displayed in the form's text box, as shown in Figure 9-12.

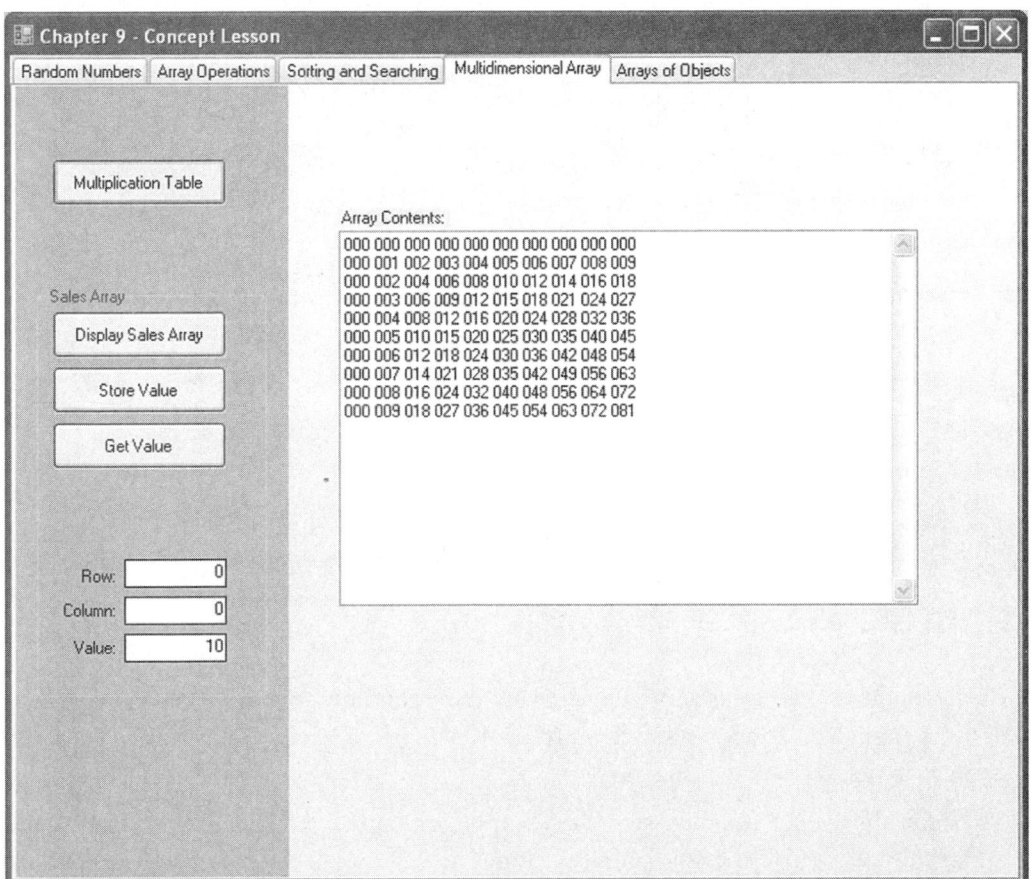

Figure 9-12: Concept lesson—Multidimensional Array tab

3. Click the **Display Sales Array** button. The sales array data shown in Table 9-1 is displayed in the form's text box.

4. The Store Value and Get Value buttons use the data stored in the text boxes to store or retrieve a value from a given row and column number. Click the **Store Value** button. The value in the text box is stored in the corresponding row and column. Enter a row and column, and then click the **Get Value** button. The value at the specified row and column is retrieved and stored in the text box.

## MINI-QUIZ 4

1. Given the following array declaration:

```
Dim QuizArray(5, 3)
```

list the number of rows and columns in the array. In addition, list the total number of array elements.

2. Given a two-dimensional array named Demo, write the statements to calculate the total of all the array elements storing the result in the variable named Total.

3. How many dimensions are in the following array?

```
Dim DemoArray(,,)
```

4. How many elements are in the following array?

```
Dim ThreeDArray(0, 0, 0)
```

# WORKING WITH ARRAYS OF OBJECTS

At this point in the discussion of arrays, you have seen how to work with arrays having data types such as `Integer` and `Double`. However, just as the `List` class can store references to objects, so too can arrays.

To begin, suppose that a form has three text boxes named txtFirstName, txtLastName, and txtAddress. Furthermore, suppose that it is necessary to perform operations on each of these text boxes as a group. In such a case, an array can be used to store references to each of these TextBox control instances, as the following statements show:

```
Dim TextBoxList(2) As TextBox
TextBoxList(0) = txtFirstName
TextBoxList(1) = txtLastName
TextBoxList(2) = txtAddress
```

As shown in the preceding statements, a one-dimensional array named TextBoxList is declared having three elements. Each element has a data type of TextBox. The remaining statements store references to the three control instances in each array element. Figure 9-13 shows how memory is allocated to store the preceding array.

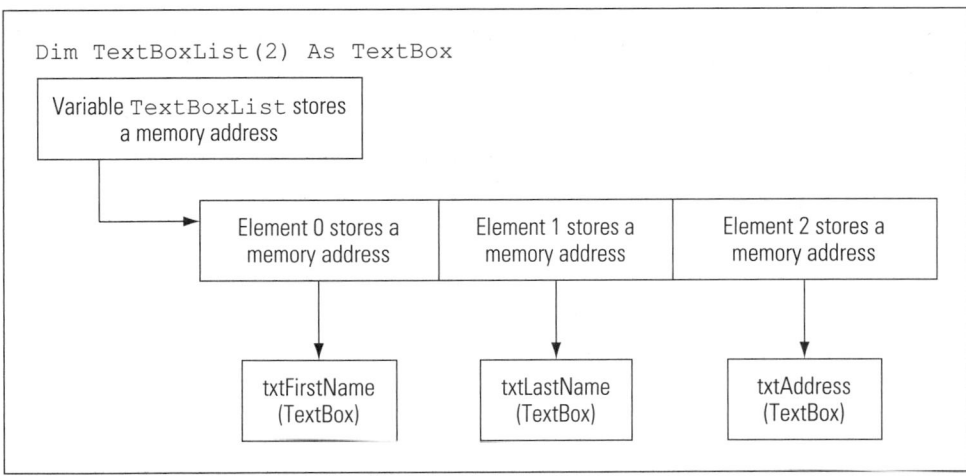

Figure 9-13: Memory allocation to store an array of text boxes

As discussed, an array is a reference type, so the array variable named TextBoxList stores a reference to the memory allocated to store the array elements. Each array element, in turn, is also a reference type. Each array element stores a reference to a TextBox control instance.

This array can then be used to perform operations on all three control instances at once. For example, a procedure named EnableTextBoxList might be useful to enable or disable a group of text boxes, as the following statements show:

```
Private Sub EnableTextBoxList(ByVal argTextBox() _
    As TextBox, ByVal argEnable As Boolean)
    Dim Counter As Integer
    For Counter = 0 To argTextBox.GetUpperBound(0)
        argTextBox(Counter).Enabled = argEnable
    Next
End Sub
```

The EnableTextBoxList procedure accepts two arguments; the first is an array of TextBox control instances. The second is a Boolean value indicating whether the control instances should be enabled or disabled. The For loop is used to enumerate the contents of the array. The statement in the For loop sets the Enabled property based on the second argument's value.

In addition to working with arrays of predefined objects, it is possible to work with arrays of class instances that you create. To illustrate, suppose that the following class has been declared:

```
Public Class LogRecord
    Public ID As Integer
    Public StartTime As DateTime
    Public EndTime As DateTime
End Class
```

The preceding class is very simple having only three members. The only purpose of the preceding class is to show how to declare and initialize an array to store multiple instances of the same class.

The following code segment shows how to declare an array, initialize class instances, and store references to those class instances in the array:

```
Dim LogRecordList() As LogRecord
Dim Count As Integer
Dim Elements As Integer
Elements = ToInt32(txtArrayElements.Text)
ReDim LogRecordList(Elements)
For Count = 0 To LogRecordList.GetUpperBound(0)
    Dim LogRecordCurrent As New LogRecord
    LogRecordCurrent.ID = Count
    LogRecordCurrent.StartTime = Now
    LogRecordCurrent.EndTime = Now
    LogRecordList(Count) = LogRecordCurrent
Next
```

The preceding code segment redimensions an array named LogRecordList. The statements in the `For` loop create a new instance of the LogRecord class and set its properties each time through the loop. The new class instance is then added to the array.

In this exploration exercise, you will work with arrays of objects. The first array contains a list of `TextBox` control instances. The second array contains a list of developer-created class instances.

1. Run the concept lesson for the chapter and click the **Arrays of Objects** tab. Figure 9-14 shows the Arrays of Objects tab.

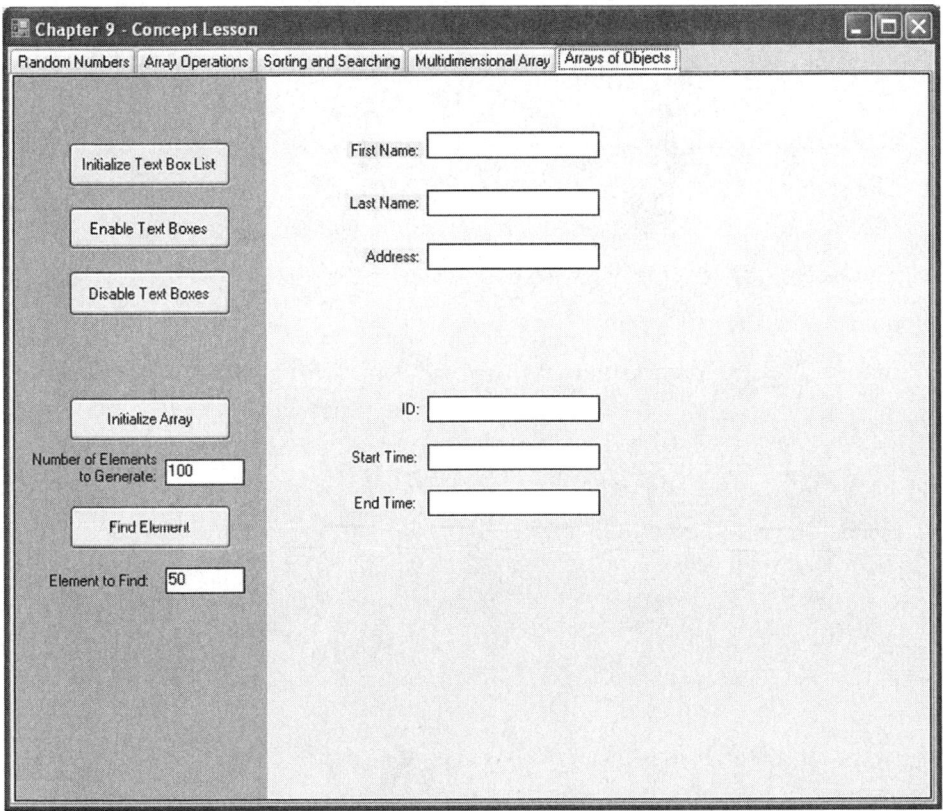

Figure 9-14: Concept lesson—Arrays of Objects tab

2. Click the **Initialize Text Box List** button. An array named TextBoxList is initialized to store references to the `TextBox` control instances appearing to the right of the group of buttons. You will not see anything change on the form.

3. Click the **Disable Text Boxes** button. The text boxes are disabled. Click the **Enable Text Boxes** button. The text boxes are enabled.

4. Click the **Initialize Array** button. An array containing instances of the LogRecord class is initialized. Again, you will not see any visible change on the form.

5. Click the **Find Element** button. The array is searched using a linear search. If the corresponding element is found, the element is displayed.

## MINI-QUIZ 5

1. Which of the following statements is correct regarding the following declaration:

   ```
   Dim LabelList(2) As Label
   ```

   a. The statement creates two instances of the Label class and stores a reference to those control instances in the array named LabelList.

   b. The statement creates three instances of the Label class and stores a reference to those control instances in the array named LabelList.

   c. The elements in the array have a data type of Label.

   d. none of the above

2. Using the Controls collection of the Form class, write the necessary statements to add references to the array named TextBoxList such that all of the TextBox control instances are added to the array. Redimension the array, as necessary.

3. Describe the error in the following statements:

   ```
   Dim ButtonList(2) As Button

   ButtonList(0).Text = "Error"
   ```

# APPLICATION LESSON

## CREATING A KENO GAME IN VISUAL STUDIO

The game of Keno is said to have originated about 200 B.C. in China and remains a popular casino game today. In fact, revenues from the game were said to have helped fund the Great Wall of China. The game consists of 80 numbers (1 through 80). A player selects between 1 and 10 numbers. Then, 20 numbers are selected at random by the casino. Depending on how many numbers the player matches (a match is often called a hit), the player wins or loses. The more numbers matched (hit), the more money the player wins.

There are several variations of the game of Keno. In this application lesson, you will implement a simple video Keno game in which a single player plays the game with the gaming device (the computer). Many casino Keno games allow several players to play the same game simultaneously.

## APPLICATION LESSON—USER INTERFACE

The application's user interface is made up of a Keno board containing 80 TextBox control instances displaying the numbers 1 through 80. The player selects the numbers to bet by clicking on the individual text boxes. As a number is selected or deselected, the background color of the corresponding text box is updated to indicate whether the number is bet or not bet. In addition, the payout table below the Keno board is updated. The payout table displays the amount won based on how many numbers are hit. A counter displaying how many numbers are bet is also updated.

The form contains the following buttons:

» The Play button begins the game. When clicked, 20 numbers are selected randomly out of the 80 possible numbers. The current game payout is calculated each time a number is selected based on how many numbers are hit. This information is displayed by updating the selected item in the list box containing the payout table. Another list box displays all of the numbers that were selected by the computer for the current game.

» The Clear button clears all of the selected numbers in preparation for a new game.

» The Exit button exits the application.

## APPLICATION LESSON—DESIGN

The design of this application works around five events, as described in the following list:

» Initialization tasks take place in the form's Load event handler. These tasks include initializing the array that stores the Keno numbers and setting default values for the form's control instances.

» When the player clicks any of the 80 TextBox control instances, a multicast event handler fires to either select or deselect the number for the purpose of wagering. In addition, the payout table is updated along with a counter indicating how many numbers are selected.

» The first Button control instance clears the board in preparation for another game. Any selected numbers are deselected.

» The second `Button` control instance plays the game. Frequently, a player bets the same numbers again and again. Thus, the game is designed so that the Play button can be clicked again and again to bet the same numbers.

» The final `Button` control instance exits the application.

Figure 9-15 shows the event handling model for the application.

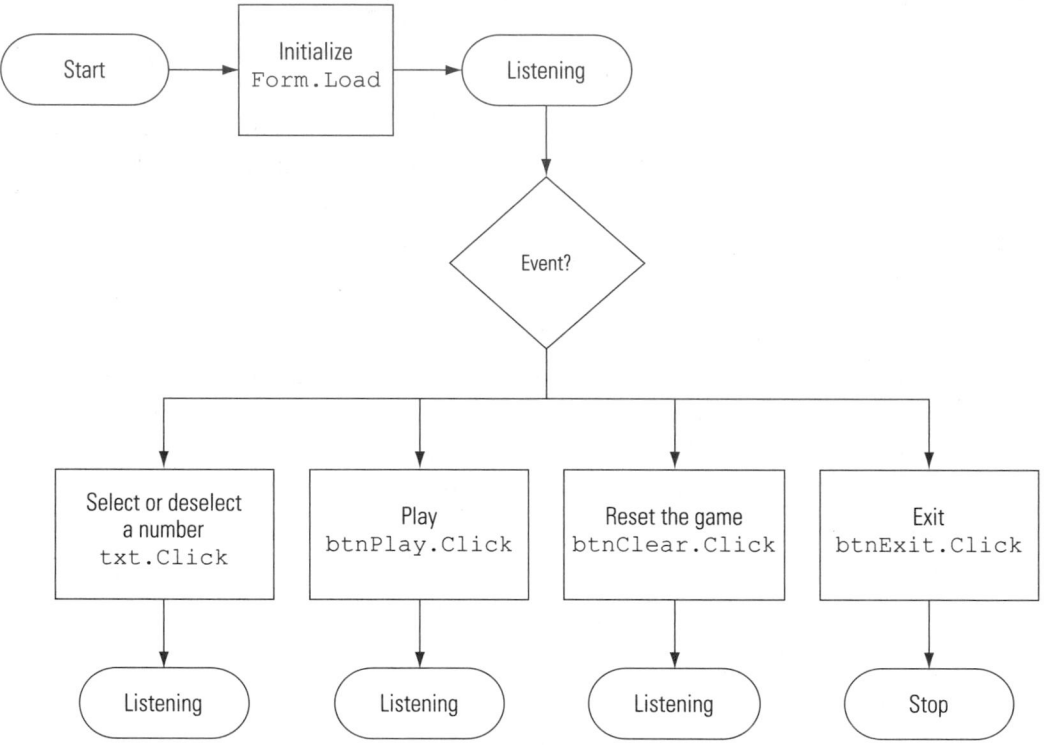

Figure 9-15: Application lesson—Event handling model

Most of the processing for this application takes place when the game is played. First, the board is reset. That is, the numbers selected by the casino for the last game are cleared. Then, 20 random numbers between 1 and 80 are selected. A `Do` loop executes performing the following tasks until 20 numbers have been selected:

» A random number between 1 and 80 is generated.

» Because a random number can repeat, an `If` statement tests whether the number has been selected already. If the number has been selected, another random number is generated.

» A counter indicating how many numbers have been selected is incremented by 1.

» The selected number is added to a list box containing a list of the selected numbers.

» If the number is bet, a counter indicating the number of hits is updated.

» The background color of the text box corresponding to the selected number is updated. The background color varies based on whether the selected number was bet.

» The list box containing the payout table is updated to reflect the numbers currently hit.

## APPLICATION LESSON—IMPLEMENTATION

Each Keno number is represented as an instance of the KenoNumber class. The following code segment shows the KenoNumber class:

```
Public Class KenoNumber
    Public Number As Integer
    Public Bet As Boolean
    Public Selected As Boolean
    Public TextBoxControl As TextBox
End Class
```

The KenoNumber class has four members. The Number member stores the Keno number (1 through 80). The Boolean Bet and Selected properties indicate whether the number was bet and whether the number was selected by the casino, respectively. Finally, the member named TextBoxControl stores a reference to a TextBox control instance created on the form.

As mentioned, the form's Load event handler contains the code to perform the initialization tasks. The following statements create instances of the KenoNumber class and store each instance in the array named KenoNumbers:

```
Dim Counter As Integer
For Counter = 1 To 80
    KenoNumbers(Counter) = New KenoNumber
Next
```

The preceding statements create 80 instances of the KenoNumber class and store each reference in an array. The first array member will not be used. Thus, array elements 1 through 80 represent the Keno numbers. In addition, the TextBoxControl property of each KenoNumber class instance is set so as to reference the corresponding TextBox control instance. The following statements show how the first two Keno numbers are initialized. The remaining statements are almost identical.

```
KenoNumbers(1).TextBoxControl = txt01
KenoNumbers(2).TextBoxControl = txt2
```

The implementation contains a two-dimensional array to store the payout table. The payout table contains 11 rows. The first row is unused so that the payout table for a one-number bet appears in the first row of the table. The following rows correspond to how many numbers are bet. That is, row 1 contains the payout table for a one-number bet, row 2 contains the payout table for a two-number bet, and so on. The columns correspond to how many numbers were hit. Table 9-2 shows the payout table.

|  | Hit 0 | Hit 1 | Hit 2 | Hit 3 | Hit 4 | Hit 5 | Hit 6 | Hit 7 | Hit 8 | Hit 9 | Hit 10 |
|---|---|---|---|---|---|---|---|---|---|---|---|
| Unused | 0 | 0 | 0 | 0 | 0 | 0 | 0 | 0 | 0 | 0 | 0 |
| Bet 1 | 0 | 2 |  |  |  |  |  |  |  |  |  |
| Bet 2 | 0 | 1 | 9 |  |  |  |  |  |  |  |  |
| Bet 3 | 0 | 0 | 3 | 39 |  |  |  |  |  |  |  |
| Bet 4 | 0 | 0 | 2 | 7 | 73 |  |  |  |  |  |  |
| Bet 5 | 0 | 0 | 0 | 5 | 20 | 448 |  |  |  |  |  |
| Bet 6 | 0 | 0 | 0 | 3 | 10 | 47 | 1010 |  |  |  |  |
| Bet 7 | 0 | 0 | 0 | 1 | 4 | 24 | 290 | 6000 |  |  |  |

Table 9-2: Keno payout table *(Continued)*

▶

|        | Hit 0 | Hit 1 | Hit 2 | Hit 3 | Hit 4 | Hit 5 | Hit 6 | Hit 7 | Hit 8 | Hit 9 | Hit 10 |
|--------|-------|-------|-------|-------|-------|-------|-------|-------|-------|-------|--------|
| Bet 8  | 0     | 0     | 0     | 0     | 2     | 15    | 125   | 1250  | 18000 |       |        |
| Bet 9  | 0     | 0     | 0     | 0     | 1     | 6     | 46    | 355   | 4700  | 20000 |        |
| Bet 10 | 0     | 0     | 0     | 0     | 1     | 5     | 21    | 130   | 850   | 4700  | 25000  |

Table 9-2: Keno payout table

The declaration appearing in Figure 9-16 shows the two-dimensional array for the preceding payout table.

```
Private PayTable(,) As Double = { _
    { 0, 0, 0, 0, 0, 0, 0, 0, 0, 0, 0}, _
    { 0, 2.0, -1, -1, -1, -1, -1, -1, -1, -1, -1}, _
    { 0, 1.0, 9.0, -1, -1, -1, -1, -1, -1, -1, -1}, _
    { 0, 0.0, 3.0, 39.0, -1, -1, -1, -1, -1, -1, -1}, _
    { 0, 0.0, 2.0, 7.0, 73.0, -1, -1, -1, -1, -1, -1}, _
    { 0, 0.0, 0.0, 5.0, 20.0, 448.0, -1, -1, -1, -1, -1}, _
    { 0, 0.0, 0.0, 3.0, 10.0, 47.0, 1010.0, -1, -1, -1, -1}, _
    { 0, 0.0, 0.0, 1.0, 4.0, 24.0, 290, 6000, -1, -1, -1}, _
    { 0, 0.0, 0.0, 0.0, 2.0, 15.0, 125.0, 1250.0, 18000.0, -1, -1}, _
    { 0, 0.0, 0.0, 0.0, 1.0, 6.0, 46.0, 355.0, 4700.0, 20000, -1}, _
    { 0, 0.0, 0.0, 0.0, 1.0, 5.0, 21.0, 130.0, 850.0, 4700, 25000.0}}
```

Figure 9-16: Keno payout table declaration

The preceding array named PayTable corresponds to the payout table. The value –1 in specific cells represent the unused elements. That is, in the second row of the table, only one number is bet. Thus, hitting one number pays two dollars. The remaining elements in the row are unused.

The following procedure updates the payout table based on how many numbers were bet:

```vb
Private Sub UpdatePayTable(ByVal numbers As Integer)
    Dim Counter As Integer
    Dim Message As String
    lstPayTable.Items.Clear()
    For Counter = 0 To PayTable.GetUpperBound(0)
        If PayTable(numbers, Counter) = -1 Then
            Exit For
        End If
        Message = "Hit=" & Counter.ToString & " pays " & _
            PayTable(numbers, Counter).ToString("c")
        lstPayTable.Items.Add(Message)
    Next
    lstPayTable.SelectedIndex = 0
End Sub
```

The UpdatePayTable procedure accepts one argument named numbers. This value contains how many Keno numbers were bet. The first statement in the procedure clears the list box containing the payout table. The For loop enumerates each column. The If statement tests whether the current column in the current row contains the value –1. If it does, the loop exits because no more numbers were selected. Otherwise, a string is created listing the numbers hit and the corresponding payout amount. The text string is then appended to the list box. Finally, the first item is selected, indicating that zero numbers have been hit.

The ResetBoard procedure examines the KenoNumbers array. If the number is bet, the background color of the TextBox control instance is updated. The background color is also reset if the number is not bet. Finally, the Selected member of the array is reset in preparation for a new game.

```vb
Private Sub ResetBoard()
    Dim Current As Integer
    For Current = 1 To 80
        If KenoNumbers(Current).Bet Then
            KenoNumbers(Current). _
                TextBoxControl.BackColor = Color.LightBlue
        Else
            KenoNumbers(Current). _
                TextBoxControl.BackColor = Color.White
        End If
        KenoNumbers(Current).Selected = False
    Next
    lstNumbersSelected.Items.Clear()
    lstPayTable.SelectedIndex = 0
End Sub
```

The preceding code segments and procedures appear in the preview application. In the following steps, you will play the game and reset the Keno board using the Preview application to see how it works.

To preview the completed application:

1. In Visual Studio, open the solution file of the same name appearing in the folder named **Chapter.09\Chapter09ApplicationLessonPreview**.

2. Run the application. Click on various numbers to place a bet. As you click each number, the corresponding text box appears with a gray-blue background. If the number (text box) is clicked again, the background color returns to normal indicating that the number is not selected (bet). Each time a number is selected or deselected, the corresponding payout table is updated in the list box. Note that it is not possible to select more than 10 numbers.

3. Click the **Play** button. The game selects 20 random numbers from the 80 possible numbers. As each number is selected, the list box containing the selected numbers is updated. If one of the selected numbers matches a number bet, the count of hits is updated in the `ListBox` control instance containing the payout table. Figure 9-17 shows the completed form for the application.

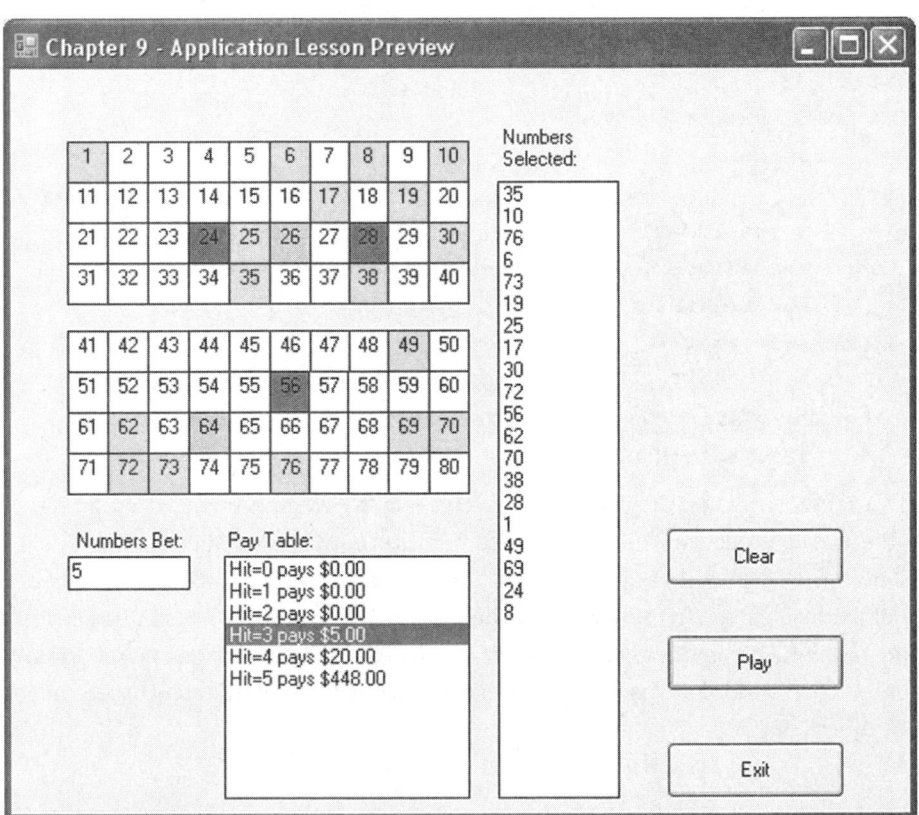

Figure 9-17: Application lesson—completed form

4. Click the **Clear** button. The Keno board is reset. That is, the selected numbers are cleared and the bet numbers are cleared.

5. Click the **Exit** button to end the application.

Much of the code has already been created for this application lesson. However, the code to update the counters as the player clicks on one of the text boxes, along with the code to play the game, has not been created.

To create the Click event handler for the TextBox control instances:

1. In Visual Studio, open the solution file in the folder named **Chapter.09\ Chapter09ApplicationLessonStartup**.

2. Activate the Code Editor for the form named frmMain, if necessary. Enter the following statements in the **Click** event handler for the text boxes. Note that the multicast event handler named **TextBoxClick** has already been created for you.

```
Dim txtCurrent As TextBox = CType(sender, TextBox)
Dim Index As Integer = ToInt32(txtCurrent.Text)

If KenoNumbers(Index).Bet Then
    KenoNumbers(Index).Bet = False
    KenoNumbers(Index).TextBoxControl.BackColor = Color.White
    NumbersBet -= 1
Else
    If NumbersBet = 10 Then
        Exit Sub
    End If
    KenoNumbers(Index).Bet = True
    KenoNumbers(Index).TextBoxControl.BackColor = _
        Color.LightBlue
    NumbersBet += 1
End If
txtNumbersBet.Text = NumbersBet.ToString
Call UpdatePayTable(NumbersBet)
```

The local variable named txtCurrent stores a reference to the text box that was clicked. The variable Index is used to reference an element in the KenoNumbers array. The If statement tests the Bet member of the current Keno number. If the number is already bet, the number is deselected. If the Keno number is not bet, a nested If statement tests whether 10 numbers have already been bet. If not, the number is marked as bet. Finally, the text box background color is updated and the payout table is updated based on the count of numbers bet.

Next, you will write the code to play the game.

To create the Click event handler for the button named btnPlay:

1. Enter the following statements in the **Click** event handler for the button named **btnPlay**:

```
Dim rndGame As New Random
Dim SelectedNumbers As Integer
Dim SelectedNumber As Integer
Dim TotalHits As Integer
Call ResetBoard()

Do Until SelectedNumbers = 20
    SelectedNumber = rndGame.Next(1, 80)
    If KenoNumbers(SelectedNumber).Selected Then
        Continue Do
    Else
        SelectedNumbers += 1
        lstNumbersSelected.Items.Add(SelectedNumber)
        KenoNumbers(SelectedNumber).Selected = True
        If KenoNumbers(SelectedNumber).Bet Then
            KenoNumbers(SelectedNumber). _
                TextBoxControl.BackColor = Color.Green
            TotalHits += 1
            lstPayTable.SelectedIndex = TotalHits
        Else
            KenoNumbers(SelectedNumber). _
                TextBoxControl.BackColor = Color.Aqua
        End If
    End If
Loop
```

The code for the Play button consists of a Do loop that iterates until 20 different numbers are selected. The first statement in the Do loop gets a random number between 1 and 80. The If statement tests whether the random number has already been selected. If it has, the loop continues without executing the remaining statements using the Continue Do statement. If the number is not already selected, the counter storing the numbers selected is updated and the selected number is added to the list box. The nested If statement checks whether the number is bet. If it is, the total number of hits is updated and the selected item in the payout table is updated.

The final step in the application's development is to create the code for the Clear button to reset the Keno board.

To create the Click event handler for the button named btnClear:

1. Enter the following statements in the **Click** event handler for the button named **btnClear**:

```
Dim Current As Integer

For Current = 1 To 80
    KenoNumbers(Current).Bet = False
    KenoNumbers(Current).Selected = False
    KenoNumbers(Current). _
        TextBoxControl.BackColor = Color.White
Next
NumbersBet = 0
txtNumbersBet.Text = "0"
lstNumbersSelected.Items.Clear()
```

The preceding code segment consists of a For loop to examine each element in the table. For each Keno number, the Bet and Selected properties are set to False. The background color of the text box is also set to white. Finally, the numbers bet is set to 0 and the list box containing the selected numbers is also reset.

Finally, you can test the application that you wrote to determine whether it is working correctly.

To test the application:

1. Run the application.

2. Bet various numbers of your choosing and click the **Play** button. As the numbers are selected, the text boxes are updated. In addition, the payout table is updated.

# CHAPTER SUMMARY

» Simulations, gaming, and other applications require the use of random numbers. The System.Random class supplies the means to generate random numbers in Visual Studio. When the constructor is called without arguments, the random number generator is seeded with a random value based on the time of day. Random number generators can also be seeded with a fixed value by passing an argument to the constructor. Calling the Next method returns a random number having a data type of Integer. The number returned is always greater than or equal to zero. Calling the NextDouble method returns a double precision random number between the range of 0.0 and 1.0.

» An array is a reference type that stores a list of values rather than a single value. An array has one or more dimensions. The number of dimensions in an array is referred to as the rank. Each data item in an array is called an element. Individual array elements are referenced using a subscript. In Visual Studio, all arrays are created using the `System.Array` class.

» An array is declared in the same way as any other variable is declared. Following the array name, however, appear opening and closing parentheses containing optional subscripts to define the array's size and shape. Arrays can be initialized when they are declared by creating an initialization list surrounded by braces ({}). Elements in the initialization list are separated by commas.

» The size of an array can be changed through a process known as redimensioning. An array is redimensioned using the `ReDim` statement. The optional `Preserve` keyword preserves the existing array contents.

» An array is referenced using an integer subscript. The smallest subscript or the lower bound of an array is 0. The `GetLowerBound` and `GetUpperBound` methods get the smallest and largest array subscript for a particular array dimension, respectively. Subscripts can be literal values or variables.

» Loops are commonly used to examine all of the elements in an array or an array dimension. Because the number of elements in an array is known in advance, a `For` loop can be used instead of a `Do` loop.

» Multidimensional arrays are arrays with two or more dimensions. A two-dimensional array has rows and columns. Two subscripts are used to reference the elements in a two-dimensional array rather than one subscript. Visual Basic also supports arrays with three or more dimensions.

» It is possible to store object references in an array element. In this case, the array works similarly to an instance of the `List` class.

# KEY TERMS

**array**—A variable that contains a list of multiple items each having the same data type.

**binary search**—A search algorithm that searches a sorted array by dividing it in half each time the array is searched.

**dimension**—Referring to an array, the number of dimensions describes the shape of an array. A one-dimensional array is similar to a list. A two-dimensional array is equivalent to a table or grid. In Visual Basic, arrays can also have three or more dimensions.

**element**—The term used to describe an item in an array. An array element is referenced using a subscript.

**random number generation**—A sequence of random numbers generated by the system. Visual Studio random numbers can be positive integers or double precision numbers between 0.0 and 1.0.

**rank**—The number of dimensions in an array. A one-dimensional array has a rank of 1. A two-dimensional array has a rank of 2, and so on.

**redimensioning**—The process of changing an array's size.

**scalar variable**—A variable that stores a single value.

**seed value**—In random number generation, the value used to initialize a random number generator. Initializing a random number generator with the same seed value causes the same sequence of random numbers to be generated.

**subscript**—The index value used to reference an array element.

# ANSWERS TO MINI-QUIZZES

## MINI-QUIZ 1

1. e. none of the above

2. b. `Dim RndCurrent As New Random(15)`

3.
```
Dim Count As Integer
For Count = 1 To 10000
    lstQuiz.Items.Add( _
        RndCurrent.Next(10000, 100000).ToString)
Next
```

## MINI-QUIZ 2

1. b. Individual array elements are referenced by a unique index value known as a subscript.

2. a. The largest subscript for the array is 4.

3. d. `Dim Quiz(9) As Integer`

4.
```
Dim Quiz(99) As Integer
Dim CurrentRandom As New Random
Dim Count As Integer
For Count = 0 To Quiz.GetUpperBound(0)
    Quiz(Count) = CurrentRandom.Next(1, 10)
Next
```

## MINI-QUIZ 3

1. b. It can only be used on a sorted array.

2. e. Both b and c

## MINI-QUIZ 4

1. There are six rows and four columns. There are 24 total elements in the array.

2.
```
Dim Rows As Integer
Dim Columns As Integer
Dim Total As Double
For Rows = 0 To Demo.GetUpperBound(0)
    For Columns = 0 To Demo.GetUpperBound(1)
        Total += Demo(Rows, Columns)
    Next
Next
```

3. 3

4. 1

## MINI-QUIZ 5

1. c. The elements in the array have a data type of Label.

2.
```
Dim TextBoxList() As TextBox
Dim CurrentControl As Control
Dim Count As Integer
For Each CurrentControl In Me.Controls
    If TypeOf CurrentControl Is TextBox Then
        ReDim Preserve TextBoxList(Count)
        TextBoxList(Count) = CurrentControl
        Count += 1
    End If
Next
```

3. The second statement causes a System.NullReferenceException because the array elements do not reference an instance of the Button control.

# REVIEW QUESTIONS

1. Which of the following statements is correct regarding random number generation?

   a. Random numbers always have a data type of `Integer`.

   b. A random number generator is initialized based on a seed value.

   c. The statement `Dim Current As New Random(1)` produces a different series of random numbers each time the statement executes.

   d. The `NextRandom` method of the `Random` class generates a random number.

   e. none of the above

2. Assuming that the variable named RndCurrent is an instance of the `Random` class, which of the following statements generates a random number between 1 and 36 and stores that value in the variable Result?

   a. `Result = RndCurrent(1, 36)`

   b. `Result = New RndCurrent.Next(1, 36)`

   c. `Result = RndCurrent.NextInteger(1, 36)`

   d. `Result = RndCurrent.Next(1, 36)`

   e. none of the above

3. Which of the following general statements about arrays is correct?

   a. The term used to describe each data item in an array is called a cell.

   b. The lower bound for an array dimension is 1. That is, the value of the first subscript for an array dimension is 1.

   c. The `ReDim` statement can be used to change the number of array dimensions along with the number of elements in a dimension.

   d. An array has one or more dimensions. The number of dimensions in an array is called the rank.

   e. none of the above

4. Which of the following statements is true regarding declaring arrays?

   a. An array must have a data type if strict type checking is enabled.

   b. When declaring an array, you must give it an initial size.

   c. Arrays cannot be declared with the `Private` keyword.

    d.  An array cannot contain more than 1000 elements.

    e.  all of the above are true

5.  Which of the following general statements is true regarding arrays?

    a.  They contain multiple elements of the same type.

    b.  An element is referenced using a subscript.

    c.  A subscript must have a data type of `String`.

    d.  both a and b

    e.  both b and c

6.  Which of the following statements declares a 10-element, one-dimensional array having a data type of `Integer`?

    a.  `Private CurrentList As Array`

    b.  `Private CurrentList(10) As Integer`

    c.  `Private CurrentList(9) As Integer`

    d.  `Private CurrentList As Integer(9)`

    e.  none of the above

7.  Given the following array declaration, which of the following statements is true?

    `Dim DemoArray(,) As Integer`

    a.  The statement causes a syntax error.

    b.  The array has two dimensions, but the array's size is undefined.

    c.  The array has one dimension, but the array's size is undefined.

    d.  The array has two dimensions. The default size of 10 rows and 10 columns is used for the array.

    e.  none of the above

8.  Which of the following statements correctly declares and initializes a one-dimensional array named Question?

    a.  `Dim Question() As Integer = {1, 2, 3, 4}`

    b.  `Dim Question As Integer = {1, 2, 3, 4}`

    c.  `Dim Question(3) As Integer = 1, 2, 3, 4`

    d.  `Dim Question(1, 2, 3, 4) As Integer`

    e.  none of the above

9. Which of the following statements is correct related to redimensioning arrays?

   a. The `ReDim` statement can be used to change the number of dimensions in an array only when the `Preserve` keyword is used.

   b. The `ReDim` statement can be used to change the size of a particular dimension.

   c. When an array is redimensioned, the contents of the array are destroyed and cannot be preserved.

   d. One-dimensional arrays can be redimensioned but two-dimensional arrays cannot.

   e. none of the above

10. Which of the following statements correctly redimensions the one-dimensional array named ArrayDemo and preserves its contents?

   a. `ReDim ArrayDemo(10)`

   b. `ReDim Preserve ArrayDemo(10)`

   c. `ReDim ArrayDemo(10) Preserve`

   d. `ReDim ArrayDemo(10, Preserve)`

   e. none of the above

11. Given the following declarations:

   `Dim Array1(10) As Integer`

   `Dim Array2(10, 10) As Integer`

   which of the following statements is legal?

   a. `ReDim Preserve Array2(10)`

   b. `ReDim Preserve Array2(10, 15)`

   c. `Redim Preserve Array2(15, 10)`

   d. `Redim Array1(-1)`

   e. none of the above are legal

12. Given the following declarations:

   `Dim Array1(20) As Integer`

   `Dim Array2(10, 2) As Integer`

   how many elements exist in the two arrays combined?

   a.  40

   b.  32

   c.  54

   d.  none of the above

13.  How many elements are in the following array?

```
Dim DemoArray(2, 2, 2) As String
```
   a.  6

   b.  8

   c.  27

   d.  The preceding array declaration is illegal.

   e.  none of the above

14.  Given the following declaration:

```
Dim TableX(2, 3) As Integer
```

what value is stored in the variable Count after the loops have executed?

```
Dim Row, Column As Integer
Dim Count As Integer = 0
For Row = 0 to TableX.GetUpperBound(0)
    For Column = 0 to TableX.GetUpperBound(1)
        Count += 1
    Next
Next
```

15.  Which of the following statements correctly declares a dynamic, three-dimensional array named List3D having a data type of Integer?

   a.  `Dim List3D(,,) As Integer`

   b.  `Dim List3D(0,0,0) As Integer`

   c.  `Dim List3D() As Integer(,,)`

   d.  `Dim List3D() As Dynamic`

   e.  none of the above

16. Describe the role of a seed value related to random number generation. In your answer, discuss the random number sequences generated using fixed seed values and random seed values.

17. Assuming that ListItem is a class and CurrentList is declared as follows:

```
Private CurrentList(10) As ListItem
```

describe the error in the following For loop.

```
For Count = 0 To 10
    Dim CurrentItem As ListItem
    CurrentList(Count) = CurrentItem
Next
```

18. The Preserve keyword is used to preserve any existing array contents when redimensioning arrays. List the restrictions related to using the Preserve keyword.

19. Compare and contrast arrays and the List class.

20. Describe the data types that can be stored in an array.

# PROGRAMMING QUESTIONS

1. Write the statements to declare a one-dimensional array named CountingNumbers having a data type of Integer so that it has 10 elements. Initialize the value of each element so that its value is the same as the element's index value. That is, the first array element should have a value of 0. The second array element should have a value of 1, and so on. Use a For loop to initialize the array.

2. Write the statements to declare a one-dimensional array named RandomList having a data type of Double having 10,000 elements. Write the statements to initialize the array to random double precision values. Create an instance of the Random class named RandCurrent using a random seed value.

3. Write the statements to declare a two-dimensional array having three columns and three rows. The array should have a data type of String and be named Subscripts. Initialize the array elements such that the element at row 0, column 0 is initialized to the string "(0,0)", the element at row 1, column 0 is initialized to the string "(1,0)", and so on. Use nested For loops to initialize the array elements and declare any local variables as necessary.

4. Write a `For` loop to examine each element of the one-dimensional array named Values. Use an accumulator named Total to tally the values contained in each array element. Assume that the array has a data type of `Double`.

5. Assume that two one-dimensional arrays exist named InputList and OutputList having the same size and data types of `Double`. Write the statements to copy the data from the array named InputList to the array named OutputList. Use the `GetUpperBound` method to determine the size of the input array. Do not use the `Copy` method of the `Array` class to copy the data. Then write the statements to increase the values of the elements in the array named OutputList by 10%. Declare any local variables, as necessary.

6. Assume that a two-dimensional array exists named Grid. Write the statements to total the values for all of the array elements. Use the `GetUpperBound` method to get the number of elements in each array dimension. Store the total of all array elements in the variable Total. Declare any local variables, as necessary.

7. Write the statement(s) to sort the one-dimensional array named IntegerList in descending order.

8. Assume that a scalar variable exists named Words having a data type of `String`. Assume that a one-dimensional array exists named LetterCount having a data type of `Integer` having 26 elements (one element for each letter of the alphabet). Write the statements to count the number of instances of each letter of the alphabet by examining each character in the string. If the character is the letter "a," increment the value of the first element in the second array. If the character is the letter "b," increment the value of the second element in the second array, and so on. Perform the count in a case-insensitive way. Assume that the string contains only letters.

9. Assume that a one-dimensional dynamic array named Items exists having a data type of `Integer` along with a list box named lstItems. Write the statements to copy the data from the list box to the array. Redimension the array named Items, as necessary.

10. Assume that three two-dimensional arrays exist named Sales2003, Sales2004, and Sales2005 each having a data type of `Double`, each having the same shape. Write the statements to tally the values from these three arrays storing the results in an array named SalesTotal having the same shape as the other three arrays. Tally the values such that row 0 and column 0 from the three input arrays are stored in row 0 and column 0 in the array named SalesTotal.

11. Write the statements to declare and initialize a two-dimensional array with four rows and three columns as follows. The array should have a data type of Double and be named RegionalSales.

| | 2004 | 2005 | 2006 |
|---|---|---|---|
| North | 1824.33 | 1922.81 | 2133.34 |
| South | 1855.84 | 1891.24 | 1926.83 |
| East | 1044.38 | 1193.24 | 1927.43 |
| West | 1734.79 | 1799.28 | 1804.33 |

Write the statements to declare a second one-dimensional array named YearlySales having three elements. In the first element, store the total sales for 2004. In the second and third elements, store the sales totals for 2005 and 2006, respectively. Use the previous table for the input data.

12. Assume that a two-dimensional array named Budget exists. Write the statements to declare a second two-dimensional array named BudgetForecast having the same dimensions as the first array named Budget and a data type of Double. Copy the contents of the array named Budget to the array named BudgetForecast. In the array named BudgetForecast, increase the value of each element by 15%.

13. Assume that a form has some number of TextBox control instances. Write the statements to declare an array named TextBoxList having a data type of TextBox. Write the statements to enumerate the Controls collection of the form. If the current control instance has a data type of TextBox, add a reference to the control instance to the array. Redimension the array as necessary.

14. Assume that the following class declaration exists:

```
Public Class Log
    Public CurrentDate As DateTime
    Public StartTime As DateTime
    Public EndTime As DateTime
End Class
```

Write the statements to declare a one-dimensional array named LogList. Redimension the array such that it has 365 elements. Create instances of the Log class such that one instance exists for each day of the year.

15. Write the statements to store the capital letters "A" to "Z" in the array named Letters having a data type of Char. Declare the array, as necessary.

# HANDS-ON PROJECTS

1. In this hands-on project, you will enhance the completed application lesson to support the following features:

    » The player should be able to wager an amount. Each time that the game is played, the amount won will be calculated based on the payout table. The payout table must also be updated based on the amount wagered. The player should be able to bet between $1.00 and $3.00 in 25-cent increments.

    » The application should keep track of the money in the player's bank. That is, if the player loses, deduct the wager from the bank. If the player wins, add the amount won to the bank. When the application is first run, the player's bank should have an initial value of $100.00.

    » Keep track of the games won and lost using two accumulators. Each time a game is played, display the total number of games won and the total number of games lost.

    » Modify the existing data structure or create a second array to store a count of each number selected by the casino. That is, each time the game is played, counters for each number selected should be incremented. Display this information to the player in another list box.

    a. A preview of this completed hands-on project can be found in the file **Chapter.09\HandsOnProjects\Ch09HandsOnProject1.exe**.

    b. Create a new solution named **Ch09HandsOnProject1.sln**.

    c. Copy the control instances and code from the completed application lesson, as necessary.

    d. Create a combo box allowing the player to select an amount to wager. Again, the amount wagered should be between $1.00 and $3.00 in 25-cent increments.

    e. Update the current payout table based on how many numbers are selected and the wager amount.

    f. When the game is played, update the player's bank, as necessary, based on the amount won or lost.

    g. Keep track of and display the total number of games won and the total number of games lost.

    h. When the game is played, update the cumulative counter of numbers selected. Display these counters in a list box.

    i. Validate the input as necessary.

2. In this hands-on project, you will work with simulated time series data. A one-dimensional array will store references to an object named Sample having the following members:

    » SampleDate—The date that a chemical sample was taken

    » ChemicalName—An abbreviation containing the name of the chemical being sampled

    » ChemicalAmount—A double precision value indicating the amount of the chemical in the sample

In practice, this data would be obtained from remote sensors. However, for the purpose of this project and to test the application, the data should be generated randomly as follows:

    » The end user will specify a range of dates using a starting and ending date. One record will be generated for each hour of each day between the starting date and the ending date.

    » Random data should be generated for four chemicals having the following names and abbreviations: Arsenic (AR), Chromium (CR), Carbon Tetrachloride (CT), and Benzine (BZ).

    » For each record generated, a random sample value should be generated for the ChemicalAmount field. Thus, if samples were generated for one year, there would be (365 * 24 * 4) samples (records).

    a. A preview of this completed hands-on project can be found in the file **Chapter.09\HandsOnProjects\Ch09HandsOnProject2.exe**.

    b. Create a new solution named **Ch09HandsOnProject2.sln**.

c. Create the application's user interface consisting of DateTimePicker controls with which the end user will select starting and ending dates from which the sample data will be generated.

d. Create the Sample class to store the data items. Create other classes as necessary to store any sample results or selection criteria.

e. Create a class named ArrayStats similar to the one discussed in the concept lesson. Modify the Total, Minimum, Maximum, and Average methods so that they operate with arrays with elements having a data type of Sample instead of a Double data type. Create an additional method named Count that will count the number of items in the list.

f. Create a button that contains the code to generate the sample data. Create the necessary class instance for each record generated. For each class instance, store a random value in the ChemicalAmount field. Generate one random record for each chemical for each hour of the day. Add each class instance to an array of samples. The chemical name should be generated randomly from the four different chemicals.

g. The end user should be able to query the randomly generated data. As input, the end user should be able to specify a date range that is within the date range of the sample data generated in the previous steps, along with a selected chemical name.

h. Using that input, the application should calculate the minimum, maximum, average, and count of chemical values and display those records on a second form displayed as a modal dialog box. Use the methods of the ArrayStats class to perform these calculations. Again, use the ArrayStats class, as necessary, to work with the Sample data type and to select only specific records based on the sample date and a specific chemical.

i. Validate the input where possible.

3. In this hands-on project, you will implement the popular children's card game Go Fish.

a. Create a new solution named **Ch09HandsOnProject3.sln**.

b. Create a class to represent a card. Each card has a suit and a value. Create an array to store the deck of cards. Initialize the array as necessary to create a standard 52-card deck. Implement the Deck as a class.

c. Create a method named Shuffle that will shuffle the array (deck of cards). To shuffle the deck of cards, simply exchange two random array elements between 1 and 52. Shuffling should begin when the class instance is created. Shuffling should stop when the first card is dealt. Use a timer and a corresponding event handler to shuffle the cards.

d. Create a method to deal a card. This method should be implemented in the Deck class.

e. The game of Fish is played by dealing seven cards to each player. For this game, assume that there is one player playing against the computer. The game is played as follows: The player asks the other player for cards having a specific rank (Jacks, for example). If the opposing player has Jacks, he gives those cards to the player. If the opposing player has no Jacks, he says "Go Fish." If the card drawn is of the requested rank, the player gets another turn. If the card drawn is not of the requested rank, the turn passes to the next player. When a player has four cards of the same rank, those cards are set down. The game ends when the stock of cards are exhausted or a player has no cards.

f. Implement the "Go Fish" game so that there are two players—the player and the computer. The computer should randomly select cards to "Fish." The end user should decide which cards to fish.

g. Create the user interface for the application as you see fit. One easy way to create the user interface is to store each player's hand in list boxes.

4. In this hands-on project, you will create a simulation using randomly generated data. The simulation should be based on the following guidelines:

» Customers enter a bank at random intervals between one and three minutes apart.

» Tellers service customers. The time to service a customer is based on the type of transaction. Deposits take one minute to process. It takes two minutes to cash a check. It takes five minutes to close an account. It takes 10 minutes to open an account. Customer transactions should be selected randomly.

a. Create a new solution named **Ch09HandsOnProject4.sln**.

b. When the application starts, allow the end user to define the number of tellers in the simulation.

c. The application should randomly have a customer enter the bank with a random transaction type. Use `Timer` control instances to build the simulation.

d. Create a user interface so that the user can visually see customers entering the bank and transactions being processed. Again, create the user interface as you see fit.

# 10

# SEQUENTIAL FILES AND STRUCTURES

**After completing this chapter, you will be able to:**

Use the `OpenFileDialog`, `SaveFileDialog`, and `FolderBrowserDialog` controls, which allow the end user to select disk files and folders

Work with different types of sequential files

Read sequential files based on the type of data stored in a text file

Write sequential files

Use structures to store and group data together

# CONCEPT LESSON

In the preceding chapters of this book, you have created applications in which the end user enters data. Calculations were performed on the input data to produce some output. However, you have not created applications that allowed the end user to save data to the disk or to read data from the disk. To help you develop applications that read and write disk files, the following topics are discussed in this chapter:

» You will learn about additional features of the `OpenFileDialog` control. In addition, you will learn how to use the similar `SaveFileDialog` and `FolderBrowserDialog` controls. These two controls allow the end user to select a file to save and to select a folder, respectively.

» The second topic presented in this chapter is how to read and write disk files with the `StreamReader` and `StreamWriter` classes.

» The final topic of the chapter introduces the concept of a structure and how to create a structure. In this chapter, you will learn how to create arrays of structures and how to read and write those arrays from and to the disk. The `With` statement is also introduced as a way to efficiently reference class and structure members.

## DOING MORE WITH THE OPENFILEDIALOG AND SAVEFILEDIALOG CONTROLS

You have already used the `OpenFileDialog` control to obtain a filename from the end user. This chapter discusses additional properties of the `OpenFileDialog` control. These additional properties allow you to specify the folder in which Visual Studio initially searches for files. These properties also let you specify a file suffix to determine which file extensions appear in the Files of type list box. In addition, you will learn how to use the `SaveFileDialog` control, which allows the end user to select a file to save.

Visual Studio supports a class named `CommonDialog`. The controls appearing in the Dialogs tab of the Toolbox are derived from the `CommonDialog` class, as shown in Figure 10-1. The controls discussed in this chapter appear in Figure 10-1.

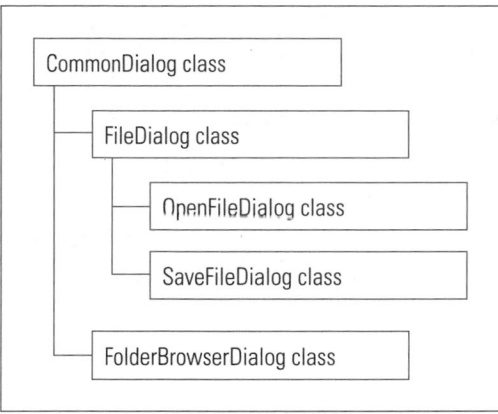

Figure 10-1: Hierarchical relationships among dialog classes

The SaveFileDialog control works nearly the same as the OpenFileDialog control. In fact, it supports almost the same properties and methods, so the members of the two controls are discussed together.

## Syntax

```
System.Windows.Forms.OpenFileDialog class

System.Windows.Forms.SaveFileDialog class
```

## Public Properties

» The Boolean CheckFileExists and CheckPathExists properties define whether the end user can select a file or directory path that does not exist from the dialog box.

» The FileName property stores a string containing the filename to open or save. The FileName property contains both the path (with the drive designator) and the filename.

» The Filter property is used to define the types of files that will be displayed for selection in the dialog box.

» The FilterIndex property works in conjunction with the Filter property. It is used to define which filter from a list of filters is active. The FilterIndex property is 1-based. That is, the first filter has an index of 1, the second filter has an index of 2, and so on.

» The InitialDirectory property stores the initial folder in which the OpenFileDialog or SaveFileDialog controls will search for a file to open or save, respectively.

» The Boolean OverwritePrompt property is used only with the SaveFileDialog control. If set to True, a message box appears prompting the end user to overwrite an existing file. If set to False, the file is overwritten without the end user being prompted.

(Continued)   ▶

» The `Boolean` `RestoreDirectory` property, if set to `True`, causes the current directory to be restored to the original directory after the dialog box closes. Otherwise, the next time the control instance is displayed, the initial directory is set to the previously selected directory.

» The `Title` property stores the text that will appear on the title bar of the dialog box.

## Public Methods

» The `ShowDialog` method displays an instance of the `OpenFileDialog` or `SaveFileDialog` controls. The methods return a value having a data type of `DialogResult`. This value is used to determine whether the end user clicked the Cancel button.

Figure 10-2 shows the visual elements of the Open dialog box.

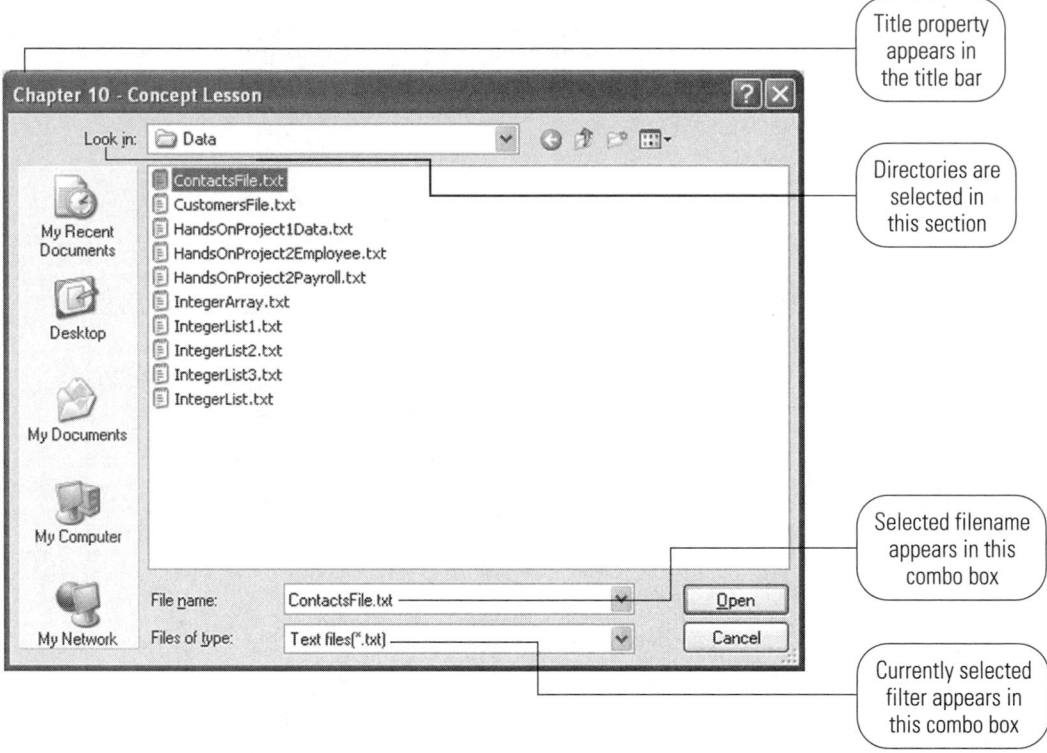

Figure 10-2: Visual elements of the Open dialog box

As shown in Figure 10-2, the contents of the `Title` property appear in the title bar of the dialog box. The Look in combo box displays the initial directory. The Files of type combo box displays the current filters. When a filename is selected, it appears in the File name combo box.

## SETTING THE FILTER FOR AN OPENFILEDIALOG

A filter is used to restrict the types of files that the end user can select in an instance of the `OpenFileDialog` control. Correctly setting this property improves the user interface by displaying only those files having a specific file extension.

A filter consists of a description, followed by a vertical bar (|), followed by the filter criteria. The filter criteria and its corresponding description work as a pair. Each filter description and criteria pair is also separated by a vertical bar. Multiple filters can be created, as necessary. The `Filter` property has the following syntax:

### Syntax

*Object*.Filter = [*description1*|*filter1*|*description2*|*filter2* ...]

### Definition

The `Filter` property contains the text string that will be used as the filter.

### Parameters

» The *object* must be an instance of the `OpenFileDialog` or `SaveFileDialog` controls.

» The *description* contains descriptive text that identifies the file type.

» *filter1* and *filter2* contain the three-character file extension of the filter preceded by the '*.' characters so that all files having a particular extension will be selected. File extensions can have a different number of characters, but nearly all Windows file extensions have three characters.

» Vertical bars separate each description and filter. Do not embed spaces between the vertical bars that separate the description and filter because the spaces are embedded either into the description or into the filter criteria itself. Embedding a space in the filter criteria causes the filter not to display any filenames.

### Code Example

```
ofdMain.Filter = "Text files (*.txt)|*.txt|" _
    "Rich text files (*.rtf)|*.rtf|All files (*.*)|*.*"
ofdMain.FilterIndex = 2
```

### Code Dissection

The preceding example contains three filters for the `OpenFileDialog` control instance named ofdMain. The first filter criteria defines files with the extension ".txt" to be displayed. The second filter causes files with the extension ".rtf" to be displayed, and the final filter causes all of the files in the current folder to be displayed. Setting the `FilterIndex` property to 2 makes the default filter ".rtf" (the second filter).

## USING THE SAVEFILEDIALOG CONTROL

The `SaveFileDialog` control works the same way as the `OpenFileDialog` control. Within the control instance, the `OverwritePrompt` property should be set to `True` so that the end user will not accidentally overwrite an existing file. If the end user attempts to overwrite a file, the dialog box shown in Figure 10-3 opens.

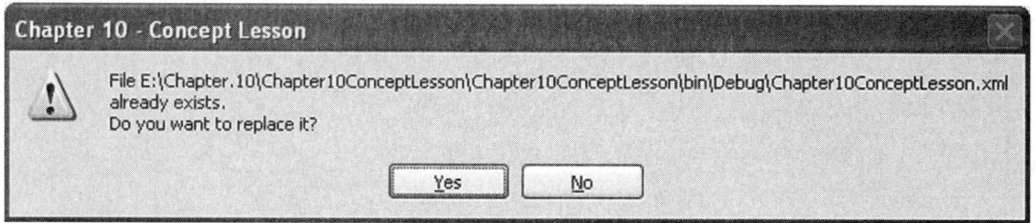

Figure 10-3: Overwrite prompt message

The following code segment shows how to display a `SaveFileDialog` and get the file-name specified by the end user:

```
Dim Result As DialogResult
sfdMain.OverwritePrompt = True
Result = sfdMain.ShowDialog()
If Result = Windows.Forms.DialogResult.OK Then
    txtFileName.Text = sfdMain.FileName
End If
```

The preceding statements display an instance of the `SaveFileDialog` control. They are nearly identical to the statements to display an `OpenFileDialog` control. The `OverwritePrompt` property is set such that the end user is prompted before a file is overwritten. The `ShowDialog` method is called to display the dialog box. If the end user clicks the OK button, the name of the selected file, which is stored in the `FileName` property, is stored in a text box named txtFileName. Again, code is usually written to save data to the specified file.

# INTRODUCTION TO THE FOLDERBROWSERDIALOG CONTROL

The FolderBrowserDialog control is used to browse and select folders instead of files. The FolderBrowserDialog control works much like the OpenFileDialog and SaveFileDialog controls and inherits from the System.Windows. Forms.CommonDialog class.

Figure 10-4 shows a FolderBrowserDialog control instance.

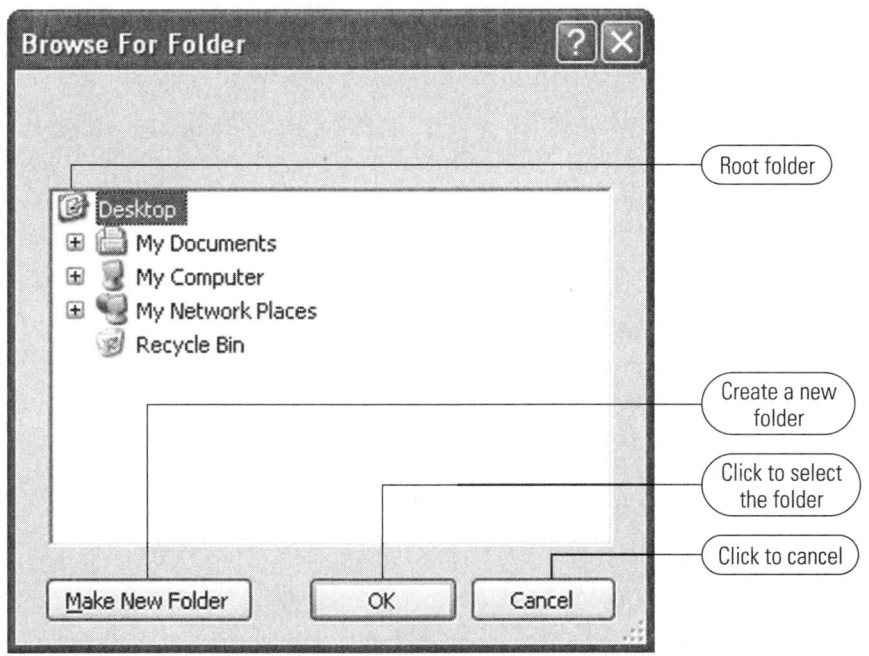

Figure 10-4: The FolderBrowserDialog control instance

As shown in Figure 10-4, the dialog box contains a region that displays folders. Navigating from folder to folder is accomplished in the same way that folder navigation is accomplished using Windows Explorer. Clicking the Make New Folder button causes a folder named "New Folder" to be created. It's also possible to rename folders and delete them using the dialog box. Clicking the OK button selects a folder. No folder is selected if the Cancel button is clicked.

The FolderBrowserDialog control supports the following properties:

» The Description property contains the text that appears in the title bar of the dialog box.

» The RootFolder property defines the topmost folder that will appear in the dialog box when it is displayed.

» The SelectedPath property contains the folder selected by the end user.

» The dialog box is displayed by calling the ShowDialog method.

The following code segment shows how to display an instance of the FolderBrowserDialog control and retrieve the folder selected by the end user:

```
Dim Result As DialogResult
Result = fbdMain.ShowDialog()
If Result = Windows.Forms.DialogResult.OK Then
    txtPathName.Text = fbdMain.SelectedPath
End If
```

The preceding statements are similar to those used to display instances of the OpenFileDialog and SaveFileDialog controls. First, the dialog box is displayed. The If statement then tests whether the user clicked the OK button. If so, the name of the selected folder is stored in the TextBox control instance named txtPathName.

To create the best possible user interface, initial directories and folders should be specified for the various file-related dialog boxes. Literal strings containing absolute directories and filenames should be avoided because it is possible that the specified directory does not exist. Windows provides classes that get directory information dynamically, based on paths defined by Windows itself, or paths related to the application. The members of these classes are discussed next.

## USING WINDOWS DEFINED DIRECTORIES

The members of the System.Environment class are used to get various directories. The read-only SystemDirectory property, as its name implies, returns the directory designated as the system directory. The value of this property is typically the directory named C:\Windows\System, but might vary based on the operating system version and the folder where the operating system is installed. Note that when an application starts, Windows assigns a value to the CurrentDirectory property. The directory is set to the same directory from which the application was started.

Windows also supports folders referred to as *system special folders*. These folders include the Desktop, My Computer, and My Documents, among others. The physical folder corresponding to these special folders can be read by calling the GetFolderPath method of the System.Environment class. The method accepts one argument, which is one of the enumerated values shown in Table 10-1.

| Enumerated value | Description |
|---|---|
| Desktop | The folder that stores the files appearing on the Desktop |
| MyComputer | The folder corresponding to My Computer |
| MyDocuments | The folder corresponding to My Documents |
| Recent | The user's recently opened files folder |

Table 10-1: The enumerated values of the Windows special folders

**» NOTE**

Table 10-1 contains only a partial list of the supported enumerated values. See the Help system for a complete list.

The following code segment shows how to get a directory corresponding to one of these special folders:

```
Dim DirectoryString As String
DirectoryString = Environment.GetFolderPath( _
    Environment.SpecialFolder.Desktop)
```

The second of the preceding statements calls the GetFolderPath method of the System.Environment class to get the physical directory corresponding to the Desktop. You can use the other enumerations to get the physical directory corresponding to the special folder name.

## USING APPLICATION-DEFINED DIRECTORIES

In addition to directories defined by Windows itself, other directories apply to a Visual Studio .NET application as it runs. The Application class, which contains members that apply to the running application itself, are described in the following list:

» The read-only StartupPath property contains the directory from which the application was started. The application name itself does not appear in the property's value.

» The read-only ExecutablePath property returns the same directory as the StartupPath property, but the executable filename is included in the string.

» The UserAppDataPath and LocalUserAppDataPath properties return the path intended for application data for all users and application data for the local user.

The following code segment shows how to read the `StartupPath` and `ExecutablePath` properties and store those values in text boxes:

```
txtStartupPath.Text = Application.StartupPath
txtExecutablePath.Text = Application.ExecutablePath
```

In this exploration exercise, you will see how to select folders and files using the `FolderBrowserDialog`, the `OpenFileDialog`, and the `SaveFileDialog` controls.

1. Start Visual Studio and open the solution file stored in the folder named **Chapter.10\Chapter10ConceptLesson**. Run the solution, and click the **Folder and File Dialogs** tab, if necessary.

2. Click the **Reset Dialogs** button. The `Reset` method is called on each of the folder and file dialogs. In addition, methods of the `System.Environment` and `Application` classes are called to get the current directory, system directory, startup path, and executable path. Figure 10-5 shows the Folder and File Dialogs tab.

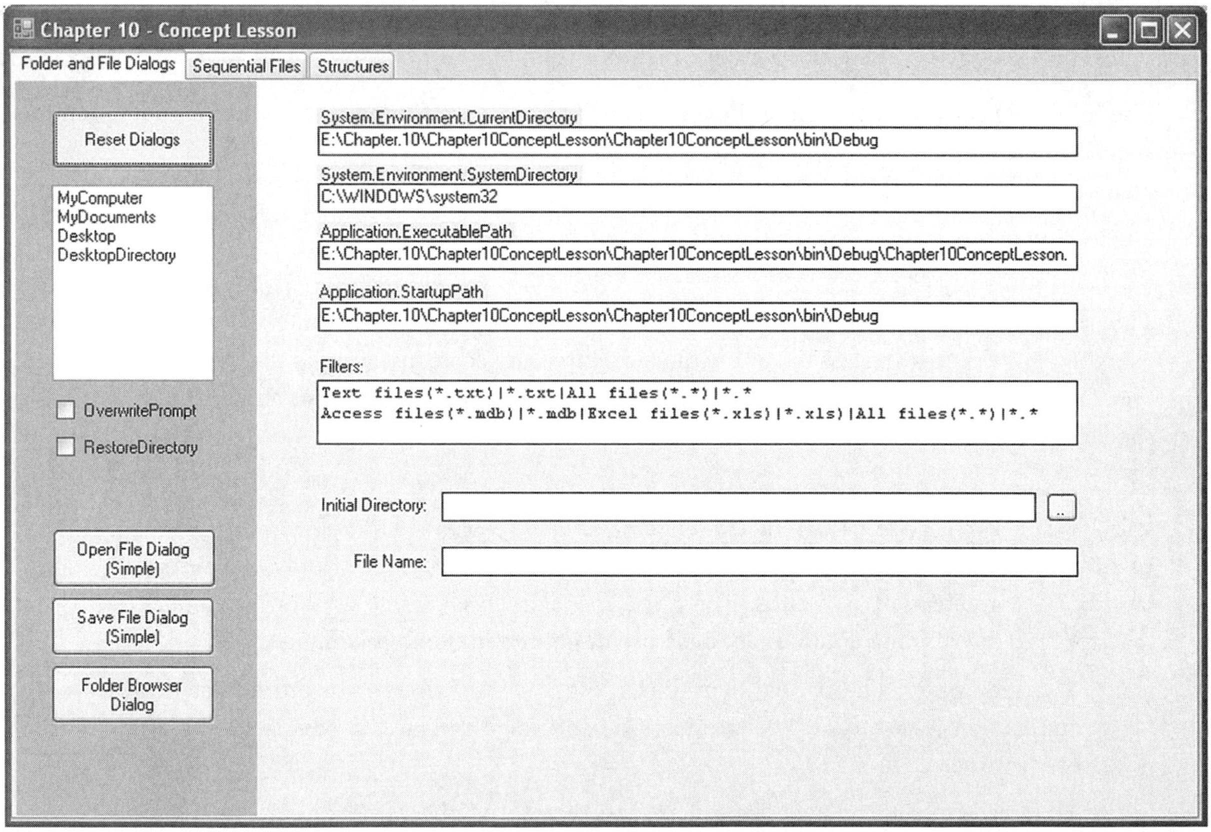

Figure 10-5: Concept lesson—Folder and File Dialogs tab

3. Select a filter from the Filters list box. Click the **Open File Dialog (Simple)** button. The dialog box is configured and displayed. Select a filename of your choosing, and click **Open**. The selected filename appears in the text box titled File Name.

4. Click the **Save File Dialog (Simple)** button. The SaveFileDialog control instance is configured and the dialog box is displayed. Select a file of your choosing. Click **Save**. Again, the selected file appears in the text box. Note that the check boxes titled OverwritePrompt and RestoreDirectory set the corresponding properties for the dialog boxes.

5. Click the **Folder Browser Dialog** button. The control instance is again configured and the dialog box displayed. Select a folder of your choosing and click **OK**. The folder you selected appears in the File Name text box.

## MINI-QUIZ 1

1. Which of the following statements is correct regarding the OpenFileDialog control?

   a. It allows the end user to select a single file or directory.

   b. To display the dialog box, the Show method should be called.

   c. The OpenFileDialog opens the selected file based on the application name, which is stored in the FileType property.

   d. If the end user clicks the Cancel button, the Canceled property is set to True.

   e. none of the above

2. Describe the error(s) in the following statement, which is designed to set the Filter property of the OpenFileDialog control instance named ofdMain. Explain how to fix the error(s).

   ```
   ofdMain.Filter = "Excel (*.xls) | *.xls | " _
       "All files (*.*) | (*.*)"
   ```

(Continued) ▶

3. Which of the following statements correctly describes the guidelines for setting the initial directory for the `OpenFileDialog` and `SaveFileDialog` controls?

a. The initial directory should always be the root directory on the C drive.

b. The initial directory should be set using a hard-coded pathname.

c. The initial directory should be set using members of the `Environment` or `Application` classes.

d. By default, the initial directory is set to the directory C:\Windows and should never be changed.

e. none of the above

4. Which of the following statements is correct regarding a `FolderBrowserDialog` control?

a. With it, the end user can select either folders or files.

b. It is derived from the `SaveFileDialog` control.

c. The folder selected by the end user appears in the `SelectedPath` property.

d. The end user can select multiple folders if the `MultiSelect` property is set to `True`.

e. none of the above

# INTRODUCTION TO PROCESSING TEXTUAL DATA

Many applications save data in the form of text files. These text files can be modified using any editor such as Notepad or WordPad. Text files can also be processed by other applications, including those that you create in Visual Studio.

**>> NOTE** When using WordPad or other word-processing applications, make sure that files are saved as text files. Many editors store files in an internal format unique to the application. For example, a WordPad document is not saved as a text file by default; you have to choose to save the file in text (.txt) format.

One way to process text files is to read or write them from beginning to end. This way of working with text files is called **sequential access**. When a file is read sequentially, the file is referred to as a **sequential file**. Textual files, can be roughly categorized into three types:

» **Freeform files** have no particular format. A mail message or a letter containing text is considered a freeform file.

» Most word-processing, spreadsheet, and database applications can read and write a type of sequential file called a **delimited file**.

» In a **fixed-field file**, each field occupies the same character positions in each record of the file.

Each of these file types are discussed in the following sections.

## UNDERSTANDING THE FORMAT OF FREEFORM FILES

Freeform files, as their name implies, have no particular format. They merely contain one or more textual characters appearing on one or more lines. The number of lines in the file is not important, and the format of each line is not important. When reading a freeform file, the file can be read character by character, or the file can be read all at once. When writing a freeform file, the file can also be written character by character, or all at once.

## UNDERSTANDING THE FORMAT OF DELIMITED FILES

All delimited sequential files have a well-defined structure and several characteristics as follows:

» The contents of sequential files are separated into lines. Each line ends with a carriage return. Pressing the Enter key embeds a carriage return in most text-processing applications. A carriage return is commonly called a **hard return** and is usually not visible to the end user.

» Each line in a sequential file is called a record. A **record** contains a logical group of items such as the information pertaining to a customer or a payment transaction. Again, a carriage return, or hard return, separates each record. Additional hard returns must not appear within records, between records, or after the last line.

» A record contains one or more fields. Each **field** is a unique piece of information contained in a record, such as a name, an address, or a telephone number. Each record in a delimited file must have the same number of fields.

» A **delimiter** is typically a single character, often a comma, which separates one field in a record from the next. A space, tab, or other character can be used as a delimiter. Multiple characters can also be combined together to form a delimiter.

Figure 10-6 shows a delimited sequential file.

Figure 10-6: Delimited sequential file

As shown in Figure 10-6, the sequential file contains four fields and three records. The comma character is used as the delimiter character. A carriage return character is embedded at the end of each record, including the last record, even though the character is not visible.

> **»TIP** When creating a delimited file, make sure that each record contains the correct number of fields. If a particular field in a record contains no information, create a blank entry by placing two delimiters next to one another. Note that these delimiters can appear at the end of a record just before the carriage return character. Also, each record in a delimited file must end with a carriage return, including the last record. Finally, make sure that no blank lines appear at the beginning of the file (before the first record) or after the last record. Typically, if the input file is not correct, an exception is thrown indicating that an attempt was made to read past the end of the file.

## INTRODUCTION TO FIXED-FIELD FILES

Another form of sequential file is called a fixed-field file. Like a delimited file, both types of files contain textual characters. However, instead of separating each field with a delimiter character, a specific character position marks the start and end of each field. There is no delimiter character. Each line in a fixed-field file is terminated with a carriage return character. Figure 10-7 shows the same data shown in Figure 10-6 expressed as a fixed-field file.

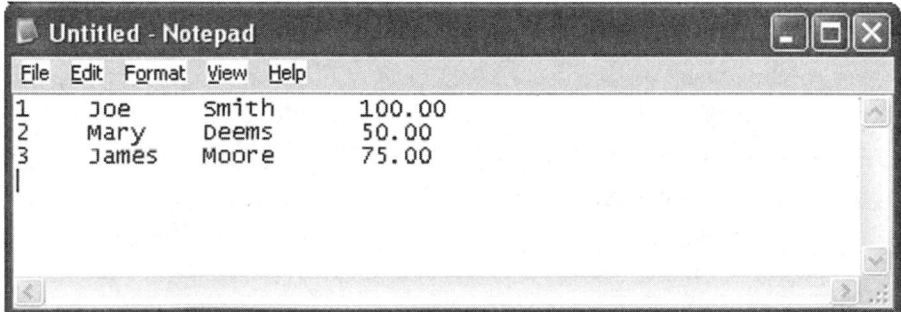

Figure 10-7: Fixed-field file

As shown in Figure 10-7, each field begins at the same character position. The delimiter character does not appear.

# OPENING AND CLOSING SEQUENTIAL FILES WITH THE STREAMREADER CLASS

The `System.IO` namespace contains the `StreamReader` and `StreamWriter` classes to read and write the sequential files.

Opening a sequential file establishes a connection between an application and the physical file. If the sequential file is used for input, the file must already exist. After the file has been opened, it can be read one character at a time, one line (record) at a time, or all at once.

Sequential files are read into memory. For example, a sequential file could be read into a string, into an array, or into an array of class instances. After a sequential file has been read, it should be explicitly closed. Closing a file disconnects the application from the file. The topics of opening, closing, and reading a sequential file are discussed in the following sections.

## OPENING A SEQUENTIAL FILE

A sequential file is opened when an instance of the `StreamReader` class is created. The `StreamReader` constructor has the following syntax:

**Syntax**

`Public Sub New(ByVal path As String)`

**Definition**

The overloaded `StreamReader` constructor opens a sequential file for reading. The preceding syntax diagram shows only one version of the overloaded constructor. Other arguments allow you to specify the Unicode character set of the file.

**Parameters**

» The constructor accepts one argument, the *path* and filename to open. The argument has a data type of `String`.

*(Continued)*

**Code Example**

```
Dim CurrentReader As System.IO.StreamReader = _
    New System.IO.StreamReader("C:\Demo.txt")
```

**Code Dissection**

The preceding statement declares a variable named CurrentReader having a data type of StreamReader. The statement creates an instance of the StreamReader class using the literal value "C:\Demo.txt", which contains the path and filename. The argument could also contain a string variable or the FileName property of an OpenFileDialog control instance.

When creating an instance of the StreamReader class, or any other class instance for that matter, it is possible to write a single statement or split the task into two statements, as shown in the following code segment:

```
Dim CurrentReader As System.IO.StreamReader
CurrentReader = New System.IO.StreamReader("C:\Demo.txt")
```

The first of the preceding statements declares a variable named CurrentReader having a data type of StreamReader, but does not create an instance of the StreamReader class because the New keyword is omitted. The second statement creates an instance of the StreamReader class, thereby calling the constructor and opening the file.

## CLOSING A SEQUENTIAL FILE

After creating an instance of the StreamReader class to open a sequential file and reading the file's contents, the file must be explicitly closed. Explicitly closing a file is necessary to prevent corruption of the file and to release any resources allocated by the operating system. To close an open file, the Close method of the StreamReader class is called, as shown in the following statement:

```
CurrentReader.Close()
```

The preceding statement closes the StreamReader class instance named CurrentReader.

# READING A FILE USING THE MEMBERS OF THE STREAMREADER CLASS

After opening a sequential file by creating an instance of the StreamReader class, methods can be called to read the file's contents. The StreamReader class supports the following members:

The following sections discuss how to read a file all at once, read a file character by character, and read a file one line at a time.

## READING THE ENTIRE CONTENTS OF A FILE

When a file contains unstructured (freeform) text, the `ReadToEnd` method of the `StreamReader` class is used to read the contents of a file all at once, as shown in the following statements:

```
Dim CurrentString As String
Dim CurrentReader As New StreamReader("C:\Demo.txt")
CurrentString = CurrentReader.ReadToEnd()
CurrentReader.Close()
```

The second of the preceding statements opens the file Demo.txt appearing in the root folder of the C drive for reading. The third statement calls the `ReadToEnd` method to read the contents of the file. The file's contents are stored in a string variable named CurrentString. After the file has been read, it is closed.

## READING A SEQUENTIAL FILE CHARACTER BY CHARACTER

In addition to reading a sequential file all at once, it's possible to read a file one character at a time. For example, if tab characters were being replaced with spaces, the file would be read and written one character at a time, replacing each character, as necessary.

As is the case with all sequential files, no processing can take place until the file has been opened. The logic to then read a sequential file one character at a time requires that the first character be read. Reading the first character in this way is often called a *priming read*. A pre-test loop then executes until each character has been read. If the file is empty, the statements in the loop never execute. Thus, an empty file does not cause an exception to be thrown. The statements in the loop process each character in some way, and then read the next character. After all of the characters have been read, the loop exits and the file is closed. Figure 10-8 shows the flowchart to read a sequential file character by character.

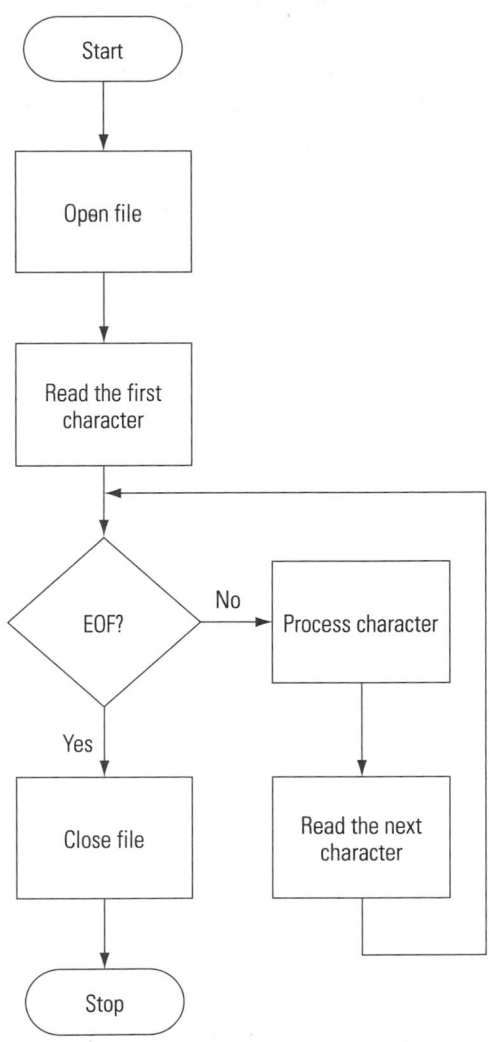

Figure 10-8: Flowchart to read a sequential file character by character

To read a file one character at a time, the Read method should be called instead of the ReadToEnd method.

The following Do loop shows the general logic to read a file one character at a time:

```
Dim CurrentChar As Integer
Dim CurrentReader As New StreamReader("C:\Demo.txt")
CurrentChar = CurrentReader.Read()
Do Until CurrentChar = -1
    ' Statements to process the character.
    CurrentChar = CurrentReader.Read()
Loop
CurrentReader.Close()
```

The second of the preceding statements creates an instance of the `StreamReader` class as before. The third statement reads the first character in the file. The `Read` method returns the integer character code of the character that was read. If there are no more characters in the file, the method returns –1. Thus, if the file is empty, the statements in the loop do not execute, and the empty file is closed. The condition in the `Do` loop tests whether the character read contains the value –1. If it does, the end of file has been reached and the loop exits. Note that a `For` loop cannot be used in place of a `Do` loop because the number of characters in the file is not known in advance. The last statement in the loop then reads the next character.

To illustrate the usefulness of reading a file one character at a time, examine the following code segment, which counts the number of characters, words, and lines in a file:

```
Dim CurrentChar, CharCount, WordCount, LineCount As Integer
Dim CurrentReader As New StreamReader(ofdMain.FileName)
CurrentChar = CurrentReader.Read()
Do Until CurrentChar = -1
    CharCount += 1
    Select Case CurrentChar
        Case 32
            WordCount += 1
        Case 10
            WordCount += 1
            LineCount += 1
    End Select
    CurrentChar = CurrentReader.Read()
Loop
CurrentReader.Close()
```

The variables CharCount, WordCount, and LineCount are accumulators used to store the number of characters, words, and lines in the file, respectively. The structure of this `Do` loop is the same as the structure of the preceding `Do` loop to read a file character by character. The only addition is the `Select Case` statement, which tests each character that was read. If the character is a space (32), the WordCount accumulator is incremented. If the character is a carriage return (10), the WordCount and LineCount accumulators are incremented. Each time through the loop, the CharCount (character count) accumulator is incremented.

## READING A SEQUENTIAL FILE ONE RECORD AT A TIME

Delimited files have a structure such that each line makes up a record containing one or more fields. The logic to read a delimited file requires the following steps be performed after an instance of the `StreamReader` class has been created:

» Call the `ReadLine` method to read the first record (line) of the file. If the file is empty, the method returns `Nothing` (an empty string).

» Using a `Do` loop, process the record that was read, and read the next record by calling the `ReadLine` method. The loop exits when there are no more records to be read.

» After all of the records have been read, close the file.

Figure 10-9 shows a sample flowchart to read a sequential file one record at a time.

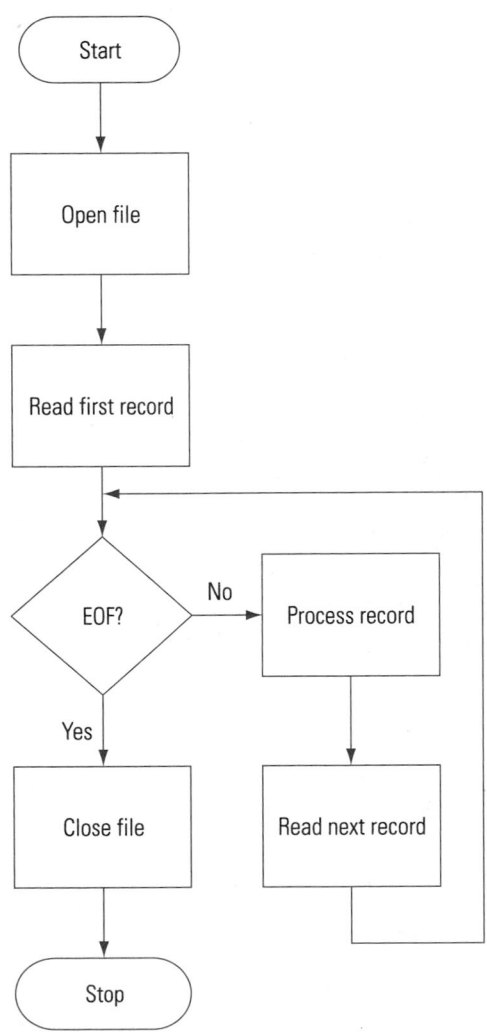

> **» NOTE**
> The logic to read a file character by character or record by record is identical. Thus, the flowcharts shown in Figures 10-8 and 10-9 are nearly identical.

Figure 10-9: Reading a sequential file as a list of records

The following code segment shows how to read a sequential file one record at a time:

```
Dim CurrentReader As New System.IO.StreamReader("C:\Demo.txt")
Dim CurrentRecord As String
CurrentRecord = CurrentReader.ReadLine()
Do Until CurrentRecord = Nothing
    ' Statements to process the current record.
    CurrentRecord = CurrentReader.ReadLine()
Loop
CurrentReader.Close()
```

The preceding statements first create an instance of the StreamReader class as before. Calling the ReadLine method the first time reads the first record. If the file is empty, the string contains the value Nothing, and the statements in the loop do not execute. An exception is not thrown if the file is empty. The statements in the Do loop process the file, and then attempt to read the next record. After all of the records have been read, the file is closed.

## PROCESSING THE RECORDS IN A SEQUENTIAL FILE

Referring back to Chapter 9 and arrays, suppose that a file containing integer values needed to be read from the file. Furthermore, suppose that each integer value appeared on a single line (record). The following code segment shows a class named ArrayFile having a method named ReadIntegerArray that reads the file into an integer array:

```
Public Class ArrayFile
    Public Shared Function ReadIntegerArray( _
        ByVal argFile As String) As Integer()
        Dim CurrentStream As New StreamReader(argFile)
        Dim CurrentRecord As String
        Dim CurrentIndex As Integer
        Dim LocalArray(0) As Integer
        CurrentRecord = CurrentStream.ReadLine()
        Do Until CurrentRecord Is Nothing
            ReDim Preserve LocalArray(CurrentIndex)
            LocalArray(CurrentIndex) = ToInt32(CurrentRecord)
            CurrentIndex += 1
            CurrentRecord = CurrentStream.ReadLine()
        Loop
        CurrentStream.Close()
        Return LocalArray
    End Function
End Class
```

The ReadIntegerArray function accepts one argument, a string containing the file to read, and returns an array having a data type of `Integer`. First, the `StreamReader` class instance is created. The array, which is declared as a local variable in the procedure, is then redimensioned to have one element. This step is performed to initialize the array. The first record is then read by calling the `ReadLine` method. The statements in the `Do` loop redimension the array increasing its size by 1. The current record is stored in the newly created array element. Then, the array index value is incremented and the next line is read. The process continues until all the records in the file have been read. Finally, the array is returned from the procedure.

Suppose that the sequential file discussed in the preceding section was formatted such that each field appeared on the same line separated by a comma as follows:

```
100,200,300,400,500
```

In this case, the file cannot be read one record at a time. As you will see in the next section, at times a string containing a record must be broken down into individual fields. The process of splitting text into individual fields or parts is called **parsing**.

## UNDERSTANDING THE SPLIT METHOD

The `Split` method of the `String` class divides (parses) a string into an array based on a certain character or characters called a delimiter. Common delimiter characters include the comma or tab character, although any character can be used as a delimiter.

The `Split` method accepts two arguments. The first argument contains the string to parse, and the second argument contains the delimiter. The delimiter character(s) are stored in an array having a data type of `Char`. The character(s) in the array makes up the delimiter. If the array contains one character, the delimiter is a single character. If the array contains multiple characters, the delimiter contains multiple characters.

To store a character in a variable having the `Char` data type, call the `ToChar` method of the `System.Convert` class, as shown in the following statements:

```
Dim DelimiterChar As Char
DelimiterChar = System.Convert.ToChar(",")
```

The second of the preceding statements converts a string containing one character, a comma, into a `Char` data type, and stores the value in the variable DelimiterChar.

Because the delimiter consists of a single character, you might be tempted to use the following statement to store the single character into a variable of type `Char`:

```
Dim DelimiterChar As Char = ","
```

However, if strict type checking is enabled, the preceding statement causes a syntax error because the literal value "," is considered a string, and a string cannot be implicitly converted to a `Char` data type because the `Char` data type is a more restrictive data type than the `String` data type.

The `Split` method requires that the delimiter character is stored in an array of type `Char`, rather than a scalar `Char` variable, as shown in the following statement:

```
Dim DelimiterChars() As Char
```

The preceding declaration has the same syntax as any other array declaration. The variable DelimiterChars is a dynamic array of type `Char`. Note that an array of type `Char` can be initialized, just as other arrays can be initialized, as shown in the following statements:

```
Dim DelimiterChar As Char = ToChar(",")
Dim DelimiterChars() As Char = {DelimiterChar}
```

The second of the preceding statements declares a dynamic array of type `Char`, and then initializes the array to the scalar variable named DelimiterChar, which stores the delimiter. The syntax is the same as the syntax to declare and initialize any other array. The preceding statements and variables used to declare and initialize the character array can be reduced to the following declaration:

```
Dim DelimiterChar() As Char = {ToChar(",")}
```

The preceding statement declares an array named DelimiterChar having a data type of `Char`. The array is initialized by calling the `ToChar` method of the `System.Convert` class. The returned character is used as the array initialization value.

Having seen how to initialize an array of type `Char`, you can use the `Split` method of the `String` class to parse a string into an array using the delimiter character. The method has the following syntax:

## Syntax
```
Public Function Split(ByVal separator() As Char) As String()
```

## Definition
The `Split` method of the `String` class parses a string into an array of strings. The `Split` method returns an array containing one element for each field in the string being parsed. The resulting array is automatically redimensioned and each field is stored in an array element. The `Split` method accepts one argument, the array of characters used as the delimiter, and returns an array of strings.

## Parameters
» The *separator* argument contains an array of type `Char`. The character(s) in the *separator* array defines the delimiter character(s) separating each field.

» The `Split` method returns an array of strings.

*(Continued)* ▶

## Code Example

```
Dim CurrentRecord As String = "Field1, Field2, Field3"
Dim Fields() As String
Dim Delimiter() As Char = {ToChar(",")}
Fields = CurrentRecord.Split(Delimiter)
```

## Code Dissection

The preceding statements declare a string variable named CurrentRecord and an array of strings named Fields. The variable Delimiter contains the delimiter character, a comma, which the `Split` method uses to parse the string into fields. The call to the `Split` method parses the string stored in the variable CurrentRecord into an array so that each field is stored in an array element.

Figure 10-10 illustrates how a line is parsed into fields.

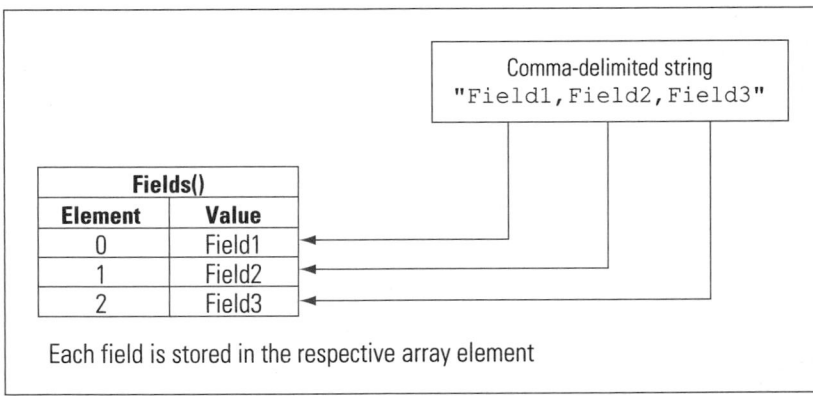

Figure 10-10: Splitting a text line

As shown in Figure 10-10, the input line contains three fields. Using a comma (,) as the delimiter, the `Split` method parses the line into a three-element array.

Suppose that a comma-delimited file containing a list of integers needed to be read and written from and to an array. To perform the read, you could use the following code segment, which shows a method named ReadIntegerList that produces the same result as the ReadIntegerArray method discussed previously. However, each field appears on the same line and a delimiter character is used to separate each field.

```
Public Class ArrayFile
    Public Shared Function ReadIntegerList( _
        ByVal argFile As String) As Integer()
        Dim CurrentStream As New StreamReader(argFile)
        Dim CurrentFileString As String
        Dim CurrentIndex As Integer
        Dim DelimiterChar As Char = ToChar(",")
        Dim DelimiterChars() As Char = {DelimiterChar}
        Dim StringArray() As String
        CurrentFileString = CurrentStream.ReadToEnd()
        StringArray = CurrentFileString.Split(DelimiterChars)
        Dim LocalArray(StringArray.GetUpperBound(0)) As Integer

        For CurrentIndex = 0 To StringArray.GetUpperBound(0)
            LocalArray(CurrentIndex) = _
                ToInt32(StringArray(CurrentIndex))
        Next

        CurrentStream.Close()
        Return LocalArray
    End Function
End Class
```

The logic of the ReadIntegerList procedure is made up of the following steps:

1. Create an instance of the StreamReader class.

2. Read the file contents into a string by calling the ReadToEnd method. The file is read into the variable named CurrentFileString.

3. Call the Split method to parse the string storing the result in an array of strings named StringArray.

4. Declare an array of integers named LocalArray to match the size of the array of strings.

5. Using a For loop, copy each element from the string array to the integer array converting the data type of each element, as necessary. Again, a For loop can be used because the number of array elements is known in advance.

6. Return the array from the procedure.

## COMMON SEQUENTIAL FILE ERRORS

Common errors are made when reading sequential files. One such error is neglecting to read the next record inside of the loop after the current record has been processed, as the following statements show:

```
Dim CurrentReader As New System.IO.StreamReader("C:\Demo.txt")
Dim CurrentRecord As String
CurrentRecord = CurrentReader.ReadLine()
Do Until CurrentRecord = Nothing
    ' Statements to process the current record.
Loop
```

The preceding loop executes indefinitely. In other words, the loop is an infinite loop. The first record (line) is read by calling the ReadLine method. If the file contains at least one record, the statements in the loop execute. However, because the loop does not contain a statement to read the next record, the variable CurrentRecord always stores the data for the first record and the loop executes indefinitely.

The following statements illustrate a second error. The statements in the loop read the next input record before processing the current record.

```
Dim CurrentReader As New System.IO.StreamReader("C:\Demo.txt")
Dim CurrentRecord As String
CurrentRecord = CurrentReader.ReadLine()
Do Until CurrentRecord = Nothing
    CurrentRecord = CurrentReader.ReadLine()
    ' Statements to process the current record.
Loop
```

The preceding loop contains a logic error. The input file is opened and the initial read is performed correctly, so everything appears to be in order. However, examine the statements in the loop carefully. The first statement in the loop reads the next input record, and then processes that record. Thus, because of the order in which the loop statements are written, the contents of the first record are not processed.

Another common loop error is neglecting to perform the priming read, as shown in the following code segment:

```
Dim CurrentReader As New System.IO.StreamReader("C:\Demo.txt")
Dim CurrentRecord As String
Do Until CurrentRecord = Nothing
    ' Statements to process the current record.
    CurrentRecord = CurrentReader.ReadLine()
Loop
```

In the preceding code segment, the first record is not read before the condition in the loop is tested the first time. Thus, the variable CurrentRecord contains Nothing, and the statements in the loop never execute—even if the file contains records.

In this exploration exercise, you will see how to read a file character by character, record by record, and all at once. The code is implemented such that the input and output is performed by methods appearing in the class named ArrayFile. These methods are nearly identical to the ones presented in the chapter. The code in the various event handlers call these methods. Examine the commented code in the ArrayFile class for a completed description of each method.

1. Run the solution for the concept lesson. Click the **Sequential Files** tab. Figure 10-11 shows the Sequential Files tab.

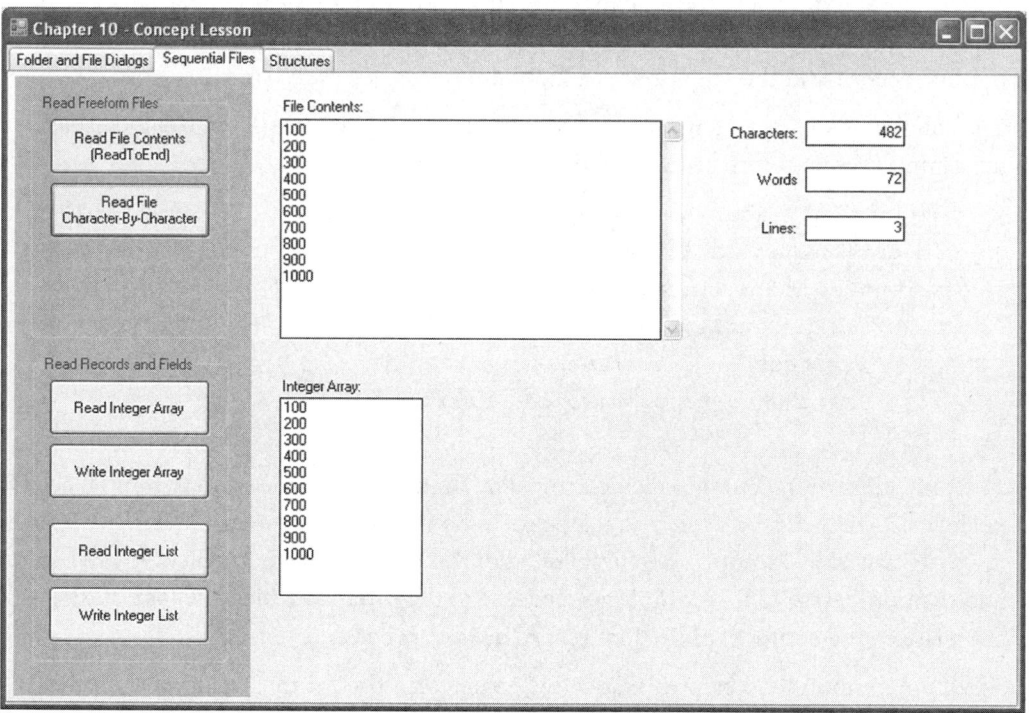

Figure 10-11: Concept lesson—Sequential Files tab

2. Click the **Read File Contents (ReadToEnd)** button. In the Open dialog box, select the file named **Chapter.10\Data\FreeForm.txt**. Click **Open** to close the dialog box. The file is read into the form's text box.

3. Click the **Read File (Character-By-Character)** button. Open the same **FreeForm.txt** file you opened in the previous step. The file is read one character at a time. The same code discussed in this section calculates the number of characters, words, and lines in the file.

4. Click the **Read Integer Array** button. In the Open dialog box, select the file named **Chapter.10\Data\IntegerArray.txt**. The ReadIntegerArray method discussed in this section is called to read the file. The file is read into an array. A For loop enumerates the array's contents and displays them in the list box.

5. Click the **Read Integer List** button. In the dialog box, select the file named **Chapter.10\Data\IntegerList.txt**. The ReadIntegerList method discussed in this section is called to read the file.

## MINI-QUIZ 2

1. Which of the following statements is correct regarding sequential files?

   a. Sequential files can be roughly categorized into freeform, delimited, and fixed-field files.

   b. The character or characters that separate each field in a delimited file are called delimiters.

   c. The delimiter character must be a comma. Also, only one character can be designated as a delimiter.

   d. both a and b

   e. all of the above

2. What is the name of the method that should be used to read a delimited file with one record appearing on each line? _____

3. Describe the error in the following statements, which are intended to read the contents of a sequential file one character at a time.

```
Dim CharCount As Integer
Dim CurrentChar As String
Dim CurrentReader As New StreamReader("C:\Quiz.txt")
CurrentChar = CurrentReader.Read()
Do Until CurrentChar Is Nothing
    CharCount += 1
    CurrentChar = CurrentReader.Read()
Loop
```

# WRITING A SEQUENTIAL FILE WITH THE STREAMWRITER CLASS

Just as the methods of the StreamReader class are used to read sequential files, the methods of the StreamWriter class are used to write sequential files.

The syntax to call the constructor is the same for both the StreamReader and StreamWriter classes. One argument is passed to the constructor, the name of the file to write. The following code segment illustrates how to open a file for writing using the StreamWriter class:

```
Dim CurrentWriter As New System.IO.StreamWriter("C:\Demo.txt")
' Statements to write the file.
CurrentWriter.Close()
```

The preceding statements first create an instance of the StreamWriter class, thereby opening the file. Placeholder statements appear for the statements that will write the file. Finally, after the file is written, it is closed by calling the Close method. The StreamWriter class supports the following members to write a file:

---

### Syntax
`System.IO.StreamWriter class`

---

### Public Properties
» The NewLine property has a data type of String and contains the character(s) that mark the end of a line. By default, these characters consist of a carriage return, followed by a line feed. When calling the WriteLine method, the line is automatically terminated by the character(s) defined by the NewLine property.

---

### Public Methods
» The Close method closes the output file. Its effect is the same as calling the Close method of the StreamReader class.

» The Write method writes a character, character array, or string to a file. The Write method accepts one argument, a primary data type, which the method converts to a string.

» Similar to the Write method, the WriteLine method writes data to a file, and the purpose of the argument is the same. However, a line terminator is written to the file after the data is written. The value of the line terminator is stored in the NewLine property.

---

## WRITING A FREEFORM FILE

Remember that a freeform file can be read into a string by calling the `ReadToEnd` method. The following code segment shows how to write a freeform file whose contents are contained in a string:

```
Dim StringData As String = "Freeform text"
Dim CurrentWriter As New System.IO.StreamWriter("C:\Demo.txt")
CurrentWriter.Write(StringData)
CurrentWriter.Close()
```

The preceding statements create an instance of the `StreamWriter` class. The third statement writes the contents of the variable named StringData. After the file contents have been written, the file is closed. Of course, any string could be written in this way, such as the `Text` property of a text box.

## WRITING A DELIMITED FILE

You saw how to read a file containing a list of integer values. Each value was stored as a separate record. The process of writing the contents of an array to a file is similar to the process of reading the file, as described in the following steps:

1. Create an instance of the `StreamWriter` class.

2. Using a `For` loop, call the `WriteLine` method to write each record. A `For` loop can be used because the number of records is known in advance.

3. After the file has been written, call the `Close` method to close the file.

The following statements show how to write a one-dimensional array to a sequential file:

```
Public Shared Sub WriteIntegerArray _
    (ByRef argArray() As Integer, ByVal argFile As String)
    Dim CurrentStream As New StreamWriter(argFile)
    Dim CurrentIndex As Integer
    For CurrentIndex = 0 To argArray.GetUpperBound(0)
        CurrentStream.WriteLine(argArray(CurrentIndex))
    Next
    CurrentStream.Close()
End Sub
```

The preceding `Sub` procedure accepts two arguments: the array to be written and a string containing the name of the file to be written. The `StreamWriter` class instance is then created, and the `For` loop examines each array element. Each time through the loop, the current array element is written to the sequential file followed by a carriage return by calling the `WriteLine` method. Thus, each line contains one record.

In addition to writing a file such that each item appears on a separate line, the `Write` method can be used to write a list such that each item is separated by a delimiter character, as the following procedure shows:

```
Public Shared Sub WriteIntegerList( _
    ByRef argArray() As Integer, ByVal argFile As String)
    Dim CurrentStream As New StreamWriter(argFile)
    Dim CurrentIndex As Integer
    For CurrentIndex = 0 To argArray.GetUpperBound(0)
        CurrentStream.Write(argArray(CurrentIndex))
        If CurrentIndex <> argArray.GetUpperBound(0) Then
            CurrentStream.Write(",")
        End If
    Next
    CurrentStream.Close()
End Function
```

The preceding `Sub` procedure accepts two arguments. The first argument contains the array to be written and the second argument contains the name of the file to write. The `StreamWriter` class instance is then created. The `For` loop contains the statements to write each array element. The first statement in the loop writes the array element. The `If` statement tests that the current element being written is the last element. If the current array element is not the last element, a comma character is written as the delimiter character.

In this exploration exercise, you will see how to write freeform data to sequential files and how to write arrays to sequential files.

1. Run the solution for the concept lesson. Click the **Sequential Files** tab. Note that this is the same tab used in the previous exploration exercise and shown in Figure 10-11.

2. Click the **Read Integer Array** button. In the Open dialog box, select the file named **Chapter.10\Data\IntegerArray.txt**, and click **Open** to close the dialog box. The ReadIntegerArray method discussed previously is called to read the file.

3. Click the **Write Integer Array** button. In the dialog box that opens, enter the file named **IntegerArrayOutput.txt**, and click **Save** to close the dialog box. The WriteIntegerArray method discussed in this section is called to write the file.

4. Click the **Read Integer List** button. In the Open dialog box, select the file named **Chapter.10\Data\IntegerList.txt**, and click **Open** to close the dialog box. The ReadIntegerList method discussed in the previous section is called to read the file.

5. Click the **Write Integer List** button. In the dialog box, enter the file named **IntegerListOutput.txt**, and click **Save** to close the dialog box. The WriteIntegerList method discussed in this section is called to write the file.

## MINI-QUIZ 3

1. Which of the following statements is correct regarding writing sequential files?

   a. The `WriteLine` method is used to write a file character by character.

   b. The `WriteDelimiter` method is used to write a delimiter to a sequential file.

   c. The `Write` method can be used to write a single character or a string to a sequential file.

   d. The `WriteHardReturn` method is used to write a carriage return to a sequential file.

   e. none of the above

2. Assume that an array named StringArray exists. Write the statements to write the array to a sequential file such that each array element appears on its own line. Write the array to the file named C:\Quiz.txt.

3. Write the statements to write the counting numbers 1 through 100 to the sequential file named C:\Quiz.txt.

# INTRODUCTION TO STRUCTURES

Chapter 9 discussed how to manage an array of class instances used to store repeating data. Visual Basic supports another type called a `Structure`, which is used to store related data items. A structure groups related data items together logically. For example, an individual card in a telephone card index might contain a person's first name, last name, telephone number, and date added. Rather than declaring individual variables to store each related item, all of the items can be grouped together and operations performed on the entire structure.

A structure is similar to a class in that both have properties and methods. However, structures are value types rather than reference types. The Structure keyword is used to create a new data type containing elements made up of other data types and has the following syntax:

## Syntax

```
[Public|Friend] Structure name

    variableDeclarations

    [procedureDeclarations]

End Structure
```

## Definition

The Structure and End Structure keywords are used to declare a structure block containing one or more members.

## Dissection

» The Public and Friend access modifiers define the accessibility of the structure. The meaning of these access modifiers is the same as their meaning when declaring variables and procedures. Note that the Private keyword cannot be used to declare a structure.

» name defines the name of the structure (type). The name must conform to the standard naming conventions for identifiers. Pascal case should be used for structure names.

» The variableDeclarations contains the members of the structure. The syntax of each variableDeclaration is the same as the syntax to declare a variable. A structure must contain at least one Public member.

» Structures can contain Function and Sub procedures identified by procedureDeclarations.

## Code Example

```
Public Structure Contact

    Public FirstName As String

    Public LastName As String

    Public TelephoneNumber As String

    Public DateAdded As DateTime

End Structure
```

## Code Dissection

The preceding structure contains three members having a data type of String and a fourth member having a data type of DateTime. The syntax to declare a Structure member is the same as the syntax to declare any other variable. That is, each variable declaration has an access modifier, a name, and a data type. A structure member can have any data type.

Just as there are rules that describe where a `Class` block can be declared, there are rules that describe where a `Structure` block can be declared, as follows:

» A `Structure` can be declared inside of a `Class` or `Module` block. A `Structure` can also be declared at the file level (outside of a `Class` or `Module` block).

» A `Structure` block can contain a nested `Structure` block.

» A `Structure` block cannot appear inside of a procedure block.

## DECLARING A STRUCTURE VARIABLE

Declaring a `Structure` block creates a new data type. It does not declare a variable having that data type. Conceptually, this is similar to declaring a class. Declaring a class creates a type, but it does not create an instance of that class. Just as variables of type `Integer` and `Single` must be declared, variables having a `Structure` data type must be declared. The following statements show the syntax to declare two variables having a data type of `Contact`:

```
Dim CurrentContact As Contact
Dim PreviousContact As Contact
```

The preceding statements declare two variables named CurrentContact and PreviousContact, each having a data type of `Contact`. The syntax is no different than the syntax to declare a scalar variable.

It is also possible to declare an array of structures, as the following statements show:

```
Public ContactList() As Contact
ReDim ContactList(9) As Contact
```

The first of the preceding statements declares an array named ContactList having no initial size. Each element in the array has a data type of `Contact`. The second statement redimensions the array so that is has 10 elements.

## STORING AND RETRIEVING DATA FROM A STRUCTURE

After declaring a structure variable, assignment statements can be used to store information into individual structure members. The syntax to reference a structure member is the same as the syntax to reference the property of an object. A period separates the structure variable name and the member name. The following statements illustrate how to store data in structure members:

```
CurrentContact.FirstName = "Joe"
CurrentContact.LastName = "Smith"
CurrentContact.Telephone = "775-555-1288"
CurrentContact.DateAdded = #3/22/2006#
```

The preceding assignment statements store literal values in each of the structure members described previously. Again, the variable name and member name are separated by a period.

Note also that assignment statements can be written to assign the value of one structure member to another, as shown in the following statements:

```
PreviousContact.FirstName = CurrentContact.FirstName
PreviousContact.LastName = CurrentContact.LastName
PreviousContact.Address = CurrentContact.Address
PreviousContact.DateAdded = CurrentContact.DateAdded
```

The preceding statements copy the contents of the variable named CurrentContact to the variable named PreviousContact one member at a time.

If two structure variables have the same data type, the entire structure can be assigned in a single statement, as the following statement shows:

```
PreviousContact = CurrentContact
```

The preceding statement copies all of the members of the variable CurrentContact to the variable named PreviousContact. Thus, the preceding statement has the same effect as the previous code segment that assigned all of the structure members individually.

Note that assignment statements involving structures work differently than assignment statements involving classes. Structures are value types so when a structure is assigned, as shown in the preceding statement, the structure's data is assigned. As you know, classes are reference types. Thus, instead of assigning the class' data, only the object reference is assigned.

## USING THE WITH STATEMENT TO REFERENCE STRUCTURE MEMBERS

Assignment statements using individual structure members can quickly become tedious as the structure variable name must be entered again and again. The With statement provides a convenient shorthand way of referencing several structure members. To use the With statement, you create a With block, as the following statements show:

```
With CurrentContact
    .FirstName = "Joe"
    .LastName = "Smith"
    .Telephone = "775-555-1288"
    .DateAdded = #3/22/2006#
End With
```

As shown in the preceding code segment, a `With` block is made up of a `With` statement and an `End With` statement. The name of the structure follows the `With` statement, and member names appear inside of the `With` block.

**>>TIP**

The `With` statement can also be used with classes.

## CONTROL STRUCTURES AND WITH BLOCKS

The `With` statement does have a few limitations. Most notably, a decision-making statement cannot break up a `With` block. Thus, the following code segment is illegal:

```
If True Then
    With CurrentContact
        .FirstName = "Joe"
        .LastName = "Smith"
End If
        .Telephone = "775-555-1288"
    End With
```

The same limitation applies to repetition structures. That is, a repetition structure cannot break up a `With` block. Thus, the following loop causes syntax errors:

```
Do While True
    With CurrentContact
        .FirstName = "Joe "
        .LastName = "Smith"
Loop
        .Telephone = "775-555-1288"
    End With
```

**>>NOTE**

Increasingly complex data types can be created by nesting structures. That is, it is possible to create a structure member having a data type that is itself a structure.

## USING ARRAYS OF STRUCTURES

As mentioned, it's possible to declare an array of structures. Storing and retrieving data to and from an array of structures requires that you specify the structure variable name, followed by an array subscript in parentheses, a period, and then the structure member name. The following statements illustrate how to store data in an array of structures:

```
Private ContactList(99) As Contact
ContactList(0).FirstName = "Joe"
ContactList(0).LastName = "Smith"
ContactList(0).Telephone = "775-555-1288"
ContactList(0).DateAdded = #3/22/2006#
```

The first of the preceding statements declares an array having 100 elements. Each element has a data type of `Contact`, which is a structure. The second and third statements store values in the FirstName and LastName members. The fourth statement stores a value in the Telephone member, and the final statement stores a value in the DateAdded member. In all cases, the statements store values in the first array element.

The `With` statement can also be used with arrays of structures, as shown in the following statements:

```
With ContactList(0)
    .FirstName = "Joe"
    .LastName = "Smith"
    .Telephone = "775-555-1288"
    .DateAdded = #3/22/2006#
End With
```

## PROCESSING DELIMITED FILES USING ARRAYS OF STRUCTURES

Previously in the chapter, you saw how to read a sequential file having one field per record into an array. Reading a sequential file into an array of structures requires that each record be read, parsed, and then stored in an array of structures. The following code segment shows a class named ContactReader with a method to open a file using the `StreamReader` class, another method to read one record, a third method to determine if end of file has been reached, and a final method to close the file. The file processed by the class is made up of four fields, as shown in the following code segment:

```
Paul,Brown,775-555-1288,3/22/2006
Mary,Deems,775-555-9444,4/21/2006
James,Smith,702-555-8334,5/17/2005
```

As shown in the preceding code segment, there are four fields separated by a delimiter, which is a comma.

The following code segment shows the ContactReader class.

```
Public Class ContactReader

    Private CurrentReader As StreamReader

    Public Sub New(ByVal argFile As String)
        CurrentReader = New StreamReader(argFile)
    End Sub

    Public Function ReadContact() As Contact
        Dim CurrentContact As Contact
        Dim Fields() As String
        Dim CurrentRecord As String
        Dim DelimiterChars() As Char = {ToChar(",")}
```

```
        CurrentRecord = CurrentReader.ReadLine()
        Fields = CurrentRecord.Split(DelimiterChars)
        With CurrentContact
            .FirstName = Fields(0)
            .LastName = Fields(1)
            .Telephone = Fields(2)
            .DateAdded = ToDateTime(Fields(3))
        End With
        Return CurrentContact
    End Function

    Function EndOfFile() As Boolean
        Dim NextCharacter As Integer
        NextCharacter = CurrentReader.Peek()
        If NextCharacter = -1 Then
            Return True
        End If
    End Function

    Public Sub Close()
        CurrentReader.Close()
    End Sub
End Class
```

The constructor accepts one argument, the name of the file to read. The statement in the constructor opens the file. The variable named CurrentReader stores the instance of the StreamReader class.

Most of the processing takes place in the ReadContact method. The ReadLine method is called to read a record. Then, the Split method is called to break the record into the individual fields. The statements in the With block copy the fields to the variable named CurrentContact. This is the value that is returned by the method.

The EndOfFile method returns a Boolean value to indicate whether there are more records in the file to be read. The final method named Close closes the file.

In this exploration exercise, you will see how structures and structure variables are declared, how to assign structure variables, and how to work with arrays of structures. The file named Contact.vb contains the ContactReader class just discussed. The buttons on the Structures tab use the ContactReader class to read the data into an array of structures named CurrentContactList. Again, examine the commented code in the concept lesson for a detailed explanation of the procedures.

1. Run the solution for the concept lesson. Click the **Structures** tab. Figure 10-12 shows the Structures tab after the sequential file has been read.

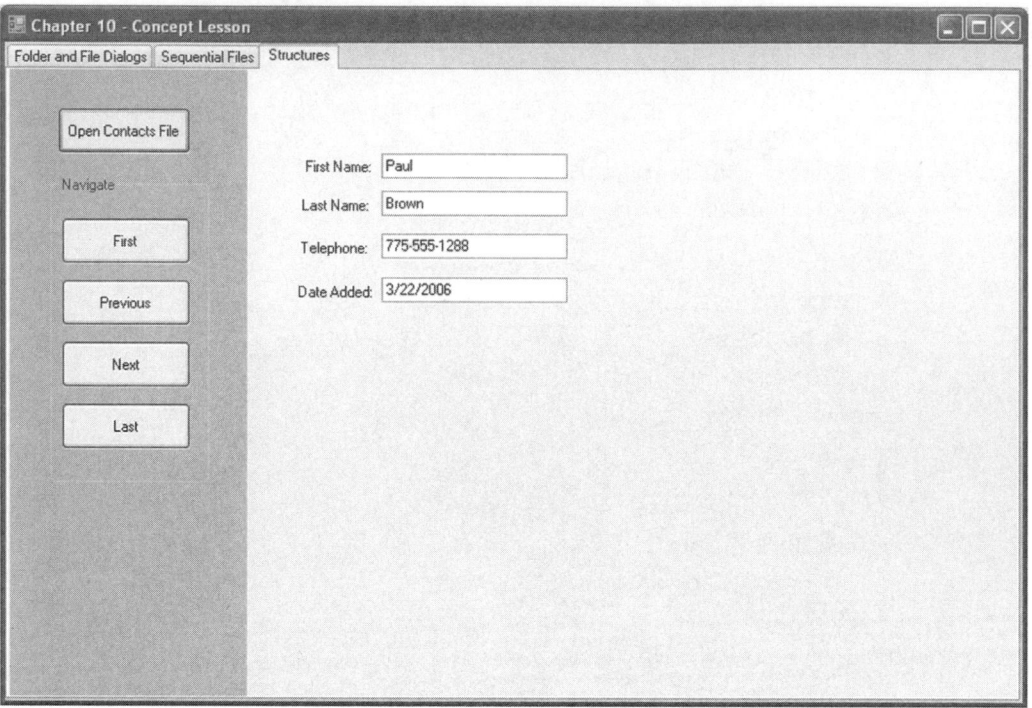

Figure 10-12: Concept lesson—Structures tab

2. Click the **Open Contacts File** button. In the dialog box that opens, select the file named **Chapter.10\Data\ContactsFile**, and then click **Open**. The code in the event handler for the Open File button uses the Contacts class to open and read the file into an array of structures. The first record is displayed in the form's text boxes.

3. Click the various navigational buttons on the left side of the form. A counter is used to keep track of the current record in the array of structures. The counter is updated accordingly and a Function procedure named DisplayCurrentRecord is called to display the current record.

# APPLICATION LESSON

## CREATING A CUSTOMER LIST MANAGER

In this application lesson, you will create the code to read and write delimited files containing a list of customers. The delimited file will be read into an array of structures. The application has a user interface with which the end user can read and write the sequential file containing the customers and click buttons to navigate from customer to customer. In addition, the end user will be able to add, change, and delete customers from the list. The user interface relies on a class named CustomerList to manage the list of customers.

## APPLICATION LESSON—USER INTERFACE

The application's user interface has buttons to read and write the sequential file containing the customers. After the file has been opened, the end user can navigate from customer record to customer record, displaying the current customer record in the form's text boxes. Using the `OpenFileDialog` and `SaveFileDialog` controls, the end user will be able to select the file to open or save. Finally, there is another group of buttons allowing the end user to add a new customer, change an existing customer, or delete the current customer. Figure 10-13 shows a segment of the sequential file managed by this application.

Figure 10-13: Application lesson—Data file

As shown in Figure 10-13, the data file is a delimited file and the comma is designated as the delimiter character. The file shown in Figure 10-13 contains three records.

## APPLICATION LESSON—DESIGN

The design of the application involves a structure named Customer having members named Name, Address, City, State, ZipCode, CreditLimit, and BalanceDue. A class named CustomerList manages a list of customers. Figure 10-14 shows the UML class diagrams for the structure and class.

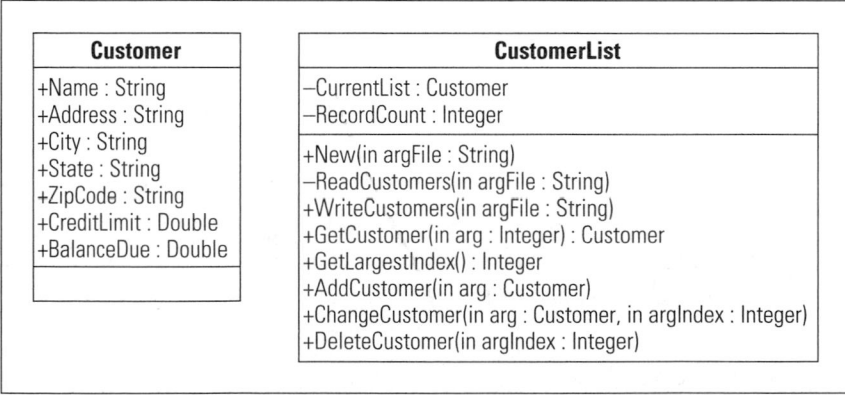

Figure 10-14: Application lesson—UML class diagram

As shown in Figure 10-14, the Customer structure contains data. The CustomerList class has members to manage the list of customers. The following list describes the members of the CustomerList class:

» The constructor for the CustomerList class creates an instance of the `StreamReader` class, calls the hidden ReadCustomers procedure, and, finally, closes the file. The constructor accepts one argument, a string containing the name of the sequential file.

» The WriteCustomers method is used to write the sequential file. The code in the method creates an instance of the `StreamWriter` class, writes each customer stored in the array of structures, and then closes the sequential file. The filename is passed as an argument to the method.

» A method named GetCustomer accepts one argument, an integer containing the index of the customer contained in the array. The method returns that customer.

» A method named GetLargestIndex returns the largest integer index from the list of customers. In other words, the method returns the upper bound of the hidden array.

» Methods named AddCustomer, ChangeCustomer, and DeleteCustomer add a new customer, modify an existing customer, and remove a customer from the list, respectively.

The form is made up of buttons that allow the end user to open and save the file. In addition, a group of navigational buttons allow the end user to locate the first, previous, next, and last records in the list. Finally, another group of buttons allow the end user to add, change, and delete items from the list.

## APPLICATION LESSON—IMPLEMENTATION

As always, a completed preview of the application lesson is provided so that you can see the results of completing the lesson's hands-on steps, and correct any mistakes that you might make.

To preview the completed application:

1. Start Visual Studio, if necessary, and open the solution file stored in the folder **Chapter.10\Chapter10ApplicationLessonPreview**. Run the application.

2. Click the **Open File** button. In the Open dialog box, select the file named **Chapter10\Data\CustomersFile.txt**, and click the **Open** button. The file is read and the first record is displayed, as shown in Figure 10-15.

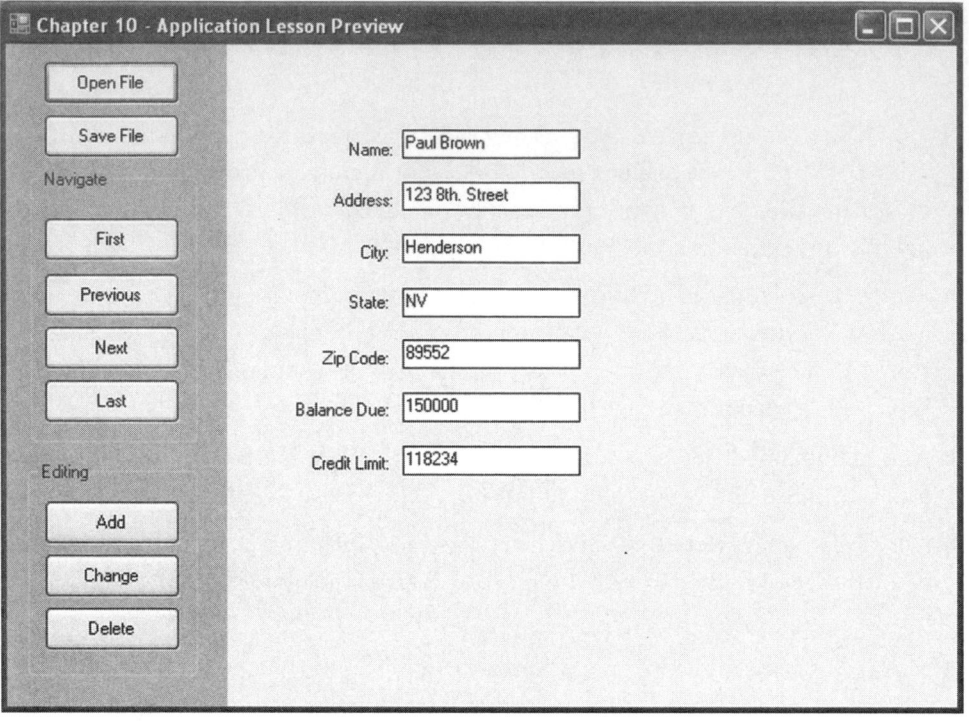

Figure 10-15: Application lesson—Completed form

3. Click the various navigation buttons to navigate from record to record. As you click the buttons, the current record is displayed.

4. Navigate to the last record. Modify the contents of the last record. Click the **Add** button to add a new record to the list.

5. Select a record of your choosing and edit the record. Click the **Change** button to save the changes to the list.

6. Finally, click the **Delete** button. The record is deleted from the list.

The user interface for this application lesson has already been completed. You will begin by first implementing the methods in the Customer class to read and write the sequential file.

To create the implementation of the Customer class:

1. Open the solution file of the same name stored in the folder **Chapter.10\Chapter10ApplicationLessonStartup**.

2. Activate the Code Editor for the class named **Customer**. Notice that the Customer structure has already been created along with the variables to store the hidden data.

Like the constructor for the `StreamReader` class, the constructor for the Customer class opens the sequential file, calls a hidden method to read the file, and then closes the file. Enter the following statements (shown in bold) in the constructor for the CustomerList class:

```
Public Sub New(ByVal argFile As String)
    CurrentReader = New StreamReader(argFile)
    Call ReadCustomers(argFile)
    CurrentReader.Close()
End Sub
```

3. The logic to read the input file involves reading and parsing each record. For each record read, the record is copied to a Customer structure, and then added to the array of customers named CurrentList. Enter the following statements in the **ReadCustomers** procedure. Refer to the application preview for a commented version of this procedure.

```
Private Sub ReadCustomers(ByVal argFile As String)
    Dim CurrentCustomer As Customer
    Dim Fields() As String
    Dim CurrentRecord As String
    Dim DelimiterChars() As Char = {ToChar(",")}
    CurrentRecord = CurrentReader.ReadLine()
    Do Until CurrentRecord Is Nothing
        Fields = CurrentRecord.Split(DelimiterChars)
        With CurrentCustomer
            .Name = Fields(0)
            .Address = Fields(1)
            .City = Fields(2)
            .State = Fields(3)
            .ZipCode = Fields(4)
            .CreditLimit = ToDouble(Fields(5))
            .BalanceDue = ToDouble(Fields(6))
        End With
        ReDim Preserve CurrentList(RecordCount)
        CurrentList(RecordCount) = CurrentCustomer
        CurrentRecord = CurrentReader.ReadLine()
        RecordCount += 1
    Loop
    RecordCount -= 1
End Sub
```

4. The WriteCustomers method accepts one argument, a string containing the filename to write. The method creates an instance of the `StreamWriter` class, and writes the hidden array named CurrentList as a delimited file. Enter the following statements (shown in bold) in the **WriteCustomers** method:

```
Public Sub WriteCustomers(ByVal argFile As String)
        CurrentWriter = New StreamWriter(argFile)
        Dim CurrentRecord As Integer
        For CurrentRecord = 0 To RecordCount
            With CurrentList(CurrentRecord)
                CurrentWriter.Write(.Name)
                CurrentWriter.Write(",")
                CurrentWriter.Write(.Address)
                CurrentWriter.Write(",")
                CurrentWriter.Write(.City)
                CurrentWriter.Write(",")
                CurrentWriter.Write(.State)
                CurrentWriter.Write(",")
                CurrentWriter.Write(.ZipCode)
                CurrentWriter.Write(",")
                CurrentWriter.Write(.CreditLimit.ToString)
                CurrentWriter.Write(",")
                CurrentWriter.Write(.BalanceDue.ToString)
                CurrentWriter.WriteLine()
            End With
        Next
        CurrentWriter.Close()
End Sub
```

5. The GetLargestIndex method returns the value of the largest array index. Enter the following statement (shown in bold) in the **GetLargestIndex** method:

```
Public Function GetLargestIndex() As Integer
        Return CurrentList.GetUpperBound(0)
End Function
```

6. The GetCustomer method accepts one argument, the index of the customer to return. The method returns a Customer structure. Enter the following statement, shown in bold, in the **GetCustomer** method:

```
Public Function GetCustomer(ByVal arg As Integer) As Customer
        Return CurrentList(arg)
End Function
```

7. The AddCustomer method increases the size of the array by one element, and stores the customer, passed as an argument, in the newly created array element. Enter the following statements (shown in bold) in the **AddCustomer** method:

```
Public Sub AddCustomer(ByVal arg As Customer)
    RecordCount += 1
    ReDim Preserve CurrentList(RecordCount)
    CurrentList(RecordCount) = arg
End Sub
```

8. The ChangeCustomer method accepts two arguments, the index of the customer and a structure containing the customer data to be replaced. The statements in the method store the customer passed as an argument into the array. Enter the following statement (shown in bold) in the **ChangeCustomer** method.

```
Public Sub ChangeCustomer(ByVal arg As Customer, _
    ByVal argIndex As Integer)
    CurrentList(argIndex) = arg
End Sub
```

9. The DeleteCustomer method accepts one argument, the index of the customer to delete. The customer is deleted by shifting all of the array elements, starting with the array element containing the current customer, to the last array element. When the process is complete, the array is redimensioned and its size decreased by 1 element. Enter the following statements (shown in bold) in the **DeleteCustomer** method:

```
Public Sub DeleteCustomer(ByVal argIndex As Integer)
    Dim Count As Integer
    For Count = argIndex To CurrentList.GetUpperBound(0) - 1
        CurrentList(Count) = CurrentList(Count + 1)
    Next
    ReDim Preserve CurrentList( _
        CurrentList.GetUpperBound(0) - 1)
    RecordCount -= 1
End Sub
```

Having completed the classes that will manage the customer records, the next step in the application's development is to create the code that will execute as the end user interacts with the form's buttons. The form contains the following Click event handlers:

» The button named btnOpen uses the methods of the CustomerList constructor to open and read the sequential file.

» The button named btnSave calls the WriteCustomers method of the CustomerList class instance to write the data back to the sequential file.

» The buttons named btnFirst, btnPrevious, btnNext, and btnLast navigate from record to record.

» The buttons named btnAdd, btnChange, and btnDelete contain code to add, change, and delete a customer, respectively.

The code for the Open button creates an instance of the CustomerList class to read the sequential file. The code for the Save File button calls the WriteCustomers method of the CustomerList class to write the sequential file.

To create the code for the Open File and Save File buttons:

1. Enter the following statements in the **Click** event handler for the button named **btnOpen**:

```
Dim Result As DialogResult
ofdMain.Filter = "Text Files(*.txt)|*.txt|All Files(*.*)|*.*"
Result = ofdMain.ShowDialog
If Result = Windows.Forms.DialogResult.OK Then
    CurrentCustomerList = New CustomerList(ofdMain.FileName)
End If
Call DisplayCustomer(0)
```

2. Enter the following statements in the **Click** event handler for the button named **btnSave**:

```
Dim Result As DialogResult
sfdMain.Filter = "Text Files(*.txt)|*.txt|All Files(*.*)|*.*"
Result = sfdMain.ShowDialog
If Result = Windows.Forms.DialogResult.OK Then
    CurrentCustomerList.WriteCustomers(sfdMain.FileName)
End If
```

The variable named CurrentCustomerList contains a reference to the list of customers. The variable named CurrentRecord declared in the form keeps track of the current customer. As the end user navigates from customer to customer, the value of this variable is updated, the customer is retrieved from the list, and the customer is displayed.

To add navigation support:

1. To locate the first record, the current record pointer is set to 0, and the corresponding record is displayed. Enter the following statements in the **Click** event handler named **btnFirst**:

```
CurrentRecord = 0
DisplayCustomer(CurrentRecord)
```

2. To locate the previous record, a decision-making statement is used to verify that the current record is not the first record and the current record is decremented accordingly. Enter the following statements in the **Click** event handler for the button named **btnPrevious**:

```
If CurrentRecord > 0 Then
    CurrentRecord -= 1
    DisplayCustomer(CurrentRecord)
End If
```

3. To locate the next record, a decision-making statement is used to verify that the current record is not the last record and the current record is incremented accordingly. Enter the following statements in the **Click** event handler for the button named **btnNext**:

```
If CurrentRecord < CurrentCustomerList.GetLargestIndex Then
    CurrentRecord += 1
    DisplayCustomer(CurrentRecord)
End If
```

4. To locate the last record, the current record pointer is set to the maximum index value in the customer list and the current record is displayed. Enter the following statements in the **Click** event handler for the button named **btnLast**:

```
CurrentRecord = CurrentCustomerList.GetLargestIndex
DisplayCustomer(CurrentRecord)
```

For brevity, the code to add, change, and delete a customer has already been completed. The code for the Add button copies data from the form's text boxes into a customer structure. The AddCustomer method is then called to add the customer. The Change button works similarly. The Delete button calls the DeleteCustomer method to delete the current customer record.

5. Test the application.

# CHAPTER SUMMARY

» The `OpenFileDialog` and `SaveFileDialog` controls are used to display dialog boxes with which the end user can select a file to open or save. The controls do not actually open or save files. That task is the responsibility of the developer. Filenames with specific file extensions are displayed by setting the `Filter` property. Filters are made up of description/value pairs separated by a vertical bar (|). The `FilterIndex` property is a 1-based value that defines the currently selected filter. The initial folder displayed is defined by the `InitialDirectory` property. Calling the `ShowDialog` method displays the dialog box.

» The initial directory for the `OpenFileDialog` and `SaveFileDialog` controls should be set dynamically using the members of the `System.Environment` and `Application` classes.

» The `FolderBrowserDialog` allows the end user to select a folder. The root directory displayed is defined using the `RootFolder` property. The directory (folder) selected by the end user is stored in the `SelectedPath` property.

» The `StreamReader` class is used to process textual files having a freeform, delimited, or fixed-field format. The constructor accepts one argument, the name of the file to open. The `Read`, `ReadLine`, and `ReadToEnd` methods are used to read the file. After a sequential file has been read, it should be explicitly closed by calling the `Close` method.

» One type of sequential file is a delimited file. One or more characters, called a delimiter, separates each field in the file. To parse a delimited string, the `Split` method of the `String` class should be called. The `Split` method accepts one argument, an array of type `Char`, which stores the delimiter character(s).

» Writing a sequential file is accomplished by creating an instance of the `StreamWriter` class. The `Write` method writes one or more characters to the sequential file. The `WriteLine` method also writes one or more characters but appends a carriage return to the end of the line. After writing the sequential file, call the `Close` method to close the file.

» The `Structure` keyword is used to declare a structure. Structures can contain variable declarations and procedures. Structures can have members, which are themselves structures. A structure must have at least one public member. Structures are value types so when assigning structures, the data is copied instead of just the reference. Members of a structure are referenced using the same dot notation used to reference the properties of an object.

» The `With` statement simplifies the process of referencing multiple structure or class members. To use the `With` statement, the structure or class variable appears on the same line as the `With` statement itself. The member names appear in the `With` block. A `With` block cannot break up a decision-making or repetition statement.

# KEY TERMS

**delimited file**—A sequential file containing a character to separate individual fields.

**delimiter**—Typically a single character, which separates one field in a record from the next. Common delimiters include the comma or tab character.

**field**—A unique piece of information contained in a record.

**fixed-field file**—A sequential file in which a field in each record occupies the same character positions.

**freeform files**—A type of sequential file containing textual characters having no particular format.

**hard return**—A character, typically a carriage return, that is embedded at the end of a record in a sequential file.

**parsing**—The process of splitting text into individual fields or parts.

**record**—A logical group of items appearing on one line in a sequential file.

**sequential access**—The process of reading a file from beginning to end.

**sequential file**—A type of data file that is read from beginning to end.

# ANSWERS TO MINI-QUIZZES

### MINI-QUIZ 1

1. e. none of the above

2. Spaces appear between the descriptions and values. Those spaces must be removed. In addition, parentheses surround the All files "*.*" filter. These characters must also be removed.

3. c. The initial directory should be set using members of the `Environment` or `Application` classes.

4. c. The folder selected by the user appears in the `SelectedPath` property.

### MINI-QUIZ 2

1. d. both a and b

2. The `ReadLine` method.

3. First, the variable CurrentChar should have a data type of `Integer`. Second, the `Do` loop should be modified as follows: `Do Until CurrentChar = -1`.

**MINI-QUIZ 3**

1. c. The `Write` method can be used to write a single character or a string to a sequential file.

2.
```
Dim CurrentWriter As New StreamWriter("C:\Quiz.txt")
Dim StringArray() As String
Dim Counter As Integer
For Counter = 0 To StringArray.GetUpperBound(0)
    CurrentWriter.WriteLine(StringArray(Counter))
Next
CurrentWriter.Close()
```

3.
```
Dim Count As Integer
Dim CurrentWriter As New StreamWriter("C:\Quiz.txt")
For Count = 1 to 100
    CurrentWriter.WriteLine(Count.ToString)
Next
CurrentWriter.Close()
```

**MINI-QUIZ 4**

1. b. The `Structure` statement creates a structure but does not declare a variable.

2.
```
Public Structure Sample
    Public SampleDate As DateTime
    Public Amount As Double
End Structure
```

3.
```
Dim CurrentSample As Sample
CurrentSample.SampleDate = #3/22/2005#
CurrentSample.Amount = 104.23
```

# REVIEW QUESTIONS

1. Which of the following statements is correct regarding the `OpenFileDialog` and `SaveFileDialog` controls?

   a. Both controls support the `MultiSelect` properties allowing the user to open and save multiple files.

   b. The `OpenFileDialog` control supports the `Filter` property, but the `SaveFileDialog` does not.

   c. Both controls derive from the `FileDialog` class, which, in turn, derives from the `CommonDialog` class.

   d. The controls open and save files.

   e. none of the above

2. Assuming that an `OpenFileDialog` control instance exists named ofdMain, which of the following filters is correct?

   a. `ofdMain.Filter = "Excel (*.xls) | *.xls | "` _
       `"All files (*.*) | (*.*)"`

   b. `ofdMain.Filter = "Excel (*.xls)|*.xls|"` _
       `"All files (*.*)|(*.*)"`

   c. `ofdMain.Filter = "Excel (*.xls)&*.xls&"` _
       `"All files (*.*)& (*.*)"`

   d. `ofdMain.Filter = "|Excel (*.xls)|*.xls"` _
       `"All files (*.*)|(*.*)|"`

   e. none of the above

3. Which of the following statements is correct regarding the `FolderBrowserDialog` control?

   a. It inherits from the `FileDialog` control.

   b. The name of the folder selected by the end user is stored in the `FolderName` property.

   c. It is possible to set the topmost folder that will appear in the dialog box by setting the `RootFolder` property.

   d. The text appearing in the title bar is specified using the `Text` property.

   e. none of the above

4. Which of the following statements regarding a delimited sequential file is true?

   a. Delimited sequential files are divided into lines called records, and each record ends with a carriage return.

   b. A record contains one or more fields.

   c. A delimiter separates each field. A delimiter can be made up of a single character or can contain multiple characters.

   d. all of the above

   e. none of the above

5. Which of the following statements correctly opens a sequential file for reading?

   a. ```
      Dim CurrentReader As New _
          StreamReader("C:\Questions.txt")
      ```

   b. ```
      Dim CurrentReader As New StreamReader( _
          "C:\Questions.txt", Read)
      ```

   c. ```
      Dim CurrentReader As _
          StreamReader("C:\Questions.txt")
      ```

   d. ```
      CurrentReader = _
          StreamReader.Open("C:\Questions.txt")
      ```

   e. ```
      Dim CurrentReader As New _
          InputStream("C:\Questions.txt")
      ```

6. Which of the following statements is correct regarding reading files with the `StreamReader` class?

   a. To read a file all at once, the `ReadAll` method should be called.

   b. The `ReadLine` method reads a record terminated by a carriage return.

   c. The `ReadLine` method is used to read a field from a sequential file.

   d. The `ReadChar` method reads a single character.

   e. none of the above

7. Which of the following statements correctly describes how to read a delimited sequential file?

   a. Open a file using an instance of the `OpenFileDialog` control. Then, using a loop, call the `ReadLine` method of the `OpenFileDialog` class.

   b. Create an instance of the `Stream` control on the form. Use the `Read` method to read the file.

   c. Open a file using the `Stream` constructor. Using a loop, call the `Read` method to read each record in the file. For each record read, call the `Divide` method to divide the record into fields.

   d. Open a file using the `StreamReader` constructor. Using a loop, call the `ReadLine` method to read each record in the file. For each record read, call the `Split` method to divide the record into fields.

   e. none of the above
      ```

8. Which of the following statements correctly declares a delimiter suitable for use with the `Split` method of the `String` class?

   a. `Dim Delim() As Char = ToChar(",")`

   b. `Dim Delim As Char = {ToChar(",")}`

   c. `Dim Delim() As Char = {ToChar(",")}`

   d. `Dim Delim() As String = ","`

   e. `Dim Delim() As Char = {ToDelimiter(",")}`

9. Which of the following statements is true regarding the `Split` method of the `String` class?

   a. It divides a string into fields using a delimiter.

   b. The delimiter consists of an array having a data type of `Char`.

   c. The method returns an array of strings such that one array element exists for each field.

   d. The delimiter can consist of a single character or multiple characters.

   e. all of the above

10. When writing a file, what is the difference between the `Write` method and the `WriteLine` method?

    a. The `Write` method can write only a single character at a time.

    b. The `Write` method does not write a carriage return, whereas the `WriteLine` method does.

    c. The `Write` method can be used to write a blank line, whereas the `WriteLine` method cannot.

    d. There is no difference between the `Write` and the `WriteLine` methods. The `Write` method is supplied for backward compatibility with previous Visual Basic versions.

    e. none of the above

11. Which of the following statements apply to structures?

    a. The `Structure` statement declares a new data type.

    b. The `Structure` statement declares a variable and stores data in the structure.

    c. To reference a structure member with code, you use the structure variable name, followed by the member name separated by an ampersand (&).

    d. A `Structure` block can be declared inside of a `Class` block but cannot be declared inside of a `Module` block.

    e. none of the above

12. Which of the following statements is correct related to classes and structures?

    a. A structure is a reference type, whereas a class is a value type.

    b. Both structures and classes are reference types.

    c. If a structure and class have the same members, assignment statements are legal between any structure and class variables.

    d. A structure is a value type, whereas a class is a reference type.

    e. none of the above

13. Which of the following statements is correct, given the following structure declaration?

```
Public Structure Coordinate
     Public X As Integer
     Public Y As Integer
End Structure
```

    a. The declaration is illegal because structure members cannot be declared with the `Public` access modifier.

    b. The declaration is not legal because the name of the structure (Coordinate) must also appear as in `End Structure Coordinate`.

    c. The structure contains two members having a data type of `Integer`.

    d. none of the above

14. Given the following declarations:

```
Public Structure Person
     Public Name As String
     Public Address As String
End Structure
Public Person1, Person2 As Person
```

which of the following statements is legal?

    a. `Person1 = Person2`

    b. `Person1.Name = Person2`

    c. `Person1 = Person`

    d. `Person2.Namc = Person1`

    e. none of the above are legal

15. Which of the following statements is correct related to the `With` statement?

    a. Decision-making and repetition statements cannot appear inside of a `With` block.

    b. When creating a `With` block, the `End With` statement is optional.

    c. When using the `With` statement, the structure or class name to be referenced appears on the same line as the `With` statement.

    d. `With` statements can be used with classes but cannot be used with structures.

    e. none of the above

16. Describe the characteristics of a sequential file. Your description should include the meaning of such terms as field and record, and the purpose of a delimiter. In addition, describe the differences between a delimited file and a fixed-field file.

17. Describe the process of reading a sequential file. Describe how to open the file, how to determine whether the file contains data, and how to create a loop that will read the contents of the file and parse each line into the individual fields.

18. Describe the difference between the `Write` and `WriteLine` methods of the `StreamWriter` class.

19. Compare and contrast a `Structure` declaration with a `Class` declaration.

20. Describe the purpose of the `With` statement. In your answer, also describe restrictions that apply to the `With` statement.

# PROGRAMMING QUESTIONS

1. Assume that an instance of the OpenFileDialog control exists named ofdMain. Write the statements to set the initial directory to the Windows system directory. Create a filter so that the user can select files with the extension .dll or .exe. Use the description "Dynamic Link Library" and "Executable File", respectively. Display the dialog box. If the end user clicks the OK button, display the selected file(s) in a message box.

2. Write the statement to open the file named C:\Question.txt for reading. Declare a variable named CurrentReader to store the open file.

3. Write the statements to open the file named C:\Unstructured.txt for reading. Read the file's contents into a variable named CurrentFile having a data type of String. Finally, close the file.

4. Assume that an input file C:\Data.txt contains the following data:

   ```
   100,84,22,184,33
   18,22,87,5,16
   204,16,94,7,93
   ```

   Write the statements to read the file into a two-dimensional array named Values having a data type of Integer. Declare and redimension the array as necessary.

5. Write the statements to open the file named Letter.txt for reading. Read the file one character at a time. Using an accumulator named CharacterCount, store the total number of characters read. Using an accumulator named SpaceCount, store the total number of spaces read.

6. Create a Sub procedure named ReplaceTabsWithSpaces that accepts two arguments having a data type of String. Assume that these arguments will contain filenames. The statements in the procedure should create instances of the StreamReader and StreamWriter classes. The procedure should read the input file character by character replacing any tab characters found with the space character. As each character is read from the input file, the character or replacement character should be written to the output file.

7. Create a `Do` loop to read the input stream referenced by the `StreamReader` class instance named CurrentQuestion. Assume that the file has one field and that the field has a data type of `Integer`. Read the data into the dynamic array named QuestionList. Resize the array as necessary. Declare any variables as necessary.

8. Write the statements to create an instance of the `StreamWriter` class named CurrentWriter, and a one-dimensional array named Values having a data type of `Double`. Write a loop to save the array to the file named C:\Output.txt. Write each array element on a separate line. The loop should determine the size of the array.

9. Write the statements to declare a structure named InventoryItem. The structure should have members named PartNumber having a data type of `String`, QuantityOnHand and QuantitySold having a data type of `Integer`, and Price having a data type of `Single`. Declare each member so that it is publicly accessible.

10. Using the structure you declared in the previous question, declare a `Private` variable named Disk60GB. Store values in each member having the proper data type.

11. Assume that a structure named Position has been declared. Write the statements to declare two variables named StartPosition and EndPosition having a data type of Position.

12. Given an array of structures named Customers having string members of Name, Address, City, and State, write the statements to create an instance of the `StreamWriter` class and write the contents of the array to the file named C:\Output.txt. Use the `GetUpperBound` method of the `Array` class to determine the array's size.

13. Given the same array of structures named Customers described in the previous question, create an instance of the `StreamReader` class. Read a delimited file named C:\Output.txt into the array of structures.

14. Given an array of structure variables named Customers having string members of Name, Address, City, and State, write the statements to print the value of each member to the Immediate window. Use the `With` statement.

# HANDS-ON PROJECTS

1. In this hands-on project, you will create an application that reads the contents of a sequential file, summarizes those contents, and saves the summarized data to a new file. The input file used in this hands-on project contains simulated data produced by an automatic sensor that monitors the temperature of a refrigerator. Sensors commonly monitor critical data for later analysis.

   The application you create will calculate the average, minimum, and maximum temperature. The input file was created such that the sensor takes one sample every 10 minutes. For each sample taken, the sensor writes one record containing the current date, time, and temperature. Thus, the input file contains two fields.

   a. A completed executable version of this hands-on project can be found in the file **Chapter.10\HandsOnProjects\Ch10HandsOnProject1.exe**. The sample data files for the application are named **Chapter.10\Data\HandsOnProject1Data.txt**.

   b. Start Visual Studio and create a new solution named **Ch10HandsOnProject1.sln**.

   c. Create the control instances, using the preview application as a template. The form contains a combo box displaying dates. Two list boxes appear below the combo box to display the detailed date/time information and the corresponding temperature for the selected date. Three buttons open a text file, save the file, and exit the solution.

   d. Declare a structure with two members to store each record from the input file. The first member should be a date, and the second member should be a single precision number. Declare a dynamic array of structures to store the file.

   e. Create the `Click` event handler for the Open Input File button. The code in the event handler should display an instance of the `OpenFileDialog` control allowing the end user to select a file. Open the input file and read the contents. Store each record in the dynamic array you declared in the previous steps, redimensioning the array, as necessary. After reading the input file, load the data from each array member into the combo box. When adding the date to the combo box, remove the time part of the value so that only the date appears. Use the `ToShortDateString` method to convert the date value. Samples are taken every 10 minutes. Thus, the array will contain duplicate date values for a particular day. Remove the duplicate values from the combo box so that only one entry appears in the combo box for each day.

f. Create the necessary event handler so that when the end user clicks on a combo box item, all the records for the selected date will appear in the two list boxes. In addition, calculate and display the minimum, maximum, and average temperature for the selected date, and display those values in the labels appearing on the form. Format the output to four decimal places. The output values should also be right-justified in the labels.

g. Create the code for the Write Output File button. Display a `SaveFileDialog` control instance allowing the user to select a file to save. The array of structures will contain several records for one day. Calculate the average temperature for each day, and write one record containing the date and average temperature to the file.

h. Create a second form to display the summarized file you generated in the previous step. The form should contain a multiline text box. Modify the form's constructor to accept one string argument. Display the string in the text box.

i. Create the code for the Exit button.

2. In this hands-on project, you will create an application that reads two sequential files. The first contains employee information and the second contains detailed payroll information for each employee. Tables 10-2 and 10-3 describe the record format for the two sequential files.

| Description | Data type |
|---|---|
| ID number | Integer |
| Name | String |
| Address | String |
| Social Security number | String |

Table 10-2: Employee file

| Description | Data type |
|---|---|
| ID number | Integer |
| Payroll date | Date |
| Gross pay | Single |
| Withholding taxes | Single |
| FICA | Single |
| Net pay | Single |

Table 10-3: Payroll file

a. A completed executable version of this hands-on project can be found in the file **Chapter.10\HandsOnProjects\Ch10HandsOnProject2.exe**. The sample data files for the application are named **Chapter.10\Data\HandsOnProject2Employee.txt** and **Chapter.10\Data\HandsOnProject2Payroll.txt**.

b. Start Visual Studio and create a new solution named **Ch10HandsOnProject2.sln**.

c. Create the control instances, using the preview application as a template.

d. Create two structures and module-level dynamic arrays to store the data described in Tables 10-2 and 10-3.

e. In the Click event handler for the Open Files button, write the code to open the employee and the payroll file, and store the records in the corresponding array. The end user should select both files using the OpenFileDialog control instance. The files should be selected one after the other.

f. Next, write the code to open and read the employee and payroll files into the two arrays of structures. As you read each employee record, write the statement(s) to add the employee ID numbers to the combo box.

g. Write the code so that when the end user clicks an item in the combo box, the employee name, address, and Social Security number appear in the labels below the combo box. To accomplish this task, you will need to write a loop that searches through the employee array to find the selected employee ID.

h. Next, write the code to display the payroll information for the selected employee ID. First, remove any existing contents from the output list boxes. Next, write a loop that searches through the array of payroll records. When a payroll record is found that matches the selected employee, add the payroll record to the output list boxes.

i. Write the statements to calculate the totals for each list box and display the values in labels below the list boxes. *Hint*: You can perform this task as a separate loop or accumulate the totals as you locate the payroll records corresponding to the selected employee.

j. Write the statements to synchronize the five output list boxes. When the end user selects a record in one output list box, the corresponding records should be displayed in the other four list boxes.

3. In this hands-on project, you will create an application that generates sequential files containing randomly generated test data for simulated customer transactions.

a. Start Visual Studio and create a new solution named **Ch10HandsOnProject3.sln**.

b. Create list boxes to store the test data along with any other necessary control instances.

c. Create a structure to store the test data. The structure should contain an ID number, a last name, a first name, a count of transactions, and a sample date. The ID number and transaction count should have a data type of `Integer`. The data type of the sample date should be `DateTime`. The data type of the other fields should be `String`.

d. Write the code to generate the sample records. To generate the unique ID number, use a counter that begins numbering at 0 and increments by 1 for each record read. The code to generate the names requires some thought. Declare and initialize two arrays with six names (elements) each. One array will store a list of first names and the other will store a list of last names. When you generate the names, use counters to cycle through the list of names.

e. To generate the transaction count, call the appropriate method of the `Random` class to generate random numbers between 1 and 100. Generate random date values, as necessary, using a technique of your choosing.

f. Write the statements to save the sample data file as a delimited file. Use an instance of the `SaveFileDialog` control to save the files. The comma character should be used as the delimiter.

4. In this hands-on project, you will create a solution that uses two types of records appearing in a single file. The first type of record contains an address, the depth of a water well, and an integer containing the number of samples. The samples appear in the second record type and contain a sample date and a water level.

a. Start Visual Studio and create a new solution named **Ch10HandsOnProject4.sln**.

b. The input file for this hands-on project differs from the other hands-on projects in this chapter. The first type of record is a header record containing three fields: an address, the depth of a well, and the number of detail records that follow. These detail records contain sample water levels. This second type of record contains two fields storing the date the water sample was taken and the water level when the sample was taken. Declare two structures and dynamic arrays to store this information. A sample input file appears in the folder **Chapter.10\Data\HandsOnProject4Data.txt**.

c. Create the input objects, as necessary, based on the information provided in the previous step.

d. In the `Click` event handler for the Open Input File button, write the statements to open the input file and read the file into two dynamic arrays. The logic to read the file is different from the logic you have used previously. When you read the address record, a field exists containing the number of detail records that follow. Thus, you will not read all of the detail records until the end of file has been reached. Rather, you will read a fixed number of detail records, and then try to read another address record. Also, as you read each address record, store it in the appropriate list box on the form.

e. Write the necessary statements so that when the end user selects an address record in the list box, the corresponding sample records appear in the other two list boxes. In addition, write the code to display the minimum and maximum water levels for the selected address.

# 11

# INTRODUCTION TO DATABASE PROCESSING

## After completing this chapter, you will be able to:

Use terminology to describe a database and the elements of a database

Use a Visual Studio Wizard to establish a database connection used to load database data into the project, and edit that data using control instances created on a form

Understand the code generated by the Visual Studio Data Source Configuration Wizard

Perform specialized database processing tasks beyond those performed by the Data Source Configuration Wizard

Work with database data programmatically

# CONCEPT LESSON

# CHARACTERISTICS OF A DATABASE AND DATABASE MANAGEMENT SYSTEMS

In Chapter 10, you learned how to process data using sequential files, which provide but one way to read and write data to the disk. Another common way to read and write data is to use a database combined with a database management system. A **database** contains a set of data related to a particular topic or purpose. Some databases are small and store the data for a particular business function, such as maintaining a simple mailing list. Large databases can store all of an organization's data and can be several terabytes in size. For example, the database to store all of the student information for a university would be quite large.

There are a variety of different types of databases, including relational, networked, and object-oriented databases. This chapter discusses the use of relational databases, such as those used in the Microsoft Access DBMS, Microsoft SQL Server DBMS, and Oracle.

The data stored in a relational database is organized into one or more tables, each made up of rows and columns. A **table** is represented as a grid made up of rows and columns. The data stored in each row of a table is called a **record**. For example, each student admitted to a university would have a record in a student table. A record is made up of multiple data items called **fields** such as a student ID or student last name.

Just as a variable has a data type, so too does a database field. Database fields have data types that correspond to the data types supported by the .NET Framework class library. From record to record, the data stored in a field has the same data type and characteristics.

## DATABASE TABLES AND FIELDS

Just as this book uses a standard prefix for controls, standard prefixes are also used for database elements. The prefix "tbl" is used to denote a database table, and the prefix "fld" is used to denote a field in a table. The application in this concept lesson uses a database named Employees with one table named tblEmployees containing the following fields:

» fldEmployeeID has an Integer data type storing a unique employee identification number.

» fldFirstName and fldLastName store an employee's first and last name, respectively. The data type of these fields is String.

» fldTelephone stores the employee's telephone number and has a data type of `String`.

» fldDateHired stores the date that the employee was hired and has a data type of `DateTime`.

» fldWage contains the hourly wage for the employee and stores a floating-point value.

» fldDeductions contains the number of tax deductions claimed by the employee and stores a floating-point value.

» fldNotes is a string containing notes pertaining to the employee.

» fldStatus has a `Boolean` data type. If `True`, the employee is currently employed. If `False`, the employee is a former employee.

» fldType is a string containing the type of employee. Valid values are Full time and Part time.

This chapter's concept lesson uses a database that has already been created for you. The database contains a populated table, as shown in Figure 11-1. (A populated table is one that contains data.)

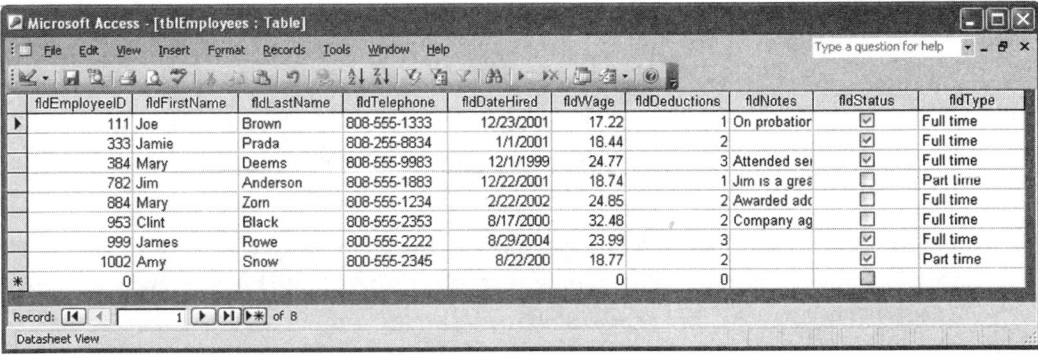

Figure 11-1: Populated database table

Figure 11-1 shows the table named tblEmployees having 10 fields and eight records. The field names appear in the column headers. Each record appears as a separate row in the table.

## INTRODUCTION TO DATABASE MANAGEMENT SYSTEMS (DBMS)

By accessing a database through a **database management system (DBMS)**, you and other users can simultaneously read and write the data contained in the database. If two users attempt to add records at the same time, the DBMS keeps track of each request without causing an error or overwriting either user's information.

Visual Studio and Visual Basic provide numerous tools making it easy to work with different database management systems, which are described in the following list:

» The Microsoft Jet Database Engine (Jet) is the DBMS used with the Microsoft Access DBMS. The term Jet is an acronym for Joint Engine Technology. In this chapter, you will learn how to use Visual Studio with a Jet database.

» SQL Server is the Microsoft flagship DBMS product. It supports security features beyond those supported by the Jet Database Engine, along with improved multi-user access and transaction-processing capabilities.

» Oracle is one of the largest companies that manufacture database management systems. Visual Studio and Visual Basic also work with Oracle databases.

Nearly all databases in use today are **relational databases**. That is, they can combine or relate data stored in different tables based on the value of a particular field. Suppose, for example, that the table named tblEmployees is only one of the tables contained in the Employees database, and that a second table named tblPayroll contains payroll records for each employee. In such a case, the data in these two tables could be tied together based on the value of the shared field named fldEmployeeID. This type of relationship is called a one-to-many relationship. That is, for any one employee, there can be many payroll records.

All relational database management systems use the same language to retrieve, insert, update, and delete records. This standard language is called the **Structured Query Language (SQL)**. The following SQL statements are used to manage the data stored in a database:

» The SELECT statement is used to select one or more rows from a table. It is possible to select all the rows in a table or restrict the selected rows based on some criteria. The selected rows can be sorted in any order that you choose.

» The INSERT statement is used to insert a new row or rows into a database table.

» The UPDATE statement is used to change the contents of one or more rows in a database table.

» The DELETE statement is used to remove one or more rows from a database table.

**» NOTE**

Although SQL is not case sensitive, the common practice is to capitalize SQL statements.

The following code segment shows a sample SELECT statement:

```
SELECT * FROM tblCustomers ORDER BY fldLastName, fldFirstName
```

The preceding SELECT statement selects all of the records from the table named tblCustomers. The FROM keyword, along with the table name, defines the table from which the rows will be selected. The records are sorted in ascending order by the field named fldLastName using the ORDER BY clause. If two records have the same last name, those records are further sorted by the field named fldFirstName.

The SELECT statement can be used to select specific fields from a table instead of selecting all the fields. To select specific fields, remove the asterisk (*) after the SELECT statement. In place of the asterisk, enter the field names separated by commas. The following SELECT statement selects two fields named fldLastName and fldFirstName from the table named tblCustomers. Even though the statement appears on multiple lines, it is a single statement.

```
SELECT fldLastName, fldFirstName FROM tblCustomers
ORDER BY fldLastName, fldFirstName
```

> **»NOTE**
> This chapter introduces only the most basic of SQL statements because the Visual Studio tools write most of the SQL statements for you.

# AN OVERVIEW OF ADO.NET

Visual Studio provides database access through the classes of the `System.Data` and `System.Data.OleDb` namespaces. The classes in these namespaces are collectively referred to as **ActiveX Data Objects (ADO.NET) 2.0**.

> **»NOTE** ADO has existed since early versions of Visual Basic. ADO.NET 1.0 was introduced with the first version of Visual Studio .NET, and differed significantly from the previous ADO versions. ADO.NET 2.0 is new to Visual Studio 2005 and has several new features not supported by ADO.NET 1.0. Those features that are new to ADO.NET 2.0 and Visual Studio 2005 are pointed out in this chapter.

Working with databases using the tools provided by ADO.NET involves performing the following sequence of steps:

1. First, a database connection is established.

2. Second, a command is sent over the open connection to retrieve the selected data. This command is a SQL SELECT statement.

3. ADO.NET then builds an in-memory representation of the returned data, which is accessible to your application.

4. After the data has been retrieved from the database, the database connection is closed.

5. Changes can then be made to the in-memory representation of the data.

6. If changes are made to the in-memory representation of the data, those changes are saved to the database by reopening the connection, saving the modified data, and then closing the connection again. Any added, changed, or deleted records are saved back to the database using SQL INSERT, UPDATE, and DELETE statements.

# USING A VISUAL STUDIO WIZARD TO WORK WITH A DATABASE

Because of the number of classes involved in performing database processing, and the interaction between them, working with a database can be complex. Fortunately, Visual Studio supplies a Wizard and other tools to simplify common database processing tasks.

The easiest way to establish a database connection is to use the Data Source Configuration Wizard. This Wizard, like all Wizards, is made up of a series of dialog boxes. After completing the information in these dialog boxes, the Data Source Configuration Wizard performs the following two tasks:

» It creates the connection between a database and an application based on information that you specify.

» It is used to select the tables and fields that will be included in the data source.

## UNDERSTANDING THE CONCEPT OF A DATA SOURCE

The first step in retrieving data from a database is to define a **data source**. A data source is a connection between a Visual Studio project and a server database, such as SQL Server, or a local database file, such as a Microsoft Access .mdb file. Figure 11-2 illustrates the relationship between an application, a data source, and the underlying database.

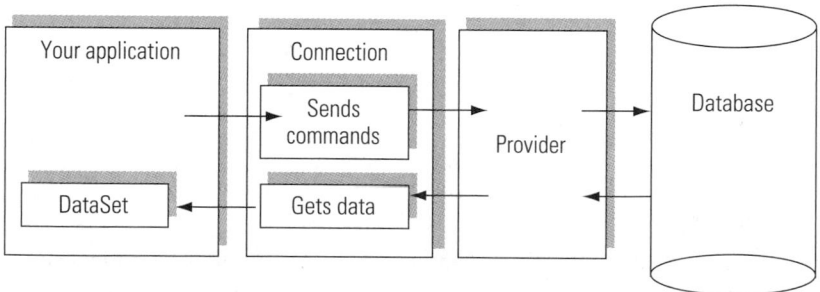

Figure 11-2: Connecting to a database

As shown in Figure 11-2, an application establishes a connection with the DBMS. Then, commands (SQL statements) are sent over that connection to retrieve selected data from the database. The data is then made available to the application.

The Data Sources window (shown in Figure 11-3) is used to manage the data sources associated with a Visual Studio project. A project can have one or many data sources. That is, it is possible for an application to work with a single database or work with multiple databases at the same time. The Data Sources window shown in Figure 11-3 is empty because no data sources have been defined.

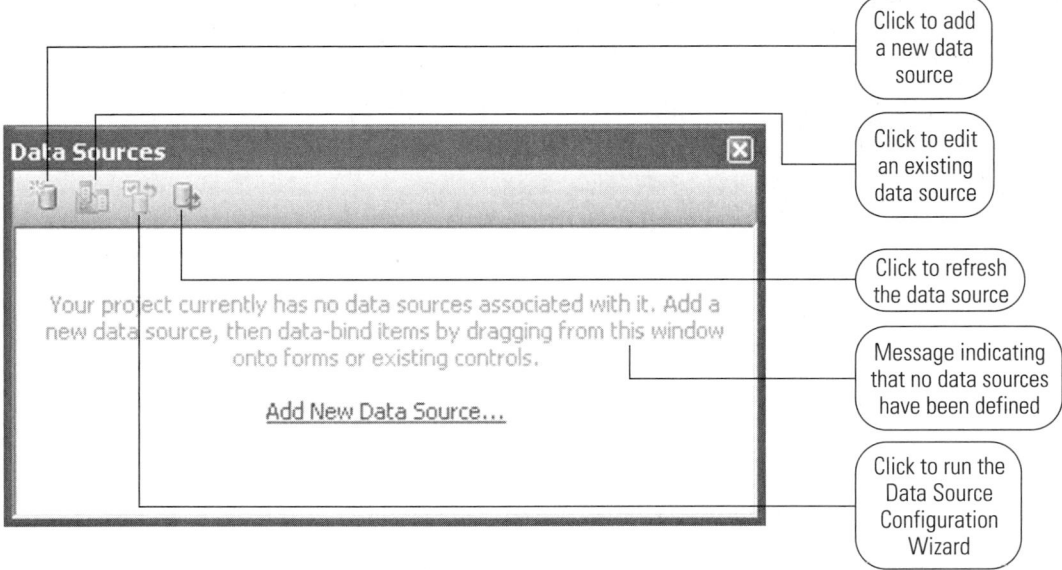

Click to add a new data source

Click to edit an existing data source

Click to refresh the data source

Message indicating that no data sources have been defined

Click to run the Data Source Configuration Wizard

Figure 11-3: Data Sources window

## CREATING A CONNECTION WITH THE DATA SOURCE CONFIGURATION WIZARD

The Data Source Configuration Wizard is used to create a new data source. To run the Data Source Configuration Wizard, click Data, Add New Data Source on the Visual Studio menu bar and complete the subsequent dialog boxes. As you complete these steps, the Data Source Configuration Wizard creates what is called a **connection string**, which ADO.NET uses to establish the database connection.

## CREATING AND BINDING CONTROL INSTANCES USING THE DATA SOURCE CONFIGURATION WIZARD

After a database connection has been established using the Data Source Configuration Wizard, the Data Sources window displays the tables and fields in the data source using a drill-down interface. Figure 11-4 shows the Data Sources window with data from one table named tblEmployees.

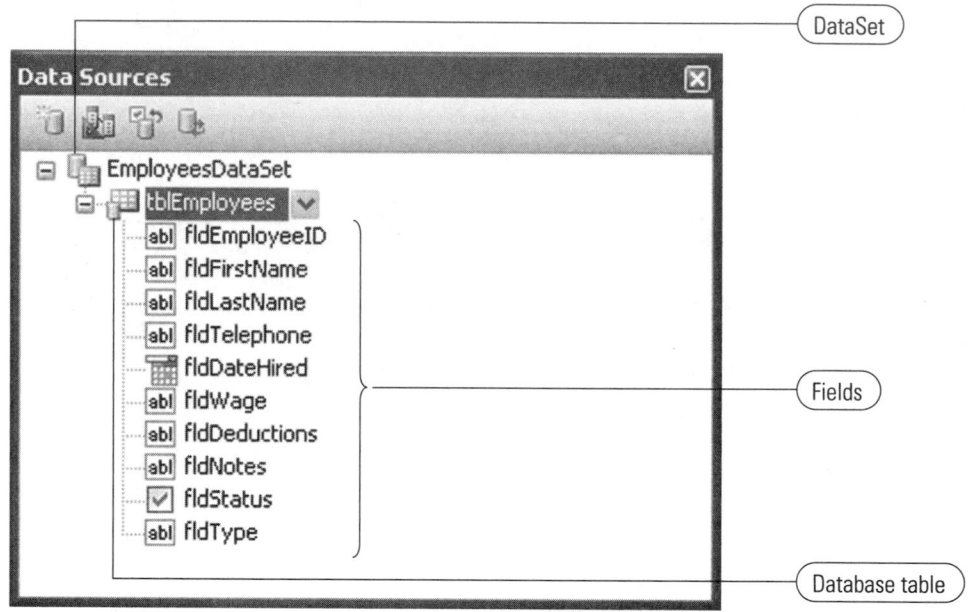

Figure 11-4: Data Sources window with a table and fields

As shown in Figure 11-4, there exists one root object named EmployeesDataSet containing one table named tblEmployees. The table named tblEmployees has 10 fields.

The Visual Studio IDE, along with the Data Sources window and the Windows Forms Designer, supply the means to create control instances on a form, and bind those control instances to a data source so that the end user can navigate from record to record. As the developer, all you need to do is drag the fields from the Data Sources window to the Windows Forms Designer. Figure 11-5 shows the Visual Studio IDE with control instances created using the Data Sources window. The prompts were created automatically when the fields were dragged from the Data Sources window to the Windows Forms Designer. Figure 11-5 shows the prompts with the automatically generated names.

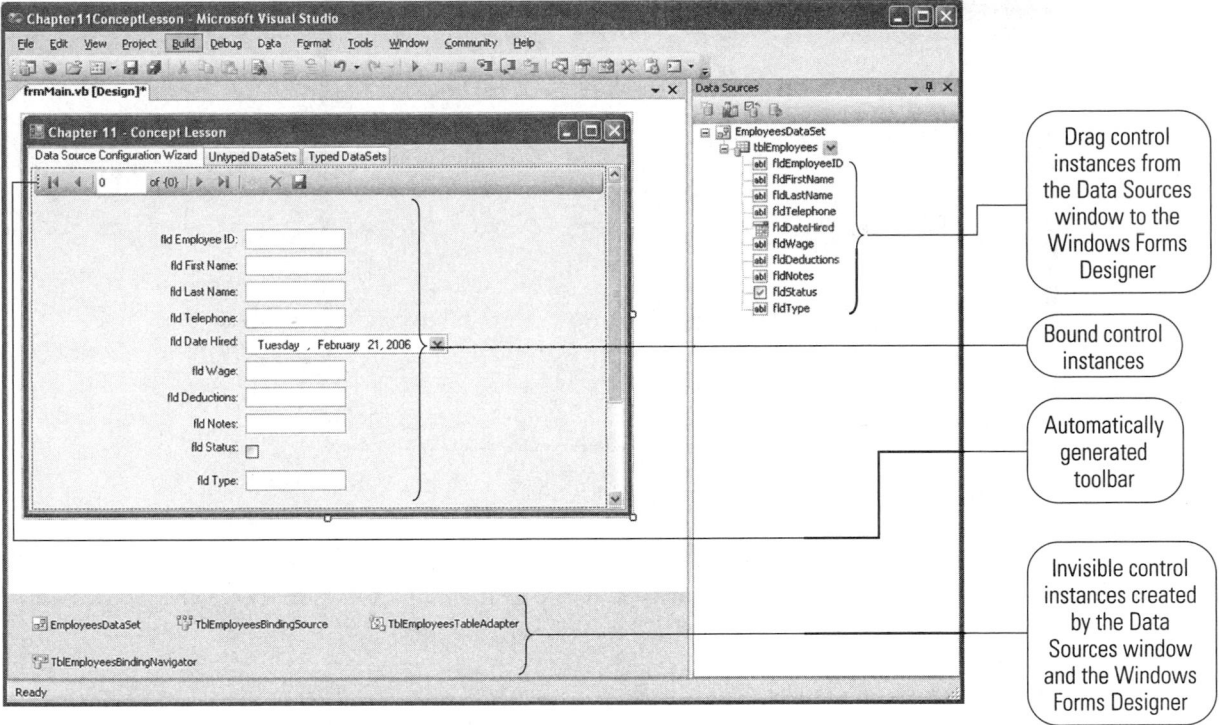

Figure 11-5: Control instances bound to a DataSet

As shown in Figure 11-5, a navigation toolbar appears across the top of the form. The toolbar and its buttons are automatically created on the form by dragging the fields from the Data Sources window to the Windows Forms Designer. In addition, the text boxes that display the data along with the descriptive prompts are automatically added as each field is dragged to the Windows Forms Designer. Several invisible control instances were created in the resizable tray below the Windows Forms Designer. These control instances are generated automatically when the first field is dragged from the Data Sources window to the Windows Forms Designer.

The following exploration exercise differs from most other exploration exercises found in this book. Instead of examining sample code, you will create a fully functional database application using the Data Source Configuration Wizard, along with the Data Sources window and the Windows Forms Designer.

1. Start Visual Studio and open the solution file in the folder named **Chapter.11\ Chapter11ConceptLessonStartup**. The application contains a blank form.

2. Open the Windows Forms Designer, if necessary, and then view the Data Sources window by clicking **Data**, **Show Data Sources** on the menu bar. Note that the Windows Forms Designer must be active for the Show Data Sources menu item to be active. The Data Sources window opens, as shown in Figure 11-6. Note that the Data Sources window may appear docked or as a floating window.

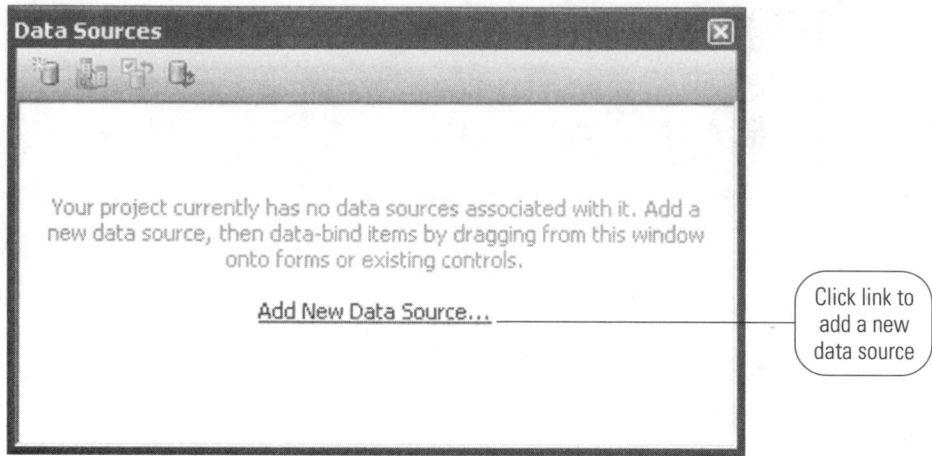

Figure 11-6: Data Sources window with no configured data sources

3. Click the **Add New Data Source** link shown in Figure 11-6. The Data Source Configuration Wizard appears, as shown in Figure 11-7.

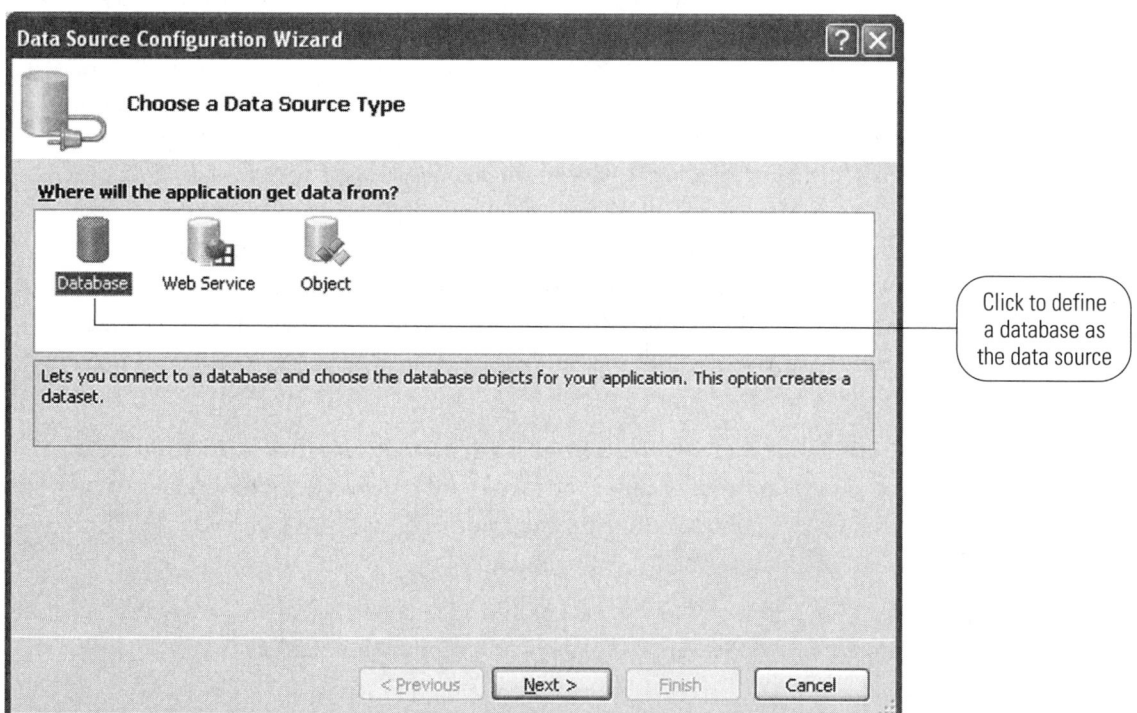

Figure 11-7: Data Source Configuration Wizard—Choose a Data Source Type

4. The first dialog box displays the data sources available on the computer, and might vary depending on your computer's configuration. Click the **Database** icon to select it, if necessary. Click **Next** to activate the dialog box shown in Figure 11-8.

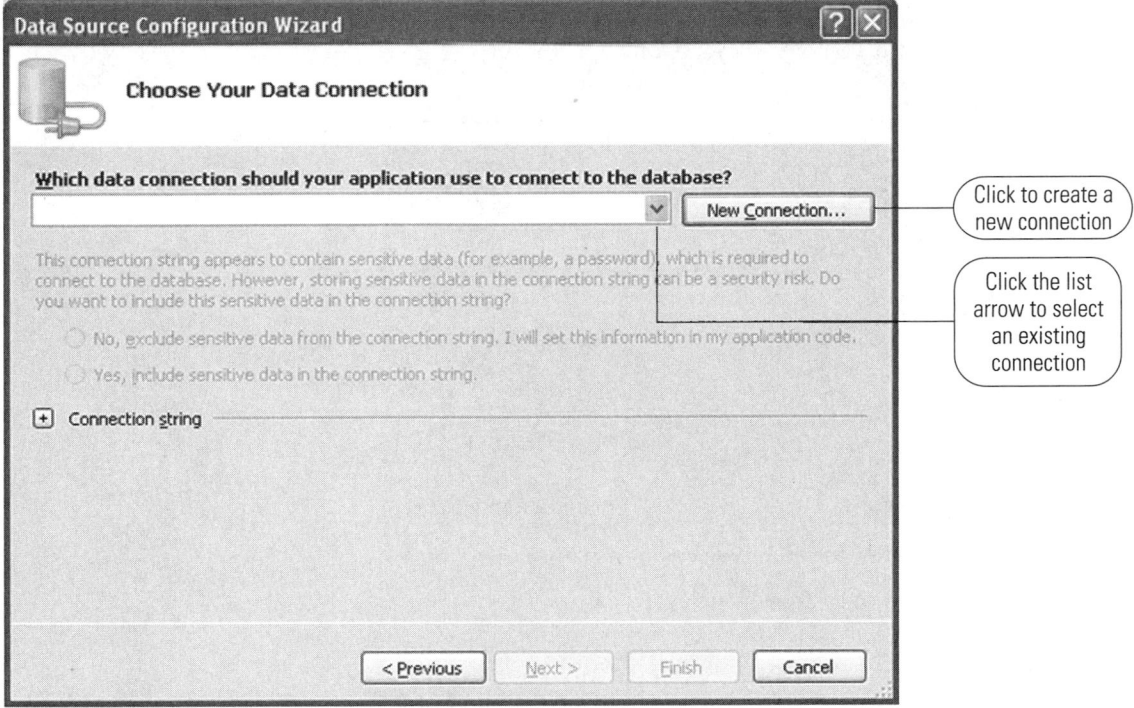

Figure 11-8: Data Source Configuration Wizard—Choose Your Data Connection

5. The dialog box in Figure 11-8 has a combo box from which existing connections can be selected. If there are no existing connections, the combo box is blank. The New Connection button is used to create a new database connection. Click the **New Connection** button in the dialog box shown in Figure 11-8 to display the Add Connection dialog box shown in Figure 11-9.

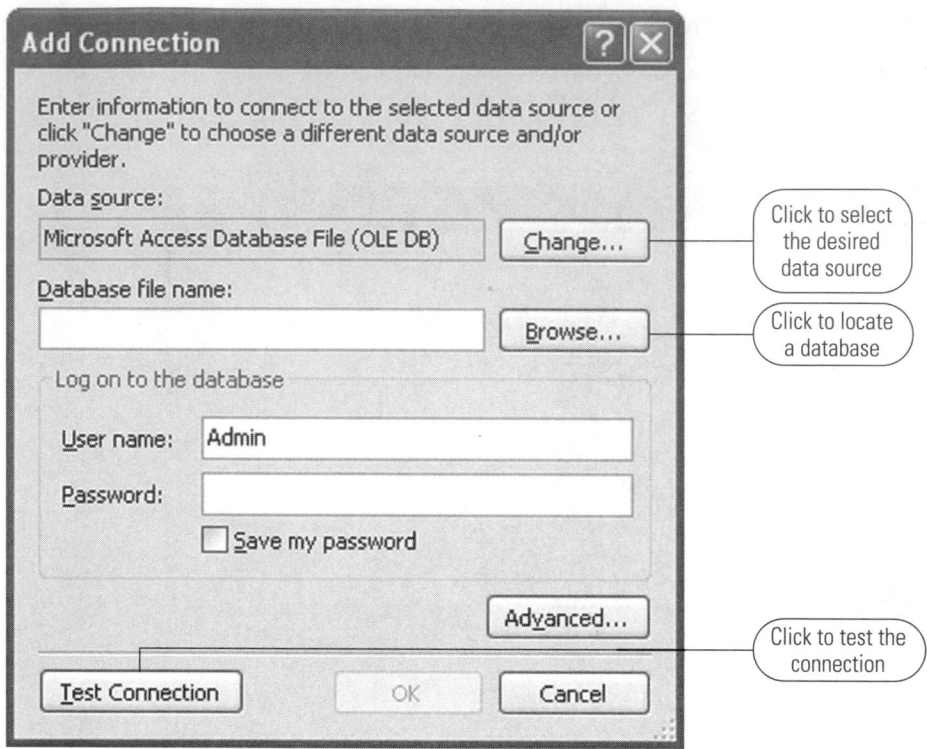

Figure 11-9: Add Connection dialog box

**»NOTE** If the Add Connection dialog box does not appear on your screen, this is the first time your system has been used to establish a database connection. Click **Microsoft Access Database File**, and then click **Continue**. You will then see the Add Connection dialog box on your screen.

6. The Add Connection dialog box is used to establish connections to Microsoft Access or SQL Server databases. Click the **Change** button to display the Change Data Source dialog box shown in Figure 11-10.

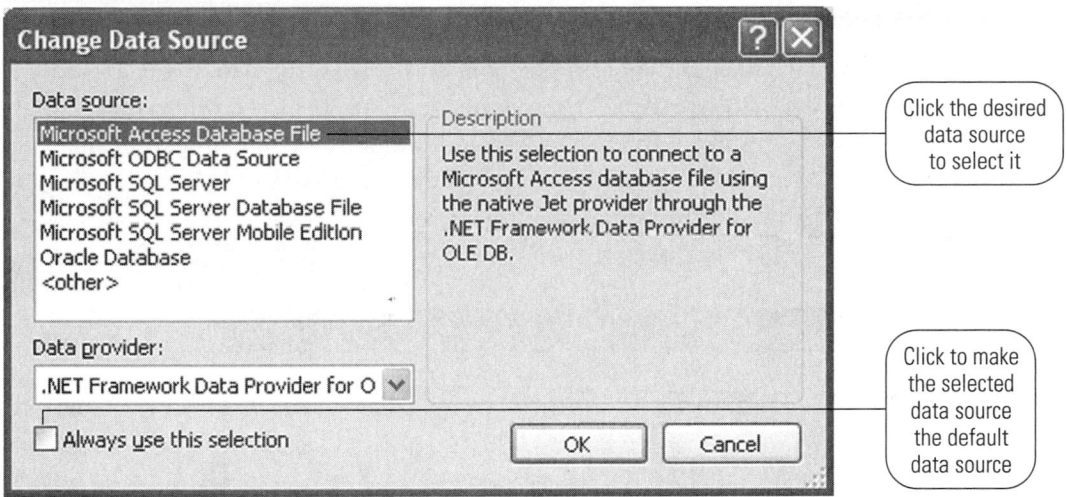

Figure 11-10: Change Data Source dialog box

7. Figure 11-10 lists several possible data sources. The list of possible data sources will vary based on the configuration of your computer and the edition of Visual Studio 2005 you are running. Click the **Microsoft Access Database File** data source, if necessary. Click the **OK** button to close the dialog box and return to the Add Connection dialog box. The data source appears in the Add Connection dialog box.

8. Next, the database must be selected. In the Add Connection dialog box, click **Browse**. An Open dialog box opens, allowing the Access database to be selected. Select the file named **Chapter.11\Data\Employees.mdb**. The database filename appears in the Add Connection dialog box.

9. Test the connection by clicking the **Test Connection** button. If Visual Studio could establish a database connection, the message box shown in Figure 11-11 appears.

Figure 11-11: Test connection message box

10. Click **OK** to return to the Add Connection dialog box.

11. In the Add Connection dialog box, click **OK** to return to the Data Source Configuration Wizard. After the connection has been configured, the Data Source Configuration Wizard displays the connection and connection string, as shown in Figure 11-12. You might have to click the + sign next to "Connection string" to see the entire display of information.

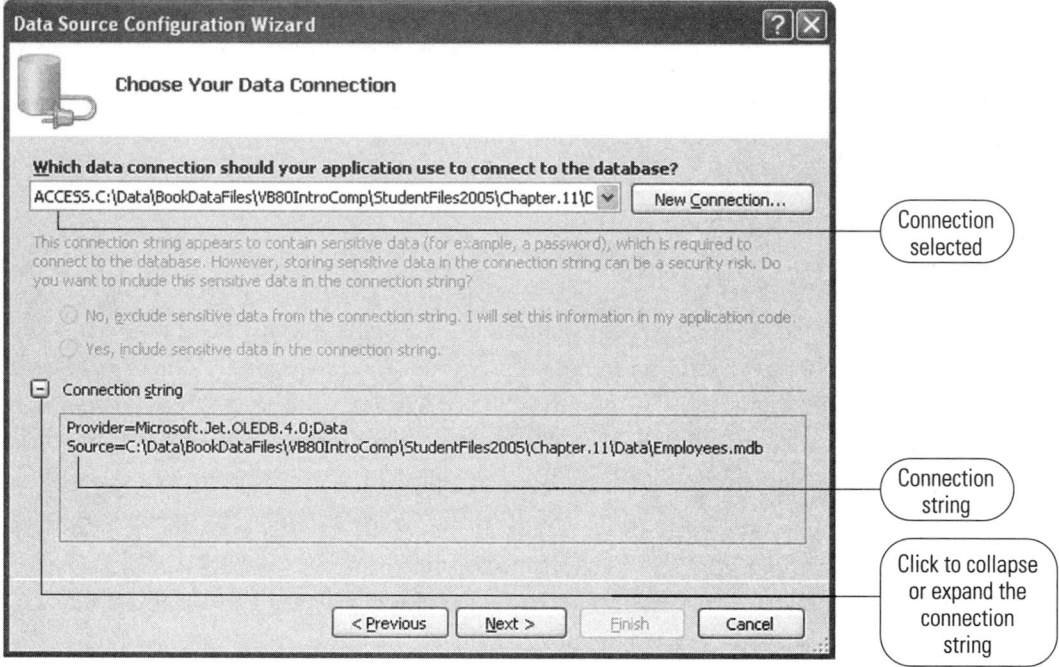

Figure 11-12: Data Source Configuration Wizard displaying the connection string

12. Click the **Next** button to create and configure the database connection. The message box that appears indicates that the newly created connection has not been added to the project, as shown in Figure 11-13.

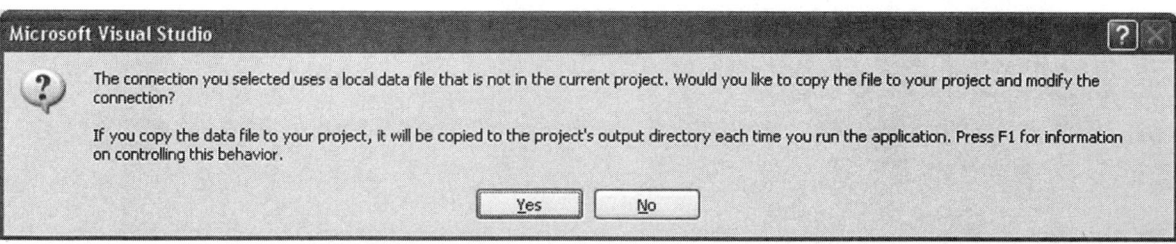

Figure 11-13: Local database file message box

13. Click **Yes** to add the database to the project and display the dialog box shown in Figure 11-14.

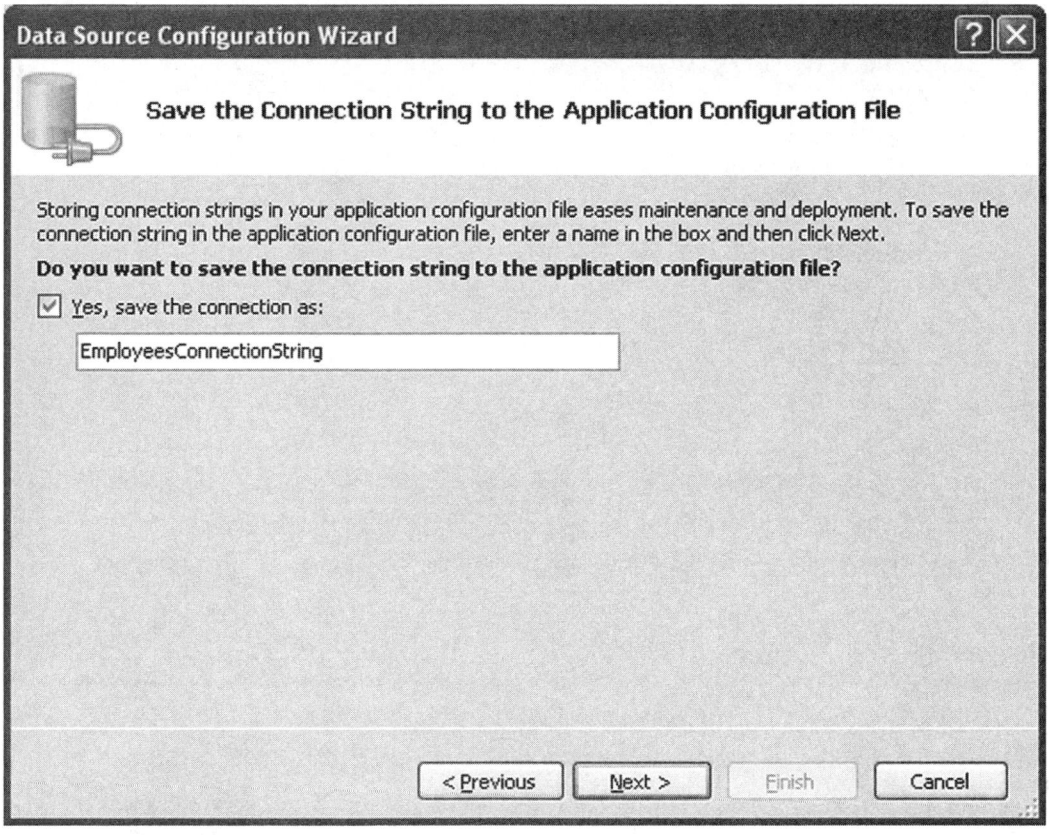

Figure 11-14: Data Source Configuration Wizard—Save the Connection String to the Application Configuration File

14. The dialog box in Figure 11-14 allows the connection string to be saved as part of the application's configuration file. Check the **Yes, save the connection as** check box, if necessary. Note that a default name of EmployeesConnectionString is used for the connection string. There is no need to change the default name. Click **Next** to display the dialog box shown in Figure 11-15.

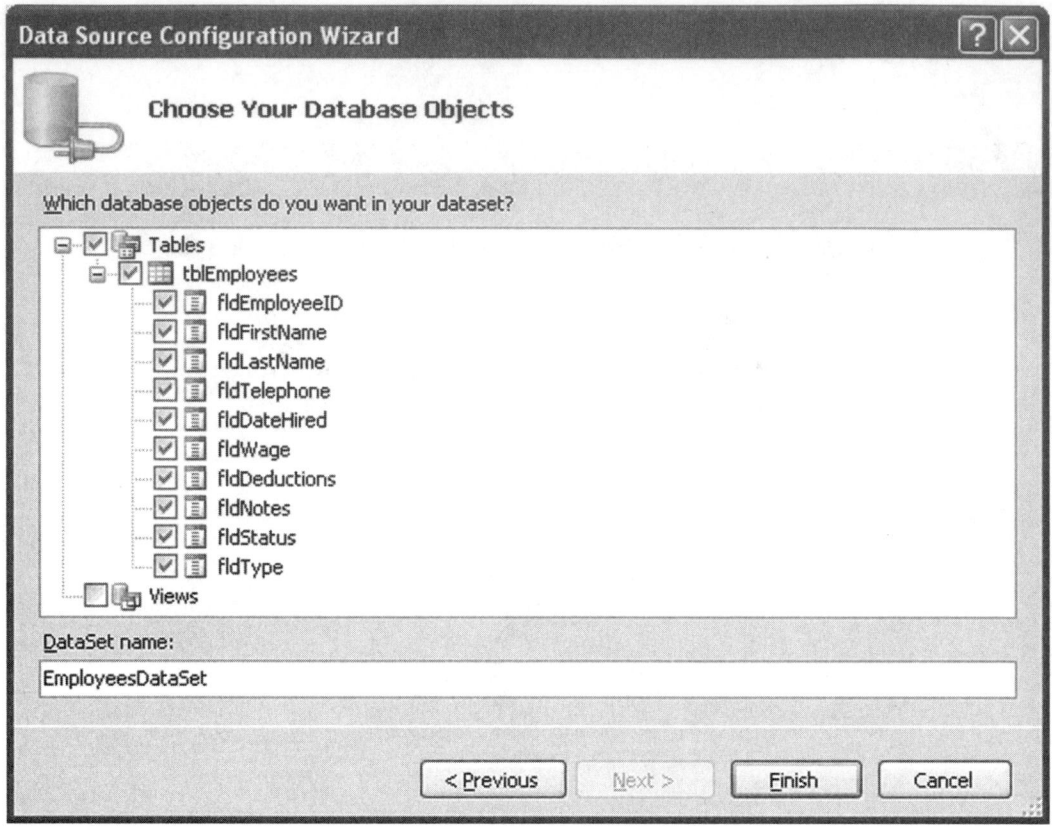

Figure 11-15: Data Source Configuration Wizard—Choose Your Database Objects

15. Figure 11-15 shows the Wizard with the Tables folder expanded. Clicking the plus and minus signs causes a folder to be expanded and collapsed, respectively. Expand the **Tables** folder along with the folder titled **tblEmployees**, if necessary. Click the adjacent check boxes to select the table and each field in the table. A default name of EmployeesDataSet is assigned to the DataSet.

16. Click **Finish** to add the data source to the project and configure it. The Data Sources window displays the data sources, table, and fields. Expand all of the folders, as necessary.

Having established the database connection and defined the data source using the Data Source Configuration Wizard, it is possible to create the form's control instances and bind them to that data source. By dragging a field from the Data Sources window to the Windows Forms Designer, Visual Studio creates the appropriate control instance along with a descriptive prompt. Depending on the data type of the bound field, Visual Studio creates the following control instances:

» For numeric and string data types, a TextBox control instance is created.

» For Boolean data types, a CheckBox control instance is created.

» For DateTime data types, a DateTimePicker control instance is created.

When using the Data Sources window to create control instances on the form, an icon appears next to each field indicating the type of the control that will be created. When a control instance is created, the Data Sources window and the Windows Forms Designer automatically generate the necessary statements to bind the control instance to the data source.

Next, you will continue the exploration exercise and create the control instances on the form.

1.  Using the Data Sources window, drag each field to the Windows Forms Designer. The first time you drag a field to the Windows Forms Designer, Visual Studio creates several invisible control instances in the resizable tray below the Windows Forms Designer. In addition, it creates a toolbar used for record navigation. As you create control instances on the form, default prompts are created to the left of each control instance. Figure 11-16 shows the Windows Forms Designer with the control instances created.

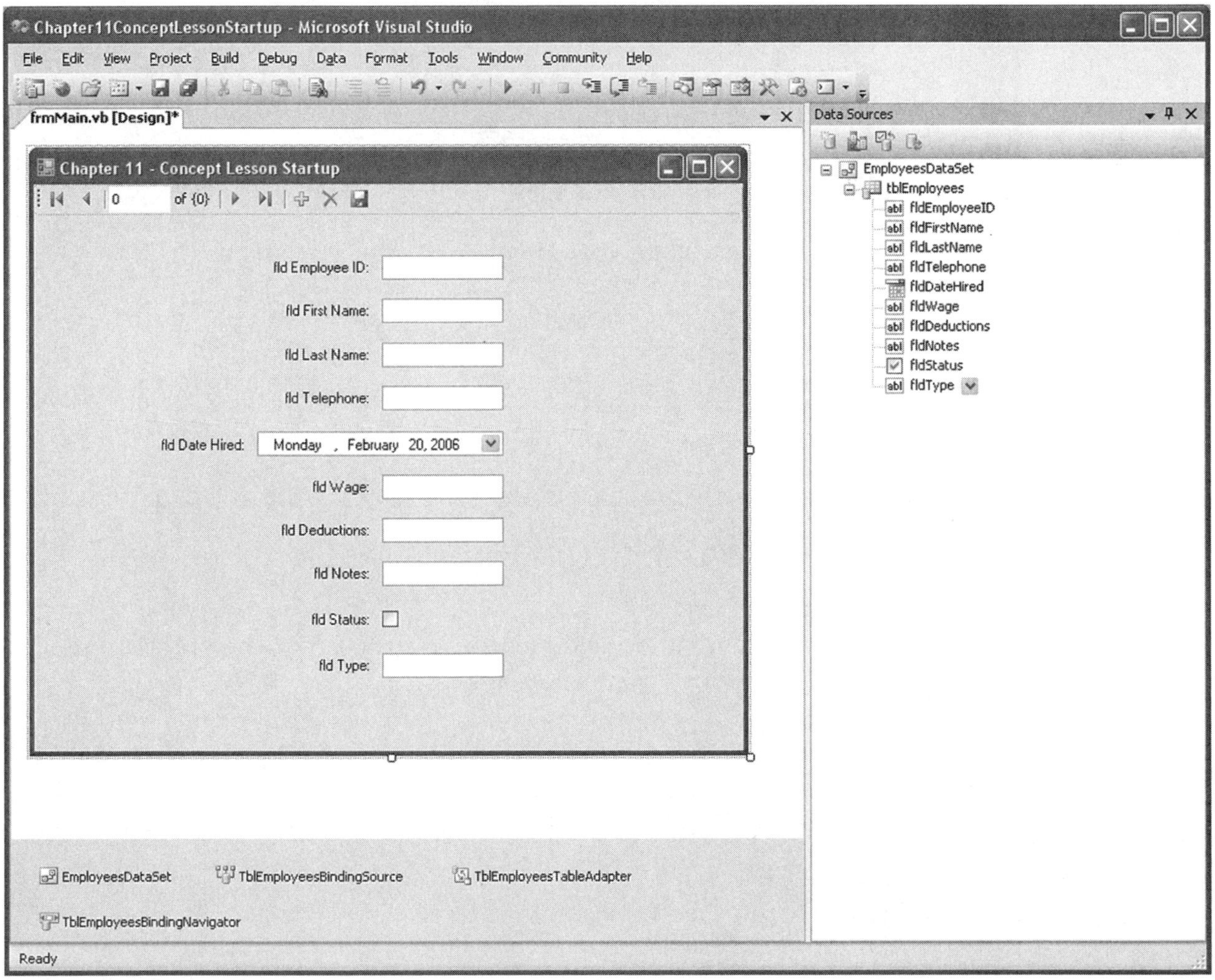

Figure 11-16: Windows Forms Designer displaying bound control instances at design time

2. That's it; you have just created your first database application. Run the application. The data from the table appears in the form's control instances, as shown in Figure 11-17.

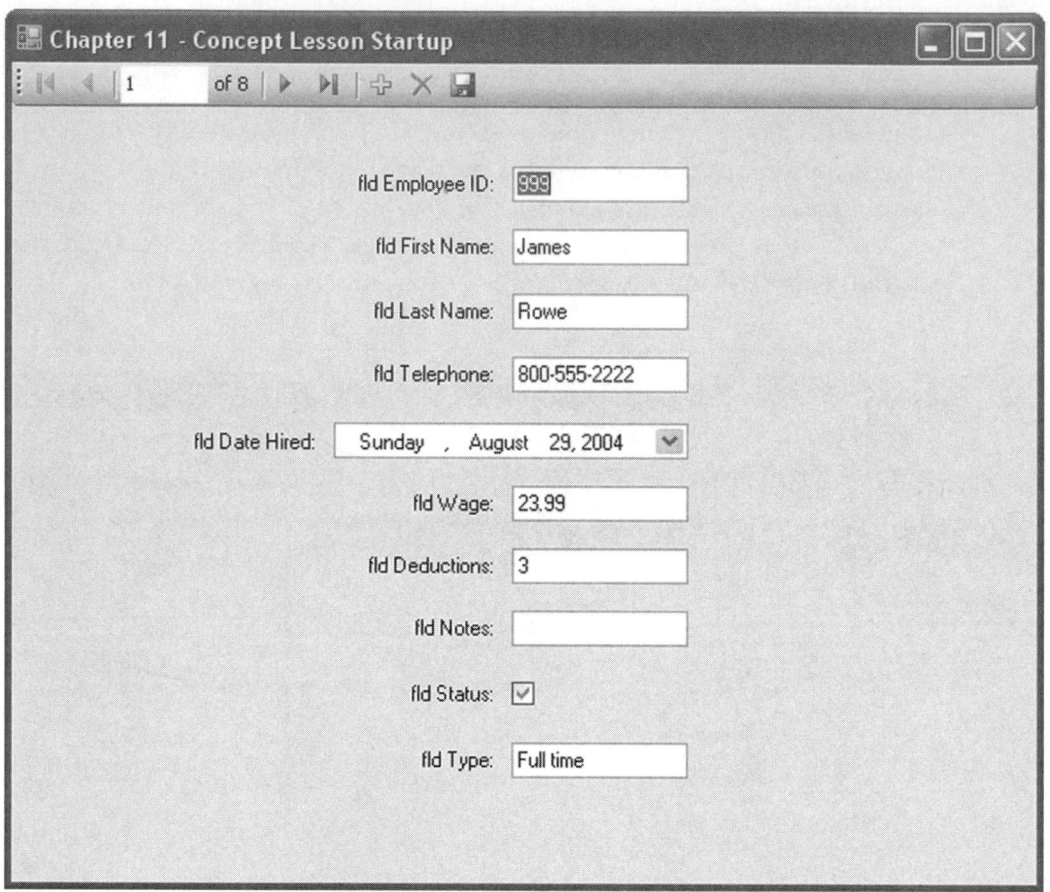

Figure 11-17: Windows form displaying bound control instances at run time

3. Click the navigation buttons on the toolbar. As you do, different records are selected and appear in the form's control instances.

4. End the application.

## MINI-QUIZ 1

1. Is a database made up of one or more tables containing one or more fields?

2. Which of the following statements is correct regarding the Data Source Configuration Wizard?

   a. Supported data sources include Microsoft Access and SQL Server.

   b. The Wizard creates a connection string, which is used to establish a connection with the data source.

   c. After configuring a data source, the Data Sources window displays a table and the fields in the table.

   d. The Data Source Configuration Wizard can be used to select all fields from a database table or selected fields from a table.

   e. all of the above

3. Which of the following statements is correct regarding the Data Sources window?

   a. Dragging a field from the Data Sources window to the Windows Forms Designer causes a bound control instance to be created on a form.

   b. The Data Sources window always displays exactly one and only one data source at a time.

   c. The Data Sources window is used to configure the properties of a particular data source.

   d. none of the above

4. List two databases supported by Visual Studio .NET.

# UNDERSTANDING HOW THE DATA SOURCE CONFIGURATION WIZARD CREATES AND MANAGES A DATA SOURCE

In the previous exploration exercise, you used the Data Source Configuration Wizard to establish a database connection, to retrieve data from the database, and to bind control instances to the data that was retrieved. In this section, you will learn about the underlying actions performed by the Data Source Configuration Wizard. These actions can be grouped into the following categories:

» The Data Source Configuration Wizard creates a connection string over which commands (SQL statements) are sent to the database for processing.

» In addition, the Data Source Configuration Wizard creates a TableAdapter class, which uses the connection and its connection string to retrieve data from the underlying database. The TableAdapter class works in conjunction with another class called the `OleDbDataAdapter` to accomplish this task.

» The `BindingSource` class supplies the means for the end user to navigate through the records in a data source.

» The `BindingNavigator` class works in conjunction with the `BindingSource` class. Its purpose is to supply a toolbar so that the end user can click buttons to navigate from record to record.

» As the fields are dragged from the Data Sources window to the form, the control instances are created and bound to the data source using the `Binding` class. The Data Sources window and the Windows Forms Designer perform this task automatically.

Each of these steps is discussed in turn, along with selected code automatically generated by the Wizard.

## INTRODUCTION TO CONNECTION STRINGS

As you saw in the previous exploration exercise, one of the steps performed by the Data Source Configuration Wizard was to create the connection string and configure that connection string so that the current project could establish a connection between a database (an external file) and a data source. A connection string is a string made up of key-value pairs. A semicolon (;) separates each key-value pair and an equal sign separates a key from its value. The following code segment shows the connection string created by the Data Source Configuration Wizard used to connect to the Access database corresponding to this concept lesson:

```
Dim ConnectionString As String
ConnectionString = "Provider=Microsoft.Jet.OLEDB.4.0;" _
    "Data Source= |DataDirectory|\Employees.mdb"
```

The preceding connection string contains two keys named Provider and Data Source. These two keys have values of Microsoft.Jet.OLEDB.4.0 and |DataDirectory|\Employees.mdb, respectively. The Provider key defines the database provider, which, in this case, is Microsoft Access. The database version number (4.0) also appears in the provider's value. The Data Source key defines the directory containing the database file and the name of the file.

> **NOTE** Connection strings vary based on database providers. In other words, the key-value pairs that make up a connection string vary depending on whether Access or SQL Server is being used. In addition, connection strings support additional key-value pairs that are used to enforce security and perform other tasks.

When you add the connection string to the project, the Data Source Configuration Wizard adds this connection string to two files. The application configuration file named App.config stores configuration information for the application and is read when the application is run. This file is an XML document, which you do not edit directly.

In addition to the configuration settings, the Data Source Configuration Wizard also adds the connection string to the resource file named Settings.settings, as shown in Figure 11-18.

> **NOTE**
> To load the connection string into the application, the Data Source Configuration Wizard generates statements in the file named EmployeesDataSet.Designer.vb.

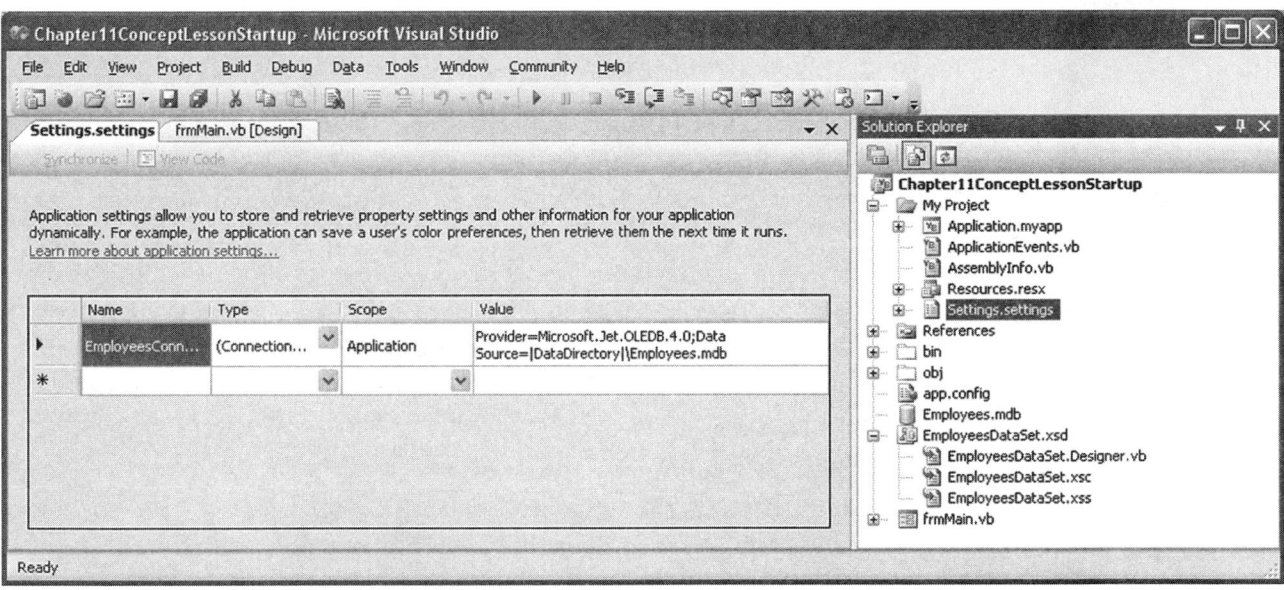

Figure 11-18: Connection string appearing in the application's resource file

The ADO.NET class which stores a database connection is named `System.Data.OleDb.OleDbConnection`, and it has the following members:

» The `ConnectionString` property stores the connection string. In the previous code segment, the connection string was read from the file Settings.settings.

» The `Open` method opens a connection, making it available for use.

» The `Close` method closes an open connection. It is not usually necessary to open and close a connection directly. This task is automatically handled by the various classes generated by the Data Source Configuration Wizard.

## INTRODUCTION TO THE TABLEADAPTER AND OLEDBDATAADAPTER CLASSES

The **TableAdapter class** is used to send requests over a connection, retrieve the data from a database table, and create the objects to store the in-memory representation of the data. The following list describes the functions performed by the TableAdapter class:

» Using a connection string, the TableAdapter class opens a connection to the database using the connection discussed previously.

» Using that open connection, the TableAdapter class sends a request (SQL SELECT statement) to retrieve data from the database.

» The database provider returns the data to the TableAdapter class.

» The data source is exposed to the application in the form of a `DataSet` object, containing one or more `DataTable` objects representing each table in the `DataSet`. Use of these two objects is discussed later in the chapter.

> **» NOTE** The TableAdapter class is not part of the .NET Framework class library. Therefore, it does not appear in the Object Browser. Rather, the TableAdapter class is created at design time by a Wizard. The TableAdapter class is also new to Visual Studio 2005.

The Data Source Configuration Wizard and the Data Sources window created a class named TblEmployeesTableAdapter inside of the file named EmployeesDataSet.Designer.vb. This class represents the TableAdapter. If you examine this class, you will find that there are methods exposed to the developer. The following code segment illustrates the declaration for the TableAdapter class appearing in the file named EmployeesDataSet.Designer.vb:

```
Namespace EmployeesDataSetTableAdapters
    Partial Public Class TblEmployeesTableAdapter
        Inherits System.ComponentModel.Component
        Private WithEvents Adapter As _
            System.Data.OleDb.OleDbDataAdapter
        ' Statements and procedures
    End Class
End Namespace
```

As shown in the preceding code segment, the class named TblEmployeesTableAdapter has a variable named Adapter having a data type of `System.Data.OleDb.OleDbDataAdapter`. The `OleDbDataAdapter` object is used to send commands (SQL statements) to the database provider that will select, insert, update, and delete records using the connection discussed previously.

The `OleDbDataAdapter` class of the `System.Data.OleDb` namespace supplies the methods to send requests that retrieve, insert, update, and delete data from a database provider. All of these requests are SQL statements. Thus, there are four SQL statements: one to select, insert, update, and delete database data.

When the Wizard generated the TableAdapter class named TblEmployeesTableAdapter, it created and configured an instance of the `OleDbDataAdapter` class named Adapter to add, change, and delete database records. The `OleDbDataAdapter` class supports the following members:

## Syntax
`System.Data.OleDbDataAdapter class`

## Public Properties
» The `SelectCommand` property has a data type of `OleDbCommand`. The `OleDbCommand` object, in turn, contains a SQL SELECT statement. When a method named `Fill` is called, the `OleDbDataAdapter` sends this statement to the database provider, through the connection, for execution. The database provider then executes the statement and returns the data.

» The `InsertCommand`, `UpdateCommand`, and `DeleteCommand` properties contain references to instances of the `OleDbCommand` class, which, in turn, contain SQL INSERT, UPDATE, and DELETE statements, respectively. The `OleDbDataAdapter` sends these statements to the provider to add, change, and delete database records that were changed.

The data type of the `SelectCommand`, `InsertCommand`, `UpdateCommand`, and `DeleteCommand` properties is `System.Data.OleDb.OleDbCommand`. The `OleDbCommand` class has three properties used to describe a command that the `OleDbDataAdapter` sends to the database provider for execution:

» The `Connection` property contains a reference to an instance of an `OleDbConnection` class. This is the same connection discussed previously.

» The `CommandText` property contains a SQL statement.

» The `CommandType` property defines the type of command that is sent to the database for processing. If the `CommandText` property contains a SQL statement, the `CommandType` property is set to `Text`.

To illustrate how the TableAdapter class creates and configures an instance of the `OleDbDataAdapter` class, examine the following groups of statements appearing in the class named tblEmployeesTableAdapter in the file named EmployeesDataSet.Designer.vb:

```
Me.m_commandCollection = New _
    System.Data.OleDb.OleDbCommand(0) {}
Me.m_commandCollection(0) = New System.Data.OleDb.OleDbCommand
```

The preceding statements create an instance of the OleDbCommand class that will store the SQL statement. The reason that the Wizard generates an array is that it is possible for a TableAdapter to have multiple queries (SQL SELECT statements). Each separate query is stored as a separate collection object.

The following statements configure the OleDbCommand object stored in the collection:

```
Me.m_commandCollection(0).Connection = Me.Connection
Me.m_commandCollection(0).CommandText = "SELECT " & _
    "fldEmployeeID, fldFirstName, fldLastName, " & _
    "fldTelephone, fldDateHired, fldWage, " & _
    "fldDeductions, fldNotes, fldType FROM tblEmployees"
Me.m_commandCollection(0).CommandType = _
    System.Data.CommandType.Text
Me.Adapter.SelectCommand = Me.CommandCollection(0)
```

The first of the preceding statements associates the OleDbCommand object with the connection. This is the same connection that was generated by the Data Source Configuration Wizard. The second statement contains the SQL SELECT statement. The statement selects all of the fields from the table named tblEmployees. The next statement indicates that the CommandText property contains a SQL statement. The final statement sets the SelectCommand property of the OleDbDataAdapter to the OleDbCommand object configured in the preceding statements.

In addition to configuring the TableAdapter, OleDbDataAdapter, and OleDbCommand objects, the Wizard created a method named Fill, as the following statements show:

```
Partial Public Class tblEmployeesTableAdapter
    Public Overloads Overridable Function Fill( _
        ByVal dataTable As _
        EmployeesDataSet.tblEmployeesDataTable) As Integer
        Dim returnValue As Integer = Me.Adapter.Fill(dataTable)
        Return returnValue
    End Function
End Class
```

The Fill method of the TableAdapter class calls the Fill method of the underlying OleDbDataAdapter. When the Fill method is called, the OleDbDataAdapter establishes a database connection, selects records based on some criteria using the OleDbCommand object referenced by the OleDbDataAdapter and the SelectCommand property, and returns those records into a DataTable contained in a DataSet.

In addition to the `Fill` method, the Wizard generates the following `Update` method in the TableAdapter class:

```
Public Overloads Overridable Function Update( _
    ByVal dataTable As _
    EmployeesDataSet.tblEmployeesDataTable) As Integer
    Return Me.Adapter.Update(dataTable)
End Function
```

The `Update` method is used to record any changes made to the data back to the database. Again, the work is actually performed by the `OleDbDataAdapter`. The `OleDbDataAdapter` creates a SQL UPDATE statement based on the `OleDbCommand` object referenced by the `UpdateCommand` property.

Figure 11-19 shows the relationships between the TableAdapter, the `OleDbDataAdapter`, and the `OleDbCommand` objects, and how they are used to send requests over a connection.

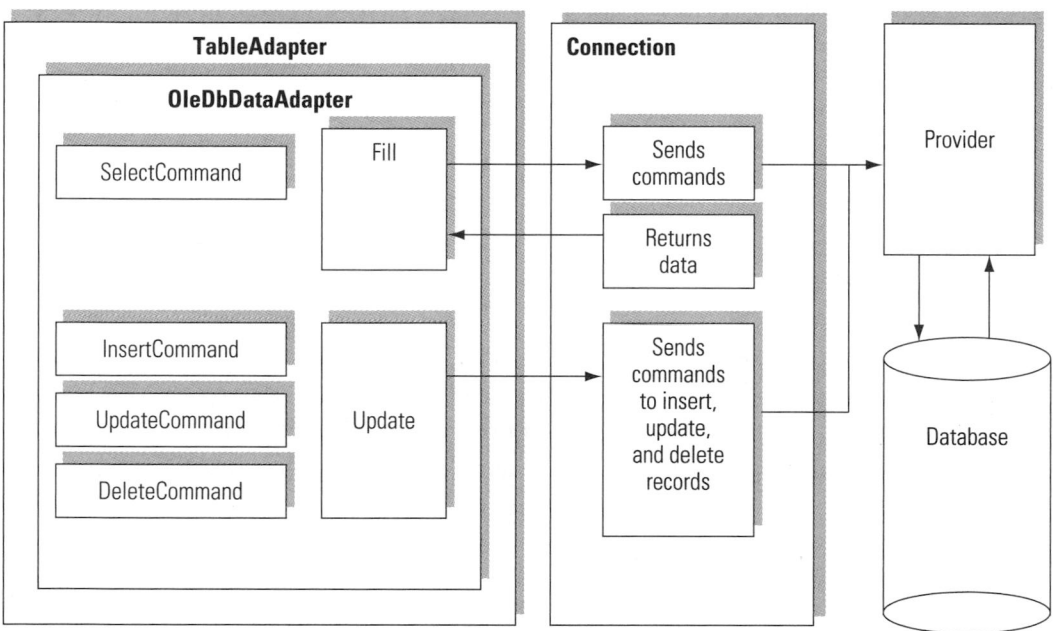

Figure 11-19: Using the TableAdapter to select and update database data

When the Data Source Configuration Wizard configures the data source, it generates the following statements in the form's Load event handler:

```
Private Sub frmMain_Load(ByVal sender As System.Object, _
    ByVal e As System.EventArgs) Handles MyBase.Load
    Me.TblEmployeesTableAdapter.Fill( _
        Me.EmployeesDataSet.tblEmployees)
End Sub
```

The TableAdapter class instance is named TblEmployeesTableAdapter. This name was automatically chosen based on the underlying table name, which was tblEmployees, and corresponds to the class named TblEmployeesTableAdapter just discussed. Calling the Fill method populates the underlying DataTable, which is passed as an argument to the Fill method. In this case, the DataTable is named tblEmployees and appears inside of the DataSet named EmployeesDataSet. The DataTable represents an in-memory view of the underlying database data. If changes are made to the data in the DataTable, those changes must be sent back to the database. This task is accomplished by calling the Update method of the TableAdapter. This method accepts one argument, the name of the DataTable containing the changed records.

The following statement shows how to update the DataTable named tblEmployees in the DataSet named EmployeesDataSet:

```
Me.TblEmployeesTableAdapter.Update( _
    Me.EmployeesDataSet.tblEmployees)
```

By executing the preceding statement, the TableAdapter object establishes a connection with the database using the underlying OleDbDataAdapter. Then, the records in the DataTable are examined to determine if a change was made. It is possible that a new record was added, an existing record was changed, or an existing record was deleted. Records are added to the database, changed, or deleted from the database, as necessary, by executing the SQL statements stored in the various OleDbCommand objects. All of these tasks are performed automatically when the Update method is called.

## INTRODUCTION TO THE BINDINGSOURCE CLASS

The TableAdapter class takes care of establishing the database connection and retrieving the data into a DataTable. It also takes care of saving any changes made to the DataTable back to the database. The TableAdapter class is not used to display any records in the control instances created on a form. Nor is the TableAdapter class used to keep track of the current record as the end user navigates from record to record. These tasks are performed using the concept of data binding and the BindingSource class.

To understand the purpose of the `BindingSource` class, it is important to know that the `DataTable` does not provide a way to keep track of the current record, or a way to navigate from record to record. The `BindingSource`, however, when bound to a `DataTable`, provides this capability.

The purpose of the `BindingSource` class is to supply methods used to navigate through the records in a data source, which, in this case, is a `DataTable`. Together, two properties are used to associate (bind) an underlying `DataTable` with a `BindingSource`:

» The `DataSource` property of the `BindingSource` class contains the name of the `DataSet` being bound. This property has a data type of `DataSet`.

» The `DataMember` property contains the name of the `DataTable` being bound. This property has a data type of `String`. The string contains the name of the table in the `DataSet`.

The Data Source Configuration Wizard generates the following statements in the file named frmMain.Designer.vb to create an instance of the `BindingSource` class and binds the class instance to the data source:

```
Friend WithEvents TblEmployeesBindingSource As _
    System.Windows.Forms.BindingSource
Me.TblEmployeesBindingSource.DataSource = Me.EmployeesDataSet
Me.TblEmployeesBindingSource.DataMember = "tblEmployees"
```

As shown in the preceding statements, the Data Source Configuration Wizard declared a variable named TblEmployeesBindingSource having a data type of `BindingSource`. Again, the variable name was chosen based on the name of the underlying database table, which is tblEmployees. The `DataSource` property is set to the name of the `DataSet`, which is EmployeesDataSet. The `DataMember` property is set to the name of the table in the `DataSet`, which is tblEmployees. Thus, the `BindingSource` named TblEmployeesBindingSource is bound to the `DataTable` named tblEmployees.

After a `BindingSource` has been configured, the following methods of the `BindingSource` class can be called to determine information about the records in the data source:

» The 1-based `Count` property gets the total number of items (records) contained in the data source.

» The `Current` property gets the current item (record) from the list.

» The 0-based `Position` property gets the index of the current list item.

The following statements illustrate how to use a `BindingSource` to read the index of the current record and the total number of records contained in a data source:

```
Dim Current, Count As Integer
Current = TblEmployeesBindingSource.Position
Count = TblEmployeesBindingSource.Count
```

Assuming that TblEmployeesBindingSource is an instance of the `BindingSource` class, the second and third statements return the index of the current record and the number of records, respectively.

In addition to determining information about the underlying data source, the methods of the `BindingSource` class are also used to navigate from one record in the data source to another. Calling any of these methods causes the `Position` property of the `BindingSource` to be updated accordingly. The following list describes the navigational methods of the `BindingSource` class:

» The `MoveFirst` method sets the current record to the first record, thereby setting the `Position` property to 0.

» The `MoveNext` method sets the current record to the next record, and increments the value of the `Position` property by 1.

» The `MovePrevious` method sets the current record to the previous record, and decrements the value of the `Position` property by 1.

» The `MoveLast` method sets the current record to the last record.

In addition to creating an instance of the `BindingSource` class, the Data Source Configuration Wizard also creates an instance of the `BindingNavigator` class, which is discussed next.

## INTRODUCTION TO THE BINDINGNAVIGATOR CLASS

The `BindingNavigator` class works in conjunction with the `BindingSource` class to supply a standardized way for the end user to navigate through the bound data on a form. Whereas the `BindingSource` class supplies the means to navigate through the records in a data source, the `BindingNavigator` class supplies the visual user interface elements that, in turn, call upon the members of the `BindingSource` class to perform the actual record navigation. That is, the end user clicks a button on the `BindingNavigator` toolbar. The `BindingNavigator`, in turn, calls a method of the `BindingSource` to perform the actual record navigation.

When the Data Source Configuration Wizard created the form's control instances, it created an instance of the `BindingNavigator` class named TblEmployeesBindingNavigator. Again, the name of the control instance was derived from the underlying table name. The control instance appears as a toolbar along the top of the form. The `BindingNavigator` control instance, in turn, contains buttons used to navigate through the records in the data source, along with other control instances used to display the current record number. There exists a one-to-one correspondence between selected members of the BindingNavigator and BindingSource classes, as shown in Table 11-1.

| Purpose | BindingNavigator member | BindingSource member |
|---|---|---|
| Move First | MoveFirstItem | MoveFirst |
| Move Next | MoveNextItem | MoveNext |
| Move Previous | MovePreviousItem | MovePrevious |
| Move Last | MoveLastItem | MoveLast |
| Current Position | PositionItem | Position |
| Count | CountItem | Count |
| Add | AddNewItem | AddNew |
| Delete | DeleteItem | Delete |

Table 11-1: Relationship between BindingNavigator and BindingSource members

## BINDING THE FORM'S CONTROL INSTANCES WITH THE BINDING CLASS

The final step in the binding process is to bind the form's control instances so that they will display the current record from the underlying data source. By binding a control instance to a BindingSource, it automatically displays the current record as the end user navigates from record to record.

To illustrate how to bind a control instance to a data source, assume that the text box named FldEmployeeIDTextBox should be bound to the field named fldEmployeeID in the underlying data source (DataTable). The following statement accomplishes this task:

```
Me.FldEmployeeIDTextBox.DataBindings.Add( _
    New System.Windows.Forms.Binding("Text", _
    Me.TblEmployeesBindingSource, "fldEmployeeID", True))
```

The preceding statement performs two tasks. First, it creates an instance of the Binding class. Second, it adds that Binding class instance to the DataBindings collection of the text box.

The purpose of the Binding class is to bind a property of a control instance, such as the Text property of a TextBox, to the property of another object. In the case of binding a control instance to a database field, the Data Source Configuration Wizard binds the control instance to the instance of the BindingSource class just discussed.

Examining the preceding statement, a new instance of the Binding class is created. Four arguments are passed to the constructor, as described in the following list:

» The first argument contains the name of the property to bind. In the previous code segment, the Text property is being bound. When using other types of controls, such as a scroll bar, other properties, such as the Value property, would likely be bound.

» The second argument contains the name of the BindingSource class instance to which the control instance should be bound. This is the BindingSource named TblEmployeesBindingSource, which is bound to the table named tblEmployees in the DataSet named EmployeesDataSet.

» The third argument contains the name of the data member. In the preceding code segment, the data member is the field named fldEmployeeID from the database table named tblEmployees. Thus, the Text property is bound to a field in a DataTable.

» The final argument indicates that the data should be formatted in the visible control instance.

Creating an instance of the `Binding` class does not associate a control instance with a particular binding. It merely creates an object that can exchange data between a control instance and the data source. To bind a control instance to a data source, the `Binding` instance must be added to the `DataBindings` collection of the control instance to be bound. Thus, in the preceding code segment, the `Binding` instance is added to the `DataBindings` collection of the text box named FldEmployeeIDTextBox.

These are all of the steps completed by the Data Source Configuration Wizard and the Data Sources window to create the data source and bind control instances to that data source.

In this exploration exercise, you will examine selected code generated by the Data Source Configuration Wizard and see how to perform record navigation using bound data.

1. Start Visual Studio, if necessary, and open the solution file stored in the folder **Chapter.11\Chapter11ConceptLesson**.

2. Activate the Solution Explorer, and click the **Show All Files** button. Expand the **My Project** folder.

3. Double-click the file named **Settings.settings**. Remember that the connection string is stored in this resource file. The connection string appears in the Resource Editor. Close the Settings.settings file that appears in the Resource Editor.

4. In the Solution Explorer, expand the folder named **EmployeesDataSet.xsd**. Open the file named **EmployeesDataSet.Designer.vb**. Scroll through the file to view the partial class named tblEmployeesTableAdapter. Scroll through the code to find the `Update` and `Fill` methods.

The `BindingSource` class supports an event named `PositionChanged`, which fires whenever the position of the current record changes. The following statements appear in the `TblEmployeesBindingSource_PositionChanged` event handler created on the main form named frmMain.vb:

```
txtBindingNavigatorPositionItem.Text= _
    TblEmployeesBindingNavigator.PositionItem.Text
txtBindingNavigatorCountItem.Text = _
    TblEmployeesBindingNavigator.CountItem.Text
txtBindingSourcePositionItem.Text = _
    TblEmployeesBindingSource.Position.ToString
txtBindingSourceCountItem.Text = _
    TblEmployeesBindingSource.Count.ToString
```

The preceding statements display the position and count of both the `BindingNavigator` and the `BindingSource` classes in corresponding text boxes.

5. Run the application. The values of these properties appear on the form's text boxes, as shown in Figure 11-20.

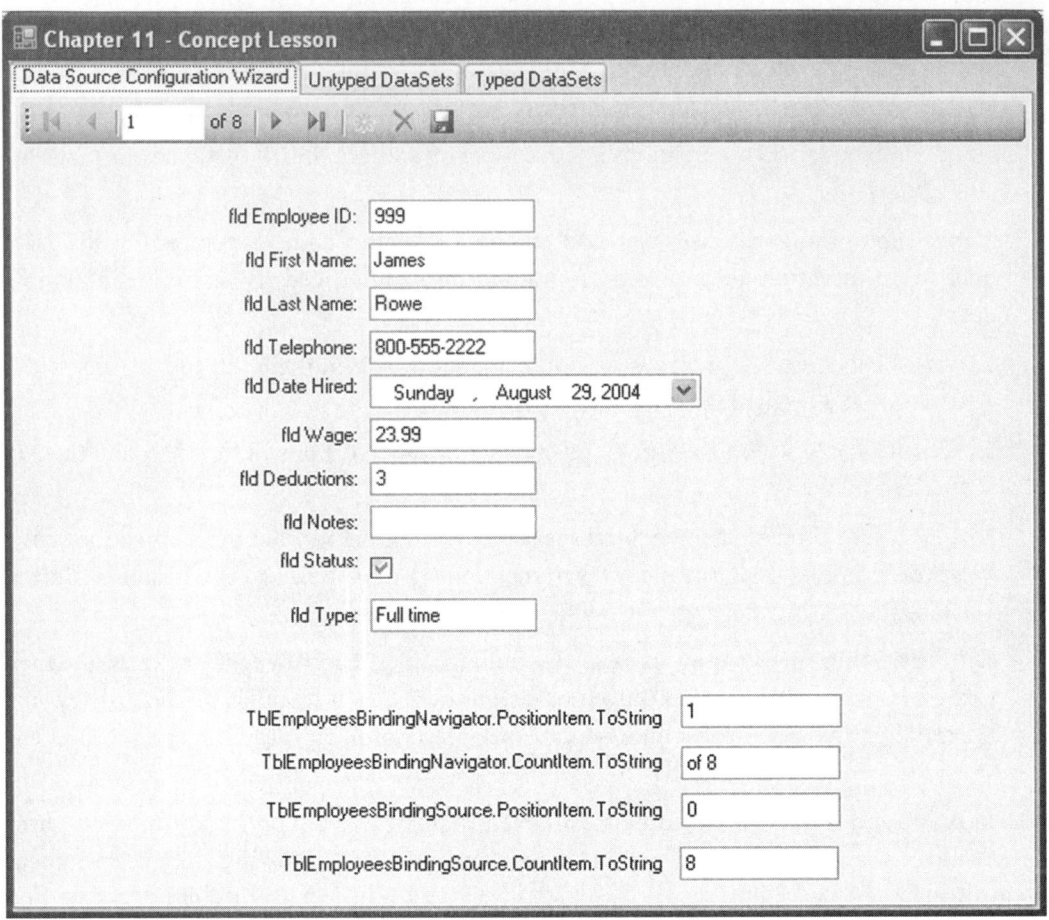

Figure 11-20: Displaying property values of the BindingNavigator and the BindingSource

Note that the properties corresponding to the `BindingNavigator` have different values than those of the `BindingSource`. This is because the `BindingNavigator` displays visual properties to the end user, whereas the `BindingSource` keeps track of the current record.

# MINI-QUIZ 2

1. Which of the following statements is correct regarding a connection string?

   a. It has a data type of `ConnectionString`. The various properties are used to set the provider and the name of the database.

   b. It has a data type of `String`. The property stores connection information as a series of key-value pairs.

   c. A connection is always open when a program that uses a database is running.

   d. An application can have at most one database connection.

   e. none of the above

2. What is the name of the class generated by the Data Source Configuration Wizard that is used to send commands over a connection to retrieve database data and update data?

3. Assuming that the variable TblEmployeesTableAdapter is a TableAdapter, what is the purpose of the following statement?

   ```
   Me.TblEmployeesTableAdapter.Fill( _
       Me.EmployeesDataSet.tblEmployees)
   ```

   a. It populates the `DataTable` named tblEmployees with data.

   b. Any changes made to the `DataTable` named tblEmployees are saved to the database automatically.

   c. It binds the TableAdapter to the `DataTable` named tblEmployees.

   d. none of the above

4. What is the name of the TableAdapter method used to record changes back to the database?

5. Which of the following statements is correct regarding the `BindingNavigator` class?

   a. It works in conjunction with the `BindingSource`.

   b. It contains methods to navigate from record to record.

   c. It contains a method to determine the current position.

   d. It contains methods to add and delete records.

   e. all of the above

# INTRODUCTION TO THE UNTYPED DATASET AND DATATABLE CLASSES

In addition to the other work performed by the Data Source Configuration Wizard, the Wizard generates two other objects called a `DataSet` and a `DataTable`. As mentioned, the `DataSet` class represents an in-memory disconnected view of the data from one or more database tables. Each table in a `DataSet` is represented as a `DataTable` object.

When you used the Data Source Configuration Wizard to configure the database connection and the Data Sources window to create the bound control instances on the form, Visual Studio also generates a class named EmployeesDataSet, which is stored in the file named EmployeesDataSet.Designer.vb. Conceptually, this class works similarly to the TableAdapter and underlying OleDbDataAdapter. That is, the EmployeesDataSet class supplies additional methods that make it easier to work with the underlying tables and fields.

Visual Studio supports a class named `System.Data.DataSet`. The `DataSet` class, in turn, has properties to get the tables stored in the `DataSet`. Each table in a `DataSet` has a data type of `DataTable`. The `DataSet` and `DataTable` classes are generic in that they are designed to operate with any database and any tables in a database regardless of the number of tables or the data types of the fields in those tables. Used in this way, the `DataSet` is called an **untyped DataSet**.

To begin, the `DataSet` class has a property named tables. The `Tables` property gets the collection of tables stored in a `DataSet`. A `DataSet` can have a single table or many tables. An individual table is referenced using a 0-based index or a string key corresponding to the table's name. In this chapter, you are working with a `DataSet` named EmployeesDataSet containing a single table (`DataTable`). The following code segment shows how to reference the first `DataTable` in the `DataSet`:

```
Dim CurrentTable As System.Data.DataTable
CurrentTable = EmployeesDataSet.Tables(0)
```

The preceding statements store a reference to the first `DataTable` in the `DataSet` in the variable named CurrentTable.

The `DataSet` class works in conjunction with the `DataTable` class, which is discussed next.

## INTRODUCTION TO THE UNTYPED DATATABLE CLASS

As mentioned, a `DataSet` stores references to one or more objects having a data type of `DataTable`, representing the data from a database table. In addition to referencing a `DataTable` using the 0-based index value of the `Tables` collection, it's possible to reference a table using the name of the table. The following statements reference the table named tblEmployees:

```
Dim CurrentTable As System.Data.DataTable
CurrentTable = EmployeesDataSet.Tables("tblEmployees")
```

As shown in the preceding statements, a variable is declared having a data type of DataTable. The second statement references a DataTable in the collection. To reference a table in the Tables collection, an index is supplied as an argument. The index contains a string having the same name as the database table, which is tblEmployees.

The DataTable class has members to reference a table's fields and rows and to get information about the table itself. For example, the TableName property is a string containing the table name.

```
Debug.WriteLine(CurrentTable.TableName)
```

The preceding statement writes the name of the DataTable object named CurrentTable.

Just as a relational database table is made up of rows and columns, the DataTable class has collections named Rows and Columns.

## INTRODUCTION TO THE UNTYPED DATAROW CLASS

The Rows property of the DataTable class references a collection of rows that make up the DataTable. One row exists in the collection for each row (record) in the DataTable. Each row in the DataTable has a data type of DataRow. The following code segment shows how to get the number of rows from the DataTable stored in the variable named CurrentTable:

```
Dim RowCount As Integer
RowCount = CurrentTable.Rows.Count
```

The Rows collection of the DataTable class, along with a numeric index, is used to reference a specific row. Each row in a DataTable has a data type of DataRow. The following code segment illustrates how to reference the first DataRow in a DataTable named tblEmployees:

```
Dim CurrentRow As System.Data.DataRow
CurrentRow = EmployeesDataSet.Tables("tblEmployees").Rows(0)
```

Assuming that EmployeesDataSet is an instance of the DataSet class, the preceding statements get the first row from the DataTable named tblEmployees and store a reference to that row in the variable named CurrentRow, which has a data type of DataRow. Examining the syntax of the statement, the statement fragment EmployeesDataSet.Tables references the Tables collection of the DataSet class. Thus, the statement fragment

`EmployeesDataSet.Tables("tblEmployees")` references the table named tblEmployees from the `Tables` collection. The `DataTable` class has a collection named `Rows`, which is used to reference a particular `DataRow` in the `DataTable`. Thus, the preceding statement returns the first row from the `DataTable` named tblEmployees in the `DataSet` named EmployeesDataSet. A reference to the `DataRow` is then stored in the variable CurrentRow.

Having referenced a `DataRow`, it is possible to reference the fields in that row. The `DataRow` class has a member named `Item` that references a field in a `DataRow`, as shown in the following statement:

```
Dim CurrentID As String
CurrentID = CurrentRow.Item("fldEmployeeID").ToString
```

Assuming that the variable CurrentRow has a data type of `DataRow`, the preceding statement retrieves the contents of the field named fldEmployeeID from the current row, converts that value to a string, and stores the result in the variable named CurrentID.

Putting the pieces together, it is possible to work with an untyped `DataTable` programmatically to examine a field in each row, and to perform calculations on that field. Each row in the table is examined and a total is calculated for the field named fldWage. Then, the average wage is calculated and displayed in a text box. The following code segment shows how to calculate the average employee wage:

```
Dim CurrentRow As System.Data.DataRow
Dim TotalWage, AverageWage As Double
Dim Count As Integer
txtUntypedOutput.Clear()
For Count = 0 To _
    EmployeesDataSet.Tables("tblEmployees").Rows.Count - 1
    CurrentRow = _
        EmployeesDataSet.Tables("tblEmployees").Rows(Count)
    txtUntypedOutput.Text &= _
        CurrentRow.Item("fldFirstName").ToString & " " & _
        CurrentRow.Item("fldLastName").ToString & " " & _
        CurrentRow.Item("fldWage").ToString & CrLf
    TotalWage += ToDouble(CurrentRow.Item("fldWage"))
Next
AverageWage = TotalWage / _
    EmployeesDataSet.Tables("tblEmployees").Rows.Count
txtUntypedOutput.Text &= "Average wage =" _
    AverageWage.ToString("c")
```

Examining the preceding code segment, the `For` loop examines each row in the `DataTable` named tblEmployees. The first statement in the `For` loop stores a reference to the current row in the variable named CurrentRow. The fields named fldFirstName, fldLastName, and fldWage are appended to the multiline text box named txtUntypedOutput. An accumulator named TotalWage is then used to tally the value of the field named fldWage. The statement following the `For` loop calculates the average wage by dividing the total wage by the number of rows in the `DataTable`. The result is then displayed in the same multiline text box.

## INTRODUCTION TO THE DATACOLUMN CLASS

Remember that a database table contains one or more columns. The `DataTable` class has a `Columns` collection. Each item in the collection has a data type of `DataColumn`, which stores information about the column. The `DataColumn` class has the following members:

### Syntax

`System.Data.DataColumn class`

### Properties

» The `ColumnName` property contains the name of the column.

» A column can have a caption that differs from the column name. A column's caption is stored in the `Caption` property.

» Each column has a data type, which is stored in the `DataType` property.

» For columns containing text, the `MaxLength` property contains the maximum number of characters that can be stored in the column. For columns having numeric data types, the `MaxLength` property has a value of −1 because the column's size is determined by the underlying data type.

The following code segment illustrates the process of examining a column in a `DataTable`:

```
Dim CurrentTable As DataTable
Dim CurrentColumn As DataColumn
CurrentTable = EmployeesDataSet.tblEmployees
CurrentColumn = CurrentTable.Columns(0)
txtColumnName.Text = CurrentColumn.ColumnName
txtUntypedOutput.Text = CurrentColumn.DataType.ToString
```

The preceding statements store a reference to a `DataTable` in the variable named CurrentTable. The fourth statement returns the first `DataColumn` from the `DataTable` and stores a reference to the column in the variable CurrentColumn. The next statement reads the `ColumnName` property and the final statement reads the `DataType` property.

Again, putting the pieces together, the following code segment shows how to examine all of the fields in a DataTable and display the results in a multiline text box:

```
Dim CurrentTable As DataTable
Dim CurrentColumn As DataColumn
Dim Count As Integer
txtUntypedOutput.Clear()
CurrentTable = EmployeesDataSet.tblEmployees
For Count = 0 To CurrentTable.Columns.Count - 1
    CurrentColumn = CurrentTable.Columns(Count)
    txtUntypedOutput.Text &= "DataType=" & _
        CurrentColumn.DataType.ToString & CrLf
    txtUntypedOutput.Text &= "Caption=" & _
        CurrentColumn.Caption.ToString & CrLf
    txtUntypedOutput.Text &= "ColumnName=" & _
        CurrentColumn.ColumnName & CrLf
    txtUntypedOutput.Text &= CrLf
Next
```

The preceding code segment uses a For loop to enumerate the Columns collection of the DataTable. Selected properties applicable to the current column are displayed in a multiline text box.

In this exploration exercise, you will apply what you have learned in this section of the chapter.

1. Run the solution file appearing in the folder named **Chapter.11\ Chapter11ConceptLesson**.

2. Click the **Untyped DataSets** tab.

3. Click the **Get Table Information (Untyped)** button. The information about the DataTable is retrieved and displayed in the form's text boxes.

4. Click the **Calculate Average Wage (Untyped)** button. Each row in the DataTable is examined. For each row examined, the employee's first name, last name, and hourly wage are displayed. After all of the rows have been examined, the average hourly wage is displayed. All of the output is displayed to the form's multiline text box. Figure 11-21 shows the Untyped DataSets tab with the results from the average wage calculation.

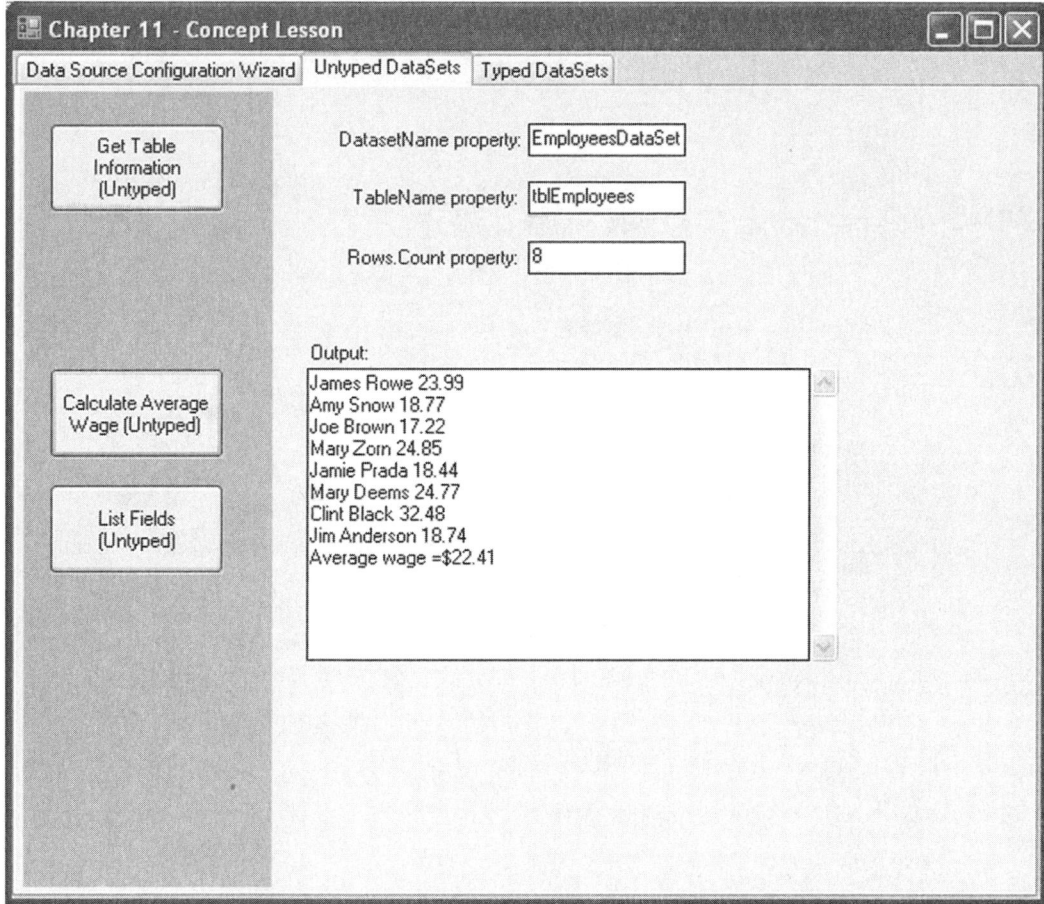

Figure 11-21: Concept lesson—Untyped DataSets tab

5. Click the **List Fields (Untyped)** button. The statements in this event handler examine each field in the table and display the information about each field. Again, the data is displayed in the form's multiline text box.

# MINI-QUIZ 3

1. Which of the following statements is correct regarding the `DataSet` class?

   a. It must contain exactly one `DataTable`.

   b. It can have one or more `DataTables`.

   c. The `Fields` collection contains a reference to `Field` objects. Each `Field` object represents a field in the `DataSet`.

   d. The `Count` property of the `DataSet` class returns the number of tables in the `DataSet`.

   e. none of the above

2. Which of the following statements is correct regarding the `DataTable` class?

   a. To get the data from each row in the `DataTable`, you would use the `DataColumn` class.

   b. Assuming that CurrentTable is a `DataTable`, the statement `CurrentTable.Rows` would return the number of rows in the table.

   c. Each row in a `DataTable` has a data type of `DataRow`.

   d. If a `DataTable` had 10 rows, the `Rows` property would have a value of 10.

   e. all of the above

3. Assuming that dsCurrent is a `DataSet` and tblDemo is a `DataTable` in that `DataSet`, describe the error(s) in the following statements:

```
Dim CurrentRow As DataRow
Dim Count As Integer
For Count = 0 to dsCurrent.Tables(tblDemo).Rows.Count
    CurrentRow = dsCurrent.Tables(tblDemo).Rows(Count)
Next
```

4. Assume that a `DataSet` exists having one `DataTable` named tblQuiz. Write the statements to declare a variable named CurrentRow having a data type of `DataRow`. Using a loop, examine each row. For each row examined, append the contents of the field fldName to the `TextBox` control instance named txtOutput.

# INTRODUCTION TO STRONGLY TYPED DATASETS, DATATABLES, AND DATAROWS

The code discussed so far in this chapter used the generic `DataSet`, `DataTable`, and `DataRow` classes to navigate through the rows in a table. These `DataSets` and `DataTables` are considered untyped. That is, the data types are the same no matter the data contained in the `DataTable`, or the `DataTables` contained in the `DataSet`. In addition to an untyped `DataSet`, Visual Studio supports what is called a strongly typed `DataSet`, which is automatically generated by a Wizard.

## STRONGLY TYPED DATASETS AND DATATABLES

To simplify the development of applications using the `DataSet` and `DataTable` classes, Visual Studio uses what is called a **strongly typed DataSet**. One of the benefits of using a strongly typed `DataSet` is that Visual Studio's Intellisense technology displays the tables stored in the `DataSet` and the fields in those tables. Thus, syntax errors are far less common.

A strongly typed DataSet is a `DataSet` generated by a Wizard. The class created by the Wizard inherits from the base `System.Data.DataSet` class. This class is stored in the project and should never be modified directly. The strongly typed DataSet is made up of two important files. The file named EmployeesDataSet.xsd is known as a schema definition file. This file is an XML document that describes the tables in the `DataSet` and the fields in those tables. The file named EmployeesDataSet.Designer.vb contains the code for the strongly typed `DataSet`, along with the code for the TableAdapter discussed previously in this chapter. Figure 11-22 shows the files that make up the strongly typed DataSet appearing in the Solution Explorer.

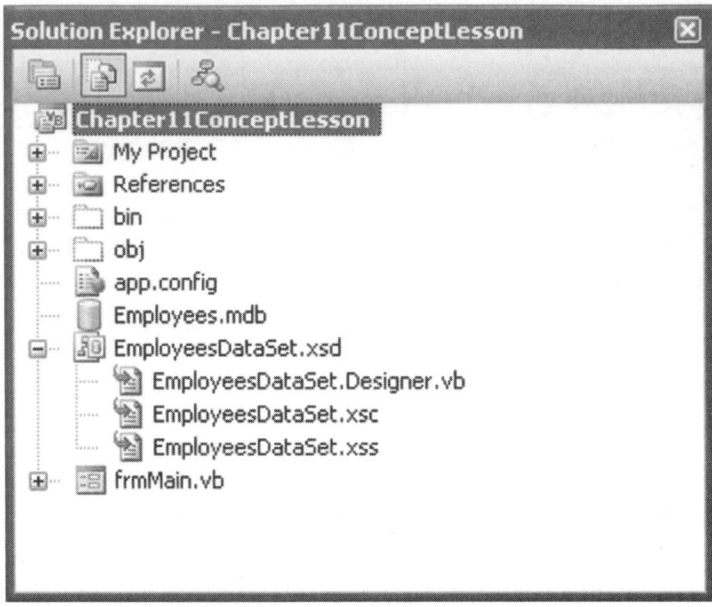

Figure 11-22: DataSet files appearing in the Solution Explorer

To illustrate the difference between untyped and strongly typed `DataSet`, `DataTable`, and `DataRow` classes, the following equivalent statement groups compare the two implementations. The following statement group shows the difference between referencing an untyped `DataTable` and a strongly typed `DataTable`:

```
' Untyped
Dim CurrentTableUntyped As System.Data.DataTable
CurrentTableUntyped = EmployeesDataSet.Tables("tblEmployees")
' Strongly typed
Dim CurrentTableTyped As Chapter11ConceptLesson. _
    EmployeesDataSet.tblEmployeesDataTable
CurrentTableTyped = EmployeesDataSet.tblEmployees
```

The first group of statements, which was discussed previously in this chapter, references the table named tblEmployees. The second group of statements accomplishes the same task. However, in the second statement group, the strongly typed `DataSet` class is used. The strongly typed `DataSet` belongs to the project's root namespace, which is Chapter11ConceptLesson. This strongly typed `DataSet` has one strongly typed `DataTable` named tblEmployeesDataTable. The final statement stores a reference to the `DataTable` in the variable named CurrentTableTyped.

To understand how a strongly typed `DataSet` works, it is necessary to examine the EmployeesDataSet.Designer.vb file generated by the Data Source Configuration Wizard. Looking at this class, you will see that a `DataSet` is generated that derives from the `System.Data.DataSet` class as the following statements show:

```
Partial Public Class EmployeesDataSet
    Inherits System.Data.DataSet
End Class
```

As shown in the preceding code segment, the `DataSet` named EmployeesDataSet inherits from the base `System.Data.DataSet` class. This class contains members to reference the `DataTable` object(s) in the `DataSet`. The following code segment shows the read-only `Property` procedure to reference the table named tblEmployees:

```
Public ReadOnly Property tblEmployees() As tblEmployeesDataTable
    Get
        Return Me.tabletblEmployees
    End Get
End Property
```

The preceding statement returns a reference to a `DataTable` named tblEmployeesDataTable. This `DataTable` is a strongly typed version of the `DataTable` class, as the following statements show:

```
Partial Public Class tblEmployeesDataTable
    Inherits System.Data.DataTable
End Class
```

As shown in the preceding code segment, the class tblEmployeesDataTable inherits from the base `System.Data.DataTable` class.

## STRONGLY TYPED DATAROWS

Continuing the comparison, the following statement group shows how to reference an untyped and strongly typed `DataRow`:

```
' Untyped
Dim CurrentRowUntyped As System.Data.DataRow
CurrentRowUntyped = _
    EmployeesDataSet.Tables("tblEmployees").Rows(0)
' Strongly typed
Dim CurrentRowTyped As _
    Chapter11ConceptLesson.EmployeesDataSet.tblEmployeesRow
CurrentRowTyped = EmployeesDataSet.tblEmployees.Item(0)
```

The preceding statement groups show how to reference the first row in a DataTable using both untyped and strongly typed methods. The strongly typed DataSet named EmployeesDataSet contains a class named tblEmployeesRow. This class is a strongly typed class that defines the fields in the row and inherits from the System.Data.DataRow class, as the following statements show:

```
Partial Public Class tblEmployeesRow
    Inherits System.Data.DataRow
End Class
```

The rows in a DataTable have a data type of DataRow. When the Data Source Configuration Wizard generated the strongly typed DataSet and DataTable classes, it also generated a strongly typed DataRow class used to represent a row in the DataTable.

Finally, it is possible to reference a field in a strongly typed DataRow, as the following statement group shows:

```
' Untyped
Dim CurrentID As String
CurrentID = CurrentRowUnTyped.Item("fldEmployeeID").ToString
' Strongly typed
CurrentID = CurrentRowTyped.fldEmployeeID.ToString
```

The preceding statements both read the field named fldEmployeeID, convert the data type to a String, and store the result in the variable CurrentID.

The strongly typed DataTable class, in turn, has Property procedures to reference the individual fields in the DataTable, as the following statements show:

```
Public ReadOnly Property fldEmployeeIDColumn() _
    As System.Data.DataColumn
    Get
        Return Me.columnfldEmployeeID
    End Get
End Property
```

The preceding Property procedure reads the column named fldEmployeeID from the DataTable.

Inside of the strongly typed `DataRow` class are properties used to reference each field in the row as the following `Property` procedure shows:

```
Public Property fldEmployeeID() As Integer
    Get
        Return CType(Me(Me.tabletblEmployees. _
        fldEmployeeIDColumn), Integer)
    End Get
    Set
        Me(Me.tabletblEmployees.fldEmployeeIDColumn) = value
    End Set
End Property
```

The preceding `Property` procedure references the field named fldEmployeeID. The `Property` procedure has the same data type as the data type of the underlying field. Nearly identical `Property` procedures reference the other fields. Each `Property` procedure has a data type that corresponds to the data type of the underlying field.

Again, putting the pieces together, the following statements show how to enumerate each strongly typed row in a `DataTable`:

```
Dim CurrentRow As EmployeesDataSet.tblEmployeesRow
Dim TotalWage, AverageWage As Double
Dim Count As Integer
txtTypedOutput.Clear()
For Count = 0 To _
    EmployeesDataSet.tblEmployees.Rows.Count - 1
    CurrentRow = _
        EmployeesDataSet.tblEmployees.Item(Count)
    txtTypedOutput.Text &= _
        CurrentRow.fldFirstName & " " & _
        CurrentRow.fldLastName & " " & _
        CurrentRow.fldWage & CrLf
    TotalWage += CurrentRow.fldWage
Next
AverageWage = TotalWage / _
    EmployeesDataSet.tblEmployees.Rows.Count
txtTypedOutput.Text &= "Average wage =" &
AverageWage.ToString("c")
```

The preceding statement block enumerates the rows in the table named tblEmployees using strongly typed members instead of untyped members. Each row is examined and the first name, last name, and wage are displayed in a multiline text box. The variable

TotalWage is used as an accumulator to store the total wage. Finally, the average wage is calculated.

In this exploration exercise, you will look at various code segments that examine the rows in a DataTable using typed DataSets and DataTables, rather than untyped DataSets and DataTables.

1. Activate the Solution Explorer, if necessary, and click the **Show All Files** button. Expand the **EmployeesDataSet.xsd** folder. Open the file named **EmployeesDataSet. Designer.vb** in the Code Editor. Scroll through the file to discover the tables and fields in the DataSet.

2. Run the solution file stored in the folder named **Chapter.11\ Chapter11ConceptLesson**.

3. Click the **Typed DataSets** tab. The visual appearance is nearly identical to the Untyped DataSets tab.

4. Click the **Get Table Information (Typed)** button. The information is retrieved using strongly typed methods instead of untyped methods.

5. Click the **Calculate Average Wage (Typed)** button. The average wage is calculated using typed members instead of untyped members and the results are displayed in the multiline text box.

# MINI-QUIZ 4

1. Which of the following statements is correct regarding a strongly typed DataSet?

   a. A strongly typed DataSet cannot be used when strict type checking is disabled (Option Strict Off).

   b. All DataSets are strongly typed.

   c. A strongly typed DataSet is derived from the System.Data. TypedDataSet class.

   d. A strongly typed DataSet inherits from the System.Data.DataSet class.

   e. none of the above

2. Where is the code for a strongly typed DataSet stored?

*(Continued)* ▶

3. Assume that a strongly typed `DataSet` exists. It is named Exam and has a table named Questions with a field named CorrectAnswer. Which of the following statements correctly references the field in the database table?

a. `Exam.Questions.Rows(0).Fields(0).CorrectAnswer`

b. `Exam.Questions.Item(0).CorrectAnswer`

c. `Exam.Questions.CorrectAnswer`

d. `Exam.Questions.DataRow(0).CorrectAnswer`

e. `StronglyTyped(Exam.Questions.Rows(0).CorrectAnswer)`

# APPLICATION LESSON

## CREATING AN ACCOUNTS RECEIVABLE AGING SYSTEM

In this application lesson, you will create an accounts receivable aging system using data from an Access database. The application will allow the end user to view the account balances of the customers in the database along with displaying a report listing the total past due balances of all customer accounts.

Table 11-2 shows the structure of the table used in this application lesson.

| Field name | Description | Data type |
|---|---|---|
| fldCustomerID | Unique identification number | Integer |
| fldCustomerName | Customer name | String |
| fldCustomerAddress | Customer address | String |
| fldCity | City | String |
| fldState | State | String |
| fldZipCode | Zip code | String |
| fldCurrentBalance | Balance due between 0 and 30 days old | Double |
| fld30DayBalance | Balance due between 31 and 60 days old | Double |
| fld60DayBalance | Balance due between 61 and 90 days | Double |
| fld90DayPlusBalance | Balance due over 90 days old | Double |
| fldCreditLimit | Customer's credit limit | Double |
| fldActive | True if the customer is active and False otherwise | Boolean |

Table 11-2: Fields in the tblAccounts table

## APPLICATION LESSON—USER INTERFACE

The application's user interface is made up of two forms. The first form allows the end user to navigate through the records in the database table. Most of the control instances are created using the Data Source Configuration Wizard and the Data Sources window using the same techniques discussed in the chapter. Most of the form's control instances are bound controls. In addition, unbound text boxes display data values that are calculated based on information contained in the current record. The following list describes these values:

» The total past due amount is calculated by adding the balance due over 30, 60, and 90 days old.

» Total balance due is calculated by adding the total past due amount to the current balance due.

» The available credit is calculated by subtracting the total balance due from the credit limit.

The application contains a second form that is used to display the current balance due and past due balances for all accounts rather than for a single account. The past due balance is displayed for each overdue category. In addition, the total credit limit and total available balances are displayed.

## APPLICATION LESSON—DESIGN

The application's design contains an instance of the `BindingNavigator` class on the main form, which allows the end user to navigate through the database records. In addition, the main form contains the following three buttons:

» The button titled Display Aging Form displays the accounts receivable aging form. The `DataTable` containing the data is passed as an argument to the form's constructor.

» The button titled Active/Inactive Customers displays a message box containing a count of the active and inactive customers.

» The button titled Exit exits the application.

In addition, the main form contains a `PositionChanged` event handler used to calculate the values for the unbound fields each time the end user changes the current record position.

## APPLICATION LESSON—IMPLEMENTATION

The implementation for this application lesson uses a strongly typed `DataSet` and `DataTable` generated using the Data Source Configuration Wizard and the Data Sources window. Thus, most of the application's code is generated by the Wizard. The Wizard created two event handlers and their code, as described in the following list:

» The `Click` event handler for the `BindingNavigator`'s Save button calls the `Update` method of the TableAdapter to save any changes made by the end user.

» The form's `Load` event handler calls the `Fill` method of the TableAdapter to populate the `DataSet` and `DataTable`.

The code for the application's main form all appears in the following event handlers:

» The `PositionChanged` event handler of the `BindingSource` gets the current row from the `DataTable` using the position of the `BindingSource`. The code in the event handler calculates and displays the total past due amount, the total amount due, and the available credit for the current customer.

» The `Click` event handler for the button named btnAgingReport creates an instance of the form named frmAging, and displays it. The strongly typed `DataTable` named tblAccounts is passed as an argument to the form's constructor.

» The `Click` event handler for the button named btnActiveInactive examines each row in the `DataTable` and counts the number of active and inactive customers. These counters are displayed in a message box.

» The Exit button exits the application.

The constructor for the form named frmAging contains the code to calculate the total current, 30 day, 60 day, and 90 day customer balances for all customers.

As usual, a completed version of the application lesson has been provided. In the following steps, you will preview the application lesson.

To preview the completed application lesson:

1. Start Visual Studio and open the solution file stored in the folder **Chapter.11\Chapter11ApplicationLessonPreview**. Run the application lesson. The completed main form appears as shown in Figure 11-23.

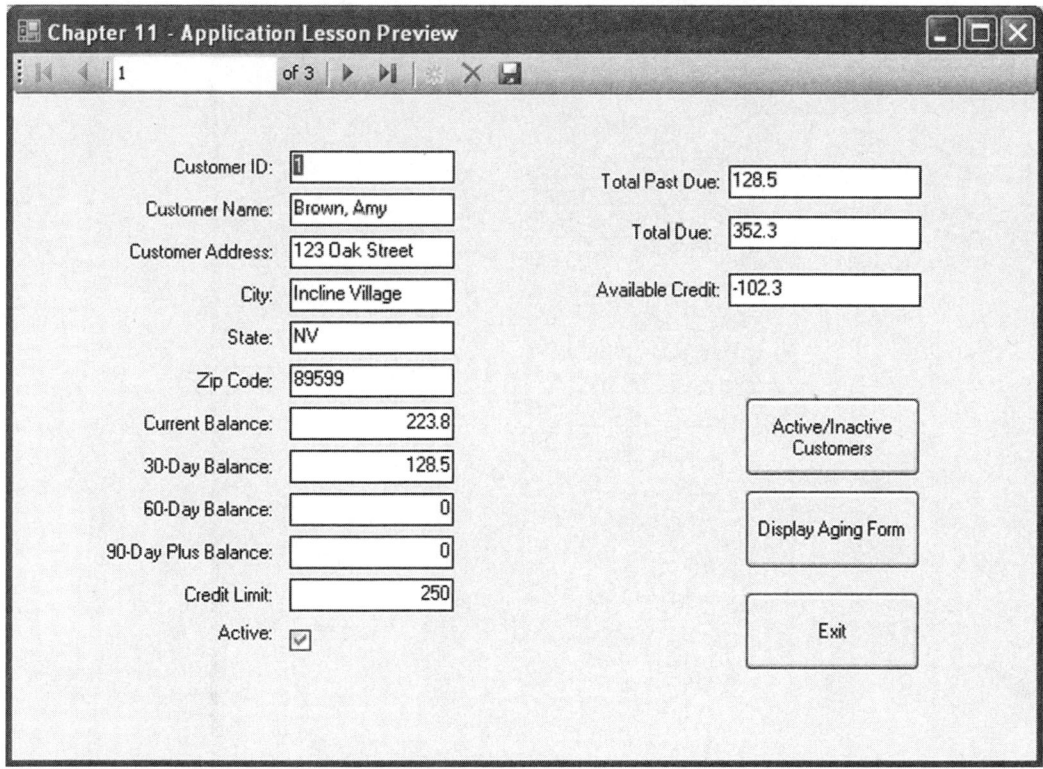

Figure 11-23: Application lesson—main form at run time

2. Navigate from record to record using the toolbar buttons. As you do, the current record is displayed and the calculated totals are updated.

3. Click the **Display Aging Form** button. The aging form appears with the calculated summary values, as shown in Figure 11-24.

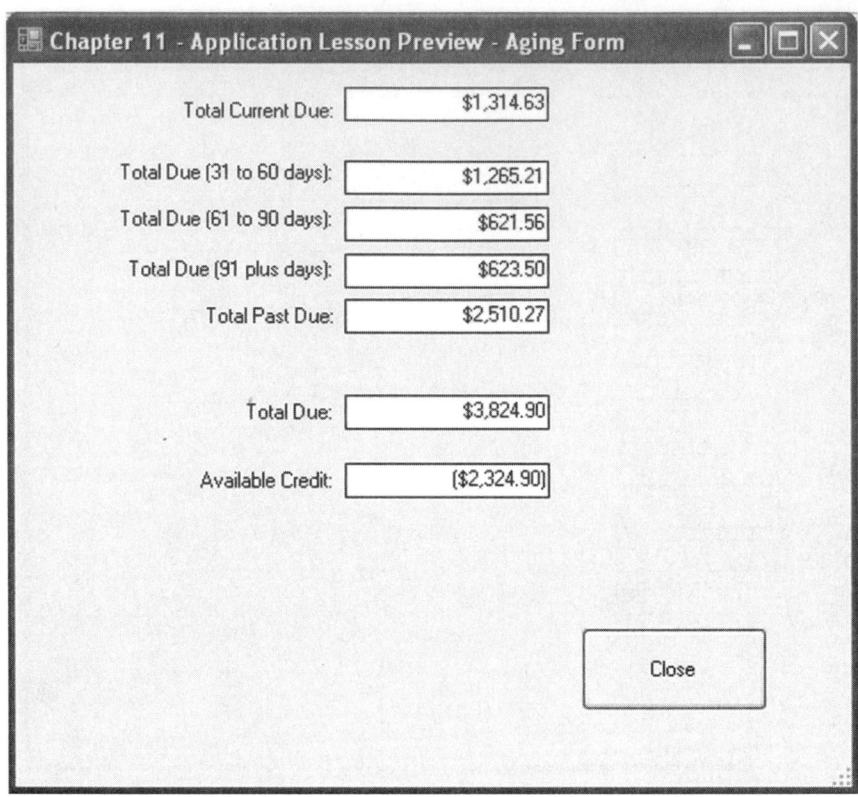

**Chapter 11 - Application Lesson Preview - Aging Form**

| | |
|---|---|
| Total Current Due: | $1,314.63 |
| Total Due (31 to 60 days): | $1,265.21 |
| Total Due (61 to 90 days): | $621.56 |
| Total Due (91 plus days): | $623.50 |
| Total Past Due: | $2,510.27 |
| Total Due: | $3,824.90 |
| Available Credit: | ($2,324.90) |

Close

Figure 11-24: Application lesson—aging form at run time

4. Close the accounts receivable aging form.

5. Click the **Active/Inactive Customers** button. The total number of active and inactive customers is displayed in a message box.

6. Exit the application and Visual Studio.

In the following steps, you will create and configure the data source.

To create and configure the application's data source:

1. Start Visual Studio and open the solution file stored in the folder **Chapter.11\Chapter11ApplicationLessonStartup**. The application contains two blank forms.

2. Activate the Windows Forms Designer for the form named frmMain.vb, if necessary. Click **Data**, **Add New Data Source** to begin adding a data source to the application.

3. In the Choose a Data Source Type dialog box, select **Database**, and then click **Next**.

4. Create a new connection such that Access will be used as the database provider, and select the database named **Chapter.11\Data\AccountsReceivable.mdb**. Test the connection.

5. Add the connection to the project and to the application settings.

6. In the Choose Your Database Objects dialog box, select all of the fields from the table named tblAccounts. Click **Finish** so that the Wizard will create the data source and display it in the Data Sources window.

7. Using the Data Sources window, drag each field to the Windows Forms Designer in the order that the field appears. When the first control instance is created on the form, the Wizard generates the invisible control instances along with the toolbar appearing across the top of the form.

8. Modify the prompts so that they are the same as the ones shown in Figure 11-23.

The total past due balance, total balance, and available credit are not stored in the database. Thus, each time the end user selects a different record, these values must be calculated.

To calculate the total balance for a customer's account:

1. Create the **PositionChanged** event handler for the binding source named **TblAccountsBindingSource**. Enter the following statements in the event handler:

```
Dim TotalPastDue As Double
Dim TotalDue As Double
Dim AvailableCredit As Double
Dim CurrentPosition As Integer
Dim CurrentRow As _
    Chapter11ApplicationLessonStartup. _
    AccountsReceivableDataSet.tblAccountsRow

CurrentPosition = TblAccountsBindingSource.Position
CurrentRow = AccountsReceivableDataSet. _
    tblAccounts.Item(CurrentPosition)

TotalPastDue = CurrentRow.fld30DayBalance + _
    CurrentRow.fld60DayBalance + CurrentRow.fld90DayPlusBalance
TotalDue = TotalPastDue + CurrentRow.fldCurrentBalance
AvailableCredit = CurrentRow.fldCreditLimit - TotalDue

txtTotalPastDue.Text = TotalPastDue.ToString()
txtTotalDue.Text = TotalDue.ToString
txtAvailableCredit.Text = AvailableCredit.ToString
```

The `PositionChanged` event fires each time the end user selects a different record. Using a strongly typed `DataSet`, the variable CurrentRow is declared so as to reference the current row. The variable CurrentPosition stores the 0-based current record position. The value is read from the `Position` property of the `BindingSource`. Next, the current row is stored in the variable named CurrentRow. Using the fields from the current row, the TotalPastDue, TotalDue, and available credit are calculated. Finally, these values are displayed in the form's text boxes.

Customers are categorized as active and inactive customers. The user interface contains a button that, when clicked, calculates the number of active and inactive customers and displays the result in a message box.

To calculate the number of active and inactive customers:

1. Create the **Click** event handler for the Button control instance named **btnActiveInactive**. Enter the following statements in the event handler:

```
Dim ActiveCount, InactiveCount As Integer
Dim CurrentPosition As Integer
Dim Message As String

Dim CurrentRow As _
    Chapter11ApplicationLessonStartup. _
    AccountsReceivableDataSet.tblAccountsRow
For CurrentPosition = 0 To _
    AccountsReceivableDataSet.tblAccounts.Count - 1
    CurrentRow = AccountsReceivableDataSet.tblAccounts. _
        Item(CurrentPosition)
    If CurrentRow.fldActive = True Then
        ActiveCount += 1
    Else
        InactiveCount += 1
    End If
Next
Message = "There are " & ActiveCount.ToString & " active and " _
    & InactiveCount.ToString & " inactive customers."
MessageBox.Show(Message, "Customer Totals", _
    MessageBoxButtons.OK, MessageBoxIcon.Information)
```

The preceding statements declare a variable named CurrentRow to store the current row in the `DataTable`. Again, strongly typed methods are used in this procedure. The `For` loop examines each `DataRow`. If the field named fldActive has a value of `True`, the counter named ActiveCount is incremented. Otherwise, the counter named InactiveCount is incremented. Finally, the results are displayed in a message box.

A second form exists in the project, which displays the accounts receivable aging data. The DataTable is passed as an argument to the form's constructor, thereby making the DataTable available to the second form. The code to display the aging form has not yet been created.

To display the aging form:

1. Enter the following statements in the **Click** event handler for the Button control instance named **btnAgingReport**:

```
Dim CurrentAgingForm As New _
    frmAging(AccountsReceivableDataSet.tblAccounts)
CurrentAgingForm.ShowDialog()
```

The first of the preceding statements creates an instance of the form named frmAging passing the DataTable named tblAccounts as an argument to the form's constructor. The second statement displays the form as a modal dialog box.

All of the code for the accounts receivable aging report appears in the form's constructor. Each row in the DataTable and totals are calculated and displayed to the end user.

To create the accounts receivable aging report:

1. Activate the Code Editor for the form named **frmAging**, and then enter the following statements, shown in bold, in the form's constructor. Note that the statements add an argument to the constructor:

```
Public Sub New(ByVal CurrentTable As _
        Chapter11ApplicationLessonStartup. _
        AccountsReceivableDataSet.tblAccountsDataTable)
    InitializeComponent()
    Dim TotalCurrentDue As Double
    Dim Total31To60Due As Double
    Dim Total61To90Due As Double
    Dim Total91PlusDue As Double
    Dim TotalPastDue As Double
    Dim TotalDue As Double
    Dim AvailableCredit As Double
    Dim TotalCreditLimit As Double
    Dim CurrentPosition As Integer
    Dim CurrentRow As Chapter11ApplicationLessonStartup. _
        AccountsReceivableDataSet.tblAccountsRow
    For CurrentPosition = 0 To CurrentTable.Count - 1
        CurrentRow = CurrentTable.Item(CurrentPosition)
        TotalCurrentDue += CurrentRow.fldCurrentBalance
        Total31To60Due += CurrentRow.fld30DayBalance
        Total61To90Due += CurrentRow.fld60DayBalance
```

```
            Total91PlusDue += CurrentRow.fld90DayPlusBalance
            TotalPastDue += CurrentRow.fld30DayBalance + _
                CurrentRow.fld60DayBalance + _
                CurrentRow.fld90DayPlusBalance
            TotalCreditLimit += CurrentRow.fldCreditLimit
        Next
        TotalDue += TotalPastDue + TotalCurrentDue
        AvailableCredit = TotalCreditLimit - TotalDue
        txtTotalCurrentDue.Text = TotalCurrentDue.ToString("c")
        txtTotal31To60Due.Text = Total31To60Due.ToString("c")
        txtTotal61To90Due.Text = Total61To90Due.ToString("c")
        txtTotal91PlusDue.Text = Total91PlusDue.ToString("c")
        txtTotalPastDue.Text = TotalPastDue.ToString("c")
        txtTotalDue.Text = TotalDue.ToString("c")
        txtAvailableCredit.Text = AvailableCredit.ToString("c")
    End Sub
```

The preceding code segment examines each row in the `DataTable`. Accumulators are used to tally the total past due amounts from each category. After all of the values have been calculated, they are displayed in the form's text boxes.

You have completed the steps to implement the accounts receivable application. The only step that remains is to test it.

To test the accounts receivable application:

1. Run the application lesson.

2. Navigate from record to record.

3. Display the aging form.

# CHAPTER SUMMARY

» A database contains a set of data related to a particular topic or purpose. The data stored in a database is organized into one or more tables made up of rows and columns. The data stored in each row is called a record. A record is made up of multiple data items called fields.

» A database management system is used to manage the data in a database. Common database management systems include the Microsoft Jet Database Engine, SQL Server, and Oracle. All of these database management systems are relational.

» Relational databases use a language called the Structured Query Language (SQL) to select database records, and to insert, update, and delete records. These tasks are performed by the SELECT, INSERT, UPDATE, and DELETE statements, respectively.

» Database operations using Visual Basic and other .NET languages are performed using ADO.NET. Using ADO.NET, a connection is made to the database. Data is then retrieved from the database, and then the connection is closed. If data needs to be saved back to the database, the connection must be reopened.

» The Data Source Configuration Wizard is used to create a database connection, and to select the table(s) and fields that will be retrieved from the database. To do this, the Data Source Configuration Wizard creates a connection string based on the information you specify in various dialog boxes.

» The Data Sources window displays the tables and fields that make up the data source configured by the Data Source Configuration Wizard. By dragging the fields from the Data Sources window to the Windows Forms Designer, control instances are created and bound to the data source. A `DataSet` and `DataTable` are automatically created when the first bound control instance is created.

» The Data Source Configuration Wizard creates a TableAdapter class, which uses the underlying connection to retrieve data from the database. The TableAdapter class operates with another class called the `OleDbDataAdapter`, which contains the SQL statements to select, insert, update, and delete database data.

» Another class called the `BindingSource` supplies the means to navigate through the records in the data source. The `BindingSource` works in conjunction with the `BindingNavigator` class. The `BindingNavigator` class supplies the user interface with which the end user navigates from record to record. As fields are dragged from the Data Sources window, the control instances are created and bound to the data source using the `Binding` class.

» Connections are implemented with the `OleDbConnection` class. The `ConnectionString` property contains a connection string that is made up of key-value pairs.

» The TableAdapter class and the underlying `OleDbDataAdapter` class instance open the connection, and send SQL SELECT statements to the database to retrieve data into a `DataSet` and `DataTable`.

» The `OleDbDataAdapter` class has properties named `SelectCommand`, `InsertCommand`, `UpdateCommand`, and `DeleteCommand`, each having a data type of `OleDbCommand`. These `OleDbCommand` objects, in turn, contain SQL statements in the `CommandText` property.

» The `Fill` method of the `OleDbDataAdapter` is used to populate the `DataSet` and `DataTable`. The `Update` method is used to save any changes made to the `DataTable` back to the database.

» The `BindingSource` class provides navigational capabilities to a `DataTable` through the `DataSource` and `DataMember` properties. The `BindingSource` class supports methods to determine the current record position, and to navigate to the first, next, previous, and last record. The `BindingSource` is typically used in conjunction with the `BindingNavigator` class. The `BindingNavigator` appears as a toolbar across the top of the form.

» The `DataSet` class is an in-memory representation of one or more database tables. Each database table in a `DataSet` is stored as an instance of the `DataTable` class.

» The `DataTable` class has members to reference the fields in a database table along with the rows in a table. To reference a specific row, use the `Rows` property with a 0-based index containing the row to reference. Each row in a database table has a data type of `DataRow`. The `Fields` collection of the `DataRow` class is used to reference the individual fields in the row.

» The `DataTable` class has a collection named `Columns`, which is used to get the name, data type, and size of a particular column in the table. Each column in the collection has a data type of `DataColumn`.

» In addition to an untyped `DataSet` and `DataTable`, it is possible to create strongly typed `DataSet` and `DataTable` objects. Strongly typed `DataSets` are automatically generated by the Data Sources window and the Windows Forms Designer. A strongly typed `DataSet` derives from the `System.Data.DataSet` class. This class contains procedures used to reference the specific `DataTables` and the fields in those `DataTables`.

# KEY TERMS

**ActiveX Data Objects (ADO.NET) 2.0**—A group of classes that supplies the means by which Visual Studio and Visual Basic applications can interact with a database management system.

**connection string**—A string made up of key-value pairs that vary from one database management system to another. It is used by ADO.NET to establish a connection between a Visual Basic application and a database.

**data source**—A connection between a Visual Studio project and a database.

**database**—A database consists of a set of information related to a particular topic or purpose.

**database management system (DBMS)**—The software component used to manage a database.

**field**—A data item in a database table.

**record**—A row in a database table.

**relational database**—A type of database that combines tables made up of rows and columns.

**strongly typed DataSet**—A class generated by a Wizard. The class appears in the file named *datasetname*.Designer.vb and contains strongly typed properties and methods that correspond to the underlying database tables and fields. *datasetname* is a place-holder for the actual name of the DataSet.

**Structured Query Language (SQL)**—The standard language used to select, insert, update, and delete data stored in a database management system.

**table**—The data stored in a database is organized into one or more tables having rows and columns.

**TableAdapter class**—A class used to open a connection to a database, retrieve records in a DataSet, and perform updates on the disconnected DataSet.

**untyped DataSet**—Generic DataSet and DataTable classes.

# ANSWERS TO MINI-QUIZZES

### MINI-QUIZ 1

1. Yes

2. e. all of the above

3. a. Dragging a field from the Data Sources window to the Windows Forms Designer causes a bound control instance to be created on a form.

4. Microsoft Access and SQL Server

### MINI-QUIZ 2

1. b. It has a data type of `String`. The property stores connection information as a series of key-value pairs.

2. TableAdapter

3. a. It populates the `DataTable` named tblEmployees with data.

4. `Update`

5. e. all of the above

### MINI-QUIZ 3

1. b. It can have one or more `DataTables`.

2. c. Each row in a `DataTable` has a data type of `DataRow`.

3. First, the table named tblDemo should appear in quotation marks. Second, the loop should iterate from 0 to Count – 1. Thus, the `For` loop should be written as

   ```
   For Count = 0 to dsCurrent.Tables(tblDemo).Rows.Count -1
   ```

4. ```
   Dim CurrentRow As DataRow
   Dim Count As Integer
   For Count = 0 to tblQuiz.Rows.Count - 1
       txtOutput.Text &= tblQuiz.Rows(Count).Item("fldName")
   Next
   ```

### MINI-QUIZ 4

1. d. A strongly typed `DataSet` inherits from the `System.Data.DataSet` class.

2. The code for a strongly typed `DataSet` is stored in a file named *datasetname*.Designer.vb, where *datasetname* is the name of the strongly typed `DataSet`.

3. b. `Exam.Questions.Item(0).CorrectAnswer`

# REVIEW QUESTIONS

1. Which of the following statements is true regarding a database?

   a. A table consists of rows and columns.

   b. The columns in a table are called fields.

   c. The rows in a table are called records.

   d. A database can have multiple tables.

   e. all of the above

2. Which of the following lists valid SQL statements?

   a. DATABASE, TABLE, RECORD, FIELD

   b. SELECT, INSERT, UPDATE, DELETE

   c. GET, ADD, CHANGE, REMOVE

   d. READTABLE, WRITETABLE

   e. SELECTDATASET, FILL, WRITEDATASET
   ```

3. Assuming that a database contains a table named Customer having a field named CustomerID, which of the following statements correctly selects all of the data from the table and sorts that data based on the contents of the CustomerID field?

   a. `SELECT ROWS FROM Customer SORTED BY CustomerID`

   b. `SELECT * FROM Customer ORDER BY CustomerID`

   c. `SELECT DATA FROM Customer SORT BY CustomerID`

   d. `SELECT FROM Customer SORT BY CustomerID ASCENDING`

   e. `SELECT * FROM Customer SORT RECORDS BY CustomerID`

4. What two classes are used to provide navigational methods for a bound data source?

   a. `BindingSource, BindingNavigator`

   b. `DataSourceNavigator, DataSourceUserInterface`

   c. `DataSet, DataTable`

   d. `BoundTable, BoundField`

   e. none of the above

5. Which of the following statements is correct regarding a connection string?

   a. The `ConnectionString` class supports a property named `Provider`, which contains the name of the database provider. The name of the database is stored in the `DataBaseName` property.

   b. It consists of key-value pairs, which vary based on the database management system. That is, a connection string differs for a SQL Server database and a Microsoft Access database.

   c. Connection strings contain the same values no matter the database management system being used. This allows maximum flexibility when connecting to different types of databases.

   d. A connection string can be created using the Connection String Wizard.

   e. The `DataSet` class uses the `ConnectionString` class to establish a database connection.

6. Which of the following statements is correct regarding the TableAdapter?

    a. The class does not belong to the .NET Framework class library. The TableAdapter class and its code is automatically generated by the Data Source Configuration Wizard when a strongly typed `DataSet` is generated.

    b. It is a class supported by the .NET Framework class library and belongs to the `System.Data` namespace.

    c. The `TableAdapter` class inherits from the `DatabaseAdapter` class.

    d. The `TableAdapter` class is stored in a project in a file named TableAdapter.Designer.vb.

    e. none of the above

7. What is the purpose of the `System.Data.OleDbDataAdapter` class?

    a. It is used to convert data types from those compatible with Microsoft Access to those compatible with Visual Studio .NET.

    b. It is used to make different types of databases compatible with each other.

    c. It is used to make databases created in older versions of Microsoft Access or SQL Server compatible with Visual Studio .NET.

    d. It is used to retrieve records from a data source and populate a `DataSet` and `DataTable`, and to save changed data back to the database.

    e. It is used to import and export database data between ASCII files.

8. What is the purpose of the `OleDbCommand` object used by the `OleDbDataAdapter` class?

    a. It is used to establish a connection to the database.

    b. It stores a SQL statement that is sent to a database provider for execution.

    c. There is no relationship between the `OleDbCommand` class and the `OleDbDataAdatper` class.

    d. none of the above

9. Which of the following statements correctly describes how to bind a control instance to a data source?

    a. Set the `Bound` property of the control instance to `True`. Set the `BindingSource` property to the field in the `DataTable` to be bound.

    b. Set the `Binding` property of the control instance to a field in the data source.

    c. First, create an instance of the `DataBinding` class. Set the `Binding` property of the control instance to be bound to the instance of the `DataBinding` class.

    d. Create an instance of the `Binding` class and add that class instance to the `DataBindings` collection of the control instance to be bound.

    e. none of the above

10. Which of the following statements correctly stores a reference to the table named tblInventory appearing in the untyped `DataSet` named dsData, into the variable CurrentTable?

    a. `CurrentTable = dsData.Tables(tblInventory)`

    b. `CurrentTable = dsData.Tables("tblInventory")`

    c. `CurrentTable = dsData.tblInventory`

    d. `CurrentTable = dsData.Tables.tblInventory`

    e. none of the above

11. Which of the following are properties of the `DataTable` class?

    a. `Add, Change, Delete`

    b. `GetData, SaveData`

    c. `Rows, Columns`

    d. `CurrentRow, CurrentColumn`

    e. `RowCount, ColumnCount`

12. Which of the following statements gets the data type of the first column of the `DataTable` named tblClassroom?

    a. `Result = tblClassroom.Columns(1).Type`

    b. `Result = tblClassroom.Fields(0).DataType`

    c. `Result = tblClassroom.Column0.Type`

    d. `Result = tblClassroom.Fields(0).Type`

    e. `Result = tblClassroom.Columns(0).DataType`

13. Assume that a strongly typed `DataSet` exists named dsAccount having a `DataTable` named tblAccountNumber with a field named fldAccountBalance. Which of the following statements correctly references the field in the last row of the `DataTable`?

    a. `dsAccount.tblAccountNumber.Rows(Count). _`
        `fldAccountBalance`

    b. `dsAccount.tblAccountNumber.Rows(Count - 1). _`
        `fldAccountBalance`

    c. `dsAccount.tblAccountNumber.Rows.Last.fldAccountBalance`

    d. `dsAccount.tblAccountNumber.LastRow.fldAccountBalance`

    e. `dsAccount.tblAccountNumber.Rows(GetUpperBound). _`
       `fldAccountBalance`

14. Describe the steps to use the Data Source Configuration Wizard so as to configure a data source.

15. What is the purpose of the `Columns` collection of the `DataTable` class and the `DataColumn` object?

16. What is the relationship between a TableAdapter and the `OleDbDataAdapter`?

17. What is the relationship between a `DataSet`, a `DataTable`, and a `DataRow` class?

18. Describe the similarities and differences between an untyped `DataSet` and `DataTable` and a typed `DataSet` and `DataTable`.

# PROGRAMMING QUESTIONS

1. Assume that an instance of the `BindingSource` class exists named CurrentBindingSource. Write the statements to bind the class instance to the `DataSet` named dsAccounts containing the `DataTable` named tblTransactions.

2. Write the statement to populate the `OleDbDataAdapter` named odbDemo. Assume that the `DataTable` is named dtDemo.

3. Assume that a `BindingSource` exists named CurrentBindingSource. Write the statements to locate the first, next, previous, and last record.

4. Assume that a `BindingSource` exists named TblInventoryBindingSource. Write the statements to create a `PositionChanged` event handler for the class instance. In the event handler, display the current position and the number of records in the text boxes named txtPosition and txtCount, respectively.

5. Write the statement(s) to create an instance of the `Binding` class named CurrentBinding. Bind the `Text` property. Assume that the `BindingSource` is named TblAccountBindingSource and the field to be bound is named fldAccountDescription.

6. Assume that a `DataSet` exists named CurrentDataSet. Write the statements to print the name of all of the tables in the `DataSet` along with the number of rows in each table to the Console window.

7. Assume that an untyped `DataSet` named Payroll has a `DataTable` named tblPayroll with a field named fldGrossPay. Write the statements to examine all of the rows in the table. Using an accumulator named TotalGrossPay, tally the value of the field named fldGrossPay for all of the rows in the table. Also, calculate the average gross pay and store the result in the variable named AverageGrossPay.

8. Assume that an untyped `DataSet` exists named CustomersDataSet with a `DataTable` named tblCustomers having a `Boolean` field named fldActive. Using variables named Active and Inactive, accumulate the number of records (rows) having a value of `True` and `False` for the field's value.

9. Assume that an untyped `DataTable` exists named tblCustomer. Write the statements to print all of the field names to the Output window.

10. Assume that an untyped `DataTable` exists named tblCustomer. Write the statements to examine each of the table's columns. In accumulators named NumericFields, BooleanFields, and TextFields, count the number of numeric fields, `Boolean` fields, and textual fields, respectively. Numeric fields are those having a data type of Int16, Int32, Int64, Single, and Double.

11. Assume that a strongly typed `DataSet` exists named AccountsPayableDataSet having a `DataTable` named tblAccounts with a numeric field named fldBalance and a `Boolean` field named fldActive. Examine each record. If the field named fldActive has a value of `True`, add the value of the field named fldBalance to the accumulator named TotalActiveBalance. If the field named fldActive has a value of `False`, add the value of the field named fldBalance to the accumulator named TotalInactiveBalance.

12. Assume that a strongly typed `DataSet` exists named LoansDataSet having a table named tblLoans with fields named fldInterestRate and fldBalance. Write the statement to examine each row in the `DataTable`. Calculate the average interest rate storing the result in the variable AverageInterestRate. In addition, calculate the total of all balances storing the result in the accumulator named TotalBalance.

13. Assume that a strongly typed `DataSet` exists named PayrollDataSet having a `DataTable` named tblPayroll. Assume that the `DataTable` has two fields named fldHoursWorked and fldWage. Write the statements to multiply the two fields

together to calculate the gross pay. Using two accumulators, calculate the total gross pay for all rows and the total hours worked for all rows.

14. Write the statement to fill the TableAdapter named TblPayrollTableAdapter using the `DataSet` named PayrollDataSet and the `DataTable` named tblPayroll.

15. Write the statement to update the TableAdapter named TblPayrollTableAdapter using the `DataSet` named PayrollDataSet and the `DataTable` named tblPayroll.

# HANDS-ON PROJECTS

1. In this hands-on project, you will create an application that allows the end user to view database records and add, change, and delete those records.

   The database is named Inventory.mdb and contains a table named tblParts having the fields shown in Table 11-3.

| Field name | Description | Data type |
|---|---|---|
| fldPartNumber | Unique identification number | Integer |
| fldPartDescription | Description of part | String |
| fldCost | Cost of part | Single |
| fldSalesPrice | Sales price of part | Single |
| fldQuantityOnHand | Number of items in inventory | Integer |
| fldDiscontinued | True if the item is discontinued | Boolean |

Table 11-3: Fields in the tblParts table

a. A completed version of the solution appears in the file **Chapter.11\HandsOnProjects\Ch11HandsOnProject1.exe**.

b. Create a new solution named **Ch11HandsOnProject1.sln**.

c. Using the Data Source Configuration Wizard, establish a connection to the database. The connection you create should select all of the fields from the database table named tblParts.

d. Create the bound control instances on the form using the Data Sources window. Change the prompts as shown in the preview application.

e. Create an unbound control instance to calculate the gross profit for the current item. The gross profit is determined by subtracting the cost from the sales price. The value should be updated whenever the current record changes.

f. Create two unbound control instances to calculate the total value in inventory of the selected part at cost and the sales price. Multiply the cost by the quantity on hand to determine the total cost. Multiply the sales price by the quantity on hand to calculate the total sales value. These values should be updated whenever the current record changes.

g. Using the strongly typed `DataSet` and `DataTable` classes generated by the Data Source Configuration Wizard, examine each record in the DataTable. Calculate the following values and display the results on a second form:

» Calculate the total number of items in inventory.

» Calculate the total value of inventory at cost.

» Calculate the total value of inventory at the sales price.

» Calculate the total value of discontinued items both at cost and at the sales price.

h. On the main form, create the code for the button to display the form you created in the previous step.

i. On the main form, create a button and corresponding `Click` event handler that will allow you to write the contents of the `DataTable` to a sequential file. The file should be created such that a comma separates each record.

j. Create a button that will display a message box containing the number of discontinued inventory items, the number of inventory items that are not discontinued, and the total count of all inventory items.

2. In this hands-on project, you will create an application that allows the user to add, change, and delete records from a database table. The database is named Customers and contains a single table named tblCustomers.

Table 11-4 describes the fields on the table named tblCustomers.

| Field name | Description | Data type |
|---|---|---|
| fldID | Unique identification number | Integer |
| fldFirstName | First name | String |
| fldLastName | Last name | String |
| fldAddress | Customer address | String |
| fldCity | Customer city | String |
| fldState | Customer state | String |
| fldZipCode | Customer zip code | String |
| fldAnnualSales | Annual sales amount | Double |
| fldBalanceDue | Balance due on account | Double |
| fldCreditLimit | Customer credit limit | Double |

Table 11-4: Fields in the tblCustomers table

a. A completed version of the solution appears in the file **Chapter.11\HandsOnProjects\Ch11HandsOnProject2.exe**.

b. Create a new solution named **Ch11HandsOnProject2.sln**.

c. Using the Data Source Configuration Wizard, establish a connection to the database. The connection you create should select all of the fields from the database table named tblCustomers.

d. Create the bound control instances on the form using the Data Sources window. Change the prompts to match the preview application.

e. Create an unbound control instance to calculate available credit for the current record. Subtract the credit limit from the balance due to determine the available credit.

f. Based on the annual sales, calculate the monthly sales. Divide the annual sales by 12 to determine the monthly sales. This value should be updated whenever the current record changes.

g. If the customer is over their credit limit, display a message in a `Label` control instance.

h. On a second form display the total outstanding credit (balance due) for all customers along with the total outstanding credit limits for all customers. Create a button on the main form to display this second form as a modal dialog box.

i. Create a button on the main form and a `Click` event handler that will write the database table to a comma-separated ASCII file. The end user should specify the filename using an instance of the `SaveFileDialog` control.

3. In this hands-on project, you will create an application that works with data involving date and time values. The database for this hands-on project is named Telephone.mdb.

Table 11-5 describes the fields in the table named tblPhoneLogs.

| Field name | Description | Data type |
| --- | --- | --- |
| fldCallID | Unique identification number | Integer |
| fldCallIn | Call originator | String |
| fldCallOut | Call destination | String |
| fldStartTime | Starting date and time of call | DateTime |
| fldEndTime | Ending date and time of call | DateTime |
| fldPeakNonPeak | Peak call time | Boolean |

Table 11-5: Fields in the tblPhoneLogs table

a. A completed version of the solution appears in the file **Chapter.11\HandsOnProjects\Ch11HandsOnProject3.exe**.

b. Create a new solution named **Ch11HandsOnProject3.sln**.

c. Using the Data Source Configuration Wizard, establish a connection to the database. The connection you create should select all of the records from the table named tblPhoneLogs.

d. Create the bound control instances on the form using the Data Sources window.

e. Create the necessary unbound control instances on the form to display the elapsed number of hours, minutes, and seconds for the current call record.

f. Create the necessary event handler to display the number of elapsed hours, minutes, and seconds, based on the starting and ending time of the call.

g. Create an input box in which the end user will enter a Call ID number. Based on the value entered by the end user, search through the rows in the `DataTable`. When the corresponding row is found, make this record the current record.

h. Create a button that will display the total duration of all peak time and non–peak time calls. Display the result in a message box.

4. In this hands-on project, you will create an application that works with payroll data. The database for this hands-on project is named Payroll.mdb

a. Create a new solution named **Ch11HandsOnProject4.sln**.

b. Using the Data Source Configuration Wizard, establish a connection to the database named **Chapter.11\Data\Payroll.mdb**. The connection you create should select all of the records from the table named tblEmployees. The table has the following fields and data types: fldID – Integer, fldFirstName – String, fldLastName – String, fldDepartment – String, fldEmployeeType – String, fldDeductions – Integer, fldWage – Double, fldPension– Boolean.

c. Create the bound control instances on the main form using the Data Sources window.

d. Create a second form that will display the payroll records corresponding to the currently selected employee. In this second form, create an unbound `DataGridView` control instance. Using the `DataTable`, search each record, and add only those records to the `DataGridView` that have the corresponding ID number. For each row, calculate the gross pay by multiplying the employee's wage by the number of hours worked by the employee for the pay period.

e. Display in a `TextBox` the total gross pay for all of the payroll records.

# 12

# DRAWING AND MOUSE EVENTS

**After completing this chapter, you will be able to:**

Describe the purpose of the graphics device interface (GDI)

Create custom colors and use the `ColorDialog` control

Use named pens and brushes and create custom pens
   and brushes

Create shapes and paint them on the screen

Create event handlers for mouse events

# CONCEPT LESSON

# INTRODUCTION TO DRAWING

Windows supplies a set of drawing services collectively referred to as the **graphics device interface (GDI)**. The GDI is made up of several classes used to define shapes, such as lines, rectangles, ellipses, arcs, and pies. It also supplies methods to draw those shapes to an output device such as a monitor or printer. To understand the purpose of the GDI, think of the task of drawing a line between two points. As you are likely aware, a computer monitor displays many dots called **pixels**. Each pixel has an $x$ and $y$ coordinate value. Personal computers are often configured to display 1280 pixels along one axis and 1024 pixels along the other axis, but many other screen resolutions are possible. Thus, a computer displaying 1280 by 1024 pixels would display a total of 1,310,720 pixels.

Without the GDI, drawing a line would require you to calculate the position of each pixel on the line and draw it one pixel at a time. Instead of drawing shapes pixel by pixel, the GDI defines the characteristics of various shapes, such as a line, and provides methods to draw those shapes to a **graphics surface**. In Visual Studio, a graphics surface is an object that supplies the interface to draw graphical shapes. This object can be connected to a form, a `PictureBox` control instance, or a printer. For example, using the GDI, it is possible to define the endpoints of a line, and then draw that line to a graphics surface by specifying the line's endpoints, the color, and the thickness of the line.

## INTRODUCTION TO THE PAINT EVENT

As you know, control instances are visible objects that are created on a form using the Toolbox. Visual Studio renders those control instances on the form, and handles their events. The process of drawing shapes with the GDI works much differently, as described in the following list:

» GDI shapes are always drawn on a graphics surface programmatically. There is no visual design-time mechanism to draw GDI shapes on a graphics surface.

» GDI shapes have no events. That is, when a graphical shape is drawn on a graphics surface using the GDI, the end user has no interaction with that shape.

» GDI shapes can only be drawn directly on a graphics surface, such as a form, or in an instance of the `PictureBox` control. It's also possible to draw graphical shapes in selected container controls.

**»NOTE**
The GDI draws two-dimensional shapes. It does not support three-dimensional graphics.

## THE CLASSES AND STRUCTURES OF THE GDI

Creating and drawing shapes is accomplished using the following types supported by the .NET Framework class library. Collectively, these types form the GDI.

» The `System.Drawing` namespace contains classes and structures used to define two-dimensional shapes and elements used by those two-dimensional shapes. These classes do not draw shapes to an output device. They merely define a shape, such as a rectangle, or the visual characteristics of a shape, such as the shape's color.

» The `System.Drawing.Drawing2D` namespace contains classes and structures that define additional graphical shapes. This namespace and its methods are not supported by Windows 95 or Windows 98.

» The `System.Drawing.Graphics` class is part of the `System.Drawing` namespace and contains the methods used to draw graphical shapes, such as lines and rectangles, to a graphics surface.

The purpose of the types that make up the `System.Drawing` namespace is threefold, as described in the following list:

» The `System.Drawing` namespace contains structures used to create a few graphical shapes, such as a `Rectangle` and a `Point`.

» It contains other structures and classes used to describe the visual characteristics of graphical shapes. For example, the `System.Drawing.Color` structure is used to describe the color of another object, such as a `Pen`, which is used to draw lines.

» It contains the `System.Drawing.Graphics` class, which is used to draw various graphical shapes to a graphics surface.

## DRAWING A FIRST SHAPE ON A FORM

The topics of graphics and drawing are interrelated. Thus, to get the process started, you will see how to draw the simplest of shapes, a line, on a form. The following code segment shows how to draw a red line on a form:

```
Private Sub frmMain_Paint(ByVal sender As Object, _
    ByVal e As System.Windows.Forms.PaintEventArgs) _
    Handles Me.Paint
    e.Graphics.DrawLine(Pens.Red, 10, 10, 150, 150)
End Sub
```

The preceding statements are all that is required to draw a red line inside the visible region of a form. Figure 12-1 shows the line drawn by the preceding statements.

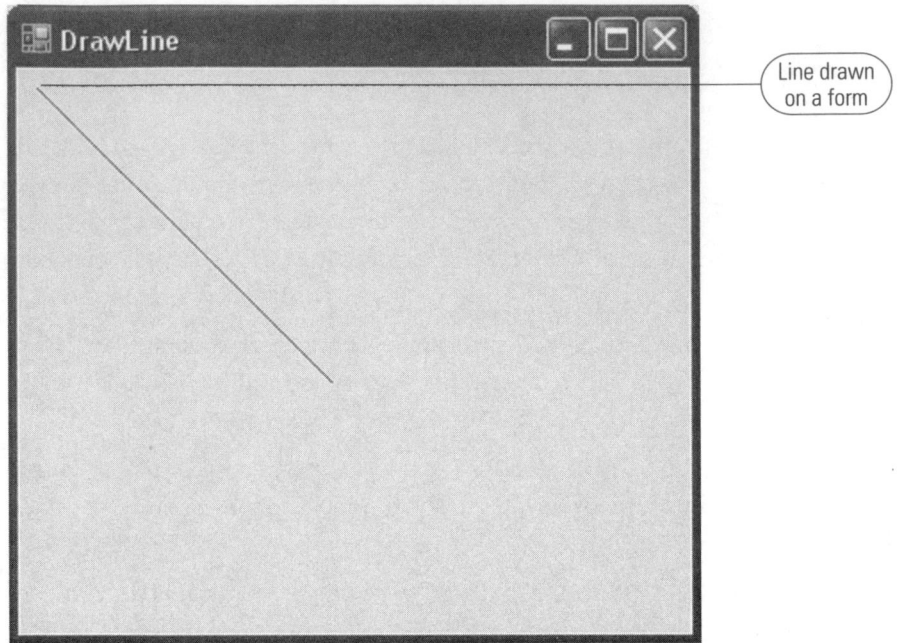

Figure 12-1: Drawing a line

The following points can be made about the preceding event handler:

» The code handles the `Paint` event. Windows fires the `Paint` event when rendering a form. All drawing operations are performed in the `Paint` event handler.

» The data type of the second argument is `System.Windows.Forms.PaintEventArgs`. This argument contains a reference to the `Graphics` class. The methods of the `Graphics` class perform all drawing operations. Thus, the statement fragment `e.Graphics` references an instance of the `Graphics` class.

» The call to the `DrawLine` method draws a line on the form. The arguments to the `DrawLine` method include a named pen (`Pens.Red`). Pens are used to draw lines and create an outline of other shapes, such as a rectangle. The final four arguments to the `DrawLine` method define the line's endpoints.

Having seen the process to draw the most simple of graphical shapes, you will now explore, in detail, the classes and structures that make up the GDI, and how to use them.

# UNDERSTANDING THE PAINT EVENT

When Windows begins to draw a form on the screen, the Paint event fires. The Paint event also applies to the PictureBox control. Thus, graphical shapes are drawn directly on the form or to an instance of the PictureBox control. Windows redraws a form (fires the Paint event) in the following situations:

» The Paint event fires when the form is drawn on the screen the first time.

» The Paint event fires when the end user resizes a form.

» The Paint event also fires when a minimized form is restored or maximized.

» The Paint event fires if an obscured or partially obscured form is no longer obscured.

» The Paint event fires when the Invalidate method of the underlying form or PictureBox control instance is called.

The second argument to the Paint event handler has a data type of PaintEventArgs. It also has a property named Graphics. The Graphics object referenced by the Graphics property provides the link to the GDI.

# UNDERSTANDING COLOR

Computer monitors display different colors by combining varying intensities of red, green, and blue. Because colors are made from red, green, and blue components, the term **RGB** is used.

Each RGB value ranges from 0 to 255. A value of zero indicates that none of the color is applied. A value of 255 indicates that the color is applied at its full intensity. Table 12-1 lists selected RGB values and the colors created. As shown in Table 12-1, setting all three RGB values to zero produces black and setting all three values to 255 produces white.

> **» NOTE**
>
> In addition to the RGB values, a fourth value, called the *alpha value*, defines the transparency or opacity of a color.

| Red value | Green value | Blue value | Color created by the combination of the values |
|:---:|:---:|:---:|---|
| 0 | 0 | 0 | Black |
| 255 | 255 | 255 | White |
| 255 | 0 | 0 | Red |
| 0 | 255 | 0 | Green |
| 0 | 0 | 255 | Blue |
| 238 | 130 | 255 | Violet |

Table 12-1: Sample RGB colors

Because each part of a color is a value between 0 and 255, each RGB component can be stored in an unsigned byte. A color is stored in 4 bytes or as an unsigned integer (UInteger) data type.

One way to define a color is to use named properties supplied by the Color structure. Each named color stores a color and there is a named color for each of the Web colors. To illustrate, the following statements show how to use named colors to set the background and foreground color of a Label control instance named lblDemo:

```
lblDemo.BackColor = Color.Gray
lblDemo.ForeColor = Color.DarkBlue
```

The preceding statements store the colors gray and dark blue in the BackColor and ForeColor properties of a label. Both properties have a data type of Color.

## CREATING CUSTOM COLORS

In addition to using named colors, the Color structure and its members can be used to create custom colors. The Color structure has the following members:

## Syntax

The `System.Drawing.Color` structure has properties to get the RGB components of a color and to create a custom color from RGB values.

### Public Properties

» The `R` property gets the red component of a color.

» The `G` property gets the green component of a color.

» The `B` property gets the blue component of a color.

### Public Methods

» The `FromArgb` method creates a color from its component RGB values.

» The `ToArgb` method returns the 32-bit `Integer` value representing a color.

To illustrate how to work with a color, the following code segment prints the RGB values for the named color `Color.Azure`:

```
Dim CurrentColor As Color = System.Drawing.Color.Azure
Console.WriteLine(CurrentColor.R.ToString)
Console.WriteLine(CurrentColor.G.ToString)
Console.WriteLine(CurrentColor.B.ToString)
```

The `FromArgb` method of the `Color` structure is used to create a custom color and has the following syntax:

## Syntax

```
Public Shared Function FromArgb(ByVal red As Integer, ByVal
green As Integer, ByVal blue As Integer) As Color
```

### Definition

The static `FromArgb` method creates a color from an RGB value. Valid RGB values range from 0 to 255. The method returns a `Color` structure.

### Parameters

» The method creates a new color using the *red*, *green*, and *blue* values, respectively.

### Code Example

```
Dim CustomColor As Color = _
    System.Drawing.Color.FromArgb(18, 127, 222)
lblDemo.BackColor = CustomColor
```

### Code Dissection

The first statement creates a custom color using RGB values and stores the color in the variable named CustomColor. The final statement sets the `BackColor` property of a label to the color stored in the variable named CustomColor.

## THE COLORDIALOG CONTROL

The `ColorDialog` control displays a standard dialog box from which the end user can select a color. The `ColorDialog` control works the same way as the other Visual Basic common dialog controls. That is, the `ShowDialog` method is called to display the dialog box. The control instance is not visible to the end user so it appears in the tray below the Windows Forms Designer. Figure 12-2 shows the Color dialog box.

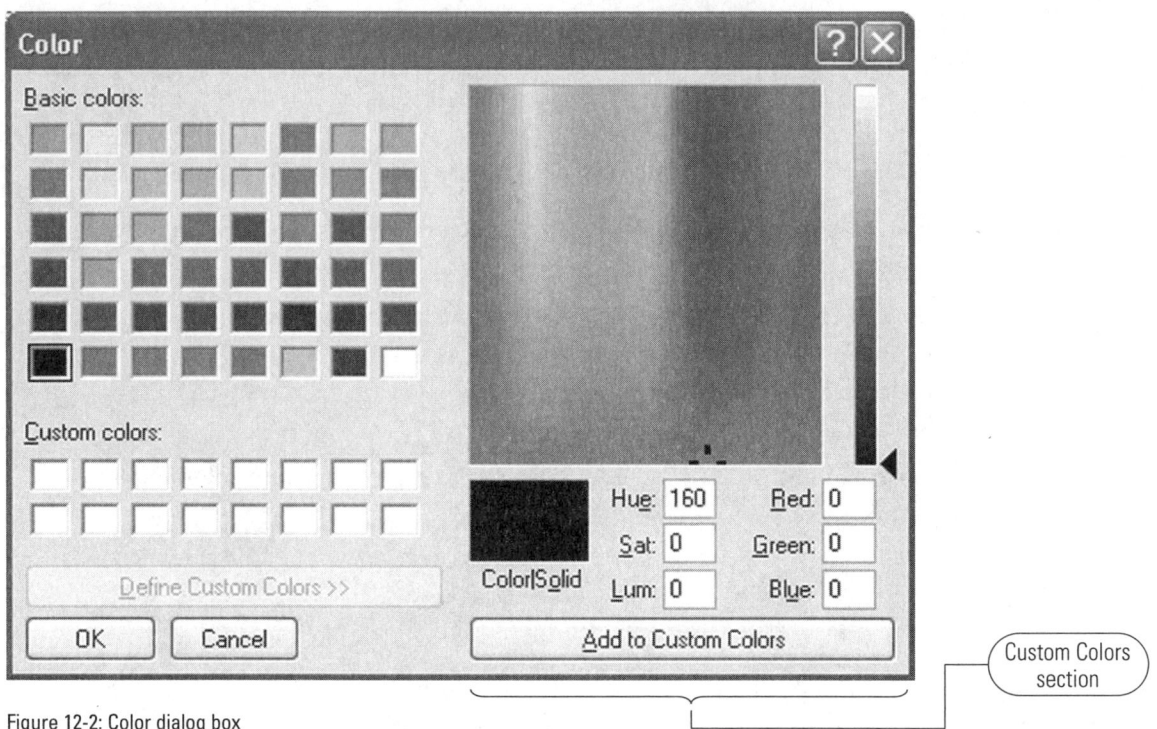

Figure 12-2: Color dialog box

Figure 12-2 shows the Color dialog box with the Custom Colors section expanded. By clicking OK, the end user selects a color, which is stored in the `Color` property. The data type of the `Color` property is `System.Drawing.Color`.

The following code segment shows how to display a `ColorDialog` control instance named cdCurrent and set a color:

```
Dim Result As DialogResult
Result = cdCurrent.ShowDialog()
If Result = Windows.Forms.DialogResult.OK Then
    picColor.BackColor = cdCurrent.Color
End If
```

As shown in the preceding code segment, the `ColorDialog` is displayed by calling the `ShowDialog` method. If the end user clicks OK, the `BackColor` property of the `PictureBox` control instance named picColor is set to the color selected by the end user.

In this exploration exercise, you will examine the RGB components of a specific color, and see how to create custom colors:

1. Start Visual Studio and open the solution file in the folder named **Chapter.12\Chapter12ConceptLesson**.

2. Run the application and click the **Color** tab, if necessary. Figure 12-3 shows the Color tab with selections already made.

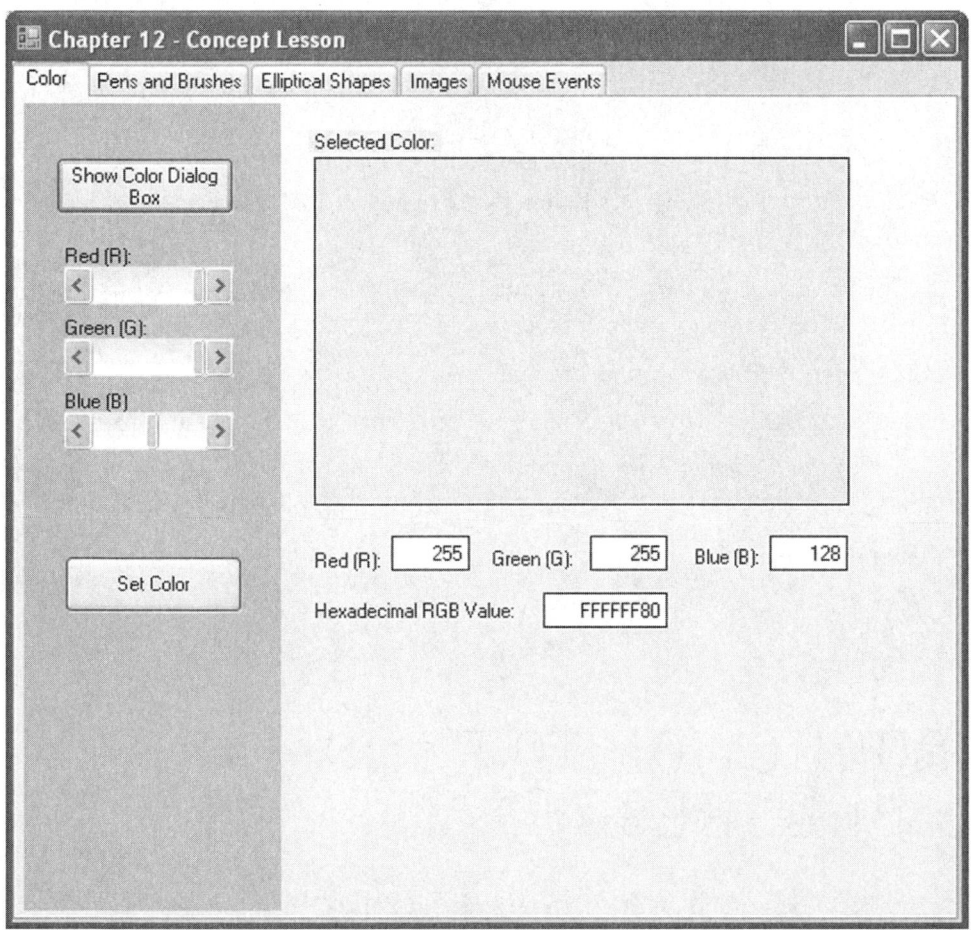

Figure 12-3: Concept lesson—Color tab

3. Click the **Show Color Dialog Box** button. The Color dialog box opens. Select a color or create a custom color, and then click **OK**. To create a custom color, you must click **Define Custom Colors**, select the color, and then click the **Add to Custom Colors** button. Finally, select the custom color to use it. The selected color appears as the background color in the picture box. In addition, the labels display the corresponding RGB values, along with the hexadecimal value of the color.

4. Using the scroll bars, select different RGB values, and then click the **Set Color** button. The RGB values are used to set the color. The background color of the picture box is updated along with the RGB values appearing in the output labels.

## MINI-QUIZ 1

1. What are the minimum and maximum values for an RGB color component?

2. Which of the following statements is correct regarding the `FromArgb` method?

   a. The `FromArgb` method of the `Graphics` class is used to get the RGB colors supported by the computer system.

   b. The method is used to create named colors.

   c. The `FromArgb` method accepts one argument—a color—and returns the composite RGB values from that color.

   d. The method is used to create a custom color from composite RGB values.

   e. none of the above

3. What RGB values would you use to create the color white?

# INTRODUCTION TO PENS AND BRUSHES

The `System.Drawing` and `System.Drawing.Drawing2D` namespaces have classes that describe how a shape will be drawn on a graphics surface. The following list introduces these classes:

» The `Pens` class is made up of members that define named pens representing each of the standard system and Web colors. For example, the named red pen is `Pens.Red`. Named pens use named colors.

» The Pen class is used to create custom pens. A custom Pen has a color and a width.

» The Brushes class is made up of members to define named brushes. Named brushes represent each of the standard system and Web colors. For example, the named red brush is Brushes.Red.

» The SolidBrush class defines a brush made up of a single color. A SolidBrush is used to fill the interior region of a shape, such as a rectangle, instead of drawing an outline of the shape. There are also custom brushes that belong to the System.Drawing.Drawing2D namespace.

## USING PENS TO OUTLINE SHAPES

A Pen can be categorized as a named pen or a custom pen. Named pens use standard Web colors. Custom pens typically use custom colors and can have custom line characteristics.

The following code segment shows how to use a named pen to draw a line:

```
e.Graphics.DrawLine(Pens.Red, 10, 10, 150, 150)
```

The preceding statement draws a line using a named pen (Pens.Red).

The System.Drawing.Pen constructor is used to create a custom pen, which you use to draw lines and outline rectangles and other shapes, and has the following syntax:

### Syntax

```
Public Sub New(ByVal color As Color)
Public Sub New(ByVal color As Color, ByVal width As Single)
```

### Definition

The Pen constructor creates a Pen object using an existing *color*. This existing color can be a named color or a custom color created by calling the FromArgb method.

### Parameters

» The first constructor creates a new Pen object using an existing *color* structure as an argument. The Pen is 1 pixel wide.

» The second constructor creates a new Pen using an existing *color*. The thickness of the pen is defined by the *width* argument, which is measured in pixels.

*(Continued)* ▶

### Code Example

```
Dim CurrentColor As Color = Color.FromArgb(122, 89, 94)
Dim CurrentPen1Pixel As New Pen(CurrentColor)
Dim CurrentPen2Pixel As New Pen(CurrentColor, 2)
e.Graphics.DrawLine(CurrentPen1Pixel, 10, 10, 150, 150)
e.Graphics.DrawLine(CurrentPen2Pixel, 10, 10, 150, 150)
```

### Code Dissection

The first of the preceding statements creates a custom color using the `FromArgb` method of the `Color` structure. The second statement creates a custom `Pen` using the color created in the first statement. The `Pen` has a default width of 1 pixel. The third statement also creates a custom `Pen` using the same custom color but the `Pen` is 2 pixels wide instead of 1 pixel wide. The final two statements draw a line on the graphics surface using the two different pens.

> **» NOTE**
>
> There are many other configurable options related to pens that are not discussed in this chapter. For example, it's possible to create pens that draw lines having custom patterns and to configure the endpoints of the line drawn with a Pen.

When working with a custom `Pen` instead of a named `Pen`, it is important to dispose of the `Pen` when you are finished using it. Calling the `Dispose` method destroys the `Pen` and the resources allocated to it so that those resources can be used for other purposes.

The following code segment shows how to dispose of a custom `Pen`:

```
Dim CurrentColor As Color = Color.FromArgb(122, 89, 94)
Dim CurrentPen1Pixel As New Pen(CurrentColor)
' Statements that use the Pen.
CurrentPen1Pixel.Dispose()
```

## USING BRUSHES TO FILL SHAPES

A `Pen` is used to draw the outline of a shape, whereas a `Brush` is used to fill the region of a shape. Just as you can use a named `Pen` and create custom ones, it is also possible to use a named `Brush` and to create custom ones.

Brushes have different types. That is, the .NET Framework supports several classes that are derived from the abstract `Brush` class, as shown in Figure 12-4.

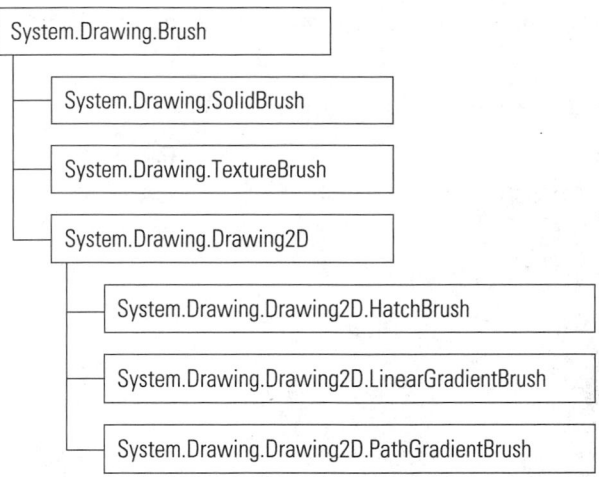

Figure 12-4: Hierarchical organization of the Brush classes

As shown in Figure 12-4, six classes inherit from the System.Drawing.Brush class. Only the HatchBrush and SolidBrush classes are discussed in this chapter.

## FILLING SHAPES WITH THE SOLIDBRUSH CLASS

A named Brush has a data type of SolidBrush and works the same way as a named Pen, as the following statements show:

```
Dim CurrentBrush As SolidBrush
CurrentBrush = System.Drawing.Brushes.Red
```

The preceding statements declare a variable named CurrentBrush and store a named Brush in the variable. The statement is redundant as the named Brush could just as well be used. The same colors are defined for both named Pens and named Brushes.

The System.Drawing.SolidBrush constructor is used to create an instance of the SolidBrush class, which can then be used to fill rectangles or other shapes. The constructor accepts one argument: a Color structure.

The following statements show how to create a solid brush using a custom color:

```
Dim CustomBrush As New System.Drawing.SolidBrush( _
    System.Drawing.Color.FromArgb(17, 22, 84))
    ' Statements that use the brush.
CustomBrush.Dispose()
```

The first statement creates a SolidBrush using a custom color created from the FromArgb method of the Color structure. Just as a custom Pen should be disposed, so too should a custom SolidBrush. The final statement takes care of this task.

In addition to using a `SolidBrush` to fill a shape, it's possible to use another kind of brush, called a `HatchBrush`.

## FILLING SHAPES WITH THE HATCHBRUSH CLASS

The `HatchBrush` class applies to the `System.Drawing.Drawing2D` namespace instead of the `System.Drawing` namespace. The class is used to define a brush containing a pattern called a hatch pattern.

The `HatchBrush` constructor has the following syntax:

### Syntax

```
Public Sub New(hatchStyle As HatchStyle, foreColor As Color)
Public Sub New(hatchStyle As HatchStyle, foreColor As Color,
backColor As Color)
```

### Definition

The `HatchBrush` constructor creates a hatched brush with a particular hatch pattern.

### Parameters

» The first argument named *hatchStyle* defines the hatch pattern that will be applied to the brush. In total, about 50 different styles can be applied. The `HatchStyle` enumeration of the `System.Drawing.Drawing2D` namespace contains the enumerated values.

» The *foreColor* argument defines the color of the brush (hatch pattern). By default, the hatch pattern is white.

» The *backColor* argument defines the background color of the brush itself. By default, the background color is black.

### Code Example

```
Dim CurrentBrush As New _
    System.Drawing.Drawing2D.HatchBrush( _
    System.Drawing.Drawing2D.HatchStyle.Cross, _
    Color.Aqua, Color.DarkGreen)
```

### Code Dissection

The preceding statement creates a new `HatchBrush` and stores it in the variable named CurrentBrush. The brush is created using a `Cross` style. The foreground and background colors are specified using the named colors `Color.Aqua` and `Color.DarkGreen`, respectively.

Having seen how to use colors to create pens and different types of brushes, you will now see how they are used in the process of creating and drawing shapes.

# CREATING AND DRAWING LINES AND RECTANGLES

Three shapes supported by the .NET Framework appear in the System.Drawing namespace, as described in the following list:

» The Point structure defines the *x* and *y* coordinates of a point on the drawing surface. Points are used to define the endpoints of a line and the position of a rectangle.

» The Size structure is used to define the width and height of another graphical shape, such as a Rectangle.

» The Rectangle structure is used to define the origin of a rectangle on the drawing surface and the size of the rectangle. The Rectangle structure is also used as the basis for many other graphical shapes, such as arcs and ellipses. There is no Square structure. To create a square, create a Rectangle with the same height and width.

Each of the preceding types is interrelated, along with the pens and brushes discussed previously. To help understand the role of these types and their relationships, examine the following code segment:

```
Private Sub frmMain_Paint(ByVal sender As Object, _
    ByVal e As System.Windows.Forms.PaintEventArgs) _
    Handles Me.Paint
    Dim Origin As New Point(10, 10)
    Dim CurrentSize As New Size(150, 150)
    Dim CurrentBrush As New _
        System.Drawing.Drawing2D.HatchBrush( _
        System.Drawing.Drawing2D.HatchStyle.Cross, _
        Color.Aqua, Color.DarkGreen)
    Dim CurrentRectangle As New Rectangle(Origin, CurrentSize)
    e.Graphics.FillRectangle(CurrentBrush, CurrentRectangle)
    e.Graphics.DrawRectangle(Pens.Black, CurrentRectangle)
End Sub
```

The preceding Paint event handler fills a rectangle with a hatch brush and then outlines the rectangle with a named black pen. The following list briefly describes the statements in the event handler:

» The first statement defines a point.

» The second statement defines a size that is 150 by 150 pixels.

» The third statement creates a new `HatchBrush`.

» The fourth statement creates a new `Rectangle`. The arguments to the `Rectangle` constructor define the position of the rectangle and the size of the rectangle, respectively.

» The fifth statement paints a filled rectangle using the brush.

» The final statement draws an outline of the rectangle using a named pen (`Pens.Black`).

Figure 12-5 shows the rectangle created by executing the statements in the preceding code segment.

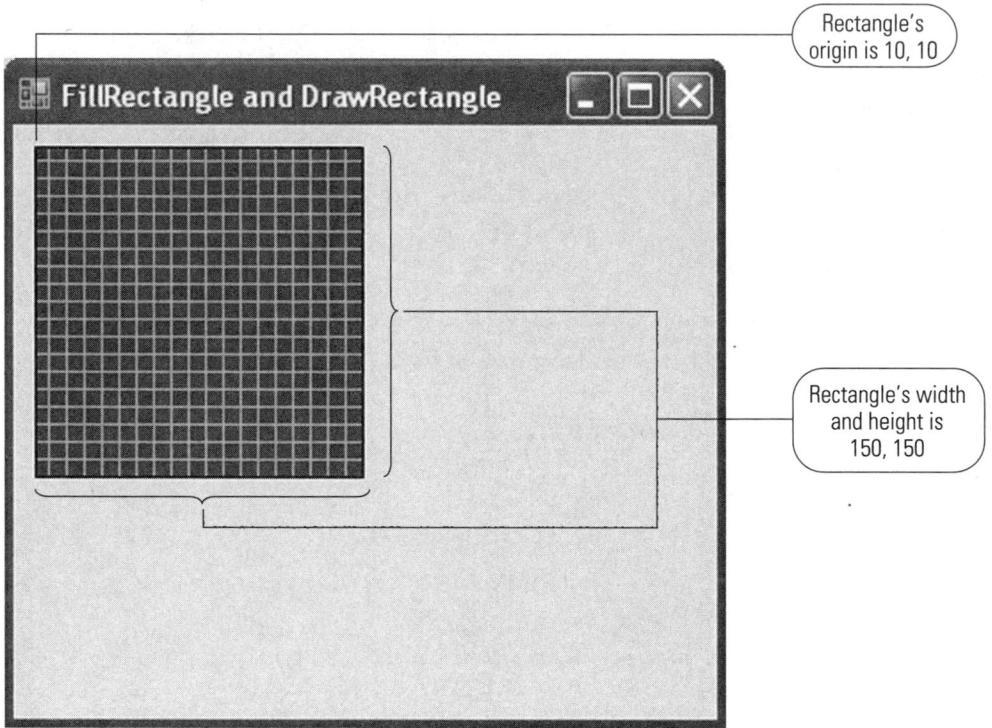

Figure 12-5: Filling and outlining a rectangle

## THE POINT AND SIZE STRUCTURES

The purpose of the `System.Drawing.Point` structure is simple: It specifies a point (pixel) on the drawing surface. The `Point` structure has the following uses:

» One `Point` structure is used to specify the origin of a rectangle or other shape.

» Two `Point` structures are used to specify the endpoints of a line.

The `Point` constructor has the following syntax:

### Syntax
```
Public Sub New(ByVal x As Integer, ByVal y As Integer)
```

### Definition
The `Point` constructor accepts two arguments containing the *x* and *y* coordinates of the point. The coordinate values are measured in pixels.

### Parameters
» The *x* argument defines the horizontal distance from the left side of the form's client area to the point. The client area of a form is that part of the form below the title bar and inside the form's borders.

» The *y* argument defines the vertical distance from the top of the form's client area to the point.

### Code Example
```
Dim CurrentPoint As New Point(10, 10)
```

### Code Dissection
The preceding statement defines a point 10 pixels to the right and 10 pixels down from the origin of the form or `PictureBox` control instance.

## THE SIZE STRUCTURE

The `Size` structure is commonly used with the `Point` structure to define the size of a rectangle or other shape. The constructor has the following syntax:

### Syntax
```
Public Sub New(ByVal width As Integer, ByVal height As Integer)
```

### Definition
The `Size` structure defines the size of a rectangle.

### Parameters
» The *width* argument defines the horizontal distance of the rectangle. The unit of measure is pixels.

» The *height* argument defines the vertical distance of the rectangle. The unit of measure is pixels.

### Code Example
```
Dim CurrentSize As New Size(150, 150)
```

### Code Dissection
The preceding statement creates a rectangular `Size` about 2 inches wide and 2 inches high.

As you know, a form has a property named `Size` that defines the size of the form, including the border and the title bar. When drawing graphics, it is often necessary to determine the size of the form's client area. A form's **client area** is that region of the form excluding the form's border and title bar. The size of a form's client area is stored in the form's `ClientSize` property, which has a data type of `Size`.

The following statement illustrates the use of the `ClientSize` property:

```
btnFill.Size = Me.ClientSize
btnFill.Height = Me.ClientSize.Height
btnFill.Width = Me.ClientSize.Width
```

The first of the preceding statements reads the client size of the form using the `Me` object. The form's client size is stored in the `Size` property of the button named btnFill, thereby making the button the same size as the form. The second and third statements have the same effect as the first statement.

## DRAWING RECTANGLES

Having seen the elements that make up a shape, you will now see how a rectangle is drawn to a graphics surface. The `System.Drawing.Rectangle` structure is used to define a rectangular shape. There are two ways to create a `Rectangle` and paint it to the graphics surface.

One way to define the shape of a `Rectangle` is to create an instance of both the `Point` and `Size` structures. The `Point` structure defines the upper-left corner of the `Rectangle`. The `Size` structure defines the size of the `Rectangle`. It is also possible to create the rectangle using coordinate values. The `Rectangle` created is used as an argument to the `DrawRectangle` and `FillRectangle` methods of the `Graphics` class.

```
Dim CurrentPoint As New Point(10, 10)
Dim CurrentSize As New Size(150, 150)
Dim FirstRectangle As New Rectangle(CurrentPoint, CurrentSize)
Dim SecondRectangle As New Rectangle(10, 10, 150, 150)
```

The first two statements create `Point` and `Size` structures. The third statement creates a new `Rectangle` using those structures. The final statement declares a variable and creates an instance of the `Rectangle` using the *x* and *y* coordinates followed by the *width* and the *height*. Both rectangles have the same origin and the same size.

Using the second technique, the `DrawRectangle` and `FillRectangle` methods of the `Graphics` class are also used. However, their arguments contain *x* and *y* coordinate values along with the rectangle's height and width.

After a `Rectangle` has been created, it can be painted on the drawing surface.

## PAINTING RECTANGLES ON A DRAWING SURFACE

The DrawRectangle method is used to draw the outline of a Rectangle using a named or custom Pen.

The following code segment shows two ways to draw a rectangle outline by calling the overloaded DrawRectangle method:

```
Private Sub frmMain_Paint(ByVal sender As Object, _
    ByVal e As System.Windows.Forms.PaintEventArgs) _
    Handles Me.Paint
    Dim CurrentRectangle As New Rectangle(10, 10, 150, 150)
    e.Graphics.DrawRectangle(Pens.Black, CurrentRectangle)
    e.Graphics.DrawRectangle(Pens.Black, 10, 10, 150, 150)
End Sub
```

The preceding event handler contains statements to draw a Rectangle using a named Pen. The first statement in the event handler creates a rectangle. The second statement uses the Graphics object supplied as an argument to the Paint event handler to draw the rectangle outline.

The first call to the DrawRectangle method uses an existing Pen and Rectangle as the first and second arguments, respectively. The second call to the DrawRectangle method uses an existing Pen, but the Rectangle is created using the *x*, *y*, *width*, and *height* arguments.

The arguments to the DrawRectangle method cause a 2-inch square rectangle to be drawn 10 pixels from the upper-left corner of the form.

The FillRectangle method fills the region of a Rectangle using a Brush. Other than replacing the Pen with a Brush, the arguments to the FillRectangle method are the same as the arguments to the DrawRectangle method.

```
Private Sub frmMain_Paint(ByVal sender As Object, _
    ByVal e As System.Windows.Forms.PaintEventArgs) _
    Handles Me.Paint
    Dim CurrentRectangle As New Rectangle(10, 10, 150, 150)
    e.Graphics.FillRectangle(Brushes.Black, CurrentRectangle)
    e.Graphics.FillRectangle(Brushes.Black, 10, 10, 150, 150)
End Sub
```

As shown in the preceding Paint event handler, the arguments to the FillRectangle method are nearly the same as the arguments to the DrawRectangle method. The first argument contains a Brush instead of a Pen, however.

## DRAWING LINES

The DrawLine method of the System.Graphics class draws a line between two points using two Point structures or a pair of *x* and *y* coordinates, as shown in the following statements:

```
Dim StartPoint As New Point(10, 10)
Dim EndPoint As New Point(150, 150)
e.Graphics.DrawLine(Pens.Red, StartPoint, EndPoint)
e.Graphics.DrawLine(Pens.Red, 10, 10, 150, 150)
```

The first call to the DrawLine method draws a line using existing Pen and Point objects. The second and third arguments define the line's starting point and the line's endpoint. Both arguments contain existing Point structures.

The second call to the DrawLine method also uses an existing Pen object as its first argument. However, instead of using existing Point structures, the second and third arguments contain the *x, y* coordinates of the line's starting point. The fourth and fifth arguments contain the *x, y* coordinates of the line's endpoint. Figure 12-6 shows the line created by executing the statements in the preceding Paint event handler.

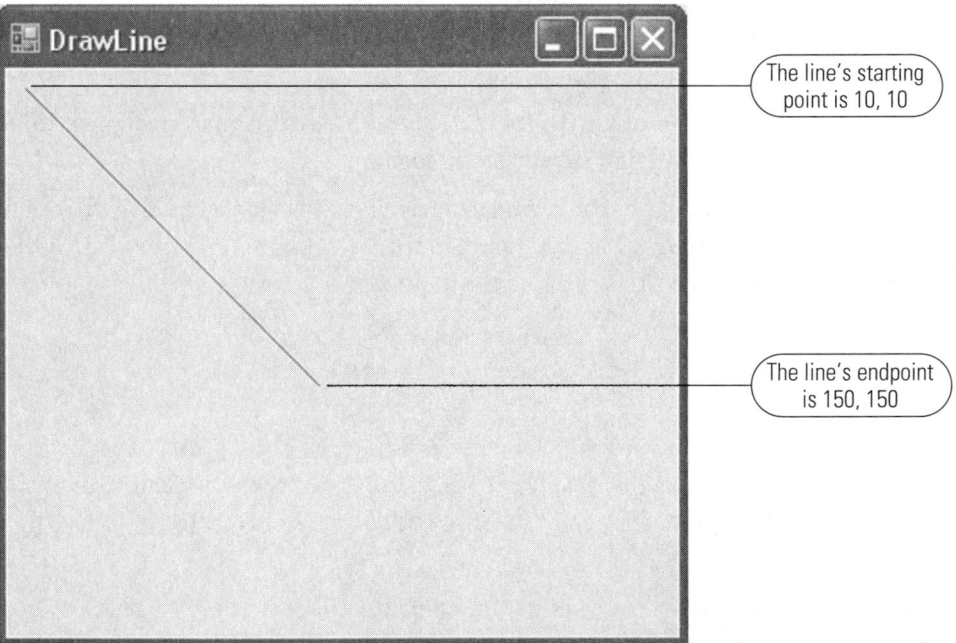

Figure 12-6: Drawing a line on a form

In this exploration exercise, you will see how to work with custom pens and brushes and how they are used to outline the region of a rectangle or fill the region of a rectangle. If you examine the code for the buttons that draw the shapes, you will see that they each store a value in a module-level variable, and call the `Invalidate` method of the picture box. The `Paint` event handler uses the module-level variable to determine the shape that will be drawn.

1. Run the chapter's concept lesson. Click the **Pens and Brushes** tab. Figure 12-7 shows the Pens and Brushes tab with a line already drawn.

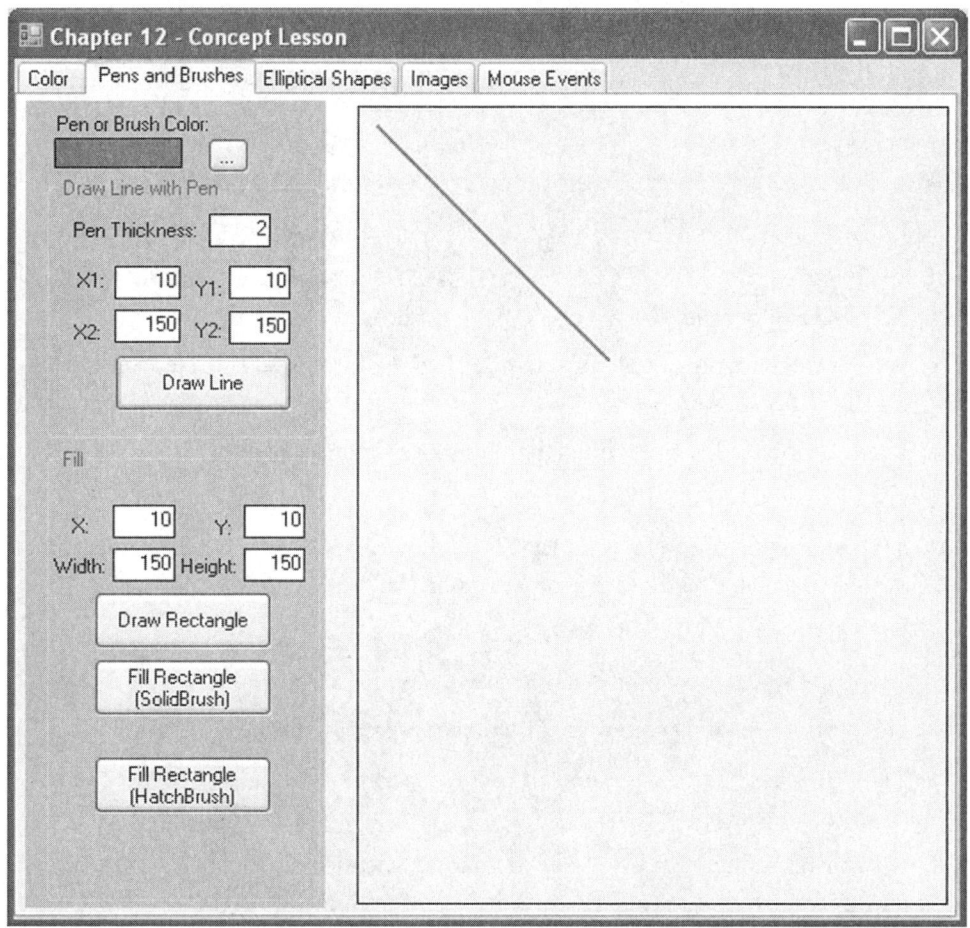

Figure 12-7: Concept lesson—Pens and Brushes tab

2. Click the button containing the ellipsis (...) to display the `ColorDialog` control instance. Select a color of your choosing, and then click **OK**. The selected color appears in the corresponding label.

3. Click the **Draw Line** button. The input is read from the form's text boxes and a line is drawn using the selected color.

4. Click the **Draw Rectangle** button. A rectangle outline is drawn. The rectangle's size is defined by the form's text boxes.

5. Click the **Fill Rectangle (SolidBrush)** button. The rectangle is filled using a solid brush. The rectangle's size is defined by the form's text boxes.

6. Click the **Fill Rectangle (HatchBrush)** button. A rectangle is filled using a hatch brush. Again, the rectangle's size is defined by the form's text boxes. The `HatchBrush` used has a `Cross` style.

## MINI-QUIZ 2

1. Which of the following statements is correct regarding pens and brushes?

   a. Both the `Pen` and `Brush` class are members of the `System.Drawing.Graphics` class.

   b. All pens and brushes are exactly 1 pixel in width.

   c. Pens are used to draw the outline of a shape, whereas brushes are used to fill the region of a shape.

   d. Brushes are used to draw lines that are more than 1 pixel wide.

   e. none of the above

2. What is the name of the method that should be called to release the memory allocated to a custom `Pen` or a custom `Brush`?

3. Describe the error in the following statement:

   ```
   Dim CustomBrush As New System.Drawing.Brush(Color.Red)
   ```

4. Which of the following statements is correct regarding filling a rectangle?

   a. The `FillRectangle` method of the `Graphics` class fills a rectangular shape on a drawing surface.

   b. When calling the `FillRectangle` method, the method can be called with an existing `Rectangle` structure or by specifying the origin, width, and height of the `Rectangle`.

   c. A `Rectangle` can be filled with a `SolidBrush` or a `HatchBrush`.

   d. all of the above

   e. none of the above

5. Write the statement to draw a line from the form's origin to the lower-right corner of the form. Use `Pens.Red` as the named `Pen`. Assume that e.Graphics is an instance of the `Graphics` class.

# CREATING AND DRAWING ELLIPTICAL SHAPES

In the preceding sections, you saw how to create and draw lines and rectangles. However, some shapes are elliptical, as introduced in the following list. Each of these shapes is drawn on the graphics surface by calling a method of the `System.Drawing.Graphics` class.

» The `DrawEllipse` method uses a bounding rectangle to define the shape and size of the ellipse. If the rectangle is square, the ellipse is a circle. The `FillEllipse` method fills an ellipse rather than drawing an outlined border around the ellipse.

» The `DrawArc` method uses a rectangle and an ellipse to draw an arc along part of the ellipse using a `Pen`.

» The `DrawPie` method uses an arc along an ellipse to draw a pie shape. The `FillPie` method fills the same pie shape using a brush.

Each of these shapes is discussed in the following sections.

## DRAWING AND FILLING ELLIPSES

Drawing an ellipse involves defining a bounding rectangle. The shape of the bounding rectangle defines the shape of the ellipse. After the shape of the rectangle has been defined, the `DrawEllipse` or `FillEllipse` methods of the `System.Drawing.Graphics` class can be called to draw an outline of the ellipse or fill the region of the ellipse, respectively. As with all shapes, an outline of an ellipse is drawn with a `Pen` and an ellipse is filled with a `SolidBrush` or a `HatchBrush`. The arguments to the `DrawEllipse` and `FillEllipse` methods are the same as the arguments to the `DrawRectangle` and `FillRectangle` methods.

The following statements draw an outline of an ellipse:

```
Dim CurrentRectangle As New Rectangle(10, 10, 150, 150)
e.Graphics.DrawEllipse(Pens.Black, CurrentRectangle)
e.Graphics.DrawEllipse(Pens.Black, 10, 10, 150, 150)
```

The first of the preceding statements defines the bounding rectangle for the ellipse. The second statement draws the ellipse with a named black pen (`Pens.Black`). The final statement draws the same ellipse using the *x* and *y* coordinates along with the *width* and the *height*.

The statements to fill an ellipse are nearly identical to those that draw an outline of an ellipse. The `FillEllipse` method is called instead of the `DrawEllipse` method. A `Brush` is used instead of a `Pen`. The following statements show how to fill an ellipse with a named brush:

```
Dim CurrentRectangle As New Rectangle(10, 10, 150, 150)
e.Graphics.FillEllipse(Brushes.Red, CurrentRectangle)
```

Figure 12-8 shows the preceding ellipse filled and drawn within a bounding rectangle. The bounding rectangle appears in the figure.

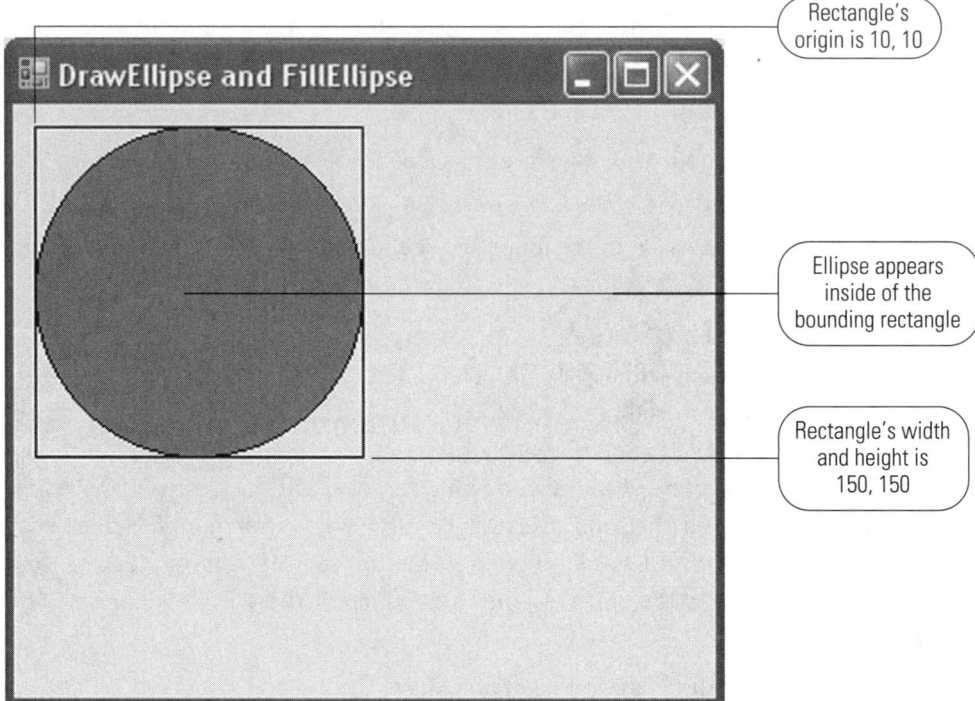

Figure 12-8: Drawing and filling an ellipse

As shown in Figure 12-8, the ellipse drawn is a circle because the width and height of the bounding rectangle is the same (150 pixels). The origin of the ellipse is 10, 10.

## DRAWING ARCS

The steps to draw an arc require that you define a bounding rectangle for an ellipse, along with an angle that encompasses a portion of the ellipse. The origin of the angle, which is measured in degrees, begins along the *x* axis. The arc drawn along the ellipse is defined by the *sweep angle*, which is measured in degrees. The arc is created clockwise from the origin if the sweep angle is positive and counterclockwise from the origin if the sweep angle is negative.

The `DrawArc` method is used to draw an arc. A corresponding `FillArc` method does not exist because it makes no sense to fill an arc, just as it makes no sense to fill a line. The following statements declare a bounding rectangle and draw an arc:

```
Dim CurrentEllipse As New Rectangle(10, 10, 150, 150)
e.Graphics.DrawArc(Pens.Red, CurrentEllipse, 0, 90)
```

The first of the preceding statements defines a bounding rectangle. The ellipse formed by the preceding rectangle is a circle. The `DrawArc` method draws an arc along the circle starting with an angle of 0. The sweep angle of the arc is 90 degrees in the clockwise direction. Thus, the arc will be drawn along one-quarter of the ellipse. Figure 12-9 shows how the arc shown in the preceding statements is drawn.

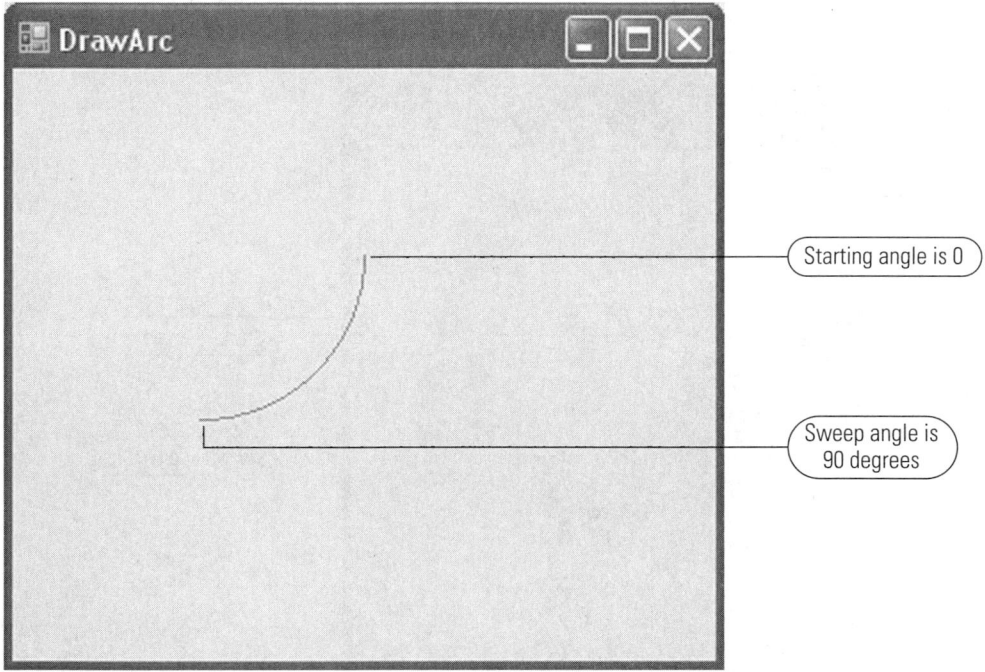

Figure 12-9: Drawing an arc

As shown in Figure 12-9, the bounding rectangle defines the shape of the ellipse. The starting angle identifies the starting point of the arc along the ellipse. The sweep angle defines the number of degrees of rotation along the ellipse.

## CREATING A PIE SHAPE

Having seen how to draw an ellipse and how to draw an arc from an ellipse, the steps to create a pie shape are nearly the same. First, a rectangle is created that defines the bounds of the ellipse. Second, the `DrawPie` method is called to draw the outline of a pie shape, or the `FillPie` method is called to fill the region of a pie shape using the same start angle and sweep angle used to create an arc.

The following statements illustrate how to fill a pie shape with a named `SolidBrush` and draw an outline of that same pie shape with a named `Pen`:

```
Dim CurrentCircle As New Rectangle(10, 10, 150, 150)
e.Graphics.FillPie(Brushes.Red, CurrentCircle, 0, 45)
e.Graphics.DrawPie(Pens.Black, CurrentCircle, 0, 45)
```

The first of the preceding statements declares the rectangle that will define the shape and size of the ellipse. The second and third statements fill the pie and draw an outline around the pie, respectively. The starting angle is 0 and the sweep angle is 45 degrees. Figure 12-10 shows the pie shape created in the preceding code segment.

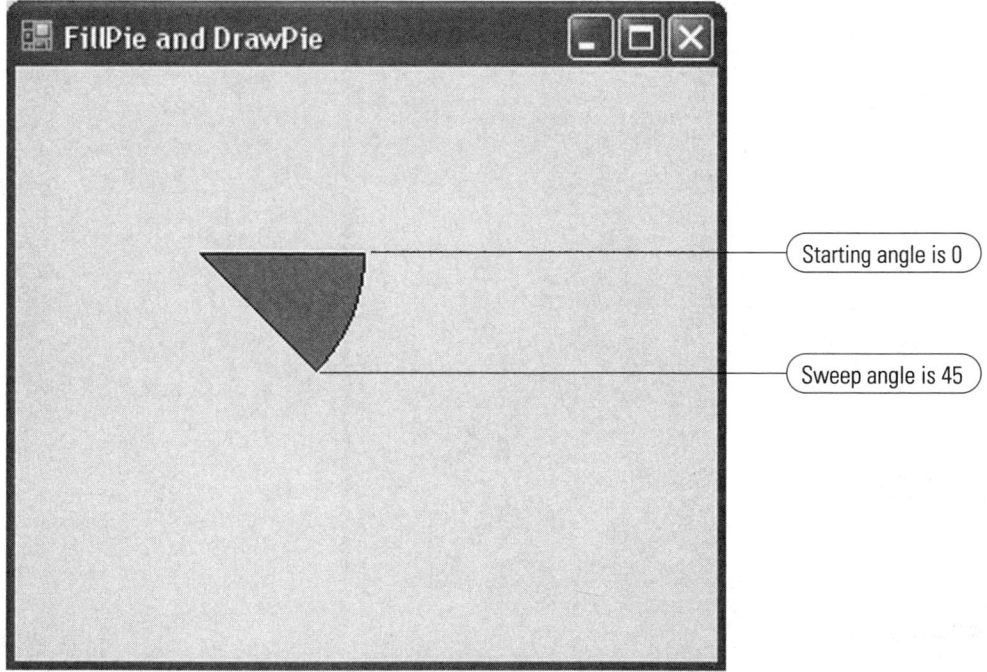

Figure 12-10: Filling and drawing a pie

In this exploration exercise, you will see how to draw elliptical shapes, such as an ellipse, an arc, and a pie. The code to draw the shapes is similar to the code for the preceding exploration exercise.

1. Run the concept lesson for the chapter. Click the **Elliptical Shapes** tab. Figure 12-11 shows the Elliptical Shapes tab.

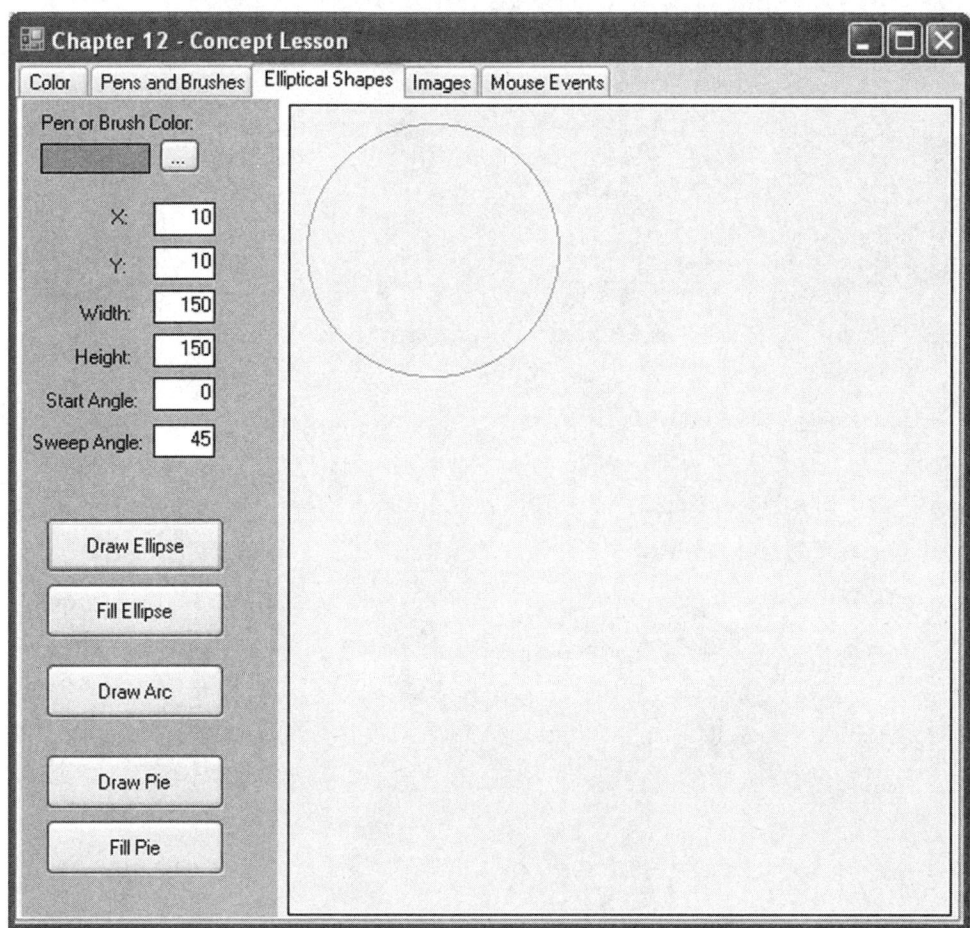

Figure 12-11: Concept lesson—Elliptical Shapes tab

2. Text boxes containing default values appear. Text boxes also appear allowing you to define the starting angle and the sweep angle for the arc and pie shapes. Using the default values or values of your choosing, click each button on the form to draw the respective shape. The shape appears in the corresponding `PictureBox` control instance.

# MINI-QUIZ 3

1. Which of the following statements correctly describes how to fill an ellipse?

   a. The `FillEllipse` method of the `Graphics` class is used to fill an elliptical shape inside of a bounding rectangle.

   b. The `FillEllipse` method of the `Graphics` class accepts two arguments: a `Point` that defines the origin of the ellipse and the radius of the ellipse.

   c. If the shape to be drawn is a circle, call the `FillCircle` method of the `Graphics` class to draw a circle.

   d. none of the above

2. Which of the following statements is correct regarding drawing an arc?

   a. The region of an arc is filled by calling the `FillArc` method of the `Graphics` class.

   b. The *x* and *y* arguments to the `DrawArc` method define the points along an ellipsis that form the arc.

   c. An arc has a starting position (angle) along an ellipse, along with a sweep angle.

   d. The radius of an arc is specified using the `Radius` property.

   e. none of the above

3. Describe the error in the following statements:

```
Dim CurrentArc As New Rectangle(5, 5, 100, 100)
e.Graphics.DrawArc(Brushes.Red, CurrentArc, 0, 90)
```

# DRAWING IMAGES

Just as the members of the `Graphics` class are used to draw shapes such as lines and rectangles, the members of the `Graphics` class can also be used to draw images to a graphics device.

Drawing an image requires that the image first be loaded into memory. The `FromFile` method of the `System.Drawing.Image` class loads an image into memory, as discussed in Chapter 3. The method accepts one argument: the filename containing the image. Valid file formats for images are bitmaps, icons, and Windows metafiles. The following statements load an image:

```
Dim CurrentImage As Image
CurrentImage = System.Drawing.Image.FromFile("C:\Image.bmp")
```

After an image has been loaded into memory, it can be painted to a drawing surface by calling the DrawImage method of the Graphics class. The first argument to the DrawImage method is an image. The second argument can be either a Point structure or a Rectangle structure, as the following statements show:

```
Dim CurrentImage As Image
Dim PointOrigin As New Point(10, 10)
Dim ImageRectangle As New Rectangle(10, 10, 150, 150)
CurrentImage = Image.FromFile("C:\Image.bmp")
e.Graphics.DrawImage(CurrentImage, PointOrigin)
e.Graphics.DrawImage(CurrentImage, ImageRectangle)
```

The preceding statements create instances of the Point and Rectangle structures. The image is read into the variable named CurrentImage. The first call to the DrawImage method draws the unscaled image at the Point specified by PointOrigin. The second call to the DrawImage method stretches the image so that it is scaled and drawn within the region of the Rectangle structure defined by ImageRectangle.

Figure 12-12 shows how an image is rendered when drawn at a Point. The image appears its normal size.

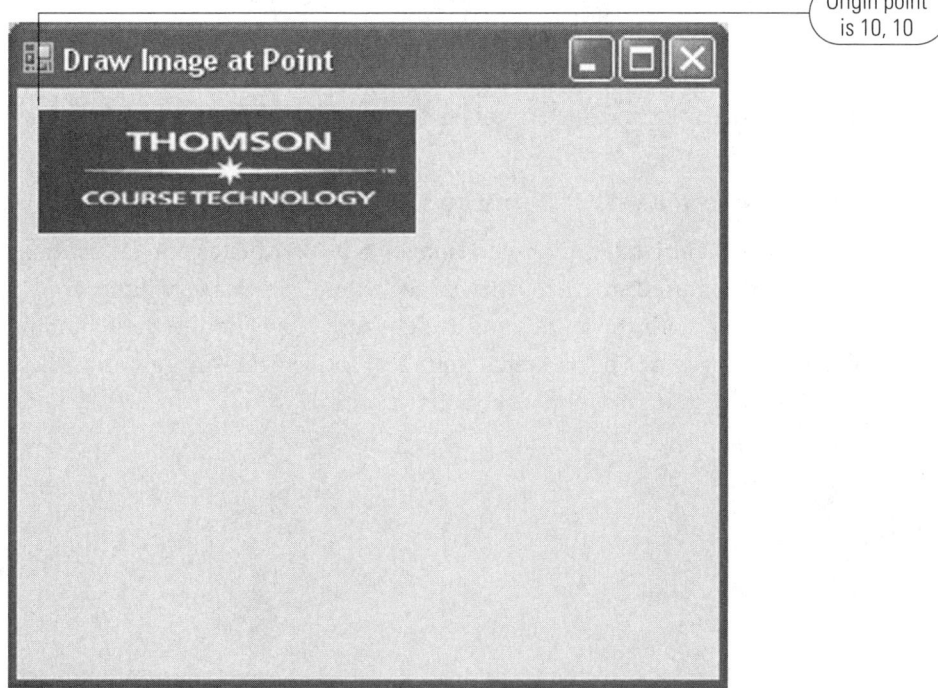

Figure 12-12: Rendering an image at a point

When rendered inside of a `Rectangle` structure, the image is scaled to fit inside of the `Rectangle`, as shown in Figure 12-13.

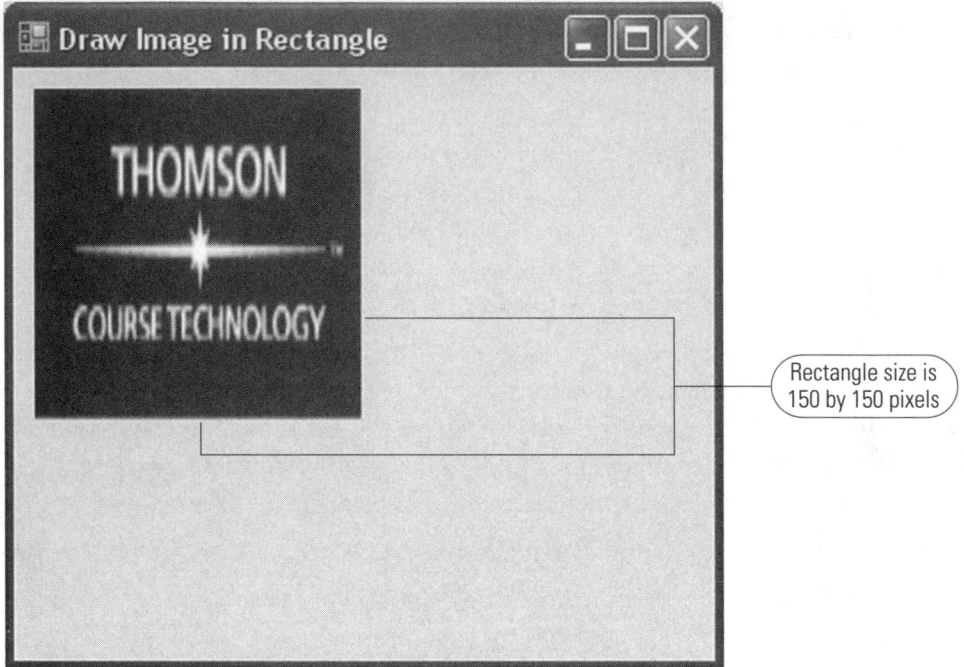

Figure 12-13: Rendering an image in a rectangle

As shown in Figure 12-13, the image is stretched to fit inside of the 150 by 150 pixel `Rectangle`.

In this exploration exercise, you will see how images can be painted to a drawing surface.

1. Run the chapter's concept lesson. Click the **Images** tab. Text boxes appear containing *x* and *y* coordinates used to create the `Point` where the image will be drawn. These text boxes along with the Width and Height text boxes define the bounding rectangle where the image will be painted. Figure 12-14 shows the Images tab with an image loaded into an instance of the `PictureBox` control.

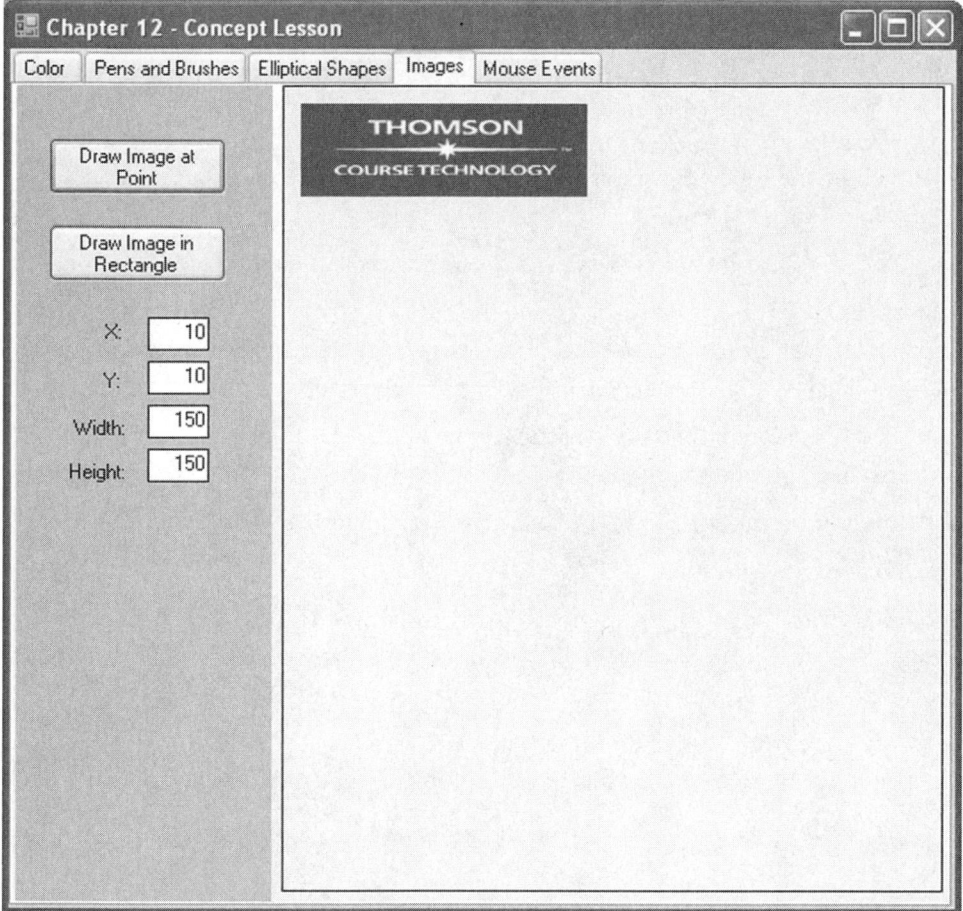

Figure 12-14: Concept lesson—Images tab

2. Click the **Draw Image at Point** button. In the Open dialog box, select the file **Chapter.12\Data\CourseImage.bmp**. The image appears in the `PictureBox` control instance at the specified point. The image appears with its actual size.

3. Click the **Draw Image in Rectangle** button. In the Open dialog box, select the file **Chapter.12\Data\CourseImage.bmp**. The image is drawn in a bounding `Rectangle` structure and scaled to fit within the rectangle.

## MINI-QUIZ 4

1. Which of the following statements is correct regarding drawing images to a graphical output device?

   a. The `FillImage` method of the `Graphics` class is used to fill an image in a `Rectangle`.

   b. The `Stretch` argument of the `FillImage` method controls how the image is scaled within a rectangle.

   c. The `DrawImage` method is used to draw an image at a particular point or inside a bounding rectangle.

   d. To draw an image, call the `FillImage` method with a `Brush`.

   e. none of the above

2. Which of the following statements correctly draws an image such that the image is drawn at the origin of the drawing surface and the size is not changed?

   a.
   ```
   e.Graphics.DrawImage(Image.FromFile( _
       "C:\Img.bmp"), New Point(0, 0))
   ```

   b.
   ```
   e.Graphics.DrawImage(Image.FromFile( _
       "C:\Img.bmp"), Size.NoResize)
   ```

   c.
   ```
   e.Graphics.DrawImage(Image.FromFile( _
       "C:\Img.bmp"), New Rectangle(0, 0, 150, 150))
   ```

   d.
   ```
   e.Graphics.DrawImage(Image.FromFile( _
       "C:\Img.bmp"), Me.ClientSize.Width, _
       Me.ClientSize.Height)
   ```

# INTRODUCTION TO MOUSE EVENTS

The Visual Studio event model supports additional categories of events beyond those you have learned thus far in the chapter. Some of these events are applicable to the mouse and are discussed next.

There are a group of events that apply to the mouse. These events fire as the end user moves the mouse across a form or control instance or presses and releases the mouse buttons. The following list describes selected mouse events:

» The `MouseClick` event is similar to the `Click` event and fires when the end user clicks the mouse on the form or a control instance created on the form.

» There are actually two events that fire when the end user clicks a mouse button. The `MouseDown` event fires when the end user presses a mouse button, and the `MouseUp` fires when a mouse button is released.

» When the mouse enters the region of a visible control instance, the `MouseEnter` event fires. When the mouse leaves the visible region of a control instance, the `MouseLeave` event fires. These events also fire for the form itself.

» The `MouseHover` event fires when the mouse hovers over a control instance for a few seconds. The `MouseHover` event is commonly used to display a ToolTip or other information.

» The `MouseMove` event fires whenever the mouse is moved. Thus, as the mouse moves across the form, several `MouseMove` events fire.

Now that you have seen the various mouse events, you will learn how to create event handlers for them. When working with mouse events, it is often necessary to determine information about the mouse, as described in the following list:

» In many graphical applications, it is necessary to get the position of the mouse to determine where to draw a line or other shape.

» Most mice have two buttons but some have three buttons. Sometimes, it is necessary to determine which mouse button was pressed. Many applications perform different actions when a different mouse button is clicked.

» Some applications use keyboard modifier keys (Ctrl, Alt, and Shift) to change the action performed when the mouse is clicked.

» Most new mice have a mouse wheel. It is often necessary to handle events fired by clicking the mouse wheel or as the end user scrolls the mouse wheel.

All of this information can be determined using the `MouseEventArgs` class, which is the data type of the second argument for all mouse-related event handlers. The following properties of the `MouseEventArgs` class are used to find out information about the mouse:

» The `Button` property is used to determine which mouse button was clicked and has a data type of `MouseButton`. Valid enumeration values are `MouseButtons.Left`, `MouseButtons.Middle`, and `MouseButtons.Right`. Note that although most personal computers have two mouse buttons, some mice have three buttons. Visual Studio does provide support for a third middle button.

» Together, the `X` and `Y` properties describe the position of the mouse when it was clicked.

» New to Visual Studio 2005, the `Location` property has a data type of `Point`, and identifies the position where the mouse was clicked.

» As a mouse wheel is rotated, small clicks can be felt. Each one of these clicks is called a *detent*. The `Delta` property contains a counter of the number of detents.

Two common tasks must be performed when handling mouse events. One is to determine the position of the mouse. The other is to test which mouse button was clicked. Each of these scenarios is discussed in the following sections.

## DETERMINING THE POSITION OF THE MOUSE

The `MouseMove` event fires repeatedly as the end user moves the mouse across the screen or a control instance. By handling the `MouseMove` event, it's possible to determine the position of the mouse, as shown in the following event handler:

```
Private Sub picMouse_MouseMove(ByVal sender As Object, _
    ByVal e As System.Windows.Forms.MouseEventArgs) _
    Handles picMouse.MouseMove
    lblMousePosition.Text = "X= " & e.X.ToString & _
        "  Y= " & e.Y.ToString
End Sub
```

The preceding event handler fires whenever the mouse is moved on the `PictureBox` control instance named picMouse. The position of the mouse is retrieved from the event handler's second argument and displayed in the `Label` control instance named lblMousePosition.

## DETERMINING WHICH MOUSE BUTTON WAS CLICKED

It's often necessary to determine which mouse button was clicked or pressed, and perform some conditional action accordingly. The following event handler illustrates how to determine which mouse button was clicked and execute conditional statements:

```
Private Sub picMouse_MouseClick(ByVal sender As Object, _
    ByVal e As System.Windows.Forms.MouseEventArgs) _
    Handles picMouse.MouseClick
    Select Case e.Button
        Case Windows.Forms.MouseButtons.Left
            lblButtonClicked.Text = "MouseButtons.Left"
        Case Windows.Forms.MouseButtons.Middle
            lblButtonClicked.Text = "MouseButtons.Middle"
        Case Windows.Forms.MouseButtons.Right
            lblButtonClicked.Text = "MouseButtons.Right"
    End Select
End Sub
```

The preceding event handler executes when the mouse is clicked on the PictureBox control instance named picMouse. The clicked button is retrieved from the event's second argument. The Select Case statement executes to determine which button was clicked and updates the contents of a Label control instance accordingly. Of course, most applications would perform some meaningful task as a result of a particular mouse button being clicked.

## HANDLING THE MOUSEENTER EVENT

Suppose that you wanted a control instance to appear emphasized when the mouse is positioned over the control instance. In this case, handling the MouseEnter and MouseLeave events can be useful, as the following statements show:

```
Private Sub ButtonList_MouseEnter(ByVal sender As Object, _
    ByVal e As System.EventArgs) Handles Button1.MouseEnter, _
    Button2.MouseEnter, Button3.MouseEnter
    CType(sender, Button).BackColor = Color.Green
End Sub

Private Sub ButtonList_MouseLeave(ByVal sender As Object, _
    ByVal e As System.EventArgs) Handles Button1.MouseLeave, _
    Button2.MouseLeave, Button3.MouseLeave
    CType(sender, Button).BackColor = Color.WhiteSmoke
End Sub
```

The preceding multicast event handlers handle the MouseEnter and MouseLeave events for three buttons named Button1, Button2, and Button3. When the mouse passes over the control instance, the MouseEnter event fires. When the mouse passes off of the control instance, the MouseLeave event fires. The code in the event handlers sets the background color of the control instance as the mouse passes over and off the respective control instance.

In this exploration exercise, you will see how mouse event handlers operate.

1. Run the chapter's completed concept lesson, and click the **Mouse Events** tab. Figure 12-15 shows the Mouse Events tab. Note that your Mouse Position values will not match the figure's.

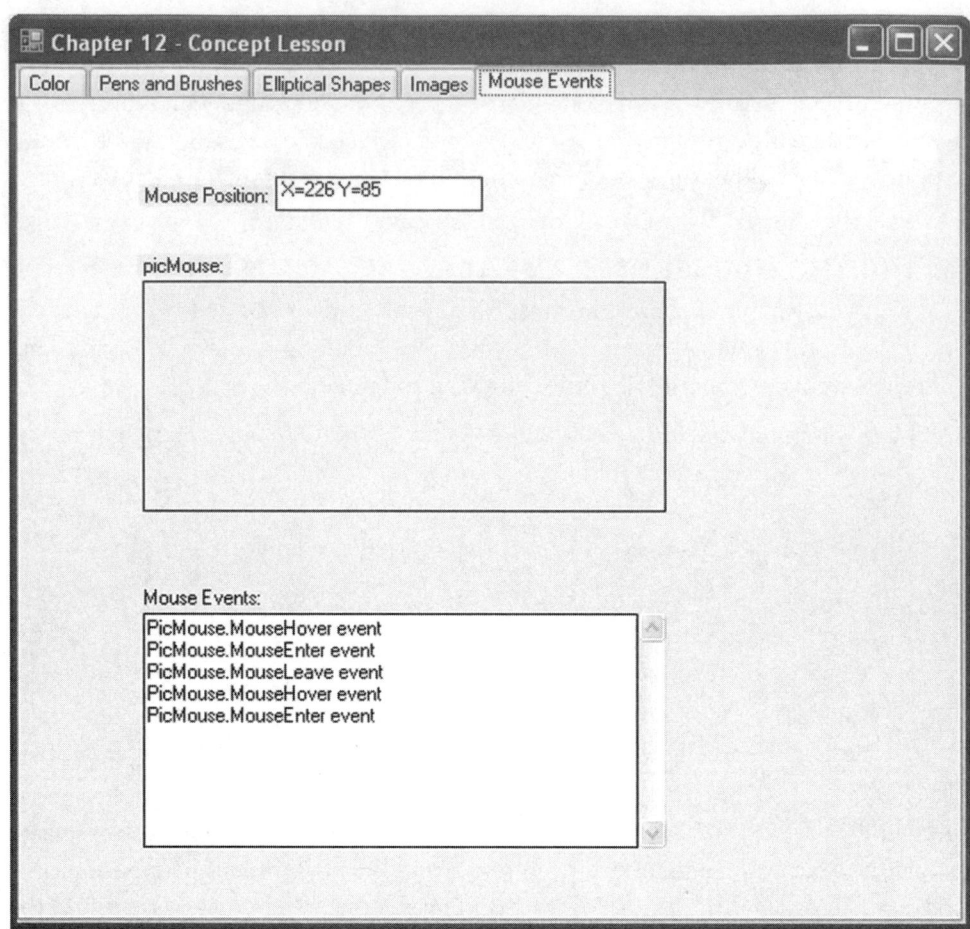

Figure 12-15: Concept lesson—Mouse Events tab

2. Move the mouse over the PictureBox control instance. Mouse events fire and the values in the Mouse Position text box change accordingly; in addition, related information is written to the Mouse Events list box, which contains the log of events.

# APPLICATION LESSON

## CREATING A DRAWING APPLICATION

In this application lesson, you will create a simple drawing program that will allow the end user to create various shapes on a form. The end user will be able to select the color for the shapes and use the mouse to define the region of the selected shape.

### APPLICATION LESSON—USER INTERFACE

The user interface for the application lesson is made up of several control instances that define the shapes that will be drawn on the graphics surface.

» A group of radio buttons is used to select the shape that will be painted on the graphics surface.

» A second group of control instances allows the end user to select the Pen and Brush color for the selected shape.

The actual task of drawing the various shapes is accomplished by handling two mouse events:

» The starting point of the shape is set when the end user presses the left mouse button. That is, the starting point of the shape is set in the MouseDown event handler.

» The ending point of the shape is set when the end user releases the left mouse button. That is, the ending point of the shape is set in the MouseUp event handler.

Instead of drawing a single shape inside of a PictureBox control instance, multiple shapes are drawn. Each shape is drawn in the same order that the shape was created. To do this, a list of the shapes created is stored and managed by the application in an instance of the List class.

## APPLICATION LESSON—DESIGN

The design of the application includes an enumeration that specifies the supported shapes. This enumeration appears in the file Shapes.vb. Thus, if the application were enhanced to support additional shapes, this enumeration could be modified to support those new shapes. The following code segment shows the enumeration that defines the supported shapes:

```
Public Enum SupportedShapes
    Line
    RectangleOutline
    RectangleFilledSolidBrush
    EllipseOutline
    EllipseFilledSolidBrush
End Enum
```

A module-level variable named SelectedShape having the same data type as the enumeration stores the shape being painted.

In addition, there is a class that describes each particular shape, as shown in the following code segment. This class also appears in the Shapes.vb file.

```
Public Class Shape
    Public ShapeType As SupportedShapes
    Public StartPoint As Point
    Public EndPoint As Point
    Public CurrentSize As Size
    Public CurrentPen As Pen
    Public CurrentBrush As SolidBrush
End Class
```

The purpose of each property is straightforward. The ShapeType member stores information about the current shape. The members named StartPoint and EndPoint are used to store a line's endpoints. The CurrentSize member is used to store the size of a rectangle or other shape. The final two statements contain the Pen or Brush used to draw the shape.

Only selected properties are used for each shape. That is, depending on the shape that is defined in a class instance, only specific properties applicable to that shape are used. Another design option would have been to declare a separate class for each shape that is drawn.

All of the event handling for the chapter's application lesson is performed in the following six event handlers:

» There is a multicast CheckedChanged event handler for the radio buttons that define the shape to be drawn. In this event handler, the enumeration variable named CurrentShape is set to the selected shape.

» There is a MouseDown event handler for the PictureBox control instance named picOutput. The position of the mouse is saved to a module-level variable in this event handler.

» There is also a MouseUp event handler for the same PictureBox control instance. The position of the mouse is saved to another module-level variable in this event handler. In addition, the shape is created based on the shape specified in the radio buttons. This shape is then added to the list of shapes.

» Much of the processing takes place in the Paint event for the PictureBox control instance named picOutput. The list of shapes is enumerated. Based on the type of shape, it is rendered to the PictureBox control instance.

» There is a button on the form to set the color of the current Pen. A ColorDialog control instance is used to get the color, which is stored in the BackColor property of a Label control instance.

» There is a button on the form to set the color of the current Brush. This button works the same way as the preceding button.

## APPLICATION LESSON—IMPLEMENTATION

Again, in this application lesson, you will finish a partially completed solution. However, before doing so, you will preview the completed application.

To preview the completed application:

1. In Visual Studio, open the solution file in the folder named **Chapter.12\ Chapter12ApplicationLessonPreview**.

2. Run the solution. Select a shape, and then select the colors for the pen and brush. Draw the selected shape by clicking and dragging on the right side of the form. Figure 12-16 shows the completed application lesson with various shapes drawn.

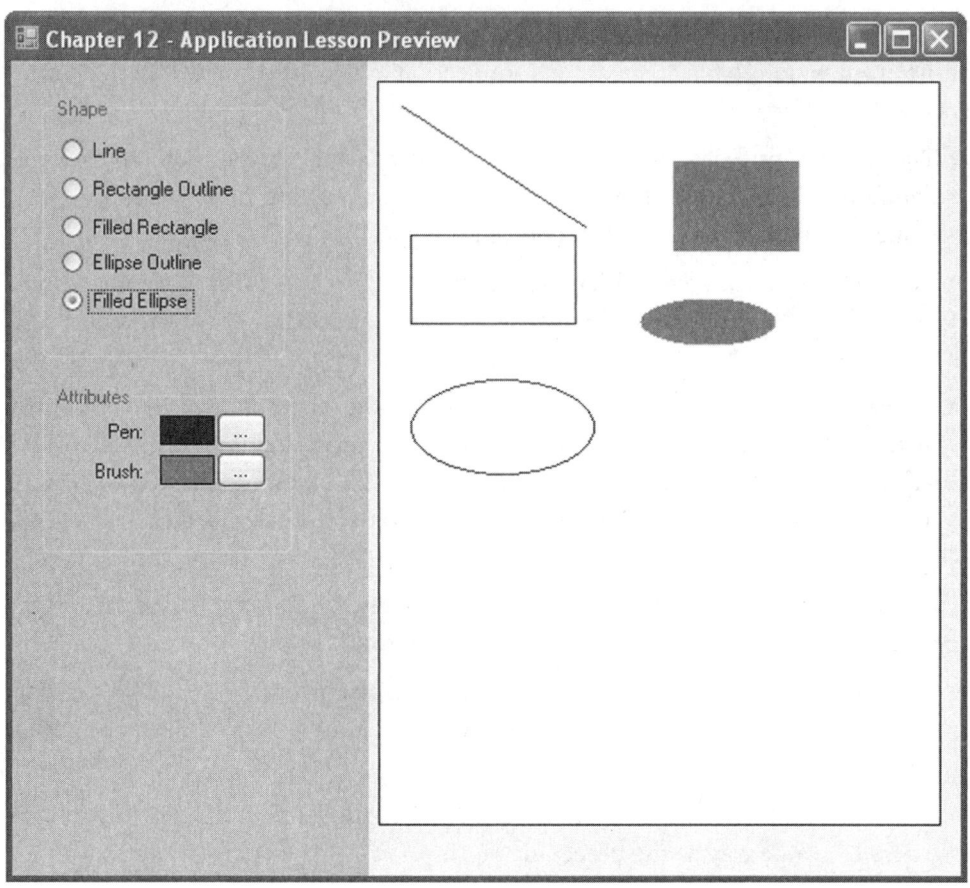

Figure 12-16: Previewing the completed application

3. Continue to draw different shapes.

Next, you will create the application from a partially completed solution file. The partially completed solution file contains the control instances but does not contain the code to paint the shapes. The class to store the shapes, along with the enumeration to define the supported shapes, has already been created.

To open the partially completed solution file:

1. In Visual Studio, open the solution file in the folder **Chapter.12\Chapter12ApplicationLessonStartup**.

2. Activate the Windows Forms Designer. As you can see, all of the control instances have been created on the form.

First, module-level variables need to be declared that will store the current shape being created, the starting point and ending point of the shape, and the stored list of shapes.

To declare the application's module-level variables:

1. Activate the Code Editor for the form named **frmMain**, and enter the following statements in the class to declare the module-level variables:

```
Private SelectedShape As SupportedShapes
Private StartPoint As Point
Private EndPoint As Point
Private ShapeList As New List(Of Shape)
```

The first of the preceding statements declares the variable SelectedShape to store the current shape. The second and third statements declare variables to store the starting and ending point of the shape. The final statement declares a List class instance named ShapeList to store references to the created shapes. Thus, the variable ShapeList will store references to an instance of the Shape class.

The form contains five radio buttons that define the supported shapes. Based on the radio button that is selected, the module-level variable named SelectedShape must be set to the desired shape.

To create the multicast event handler to set the current shape:

1. Create the multicast event handler named **radShape_CheckedChanged**, as shown in the following statements:

```
Private Sub radShape_CheckedChanged( _
    ByVal sender As System.Object, _
    ByVal e As System.EventArgs) _
    Handles radLine.CheckedChanged, _
    radRectangleOutline.CheckedChanged, _
    radFilledRectangle.CheckedChanged, _
    radEllipseOutline.CheckedChanged, _
    radFilledEllipse.CheckedChanged
```

```
Dim CurrentRadioButton As RadioButton
CurrentRadioButton = CType(sender, RadioButton)
Select Case CurrentRadioButton.Name
    Case "radLine"
        SelectedShape = SupportedShapes.Line
    Case "radRectangleOutline"
        SelectedShape = SupportedShapes.RectangleOutline
    Case "radFilledRectangle"
        SelectedShape = _
            SupportedShapes.RectangleFilledSolidBrush
    Case "radEllipseOutline"
        SelectedShape = SupportedShapes.EllipseOutline
    Case "radFilledEllipse"
        SelectedShape = _
            SupportedShapes.EllipseFilledSolidBrush
End Select
End Sub
```

The preceding event handler determines which radio button was clicked. The `Select Case` statement examines the `Name` property of the control instance and sets the SelectedShape variable accordingly.

Next, the `Click` event handlers can be created for the form's buttons. The code in these two `Click` event handlers specify the characteristics of the `Pen` and `Brush`.

To create the button's Click event handlers:

1. Create the **Click** event handler for the button named **btnSetPenColor**, and then enter the following statements:

```
Dim Result As DialogResult
Result = cdCurrent.ShowDialog
If Result = Windows.Forms.DialogResult.OK Then
    lblPenColor.BackColor = cdCurrent.Color
End If
```

2. Create the **Click** event handler for the button named **btnSetBrushColor**, and then enter the following statements:

```
Dim Result As DialogResult
Result = cdCurrent.ShowDialog
If Result = Windows.Forms.DialogResult.OK Then
    lblBrushColor.BackColor = cdCurrent.Color
End If
```

The preceding event handlers set the background color of the `Label` control instances. These control instances are used to define the color of a `Pen` or `Brush`.

Next, the `MouseDown` and `MouseUp` event handlers need to be created. The code in the `MouseDown` event handler sets the starting position of the mouse. The code for the `MouseUp` event handler is more complex. First, the mouse position is stored in a module-level variable. Then, a `Select Case` statement is used to determine the current shape. Based on the shape selected, an instance of the Shape class is created and configured to store the shape. The shape is then added to the instance of the `List` class.

To create the mouse event handlers:

1. Create the **MouseDown** event handler for the PictureBox control instance named **picOutput**, and then enter the following statement to save the starting mouse position to a module-level variable:

```
StartPoint = New Point(e.X, e.Y)
```

2. Create the **MouseUp** event handler for the PictureBox control instance named **picOuptut**, and then enter the following statements to save the mouse position, create the shape, and call the `Invalidate` method on the `PictureBox` control instance, thereby causing the `Paint` event to fire.

```
EndPoint = New Point(e.X, e.Y)
Select Case SelectedShape

    Case SupportedShapes.Line
        Dim CurrentShape As New Shape
        With CurrentShape
            .ShapeType = SupportedShapes.Line
            .CurrentPen = New Pen(lblPenColor.BackColor)
            .StartPoint = StartPoint
            .EndPoint = EndPoint
        End With
        ShapeList.Add(CurrentShape)

    Case SupportedShapes.RectangleOutline
        Dim CurrentShape As New Shape
        With CurrentShape
            .ShapeType = SupportedShapes.RectangleOutline
            .CurrentPen = New Pen(lblPenColor.BackColor)
            .StartPoint = StartPoint
            .CurrentSize = New Size(EndPoint.X - _
                StartPoint.X, EndPoint.Y - StartPoint.Y)
        End With
        ShapeList.Add(CurrentShape)
```

```
        Case SupportedShapes.RectangleFilledSolidBrush
            Dim CurrentShape As New Shape
            With CurrentShape
                .ShapeType = _
                    SupportedShapes.RectangleFilledSolidBrush
                .CurrentBrush = New _
                    SolidBrush(lblBrushColor.BackColor)
                .StartPoint = StartPoint
                .CurrentSize = New Size(EndPoint.X - _
                    StartPoint.X, EndPoint.Y - StartPoint.Y)
            End With
            ShapeList.Add(CurrentShape)

        Case SupportedShapes.EllipseOutline
            Dim CurrentShape As New Shape
            With CurrentShape
                .ShapeType = SupportedShapes.EllipseOutline
                .CurrentPen = New Pen(lblPenColor.BackColor)
                .StartPoint = StartPoint
                .CurrentSize = New Size(EndPoint.X - _
                    StartPoint.X, EndPoint.Y - StartPoint.Y)
            End With
            ShapeList.Add(CurrentShape)

        Case SupportedShapes.EllipseFilledSolidBrush
            Dim CurrentShape As New Shape
            With CurrentShape
                .ShapeType = _
                    SupportedShapes.EllipseFilledSolidBrush
                .CurrentBrush = _
                    New SolidBrush(lblBrushColor.BackColor)
                .StartPoint = StartPoint
                .CurrentSize = New Size(EndPoint.X - _
                StartPoint.X, EndPoint.Y - StartPoint.Y)
            End With
            ShapeList.Add(CurrentShape)
    End Select
    picOutput.Invalidate()
```

The preceding event handler has a `Select Case` statement to determine the current shape. Based on the current shape, an instance of the Shape class is created and configured to store the data necessary to draw the shape. Finally, the Shape class instance is added to the list named ShapeList.

Finally, the code needs to be created in the `Paint` event handler for the `PictureBox` control instance. Here, the list of shapes is enumerated. Another `Select Case` statement determines the type of shape to be painted, and then paints the shape accordingly.

To create the Paint event handler:

1. Activate the Code Editor, if necessary. Create the **Paint** event handler for the picture box named **picOutput**, and then enter the following statements:

```
Dim CurrentShape As Shape
For Each CurrentShape In ShapeList
    Select Case CurrentShape.ShapeType
        Case SupportedShapes.Line
            e.Graphics.DrawLine(CurrentShape.CurrentPen, _
                CurrentShape.StartPoint, CurrentShape.EndPoint)

        Case SupportedShapes.RectangleOutline
            Dim CurrentRectangle As New Rectangle( _
                CurrentShape.StartPoint, _
                CurrentShape.CurrentSize)
            e.Graphics.DrawRectangle(CurrentShape.CurrentPen, _
                CurrentRectangle)

        Case SupportedShapes.RectangleFilledSolidBrush
            Dim CurrentRectangle As New Rectangle( _
                CurrentShape.StartPoint, _
                CurrentShape.CurrentSize)
            e.Graphics.FillRectangle( _
                CurrentShape.CurrentBrush, CurrentRectangle)

        Case SupportedShapes.EllipseOutline
            Dim CurrentRectangle As New Rectangle( _
                CurrentShape.StartPoint, _
                CurrentShape.CurrentSize)
            e.Graphics.DrawEllipse( _
                CurrentShape.CurrentPen, CurrentRectangle)

        Case SupportedShapes.EllipseFilledSolidBrush
            Dim CurrentRectangle As New Rectangle( _
                CurrentShape.StartPoint, _
                CurrentShape.CurrentSize)
            e.Graphics.FillEllipse(CurrentShape.CurrentBrush, _
                CurrentRectangle)
    End Select
Next
```

The `Paint` event handler examines all of the items in the list named ShapeList. The `Select Case` statement executes to determine the shape to be drawn. The statements in each case draw the selected shape.

2. Test the application. Select different colored pens and brushes and paint different shapes.

# CHAPTER SUMMARY

» Windows supplies a set of drawing services referred to as the graphics device interface (GDI). Collectively, the GDI is made up of classes and structures to define colors, pens, and brushes, and to create and draw two-dimensional shapes, such as lines, rectangles, ellipses, arcs, pies, and other shapes.

» Using the GDI, all objects are drawn using a color represented as a `Color` structure. A color consists of red, green, and blue components called an RGB value. Each component has a value between 0 and 255. Visual Basic supports several named colors along with the ability to create custom colors using the `FromArgb` method of the `System.Color` structure.

» The `ColorDialog` control is a standard dialog control from which the end user can select a color. The `Color` property contains the color selected by the end user.

» The `Pen` class is used to draw lines and to outline other shapes. A `Pen` can be categorized as a named pen or a custom pen.

» The `SolidBrush` class is used to fill the region of a shape. Like a `Pen`, it is possible to use a named brush or to create a custom brush. There is another type of brush called a `HatchBrush`.

» The `HatchBrush` works similarly to the `SolidBrush`. However, instead of filling a region with a solid color, the `HatchBrush` fills a region with a background color and a pattern. In all, over 50 brush patterns are supported.

» The `Graphics` class supports a method named `DrawLine`. The method accepts a named or custom `Pen`, which describes the color and thickness of the line. The line is drawn using *x* and *y* coordinates or two instances of the `Point` class.

» The `Rectangle` structure is used to define the shape and size of a `Rectangle`. A rectangle can be created using the *x* and *y* coordinates of the rectangle's origin, along with the rectangle's *width* and *height*. In addition, a `Rectangle` can be created using `Point` and `Size` structures. A `Rectangle` is created on the drawing surface by calling the `DrawRectangle` and `FillRectangle` methods of the `Graphics` class.

» Visual Basic also supports elliptical shapes. The `DrawEllipse` and `FillEllipse` methods of the `Graphics` class draw and fill an ellipse, respectively. The `DrawArc` method draws an arc along an ellipse. The `DrawPie` and `FillPie` methods are used to draw and fill pie shapes.

» The `DrawImage` method is used to draw an image that has been loaded into memory. One version of the method draws the image at a specific `Point`. The image appears its actual size. A second version of the method draws the image inside the region of a bounding rectangle. The image is stretched to fill the region of the bounding rectangle.

» Graphics applications and other types of applications must often handle events generated by the mouse. The `MouseMove` event fires whenever the mouse is moved on the form or control instance. The `MouseEnter` and `MouseLeave` events fire as the mouse passes over a control instance and as the mouse passes off a control instance, respectively. The `MouseDown` and `MouseUp` events fire when the mouse is pressed and released, respectively. The data type of the second argument for mouse events is `MouseEventArgs`. This class has properties that return the state of modifier keys, along with determining which mouse button was used.

# KEY TERMS

**client area**—The part of a form used for drawing, excluding the form's border and title bar.

**graphics device interface (GDI)**—A group of types that contains members used to define shapes and to draw those shapes to a graphics surface, such as the screen or printer.

**graphics surface**—An endpoint for graphics output, such as a screen or printer.

**pixel**—An individual dot displayed on a screen.

**RGB**—A value that defines the amount of the colors red, green, and blue applied to create a color.

# ANSWERS TO MINI-QUIZZES

### MINI-QUIZ 1

1. The minimum RGB value is 0 and the maximum RGB value is 255.

2. d. The method is used to create a custom color from composite RGB values.

3. 255, 255, 255

### MINI-QUIZ 2

1. c. Pens are used to draw the outline of a shape, whereas brushes are used to fill the region of a shape.

2. `Dispose()`

3. The class to create a brush is named `SolidBrush` not `Brush`. The `Brush` class is an abstract class, which cannot be instantiated.

4. d. all of the above

5. e.`Graphics.DrawLine(Pens.Red, 0, 0, _`
   `Me.ClientSize.Width, Me.ClientSize.Height)`

### MINI-QUIZ 3

1. a. The `FillEllipse` method of the `Graphics` class is used to fill an elliptical shape inside of a bounding rectangle.

2. c. An arc has a starting position (angle) along an ellipse, along with a sweep angle.

3. The `DrawArc` method should be called with a `Pen` rather than a `Brush`.

### MINI-QUIZ 4

1. c. The `DrawImage` method is used to draw an image at a particular point or inside a bounding rectangle.

2. a. e.`Graphics.DrawImage(Image.FromFile( _`
   `"C:\Img.bmp"), New Point(0, 0))`

### MINI-QUIZ 5

1. b. `MouseMove`

2. X, Y, `Location`

# REVIEW QUESTIONS

1. Which of the following statements is true regarding the `System.Drawing.Graphics` class?

   a. It provides the interface to the GDI.

   b. Its methods are used to draw rectangles, lines, and other shapes on a form or other output device.

c. A reference to an instance of the `System.Drawing.Graphics` class is supplied through the `PaintEventArgs` class in a form's `Paint` event handler.

d. all of the above

e. none of the above

2. Which of the following statements applies to the `Color` structure?

a. The `FromArgb` method creates a color from RGB values.

b. The `Color` structure supports named properties such as `Color.Blue` and `Color.Black`.

c. Colors are used with brushes and pens.

d. It is possible to create custom colors using RGB values.

e. all of the above

3. Which of the following statements is true regarding the `Pen` class?

a. Pens are used to draw lines and outline other shapes such as rectangles.

b. Pens are used to fill rectangles along with other shapes.

c. A pen is used to draw a text string inside of a rectangle.

d. A pen is always 1 pixel wide.

e. none of the above

4. Assuming that the following color has been declared:

```
Dim MyColor As Color = Color.FromArgb(33, 44, 55)
```

which of the following statements will cause a syntax error:

a. `Dim CurrentBrush1 As New SolidBrush(MyColor)`

b. `Dim CurrentBrush2 As New Brushes(MyColor)`

c. `Dim CurrentBrush3 As New _`
      `System.Drawing.Drawing2D.HatchBrush( _`
      `Drawing2D.HatchStyle.Cross, MyColor)`

d. `Dim CurrentBrush4 As Brush = Brushes.Red`

e. all of the above are valid

5. Which of the following statements is true regarding rectangles?

   a. The `Rectangle` structure appears in the `System.Drawing` namespace.

   b. Calling the `Rectangle` constructor causes a rectangle to be drawn on a form.

   c. To fill a rectangle with a brush, you call the `DrawRectangle` method.

   d. The size of a rectangle is determined by the `Top`, `Left`, `Bottom`, and `Right` properties.

   e. none of the above

6. Which of the following statements creates a rectangle that is the same size as the form?

   a. `Dim CurrentRectangle1 As New Rectangle(Me.ClientSize)`

   b. `Dim CurrentRectangle2 As New Rectangle( _`
       `0, 0, Me.ClientSize.X, Me.ClientSize.Y)`

   c. `Dim CurrentRectangle3 As New Rectangle( _`
       `0, 0, Me.ClientSize)`

   d. `Dim CurrentRectangle4 As New Rectangle(0, 0, _`
       `Me.ClientSize.Width, Me.ClientSize.Height)`

   e. none of the above are correct

7. Which of the following statements correctly describes how to draw an ellipse?

   a. An ellipse is drawn by specifying the point at the center of the ellipse, along with the lines along the x and y axis that define the bounds of the ellipse.

   b. An ellipse is drawn using two lines.

   c. An ellipse is drawn inside of a bounding rectangle.

   d. An ellipse is drawn by setting the `Stretch` property of a circle to describe the shape of the ellipse.

   e. none of the above

8. What is the name of the method that you would call to display an image on a form?

   a. `FillImage`

   b. `FillImageRectangle`

   c. `DrawImage`

   d. `PaintImageImage`

   e. `PaintPicture`

9. Which of the following statements correctly draws a circle?

   a. `e.Graphics.DrawEllipse(Pens.Red, 0, 0, 150, 150)`

   b. `e.Graphics.DrawEllipse(Pens.Red, 0, 360)`

   c. `e.Graphics.DrawCircle(Pens.Red, 0, 0, 150, 150)`

   d. `e.Graphics.DrawCircle(Pens.Red, 0, 360)`

   e. `e.Graphics.DrawRectangle( _`
       `Pens.Red, 0, 0, 150, 150, Shape.Circle)`

10. Which of the following statements is correct related to filling a pie shape on a graphics surface?

   a. To define the position and size of the pie slice, the constructor for the `Pie` class must be called, which is then passed to the `FillPie` method.

   b. A pie slice is filled with a `Pen`.

   c. A pie shape is filled inside of a bounding ellipse by calling the `FillPie` method of the `Graphics` class.

   d. all of the above

   e. none of the above

11. Referring to color, describe the purpose of the RGB values.

12. List and describe the different actions that will cause a `Paint` event to fire.

13. Describe the purpose of the `Rectangle` structure when drawing and filling elliptical shapes such as arcs and pie slices.

14. List and describe the two ways an image can be drawn to a form. Describe how the image will be scaled depending on how the image is drawn.

15. Describe the error in the following statements and correct the error:

```
Dim CurrentBrush As New _
    SolidBrush(Color.FromArgb(255, 50, 255))
e.Graphics.DrawArc(CurrentBrush, 0, 0, 150, 150)
```

# PROGRAMMING QUESTIONS

1. Write the statement to create a color using the `FromArgb` method. Use a red value of 255, a green value of 128, and a blue value of 128. Store the result in a variable named CurrentColor having a data type of `Color`.

2. Assume that a form named frmDemo exists. Write the necessary statements to define a rectangle named CurrentRectangle that is the same size as a form's client area. Using the named color `Color.Blue`, fill the rectangle, and draw it on the form. Assume that e.Graphics represents an instance of the `Graphics` class.

3. Write the statements to draw two diagonal lines on a form. The first line should be drawn from the upper-left corner of the form to the lower-right corner of the form. The second line should be drawn from the lower-left corner of the form to the upper-right corner of the form. Use the named pen `Pens.Red` to draw the lines. Assume that e.Graphics represents an instance of the `Graphics` class.

4. Write the statements to declare a `Point` structure named CenterPoint whose location is the center of the form's client area.

5. A chessboard has 64 squares: 8 rows and 8 columns. Write the necessary statements to create a black, filled rectangle the same size as the form. Draw white lines in the rectangle to form 64 squares. When complete, seven horizontal and seven vertical lines will be drawn on the form. *Hint:* Use one `For` loop to draw the horizontal lines and another to draw the vertical lines. Assume that the variable e.Graphics references an instance of the `Graphics` class.

6. Again assuming the chessboard example from the previous question, write the statements to create 64 alternating rectangles having colors of white and black to mimic the appearance of the chessboard. Assume that e.Graphics represents an instance of the `Graphics` class.

7. Write the statements to create a right triangle on the form. The left side and base of the right triangle should be 250 pixels in size. The hypotenuse should connect the left side and the base. Place the right triangle on the form such that the left side appears 100 pixels from the left border of the form and the base appears 100 pixels from the bottom of the form. Assume that the variable e.Graphics references an instance of the `Graphics` class. Use a blue pen that is 3 points in width.

8. Assume that a form has a height and width of 255. Write the statements to declare a color named CurrentColor and a pen named PenCurrent. Create a For loop that will draw 255 horizontal lines on the form. Each line should have a different color. Use 0 for the red and green values. Increment the blue value for the color by 1 each time through the loop. Thus, the first line will be black. Assume that the variable e.Graphics references an instance of the Graphics class.

9. Write the statements to create an ellipse on the form that is the size of the form's client area. Use a blue hatched brush with a cross pattern to fill the ellipse.

10. Write the statements to draw an arc from the center of the form to the lower-left corner of the form's client area. Use a named blue pen.

11. Write the statements to create four pie shapes on the form such that the bounding ellipse is the same size as the form's client area. The first pie slice should fill 10% of the ellipse. The second pie slice should fill 30% of the ellipse. The third and fourth pie slices should fill 40% and 20% of the ellipse, respectively. Use the named brushes Brushes.Red, Brushes.Green, Brushes.Blue, and Brushes.Orange for the pie slices.

12. Write the statements to load the image named C:\CurrentImage.bmp. Draw the image so that it fills the client area of the form.

13. Create two multicast mouse event handlers that will fire when the mouse moves over the text boxes named txtName, txtAddress, and txtStreet. Set the background color to light blue when the mouse passes over the control instances and to white when the mouse passes off of the control instances.

14. Create a MouseMove event handler that will display the mouse position in the form's title bar.

# HANDS-ON PROJECTS

1. In this hands-on project, you will create an application that shows the effect of various RGB values on the color produced. To define the RGB values, you will create one scroll bar for each color component. Thus, the application will require three scroll bars for the red, green, and blue values, respectively. Each time the value of one of the scroll bars changes, the output color should be displayed in a filled rectangle.

    a. A preview of the application appears in the file **Chapter.12\HandsOnProjects\ Ch12HandsOnProject1.exe**.

    b. Start Visual Studio, if necessary, and create a new solution named **Ch12HandsOnProject1.sln**.

    c. Create three scroll bars on the form setting the minimum value to 0 and the maximum value to 255. Set the name of each scroll bar as appropriate.

    d. Create three labels to describe the scroll bars you just created. Position these labels directly above the scroll bars.

    e. Create three more labels below the scroll bars. These labels will display the current value of the respective scroll bar.

    f. Create an instance of the `PictureBox` control on the form.

    g. In the `ValueChanged` event for each scroll bar, write the necessary statements to update the label containing the value of the respective scroll bar. Also write the statements to create a color. The background of the picture box should be set to that color.

    h. Using the `Color` dialog box, allow the end user to select a color. When the end user selects a color, update the RGB values in the scroll bars, labels, and the displayed color.

    i. Create a button to exit the solution.

2. In this hands-on project, you will create an application that will print a bar chart based on several input values. The input for the bar chart will be read from a sequential file.

   a. A preview of the application appears in the file **Chapter.12\HandsOnProjects\ Ch12HandsOnProject2.exe**. Run the preview application. Click the **Open File** button and open the file named **Chapter.12\Data\Sales.txt**. The graph appears in the picture box on the main form.

   b. Start Visual Studio and create a new solution named **Ch12HandsOnProject2.sln**.

   c. Crease a splash screen for the solution using drawing objects of your choice to create an interesting user interface.

   d. Create the main form and its control instances, as shown in the preview application.

   e. Create the code for the Open File button to display the graph. Write the code to read the file Sales.txt. Each record in the file contains two fields. The first field contains the year. The second field contains the sales amount.

   f. Create the x and y axis. Use the Help system to learn about the DrawString method. Use the DrawString method to display the labels along the y axis.

   g. Create the bars in the bar chart to graphically display the sales data. The graph that you create should work properly for between three and 10 years of sales data.

3. In this hands-on project, you will create an animation. This animation will repeatedly draw shapes at regular intervals using an instance of the Timer control.

   a. A preview of the application appears in the file **Chapter.12\HandsOnProjects\ Ch12HandsOnProject3.exe**.

   b. Create a new solution named **Ch12HandsOnProject3.sln**.

   c. The end user should be able to create the animation using either outlined shapes or filled shapes. In addition to specifying whether the shape is filled or outlined, the end user should be able to select the color for the shape. Create the control instances that will allow the user to select a shape.

   d. The end user should be able to draw two different shapes: a rectangle and an ellipse. The shapes drawn should be outlined or filled. The shape that is drawn should be selected by the end user by clicking on one of the radio button's appearing on the form. The shapes should be 50 by 50 pixels.

   e. Create buttons on the form to start and stop the animation. The animation should be started and stopped by enabling and disabling the Timer control instance.

   f. Create a button to exit the application.

   g. Create a scroll bar on the form that will adjust the speed of the animation. To change the speed of the animation, change the value of the Interval property of the Timer control instance.

h. The animation itself should be drawn inside an instance of the `PictureBox` control. The selected shape should move one pixel at a time from the top of the control instance to the bottom of the control instance. The animation should be created to repeat indefinitely.

i. Create the necessary event handler that will move the shape to the position of the mouse when the mouse is clicked inside of the `PictureBox` control instance.

4. In this hands-on project, you will extend the application lesson completed in the chapter.

   a. Create a new solution named **Ch12HandsOnProject4.sln**.

   b. Copy the control instances and the code from the application lesson into this project as a basis for this hands-on project.

   c. In the application lesson, the `Pen` selected by the end user is always 1 pixel wide. Modify the class and change the form so that pens of different widths are supported.

   d. In addition to filling shapes with a `SolidBrush`, the end user should be able to fill shapes with at least four different `HatchBrushes`. Choose the brushes as you see fit.

   e. The shapes drawn in the chapter's application are drawn in the order that they are created on the drawing surface. Using the controls of your choice, allow the end user to change the order in which each shape is drawn. In addition, allow the end user to remove a shape from the list of shapes that are drawn.

# 13

# ADDITIONAL WINDOWS CONTROLS

**After completing this chapter, you will be able to:**

Describe the purpose of container controls and the relationships between them

Create a menu system for a form

Create a toolbar on a form

Display informational messages using the `StatusStrip` control

Restrict character input using the `MaskedTextBox` control

Use the `RichTextBox` control to work with formatted text

# CONCEPT LESSON

# WORKING WITH ADDITIONAL WINDOWS CONTROLS

Although you have worked with several types of controls throughout this book, there are many more controls that remain to be explored. These controls can be used to "round out" a user interface and are described in the following list:

» The `MenuStrip` control is used to create a menu system for a form. This control is used in conjunction with other controls that appear on the `MenuStrip`.

» The `ContextMenuStrip` control is used to create pop-up (context) menus. Again, this control is used in conjunction with other controls that appear on the `ContextMenuStrip`.

» The `ToolStrip` control is used to create a toolbar. Again, the `ToolStrip` control is used in conjunction with other controls that make up the items appearing on the `ToolStrip`.

» The `StatusStrip` control is used to create a status bar, which typically appears across the bottom of a form.

» The `MaskedTextBox` control is similar to a `TextBox` control, but restricts valid input by forcing the end user to enter specific characters into specific character positions.

» The `RichTextBox` control is a superset of the `TextBox` control, and supplies additional text formatting capabilities.

# UNDERSTANDING THE PURPOSE OF CONTAINER CONTROLS

You have seen how a control like a `GroupBox` operates as a container for other controls, such as radio buttons. Visual Studio supports many other container controls in addition to the `GroupBox` control.

This concept lesson uses many container controls, which are related together hierarchically. For example, in this concept lesson, there is a single instance of the `TabControl` control, which is a container control. The `TabControl`, in turn, contains instances of the `TabPage` control, which form the individual pages on the `TabControl`. These `TabPage` control instances, in turn, contain other container control instances, such as the `MenuStrip`, `ToolStrip`, and `StatusStrip` controls. These controls, in turn, contain other control instances, such as the boxes and buttons that appear on the `ToolStrip` or `StatusStrip`. Figure 13-1 shows the hierarchical relationship between the container controls in this concept lesson.

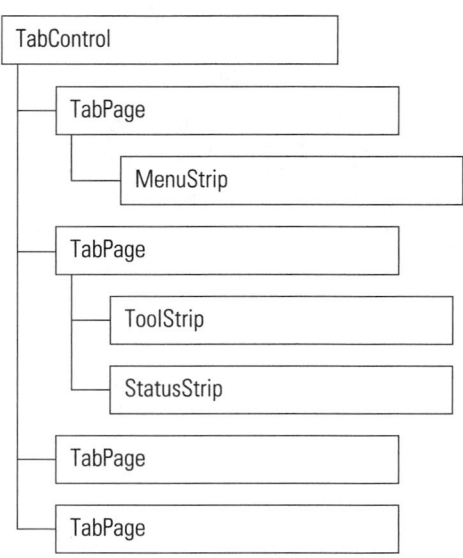

Figure 13-1: Hierarchical relationship between container control instances

As shown in Figure 13-1, each `TabPage` control instance is contained by the `TabControl`. One `TabPage` control contains a `MenuStrip` control instance. Another `TabPage` control instance contains the `ToolStrip` and `StatusStrip` control instances. The last two `TabPage` control instances have no subordinate containers.

# CREATING MENUS

A menu system in Visual Basic gives the end user a way to perform tasks and provides an alternative to clicking buttons on a form. A menu system that you create works the same way as any menu system that you have used. A menu system consists of a menu bar that displays drop-down menus. Drop-down menus contain menu items alone or submenus. In addition, it's possible to create context menus (pop-up menus) that are activated when the end user right-clicks the mouse on a form or control instance. A menu system has several parts, as shown in Figure 13-2.

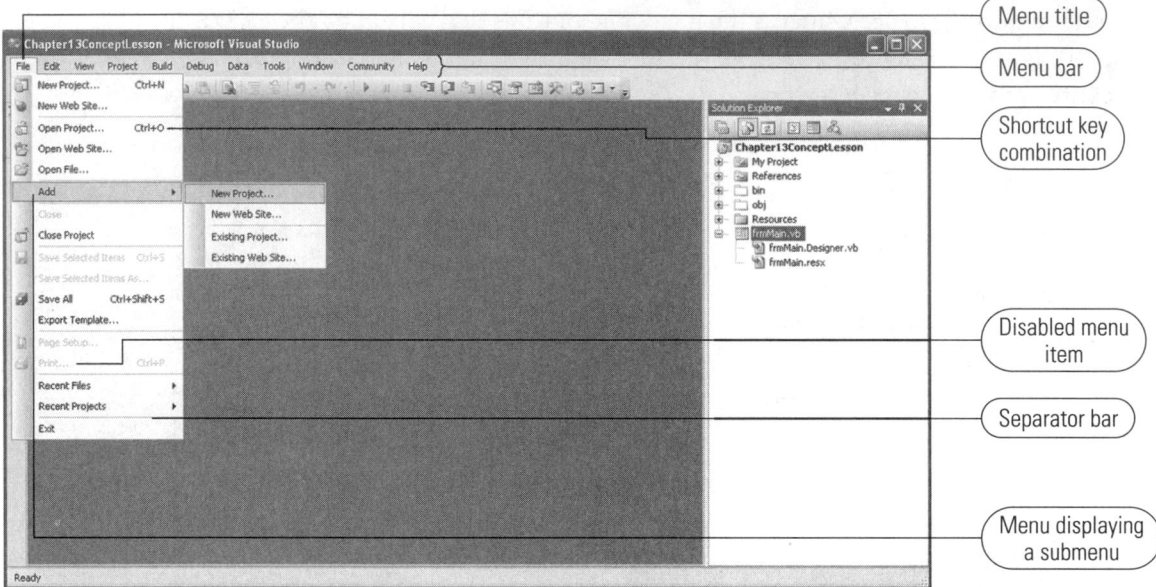

Figure 13-2: Anatomy of a menu

As shown in Figure 13-2, a menu bar appears across the top of a form, just below the form's title bar. A menu can appear in a container control too. For example, in this concept lesson, the menu bar appears on a `TabPage` control instance. Each menu title appearing on the menu bar displays a drop-down menu when clicked. A drop-down menu can contain menu items, which can be either enabled or disabled. Menu items can display submenus (additional drop-down menus). A drop-down menu can also contain separator bars to visually group menu items. Finally, each menu item can have a hot key, a shortcut key, or an associated icon.

Together, the following classes are used to create a menu system:

» The `MenuStrip` class provides the container for the menu.

» The `ToolStripMenuItem` class is used to create individual items on a menu.

» The `ToolStripComboBox` class is used to create a drop-down combo box on a menu.

» The `ToolStripTextBox` class is used to create a text box on a menu.

» The `ToolStripSeparator` class is used to create a separator bar to visually group menu items.

Only the more commonly used menu classes are discussed in this section.

> **NOTE** The `MenuStrip` and `ToolStripMenuItem` classes replace the `MainMenu` and `MenuItem` classes found in previous Visual Studio .NET versions. However, the `MainMenu` and `MenuItem` classes remain supported for backward compatibility. The `ToolStripComboBox`, `ToolStripTextBox`, and `ToolStripSeparator` classes are also new to Visual Studio 2005.

## INTRODUCTION TO THE MENUSTRIP CLASS

By itself, the `MenuStrip` class does very little. The `MenuStrip` class is responsible for the layout of menu items. It also defines whether ToolTips are displayed and the behavior of shortcut keys. The Hungarian prefix used in this chapter for the `MenuStrip` class is "ms".

The following properties are commonly used with the `MenuStrip` class:

» The `Items` property is a collection. The collection contains a reference to the items appearing on the menu.

» The `ShowItemToolTips` property defines whether ToolTips appear when the mouse hovers over a menu item. ToolTips work the same way with menu items as they do with any other control instance.

» The `TextDirection` property allows the text displayed on the menus to be rotated. For example, it's possible, although uncommon, to create a menu system that appears along the left or right side of the form with the text rotated 90 or 270 degrees.

» The `Visible` property makes a menu and its menu items visible or invisible.

## INTRODUCTION TO THE TOOLSTRIPMENUITEM CLASS

Different types of menu items can be created on a `MenuStrip`. The `ToolStripComboBox` control works similarly to the `ComboBox` control, and the `ToolStripTextBox` control works similarly to the `TextBox` control.

The primary control appearing on a `MenuStrip` is the `ToolStripMenuItem`, which supports the following members:

---

### Syntax
`System.Windows.Forms.ToolStripMenuItem class`

---

### Public Properties

» The `Checked` property defines a checked menu item, which is a menu item that displays a check mark to the left of the menu text. Valid values for the `Checked` property are `True` and `False`.

» The `Boolean Enabled` property defines whether the `ToolStripMenuItem` is enabled or disabled. Windows fires a `Click` event for enabled menu items. Windows does not fire a `Click` event for a disabled menu item. The text of a disabled menu item appears shaded. Thus, a disabled menu item works the same way as a disabled button.

» The `Image` property contains a reference to an image that appears on the menu item to the left of the menu text.

» The `Name` property defines the name for a `ToolStripMenuItem`. As with any other control instance, you use the `Name` property to reference the `ToolStripMenuItem` with code.

» The `ShowShortcutKeys` property defines whether the shortcut key for a menu item appears at run time. The shortcut key assigned to a menu item always appears to the right of the menu text.

» The `ShortcutKeys` property allows you to define a shortcut key for a menu item. This property works in tandem with the `ShowShortcutKeys` property.

» The `Text` property defines the text that appears on the menu item. Placing an ampersand (&) character in the text creates a hot key. This hot key works the same way as a hot key for a button.

» The `Visible` property determines whether a menu item is visible.

---

### Public Events

» Windows fires a `Click` event for a menu item when the end user clicks it, just as Windows fires a `Click` event for a button when the end user clicks the button.

---

Having discussed the classes used to create a menu system, you will now see how to implement one.


## CREATING MENU TITLES

To create a menu system, you first create an instance of the `MenuStrip` control on a form. As with any other control, when you create the `MenuStrip` control instance on a form, the Windows Forms Designer writes the necessary statements in the corresponding module file to create the control instance from its underlying class. As you create the menus, menu items, and submenus, the Windows Forms Designer writes additional statements to create instances of the `ToolStripMenuItem` class. The `MenuStrip` control appears in the resizable tray below the Windows Forms Designer.

Visual Studio makes the process of creating a form's menu system easy because it can be created in a visual way directly on a form. When you select an instance of the `MenuStrip` control, the Windows Forms Designer displays an in-place editor with which you create the individual menu items (`ToolStripMenuItem` control instances). Figure 13-3 shows the Windows Forms Designer and the corresponding in-place editor before any menus or menu items have been created.

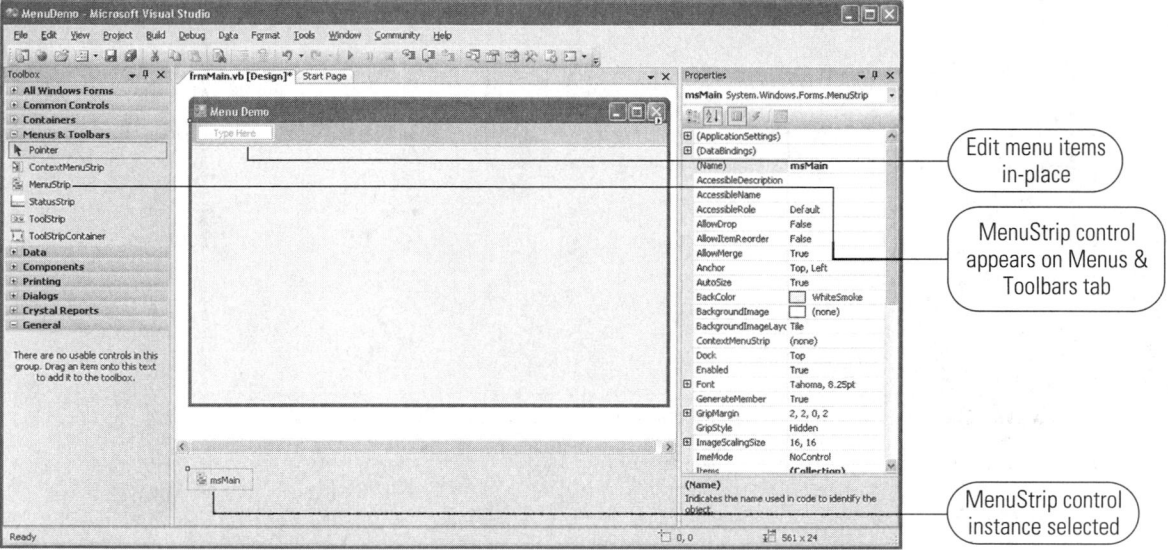

Figure 13-3: Menu visual designer

As shown in Figure 13-3, the `MenuStrip` control appears on the Menus & Toolbars tab of the Toolbox. The `MenuStrip` control instance appears in the resizable tray below the Windows Forms Designer. When the control instance is selected, the visual designer and in-place editor shown in Figure 13-3 allow you to create the menu system as it will appear to the end user. The menu system is created by typing menu captions in the same position that they will appear to the end user. Menu captions are entered in the boxes titled "Type Here." The properties applicable to each `ToolStripMenuItem` can be edited using the Properties window, just as the Properties window is used to edit properties for any other control instance. Figure 13-4 shows the visual designer and in-place editor with several menu items created.

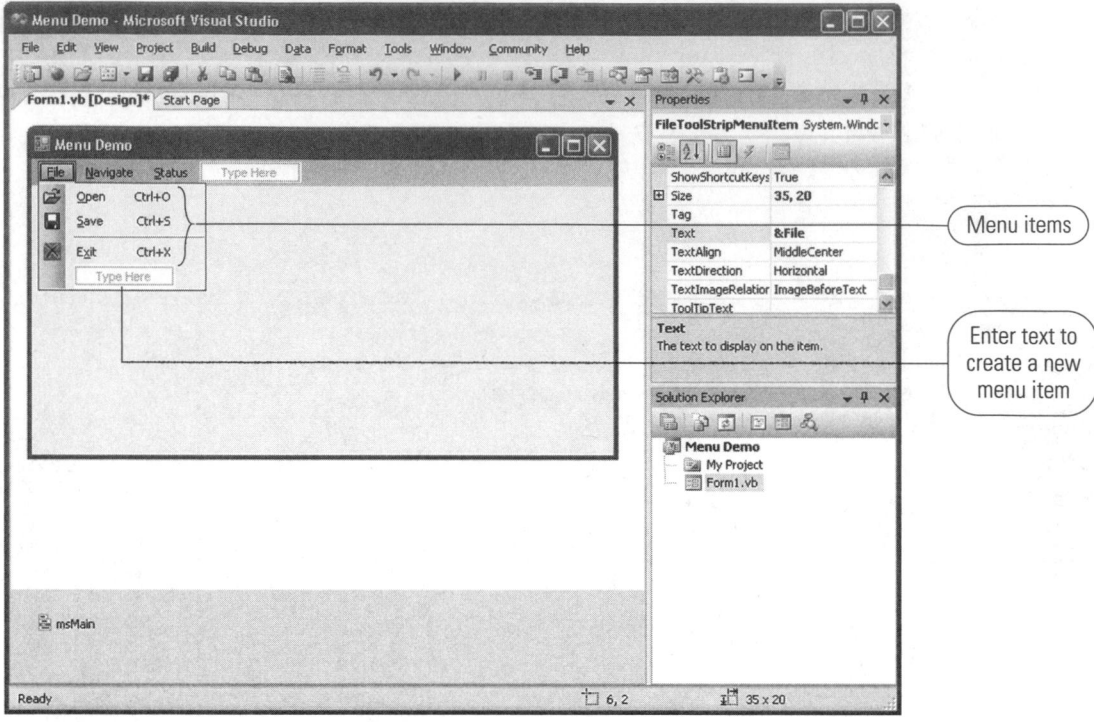

Figure 13-4: Menu visual designer with menu items created

As shown in Figure 13-4, the MenuStrip control instance contains menus named File, Navigate, and Status. A hot key is defined for each menu. The File menu contains three menu items named Open, Save, and Exit. A horizontal line called a separator bar appears between the Save and Exit menu items. Hot keys and shortcut key combinations have been defined for each menu item. Entering text in the prompt "Type Here" creates a new menu item.

Each ToolStripMenuItem on a menu has a Name property and a Text property. The Name property has the same purpose as it does for any other control instance. When writing code, the menu item is referenced by its name. The value of the Text property contains the text that the end user sees on the menu or menu item. Because a menu system is bound to a form, each form in an application can have a unique menu system associated with it. An instance of the MenuStrip control is associated with a form by setting the form's MainMenuStrip property to an instance of the MenuStrip control. The MainMenuStrip property is set automatically when the MenuStrip control instance is created on the form.

The following statement illustrates how to associate a `MenuStrip` control instance named msDemo with the form using the `Me` keyword:

```
Me.MainMenuStrip = msDemo
```

> **» NOTE** This book typically uses Hungarian notation to name control instances. However, Visual Studio assigns meaningful default names to the menu items that make up a menu. This descriptive name is the same as the menu item's caption with all the spaces removed, followed by the string "ToolStripMenuItem." Default names for menu items are used in this chapter for brevity.

> **» TIP** The order in which a form's menu system is created is a matter of personal choice. It is possible to create all the menu titles first, and then create the menu items that correspond to those menu titles. It is also possible to create a menu title, and then create all of the menu items that appear beneath it before proceeding to the next menu title.

## MODIFYING A MENU SYSTEM

Visual Studio makes it easy to change the appearance and organization of menu items on an existing menu. You need only right-click the menu in the Windows Forms Designer, and then select items from the context menu, as discussed in the following list:

» Clicking *Delete* on the context menu removes the selected menu title or menu item. If a menu title is selected, a dialog box opens indicating that the menu items below the menu title or menu item will be deleted.

» If a menu title is selected, clicking *Insert* on the context menu inserts a new menu item, combo box, or text box, before the selected menu title, depending on the option selected. If a menu item is selected, a new menu item, combo box, or text box is inserted above the selected menu item.

» The *Insert, Separator* command applies only to menu items. Clicking this command inserts a separator bar before the selected menu item. A **separator bar** is a horizontal line that divides two items on a menu. Its only purpose is to visually group or separate menu items. Like all components of a menu, a separator bar must have a unique name (which is the value of the `Name` property). The data type of a separator bar is `ToolStripSeparator`.

» Clicking the *Edit DropDownItems* command on the context menu allows you to edit the menu items using the Items Collection Editor.

» Clicking the *View Code* command activates the Code Editor and selects or creates the `Click` event handler for the selected menu item.

» Clicking the *Properties* command activates the Properties window for the selected menu title or menu item.

» Clicking the *Set Image* button activates the Select Resource dialog box, which is used to add an image to the application's resource file.

## THE ITEMS COLLECTION EDITOR

In addition to editing menu items in place, it is possible to edit menu items using the Items Collection Editor, which is shown in Figure 13-5.

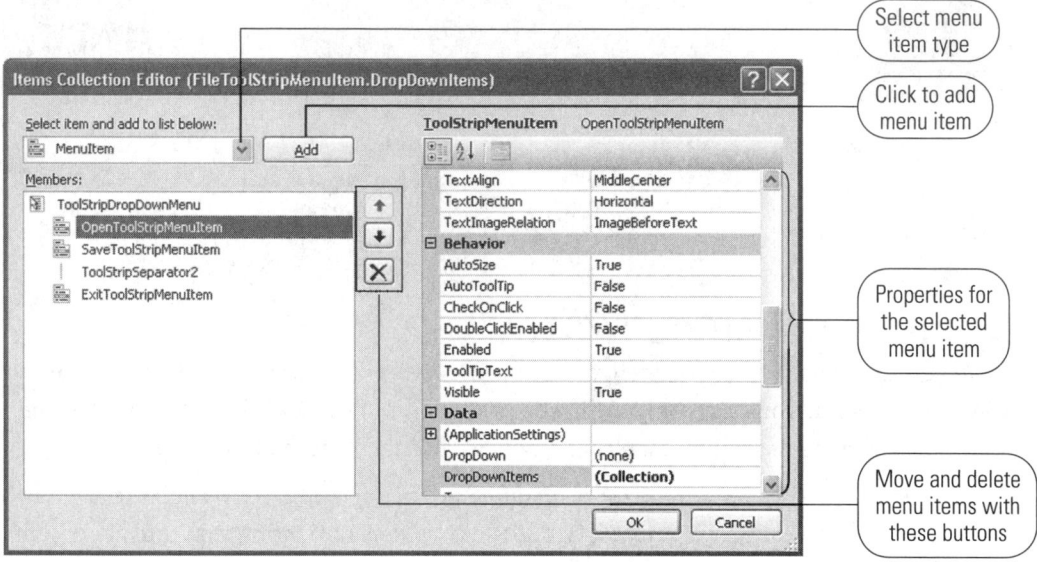

Figure 13-5: Items Collection Editor

The Items Collection Editor can only be used to edit part of a menu at one time. That is, it's only possible to edit the menu titles or the menu items on a single submenu. Figure 13-5 shows the Items Collection Editor editing the menu items for the File menu.

The following list describes features of the Items Collection Editor:

» In the combo box appearing in the upper-left corner of the Items Collection Editor, you select the type of control instance to create on the menu.

» Clicking the Add button creates the control instance. The control instances appear in the Members area. When a control instance is added, it is added to the end of the list appearing in the Members area.

» The three buttons appearing in the Members area are used to move a menu item up or down in the order of menu items, and to delete an existing menu item, respectively.

» The properties for the selected member appear in the Properties section appearing on the right side of the dialog box. This section works just like the Properties window and is used to edit the same properties. Menu properties can also be edited by selecting a menu item and activating the Properties window to set the menu items' properties.

## SHORTCUT KEYS

Shortcut keys should be created for the more frequently used menu items to allow the end user to execute the menu item directly without navigating through the menu. Furthermore, by allowing both mouse and keyboard input for a menu item, the interface appeals to the broadest number of users.

When selecting characters for a shortcut key, most developers use the first character of the menu caption. The Items Collection Editor or the Properties window can be used to define a shortcut key. To define a shortcut key for a menu item, you set the `ShortcutKeys` property, as shown in Figure 13-6.

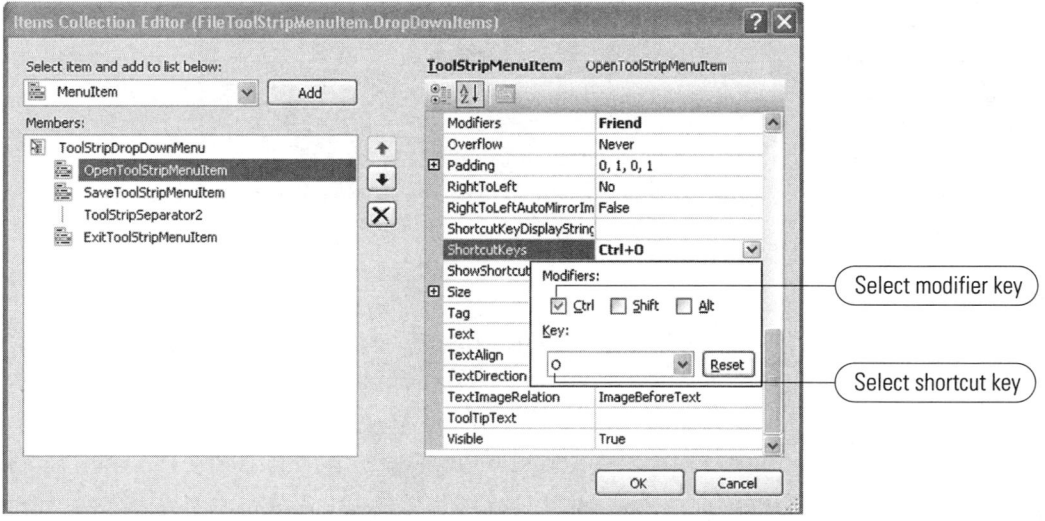

Figure 13-6: Creating a shortcut key for a menu item

As shown in Figure 13-6, the `ShortcutKeys` property is set using a visual editor. The check boxes allow you to select the modifier key that will be used. The Ctrl, Shift, and Alt keys are the valid modifier keys. The Key combo box allows you to select the keyboard key. The combo box lists the keys alphabetically. The shortcut key defined in Figure 13-6 is Ctrl+O.

## ADDING IMAGES TO MENU ITEMS

Each menu item can display an image. In addition, images are used by other control instances, including the `ToolStrip` and the `StatusStrip` controls discussed later in this chapter. Because several different control instances might need to use a particular image, the images are not stored in the control instance itself. Rather, the image is stored in an application-wide resource file. Images are added to a resource file using the Select Resource dialog box shown in Figure 13-7.

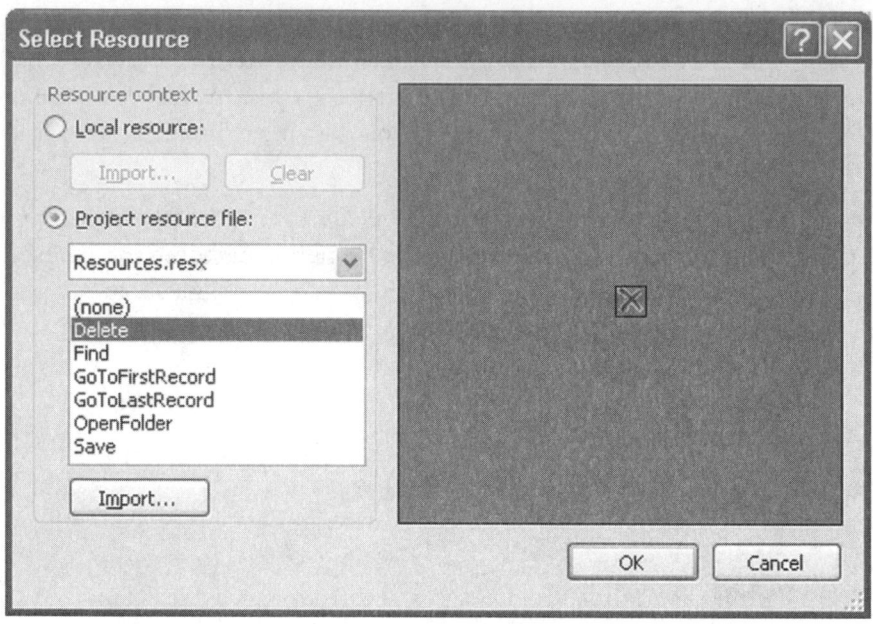

Figure 13-7: Select Resource dialog box

As shown in Figure 13-7, the Select Resource dialog box has two radio buttons. These radio buttons define how the images are added to the application, as follows:

» The Local resource radio button causes an image to be added to the resource file associated with the form. In the Solution Explorer, this file appears as a subfolder of the form with a file extension of .resx. Thus, if the form were named frmMain, the corresponding resource file would be named frmMain.resx. If images are added to the resource file for a form, they can be used only by that form.

» The Project resource file radio button causes an image to be added to the resource file associated with the project itself. Thus, any images added to the project's resource file can be used by all of the forms in a project. When a resource is added to the project, the resource is added to the project's resource file named Resources.resx.

In this chapter, images are added to the project's resource file. Importing an image into a resource file involves selecting the resource context, and then clicking the Import button. When the Import button is clicked, an Open dialog box opens, allowing you to select the image file to import.

## CREATING EVENT HANDLERS FOR MENUS

When the end user clicks a menu item or activates it using a hot key or shortcut key, Windows fires a `Click` event for that menu item, causing the corresponding `Click` event handler to execute. Thus, the event handler for a menu item works the same way as the event handler for a button.

The easiest way to create a `Click` event handler for a menu item is to double-click the menu item in the Windows Forms Designer. Visual Studio automatically opens the Code Editor and creates an event handler prototype for you. It's also possible to use the Class Name and Method Name combo boxes in the Code Editor to create or select the event handler.

The following code segment illustrates the `Click` event handler for the `ToolStripMenuItem` control instance named OpenToolStripMenuItem:

```
Private Sub OpenToolStripMenuItem_Click( _
    ByVal sender As System.Object, _
    ByVal e As System.EventArgs) _
    Handles OpenToolStripMenuItem.Click
    . . .
End Sub
```

As you can see from the preceding code segment, the `Click` event handler for a `ToolStripMenuItem` has the same syntax as the `Click` event handler for an instance of the `Button` control.

When working with a checked menu item, the `Click` event handler works the same way. However, additional code must be written to check or uncheck the menu item, as shown in the following statements:

```
Private Sub EnabledToolStripMenuItem_Click( _
    ByVal sender As System.Object, _
    ByVal e As System.EventArgs) _
    Handles EnabledToolStripMenuItem.Click

    If EnabledToolStripMenuItem.Checked Then
        EnabledToolStripMenuItem.Checked = False
        ' Statements
    Else
        EnabledToolStripMenuItem.Checked = True
        ' Statements
    End If
End Sub
```

The preceding code segment causes a menu item to operate as a toggle switch that is either checked or unchecked. The `If` statement determines whether the menu item is currently checked. If it is, the `Checked` property is set to `False`. If the menu item is not checked, the `Checked` property is set to `True`.

## CREATING CONTEXT MENUS

Context menus work similarly to ordinary menus appearing on a form. However, instead of using the `MenuStrip` control, the `ContextMenuStrip` control is used. To create multiple context menus, create multiple instances of the `ContextMenuStrip` control. Like the `MenuStrip` control, the `ContextMenuStrip` control is an invisible control so it appears in the resizable tray below the Windows Forms Designer.

Menu items are created on a context menu in the same way that they are created on ordinary menus. That is, you select the context menu, and then edit the menu items in-place in the Windows Forms Designer or using the Items Collection Editor. `Click` event handlers are also created the same way. Figure 13-8 shows a context menu in the Windows Forms Designer.

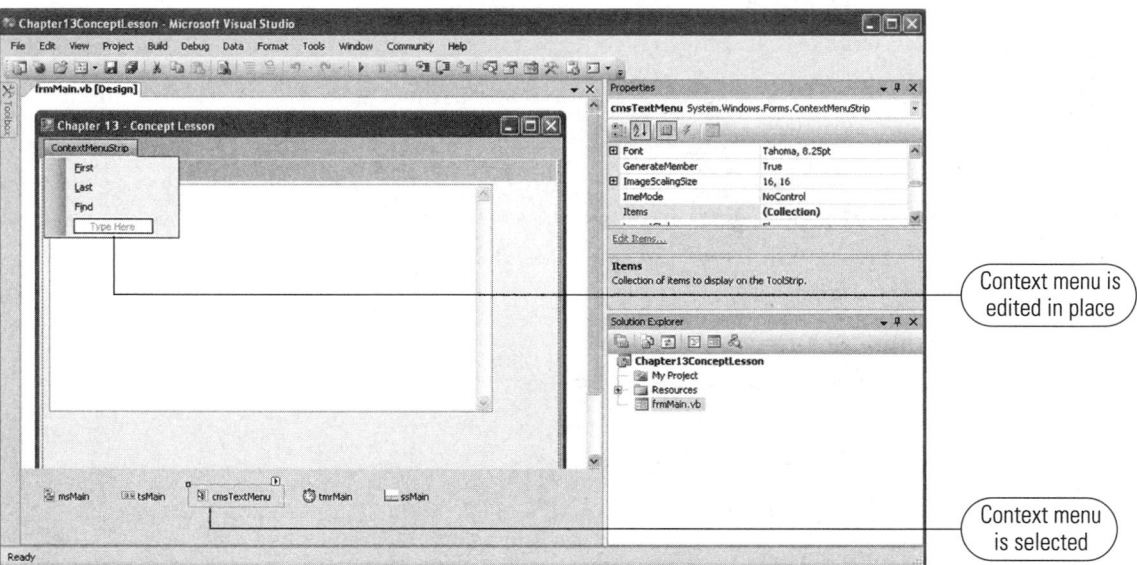

Figure 13-8: Creating a context menu

After a context menu has been created, it must be associated with a form or control instance on the form. To associate a `ContextMenuStrip` with another control instance, you set the `ContextMenuStrip` property of the control instance to an existing `ContextMenuStrip`. This property can be set at design time using the Properties window, or by writing an executable statement, as shown in the following code segment:

```
txtDemo.ContextMenuStrip = cmsDemo
```

The preceding statement causes the text box named txtDemo to be associated with the ContextMenuStrip control instance named cmsDemo. It is possible to change the association of a context menu strip and a control instance while an application runs.

When the end user right-clicks the mouse on the control instance at run time, the applicable ContextMenuStrip appears.

In this exploration exercise, you will examine a menu system for a form and how to configure different menu items.

1. Start Visual Studio and open the chapter's concept lesson located in the folder **Chapter.13\Chapter13ConceptLesson**. Activate the **Windows Forms Designer** for the form named frmMain, if necessary.

2. At design time, click the control instance named **msMain** in the resizable tray below the Windows Forms Designer. The Windows Forms Designer allows you to edit the control instance in place. Select different menu items and examine the property settings in the Properties window. Figure 13-9 shows the MenuStrip Control tab activated.

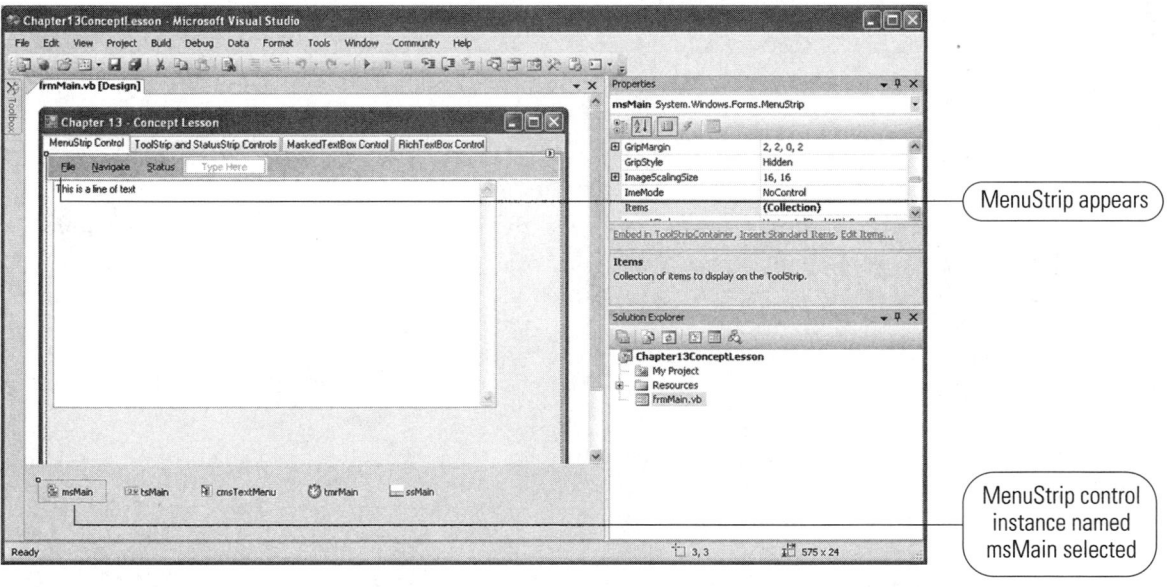

Figure 13-9: Concept lesson—MenuStrip Control tab

3. Using the in-place editor in the Windows Forms Designer, click **File** on the menu bar, and then double-click the **Open** menu item on the File menu. Note that the Click event handler is activated in the Code Editor in the same way that a Click event handler would be activated for a Button control instance.

4. Activate the Windows Forms Designer, and select the `ContextMenuStrip` control instance named **cmsTextMenu**. As you can see, the context menu can be edited in place in the Windows Forms Designer in the same way as any other menu.

5. Run the application.

6. Click **File**, **Open** and open a text file of your choosing. The file is read into the `TextBox` control instance on the form. Click the menu items on the **Navigate** menu to select the start of the text and the end of the text. Finally, click the **Enabled** and **Locked** menu items on the Status menu. These two menu items are configured to operate as checked menu items.

## MINI-QUIZ 1

1. Which of the following statements is correct regarding creating a menu?

   a. The `MainMenu` control is new to Visual Studio 2005 and is used to create the menu system for a form.

   b. The `MenuStrip` control is new to Visual Studio 2005 and replaces the `MainMenu` control.

   c. To create the menu items on a form, you use the Menu Items Editor.

   d. Menu items on a menu are always visible and enabled. That is, a menu item cannot be made invisible or be disabled.

   e. none of the above

2. Which of the following statements is correct regarding a context menu?

   a. A form can have at most one context menu.

   b. A context menu is associated with a form or control instance by setting the `PopUpMenu` property.

   c. A form can have multiple context menus. Different control instances on the form can be associated with different context menus.

   d. To create a context menu, you use the Context Menu Editor.

   e. none of the above

3. What is meant by the term container control? In your answer, list three or more container controls.

# CREATING A TOOLBAR

The topics of menus and toolbars are closely related. Most applications that you use supply both a menu system and equivalent toolbar buttons. That is, many applications allow you to click File, Open to open a file, or click an equivalent toolbar button to accomplish the same task. A well-designed user interface should provide a menu system and a toolbar to perform equivalent tasks so as to appeal to the broadest number of users.

The process to create a toolbar is very similar to the process to create a menu system. The `ToolStrip` control supplies the container for the buttons that appear on the toolbar in the same way that the `MenuStrip` control supplies the container for the menu items that appear on the menu. The `ToolStrip` control instance appears in the resizable tray below the Windows Forms Designer.

After a `ToolStrip` control instance has been created on a form, you create other control instances on the container (`ToolStrip`). The following list describes the control instances that can be created on the `ToolStrip` container:

» The `ToolStripButton` class works the same way as the `Button` class and provides a clickable button. The Hungarian prefix used in this book for the `ToolStripButton` is "tsb".

» The `ToolStripSeparator` class displays a separator bar between two items on the `ToolStrip`.

» The `ToolStripLabel` class works the same way as the `Label` class and displays a textual message. The Hungarian prefix used in this book for the `ToolStripLabel` is "tsl".

» The `ToolStripDropDownButton` class is used to create a drop-down menu on the toolbar. The Hungarian prefix used in this book for the `ToolStripDropDownButton` is "tsdd".

» The `ToolStripComboBox` class works the same way as the `ComboBox` class and displays a drop-down list of items. The Hungarian prefix used in this book for the `ToolStripComboBox` is "tscbo".

» The `ToolStripTextBox` class works the same way as the `TextBox` class supplying an editable field. The Hungarian prefix used in this book for the `ToolStripTextBox` is "tstxt".

Figure 13-10 shows a sample toolbar with the various types of buttons.

> **»NOTE**
>
> The `ToolStrip` control replaces the `ToolBar` control supported by previous versions of Visual Studio .NET. The `ToolBar` control remains supported for backward compatibility with previous Visual Studio .NET versions.

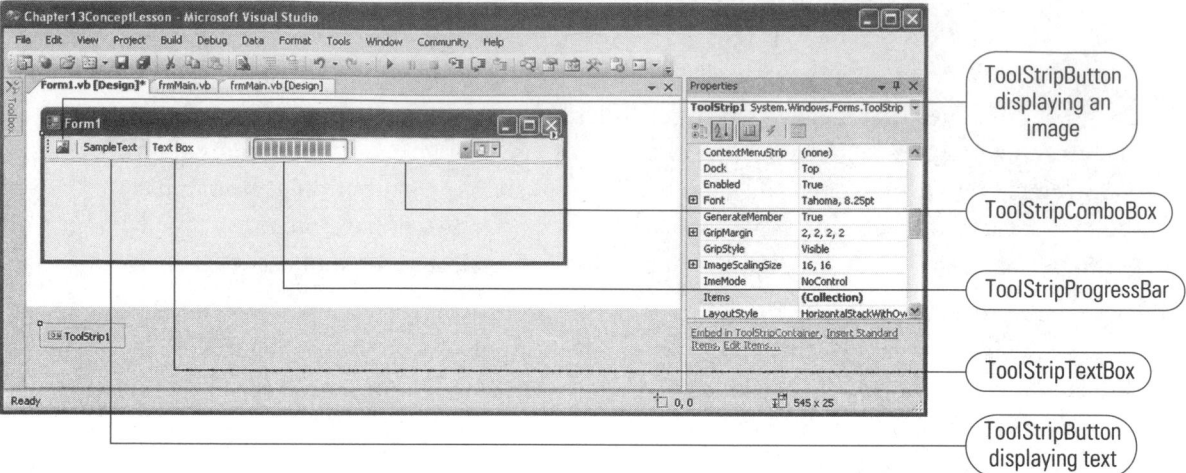

Figure 13-10: Toolbar with sample buttons

The steps to create the buttons on a toolbar involve using the Items Collection Editor shown in Figure 13-11. This is the same Items Collection Editor used to create items on a menu.

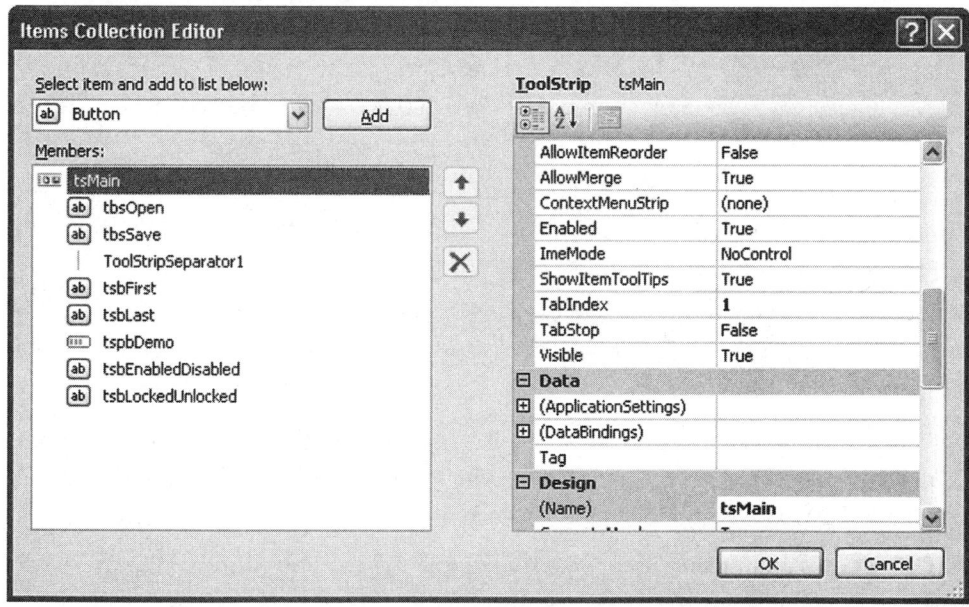

Figure 13-11: Items Collection Editor

As shown in Figure 13-11, the Items Collection Editor works the same way for a toolbar as it works for a menu. The combo box is used to select the type of control instance to add. The control instances appear in the Members section. Buttons can be reordered and deleted by clicking the buttons in the Members area. The Properties section is used to edit the properties for the selected member.

## THE TOOLSTRIPBUTTON CLASS

The `ToolStripButton` class represents a button on a toolbar and works similarly to an instance of the `Button` control. It has the following properties:

» The `Checked` property denotes whether the button appears raised or recessed. Values for the `Checked` property are `True` or `False`.

» If the `CheckOnClick` property is set to `True`, the button is automatically pressed or raised as the button is clicked. Thus, the button operates as a toggle switch.

» The `DisplayStyle` property specifies whether text, an image, or both appear on the button. Typically, toolbar buttons display images.

» The `Image` property is used to specify the image that appears on the button. Again, the Image Collection Editor is used to set the `Image` property.

» The `Text` property controls the text displayed on the button.

The `ToolStripButton` class handles a `Click` event in the same way that a `Button` control instance handles a `Click` event. The following statements illustrate the `Click` event handler for the `ToolStripButton` named tsbFirst:

```
Private Sub tsbFirst_Click(ByVal sender As System.Object, _
    ByVal e As System.EventArgs) Handles tsbFirst.Click
    ' Statements
End Sub
```

## THE TOOLSTRIPSEPARATOR CLASS

In addition to clickable buttons, it is possible to create a vertical separator bar to visually identify groups of buttons or other control instances appearing on the toolbar. Two properties are useful when creating separator bars:

» The `ForeColor` property defines the foreground color of the separator bar.

» The `Visible` property specifies whether the separator bar is visible or hidden. Separator bars are often hidden when the surrounding toolbar control instances are hidden.

Other than seeing that the separator bar visually separates the buttons on a toolbar, the end user has no interaction with the separator bar.

## THE TOOLSTRIPPROGRESSBAR CLASS

The `ToolStrip` control can also be configured to display a progress bar. A progress bar displays the relative completion of a long-running task. The relative progress is defined by the following properties and methods of the `ToolStripProgressBar` class:

» The `Minimum` property defines the minimum value of the progress bar. The default value is 0.

» The `Maximum` property defines the maximum value of the progress bar. The default value is 100.

» The `Value` property defines the current value of the progress bar. This value must be between the minimum value and the maximum value.

» The `Increment` method accepts one argument, the value to increment the progress bar. In other words, the `Value` property is incremented using the `Increment` method. It is also possible to set the `Value` property directly.

The following code segment illustrates how to update a progress bar:

```
Dim Count As Integer
For Count = 1 To 100000000
    If Count Mod 1000000 = 0 Then
        tspbDemo.Increment(1)
    End If
Next
```

The preceding statements illustrate a long-running loop. The `If` statement causes the value of the progress bar to be incremented by 1 every 1,000,000 iterations. Thus, the progress bar is incremented from 1 to 100.

A progress bar can be reset by setting the value of the progress bar to 0 (the value of the `Minimum` property), as shown in the following statement:

```
tspbDemo.Value = 0
```

## THE TOOLSTRIPCOMBOBOX, TOOLSTRIPTEXTBOX, AND TOOLSTRIPLABEL CLASSES

The `ToolStripComboBox`, `ToolStripTextBox`, and `ToolStripLabel` classes work just like the `ComboBox`, `TextBox`, and `Label` classes with which you are familiar. It is common to use a `ToolStripComboBox` to create a drop-down list. For example, Microsoft Word uses a drop-down combo box with which the end user selects font sizes and selects the magnification.

# INTRODUCTION TO THE STATUSSTRIP

Most well-designed applications display status information in a status bar that appears across the bottom of the form. For example, Microsoft Word displays the current editing position along with other information in a status bar. To create a status bar, you use the `StatusStrip` control. The implementation of the `StatusStrip` control is similar to the implementation of the `ToolStrip` control. That is, the `StatusStrip` control is a container for the other control instances created in the status bar. This book uses a Hungarian prefix of "ss" for the `StatusStrip` control.

Like the other controls discussed in this chapter, the `StatusStrip` control is a container control. The following list describes the control instances that can be created on an instance of the `StatusStrip` control:

» The `ToolStripStatusLabel` class displays descriptive text in the same way that the `Label` control displays descriptive text. However, additional properties of the `ToolStripStatusLabel` are used to define how the control instance is resized when the form is resized.

» The `ToolStripProgressBar` class, as its name implies, displays a progress bar to show the relative progress of a long-running operation. This class works the same way as a progress bar appearing on a toolbar.

» The `ToolStripDropDownButton` class is used to create a button that drops down. Drop-down buttons are not commonly used on a status bar.

Figure 13-12 shows an instance of the `StatusStrip` control with sample control instances.

> **» NOTE**
>
> The `StatusStrip` control replaces the `StatusBar` control found in previous versions of Visual Studio .NET. However, the `StatusBar` control remains supported for backward compatibility.

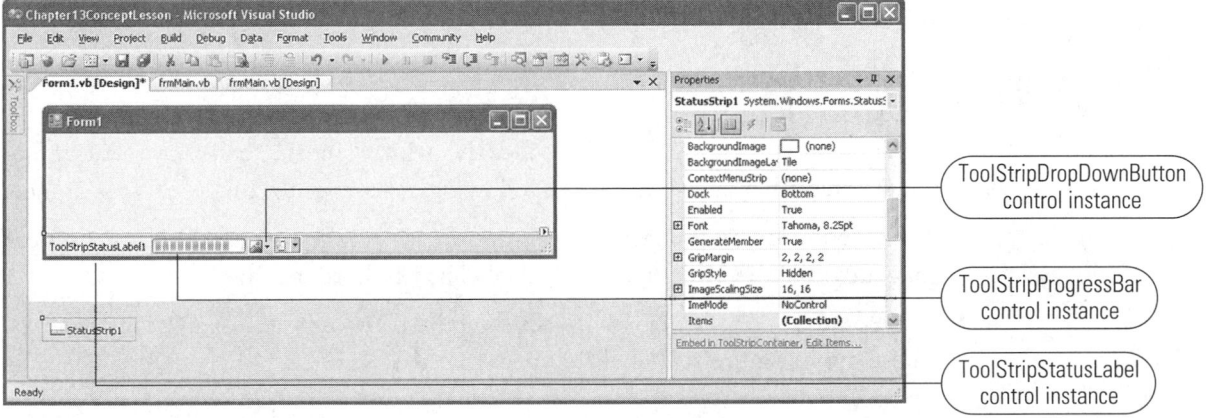

Figure 13-12: StatusStrip with sample control instances

All of these control instances are created using the Items Collection Editor shown in Figure 13-13.

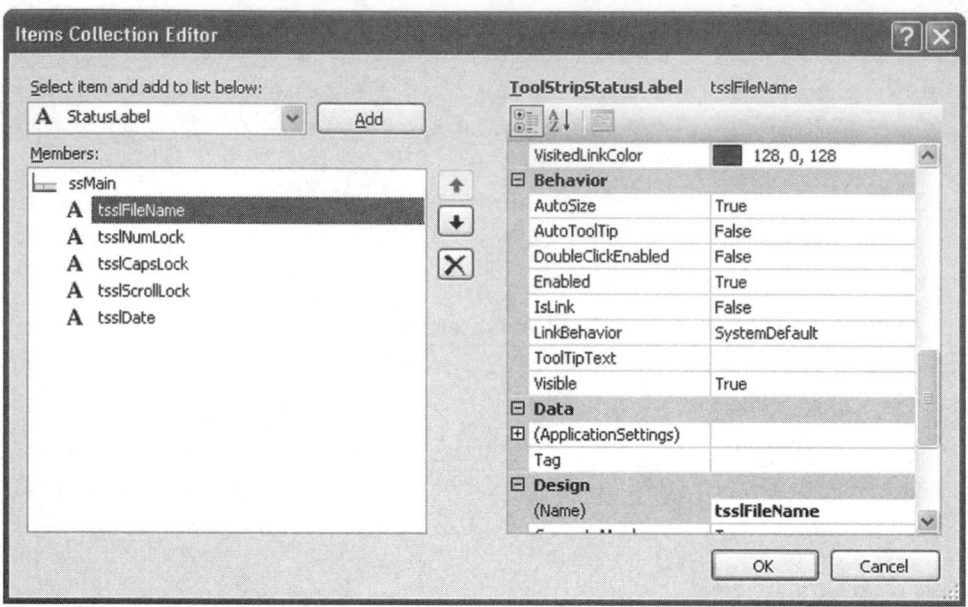

Figure 13-13: Items Collection Editor for the StatusStrip

As shown in Figure 13-13, the Items Collection Editor works the same way for the `StatusStrip` control, the `ToolStrip` control, and the `MenuStrip` control. The control instances that can appear in the container appear in the drop-down box found in the upper-left corner of the dialog box. The Members box displays the control instances that have been created. The Properties section displays the applicable properties for the currently selected member.

## THE TOOLSTRIPSTATUSLABEL CLASS

The `ToolStripStatusLabel` class provides the primary means to display status information in the status bar and supports the following properties to control its appearance:

» The `BorderSides` property defines optional top, left, right, and bottom borders that surround the label. By default, a label has no borders.

» The `BorderStyle` property defines how the three-dimensional border appears. These options allow the label to appear raised or sunken.

» The `Padding` property contains the number of pixels of white space that appear between the control instance and the text or image appearing in the control instance.

» The `Spring` property causes the label to resize to fill the available region of the status bar.

» If the `AutoSize` property is set to `True`, the control instance resizes based on its contents. If set to `False`, the size of the control instance is fixed on the `StatusStrip`.

## DISPLAYING THE STATUS OF KEYBOARD KEYS ON A STATUS BAR

The `Keyboard` class supported by the `My.Computer` object is used to get information about the keyboard, including the status of modifier keys and other keys such as the Num Lock, Caps Lock, and Scroll Lock keys. The following code segment shows how to determine whether the Num Lock key is enabled:

```
If My.Computer.Keyboard.NumLock = True Then
    tsslNumLock.Text = "Num enabled"
Else
    tsslNumLock.Text = "Num disabled"
End If
```

In the preceding code segment, if the Num Lock key is enabled, the text "Num enabled" appears in the `ToolStripStatusLabel` named tsslNumLock. Otherwise, the text "Num disabled" appears in the control instance. The following properties return the status of other keyboard keys:

» The `Keyboard.CapsLock` property indicates whether the Caps Lock key is enabled.

» The `Keyboard.ScrollLock` property indicates whether the Scroll Lock key is enabled.

In this exploration exercise, you will see how to work with the `ToolStrip` and `StatusStrip` controls.

1. Activate the Windows Forms Designer for the chapter's main form. Click the **ToolStrip and StatusStrip Controls** tab, as shown in Figure 13-14. Figure 13-14 shows the form at run time.

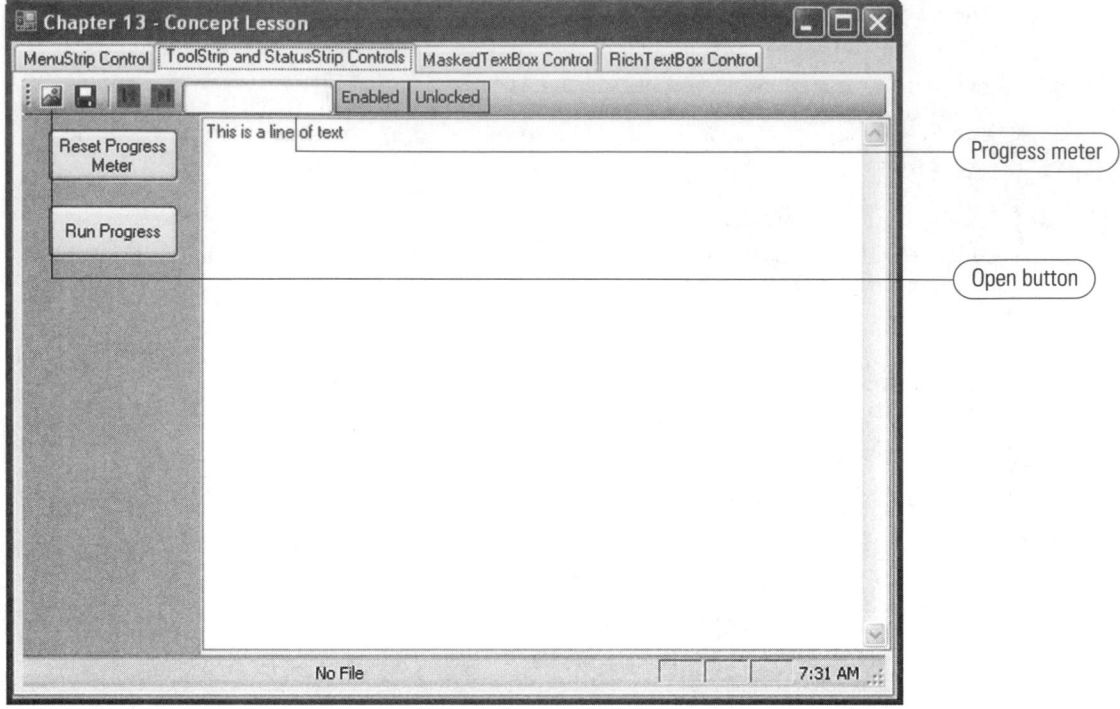

Figure 13-14: Concept lesson—ToolStrip and StatusStrip Controls tab

As shown in Figure 13-14, a `ToolStrip` control instance appears at the top of the form and a `StatusStrip` control instance appears along the bottom of the form.

2. Activate the Properties window for the `ToolStrip` control instance named tsMain. Locate the `Items` property and click the **Value** column to display the Build button. Click the **Build** button to display the Items Collection Editor. Examine the buttons that make up the `ToolStrip` and how they are configured.

3. Run the application and click the **ToolStrip and StatusStrip Controls** tab. Click the **Open** button shown in Figure 13-14. The button's `Click` event handler executes. This `Click` event handler has the same syntax as any other `Click` event handler. Open a text file of your choosing.

4. Click the navigation buttons to position the insertion point at the beginning of the text box and at the end of the text box.

5. The Enabled and Unlocked buttons are configured to operate as check boxes. Click the **Enabled** and **Unlocked** buttons to disable and lock the text box, respectively.

6. Click the **Run Progress** button. The same long-running loop as the one presented in this chapter executes and updates the progress meter appearing in the toolbar. Click the **Reset Progress Meter** button to reset the progress meter. The code in the button's `Click` event handler resets the `Value` property to 0.

7. Note that a `StatusStrip` appears on the screen when the ToolStrip and StatusStrip Controls tab is visible. End the application. Again, using the Properties window, activate the Items Collection Editor for the control instance to view the control instances appearing on the `StatusStrip` and their configuration.

8. Run the application again, and then click the **ToolStrip and StatusStrip Controls** tab.

9. Press each of the **Num Lock**, **Caps Lock**, and **Scroll Lock** keys twice. The status bar is updated to display the status of these keys. To do so, the form's `KeyUp` event handler contains the code to check the status of these keyboard keys and update the status bar accordingly.

## MINI-QUIZ 2

1. Which of the following general statements is correct regarding a toolbar?

   a. An application can have a menu or a toolbar but not both.

   b. By definition, a toolbar must appear at the top of a form, just above the menu if one exists.

   c. Toolbar buttons are typically created to mimic equivalent menu items.

   d. All toolbar buttons work the same way. That is, it is not possible to configure toolbar buttons differently.

   e. none of the above

2. Describe how to create a separator bar on a toolbar and the purpose of a separator bar.

3. What is the name of the property you set to make a `ToolStripStatusLabel` resize to fit the unoccupied region of the status bar control instance?

   a. `Resize`

   b. `Grow`

   c. `AdjustSize`

   d. `Spring`

   e. none of the above

*(Continued)* ▶

4. Which of the following controls can be contained by a `StatusStrip`?

   a. `StatusLabel, StatusProgressBar, StatusButton`

   b. `ToolStripStatusLabel, ToolStripProgressBar,`
      `ToolStripDropDownButton`

   c. `Label, ProgressBar, DropDownButton`

   d. `ContainerTextBox, ContainerLabel, ContainerButton`

   e. none of the above

# ADVANCED TEXT PROCESSING CONTROLS

Visual Studio supports two additional text-based controls that have capabilities to extend those of the `TextBox` control, as follows:

» The `MaskedTextBox` control supplies specialized editing capabilities by restricting the allowable characters in each character position. Thus, the `MaskedTextBox` control can be used to simplify the process of input validation.

» The `RichTextBox` control supports editing of a file format called rich text format. This type of file supports custom formatting of fonts and colors.

These two controls are discussed in the following sections of the chapter.

## THE MASKEDTEXTBOX CONTROL

Visual Studio supports a control called the `MaskedTextBox` control that makes input validation surprisingly easy. Like the `TextBox` control, the `MaskedTextBox` control inherits from the `TextBoxBase` class, so it supports nearly the same properties. One important property related to the `MaskedTextBox` control is the `Mask` property.

### PLACEHOLDER AND LITERAL CHARACTERS

The `Mask` property works similarly to the Format argument of the `ToString` method applicable to numeric data types. That is, placeholder and literal characters describe how data should be formatted. The `Mask` property is used to define the number of required and optional input characters and the position at which those characters must appear. It is also used to specify the type of input that must appear at a particular character position along with any literal values that must appear. Conceptually, these input masks work similarly to masks you have used when formatting strings. Table 13-1 illustrates selected mask characters and their purposes.

| Mask character | Description |
|---|---|
| 0 | A required digit between 0 and 9 |
| 9 | An optional digit or space |
| # | An optional digit or space; if the position is left blank, a space is rendered |
| L | A required letter |
| ? | An optional letter |
| A | An optional alphanumeric entry |
| . | The decimal placeholder |
| , | The thousands placeholder |
| : | The time separator |
| / | The date separator |
| $ | The currency placeholder |

Table 13-1: Mask characters

So that you don't have to create common input masks by hand, a dialog box is supplied that allows common input masks to be selected, as shown in Figure 13-15.

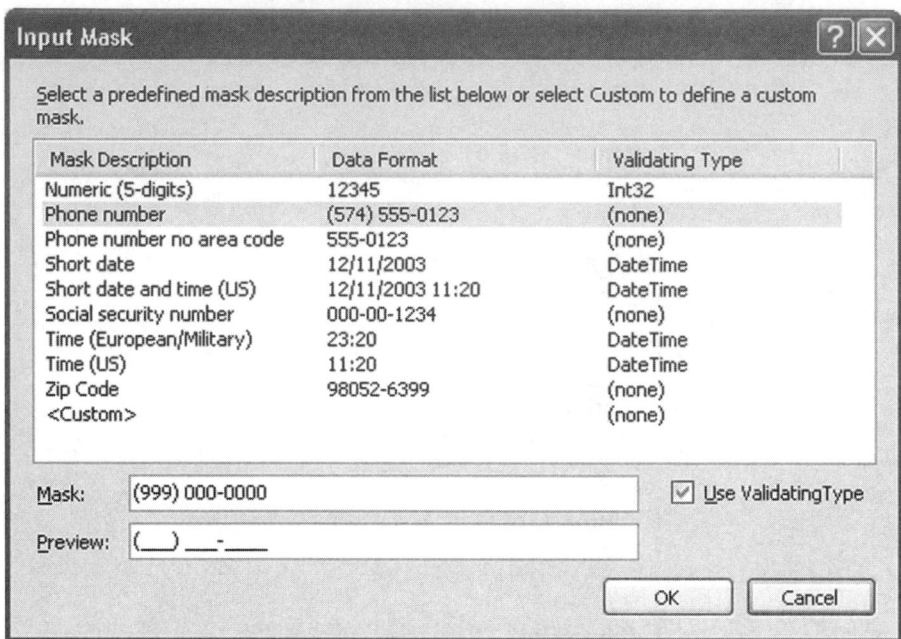

Figure 13-15: Input Mask dialog box

As shown in Figure 13-15, the Input Mask dialog box contains three columns. The first column lists the description of the mask. The second column contains a sample of the mask, and the final column contains the data type of the mask. It's also possible to create a custom mask by setting the `Mask` property directly. A preview of the input mask also appears in the dialog box.

In addition to setting the `Mask` property at design time, it's also possible to set the `Mask` property at run time, as the following statement shows:

```
mtbDemo.Mask = "LLL000"
```

The preceding mask requires that the input contain three letters followed by three digits.

## ADDITIONAL PROPERTIES OF THE MASKEDTEXTBOX CONTROL

In addition to the `Mask` property, there are additional properties related to the `MaskedTextBox`, as described in the following list:

» The `PromptChar` property stores a character that will be displayed in the absence of input by the end user. The underscore character is commonly used as the prompt character.

» The `BeepOnError` property defines whether an audible beep will sound when an invalid character is entered. Valid values for the property are `True` or `False`.

» The `MaskInputRejected` event fires each time an invalid mask character is entered into a field (character position).

It is common to handle the `MaskInputRejected` event to display a message about the error and how the end user can correct it. To illustrate, Canadian zip codes have the format (mask) of L0L-0L0. Thus, a valid Canadian zip code format would be A1A-2B2. The following code segment illustrates a possible `MaskInputRejected` event handler:

```
Private Sub mtbCanadaZipCode_MaskInputRejected( _
    ByVal sender As System.Object, ByVal e As _
    System.Windows.Forms.MaskInputRejectedEventArgs) _
    Handles mtbCanadaZipCode.MaskInputRejected
    Select Case e.Position
        Case 0, 2, 5
            txtMessage.Text = "Character at position " _
                & e.Position.ToString & " must be a letter." & _
                CrLf & txtMessage.Text
        Case 1, 4, 6
            txtMessage.Text = "Character at position " _
                & e.Position.ToString & " must be a digit." & _
                CrLf & txtMessage.Text
    End Select
End Sub
```

The preceding code segment displays a different error message based on the character position containing the error. Character positions 0, 2, and 5 must contain a letter, and character positions 1, 4, and 6 must contain a digit.

In this exploration exercise, you will see how to use the `MaskedTextBox` control and explore different input masks.

1. Run the concept lesson named **Chapter13ConceptLesson**. Click the **MaskedTextBox Control** tab, as shown in Figure 13-16.

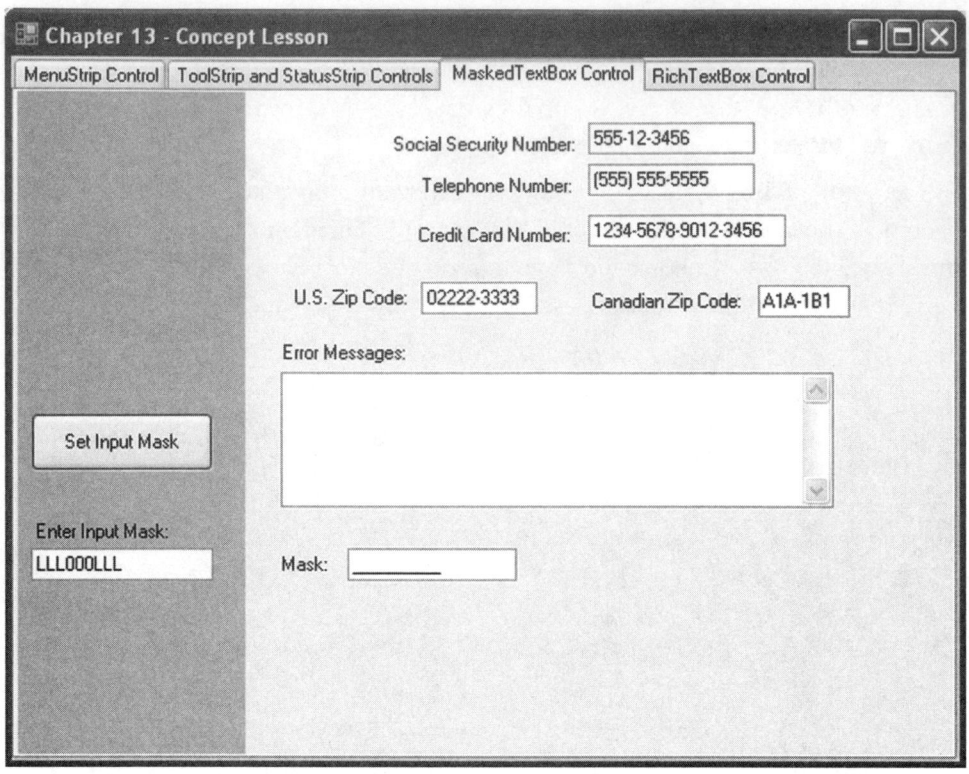

Figure 13-16: Concept lesson—MaskedTextBox Control tab

As shown in Figure 13-16, there are multiple `MaskedTextBox` control instances to test Social Security numbers, telephone numbers, credit card numbers, and U.S. and Canadian zip codes.

2. Enter valid and invalid input into these control instances. When an invalid character is entered at a character position, a message is written to the multiline text box.

3. The Enter Input Mask text box allows you to dynamically set an input mask to explore how different input masks work. Use the default input mask in the control instance or create other custom input masks. Click the **Set Input Mask** button. The `MaskedTextBox` control instance is updated with the new input mask.

# MINI-QUIZ 3

1. Referring to the `MaskedTextBox` control, what is the name of the property that contains the input mask?

   a. `InputMask`

   b. `Mask`

   c. `Format`

   d. `InputFormat`

   e. none of the above

2. Given an input mask of 00000-9999, which of the following inputs is valid?

   a. 12345-1234

   b. 12345

   c. 1234

   d. both a and b

   e. all of the above are valid

3. Write the statement to set the `Mask` property for the `MaskedTextBox` control instance named mtbPartNumber such that the first three characters must contain a letter. The fourth character is a dash. Characters 5 through 8 must contain digits.

4. Given an input mask of ###-000-????, which of the following statements is correct?

   a. The first three characters are required digits.

   b. The last four characters are optional letters.

   c. The first three characters are required uppercase letters.

   d. The last four characters are required letters.

   e. none of the above

## USING THE RICHTEXTBOX CONTROL

The `RichTextBox` control allows the end user to edit files having a standardized file format called **Rich Text Format (RTF)**. Embedded inside RTF files are formatting directives. The rich text box does not display these directives. Rather, the control instance interprets them and performs the specified formatting task. Figure 13-17 shows a short RTF file with formatting directives.

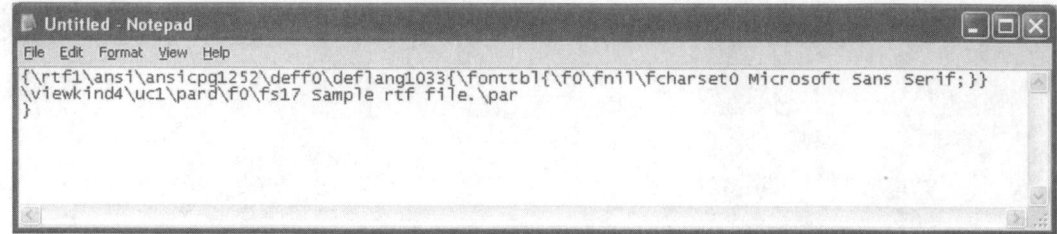

Figure 13-17: Rich text file

As shown in Figure 13-17, directives specify the font, font size, and font attributes. The text displayed in the RichTextBox control instance is embedded in the directives. As the developer, you do not have to worry about these directives as the RichTextBox control interprets them automatically. In addition, when formatting is applied to specific text, the RichTextBox control stores the relevant directives in the file. The RichTextBox control can read and write ordinary text files as well as process rich text files. The text shown in Figure 13-17 appears formatted in Figure 13-18.

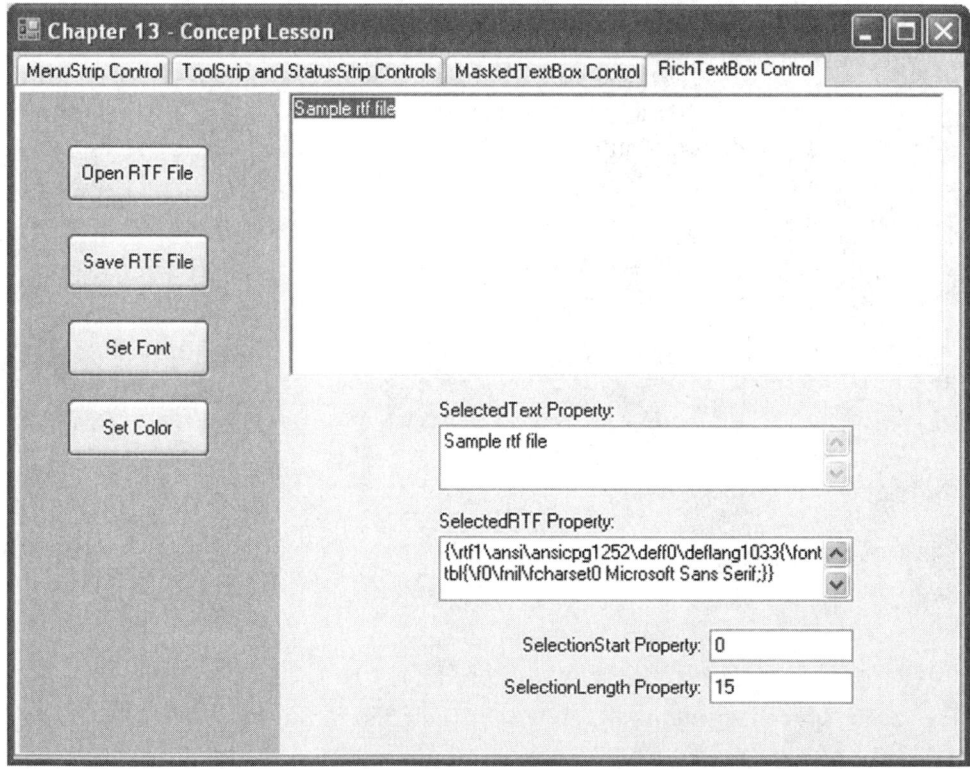

Figure 13-18: Formatted text in a RichTextBox control instance

## CONFIGURING THE APPEARANCE OF THE RICHTEXTBOX CONTROL

The RichTextBox control supports the following properties to define how the text is displayed in the control instance:

» The AcceptsTab property defines what happens when the end user presses the Tab key. If set to True, a Tab character is inserted into the control instance. If set to False, pressing the Tab key causes the next control instance in the form's tab order to get focus.

» The DetectUrls property causes the RichTextBox control instance to recognize URLs. The text of a recognized URL appears as a link. When the end user clicks the link, the LinkClicked event fires. The RichTextBox control detects that a string contains a URL when the text "www" or "http" is found. In addition, "ftp" (File Transfer Protocol) and "https" (HTTP secure) are also recognized as valid URLs. The control cannot detect whether the URL itself references an actual address on the Web. An RTF file can contain multiple links.

» The MultiLine property has the same purpose as it does for the TextBox control. When set to True, the text spans multiple lines. The Lines property is an array of strings. Each line is stored in an array element.

» The RightMargin property sets the rightmost limit for the text that appears on a line. This property is measured in pixels. The property value must contain the value zero or a positive integer.

» The ScrollBars property has the same purpose as it does for the TextBox control. That is, it defines whether horizontal or vertical scroll bars appear.

## READING AND WRITING FILES WITH THE RICHTEXTBOX CONTROL

One function supported by the RichTextBox control is the capability to read and write text and RTF files. Instead of writing statements to open, read or write, and then close a file, all of the necessary functionality to read and write files is built in to the RichTextBox control itself. Thus, you do not need to read a file by creating an instance of the StreamReader class, reading each line, and storing the lines read in the control instance.

The LoadFile and SaveFile methods have the following syntax:

### Syntax

```
Public Sub LoadFile(path As String, fileType As
RichTextBoxStreamType)

Public Sub SaveFile(path As String, fileType As
RichTextBoxStreamType)
```

*(Continued)* ▶

## MANAGING THE TEXT IN AN INSTANCE OF THE RICHTEXTBOX CONTROL

When working with the text in an instance of the `RichTextBox` control, two concepts are important: the insertion point and the selection, as follows:

» When no text is selected in the control instance, the cursor position is referred to as the **insertion point**. If the end user applies formatting attributes, such as boldface or a different font, the characters typed by the end user at the insertion point appear in boldface and have that selected font.

» When the end user selects text, the selected text is called the **selection**. Any formatting attributes chosen by the end user are applied to the selection. The selection must be a contiguous range of characters.

Several properties work with the insertion point and the selection, as described in the following list:

» The `SelectedRTF` property contains the selected text, including all rich text formatting directives.

» The `SelectedText` property contains the selected text. However, only the selected text is stored in the property. The formatting directives are removed.

» The `SelectionColor` property defines the color of the selected text or insertion point. The property has a data type of `Color`.

» The `SelectionFont` property defines the font of the selected text or insertion point.

» The `SelectionStart` property contains an integer and defines the position of the starting character of the selection. If the property's value is 0, text is inserted at the first character. Thus, the property is 0-based.

» The `SelectionLength` property contains the number of characters in the selection.

As the end user changes or updates the selection or modifies the text appearing in the rich text box, events fire as described in the following list:

» The `LinkClicked` event fires only when the `DetectUrls` property is set to `True`. The event fires when the end user clicks a link.

» The `TextChanged` event fires when the end user modifies the contents of the control instance.

» The `SelectionChanged` event fires when the end user selects different text or moves the insertion point.

The `RichTextBox` control supports several properties that work with the insertion point and the selection. For example, the `SelectionFont` property returns the font of the insertion point or the selection. The `SelectionFont` property, in turn, has properties to describe font attributes.

In this exploration exercise, you will see how to use the `RichTextBox` control.

1. Run the concept lesson for the chapter. Click the **RichTextBox Control** tab.

2. Enter text in the `RichTextBox` control instance (the large white box in the middle of the form). As you do, note that the text boxes at the bottom of the form are updated to display information about the selected text. (You can examine the code in the `SelectionChanged` event handler to see how the process works.)

3. Click the **Open RTF File** button to open a rich text file. Select the file named **Chapter.13\Data\demo.rtf**. Select some text.

4. Click the **Set Font** button. Select a font in the Font dialog box, and then click **OK**. The font is applied to the selection.

5. Click the **Set Color** button. Select a color in the Color dialog box and click **OK**. The color is applied to the selection.

# APPLICATION LESSON

## CREATING A BASIC WORD PROCESSOR

In this application lesson, you will create a word processor made up of a menu, a toolbar, a status bar, and an instance of the `RichTextBox` that works as the word processor.

### APPLICATION LESSON—USER INTERFACE

The user interface for this application lesson contains a menu with which the end user can open and save RTF files. These RTF files are displayed in an instance of the `RichTextBox` control. In addition, there are menu items with which the end user can format the file currently displayed in the `RichTextBox` control instance. There is a toolbar that duplicates many of the items found on the menu. The status bar displays the currently open document and information about the currently open document.

### APPLICATION LESSON—DESIGN

The design of the application is made up of procedures that are called from the various menu items and toolbar buttons. This way, the task performed by a toolbar button and menu item is equivalent. Note that all menu items do not have equivalent toolbar buttons. All event handling is performed through the menu and toolbar. The form contains no buttons. Status information is updated by handling the various events of the `RichTextBox` control.

## APPLICATION LESSON—IMPLEMENTATION

Most of the code for the application appears in the event handlers for the various control instances. In addition, general procedures exist for those tasks that are duplicated by a menu item and an equivalent toolbar button. The following list describes the event handlers for this application:

» Two event handlers, named OpenToolStripMenuItem and tsbOpen, call a procedure named OpenFile to open an RTF file.

» Two event handlers, named SaveToolStripMenuItem and tsbSave, call a procedure named SaveFile to save the current RTF file.

» Two event handlers, named FirstToolStripMenuItem and tsbFirst, call a procedure named NavigateFirst to position the insertion point at the first character in the rich text box.

» Two event handlers, named LastToolStripMenuItem and tsbLast, call a procedure named NavigateLast to position the insertion point at the last character position in the rich text box.

» The menu contains menu items named ColorToolStripMenuItem and FontToolStripMenuItem. Click event handlers are used to set the color and font of the selection or insertion point, respectively.

» A SelectionChanged event handler appears for the rich text box to update the position of the insertion point in the status bar.

» A KeyUp event handler appears to update the status bar after each key is released.

To preview the completed application:

1. Open the solution file appearing in the folder named **Chapter.13\ Chapter13ApplicationLessonPreview**. Run the application lesson.

2. Open the file named **Chapter.13\Data\Demo.rtf** using the appropriate toolbar button or menu item. The filename appears in the status bar appearing along the bottom of the form, as shown in Figure 13-19. Note that the text "Caps" and "Scroll" will appear in the status bar only if the Caps Lock and Scroll Lock keys are enabled.

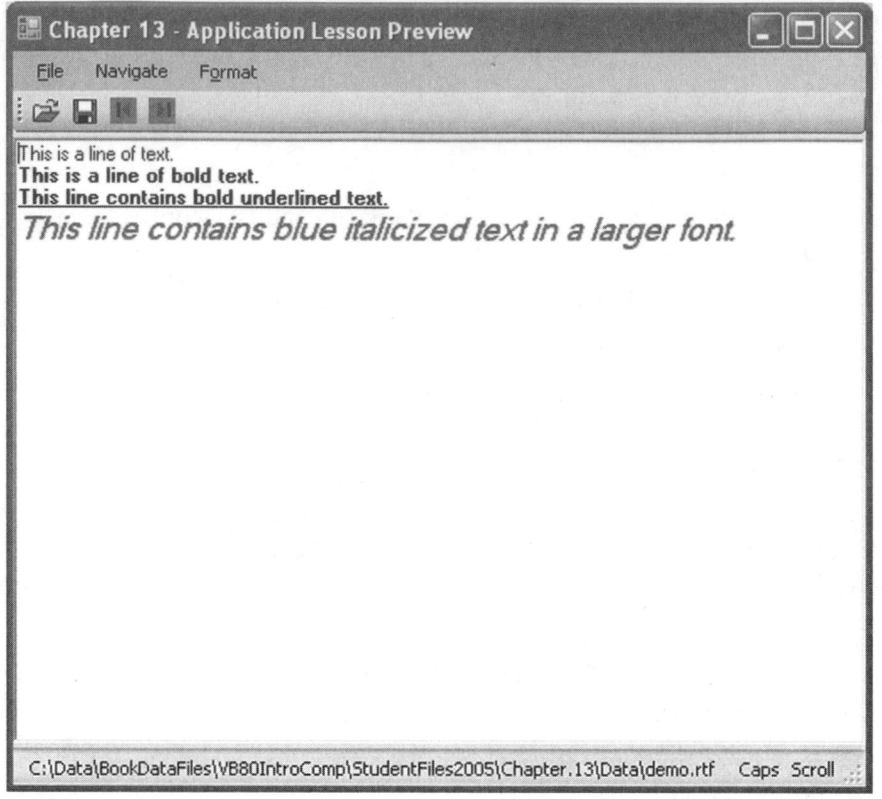

Figure 13-19: Application lesson preview

3. Select text and apply formatting as you see fit.

4. Exit the application.

First, you will create the MenuStrip, ToolStrip, and StatusStrip control instances on the form.

To create the control instances on the form:

1. Open the solution file in the folder named **Chapter.13\ Chapter13ApplicationLessonStartup**.

2. Create an instance of the MenuStrip control on the form. Set its Name property to **msMain**.

3. Create menu titles named **File**, **Navigate**, and **Format**. Create the menu items shown in Table 13-2.

| Menu | Menu item | Name (these names will be set automatically) |
|------|-----------|----------------------------------------------|
| File | Open | `OpenToolStripMenuItem` |
| File | Save | `SaveToolStripMenuItem` |
| File | Exit | `ExitToolStripMenuItem` |
| Navigate | First | `FirstToolStripMenuItem` |
| Navigate | Last | `LastToolStripMenuItem` |
| Format | Color | `ColorToolStripMenuItem` |
| Format | Font | `FontToolStripMenuItem` |

Table 13-2: Menu items

4. Create an instance of the `ToolStrip` control on the form. Set its name to **tsMain**. Using the Items Collection Editor, create buttons on the control instance, as described in Table 13-3. Set the images using the project's resource file.

| Button name | Image |
|---|---|
| tsbOpen | Chapter.13\Data\OpenFolder |
| tsbSave | Chapter.13\Data\Save |
| tsbFirst | Chapter.13\Data\GoToFirstRecord |
| tsbLast | Chapter.13\Data\GoToLastRecord |

Table 13-3: Toolbar buttons

5. Create an instance of the StatusStrip control on the form. Set its name to **ssMain**. Create instances of the ToolStripStatusLabel on the control instance, as described in Table 13-4.

| Label name | Property |
|---|---|
| tsslFileName | Spring = True<br>Text = No File Open |
| tsslNumLock | Spring = False |
| tsslCapsLock | Spring = False |
| tsslScrollLock | Spring = False |
| tsslPosition | Spring = False |

Table 13-4: Status bar labels

Having created the form's control instances, you can now create the code that will execute as the end user runs the application. First, you will create the procedures that will be shared by the menu items and the buttons on the toolbar.

To create the application's procedures:

1. Create the following procedure named **OpenFile** to read an RTF file:

```
Private Sub OpenFile()
    Dim Result As DialogResult
    Result = ofdMain.ShowDialog
    If Result = Windows.Forms.DialogResult.OK Then
        rtbMain.LoadFile(ofdMain.FileName, _
            RichTextBoxStreamType.RichText)
    End If
    tsslFileName.Text = ofdMain.FileName
End Sub
```

2. Create the following procedure named **SaveFile** to write an RTF file:

```
Private Sub SaveFile()
    Dim Result As DialogResult
    Result = sfdMain.ShowDialog
    If Result = Windows.Forms.DialogResult.OK Then
        rtbMain.SaveFile(sfdMain.FileName, _
            RichTextBoxStreamType.RichText)
    End If
End Sub
```

3. Create the following procedure named **NavigateFirst** to locate the first character in the RichTextBox control instance:

```
Private Sub NavigateFirst()
    rtbMain.SelectionStart = 0
    rtbMain.SelectionLength = 0
End Sub
```

4. Create the following procedure named **NavigateLast** to locate the last character in the RichTextBox control instance.

```
Private Sub NavigateLast()
    rtbMain.SelectionStart = rtbMain.Text.Length - 1
End Sub
```

Next, you can write the code for the menu items so as to call the general procedures that you just created.

To create the procedures for the menu items:

1. Create the **Click** event handler for the menu item named **OpenToolStripMenuItem**, and enter the following statement:

```
Call OpenFile()
```

2. Create the **Click** event handler for the menu item named **SaveToolStripMenuItem**, and enter the following statement:

```
Call SaveFile()
```

3. Create the **Click** event handler for the menu item named **FirstToolStripMenuItem**, and enter the following statement:

```
Call NavigateFirst()
```

4. Create the **Click** event handler for the menu item named **LastToolStripMenuItem**, and enter the following statement:

```
Call NavigateLast()
```

5. Create the **Click** event handler for the menu item named **ExitToolStripMenuItem**, and enter the following statement:

```
Me.Close()
```

6. Create the **Click** event handler for the menu item named **ColorToolStripMenuItem**, and enter the following code:

```
Dim Result As DialogResult
Result = cdMain.ShowDialog
If Result = Windows.Forms.DialogResult.OK Then
    rtbMain.SelectionColor = cdMain.Color
End If
```

7. Create the **Click** event handler for the menu item named **FontToolStripMenuItem**, and enter the following code:

```
Dim Result As DialogResult
Result = fdMain.ShowDialog
If Result = Windows.Forms.DialogResult.OK Then
    rtbMain.SelectionFont = fdMain.Font
End If
```

Next, you need to create the statements to call the appropriate procedure when the end user clicks a button on the toolbar.

To create the code for the toolbar buttons:

1. Create the **Click** event handler for the ToolStripButton named **tsbOpen** using the following statement:

```
Call OpenFile()
```

2. Create the **Click** event handler for the ToolStripButton named **tsbSave** using the following statement:

```
Call SaveFile()
```

3. Create the **Click** event handler for the ToolStripButton named **tsbFirst** using the following statement:

```
Call NavigateFirst()
```

4. Create the **Click** event handler for the ToolStripButton named **tsbLast** using the following statement:

```
Call NavigateLast()
```

Next, you need to create the code to display the position of the insertion point in the status bar.

To update the character position display:

1. Create the **SelectionChanged** event handler for the `RichTextBox` control instance named **rtbMain** and enter the following statement:

```
tsslPosition.Text = "Position= " & _
    rtbMain.SelectionStart.ToString
```

Finally, you need to create the keyboard event handler to display the status of various keyboard keys:

1. Create the **KeyUp** event handler for the form and enter the following statements:

```
If My.Computer.Keyboard.NumLock = True Then
    tsslNumLock.Text = "Num"
Else
    tsslNumLock.Text = ""
End If

If My.Computer.Keyboard.CapsLock = True Then
    tsslCapsLock.Text = "Caps"
Else
    tsslCapsLock.Text = ""
End If

If My.Computer.Keyboard.ScrollLock = True Then
    tsslScrollLock.Text = "Scroll"
Else
    tsslScrollLock.Text = ""
End If
```

2. Test the application. Open an RTF file. Test the navigational buttons on the toolbar and menu bar. Test the formatting menu items. Finally, make sure that the status bar is updated as the selection changes and as the Num Lock, Scroll Lock, and Caps Lock keys are pressed.

# CHAPTER SUMMARY

» A menu system gives the end user a way to perform tasks via a menu that appears just below a form's title bar. The `MenuStrip` class forms the container for the menu items that appear on the menu. Each menu item has a data type of `ToolStripMenuItem`. A menu item can be configured to operate as a checked menu item or as a clickable button. Shortcut keys can also be assigned to a menu item. Individual menu items can be made visible or invisible, enabled or disabled. Separator bars can also be created to visually group or separate the items on a menu.

» Context menus are typically displayed when the end user right-clicks the mouse on the form or control instance. Context menus are created with the `ContextMenuStrip` control. It is possible to have multiple context menus on a form. In addition, a context menu can be bound to a form or control instance dynamically at run time.

» A toolbar is another common user interface element. A toolbar typically contains buttons that mimic the functionality of an equivalent menu item. The `ToolStrip` control is used to implement a toolbar and works similarly to a `MenuStrip` control. After a `ToolStrip` has been created, other control instances are created on the `ToolStrip`.

» Many applications include a status bar as a user interface element to display information about the application. Visual Studio implements a status bar using the `StatusStrip` control. After an instance of the `StatusStrip` control has been created, other control instances can be created on the `StatusStrip` to display status information.

» The `MaskedTextBox` control is derived from the `TextBoxBase` class and works similarly to the `TextBox` control. However, the `MaskedTextBox` control has additional properties that restrict the possible characters and positions that can be entered into the control instance.

» The `RichTextBox` control allows the end user to edit files containing either plain text or rich text. The `LoadFile` method reads a file and the `SaveFile` method saves a file.

» The contents of the `RichTextBox` are formatted based on the selection or the insertion point. The `SelectionFont` property allows you to define the font of the selection or insertion point. The `SelectionColor` property allows you to define the color of the selected text or the insertion point.

# KEY TERMS

**insertion point**—The cursor position when no text is currently selected by the end user.

**Rich Text Format (RTF)**—A file format containing embedded directives, which are used to format text.

**selection**—The text that the end user selects in a rich text box.

**separator bar**—A horizontal line that divides two items on a menu.

# ANSWERS TO MINI-QUIZZES

### MINI-QUIZ 1

1. b. The `MenuStrip` control is new to Visual Studio 2005 and replaces the `MainMenu` control.

2. c. A form can have multiple context menus. Different control instances on the form can be associated with different context menus.

3. A container control, as its name implies, is used to contain other control instances. For example, the `TabStrip` and `TabPage` are both container controls. The `MenuStrip` control is also a container control.

### MINI-QUIZ 2

1. c. Toolbar buttons are typically created to mimic equivalent menu items.

2. A separator bar can be created using the Items Collection Editor. The only purpose of a separator bar is to visually separate the items on the toolbar.

3. d. `Spring`

4. b. `ToolStripStatusLabel`, `ToolStripProgressBar`, `ToolStripDropDownButton`

### MINI-QUIZ 3

1. b. `Mask`

2. d. both a and b

3. `mtbPartNumber.Mask = "LLL-0000"`

4. b. The last four characters are optional letters.

### MINI-QUIZ 4

1. `LoadFile`

2. The insertion point

3. `rtbDemo.SelectionStart = 0`
   `rtbDemo.SelectionLength = rtbDemo.Text.Length`

# REVIEW QUESTIONS

1. Which of the following controls is considered a container control?

   a. `StatusStrip`          b. `RadioButton`

   c. `CheckBox`            d. `RichTextBox`

   e. none of the above are container controls

2. Which of the following statements is correct regarding a menu?

   a. The `FormMenu` control is a container control. It contains the menus and menu items appearing on the menu.

   b. A menu item can have a shortcut key assigned along with an optional image.

   c. A menu is associated with a form by setting the form's `MainMenuStrip` property to the name of a `FormMenu` control instance created on the form.

   d. all of the above

   e. none of the above

3. What is the name of the event that fires when the end user clicks a menu item?

   a. `MenuClick`           b. `Click`

   c. `ItemClick`           d. `MenuItemClick`

   e. none of the above

4. What is the data type of an item appearing on a menu?

   a. `MenuItem`            b. `Menu`

   c. `ToolStripMenuItem`   d. `TextBox`

   e. none of the above

5. Which of the following statements is correct regarding a context menu?

   a. Both a form's menu system and context menus are created using the `MainMenu` control.

   b. Unlike ordinary menus, context menus cannot have shortcut keys.

   c. A form can have at most one context menu.

   d. After a context menu is associated with a control instance at design time, it cannot be changed while an application runs.

   e. none of the above

6. Which of the following statements describes how to associate a context menu with a control instance created on a form?

   a. Set the `ContextMenuList` property of the control instance to the items that will appear on the context menu.

   b. Create an instance of the `ListBox` control. Set the `Type` property of the `ListBox` to ContextMenu.

   c. Set the `ContextMenuStrip` property of a control instance to an instance of the `ContextMenuStrip` control.

   d. Set the `MainMenu` property of a control instance to an instance of the `MainMenu` control.

   e. none of the above

7. Which of the following statements is correct regarding the `ToolStrip` control?

   a. A form can have at most one instance of the `ToolStrip` control.

   b. The buttons appearing on an instance of the `ToolStrip` control have a data type of `Button`.

   c. To create a button that can be checked or unchecked, you create an instance of the `CheckedButton` control on an instance of the `ToolStrip` control.

   d. Control instances that can be created on the `ToolStrip` include the `ToolStripButton`, `ToolStripComboBox`, and `ToolStripTextBox`.

   e. none of the above

8. Which of the following statements describes the event that fires when the end user clicks on a toolbar button?

   a. The `ToolStrip` control fires a `ButtonClick` event for all buttons on the toolbar. The second argument to the event handler contains a reference to the button that was clicked.

   b. Each `ToolBarButton` causes a `Click` event to fire.

   c. By definition, a multicast event handler handles the `Click` event for the various toolbar buttons.

   d. Each button fires a `ButtonClick` event.

   e. none of the above

9. Which of the following statements is correct regarding the `StatusStrip` control?

   a. By definition, the `StatusStrip` control must appear at the bottom of a form.

   b. The `StatusStrip` control is divided into regions called `StatusAreas`. Each `StatusArea` object displays a particular status item.

   c. All of the control instances contained in a `StatusStrip` must be of the same size.

   d. The `StatusStrip` control can contain other control instances such as a `ToolStripStatusLabel` or a `ToolStripProgressBar`.

   e. none of the above

10. Referring to the `ToolStripStatusLabel`, what is the name of the property that you would set to cause the label to resize so that it fills the region of the `StatusStrip`?

    a. `Spring`    b. `Expand`

    c. `AutoSize`    d. `Fill`

    e. `Resize`

11. Which of the following masks correctly forms a telephone number as (*xxx*) *xxx-xxxx*, where *x* is a digit? Assume that the area code in the parentheses is optional and the other fields are required.

    a. (###) 000-0000    b. (000) 999-9999

    c. (999) 000-0000    d. (###) 999-9999

    e. (***) ###-####

12. What is the name of the event pertaining to the `MaskedTextBox` control that fires when an invalid character is entered into the control instance?

    a. `Validating`    b. `DataError`

    c. `FieldError`    d. `InvalidInput`

    e. `MaskInputRejected`

13. Which of the following statements is correct regarding the `RichTextBox` control?

   a. As well as reading and writing RTF files, the `RichTextBox` control can read and write HTML files.

   b. The `RichTextBox` control can read and write text files and RTF files.

   c. A file read as an RTF file cannot be saved as a text file.

   d. Although it is possible to set formatting attributes, it is not possible to change the color of RTF text because the RTF format does not support color.

   e. none of the above

14. Which of the following statements is correct regarding the formatting capabilities supplied by the `RichTextBox` control?

   a. It is possible to set the color of text.

   b. It is possible to change fonts and font sizes.

   c. It is possible to configure an instance of the `RichTextBox` control to recognize URLs.

   d. all of the above

   e. none of the above

15. What is the name of the property applicable to the `RichTextBox` control that causes the control instance to recognize URLs?

   a. `URLEnabled`                    b. `WebFormat`

   c. `DetectURLs`                    d. `HTML`

   e. none of the above

16. Referring to the `MenuStrip`, `ToolStrip`, and `StatusStrip` controls, what is the purpose of the Items Collection Editor?

17. Describe how to configure shortcut keys for a menu.

18. What is the purpose of a container control?

19. Describe the role of resource files in storing images.

20. Referring to the `RichTextBox` control, what is meant by the terms insertion point and selection?

# PROGRAMMING QUESTIONS

1. Write the statement to associate the `MenuStrip` control instance named msMain with the form named frmMain.

2. Write the statement to check the menu item named BoldMenuItem.

3. Write the statement to associate the `ContextMenuStrip` control instance named cmsFormat with the `RichTextBox` control instance named rtbMain.

4. Create the event handler for the `ToolStripButton` control instance named tsbExit that will fire when the button is clicked. In the event handler, write the statement to close the current form.

5. Assume that a checked `ToolStripButton` is named tsbBold, and that a `ToolStripMenuItem` is named tsmiBold. Create the necessary event handlers to synchronize the `Checked` property of the two control instances.

6. Assume that a `ToolStrip` control instance has three `ToolStripButton` control instances named tsbLeft, tsbRight, and tsbCenter. Write the statements to create a multicast `Click` event handler for the three control instances. In the event handler, write the statements to determine which button was clicked. Check the clicked button and uncheck the other two buttons. The event handler should be named tsbJustify.

7. Create the event handler that will fire when the end user clicks the `ToolStripMenuItem` named LockToolStripMenuItem. The code in the event handler should check the menu item if it is not checked and uncheck the menu item if it is checked. That is, configure the menu item to operate as a toggle switch.

8. Assume that a `ToolStripStatusLabel` exists named tsslAlt. Write the statements to store the string "Alt" in the control instance if the Alt modifier key is pressed. Store nothing in the control instance if the Alt modifier is not pressed.

9. Write the appropriate input mask, for a zip-plus-four zip code having the following format: *xxxxx-xxxx*, where each positional character is a required digit. Assume that the `MaskedTextBox` is named mtbMain.

10. Create the event handler for an instance of the `MaskedTextBox` control named mtbQuestion that will fire if the end user enters an invalid character. Display the character position of the error in a message box.

11. Assume that an instance of the `RichTextBox` control exists named rtbMain. Write the statement(s) to select all of the characters in the control instance.

12. Assume that an instance of the `RichTextBox` control exists named rtbMain. Write the statements to load and save the file named C:\Question.rtf as an RTF file.

13. Assume that an instance of the `RichTextBox` control exists named rtbMain. Write the statements to display an instance of the `FontDialog` control named fdCurrent. If the end user clicks the OK button, apply the font to the selected text in the `RichTextBox` control instance.

14. Assume that an instance of the `RichTextBox` control named rtbMain exists. Write the statements to examine each line appearing in the control instance. If the line contains more than 80 characters, increment the value of the integer counter named LongLineCount.

15. Assume that an instance of the `RichTextBox` control named rtbMain exists. Create the necessary event handler that will execute when the insertion point or selection changes. In the event handler, display the position of the insertion point in the `ToolStripStatusLabel` control instance named tsslPosition.

# HANDS-ON PROJECTS

1. In this hands-on project, you will expand on the word processor that you implemented in the chapter's application lesson. The end user will be able to dynamically adjust the right margin of the text appearing in the control instance, apply default formatting, and perform many other tasks.

   a. A preview of the completed hands-on project appears in the file **Chapter.13\ HandsOnProjects\Ch13HandsOnProject1.exe**.

b. Start Visual Studio, if necessary, and create a new solution named **Ch13HandsOnProject1.sln**.

c. Use the preview version of the application lesson as a template for this hands-on project.

d. Modify the project so that a message box will be displayed when the end user attempts to exit the application if there have been changes to the text in the RichTextBox control instance since the file was last saved.

e. Create a toolbar button to reset the formatting of the RichTextBox control instance to default values. Use a 10 point Times New Roman font. The default text color should be black. The button should display the text "Default."

f. Create a means for the end user to set the right margin of the RichTextBox to a user-specified value. Create a menu item on the Format menu that will allow the user to set the right margin. Get the input value using an input box. The value is measured in pixels; thus, a value of 250 would cause the line to be 250 pixels wide.

g. Allow the end user to save an RTF file as a plain text file.

h. In an instance of the StatusStrip control, display the color of the selected text along with the font name of the selected text.

2. In this hands-on project, you will create an application that reads and writes a sequential file. The sequential file that you will process contains a rolodex with a notes field. The notes field contains RTF text instead of plain text. The sequential file corresponding to this hands-on project is named Chapter.13\Data\HandsOnProject2DataFile.txt. The fields contain the following data: last name, first name, address, city, state, zip code, last contact date, and notes. With the exception of the notes field, all of the other fields contain text.

a. A preview of the completed hands-on project appears in the file **Chapter.13\ HandsOnProjects\Ch13HandsOnProject2.exe**.

b. Start Visual Studio, if necessary, and create a new solution named **Ch13HandsOnProject2.sln**.

c. Create a structure or class to store each record in the sequential file. Use appropriate data types for each field.

d. Create the necessary code to store a list of the records you defined in the preceding step. Use an array or List class to store the data in memory.

e. Create the control instances on the main form, as shown in the preview application. Use a MaskedTextBox control instance for the zip code field. Use a RichTextBox control instance to display the notes.

    f.  Create a menu system for the application. Create a File menu with menu items to open and save the data file, and to exit the application. Create a Navigate menu with menu items to locate the first, next, previous, and last records. Create an Edit menu with menu items that will allow the end user to add, change, and delete records.

    g.  Create a toolbar for the application. The toolbar should contain buttons to open and save the data file, and to perform record navigation. These toolbar buttons should mimic the functionality of the corresponding menu items. The toolbar need not contain buttons to add, change, or delete records.

    h.  Create the code to open and save the file. This code requires some thought. The sequential file is structured such that each field appears on a single line, with the exception of the notes data, which can appear on multiple lines. The notes appear on multiple lines because RTF data can have embedded carriage return characters. Each record is separated by the pattern "\\\". Examine the sample data file for the file format.

    i.  Create a status bar on the form. Configure the status bar so that it will display the index of the current record (record number) and a count of the total number of records. In addition, display the filename selected by the end user. Display the status of the Num Lock, Caps Lock, and Scroll Lock keys.

3.  In this hands-on project, you will create an application that processes database files similar to the ones found in Chapter 11. The `MaskedTextBox` will be used to edit text. In addition, one of the database fields contains RTF text. This text will be displayed in an instance of the `RichTextBox` control. Table 13-5 describes the fields in the table named tblNotes. The database is named Notes.

| Field name | Description | Data type |
|---|---|---|
| fldIDNumber | Unique identification number | Integer |
| fldFirstName | First name | String |
| fldLastName | Last name | String |
| fldAddress | Customer address | String |
| fldCity | Customer city | String |
| fldState | Customer state | String |
| fldZipCode | Customer zip code | String |
| fldAnnualSales | Annual sales amount | Double |
| fldNotes | Notes in RTF format | String |

Table 13-5: Fields in the tblNotes table

a. Start Visual Studio, if necessary, and create a new solution named **Ch13HandsOnProject3.sln**.

b. Using the Data Source Configuration Wizard, establish a connection to the database. The connection you create should select all of the fields from the database table named tblCustomers.

c. Create the bound control instances on the form using the Data Sources window. Again, an instance of the `BindingNavigator` class is automatically generated.

d. Instead of binding the field named fldZipCode to an instance of the `TextBox` control, bind the field to an instance of the `MaskedTextBox` control.

e. Create a menu system for the application. Create a Navigate menu with menu items to locate the first, next, previous, and last records. Create a Format menu with menu items to format the contents of the RichTextBox.

f. Create a status bar on the form. Configure the status bar so that it will display the index of the current record and a count of the total number of records. In addition, display the database filename selected by the end user.

# DEBUGGING

**After completing this appendix, you will be able to:**

Describe the types of programming errors

Trace statement execution

Set breakpoints in code

Use the Immediate window to evaluate expressions

Add watch expressions

Trace cascading events with the Call Stack window

Use the Locals window

# DEBUGGING APPLICATIONS

This appendix describes how to use the Visual Studio debugging tools. In any application that you create, you will likely make mistakes. Finding those mistakes and being able to effectively correct them is an important part of the development process. This appendix discusses numerous techniques to help you locate and fix common programming errors.

# TYPES OF PROGRAMMING ERRORS

Any error that causes an application to end abnormally or to produce unexpected results is considered a programming error. The process of locating and fixing programming errors in an application is called **debugging**. Visual Studio supports numerous built-in tools that help you to debug the applications that you create.

Many developers feel that debugging an application is part science and part art. The science involves being able to use the Visual Studio debugging tools effectively. These tools include windows that allow you to watch statements as they execute, to examine the current value of variables, and to use the commands that execute statements one at a time. The art involves deciding where to search for the exact cause of an error and choosing which Visual Studio tools to use to find the error.

Programming errors can be categorized into three different types: syntax errors, run-time errors, and logic errors, which are discussed in the following sections.

> **» NOTE**
> A common term used to describe any kind of programming error is "a bug."

## SYNTAX ERRORS

As each statement of an application is entered into the Code Editor, the Visual Basic compiler examines the statement for syntax errors (violations of the rules of a programming language) as the insertion point is moved from one statement to the next. A syntax error occurs when the Visual Basic compiler cannot understand a statement that you have written. If an application has syntax errors, the application cannot be compiled or executed.

You can find syntax errors in two ways:

» The Visual Basic compiler underlines syntax errors with a ragged blue line in the Code Editor.

» Syntax errors are listed in the Error List window.

Figure A-1 shows the Code Editor and Error List windows displaying various syntax errors.

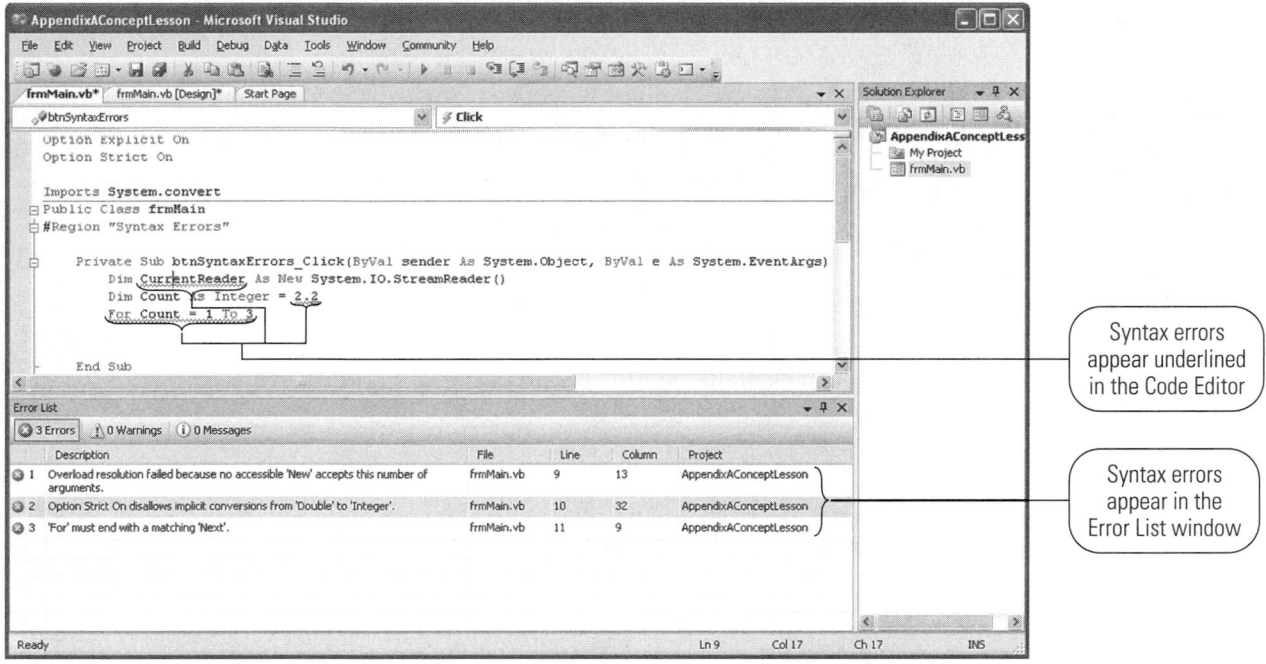

Figure A-1: Syntax errors appearing in the Code Editor and Error List windows

As shown in Figure A-1, three syntax errors appear in the Code Editor with ragged underlines. The same syntax errors appear in the Error List window. The columns appearing in the Error List window provide the following information:

» The first column displays an icon showing the severity of the error. In Figure A-1, all three errors are critical and prevent the application from compiling.

» The second column shows the error number. Errors are numbered sequentially.

» The third column contains a description of the syntax error.

» The fourth column displays the name of the file that contains the syntax error.

» The fifth and sixth columns display the line and column position where the error was detected.

» The final column displays the project where the error appeared.

**»NOTE**

The Error List window also displays warning errors. For example, if you declare a variable but do not use that variable, a warning error appears in the Error List window. Warning errors do not prevent an application from compiling.

In this exploration exercise, you will use the Code Editor and Error List windows to locate and correct syntax errors.

1. Start Visual Studio, if necessary, and open the solution appearing in the folder named **Appendix.A\AppendixAConceptLesson**.

2. Activate the Code Editor for the form named **frmMain**.

3. Activate the Error List window by clicking **View**, **Error List** on the menu bar. By default, the Error List window is docked along the bottom of the Visual Studio IDE.

4. Expand the Syntax Errors region, if necessary. At the beginning of the module, modify the statement that reads `Private Count1 As Integer` so that it reads **Pirvite Count1 As Integer** (misspelling the keyword Private).

5. Move the insertion point to the next line so that Visual Studio checks the syntax of the statement you just modified. In the Code Editor, the statement with the incorrect syntax appears underlined. In addition, a message appears in the Error List window with the description "Declaration expected." indicating that only declaration statements can appear at the module level.

6. Correct the error by spelling the keyword **Private** correctly, and then move the insertion point to the next line. The syntax of the statement is checked. Because the syntax of the statement is correct, the error is removed from both the Code Editor and the Error List window.

## RUN-TIME ERRORS

Unlike syntax errors, run-time errors are not detected by the Visual Basic compiler when the application is compiled. Rather, these errors occur as an application executes and an exception is thrown.

Chapter 7 describes exceptions and how to handle them. Exceptions can be thrown for many reasons, such as the following:

» Trying to store data of an incompatible data type in a property or variable

» Calling functions with arguments having invalid data

» Trying to store too large or too small a value into a variable (numeric overflow)

» Trying to reference an object before creating an instance of the class with the New keyword

If a statement that is not enclosed in an exception handler executes and causes an exception to be thrown, a run-time error occurs. When an exception is thrown, Visual Studio displays a message box to help explain the cause of the exception and to help you locate the statement that caused the exception. Figure A-2 shows an unhandled exception appearing in a dialog box.

**»TIP**

Syntax errors can cascade. That is, one syntax error can cause Visual Studio to identify additional syntax errors. Thus, when an application contains multiple syntax errors, fix the first syntax error in the list first, as it might be the cause of subsequent syntax errors.

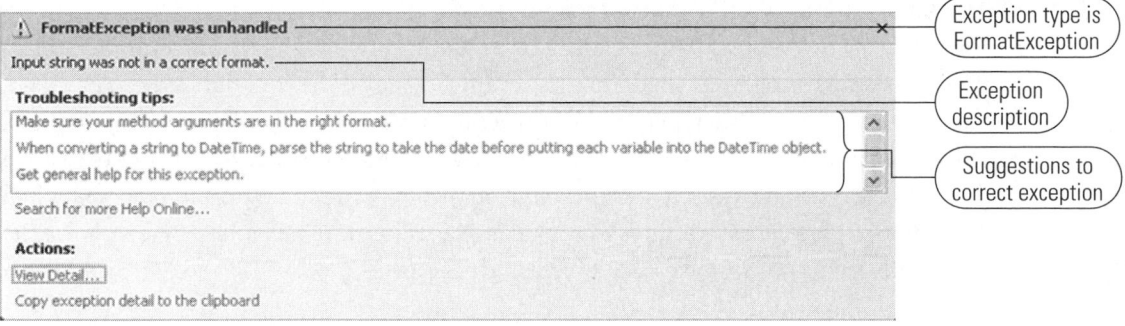

Figure A-2: Unhandled exception message

As shown in Figure A-2, the dialog box shows the exception type, which, in this case, is a `System.FormatException`. It means that Visual Studio executed a statement but could not convert the textual input data to a numeric value. The dialog box displays a descriptive message, along with tips to solve the problem.

> **>>NOTE** In some cases, the statement that caused an exception might be only a symptom of the underlying problem. Instead, the exception might be thrown at a later point during the execution of the program. In such cases, you might want to examine the statements that lead up to an exception, even though these statements themselves are not directly responsible for the exception.

Exceptions can be thrown when an application is running and are often caused by type mismatch errors and numeric overflow and underflow errors. These errors are discussed in the following sections.

## TYPE MISMATCH AND FORMATEXCEPTION ERRORS

Calling a method of the `System.Convert` class with incorrect data causes an exception to be thrown. For example, a `FormatException` is thrown if a string cannot be converted to a numeric value, as shown in the following code segment:

```
Dim StringDemo As String = "$1234.56"
Dim DoubleDemo As Double = _
    System.Convert.ToDouble(StringDemo)
```

The second of the preceding statements causes a `FormatException` to be thrown because the value stored in the variable StringDemo cannot be converted to the `Double` data type.

This type of error can be corrected in two ways. First, you can write code to validate the contents of a string variable or text box using the `IsNumeric` and `IsDate` functions. Second, any statements that might cause a type mismatch error or format error can be enclosed in a structured exception handler.

> **»NOTE**
>
> When performing arithmetic operations on floating-point numbers, Visual Studio does not raise an exception in the case of numeric overflow. Rather, Visual Studio stores a special value (not a number) in the variable.

## NUMERIC OVERFLOW ERRORS

Numeric overflow exceptions are caused by executing statements that attempt to store a value that is too large or too small into a variable having an integral data type. The Long, Integer, and Short data types are all subject to numeric overflow errors. For example, the largest value that can be stored in the Short data type is 32,767. Trying to store a value larger than that causes an exception to be thrown. The same problem occurs when an attempt is made to store too large a negative value in a variable. For example, the Short data type cannot store a negative value beyond –32,768.

Numeric overflow and underflow errors are resolved by creating structured exception handlers. In this exploration exercise, you will examine how execution of a statement can cause an exception to be thrown.

1. Run the solution for this appendix. By default, the Run-Time Errors tab should be active. Figure A-3 shows the Run-Time Errors tab.

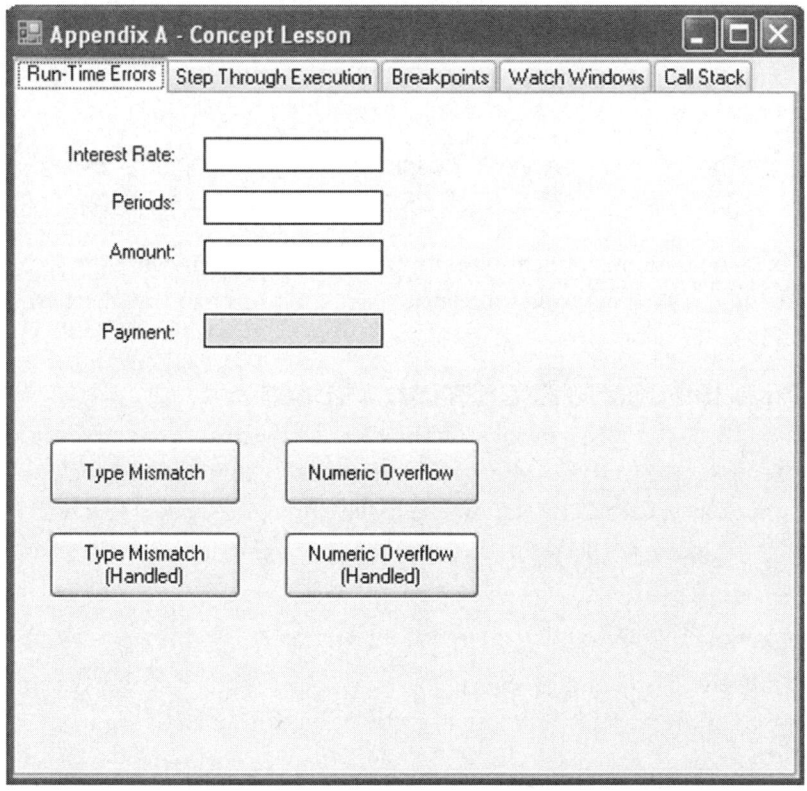

Figure A-3: Concept lesson—Run-Time Errors tab

2. Enter the value **.25A** for the interest rate, **15000A** for the period, and **10000A** for the amount. Each of these values is invalid and causes an exception to be thrown when the executing statement tries to convert the invalid value to a numeric data type.

3. Click the **Type Mismatch** button. A dialog box opens describing the error. The error is categorized as a `System.FormatException` error because the value of an argument is not valid. The statement causing the exception is also highlighted in the Code Editor.

4. End the program and run it again. Enter the same invalid input into the text boxes. Click the **Type Mismatch (Handled)** button. This time, an exception handler appears in the event handler. This exception handler displays a message box describing the nature of the error. Click **OK** to close the message box.

5. Click the **Numeric Overflow** button. A multiplication operation is performed causing a `System.OverflowException` to be thrown.

6. End the program and run it again. Reenter the invalid values from Step 2. Click the **Numeric Overflow (Handled)** button. The same multiplication operation is performed, but this time, the statement that causes the exception is enclosed in an exception handler. The statement in the exception handler displays a message box to the end user.

7. End the application.

## LOGIC ERRORS

A **logic error** occurs when an application does not perform as it is expected to perform, but instead produces incorrect results. In such a situation, logic errors will surface while an application is running. For example, if you intended to compute the area of a rectangle, you would multiply the length of the rectangle by its width. If you added the numbers instead of multiplying them, the application would produce an incorrect answer, and a logic error would have been created. The Visual Studio debugging tools cannot solve logic errors directly. That is, the debugging tools cannot tell you that a statement contains a logic error. Rather, you must use the debugging tools to locate and correct any logic errors that you yourself create.

> **»NOTE** The distinction between logic and run-time errors is sometimes unclear to those new to programming. For example, a logic error would occur if you added two values together instead of multiplying them. If this error causes a numeric overflow exception to be thrown, the logic error would, in turn, cause a run-time error.

For example, if you called the `PMT` method with incorrect argument values, the method call might cause an exception to be thrown. You would first need to determine which argument was incorrect, and then locate the statement that set the value of the erroneous argument.

# INTRODUCING THE VISUAL STUDIO DEBUGGING TOOLS

Visual Studio's debugging tools consist of commands that allow you to temporarily suspend the execution of an application by entering *break mode*. You can then trace the execution of statements and procedures as they are called by Visual Studio. Statements can be executed line-by-line with Visual Studio suspending execution as each statement executes. It is also possible to suspend execution just before executing a specific statement or when the value of a variable or a property's value changes.

"Stepping through the statements" in an application means that the Visual Studio run-time system executes each statement in a procedure line-by-line, highlighting each statement just before executing it. As you step through the statements in an application, you typically examine the variables and object properties to locate the cause of logic or run-time errors.

The Visual Studio debugging tools are made up of several windows that are used together to find errors in an application and to subsequently correct them. These windows are collectively referred to as **debugging windows**. The following list identifies selected debugging windows that are discussed in this appendix. These debugging windows are all tool windows and can be docked or Auto Hidden along an edge of the IDE. The debugging tool windows can also appear as floating windows.

» The *Breakpoints window* is used to define the locations (executable statements) in an application where Visual Studio will suspend execution. After execution is suspended, it is common to examine the values of variables so as to determine the cause of a particular error. In addition, the Code Editor and the buttons on the Debug toolbar can be used to execute statements one at a time.

» In the *Immediate window*, expressions can be entered that display the values of variables and object properties. It is also possible to call procedures using the Immediate window.

» *Watch windows* are used to examine the values of expressions.

» The *Call Stack* window is used to examine the procedures that have been called and the order in which those procedures have been called.

» The *Locals window* is used to examine the values of local variables, or for example, the properties of a form, its control instances, and the variables declared in the form.

> **»TIP** When debugging an application, you will likely have several windows open simultaneously, which might cause windows to obscure one another. Consider Auto Hiding the debugging windows along the bottom of the IDE. To Auto Hide a window, dock the window along an edge of the IDE. Right-click the window's title bar, and then click Auto Hide.

## TRACING EXECUTION AND SETTING BREAKPOINTS WITH THE BREAKPOINTS WINDOW

Often, the applications you create contain logic errors. That is, the application produces incorrect results but does not cause any exceptions to be thrown. When an application produces incorrect results, but the reason is not clear, it might prove helpful to step through the statements; that is, it might be helpful to follow the execution of each statement line-by-line until the problem is found. It might also be helpful to execute statements line-by-line to help determine why an exception is thrown.

The following list describes the toolbar buttons used to step through statements as Visual Studio executes them.

» Visual Studio executes one statement, and then enters break mode when the Step Into button is clicked. The *Step Into* button traces execution as procedures are called and as they complete. If a statement is a procedure call, the statements in the called procedure are executed line-by-line.

» The *Step Over* button works similarly to the Step Into button. If the statement is a procedure call, however, Visual Studio executes all of the statements in the procedure, and then enters break mode just before executing the statement following the procedure call.

» The *Step Out* button works similarly to the Step Over button. When clicked, Visual Studio executes all of the remaining statements in the current procedure, and then enters break mode at the statement following the statement that called the procedure.

In this exploration exercise, you will trace the execution of statements line-by-line using the Step Into button. The `Click` event handler for this button contains the following code to determine whether a number is even or odd:

```
Dim Count As Integer
For Count = 1 To 10
    txtLog.Text &= CrLf & "Count=" & Count.ToString()
    Select Case Count
        Case 1, 3, 5, 7, 9
            txtLog.Text &= CrLf & "Count is odd"
        Case 2, 4, 6, 8, 10
            txtLog.Text &= CrLf & "Count is even"
    End Select
Next
```

1. Click **View**, **Toolbars**, **Debug**, if necessary, to display the Debug toolbar. Click the **Step Into** button or press **F11** to begin executing the application.

2. Click the **Step Through Execution** tab. Click the **Single Step** button on the form. The Code Editor appears and the procedure declaration appears highlighted in yellow, indicating that the procedure is about to execute.

3. Press **F11** several times to execute each statement line-by-line. Pay particular attention to the fact that the statement that will execute next is highlighted in the Code Editor. Watch the statements in the loop as they execute. Furthermore, watch when the different `Case` blocks execute depending on whether the value of the variable Count is even or odd. Figure A-4 shows the Code Editor while single stepping through an application. Note that the Output Log text box on the main form shows the results of statements as they execute.

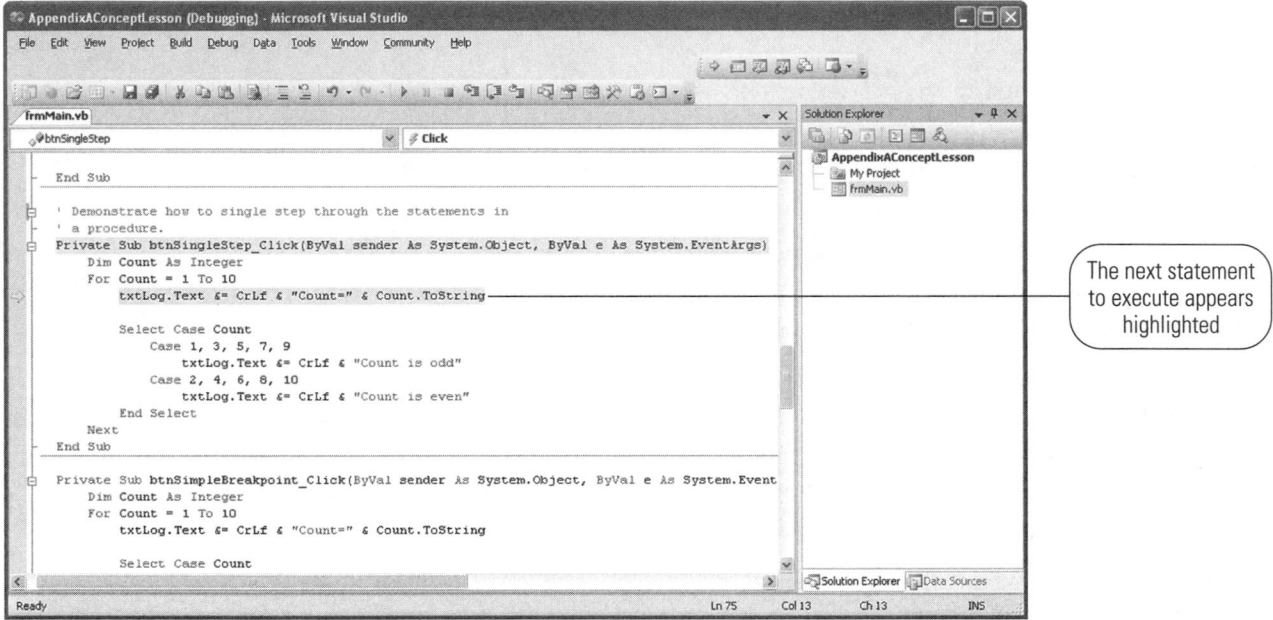

Figure A-4: Line-by-line statement execution in the Code Editor

4. As you watch the statements execute, highlight the variable **Count** by moving the cursor over the variable. Note that the value of the variable appears in a ToolTip.

5. Press **F5** or click the **Step Out** button. The process of single stepping ends and execution continues as normal.

6. End the application.

Clicking the Step Into button causes Visual Studio to step through the statements in a procedure. If a statement is a procedure call, Visual Studio single steps into the procedure, and then continues executing the statements in that procedure one statement at a time.

In addition to stepping through every statement in every procedure in an application, it is possible to step through parts of an application or pause the application (enter break mode), and then continue executing statements one at a time. When debugging a procedure that calls other procedures, for instance, it is not necessary to trace through the statements in a called procedure after it is known to work correctly. Instead, the Step Over button can be used to execute all of the statements in a procedure, and then suspend execution at the statement following the one that called the procedure. Furthermore, execution can be suspended at any time by clicking the Break All button while the application is running.

## TYPES OF BREAKPOINTS

When you suspect that a problem is occurring in a particular procedure or that a particular statement is incorrect, it is possible to suspend execution at any executable statement by setting a breakpoint. A **breakpoint** is an executable statement where Visual Studio suspends execution and enters break mode, just before executing the marked statement.

Breakpoints are one of the most common and easy to use of the Visual Studio debugging tools. Breakpoints can be created and deleted as needed so as to examine the values of variables at a particular point in an application's execution. Visual Studio supports different types of breakpoints. In this appendix, you will examine a type of breakpoint called a file breakpoint. A file breakpoint is an executable statement in an application where execution will be suspended.

Visual Studio lists the current breakpoints in a project in different ways. First, an icon appears in the left margin of the Code Editor to indicate that a breakpoint is set. In addition, a list of breakpoints appears in another window called the Breakpoints window. Figure A-5 shows the Code Editor and Breakpoints window with two breakpoints set.

> **» TIP**
>
> While debugging an application, it is often useful to enter break mode, and then step through each statement that you suspect is in error. When a procedure appears to work correctly, you can step over it and move on to the next statement. This is where setting breakpoints comes into play.

> **» NOTE**
>
> Breakpoints cannot be set on declaration statements because they are not executable statements.

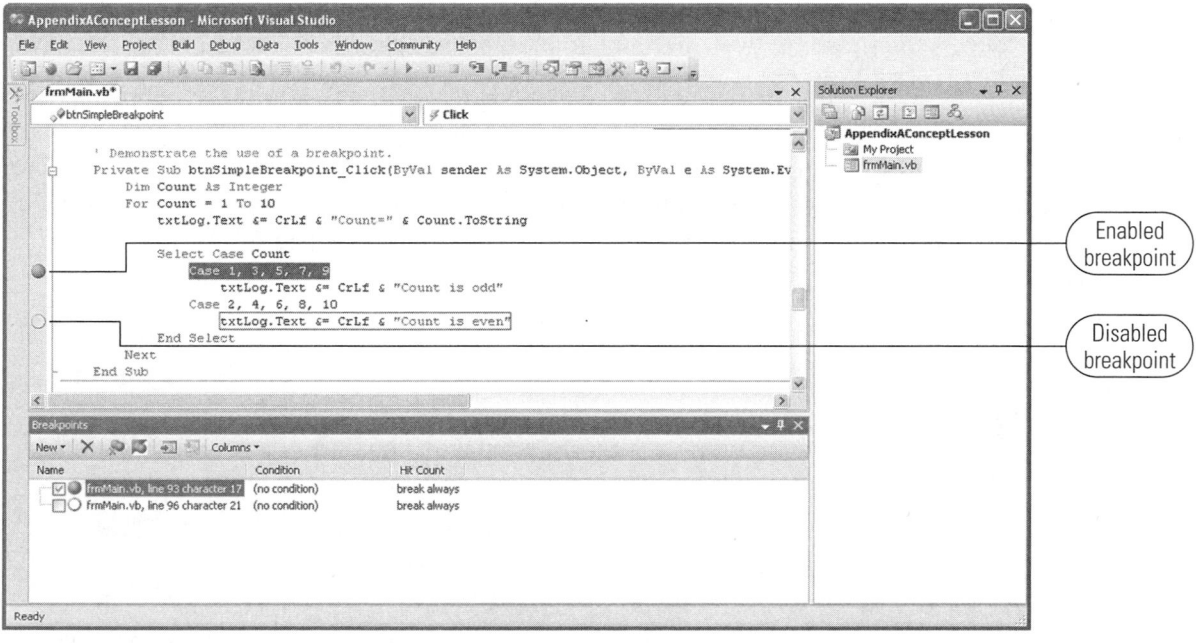

Figure A-5: Breakpoints appearing in the Code Editor and the Breakpoints window

Note the following about the breakpoints appearing in Figure A-5:

» A filled circle denotes an enabled breakpoint. Visual Studio suspends execution just before executing the statement containing the enabled breakpoint. If the breakpoint is set on a procedure declaration, execution is suspended just before executing the first statement in the procedure. Note that the breakpoints appear in both the Breakpoints window and the Code Editor.

» An outlined circle indicates that a breakpoint is disabled. Breakpoints are enabled and disabled by right-clicking the breakpoint in the Code Editor, and then clicking Disable Breakpoint or Enable Breakpoint from the pop-up menu. Visual Studio does not suspend execution on breakpoints that are disabled.

## CREATING A BREAKPOINT

A breakpoint can be created in one of two ways. First, you can locate an executable statement in the Code Editor, and then click in the left margin. A filled circle appears in the margin indicating that a breakpoint is set and enabled. Using the second technique, right-click an executable statement in the Code Editor, and then click Breakpoint, Insert Breakpoint from the pop-up menu.

To remove a breakpoint, right-click the statement in the Code Editor containing the breakpoint, and then click Breakpoint, Delete Breakpoint from the pop-up menu. It is also possible to remove a breakpoint by selecting the breakpoint in the Breakpoints window, and then clicking the Delete button. Clicking Debug, Delete All Breakpoints removes all of the breakpoints in an application. A breakpoint can also be removed by clicking the filled circle in the Code Editor.

In addition to setting simple breakpoints that suspend execution just before a statement executes, it is possible to set hit count breakpoints and conditional breakpoints, as follows:

» A *hit count* breakpoint causes execution to be suspended after the statement containing the breakpoint has executed a certain number of times. For example, a hit count breakpoint is often useful with a `For` loop. After the statement(s) in the loop has executed some number of times, Visual Studio suspends execution. The dialog box shown in Figure A-6 is used to set a hit count breakpoint.

**» NOTE**

It's possible to create as many breakpoints as you need. In addition, breakpoints are persistent from one invocation of Visual Studio to the next. That is, if breakpoints exist and you exit Visual Studio, those breakpoints will continue to exist the next time the application is loaded into Visual Studio.

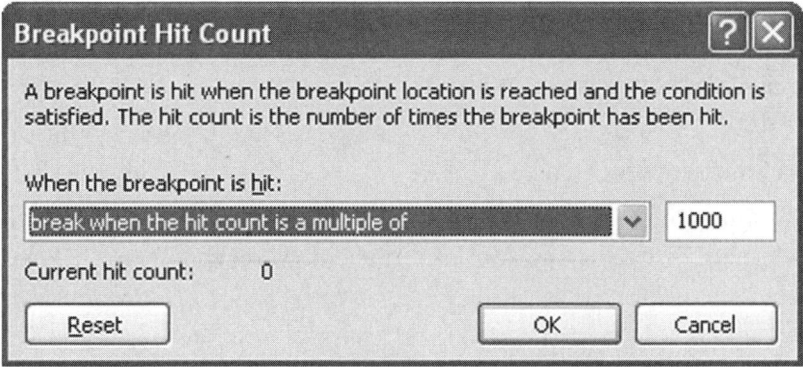

Figure A-6: Breakpoint Hit Count dialog box

As shown in Figure A-6, a list box is used to define how the hit count breakpoint will operate. In Figure A-6, execution will be suspended every 1000 times the statement executes.

» A *conditional breakpoint*, as its name implies, suspends execution when some condition is met. The condition in a conditional breakpoint has the same syntax as the condition in an If statement. The dialog box shown in Figure A-7 is used to set a conditional breakpoint.

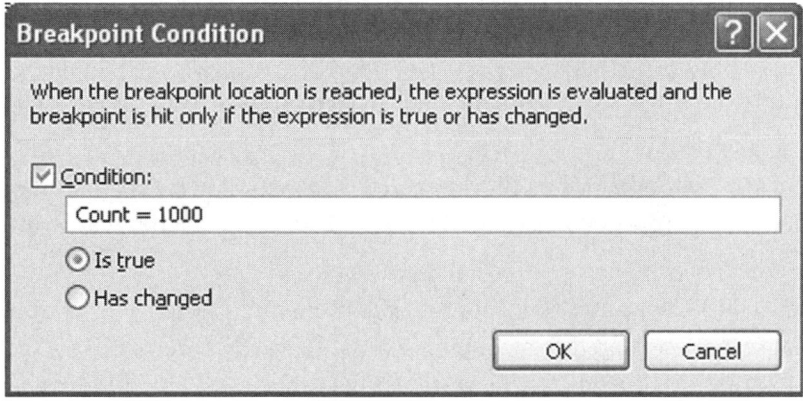

Figure A-7: Breakpoint Condition dialog box

As shown in Figure A-7, the Breakpoint Condition dialog box contains a text box in which a condition is entered. The Is true radio button, when selected, causes execution to be suspended when the condition is true. The Has changed radio button, when selected, causes execution to be suspended when the value of the condition changes. Using the breakpoint shown in Figure A-7, execution will be suspended when the variable Count is equal to 1000.

In this exploration exercise, you will see how to set breakpoints and use breakpoints to trace the execution of program statements.

1. Activate the Code Editor for the form named **frmMain**. Locate the procedure named **btnSimpleBreakpoint_Click**. Set breakpoints on the following statements (shown in bold):

```
Case 1, 3, 5, 7, 9
    txtLog.Text &= CrLf & "Count is odd"
Case 2, 4, 6, 8, 10
    txtLog.Text &= CrLf & "Count is even"
```

2. Run the application. Click the **Breakpoints** tab. Click the **Simple Breakpoint** button. When the breakpoint is reached, the Code Editor appears and the statement that will be executed next is highlighted. While in break mode, highlight the variable named **Count** and the **Text** property of the text box named **txtLog**. As you do, the value of the variable and object property appears in a ToolTip.

3. Press **F5** to continue execution. Execution continues until the next breakpoint is hit.

4. Remove the two breakpoints and end the application.

5. Next, activate the Code Editor, and locate the **Click** event handler for the button named **btnHitCountBreakPoint**. Set a breakpoint on the following line:

```
Do Until Count > 10000000
```

6. In the Code Editor, right-click the breakpoint, and click **Hit Count** from the shortcut menu.

7. In the Breakpoint Hit Count dialog box that opens, select **Break when the hit count is a multiple of** from the drop-down list, and then enter **100** in the text box. Click **OK** to close the dialog box.

8. Run the application. Click the **Breakpoints** tab. Click the **Hit Count Breakpoint** button. The breakpoint is activated every 100 iterations. To see this, move the cursor over the variable Count in the Code Editor. Note that its value is 99. The value of the breakpoint will be 199, 299, and so on when the breakpoint is subsequently hit. Thus, the breakpoint is hit every 100 iterations.

9. Remove the breakpoint and end the application.

**▶▶ NOTE**

Hit count breakpoints are not available in the Visual Basic Express edition.

## USING THE IMMEDIATE WINDOW

The Immediate window is used to examine the values of variables, change those values, and call procedures. Typing a question mark (?) followed by an expression causes Visual Studio to evaluate that expression and display the result on the line following the expression. The expression following the question mark can be a variable, object property, or any other expression that is valid on the right side of an assignment statement. Expressions containing variables or object properties are valid only in break mode because variables only have values while a Visual Studio program is running. It is also possible to set the value of a variable or object property using an assignment statement. Figure A-8 shows the Immediate window with various expressions.

Figure A-8: Immediate window

As shown in Figure A-8, expressions are entered in the Immediate window by entering a question mark (?) followed by the expression name. The expression is evaluated, and the result is then displayed.

In this exploration exercise, you will see how to use the Immediate window to examine the value of variables and object properties.

1. Activate the Code Editor, and locate the **Click** event handler for the button named **btnImmediateWindow**. Set a breakpoint on the following line:

```
txtSquared.Text = Squared.ToString
```

2. Run the application, and click the **Breakpoints** tab. Enter the value **42** in the Enter a Number text box. Click the **Immediate Window** button. The breakpoint you specified in the previous step is hit and execution is suspended. Again, the statement is highlighted in the Code Editor.

3. View the Immediate window by clicking **Debug**, **Windows**, **Immediate**.

4. Enter the following statement in the Immediate window, and then press **Enter**:
   `?Input`

   The value of the variable 42.0 appears in the Immediate window. This is the value stored in the variable Input.

**»NOTE**

Equivalent results can be obtained by highlighting a variable in the Code Editor or entering a comparable expression in the Immediate window. Both display the value of a variable. Which technique to use is a matter of personal preference.

5. Enter the following statement in the Immediate window, and then press **Enter**:
   `?Squared`

   The value of the variable (1764.0) appears in the Immediate window.

6. Enter the following statement in the Immediate window, and then press **Enter**:
   `?txtSquared.Text`

   An empty string is displayed because a value has yet to be stored in this control instance.

7. Clear the breakpoint and end the application.

## SETTING WATCH EXPRESSIONS WITH THE WATCH WINDOWS

To examine the value of the same variable repeatedly, you can use watch expressions. Watch expressions provide a useful alternative to entering the same expression again and again in the Immediate window. Each time Visual Studio enters break mode, the values of watch expressions appear in one of four Watch windows. Watch expressions can be created, changed, or deleted while a project is in break mode. Like breakpoints, watch expressions are persistent from one invocation of Visual Studio to the next.

To add a watch expression to a project, one of four Watch windows is used. Each Watch window works exactly the same way. Visual Studio supplies four Watch windows so that you can organize the variables or expressions that you want to watch into functional or logical groupings. The contents of Watch windows can only be edited while Visual Studio is in break mode. Figure A-9 shows the first Watch window with four watch expressions.

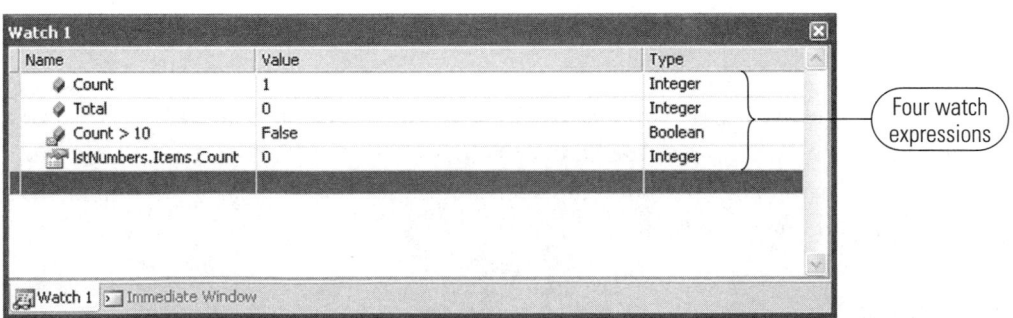

Figure A-9: Watch window

As shown in Figure A-9, you can watch a variable, or create more complex expressions such as `Count > 10`. Furthermore, it is possible to examine the properties of control instances such as a list box.

Each of the four Watch windows contains the following three columns:

» In the *Name* column, you enter the expression that you want Visual Studio to evaluate. To avoid typographical errors, you can copy the expression or variable from the Code Editor to a Watch window by means of the Windows Clipboard. The watch expression can consist of a variable, object, property, or more complex expressions.

» The *Value* column contains the current value of the watch expression.

» The *Type* column contains the data type of the watch expression.

A watch expression can be created, edited, or deleted only when Visual Studio is in break mode. To edit a watch expression, click on the expression to be edited in the desired Watch window, and then change the expression, as necessary.

In this exploration exercise, you will see how to work with a Watch window to examine expressions as an application executes.

1. Activate the Code Editor and select the **Click** event handler for the button named **btnWatch**, which is located in the Watch Windows region. Set a breakpoint on the following line:

```
lstNumbers.Items.Add(Count.ToString)
```

2. Run the application. Click the **Watch Windows** tab. Click the **Watch** button to execute the event handler for which you set a breakpoint in the previous step. Execution is suspended at the breakpoint you just created.

3. Click **Debug** on the menu bar, point to **Windows**, point to **Watch**, and then click **Watch 1** to display the first Watch window. Note that the Visual Basic Express edition has only one Watch window named Watch.

4. Type **Count** in the first row of the Name column.

5. Type **Total** in the second row of the Name column.

6. Type **Count > 10** in the third row of the Name column.

7. Press **F11** several times. Each time the value of one of the watched variables changes, the value is updated in the Watch window. Clear the breakpoint and end the application.

## THE CALL STACK WINDOW

The Call Stack window allows you to view which event handlers or other procedures have been called and the order in which those procedures were called. One use of the Call Stack window is to detect a phenomenon called cascading events. Cascading events and the Call Stack window are discussed in the following sections.

---

**» TIP**

Use care when creating watch expressions. Visual Studio must check and evaluate each watch expression every time a statement executes. Thus, if you create too many watch expressions at once, program execution becomes very slow.

**» NOTE**

Although not a Visual Studio debugging tool, a message box can be used to display the value of a variable or object property. It's also possible to call the `Console.WriteLine` and `Debug.WriteLine` methods. Of course, when the application is known to be working correctly, this code must be removed.

## CASCADING EVENTS

In event-driven applications, improper logic can cause one event to raise another event indefinitely. Such a problem can arise when a statement fires a `TextChanged` event for one control instance. That control instance, in turn, fires a `TextChanged` event in a second control instance, and so on. If a control instance down the line fires a `TextChanged` event for the first control instance, the execution path becomes circular; that is, the events continue firing each other indefinitely. This phenomenon is called **cascading events**.

Consider a simple example involving two text boxes. After each text box gets input focus, it sets the focus to the other text box, and focus switches back and forth between the two text boxes indefinitely. The application seems to "lock up," and you cannot click any other control instance on the form while the text boxes continue updating one another. Whenever an application seems to lock up because of cascading events, it's possible to press the Break All button on the Debug toolbar, and then check the relationship between the events in the program.

## VIEWING THE CALL STACK WINDOW

The Call Stack window lists both the procedures you create and those procedures that Visual Studio executes internally to create objects and handle events. Figure A-10 shows the Call Stack window demonstrating the cascading event problem discussed in the preceding section.

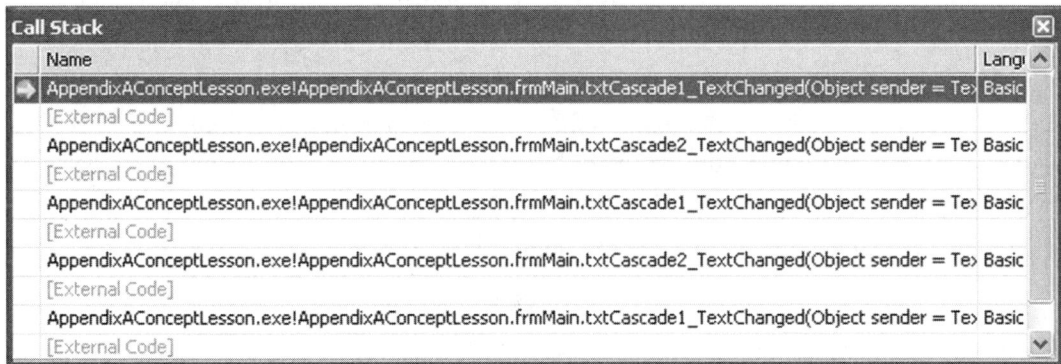

Figure A-10: Call Stack window

The Call Stack window displays procedures in the order in which they were called, that is, from the most recently called procedure to the least recently called procedure. The lines that appear dimmed contain procedures that Visual Studio executes internally.

These procedures set up event handlers and allow Visual Studio to call the event handlers and procedures that you create.

Figure A-10 shows that the event procedure `txtCascade1_TextChanged` was the procedure most recently called. The contents of this line say that the executable file named AppendixAConceptLesson.exe contains an executing event handler named `txtCascade1_TextChanged` in the form module named `frmMain`. Note that any arguments supplied to the event handler also appear in the Call Stack window. The Call Stack window can be helpful to locate cascading events as it lists each event handler that Visual Studio called.

In this exploration exercise, you will use the Call Stack window to examine cascading events.

1. Run the solution and click the **Call Stack** tab. Enter the value **5** in the top text box.

2. Press **F11** to fire the cascading `TextChanged` events. The cascading events will continue to fire until an exception is thrown.

3. On the menu bar, click **Debug**, **Windows**, **Call Stack** to view the Call Stack window. The cascading events appear in the Call Stack window.

4. End the application.

In addition to locating cascading events, the Call Stack window can be used to examine the order in which Visual Studio called the various procedures and which procedures are executing.

## THE LOCALS WINDOW

The Locals window displays the local variables pertaining to the currently executing event handler or any other executing procedure. As one procedure calls another procedure, Visual Studio updates the contents of the Locals window to display the information pertaining to the currently executing procedure.

The Locals window can be displayed only while Visual Studio is in break mode. In addition, the Locals window is useful only when an event handler or other procedure is executing. Although it is possible to display the Locals window while Visual Studio is waiting for an event handler to execute, the Locals window will display nothing. Figure A-11 shows the Locals window while the event handler named btnTypeMismatch is executing.

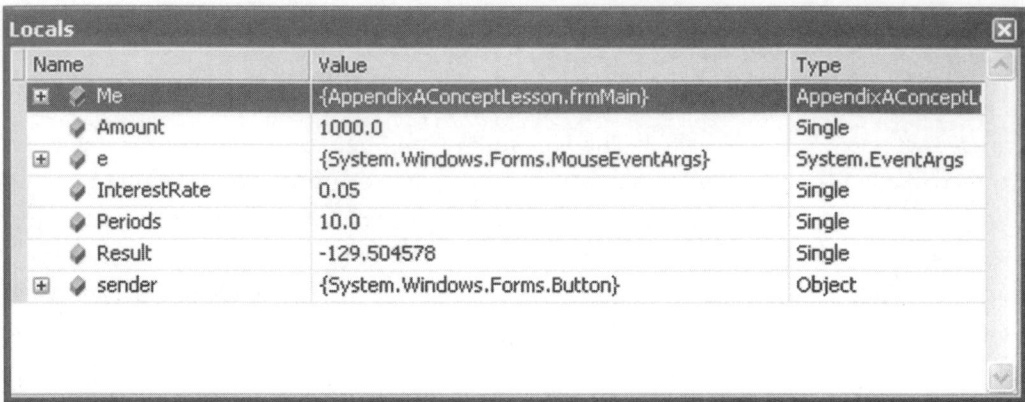

Figure A-11: Locals window

As shown in Figure A-11, a reference to the form, its objects, and the form-level variables appears in the Locals window through a reference to the Me keyword. Sender and e provide the reference to the event handler's arguments. As these variables are objects supporting properties, they can be expanded and collapsed. Finally, the variables Amount, InterestRate, Periods, and Result are the local variables declared in the event handler. Note that if the current procedure is not an event handler, Me does not appear, and no reference to the form exists.

Note that the Locals window has a drill-down interface. Clicking the plus sign expands an object and clicking the minus sign collapses the object. The object supplied by the Me keyword is hierarchical. That is, Me (the form) might contain a text box, which, in turn, supports properties.

# OTHER DEBUGGING WINDOWS

Visual Studio supplies several other debugging windows. The following list briefly describes the purpose of these windows:

- » The Autos window displays the variables and objects in the current statement and the statements surrounding the currently executing statement.

- » The Memory window displays blocks of memory in both text and hexadecimal format.

- » The Processes window is useful to debug applications that communicate with each other.

» The Disassembly window allows you to view the intermediate language (IL) code for the program and is generated by the Visual Basic compiler.

» The Registers window allows you to view the CPU registers and their contents.

# APPENDIX SUMMARY

This appendix presented an overview of the tools that can be used to debug applications. When and how to use these tools is up to the developer.

» To trace the execution of the statements in an application, use the Step Into, Step Over, and Step Out buttons.

» Breakpoints cause execution to be suspended when a particular statement is reached. Breakpoints can be set by clicking the left margin in the Code Editor. It is possible to set several breakpoints at the same time. Just before executing the statement containing the breakpoint, Visual Studio enters break mode, allowing you to examine the values of variables and properties. In addition to simple breakpoints, it is also possible to set hit count breakpoints and conditional breakpoints.

» The Immediate window is used to evaluate expressions while Visual Studio is in break mode. To evaluate an expression, enter a question mark, followed by the expression to evaluate.

» Four Watch windows allow you to examine the values of variables and expressions while Visual Studio is in break mode. Each Watch window works the same way.

» The Call Stack window is used to examine the order in which procedures are called. It can be useful to detect cascading events.

# KEY TERMS

**breakpoint**—An executable statement where execution will be suspended.

**cascading events**—A phenomenon that occurs when one event causes another event to fire indefinitely.

**debugging**—The process of locating and fixing programming errors.

**debugging windows**—A collection of windows supplied by the Visual Studio IDE designed to help you correct errors in the applications you write.

**logic error**—A type of error that occurs when an application produces unexpected results.

# ASCII CHART

| Ctrl | Dec | Code | Dec | Char | Dec | Char | Dec | Char |
|------|-----|------|-----|------|-----|------|-----|------|
| ^@ | 0 | NUL | 32 | Sp | 64 | @ | 96 | ` |
| ^A | 1 | SOH | 33 | ! | 65 | A | 97 | a |
| ^B | 2 | STX | 34 | " | 66 | B | 98 | b |
| ^C | 3 | ETX | 35 | # | 67 | C | 99 | c |
| ^D | 4 | EOT | 36 | $ | 68 | D | 100 | d |
| ^E | 5 | ENQ | 37 | % | 69 | E | 101 | e |
| ^F | 6 | ACK | 38 | & | 70 | F | 102 | f |
| ^G | 7 | BEL | 39 | ' | 71 | G | 103 | g |
| ^H | 8 | CS | 40 | ( | 72 | H | 104 | h |
| ^I | 9 | HT | 41 | ) | 73 | I | 105 | i |
| ^J | 10 | LF | 42 | * | 74 | J | 106 | j |
| ^K | 11 | VT | 43 | + | 75 | K | 107 | k |
| ^L | 12 | FF | 44 | , | 76 | L | 108 | l |
| ^M | 13 | CR | 45 | - | 77 | M | 109 | m |
| ^N | 14 | SO | 46 | . | 78 | N | 110 | n |
| ^O | 15 | SI | 47 | / | 79 | O | 111 | o |
| ^P | 16 | DLE | 48 | 0 | 80 | P | 112 | p |

*(Continued)* ▶

| Ctrl | Dec | Code | Dec | Char | Dec | Char | Dec | Char |
|------|-----|------|-----|------|-----|------|-----|------|
| ^Q | 17 | DC1 | 49 | 1 | 81 | Q | 113 | q |
| ^R | 18 | DC2 | 50 | 2 | 82 | R | 114 | r |
| ^S | 19 | DC3 | 51 | 3 | 83 | S | 115 | s |
| ^T | 20 | DC4 | 52 | 4 | 84 | T | 116 | t |
| ^U | 21 | NAK | 53 | 5 | 85 | U | 117 | u |
| ^V | 22 | SYN | 54 | 6 | 86 | V | 118 | v |
| ^W | 23 | STB | 55 | 7 | 87 | W | 119 | w |
| ^X | 24 | CAN | 56 | 8 | 88 | X | 120 | x |
| ^Y | 25 | EM | 57 | 9 | 89 | Y | 121 | y |
| ^Z | 26 | SUB | 58 | : | 90 | Z | 122 | z |
| ^[ | 27 | ESC | 59 | ; | 91 | [ | 123 | { |
| ^\ | 28 | FS | 60 | < | 92 | \ | 124 | \| |
| ^] | 29 | GS | 61 | = | 93 | ] | 125 | } |
| ^^ | 30 | RS | 62 | > | 94 | ^ | 126 | ~ |
| ^_ | 31 | US | 63 | ? | 95 | _ | 127 | DEL |

# INDEX

# T

# X

# Y